Broadview Public Library District
2226 S 16th Avenue
Broadview IL 60155-4000
708-345-1325
www.broadviewlibrary.org

CRIME IN THE UNITED STATES

2024

EIGHTEENTH EDITION

EDITED BY SHANA HERTZ HATTIS

Lanham • Boulder • New York • London

Published by Bernan Press
An imprint of The Rowman & Littlefield Publishing Group, Inc.
4501 Forbes Boulevard, Suite 200, Lanham, Maryland 20706
www.rowman.com

86-90 Paul Street, London EC2A 4NE

Library of Congress Cataloging-in-Publication Data available

ISBN 979-8-89205-006-7 (hardcover) | ISBN 979-8-89205-007-4 (ebook)

CONTENTS

SECTION I: SUMMARY OF THE UNIFORM CRIME REPORTING (UCR) PROGRAM...1

SECTION II: OFFENSES KNOWN TO POLICE 9
(*Violent Crime*: Murder, Rape, Robbery, Aggravated Assault)
(*Property Crime*: Burglary, Larceny-Theft, Motor Vehicle Theft, Arson)

Table 1.	Crime in the United States, by Volume and Rate Per 100,000 Inhabitants, 2003–2022	35
Table 2.	Crime, by Community Type, 2022	37
Table 3.	Crime in the United States, Population and Offense Distribution, by Region, 2022	37
Table 4.	Crime in the United States, by Region, Geographic Division, and State 2021–2022	38
Table 5.	Crime in the United States, by State and Area, 2022	46
Table 6.	Crime in the United States, by Selected Metropolitan Statistical Area, 2022	54
Table 7.	Offense Analysis, United States, 2018–2022	83
Table 8.	Offenses Known to Law Enforcement, by Selected State and City, 2022	84
Table 9.	Offenses Known to Law Enforcement, by Selected State and University and College, 2022	181
Table 10.	Offenses Known to Law Enforcement, by Selected State Metropolitan and Nonmetropolitan Counties, 2022	190
Table 11.	Offenses Known to Law Enforcement, by Selected State, Tribal, and Other Agencies, 2022	222
Table 12.	Crime Trends, by Population Group, 2021–2022	247
Table 13.	Crime Trends, by Suburban and Nonsuburban Cities, by Population Group, 2021–2022	248
Table 14.	Crime Trends, by Metropolitan and Nonmetropolitan Counties, by Population Group, 2021–2022	249
Table 15.	Crime Trends, Additional Information About Selected Offenses, by Population Group, 2021–2022	250
Table 16.	Rate: Number of Crimes Per 100,000 Population, by Population Group, 2022	252
Table 17.	Rate: Number of Crimes Per 100,000 Inhabitants, by Suburban and Nonsuburban Cities, by Population Group, 2022	254
Table 18.	Rate: Number of Crimes Per 100,000 Inhabitants, by Metropolitan and Nonmetropolitan Counties, by Population Group, 2022	255
Table 19.	Rate: Number of Crimes Per 100,000 Inhabitants, Additional Information About Selected Offenses, by Population Group, 2022	257
Table 20.	Murder, by Selected State and Type of Weapon, 2022	259
Table 21.	Robbery, by State and Type of Weapon, 2022	260
Table 22.	Aggravated Assault, by State and Type of Weapon, 2022	261
Table 23.	Offense Analysis, Number and Percent Distribution, 2021–2022	262
Table 24.	Property Stolen and Recovered, by Type and Value, 2022	263

SECTION III: OFFENSES CLEARED 265

Table 25.	Incidents Cleared, by Offense Category, 2022	269
Table 25A.	Number and Percent of Offenses Cleared by Arrest or Exceptional Means, by Population Group, 2022	270
Table 26.	Number and Percent of Offenses Cleared by Arrest or Exceptional Means, by Region and Geographic Division, 2022	271
Table 27.	Number and Percent of Offenses Cleared by Arrest or Exceptional Means, Additional Information About Selected Offenses, by Population Group, 2022	272
Table 28.	Number of Offenses Cleared by Arrest or Exceptional Means and Percent Involving Persons Under 18 Years of Age, by Population Group, 2022	274

SECTION IV: PERSONS ARRESTED..**275**

  Table 29.   Estimated Number of Arrests, 2022..283
  Table 30.   Number and Rate of Arrests, by Geographic Region, 2022...284
  Table 31.   Number and Rate of Arrests, by Population Group, 2022 285
  Table 32.   Ten-Year Arrest Trends, 2013 and 2022 287
  Table 33.   Ten-Year Arrest Trends, by Age and Sex, 2013 and 2022 288
  Table 34.   Five-Year Arrest Trends, by Age, 2018 and 2022 289
  Table 35.   Five-Year Arrest Trends, by Age and Sex, 2018 and 2022 290
  Table 36.   Year Over Previous Year Arrest Trends, 2021–2022 291
  Table 37.   Year Over Previous Year Arrest Trends, by Age and Sex, 2021–2022 292
  Table 38.   Arrests, Distribution by Age, by Arrest Offense Category, 2022.......................................293
  Table 39.   Male Arrests, Distribution by Age, 2022 296
  Table 40.   Female Arrests, Distribution by Age, 2022...299
  Table 41.   Arrests of Persons Under 15, 18, 21, and 25 Years of Age, 2022 302
  Table 42.   Arrests, Distribution by Sex, 2022..303
  Table 43.   Arrests, Distribution by Race, by Offense Category, 2022..304
  Table 43A.   Arrests, Distribution by Ethnicity, 2022 307
  Table 44.   Arrest Trends, Cities, 2021–2022 309
  Table 45.   Arrest Trends, Cities, by Age and Sex, 2021–2022 310
  Table 46.   Arrests, Cities, Distribution by Age, 2022..311
  Table 47.   Arrests, Cities, Persons Under 15, 18, 21, and 25 Years of Age, 2022 313
  Table 48.   Arrests, Cities, Distribution by Sex, 2022 314
  Table 49.   Arrests, Cities, Distribution by Race, 2022 315
  Table 49A.   Arrests, Cities, Distribution by Ethnicity, 2022 318
  Table 50.   Arrest Trends, Metropolitan Counties, 2021–2022 320
  Table 51.   Arrest Trends, Metropolitan Counties, by Age and Sex, 2021–2022 321
  Table 52.   Arrests, Metropolitan Counties, Distribution by Age, 2022 322
  Table 53.   Arrests, Metropolitan Counties, Persons Under 15, 18, 21, and 25 Years of Age, 2022 324
  Table 54.   Arrests, Metropolitan Counties, Distribution by Sex, 2022..325
  Table 55.   Arrests, Metropolitan Counties, Distribution by Race, 2022...326
  Table 55A.   Arrests, Metropolitan Counties, Distribution by Ethnicity, 2022 329
  Table 56.   Arrest Trends, Nonmetropolitan Counties, 2021–2022 331
  Table 57.   Arrest Trends, Nonmetropolitan Counties, by Age and Sex, 2021–2022.........................332
  Table 58.   Arrests, Nonmetropolitan Counties, Distribution by Age, 2022..333
  Table 59.   Arrests, Nonmetropolitan Counties, Persons Under 15, 18, 21, and 25 Years of Age, 2022...............335
  Table 60.   Arrests, Nonmetropolitan Counties, Distribution by Sex, 2022 336
  Table 61A.   Arrests, Nonmetropolitan Counties, Distribution by Ethnicity, 2022...............................337
  Table 61.   Arrests, Nonmetropolitan Counties, Distribution by Race, 2022 339
  Table 62.   Arrest Trends, Suburban Areas, 2021–2022 342
  Table 63.   Arrest Trends, Suburban Areas, by Age and Sex, 2021–2022 343
  Table 64.   Arrests, Suburban Areas, Distribution by Age, 2022..344
  Table 65.   Arrests, Suburban Areas, Persons Under 15, 18, 21, and 25 Years of Age, 2022 346
  Table 66.   Arrests, Suburban Areas, Distribution by Sex, 2022 347
  Table 67.   Arrests, Suburban Areas, Distribution by Race, 2022 348
  Table 67A.   Arrests, Suburban Areas, Distribution by Ethnicity, 2022 351
  Table 68.   Police Disposition of Juvenile Offenders Taken into Custody, 2022 353
  Table 69.   Arrests, by State, 2022 354

SECTION V: LAW ENFORCEMENT PERSONNEL..**359**

  Table 70.   Full-Time Law Enforcement Employees, by Region and Geographic Division and
                  Population Group, 2022..364
  Table 71.   Full-Time Law Enforcement Officers, by Region, Geographic Division, and Population
                  Group, 2022 365

Table 72.   Full-Time Law Enforcement Employees, Range in Rate, by Population Group, 2022........................366
Table 73.   Full-Time Law Enforcement Officers, Range in Rate, by Population Group, 2022...........................367
Table 74.   Full-Time Law Enforcement Employees, by Population Group, Percent Male
              and Female, 2022 368
Table 75.   Full-Time Civilian Law Enforcement Employees, by Population Group, 2022...............................369
Table 76.   Full-Time State Law Enforcement Employees, by Selected State, 2022 370
Table 77.   Full-Time Law Enforcement Employees, by State, 2022...373
Table 78.   Full-Time Law Enforcement Employees, by Selected State and City, 2022 374
Table 79.   Full-Time Law Enforcement Employees, by Selected State and University or
              College, 2022 487
Table 80.   Full-Time Law Enforcement Employees, by Selected State Metropolitan and
              NonMetropolitan Counties, 2022..498
Table 81.   Full-Time Law Enforcement Employees, by Selected State and Agency, 2022 533

SECTION VI: HATE CRIMES...**549**
Table 82.   Incidents, Offenses, Victims, and Known Offenders, by Bias Motivation, 2022 554
Table 83.   Incidents, Offenses, Victims, and Known Offenders, by Offense Type, 2022................................555
Table 84.   Offenses, Known Offender's Race and Ethnicity, by Offense Type, 2022 556
Table 85.   Offenses, Offense Type, by Bias Motivation, 2022..557
Table 86.   Offenses, Known Offender's Race and Ethnicity, by Bias Motivation, 2022.................................559
Table 87.   Offenses, Victim Type, by Offense Type, 2022...560
Table 88.   Victims, Offense Type, by Bias Motivation, 2022...561
Table 89.   Incidents, Victim Type, by Bias Motivation, 2022..563
Table 90.   Known Offenders, by Known Offender's Race, Ethnicity, and Age, 2022....................................564
Table 91.   Incidents, Bias Motivation, by Location, 2022..565
Table 92.   Offenses, Offense Type, by Participating State, Territory, and Federal, 2022 566
Table 93.   Agency Hate Crime Reporting, by Participating State, Territory, and Federal, 2022.......................567
Table 94.   Hate Crime Incidents Per Bias Motivation and Quarter, by Selected State, Territory,
              Federal, and Agency, 2022 569

APPENDIXES..**615**
Appendix I. Methodology 617
Appendix II. Offense Definitions...621
Appendix III. Geographic Area Definitions..623
Appendix IV. The Nation's Two Crime Measures 625
Appendix V. Calculations by Population, Tables 16, 17, 18, 19 627

INDEX... **629**

LIST OF FIGURES

SECTION II: OFFENSES KNOWN TO POLICE **9**

Figure 2-1. Violent Crime Rates, by Offense and Region, 2022 11
Figure 2-2. Murder Victim, Known Relationship to Offender, 2022 15
Figure 2-3. Number of Rapes and Rate Per 100,000 Inhabitants, 2013–2022 19
Figure 2-4. Robberies, by Location and Percent Distribution, 2022 21
Figure 2-5. Number and Rate of Aggravated Assaults, 1992–2022 23
Figure 2-6. Percent Change in Property Crimes, 1992–2022...25
Figure 2-7. Burglary, by Location and Time, 2022 27
Figure 2-8. Larceny-Theft, Percent Distribution, 2022 29
Figure 2-9. Number and Rate of Motor Vehicle Theft, 1992–2022..31
Figure 2-10. Arson Sites, Percent Distribution, 2022...33

SECTION III: OFFENSES CLEARED **265**

Figure 3-1. Percent of Selected Crimes Cleared by Arrest or Exceptional Means, 2022 267

SECTION IV: PERSONS ARRESTED **275**

Figure 4.1.   Percent Change in the Number of Persons Arrested, by Offense, 2013–2022 277
Figure 4-2A. Arrest Distribution, Violent Crime, by Age, 2022 279
Figure 4-2B. Arrest Distribution, Property Crime, by Age, 2022 280

SECTION V: LAW ENFORCEMENT PERSONNEL **359**

Figure 5-1. Average Number of Officers and Employees in Cities Per 1,000 Inhabitants, by Region, 2022..........361

SECTION VI. HATE CRIMES **549**

Figure 6-1. Percent Distribution of Single-Bias Hate Crime Incidents, 2022 551
Figure 6-2. Hate Crimes, by Type of Victim, 2022..553

SECTION I

SUMMARY OF THE UNIFORM CRIME REPORTING (UCR) PROGRAM

SUMMARY OF THE UNIFORM CRIME REPORTING (UCR) PROGRAM

Bernan Press is proud to present its eighteenth edition of *Crime in the United States*. This title was formerly published by the Federal Bureau of Investigation (FBI) but is no longer available in printed form from the government. This edition contains final data from 2022, the most current year for which data is available.

Transition to NIBRS

As of January 1, 2021, the FBI's National Incident-Based Reporting System (NIBRS) became the national standard for law enforcement crime data reporting in the United States. The 2021 data year will mark the first time that the FBI and BJS estimate reported crime in the United States based solely on NIBRS data.

As of June 2022, all 50 U.S. states and the District of Columbia were certified to report crime data to NIBRS. Just under two-thirds of the U.S. population is covered by NIBRS-reporting law enforcement agencies, and 62 NIBRS-certified agencies serve cities with a population of 250,000 or more; these agencies cover a total population of more than 37 million.

Due to a system upgrade in 2019, the FBI now calculates rates for each offense based on the individual offenses and population published for each agency in tables 8–11. (Previous to 2019, when agencies were published in tables 8–11, but they had one or two offenses removed from publication due to not meeting UCR publication guidelines, the agency's data was not used to calculate rates for this table.) The FBI derived the offense rates by dividing the individual offense counts by the individual populations covered by contributing agencies for which 12 months of publishable data were supplied and then multiplying the resulting figure by 100,000. See Appendix V for the agency and population counts.

About the UCR Program

The UCR program's primary objective is to generate reliable information for use in law enforcement administration, operation, and management; however, over the course of the program, its data has stood out as one of the country's leading social indicators.

The UCR program is a nationwide, cooperative statistical effort of (typically) more than 18,000 city, university and college, county, state, tribal, and federal law enforcement agencies voluntarily reporting data on crimes brought to their attention. Since 1930, the FBI has administered the UCR program and continued to assess and monitor the nature and type of crime in the nation. Criminologists, sociologists, legislators, municipal planners, the media, and other students of criminal justice use the data for varied research and planning purposes.

Note for Users

To ensure that data are uniformly reported, the FBI provides contributing law enforcement agencies with guidelines that explain how to classify and score offenses and provides uniform crime offense definitions. Acknowledging that offense definitions may vary from state to state, the FBI cautions agencies to report offenses according to the guidelines provided in the handbook, rather than by local or state statutes. Most agencies make a good faith effort to comply with established guidelines.

The UCR program publishes the statistics most commonly requested by data users.

Considering Other Characteristics of a Jurisdiction

To assess criminality and law enforcement's response from jurisdiction to jurisdiction, data users must consider many variables, some of which (despite having significant impact on crime) are not readily measurable or applicable among all locales. Geographic and demographic factors specific to each jurisdiction must be considered and applied in order to make an accurate and complete assessment of crime in that jurisdiction. Several sources of information are available to help the researcher explore the variables that affect crime in a particular locale. For example, U.S. Census Bureau data can help users better understand the makeup of a locale's population. The transience of the population, its racial and ethnic makeup, and its composition by age and gender, educational levels, and prevalent family structures are all key factors in assessing and understanding crime.

Local chambers of commerce, planning offices, and similar entities provide information regarding the economic and cultural makeup of cities and counties. Understanding a jurisdiction's industrial/economic base, its dependence upon neighboring jurisdictions, its transportation system, its economic dependence on nonresidents (such as tourists and convention attendees), and its proximity to military installations, correctional institutions, and other types of facilities all contribute to accurately gauging and interpreting the crime known to and reported by law enforcement.

The strength (including personnel and other resources) and aggressiveness of a jurisdiction's law enforcement agency are also key factors in understanding the nature and extent of crime occurring in that area. Although information pertaining to the number of sworn and civilian employees can be found in this publication, it cannot be used alone as an assessment of the emphasis that a community places on enforcing the law. For example, one city may report more crime than another comparable city because its law enforcement agency identifies more offenses. Attitudes of citizens toward crimes and their subsequent crime reporting practices (especially for minor offenses) also impact the volume of crimes known to police.

Making Valid Crime Assessments

It is essential for all data users to become as well educated as possible about understanding and quantifying the nature and extent of crime in the United States and in the jurisdictions represented by law enforcement contributors to the UCR program. Valid assessments are possible only with careful study and analysis of the various unique conditions that affect each local law enforcement jurisdiction.

Some factors that are known to affect the volume and type of crime occurring from place to place are:

- Population density and degree of urbanization

- Variations in composition of population, particularly in the concentration of youth

- Stability of the population with respect to residents' mobility, commuting patterns, and transient factors

- Modes of transportation and highway systems

- Economic conditions, including median income, poverty level, and job availability

- Cultural factors and educational, recreational, and religious characteristics

- Family conditions, with respect to divorce and family cohesiveness

- Climate

- Effective strength of law enforcement agencies

- Administrative and investigative emphases of law enforcement

- Policies of other components of the criminal justice system (that is, prosecutorial, judicial, correctional, and probational policies)

- Residents' attitudes toward crime

- Crime reporting practices of residents

Although many of the listed factors equally affect the crime of a particular area, the UCR program makes no attempt to relate them to the data presented. The data user is therefore cautioned against comparing statistical data of individual reporting units from cities, counties, metropolitan areas, states, or colleges or universities solely on the basis on their population coverage or student enrollment. Until data users examine all the variables that affect crime in a town, city, county, state, region, or college or university, they can make no meaningful comparisons.

Historical Background

Since 1930, the FBI has administered the UCR program; the agency continues to assess and monitor the nature and type of crime in the nation. Data users look to the UCR program for various research and planning purposes.

Recognizing a need for national crime statistics, the International Association of Chiefs of Police (IACP) formed the Committee on Uniform Crime Records in the 1920s to develop a system of uniform crime statistics. After studying state criminal codes and making an evaluation of the record-keeping practices in use, the committee completed a plan for crime reporting that became the foundation of the UCR program in 1929. The plan included standardized offense definitions for seven main offense classifications known as Part I crimes to gauge fluctuations in the overall volume and rate of crime. Developers also instituted the Hierarchy Rule as the main reporting procedure for what is now known as the Summary Reporting System of the UCR program.

Seven main offense classifications, known as Part I crimes, were chosen to gauge the state of crime in the nation. These seven offense classifications included the violent crimes of murder and nonnegligent manslaughter, rape, robbery, and aggravated assault; also included were the property crimes of burglary, larceny-theft, and motor vehicle theft. By congressional mandate, arson was added as the eighth Part I offense category. Data collection for arson began in 1979.

During the early planning of the program, it was recognized that the differences among criminal codes precluded a mere aggregation of state statistics to arrive at a national total. Also, because of the variances in punishment for the same offenses in different states, no distinction between felony and misdemeanor crimes was possible. To avoid these problems and provide nationwide uniformity in crime reporting, standardized offense definitions were developed. Law enforcement agencies use these to submit data without regard for local statutes. UCR program offense definitions can be found in Appendix I.

In January 1930, 400 cities (representing 20 million inhabitants in 43 states) began participating in the UCR program. Congress enacted Title 28, Section 534, of the *United States Code* that same year, which authorized the attorney general to gather crime information. The attorney general, in turn, designated the FBI to serve as the national clearinghouse for the collected crime data. Since then, data based on uniform classifications and procedures for reporting have been obtained annually from the nation's law enforcement agencies.

Advisory Groups

Providing vital links between local law enforcement and the FBI for the UCR program are the Criminal Justice Information Systems Committees of the IACP and the National Sheriffs' Association (NSA). The IACP represents the thousands of police departments nationwide, as it has since the program began. The NSA encourages sheriffs throughout the country to participate fully in the program. Both committees serve the program in advisory capacities.

In 1988, a Data Providers' Advisory Policy Board was established. This board operated until 1993, when it combined with the National Crime Information Center Advisory Policy Board to form a single Advisory Policy Board (APB) to address all FBI criminal justice information services. The current APB works to ensure continuing emphasis on UCR-related issues. The Association of State Uniform Crime Reporting Programs (ASUCRP) focuses on UCR issues within individual state law enforcement associations and also promotes interest in the UCR program. These organizations foster widespread and responsible use of uniform crime statistics and lend assistance to data contributors.

Redesign of UCR

Although UCR data collection was originally conceived as a tool for law enforcement administration, the data were widely used by other entities involved in various forms of social planning by the 1980s. Recognizing the need for more detailed crime statistics, law enforcement called for a thorough evaluative study to modernize the UCR program. The FBI formulated a comprehensive three-phase redesign effort. The Bureau of Justice Statistics (BJS) agency in the Department of Justice responsible for funding criminal justice information projects, agreed to underwrite the first two phases. These phases were conducted by an independent contractor and structured to determine what, if any, changes should be made to the current program. The third phase would involve implementation of identified changes.

The final report, the *Blueprint for the Future of the Uniform Crime Reporting Program,* was released in the summer of 1985. It specifically outlined recommendations for an expanded, improved UCR program to meet future informational needs. There were three recommended areas of enhancement to the UCR program:

- Offenses and arrests would be reported using an incident-based system

- Data would be collected on two levels. Agencies in level one would report important details about those offenses comprising the Part I crimes, their victims, and arrestees. Level two would consist of law enforcement agencies covering populations of more than 100,000 and a sampling of smaller agencies that would collect expanded detail on all significant offenses

- A quality assurance program would be introduced

In January 1986, Phase III of the redesign effort began, guided by the general recommendations set forth in the *Blueprint.* The FBI selected an experimental site to implement the redesigned program, while contractors developed new data guidelines and system specifications. Upon selecting the South Carolina Law Enforcement Division (SLED), which enlisted the cooperation of nine local law enforcement agencies, the FBI developed automated data capture specifications to adapt the SLED's state system to the national UCR program's standards, and the BJS funded the revisions. The pilot demonstration ran from March 1 through September 30, 1987, and resulted in further refinement of the guidelines and specifications.

From March 1 through March 3, 1988, the FBI held a national UCR conference to present the new system to law enforcement and to obtain feedback on its acceptability. Attendees of the conference passed three overall recommendations without dissent: first, that there be established a new, incident-based national crime reporting system; second, that the FBI manage this program, and third, that an Advisory Policy Board composed of law enforcement executives be formed to assist in directing and implementing the new program. Furthermore, attendees recommended that the implementation of national incident-based reporting proceed at a pace commensurate with the resources and limitations of contributing law enforcement agencies.

Establishing the NIBRS

From March 1988 through January 1989, the FBI developed and assumed management of the UCR program's National Incident-Based Reporting System (NIBRS), and by April 1989, the first test of NIBRS data was submitted to the national UCR program. Over the next few years, the national IUCR program published information about the redesigned program in five documents:

- *Uniform Crime Reporting Handbook*, NIBRS Edition (1992) provides a nontechnical program overview focusing on definitions, policies, and procedures of the IBRS

- *Data Submission Specifications* (May 1992) is used by local and state systems personnel, who are responsible for preparing magnetic media for submission to the FBI

- *Approaches to Implementing an Incident-Based System* (July 1992) is a guide for system designers

- *Error Message Manual* (revised December 1999) contains designations of mandatory and optional data elements, data element edits, and error messages

- *Data Collection Guidelines* (revised August 2000) contains a system overview and descriptions of the offense codes, reports, data elements, and data values used in the system

As more agencies inquired about the NIBRS, the FBI, in May 2002, made the *Handbook for Acquiring a Records Management System (RMS) That Is Compatible with the NIBRS* available to agencies considering or developing automated incident-based records management systems. The handbook, developed under the sponsorship of the FBI and the BJS, provides instructions for planning and conducting a system acquisition and offers guidelines on preparing an agency for conversion to the new system and to the NIBRS.

Originally designed with 52 data elements, the redesigned NIBRS captures up to 57 data elements via 6 types of data segments: administrative, offense, victim property, offender, and arrestee. Although, in the late 1980s, the FBI committed to hold all changes to the NIBRS in abeyance until a substantial amount of contributors implemented the system, modifications have been necessary. The system's flexibility has allowed the collection of four additional pieces of information to be captured within an incident: bias-motivated offenses (1990), the presence of gang activity (1997), data for law enforcement officers killed and assaulted (2003), and data on cargo theft (2005). The system has also allowed the addition of new codes to further specify location and property types (2010).

The FBI began accepting NIBRS data from a handful of agencies in January 1989. As more contributing law enforcement agencies become educated about the rich data available through incident-based reporting and as resources permit, more agencies are implementing the NIBRS. Based on the 2012 data submissions, 15 states submit all their data via the NIBRS and 32 state UCR Programs are certified for NIBRS participation.

Suspension of the *Crime Index* and the *Modified Crime Index*

In June 2004, the CJIS APB approved discontinuing the use of the *Crime Index* in the UCR program and its publications and directed the FBI to publish a violent crime total and a property crime total. The *Crime Index*, first published in *Crime in the United States* in 1960, was the title used for a simple aggregation of the seven main offense classifications (Part I offenses) in the Summary Reporting System. The Modified Crime Index was the number of Crime Index offenses plus arson.

For several years, the CJIS Division studied the appropriateness and usefulness of these indices and brought the matter before many advisory groups including the UCR Subcommittee of the CJIS APB, the ASUCRP, and a meeting of leading criminologists and sociologists hosted by the BJS. In short, the *Crime Index* and the *Modified Crime Index* were not true indicators of the degrees of criminality because they were always driven upward by the offense with the highest number, typically larceny-theft. The sheer volume of those offenses overshadowed more serious but less frequently committed offenses, creating a bias against a jurisdiction with a high number of larceny-thefts but a low number of other serious crimes such as murder and rape.

Recent Developments in UCR Program

In the fall of 2011, the APB recommended, and FBI Director Robert Mueller III approved, changing the definition of rape. Since 1929, in the SRS, rape had been defined as "the carnal knowledge of a female forcibly and against her will," (*UCR Handbook*, 2004, p.19). Beginning with the 2013 data collection, the SRS definition for the violent crime of rape will be: "Penetration, no matter how slight, of the vagina or anus with any body part or object, or oral penetration by a sex organ of another person, without the consent of the victim." This definition can be found in the *Summary Reporting System [SRS] User Manual*, Version 1.0, dated June 20, 2013. The FBI is developing reporting options for law enforcement agencies to meet this requirement, which will be built into the redeveloped data collection system.

In addition to approving the new definition of rape for the SRS, the APB and Director Mueller approved removing the word "forcible" from the name of the offense and also replacing the phrase "against the person's will" with "without the consent of the victim" in other sex-related offenses in the SRS, the NIBRS, the Hate Crime Statistics Program, and Cargo Theft.

In response to a directive by the U.S. Government's Office of Management and Budget, the national UCR Program has expanded its data collection categories for race from four (White, Black, American Indian or Alaska Native, and Asian or Other Pacific Islander) to five (White, Black or African American, American Indian or Alaska Native, Asian, and Native Hawaiian or Other Pacific Islander). Also, the ethnicity categories have changed from "Hispanic" to "Hispanic or Latino" and from "Non-Hispanic" to "Not Hispanic or Latino." These changes are reflected in data presented from 2012.

The national UCR Program staff continues to develop data collection methods to comply with both the William Wilberforce Trafficking Victims Protection Reauthorization Act of 2008 and the Matthew Shepard and James Byrd, Jr. Hate Crime Prevention Act of 2009. As a result, the FBI began accepting data on human trafficking as well as data on crimes motivated by "gender and gender identity" bias and "crimes committed by, and crimes directed against, juveniles" from contributors in January 2013.

Uniform Crime Reporting Program Changes Definition of Rape

For the first time in the more than 80-year history of the Uniform Crime Reporting (UCR) Program, the FBI has changed the definition of a Part 1 offense. In December 2011, then FBI Director Robert S. Mueller, III, approved revisions to the UCR Program's definition of rape as recommended by the FBI's Criminal Justice Information Services (CJIS) Division Advisory Policy Board (APB), which is made up of representatives from all facets of law enforcement.

Beginning in 2013, rape is defined for Summary UCR purposes as, "Penetration, no matter how slight, of the vagina or anus with any body part or object, or oral penetration by a sex organ of another person, without the consent of the victim." The new definition updated the 80-year-old historical definition of rape which was "carnal knowledge of a female forcibly and against her will." Effectively, the revised definition expands rape to include both male and female victims and offenders, and reflects the various forms of sexual penetration understood to be rape, especially nonconsenting acts of sodomy, and sexual assaults with objects. Beginning in 2017, only this revised definition of rape was used.

"This new, more inclusive definition will provide us with a more accurate understanding of the scope and volume of these crimes," said Attorney General Eric Holder. Proponents of the new definition and of the omission of the term "forcible" say that the changes broaden the scope of the previously narrow definitions by capturing (1) data without regard to gender, (2) the penetration of any bodily orifice, penetration by any object or body part, and (3) offenses in which physical force is not involved. Now, for example, instances in which offenders use drugs or alcohol or incidents in which offenders sodomize victims of the same gender will be counted as rape for statistical purposes.

It has long been the UCR Program's mission to collect and publish data regarding the scope and nature of crime in the nation, including those for rape. Since the FBI began collecting data using the revised definition of rape in January 2013, program officials expected that the number of reported rapes would rise. According to David Cuthbertson, former FBI Assistant Director of the CJIS Division, "As we implement this change, the FBI is confident that the number of victims of this heinous crime will be more accurately reflected in national crime statistics."

About the Editor

Shana Hertz Hattis is a consulting writer-editor for Bernan Press. She holds a master of science in education degree in from Northwestern University and a bachelor's degree in journalism from the same university. She has previously edited *Vital Statistics of the United States: Births, Life Expectancy, Deaths, and Selected Health Data* and several volumes of *Crime in the United States* for Bernan.

SECTION II

OFFENSES KNOWN TO POLICE

VIOLENT CRIME

- MURDER

- RAPE

- ROBBERY

- AGGRAVATED ASSAULT

PROPERTY CRIME

- BURGLARY

- LARCENY-THEFT

- MOTOR VEHICLE THEFT

- ARSON

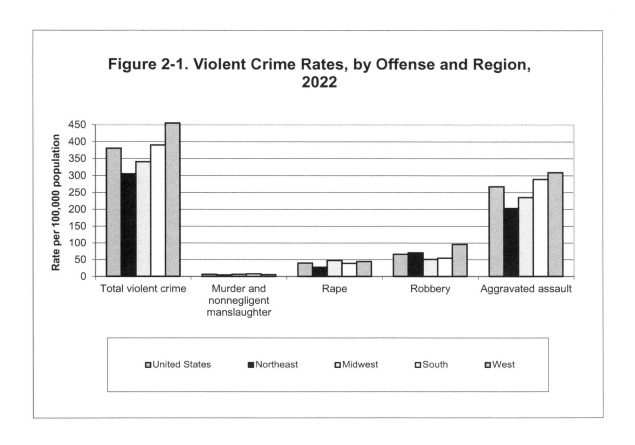

Figure 2-1. Violent Crime Rates, by Offense and Region, 2022

Definition

Violent crime consists of four offenses: murder and nonnegligent manslaughter, rape, robbery, and aggravated assault. According to the Uniform Crime Reporting (UCR) program, run by the Federal Bureau of Investigation (FBI), violent crimes involve either the use of force or the threat of force.

Data Collection

The data presented in *Crime in the United States* reflect the Hierarchy Rule, which counts only the most serious offense in a multiple-offense criminal incident. In descending order of severity, the violent crimes are murder and nonnegligent manslaughter, rape, robbery, and aggravated assault; these are followed by the property crimes of burglary, larceny-theft, and motor vehicle theft. Arson is also considered a property crime, but the Hierarchy Rule does not apply to the arson offense. In cases in which arson occurs in conjunction with another violent or property crime, the arson and the additional crime are reported. More information on the expanded violent crime tables (which are available online but not included in this publication) can be found in Section I.

Important Note: Transition to NIBRS

As of January 1, 2021, the FBI's National Incident-Based Reporting System (NIBRS) became the national standard for law enforcement crime data reporting in the United States. The 2021 data year will mark the first time that the FBI and BJS estimate reported crime in the United States based solely on NIBRS data. As of June 2022, all 50 U.S. states and the District of Columbia were certified to report crime data to NIBRS.

National Volume, Trends, and Rate

In 2022, an estimated 1,232,428 violent crimes occurred in the United States, a decrease of 1.7 percent from the 2021 estimate. An estimated 369.8 violent crimes were committed per 100,000 inhabitants in 2022, a decrease of 2.1 percent from 2021. Aggravated assaults accounted for 72.5 percent of violent crimes, the highest percentage of violent crimes reported to law enforcement. Robbery accounted for 17.9 percent of violent crimes, rape accounted for 7.9 percent of violent crimes, and murder accounted for 1.7 percent of violent crimes. (Table 1)

Occurrences of murder, rape, and aggravated assault incidents decreased from 2022 to 2021, with murder decreasing by 6.1 percent, rape by 8.2 percent, and aggravated assault by 1.1 percent. Robbery occurrences increased 1.3 percent. (Table 1)

In 2022, offenders used firearms in 77.0 percent of the nation's murders. (Expanded Homicide data)

Many violent crimes are committed by people in known relationships. Figure 2 shows the number of murder victims who knew their offender. In the figure, the relationship categories of husband and wife include common-law spouses and ex-spouses. The categories of mother, father, sister, brother, son, and daughter include stepparents, stepchildren, and stepsiblings. The category of "acquaintance" includes homosexual relationships and the composite category of other known-to-victim offenders.

Regional Offense Trends and Rate

The UCR program divides the United States into four regions: the Northeast, the South, the Midwest, and the West. (More details concerning geographic regions are provided in Appendix IV.) The population distribution of the regions can be found in Table 3, and the estimated volume and rate of violent crime by region are provided in Table 4.

The Northeast

The Northeast accounted for an estimated 17.1 percent of the nation's population in 2022 and an estimated 13.7 percent of its violent crimes. The estimated number of violent crimes increased 16.9 percent from 2021 to 2022. Murders decreased 8.9 percent in the Northeast. Rapes decreased 0.3 percent. Robberies increased 13.3 percent. Aggravated assaults rose 21.8 percent from 2021 to 2022. In 2022, there were an estimated 305.0 violent crimes per 100,000 inhabitants, a 17.3 percent increase from 2021. (Tables 3 and 4)

The Midwest

With an estimated 20.6 percent of the total population of the United States, the Midwest accounted for 18.4 percent of the nation's estimated number of violent crimes in 2022. The region had an 8.6 percent decrease in violent crime from 2021 to 2022. The estimated number of aggravated assaults decreased 8.9 percent, while the estimated number of robberies fell 8.3 percent. The estimated number of murders fell 10.6 percent. The estimated number of rapes decreased 7.5 percent. The rate of violent crime per 100,000 inhabitants in the Midwest was 387.8, a decrease of 8.6 percent from 2021 to 2022. (Tables 3 and 4)

The South

The South, the nation's most populous region, accounted for 38.6 percent of the nation's population in 2022. Approximately 38.6 percent of violent crimes in 2022 occurred in the South. Violent crime decreased 5.5 percent from 2021 to 2022. The estimated number of murders fell 5.4 percent and the estimated number of aggravated assaults fell 5.6 percent. Robberies dropped 4.7 percent, while rapes decreased by 5.5 percent. The estimated rate of violent crime in the South was 390.5 incidents per 100,000 inhabitants in 2022, a 6.5 percent increase from 2021. (Tables 3 and 4)

The West

With 23.6 percent of the nation's population in 2022, the West accounted for an estimated 23.6 percent of the nation's violent crime. Violent crime in the West increased 2.9 percent from 2021 to 2022. Murders dropped 1.3 percent, rapes decreased by 5.4 percent; however, robberies dropped increased by 6.8 percent, and aggravated assault increased by 3.2 percent. The region's violent crime rate in 2022 was 454.9 per 100,000 inhabitants, a 2.7 percent rise from 2021. (Tables 3 and 4)

Community Types

The UCR program aggregates crime data into three community types: metropolitan statistical areas (MSAs), cities outside MSAs, and nonmetropolitan counties outside MSAs. Appendix IV provides additional information regarding community types. In 2022, approximately 86.1 percent of the nation's population lived in MSAs. Residents of cities outside MSAs accounted for 5.7 percent of the country's population, and residents living in nonmetropolitan counties accounted for 8.2 percent of the population. (Table 2)

In the areas reporting violent crimes to the UCR Program, approximately 90.3 percent of these crimes occurred in MSAs, while 5.3 percent occurred in cities outside MSAs and 4.4 percent occurred in nonmetropolitan counties. By community type, the violent crime rates were estimated at 399.2 incidents per 100,000 inhabitants in MSAs, 353.9 incidents per 100,000 inhabitants in cities outside MSAs, and 205.2 incidents per 100,000 inhabitants in nonmetropolitan counties. (Table 2)

Population Groups: Trends and Rates

In the UCR program, data are also aggregated into population groups; these groups are described in more detail in Appendix IV. The nation's cities had an overall decrease of 2.4 percent in the estimated number of violent crimes from 2021 to 2022. By city population group, cities with 500,000 to

999,999 inhabitants had the largest decrease in the estimated number of violent crimes (−5.9 percent). Metropolitan counties experienced a 0.7 percent decrease in violent crimes from 2021 to 2022, while nonmetropolitan counties saw a 4.9 percent decrease and suburban areas saw a 0.6 percent decrease. (Table 12)

The law enforcement agencies in the nation's cities collectively reported a rate of 485.5 violent crimes per 100,000 inhabitants in 2022. Law enforcement agencies in the subset of cities with 500,000 to 999,999 inhabitants reported the highest violent crime rate, 878.2 violent crimes per 100,000 inhabitants; the violent crime rate for all cities with 250,000 or more inhabitants was 781.77 per 100,000 inhabitants. Agencies in cities with less than 10,000 inhabitants reported the lowest violent crime rate (261.6 incidents per 100,000 inhabitants). Law enforcement agencies in the nation's metropolitan counties reported a collective violent crime rate of 261.9 per 100,000 inhabitants, while agencies in nonmetropolitan counties reported a collective rate of 216.5 violent crimes per 100,000 inhabitants and suburban areas reported a violent crime rate of 252.4 violent crimes per 100,000 inhabitants. (Table 16)

MURDER AND NONNEGLIGENT MANSLAUGHTER

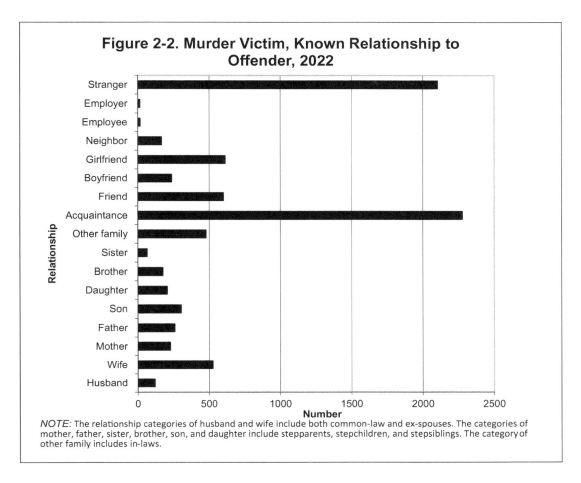

Figure 2-2. Murder Victim, Known Relationship to Offender, 2022

NOTE: The relationship categories of husband and wife include both common-law and ex-spouses. The categories of mother, father, sister, brother, son, and daughter include stepparents, stepchildren, and stepsiblings. The category of other family includes in-laws.

Definition

The UCR program defines murder and non-negligent manslaughter as the willful (non-negligent) killing of one human being by another. The classification of this offense is based solely on police investigation, rather than on the determination of a court, medical examiner, coroner, jury, or other judicial body. The UCR program does not include the following situations under this offense classification: deaths caused by negligence, suicide, or accident; justifiable homicides; and attempts to murder or assaults to murder, which are considered aggravated assaults.

Data Collection/Supplementary Homicide Data

The UCR provides supplementary information about murder victims and offenders by age, sex, and race; the types of weapons used in the murders; the relationships of the victims to the offenders; and the circumstances surrounding the incident. Law enforcement agencies are asked to provide this data for each murder reported to the UCR program. Data can be viewed in the Expanded Homicide Data section on the FBI's

Crime Explorer data page: https://crime-data-explorer.app.cloud.gov/pages/home. Some highlights from these tables have been included below.

National Volume, Trends, and Rates

An estimated 21,156 persons were murdered nationwide in 2022. This number was a 6.1 percent increase from the 2021 estimate, a 24.9 percent increase from 2018, and a 47.7 percent increase from 2013. The 2022 murder rate, 6.3 offenses per 100,000 inhabitants, was a 7.4 percent decrease from the 2021 rate, a 21.2 percent increase from 2018, and a 40.0 percent increase from 2013. Murder accounted for 1.7 percent of the overall estimated number of violent crimes in 2022. (Table 1)

Regional Offense Trends and Rates

The UCR program divides the United States into four regions: the Northeast, the South, the Midwest, and the West. (More details concerning geographic regions are provided in Appendix IV.) In 2022, 47.2 percent of murders were reported in the

South, the country's most populous region. The West reported 21.0 percent of all murders, while the Midwest reported 20.1 percent of all murders. The Northeast reported 11.7 percent of murders. (Table 3)

The Northeast

In 2022, the Northeast accounted for an estimated 17.1 percent of the nation's population and 11.7 percent of its estimated number of murders. With an estimated 2,466 murders, the Northeast saw an 8.9 percent decrease from the 2021 figure. The offense rate for the Northeast was 4.3 murders per 100,000 inhabitants in 2022, an 8.6 percent drop from 2021. (Tables 3 and 4)

The Midwest

The Midwest accounted for an estimated 20.6 percent of the nation's total population and 20.1 percent of the country's estimated number of murders in 2022. The Midwest reported an estimated 4,257 murders in 2022, down 10.6 percent from 2021. The region experienced a rate of 6.2 murders per 100,000 inhabitants in 2022, 10.5 percent below its 2021 rate of 6.9. (Tables 3 and 4)

The South

The South accounted for an estimated 38.6 percent of the nation's population in 2022 and 47.2 percent of the nation's murders, the highest proportion among the four regions. The estimated 9,994 murders represented a 5.4 percent decrease from the 2021 figure. The region's estimated rate of 7.8 murders per 100,000 inhabitants represented a decrease of 6.5 percent from the estimated rate for 2021. (Tables 3 and 4)

The West

The West accounted for an estimated 23.6 percent of the nation's population and 21.0 percent of the estimated number of murders in 2022. The West experienced an estimated 4,439 murders, a 1.3 percent decrease from the 2021 estimate. The region's murder rate was 5.6 per 100,000 inhabitants, down 1.5 percent from 2021. (Tables 3 and 4)

Community Types

The UCR program aggregates data for three community types: metropolitan statistical areas (MSAs), cities outside MSAs, and nonmetropolitan counties outside MSAs. (See Appendix IV for definitions.) In 2022, MSAs accounted for 86.1 percent of the nation's population and 85.6 percent of the estimated total number of murders. MSAs experienced a rate of 6.6 murders per 100,000 inhabitants in 2022. Cities outside MSAs accounted for 5.7 percent of the U.S. population and 4.7 percent of the estimated murders in the nation. The murder rate for cities outside MSAs was 5.8 per 100,000

inhabitants. In 2022, approximately 8.2 percent of the nation's population lived in nonmetropolitan counties outside MSAs. An estimated 1,208 murders took place in these counties, accounting for 6.4 percent of the nation's estimated total. The murder rate in nonmetropolitan counties was 4.4 per 100,000 inhabitants. (Table 2)

Population Groups: Trends and Rates

The UCR program uses the following population group designations in its data presentations: cities (grouped according to population size) and counties (classified as either metropolitan or nonmetropolitan). A breakdown of these classifications is provided in Appendix IV.

From 2021 to 2022, the nation's cities experienced a 5.0 percent decrease in homicides, with only cities with less than 10,000 inhabitants experiencing an increase. Cities with 10,000 to 24,999 residents experienced the smallest decrease, 0.7 percent, while cities with 500,000 to 999,999 residents experienced the biggest decrease, 8.7 percent. Metropolitan counties experienced a 9.9 percent decrease from 2021 to 2022, while nonmetropolitan counties experienced a decrease of 7.8 percent. Suburban areas experienced a decrease of 8.1 percent. (Table 12)

In 2022, cities collectively had a rate of 7.8 murders per 100,000 inhabitants. Cities with 500,000 to 999,999 inhabitants had the highest murder rate (16.2 murders per 100,000 inhabitants). Cities with 10,000 to 24,999 inhabitants had the lowest murder rate, with 4.0 murders per 100,000 inhabitants. The homicide rate for metropolitan counties was 4.3 murders per 100,000 inhabitants, while the rate for nonmetropolitan counties was 4.8 murders per 100,000 inhabitants. Suburban areas had a homicide rate of 3.9 per 100,000 inhabitants. (Table 16)

Supplementary Homicide Reports Data

VICTIMS/OFFENDERS

Based on 2022 supplemental homicide data (where the ages, sexes, or races of the murder victims were identified), 83.5 percent of victims were 20 years of age or over, 16.5 percent were 19 years of age or less, and the age of 0.9 percent of the victims was unknown. Of the 19,200 murder victims represented in the 2022 expanded tables whose gender was identified, 78.1 percent were male. Concerning race among the 18,746 victims for whom race was identified, 41.1 percent of victims were White, 55.9 percent were Black or African American, and 3.0 percent were of other races. Race was unknown for 454 victims. Approximately 16.7 percent of victims were of Hispanic origin. For murders in which the gender of the offender was identified, 76.1 percent were males; the sex of offenders for 13.3 percent of homicides was unknown. For the offenders for whom race was identified,

57.6 percent were Black or African American, 39.5 percent were White, and 2.8 percent were other races; 3,076 offenders (15.6 percent) were of unknown race. Approximately 13.3 percent of offenders were of Hispanic origin. (Expanded Homicide Data)

VICTIM-OFFENDER RELATIONSHIPS

For incidents in which the victim-offender relationship was specified (including the designation of "unknown"), 11.5 percent of victims were slain by family members, 10.5 percent were murdered by strangers, and 23.7 percent were killed by someone they knew other than family members (acquaintances, neighbors, friends, employers, romantic partners, employees, etc.). The victim-offender relationship was unknown in 51.2 percent of incidents. (Expanded Homicide Data)

CIRCUMSTANCES/WEAPONS

Concerning the known circumstances surrounding murders, and including murders with unknown circumstances, 3.1 percent of victims were murdered during gang killings in 2022. Circumstances of rape, robbery, burglary, larceny-theft, motor vehicle theft, and arson accounted for 3.7 percent of murders. Circumstances were unknown for 48.5 percent of reported homicides. Of the homicides for which the type of weapon was specified, 77.0 percent involved the use of firearms. Of the identified firearms used, handguns comprised 53.7 percent of the total. (Expanded Homicide Data)

RAPE

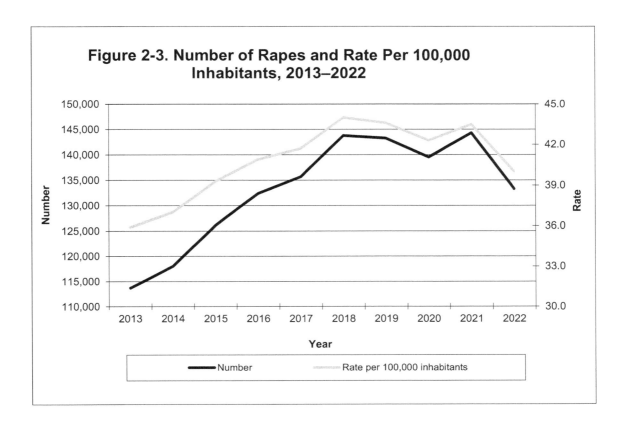

Figure 2-3. Number of Rapes and Rate Per 100,000 Inhabitants, 2013–2022

Definition

In 2013, the FBI UCR Program began collecting rape data under a revised definition within the Summary Reporting System. Previously, offense data for forcible rape were collected under the legacy UCR definition: the carnal knowledge of a female forcibly and against her will. Beginning with the 2013 data year, the term "forcible" was removed from the offense title, and the definition was changed. The revised UCR definition of rape is: penetration, no matter how slight, of the vagina or anus with any body part or object, or oral penetration by a sex organ of another person, without the consent of the victim. Attempts or assaults to commit rape are also included in the statistics presented here; however, statutory rape and incest are excluded.

In 2016, the FBI Director approved the recommendation to discontinue the reporting of rape data using the UCR legacy definition beginning in 2017. However, to maintain the 20-year trend in Table 1, national estimates for rape under the legacy definition are provided along with estimates under the revised definition. The UCR Program counts one offense for each victim of a rape, attempted rape, or assault with intent to rape, regardless of the victim's age. Non-consensual sexual relations involving a familial member is considered rape, not incest. All other crimes of a sexual nature are considered to be Part II offenses; as such, the UCR Program collects only arrest data for those crimes. The offense of statutory rape, in which no force is used but the female victim is under the age of consent, is included in the arrest total for the sex offenses category.

National Volume, Trends, and Rates

In 2022, the estimated number of rapes (revised definition), 133,294, decreased 5.4 percent from the 2021 estimate. The estimated volume of rapes in 2022 was 9.0 percent lower than the 2018 estimate. (Table 1)

Regional Offense Trends and Rates

The UCR program divides the United States into four regions: the Northeast, the South, the Midwest, and the West. (More details concerning geographic regions are provided in Appendix IV) Regional analysis offers estimates of the volume of rapes, the percent change from the previous year's estimate, and the rate of rape per 100,000 inhabitants in each region.

NORTHEAST

The Northeast made up 17.1 percent of the U.S. population in 2022. An estimated 15,530 rapes—11.7 percent of the national total—occurred in the Northeast. This was a decrease of 0.3 percent from the 2021 estimated figure. The region's rate of rape occurrences—27.2 per 100,000 inhabitants—was a 0.1 percent rise from 2021. (Tables 3 and 4)

MIDWEST

The Midwest accounted for 20.6 percent of the U.S. population in 2022. Of all the rapes in the nation, 24.6 percent occurred in the Midwest in 2022. The 2022 estimate (32.847 rapes) represented a decrease of 7.5 percent from the 2021 estimate. The region's rate of rape occurrences—47.8 per 100,000 inhabitants—was a 7.4 percent drop from 2021. (Tables 3 and 4)

SOUTH

The South, the nation's most populous region, accounted for an estimated 38.6 percent of the nation's population in 2022; the region also accounted for an estimated 37.6 percent of the nation's estimated number of rapes. An estimated 50,097 victims reported rape in the South in 2022, down 5.5 percent from 2021. The region's rate of rape occurrences—38.9 per 100,000 inhabitants—was a 6.5 percent drop from 2021. (Tables 3 and 4)

WEST

The West accounted for 23.6 percent of the nation's population in 2022. The region also accounted for 26.1 percent of the nation's total number of estimated rapes with an estimated 34,820 offenses. The West saw a 5.4 percent decrease in rapes from 2021 to 2022. The region's rate of rape occurrences—44.2 per 100,000 inhabitants—was a 5.5 percent drop from 2021. (Tables 3 and 4)

Community Types

Using the U.S. Office of Management and Budget's designations, the UCR program aggregates crime data by type of community in which the offenses occur: metropolitan statistical areas (MSAs), cities outside MSAs, and nonmetropolitan counties outside MSAs. (Appendix IV provides more detailed information about community types.)

MSAS

In 2022, MSAs accounted for 86.1 percent of the nation's population and 80.2 percent of the nation's estimated number of rapes (revised definition). An estimated 112,744 victims were forcibly raped in metropolitan areas. MSAs had a rape rate of 39.3 per 100,000 inhabitants. (Table 2)

CITIES OUTSIDE MSAS

Cities outside MSAs are mostly incorporated areas that are served by city law enforcement agencies. Although accounting for only 5.7 percent of the U.S. population in 2022, cities outside MSAs accounted for 6.8 percent of the nation's estimated rapes. Cities outside MSAs had a rate of 53.3 rapes per 100,000 inhabitants. (Table 2)

NONMETROPOLITAN COUNTIES

In 2022, approximately 8.2 percent of the nation's population lived in nonmetropolitan counties outside MSAs (counties made up of mostly non-incorporated areas that are served by noncity law enforcement agencies). Collectively, these areas had an estimated 10,506 rapes, representing 7.1 percent of the nation's estimated total. Nonmetropolitan counties had a rate of 38.4 rapes per 100,000 inhabitants. (Table 2)

POPULATION GROUPS: TRENDS AND RATES

The UCR program uses the following population group designations in its data presentations: cities (grouped according to population size) and counties (classified as either metropolitan or nonmetropolitan). A breakdown of these classifications is provided in Appendix IV.

From 2021 to 2022, the nation's cities experienced a 7.0 percent decrease in rapes. Cities with 500,000 to 999,999 inhabitants experienced the greatest decrease (10.0 percent). Metropolitan counties experienced a 7.7 percent decrease from 2021 to 2022, while nonmetropolitan counties experienced a 9.0 percent decrease and suburban areas experienced a 7.1 percent decrease. (Table 12)

In 2022, cities collectively had a rate of 45.9 rapes per 100,000 inhabitants. Cities with 500,000 to 999,999 inhabitants had the highest rate of rape (60.0 rapes per 100,000 inhabitants). Cities with 25,000 to 49,999 inhabitants had the lowest rate, with 38.0 rapes per 100,000 inhabitants. The rape rate for metropolitan counties was 31.2 per 100,000 inhabitants, and for nonmetropolitan counties, it was 40.8 per 100,000 inhabitants. Suburban areas had a rape rate of 32.2 per 100,000 inhabitants. (Table 16)

Due to a system upgrade in 2019, the FBI now calculates rates for each offense based on the individual offenses and population published for each agency in tables 8–11. (Previous to 2019, when agencies were published in tables 8–11, but they had one or two offenses removed from publication due to not meeting UCR publication guidelines, the agency's data was not used to calculate rates for this table.) The FBI derived the offense rates by dividing the individual offense counts by the individual populations covered by contributing agencies for which 12 months of publishable data were supplied and then multiplying the resulting figure by 100,000. See Appendix V for the agency and population counts.

ROBBERY

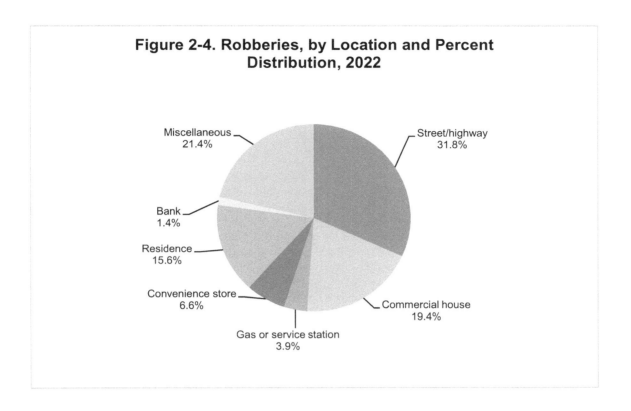

Figure 2-4. Robberies, by Location and Percent Distribution, 2022

- Miscellaneous 21.4%
- Street/highway 31.8%
- Bank 1.4%
- Residence 15.6%
- Convenience store 6.6%
- Gas or service station 3.9%
- Commercial house 19.4%

Definition

The UCR program defines robbery as the taking or attempt to take anything of value from the care, custody, or control of a person or persons by force or threat of force or violence and/ or by putting the victim in fear.

National Volume, Trends, and Rates

In 2022, the estimated robbery total (220,450) increased 1.3 percent from the 2021 estimate. The 5-year robbery trend (2018 data compared with 2022 data) showed a decrease of 21.9 percent, and the decrease since 2013 (10-year estimates) was 36.4 percent. The 2022 estimated robbery rate (66.1 per 100,000 inhabitants) showed an increase of 0.9 percent when compared with the 2021 rate, while the 5-year trend showed a 23.3 percent decreased and the 10-year trend showed a 39.7 percent decrease. (Table 1)

Regional Offense Trends and Rates

The UCR program divides the United States into four regions: the Northeast, the South, the Midwest, and the West. (More details concerning geographic regions are provided in Appendix IV.)

NORTHEAST

The Northeast, with an estimated 17.1 percent of the nation's population in 2022, accounted for 18.3 percent of the nation's estimated number of robberies. The estimated number of robberies (40,256) increased 13.3 percent from 2021. The rate for this region was 70.6 robberies per 100,000 inhabitants, up 13.7 percent from the 2021 figure. (Tables 3 and 4)

MIDWEST

The Midwest accounted for 20.6 percent of the total population of the United States and 15.9 percent of its estimated number of robberies in 2022. An estimated 35,044 robberies occurred in the Midwest in 2022, an 8.3 percent decrease from the estimated figure from 2021. The region's robbery rate was 50.9 robberies per 100,000 inhabitants in 2022, down 8.2 percent from 2021. (Tables 3 and 4)

SOUTH

The South, the nation's most highly populated region, accounted for an estimated 38.6 percent of the nation's population and 31.7 percent of the nation's estimated number of robberies in 2022. Robberies accounted for an estimated 69.846 violent crimes in this region in 2022, representing a

4.7 percent decrease from the 2021 figure. The 2022 robbery rate in the South was 54.3 per 100,000 inhabitants, down 5.7 percent from 2021. (Tables 3 and 4)

WEST

The West was home to an estimated 23.6 percent of the nation's population and accounted for 34.2 percent of the nation's estimated number of robberies in 2022. The estimated number of robberies (75,304) in the region in 2022 represented a 6.8 percent increase from the 2021 figure. The rate of robberies per 100,000 inhabitants in the West was 95.6, a 6.6 percent increasefrom the 2021 rate. (Tables 3 and 4)

Community Types

The UCR program aggregates data for three community types: metropolitan statistical areas (MSAs), cities outside MSAs, and nonmetropolitan counties outside MSAs. MSAs include a central city or urbanized area with at least 50,000 inhabitants, as well as the county that contains the principal city and other adjacent counties that have, as defined by the U.S. Office of Management and Budget, a high degree of social and economic integration as measured through commuting. Cities outside MSAs are mostly incorporated areas, and nonmetropolitan counties are made up of mostly unincorporated areas served by non-city law enforcement.

In 2022, MSAs were home to an estimated 86.1 percent of the nation's population, and 94.5 percent of the nation's estimated number of robberies took place in these areas. Robberies in MSAs occurred at a rate of 74.5 per 100,000 inhabitants. Cities outside MSAs accounted for 5.7 percent of the U.S. population and 1.9 percent of the estimated number of robberies in the nation. The robbery rate for cities outside MSAs was 24.1 per 100,000 inhabitants. Nonmetropolitan counties made up 8.2 percent of the nation's estimated population and 0.8 percent of the nation's estimated robberies, with a rate of 7.2 robberies per 100,000 inhabitants. (Table 2)

Population Groups: Trends and Rates

The national UCR program aggregates data by various population groups, which include cities, metropolitan counties, and nonmetropolitan counties. A definition of these groups can be found in Appendix IV.

The number of robberies in cities as a whole decreased by 1.4 percent between 2021 and 2022. Among the population groups and subsets labeled *city*, those cities with 500,000 to 999,999 inhabitants had the greatest decrease in the number of robberies (6.9 percent). Metropolitan counties had a 4.4 percent increase in the estimated number of robberies, while nonmetropolitan counties showed a 6.3 percent decrease. The number of robberies in suburban areas rose 2.3 percent. (Table 12)

Among the population groups, the nation's cities collectively had a rate of 96.0 robberies per 100,000 inhabitants. Of the population groups and subsets designated *city*, those with 1,000,000 or more inhabitants had the highest rate (224.0 per 100,000 inhabitants), while those with fewer than 10,000 inhabitants had the lowest rate (27.2 per 100,000 inhabitants) of robberies. Of the two county groups, metropolitan counties had a rate of 31.1 robberies per 100,000 inhabitants, while nonmetropolitan counties had a rate of 7.5 robberies per 100,000 inhabitants. Suburban areas had a robbery rate of 32.0 per 100,000 inhabitants. (Table 16)

Due to a system upgrade in 2019, the FBI now calculates rates for each offense based on the individual offenses and population published for each agency in tables 8–11. (Previous to 2019, when agencies were published in tables 8–11, but they had one or two offenses removed from publication due to not meeting UCR publication guidelines, the agency's data was not used to calculate rates for this table.) The FBI derived the offense rates by dividing the individual offense counts by the individual populations covered by contributing agencies for which 12 months of publishable data were supplied and then multiplying the resulting figure by 100,000. See Appendix V for the agency and population counts.

OFFENSE ANALYSIS

The UCR program collects supplemental data about robberies to document the use of weapons, the dollar loss associated with the offense, and the location types.

ROBBERY BY WEAPON

Firearms were used in 37.1 percent of robberies in 2022. Offenders used knives or cutting instruments in 8.5 percent of these crimes, strong-arm tactics in 42.5 percent of incidents, and other dangerous weapons in 11.8 percent of offenses. (Table 19)

ROBBERY TRENDS BY LOCATION

Among the location types, residence robberies had the greatest percentage decrease from 2021 to 2022, declining 5.2 percent. Robberies that occurred on streets and highways decreased 1.5 percent, while bank robberies increased 6.5 percent. (Table 23)

By location type, the greatest proportion of robberies in 2022 occurred on streets and highways (31.8 percent). Robbers targeted commercial houses in 19.4 percent of offenses and struck residences in 15.6 percent of offenses. Convenience stores accounted for 6.6 percent of robberies, followed by gas and service stations (3.9 percent) and banks (1.4 percent). (Table 23)

AGGRAVATED ASSAULT

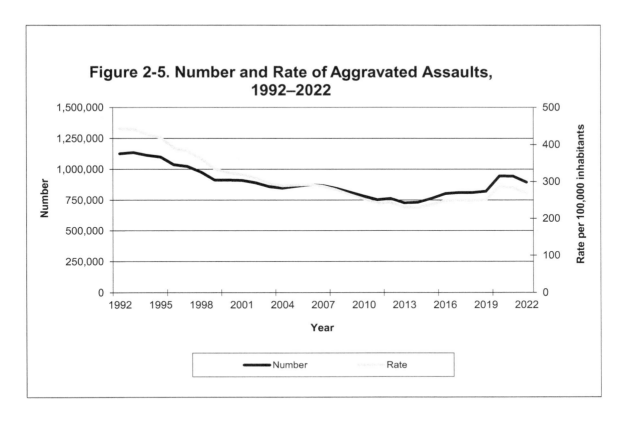

Figure 2-5. Number and Rate of Aggravated Assaults, 1992–2022

Definition

The UCR program defines aggravated assault as an unlawful attack by one person upon another for the purpose of inflicting severe or aggravated bodily injury. This type of assault is usually accompanied by the use of a weapon or by other means likely to produce death or great bodily harm. Attempted aggravated assaults that involve the display or threat of a gun, knife, or other weapon are included in this crime category because serious personal injury would likely result if these assaults were completed. When aggravated assault and larceny-theft occur together, the offense falls under the category of robbery.

National Volume, Trends, and Rates

In 2022, estimated occurrences of aggravated assaults totaled 893,980, a 1.1 percent decrease from the 2021 figure, a 9.2 percent increase when compared with the estimate for 2018, and a 22.6 percent increase when compared to 2013. The estimated rate of aggravated assault in 2022 was 268.2 per 100,000 inhabitants, a 1.5percent decrease from 2021, a 7.2 percent increase from 2018, and a 16.3 percent increase from 2013. (Table 1)

Among the four types of violent crime offenses (murder, rape, robbery, and aggravated assault), aggravated assault typically has the highest rate of occurrence. This trend continued in 2022. (Table 1)

Regional Offense Trends and Rates

The UCR program divides the United States into four regions: the Northeast, the South, the Midwest, and the West. (More details concerning geographic regions are provided in Appendix IV.)

NORTHEAST

The region with the smallest proportion of the nation's population (an estimated 17.1 percent in 2022) also accounted for the smallest proportion of the nation's estimated number of aggravated assaults (12.9 percent). Occurrences of aggravated assault increased 21.8 percent from 2021 to 2022, rising to an estimated 115,747 incidents. The region continued to have the lowest aggravated assault rate in the nation, at 202.9 incidents per 100,000 inhabitants, although this represented a 22.3 percent increase from the rate in 2021. (Tables 3 and 4)

MIDWEST

With 20.6 percent of the nation's total population in 2022, the Midwest accounted for approximately 18.1 percent of the nation's estimated number of aggravated assaults. Occurrences of this offense dropped 8.9 percent from the estimated total for 2021, falling to an estimated 161,914 incidents. The region's aggravated assault rate, at 289.6 incidents per 100,000 inhabitants, represented an 8.8 percent decrease from the 2021 rate. (Tables 3 and 4)

SOUTH

The South, the nation's most highly populated region, accounted for an estimated 38.6 percent of the nation's population in 2022 and the largest amount of the nation's estimated number of aggravated assaults (41.7 percent). From 2021 to 2022, the estimated number of aggravated assaults decreased 5.6 percent to a total of 372,717 incidents. The rate of aggravated assaults fell 6.7 percent to 289.6 incidents per 100,000 inhabitants. (Tables 3 and 4)

WEST

In 2022, the West was home to an estimated 23.6 percent of the nation's population. The region accounted for 27.2 percent of the nation's estimated number of aggravated assaults. From 2021 to 2022, the estimated number of offenses increased 3,2 percent to a total of 243,602 incidents. The rate of aggravated assaults increased 3.0 percent to 309.4 incidents per 100,000 inhabitants. (Tables 3 and 4)

Community Types

The UCR program aggregates data for three community types: metropolitan statistical areas (MSAs), cities outside MSAs, and nonmetropolitan counties outside MSAs. MSAs include a central city or urbanized area with at least 50,000 inhabitants, as well as the county that contains the principal city and other adjacent counties that have a high degree of social and economic integration as measured through commuting. Cities outside MSAs are mostly incorporated areas, and nonmetropolitan counties are made up of mostly unincorporated areas. (For additional information about community types, see Appendix IV.)

In 2022, 86.1 percent of the nation's population lived in MSAs, where the rate of aggravated assault was an estimated 278.8 per 100,000 inhabitants. Approximately 86.1 percent of all aggravated assaults occurred in MSAs. Cities outside MSAs (with 5.7 percent of the U.S. population and 5.0 percent of aggravated assaults) had a rate of aggravated assault of 270.8 offenses per 100,000 inhabitants. Nonmetropolitan

counties accounted for 8.2 percent of the U.S. population and 4.2 percent of aggravated assaults. Nonmetropolitan counties had an offense rate of 155.2 aggravated assaults per 100,000 inhabitants. (Table 2)

Population Groups: Trends and Rates

Cities experienced a collective drop of 1.9 percent in aggravated assaults from 2021 to 2022.Cities with 250,000 to 499,99 and cities with 500,000 to 999,999 inhabitants experienced the greatest decrease in aggravated assaults from 2021 to 2022 (16.9 percent). Cities with under 10,000 inhabitants experienced the only increase among cities, 0.5 percent. In metropolitan counties, the number of aggravated assaults rose 0.2 percent; in nonmetropolitan counties, this number fell 3.6 percent. Aggravated assaults in suburban areas increased 0.5 percent from 2021 to 2022. (Table 12)

Aggravated assault occurred at an estimated rate of 287.3 offenses per 100,000 inhabitants nationwide in 2022. The collective rate for cities was 335.8 aggravated assaults per 100,000 inhabitants. Among city population groups and subsets, rates ranged from a high of 614.1 offenses per 100,000 inhabitants (in cities with 500,000 to 999,999 inhabitants) to a low of 189.8 offenses per 100,000 inhabitants (in cities with 10,000 to 24,999 inhabitants). The aggravated assault rate was 195.2 in metropolitan counties and 163.5 in nonmetropolitan counties. It was 184.4 in suburban areas. (Table 16)

Due to a system upgrade in 2019, the FBI now calculates rates for each offense based on the individual offenses and population published for each agency in tables 8–11. (Previous to 2019, when agencies were published in tables 8–11, but they had one or two offenses removed from publication due to not meeting UCR publication guidelines, the agency's data was not used to calculate rates for this table.) The FBI derived the offense rates by dividing the individual offense counts by the individual populations covered by contributing agencies for which 12 months of publishable data were supplied and then multiplying the resulting figure by 100,000. See Appendix V for the agency and population counts.

Offense Analysis

AGGRAVATED ASSAULT BY WEAPON

Of the aggravated assault offenses for which law enforcement agencies provided expanded data in 2022, 36.6 percent were committed with firearms; 19.8 percent involved hands, feet, and/or fists; 15.7 percent involved knives or other cutting instruments; and 27.9 percent involved other weapons. (Table 19)

PROPERTY CRIME

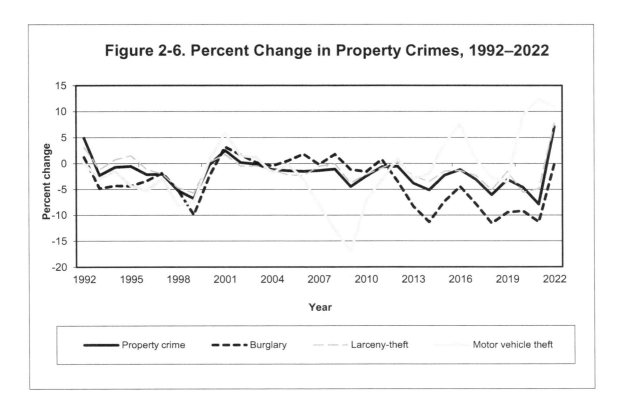

Figure 2-6. Percent Change in Property Crimes, 1992–2022

Definition

The UCR program's definition of property crime includes the offenses of burglary, larceny-theft, motor vehicle theft, and arson. The object of theft-type offenses is the taking of money or property without the use of force or threat of force against the victims. Property crime includes arson because the offense involves the destruction of property; however, arson victims may be subjected to force. Because of limited participation and the varying collection procedures conducted by local law enforcement agencies, only limited data are available for arson. More information on the expanded arson tables (which are available online but not included in this publication) can be found in Section I.

Data Collection

The data presented in *Crime in the United States* reflect the Hierarchy Rule, which counts only the most serious offense in a multiple-offense criminal incident. In descending order of severity, the violent crimes are murder and nonnegligent manslaughter, rape, robbery, and aggravated assault; these are followed by the property crimes of burglary, larceny-theft, and motor vehicle theft. The Hierarchy Rule does not apply to the offense of arson.

National Volume, Trends, and Rates

An estimated 6,513,829 property crimes were committed in the United States in 2022, representing a 7.1 percent increase from the 2021 (2-year trend) estimate, a 12.0 percent decrease from the 2018 (5-year trend) estimate, and a 24.9 percent decrease from the 2013 (10-year trend) estimate. (Table 1)

From 2021 to 2022, motor vehicle theft increased 10.9 percent; from 2018 to 2022, it increased 22.9 percent, and from 2013 to 2022, it increased 33.8 percent. Larceny-theft decreased 22.6 percent from 2013 to 2022, decreased 12.9 percent from 2018 to 2022, and increased 7.8 percent from 2021 to 2022. Burglary remained static from 2021, declined 29.1 percent from 2018, and 53.5 percent from 2013. (Table 1)

The estimated property crime rate per 100,000 inhabitants in 2022 was 1,954.4 incidents per 100,000 people, a 6.7 percent increase from the 2021 rate, a 13.6 percent decrease from the 2018 rate, and a 28.8 percent decrease from the 2013 rate. The rate of burglaries per 100,000 residents fell 55.9 percent from 2013 to 2022. The motor vehicle theft rates per 100,000 residents rose 26.9 percent from 2013 to 2022, and the larceny-theft rate declined 26.6 percent in that same timeframe. (Table 1)

Regional Offense Trends and Rates

The UCR program separates the United States into four regions: the Northeast, the Midwest, the South, and the West. (Geographic breakdowns can be found in Appendix IV.) Property crime data collected by the UCR program and aggregated by region reflected the following results.

NORTHEAST

The Northeast region accounted for 17.1 percent of the nation's population in 2022. The region also accounted for 13.0 percent of the nation's estimated number of property crimes in 2022. Law enforcement in the Northeast saw a 30.2 percent increase in the estimated number of property crimes from 2021 to 2022. The property crime rate for the Northeast, estimated at 1,484.8 incidents per 100,000 inhabitants, was 30.7 percent more than the 2021 rate. (Tables 3 and 4)

MIDWEST

The Midwest, with 20.6 percent of the U.S. population in 2022, accounted for 18.3 percent of the nation's estimated number of property crimes. Law enforcement in the Midwest saw the number of property crimes rise 2.9 percent from 2021 to 2022. The rate of property crime in the Midwest in 2022, estimated at 1,728.9 incidents per 100,000 inhabitants, represented a 3.0 percent increase from the 2021 rate. (Tables 3 and 4)

SOUTH

The South, the nation's most populous region, accounted for 39.0 percent of the U.S. population in 2022. The region also accounted for an estimated 41.4 percent of the nation's property crimes. The South experienced a 4.1 percent increase in its estimated number of property crimes from 2021 to 2022. The 2022 property crime rate, an estimated 2,458.0 incidents per 100,000 inhabitants, increased 2.9 percent from the 2021 rate. (Tables 3 and 4)

WEST

In 2022, the West accounted for 23.6 percent of the nation's population. The West also accounted for 29.7 percent of the nation's estimated number of property crimes. From 2021 to 2022, the estimated number of property crimes in this region increased 5.6 percent. The estimated property crime rate in the West in 2022, 2,458.0 incidents per 100,000 inhabitants, was a 5.4 percent increase from the 2021 rate. (Tables 3 and 4)

Community Types

The UCR program aggregates data by three community types: metropolitan statistical areas (MSAs), cities outside metropolitan areas, and nonmetropolitan counties. (Additional in-depth information regarding community types can be found in Appendix IV.) In 2022, 86.1 percent of the U.S. population lived in MSAs and had 86.6 percent of all property crimes. The property crime rate for MSAs was 2,059.8 per 100,000 inhabitants. Cities outside metropolitan areas, which accounted for 5.7 percent of the total population in 2022 and 5.1 percent of property crimes, had a property crime rate of 1,983.9 per 100,000 inhabitants. Nonmetropolitan counties, with 8.2 percent of the nation's population in 2022 and 3.1 percent of property crimes, had a property crime rate of 828.4 per 100,000 inhabitants. (Table 2)

Population Groups: Trends and Rates

The UCR program organizes the agencies that contribute data into population groups, which include cities, metropolitan counties, and nonmetropolitan counties. (Appendix IV provides further details about these groups.)

From 2021 to 2022, law enforcement in the nation's cities collectively reported a 5.8 percent increase in the number of property crimes. All city groups experienced increases in the number of property crimes; cities with 1,000,00 or more residents had the greatest increase at 12.4 percent. Metropolitan counties also experienced an increase of 3.2 percent from 2021 to 2022, while property crime in nonmetropolitan counties dropped 7.1 percent. Property crime in suburban areas rose 5.3 percent. (Table 12)

The nation's cities collectively had a property crime rate of 2,484.8 incidents per 100,000 inhabitants in 2022, ranging from a high of 3,801.2 per 100,000 inhabitants in cities with 500,000 to 999,999 residents to a low of 1,808.5 per 100,000 inhabitants in cities with 10,000 to 24,999 residents. Metropolitan counties had a rate of 1,255.4 incidents per 100,000 inhabitants, and nonmetropolitan counties had a rate of 857.6 incidents per 100,000 inhabitants. The rate was 1,463.8 in suburban areas. (Table 16)

Due to a system upgrade in 2019, the FBI now calculates rates for each offense based on the individual offenses and population published for each agency in tables 8–11. (Previous to 2019, when agencies were published in tables 8–11, but they had one or two offenses removed from publication due to not meeting UCR publication guidelines, the agency's data was not used to calculate rates for this table.) The FBI derived the offense rates by dividing the individual offense counts by the individual populations covered by contributing agencies for which 12 months of publishable data were supplied and then multiplying the resulting figure by 100,000. See Appendix V for the agency and population counts.

BURGLARY

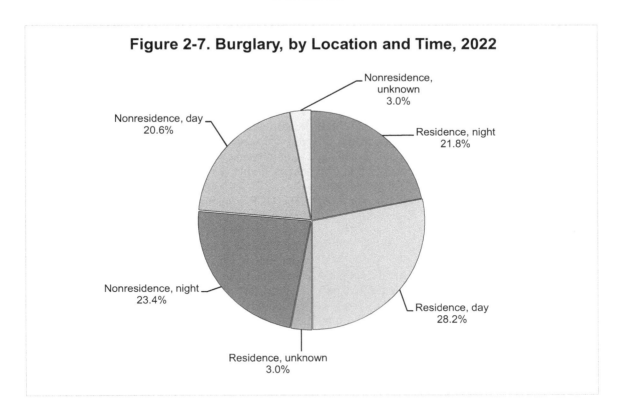

Figure 2-7. Burglary, by Location and Time, 2022

Nonresidence, unknown
3.0%

Residence, night
21.8%

Nonresidence, day
20.6%

Nonresidence, night
23.4%

Residence, day
28.2%

Residence, unknown
3.0%

Definition

The UCR program defines burglary as the unlawful entry of a structure to commit a felony or theft. To classify an offense as a burglary, the use of force to gain entry need not have occurred. The program has three subclassifications for burglary: forcible entry, unlawful entry where no force is used, and attempted forcible entry. The UCR definition of "structure" includes, but is not limited to, apartments, barns, house trailers or houseboats (when used as permanent dwellings), offices, railroad cars (but not automobiles), stables, and vessels (such as ships).

National Volume, Trends, and Rate

In 2022, there were an estimated 899,293 burglaries—a statistically insignificant change from 2021. There was a decrease of 29.1 percent in the number of burglaries in 2022 when compared with the 2018 estimate, and a decrease of 53.5 percent when compared with the 2013 estimate. Burglary accounted for 13.8 percent of the estimated number of property crimes committed in 2022. The burglary rate for the United States in 2022 was 269.8 incidents per 100,000 inhabitants, a 0.4 percent decrease from the 2021 rate, a 30.4 percent decrease

from the 2018 rate, and a 55.9 percent decrease from the 2013 rate. (Table 1)

Regional Offense Trends and Rates

The UCR program divides the United States into four regions: the Northeast, the Midwest, the South, and the West. (Details regarding these regions can be found in Appendix IV.) An analysis of burglary data by region showed the following details.

NORTHEAST

In 2022, 17.1 percent of the nation's population lived in the Northeast. This region accounted for 9.4 percent of the estimated total number of burglary offenses in the nation in 2022. The region's burglary rate, an estimated 148.3 offenses per 100,000 inhabitants, represented an increase of 6.1 percent from the 2021 rate. The number of incidents rose 5.7 percent to 84,614 from 2021 to 2022. (Tables 3 and 4)

MIDWEST

The Midwest accounted for 20.6 percent of the nation's population in 2022. This region accounted for 17.4 percent of the nation's estimated number of burglaries. In this region, the estimated number of burglaries dropped 4.76 percent to 156,574 from 2021 to 2022. The Midwest had a burglary rate of 227.6 offenses per 100,000 inhabitants, another 4.7 percent decrease from the 2021 rate. (Tables 3 and 4)

SOUTH

The South, the nation's most highly populated region (38.6 percent of all inhabitants), had the most burglaries in 2022 (an estimated 365,113 incidents); however, this represented q 1.6 percent drop from its estimate in 2021. This region accounted for 40.6 percent of all burglaries in the United States. The estimated rate of burglary in the South was 283.7 incidents per 100,000 inhabitants, a 2.7 percent decrease from the 2021 rate. (Tables 3 and 4)

WEST

The West accounted for 23.6 percent of the nation's population in 2022. This region accounted for an estimated 32.6 percent of the nation's burglaries. The region's burglary rate was 372.1, a 3.0 percent increase from the 2021 rate. The total number of burglaries (292,992) represented a 3.2 percent increase from the 2021 estimate. (Tables 3 and 4)

Community Types

The UCR program aggregates data by three community types: metropolitan statistical areas (MSAs), cities outside MSAs, and nonmetropolitan counties. (See Appendix IV for more information regarding community types.)

In 2022, 86.1 percent of the U.S. population lived in MSAs, and an estimated 83.6 percent of all burglaries occurred in this type of community. Inhabitants of cities outside MSAs accounted for 5.7 percent of the total population in 2022 and 5.7 percent of the estimated number of burglaries; nonmetropolitan counties, with 8.2 percent of the U.S. population, accounted for the remaining 5.3 percent of all burglaries. The burglary rates per 100,000 inhabitants were 273.9 in MSAs, 310.5 in cities outside MSAs, and 199.1 in nonmetropolitan counties. (Table 2)

Population Groups: Trends and Rates

In addition to analyzing data by region and community type, the UCR program aggregates crime statistics by population groups. Cities are categorized into six groups based on the number of inhabitants; counties are categorized into two groups, metropolitan and nonmetropolitan. (Appendix IV offers further details regarding these population groups.)

An examination of data from law enforcement agencies showed that the nation's cities experienced a collective 0.7 percent decrease in burglaries from 2021 to 2022. Burglaries decreased in most city groups and subsets, with cities with 500,000 to 999,999 inhabitants posting the greatest decrease (5.9 percent). Cities with 1,000,000 or more inhabitants experienced a 6.7 percent increase. The volume of burglaries decreased 2.0 percent in metropolitan counties, 11.4 percent in nonmetropolitan counties, and 1.0 percent in suburban areas. (Table 12)

The UCR program calculates burglary rates for population groups from the information provided by participating agencies that submitted all 12 months of offense data for the year. In 2022, the nation's cities had 327.8 offenses per 100,000 inhabitants. Cities with 500,000 to 999,999 inhabitants had the highest burglary rate at 536.4 incidents per 100,000 inhabitants. Cities with 10,000 to 24,999 inhabitants had the lowest burglary rate—241.5 incidents per 100,000 inhabitants. Metropolitan counties had a rate of 197.4 per 100,000 inhabitants, and nonmetropolitan counties had a rate of 208.2 per 100,000 inhabitants. The rate in suburban areas was 202.1 per 100,000 inhabitants. (Table 16)

Due to a system upgrade in 2019, the FBI now calculates rates for each offense based on the individual offenses and population published for each agency in tables 8–11. (Previous to 2019, when agencies were published in tables 8–11, but they had one or two offenses removed from publication due to not meeting UCR publication guidelines, the agency's data was not used to calculate rates for this table.) The FBI derived the offense rates by dividing the individual offense counts by the individual populations covered by contributing agencies for which 12 months of publishable data were supplied and then multiplying the resulting figure by 100,000. See Appendix V for the agency and population counts.

Offense Analysis

The UCR program requests that participating law enforcement agencies provide details regarding the nature of burglaries in their jurisdictions, such as type of entry, type of structure, time of day, and dollar loss associated with each offense.

Of all burglaries in 2022, 56.9 percent involved forcible entry, 36.9 percent were unlawful entries (without force), and 6.2 percent comprised forcible entry attempts. (Table 19)

LARCENY-THEFT

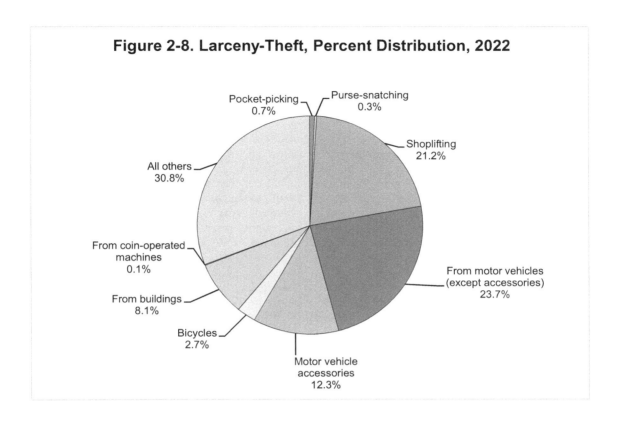

Figure 2-8. Larceny-Theft, Percent Distribution, 2022

Pocket-picking
0.7%

Purse-snatching
0.3%

Shoplifting
21.2%

All others
30.8%

From motor vehicles
(except accessories)
23.7%

From coin-operated
machines
0.1%

From buildings
8.1%

Bicycles
2.7%

Motor vehicle
accessories
12.3%

Definition

The UCR program defines larceny-theft as the unlawful taking, carrying, leading, or riding away of property from the possession or constructive possession of another. Examples are thefts of bicycles, motor vehicle parts and accessories, shoplifting, pocket picking, or the stealing of any property or article not taken by force and violence or by fraud. Attempted larcenies are included. Embezzlement, confidence games, forgery, check fraud, and so on, are excluded from this category.

National Volume, Trends, and Rates

Larceny-thefts accounted for an estimated 71.7 percent of property crimes in 2022, with an estimated 4,672,363 larceny-thefts nationwide. The estimated number of larceny-thefts rose 7.8 percent from 2021 to 2022. The 2022 estimate showed a 12.9 percent decline from the 2018 data and a 22.6 percent decrease from the 2013 estimate. The trend data also showed similar patterns in the larceny-theft rates per 100,000 inhabitants during these periods. The rate of larceny-thefts

(1,401.9 per 100,000 inhabitants in 2022) rose 7.4 percent from 2021 to 2022, declined 14.5 percent from 2018 to 2022, and declined 26.6 percent from 2013 to 2022. (Table 1)

Regional Offense Trends and Rates

The UCR program defines four regions within the United States: the Northeast, the Midwest, the South, and the West. (See Appendix IV for a geographical description of each region.)

NORTHEAST

The Northeast was the region with the smallest proportion (17.1 percent) of the U.S. population in 2022. The region also experienced the fewest larceny-thefts in the country, accounting for only 14.6 percent of all larceny-thefts. The estimated number of offenses in 2022 (681,113) represented a 36.0 percent increase from 2021, and the estimated rate—1,194.1 incidents per 100,000 inhabitants—represented a 36.5 percent increase from 2021. (Tables 3 and 4)

MIDWEST

With 20.6 percent of the U.S. population in 2022, the Midwest accounted for an estimated 18.1 percent of the nation's larceny-thefts. The estimated number of offenses (846,896) rose 1.8 percent from the 2021 total, and the estimated rate of occurrence (1,231.2 incidents per 100,000 inhabitants) also rose 1.8 percent. (Tables 3 and 4)

SOUTH

With nearly two-fifths of the U.S. population in 2022 (38.6 percent), the South had the nation's highest proportion of larceny-theft offenses: an estimated 40.0 percent. Estimated offenses in this region in 2022 totaled 1,869,989, a 4.4 percent increase from the 2021 estimate. The South's larceny-theft rate—estimated at 1,452.8 offenses per 100,000 inhabitants—increased 3.3 percent from the 2021 estimate. (Tables 3 and 4)

WEST

In 2022, an estimated 23.6 percent of the U.S. population lived in the West. This region was also where 27.3 percent of the nation's estimated number of larceny-thefts took place. Occurrences of larceny-theft increased 5.3 percent from 2021 to 2022, rising to an estimated total of 1,274,365 offenses. The region's larceny-theft rate, estimated at 1,618.4 offenses per 100,000 inhabitants, represented an increase of 5.1 percent from the 2021 rate. (Tables 3 and 4)

Community Types

The UCR program aggregates data for three community types: metropolitan statistical areas (MSAs), cities outside MSAs, and nonmetropolitan counties outside MSAs. MSAs include a central city or urbanized area with at least 50,000 inhabitants, as well as the county that contains the principal city and other adjacent counties that share a high degree of social and economic integration as measured through commuting. Cities outside MSAs are mostly incorporated areas, and nonmetropolitan counties are composed of unincorporated areas. (See Appendix IV for more information regarding community types.)

In 2022, MSAs were home to an estimated 86.1 percent of the nation's population and experienced 86.4 percent of the nation's larceny-theft incidents. Cities outside MSAs

accounted for 5.7 percent of the U.S. population and 5.4 percent of larceny-theft offenses. Nonmetropolitan counties, which were home to 8.2 percent of the nation's population, accounted for 2.7 percent of the estimated number of larceny-theft offenses. The larceny-theft rates per 100,000 inhabitants were 1,478.7 in MSAs, 1,507.7 in cities outside MSAs, and 523.4 in nonmetropolitan counties. (Table 2)

Population Groups: Trends and Rates

In cities, collectively, occurrences of larceny-theft rose 5.1 percent between 2021 and 2022, with all city groups and subsets experiencing increases. Cities with 1,000,00 or more inhabitants experienced the greatest increase (11.7 percent). Metropolitan counties experienced an increase of 3.9 percent in larceny theft, while the number of incidents nonmetropolitan counties decreased 5.0 percent but rose 6.1 percent in suburban areas. (Table 12)

Based on reports of larceny-theft offenses from U.S. law enforcement agencies that submitted 12 months of complete data for 2022, this offense occurred at a rate of 1,459.2 offenses per 100,000 inhabitants. The collective rate for cities was 1,776.2 offenses per 100,000 inhabitants. Among city population groups and subsets, cities with 500,000 to 999,000 inhabitants had the highest larceny-theft rate, 2,478.1 incidents per 100,000 inhabitants. Cities with 10,000 to 24,999 inhabitants had the lowest rate, at 1,385.5. In metropolitan counties, the rate was 890.5 incidents per 100,000 inhabitants; in nonmetropolitan counties, the rate was 538.9 incidents per 100,000 inhabitants. The rate in suburban areas was 1,078.4 incidents per 100,000 inhabitants. (Table 16)

Due to a system upgrade in 2019, the FBI now calculates rates for each offense based on the individual offenses and population published for each agency in tables 8–11. (Previous to 2019, when agencies were published in tables 8–11, but they had one or two offenses removed from publication due to not meeting UCR publication guidelines, the agency's data was not used to calculate rates for this table.) The FBI derived the offense rates by dividing the individual offense counts by the individual populations covered by contributing agencies for which 12 months of publishable data were supplied and then multiplying the resulting figure by 100,000. See Appendix V for the agency and population counts.

MOTOR VEHICLE THEFT

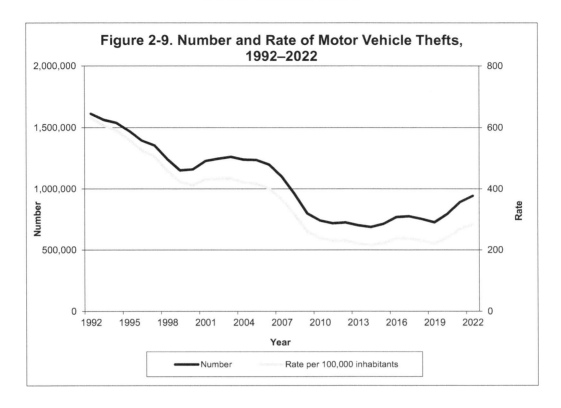

Figure 2-9. Number and Rate of Motor Vehicle Thefts, 1992–2022

Number — Rate per 100,000 inhabitants

Definition

The UCR program defines motor vehicle theft as the theft or attempted theft of a motor vehicle. The offense includes the stealing of automobiles, trucks, buses, motorcycles, snowmobiles, etc. The taking of a motor vehicle for temporary use by a person or persons with lawful access is excluded.

National Volume, Trends, and Rates

In 2022, an estimated 942,173 motor vehicle thefts took place in the United States. The estimated number of motor vehicle thefts increased 10.9 percent when compared with data from 2021, increased 22.9 percent when compared with 2018 data, and increased 33.8 percent when compared with 2013 data. (Table 1)

The estimated rate of motor vehicle theft in 2022 was 282.7 incidents per 100,000 inhabitants. The 2022 rate was 10.5 percent more than the 2021 rate, 20.7 percent more than the 2018 rate, and 26.9 percent more than the 2013 rate. (Table 1)

Regional Offense Trends and Rates

In order to analyze crime by geographic area, the UCR program divides the United States into four regions: the Northeast, the Midwest, the South, and the West. (Appendix IV provides a map delineating the regions.) This section provides a regional overview of motor vehicle theft.

NORTHEAST

The Northeast accounted for an estimated 17.1 percent of the nation's population in 2022. The region also accounted for an estimated 8.6 percent of its motor vehicle thefts. An estimated 81,226 motor vehicle thefts occurred in the Northeast in 2022, a 16.7 percent rise in occurrences from 2021. The estimated rate of 142.4 motor vehicle thefts per 100,000 inhabitants in the Northeast in 2022 represented a 17.1 percent increase from the 2021 rate. (Tables 3 and 4)

MIDWEST

An estimated 20.6 percent of the country's population resided in the Midwest in 2022. The region accounted for 19.7 percent of the nation's motor vehicle thefts. The Midwest had an estimated 185,820 motor vehicle thefts in 2022, an increase of 16.6 percent from the previous year's total. The motor vehicle theft rate was estimated at 270.1 motor vehicles stolen per 100,000 inhabitants, an increase of 16.7 percent from the 2021 rate. (Tables 3 and 4)

SOUTH

The South, the nation's most populous region, was home to an estimated 38.6 percent of the U.S. population in 2022 and accounted for 32.6 percent of the nation's motor vehicle thefts. The estimated 306,901 motor vehicle thefts in the South represented a 9.0 percent increase from the 2021 estimate. Motor vehicles in the South were stolen at an estimated rate of 238.5 offenses per 100,000 inhabitants in 2022, a rate that was up 7.8 percent from the 2021 rate. (Tables 3 and 4)

WEST

With approximately 23.6 percent of the U.S. population in 2022, the West accounted for 39.1 percent of all motor vehicle thefts in the nation. An estimated 368,166 motor vehicle thefts occurred in the West, the most of any region. This number represented an 8.6 percent increase from the previous year's estimate. The region's 2022 rate of 467.6 motor vehicles stolen per 100,000 inhabitants was 8.43 percent higher than the 2021 rate. (Tables 3 and 4)

Community Types

The UCR program aggregates data by three community types: metropolitan statistical areas (MSAs), cities outside MSAs, and nonmetropolitan counties. MSAs are areas that include a principal city or urbanized area with at least 50,000 inhabitants and the county that contains the principal city and other adjacent counties that have, as defined by the U.S. Office of Management and Budget, a high degree of economic and social integration.

In 2022, the vast majority (86.1 percent) of the U.S. population resided in MSAs, where approximately 90.8 percent of motor vehicle thefts occurred. For 2022, the UCR program estimated an overall rate of 307.2 motor vehicles stolen per 100,000 MSA inhabitants. Cities outside MSAs, with 5.7 percent of the U.S. population, accounted for 3.0 percent of motor vehicle thefts, and nonmetropolitan counties, with 8.2 percent of the population, accounted for 2.7 percent of motor vehicle thefts. The UCR program estimated a 2022 rate of 165.8 motor vehicles stolen for every 100,000 inhabitants in cities outside MSAs and a rate of 105.9 motor vehicles stolen per 100,000 inhabitants in nonmetropolitan counties. (Table 2)

Population Groups: Trends and Rates

The UCR program aggregates data by various population groups, which include cities, metropolitan counties, and nonmetropolitan counties. (A definition of these groups can be found in Appendix IV.)

In cities, collectively, the number of motor vehicle thefts increased 10.5 percent from 2021 to 2022. Occurrences rose in all groups and. subsets. Cities with 1,000,000 or more residents experienced the greatest increase at 19.2 percent. Metropolitan counties experienced an increase of 6.3 percent, nonmetropolitan counties experienced a decrease of 8.9 percent, and suburban areas experienced an increase of 8.1 percent. (Table 12)

In 2022, cities had a collective motor vehicle theft rate of 380.7 per 100,000 inhabitants. Among the population groups and subsets, cities with 500,000 to 999,999 inhabitants experienced the highest rate of motor vehicle thefts with 786.7 motor vehicle thefts per 100,000 inhabitants. Cities with populations of 10,000 to 24,999 residents had the lowest rate of motor vehicle theft with 181.5 incidents per 100,000 in population. Within the county groups, metropolitan counties had a rate of 167.5 motor vehicles stolen per 100,000 inhabitants, while nonmetropolitan counties had a rate of 110.5 incidents per 100,000 inhabitants. Suburban areas had a rate of 183.2 per 100,000 inhabitants. (Table 16)

Due to a system upgrade in 2019, the FBI now calculates rates for each offense based on the individual offenses and population published for each agency in tables 8–11. (Previous to 2019, when agencies were published in tables 8–11, but they had one or two offenses removed from publication due to not meeting UCR publication guidelines, the agency's data was not used to calculate rates for this table.) The FBI derived the offense rates by dividing the individual offense counts by the individual populations covered by contributing agencies for which 12 months of publishable data were supplied and then multiplying the resulting figure by 100,000. See Appendix V for the agency and population counts.

Offense Analysis

By type of vehicle, automobiles were stolen at a rate of 234.9 cars per 100,000 inhabitants in 2022. Trucks and buses were stolen at a rate of 46.6 vehicles per 100,000 inhabitants, and other types of vehicles were stolen at a rate of 25.0 vehicles per 100,000 inhabitants. (Table 19)

ARSON

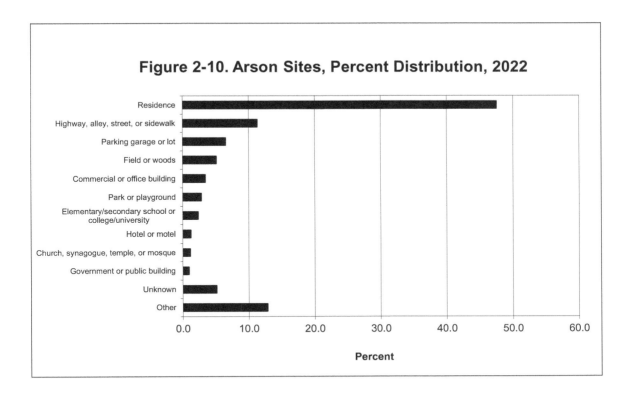

The UCR program defines arson as any willful or malicious burning or attempt to burn (with or without intent to defraud) a dwelling house, public building, motor vehicle, aircraft, or personal property of another, etc.

Data Collection

Only fires that investigators determined were willfully set (not fires labeled as "suspicious" or "of unknown origin") are included in this arson data collection. Points to consider regarding arson statistics include:

National offense rates per 100,000 inhabitants (found in Tables 1, 2, and 4) do not include arson data; the FBI presents rates for arson separately. Arson rates are calculated based upon data received from all law enforcement agencies that provide the UCR program with data for 12 complete months.

Arson data collection does not include estimates for arson, because the degree of reporting arson offenses varies from agency to agency. Because of this unevenness of reporting,

arson offenses are excluded from Tables 1 through 7, all of which contain offense estimations.

The number of arsons reported by individual law enforcement agencies is available in Tables 8 through 11. Arson trend data (which indicate year-to-year changes) can be found in Tables 12 through 15.

Population Groups: Trends and Rates

The number of arsons reported in cities 2022 was 4.6 percent lower than the number reported in 2021. Among the population groups labeled *city,* the group with 25,000 to 49,999 inhabitants reported the largest increase (8.0 percent). Cities with 500,000 to 999,999 inhabitants showed the largest decrease (13.4 percent). Agencies in the nation's metropolitan counties reported a 9.6 percent decrease in the number of arsons, while those in nonmetropolitan counties reported an 8.7 percent decrease from 2021 to 2022. Agencies in suburban areas reported a 3.3 percent drop in arsons. (Table 12)

Offense Analysis

The UCR program breaks down arson offenses into three property categories: structural, mobile, and other. In addition, the structural property type is broken down into seven types of structures, and the mobile property type consists of two sub-groupings. The program also collects information on the estimated dollar value of the damaged property. Arson rates were based on information received from 13,159 agencies that provided 12 months of complete arson data to the UCR program.

Property Type

Arsons of structures comprised 37.4 percent of arsons, while arsons of mobile properties comprised 20.5 percent of arsons. (Table 15)

Table 1. Crime in the United States, by Volume and Rate Per 100,000 Inhabitants, 2003–2022

(Number, rate per 100,000 population.)

Year	Population[1]	Violent crime[2]		Murder and nonnegligent manslaughter		Rape (revised definition)[3]		Rape (legacy definition)[4]		Robbery		Aggravated assault	
		Number	Rate	Number	Rate	Number	Rate	Number	Rate	Number	Rate	Number	Rate
2003	290,809,777	1,459,416	501.8	17,716	6.1	X	X	92,024	31.6	451,480	155.2	898,196	308.9
2004	293,655,404	1,428,745	486.5	16,930	5.8	X	X	92,126	31.4	430,308	146.5	889,381	302.9
2005	296,410,404	1,460,666	492.8	17,750	6.0	X	X	92,002	31.0	453,165	152.9	897,749	302.9
2006	299,398,484	1,433,310	478.7	17,241	5.8	X	X	89,554	29.9	451,574	150.8	874,941	292.2
2007	301,621,157	1,437,800	476.7	17,374	5.8	X	X	87,624	29.1	455,900	151.1	876,902	290.7
2008	304,059,724	1,398,219	459.9	16,554	5.4	X	X	85,582	28.1	448,057	147.4	848,026	278.9
2009	307,006,550	1,333,418	434.3	15,511	5.1	X	X	86,290	28.1	414,441	135.0	817,176	266.2
2010	308,745,538	1,271,312	411.8	14,851	4.8	X	X	87,393	28.3	375,695	121.7	793,373	257.0
2011	311,591,917	1,213,343	389.4	14,754	4.7	X	X	84,630	27.2	356,845	114.5	757,114	243.0
2012	313,914,040	1,217,562	387.9	14,975	4.8	X	X	84,946	27.1	355,047	113.1	762,594	242.9
2013	316,128,839	1,170,770	370.3	14,322	4.5	114,927	36	80,775	25.6	346,749	109.7	728,924	230.6
2014	318,857,056	1,159,239	363.6	14,220	4.5	118,466	37	83,641	26.2	325,121	102.0	736,257	230.9
2015	321,418,820	1,197,119	372.4	15,894	4.9	125,398	39	88,949	27.7	326,567	101.6	765,709	238.2
2016	323,127,513	1,259,739	389.9	17,445	5.4	132,231	40.9	98,547	30.5	334,755	103.6	808,992	250.4
2017	325,719,178	1,230,368	377.7	18,206	5.6	137,124	42.1	95,945	29.5	311,447	95.6	804,770	247.1
2018	327,167,434	1,221,594	373.4	16,937	5.2	146,519	44.8	103,852	31.7	282,180	86.2	818,625	250.2
2019	328,239,355	1,194,626	363.9	16,952	5.2	144,593	44.1	101,823	31.0	263,474	80.3	812,377	247.5
2020	329,484,123	1,269,217	385.2	22,414	6.8	131,868	40.0	92,721	28.1	240,837	73.1	913,245	277.2
2021[5]	332,031,554	1,253,716	377.6	22,536	6.8	140,902	42.4	109,733	33.0	217,550	65.5	903,897	272.2
2022	333,287,557	1,232,428	369.8	21,156	6.3	133,294	40.0	96,842	29.1	220,450	66.1	893,980	268.2

Table 1. Crime in the United States, by Volume and Rate Per 100,000 Inhabitants, 2003–2022—Continued

(Number, rate per 100,000 population.)

Year	Property crime Number	Property crime Rate	Burglary Number	Burglary Rate	Larceny-theft Number	Larceny-theft Rate	Motor vehicle theft Number	Motor vehicle theft Rate
2003	10,755,844	3,698.6	2,221,300	763.8	7,217,863	2,482.0	1,316,681	452.8
2004	10,542,192	3,590.0	2,183,644	743.6	7,079,679	2,410.9	1,278,869	435.5
2005	10,413,836	3,513.3	2,209,340	745.4	6,916,776	2,333.5	1,287,720	434.4
2006	10,023,262	3,347.8	2,198,214	734.2	6,626,132	2,213.1	1,198,916	400.4
2007	9,968,661	3,305.0	2,213,816	734.0	6,644,814	2,203.0	1,110,031	368.0
2008	9,832,319	3,233.7	2,249,231	739.7	6,616,959	2,176.2	966,129	317.7
2009	9,405,612	3,063.7	2,223,277	724.2	6,379,794	2,078.1	802,541	261.4
2010	9,230,978	2,989.8	2,197,231	711.7	6,277,390	2,033.2	756,357	245.0
2011	9,073,857	2,912.1	2,196,509	704.9	6,153,892	1,975.0	723,456	232.2
2012	8,980,695	2,860.9	2,111,369	672.6	6,146,429	1,958.0	722,897	230.3
2013	8,674,132	2,743.9	1,935,614	612.3	6,034,252	1,908.8	704,266	222.8
2014	8,255,751	2,589.2	1,724,618	540.9	5,837,470	1,830.7	693,663	217.5
2015	7,974,900	2,481.2	1,579,920	491.5	5,684,715	1,768.6	710,265	221.0
2016	7,973,238	2,467.5	1,524,780	471.9	5,675,800	1,756.5	772,658	239.1
2017	7,692,710	2,361.8	1,397,148	428.9	5,526,199	1,696.6	769,363	236.2
2018	7,398,241	2,261.3	1,267,920	387.5	5,363,735	1,639.4	766,586	234.3
2019	6,999,989	2,132.6	1,112,338	338.9	5,162,288	1,572.7	725,363	221.0
2020	6,470,751	1,963.9	1,026,234	311.5	4,628,945	1,404.9	815,572	247.5
2021[5]	6,083,874	1,832.3	899,369	270.9	4,334,764	1,305.5	849,741	255.9
2022	6,513,829	1,954.4	899,293	269.8	4,672,363	1,401.9	942,173	282.7

NOTE: Although arson data are included in the trend and clearance tables, sufficient data are not available to estimate totals for this offense. Therefore, no arson data are published in this table.
X = Not applicable.
1 Populations are U.S. Census Bureau provisional estimates as of July 1 for each year except 2000 and 2010, which are decennial census counts.   2 The violent crime figures include the offenses of murder, rape (legacy definition), robbery, and aggravated assault.   3 The figures shown in this column for the offense of rape were estimated using the revised UCR definition of rape.   4 The figures shown in this column for the offense of rape were estimated using the legacy UCR definition of rape.   5 The crime figures have been adjusted.

Table 2. Crime, by Community Type, 2022

(Number, rate per 100,000 population, percent.)

Area	Population[1]	Violent crime	Murder and nonnegligent manslaughter	Rape	Robbery	Aggravated assault	Property crime	Burglary	Larceny-theft	Motor vehicle theft
United States	333,287,557	1,268,880	21,156	133,294	220,450	893,980	6,513,829	899,293	4,672,363	942,173
Rate per 100,000 inhabitants		380.7	6.3	40.0	66.1	268.2	1,954.4	269.8	1,401.9	282.7
Metropolitan Statistical Area	287,070,738									
Area actually reporting[2]	93.7%	1,102,990	18,112	106,924	208,243	769,711	5,642,018	751,909	4,034,643	855,466
Estimated total	100.00%	1,145,995	18,863	112,744	213,927	800,461	5,913,026	786,281	4,244,820	881,925
Rate per 100,000 inhabitants		399.2	6.6	39.3	74.5	278.8	2,059.8	273.9	1,478.7	307.2
Cities Outside Metropolitan Areas	18,861,854									
Area actually reporting[2]	86.8%	59,233	984	9,084	4,102	45,063	330,726	51,142	251,695	27,889
Estimated total	100.00%	66,744	1,085	10,044	4,546	51,069	374,202	58,558	284,377	31,267
Rate per 100,000 inhabitants		353.9	5.8	53.3	24.1	270.8	1,983.9	310.5	1,507.7	165.8
Nonmetropolitan counties	27,354,965									
Area actually reporting[2]	87.8%	49,981	1,109	9,441	1,707	37,724	199,279	47,898	125,757	25,624
Estimated total	100.00%	56,141	1,208	10,506	1,977	42,450	226,601	54,454	143,166	28,981
Rate per 100,000 inhabitants		205.2	4.4	38.4	7.2	155.2	828.4	199.1	523.4	105.9

NOTE: Although arson data are included in the trend and clearance tables, sufficient data are not available to estimate totals for this offense. Therefore, no arson data are published in this table.
1 Population figures are U.S. Census Bureau provisional estimates as of July 1, 2020.   2 The percentage reported under "Area actually reporting" is based upon the population covered by agencies providing 3 months or more of crime reports to the FBI.

Table 3. Crime in the United States, Population and Offense Distribution, by Region, 2022

(Percent distribution.)

Region	Population	Violent crime	Murder and nonnegligent manslaughter	Rape	Robbery	Aggravated assault	Property crime	Burglary	Larceny-theft	Motor vehicle theft
United States[1]	100.0	100.0	100.0	100.0	100.0	100.0	100.0	100.0	100.0	100.0
Northeast	17.1	13.7	11.7	11.7	18.3	12.9	13.0	9.4	14.6	8.6
Midwest	20.6	18.4	20.1	24.6	15.9	18.1	18.3	17.4	18.1	19.7
South	38.6	39.6	47.2	37.6	31.7	41.7	39.0	40.6	40.0	32.6
West	23.6	28.2	21.0	26.1	34.2	27.2	29.7	32.6	27.3	39.1

NOTE: Although arson data are included in the trend and clearance tables, sufficient data are not available to estimate totals for this offense. Therefore, no arson data are published in this table.
1 Because of rounding, percentages may not sum to 100.0.

Table 4. Crime in the United States,[1] by Region, Geographic Division, and State 2021–2022

(Number, rate per 100,000 population, percent.)

Area	Population[2]	Violent crime		Murder and nonnegligent manslaughter		Rape		Robbery	
		Number	Rate	Number	Rate	Number	Rate	Number	Rate
UNITED STATES[3,4]									
2021	332,031,554	1,284,885	387.0	22,536	6.8	140,902	42.4	217,550	65.5
2022	333,287,557	1,268,880	380.7	21,156	6.3	133,294	40.0	220,450	66.1
Percent change		-1.2	-1.6	-6.1	-6.5	-5.4	-5.8	+1.3	+1.0
NORTHEAST									
2021	57,259,257	148,855	260.0	2,707	4.7	15,573	27.2	35,539	62.1
2022	57,040,406	173,999	305.0	2,466	4.3	15,530	27.2	40,256	70.6
Percent change		+16.9	+17.3	-8.9	-8.6	-0.3	+0.1	+13.3	+13.7
New England									
2021	15,121,745	33,961	224.6	368	2.4	4,827	31.9	5,283	34.9
2022	15,129,548	34,429	227.6	377	2.5	4,340	28.7	4,977	32.9
Percent change		+1.4	+1.3	+2.4	+2.4	-10.1	-10.1	-5.8	-5.8
Connecticut									
2021	3,623,355	6,109	168.6	155	4.3	805	22.2	1,968	54.3
2022	3,626,205	5,441	150.0	136	3.8	656	18.1	1,629	44.9
Percent change		-10.9	-11.0	-12.3	-12.3	-18.5	-18.6	-17.2	-17.3
Maine									
2021	1,377,238	1,555	112.9	20	1.5	522	37.9	161	11.7
2022	1,385,340	1,431	103.3	30	2.2	444	32.0	139	10.0
Percent change		-8.0	-8.5	+50.0	+49.1	-14.9	-15.4	-13.7	-14.2
Massachusetts									
2021	6,989,690	21,043	301.1	134	1.9	2,056	29.4	2,616	37.4
2022	6,981,974	22,484	322.0	148	2.1	2,033	29.1	2,630	37.7
Percent change		+6.8	+7.0	+10.4	+10.6	-1.1	-1.0	+0.5	+0.6
New Hampshire									
2021	1,387,505	1,800	129.7	13	0.9	700	50.5	192	13.8
2022	1,395,231	1,752	125.6	25	1.8	553	39.6	224	16.1
Percent change		-2.7	-3.2	+92.3	+91.2	-21.0	-21.4	+16.7	+16.0
Rhode Island									
2021	1,096,985	2,199	200.5	37	3.4	461	42.0	277	25.3
2022	1,093,734	1,885	172.3	16	1.5	416	38.0	269	24.6
Percent change		-14.3	-14.0	-56.8	-56.6	-9.8	-9.5	-2.9	-2.6
Vermont									
2021	646,972	1,255	194.0	9	1.4	283	43.7	69	10.7
2022	647,064	1,436	221.9	22	3.4	238	36.8	86	13.3
Percent change		+14.4	+14.4	+144.4	+144.4	-15.9	-15.9	+24.6	+24.6
Middle Atlantic									
2021	42,137,512	114,894	272.7	2,339	5.6	10,746	25.5	30,256	71.8
2022	41,910,858	139,570	333.0	2,089	5.0	11,190	26.7	35,279	84.2
Percent change		+21.5	+22.1	-10.7	-10.2	+4.1	+4.7	+16.6	+17.2
New Jersey									
2021	9,267,961	17,003	183.5	381	4.1	1,517	16.4	4,049	43.7
2022	9,261,699	18,794	202.9	286	3.1	1,557	16.8	4,410	47.6
Percent change		+10.5	+10.6	-24.9	-24.9	+2.6	+2.7	+8.9	+9.0
New York									
2021	19,857,492	61,227	308.3	871	4.4	4,920	24.8	18,000	90.6
2022	19,677,151	84,469	429.3	783	4.0	5,805	29.5	22,040	112.0
Percent change		+38.0	+39.2	-10.1	-9.3	+18.0	+19.1	+22.4	+23.6
Pennsylvania[3]									
2021	13,012,059	36,664	281.8	1087	8.4	4,309	33.1	8,207	63.1
2022	12,972,008	36,307	279.9	1,020	7.9	3,828	29.5	8,829	68.1
Percent change		-1.0	-0.7	-6.2	-5.9	-11.2	-10.9	+7.6	+7.9
MIDWEST									
2021	68,836,505	256,158	372.1	4,762	6.9	35,499	51.6	38,213	55.5
2022	68,787,595	234,062	340.3	4,257	6.2	32,847	47.8	35,044	50.9
Percent change		-8.6	-8.6	-10.6	-10.5	-7.5	-7.4	-8.3	-8.2
East North Central									
2021	47,181,948	172,170	364.9	3,616	7.7	24,164	51.2	27,757	58.8
2022	47,097,779	155,343	329.8	3,136	6.7	22,762	48.3	25,829	54.8
Percent change		-9.8	-9.6	-13.3	-13.1	-5.8	-5.6	-6.9	-6.8
Illinois[3]									
2021	12,686,469	43,739	344.8	1150	9.1	6,641	52.3	10,860	85.6
2022	12,582,032	36,149	287.3	982	7.8	6,052	48.1	10,655	84.7
Percent change		-17.4	-16.7	-14.6	-13.9	-8.9	-8.1	-1.9	-1.1
Indiana									
2021	6,813,532	22,661	332.6	490	7.2	2,444	35.9	3,189	46.8
2022	6,833,037	20,925	306.2	427	6.2	2,241	32.8	2,936	43.0
Percent change		-7.7	-7.9	-12.9	-13.1	-8.3	-8.6	-7.9	-8.2

Table 4. Crime in the United States,[1] by Region, Geographic Division, and State 2021–2022—Continued

(Number, rate per 100,000 population, percent.)

Area	Aggravated assault		Property crime		Burglary		Larceny-theft		Motor vehicle theft	
	Number	Rate	Number	Rate	Number	Rate	Number	Rate	Number	Rate
UNITED STATES[3,4]										
2021	903,897	272.2	6,083,874	1,832.3	899,369	270.9	4,334,764	1,305.5	849,741	255.9
2022	893,980	268.2	6,513,829	1,954.4	899,293	269.8	4,672,363	1,401.9	942,173	282.7
Percent change	-1.1	-1.5	+7.1	+6.7	*	-0.4	+7.8	+7.4	+10.9	+10.5
NORTHEAST										
2021	95,036	166.0	650,424	1,135.9	80,063	139.8	500,737	874.5	69,624	121.6
2022	115,747	202.9	846,953	1,484.8	84,614	148.3	681,113	1,194.1	81,226	142.4
Percent change	+21.8	+22.3	+30.2	+30.7	+5.7	+6.1	+36.0	+36.5	+16.7	+17.1
New England										
2021	23,483	155.3	177,380	1,173.0	20,338	134.5	138,567	916.3	18,475	122.2
2022	24,735	163.5	184,676	1,220.6	19,699	130.2	146,654	969.3	18,323	121.1
Percent change	+5.3	+5.3	+4.1	+4.1	-3.1	-3.2	+5.8	+5.8	-0.8	-0.9
Connecticut										
2021	3,181	87.8	55,018	1,518.4	5,297	146.2	42,073	1,161.2	7,648	211.1
2022	3,020	83.3	54,175	1,494.0	4,716	130.1	42,359	1,168.1	7,100	195.8
Percent change	-5.1	-5.1	-1.5	-1.6	-11.0	-11.0	+0.7	+0.6	-7.2	-7.2
Maine										
2021	852	61.9	15,621	1,134.2	1,739	126.3	12,985	942.8	897	65.1
2022	818	59.0	16,811	1,213.5	1,605	115.9	14,224	1,026.8	982	70.9
Percent change	-4.0	-4.6	+7.6	+7.0	-7.7	-8.2	+9.5	+8.9	+9.5	+8.8
Massachusetts										
2021	16,237	232.3	69,918	1,000.3	9,596	137.3	53,513	765.6	6,809	97.4
2022	17,673	253.1	74,714	1,070.1	9,968	142.8	57,784	827.6	6,962	99.7
Percent change	+8.8	+9.0	+6.9	+7.0	+3.9	+4.0	+8.0	+8.1	+2.2	+2.4
New Hampshire										
2021	895	64.5	14,396	1,037.5	1,023	73.7	12,382	892.4	991	71.4
2022	950	68.1	14,105	1,010.9	1,025	73.5	12,152	871.0	928	66.5
Percent change	+6.1	+5.6	-2.0	-2.6	+0.2	-0.4	-1.9	-2.4	-6.4	-6.9
Rhode Island										
2021	1,424	129.8	13,474	1,228.3	1,507	137.4	10,315	940.3	1,652	150.6
2022	1,184	108.3	14,058	1,285.3	1,401	128.1	10,911	997.6	1,746	159.6
Percent change	-16.9	-16.6	+4.3	+4.6	-7.0	-6.8	+5.8	+6.1	+5.7	+6.0
Vermont										
2021	894	138.2	8,953	1,383.8	1,176	181.8	7,299	1,128.2	478	73.9
2022	1,090	168.5	10,813	1,671.1	984	152.1	9,224	1,425.5	605	93.5
Percent change	+21.9	+21.9	+20.8	+20.8	-16.3	-16.3	+26.4	+26.4	+26.6	+26.6
Middle Atlantic										
2021	71,553	169.8	473,044	1,122.6	59,725	141.7	362,170	859.5	51,149	121.4
2022	91,012	217.2	662,277	1,580.2	64,915	154.9	534,459	1,275.2	62,903	150.1
Percent change	+27.2	+27.9	+40.0	+40.8	+8.7	+9.3	+47.6	+48.4	+23.0	+23.6
New Jersey										
2021	11,056	119.3	102,821	1,109.4	11,529	124.4	79,052	853.0	12,240	132.1
2022	12,541	135.4	131,209	1,416.7	13,708	148.0	102,718	1,109.1	14,783	159.6
Percent change	+13.4	+13.5	+27.6	+27.7	+18.9	+19.0	+29.9	+30.0	+20.8	+20.9
New York										
2021	37,436	188.5	208,058	1,047.8	29,702	149.6	156,745	789.3	21,611	108.8
2022	55,841	283.8	338,757	1,721.6	31,976	162.5	279,810	1,422.0	26,971	137.1
Percent change	+49.2	+50.5	+62.8	+64.3	+7.7	+8.6	+78.5	+80.1	+24.8	+25.9
Pennsylvania[3]										
2021	23,061	177.2	162,165	1,246.3	18,494	142.1	126,373	971.2	17,298	132.9
2022	22,630	174.5	192,311	1,482.5	19,231	148.2	151,931	1,171.2	21,149	163.0
Percent change	-1.9	-1.6	+18.6	+19.0	+4.0	+4.3	+20.2	+20.6	+22.3	+22.6
MIDWEST										
2021	177,684	258.1	1,155,853	1,679.1	164,347	238.7	832,168	1,208.9	159,338	231.5
2022	161,914	235.4	1,189,290	1,728.9	156,574	227.6	846,896	1,231.2	185,820	270.1
Percent change	-8.9	-8.8	+2.9	+3.0	-4.7	-4.7	+1.8	+1.8	+16.6	+16.7
East North Central										
2021	116,633	247.2	712,546	1,510.2	102,595	217.4	512,142	1,085.5	97,809	207.3
2022	103,616	220.0	762,624	1,619.2	102,255	217.1	542,184	1,151.2	118,185	250.9
Percent change	-11.2	-11.0	+7.0	+7.2	-0.3	-0.2	+5.9	+6.1	+20.8	+21.0
Illinois[3]										
2021	25,088	197.8	176,763	1,393.3	24,989	197.0	129,894	1,023.9	21,880	172.5
2022	18,460	146.7	211,721	1,682.7	26,229	208.5	150,061	1,192.7	35,431	281.6
Percent change	-26.4	-25.8	+19.8	+20.8	+5.0	+5.8	+15.5	+16.5	+61.9	+63.3
Indiana										
2021	16,538	242.7	105,814	1,553.0	14,441	211.9	77,079	1,131.3	14,294	209.8
2022	15,321	224.2	105,514	1,544.2	15,449	226.1	76,437	1,118.6	13,628	199.4
Percent change	-7.4	-7.6	-0.3	-0.6	+7.0	+6.7	-0.8	-1.1	-4.7	-4.9

Table 4. Crime in the United States,[1] by Region, Geographic Division, and State 2021–2022—Continued

(Number, rate per 100,000 population, percent.)

Area	Population[2]	Violent crime		Murder and nonnegligent manslaughter		Rape		Robbery	
		Number	Rate	Number	Rate	Number	Rate	Number	Rate
Michigan									
2021	10,037,504	49,295	491.1	761	7.6	6,787	67.6	4,039	40.2
2022	10,034,113	46,257	461.0	695	6.9	6,504	64.8	3,672	36.6
Percent change		-6.2	-6.1	-8.7	-8.6	-4.2	-4.1	-9.1	-9.1
Ohio									
2021	11,764,342	37,341	317.4	883	7.5	5,649	48.0	6,977	59.3
2022	11,756,058	34,510	293.6	718	6.1	5,692	48.4	6,243	53.1
Percent change		-7.6	-7.5	-18.7	-18.6	+0.8	+0.8	-10.5	-10.5
Wisconsin									
2021	5,880,101	19,134	325.4	332	5.6	2,643	44.9	2,692	45.8
2022	5,892,539	17,502	297.0	314	5.3	2,273	38.6	2,323	39.4
Percent change		-8.5	-8.7	-5.4	-5.6	-14.0	-14.2	-13.7	-13.9
West North Central									
2021	21,654,557	83,988	387.9	1,146	5.3	11,335	52.3	10,456	48.3
2022	21,689,816	78,719	362.9	1,121	5.2	10,085	46.5	9,215	42.5
Percent change		-6.3	-6.4	-2.2	-2.3	-11.0	-11.2	-11.9	-12.0
Iowa									
2021	3,197,689	9,434	295.0	73	2.3	1,552	48.5	692	21.6
2022	3,200,517	9,170	286.5	53	1.7	1,361	42.5	692	21.6
Percent change		-2.8	-2.9	-27.4	-27.5	-12.3	-12.4	0.0	-0.1
Kansas									
2021	2,937,922	13,071	444.9	142	4.8	1,484	50.5	979	33.3
2022	2,937,150	12,178	414.6	134	4.6	1,335	45.5	859	29.2
Percent change		-6.8	-6.8	-5.6	-5.6	-10.0	-10.0	-12.3	-12.2
Minnesota									
2021	5,711,471	17,643	308.9	203	3.6	2,602	45.6	3,999	70.0
2022	5,717,184	16,044	280.6	182	3.2	2,327	40.7	3,260	57.0
Percent change		-9.1	-9.2	-10.3	-10.4	-10.6	-10.7	-18.5	-18.6
Missouri									
2021	6,169,823	32,348	524.3	630	10.2	3,466	56.2	3,782	61.3
2022	6,177,957	30,149	488.0	624	10.1	3,023	48.9	3,387	54.8
Percent change		-6.8	-6.9	-1.0	-1.1	-12.8	-12.9	-10.4	-10.6
Nebraska									
2021	1,963,554	5,831	297.0	57	2.9	1,204	61.3	623	31.7
2022	1,967,923	5,565	282.8	62	3.2	1,089	55.3	572	29.1
Percent change		-4.6	-4.8	+8.8	+8.5	-9.6	-9.8	-8.2	-8.4
North Dakota									
2021	777,934	2,150	276.4	14	1.8	436	56.0	205	26.4
2022	779,261	2,179	279.6	27	3.5	442	56.7	215	27.6
Percent change		+1.3	+1.2	+92.9	+92.5	+1.4	+1.2	+4.9	+4.7
South Dakota									
2021	896,164	3,511	391.8	27	3.0	591	65.9	176	19.6
2022	909,824	3,434	377.4	39	4.3	508	55.8	230	25.3
Percent change		-2.2	-3.7	+44.4	+42.3	-14.0	-15.3	+30.7	+28.7
SOUTH									
2021	127,346,029	531,942	417.7	10,570	8.3	53,036	41.6	73,315	57.6
2022	128,716,192	502,654	390.5	9,994	7.8	50,097	38.9	69,846	54.3
Percent change		-5.5	-6.5	-5.4	-6.5	-5.5	-6.5	-4.7	-5.7
South Atlantic									
2021	66,666,348	244,557	366.8	5,105	7.7	22,590	33.9	35,297	52.9
2022	67,452,940	226,120	335.2	4,951	7.3	21,777	32.3	33,784	50.1
Percent change		-7.5	-8.6	-3.0	-4.1	-3.6	-4.7	-4.3	-5.4
Delaware									
2021	1,004,807	4,212	419.2	97	9.7	323	32.1	565	56.2
2022	1,018,396	3,906	383.5	49	4.8	224	22.0	580	57.0
Percent change		-7.3	-8.5	-49.5	-50.2	-30.7	-31.6	+2.7	+1.3
District of Columbia[4]									
2021	668,791	6,362	951.3	274	41.0	307	45.9	2,618	391.5
2022	671,803	5,457	812.3	197	29.3	279	41.5	2,402	357.5
Percent change		-14.2	-14.6	-28.1	-28.4	-9.1	-9.5	-8.3	-8.7
Florida[3]									
2021	21,828,069	73,632	337.3	937	4.3	6,771	31.0	8,432	38.6
2022	22,244,823	57,587	258.9	1,113	5.0	6,714	30.2	7,477	33.6
Percent change		-21.8	-23.3	+18.8	+16.6	-0.8	-2.7	-11.3	-13.0

Table 4. Crime in the United States,[1] by Region, Geographic Division, and State 2021–2022—Continued

(Number, rate per 100,000 population, percent.)

Area	Aggravated assault		Property crime		Burglary		Larceny-theft		Motor vehicle theft	
	Number	Rate	Number	Rate	Number	Rate	Number	Rate	Number	Rate
Michigan										
2021	37,708	375.7	137,199	1,366.9	20,654	205.8	94,899	945.4	21,646	215.7
2022	35,386	352.7	154,203	1,536.8	21,503	214.3	105,887	1,055.3	26,813	267.2
Percent change	-6.2	-6.1	+12.4	+12.4	+4.1	+4.1	+11.6	+11.6	+23.9	+23.9
Ohio										
2021	23,832	202.6	202,361	1,720.1	32,044	272.4	148,792	1,264.8	21,525	183.0
2022	21,857	185.9	209,575	1,782.7	30,015	255.3	151,994	1,292.9	27,566	234.5
Percent change	-8.3	-8.2	+3.6	+3.6	-6.3	-6.3	+2.2	+2.2	+28.1	+28.2
Wisconsin										
2021	13,467	229.0	90,409	1,537.5	10,467	178.0	61,478	1,045.5	18,464	314.0
2022	12,592	213.7	81,611	1,385.0	9,059	153.7	57,805	981.0	14,747	250.3
Percent change	-6.5	-6.7	-9.7	-9.9	-13.5	-13.6	-6.0	-6.2	-20.1	-20.3
West North Central										
2021	61,051	281.9	443,307	2,047.2	61,752	285.2	320,026	1,477.9	61,529	284.1
2022	58,298	268.8	426,666	1,967.1	54,319	250.4	304,712	1,404.9	67,635	311.8
Percent change	-4.5	-4.7	-3.8	-3.9	-12.0	-12.2	-4.8	-4.9	+9.9	+9.7
Iowa										
2021	7,117	222.6	48,232	1,508.3	8,515	266.3	33,661	1,052.7	6,056	189.4
2022	7,064	220.7	42,614	1,331.5	6,997	218.6	30,899	965.4	4,718	147.4
Percent change	-0.7	-0.8	-11.6	-11.7	-17.8	-17.9	-8.2	-8.3	-22.1	-22.2
Kansas										
2021	10,466	356.2	66,020	2,247.2	9,770	332.5	48,381	1,646.8	7,869	267.8
2022	9,850	335.4	58,515	1,992.2	8,029	273.4	43,725	1,488.7	6,761	230.2
Percent change	-5.9	-5.9	-11.4	-11.3	-17.8	-17.8	-9.6	-9.6	-14.1	-14.1
Minnesota										
2021	10,839	189.8	116,831	2,045.6	14,735	258.0	87,732	1,536.1	14,364	251.5
2022	10,275	179.7	112,448	1,966.8	12,244	214.2	83,747	1,464.8	16,457	287.9
Percent change	-5.2	-5.3	-3.8	-3.8	-16.9	-17.0	-4.5	-4.6	+14.6	+14.5
Missouri										
2021	24,470	396.6	144,792	2,346.8	19,255	312.1	101,171	1,639.8	24,366	394.9
2022	23,115	374.2	144,569	2,340.1	18,276	295.8	96,202	1,557.2	30,091	487.1
Percent change	-5.5	-5.7	-0.2	-0.3	-5.1	-5.2	-4.9	-5.0	+23.5	+23.3
Nebraska										
2021	3,947	201.0	35,709	1,818.6	3,956	201.5	27,150	1,382.7	4,603	234.4
2022	3,842	195.2	37,171	1,888.8	3,591	182.5	28,168	1,431.4	5,412	275.0
Percent change	-2.7	-2.9	+4.1	+3.9	-9.2	-9.4	+3.7	+3.5	+17.6	+17.3
North Dakota										
2021	1,495	192.2	16,685	2,144.8	3,104	399.0	11,403	1,465.8	2,178	280.0
2022	1,495	191.8	15,545	1,994.8	2,789	357.9	10,764	1,381.3	1,992	255.6
Percent change	+0.0	-0.2	-6.8	-7.0	-10.1	-10.3	-5.6	-5.8	-8.5	-8.7
South Dakota										
2021	2,717	303.2	15,038	1,678.0	2,417	269.7	10,528	1,174.8	2,093	233.6
2022	2,657	292.0	15,804	1,737.0	2,393	263.0	11,207	1,231.8	2,204	242.2
Percent change	-2.2	-3.7	+5.1	+3.5	-1.0	-2.5	+6.4	+4.9	+5.3	+3.7
SOUTH										
2021	395,021	310.2	2,444,316	1,919.4	371,088	291.4	1,791,505	1,406.8	281,723	221.2
2022	372,717	289.6	2,542,063	1,974.9	365,113	283.7	1,869,989	1,452.8	306,961	238.5
Percent change	-5.6	-6.7	+4.0	+2.9	-1.6	-2.7	+4.4	+3.3	+9.0	+7.8
South Atlantic										
2021	181,565	272.3	1,144,300	1,716.5	149,095	223.6	887,035	1,330.6	108,170	162.3
2022	165,608	245.5	1,189,523	1,763.5	150,009	222.4	917,102	1,359.6	122,412	181.5
Percent change	-8.8	-9.9	+4.0	+2.7	+0.6	-0.6	+3.4	+2.2	+13.2	+11.8
Delaware										
2021	3,227	321.2	18,904	1,881.4	2,394	238.3	14,844	1,477.3	1,666	165.8
2022	3,053	299.8	20,002	1,964.1	2,068	203.1	16,204	1,591.1	1,730	169.9
Percent change	-5.4	-6.7	+5.8	+4.4	-13.6	-14.8	+9.2	+7.7	+3.8	+2.5
District of Columbia[4]										
2021	3,163	472.9	27,669	4,137.2	1,831	273.8	21,755	3,252.9	4,083	610.5
2022	2,579	383.9	23,926	3,561.5	1,352	201.2	18,696	2,783.0	3,878	577.3
Percent change	-18.5	-18.8	-13.5	-13.9	-26.2	-26.5	-14.1	-14.4	-5.0	-5.4
Florida[3]										
2021	57,492	263.4	331,252	1,517.6	32,959	151.0	276,677	1,267.5	21,616	99.0
2022	42,283	190.1	348,403	1,566.2	38,594	173.5	279,116	1,254.7	30,693	138.0
Percent change	-26.5	-27.8	+5.2	+3.2	+17.1	+14.9	+0.9	-1.0	+42.0	+39.3

Table 4. Crime in the United States,[1] by Region, Geographic Division, and State 2021–2022—Continued

(Number, rate per 100,000 population, percent.)

Area	Population[2]	Violent crime		Murder and nonnegligent manslaughter		Rape		Robbery	
		Number	Rate	Number	Rate	Number	Rate	Number	Rate
Georgia									
2021	10,788,029	37,741	349.8	851	7.9	3,595	33.3	4,577	42.4
2022	10,912,876	40,048	367.0	893	8.2	3,977	36.4	4,753	43.6
Percent change		+6.1	+4.9	+4.9	+3.7	+10.6	+9.4	+3.8	+2.7
Maryland[3]									
2021	6,174,610	26,866	435.1	680	11.0	2,196	35.6	7,425	120.3
2022	6,164,660	24,565	398.5	526	8.5	1,885	30.6	7,038	114.2
Percent change		-8.6	-8.4	-22.6	-22.5	-14.2	-14.0	-5.2	-5.1
North Carolina									
2021	10,565,885	44,328	419.5	995	9.4	3,295	31.2	5,970	56.5
2022	10,698,973	43,344	405.1	862	8.1	3,267	30.5	5,875	54.9
Percent change		-2.2	-3.4	-13.4	-14.4	-0.8	-2.1	-1.6	-2.8
South Carolina									
2021	5,193,266	26,685	513.8	590	11.4	2,307	44.4	2,580	49.7
2022	5,282,634	25,955	491.3	592	11.2	2,019	38.2	2,145	40.6
Percent change		-2.7	-4.4	+0.3	-1.4	-12.5	-14.0	-16.9	-18.3
Virginia									
2021	8,657,365	19,526	225.5	573	6.6	2,851	32.9	2,920	33.7
2022	8,683,619	20,324	234.0	638	7.3	2,623	30.2	3,336	38.4
Percent change		+4.1	+3.8	+11.3	+11.0	-8.0	-8.3	+14.2	+13.9
West Virginia									
2021	1,785,526	5,205	291.5	108	6.0	945	52.9	210	11.8
2022	1,775,156	4,934	277.9	81	4.6	789	44.4	178	10.0
Percent change		-5.2	-4.7	-25.0	-24.6	-16.5	-16.0	-15.2	-14.7
East South Central									
2021	19,474,372	84,056	431.6	1,833	9.4	7,304	37.5	9,557	49.1
2022	19,578,002	81,455	416.1	1,695	8.7	6,715	34.3	8,955	45.7
Percent change		-3.1	-3.6	-7.5	-8.0	-8.1	-8.6	-6.3	-6.8
Alabama									
2021	5,049,846	17,590	348.3	476	9.4	1,369	27.1	1,570	31.1
2022	5,074,296	20,759	409.1	552	10.9	1,504	29.6	1,750	34.5
Percent change		+18.0	+17.4	+16.0	+15.4	+9.9	+9.3	+11.5	+10.9
Kentucky									
2021	4,506,589	12,121	269.0	374	8.3	1,716	38.1	2,227	49.4
2022	4,512,310	9,663	214.1	306	6.8	1,527	33.8	1,720	38.1
Percent change		-20.3	-20.4	-18.2	-18.3	-11.0	-11.1	-22.8	-22.9
Mississippi									
2021	2,949,586	7,532	255.4	274	9.3	1,202	40.8	820	27.8
2022	2,940,057	7,204	245.0	228	7.8	990	33.7	754	25.6
Percent change		-4.4	-4.0	-16.8	-16.5	-17.6	-17.4	-8.0	-7.8
Tennessee									
2021	6,968,351	46,813	671.8	709	10.2	3,017	43.3	4,940	70.9
2022	7,051,339	43,829	621.6	609	8.6	2,694	38.2	4,731	67.1
Percent change		-6.4	-7.5	-14.1	-15.1	-10.7	-11.8	-4.2	-5.4
West South Central									
2021	41,205,309	203,329	493.5	3,632	8.8	23,142	56.2	28,461	69.1
2022	41,685,250	195,079	468.0	3,348	8.0	21,605	51.8	27,107	65.0
Percent change		-4.1	-5.2	-7.8	-8.9	-6.6	-7.7	-4.8	-5.9
Arkansas									
2021	3,028,122	21,271	702.4	334	11.0	2,461	81.3	1,282	42.3
2022	3,045,637	19,654	645.3	312	10.2	2,315	76.0	1,208	39.7
Percent change		-7.6	-8.1	-6.6	-7.1	-5.9	-6.5	-5.8	-6.3
Louisiana									
2021	4,627,098	30,666	662.7	907	19.6	1,881	40.7	2,778	60.0
2022	4,590,241	28,852	628.6	740	16.1	1,975	43.0	3,091	67.3
Percent change		-5.9	-5.2	-18.4	-17.8	+5.0	+5.8	+11.3	+12.2
Oklahoma									
2021	3,991,225	17,483	438.0	304	7.6	2,519	63.1	1,795	45.0
2022	4,019,800	16,871	419.7	270	6.7	2,313	57.5	1,632	40.6
Percent change		-3.5	-4.2	-11.2	-11.8	-8.2	-8.8	-9.1	-9.7
Texas									
2021	29,558,864	133,909	453.0	2,087	7.1	16,281	55.1	22,606	76.5
2022	30,029,572	129,702	431.9	2,026	6.7	15,002	50.0	21,176	70.5
Percent change		-3.1	-4.7	-2.9	-4.4	-7.9	-9.3	-6.3	-7.8

Table 4. Crime in the United States,[1] by Region, Geographic Division, and State 2021–2022—Continued

(Number, rate per 100,000 population, percent.)

Area	Aggravated assault		Property crime		Burglary		Larceny-theft		Motor vehicle theft	
	Number	Rate	Number	Rate	Number	Rate	Number	Rate	Number	Rate
Georgia										
2021	28,718	266.2	172,761	1,601.4	21,980	203.7	130,062	1,205.6	20,719	192.1
2022	30,425	278.8	184,513	1,690.8	23,772	217.8	138,207	1,266.5	22,534	206.5
Percent change	+5.9	+4.7	+6.8	+5.6	+8.2	+6.9	+6.3	+5.0	+8.8	+7.5
Maryland[3]										
2021	16,565	268.3	93,975	1,522.0	13,022	210.9	69,005	1,117.6	11,948	193.5
2022	15,116	245.2	100,818	1,635.4	11,728	190.2	75,539	1,225.4	13,551	219.8
Percent change	-8.7	-8.6	+7.3	+7.5	-9.9	-9.8	+9.5	+9.6	+13.4	+13.6
North Carolina										
2021	34,068	322.4	220,527	2,087.2	42,437	401.6	158,194	1,497.2	19,896	188.3
2022	33,340	311.6	220,841	2,064.1	39,668	370.8	159,845	1,494.0	21,328	199.3
Percent change	-2.1	-3.4	+0.1	-1.1	-6.5	-7.7	+1.0	-0.2	+7.2	+5.9
South Carolina										
2021	21,208	408.4	129,509	2,493.8	20,125	387.5	94,584	1,821.3	14,800	285.0
2022	21,199	401.3	121,935	2,308.2	18,632	352.7	90,137	1,706.3	13,166	249.2
Percent change	*	-1.7	-5.8	-7.4	-7.4	-9.0	-4.7	-6.3	-11.0	-12.5
Virginia										
2021	13,182	152.3	125,478	1,449.4	10,508	121.4	103,506	1,195.6	11,464	132.4
2022	13,727	158.1	147,249	1,695.7	10,818	124.6	122,473	1,410.4	13,958	160.7
Percent change	+4.1	+3.8	+17.4	+17.0	+3.0	+2.6	+18.3	+18.0	+21.8	+21.4
West Virginia										
2021	3,942	220.8	24,225	1,356.7	3,839	215.0	18,408	1,031.0	1,978	110.8
2022	3,886	218.9	21,836	1,230.1	3,377	190.2	16,885	951.2	1,574	88.7
Percent change	-1.4	-0.8	-9.9	-9.3	-12.0	-11.5	-8.3	-7.7	-20.4	-20.0
East South Central										
2021	65,362	335.6	359,512	1,846.1	62,120	319.0	250,267	1,285.1	47,125	242.0
2022	64,090	327.4	367,313	1,876.2	58,247	297.5	258,469	1,320.2	50,597	258.4
Percent change	-1.9	-2.5	+2.2	+1.6	-6.2	-6.7	+3.3	+2.7	+7.4	+6.8
Alabama										
2021	14,175	280.7	74,271	1,470.8	13,584	269.0	50,982	1,009.6	9,705	192.2
2022	16,953	334.1	88,240	1,739.0	14,408	283.9	63,566	1,252.7	10,266	202.3
Percent change	+19.6	+19.0	+18.8	+18.2	+6.1	+5.6	+24.7	+24.1	+5.8	+5.3
Kentucky										
2021	7,804	173.2	73,175	1,623.7	13,063	289.9	49,080	1,089.1	11,032	244.8
2022	6,110	135.4	65,375	1,448.8	11,044	244.8	44,664	989.8	9,667	214.2
Percent change	-21.7	-21.8	-10.7	-10.8	-15.5	-15.6	-9.0	-9.1	-12.4	-12.5
Mississippi										
2021	5,236	177.5	54,873	1,860.4	11,851	401.8	37,367	1,266.9	5,655	191.7
2022	5,232	178.0	51,356	1,746.8	10,296	350.2	35,946	1,222.6	5,114	173.9
Percent change	-0.1	+0.2	-6.4	-6.1	-13.1	-12.8	-3.8	-3.5	-9.6	-9.3
Tennessee										
2021	38,147	547.4	157,193	2,255.8	23,622	339.0	112,838	1,619.3	20,733	297.5
2022	35,795	507.6	162,342	2,302.3	22,499	319.1	114,293	1,620.9	25,550	362.3
Percent change	-6.2	-7.3	+3.3	+2.1	-4.8	-5.9	+1.3	+0.1	+23.2	+21.8
West South Central										
2021	148,094	359.4	940,504	2,282.5	159,873	388.0	654,203	1,587.7	126,428	306.8
2022	143,019	343.1	985,227	2,363.5	156,857	376.3	694,418	1,665.9	133,952	321.3
Percent change	-3.4	-4.5	+4.8	+3.5	-1.9	-3.0	+6.1	+4.9	+6.0	+4.7
Arkansas										
2021	17,194	567.8	76,580	2,529.0	14,662	484.2	53,436	1,764.7	8,482	280.1
2022	15,819	519.4	74,664	2,451.5	14,204	466.4	52,824	1,734.4	7,636	250.7
Percent change	-8.0	-8.5	-2.5	-3.1	-3.1	-3.7	-1.1	-1.7	-10.0	-10.5
Louisiana										
2021	25,100	542.5	117,013	2,528.9	22,887	494.6	81,029	1,751.2	13,097	283.0
2022	23,046	502.1	126,147	2,748.2	22,850	497.8	89,052	1,940.0	14,245	310.3
Percent change	-8.2	-7.4	+7.8	+8.7	-0.2	+0.6	+9.9	+10.8	+8.8	+9.6
Oklahoma										
2021	12,865	322.3	104,908	2,628.5	23,937	599.7	65,530	1,641.9	15,441	386.9
2022	12,656	314.8	93,756	2,332.4	19,401	482.6	61,734	1,535.7	12,621	314.0
Percent change	-1.6	-2.3	-10.6	-11.3	-18.9	-19.5	-5.8	-6.5	-18.3	-18.8
Texas										
2021	92,935	314.4	642,003	2,171.9	98,387	332.9	454,208	1,536.6	89,408	302.5
2022	91,498	304.7	690,660	2,299.9	100,402	334.3	490,808	1,634.4	99,450	331.2
Percent change	-1.5	-3.1	+7.6	+5.9	+2.0	+0.4	+8.1	+6.4	+11.2	+9.5

Table 4. Crime in the United States,[1] by Region, Geographic Division, and State 2021–2022—Continued

(Number, rate per 100,000 population, percent.)

Area	Population[2]	Violent crime		Murder and nonnegligent manslaughter		Rape		Robbery	
		Number	Rate	Number	Rate	Number	Rate	Number	Rate
WEST									
2021	78,589,763	347,930	442.7	4,497	5.7	36,794	46.8	70,483	89.7
2022	78,743,364	358,165	454.9	4,439	5.6	34,820	44.2	75,304	95.6
Percent change		+2.9	+2.7	-1.3	-1.5	-5.4	-5.5	+6.8	+6.6
Mountain									
2021	25,268,390	109,536	433.5	1,548	6.1	15,331	60.7	16,094	63.7
2022	25,514,320	110,157	431.7	1,529	6.0	13,901	54.5	15,943	62.5
Percent change		+0.6	-0.4	-1.2	-2.2	-9.3	-10.2	-0.9	-1.9
Arizona									
2021	7,264,877	30,922	425.6	485	6.7	3,319	45.7	5,269	72.5
2022	7,359,197	31,754	431.5	500	6.8	3,246	44.1	5,160	70.1
Percent change		+2.7	+1.4	+3.1	+1.8	-2.2	-3.5	-2.1	-3.3
Colorado									
2021	5,811,297	27,916	480.4	360	6.2	4,286	73.8	4,328	74.5
2022	5,839,926	28,759	492.5	375	6.4	3,700	63.4	4,241	72.6
Percent change		+3.0	+2.5	+4.2	+3.7	-13.7	-14.1	-2.0	-2.5
Idaho									
2021	1,904,314	4,585	240.8	43	2.3	1,091	57.3	158	8.3
2022	1,939,033	4,681	241.4	53	2.7	945	48.7	159	8.2
Percent change		+2.1	+0.3	+23.3	+21.0	-13.4	-14.9	+0.6	-1.2
Montana									
2021	1,106,227	5,197	469.8	36	3.3	720	65.1	289	26.1
2022	1,122,867	4,693	417.9	50	4.5	611	54.4	262	23.3
Percent change		-9.7	-11.0	+38.9	+36.8	-15.1	-16.4	-9.3	-10.7
Nevada									
2021	3,146,402	13,592	432.0	239	7.6	1,924	61.1	2,364	75.1
2022	3,177,772	14,427	454.0	216	6.8	1,871	58.9	2,735	86.1
Percent change		+6.1	+5.1	-9.6	-10.5	-2.8	-3.7	+15.7	+14.6
New Mexico									
2021	2,116,677	17,374	820.8	273	12.9	1,408	66.5	2,513	118.7
2022	2,113,344	16,494	780.5	253	12.0	1,153	54.6	2,338	110.6
Percent change		-5.1	-4.9	-7.3	-7.2	-18.1	-18.0	-7.0	-6.8
Utah									
2021	3,339,113	8,653	259.1	94	2.8	2,177	65.2	1,103	33.0
2022	3,380,800	8,175	241.8	67	2.0	2,010	59.5	1,002	29.6
Percent change		-5.5	-6.7	-28.7	-29.6	-7.7	-8.8	-9.2	-10.3
Wyoming									
2021	579,483	1,297	223.8	18	3.1	406	70.1	70	12.1
2022	581,381	1,174	201.9	15	2.6	365	62.8	46	7.9
Percent change		-9.5	-9.8	-16.7	-16.9	-10.1	-10.4	-34.3	-34.5
Pacific									
2021	53,321,373	238,394	447.1	2,949	5.5	21,463	40.3	54,389	102.0
2022	53,229,044	248,008	465.9	2,910	5.5	20,919	39.3	59,361	111.5
Percent change		+4.0	+4.2	-1.3	-1.2	-2.5	-2.4	+9.1	+9.3
Alaska									
2021	734,182	5,573	759.1	45	6.1	1168	159.1	540	73.6
2022	733,583	5,567	758.9	70	9.5	983	134.0	551	75.1
Percent change		-0.1	*	+55.6	+55.7	-15.8	-15.8	+2.0	+2.1
California									
2021	39,142,991	188,343	481.2	2,346	6.0	14,639	37.4	44,649	114.1
2022	39,029,342	194,935	499.5	2,231	5.7	14,613	37.4	48,192	123.5
Percent change		+3.5	+3.8	-4.9	-4.6	-0.2	+0.1	+7.9	+8.2
Hawaii									
2021	1,447,154	3,965	274.0	23	1.6	676	46.7	888	61.4
2022	1,440,196	3,739	259.6	30	2.1	546	37.9	952	66.1
Percent change		-5.7	-5.2	+30.4	+31.1	-19.2	-18.8	+7.2	+7.7
Oregon									
2021	4,256,301	14,526	341.3	204	4.8	1,875	44.1	2,579	60.6
2022	4,240,137	14,520	342.4	192	4.5	1,722	40.6	2,910	68.6
Percent change		*	+0.3	-5.9	-5.5	-8.2	-7.8	+12.8	+13.3
Washington									
2021	7,740,745	25,987	335.7	331	4.3	3,105	40.1	5,733	74.1
2022	7,785,786	29,247	375.6	387	5.0	3,055	39.2	6,756	86.8
Percent change		+12.5	+11.9	+16.9	+16.2	-1.6	-2.2	+17.8	+17.2

Table 4. Crime in the United States,[1] by Region, Geographic Division, and State 2021–2022—Continued

(Number, rate per 100,000 population, percent.)

Area	Aggravated assault		Property crime		Burglary		Larceny-theft		Motor vehicle theft	
	Number	Rate	Number	Rate	Number	Rate	Number	Rate	Number	Rate
WEST										
2021	236,156	300.5	1,833,281	2,332.7	283,871	361.2	1,210,354	1,540.1	339,056	431.4
2022	243,602	309.4	1,935,523	2,458.0	292,992	372.1	1,274,365	1,618.4	368,166	467.6
Percent change	+3.2	+3.0	+5.6	+5.4	+3.2	+3.0	+5.3	+5.1	+8.6	+8.4
Mountain										
2021	76,563	303.0	586,094	2,319.5	86,161	341.0	402,557	1,593.1	97,376	385.4
2022	78,784	308.8	587,035	2,300.8	83,001	325.3	400,888	1,571.2	103,146	404.3
Percent change	+2.9	+1.9	+0.2	-0.8	-3.7	-4.6	-0.4	-1.4	+5.9	+4.9
Arizona										
2021	21,849	300.7	153,641	2,114.8	20,717	285.2	115,305	1,587.2	17,619	242.5
2022	22,848	310.5	151,421	2,057.6	19,941	271.0	113,508	1,542.4	17,972	244.2
Percent change	+4.6	+3.2	-1.4	-2.7	-3.7	-5.0	-1.6	-2.8	+2.0	+0.7
Colorado										
2021	18,942	326.0	182,850	3,146.5	24,429	420.4	117,067	2,014.5	41,354	711.6
2022	20,443	350.1	183,816	3,147.6	23,077	395.2	114,856	1,966.7	45,883	785.7
Percent change	+7.9	+7.4	+0.5	*	-5.5	-6.0	-1.9	-2.4	+11.0	+10.4
Idaho										
2021	3,293	172.9	18,371	964.7	3,090	162.3	13,557	711.9	1,724	90.5
2022	3,524	181.7	17,972	926.9	3,075	158.6	13,129	677.1	1,768	91.2
Percent change	+7.0	+5.1	-2.2	-3.9	-0.5	-2.3	-3.2	-4.9	+2.6	+0.7
Montana										
2021	4,152	375.3	22,449	2,029.3	2,736	247.3	16,674	1,507.3	3,039	274.7
2022	3,770	335.7	21,543	1,918.6	2,249	200.3	16,795	1,495.7	2,499	222.6
Percent change	-9.2	-10.5	-4.0	-5.5	-17.8	-19.0	+0.7	-0.8	-17.8	-19.0
Nevada										
2021	9,065	288.1	70,236	2,232.3	12,783	406.3	43,850	1,393.7	13,603	432.3
2022	9,605	302.3	75,635	2,380.1	13,859	436.1	46,188	1,453.5	15,588	490.5
Percent change	+6.0	+4.9	+7.7	+6.6	+8.4	+7.3	+5.3	+4.3	+14.6	+13.5
New Mexico										
2021	13,180	622.7	58,682	2,772.4	12,853	607.2	35,661	1,684.8	10,168	480.4
2022	12,750	603.3	63,063	2,984.0	12,764	604.0	38,851	1,838.4	11,448	541.7
Percent change	-3.3	-3.1	+7.5	+7.6	-0.7	-0.5	+8.9	+9.1	+12.6	+12.8
Utah										
2021	5,279	158.1	70,096	2,099.2	7,988	239.2	53,536	1,603.3	8,572	256.7
2022	5,096	150.7	64,069	1,895.1	6,818	201.7	50,207	1,485.1	7,044	208.4
Percent change	-3.5	-4.7	-8.6	-9.7	-14.6	-15.7	-6.2	-7.4	-17.8	-18.8
Wyoming										
2021	803	138.6	9,769	1,685.8	1,565	270.1	6,907	1,191.9	1,297	223.8
2022	748	128.7	9,516	1,636.8	1,218	209.5	7,354	1,264.9	944	162.4
Percent change	-6.8	-7.2	-2.6	-2.9	-22.2	-22.4	+6.5	+6.1	-27.2	-27.5
Pacific										
2021	159,593	299.3	1,247,187	2,339.0	197,710	370.8	807,797	1,515.0	241,680	453.3
2022	164,818	309.6	1,348,488	2,533.4	209,991	394.5	873,477	1,641.0	265,020	497.9
Percent change	+3.3	+3.5	+8.1	+8.3	+6.2	+6.4	+8.1	+8.3	+9.7	+9.8
Alaska										
2021	3,820	520.3	13,456	1,832.8	2,312	314.9	9,355	1,274.2	1,789	243.7
2022	3,963	540.2	13,124	1,789.0	1,973	269.0	9,350	1,274.6	1,801	245.5
Percent change	+3.7	+3.8	-2.5	-2.4	-14.7	-14.6	-0.1	*	+0.7	+0.8
California										
2021	126,709	323.7	847,567	2,165.3	134,873	344.6	534,827	1,366.3	177,867	454.4
2022	129,899	332.8	914,517	2,343.2	145,141	371.9	585,181	1,499.3	184,195	471.9
Percent change	+2.5	+2.8	+7.9	+8.2	+7.6	+7.9	+9.4	+9.7	+3.6	+3.9
Hawaii										
2021	2,378	164.3	36,660	2,533.2	4,808	332.2	25,555	1,765.9	6,297	435.1
2022	2,211	153.5	35,065	2,434.7	3,745	260.0	25,459	1,767.7	5,861	407.0
Percent change	-7.0	-6.6	-4.4	-3.9	-22.1	-21.7	-0.4	+0.1	-6.9	-6.5
Oregon										
2021	9,868	231.8	114,532	2,690.9	14,395	338.2	80,025	1,880.2	20,112	472.5
2022	9,696	228.7	124,459	2,935.3	15,295	360.7	85,778	2,023.0	23,386	551.5
Percent change	-1.7	-1.4	+8.7	+9.1	+6.3	+6.7	+7.2	+7.6	+16.3	+16.7
Washington										
2021	16,818	217.3	234,972	3,035.5	41,322	533.8	158,035	2,041.6	35,615	460.1
2022	19,049	244.7	261,323	3,356.4	43,837	563.0	167,709	2,154.0	49,777	639.3
Percent change	+13.3	+12.6	+11.2	+10.6	+6.1	+5.5	+6.1	+5.5	+39.8	+39.0

NOTE: Although arson data are included in the trend and clearance tables, sufficient data are not available to estimate totals for this offense. Therefore, no arson data are published in this table.
* = Less than one-tenth of one percent.
1 The previous year's crime figures have been adjusted.   2 Population figures are U.S. Census Bureau provisional estimates as of July 1, 2020.   3 Limited data for 2022 were available for Florida, Illinois, Maryland, and Pennsylvania.   4 Includes offenses reported by the Metro Transit Police and the District of Columbia Fire and Emergency Medical Services: Arson Investigation Unit.

Table 5. Crime in the United States, by State and Area, 2022

(Number, percent, rate per 100,000 population.)

Area	Population[1]	Violent crime	Murder and nonnegligent manslaughter	Rape	Robbery	Aggravated assault	Property crime	Burglary	Larceny-theft	Motor vehicle theft
Alabama										
Metropolitan statistical area	3,884,161									
Area actually reporting	87.4%	14,997	386	1,053	1,329	12,229	62,063	9,518	45,354	7,191
Estimated total	100.0%	17,488	451	1,198	1,559	14,280	70,795	10,986	51,485	8,324
Cities outside metropolitan areas	540,433									
Area actually reporting	92.1%	2,205	62	193	144	1,806	12,097	2,244	8,683	1,170
Estimated total	100.0%	2,409	67	210	157	1,975	13,221	2,448	9,498	1,275
Nonmetropolitan counties	649,702									
Area actually reporting	95.5%	816	32	92	33	659	4,033	928	2,468	637
Estimated total	100.0%	862	34	96	34	698	4,224	974	2,583	667
State total	5,074,296	20,759	552	1,504	1,750	16,953	88,240	14,408	63,566	10,266
Rate per 100,000 inhabitants		409.1	10.9	29.6	34.5	334.1	1,739.0	283.9	1,252.7	202.3
Alaska										
Metropolitan statistical area	337,055									
Area actually reporting	100.0%	3,653	39	538	477	2,599	9,875	1,331	7,196	1,348
Cities outside metropolitan areas	123,785									
Area actually reporting	95.5%	567	7	134	32	394	1,287	138	1,038	111
Estimated total	100.0%	574	7	134	32	401	1,308	144	1,052	112
Nonmetropolitan counties	272,743									
Area actually reporting	100.0%	1,340	24	311	42	963	1,941	498	1,102	341
State total	733,583	5,567	70	983	551	3,963	13,124	1,973	9,350	1,801
Rate per 100,000 inhabitants		758.9	9.5	134.0	75.1	540.2	1,789.0	269.0	1,274.6	245.5
Arizona										
Metropolitan statistical area	7,018,141									
Area actually reporting	87.0%	26,890	430	2,807	4,725	18,928	131,966	17,042	99,174	15,750
Estimated total	100.0%	29,904	476	3,114	5,126	21,188	147,238	19,110	110,729	17,399
Cities outside metropolitan areas	124,487									
Area actually reporting	85.2%	1,432	15	94	26	1,297	2,842	550	1,905	387
Estimated total	100.0%	1,537	15	98	32	1,392	3,220	611	2,192	417
Nonmetropolitan counties	216,569									
Area actually reporting	100.0%	313	9	34	2	268	963	220	587	156
State total	7,359,197	31,754	500	3,246	5,160	22,848	151,421	19,941	113,508	17,972
Rate per 100,000 inhabitants		431.5	6.8	44.1	70.1	310.5	2,057.6	271.0	1,542.4	244.2
Arkansas										
Metropolitan statistical area	1,959,160									
Area actually reporting	99.6%	13,860	222	1,525	1,019	11,094	54,997	9,923	39,217	5,857
Estimated total	100.0%	13,891	222	1,531	1,019	11,119	55,110	9,946	39,296	5,868
Cities outside metropolitan areas	486,439									
Area actually reporting	97.1%	3,294	61	398	143	2,692	12,762	2,575	9,334	853
Estimated total	100.0%	3,390	63	408	148	2,771	13,141	2,654	9,610	877
Nonmetropolitan counties	600,038									
Area actually reporting	91.5%	2,181	23	349	36	1,773	5,913	1,472	3,615	826
Estimated total	100.0%	2,373	27	376	41	1,929	6,413	1,604	3,918	891
State total	3,045,637	19,654	312	2,315	1,208	15,819	74,664	14,204	52,824	7,636
Rate per 100,000 inhabitants		645.3	10.2	76.0	39.7	519.4	2,451.5	466.4	1,734.4	250.7
California										
Metropolitan statistical area	38,539,958									
Area actually reporting	99.9%	170,104	2,158	12,997	44,286	110,663	827,403	141,667	519,418	166,318
Estimated total	100.0%	170,131	2,158	13,000	44,291	110,682	827,545	141,689	519,521	166,335
Cities outside metropolitan areas	268,242									
Area actually reporting	100.0%	1,583	9	149	281	1,144	6,887	1,501	4,407	979
Nonmetropolitan counties	559,878									
Area actually reporting	89.5%	2,376	16	334	141	1,885	4,992	1,760	3,088	144
Estimated total	100.0%	2,648	18	375	160	2,095	5,556	1,950	3,450	156
State total	39,029,342	194,935	2,231	14,613	48,192	129,899	914,517	145,141	585,181	184,195
Rate per 100,000 inhabitants		499.5	5.7	37.4	123.5	332.8	2,343.2	371.9	1,499.3	471.9
Colorado										
Metropolitan statistical area	5,116,793									
Area actually reporting	99.8%	27,257	347	3,384	4,183	19,343	173,502	21,442	107,226	44,834
Estimated total	100.0%	27,287	347	3,392	4,186	19,362	173,848	21,474	107,468	44,906
Cities outside metropolitan areas	349,382									
Area actually reporting	98.5%	957	11	194	46	706	7,226	940	5,701	585
Estimated total	100.0%	963	11	194	46	712	7,273	952	5,731	590
Nonmetropolitan counties	373,751									
Area actually reporting	98.3%	501	17	113	9	362	2,639	636	1,624	379
Estimated total	100.0%	509	17	114	9	369	2,695	651	1,657	387
State total	5,839,926	28,759	375	3,700	4,241	20,443	183,816	23,077	114,856	45,883
Rate per 100,000 inhabitants		492.5	6.4	63.4	72.6	350.1	3,147.6	395.2	1,966.7	785.7
Connecticut										
Metropolitan statistical area	3,001,920									
Area actually reporting	100.0%	5,192	124	594	1,585	2,889	51,473	4,429	40,302	6,742
Cities outside metropolitan areas	114,979									
Area actually reporting	100.0%	42	0	10	16	16	1,117	97	920	100
Nonmetropolitan counties	509,306									
Area actually reporting	100.0%	207	12	52	28	115	1,585	190	1,137	258
State total	3,626,205	5,441	136	656	1,629	3,020	54,175	4,716	42,359	7,100
Rate per 100,000 inhabitants		150.0	3.8	18.1	44.9	83.3	1,494.0	130.1	1,168.1	195.8

Table 5. Crime in the United States, by State and Area, 2022—Continued

(Number, percent, rate per 100,000 population.)

Area	Population[1]	Violent crime	Murder and nonnegligent manslaughter	Rape	Robbery	Aggravated assault	Property crime	Burglary	Larceny-theft	Motor vehicle theft
Delaware										
Metropolitan statistical area	1,018,396									
Area actually reporting	99.7%	3,890	49	222	578	3,041	19,914	2,059	16,130	1,725
	100.0%	3,905	49	223	580	3,053	19,997	2,068	16,199	1,730
Cities outside metropolitan areas	None									
Nonmetropolitan counties	None									
State total	1,018,396	3,906	49	224	580	3,053	20,002	2,068	16,204	1,730
Rate per 100,000 inhabitants		383.5	4.8	22.0	57.0	299.8	1,964.1	203.1	1,591.1	169.9
Estimated total										
District of Columbia[2]										
Metropolitan statistical area	671,803									
Area actually reporting	100.0%	5,457	197	279	2,402	2,579	23,926	1,352	18,696	3,878
Cities outside metropolitan areas	None									
Nonmetropolitan counties	None									
District total	671,803	5,457	197	279	2,402	2,579	23,926	1,352	18,696	3,878
Rate per 100,000 inhabitants		812.3	29.3	41.5	357.5	383.9	3,561.5	201.2	2,783.0	577.3
Florida[3]										
Metropolitan statistical area	21,541,770									
Area actually reporting	63.1%	40,285	727	4,190	5,058	30,310	219,143	24,116	174,549	20,478
Estimated total	100.0%	55,967	1,083	6,516	7,372	40,996	340,798	37,259	273,665	29,874
Cities outside metropolitan areas	141,387									
Area actually reporting	56.8%	208	4	38	23	143	1,464	178	1,156	130
Estimated total	100.0%	451	5	64	44	338	2,598	348	2,026	224
Nonmetropolitan counties	561,666									
Area actually reporting	43.8%	486	11	56	25	394	2,089	413	1,428	248
Estimated total	100.0%	1,169	25	134	61	949	5,007	987	3,425	595
State total	22,244,823	57,587	1,113	6,714	7,477	42,283	348,403	38,594	279,116	30,693
Rate per 100,000 inhabitants		258.9	5.0	30.2	33.6	190.1	1,566.2	173.5	1,254.7	138.0
Georgia										
Metropolitan statistical area	9,079,272									
Area actually reporting	92.7%	32,397	744	3,105	4,130	24,418	145,175	17,663	108,566	18,946
Estimated total	100.0%	34,528	786	3,329	4,358	26,055	155,235	18,917	116,201	20,117
Cities outside metropolitan areas	646,712									
Area actually reporting	76.9%	2,415	56	235	228	1,896	13,713	1,861	11,020	832
Estimated total	100.0%	3,003	65	278	267	2,393	17,220	2,353	13,805	1,062
Nonmetropolitan counties	1,186,892									
Area actually reporting	82.6%	2,071	38	302	104	1,627	9,950	2,066	6,774	1,110
Estimated total	100.0%	2,517	42	370	128	1,977	12,058	2,502	8,201	1,355
State total	10,912,876	40,048	893	3,977	4,753	30,425	184,513	23,772	138,207	22,534
Rate per 100,000 inhabitants		367.0	8.2	36.4	43.6	278.8	1,690.8	217.8	1,266.5	206.5
Hawaii										
Metropolitan statistical area	1,159,680									
Area actually reporting	100.0%	3028	30	353	884	1,761	30,284	3,113	21,760	5,411
Estimated total	None									
Cities outside metropolitan areas	280,516									
Nonmetropolitan counties	0	188	0	51	18	119	1,264	167	978	119
Area actually reporting	100.0%	711	0	193	68	450	4,781	632	3,699	450
State total	1,440,196	3,739	30	546	952	2,211	35,065	3,745	25,459	5,861
Rate per 100,000 inhabitants		259.6	2.1	37.9	66.1	153.5	2,434.7	260.0	1,767.7	407.0
Idaho										
Metropolitan statistical area	1,438,718									
Estimated total	99.9%	3,678	29	769	137	2,743	14,399	2,391	10,599	1,409
Area actually reporting	100.0%	3,680	29	770	137	2,744	14,404	2,393	10,601	1,410
Cities outside metropolitan areas	200,715									
Area actually reporting	100.0%	451	9	73	14	355	1,980	374	1,436	170
Nonmetropolitan counties	299,600									
Area actually reporting	100.0%	550	15	102	8	425	1,588	308	1,092	188
State total	1,939,033	4,681	53	945	159	3,524	17,972	3,075	13,129	1,768
Rate per 100,000 inhabitants		241.4	2.7	48.7	8.2	181.7	926.9	158.6	677.1	91.2
Illinois[3]										
Metropolitan statistical area	11,176,811									
Area actually reporting	77.5%	27,977	868	4,239	9,804	13,066	168,230	19,491	117,941	30,798
Estimated total	100.0%	33,850	949	5,382	10,551	16,968	200,224	23,968	141,715	34,541
Cities outside metropolitan areas	785,696									
Area actually reporting	49.3%	740	4	203	56	477	4,418	684	3,455	279
Estimated total	100.0%	1,354	4	363	91	896	8,340	1,337	6,455	548
Nonmetropolitan counties	619,525									
Area actually reporting	57.6%	678	28	209	13	428	1,896	535	1,164	197
Estimated total	100.0%	945	29	307	13	596	3,157	924	1,891	342
State total	12,582,032	36,149	982	6,052	10,655	18,460	211,721	26,229	150,061	35,431
Rate per 100,000 inhabitants		287.3	7.8	48.1	84.7	146.7	1,682.7	208.5	1,192.7	281.6
Indiana										
Metropolitan statistical area	5,363,952									
Area actually reporting	87.5%	17,714	373	1,713	2,736	12,892	84,497	12,265	61,450	10,782
Estimated total	100.0%	19,051	388	1,868	2,878	13,917	92,124	13,533	66,832	11,759
Cities outside metropolitan areas	574,733									
Area actually reporting	54.6%	456	9	91	27	329	4,557	486	3,637	434
Estimated total	100.0%	832	12	140	40	640	8,589	899	6,787	903

Table 5. Crime in the United States, by State and Area, 2022—Continued

(Number, percent, rate per 100,000 population.)

Area	Population[1]	Violent crime	Murder and nonnegligent manslaughter	Rape	Robbery	Aggravated assault	Property crime	Burglary	Larceny-theft	Motor vehicle theft
Nonmetropolitan counties	894,352									
Area actually reporting	52.8%	685	27	164	15	479	2,634	457	1,633	544
Estimated total	100.0%	1,042	27	233	18	764	4,801	1,017	2,818	966
State total	6,833,037	20,925	427	2,241	2,936	15,321	105,514	15,449	76,437	13,628
Rate per 100,000 inhabitants		306.2	6.2	32.8	43.0	224.2	1,544.2	226.1	1,118.6	199.4
Iowa										
Metropolitan statistical area	1,976,994									
Area actually reporting	94.6%	5,640	37	819	583	4,201	28,782	4,324	21,101	3,357
Estimated total	100.0%	5,850	37	853	594	4,366	29,779	4,467	21,851	3,461
Cities outside metropolitan areas	580,986									
Area actually reporting	89.1%	2,205	8	337	85	1,775	9,204	1,537	6,876	791
Estimated total	100.0%	2,424	8	365	86	1,965	10,032	1,677	7,499	856
Nonmetropolitan counties	642,537									
Area actually reporting	88.2%	795	8	127	12	648	2,456	748	1,355	353
Estimated total	100.0%	896	8	143	12	733	2,803	853	1,549	401
State total	3,200,517	9,170	53	1,361	692	7,064	42,614	6,997	30,899	4,718
Rate per 100,000 inhabitants		286.5	1.7	42.5	21.6	220.7	1,331.5	218.6	965.4	147.4
Kansas										
Metropolitan statistical area	2,052,847									
Area actually reporting	91.2%	8,584	103	840	667	6,974	40,590	4,925	30,771	4,894
Estimated total	100.0%	9,288	110	901	730	7,547	44,605	5,395	33,765	5,445
Cities outside metropolitan areas	559,266									
Area actually reporting	85.7%	1,854	16	282	105	1,451	9,706	1,586	7,331	789
Estimated total	100.0%	2,126	17	316	111	1,682	11,024	1,823	8,291	910
Nonmetropolitan counties	325,037									
Area actually reporting	92.5%	707	7	106	18	576	2,658	742	1,541	375
Estimated total	100.0%	764	7	118	18	621	2,886	811	1,669	406
State total	2,937,150	12,178	134	1,335	859	9,850	58,515	8,029	43,725	6,761
Rate per 100,000 inhabitants		414.6	4.6	45.5	29.2	335.4	1,992.2	273.4	1,488.7	230.2
Kentucky										
Metropolitan statistical area	2,691,144									
Area actually reporting	99.9%	7,629	238	873	1,537	4,981	50,906	7,958	35,439	7,509
Estimated total	100.0%	7,629	238	873	1,537	4,981	50,917	7,960	35,446	7,511
Cities outside metropolitan areas	537,419									
Area actually reporting	99.8%	802	13	194	123	472	8,279	1,373	6,026	880
Estimated total	100.0%	802	13	194	123	472	8,287	1,375	6,031	881
Nonmetropolitan counties	1,283,747									
Area actually reporting	100.0%	1,232	55	460	60	657	6,171	1,709	3,187	1,275
State total	4,512,310	9,663	306	1,527	1,720	6,110	65,375	11,044	44,664	9,667
Rate per 100,000 inhabitants		214.1	6.8	33.8	38.1	135.4	1,448.8	244.8	989.8	214.2
Louisiana										
Metropolitan statistical area	3,881,793									
Area actually reporting	93.4%	23,473	650	1,638	2,836	18,349	107,700	19,249	75,693	12,758
Estimated total	100.0%	24,986	672	1,724	2,939	19,651	114,123	20,371	80,538	13,214
Cities outside metropolitan areas	254,178									
Area actually reporting	49.7%	1,184	28	66	66	1,024	3,933	743	2,928	262
Estimated total	100.0%	2,166	43	124	110	1,889	7,056	1,339	5,255	462
Nonmetropolitan counties	454,270									
Area actually reporting	72.1%	1,225	18	90	30	1,087	3,547	808	2,335	404
Estimated total	100.0%	1,700	25	127	42	1,506	4,968	1,140	3,259	569
State total	4,590,241	28,852	740	1,975	3,091	23,046	126,147	22,850	89,052	14,245
Rate per 100,000 inhabitants		628.6	16.1	43.0	67.3	502.1	2,748.2	497.8	1,940.0	310.3
Maine										
Metropolitan statistical area	828,104									
Area actually reporting	100.0%	835	13	234	111	477	10,351	828	8,957	566
Cities outside metropolitan areas	258,849									
Area actually reporting	97.9%	329	4	101	24	200	4,191	361	3,617	213
Estimated total	100.0%	333	4	102	24	203	4,252	367	3,669	216
Nonmetropolitan counties	298,387									
Area actually reporting	100.0%	263	13	108	4	138	2,208	410	1,598	200
State total	1,385,340	1,431	30	444	139	818	16,811	1,605	14,224	982
Rate per 100,000 inhabitants		103.3	2.2	32.0	10.0	59.0	1,213.5	115.9	1,026.8	70.9
Maryland[3]										
Metropolitan statistical area	6,012,707									
Area actually reporting	97.7%	23,865	517	1,795	6,927	14,626	97,419	11,170	72,907	13,342
Estimated total	100.0%	24,347	523	1,854	7,011	14,959	99,340	11,466	74,401	13,473
Cities outside metropolitan areas	53,923									
Area actually reporting	71.9%	70	1	11	16	42	592	69	498	25
Estimated total	100.0%	87	2	15	21	49	783	89	661	33
Nonmetropolitan counties	98,030									
Area actually reporting	100.0%	131	1	16	6	108	695	173	477	45
State total	6,164,660	24,565	526	1,885	7,038	15,116	100,818	11,728	75,539	13,551
Rate per 100,000 inhabitants		398.5	8.5	30.6	114.2	245.2	1,635.4	190.2	1,225.4	219.8
Massachusetts										
Metropolitan statistical area	6,945,429									
Area actually reporting	99.5%	22,298	147	2,014	2,629	17,508	74,119	9,868	57,334	6,917
Estimated total	100.0%	22,339	147	2,019	2,629	17,544	74,266	9,891	57,443	6,932

Table 5. Crime in the United States, by State and Area, 2022—Continued

(Number, percent, rate per 100,000 population.)

Area	Population[1]	Violent crime	Murder and nonnegligent manslaughter	Rape	Robbery	Aggravated assault	Property crime	Burglary	Larceny-theft	Motor vehicle theft
Cities outside metropolitan areas	36,545									
Area actually reporting	100.0%	144	1	14	1	128	447	77	341	29
Nonmetropolitan counties	None									
State total	6,981,974	22,484	148	2,033	2,630	17,673	74,714	9,968	57,784	6,962
Rate per 100,000 inhabitants		322.0	2.1	29.1	37.7	253.1	1,070.1	142.8	827.6	99.7
Michigan										
Metropolitan statistical area	8,215,163									
Area actually reporting	97.4%	41,006	657	4,828	3,571	31,950	134,966	18,180	91,554	25,232
Estimated total	100.0%	41,481	660	4,923	3,594	32,304	136,950	18,439	93,045	25,466
Cities outside metropolitan areas	582,445									
Area actually reporting	91.6%	1,612	10	474	49	1,079	7,619	796	6,324	499
Estimated total	100.0%	1,735	10	512	51	1,162	8,240	864	6,837	539
Nonmetropolitan counties	1,236,505									
Area actually reporting	87.3%	2,811	25	999	25	1,762	8,183	2,026	5,418	739
Estimated total	100.0%	3,041	25	1,069	27	1,920	9,013	2,200	6,005	808
State total	10,034,113	46,257	695	6,504	3,672	35,386	154,203	21,503	105,887	26,813
Rate per 100,000 inhabitants		461.0	6.9	64.8	36.6	352.7	1,536.8	214.3	1,055.3	267.2
Minnesota										
Metropolitan statistical area	4,450,468									
Area actually reporting	100.0%	13,956	165	1,865	3,195	8,731	100,043	10,464	74,045	15,534
Cities outside metropolitan areas	581,775									
Area actually reporting	99.7%	1,226	1	266	56	903	8,709	958	7,228	523
Estimated total	100.0%	1,227	1	266	56	904	8,719	959	7,237	523
Nonmetropolitan counties	684,941									
Area actually reporting	99.4%	856	x	195	9	636	3,670	818	2,454	398
Estimated total	100.0%	861	16	196	9	640	3,686	821	2,465	400
State total	5,717,184	16,044	182	2,327	3,260	10,275	112,448	12,244	83,747	16,457
Rate per 100,000 inhabitants		280.6	3.2	40.7	57.0	179.7	1,966.8	214.2	1,464.8	287.9
Mississippi										
Metropolitan statistical area	1,439,088									
Area actually reporting	64.0%	2,034	58	297	273	1,406	18,817	2,908	14,072	1,837
Estimated total	100.0%	2,908	82	450	372	2,004	26,368	4,250	19,442	2,676
Cities outside metropolitan areas	551,589									
Area actually reporting	52.9%	1,247	39	122	140	946	9,111	2,042	6,345	724
Estimated total	100.0%	2,302	69	234	255	1,744	16,769	3,766	11,662	1,341
Nonmetropolitan counties	949,380									
Area actually reporting	60.8%	1,208	45	187	75	901	4,960	1,372	2,919	669
Estimated total	100.0%	1,994	77	306	127	1,484	8,219	2,280	4,842	1,097
State total	2,940,057	7,204	228	990	754	5,232	51,356	10,296	35,946	5,114
Rate per 100,000 inhabitants		245.0	7.8	33.7	25.6	178.0	1,746.8	350.2	1,222.6	173.9
Missouri										
Metropolitan statistical area	4,663,768									
Area actually reporting	99.1%	25,516	574	2,168	3,254	19,520	121,714	14,690	79,975	27,049
Estimated total	100.0%	25,689	574	2,175	3,258	19,682	122,451	14,791	80,416	27,244
Cities outside metropolitan areas	626,309									
Area actually reporting	93.6%	2,100	25	423	100	1,552	13,865	1,846	10,859	1,160
Estimated total	100.0%	2,214	25	440	100	1,649	14,481	1,957	11,306	1,218
Nonmetropolitan counties	887,880									
Area actually reporting	96.6%	2,161	25	394	28	1,714	7,399	1,479	4,337	1,583
Estimated total	100.0%	2,246	25	408	29	1,784	7,637	1,528	4,480	1,629
State total	6,177,957	30,149	624	3,023	3,387	23,115	144,569	18,276	96,202	30,091
Rate per 100,000 inhabitants		488.0	10.1	48.9	54.8	374.2	2,340.1	295.8	1,557.2	487.1
Montana										
Metropolitan statistical area	395,085									
Area actually reporting	100.0%	2,264	18	244	207	1,795	11,842	1,251	9,245	1,346
Cities outside metropolitan areas	248,632									
Area actually reporting	100.0%	1,266	8	210	36	1,012	5,234	430	4,354	450
Nonmetropolitan counties	479,150									
Area actually reporting	99.6%	1,158	24	156	19	959	4,455	566	3,188	701
Estimated total	100.0%	1,163	24	157	19	963	4,467	568	3,196	703
State total	1,122,867	4,693	50	611	262	3,770	21,543	2,249	16,795	2,499
Rate per 100,000 inhabitants		417.9	4.5	54.4	23.3	335.7	1,918.6	200.3	1,495.7	222.6
Nebraska										
Metropolitan statistical area	1,299,398									
Area actually reporting	99.9%	4,528	47	794	539	3,148	30,971	2,782	23,343	4,846
Estimated total	100.0%	4,529	47	794	539	3,149	30,980	2,784	23,349	4,847
Cities outside metropolitan areas	355,028									
Area actually reporting	96.8%	736	5	208	31	492	4,823	548	3,882	393
Estimated total	100.0%	737	5	208	31	493	4,883	559	3,931	393
Nonmetropolitan counties	313,497									
Area actually reporting	89.1%	266	10	77	2	177	1,155	217	785	153
Estimated total	100.0%	299	10	87	2	200	1,308	248	888	172
State total	1,967,923	5,565	62	1,089	572	3,842	37,171	3,591	28,168	5,412
Rate per 100,000 inhabitants		282.8	3.2	55.3	29.1	195.2	1,888.8	182.5	1,431.4	275.0
Nevada										
Metropolitan statistical area	2,877,882									
Area actually reporting	100.0%	13,510	195	1,716	2,677	8,922	72,006	12,964	43,974	15,068

Table 5. Crime in the United States, by State and Area, 2022—Continued

(Number, percent, rate per 100,000 population.)

Area	Population[1]	Violent crime	Murder and nonnegligent manslaughter	Rape	Robbery	Aggravated assault	Property crime	Burglary	Larceny-theft	Motor vehicle theft
Cities outside metropolitan areas	50,407									
Area actually reporting	89.9%	202	5	36	15	146	949	178	630	141
Estimated total	100.0%	218	5	38	16	159	1,042	202	686	154
Nonmetropolitan counties	249,483									
Area actually reporting	95.9%	661	14	108	42	497	2,468	637	1,484	347
Estimated total	100.0%	699	16	117	42	524	2,587	693	1,528	366
State total	3,177,772	14,427	216	1,871	2,735	9,605	75,635	13,859	46,188	15,588
Rate per 100,000 inhabitants		454.0	6.8	58.9	86.1	302.3	2,380.1	436.1	1,453.5	490.5
New Hampshire										
Metropolitan statistical area	875,630									
Area actually reporting	98.9%	1,159	11	308	162	678	8,545	630	7,301	614
Estimated total	100.0%	1,164	11	310	162	681	8,589	634	7,338	617
Cities outside metropolitan areas	496,304									
Area actually reporting	98.7%	551	11	226	62	252	5,312	357	4,661	294
Estimated total	100.0%	557	11	229	62	255	5,362	361	4,704	297
Nonmetropolitan counties	23,297									
Area actually reporting	100.0%	31	3	14	0	14	154	30	110	14
State total	1,395,231	1,752	25	553	224	950	14,105	1,025	12,152	928
Rate per 100,000 inhabitants		125.6	1.8	39.6	16.1	68.1	1,010.9	73.5	871.0	66.5
New Jersey	9,261,699									
Metropolitan statistical area	1	16720	258	1377	4032	11053	119704	12367	93947	13390
Area actually reporting	100.0%	18,274	277	1,524	4,353	12,120	129,166	13,529	100,958	14,679
Cities outside metropolitan areas	None									
Nonmetropolitan counties	None									
State total	9,261,699	18,794	286	1,557	4,410	12,541	131,209	13,708	102,718	14,783
Rate per 100,000 inhabitants		202.9	3.1	16.8	47.6	135.4	1,416.7	148.0	1,109.1	159.6
New Mexico										
Metropolitan statistical area	1,417,824									
Area actually reporting	97.0%	12,449	175	793	2,042	9,439	48,219	9,268	29,633	9,318
Estimated total	100.0%	12,614	176	808	2,051	9,579	48,835	9,448	29,954	9,433
Cities outside metropolitan areas	398,625									
Area actually reporting	74.0%	2,089	23	204	175	1,687	8,373	1,805	5,498	1,070
Estimated total	100.0%	2,691	32	256	228	2,175	10,906	2,390	7,133	1,383
Nonmetropolitan counties	296,895									
Area actually reporting	47.9%	892	38	65	41	748	2,008	530	1,033	445
Estimated total	100.0%	1,189	45	89	59	996	3,322	926	1,764	632
State total	2,113,344	16,494	253	1,153	2,338	12,750	63,063	12,764	38,851	11,448
Rate per 100,000 inhabitants		780.5	12.0	54.6	110.6	603.3	2,984.0	604.0	1,838.4	541.7
New York										
Metropolitan statistical area	18,308,532									
Area actually reporting	98.9%	81,340	740	5,005	21,696	53,899	318,929	29,020	264,215	25,694
Estimated total	100.0%	81,998	754	5,048	21,865	54,331	322,376	29,505	266,739	26,132
Cities outside metropolitan areas	498,224									
Area actually reporting	93.9%	1,061	14	204	122	721	7,954	1,046	6,523	385
Estimated total	100.0%	1,104	14	211	127	752	8,329	1,095	6,830	404
Nonmetropolitan counties	870,395									
Area actually reporting	92.5%	1,342	15	541	46	740	7,808	1,336	6,050	422
Estimated total	100.0%	1,367	15	546	48	758	8,052	1,376	6,241	435
State total	19,677,151	84,469	783	5,805	22,040	55,841	338,757	31,976	279,810	26,971
Rate per 100,000 inhabitants		429.3	4.0	29.5	112.0	283.8	1,721.6	162.5	1,422.0	137.1
North Carolina										
Metropolitan statistical area	8,759,259									
Area actually reporting	96.8%	35,140	624	2,411	5,208	26,897	180,584	29,519	133,517	17,548
Estimated total	100.0%	35,635	633	2,471	5,243	27,288	184,229	30,261	136,061	17,907
Cities outside metropolitan areas	589,179									
Area actually reporting	85.8%	3,400	92	295	369	2,644	16,651	3,481	12,006	1,164
Estimated total	100.0%	3,770	100	323	407	2,940	18,971	3,893	13,770	1,308
Nonmetropolitan counties	1,350,535									
Area actually reporting	90.0%	3,524	115	426	199	2,784	15,833	4,945	9,000	1,888
Estimated total	100.0%	3,939	129	473	225	3,112	17,641	5,514	10,014	2,113
State total	10,698,973	43,344	862	3,267	5,875	33,340	220,841	39,668	159,845	21,328
Rate per 100,000 inhabitants		405.1	8.1	30.5	54.9	311.6	2,064.1	370.8	1,494.0	199.3
North Dakota										
Metropolitan statistical area	399,910									
Area actually reporting	100.0%	1,414	16	257	187	954	11,448	2,082	8,065	1,301
Cities outside metropolitan areas	184,008									
Area actually reporting	100.0%	566	5	131	23	407	2,907	473	1,997	437
Nonmetropolitan counties	195,343									
Area actually reporting	100.0%	199	6	54	5	134	1,190	234	702	254
State total	779,261	2,179	27	442	215	1,495	15,545	2,789	10,764	1,992
Rate per 100,000 inhabitants		279.6	3.5	56.7	27.6	191.8	1,994.8	357.9	1,381.3	255.6
Ohio										
Metropolitan statistical area	9,463,754									
Area actually reporting	94.1%	30,500	656	4,589	5,987	19,268	177,126	25,255	126,445	25,426
Estimated total	100.0%	31,233	662	4,744	6,062	19,765	185,611	26,110	133,502	25,999

Table 5. Crime in the United States, by State and Area, 2022—Continued

(Number, percent, rate per 100,000 population.)

Area	Population[1]	Violent crime	Murder and nonnegligent manslaughter	Rape	Robbery	Aggravated assault	Property crime	Burglary	Larceny-theft	Motor vehicle theft
Cities outside metropolitan areas	1,010,201									
Area actually reporting	78.9%	1,327	27	416	113	771	11,751	1,494	9,753	504
Estimated total	100.0%	1,705	27	508	130	1,040	14,913	1,919	12,353	641
Nonmetropolitan counties	1,282,103									
Area actually reporting	83.7%	1,373	25	377	45	926	7,613	1,666	5,166	781
Estimated total	100.0%	1,572	29	440	51	1,052	9,051	1,986	6,139	926
State total	11,756,058	34,510	718	5,692	6,243	21,857	209,575	30,015	151,994	27,566
Rate per 100,000 inhabitants		293.6	6.1	48.4	53.1	185.9	1,782.7	255.3	1,292.9	234.5
Oklahoma										
Metropolitan statistical area	2,721,256									
Area actually reporting	100.0%	12,712	201	1,714	1,413	9,384	67,617	13,422	44,876	9,319
Cities outside metropolitan areas	727,463									
Area actually reporting	99.7%	2,998	39	422	197	2,340	19,439	4,057	13,285	2,097
Estimated total	100.0%	3,002	39	422	197	2,344	19,468	4,065	13,301	2,102
Nonmetropolitan counties	571,081									
Area actually reporting	100.0%	1,157	30	177	22	928	6,671	1,914	3,557	1,200
State total	4,019,800	16,871	270	2,313	1,632	12,656	93,756	19,401	61,734	12,621
Rate per 100,000 inhabitants		419.7	6.7	57.5	40.6	314.8	2,332.4	482.6	1,535.7	314.0
Oregon										
Metropolitan statistical area	3,540,470									
Area actually reporting	96.6%	12,289	170	1,394	2,653	8,072	107,046	12,590	73,300	21,156
Estimated total	100.0%	12,545	173	1,434	2,697	8,241	109,219	12,861	74,801	21,557
Cities outside metropolitan areas	324,127									
Area actually reporting	96.2%	1,093	7	180	166	740	10,510	1,419	8,046	1,045
Estimated total	100.0%	1,123	7	183	168	765	10,749	1,457	8,220	1,072
Nonmetropolitan counties	375,540									
Area actually reporting	91.0%	788	11	95	41	641	4,072	877	2,523	672
Estimated total	100.0%	852	12	105	45	690	4,491	977	2,757	757
State total	4,240,137	14,520	192	1,722	2,910	9,696	124,459	15,295	85,778	23,386
Rate per 100,000 inhabitants		342.4	4.5	40.6	68.6	228.7	2,935.3	360.7	2,023.0	551.5
Pennsylvania[3]										
Metropolitan statistical area	11,537,031									
Area actually reporting	93.7%	32,480	954	3,008	8,497	20,021	171,123	16,227	135,005	19,891
Estimated total	100.0%	34,198	967	3,238	8,741	21,252	179,825	17,059	142,289	20,477
Cities outside metropolitan areas	629,580									
Area actually reporting	86.7%	888	22	138	37	691	4,991	651	4,199	141
Estimated total	100.0%	981	38	170	41	732	5,686	757	4,785	144
Nonmetropolitan counties	805,397									
Area actually reporting	100.0%	1,128	15	420	47	646	6,800	1,415	4,857	528
State total	12,972,008	36,307	1,020	3,828	8,829	22,630	192,311	19,231	151,931	21,149
Rate per 100,000 inhabitants		279.9	7.9	29.5	68.1	174.5	1,482.5	148.2	1,171.2	163.0
Rhode Island										
Metropolitan statistical area	1,093,734									
Area actually reporting	100.0%	1,885	16	416	269	1,184	14,058	1,401	10,911	1,746
Cities outside metropolitan areas	None									
Nonmetropolitan counties	None									
State total	1,093,734	1,885	16	416	269	1,184	14,058	1,401	10,911	1,746
Rate per 100,000 inhabitants		172.3	1.5	38.0	24.6	108.3	1,285.3	128.1	997.6	159.6
South Carolina										
Metropolitan statistical area	4,557,911									
Area actually reporting	99.8%	21,005	379	1,737	1,863	17,026	103,628	14,982	77,223	11,423
Estimated total	100.0%	21,041	379	1,739	1,865	17,058	103,850	15,017	77,390	11,443
Cities outside metropolitan areas	197,117									
Area actually reporting	98.3%	1,856	109	124	155	1,468	7,697	1,300	5,917	480
Estimated total	100.0%	1,882	109	126	157	1,490	7,794	1,318	5,989	487
Nonmetropolitan counties	527,606									
Area actually reporting	100.0%	3,032	104	154	123	2,651	10,291	2,297	6,758	1,236
State total	5,282,634	25,955	592	2,019	2,145	21,199	121,935	18,632	90,137	13,166
Rate per 100,000 inhabitants		491.3	11.2	38.2	40.6	401.3	2,308.2	352.7	1,706.3	249.2
South Dakota										
Metropolitan statistical area	451,110									
Area actually reporting	98.5%	1,976	16	252	214	1,494	10,718	1,617	7,389	1,712
Estimated total	100.0%	1,990	16	254	214	1,506	10,836	1,645	7,465	1,726
Cities outside metropolitan areas	221,422									
Area actually reporting	90.7%	1,114	22	212	16	864	3,750	508	2,909	333
Estimated total	100.0%	1,194	22	217	16	939	4,086	553	3,180	353
Nonmetropolitan counties	237,292									
Area actually reporting	74.9%	188	1	26	0	161	662	145	420	97
Estimated total	100.0%	250	1	37	0	212	882	195	562	125
State total	909,824	3,434	39	508	230	2,657	15,804	2,393	11,207	2,204
Rate per 100,000 inhabitants		377.4	4.3	55.8	25.3	292.0	1,737.0	263.0	1,231.8	242.2
Tennessee										
Metropolitan statistical area	5,524,925									
Area actually reporting	99.9%	38,620	534	2,264	4,587	31,235	140,557	18,363	99,259	22,935
Estimated total	100.0%	38,622	534	2,264	4,587	31,237	140,574	18,365	99,272	22,937

Table 5. Crime in the United States, by State and Area, 2022—Continued

(Number, percent, rate per 100,000 population.)

Area	Population[1]	Violent crime	Murder and nonnegligent manslaughter	Rape	Robbery	Aggravated assault	Property crime	Burglary	Larceny-theft	Motor vehicle theft
Cities outside metropolitan areas	505,138									
Area actually reporting	98.9%	2,653	37	219	98	2,299	12,518	1,812	9,597	1,109
Estimated total	100.0%	2,674	37	219	98	2,320	12,597	1,825	9,653	1,119
Nonmetropolitan counties	1,021,276									
Area actually reporting	100.0%	2,533	38	211	46	2,238	9,171	2,309	5,368	1,494
State total	7,051,339	43,829	609	2,694	4,731	35,795	162,342	22,499	114,293	25,550
Rate per 100,000 inhabitants		621.6	8.6	38.2	67.1	507.6	2,302.3	319.1	1,620.9	362.3
Texas										
Metropolitan statistical area	26,912,486									
Area actually reporting	99.4%	120,772	1,866	13,579	20,670	84,657	649,089	90,421	463,694	94,974
Estimated total	100.0%	121,143	1,868	13,649	20,690	84,936	651,256	90,824	465,154	95,278
Cities outside metropolitan areas	1,444,842									
Area actually reporting	93.1%	5,050	96	702	342	3,910	24,143	5,023	16,982	2,138
Estimated total	100.0%	5,296	97	729	353	4,117	25,250	5,305	17,677	2,268
Nonmetropolitan counties	1,672,244									
Area actually reporting	91.7%	3,002	58	575	125	2,244	12,957	3,911	7,309	1,737
Estimated total	100.0%	3,263	61	624	133	2,445	14,154	4,273	7,977	1,904
State total	30,029,572	129,702	2,026	15,002	21,176	91,498	690,660	100,402	490,808	99,450
Rate per 100,000 inhabitants		431.9	6.7	50.0	70.5	304.7	2,299.9	334.3	1,634.4	331.2
Utah										
Metropolitan statistical area	3,032,394									
Area actually reporting	99.1%	7,298	63	1,739	987	4,509	59,751	6,264	46,802	6,685
Estimated total	100.0%	7,326	63	1,747	989	4,527	60,037	6,308	47,015	6,714
Cities outside metropolitan areas	157,539									
Area actually reporting	89.9%	321	1	101	6	213	2,223	218	1,884	121
Estimated total	100.0%	357	1	115	6	235	2,458	243	2,083	132
Nonmetropolitan counties	190,867									
Area actually reporting	90.6%	452	3	135	7	307	1,432	242	1,010	180
Estimated total	100.0%	492	3	148	7	334	1,574	267	1,109	198
State total	3,380,800	8,175	67	2,010	1,002	5,096	64,069	6,818	50,207	7,044
Rate per 100,000 inhabitants		241.8	2.0	59.5	29.6	150.7	1,895.1	201.7	1,485.1	208.4
Vermont										
Metropolitan statistical area	227,105									
Area actually reporting	100.0%	562	12	91	34	425	5,460	367	4,649	444
Cities outside metropolitan areas	199,698									
Area actually reporting	100.0%	588	4	102	45	437	4,436	425	3,900	111
Nonmetropolitan counties	220,261									
Area actually reporting	100.0%	286	6	45	7	228	917	192	675	50
State total	647,064	1,436	22	238	86	1,090	10,813	984	9,224	605
Rate per 100,000 inhabitants		221.9	3.4	36.8	13.3	168.5	1,671.1	152.1	1,425.5	93.5
Virginia										
Metropolitan statistical area	7,628,948									
Area actually reporting	99.9%	18,230	545	2,144	3,194	12,347	134,728	9,358	112,551	12,819
Estimated total	100.0%	18,232	545	2,144	3,194	12,349	134,747	9,360	112,568	12,819
Cities outside metropolitan areas	247,905									
Area actually reporting	99.9%	662	28	131	76	427	5,523	435	4,738	350
Estimated total	100.0%	662	28	131	76	427	5,526	435	4,741	350
Nonmetropolitan counties	806,766									
Area actually reporting	100.0%	1,430	65	348	66	951	6,976	1,023	5,164	789
State total	8,683,619	20,324	638	2,623	3,336	13,727	147,249	10,818	122,473	13,958
Rate per 100,000 inhabitants		234.0	7.3	30.2	38.4	158.1	1,695.7	124.6	1,410.4	160.7
Washington	6,977,179									
Metropolitan statistical area	99.7%	27,585	349	2,714	6,569	17,953	244,332	40,019	156,515	47,798
Area actually reporting	100.0%	27,623	349	2,721	6,574	17,979	244,752	40,103	156,788	47,861
Estimated total	319,446									
Cities outside metropolitan areas	92.1%	844	19	177	125	523	9,498	1,675	6,816	1,007
Area actually reporting	100.0%	887	19	189	128	551	10,243	1,812	7,337	1,094
Estimated total	489,161									
Nonmetropolitan counties	96.6%	711	18	140	53	500	6,095	1,856	3,439	800
Area actually reporting	1	737	19	145	54	519	6,328	1,922	3,584	822
Estimated total	7,785,786	29,247	387	3,055	6,756	19,049	261,323	43,837	167,709	49,777
State total		375.6	5.0	39.2	86.8	244.7	3,356.4	563.0	2,154.0	639.3
Rate per 100,000 inhabitants										
West Virginia	1,159,305									
Metropolitan statistical area	83.5%	3,001	59	569	157	2,216	15,545	2,396	12,014	1,135
Area actually reporting	100.0%	3,275	60	601	162	2,452	16,973	2,599	13,148	1,226
Estimated total	168,778									
Cities outside metropolitan areas	67.1%	373	3	22	8	340	1,500	161	1,287	52
Area actually reporting	100.0%	652	3	46	8	595	2,569	244	2,238	87
Estimated total	447,073									
Nonmetropolitan counties	87.3%	901	18	141	8	734	2,189	497	1,440	252
Area actually reporting	100.0%	1,007	18	142	8	839	2,294	534	1,499	261
Estimated total	1,775,156	4,934	81	789	178	3,886	21,836	3,377	16,885	1,574
State total		277.9	4.6	44.4	10.0	218.9	1,230.1	190.2	951.2	88.7
Rate per 100,000 inhabitants										

Table 5. Crime in the United States, by State and Area, 2022—Continued

(Number, percent, rate per 100,000 population.)

Area	Population[1]	Violent crime	Murder and nonnegligent manslaughter	Rape	Robbery	Aggravated assault	Property crime	Burglary	Larceny-theft	Motor vehicle theft
Wisconsin										
Metropolitan statistical area	4,382,290									
Area actually reporting	98.7%	15,187	290	1,669	2,273	10,955	68,491	7,501	47,027	13,963
Estimated total	100.0%	15,248	290	1,683	2,280	10,995	69,064	7,536	47,517	14,011
Cities outside metropolitan areas	665,543									
Area actually reporting	89.6%	1,230	7	327	30	866	7,757	581	6,782	394
Estimated total	100.0%	1,357	7	362	31	957	8,572	640	7,500	432
Nonmetropolitan counties	844,706									
Area actually reporting	97.9%	878	17	223	12	626	3,879	861	2,722	296
Estimated total	100.0%	897	17	228	12	640	3,975	883	2,788	304
State total	5,892,539	17,502	314	2,273	2,323	12,592	81,611	9,059	57,805	14,747
Rate per 100,000 inhabitants		297.0	5.3	38.6	39.4	213.7	1,385.0	153.7	981.0	250.3
Wyoming										
Metropolitan statistical area	180,220									
Area actually reporting	67.8%	298	7	84	19	188	2,962	365	2,238	359
Estimated total	100.0%	459	7	140	33	279	5,074	608	3,867	599
Cities outside metropolitan areas	237,288									
Area actually reporting	85.8%	484	4	139	13	328	3,124	366	2,518	240
Estimated total	100.0%	548	4	158	13	373	3,499	452	2,780	267
Nonmetropolitan counties	163,873									
Area actually reporting	78.2%	130	3	52	0	75	742	125	555	62
Estimated total	100.0%	167	4	67	0	96	943	158	707	78
State total	581,381	1,174	15	365	46	748	9,516	1,218	7,354	944
Rate per 100,000 inhabitants		201.9	2.6	62.8	7.9	128.7	1,636.8	209.5	1,264.9	162.4

NOTE: Although arson data are included in the trend and clearance tables, sufficient data are not available to estimate totals for this offense. Therefore, no arson data are published in this table.
1 Population figures are U.S. Census Bureau provisional estimates as of July 1, 2020.   2 Includes offenses reported by the Metro Transit Police and the District of Columbia Fire and Emergency Medical Services: Arson Investigation Unit.   3 Limited data for 2022 were available for Florida, Illinois, Maryland, and Pennsylvania.

Table 6. Crime in the United States, by Selected Metropolitan Statistical Area, 2022

(Number, percent, rate per 100,000 population.)

Area	Population	Violent crime	Murder and nonnegligent manslaughter	Rape	Robbery	Aggravated assault	Property crime	Burglary	Larceny-theft	Motor vehicle theft
Abilene, TX M. S. A.	178,898									
Includes Callahan, Jones, Taylor Counties										
City of Abilene	125,186	587	7	107	82	391	2,498	446	1,854	198
Total area actually reporting	98.7%	649	8	122	84	435	2,799	543	2,020	236
Estimated total	100.0%	655	8	123	85	439	2,837	550	2,046	241
Rate per 100,000 inhabitants		366.1	4.5	68.8	47.5	245.4	1,585.8	307.4	1,143.7	134.7
Akron, OH M. S. A.	697,907									
Includes Portage, Summit Counties										
City of Akron	188,534	1,548	38	206	156	1,148	6,464	1,030	4,525	909
Total area actually reporting	98.5%	2,181	43	340	208	1,590	13,817	1,713	10,791	1,313
Estimated total	100.0%	2,190	43	342	208	1,597	14,052	1,730	11,001	1,321
Rate per 100,000 inhabitants		313.8	6.2	49.0	29.8	228.8	2,013.4	247.9	1,576.3	189.3
Albany, GA M. S. A.	147,645									
Includes Dougherty, Lee, Terrell, Worth Counties										
City of Albany	68,613	229	16	15	10	188	519	47	400	72
Total area actually reporting	87.1%	351	16	36	21	278	1,113	151	828	134
Estimated total	100.0%	411	18	42	25	326	1,357	189	1,003	165
Rate per 100,000 inhabitants		278.4	12.2	28.4	16.9	220.8	919.1	128	679.3	111.8
Albany-Lebanon, OR M. S. A.	130,407									
Includes Linn County										
City of Albany	47,684	89	2	10	28	50	1,318	124	1,041	153
City of Lebanon	19,456	35	0	1	4	30	244	20	184	40
Total area actually reporting	100.0%	239	2	28	48	162	2,911	351	2,182	378
Rate per 100,000 inhabitants		183.3	1.5	21.5	36.8	124.2	2,232.2	269.2	1,673.2	289.9
Albany-Schenectady-Troy, NY M. S. A.	906,806									
Includes Albany, Rensselaer, Saratoga, Schenectady, Schoharie Counties										
City of Albany	98,104	912	11	60	230	611	3,710	529	2,626	555
City of Schenectady	67,101	508	8	29	118	353	2,296	315	1,773	208
City of Troy	50,106	337	5	18	82	232	1,679	248	1,319	112
Total area actually reporting	99.7%	2,545	30	309	545	1,661	17,817	1,877	14,668	1,272
Estimated total	100.0%	2,547	30	309	545	1,663	17,845	1,880	14,691	1,274
Rate per 100,000 inhabitants		280.9	3.3	34.1	60.1	183.4	1,967.9	207.3	1,620.1	140.5
Albuquerque, NM M. S. A.	918,951									
Includes Bernalillo, Sandoval, Torrance, Valencia Counties										
City of Albuquerque	560,557	7,737	125	344	1,651	5,617	26,883	4,555	16,431	5,897
Total area actually reporting	95.7%	9,554	149	490	1,817	7,098	33,715	6,140	20,524	7,051
Estimated total	100.0%	9,705	150	504	1,825	7,226	34,276	6,304	20,812	7,160
Rate per 100,000 inhabitants		1,056.1	16.3	54.8	198.6	786.3	3,729.9	686.0	2,264.8	779.1
Alexandria, LA M. S. A.	149,795									
Includes Grant, Rapides Counties										
City of Alexandria	44,349	791	18	56	78	639	2,804	473	2,129	202
Total area actually reporting	85.8%	1,253	30	97	89	1,037	4,510	1,074	3,051	385
Estimated total	100.0%	1,366	31	106	97	1,132	5,125	1,168	3,535	422
Rate per 100,000 inhabitants		911.9	20.7	70.8	64.8	755.7	3,421.3	779.7	2,359.9	281.7
Amarillo, TX M. S. A.	272,284									
Includes Armstrong, Carson, Oldham, Potter, Randall Counties										
City of Amarillo	201,572	1,537	23	197	199	1,118	6,997	1,166	4,899	932
Total area actually reporting	99.7%	1,706	25	235	205	1,241	7,557	1,270	5,270	1,017
Estimated total	100.0%	1,707	25	235	205	1,242	7,571	1,272	5,280	1,019
Rate per 100,000 inhabitants		626.9	9.2	86.3	75.3	456.1	2,780.6	467.2	1,939.2	374.2
Anchorage, AK M. S. A.	301,935									
Includes Anchorage, Matanuska-Susitna Counties										
City of Anchorage	285,821	3,289	29	492	436	2,332	7,900	1,179	5,605	1,116
Total area actually reporting	100.0%	3,371	29	501	445	2,396	8,301	1,196	5,950	1,155
Rate per 100,000 inhabitants		1,116.5	9.6	165.9	147.4	793.5	2,749.3	396.1	1,970.6	382.5
Ann Arbor, MI M. S. A.	367,133									
Includes Washtenaw County										
City of Ann Arbor	120,549	371	1	49	39	282	2,069	259	1,662	148
Total area actually reporting	100.0%	1,503	12	191	115	1,186	5,557	696	4,374	487
Rate per 100,000 inhabitants		409.4	3.3	52.0	31.3	323.0	1,513.6	189.6	1,191.4	132.6
Anniston-Oxford, AL M. S. A.	116,107									
Includes Calhoun County										
City of Anniston	21,007	177	4	11	17	145	1,152	246	766	140
City of Oxford	17,860	42	0	6	4	32	520	38	460	22
Total area actually reporting	100.0%	626	4	40	22	560	2,381	440	1,756	185
Rate per 100,000 inhabitants		539.2	3.4	34.5	18.9	482.3	2,050.7	379.0	1,512.4	159.3
Appleton, WI M. S. A.	244,565									
Includes Calumet, Outagamie Counties										
City of Appleton	72,985	196	1	31	8	157	1,094	113	930	50
Total area actually reporting	97.5%	381	4	102	15	261	2,913	434	2,356	122
Estimated total	100.0%	387	4	103	16	265	2,974	438	2,408	127
Rate per 100,000 inhabitants		158.2	1.6	42.1	6.5	108.4	1,216.0	179.1	984.6	51.9

Table 6. Crime in the United States, by Selected Metropolitan Statistical Area, 2022—Continued

(Number, percent, rate per 100,000 population.)

Area	Population	Violent crime	Murder and nonnegligent manslaughter	Rape	Robbery	Aggravated assault	Property crime	Burglary	Larceny-theft	Motor vehicle theft
Asheville, NC M. S. A.	477,564									
Includes Buncombe, Haywood, Henderson, Madison Counties										
City of Asheville	93,729	879	12	61	136	670	4,811	676	3,717	418
Total area actually reporting	98.6%	1,340	18	152	160	1,010	9,248	1,715	6,612	921
Estimated total	100.0%	1,352	18	154	160	1,020	9,404	1,738	6,731	935
Rate per 100,000 inhabitants		283.1	3.8	32.2	33.5	213.6	1,969.2	363.9	1,409.4	195.8
Athens-Clarke County, GA M. S. A.	220,680									
Includes Clarke, Madison, Oconee, Oglethorpe Counties										
City of Athens-Clarke County	128,177	763	4	153	67	539	3,374	424	2,605	345
Total area actually reporting	99.5%	924	7	194	77	646	4,744	552	3,756	436
Estimated total	100.0%	925	7	194	77	647	4,757	554	3,766	437
Rate per 100,000 inhabitants		419.2	3.2	87.9	34.9	293.2	2,155.6	251.0	1,706.5	198.0
Atlanta-Sandy Springs-Alpharetta, GA M. S. A.	6,209,475									
Includes Barrow, Bartow, Butts, Carroll, Cherokee, Clayton, Cobb, Coweta, Dawson, Dekalb, Douglas, Fayette, Forsyth, Fulton, Gwinnett, Haralson, Heard, Henry, Jasper, Lamar, Meriwether, Morgan, Newton, Paulding, Pickens, Pike, Rockdale, Spalding, Walton Counties										
City of Atlanta	495,707	4,167	168	157	711	3,131	18,579	1,839	13,437	3,303
City of Sandy Springs	106,747	148	4	25	29	90	1,597	186	1,258	153
City of Alpharetta	66,629	183	0	13	6	164	868	56	771	41
City of Marietta	62,059	273	3	31	54	185	1,534	168	1,192	174
Total area actually reporting	93.1%	21,803	517	2,110	2,919	16,257	99,663	11,234	74,840	13,590
Estimated total	100.0%	23,338	549	2,262	3,104	17,423	106,911	12,103	80,361	14,448
Rate per 100,000 inhabitants		375.8	8.8	36.4	50.0	280.6	1,721.7	194.9	1,294.2	232.7
Atlantic City-Hammonton, NJ M. S. A.	275,929									
Includes Atlantic County										
City of Atlantic City	38,502	651	7	56	205	383	3,000	645	2,103	252
City of Hammonton	14,861	44	0	1	4	39	104	13	78	13
Total area actually reporting	93.0%	985	12	90	254	629	6,635	1,150	5,043	442
Estimated total	100.0%	1,049	13	96	266	674	6,993	1,198	5,303	492
Rate per 100,000 inhabitants		380.2	4.7	34.8	96.4	244.3	2,534.3	434.2	1,921.9	178.3
Auburn-Opelika, AL M. S. A.	180,539									
Includes Lee County										
City of Auburn	80,759	106	3	23	8	72	937	74	797	66
City of Opelika	32,010	259	7	23	19	210	877	90	718	69
Total area actually reporting	100.0%	586	17	77	36	455	2,728	327	2,129	272
Rate per 100,000 inhabitants		324.6	9.4	42.7	19.9	252.0	1,511.0	181.1	1,179.2	150.7
Augusta-Richmond County, GA-SC M. S. A.	622,841									
Includes Aiken, Burke, Columbia, Edgefield, Lincoln, Mcduffie, Richmond Counties										
Total area actually reporting	97.5%	822	25	120	95	582	5,802	952	4,236	614
Estimated total	100.0%	892	27	125	101	639	6,111	985	4,486	640
Rate per 100,000 inhabitants		143.2	4.3	20.1	16.2	102.6	981.1	158.1	720.2	102.8
Austin-Round Rock-Georgetown, TX M. S. A.	2,422,231									
Includes Bastrop, Caldwell, Hays, Travis, Williamson Counties										
City of Austin	964,227	5,210	69	527	938	3,675	34,614	4,811	24,455	5,347
City of Round Rock	127,349	215	2	47	42	124	2,934	166	2,597	171
City of Georgetown	83,371	133	2	44	11	76	1,048	128	865	55
City of San Marcos	69,470	445	0	106	47	292	1,811	211	1,380	220
Total area actually reporting	99.9%	8,465	113	1,200	1,237	5,915	54,544	7,354	39,856	7,335
Estimated total	100.0%	8,469	113	1,201	1,237	5,918	54,577	7,360	39,879	7,339
Rate per 100,000 inhabitants		349.6	4.7	49.6	51.1	244.3	2,253.2	303.9	1,646.4	303.0
Bakersfield, CA M. S. A.	926,446									
Includes Kern County										
City of Bakersfield	411,873	2,106	38	129	664	1,275	16,361	3,184	8,319	4,858
Total area actually reporting	100.0%	6,641	102	298	1,281	4,960	29,695	6,471	14,113	9,111
Rate per 100,000 inhabitants		716.8	11.0	32.2	138.3	535.4	3,205.3	698.5	1,523.3	983.4
Baltimore-Columbia-Towson, MD[1] M. S. A.	2,838,119									
Includes Anne Arundel, Baltimore, Baltimore City, Carroll, Harford, Howard, Queen Anne'S Counties										
City of Baltimore	570,546	8,861	287	259	3,172	5,143	18,699	3,333	11,940	3,426
Total area actually reporting	98.1%	15,211	352	924	4,421	9,514	51,609	6,435	38,813	6,361
Estimated total	100.0%	15,307	355	947	4,432	9,573	52,044	6,515	39,136	6,393
Rate per 100,000 inhabitants		539.3	12.5	33.4	156.2	337.3	1,833.7	229.6	1,378.9	225.3
Bangor, ME M. S. A.	153,862									
Includes Penobscot County										
City of Bangor	32,078	52	0	7	19	26	1,550	100	1,417	33
Total area actually reporting	100.0%	85	0	9	24	52	2,569	206	2,269	94
Rate per 100,000 inhabitants		55.2	0.0	5.8	15.6	33.8	1,669.7	133.9	1,474.7	61.1
Barnstable Town, MA M. S. A.	237,052									
Includes Barnstable County										
City of Barnstable	50,501	234	1	26	11	196	401	64	311	26
Total area actually reporting	100.0%	619	4	84	27	504	1,686	308	1,308	70
Rate per 100,000 inhabitants		261.1	1.7	35.4	11.4	212.6	711.2	129.9	551.8	29.5

Table 6. Crime in the United States, by Selected Metropolitan Statistical Area, 2022—Continued

(Number, percent, rate per 100,000 population.)

Area	Population	Violent crime	Murder and nonnegligent manslaughter	Rape	Robbery	Aggravated assault	Property crime	Burglary	Larceny-theft	Motor vehicle theft
Baton Rouge, LA M. S. A.	872,256									
Includes Ascension, Assumption, East Baton Rouge, East Feliciana, Iberville, Livingston, Pointe Coupee, St Helena, West Baton Rouge, West Feliciana Counties										
City of Baton Rouge	219,913	2,260	64	134	340	1,722	12,870	3,109	8,168	1,593
Total area actually reporting	94.9%	4,586	101	332	550	3,603	26,402	5,484	18,099	2,819
Estimated total	100.0%	4,766	104	341	559	3,762	27,093	5,612	18,605	2,876
Rate per 100,000 inhabitants		546.4	11.9	39.1	64.1	431.3	3,106.1	643.4	2,133.0	329.7
Battle Creek, MI M. S. A.	133,524									
Includes Calhoun County										
City of Battle Creek	61,347	720	10	97	33	580	1,644	346	1,153	145
Total area actually reporting	100.0%	1,027	10	151	45	821	3,475	640	2,586	249
Rate per 100,000 inhabitants		769.2	7.5	113.1	33.7	614.9	2,602.5	479.3	1,936.7	186.5
Bay City, MI M. S. A.	102,379									
Includes Bay County										
City of Bay City	32,249	179	0	29	5	145	384	59	288	37
Total area actually reporting	100.0%	296	3	60	14	219	965	133	745	87
Rate per 100,000 inhabitants		289.1	2.9	58.6	13.7	213.9	942.6	129.9	727.7	85.0
Beaumont-Port Arthur, TX M. S. A.	396,273									
Includes Hardin, Jefferson, Orange Counties										
City of Beaumont	110,898	1,198	18	105	257	818	4,305	971	2,973	361
City of Port Arthur	55,899	417	8	40	48	321	1,008	273	620	115
Total area actually reporting	100.0%	2,142	36	248	336	1,522	7,908	1,801	5,277	830
Rate per 100,000 inhabitants		540.5	9.1	62.6	84.8	384.1	1,995.6	454.5	1,331.7	209.5
Beckley, WV M. S. A.	112,621									
Includes Fayette, Raleigh Counties										
City of Beckley	16,843	125	1	15	8	101	1,297	134	1,114	49
Total area actually reporting	96.7%	309	4	64	14	227	2,470	358	1,982	130
Estimated total	100.0%	318	4	64	14	236	2,495	361	2,002	133
Rate per 100,000 inhabitants		282.4	3.6	56.8	12.4	209.6	2,215.4	320.5	1,777.6	118.1
Bellingham, WA M. S. A.	231,154									
Includes Whatcom County										
City of Bellingham	93,014	378	2	22	135	219	6,058	801	4,764	493
Total area actually reporting	100.0%	589	8	66	162	353	8,035	1,149	6,207	679
Rate per 100,000 inhabitants		254.8	3.5	28.6	70.1	152.7	3,476.0	497.1	2,685.2	293.7
Bend, OR M. S. A.	209,847									
Includes Deschutes County										
City of Bend	104,649	158	2	30	27	99	1,660	169	1,327	164
Total area actually reporting	100.0%	303	3	50	41	209	3,056	299	2,440	317
Rate per 100,000 inhabitants		144.4	1.4	23.8	19.5	99.6	1,456.3	142.5	1,162.8	151.1
Billings, MT M. S. A.	189,549									
Includes Carbon, Stillwater, Yellowstone Counties										
City of Billings	117,866	1,095	13	89	144	849	4,943	529	3,613	801
Total area actually reporting	100.0%	1,300	14	111	150	1,025	5,882	605	4,332	945
Rate per 100,000 inhabitants		685.8	7.4	58.6	79.1	540.8	3,103.2	319.2	2,285.4	498.6
Binghamton, NY M. S. A.	245,731									
Includes Broome, Tioga Counties										
City of Binghamton	47,259	318	0	21	49	248	1,746	294	1,343	109
Total area actually reporting	100.0%	670	4	117	71	478	4,840	687	3,908	245
Rate per 100,000 inhabitants		272.7	1.6	47.6	28.9	194.5	1,969.6	279.6	1,590.4	99.7
Birmingham-Hoover, AL M. S. A.	1,118,053									
Includes Bibb, Blount, Chilton, Jefferson, Shelby, St Clair Counties										
City of Birmingham	195,050	3,280	142	62	477	2,599	8,139	1,519	4,821	1,799
City of Hoover	92,491	90	2	16	13	59	1,443	114	1,251	78
Total area actually reporting	98.7%	5,929	200	276	739	4,714	22,603	3,413	15,743	3,448
Estimated total	100.0%	5,970	201	278	741	4,750	22,849	3,448	15,929	3,473
Rate per 100,000 inhabitants		534.0	18.0	24.9	66.3	424.8	2,043.6	308.4	1,424.7	310.6
Bismarck, ND M. S. A.	136,579									
Includes Burleigh, Morton, Oliver Counties										
City of Bismarck	74,604	231	6	32	43	150	2,509	383	1,870	256
Total area actually reporting	100.0%	325	9	50	46	220	3,589	566	2,614	409
Rate per 100,000 inhabitants		238.0	6.6	36.6	33.7	161.1	2,627.8	414.4	1,913.9	299.5
Blacksburg-Christiansburg, VA M. S. A.	165,068									
Includes Giles, Montgomery, Pulaski, Radford City Counties										
City of Blacksburg	45,749	20	1	11	3	5	266	21	235	10
City of Christiansburg	21,746	40	0	10	2	28	514	22	473	19
Total area actually reporting	100.0%	340	4	83	15	238	2,603	256	2,195	152
Rate per 100,000 inhabitants		206.0	2.4	50.3	9.1	144.2	1,576.9	155.1	1,329.8	92.1
Bloomington, IN M. S. A.	161,977									
Includes Monroe, Owen Counties										
City of Bloomington	80,135	407	4	60	59	284	1,874	249	1,508	117

Table 6. Crime in the United States, by Selected Metropolitan Statistical Area, 2022—Continued

(Number, percent, rate per 100,000 population.)

Area	Population	Violent crime	Murder and nonnegligent manslaughter	Rape	Robbery	Aggravated assault	Property crime	Burglary	Larceny-theft	Motor vehicle theft
Total area actually reporting	82.6%	471	5	98	66	302	2,377	288	1,923	166
Estimated total	100.0%	509	5	103	68	333	2,553	317	2,042	194
Rate per 100,000 inhabitants		314.2	3.1	63.6	42.0	205.6	1,576.1	195.7	1,260.7	119.8
Boise City, ID M. S. A.	814,807									
Includes Ada, Boise, Canyon, Gem, Owyhee Counties										
City of Boise	239,074	591	3	186	46	356	2,878	285	2,327	266
Total area actually reporting	99.9%	2,144	15	521	84	1,524	7,459	978	5,723	758
Estimated total	100.0%	2,146	15	522	84	1,525	7,464	980	5,725	759
Rate per 100,000 inhabitants		263.4	1.8	64.1	10.3	187.2	916.0	120.3	702.6	93.2
Boston-Cambridge-Newton, MA-NH M. S. A.	4,884,092									
Includes the Metro Divisions of Boston, MA; Cambridge-Newton-Framingham, MA; Rockingham County-Strafford County, NH										
City of Boston, MA	638,925	3,955	44	176	770	2,965	11,514	1,213	9,116	1,185
City of Cambridge, MA	117,044	475	0	42	96	337	2,622	278	2,205	139
City of Newton, MA	86,710	56	1	8	8	39	568	60	497	11
City of Framingham, MA	70,716	201	1	17	4	179	990	356	549	85
City of Waltham, MA	63,525	95	0	14	3	78	349	55	269	25
Total area actually reporting	99.8%	13,297	87	1,258	1,660	10,292	50,228	5,839	39,780	4,609
Estimated total	100.0%	13,302	87	1,260	1,660	10,295	50,265	5,842	39,811	4,612
Rate per 100,000 inhabitants		272.4	1.8	25.8	34.0	210.8	1,029.2	119.6	815.1	94.4
Boston, MA M. D.	2,015,569									
Includes Norfolk, Plymouth, Suffolk Counties										
Total area actually reporting	100.0%	7,542	61	606	1,052	5,823	24,076	2,762	18,817	2,497
Rate per 100,000 inhabitants		374.2	3.0	30.1	52.2	288.9	1,194.5	137.0	933.6	123.9
Cambridge-Newton-Framingham, MA M. D.	2,416,824									
Includes Essex, Middlesex Counties										
Total area actually reporting	100.0%	5,342	25	496	566	4,255	22,542	2,811	17,856	1,875
Rate per 100,000 inhabitants		221.0	1.0	20.5	23.4	176.1	932.7	116.3	738.8	77.6
Rockingham County-Strafford County, NH M. D.	451,699									
Includes Rockingham, Strafford Counties										
Total area actually reporting	98.1%	413	1	156	42	214	3,610	266	3,107	237
Estimated total	100.0%	418	1	158	42	217	3,647	269	3,138	240
Rate per 100,000 inhabitants		92.5	0.2	35.0	9.3	48.0	807.4	59.6	694.7	53.1
Boulder, CO M. S. A.	328,241									
Includes Boulder County										
City of Boulder	103,099	383	7	51	49	276	3,093	471	2,298	324
Total area actually reporting	100.0%	1,047	19	232	90	706	8,596	1,160	6,432	1,004
Rate per 100,000 inhabitants		319.0	5.8	70.7	27.4	215.1	2,618.8	353.4	1,959.5	305.9
Bowling Green, KY M. S. A.	185,136									
Includes Allen, Butler, Edmonson, Warren Counties										
City of Bowling Green	74,427	212	4	65	56	87	2,841	356	2,196	289
Total area actually reporting	100.0%	288	6	82	63	137	3,633	507	2,745	381
Rate per 100,000 inhabitants		155.6	3.2	44.3	34.0	74.0	1,962.3	273.9	1,482.7	205.8
Bremerton-Silverdale-Port Orchard, WA M. S. A.	273,907									
Includes Kitsap County										
City of Bremerton	44,256	210	1	40	44	125	1,859	316	1,191	352
City of Port Orchard	16,351	72	0	15	17	40	955	136	596	223
Total area actually reporting	100.0%	938	5	161	127	645	7,570	1,375	4,880	1,315
Rate per 100,000 inhabitants		342.5	1.8	58.8	46.4	235.5	2,763.7	502.0	1,781.6	480.1
Bridgeport-Stamford-Norwalk, CT M. S. A.	946,590									
Includes Fairfield County										
City of Bridgeport	148,395	606	15	52	277	262	1,843	303	965	575
City of Stamford	136,936	264	2	24	74	164	1,601	144	1,285	172
City of Norwalk	91,414	113	1	10	26	76	1,582	76	1,349	157
City of Danbury	87,164	120	4	19	23	74	1,138	106	931	101
City of Stratford	52,320	59	0	10	28	21	973	41	798	134
Total area actually reporting	100.0%	1,288	24	140	473	651	11,711	1,065	8,987	1,659
Rate per 100,000 inhabitants		136.1	2.5	14.8	50.0	68.8	1,237.2	112.5	949.4	175.3
Brownsville-Harlingen, TX M. S. A.	427,426									
Includes Cameron County										
City of Brownsville	188,906	817	4	71	127	615	3,467	398	2,880	189
City of Harlingen	72,047	233	3	11	52	167	2,034	260	1,646	128
Total area actually reporting	98.7%	1,629	11	165	214	1,239	7,525	959	6,066	500
Estimated total	100.0%	1,641	11	167	215	1,248	7,614	975	6,127	512
Rate per 100,000 inhabitants		383.9	2.6	39.1	50.3	292.0	1,781.4	228.1	1,433.5	119.8
Brunswick, GA M. S. A.	114,832									
Includes Brantley, Glynn, Mcintosh Counties										
City of Brunswick	14,650	204	3	16	58	127	811	108	647	56
Total area actually reporting	99.1%	474	7	52	84	331	2,395	401	1,756	238
Estimated total	100.0%	475	7	52	84	332	2,405	402	1,764	239
Rate per 100,000 inhabitants		413.6	6.1	45.3	73.2	289.1	2,094.4	350.1	1,536.2	208.1

Table 6. Crime in the United States, by Selected Metropolitan Statistical Area, 2022—Continued

(Number, percent, rate per 100,000 population.)

Area	Population	Violent crime	Murder and nonnegligent manslaughter	Rape	Robbery	Aggravated assault	Property crime	Burglary	Larceny-theft	Motor vehicle theft
Buffalo-Cheektowaga, NY M. S. A.	1,167,905									
Includes Erie, Niagara Counties										
City of Buffalo	275,710	2,030	67	110	533	1,320	8,852	1,324	6,005	1,523
City of Cheektowaga Town	79,606	220	1	12	63	144	2,610	242	2,151	217
Total area actually reporting	98.2%	3,610	88	297	815	2,410	22,242	2,720	16,805	2,717
Estimated total	100.0%	3,637	88	302	818	2,429	22,516	2,744	17,041	2,731
Rate per 100,000 inhabitants		311.4	7.5	25.9	70.0	208.0	1,927.9	235.0	1,459.1	233.8
Burlington, NC M. S. A.	176,793									
Includes Alamance County										
City of Burlington	58,132	484	4	32	62	386	2,197	331	1,648	218
Total area actually reporting	100.0%	781	5	72	79	624	3,828	595	2,850	382
Rate per 100,000 inhabitants		441.8	2.8	40.7	44.7	353.0	2,165.2	336.6	1,612.1	216.1
Burlington-South Burlington, VT M. S. A.	227,105									
Includes Chittenden, Franklin, Grand Isle Counties										
City of Burlington	44,689	183	5	14	12	152	2,291	175	1,804	312
City of South Burlington	20,307	60	1	9	4	46	810	31	740	39
Total area actually reporting	100.0%	562	12	91	34	425	5,460	367	4,649	444
Rate per 100,000 inhabitants		247.5	5.3	40.1	15.0	187.1	2,404.2	161.6	2,047.1	195.5
California-Lexington Park, MD[1] M. S. A.	115,107									
Includes St Mary'S County										
Total area actually reporting	100.0%	329	4	42	27	256	1,310	267	963	80
Rate per 100,000 inhabitants		285.8	3.5	36.5	23.5	222.4	1,138.1	232.0	836.6	69.5
Cape Girardeau, MO-IL[1] M. S. A.	97,862									
Includes Alexander, Bollinger, Cape Girardeau Counties										
City of Cape Girardeau, MO	40,067	241	4	32	11	194	984	151	732	101
Total area actually reporting	94.6%	380	6	46	11	317	1,405	223	1,025	157
Estimated total	100.0%	388	6	49	11	322	1,450	234	1,052	164
Rate per 100,000 inhabitants		396.5	6.1	50.1	11.2	329.0	1,481.7	239.1	1,075.0	167.6
Carson City, NV M. S. A.	59,377									
Includes Carson City County										
Total area actually reporting	100.0%	195	1	36	14	144	620	141	393	86
Rate per 100,000 inhabitants		328.4	1.7	60.6	23.6	242.5	1,044.2	237.5	661.9	144.8
Cedar Rapids, IA M. S. A.	274,672									
Includes Benton, Jones, Linn Counties										
City of Cedar Rapids	135,362	433	10	14	55	354	4,124	598	3,108	418
Total area actually reporting	98.2%	692	11	66	68	547	5,146	796	3,824	526
Estimated total	100.0%	705	11	68	69	557	5,206	806	3,869	531
Rate per 100,000 inhabitants		256.7	4.0	24.8	25.1	202.8	1,895.4	293.4	1,408.6	193.3
Charleston-North Charleston, SC M. S. A.	828,092									
Includes Berkeley, Charleston, Dorchester Counties										
City of Charleston	152,324	571	8	54	73	436	2,878	229	2,146	503
City of North Charleston	119,198	1,123	33	83	228	779	5,728	565	4,455	708
Total area actually reporting	99.5%	3,287	69	299	445	2,475	17,997	1,954	13,520	2,525
Estimated total	100.0%	3,308	69	301	447	2,492	18,116	1,973	13,609	2,536
Rate per 100,000 inhabitants		399.5	8.3	36.3	54.0	300.9	2,187.7	238.3	1,643.4	306.2
Charleston, WV M. S. A.	252,056									
Includes Boone, Clay, Jackson, Kanawha, Lincoln Counties										
City of Charleston	47,350	302	10	44	35	213	1,943	423	1,375	145
Total area actually reporting	79.0%	1,080	21	153	55	851	4,969	891	3,641	436
Estimated total	100.0%	1,158	21	159	55	923	5,129	921	3,753	453
Rate per 100,000 inhabitants		459.4	8.3	63.1	21.8	366.2	2,034.9	365.4	1,489.0	179.7
Charlotte-Concord-Gastonia, NC-SC M. S. A.	2,746,745									
Includes Anson, Cabarrus, Chester, Gaston, Iredell, Lancaster, Lincoln, Mecklenburg, Rowan, Union, York Counties										
City of Charlotte-Mecklenburg, NC	955,466	7,132	108	271	1,381	5,372	32,246	4,095	24,356	3,795
City of Concord, NC	109,660	116	6	15	31	64	1,079	82	863	134
City of Gastonia, NC	81,937	645	8	27	99	511	3,227	474	2,411	342
City of Rock Hill, SC	74,047	355	8	25	22	300	1,984	194	1,627	163
Total area actually reporting	99.6%	11,889	204	695	1,882	9,108	61,353	8,638	46,164	6,551
Estimated total	100.0%	11,931	206	700	1,886	9,139	61,619	8,686	46,362	6,571
Rate per 100,000 inhabitants		434.4	7.5	25.5	68.7	332.7	2,243.3	316.2	1,687.9	239.2
Charlottesville, VA M. S. A.	224,666									
Includes Albemarle, Charlottesville City, Fluvanna, Greene, Nelson Counties										
City of Charlottesville	45,089	244	2	36	35	171	1,538	126	1,249	163
Total area actually reporting	100.0%	472	15	97	55	305	4,264	295	3,565	404
Rate per 100,000 inhabitants		210.1	6.7	43.2	24.5	135.8	1,897.9	131.3	1,586.8	179.8
Chattanooga, TN-GA M. S. A.	573,413									
Includes Catoosa, Dade, Hamilton, Marion, Sequatchie, Walker Counties										
City of Chattanooga, TN	182,603	2,077	24	166	218	1,669	9,534	1,066	7,108	1,360
Total area actually reporting	86.6%	2,807	31	245	255	2,276	13,088	1,546	9,718	1,824
Estimated total	100.0%	2,959	34	266	265	2,394	13,893	1,669	10,301	1,923
Rate per 100,000 inhabitants		516.0	5.9	46.4	46.2	417.5	2,422.9	291.1	1,796.4	335.4

Table 6. Crime in the United States, by Selected Metropolitan Statistical Area, 2022—Continued

(Number, percent, rate per 100,000 population.)

Area	Population	Violent crime	Murder and nonnegligent manslaughter	Rape	Robbery	Aggravated assault	Property crime	Burglary	Larceny-theft	Motor vehicle theft
Cheyenne, WY M. S. A.	101,203									
Includes Laramie County										
City of Cheyenne	64,941	181	0	63	16	102	2,361	272	1,821	268
Total area actually reporting	100.0%	266	5	76	19	166	2,697	338	2,037	322
Rate per 100,000 inhabitants		262.8	4.9	75.1	18.8	164.0	2,664.9	334.0	2,012.8	318.2
Chico, CA M. S. A.	206,780									
Includes Butte County										
City of Chico	102,499	589	1	80	60	448	1,703	224	1,214	265
Total area actually reporting	100.0%	1,290	11	183	121	975	3,734	663	2,525	546
Rate per 100,000 inhabitants		623.9	5.3	88.5	58.5	471.5	1,805.8	320.6	1,221.1	264.0
Cincinnati, OH-KY-IN M. S. A.	2,260,046									
Includes Boone, Bracken, Brown, Butler, Campbell, Clermont, Dearborn, Franklin, Gallatin, Grant, Hamilton, Kenton, Ohio, Pendleton, Union, Warren Counties										
City of Cincinnati, OH	307,761	2,591	73	259	640	1,619	11,543	1,877	7,655	2,011
Total area actually reporting	92.0%	4,692	106	724	947	2,915	34,068	4,180	26,186	3,705
Estimated total	100.0%	4,932	109	768	972	3,083	36,185	4,439	27,855	3,894
Rate per 100,000 inhabitants		218.2	4.8	34.0	43.0	136.4	1,601.1	196.4	1,232.5	172.3
Clarksville, TN-KY M. S. A.	335,845									
Includes Christian, Montgomery, Stewart, Trigg Counties										
City of Clarksville, TN	174,738	871	11	93	68	699	3,493	514	2,537	442
Total area actually reporting	99.9%	1,134	19	138	105	872	5,624	935	4,042	647
Estimated total	100.0%	1,135	19	138	105	873	5,631	936	4,047	648
Rate per 100,000 inhabitants		338.0	5.7	41.1	31.3	259.9	1,676.7	278.7	1,205.0	192.9
Cleveland-Elyria, OH M. S. A.	2,063,662									
Includes Cuyahoga, Geauga, Lake, Lorain, Medina Counties										
City of Cleveland	363,764	5,870	145	453	1,549	3,723	15,704	3,004	8,728	3,972
City of Elyria	52,902	105	8	24	22	51	1,007	158	766	83
Total area actually reporting	90.4%	8,010	189	736	1,893	5,192	30,658	4,626	20,382	5,650
Estimated total	100.0%	8,276	191	790	1,923	5,372	33,522	4,922	22,730	5,870
Rate per 100,000 inhabitants		401.0	9.3	38.3	93.2	260.3	1,624.4	238.5	1,101.4	284.4
Cleveland, TN M. S. A.	129,945									
Includes Bradley, Polk Counties										
City of Cleveland	48,579	352	1	17	26	308	1,650	172	1,336	142
Total area actually reporting	100.0%	557	4	32	32	489	2,527	337	1,915	275
Rate per 100,000 inhabitants		428.6	3.1	24.6	24.6	376.3	1,944.7	259.3	1,473.7	211.6
Coeur d'Alene, ID M. S. A.	185,620									
Includes Kootenai County										
City of Coeur d'Alene	57,061	176	1	54	14	107	580	72	472	36
Total area actually reporting	100.0%	392	6	76	21	289	1,593	255	1,217	121
Rate per 100,000 inhabitants		211.2	3.2	40.9	11.3	155.7	858.2	137.4	655.6	65.2
Colorado Springs, CO M. S. A.	768,972									
Includes El Paso, Teller Counties										
City of Colorado Springs	487,728	3,135	45	446	365	2,279	16,583	2,686	11,164	2,733
Total area actually reporting	99.7%	3,905	64	605	433	2,803	20,266	3,292	13,701	3,273
Estimated total	100.0%	3,914	64	607	434	2,809	20,354	3,301	13,760	3,293
Rate per 100,000 inhabitants		509.0	8.3	78.9	56.4	365.3	2,646.9	429.3	1,789.4	428.2
Columbia, MO M. S. A.	214,980									
Includes Boone, Cooper, Howard Counties										
City of Columbia	127,862	603	11	91	65	436	3,343	397	2,487	459
Total area actually reporting	98.0%	805	14	119	74	598	4,540	534	3,418	588
Estimated total	100.0%	824	14	120	74	616	4,615	545	3,461	609
Rate per 100,000 inhabitants		383.3	6.5	55.8	34.4	286.5	2,146.7	253.5	1,609.9	283.3
Columbia, SC M. S. A.	850,763									
Includes Calhoun, Fairfield, Kershaw, Lexington, Richland, Saluda Counties										
City of Columbia	137,768	825	13	45	100	667	3,923	495	3,000	428
Total area actually reporting	99.9%	4,740	79	275	392	3,994	21,962	3,362	16,039	2,561
Estimated total	100.0%	4,742	79	275	392	3,996	21,977	3,364	16,050	2,563
Rate per 100,000 inhabitants		557.4	9.3	32.3	46.1	469.7	2,583.2	395.4	1,886.5	301.3
Columbus, GA-AL M. S. A.	327,116									
Includes Chattahoochee, Harris, Marion, Muscogee, Russell, Stewart, Talbot Counties										
City of Columbus, GA	204,986	1,292	19	54	157	1,062	4,819	631	3,602	586
Total area actually reporting	93.2%	1,653	28	85	187	1,354	6,895	872	5,250	772
Estimated total	100.0%	1,781	30	95	198	1,459	7,342	917	5,613	811
Rate per 100,000 inhabitants		544.5	9.2	29.0	60.5	446.0	2,244.5	280.3	1,715.9	247.9
Columbus, OH M. S. A.	2,158,693									
Includes Delaware, Fairfield, Franklin, Hocking, Licking, Madison, Morrow, Perry, Pickaway, Union Counties										
City of Columbus	907,196	4,081	127	1,005	1,276	1,675	31,609	4,288	20,028	7,293
Total area actually reporting	97.4%	5,953	151	1,464	1,552	2,789	49,553	6,355	34,394	8,805

Table 6. Crime in the United States, by Selected Metropolitan Statistical Area, 2022—Continued

(Number, percent, rate per 100,000 population.)

Area	Population	Violent crime	Murder and nonnegligent manslaughter	Rape	Robbery	Aggravated assault	Property crime	Burglary	Larceny-theft	Motor vehicle theft
Estimated total	100.0%	6,022	152	1,478	1,560	2,835	50,469	6,442	35,168	8,860
Rate per 100,000 inhabitants		279.0	7.0	68.5	72.3	131.3	2,337.9	298.4	1,629.1	410.4
Corpus Christi, TX M. S. A.	426,250									
Includes Nueces, San Patricio Counties										
City of Corpus Christi	317,694	2,512	41	240	355	1,876	9,915	1,593	7,478	844
Total area actually reporting	95.1%	2,778	47	290	372	2,069	11,501	1,942	8,583	976
Estimated total	100.0%	2,821	47	298	374	2,102	11,696	1,987	8,706	1,003
Rate per 100,000 inhabitants		661.8	11.0	69.9	87.7	493.1	2,743.9	466.2	2,042.5	235.3
Corvallis, OR M. S. A.	96,622									
Includes Benton County										
City of Corvallis	60,031	124	0	22	29	73	2,197	249	1,829	119
Total area actually reporting	100.0%	177	0	30	37	109	3,037	337	2,522	178
Rate per 100,000 inhabitants		183.2	0.0	31.0	38.3	112.8	3,143.2	348.8	2,610.2	184.2
Cumberland, MD[1]-WV M. S. A.	94,403									
Includes Allegany, Mineral Counties										
City of Cumberland, MD	18,647	114	1	11	24	78	633	115	493	25
Total area actually reporting	98.6%	204	2	37	30	135	1,044	211	784	49
Estimated total	100.0%	207	2	37	30	138	1,052	211	792	49
Rate per 100,000 inhabitants		219.3	2.1	39.2	31.8	146.2	1,114.4	223.5	839.0	51.9
Dallas-Fort Worth-Arlington, TX M. S. A.	7,908,930									
Includes the Metro Divisions of Dallas-Plano-Irving, TX; Fort Worth-Arlington-Grapevine, TX										
City of Dallas	1,286,121	10,009	157	492	2,134	7,226	49,037	6,788	28,878	13,372
City of Fort Worth	930,683	4,675	98	580	676	3,321	25,498	3,918	18,090	3,490
City of Arlington	391,591	2,272	16	336	276	1,644	9,886	1,024	7,625	1,237
City of Plano	289,847	458	1	91	86	280	5,496	682	4,293	521
City of Irving	254,141	853	12	144	164	533	6,433	748	4,698	987
City of Denton	154,230	445	7	117	45	276	3,672	450	2,780	442
City of Richardson	115,771	183	2	31	60	90	2,630	281	2,004	345
City of Grapevine	50,988	72	0	25	4	43	1,500	101	1,200	199
City of Fort Worth	17,922	90	2	11	13	64	491	75	348	67
Total area actually reporting	99.9%	27,600	415	3,313	4,637	19,236	172,812	22,151	121,156	29,507
Estimated total	100.0%	27,616	415	3,317	4,638	19,247	172,926	22,172	121,234	29,522
Rate per 100,000 inhabitants		349.2	5.2	41.9	58.6	243.4	2,186.5	280.3	1,532.9	373.3
Dallas-Plano-Irving, TX M. D.	5,321,983									
Includes Collin, Dallas, Denton, Ellis, Hunt, Kaufman, Rockwall Counties										
Total area actually reporting	99.9%	18,144	253	1,839	3,405	12,648	118,039	14,890	80,549	22,600
Estimated total	100.0%	18,154	253	1,842	3,405	12,655	118,115	14,904	80,601	22,610
Rate per 100,000 inhabitants		341.1	4.8	34.6	64.0	237.8	2,219.4	280.0	1,514.5	424.8
Fort Worth-Arlington-Grapevine, TX M. D.	2,586,947									
Includes Johnson, Parker, Tarrant, Wise Counties										
Total area actually reporting	99.9%	9,456	162	1,474	1,232	6,588	54,773	7,261	40,607	6,907
Estimated total	100.0%	9,462	162	1,475	1,233	6,592	54,811	7,268	40,633	6,912
Rate per 100,000 inhabitants		365.8	6.3	57.0	47.7	254.8	2,118.8	280.9	1,570.7	267.2
Dalton, GA M. S. A.	143,426									
Includes Murray, Whitfield Counties										
City of Dalton	34,276	127	2	18	23	84	845	79	699	67
Total area actually reporting	98.5%	517	3	67	29	418	1,843	233	1,423	187
Estimated total	100.0%	520	3	68	29	420	1,866	236	1,441	189
Rate per 100,000 inhabitants		362.6	2.1	47.4	20.2	292.8	1,301.0	164.5	1,004.7	131.8
Danville, IL[1] M. S. A.	72,445									
Includes Vermilion County										
City of Danville	28,480	500	4	42	35	419	1,373	287	1,015	71
Total area actually reporting	95.8%	608	5	74	41	488	2,088	496	1,476	116
Estimated total	100.0%	613	5	75	42	491	2,126	501	1,505	120
Rate per 100,000 inhabitants		846.2	6.9	103.5	58.0	677.8	2,934.6	691.6	2,077.4	165.6
Daphne-Fairhope-Foley, AL M. S. A.	246,518									
Includes Baldwin County										
City of Daphne	29,871	22	1	2	1	18	262	19	220	23
City of Fairhope	23,747	43	1	6	3	33	364	60	280	24
City of Foley	23,629	38	2	5	4	27	449	40	367	42
City of Gulf Shores	16,274	54	1	6	0	47	394	31	356	7
Total area actually reporting	98.2%	275	6	30	14	225	2,431	241	2,036	154
Estimated total	100.0%	288	6	31	15	236	2,512	251	2,100	161
Rate per 100,000 inhabitants		116.8	2.4	12.6	6.1	95.7	1,019.0	101.8	851.9	65.3
Davenport-Moline-Rock Island, IA-IL[1] M. S. A.	380,145									
Includes Henry, Mercer, Rock Island, Scott Counties										
City of Davenport, IA	100,437	701	4	93	97	507	3,496	659	2,358	479
City of Moline, IL	42,009	210	1	41	11	157	1,190	183	831	176
City of Rock Island, IL	36,235	204	11	3	13	177	939	164	586	189
Total area actually reporting	91.7%	1,358	17	194	143	1,004	7,842	1,322	5,407	1,113
Estimated total	100.0%	1,401	17	206	147	1,031	8,185	1,375	5,657	1,153
Rate per 100,000 inhabitants		368.5	4.5	54.2	38.7	271.2	2,153.1	361.7	1,488.1	303.3

Table 6. Crime in the United States, by Selected Metropolitan Statistical Area, 2022—Continued

(Number, percent, rate per 100,000 population.)

Area	Population	Violent crime	Murder and nonnegligent manslaughter	Rape	Robbery	Aggravated assault	Property crime	Burglary	Larceny-theft	Motor vehicle theft
Dayton-Kettering, OH M. S. A.	812,598									
Includes Greene, Miami, Montgomery Counties										
City of Dayton	137,084	1,605	34	203	259	1,109	5,875	1,339	3,096	1,440
City of Kettering	57,107	29	0	11	6	12	804	85	633	86
Total area actually reporting	93.5%	2,784	49	523	408	1,804	15,943	2,615	10,636	2,691
Estimated total	100.0%	2,858	50	539	416	1,853	16,670	2,693	11,229	2,747
Rate per 100,000 inhabitants		351.7	6.2	66.3	51.2	228.0	2,051.4	331.4	1,381.9	338.1
Decatur, IL[1] M. S. A.	101,412									
Includes Macon County										
City of Decatur	68,789	485	16	54	70	345	1,702	418	1,014	270
Total area actually reporting	96.4%	515	21	69	73	352	1,984	453	1,240	291
Estimated total	100.0%	519	21	70	73	355	2,023	459	1,270	294
Rate per 100,000 inhabitants		511.8	20.7	69.0	72.0	350.1	1,994.8	452.6	1,252.3	289.9
Denver-Aurora-Lakewood, CO M. S. A.	2,975,833									
Includes Adams, Arapahoe, Broomfield, Clear Creek, Denver, Douglas, Elbert, Gilpin, Jefferson, Park Counties										
City of Denver	705,264	7,545	90	756	1,301	5,398	45,336	5,171	24,964	15,201
City of Aurora	392,134	4,225	54	296	827	3,048	16,585	1,821	7,959	6,805
City of Lakewood	157,068	1,278	12	111	286	869	8,362	1,089	5,159	2,114
City of Centennial	105,849	209	1	14	16	178	2,233	324	1,437	472
City of Broomfield	76,137	112	3	31	12	66	1,993	208	1,395	390
City of Commerce City	65,817	467	6	60	61	340	2,502	267	1,389	846
Total area actually reporting	99.9%	17,918	207	1,957	3,108	12,645	117,946	13,395	68,919	35,632
Estimated total	100.0%	17,919	207	1,958	3,108	12,645	117,966	13,396	68,935	35,635
Rate per 100,000 inhabitants		602.2	7.0	65.8	104.4	424.9	3,964.1	450.2	2,316.5	1,197.5
Detroit-Warren-Dearborn, MI M. S. A.	4,344,753									
Includes the Metro Divisions of Detroit-Dearborn-Livonia, MI; Warren-Troy-Farmington Hills, MI										
City of Detroit	626,757	12,710	308	712	1,398	10,292	28,068	4,829	13,794	9,445
City of Warren	137,138	670	5	79	56	530	2,274	295	1,519	460
City of Dearborn	107,197	302	2	29	53	218	2,059	149	1,470	440
City of Livonia	93,517	229	0	26	19	184	1,614	111	1,257	246
City of Troy	86,548	102	2	9	20	71	1,304	67	1,104	133
City of Farmington Hills	82,806	119	0	20	7	92	962	78	718	166
City of Southfield	75,432	379	2	40	65	272	1,988	240	1,247	501
City of Novi	66,936	49	0	12	6	31	561	18	483	60
City of Taylor	61,901	386	0	44	26	316	1,129	170	774	185
City of Pontiac	60,581	620	13	34	53	520	1,072	192	718	162
Total area actually reporting	99.8%	22,959	434	1,994	2,246	18,285	72,386	9,612	45,741	17,033
Estimated total	100.0%	22,982	434	1,998	2,247	18,303	72,468	9,622	45,804	17,042
Rate per 100,000 inhabitants		529.0	10.0	46.0	51.7	421.3	1,667.9	221.5	1,054.2	392.2
Detroit-Dearborn-Livonia, MI M. D.	1,759,509									
Includes Wayne County										
Total area actually reporting	99.60%	17,251	364	1,158	1,798	13,931	45,941	6,754	26,189	12,998
Estimated total	100.0%	17,274	364	1,162	1,799	13,949	46,023	6,764	26,252	13,007
Rate per 100,000 inhabitants		981.8	20.7	66.0	102.2	792.8	2,615.7	384.4	1,492.0	739.2
Warren-Troy-Farmington Hills, MI M. D.	2,585,244									
Includes Lapeer, Livingston, Macomb, Oakland, St Clair Counties										
Total area actually reporting	100.0%	5,708	70	836	448	4,354	26,445	2,858	19,552	4,035
Rate per 100,000 inhabitants		220.8	2.7	32.3	17.3	168.4	1,022.9	110.6	756.3	156.1
Dothan, AL M. S. A.	152,773									
Includes Geneva, Henry, Houston Counties										
City of Dothan	69,647	658	14	58	43	543	2,024	377	1,541	106
Total area actually reporting	98.8%	865	21	84	50	710	2,994	616	2,143	235
Estimated total	100.0%	869	21	84	50	714	3,019	620	2,160	239
Rate per 100,000 inhabitants		568.8	13.7	55.0	32.7	467.4	1,976.1	405.8	1,413.9	156.4
Dover, DE M. S. A.	186,645									
Includes Kent County										
City of Dover	38,438	315	3	24	22	266	1,741	26	1,541	174
Total area actually reporting	100.0%	779	11	65	50	653	3,716	308	3,065	343
Rate per 100,000 inhabitants		417.4	5.9	34.8	26.8	349.9	1,990.9	165.0	1,642.2	183.8
Dubuque, IA M. S. A.	98,295									
Includes Dubuque County										
City of Dubuque	58,676	277	1	56	25	195	1,052	224	765	63
Total area actually reporting	97.9%	314	1	68	25	220	1,243	281	888	74
Estimated total	100.0%	318	1	68	25	224	1,257	284	897	76
Rate per 100,000 inhabitants		323.5	1.0	69.2	25.4	227.9	1,278.8	288.9	912.6	77.3
Duluth, MN-WI M. S. A.	290,620									
Includes Carlton, Douglas, Lake, St Louis Counties										
City of Duluth, MN	86,144	249	6	52	28	163	2,509	360	1,984	165
Total area actually reporting	100.0%	616	7	124	38	447	5,349	756	4,192	401
Rate per 100,000 inhabitants		212.0	2.4	42.7	13.1	153.8	1,840.5	260.1	1,442.4	138.0

Table 6. Crime in the United States, by Selected Metropolitan Statistical Area, 2022—Continued

(Number, percent, rate per 100,000 population.)

Area	Population	Violent crime	Murder and nonnegligent manslaughter	Rape	Robbery	Aggravated assault	Property crime	Burglary	Larceny-theft	Motor vehicle theft
Durham-Chapel Hill, NC M. S. A.	660,069									
Includes Chatham, Durham, Granville, Orange, Person Counties										
City of Durham	286,377	1,968	42	146	587	1,193	9,498	1,462	7,166	870
City of Chapel Hill	60,984	113	2	9	26	76	1,213	190	951	72
Total area actually reporting	100.0%	2,936	69	239	700	1,928	15,649	2,652	11,658	1,339
Rate per 100,000 inhabitants		444.8	10.5	36.2	106.0	292.1	2,370.8	401.8	1,766.2	202.9
East Stroudsburg, PA[1] M. S. A.	170,736									
Includes Monroe County										
Total area actually reporting	100.0%	301	2	62	25	212	2,066	254	1,733	79
Rate per 100,000 inhabitants		176.3	1.2	36.3	14.6	124.2	1,210.1	148.8	1,015.0	46.3
Eau Claire, WI M. S. A.	174,334									
Includes Chippewa, Eau Claire Counties										
City of Eau Claire	69,569	96	1	38	5	52	1,549	217	1,250	82
Total area actually reporting	100.0%	228	6	76	7	139	2,426	337	1,961	128
Rate per 100,000 inhabitants		130.8	3.4	43.6	4.0	79.7	1,391.6	193.3	1,124.9	73.4
El Centro, CA M. S. A.	180,415									
Includes Imperial County										
City of El Centro	44,076	151	4	15	29	103	919	160	641	118
Total area actually reporting	95.3%	527	11	49	69	398	2,982	616	1,785	581
Estimated total	100.0%	573	11	52	81	429	3,481	714	2,120	647
Rate per 100,000 inhabitants		317.6	6.1	28.8	44.9	237.8	1,929.4	395.8	1,175.1	358.6
Elizabethtown-Fort Knox, KY M. S. A.	157,874									
Includes Hardin, Larue, Meade Counties										
City of Elizabethtown	32,437	40	0	10	16	14	290	63	191	36
Total area actually reporting	100.0%	140	4	35	26	75	1,182	257	733	192
Rate per 100,000 inhabitants		88.7	2.5	22.2	16.5	47.5	748.7	162.8	464.3	121.6
Elkhart-Goshen, IN M. S. A.	207,189									
Includes Elkhart County										
City of Elkhart	53,947	575	8	41	57	469	1,538	300	1,029	209
City of Goshen	34,697	87	2	13	7	65	956	140	718	98
Total area actually reporting	100.0%	730	10	63	67	590	2,921	512	2,032	377
Rate per 100,000 inhabitants		352.3	4.8	30.4	32.3	284.8	1,409.8	247.1	980.7	182.0
El Paso, TX M. S. A.	878,428									
Includes El Paso, Hudspeth Counties										
City of El Paso	678,232	2,123	22	294	267	1,540	9,353	970	6,973	1,410
Total area actually reporting	100.0%	2,661	35	372	315	1,939	11,081	1,197	8,170	1,714
Rate per 100,000 inhabitants		302.9	4.0	42.3	35.9	220.7	1,261.5	136.3	930.1	195.1
Enid, OK M. S. A.	61,352									
Includes Garfield County										
City of Enid	49,990	204	0	45	13	146	1,424	360	980	84
Total area actually reporting	100.0%	219	0	51	13	155	1,533	395	1,030	108
Rate per 100,000 inhabitants		357.0	0.0	83.1	21.2	252.6	2,498.7	643.8	1,678.8	176.0
Erie, PA[1] M. S. A.	268,280									
Includes Erie County										
City of Erie	93,363	567	5	49	86	427	2,114	280	1,719	115
Total area actually reporting	98.9%	908	5	109	98	696	4,366	514	3,647	205
Estimated total	100.0%	912	5	109	98	700	4,390	516	3,667	207
Rate per 100,000 inhabitants		339.9	1.9	40.6	36.5	260.9	1,636.4	192.3	1,366.9	77.2
Evansville, IN-KY M. S. A.	314,187									
Includes Henderson, Posey, Vanderburgh, Warrick Counties										
City of Evansville, IN	115,719	832	25	82	70	655	4,359	654	3,250	455
Total area actually reporting	99.8%	1,309	32	158	98	1,021	6,207	972	4,596	639
Estimated total	100.0%	1,310	32	158	98	1,022	6,218	975	4,603	640
Rate per 100,000 inhabitants		416.9	10.2	50.3	31.2	325.3	1,979.1	310.3	1,465.1	203.7
Fairbanks, AK M. S. A.	35,120									
Includes Fairbanks North Star County										
City of Fairbanks	32,785	271	10	37	32	192	1,407	130	1,109	168
Total area actually reporting	100.0%	277	10	37	32	198	1,457	134	1,148	175
Rate per 100,000 inhabitants		788.7	28.5	105.4	91.1	563.8	4,148.6	381.5	3,268.8	498.3
Fargo, ND-MN M. S. A.	256,129									
Includes Cass, Clay Counties										
City of Fargo, ND	127,649	787	5	144	116	522	5,294	1,075	3,534	685
Total area actually reporting	100.0%	1,086	6	201	140	739	7,350	1,430	4,978	942
Rate per 100,000 inhabitants		424.0	2.3	78.5	54.7	288.5	2,869.6	558.3	1,943.6	367.8
Farmington, NM M. S. A.	120,501									
Includes San Juan County										
City of Farmington	46,249	495	4	78	29	384	1,103	164	818	121
Total area actually reporting	100.0%	802	6	131	37	628	1,715	305	1,206	204
Rate per 100,000 inhabitants		665.6	5.0	108.7	30.7	521.2	1,423.2	253.1	1,000.8	169.3
Fayetteville, NC M. S. A.	531,453									
Includes Cumberland, Harnett, Hoke Counties										

Table 6. Crime in the United States, by Selected Metropolitan Statistical Area, 2022—Continued

(Number, percent, rate per 100,000 population.)

Area	Population	Violent crime	Murder and nonnegligent manslaughter	Rape	Robbery	Aggravated assault	Property crime	Burglary	Larceny-theft	Motor vehicle theft
City of Fayetteville	208,980	2,044	35	90	242	1,677	7,224	1,298	5,381	545
Total area actually reporting	99.6%	3,710	68	209	362	3,071	13,146	2,641	9,383	1,122
Estimated total	100.0%	3,715	68	210	362	3,075	13,200	2,649	9,424	1,127
Rate per 100,000 inhabitants		699.0	12.8	39.5	68.1	578.6	2,483.8	498.4	1,773.3	212.1
Fayetteville-Springdale-Rogers, AR M. S. A.	573,153									
Includes Benton, Madison, Washington Counties										
City of Fayetteville	96,456	486	2	55	40	389	3,890	337	3,155	398
City of Rogers	72,115	285	1	82	14	188	1,539	127	1,303	109
City of Bentonville	58,871	188	1	29	2	156	686	69	575	42
City of Springdale	15,128	83	1	20	5	57	382	42	294	46
Total area actually reporting	99.4%	2,215	14	462	97	1,642	10,905	1,359	8,386	1,160
Estimated total	100.0%	2,228	14	465	97	1,652	10,952	1,370	8,417	1,165
Rate per 100,000 inhabitants		388.7	2.4	81.1	16.9	288.2	1,910.8	239.0	1,468.5	203.3
Flint, MI M. S. A.	402,767									
Includes Genesee County										
City of Flint	80,059	985	13	84	28	860	1,047	189	689	169
Total area actually reporting	100.0%	2,477	51	289	113	2,024	5,631	987	3,841	803
Rate per 100,000 inhabitants		615.0	12.7	71.8	28.1	502.5	1,398.1	245.1	953.7	199.4
Florence-Muscle Shoals, AL M. S. A.	152,753									
Includes Colbert, Lauderdale Counties										
City of Florence	40,063	233	1	31	6	195	1,060	175	787	98
City of Muscle Shoals	16,917	61	0	5	1	55	413	28	359	26
Total area actually reporting	99.8%	476	6	56	11	403	2,270	362	1,653	255
Estimated total	100.0%	477	6	56	11	404	2,274	363	1,655	256
Rate per 100,000 inhabitants		312.3	3.9	36.7	7.2	264.5	1,488.7	237.6	1,083.4	167.6
Florence, SC M. S. A.	200,039									
Includes Darlington, Florence Counties										
City of Florence	39,997	520	21	19	49	431	2,227	203	1,900	124
Total area actually reporting	99.6%	1,836	57	111	145	1,523	7,343	1,353	5,336	654
Estimated total	100.0%	1,839	57	111	145	1,526	7,367	1,357	5,354	656
Rate per 100,000 inhabitants		919.3	28.5	55.5	72.5	762.9	3,682.8	678.4	2,676.5	327.9
Fond du Lac, WI M. S. A.	104,522									
Includes Fond Du Lac County										
City of Fond du Lac	44,613	129	4	28	5	92	732	42	653	37
Total area actually reporting	97.8%	190	4	48	6	132	983	87	839	57
Estimated total	100.0%	193	4	49	6	134	1,009	89	861	59
Rate per 100,000 inhabitants		184.7	3.8	46.9	5.7	128.2	965.3	85.1	823.8	56.4
Fort Collins, CO M. S. A.	365,359									
Includes Larimer County										
City of Fort Collins	168,045	540	2	56	46	436	4,379	411	3,493	475
Total area actually reporting	100.0%	1,046	9	144	82	810	8,408	875	6,586	946
Rate per 100,000 inhabitants		286.3	2.5	39.4	22.4	221.7	2,301.3	239.5	1,802.6	258.9
Fort Smith, AR-OK M. S. A.	247,162									
Includes Crawford, Franklin, Sebastian, Sequoyah Counties										
City of Fort Smith, AR	90,013	940	3	70	66	801	4,450	733	3,293	424
Total area actually reporting	99.2%	1,466	14	160	81	1,211	6,890	1,311	4,902	677
Estimated total	100.0%	1,474	14	161	81	1,218	6,920	1,316	4,924	680
Rate per 100,000 inhabitants		596.4	5.7	65.1	32.8	492.8	2,799.8	532.4	1,992.2	275.1
Fort Wayne, IN M. S. A.	426,275									
Includes Allen, Whitley Counties										
City of Fort Wayne	267,791	702	20	120	189	373	6,393	592	5,196	605
Total area actually reporting	94.2%	815	20	135	203	457	7,230	730	5,849	651
Estimated total	100.0%	851	20	139	205	487	7,385	763	5,944	678
Rate per 100,000 inhabitants		199.6	4.7	32.6	48.1	114.2	1,732.4	179.0	1,394.4	159.1
Fresno, CA M. S. A.	1,019,353									
Includes Fresno County										
City of Fresno	546,871	4,732	61	242	963	3,466	18,862	3,980	11,748	3,134
Total area actually reporting	100.0%	7,234	83	361	1,258	5,532	27,809	5,859	17,050	4,900
Rate per 100,000 inhabitants		709.7	8.1	35.4	123.4	542.7	2,728.1	574.8	1,672.6	480.7
Gadsden, AL M. S. A.	103,313									
Includes Etowah County										
City of Gadsden	33,521	189	6	15	17	151	1,302	152	1,009	141
Total area actually reporting	98.9%	240	9	23	24	184	1,831	225	1,406	200
Estimated total	100.0%	242	9	23	24	186	1,847	228	1,417	202
Rate per 100,000 inhabitants		234.2	8.7	22.3	23.2	180.0	1,787.8	220.7	1,371.6	195.5
Gainesville, GA M. S. A.	211,946									
Includes Hall County										
City of Gainesville	44,314	247	3	33	29	182	1,233	111	1,009	113
Total area actually reporting	100.0%	554	13	87	53	401	2,838	401	2,142	296
Rate per 100,000 inhabitants		261.4	6.1	41.0	25.0	189.2	1,339.0	189.2	1,010.6	139.7
Glens Falls, NY M. S. A.	127,320									
Includes Warren, Washington Counties										

Table 6. Crime in the United States, by Selected Metropolitan Statistical Area, 2022—Continued

(Number, percent, rate per 100,000 population.)

Area	Population	Violent crime	Murder and nonnegligent manslaughter	Rape	Robbery	Aggravated assault	Property crime	Burglary	Larceny-theft	Motor vehicle theft
City of Glens Falls	14,639	22	0	9	0	13	121	6	107	8
Total area actually reporting	97.5%	170	1	87	11	71	1,221	128	1,048	45
Estimated total	100.0%	172	1	87	11	73	1,250	131	1,072	47
Rate per 100,000 inhabitants		135.1	0.8	68.3	8.6	57.3	981.8	102.9	842.0	36.9
Goldsboro, NC M. S. A.	117,012									
Includes Wayne County										
City of Goldsboro	32,464	366	6	15	38	307	1,660	241	1,302	117
Total area actually reporting	97.5%	576	12	24	46	494	2,840	601	1,945	294
Estimated total	100.0%	581	12	24	46	499	2,911	612	2,000	299
Rate per 100,000 inhabitants		496.5	10.3	20.5	39.3	426.5	2,487.8	523.0	1,709.2	255.5
Grand Forks, ND-MN M. S. A.	103,617									
Includes Grand Forks, Polk Counties										
City of Grand Forks, ND	58,620	172	2	30	19	121	1,670	284	1,263	123
Total area actually reporting	100.0%	266	2	54	22	188	2,087	365	1,564	158
Rate per 100,000 inhabitants		256.7	1.9	52.1	21.2	181.4	2,014.1	352.3	1,509.4	152.5
Grand Island, NE M. S. A.	75,546									
Includes Hall, Howard, Merrick Counties										
City of Grand Island	51,733	210	1	49	20	140	1,333	191	992	150
Total area actually reporting	100.0%	221	2	51	21	147	1,495	206	1,117	172
Rate per 100,000 inhabitants		292.5	2.6	67.5	27.8	194.6	1,978.9	272.7	1,478.6	227.7
Grand Junction, CO M. S. A.	158,724									
Includes Mesa County										
City of Grand Junction	68,126	346	4	55	28	259	2,140	274	1,677	189
Total area actually reporting	99.5%	522	5	99	37	381	3,354	484	2,536	334
Estimated total	100.0%	525	5	101	37	382	3,396	486	2,571	339
Rate per 100,000 inhabitants		330.8	3.2	63.6	23.3	240.7	2,139.6	306.2	1,619.8	213.6
Grand Rapids-Kentwood, MI M. S. A.	1,095,050									
Includes Ionia, Kent, Montcalm, Ottawa Counties										
City of Grand Rapids	196,662	1,926	19	187	267	1,453	5,912	546	3,894	1,472
City of Kentwood	53,977	241	2	32	25	182	1,203	114	798	291
Total area actually reporting	95.6%	4,276	38	882	415	2,941	16,645	1,683	12,071	2,891
Estimated total	100.0%	4,365	38	903	417	3,007	17,034	1,748	12,351	2,935
Rate per 100,000 inhabitants		398.6	3.5	82.5	38.1	274.6	1,555.5	159.6	1,127.9	268.0
Grants Pass, OR M. S. A.	88,357									
Includes Josephine County										
City of Grants Pass	39,519	146	1	20	39	86	1,563	128	1,280	155
Total area actually reporting	100.0%	344	6	44	47	247	1,956	190	1,442	324
Rate per 100,000 inhabitants		389.3	6.8	49.8	53.2	279.5	2,213.7	215.0	1,632.0	366.7
Great Falls, MT M. S. A.	84,694									
Includes Cascade County										
City of Great Falls	60,386	300	2	48	19	231	2,708	236	2,290	182
Total area actually reporting	100.0%	356	2	52	20	282	2,908	283	2,430	195
Rate per 100,000 inhabitants		420.3	2.4	61.4	23.6	333.0	3,433.5	334.1	2,869.2	230.2
Greeley, CO M. S. A.	348,899									
Includes Weld County										
City of Greeley	109,258	636	8	59	94	475	3,455	375	2,079	1,001
Total area actually reporting	98.3%	995	10	164	117	705	6,545	681	4,159	1,705
Estimated total	100.0%	1,012	10	167	119	717	6,741	701	4,291	1,749
Rate per 100,000 inhabitants		290.1	2.9	47.9	34.1	205.5	1,932.1	200.9	1,229.9	501.3
Green Bay, WI M. S. A.	330,261									
Includes Brown, Kewaunee, Oconto Counties										
City of Green Bay	106,916	456	6	67	30	353	1,844	251	1,419	174
Total area actually reporting	98.7%	663	8	150	34	471	3,558	489	2,802	267
Estimated total	100.0%	668	8	151	35	474	3,600	491	2,839	270
Rate per 100,000 inhabitants		202.3	2.4	45.7	10.6	143.5	1,090.0	148.7	859.6	81.8
Greensboro-High Point, NC M. S. A.	784,745									
Includes Guilford, Randolph, Rockingham Counties										
City of Greensboro	298,719	2,447	40	79	465	1,863	11,308	1,662	8,415	1,231
City of High Point	107,395	588	14	23	101	450	2,891	493	2,104	293
Total area actually reporting	99.6%	3,882	66	212	642	2,963	19,607	3,273	14,352	1,981
Estimated total	100.0%	3,893	66	213	643	2,972	19,679	3,287	14,405	1,986
Rate per 100,000 inhabitants		496.1	8.4	27.1	81.9	378.7	2,507.7	418.9	1,835.6	253.1
Greenville-Anderson, SC M. S. A.	957,058									
Includes Anderson, Greenville, Laurens, Pickens Counties										
City of Greenville	73,311	397	4	24	55	314	2,696	274	2,156	266
City of Anderson	29,398	181	2	11	14	154	1,614	128	1,353	133
Total area actually reporting	100.0%	3,993	44	383	333	3,233	21,754	3,207	16,157	2,390
Rate per 100,000 inhabitants		417.2	4.6	40.0	34.8	337.8	2,273.0	335.1	1,688.2	249.7
Greenville, NC M. S. A.	174,629									
Includes Pitt County										
City of Greenville	89,363	508	12	22	67	407	2,438	273	2,017	148

Table 6. Crime in the United States, by Selected Metropolitan Statistical Area, 2022—Continued

(Number, percent, rate per 100,000 population.)

Area	Population	Violent crime	Murder and nonnegligent manslaughter	Rape	Robbery	Aggravated assault	Property crime	Burglary	Larceny-theft	Motor vehicle theft
Total area actually reporting	99.2%	775	20	48	90	617	3,399	517	2,677	205
Estimated total	100.0%	777	20	48	90	619	3,433	522	2,703	208
Rate per 100,000 inhabitants		444.9	11.5	27.5	51.5	354.5	1,965.9	298.9	1,547.9	119.1
Hammond, LA M. S. A.	136,671									
Includes Tangipahoa County										
City of Hammond	20,847	256	0	13	18	225	1,373	156	1,150	67
Total area actually reporting	94.1%	912	10	54	52	796	3,333	559	2,466	308
Estimated total	100.0%	939	10	55	53	821	3,449	582	2,553	314
Rate per 100,000 inhabitants		687.1	7.3	40.2	38.8	600.7	2,523.6	425.8	1,868.0	229.7
Hanford-Corcoran, CA M. S. A.	154,435									
Includes Kings County										
City of Hanford	58,990	253	3	28	26	196	799	113	517	169
City of Corcoran	22,609	110	3	8	7	92	289	43	185	61
Total area actually reporting	100.0%	647	16	68	60	503	2,110	334	1,327	449
Rate per 100,000 inhabitants		418.9	10.4	44.0	38.9	325.7	1,366.3	216.3	859.3	290.7
Harrisonburg, VA M. S. A.	136,692									
Includes Harrisonburg City, Rockingham Counties										
City of Harrisonburg	51,363	129	1	26	8	94	929	65	812	52
Total area actually reporting	100.0%	249	4	62	16	167	1,500	171	1,242	87
Rate per 100,000 inhabitants		182.2	2.9	45.4	11.7	122.2	1,097.4	125.1	908.6	63.6
Hartford-East Hartford-Middletown, CT M. S. A.	1,024,047									
Includes Hartford, Middlesex, Tolland Counties										
City of Hartford	120,196	685	37	22	128	498	2,978	347	2,011	620
City of East Hartford	50,579	96	3	14	32	47	1,352	89	1,065	198
City of Middletown	47,256	48	0	7	9	32	771	46	628	97
Total area actually reporting	100.0%	1,659	52	179	411	1,017	19,178	1,631	15,397	2,150
Rate per 100,000 inhabitants		162.0	5.1	17.5	40.1	99.3	1,872.8	159.3	1,503.5	210.0
Hattiesburg, MS M. S. A.	173,687									
Includes Covington, Forrest, Lamar, Perry Counties										
City of Hattiesburg	46,862	161	3	29	24	105	2,099	259	1,673	167
Total area actually reporting	92.8%	320	7	63	38	212	3,224	701	2,189	334
Estimated total	100.0%	338	7	69	40	222	3,348	734	2,260	354
Rate per 100,000 inhabitants		194.6	4.0	39.7	23.0	127.8	1,927.6	422.6	1,301.2	203.8
Hickory-Lenoir-Morganton, NC M. S. A.	369,445									
Includes Alexander, Burke, Caldwell, Catawba Counties										
City of Hickory	43,756	231	8	17	22	185	1,532	267	1,142	123
City of Lenoir	18,160	38	0	13	5	20	668	172	426	70
City of Morganton	17,568	72	0	9	5	58	585	164	386	35
Total area actually reporting	97.5%	847	27	154	63	604	6,727	1,561	4,460	706
Estimated total	100.0%	875	28	158	65	625	6,947	1,599	4,626	722
Rate per 100,000 inhabitants		236.8	7.6	42.8	17.6	169.2	1,880.4	432.8	1,252.1	195.4
Hilton Head Island-Bluffton, SC M. S. A.	228,846									
Includes Beaufort, Jasper Counties										
City of Bluffton	36,064	25	1	3	4	17	211	30	160	21
Total area actually reporting	100.0%	868	11	67	69	721	3,500	514	2,655	331
Rate per 100,000 inhabitants		379.3	4.8	29.3	30.2	315.1	1,529.4	224.6	1,160.2	144.6
Homosassa Springs, FL[1] M. S. A.	163,651									
Includes Citrus County										
Total area actually reporting	100.0%	50	6	20	24	0	1,346	281	1,065	0
Rate per 100,000 inhabitants		30.6	3.7	12.2	14.7	0.0	822.5	171.7	650.8	0.0
Hot Springs, AR M. S. A.	100,683									
Includes Garland County										
City of Hot Springs	38,174	196	5	32	29	130	2,238	363	1,687	188
Total area actually reporting	100.0%	549	6	79	38	426	3,402	823	2,253	326
Rate per 100,000 inhabitants		545.3	6.0	78.5	37.7	423.1	3,378.9	817.4	2,237.7	323.8
Houma-Thibodaux, LA M. S. A.	205,261									
Includes Lafourche, Terrebonne Counties										
City of Houma	32,762	272	15	2	26	229	1,337	261	1,006	70
City of Thibodaux	15,166	71	2	4	7	58	456	41	402	13
Total area actually reporting	98.8%	907	27	35	63	782	5,324	847	4,165	312
Estimated total	100.0%	912	27	35	63	787	5,344	851	4,180	313
Rate per 100,000 inhabitants		444.3	13.2	17.1	30.7	383.4	2,603.5	414.6	2,036.4	152.5
Houston-The Woodlands-Sugar Land, TX M. S. A.	7,322,248									
Includes Austin, Brazoria, Chambers, Fort Bend, Galveston, Harris, Liberty, Montgomery, Waller Counties										
City of Houston	2,276,533	25,987	433	1,139	6,955	17,459	104,303	14,939	72,021	17,344
City of Sugar Land	107,989	97	0	12	33	52	1,745	133	1,497	115
City of Conroe	98,623	314	3	59	35	217	2,001	225	1,561	215
City of Baytown	81,477	358	2	58	68	230	3,182	438	2,225	519
City of Galveston	52,920	248	6	64	38	140	1,548	202	1,137	209
Total area actually reporting	99.8%	42,809	692	3,504	9,697	28,916	206,601	28,699	147,300	30,605
Estimated total	100.0%	42,851	692	3,512	9,699	28,948	206,897	28,747	147,510	30,643
Rate per 100,000 inhabitants		585.2	9.5	48.0	132.5	395.3	2,825.6	392.6	2,014.5	418.5

Table 6. Crime in the United States, by Selected Metropolitan Statistical Area, 2022—Continued

(Number, percent, rate per 100,000 population.)

Area	Population	Violent crime	Murder and nonnegligent manslaughter	Rape	Robbery	Aggravated assault	Property crime	Burglary	Larceny-theft	Motor vehicle theft
Huntsville, AL M. S. A.	513,507									
Includes Limestone, Madison Counties										
City of Huntsville	218,897	654	0	68	61	525	3,297	613	2,348	336
Total area actually reporting	75.9%	953	6	94	83	770	5,187	1,029	3,696	461
Estimated total	100.0%	1,298	14	131	106	1,047	6,789	1,274	4,905	609
Rate per 100,000 inhabitants		252.8	2.7	25.5	20.6	203.9	1,322.1	248.1	955.2	118.6
Idaho Falls, ID M. S. A.	166,008									
Includes Bonneville, Butte, Jefferson Counties										
City of Idaho Falls	68,162	237	2	38	9	188	935	305	529	101
Total area actually reporting	100.0%	365	3	55	10	297	1,740	522	1,033	185
Rate per 100,000 inhabitants		219.9	1.8	33.1	6.0	178.9	1,048.1	314.4	622.3	111.4
Indianapolis-Carmel-Anderson, IN M. S. A.	2,142,269									
Includes Boone, Brown, Hamilton, Hancock, Hendricks, Johnson, Madison, Marion, Morgan, Putnam, Shelby Counties										
City of Indianapolis	886,455	9,109	208	565	1,624	6,712	29,932	4,804	20,451	4,677
City of Carmel	101,670	66	2	17	5	42	821	47	704	70
City of Anderson	54,965	267	7	52	59	149	1,594	242	1,101	251
Total area actually reporting	92.8%	10,522	234	831	1,860	7,597	42,010	6,021	29,865	6,124
Estimated total	100.0%	10,728	236	855	1,873	7,764	43,253	6,229	30,734	6,290
Rate per 100,000 inhabitants		500.8	11.0	39.9	87.4	362.4	2,019.0	290.8	1,434.6	293.6
Iowa City, IA M. S. A.	179,159									
Includes Johnson, Washington Counties										
City of Iowa City	74,749	197	1	18	29	149	1,327	173	1,018	136
Total area actually reporting	99.3%	466	1	83	45	337	2,606	355	2,024	227
Estimated total	100.0%	468	1	83	45	339	2,614	357	2,029	228
Rate per 100,000 inhabitants		261.2	0.6	46.3	25.1	189.2	1,459.0	199.3	1,132.5	127.3
Ithaca, NY M. S. A.	105,711									
Includes Tompkins County										
City of Ithaca	31,576	96	2	8	16	70	1,191	185	983	23
Total area actually reporting	100.0%	176	2	36	27	111	2,158	307	1,802	49
Rate per 100,000 inhabitants		166.5	1.9	34.1	25.5	105.0	2,041.4	290.4	1,704.6	46.4
Jackson, MI M. S. A.	159,898									
Includes Jackson County										
City of Jackson	31,206	336	4	44	27	261	1,110	173	787	150
Total area actually reporting	100.0%	697	6	134	37	520	3,013	430	2,254	329
Rate per 100,000 inhabitants		435.9	3.8	83.8	23.1	325.2	1,884.3	268.9	1,409.6	205.8
Jackson, TN M. S. A.	181,719									
Includes Chester, Crockett, Gibson, Madison Counties										
City of Jackson	68,059	612	9	28	55	520	1,973	249	1,525	199
Total area actually reporting	100.0%	987	15	57	71	844	3,098	484	2,270	344
Rate per 100,000 inhabitants		543.1	8.3	31.4	39.1	464.5	1,704.8	266.3	1,249.2	189.3
Jacksonville, FL[1] M. S. A.	1,683,524									
Includes Baker, Clay, Duval, Nassau, St Johns Counties										
Total area actually reporting	84.30%	6,315	128	452	644	5,091	25,788	2,770	20,861	2,157
Estimated total	100.0%	7,075	140	527	728	5,680	29,590	3,191	23,861	2,538
Rate per 100,000 inhabitants		420.2	8.3	31.3	43.2	337.4	1,757.6	189.5	1,417.3	150.8
Janesville-Beloit, WI M. S. A.	164,921									
Includes Rock County										
City of Janesville	66,242	112	1	28	17	66	1,299	112	1,086	101
City of Beloit	36,784	225	3	22	26	174	773	98	568	107
Total area actually reporting	99.1%	398	4	57	48	289	2,453	279	1,930	244
Estimated total	100.0%	400	4	58	48	290	2,469	280	1,944	245
Rate per 100,000 inhabitants		242.5	2.4	35.2	29.1	175.8	1,497.1	169.8	1,178.7	148.6
Jefferson City, MO M. S. A.	151,105									
Includes Callaway, Cole, Moniteau, Osage Counties										
City of Jefferson City	42,653	152	2	50	7	93	728	65	542	121
Total area actually reporting	94.2%	310	3	66	11	230	1,620	209	1,192	219
Estimated total	100.0%	344	3	68	13	260	1,821	232	1,329	260
Rate per 100,000 inhabitants		227.7	2.0	45.0	8.6	172.1	1,205.1	153.5	879.5	172.1
Johnson City, TN M. S. A.	209,464									
Includes Carter, Unicoi, Washington Counties										
City of Johnson City	71,129	267	3	54	23	186	2,431	226	2,024	181
Total area actually reporting	100.0%	576	8	85	26	456	3,961	504	3,077	380
Rate per 100,000 inhabitants		275.0	3.8	40.6	12.4	217.7	1,891.0	240.6	1,469.0	181.4
Jonesboro, AR M. S. A.	135,542									
Includes Craighead, Poinsett Counties										
City of Jonesboro	79,865	516	9	83	43	381	2,655	897	1,549	209
Total area actually reporting	98.3%	781	12	144	47	578	3,632	1,137	2,183	312
Estimated total	100.0%	791	12	146	47	586	3,668	1,144	2,209	315
Rate per 100,000 inhabitants		583.6	8.9	107.7	34.7	432.3	2,706.2	844.0	1,629.8	232.4

Table 6. Crime in the United States, by Selected Metropolitan Statistical Area, 2022—Continued

(Number, percent, rate per 100,000 population.)

Area	Population	Violent crime	Murder and nonnegligent manslaughter	Rape	Robbery	Aggravated assault	Property crime	Burglary	Larceny-theft	Motor vehicle theft
Joplin, MO M. S. A.	183,577									
Includes Jasper, Newton Counties										
City of Joplin	51,989	253	8	45	35	165	3,172	495	2,323	354
Total area actually reporting	97.2%	541	9	133	43	356	5,734	877	4,118	739
Estimated total	100.0%	564	9	133	43	379	5,822	890	4,168	764
Rate per 100,000 inhabitants		307.2	4.9	72.4	23.4	206.5	3,171.4	484.8	2,270.4	416.2
Kahului-Wailuku-Lahaina, HI M. S. A.	164,881									
Includes Maui County										
Total area actually reporting	100.0%	507	5	56	51	395	4,635	486	3,360	789
Rate per 100,000 inhabitants		307.5	3.0	34.0	30.9	239.6	2,811.1	294.8	2,037.8	478.5
Kalamazoo-Portage, MI M. S. A.	260,584									
Includes Kalamazoo County										
City of Kalamazoo	72,810	1,104	10	106	125	863	3,278	633	2,251	394
City of Portage	48,811	155	8	34	10	103	1,618	114	1,394	110
Total area actually reporting	100.0%	1,824	22	205	184	1,413	8,275	1,153	6,135	987
Rate per 100,000 inhabitants		700.0	8.4	78.7	70.6	542.2	3,175.6	442.5	2,354.3	378.8
Kennewick-Richland, WA M. S. A.	313,400									
Includes Benton, Franklin Counties										
City of Kennewick	85,058	406	8	68	61	269	3,961	505	2,720	736
City of Richland	63,081	197	5	43	25	124	2,341	282	1,742	317
Total area actually reporting	100.0%	992	24	162	156	650	9,793	1,369	6,644	1,780
Rate per 100,000 inhabitants		316.5	7.7	51.7	49.8	207.4	3,124.8	436.8	2,120.0	568.0
Killeen-Temple, TX M. S. A.	498,581									
Includes Bell, Coryell, Lampasas Counties										
City of Killeen	159,546	864	19	79	85	681	2,787	560	1,808	419
City of Temple	88,484	312	5	81	34	192	1,549	191	1,220	138
Total area actually reporting	99.1%	1,596	33	266	148	1,149	6,994	1,140	5,076	778
Estimated total	100.0%	1,606	33	267	149	1,157	7,068	1,151	5,129	788
Rate per 100,000 inhabitants		322.1	6.6	53.6	29.9	232.1	1,417.6	230.9	1,028.7	158.0
Kingsport-Bristol, TN-VA M. S. A.	310,856									
Includes Bristol City, Hawkins, Scott, Sullivan, Washington Counties										
City of Kingsport, TN	55,799	439	2	42	28	367	2,271	255	1,706	310
City of Bristol, TN	27,862	140	0	16	4	120	640	85	479	76
Total area actually reporting	100.0%	1,191	9	152	51	979	5,862	848	4,215	799
Rate per 100,000 inhabitants		383.1	2.9	48.9	16.4	314.9	1,885.8	272.8	1,355.9	257.0
Kingston, NY M. S. A.	185,611									
Includes Ulster County										
City of Kingston	24,203	62	0	6	13	43	497	35	433	29
Total area actually reporting	95.4%	192	2	41	22	127	1,505	125	1,300	80
Estimated total	100.0%	200	2	41	24	133	1,583	133	1,364	86
Rate per 100,000 inhabitants		107.8	1.1	22.1	12.9	71.7	852.9	71.7	734.9	46.3
Knoxville, TN M. S. A.	907,876									
Includes Anderson, Blount, Campbell, Knox, Loudon, Morgan, Roane, Union Counties										
City of Knoxville	194,724	1,640	32	151	179	1,278	7,609	874	5,780	955
Total area actually reporting	100.0%	3,351	46	345	224	2,738	15,011	2,007	11,101	1,902
Rate per 100,000 inhabitants		369.1	5.1	38.0	24.7	301.6	1,653.4	221.1	1,222.7	209.5
Kokomo, IN M. S. A.	83,831									
Includes Howard County										
City of Kokomo	59,776	306	3	28	13	262	921	196	630	95
Total area actually reporting	98.4%	340	5	30	14	291	1,002	223	670	109
Estimated total	100.0%	344	5	30	15	294	1,030	231	686	113
Rate per 100,000 inhabitants		410.3	6.0	35.8	17.9	350.7	1,228.7	275.6	818.3	134.8
La Crosse-Onalaska, WI-MN M. S. A.	138,636									
Includes Houston, La Crosse Counties										
City of La Crosse, WI	51,727	158	3	44	16	95	1,601	114	1,394	93
City of Onalaska, WI	18,807	7	0	3	1	3	399	20	368	11
Total area actually reporting	100.0%	201	3	57	18	123	2,365	194	2,045	126
Rate per 100,000 inhabitants		145.0	2.2	41.1	13.0	88.7	1,705.9	139.9	1,475.1	90.9
Lafayette-West Lafayette, IN M. S. A.	225,950									
Includes Benton, Carroll, Tippecanoe, Warren Counties										
City of Lafayette	70,861	421	2	66	35	318	1,551	227	1,116	208
City of West Lafayette	44,891	46	0	14	2	30	457	43	383	31
Total area actually reporting	83.2%	568	3	100	42	423	2,713	355	2,047	311
Estimated total	100.0%	618	3	105	44	466	2,978	410	2,218	350
Rate per 100,000 inhabitants		273.5	1.3	46.5	19.5	206.2	1,318.0	181.5	981.6	154.9
Lake Charles, LA M. S. A.	198,972									
Includes Calcasieu, Cameron Counties										
City of Lake Charles	77,054	485	14	32	53	386	2,398	538	1,638	222
Total area actually reporting	96.3%	1,429	19	120	77	1,213	7,440	1,392	5,410	638
Estimated total	100.0%	1,460	19	122	79	1,240	7,590	1,421	5,518	651
Rate per 100,000 inhabitants		733.8	9.5	61.3	39.7	623.2	3,814.6	714.2	2,773.3	327.2

Table 6. Crime in the United States, by Selected Metropolitan Statistical Area, 2022—Continued

(Number, percent, rate per 100,000 population.)

Area	Population	Violent crime	Murder and nonnegligent manslaughter	Rape	Robbery	Aggravated assault	Property crime	Burglary	Larceny-theft	Motor vehicle theft
Lake Havasu City-Kingman, AZ M. S. A.	220,852									
Includes Mohave County										
City of Lake Havasu City	59,166	163	0	35	2	126	804	91	631	82
City of Kingman	34,803	133	1	13	15	104	1,100	112	910	78
Total area actually reporting	100.0%	719	13	134	40	532	4,483	717	3,279	487
Rate per 100,000 inhabitants		325.6	5.9	60.7	18.1	240.9	2,029.9	324.7	1,484.7	220.5
Lansing-East Lansing, MI M. S. A.	539,820									
Includes Clinton, Eaton, Ingham, Shiawassee Counties										
City of Lansing	112,567	1,440	15	99	148	1,178	3,029	579	1,797	653
City of East Lansing	46,660	124	0	31	12	81	830	101	623	106
Total area actually reporting	99.3%	2,515	19	379	210	1,907	8,533	1,241	6,058	1,234
Estimated total	100.0%	2,521	19	379	210	1,913	8,571	1,246	6,088	1,237
Rate per 100,000 inhabitants		467.0	3.5	70.2	38.9	354.4	1,587.8	230.8	1,127.8	229.2
Laredo, TX M. S. A.	270,271									
Includes Webb County										
City of Laredo	256,973	705	12	67	130	496	3,303	404	2,621	278
Total area actually reporting	98.4%	756	12	78	133	533	3,454	430	2,718	306
Estimated total	100.0%	767	12	80	134	541	3,530	441	2,773	316
Rate per 100,000 inhabitants		283.8	4.4	29.6	49.6	200.2	1,306.1	163.2	1,026.0	116.9
Las Cruces, NM M. S. A.	223,022									
Includes Dona Ana County										
City of Las Cruces	114,102	704	10	75	60	559	6,093	1,270	3,927	896
Total area actually reporting	100.0%	1,156	14	109	82	951	7,692	1,640	4,773	1,279
Rate per 100,000 inhabitants		518.3	6.3	48.9	36.8	426.4	3,449.0	735.4	2,140.1	573.5
Las Vegas-Henderson-Paradise, NV M. S. A.	2,314,295									
Includes Clark County										
City of Las Vegas Metropolitan Police Department	1,667,961	8,605	147	1,041	1,622	5,795	48,669	9,338	28,710	10,621
City of Henderson	325,332	985	3	97	234	651	6,242	950	4,421	871
Total area actually reporting	100.0%	10,889	176	1,277	2,232	7,204	60,839	11,216	36,222	13,401
Rate per 100,000 inhabitants		470.5	7.6	55.2	96.4	311.3	2,628.8	484.6	1,565.1	579.1
Lawrence, KS M. S. A.	120,068									
Includes Douglas County										
City of Lawrence	95,580	448	7	68	34	339	2,098	233	1,697	168
Total area actually reporting	100.0%	504	19	73	36	376	2,388	258	1,943	187
Rate per 100,000 inhabitants		419.8	15.8	60.8	30.0	313.2	1,988.9	214.9	1,618.2	155.7
Lawton, OK M. S. A.	128,677									
Includes Comanche, Cotton Counties										
City of Lawton	91,596	767	22	98	54	593	1,898	884	786	228
Total area actually reporting	100.0%	825	22	105	55	643	2,222	974	988	260
Rate per 100,000 inhabitants		641.1	17.1	81.6	42.7	499.7	1,726.8	756.9	767.8	202.1
Lewiston-Auburn, ME M. S. A.	111,272									
Includes Androscoggin County										
City of Lewiston	36,488	101	3	26	26	46	701	95	570	36
City of Auburn	24,122	40	2	10	4	24	624	31	568	25
Total area actually reporting	100.0%	185	5	55	34	91	1,639	166	1,389	84
Rate per 100,000 inhabitants		166.3	4.5	49.4	30.6	81.8	1,473.0	149.2	1,248.3	75.5
Lewiston, ID-WA M. S. A.	65,037									
Includes Asotin, Nez Perce Counties										
City of Lewiston, ID	34,711	63	1	19	2	41	916	171	673	72
Total area actually reporting	98.2%	125	2	33	3	87	1,463	303	1,053	107
Estimated total	100.0%	127	2	34	3	88	1,484	309	1,065	110
Rate per 100,000 inhabitants		195.3	3.1	52.3	4.6	135.3	2,281.8	475.1	1,637.5	169.1
Lexington-Fayette, KY M. S. A.	518,359									
Includes Bourbon, Clark, Fayette, Jessamine, Scott, Woodford Counties										
City of Lexington	320,983	868	33	176	225	434	8,717	1,099	6,393	1,225
Total area actually reporting	100.0%	1,100	36	233	251	580	11,952	1,623	8,817	1,512
Rate per 100,000 inhabitants		212.2	6.9	44.9	48.4	111.9	2,305.7	313.1	1,700.9	291.7
Lima, OH M. S. A.	101,162									
Includes Allen County										
City of Lima	35,633	230	3	23	30	174	1,290	301	954	35
Total area actually reporting	94.1%	341	4	46	41	250	2,232	473	1,684	75
Estimated total	100.0%	348	4	48	41	255	2,305	480	1,745	80
Rate per 100,000 inhabitants		344.0	4.0	47.4	40.5	252.1	2,278.5	474.5	1,725.0	79.1
Lincoln, NE M. S. A.	344,058									
Includes Lancaster, Seward Counties										
City of Lincoln	293,937	1,123	11	239	145	728	8,354	879	6,633	842
Total area actually reporting	100.0%	1,181	11	263	148	759	8,790	937	6,974	879
Rate per 100,000 inhabitants		343.3	3.2	76.4	43.0	220.6	2,554.8	272.3	2,027.0	255.5
Little Rock-North Little Rock-Conway, AR M. S. A.	754,876									
Includes Faulkner, Grant, Lonoke, Perry, Pulaski, Saline Counties										
City of Little Rock	201,513	3,694	79	250	429	2,936	10,778	1,926	7,775	1,077

Table 6. Crime in the United States, by Selected Metropolitan Statistical Area, 2022—Continued

(Number, percent, rate per 100,000 population.)

Area	Population	Violent crime	Murder and nonnegligent manslaughter	Rape	Robbery	Aggravated assault	Property crime	Burglary	Larceny-theft	Motor vehicle theft
City of Conway	66,487	384	7	46	15	316	1,890	138	1,628	124
City of North Little Rock	63,663	783	18	31	75	659	2,950	476	2,102	372
Total area actually reporting	100.0%	6,901	131	555	622	5,593	24,896	4,226	18,056	2,614
Rate per 100,000 inhabitants		914.2	17.4	73.5	82.4	740.9	3,298.0	559.8	2,391.9	346.3
Logan, UT-ID M. S. A.	155,726									
Includes Cache, Franklin Counties										
City of Logan, UT	56,267	100	0	40	2	58	716	82	588	46
Total area actually reporting	100.0%	205	0	63	6	136	1,227	190	963	74
Rate per 100,000 inhabitants		131.6	0.0	40.5	3.9	87.3	787.9	122.0	618.4	47.5
Longview, TX M. S. A.	291,345									
Includes Gregg, Harrison, Rusk, Upshur Counties										
City of Longview	81,811	360	13	54	71	222	2,350	477	1,659	214
Total area actually reporting	100.0%	903	24	152	107	620	4,868	1,165	3,171	532
Rate per 100,000 inhabitants		309.9	8.2	52.2	36.7	212.8	1,670.9	399.9	1,088.4	182.6
Longview, WA M. S. A.	112,510									
Includes Cowlitz County										
City of Longview	37,768	132	0	26	35	71	1,694	292	1,188	214
Total area actually reporting	100.0%	270	4	60	54	152	3,118	676	2,026	416
Rate per 100,000 inhabitants		240.0	3.6	53.3	48.0	135.1	2,771.3	600.8	1,800.7	369.7
Lubbock, TX M. S. A.	330,370									
Includes Crosby, Lubbock, Lynn Counties										
City of Lubbock	264,142	2,809	25	301	349	2,134	10,922	2,260	7,445	1,217
Total area actually reporting	98.0%	2,997	27	335	369	2,266	12,108	2,514	8,193	1,401
Estimated total	100.0%	3,010	27	337	369	2,277	12,213	2,533	8,266	1,414
Rate per 100,000 inhabitants		911.1	8.2	102.0	111.7	689.2	3,696.8	766.7	2,502.0	428.0
Lynchburg, VA M. S. A.	264,027									
Includes Amherst, Appomattox, Bedford, Campbell, Lynchburg City Counties										
City of Lynchburg	79,421	284	8	24	52	200	1,955	214	1,436	305
Total area actually reporting	100.0%	588	18	86	61	423	3,831	414	2,937	480
Rate per 100,000 inhabitants		222.7	6.8	32.6	23.1	160.2	1,451.0	156.8	1,112.4	181.8
Macon-Bibb County, GA M. S. A.	235,000									
Includes Bibb, Crawford, Jones, Monroe, Twiggs Counties										
Total area actually reporting	97.7%	2,402	68	116	253	1,965	6,496	1,358	4,139	999
Estimated total	100.0%	2,415	68	117	254	1,976	6,592	1,368	4,215	1,009
Rate per 100,000 inhabitants		1,027.7	28.9	49.8	108.1	840.9	2,805.1	582.1	1,793.6	429.4
Madera, CA M. S. A.	162,431									
Includes Madera County										
City of Madera	69,395	320	2	33	54	231	1,122	132	748	242
Total area actually reporting	100.0%	822	6	89	85	642	2,304	373	1,567	364
Rate per 100,000 inhabitants		506.1	3.7	54.8	52.3	395.2	1,418.4	229.6	964.7	224.1
Madison, WI M. S. A.	684,054									
Includes Columbia, Dane, Green, Iowa Counties										
City of Madison	269,546	810	6	85	113	606	6,459	921	4,866	672
Total area actually reporting	98.4%	1,384	12	181	156	1,035	10,464	1,328	8,112	1,024
Estimated total	100.0%	1,396	12	184	157	1,043	10,578	1,335	8,210	1,033
Rate per 100,000 inhabitants		204.1	1.8	26.9	23.0	152.5	1,546.4	195.2	1,200.2	151.0
Manchester-Nashua, NH M. S. A.	423,931									
Includes Hillsborough County										
City of Manchester	114,650	472	5	50	87	330	2,854	226	2,381	247
City of Nashua	91,027	143	4	50	21	68	973	63	845	65
Total area actually reporting	99.7%	746	10	152	120	464	4,935	364	4,194	377
Estimated total	100.0%	746	10	152	120	464	4,942	365	4,200	377
Rate per 100,000 inhabitants		176.0	2.4	35.9	28.3	109.5	1,165.8	86.1	990.7	88.9
Manhattan, KS M. S. A.	133,924									
Includes Geary, Pottawatomie, Riley Counties										
Total area actually reporting	95.8%	439	3	65	11	360	1,811	259	1,411	141
Estimated total	100.0%	452	3	67	12	370	1,912	269	1,490	153
Rate per 100,000 inhabitants		337.5	2.2	50.0	9.0	276.3	1,427.7	200.9	1,112.6	114.2
Mankato, MN M. S. A.	103,725									
Includes Blue Earth, Nicollet Counties										
City of Mankato	44,925	116	0	31	12	73	1,125	141	940	44
Total area actually reporting	100.0%	180	0	55	12	113	1,544	226	1,237	81
Rate per 100,000 inhabitants		173.5	0.0	53.0	11.6	108.9	1,488.6	217.9	1,192.6	78.1
Mansfield, OH M. S. A.	125,402									
Includes Richland County										
City of Mansfield	47,845	229	6	43	28	152	1,529	287	1,131	111
Total area actually reporting	98.5%	308	6	78	30	194	2,258	369	1,722	167
Estimated total	100.0%	309	6	78	30	195	2,309	373	1,767	169
Rate per 100,000 inhabitants		246.4	4.8	62.2	23.9	155.5	1,841.3	297.4	1,409.1	134.8

Table 6. Crime in the United States, by Selected Metropolitan Statistical Area, 2022—Continued

(Number, percent, rate per 100,000 population.)

Area	Population	Violent crime	Murder and nonnegligent manslaughter	Rape	Robbery	Aggravated assault	Property crime	Burglary	Larceny-theft	Motor vehicle theft
McAllen-Edinburg-Mission, TX M. S. A.	893,918									
Includes Hidalgo County										
City of McAllen	145,510	285	5	58	42	180	2,840	159	2,618	63
City of Edinburg	104,987	352	3	68	59	222	2,323	229	2,008	86
City of Mission	86,577	294	1	74	30	189	1,451	160	1,174	117
Total area actually reporting	99.1%	2,656	29	462	346	1,819	15,624	1,869	12,691	1,064
Estimated total	100.0%	2,675	29	465	348	1,833	15,758	1,889	12,788	1,081
Rate per 100,000 inhabitants		299.2	3.2	52.0	38.9	205.1	1,762.8	211.3	1,430.6	120.9
Medford, OR M. S. A.	223,490									
Includes Jackson County										
City of Medford	86,876	323	2	46	76	199	3,566	337	2,866	363
Total area actually reporting	100.0%	592	5	76	119	392	6,002	727	4,675	600
Rate per 100,000 inhabitants		264.9	2.2	34.0	53.2	175.4	2,685.6	325.3	2,091.8	268.5
Memphis, TN-MS-AR M. S. A.	1,337,592									
Includes Crittenden, Desoto, Fayette, Marshall, Shelby, Tate, Tipton, Tunica Counties										
City of Memphis, TN	624,944	15,129	269	397	2,324	12,139	44,783	6,022	27,837	10,924
Total area actually reporting	98.0%	17,922	319	640	2,546	14,417	57,761	7,680	37,119	12,902
Estimated total	100.0%	17,958	320	646	2,549	14,443	58,027	7,744	37,344	12,939
Rate per 100,000 inhabitants		1,342.6	23.9	48.3	190.6	1,079.8	4,338.2	579.0	2,791.9	967.3
Merced, CA M. S. A.	291,601									
Includes Merced County										
City of Merced	92,191	738	6	107	154	471	2,528	381	1,722	425
Total area actually reporting	100.0%	1,820	35	190	307	1,288	6,593	1,036	4,454	1,103
Rate per 100,000 inhabitants		624.1	12.0	65.2	105.3	441.7	2,261.0	355.3	1,527.4	378.3
Michigan City-La Porte, IN M. S. A.	112,661									
Includes La Porte County										
City of Michigan City	32,051	135	1	5	17	112	1,185	210	865	110
City of La Porte	22,371	45	1	10	5	29	372	83	242	47
Total area actually reporting	91.1%	204	4	17	26	157	2,000	484	1,304	212
Estimated total	100.0%	226	4	18	31	173	2,152	518	1,402	232
Rate per 100,000 inhabitants		200.6	3.6	16.0	27.5	153.6	1,910.2	459.8	1,244.4	205.9
Midland, MI M. S. A.	83,437									
Includes Midland County										
City of Midland	42,266	49	2	15	0	32	278	25	242	11
Total area actually reporting	100.0%	103	2	47	0	54	540	69	442	29
Rate per 100,000 inhabitants		123.4	2.4	56.3	0.0	64.7	647.2	82.7	529.7	34.8
Midland, TX M. S. A.	171,945									
Includes Martin, Midland Counties										
City of Midland	129,904	639	13	70	42	514	2,481	289	1,905	287
Total area actually reporting	100.0%	807	14	88	49	655	3,342	410	2,467	465
Rate per 100,000 inhabitants		469.3	8.1	51.2	28.5	380.9	1,943.6	238.4	1,434.8	270.4
Milwaukee-Waukesha, WI M. S. A.	1,557,605									
Includes Milwaukee, Ozaukee, Washington, Waukesha Counties										
City of Milwaukee	561,743	8,474	214	425	1,577	6,258	19,702	2,232	8,027	9,443
City of Waukesha	71,147	71	1	20	1	49	564	50	473	41
Total area actually reporting	99.0%	9,633	227	593	1,819	6,994	33,084	2,974	18,981	11,129
Estimated total	100.0%	9,650	227	597	1,821	7,005	33,241	2,984	19,115	11,142
Rate per 100,000 inhabitants		619.5	14.6	38.3	116.9	449.7	2,134.1	191.6	1,227.2	715.3
Minneapolis-St. Paul-Bloomington, MN-WI M. S. A.	3,694,557									
Includes Anoka, Carver, Chisago, Dakota, Hennepin, Isanti, Le Sueur, Mille Lacs, Pierce, Ramsey, Scott, Sherburne, St Croix, Washington, Wright Counties										
City of Minneapolis, MN	421,690	5,170	79	330	1,772	2,989	22,191	2,552	13,498	6,141
City of St. Paul, MN	277,533	2,127	34	242	413	1,438	12,900	1,505	8,206	3,189
City of Bloomington, MN	88,745	259	2	42	52	163	3,321	156	2,878	287
City of Plymouth, MN	78,585	46	4	9	10	23	986	175	727	84
City of Eagan, MN	68,518	95	0	29	11	55	1,542	108	1,299	135
City of Eden Prairie, MN	62,008	48	0	18	4	26	808	77	676	55
City of Edina, MN	53,206	49	0	7	16	26	1,052	131	847	74
City of Minnetonka, MN	52,309	47	0	7	13	27	908	102	735	71
Total area actually reporting	99.9%	12,295	157	1,494	3,056	7,588	85,976	8,574	62,886	14,516
Estimated total	100.0%	12,299	157	1,495	3,056	7,591	86,016	8,576	62,920	14,520
Rate per 100,000 inhabitants		332.9	4.2	40.5	82.7	205.5	2,328.2	232.1	1,703.0	393.0
Missoula, MT M. S. A.	120,842									
Includes Missoula County										
City of Missoula	75,705	480	2	62	31	385	2,683	259	2,260	164
Total area actually reporting	100.0%	608	2	81	37	488	3,052	363	2,483	206
Rate per 100,000 inhabitants		503.1	1.7	67.0	30.6	403.8	2,525.6	300.4	2,054.7	170.5
Mobile, AL M. S. A.	428,477									
Includes Mobile, Washington Counties										
City of Mobile	239,323	2,218	41	124	135	1,918	7,211	1,077	5,521	613
Total area actually reporting	98.7%	2,863	58	155	176	2,474	9,805	1,606	7,172	1,027

Table 6. Crime in the United States, by Selected Metropolitan Statistical Area, 2022—Continued

(Number, percent, rate per 100,000 population.)

Area	Population	Violent crime	Murder and nonnegligent manslaughter	Rape	Robbery	Aggravated assault	Property crime	Burglary	Larceny-theft	Motor vehicle theft
Estimated total	100.0%	2,879	58	156	177	2,488	9,905	1,619	7,250	1,036
Rate per 100,000 inhabitants		671.9	13.5	36.4	41.3	580.7	2,311.7	377.8	1,692.0	241.8
Modesto, CA M. S. A.	553,905									
Includes Stanislaus County										
City of Modesto	219,083	1,669	10	111	292	1,256	5,264	582	3,891	791
Total area actually reporting	100.0%	3,011	27	229	591	2,164	11,427	1,563	8,098	1,766
Rate per 100,000 inhabitants		543.6	4.9	41.3	106.7	390.7	2,063.0	282.2	1,462.0	318.8
Monroe, LA M. S. A.	202,879									
Includes Morehouse, Ouachita, Union Counties										
City of Monroe	46,908	1,284	18	18	107	1,141	3,153	662	2,280	211
Total area actually reporting	87.6%	2,459	27	88	176	2,168	7,256	1,590	5,107	559
Estimated total	100.0%	2,564	29	94	181	2,260	7,646	1,660	5,390	596
Rate per 100,000 inhabitants		1,263.8	14.3	46.3	89.2	1,114.0	3,768.7	818.2	2,656.8	293.8
Morgantown, WV M. S. A.	141,304									
Includes Monongalia, Preston Counties										
City of Morgantown	29,279	84	6	19	8	51	715	41	648	26
Total area actually reporting	91.4%	250	9	97	11	133	1,778	165	1,537	76
Estimated total	100.0%	270	9	98	11	152	1,959	181	1,695	83
Rate per 100,000 inhabitants		191.1	6.4	69.4	7.8	107.6	1,386.4	128.1	1,199.5	58.7
Morristown, TN M. S. A.	145,292									
Includes Grainger, Hamblen, Jefferson Counties										
City of Morristown	30,988	223	0	15	14	194	1,141	132	851	158
Total area actually reporting	100.0%	531	5	40	24	462	2,300	343	1,617	340
Rate per 100,000 inhabitants		365.5	3.4	27.5	16.5	318.0	1,583.0	236.1	1,112.9	234.0
Mount Vernon-Anacortes, WA M. S. A.	131,994									
Includes Skagit County										
City of Mount Vernon	35,511	96	1	9	20	66	1,047	155	737	155
City of Anacortes	17,990	16	1	6	4	5	591	82	458	51
Total area actually reporting	100.0%	240	5	22	58	155	3,951	644	2,851	456
Rate per 100,000 inhabitants		181.8	3.8	16.7	43.9	117.4	2,993.3	487.9	2,159.9	345.5
Muncie, IN M. S. A.	112,175									
Includes Delaware County										
City of Muncie	65,343	315	11	35	30	239	1,776	315	1,214	247
Total area actually reporting	100.0%	372	20	43	33	276	2,090	384	1,425	281
Rate per 100,000 inhabitants		331.6	17.8	38.3	29.4	246.0	1,863.2	342.3	1,270.3	250.5
Muskegon, MI M. S. A.	177,206									
Includes Muskegon County										
City of Muskegon	37,615	320	7	33	27	253	1,007	171	698	138
Total area actually reporting	100.0%	787	14	163	53	557	3,551	409	2,841	301
Rate per 100,000 inhabitants		444.1	7.9	92.0	29.9	314.3	2,003.9	230.8	1,603.2	169.9
Myrtle Beach-Conway-North Myrtle Beach, SC-NC M. S. A.	531,626									
Includes Brunswick, Horry Counties										
City of Myrtle Beach, SC	38,117	386	6	68	65	247	2,553	218	2,138	197
City of Conway, SC	23,664	162	5	11	11	135	643	35	548	60
City of North Myrtle Beach, SC	19,888	89	2	11	12	64	864	75	733	56
Total area actually reporting	99.7%	1,755	32	221	159	1,343	10,497	1,270	8,307	920
Estimated total	100.0%	1,759	32	221	159	1,347	10,533	1,275	8,335	923
Rate per 100,000 inhabitants		330.9	6.0	41.6	29.9	253.4	1,981.3	239.8	1,567.8	173.6
Napa, CA M. S. A.	134,970									
Includes Napa County										
City of Napa	78,586	255	2	24	44	185	1,162	151	857	154
Total area actually reporting	100.0%	454	2	59	72	321	2,042	287	1,447	308
Rate per 100,000 inhabitants		336.4	1.5	43.7	53.3	237.8	1,512.9	212.6	1,072.1	228.2
Naples-Marco Island, FL[1] M. S. A.	399,485									
Includes Collier County										
City of Naples	19,668	21	0	4	1	16	306	22	252	32
City of Marco Island	16,137	14	0	3	0	11	84	1	77	6
Total area actually reporting	100.0%	809	8	68	108	625	3,076	253	2,578	245
Rate per 100,000 inhabitants		202.5	2.0	17.0	27.0	156.5	770.0	63.3	645.3	61.3
Nashville-Davidson--Murfreesboro--Franklin, TN M. S. A.	2,036,090									
Includes Cannon, Cheatham, Davidson, Dickson, Macon, Maury, Robertson, Rutherford, Smith, Sumner, Trousdale, Williamson, Wilson Counties										
City of Metropolitan Nashville Police Department	679,562	7,491	83	385	1,224	5,799	25,991	3,470	19,534	2,987
City of Murfreesboro	161,810	827	9	114	59	645	3,415	291	2,762	362
City of Franklin	87,081	170	0	19	9	142	899	101	733	65
Total area actually reporting	100.0%	11,328	123	777	1,432	8,996	41,536	5,157	31,650	4,729
Rate per 100,000 inhabitants		556.4	6.0	38.2	70.3	441.8	2,040.0	253.3	1,554.4	232.3
New Bern, NC M. S. A.	123,156									
Includes Craven, Jones, Pamlico Counties										
City of New Bern	31,614	160	3	11	12	134	645	146	466	33

Table 6. Crime in the United States, by Selected Metropolitan Statistical Area, 2022—Continued

(Number, percent, rate per 100,000 population.)

Area	Population	Violent crime	Murder and nonnegligent manslaughter	Rape	Robbery	Aggravated assault	Property crime	Burglary	Larceny-theft	Motor vehicle theft
Total area actually reporting	89.7%	323	6	21	20	276	1,671	386	1,142	143
Estimated total	100.0%	350	6	25	22	297	1,853	424	1,269	160
Rate per 100,000 inhabitants		284.2	4.9	20.3	17.9	241.2	1,504.6	344.3	1,030.4	129.9
New Haven-Milford, CT M. S. A.	810,644									
Includes New Haven County										
City of New Haven	136,205	756	15	48	243	450	4,224	395	3,049	780
City of Milford	52,694	43	2	3	26	12	1,234	74	1,035	125
Total area actually reporting	100.0%	1,943	44	181	635	1,083	18,071	1,455	13,912	2,704
Rate per 100,000 inhabitants		239.7	5.4	22.3	78.3	133.6	2,229.2	179.5	1,716.2	333.6
New Orleans-Metairie, LA M. S. A.	1,251,216									
Includes Jefferson, Orleans, Plaquemines, St Bernard, St Charles, St James, St John The Baptist, St Tammany Counties										
City of New Orleans	370,128	5,345	266	442	1,039	3,598	17,177	1,837	11,138	4,202
Total area actually reporting	99.9%	8,177	339	609	1,397	5,832	33,870	4,849	23,155	5,866
Estimated total	100.0%	8,179	339	609	1,397	5,834	33,876	4,850	23,160	5,866
Rate per 100,000 inhabitants		653.7	27.1	48.7	111.7	466.3	2,707.4	387.6	1,851.0	468.8
New York-Newark-Jersey City, NY-NJ-PA[1] M. S. A.	11,316,953									
Includes the Metro Divisions of Nassau County-Suffolk County, NY; Newark, NJ-PA; New Brunswick-Lakewood, NJ; New York-Jersey City-White Plains, NY-NJ										
City of Newark, NJ	304,311	1,582	53	86	469	974	5,539	537	2,869	2,133
City of Jersey City, NJ	276,300	609	12	39	89	469	3,825	61	3,125	639
City of Lakewood Township, NJ	141,190	123	0	14	25	84	914	151	661	102
City of White Plains, NY	59,488	68	0	7	14	47	757	37	701	19
City of New Brunswick, NJ	55,971	480	4	47	217	212	1,211	152	959	100
Total area actually reporting	96.0%	15,766	212	1,200	3,954	10,400	125,650	10,387	101,659	13,604
Estimated total	100.0%	17,205	234	1,310	4,313	11,348	133,770	11,427	107,610	14,733
Rate per 100,000 inhabitants		152.0	2.1	11.6	38.1	100.3	1,182.0	101.0	950.9	130.2
Nassau County-Suffolk County, NY M. D.	2,938,399									
Includes Nassau, Suffolk Counties										
Total area actually reporting	99.9%	3,630	44	230	921	2,435	35,454	2,130	30,894	2,430
Estimated total	100.0%	3,632	44	230	921	2,437	35,491	2,134	30,924	2,433
Rate per 100,000 inhabitants		123.6	1.5	7.8	31.3	82.9	1,207.8	72.6	1,052.4	82.8
Newark, NJ-PA[1] M. D.	2,271,749									
Includes Essex, Hunterdon, Morris, Pike, Sussex, Union Counties										
Total area actually reporting	96.4%	4,283	88	316	1,284	2,595	27,231	2,681	19,187	5,363
Estimated total	100.0%	4,597	93	348	1,339	2,817	28,864	2,904	20,358	5,602
Rate per 100,000 inhabitants		202.4	4.1	15.3	58.9	124.0	1,270.6	127.8	896.1	246.6
New Brunswick-Lakewood, NJ M. D.	2,514,571									
Includes Middlesex, Monmouth, Ocean, Somerset Counties										
Total area actually reporting	96.9%	3,133	37	315	626	2,155	25,618	2,831	20,633	2,154
Estimated total	100.0%	3,302	39	332	660	2,271	26,871	2,984	21,597	2,290
Rate per 100,000 inhabitants		131.3	1.6	13.2	26.2	90.3	1,068.6	118.7	858.9	91.1
New York-Jersey City-White Plains, NY-NJ M. D.	3,592,234									
Includes Bergen, Bronx, Hudson, Kings, New York, Passaic, Putnam, Rockland, Westchester Counties										
Total area actually reporting	92.1%	4,720	43	339	1,123	3,215	37,347	2,745	30,945	3,657
Estimated total	100.0%	5,674	58	400	1,393	3,823	42,544	3,405	34,731	4,408
Rate per 100,000 inhabitants		158.0	1.6	11.1	38.8	106.4	1,184.3	94.8	966.8	122.7
Niles, MI M. S. A.	152,111									
Includes Berrien County										
City of Niles	11,756	69	1	10	7	51	277	25	209	43
Total area actually reporting	99.7%	876	14	146	52	664	2,928	423	2,103	402
Estimated total	100.0%	877	14	146	52	665	2,933	424	2,107	402
Rate per 100,000 inhabitants		576.6	9.2	96.0	34.2	437.2	1,928.2	278.7	1,385.2	264.3
Norwich-New London, CT M. S. A.	178,647									
Includes New London County										
City of Norwich	40,096	121	2	33	22	64	667	126	483	58
City of New London	27,667	66	2	20	25	19	467	63	328	76
Total area actually reporting	100.0%	263	4	74	59	126	1,990	258	1,546	186
Rate per 100,000 inhabitants		147.2	2.2	41.4	33.0	70.5	1,113.9	144.4	865.4	104.1
Ocean City, NJ M. S. A.	96,314									
Includes Cape May County										
City of Ocean City	11,258	14	0	0	0	14	672	22	637	13
Total area actually reporting	76.5%	208	1	17	17	173	2,155	157	1,941	57
Estimated total	100.0%	295	2	26	32	235	2,621	221	2,276	124
Rate per 100,000 inhabitants		306.3	2.1	27.0	33.2	244.0	2,721.3	229.5	2,363.1	128.7
Odessa, TX M. S. A.	157,772									
Includes Ector County										
City of Odessa	106,389	553	8	63	62	421	2,200	345	1,576	279
Total area actually reporting	100.0%	673	12	70	69	523	2,520	394	1,718	408
Rate per 100,000 inhabitants		426.6	7.6	44.4	43.7	331.5	1,597.2	249.7	1,088.9	258.6

Table 6. Crime in the United States, by Selected Metropolitan Statistical Area, 2022—Continued

(Number, percent, rate per 100,000 population.)

Area	Population	Violent crime	Murder and nonnegligent manslaughter	Rape	Robbery	Aggravated assault	Property crime	Burglary	Larceny-theft	Motor vehicle theft
Ogden-Clearfield, UT M. S. A.	713,700									
Includes Box Elder, Davis, Morgan, Weber Counties										
City of Ogden	86,870	482	3	98	44	337	2,204	272	1,661	271
City of Clearfield	32,586	77	2	18	6	51	500	67	396	37
Total area actually reporting	96.5%	1,264	6	349	94	815	9,972	1,360	7,703	909
Estimated total	100.0%	1,291	6	357	96	832	10,245	1,401	7,907	937
Rate per 100,000 inhabitants		180.9	0.8	50.0	13.5	116.6	1,435.5	196.3	1,107.9	131.3
Oklahoma City, OK M. S. A.	1,457,832									
Includes Canadian, Cleveland, Grady, Lincoln, Logan, Mcclain, Oklahoma Counties										
City of Oklahoma City	692,651	4,447	65	505	642	3,235	21,187	3,830	14,396	2,961
Total area actually reporting	100.0%	6,264	81	848	774	4,561	36,082	6,397	25,253	4,432
Rate per 100,000 inhabitants		429.7	5.6	58.2	53.1	312.9	2,475.0	438.8	1,732.2	304.0
Olympia-Lacey-Tumwater, WA M. S. A.	301,267									
Includes Thurston County										
City of Olympia	56,214	293	2	31	84	176	2,363	344	1,661	358
City of Lacey	55,101	121	2	16	32	71	1,896	257	1,362	277
City of Tumwater	26,227	60	0	8	13	39	881	143	600	138
Total area actually reporting	99.3%	751	8	87	172	484	7,068	1,242	4,780	1,046
Estimated total	100.0%	754	8	88	172	486	7,104	1,252	4,800	1,052
Rate per 100,000 inhabitants		250.3	2.7	29.2	57.1	161.3	2,358.0	415.6	1,593.3	349.2
Omaha-Council Bluffs, NE-IA M. S. A.	975,750									
Includes Cass, Douglas, Harrison, Mills, Pottawattamie, Sarpy, Saunders, Washington Counties										
City of Omaha	483,462	2,713	29	298	336	2,050	16,768	1,255	12,156	3,357
City of Council Bluffs, IA	62,206	262	1	43	54	164	1,867	349	1,200	318
Total area actually reporting	99.6%	3,523	35	541	425	2,522	22,577	2,038	16,414	4,125
Estimated total	100.0%	3,531	35	542	425	2,529	22,618	2,045	16,444	4,129
Rate per 100,000 inhabitants		361.9	3.6	55.5	43.6	259.2	2,318.0	209.6	1,685.3	423.2
Oshkosh-Neenah, WI M. S. A.	171,391									
Includes Winnebago County										
City of Oshkosh	66,521	224	1	56	14	153	1,080	147	862	71
City of Neenah	27,706	64	0	15	5	44	352	57	254	41
Total area actually reporting	100.0%	344	1	92	20	231	2,067	303	1,609	155
Rate per 100,000 inhabitants		200.7	0.6	53.7	11.7	134.8	1,206.0	176.8	938.8	90.4
Owensboro, KY M. S. A.	120,882									
Includes Daviess, Hancock, Mclean Counties										
City of Owensboro	59,839	221	3	49	39	130	2,070	261	1,545	264
Total area actually reporting	100.0%	241	3	55	42	141	2,385	334	1,738	313
Rate per 100,000 inhabitants		199.4	2.5	45.5	34.7	116.6	1,973.0	276.3	1,437.8	258.9
Panama City, FL[1] M. S. A.	186,049									
Includes Bay County										
City of Panama City	35,384	18	1	0	17	0	1,029	168	783	78
Total area actually reporting	79.0%	107	3	15	34	55	2,604	484	1,933	187
Estimated total	100.0%	192	5	27	51	109	3,338	568	2,522	248
Rate per 100,000 inhabitants		103.2	2.7	14.5	27.4	58.6	1,794.2	305.3	1,355.6	133.3
Parkersburg-Vienna, WV M. S. A.	88,140									
Includes Wirt, Wood Counties										
City of Parkersburg	29,190	129	5	26	9	89	1,011	110	825	76
City of Vienna	10,521	19	0	6	2	11	381	12	362	7
Total area actually reporting	100.0%	204	5	49	11	139	1,646	155	1,387	104
Rate per 100,000 inhabitants		231.4	5.7	55.6	12.5	157.7	1,867.5	175.9	1,573.6	118.0
Philadelphia-Camden-Wilmington, PA[1]-NJ-DE-MD[1] M. S. A.	6,229,097									
Includes the Metro Divisions of Camden, NJ; Montgomery County-Bucks County-Chester County, PA; Philadelphia, PA; Wilmington, DE-MD-NJ										
City of Philadelphia, PA	1,555,812	16,202	514	785	5,763	9,140	67,233	6,485	48,067	12,681
City of Camden County Police Department, NJ	71,616	1,125	28	52	244	801	1,970	316	1,222	432
City of Wilmington, DE	70,625	848	18	12	216	602	2,382	418	1,566	398
Total area actually reporting	96.5%	25,596	692	1,598	7,754	15,552	136,715	12,770	105,652	18,292
Estimated total	100.0%	26,096	698	1,644	7,840	15,914	139,765	13,113	108,028	18,623
Rate per 100,000 inhabitants		418.9	11.2	26.4	125.9	255.5	2,243.7	210.5	1,734.2	299.0
Camden, NJ M. D.	1,298,263									
Includes Burlington, Camden, Gloucester Counties										
Total area actually reporting	93.5%	3,136	48	228	662	2,198	21,817	2,496	17,573	1,748
Estimated total	100.0%	3,322	50	246	693	2,333	23,135	2,660	18,572	1,903
Rate per 100,000 inhabitants		255.9	3.9	18.9	53.4	179.7	1,782.0	204.9	1,430.5	146.6
Montgomery County-Bucks County-Chester County, PA[1] M. D.	2,058,300									
Includes Bucks, Chester, Montgomery Counties										
Total area actually reporting	98.3%	2,141	52	291	518	1,280	23,986	1,590	20,753	1,643
Estimated total	100.0%	2,189	52	294	524	1,319	24,255	1,613	20,981	1,661
Rate per 100,000 inhabitants		106.3	2.5	14.3	25.5	64.1	1,178.4	78.4	1,019.3	80.7

Table 6. Crime in the United States, by Selected Metropolitan Statistical Area, 2022—Continued

(Number, percent, rate per 100,000 population.)

Area	Population	Violent crime	Murder and nonnegligent manslaughter	Rape	Robbery	Aggravated assault	Property crime	Burglary	Larceny-theft	Motor vehicle theft
Philadelphia, PA[1] M. D.	2,128,581									
Includes Delaware, Philadelphia Counties										
Total area actually reporting	96.9%	17,501	551	878	6,069	10,003	75,999	7,113	55,370	13,516
Estimated total	100.0%	17,624	553	889	6,092	10,090	76,725	7,174	55,968	13,583
Rate per 100,000 inhabitants		828.0	26.0	41.8	286.2	474.0	3,604.5	337.0	2,629.4	638.1
Wilmington, DE-MD[1]-NJ M. D.	743,953									
Includes Cecil, New Castle, Salem Counties										
Total area actually reporting	95.4%	2,818	41	201	505	2,071	14,913	1,571	11,956	1,385
Estimated total	100.0%	2,961	43	215	531	2,172	15,650	1,666	12,507	1,476
Rate per 100,000 inhabitants		398.0	5.8	28.9	71.4	292.0	2,103.6	223.9	1,681.2	198.4
Pine Bluff, AR M. S. A.	85,764									
Includes Cleveland, Jefferson, Lincoln Counties										
City of Pine Bluff	39,549	644	17	34	62	531	2,025	375	1,330	320
Total area actually reporting	100.0%	849	24	68	71	686	2,860	596	1,815	449
Rate per 100,000 inhabitants		989.9	28.0	79.3	82.8	799.9	3,334.7	694.9	2,116.3	523.5
Pittsfield, MA M. S. A.	129,181									
Includes Berkshire County										
City of Pittsfield	43,496	326	3	40	32	251	693	231	390	72
Total area actually reporting	95.9%	564	6	65	52	441	1,489	362	1,009	118
Estimated total	100.0%	571	6	66	52	447	1,511	365	1,026	120
Rate per 100,000 inhabitants		442.0	4.6	51.1	40.3	346.0	1,169.7	282.5	794.2	92.9
Pocatello, ID M. S. A.	96,548									
Includes Bannock, Power Counties										
City of Pocatello	57,914	238	0	24	5	209	781	173	524	84
Total area actually reporting	100.0%	313	1	35	10	267	1,353	242	988	123
Rate per 100,000 inhabitants		324.2	1.0	36.3	10.4	276.5	1,401.4	250.7	1,023.3	127.4
Portland-South Portland, ME M. S. A.	562,970									
Includes Cumberland, Sagadahoc, York Counties										
City of Portland	68,199	126	5	31	17	73	1,149	35	1,018	96
City of South Portland	27,445	43	0	10	9	24	492	26	418	48
Total area actually reporting	100.0%	565	8	170	53	334	6,143	456	5,299	388
Rate per 100,000 inhabitants		100.4	1.4	30.2	9.4	59.3	1,091.2	81.0	941.3	68.9
Portland-Vancouver-Hillsboro, OR-WA M. S. A.	2,503,925									
Includes Clackamas, Clark, Columbia, Multnomah, Skamania, Washington, Yamhill Counties										
City of Portland, OR	630,129	4,733	94	354	1,279	3,006	39,853	4,789	24,206	10,856
City of Vancouver, WA	193,273	1,229	14	132	293	790	10,777	1,351	6,625	2,801
City of Hillsboro, OR	106,345	315	4	58	63	190	2,730	318	2,077	335
City of Beaverton, OR	98,991	303	3	37	46	217	2,707	317	2,019	371
City of Tigard, OR	56,550	202	3	17	67	115	2,080	249	1,564	267
Total area actually reporting	100.0%	9,939	152	1,126	2,297	6,364	85,429	10,296	54,952	20,179
Rate per 100,000 inhabitants		396.9	6.1	45.0	91.7	254.2	3,411.8	411.2	2,194.6	805.9
Poughkeepsie-Newburgh-Middletown, NY M. S. A.	711,561									
Includes Dutchess, Orange Counties										
City of Poughkeepsie	32,202	198	5	16	36	141	594	71	473	50
City of Middletown	30,538	109	2	8	22	77	438	42	373	23
City of Newburgh	28,819	318	3	21	70	224	714	97	550	67
City of Woodbury Town	11,705	4	0	2	1	1	408	6	398	4
Total area actually reporting	99.4%	1,299	18	212	191	878	7,460	548	6,570	342
Estimated total	100.0%	1,301	18	212	191	880	7,500	552	6,603	345
Rate per 100,000 inhabitants		182.8	2.5	29.8	26.8	123.7	1,054.0	77.6	928.0	48.5
Prescott Valley-Prescott, AZ M. S. A.	246,967									
Includes Yavapai County										
City of Prescott Valley	49,422	140	2	26	5	107	372	43	308	21
City of Prescott	47,878	192	1	21	8	162	636	127	474	35
Total area actually reporting	100.0%	752	7	80	19	646	2,299	400	1,685	213
Rate per 100,000 inhabitants		304.5	2.8	32.4	7.7	261.6	930.9	162.0	682.3	86.2
Providence-Warwick, RI-MA M. S. A.	1,670,973									
Includes Bristol, Kent, Newport, Providence, Washington Counties										
City of Providence, RI	189,064	643	7	65	136	435	4,786	385	3,687	714
City of Warwick, RI	82,966	63	0	19	6	38	1,167	82	990	95
Total area actually reporting	100.0%	4,299	23	585	547	3,144	20,028	2,298	15,388	2,342
Rate per 100,000 inhabitants		257.3	1.4	35.0	32.7	188.2	1,198.6	137.5	920.9	140.2
Provo-Orem, UT M. S. A.	716,788									
Includes Juab, Utah Counties										
City of Provo	114,120	168	0	46	14	108	1,597	159	1,301	137
City of Orem	97,430	182	6	90	10	76	1,642	129	1,363	150
Total area actually reporting	100.0%	772	13	316	62	381	7,682	689	6,353	640
Rate per 100,000 inhabitants		107.7	1.8	44.1	8.6	53.2	1,071.7	96.1	886.3	89.3
Pueblo, CO M. S. A.	170,765									
Includes Pueblo County										
City of Pueblo	112,618	1,764	29	183	301	1,251	7,196	1,336	4,154	1,706

Table 6. Crime in the United States, by Selected Metropolitan Statistical Area, 2022—Continued

(Number, percent, rate per 100,000 population.)

Area	Population	Violent crime	Murder and nonnegligent manslaughter	Rape	Robbery	Aggravated assault	Property crime	Burglary	Larceny-theft	Motor vehicle theft
Total area actually reporting	100.0%	1,825	33	183	316	1,293	8,387	1,555	4,893	1,939
Rate per 100,000 inhabitants		1,068.7	19.3	107.2	185.0	757.2	4,911.4	910.6	2,865.3	1,135.5
Racine, WI M. S. A.	196,114									
Includes Racine County										
City of Racine	76,679	333	5	30	68	230	1,154	339	647	168
Total area actually reporting	100.0%	421	5	42	73	301	1,986	416	1,344	226
Rate per 100,000 inhabitants		214.7	2.5	21.4	37.2	153.5	1,012.7	212.1	685.3	115.2
Raleigh-Cary, NC M. S. A.	1,484,502									
Includes Franklin, Johnston, Wake Counties										
City of Raleigh	469,300	2,345	44	173	438	1,690	10,956	1,203	8,556	1,197
City of Cary	174,726	139	0	12	28	99	1,932	293	1,501	138
Total area actually reporting	99.4%	3,710	57	314	634	2,705	23,154	2,912	18,077	2,165
Estimated total	100.0%	3,738	57	318	636	2,727	23,364	2,949	18,234	2,181
Rate per 100,000 inhabitants		251.8	3.8	21.4	42.8	183.7	1,573.9	198.7	1,228.3	146.9
Rapid City, SD M. S. A.	145,637									
Includes Meade, Pennington Counties										
City of Rapid City	78,063	532	5	97	65	365	2,799	475	1,921	403
Total area actually reporting	97.6%	745	7	154	71	513	3,650	676	2,463	511
Estimated total	100.0%	755	7	156	71	521	3,713	690	2,505	518
Rate per 100,000 inhabitants		518.4	4.8	107.1	48.8	357.7	2,549.5	473.8	1,720.0	355.7
Reno, NV M. S. A.	504,210									
Includes Storey, Washoe Counties										
City of Reno	273,671	1,565	11	277	300	977	6,994	1,113	4,790	1,091
Total area actually reporting	100.0%	2,401	18	400	428	1,555	10,348	1,601	7,178	1,569
Rate per 100,000 inhabitants		476.2	3.6	79.3	84.9	308.4	2,052.3	317.5	1,423.6	311.2
Richmond, VA M. S. A.	1,337,172									
Includes Amelia, Charles City, Chesterfield, Colonial Heights City, Dinwiddie, Goochland, Hanover, Henrico, Hopewell City, King And Queen, King William, New Kent, Petersburg City, Powhatan, Prince George, Richmond City, Sussex Counties										
City of Richmond	227,323	818	59	10	221	528	7,803	785	6,253	765
Total area actually reporting	100.0%	3,377	154	279	570	2,374	26,135	2,162	21,798	2,175
Rate per 100,000 inhabitants		252.5	11.5	20.9	42.6	177.5	1,954.5	161.7	1,630.2	162.7
Riverside-San Bernardino-Ontario, CA M. S. A.	4,706,541									
Includes Riverside, San Bernardino Counties										
City of Riverside	319,889	1,652	17	138	434	1,063	10,366	1,563	7,058	1,745
City of San Bernardino	222,623	2,640	72	112	675	1,781	6,578	1,244	3,608	1,726
City of Ontario	180,004	582	7	104	150	321	3,833	653	2,254	926
City of Corona	161,946	350	4	37	105	204	3,891	642	2,595	654
City of Temecula	111,611	175	1	12	65	97	2,651	438	1,903	310
City of Chino	94,611	274	0	31	59	184	2,538	314	1,942	282
City of Redlands	73,554	206	1	31	81	93	2,265	292	1,713	260
City of Palm Desert	51,918	182	2	9	32	139	2,024	303	1,477	244
Total area actually reporting	100.0%	20,813	298	1,380	4,204	14,931	99,775	17,238	63,305	19,232
Rate per 100,000 inhabitants		442.2	6.3	29.3	89.3	317.2	2,119.9	366.3	1,345.0	408.6
Roanoke, VA M. S. A.	315,040									
Includes Botetourt, Craig, Franklin, Roanoke, Roanoke City, Salem City Counties										
City of Roanoke	98,204	594	18	114	98	364	4,212	508	3,295	409
Total area actually reporting	100.0%	999	27	185	136	651	6,731	798	5,312	621
Rate per 100,000 inhabitants		317.1	8.6	58.7	43.2	206.6	2,136.6	253.3	1,686.1	197.1
Rochester, MN M. S. A.	228,145									
Includes Dodge, Fillmore, Olmsted, Wabasha Counties										
City of Rochester	121,534	271	1	69	32	169	2,276	277	1,855	144
Total area actually reporting	100.0%	336	2	92	35	207	2,813	380	2,243	190
Rate per 100,000 inhabitants		147.3	0.9	40.3	15.3	90.7	1,233.0	166.6	983.1	83.3
Rochester, NY M. S. A.	1,089,328									
Includes Livingston, Monroe, Ontario, Orleans, Wayne, Yates Counties										
City of Rochester	210,270	1,538	66	69	478	925	7,529	932	5,233	1,364
Total area actually reporting	98.9%	2,578	73	341	644	1,520	18,430	2,068	14,193	2,169
Estimated total	100.0%	2,582	73	341	644	1,524	18,532	2,077	14,279	2,176
Rate per 100,000 inhabitants		237.0	6.7	31.3	59.1	139.9	1,701.2	190.7	1,310.8	199.8
Rockford, IL[1] M. S. A.	334,983									
Includes Boone, Winnebago Counties										
City of Rockford	146,710	2,098	16	128	202	1,752	3,866	626	2,470	770
Total area actually reporting	100.0%	2,472	25	213	228	2,006	5,606	914	3,752	940
Rate per 100,000 inhabitants		737.9	7.5	63.6	68.1	598.8	1,673.5	272.8	1,120.1	280.6
Rocky Mount, NC M. S. A.	144,046									
Includes Edgecombe, Nash Counties										
City of Rocky Mount	53,668	473	19	17	89	348	1,486	312	1,026	148
Total area actually reporting	90.6%	642	27	30	96	489	2,177	522	1,462	193
Estimated total	100.0%	678	27	33	99	519	2,517	577	1,721	219
Rate per 100,000 inhabitants		470.7	18.7	22.9	68.7	360.3	1,747.4	400.6	1,194.8	152.0

Table 6. Crime in the United States, by Selected Metropolitan Statistical Area, 2022—Continued

(Number, percent, rate per 100,000 population.)

Area	Population	Violent crime	Murder and nonnegligent manslaughter	Rape	Robbery	Aggravated assault	Property crime	Burglary	Larceny-theft	Motor vehicle theft
Rome, GA M. S. A.	99,290									
Includes Floyd County										
City of Rome	37,778	319	5	33	25	256	1,479	155	1,195	129
Total area actually reporting	100.0%	496	5	74	34	383	2,151	280	1,653	218
Rate per 100,000 inhabitants		499.5	5.0	74.5	34.2	385.7	2,166.4	282.0	1,664.8	219.6
Sacramento-Roseville-Folsom, CA M. S. A.	2,426,345									
Includes El Dorado, Placer, Sacramento, Yolo Counties										
City of Sacramento	526,671	4,468	54	186	1,243	2,985	16,681	2,769	10,328	3,584
City of Roseville	155,448	254	2	38	89	125	2,930	285	2,372	273
City of Folsom	83,011	115	0	20	16	79	1,211	162	945	104
City of Rancho Cordova	81,041	382	4	23	92	263	1,809	333	1,081	395
City of West Sacramento	53,643	93	1	9	28	55	537	58	404	75
Total area actually reporting	100.0%	10,674	128	769	2,477	7,300	50,160	7,594	33,963	8,603
Rate per 100,000 inhabitants		439.9	5.3	31.7	102.1	300.9	2,067.3	313.0	1,399.8	354.6
Saginaw, MI M. S. A.	189,348									
Includes Saginaw County										
City of Saginaw	43,651	925	20	46	48	811	895	262	498	135
Total area actually reporting	99.8%	1,445	30	128	71	1,216	2,538	505	1,749	284
Estimated total	100.0%	1,445	30	128	71	1,216	2,540	505	1,751	284
Rate per 100,000 inhabitants		763.1	15.8	67.6	37.5	642.2	1,341.4	266.7	924.8	150.0
Salem, OR M. S. A.	437,378									
Includes Marion, Polk Counties										
City of Salem	179,661	866	7	44	175	640	6,506	749	4,568	1,189
Total area actually reporting	99.0%	1,439	12	147	266	1,014	12,020	1,345	8,570	2,105
Estimated total	100.0%	1,445	12	148	266	1,019	12,091	1,353	8,625	2,113
Rate per 100,000 inhabitants		330.4	2.7	33.8	60.8	233.0	2,764.4	309.3	1,972.0	483.1
Salinas, CA M. S. A.	436,640									
Includes Monterey County										
City of Salinas	162,187	845	13	91	245	496	2,720	340	1,695	685
Total area actually reporting	100.0%	1,827	23	187	385	1,232	6,216	990	4,193	1,033
Rate per 100,000 inhabitants		418.4	5.3	42.8	88.2	282.2	1,423.6	226.7	960.3	236.6
Salisbury, MD[1]-DE M. S. A.	440,369									
Includes Somerset, Sussex, Wicomico, Worcester Counties										
City of Salisbury, MD	33,063	362	1	14	65	282	854	130	684	40
Total area actually reporting	90.7%	1,585	12	83	199	1,291	6,474	933	5,180	362
Estimated total	100.0%	1,677	13	95	215	1,354	6,981	998	5,598	386
Rate per 100,000 inhabitants		380.8	3.0	21.6	48.8	307.5	1,585.3	226.6	1,271.2	87.7
Salt Lake City, UT M. S. A.	1,261,030									
Includes Salt Lake, Tooele Counties										
City of Salt Lake City	201,373	1,970	13	380	413	1,164	12,934	1,316	9,887	1,731
Total area actually reporting	99.9%	4,728	41	923	813	2,951	38,758	3,807	30,130	4,821
Estimated total	100.0%	4,729	41	923	813	2,952	38,771	3,810	30,139	4,822
Rate per 100,000 inhabitants		375.0	3.3	73.2	64.5	234.1	3,074.6	302.1	2,390.0	382.4
San Angelo, TX M. S. A.	122,414									
Includes Irion, Sterling, Tom Green Counties										
City of San Angelo	99,243	334	6	64	26	238	2,802	428	2,174	200
Total area actually reporting	100.0%	395	7	84	28	276	3,024	477	2,323	224
Rate per 100,000 inhabitants		322.7	5.7	68.6	22.9	225.5	2,470.3	389.7	1,897.7	183.0
San Antonio-New Braunfels, TX M. S. A.	2,653,896									
Includes Atascosa, Bandera, Bexar, Comal, Guadalupe, Kendall, Medina, Wilson Counties										
City of San Antonio	1,465,608	12,935	230	1,555	1,700	9,450	74,288	9,338	52,586	12,364
City of New Braunfels	107,017	201	0	30	20	151	1,513	179	1,157	177
Total area actually reporting	97.9%	15,387	258	1,851	1,955	11,321	92,248	12,264	65,144	14,838
Estimated total	100.0%	15,509	260	1,875	1,960	11,412	92,775	12,379	65,469	14,925
Rate per 100,000 inhabitants		584.4	9.8	70.7	73.9	430.0	3,495.8	466.4	2,466.9	562.4
San Diego-Chula Vista-Carlsbad, CA M. S. A.	3,278,578									
Includes San Diego County										
City of San Diego	1,377,838	5,932	53	410	1,288	4,181	25,044	3,290	15,106	6,648
City of Chula Vista	277,976	975	8	33	295	639	3,550	519	2,035	996
City of Carlsbad	115,531	241	0	29	48	164	2,047	296	1,565	186
City of Poway	48,011	83	0	3	18	62	459	73	343	43
Total area actually reporting	100.0%	12,879	108	776	2,762	9,233	54,706	7,834	34,285	12,587
Rate per 100,000 inhabitants		392.8	3.3	23.7	84.2	281.6	1,668.6	238.9	1,045.7	383.9
San Jose-Sunnyvale-Santa Clara, CA M. S. A.	1,912,522									
Includes San Benito, Santa Clara Counties										
City of San Jose	956,814	5,046	35	894	1,264	2,853	25,363	3,884	15,010	6,469
City of Sunnyvale	148,739	326	0	45	83	198	3,654	621	2,633	400
City of Santa Clara	126,877	396	1	35	86	274	4,564	646	3,394	524
City of Mountain View	80,588	223	1	22	49	151	2,386	400	1,804	182
City of Milpitas	77,790	197	2	13	71	111	2,845	353	2,123	369
City of Palo Alto	64,922	134	0	22	45	67	1,945	147	1,688	110
City of Cupertino	56,950	66	1	15	18	32	758	161	535	62

Table 6. Crime in the United States, by Selected Metropolitan Statistical Area, 2022—Continued

(Number, percent, rate per 100,000 population.)

Area	Population	Violent crime	Murder and nonnegligent manslaughter	Rape	Robbery	Aggravated assault	Property crime	Burglary	Larceny-theft	Motor vehicle theft
Total area actually reporting	100.0%	7,641	44	1,231	1,844	4,522	48,428	7,471	31,531	9,426
Rate per 100,000 inhabitants		399.5	2.3	64.4	96.4	236.4	2,532.2	390.6	1,648.7	492.9
San Luis Obispo-Paso Robles, CA M. S. A.	284,407									
Includes San Luis Obispo County										
City of San Luis Obispo	47,990	267	0	38	40	189	1,745	254	1,372	119
City of Paso Robles	31,966	98	0	13	14	71	524	42	433	49
Total area actually reporting	100.0%	1,223	3	121	105	994	5,143	949	3,757	437
Rate per 100,000 inhabitants		430.0	1.1	42.5	36.9	349.5	1,808.3	333.7	1,321.0	153.7
Santa Cruz-Watsonville, CA M. S. A.	265,551									
Includes Santa Cruz County										
City of Santa Cruz	61,650	447	1	38	122	286	2,226	253	1,782	191
City of Watsonville	51,517	302	1	31	56	214	959	137	611	211
Total area actually reporting	100.0%	1,202	2	143	225	832	5,238	754	3,881	603
Rate per 100,000 inhabitants		452.6	0.8	53.9	84.7	313.3	1,972.5	283.9	1,461.5	227.1
Santa Fe, NM M. S. A.	155,350									
Includes Santa Fe County										
City of Santa Fe	88,705	741	5	42	100	594	4,333	955	2,713	665
Total area actually reporting	97.8%	891	6	59	104	722	4,909	1,164	2,990	755
Estimated total	100.0%	905	6	60	105	734	4,964	1,180	3,023	761
Rate per 100,000 inhabitants		582.6	3.9	38.6	67.6	472.5	3,195.4	759.6	1,945.9	489.9
Santa Maria-Santa Barbara, CA M. S. A.	445,356									
Includes Santa Barbara County										
City of Santa Maria	109,518	712	10	74	209	419	3,039	393	1,504	1,142
City of Santa Barbara	87,817	400	3	45	80	272	1,795	226	1,400	169
Total area actually reporting	100.0%	1,704	21	188	384	1,111	8,670	1,177	5,618	1,875
Rate per 100,000 inhabitants		382.6	4.7	42.2	86.2	249.5	1,946.8	264.3	1,261.5	421.0
Santa Rosa-Petaluma, CA M. S. A.	483,980									
Includes Sonoma County										
City of Santa Rosa	175,999	597	10	130	98	359	2,391	439	1,560	392
City of Petaluma	59,129	302	2	37	47	216	714	89	521	104
Total area actually reporting	94.7%	1,554	19	291	220	1,024	5,571	933	3,822	816
Estimated total	100.0%	1,644	20	299	240	1,085	6,114	1,027	4,187	900
Rate per 100,000 inhabitants		339.7	4.1	61.8	49.6	224.2	1,263.3	212.2	865.1	186.0
Scranton--Wilkes-Barre, PA[1] M. S. A.	570,371									
Includes Lackawanna, Luzerne, Wyoming Counties										
City of Scranton	75,798	310	1	111	34	164	1,281	134	1,059	88
City of Wilkes-Barre	44,497	177	1	17	27	132	717	85	580	52
Total area actually reporting	84.7%	1,106	19	215	129	743	5,813	729	4,744	340
Estimated total	100.0%	1,230	19	226	143	842	6,566	788	5,389	389
Rate per 100,000 inhabitants		215.6	3.3	39.6	25.1	147.6	1,151.2	138.2	944.8	68.2
Seattle-Tacoma-Bellevue, WA M. S. A.	4,012,235									
Includes the Metro Divisions of Seattle-Bellevue-Kent, WA; Tacoma-Lakewood, WA										
City of Seattle	729,691	6,115	54	311	1,748	4,002	41,745	8,765	26,038	6,942
City of Tacoma	219,027	3,526	41	147	746	2,592	18,704	2,381	10,422	5,901
City of Bellevue	147,079	230	2	17	103	108	5,569	786	4,299	484
City of Kent	133,066	611	9	73	209	320	7,356	1,545	3,802	2,009
City of Everett	110,694	490	12	54	110	314	4,816	738	3,082	996
City of Renton	103,619	382	7	22	141	212	4,796	669	2,773	1,354
City of Redmond	79,403	94	0	16	41	37	2,520	265	2,036	219
City of Auburn	74,389	372	11	37	110	213	3,825	778	1,929	1,117
City of Lakewood	63,044	529	4	34	112	379	3,282	537	1,749	996
City of Auburn	9,890	49	2	5	15	28	509	104	257	149
Total area actually reporting	100.0%	18,360	218	1,399	4,808	11,935	154,766	25,964	95,618	33,184
Rate per 100,000 inhabitants		457.6	5.4	34.9	119.8	297.5	3,857.4	647.1	2,383.2	827.1
Seattle-Bellevue-Kent, WA M. D.	3,080,469									
Includes King, Snohomish Counties										
Total area actually reporting	100.0%	12,064	145	1,013	3,487	7,418	113,886	19,860	72,568	21,458
Rate per 100,000 inhabitants		391.6	4.7	32.9	113.2	240.8	3,697.0	644.7	2,355.7	696.6
Tacoma-Lakewood, WA M. D.	931,766									
Includes Pierce County										
Total area actually reporting	100.0%	6,296	73	386	1,321	4,517	40,880	6,104	23,050	11,726
Rate per 100,000 inhabitants		675.7	7.8	41.4	141.8	484.8	4,387.4	655.1	2,473.8	1,258.5
Sheboygan, WI M. S. A.	117,414									
Includes Sheboygan County										
City of Sheboygan	49,917	166	0	45	11	110	696	66	601	29
Total area actually reporting	100.0%	208	1	62	12	133	1,212	129	1,038	45
Rate per 100,000 inhabitants		177.2	0.9	52.8	10.2	113.3	1,032.2	109.9	884.1	38.3
Sherman-Denison, TX M. S. A.	143,596									
Includes Grayson County										
City of Sherman	45,881	161	3	25	15	118	866	272	496	98
City of Denison	25,828	73	0	12	1	60	323	60	201	62

Table 6. Crime in the United States, by Selected Metropolitan Statistical Area, 2022—Continued

(Number, percent, rate per 100,000 population.)

Area	Population	Violent crime	Murder and nonnegligent manslaughter	Rape	Robbery	Aggravated assault	Property crime	Burglary	Larceny-theft	Motor vehicle theft
Total area actually reporting	94.3%	334	8	71	18	237	1,697	485	1,004	208
Estimated total	100.0%	354	8	74	20	252	1,837	506	1,105	226
Rate per 100,000 inhabitants		246.5	5.6	51.5	13.9	175.5	1,279.3	352.4	769.5	157.4
Shreveport-Bossier City, LA M. S. A.	385,192									
Includes Bossier, Caddo, De Soto Counties										
City of Shreveport	180,763	1,466	47	137	231	1,051	6,851	1,270	4,894	687
City of Bossier City	63,078	636	6	46	44	540	2,945	358	2,305	282
Total area actually reporting	99.2%	2,380	55	230	290	1,805	11,185	1,887	8,189	1,109
Estimated total	100.0%	2,386	55	230	290	1,811	11,208	1,891	8,207	1,110
Rate per 100,000 inhabitants		619.4	14.3	59.7	75.3	470.2	2,909.7	490.9	2,130.6	288.2
Sierra Vista-Douglas, AZ M. S. A.	126,406									
Includes Cochise County										
City of Sierra Vista	45,611	128	1	19	11	97	738	83	630	25
City of Douglas	16,529	19	1	3	1	14	209	41	153	15
Total area actually reporting	95.8%	271	8	25	16	222	1,542	301	1,142	99
Estimated total	100.0%	299	8	27	19	245	1,703	323	1,269	111
Rate per 100,000 inhabitants		236.5	6.3	21.4	15.0	193.8	1,347.2	255.5	1,003.9	87.8
Sioux City, IA-NE-SD M. S. A.	149,018									
Includes Dakota, Dixon, Union, Woodbury Counties										
City of Sioux City, IA	85,577	441	1	79	60	301	2,514	342	1,893	279
Total area actually reporting	96.1%	529	2	97	65	365	3,216	417	2,444	354
Estimated total	100.0%	543	2	99	66	376	3,288	430	2,497	360
Rate per 100,000 inhabitants		364.4	1.3	66.4	44.3	252.3	2,206.4	288.6	1,675.6	241.6
Sioux Falls, SD M. S. A.	288,449									
Includes Lincoln, Mccook, Minnehaha, Turner Counties										
City of Sioux Falls	199,879	1,092	7	75	140	870	6,162	738	4,345	1,079
Total area actually reporting	99.1%	1,216	9	97	142	968	6,909	914	4,807	1,189
Estimated total	100.0%	1,219	9	97	142	971	6,952	925	4,833	1,195
Rate per 100,000 inhabitants		422.6	3.1	33.6	49.2	336.6	2,410.1	320.7	1,675.5	414.3
Spartanburg, SC M. S. A.	344,486									
Includes Spartanburg County										
City of Spartanburg	38,271	457	2	39	42	374	2,247	391	1,665	191
Total area actually reporting	99.8%	1,791	27	161	117	1,486	7,354	1,372	5,178	804
Estimated total	100.0%	1,794	27	161	117	1,489	7,374	1,375	5,193	806
Rate per 100,000 inhabitants		520.8	7.8	46.7	34.0	432.2	2,140.6	399.1	1,507.5	234.0
Spokane-Spokane Valley, WA M. S. A.	601,782									
Includes Spokane, Stevens Counties										
City of Spokane	229,292	1,541	18	194	309	1,020	13,153	1,771	9,579	1,803
City of Spokane Valley	108,076	360	3	49	71	237	4,390	593	3,230	567
Total area actually reporting	99.6%	2,248	29	301	416	1,502	21,404	3,007	15,510	2,887
Estimated total	100.0%	2,254	29	302	417	1,506	21,465	3,018	15,551	2,896
Rate per 100,000 inhabitants		374.6	4.8	50.2	69.3	250.3	3,566.9	501.5	2,584.2	481.2
Springfield, IL[1] M. S. A.	205,897									
Includes Menard, Sangamon Counties										
City of Springfield	112,549	867	7	96	147	617	4,777	909	3,361	507
Total area actually reporting	86.4%	1,095	10	136	165	784	5,636	1,107	3,927	602
Estimated total	100.0%	1,125	10	144	167	804	5,914	1,158	4,125	631
Rate per 100,000 inhabitants		546.4	4.9	69.9	81.1	390.5	2,872.3	562.4	2,003.4	306.5
Springfield, MA M. S. A.	696,028									
Includes Franklin, Hampden, Hampshire Counties										
City of Springfield	155,046	1,337	14	82	265	976	3,674	579	2,590	505
Total area actually reporting	97.6%	3,139	27	333	412	2,367	10,639	1,444	8,168	1,027
Estimated total	100.0%	3,158	27	335	412	2,384	10,708	1,455	8,219	1,034
Rate per 100,000 inhabitants		453.7	3.9	48.1	59.2	342.5	1,538.4	209.0	1,180.8	148.6
Springfield, MO M. S. A.	486,563									
Includes Christian, Dallas, Greene, Polk, Webster Counties										
City of Springfield	169,822	2,408	17	190	309	1,892	8,336	1,368	5,819	1,149
Total area actually reporting	98.9%	2,992	25	272	324	2,371	11,165	1,932	7,749	1,484
Estimated total	100.0%	3,016	25	273	324	2,394	11,255	1,945	7,800	1,510
Rate per 100,000 inhabitants		619.9	5.1	56.1	66.6	492.0	2,313.2	399.7	1,603.1	310.3
Springfield, OH M. S. A.	135,387									
Includes Clark County										
City of Springfield	58,725	707	6	58	136	507	2,651	531	1,765	355
Total area actually reporting	92.5%	748	6	66	138	538	3,238	639	2,213	386
Estimated total	100.0%	759	6	69	139	545	3,407	653	2,360	394
Rate per 100,000 inhabitants		560.6	4.4	51.0	102.7	402.5	2,516.5	482.3	1,743.2	291.0
Staunton, VA M. S. A.	126,397									
Includes Augusta, Staunton City, Waynesboro City Counties										
City of Staunton	25,611	36	1	6	3	26	478	33	425	20
Total area actually reporting	100.0%	183	2	52	14	115	1,655	220	1,310	125
Rate per 100,000 inhabitants		144.8	1.6	41.1	11.1	91.0	1,309.4	174.1	1,036.4	98.9

Table 6. Crime in the United States, by Selected Metropolitan Statistical Area, 2022—Continued

(Number, percent, rate per 100,000 population.)

Area	Population	Violent crime	Murder and nonnegligent manslaughter	Rape	Robbery	Aggravated assault	Property crime	Burglary	Larceny-theft	Motor vehicle theft
St. Cloud, MN M. S. A.	201,442									
Includes Benton, Stearns Counties										
City of St. Cloud	55,331	250	2	39	30	181	2,367	193	1,980	193
Total area actually reporting	100.0%	445	2	86	38	321	4,514	414	3,791	309
Rate per 100,000 inhabitants		220.9	1.0	42.7	18.9	159.4	2,240.8	205.5	1,881.9	153.4
St. George, UT M. S. A.	200,095									
Includes Washington County										
City of St. George	104,158	170	3	38	8	121	1,139	95	918	126
Total area actually reporting	100.0%	339	3	90	13	233	2,158	218	1,696	244
Rate per 100,000 inhabitants		169.4	1.5	45.0	6.5	116.4	1,078.5	108.9	847.6	121.9
St. Joseph, MO-KS M. S. A.	119,602									
Includes Andrew, Buchanan, Dekalb, Doniphan Counties										
City of St. Joseph, MO	70,918	536	4	150	60	322	3,068	362	2,251	455
Total area actually reporting	97.5%	622	4	175	60	384	3,488	430	2,532	526
Estimated total	100.0%	629	4	175	60	391	3,531	434	2,563	534
Rate per 100,000 inhabitants		525.9	3.3	146.3	50.2	326.9	2,952.3	362.9	2,142.9	446.5
St. Louis, MO-IL[1] M. S. A.	2,801,763									
Includes Bond, Calhoun, Clinton, Crawford, Franklin, Jefferson, Jersey, Lincoln, Macoupin, Madison, Monroe, St Charles, St Clair, St Louis, St Louis City, Warren Counties										
City of St. Louis, MO	286,053	4,212	200	151	803	3,058	19,718	2,306	11,150	6,262
City of St. Charles, MO	71,079	151	1	16	20	114	1,242	197	877	168
Total area actually reporting	95.0%	11,104	322	898	1,468	8,416	58,993	6,792	37,227	14,974
Estimated total	100.0%	11,329	325	954	1,497	8,553	60,677	7,018	38,480	15,179
Rate per 100,000 inhabitants		404.4	11.6	34.0	53.4	305.3	2,165.7	250.5	1,373.4	541.8
Stockton, CA M. S. A.	799,295									
Includes San Joaquin County										
City of Stockton	323,501	3,742	48	178	980	2,536	8,878	1,760	5,636	1,482
Total area actually reporting	87.5%	5,251	59	264	1,244	3,684	15,187	2,841	10,157	2,189
Estimated total	100.0%	5,615	62	294	1,335	3,924	17,333	3,172	11,586	2,575
Rate per 100,000 inhabitants		702.5	7.8	36.8	167.0	490.9	2,168.5	396.8	1,449.5	322.2
Sumter, SC M. S. A.	135,844									
Includes Clarendon, Sumter Counties										
City of Sumter	42,613	376	6	10	24	336	1,372	181	1,076	115
Total area actually reporting	99.4%	1,060	18	48	62	932	3,788	729	2,665	394
Estimated total	100.0%	1,063	18	48	62	935	3,808	732	2,680	396
Rate per 100,000 inhabitants		782.5	13.3	35.3	45.6	688.3	2,803.2	538.9	1,972.9	291.5
Syracuse, NY M. S. A.	660,619									
Includes Madison, Onondaga, Oswego Counties										
City of Syracuse	145,179	1,294	17	80	287	910	4,430	1,171	2,636	623
Total area actually reporting	98.3%	2,070	26	286	381	1,377	10,677	1,957	7,641	1,079
Estimated total	100.0%	2,085	26	289	383	1,387	10,827	1,970	7,770	1,087
Rate per 100,000 inhabitants		315.6	3.9	43.7	58.0	210.0	1,638.9	298.2	1,176.2	164.5
Texarkana, TX-AR M. S. A.	147,671									
Includes Bowie, Little River, Miller Counties										
City of Texarkana, TX	35,859	150	2	13	28	107	1,045	105	821	119
Total area actually reporting	99.0%	597	12	48	58	479	2,912	450	2,131	331
Estimated total	100.0%	600	12	49	58	481	2,935	454	2,147	334
Rate per 100,000 inhabitants		406.3	8.1	33.2	39.3	325.7	1,987.5	307.4	1,453.9	226.2
The Villages, FL[1] M. S. A.	142,114									
Includes Sumter County										
Total area actually reporting	87.3%	94	0	14	0	80	506	64	374	68
Estimated total	100.0%	132	1	19	7	105	847	103	647	97
Rate per 100,000 inhabitants		92.9	0.7	13.4	4.9	73.9	596.0	72.5	455.3	68.3
Toledo, OH M. S. A.	641,863									
Includes Fulton, Lucas, Ottawa, Wood Counties										
City of Toledo	266,984	3,105	61	227	494	2,323	8,225	1,505	5,564	1,156
Total area actually reporting	91.6%	3,434	62	307	532	2,533	13,287	1,871	9,842	1,574
Estimated total	100.0%	3,506	62	323	536	2,585	14,045	1,956	10,473	1,616
Rate per 100,000 inhabitants		546.2	9.7	50.3	83.5	402.7	2,188.2	304.7	1,631.7	251.8
Topeka, KS M. S. A.	232,893									
Includes Jackson, Jefferson, Osage, Shawnee, Wabaunsee Counties										
City of Topeka	125,658	1,211	13	60	117	1,021	4,659	711	3,243	705
Total area actually reporting	96.9%	1,444	14	79	124	1,227	5,769	907	4,039	823
Estimated total	100.0%	1,457	14	79	124	1,240	5,870	914	4,120	836
Rate per 100,000 inhabitants		625.6	6.0	33.9	53.2	532.4	2,520.5	392.5	1,769.1	359.0
Trenton-Princeton, NJ M. S. A.	385,299									
Includes Mercer County										
City of Trenton	90,313	960	23	66	282	589	1,690	245	1,130	315
City of Princeton	30,797	9	0	1	3	5	226	23	193	10
Total area actually reporting	100.0%	1,320	28	111	376	805	6,227	623	4,972	632
Rate per 100,000 inhabitants		342.6	7.3	28.8	97.6	208.9	1,616.1	161.7	1,290.4	164.0

Table 6. Crime in the United States, by Selected Metropolitan Statistical Area, 2022—Continued

(Number, percent, rate per 100,000 population.)

Area	Population	Violent crime	Murder and nonnegligent manslaughter	Rape	Robbery	Aggravated assault	Property crime	Burglary	Larceny-theft	Motor vehicle theft
Tulsa, OK M. S. A.	1,033,553									
Includes Creek, Okmulgee, Osage, Pawnee, Rogers, Tulsa, Wagoner Counties										
City of Tulsa	410,135	3,810	57	369	470	2,914	17,521	3,589	10,793	3,139
Total area actually reporting	100.0%	5,038	83	613	562	3,780	27,012	5,504	17,080	4,428
Rate per 100,000 inhabitants		487.4	8.0	59.3	54.4	365.7	2,613.5	532.5	1,652.6	428.4
Twin Falls, ID M. S. A.	118,335									
Includes Jerome, Twin Falls Counties										
City of Twin Falls	54,648	243	2	36	6	199	793	72	637	84
Total area actually reporting	100.0%	386	3	61	9	313	1,257	211	901	145
Rate per 100,000 inhabitants		326.2	2.5	51.5	7.6	264.5	1,062.2	178.3	761.4	122.5
Tyler, TX M. S. A.	241,794									
Includes Smith County										
City of Tyler	108,422	575	11	87	43	434	2,523	274	2,038	211
Total area actually reporting	99.2%	915	14	122	53	726	3,638	548	2,698	392
Estimated total	100.0%	919	14	123	53	729	3,670	554	2,720	396
Rate per 100,000 inhabitants		380.1	5.8	50.9	21.9	301.5	1,517.8	229.1	1,124.9	163.8
Urban Honolulu, HI M. S. A.	994,799									
Includes Honolulu County										
City of Honolulu	994,799	2,521	25	297	833	1,366	25,649	2,627	18,400	4,622
Total area actually reporting	100.0%	2,521	25	297	833	1,366	25,649	2,627	18,400	4,622
Rate per 100,000 inhabitants		253.4	2.5	29.9	83.7	137.3	2,578.3	264.1	1,849.6	464.6
Utica-Rome, NY M. S. A.	290,904									
Includes Herkimer, Oneida Counties										
City of Utica	63,906	363	1	40	82	240	2,178	274	1,749	155
City of Rome	31,834	77	0	11	18	48	481	57	399	25
Total area actually reporting	97.1%	760	1	168	115	476	5,283	607	4,375	301
Estimated total	100.0%	768	1	169	116	482	5,360	615	4,439	306
Rate per 100,000 inhabitants		264.0	0.3	58.1	39.9	165.7	1,842.5	211.4	1,525.9	105.2
Valdosta, GA M. S. A.	150,669									
Includes Brooks, Echols, Lanier, Lowndes Counties										
City of Valdosta	55,666	195	14	16	48	117	1,274	90	1,058	126
Total area actually reporting	99.5%	451	19	74	71	287	2,558	289	2,011	258
Estimated total	100.0%	451	19	74	71	287	2,566	290	2,017	259
Rate per 100,000 inhabitants		299.3	12.6	49.1	47.1	190.5	1,703.1	192.5	1,338.7	171.9
Vallejo, CA M. S. A.	450,665									
Includes Solano County										
City of Vallejo	123,940	1,207	22	90	361	734	4,967	904	2,935	1,128
Total area actually reporting	100.0%	2,509	37	247	661	1,564	11,589	1,724	7,716	2,149
Rate per 100,000 inhabitants		556.7	8.2	54.8	146.7	347.0	2,571.5	382.5	1,712.1	476.9
Victoria, TX M. S. A.	98,606									
Includes Goliad, Victoria Counties										
City of Victoria	65,165	247	7	35	36	169	1,452	269	1,107	76
Total area actually reporting	100.0%	340	7	53	41	239	1,752	352	1,288	112
Rate per 100,000 inhabitants		344.8	7.1	53.7	41.6	242.4	1,776.8	357.0	1,306.2	113.6
Vineland-Bridgeton, NJ M. S. A.	153,510									
Includes Cumberland County										
City of Vineland	61,110	280	7	28	31	214	1,566	226	1,282	58
City of Bridgeton	26,524	187	1	22	78	86	845	111	689	45
Total area actually reporting	75.0%	606	9	62	135	400	3,474	441	2,892	141
Estimated total	100.0%	761	12	78	162	509	4,259	550	3,451	258
Rate per 100,000 inhabitants		495.7	7.8	50.8	105.5	331.6	2,774.4	358.3	2,248.1	168.1
Virginia Beach-Norfolk-Newport News, VA-NC M. S. A.	1,813,114									
Includes Camden, Chesapeake City, Currituck, Franklin City, Gates, Gloucester, Hampton City, Isle Of Wight, James City, Mathews, Newport News City, Norfolk City, Poquoson City, Portsmouth City, Southampton, Suffolk City, Virginia Beach City, Williamsburg City, York Counties										
City of Virginia Beach, VA	457,556	400	21	54	139	186	7,347	352	6,194	801
City of Norfolk, VA	233,419	1,640	63	98	301	1,178	11,372	546	8,962	1,864
City of Newport News, VA	183,903	1,121	31	58	177	855	4,233	337	3,434	462
City of Hampton, VA	138,843	375	21	45	86	223	4,035	274	3,387	374
City of Portsmouth, VA	98,003	858	47	48	209	554	4,784	421	3,940	423
Total area actually reporting	100.0%	6,476	234	504	1,145	4,593	42,460	2,753	35,015	4,692
Rate per 100,000 inhabitants		357.2	12.9	27.8	63.2	253.3	2,341.8	151.8	1,931.2	258.8
Visalia, CA M. S. A.	480,931									
Includes Tulare County										
City of Visalia	144,137	716	9	71	130	506	3,421	390	2,421	610
Total area actually reporting	100.0%	2,086	44	184	383	1,475	9,878	1,512	6,230	2,136
Rate per 100,000 inhabitants		433.7	9.1	38.3	79.6	306.7	2,053.9	314.4	1,295.4	444.1
Waco, TX M. S. A.	284,594									
Includes Falls, Mclennan Counties										

Table 6. Crime in the United States, by Selected Metropolitan Statistical Area, 2022—Continued

(Number, percent, rate per 100,000 population.)

Area	Population	Violent crime	Murder and nonnegligent manslaughter	Rape	Robbery	Aggravated assault	Property crime	Burglary	Larceny-theft	Motor vehicle theft
City of Waco	140,911	906	14	117	106	669	4,550	750	3,420	380
Total area actually reporting	96.3%	1,181	16	191	126	848	6,215	1,074	4,565	576
Estimated total	100.0%	1,205	16	195	127	867	6,393	1,103	4,691	599
Rate per 100,000 inhabitants		423.4	5.6	68.5	44.6	304.6	2,246.4	387.6	1,648.3	210.5
Walla Walla, WA M. S. A.	63,004									
Includes Walla Walla County										
City of Walla Walla	33,899	126	2	27	10	87	1,037	206	741	90
Total area actually reporting	100.0%	177	3	31	13	130	1,504	332	1,018	154
Rate per 100,000 inhabitants		280.9	4.8	49.2	20.6	206.3	2,387.2	527.0	1,615.8	244.4
Washington-Arlington-Alexandria, DC-VA-MD¹-WV M. S. A.	5,691,407									
Includes the Metro Divisions of Frederick-Gaithersburg-Rockville, MD; Washington-Arlington-Alexandria, DC-VA-MD-WV										
City of Alexandria, VA	150,957	281	6	7	103	165	2,946	155	2,459	332
City of Frederick, MD	80,985	301	2	36	40	223	1,259	174	1,024	61
Total area actually reporting	99.1%	11,362	196	1,326	3,337	6,503	78,054	5,205	63,052	9,797
Estimated total	100.0%	11,648	198	1,349	3,389	6,712	79,085	5,360	63,852	9,873
Rate per 100,000 inhabitants		204.7	3.5	23.7	59.5	117.9	1,389.6	94.2	1,121.9	173.5
Frederick-Gaithersburg-Rockville, MD¹ M. D.	1,336,991									
Includes Frederick, Montgomery Counties										
Total area actually reporting	100.0%	2,198	23	368	521	1,286	16,415	1,458	13,462	1,495
Rate per 100,000 inhabitants		164.4	1.7	27.5	39.0	96.2	1,227.8	109.1	1,006.9	111.8
Washington-Arlington-Alexandria, DC-VA-MD¹-WV M. D.	4,354,416									
Includes Alexandria City, Arlington, Calvert, Charles, Clarke, Culpeper, Fairfax, Fairfax City, Falls Church City, Fauquier, Fredericksburg City, Jefferson, Loudoun, Madison, Manassas City, Manassas Park City, Prince George'S, Prince William, Rappahannock, Spotsylvania, Stafford, Warren Counties										
Total area actually reporting	98.9%	9,164	173	958	2,816	5,217	61,639	3,747	49,590	8,302
Estimated total	100.0%	9,450	175	981	2,868	5,426	62,670	3,902	50,390	8,378
Rate per 100,000 inhabitants		217.0	4.0	22.5	65.9	124.6	1,439.2	89.6	1,157.2	192.4
Watertown-Fort Drum, NY M. S. A.	117,333									
Includes Jefferson County										
City of Watertown	24,558	156	0	33	11	112	1,009	103	883	23
Total area actually reporting	100.0%	253	1	84	15	153	1,728	240	1,443	45
Rate per 100,000 inhabitants		215.6	0.9	71.6	12.8	130.4	1,472.7	204.5	1,229.8	38.4
Wausau-Weston, WI M. S. A.	165,850									
Includes Lincoln, Marathon Counties										
City of Wausau	39,349	153	0	40	7	106	504	59	409	36
Total area actually reporting	96.8%	417	4	85	11	317	1,435	189	1,145	101
Estimated total	100.0%	423	4	86	12	321	1,488	192	1,190	106
Rate per 100,000 inhabitants		255.0	2.4	51.9	7.2	193.5	897.2	115.8	717.5	63.9
Weirton-Steubenville, WV-OH M. S. A.	114,477									
Includes Brooke, Hancock, Jefferson Counties										
City of Weirton, WV	18,544	17	0	7	0	10	70	0	70	0
City of Steubenville, OH	17,869	29	2	1	6	20	616	57	544	15
Total area actually reporting	87.0%	115	7	28	6	74	844	87	731	26
Estimated total	100.0%	130	7	30	6	87	1,143	107	1,000	36
Rate per 100,000 inhabitants		113.6	6.1	26.2	5.2	76.0	998.5	93.5	873.5	31.4
Wenatchee, WA M. S. A.	124,940									
Includes Chelan, Douglas Counties										
City of Wenatchee	35,462	85	2	17	9	57	982	154	733	95
Total area actually reporting	100.0%	154	3	36	13	102	1,897	430	1,274	193
Rate per 100,000 inhabitants		123.3	2.4	28.8	10.4	81.6	1,518.3	344.2	1,019.7	154.5
Wheeling, WV-OH M. S. A.	136,423									
Includes Belmont, Marshall, Ohio Counties										
City of Wheeling, WV	26,244	323	5	25	14	279	633	187	405	41
Total area actually reporting	93.5%	544	5	48	19	472	1,123	273	769	81
Estimated total	100.0%	561	5	49	19	488	1,249	283	879	87
Rate per 100,000 inhabitants		411.2	3.7	35.9	13.9	357.7	915.5	207.4	644.3	63.8
Wichita Falls, TX M. S. A.	150,581									
Includes Archer, Clay, Wichita Counties										
City of Wichita Falls	103,337	486	14	110	53	309	2,964	516	2,147	301
Total area actually reporting	95.2%	557	15	132	56	354	3,262	596	2,334	332
Estimated total	100.0%	578	15	137	57	369	3,361	618	2,395	348
Rate per 100,000 inhabitants		383.8	10.0	91.0	37.9	245.1	2,232.0	410.4	1,590.5	231.1
Wichita, KS M. S. A.	648,748									
Includes Butler, Harvey, Sedgwick, Sumner Counties										
City of Wichita	394,286	3,670	31	272	302	3,065	13,368	1,689	10,107	1,572
Total area actually reporting	99.0%	4,255	39	369	331	3,516	17,171	2,222	13,079	1,870
Estimated total	100.0%	4,267	39	370	331	3,527	17,255	2,229	13,146	1,880
Rate per 100,000 inhabitants		657.7	6.0	57.0	51.0	543.7	2,659.7	343.6	2,026.4	289.8

Table 6. Crime in the United States, by Selected Metropolitan Statistical Area, 2022—Continued

(Number, percent, rate per 100,000 population.)

Area	Population	Violent crime	Murder and nonnegligent manslaughter	Rape	Robbery	Aggravated assault	Property crime	Burglary	Larceny-theft	Motor vehicle theft
Wilmington, NC M. S. A.	298,613									
Includes New Hanover, Pender Counties										
City of Wilmington	119,159	634	12	77	111	434	3,415	470	2,675	270
Total area actually reporting	99.1%	921	16	152	131	623	5,732	792	4,533	407
Estimated total	100.0%	926	16	153	131	627	5,795	802	4,581	412
Rate per 100,000 inhabitants		310.1	5.4	51.2	43.9	210.0	1,940.6	268.6	1,534.1	138.0
Winchester, VA-WV M. S. A.	147,926									
Includes Frederick, Hampshire, Winchester City Counties										
City of Winchester, VA	28,363	76	1	28	11	36	787	75	683	29
Total area actually reporting	99.7%	157	5	43	18	91	1,792	157	1,538	97
Estimated total	100.0%	158	5	43	18	92	1,794	157	1,540	97
Rate per 100,000 inhabitants		106.8	3.4	29.1	12.2	62.2	1,212.8	106.1	1,041.1	65.6
Winston-Salem, NC M. S. A.	689,896									
Includes Davidson, Davie, Forsyth, Stokes, Yadkin Counties										
City of Winston-Salem	251,295	2,954	30	87	282	2,555	9,785	1,796	7,070	919
Total area actually reporting	88.1%	3,631	47	142	354	3,087	15,552	2,916	11,148	1,489
Estimated total	100.0%	3,767	50	162	361	3,193	16,373	3,134	11,654	1,586
Rate per 100,000 inhabitants		546.0	7.2	23.5	52.3	462.8	2,373.3	454.3	1,689.2	229.9
Worcester, MA-CT M. S. A.	908,783									
Includes Windham, Worcester Counties										
City of Worcester, MA	206,575	1,245	11	42	166	1,026	3,444	696	2,408	340
Total area actually reporting	98.7%	2,643	15	247	242	2,139	7,834	1,297	5,814	723
Estimated total	100.0%	2,658	15	249	242	2,152	7,890	1,306	5,855	729
Rate per 100,000 inhabitants		292.5	1.7	27.4	26.6	236.8	868.2	143.7	644.3	80.2
Yakima, WA M. S. A.	256,410									
Includes Yakima County										
City of Yakima	96,267	589	12	51	121	405	3,026	545	1,975	506
Total area actually reporting	94.8%	995	21	92	191	691	6,750	1,352	4,277	1,121
Estimated total	100.0%	1,022	21	96	195	710	7,052	1,409	4,477	1,166
Rate per 100,000 inhabitants		398.6	8.2	37.4	76.1	276.9	2,750.3	549.5	1,746.0	454.7
Youngstown-Warren-Boardman, OH-PA[1] M. S. A.	536,232									
Includes Mahoning, Mercer, Trumbull Counties										
City of Youngstown, OH	59,942	411	18	36	61	296	1,721	447	1,004	270
City of Boardman, OH	39,490	90	1	21	30	38	1,440	143	1,238	59
City of Warren, OH	38,943	171	2	14	38	117	1,115	282	746	87
Total area actually reporting	94.2%	1,264	26	163	192	883	8,482	1,513	6,307	662
Estimated total	100.0%	1,301	26	172	194	909	8,932	1,554	6,691	687
Rate per 100,000 inhabitants		242.6	4.8	32.1	36.2	169.5	1,665.7	289.8	1,247.8	128.1
Yuba City, CA M. S. A.	183,790									
Includes Sutter, Yuba Counties										
City of Yuba City	69,122	380	2	46	63	269	1,565	187	1,135	243
Total area actually reporting	83.9%	662	7	79	103	473	3,100	489	1,970	641
Estimated total	100.0%	765	9	90	112	554	3,479	572	2,225	682
Rate per 100,000 inhabitants		416.2	4.9	49.0	60.9	301.4	1,892.9	311.2	1,210.6	371.1
Yuma, AZ M. S. A.	209,080									
Includes Yuma County										
City of Yuma	98,164	551	19	41	50	441	1,657	450	990	217
Total area actually reporting	100.0%	759	28	68	57	606	2,804	727	1,665	412
Rate per 100,000 inhabitants		363.0	13.4	32.5	27.3	289.8	1,341.1	347.7	796.3	197.1

NOTE: Although arson data are included in the trend and clearance tables, sufficient data are not available to estimate totals for this offense. Therefore, no arson data are published in this table.
1 Limited data for 2022 were available for Florida, Illinois, Maryland, and Pennsylvania.

Table 7. Offense Analysis, United States, 2018–2022

(Number.)

Classification	2018	2019	2020	2021[1]	2022
Murder	16,937	16,952	22,414	22,536	21,156
Rape	146,519	144,593	131,868	140,902	133,294
Robbery[2]	282,180	263,474	240,837	217,550	220,450
By location					
Street/highway	101,432	91,925	78,606	69,100	70,021
Commercial house	45,250	42,908	39,732	42,173	42,736
Gas or service station	8,497	8,020	8,806	8,438	8,550
Convenience store	19,079	17,341	17,745	14,276	14,466
Residence	45,449	42,101	42,312	33,864	34,316
Bank	4,461	3,749	2,693	3,136	3,178
Miscellaneous	58,012	57,430	50,944	46,562	47,183
Burglary[2]	1,267,920	1,112,338	1,026,234	899,369	899,293
By location					
Residence (dwelling):	832,792	703,082	575,106	476,559	476,519
Night	265,454	240,385	221,420	196,137	196,120
Day	420,381	356,653	281,699	253,850	253,829
Unknown	146,957	106,044	71,987	26,572	26,570
Nonresidence (store, office, etc.)	435,128	409,256	451,128	422,810	422,774
Night	195,232	188,937	216,529	210,436	210,418
Day	154,978	152,704	173,922	185,144	185,128
Unknown	84,918	67,614	60,676	27,230	27,228
Larceny-theft (except motor vehicle theft)[2]	5,363,735	5,162,288	4,628,945	4,334,764	4,672,363
By type					
Pocket-picking	30,039	32,057	19,911	30,700	33,091
Purse-snatching	20,447	19,118	14,574	13,475	14,524
Shoplifting	1,157,871	1,150,397	967,480	918,921	990,488
From motor vehicles (except accessories)	1,422,629	1,363,382	1,254,571	1,029,327	1,109,493
Motor vehicle accessories	330,642	325,404	391,434	532,857	574,357
Bicycles	162,409	156,108	155,785	117,988	127,177
From buildings	565,308	516,537	395,292	350,206	377,481
From coin-operated machines	11,520	11,206	8,901	6,041	6,512
All others	1,662,870	1,588,079	1,420,996	1,335,248	1,439,239
By value					
Over $200	2,495,020	2,427,883	2,228,367	2,402,342	2,589,441
$50 to $200	1,135,868	1,088,110	939,519	763,183	822,621
Under $50	1,732,843	1,646,292	1,461,117	1,169,235	1,260,347
Motor vehicle theft	766,586	725,363	815,572	849,741	942,173

1 The crime figures have been adjusted.   2 Because of rounding, the number of offenses may not add to the total.

Table 8. Offenses Known to Law Enforcement, by Selected State and City, 2022

(Number.)

State/city	Population	Violent crime	Murder and nonnegligent manslaughter	Rape	Robbery	Aggravated assault	Property crime	Burglary	Larceny-theft	Motor vehicle theft	Arson[1]
ALABAMA											
Abbeville	2,390	13	0	0	0	13	42	10	30	2	0
Adamsville	4,233	19	1	0	0	18	230	18	195	17	0
Addison	672	4	0	0	0	4	19	8	9	2	0
Alabaster	33,974	33	0	3	8	22	712	14	678	20	0
Alexander City	14,476	115	2	5	7	101	670	294	326	50	2
Aliceville	2,081	0	0	0	0	0	4	1	3	0	0
Andalusia	8,699	42	2	4	5	31	346	110	203	33	1
Anniston	21,007	177	4	11	17	145	1,152	246	766	140	4
Arab	8,550	28	0	6	3	19	290	48	210	32	1
Ardmore	1,406	5	0	0	0	5	23	5	13	5	1
Argo	4,421	3	0	0	0	3	15	2	10	3	0
Ashford	2,255	4	0	0	0	4	10	0	10	0	0
Ashland	1,962	11	0	0	0	11	31	6	24	1	1
Ashville	2,376	5	0	0	1	4	31	6	21	4	0
Athens	28,438	59	1	4	8	46	765	136	589	40	0
Atmore	8,536	127	0	7	3	117	365	53	280	32	0
Attalla	5,840	22	2	1	5	14	460	231	205	24	0
Auburn	80,759	106	3	23	8	72	937	74	797	66	0
Autaugaville	787	1	0	0	0	1	2	1	0	1	0
Bay Minette	8,000	41	0	1	1	39	129	11	112	6	0
Bayou La Batre	2,166	25	0	2	1	22	125	22	87	16	2
Bear Creek	1,047	1	0	0	0	1	20	5	13	2	0
Berry	1,193	0	0	0	0	0	6	1	5	0	0
Bessemer	25,265	460	10	15	75	360	1,872	211	1,382	279	8
Birmingham	195,050	3,280	142	62	477	2,599	8,139	1,519	4,821	1,799	134
Blountsville	1,825	3	0	1	0	2	29	7	17	5	0
Brent	2,995	18	0	1	1	16	99	9	84	6	0
Brewton	5,251	46	0	3	0	43	148	18	119	11	3
Bridgeport	2,256	8	0	0	0	8	53	11	35	7	0
Brookside	1,218	1	0	0	0	1	13	3	9	1	0
Brundidge	2,053	11	1	0	4	6	61	8	48	5	0
Butler	1,846	4	0	0	1	3	38	9	23	6	0
Camden	1,808	2	0	0	0	2	10	3	4	3	0
Camp Hill	977	3	2	0	1	0	8	0	8	0	0
Carbon Hill	1,714	3	0	1	0	2	36	7	26	3	0
Castleberry	469	0	0	0	0	0	6	3	3	0	0
Cedar Bluff	1,879	5	0	0	0	5	41	6	29	6	0
Centre	3,546	8	0	2	0	6	186	20	153	13	1
Centreville	2,803	10	0	5	0	5	42	12	30	0	0
Chatom	1,034	3	0	1	0	2	8	2	5	1	0
Cherokee	958	1	0	0	0	1	24	4	16	4	3
Chickasaw	6,333	27	2	3	2	20	118	19	87	12	2
Childersburg	4,631	9	0	0	1	8	107	44	49	14	0
Citronelle	3,916	19	2	0	1	16	48	13	31	4	0
Clanton	8,799	47	3	3	2	39	393	128	250	15	3
Clayhatchee	473	2	0	0	0	2	7	1	6	0	0
Clayton	2,258	8	0	0	0	8	17	5	11	1	0
Cleveland	1,242	2	0	0	0	2	14	2	10	2	0
Coffeeville	260	0	0	0	0	0	0	0	0	0	0
Collinsville	2,029	2	1	0	0	1	23	4	15	4	0
Columbia	691	0	0	0	0	0	1	0	1	0	0
Columbiana	4,347	19	0	0	1	18	532	450	76	6	0
Coosada	1,276	1	0	0	0	1	9	3	3	3	0
Cordova	1,663	7	0	1	0	6	57	10	43	4	0
Cottonwood	1,046	2	0	0	0	2	20	4	15	1	1
Creola	1,936	5	0	0	0	5	42	6	31	5	0
Crossville	1,810	0	0	0	0	0	3	1	0	2	0
Cullman	19,065	24	0	10	6	8	684	39	611	34	1
Dadeville	2,962	4	0	0	1	3	55	6	42	7	0
Daleville	4,876	24	0	2	4	18	99	16	76	7	3
Daphne	29,871	22	1	2	1	18	365	122	220	23	0
Dauphin Island	1,843	3	0	0	0	3	18	2	16	0	0
Decatur	57,831	242	12	21	34	175	1,501	182	1,166	153	162
Demopolis	6,885	50	1	4	2	43	224	38	175	11	0
Dora	2,281	2	0	0	0	2	58	9	40	9	0
Dothan	71,196	749	14	59	44	632	2,686	1,003	1,575	108	31
Double Springs	1,083	3	0	0	1	2	25	7	13	5	0
Douglas	765	0	0	0	0	0	20	5	11	4	0
East Brewton	2,261	8	0	0	0	8	32	3	25	4	0
Eclectic	1,234	6	0	0	0	6	19	2	14	3	0
Elba	3,398	12	1	1	0	10	119	38	70	11	3
Elberta	2,036	6	1	2	0	3	81	10	46	25	0
Enterprise	29,936	172	1	7	6	158	729	144	525	60	3
Eufaula	12,528	57	2	4	6	45	316	58	236	22	6
Eutaw	2,823	3	0	0	0	3	10	1	6	3	0
Evergreen	3,309	15	1	1	2	11	32	6	20	6	1
Excel	546	4	1	0	0	3	22	7	14	1	1
Fairhope	23,747	43	1	6	3	33	364	60	280	24	3
Fayette	4,132	7	0	0	0	7	69	8	54	7	1
Flomaton	1,455	9	1	1	0	7	61	21	36	4	1
Florala	1,904	6	0	1	0	5	56	11	30	15	0
Florence	40,063	233	1	31	6	195	1,060	175	787	98	1

Table 8. Offenses Known to Law Enforcement, by Selected State and City, 2022—Continued

(Number.)

State/city	Population	Violent crime	Murder and nonnegligent manslaughter	Rape	Robbery	Aggravated assault	Property crime	Burglary	Larceny-theft	Motor vehicle theft	Arson[1]
Foley	23,629	38	2	5	4	27	554	145	367	42	3
Fort Deposit	1,154	11	0	0	1	10	43	4	27	12	0
Fort Payne	14,845	22	0	5	2	15	265	37	202	26	3
Frisco City	1,156	4	1	0	0	3	17	6	10	1	0
Fultondale	9,699	15	0	2	4	9	271	25	197	49	2
Gadsden	33,521	189	6	15	17	151	1,302	152	1,009	141	13
Gardendale	16,861	61	0	3	8	50	366	14	325	27	1
Geneva	4,169	11	0	1	0	10	84	10	69	5	0
Georgiana	1,303	14	1	1	0	12	33	3	29	1	0
Geraldine	910	0	0	0	0	0	12	2	8	2	0
Gilbertown	721	1	0	0	0	1	7	0	7	0	0
Glencoe	5,406	4	0	0	0	4	25	3	15	7	0
Gordo	1,590	2	0	0	0	2	6	2	3	1	0
Gordon	293	0	0	0	0	0	7	1	6	0	0
Grant	1,042	1	0	1	0	0	18	5	12	1	0
Greensboro	2,179	0	0	0	0	0	0	0	0	0	0
Guin	2,158	6	0	1	1	4	23	2	11	10	0
Gulf Shores	16,274	54	1	6	0	47	394	31	356	7	2
Guntersville	8,858	29	1	8	3	17	275	45	185	45	1
Gurley	826	2	0	0	0	2	26	6	18	2	1
Hackleburg	1,430	1	0	0	0	1	8	2	6	0	0
Haleyville	4,366	23	0	2	0	21	194	74	108	12	0
Hanceville	3,261	10	0	1	0	9	66	9	48	9	0
Harpersville	1,752	6	0	0	1	5	22	3	18	1	1
Hartford	2,666	3	0	0	0	3	15	3	11	1	1
Hartselle	15,626	30	2	5	0	23	161	20	123	18	1
Hayden	1,328	2	0	0	1	1	16	4	11	1	0
Hayneville	751	3	1	0	0	2	5	0	5	0	0
Headland	5,320	2	0	0	0	2	51	15	34	2	0
Heflin	3,402	2	0	0	0	2	39	9	21	9	0
Helena	22,035	21	2	3	0	16	123	16	93	14	0
Henagar	2,293	2	0	0	0	2	20	5	13	2	0
Hillsboro	408	0	0	0	0	0	0	0	0	0	0
Hokes Bluff	4,451	2	0	0	0	2	29	4	20	5	0
Hollywood	921	2	0	0	1	1	31	3	28	0	0
Homewood	25,788	19	0	1	4	14	341	26	283	32	0
Hoover	92,491	90	2	16	13	59	1,443	114	1,251	78	1
Hueytown	16,313	70	5	4	8	53	549	122	374	53	2
Huntsville	218,897	654	0	68	61	525	3,297	613	2,348	336	6
Ider	743	1	0	0	0	1	26	5	18	3	0
Irondale	13,528	38	0	2	6	30	344	142	148	54	2
Jackson	4,576	30	0	5	0	25	116	29	81	6	0
Jacksons Gap	757	5	0	0	0	5	20	2	13	5	0
Jacksonville	13,025	120	0	6	0	114	260	58	196	6	1
Jasper	14,312	60	1	8	2	49	677	174	443	60	2
Jemison	2,662	17	0	5	2	10	69	14	46	9	0
Killen	1,043	5	0	0	0	5	16	3	11	2	0
Kimberly	4,036	6	0	0	0	6	22	2	15	5	0
Kinsey	2,290	0	0	0	0	0	1	1	0	0	0
Kinston	589	3	0	0	0	3	37	7	28	2	2
LaFayette	2,579	3	0	0	0	3	25	6	18	1	0
Lake View	3,709	3	0	1	0	2	22	6	13	3	0
Lanett	6,716	34	0	3	5	26	181	31	129	21	1
Leeds	12,206	40	1	5	2	32	231	30	183	18	1
Leesburg	914	1	0	0	0	1	6	0	5	1	0
Leighton	662	0	0	0	0	0	9	3	4	2	0
Level Plains	1,823	11	0	0	1	10	31	2	27	2	1
Lincoln	7,256	34	0	3	2	29	164	26	104	34	2
Linden	1,856	11	1	1	1	8	24	8	12	4	0
Lineville	2,469	3	0	0	0	3	10	3	7	0	0
Lipscomb	2,018	2	0	0	0	2	2	0	1	1	0
Littleville	1,041	1	0	0	1	0	8	1	5	2	0
Livingston	3,112	16	0	0	1	15	30	10	18	2	0
Lockhart	445	0	0	0	0	0	0	0	0	0	0
Luverne	2,658	12	1	3	2	6	47	5	36	6	0
Maplesville	643	1	0	0	0	1	15	4	11	0	0
Margaret	5,685	3	0	0	0	3	31	2	25	4	0
McIntosh	198	3	0	0	0	3	20	6	14	0	1
Mentone	322	0	0	0	0	0	9	4	4	1	0
Midfield	5,036	25	1	0	7	17	56	7	41	8	0
Midland City	2,285	15	0	1	3	11	64	15	45	4	1
Millbrook	17,567	32	1	5	3	23	429	20	379	30	0
Millport	960	1	0	0	1	0	3	1	2	0	0
Millry	439	1	0	0	0	1	7	2	4	1	0
Mobile	239,323	2,218	41	124	135	1,918	7,211	1,077	5,521	613	15
Monroeville	5,797	52	3	1	1	47	138	11	116	11	1
Montevallo	7,517	7	0	0	0	7	73	14	57	2	3
Moody	13,862	23	2	3	1	17	140	12	95	33	0
Morris	2,246	0	0	0	0	0	12	1	8	3	0
Moulton	3,353	13	0	1	2	10	155	17	129	9	0
Mountain Brook	21,910	6	0	1	0	5	206	36	161	9	1
Mount Vernon	1,371	6	0	0	0	6	31	19	11	1	1
Muscle Shoals	16,917	61	0	5	1	55	413	28	359	26	1

Table 8. Offenses Known to Law Enforcement, by Selected State and City, 2022—Continued

(Number.)

State/city	Population	Violent crime	Murder and nonnegligent manslaughter	Rape	Robbery	Aggravated assault	Property crime	Burglary	Larceny-theft	Motor vehicle theft	Arson[1]
Napier Field	410	2	0	0	0	2	5	3	2	0	0
New Brockton	1,453	2	0	0	0	2	21	5	13	3	0
New Hope	2,884	3	0	0	0	3	31	5	22	4	0
Newton	1,615	13	0	2	1	10	46	8	32	6	0
North Courtland	486	0	0	0	0	0	0	0	0	0	0
Northport	30,901	110	0	5	7	98	508	70	403	35	3
Notasulga	894	2	0	0	0	2	7	0	3	4	0
Odenville	5,026	11	0	1	1	9	58	9	41	8	0
Ohatchee	1,203	4	0	1	0	3	27	2	20	5	0
Oneonta	6,798	19	0	2	2	15	262	17	240	5	1
Opelika	32,010	259	7	23	19	210	877	90	718	69	5
Opp	6,641	31	0	3	4	24	140	24	109	7	0
Orange Beach	8,530	32	0	5	1	26	206	16	182	8	0
Owens Crossroads	2,648	4	0	0	0	4	32	1	25	6	0
Oxford	22,318	52	0	7	5	40	650	47	575	28	0
Ozark	14,299	75	0	5	6	64	491	65	389	37	6
Parrish	977	5	0	0	2	3	34	12	21	1	0
Pelham	24,920	33	0	1	2	30	329	25	264	40	3
Pell City	13,607	40	1	5	3	31	313	24	263	26	0
Pennington	329	0	0	0	0	0	0	0	0	0	0
Phenix City	38,076	334	10	24	31	269	1,408	186	1,047	175	4
Phil Campbell	988	2	0	0	0	2	14	5	7	2	0
Pickensville	545	0	0	0	0	0	3	0	1	2	0
Piedmont	4,779	5	0	2	0	3	10	0	7	3	0
Pine Hill	751	6	3	0	0	3	10	2	7	1	1
Pleasant Grove	9,454	22	0	3	0	19	93	20	65	8	1
Prattville	38,679	106	5	7	8	86	895	58	779	58	1
Priceville	3,822	7	0	3	0	4	19	3	13	3	0
Prichard	18,936	157	3	7	19	128	399	108	213	78	20
Ragland	1,715	2	0	0	0	2	17	1	13	3	0
Rainbow City	10,150	11	0	6	1	4	117	17	94	6	0
Rainsville	5,685	4	0	2	0	2	13	0	10	3	1
Ranburne	420	2	0	0	0	2	6	1	5	0	0
Red Bay	3,177	7	0	2	0	5	51	5	40	6	0
Red Level	431	0	0	0	0	0	1	0	1	0	0
Repton	230	0	0	0	0	0	0	0	0	0	0
Riverside	2,265	4	0	0	0	4	27	4	20	3	0
Robertsdale	7,116	24	0	2	2	20	389	115	268	6	0
Rogersville	1,370	3	0	0	0	3	18	6	9	3	1
Russellville	10,768	26	1	3	0	22	225	40	170	15	1
Samson	1,856	4	0	0	0	4	12	3	8	1	0
Saraland	16,459	23	0	2	3	18	319	21	274	24	0
Sardis City	1,787	0	0	0	0	0	22	5	15	2	0
Satsuma	6,811	4	0	0	0	4	30	2	23	5	0
Selma	17,296	133	7	7	11	108	280	91	166	23	3
Shorter	366	0	0	0	0	0	0	0	0	0	0
Silverhill	1,341	3	0	0	0	3	12	1	10	1	0
Skyline	843	0	0	0	0	0	0	0	0	0	0
Slocomb	2,099	1	0	0	0	1	10	0	9	1	0
Snead	1,023	1	0	0	0	1	17	1	9	7	0
Somerville	802	1	0	0	0	1	7	1	5	1	0
Southside	9,524	4	1	0	0	3	22	0	16	6	0
Spanish Fort	10,689	4	0	0	2	2	185	26	152	7	0
Springville	5,048	12	0	0	1	11	49	7	36	6	1
Stevenson	1,963	7	0	1	1	5	29	4	20	5	0
St. Florian	704	2	0	0	0	2	22	2	19	1	0
Sulligent	1,806	1	0	0	0	1	20	7	12	1	0
Sumiton	2,405	5	0	2	0	3	64	6	48	10	0
Summerdale	1,587	6	0	1	0	5	43	6	34	3	1
Sweet Water	221	0	0	0	0	0	0	0	0	0	0
Sylacauga	12,205	74	3	7	1	63	400	133	241	26	2
Sylvania	1,805	0	0	0	0	0	16	3	11	2	0
Talladega	15,448	100	3	11	2	84	377	65	271	41	0
Tallassee	4,816	33	1	2	2	28	225	53	141	31	1
Tarrant	5,913	149	0	3	15	131	270	58	168	44	5
Thomasville	3,518	19	0	0	0	19	86	7	70	9	1
Thorsby	2,117	4	0	0	0	4	14	5	7	2	0
Trafford	598	0	0	0	0	0	1	1	0	0	0
Triana	3,829	7	0	0	0	7	17	10	7	0	0
Trinity	2,553	8	1	0	0	7	52	7	38	7	1
Troy	17,639	73	0	11	7	55	443	77	347	19	0
Trussville	26,561	41	4	3	8	26	692	18	641	33	0
Tuscaloosa	101,280	646	12	27	60	547	2,919	356	2,312	251	4
Tuscumbia	9,081	0	0	0	0	0	28	9	12	7	0
Tuskegee	8,600	82	8	2	11	61	130	26	94	10	2
Union Springs	3,301	50	2	0	4	44	58	11	36	11	2
Valley	10,475	54	4	9	7	34	384	52	297	35	1
Vernon	1,833	5	0	0	0	5	47	6	38	3	0
Vestavia Hills	38,515	30	3	7	3	17	281	29	217	35	1
Walnut Grove	773	0	0	0	0	0	0	0	0	0	0
Warrior	3,189	5	0	1	0	4	12	2	8	2	0
Weaver	3,394	16	0	3	0	13	77	20	51	6	0
Wedowee	719	3	0	0	0	3	28	4	21	3	0

Table 8. Offenses Known to Law Enforcement, by Selected State and City, 2022—Continued

(Number.)

State/city	Population	Violent crime	Murder and nonnegligent manslaughter	Rape	Robbery	Aggravated assault	Property crime	Burglary	Larceny-theft	Motor vehicle theft	Arson[1]
Wetumpka	7,317	12	1	1	0	10	249	20	220	9	1
Winfield	4,805	6	0	2	0	4	143	22	113	8	1
Woodstock	1,691	11	0	5	0	6	55	4	43	8	0
York	2,387	1	0	0	0	1	0	0	0	0	0
ALASKA											
Anchorage	285,821	3,289	29	492	436	2,332	7,900	1,179	5,605	1,116	136
Bethel	6,267	78	1	3	2	72	17	4	8	5	2
Bristol Bay Borough	846	5	0	2	1	2	8	3	5	0	0
Cordova	2,160	4	0	0	0	4	6	2	3	1	0
Craig	1,028	2	0	0	0	2	4	1	1	2	0
Fairbanks	32,785	271	10	37	32	192	1,407	130	1,109	168	25
Haines	2,058	1	0	0	0	1	8	3	4	1	0
Homer	5,894	25	1	8	0	16	73	4	63	6	0
Juneau	31,775	197	2	81	23	91	550	56	450	44	8
Kenai	7,713	26	1	8	0	17	152	9	138	5	0
Ketchikan	7,953	13	0	3	1	9	74	5	69	0	0
Kodiak	5,357	17	0	5	0	12	44	2	35	7	0
Kotzebue	3,041	46	0	7	0	39	30	9	15	6	1
Nome	3,546	72	0	48	1	23	18	1	16	1	1
North Pole	2,335	6	0	0	0	6	50	4	39	7	0
North Slope Borough	10,959	81	2	8	1	70	61	17	28	16	5
Palmer	6,305	29	0	4	0	25	101	6	75	20	2
Petersburg	3,314	2	0	0	0	2	39	4	33	2	0
Seward	2,667	10	0	1	1	8	43	2	37	4	0
Sitka	8,392	8	0	0	1	7	36	0	31	5	0
Skagway	1,035	0	0	0	0	0	5	0	5	0	0
Soldotna	4,527	13	0	3	1	9	80	7	72	1	2
Unalaska	3,908	5	0	1	0	4	19	4	10	5	1
Valdez	3,839	4	0	2	0	2	14	4	10	0	0
Wasilla	9,809	53	0	5	9	39	300	11	270	19	1
Wrangell	1,984	4	0	0	0	4	6	1	5	0	0
ARIZONA											
Apache Junction	41,099	135	4	16	7	108	786	107	572	107	4
Avondale	91,467	384	6	40	72	266	2,888	285	2,328	275	16
Bisbee	4,909	12	1	0	1	10	34	7	20	7	1
Buckeye	110,002	205	1	53	7	144	1,141	141	885	115	5
Camp Verde	12,362	23	0	4	0	19	170	30	114	26	0
Casa Grande	61,271	353	5	39	45	264	1,635	195	1,266	174	11
Chandler	281,373	513	11	95	72	335	5,086	478	4,166	442	13
Chino Valley	13,875	14	0	0	0	14	69	11	48	10	1
Clarkdale	4,815	8	0	0	0	8	31	13	15	3	1
Coolidge	16,027	89	4	5	11	69	403	44	320	39	2
Cottonwood	12,680	43	0	5	4	34	259	21	213	25	0
Douglas	16,529	19	1	3	1	14	209	41	153	15	2
Eagar	4,448	1	0	0	0	1	19	2	17	0	0
El Mirage	36,039	119	5	6	10	98	511	38	409	64	10
Eloy	15,717	109	0	10	0	99	304	70	197	37	8
Florence	26,814	36	0	0	1	35	100	12	81	7	2
Fredonia	1,330	0	0	0	0	0	3	0	3	0	0
Gilbert	277,123	323	2	74	30	217	2,818	276	2,332	210	10
Glendale	250,466	1,365	20	156	200	989	8,115	947	6,063	1,105	39
Globe	7,155	114	0	1	5	108	359	52	283	24	
Goodyear	107,212	181	2	11	28	140	1,995	279	1,570	146	6
Huachuca City	1,622	1	0	0	0	1	21	4	16	1	0
Jerome	471	0	0	0	0	0	12	1	11	0	
Kingman	34,803	133	1	13	15	104	1,100	112	910	78	8
Lake Havasu City	59,166	163	0	35	2	126	804	91	631	82	3
Litchfield Park	6,989	19	0	0	4	15	89	15	62	12	1
Mammoth	1,135	9	0	0	0	9	35	13	22	0	
Marana	57,119	49	1	5	17	26	1,274	85	1,154	35	7
Maricopa	66,525	125	1	8	6	110	507	37	416	54	6
Mesa	513,116	2,193	27	245	311	1,610	9,081	1,098	6,918	1,065	28
Miami	1,540	24	0	1	3	20	59	6	39	14	
Nogales	19,725	48	1	0	1	46	701	95	409	197	0
Oro Valley	48,441	16	1	4	3	8	575	45	507	23	2
Page	7,328	60	1	10	2	47	327	22	285	20	0
Paradise Valley	12,663	12	0	6	0	6	181	40	129	12	0
Parker	3,263	12	0	2	2	8	57	15	35	7	0
Payson	16,638	82	0	1	2	79	270	70	184	16	1
Peoria	197,894	386	3	62	53	268	2,734	370	2,120	244	5
Phoenix	1,637,902	13,515	217	1,105	3,207	8,986	47,530	6,266	33,631	7,633	257
Pima	2,960	0	0	0	0	0	16	5	8	3	
Pinetop-Lakeside	4,179	22	0	2	2	18	106	13	87	6	0
Prescott	47,878	192	1	21	8	162	636	127	474	35	6
Prescott Valley	49,422	140	2	26	5	107	372	43	308	21	3
Queen Creek	72,229	105	0	16	1	88	717	85	602	30	4
Sahuarita	36,229	36	0	6	3	27	334	26	283	25	2
San Luis	38,528	20	0	0	1	19	212	30	141	41	1
Sedona	9,829	37	0	6	2	29	171	41	122	8	3
Show Low	12,157	80	0	13	1	66	244	30	200	14	0
Sierra Vista	45,611	128	1	19	11	97	738	83	630	25	7

Table 8. Offenses Known to Law Enforcement, by Selected State and City, 2022—Continued

(Number.)

State/city	Population	Violent crime	Murder and nonnegligent manslaughter	Rape	Robbery	Aggravated assault	Property crime	Burglary	Larceny-theft	Motor vehicle theft	Arson[1]
Snowflake-Taylor	10,834	38	1	9	1	27	153	15	124	14	1
Somerton	14,480	9	3	1	0	5	80	20	41	19	1
South Tucson	4,537	109	2	3	15	89	603	51	514	38	3
Springerville	1,706	8	0	0	0	8	4	1	1	2	0
St. Johns	3,365	20	0	3	0	17	42	12	24	6	1
Superior	2,528	12	0	0	1	11	91	14	66	11	1
Surprise	154,128	182	2	23	35	122	2,163	203	1,811	149	15
Tempe	187,473	1,095	7	156	178	754	8,126	929	6,405	792	30
Thatcher	5,369	2	0	0	0	2	34	4	30	0	0
Tombstone	1,308	4	0	0	0	4	41	9	29	3	0
Wellton	2,528	2	0	0	0	2	18	2	16	0	1
Wickenburg	7,868	8	0	1	0	7	158	29	110	19	0
Willcox	3,202	8	0	0	2	6	114	35	75	4	2
Williams	3,316	27	0	1	1	25	98	5	84	9	0
Yuma	98,164	551	19	41	50	441	1,657	450	990	217	13
ARKANSAS											
Alexander	3,798	31	0	7	0	24	79	36	34	9	1
Alma	5,874	24	0	9	0	15	156	32	117	7	0
Arkadelphia	10,233	25	0	5	2	18	195	53	133	9	1
Ashdown	4,150	5	0	1	0	4	73	9	56	8	1
Ash Flat	1,128	1	0	0	0	1	20	4	16	0	0
Atkins	2,864	15	0	1	1	13	64	12	48	4	0
Augusta	1,928	2	0	0	1	1	15	5	10	0	0
Austin	4,547	4	0	1	0	3	25	11	13	1	0
Bald Knob	2,534	16	0	7	1	8	64	14	48	2	0
Barling	4,894	24	0	7	1	16	59	5	52	2	0
Batesville	11,129	45	0	20	0	25	204	50	141	13	0
Bay	1,825	8	0	1	0	7	30	6	22	2	0
Beebe	8,683	43	0	5	1	37	191	18	158	15	0
Bella Vista	31,316	69	0	29	1	39	133	10	118	5	0
Benton	36,282	125	3	17	12	93	1,020	152	793	75	6
Bentonville	58,871	188	1	29	2	156	686	69	575	42	1
Berryville	5,727	12	0	4	1	7	191	36	150	5	2
Blytheville	12,732	123	3	6	8	106	523	48	454	21	0
Bonanza	601	11	0	0	0	11	2	0	2	0	3
Bono	2,738	0	0	0	0	0	8	0	8	0	0
Booneville	3,826	17	0	3	0	14	51	8	39	4	1
Bradford	681	0	0	0	0	0	11	4	6	1	0
Brookland	4,355	20	0	9	0	11	62	17	38	7	0
Bryant	21,407	26	2	3	5	16	744	54	657	33	4
Bull Shoals	1,948	8	0	0	0	8	16	4	12	0	0
Cabot	26,750	99	2	33	4	60	447	57	345	45	2
Caddo Valley	589	6	0	2	0	4	29	7	21	1	0
Cammack Village	756	2	0	0	0	2	4	0	3	1	0
Caraway	1,106	2	0	0	0	2	13	1	12	0	0
Carlisle	1,991	5	0	1	0	4	73	7	55	11	0
Cave Springs	6,218	7	0	6	0	1	16	6	8	2	0
Centerton	21,927	45	0	8	0	37	93	29	57	7	0
Charleston	2,642	6	0	3	0	3	44	11	31	2	0
Cherokee Village	4,944	17	0	4	0	13	59	15	42	2	0
Cherry Valley	562	1	0	0	0	1	7	0	7	0	0
Clarendon	1,476	7	0	0	0	7	73	15	56	2	3
Clarksville	9,559	21	0	8	0	13	196	31	153	12	1
Conway	66,487	384	7	46	15	316	1,890	138	1,628	124	6
Corning	3,124	14	0	1	0	13	35	4	29	2	0
Cotter	924	0	0	0	0	0	4	1	2	1	0
Crossett	4,619	33	0	4	0	29	167	56	110	1	3
Damascus	384	1	0	0	0	1	1	0	1	0	0
Danville	2,001	8	0	0	0	8	9	3	6	0	0
Dardanelle	4,485	14	0	4	0	10	80	15	55	10	1
Decatur	1,733	6	0	1	0	5	26	4	21	1	0
De Queen	6,069	29	3	4	0	22	136	29	100	7	2
Des Arc	1,844	0	0	0	0	0	13	5	8	0	0
DeWitt	2,832	27	1	3	0	23	76	11	65	0	0
Diamond City	789	5	0	0	0	5	4	3	1	0	0
Diaz	1,266	3	0	0	0	3	4	2	2	0	0
Dover	1,335	0	0	0	0	0	17	8	9	0	1
Dumas	3,796	26	2	6	3	15	68	10	50	8	0
Earle	1,758	7	0	0	0	7	26	10	13	3	0
El Dorado	17,037	295	9	6	16	264	541	218	297	26	5
Elkins	3,828	11	0	4	1	6	29	5	19	5	0
England	2,427	17	0	1	0	16	41	14	26	1	0
Etowah	243	0	0	0	0	0	5	1	3	1	0
Eudora	1,664	7	0	0	0	7	28	7	19	2	0
Eureka Springs	2,195	12	0	0	1	11	49	13	29	7	0
Fairfield Bay	2,111	5	0	4	0	1	36	7	26	3	0
Farmington	8,862	15	0	6	2	7	62	14	41	7	0
Fayetteville	96,456	486	2	55	40	389	3,890	337	3,155	398	6
Flippin	1,344	3	0	1	0	2	54	5	48	1	0
Fordyce	3,254	57	0	2	1	54	167	29	122	16	1
Forrest City	12,807	283	12	6	16	249	526	105	361	60	9
Fort Smith	90,013	940	3	70	66	801	4,450	733	3,293	424	17

Table 8. Offenses Known to Law Enforcement, by Selected State and City, 2022—Continued

(Number.)

State/city	Population	Violent crime	Murder and nonnegligent manslaughter	Rape	Robbery	Aggravated assault	Property crime	Burglary	Larceny-theft	Motor vehicle theft	Arson[1]
Gassville	2,208	3	0	0	0	3	52	5	45	2	0
Gentry	4,156	19	0	2	0	17	15	0	9	6	1
Gillett	586	0	0	0	0	0	3	1	2	0	0
Goshen	2,250	5	0	1	0	4	10	0	7	3	1
Gravette	3,721	10	0	3	0	7	60	9	43	8	0
Greenbrier	5,954	4	0	0	0	4	4	0	3	1	0
Green Forest	3,081	21	0	6	2	13	47	11	29	7	0
Greenland	1,215	2	0	0	0	2	12	1	10	1	0
Greenwood	9,705	14	0	2	0	12	39	13	22	4	1
Greers Ferry	833	1	0	0	0	1	8	2	5	1	0
Gurdon	1,847	23	0	2	1	20	18	3	14	1	0
Guy	743	2	0	2	0	0	3	0	3	0	0
Hackett	842	3	0	0	0	3	9	0	9	0	1
Hamburg	2,425	22	0	1	0	21	46	11	34	1	0
Hampton	1,191	1	0	0	0	1	13	8	4	1	0
Harrisburg	2,199	16	1	4	0	11	36	12	21	3	1
Harrison	13,350	20	0	5	1	14	280	64	200	16	0
Hartford	501	0	0	0	0	0	1	0	1	0	0
Haskell	4,061	11	0	2	0	9	45	19	22	4	0
Hazen	1,418	9	3	1	1	4	22	9	7	6	0
Heber Springs	7,353	39	0	14	2	23	188	34	143	11	0
Helena-West Helena	8,874	147	5	11	11	120	302	94	180	28	9
Highfill	2,099	4	0	0	0	4	0	0	0	0	0
Highland	1,041	2	0	1	0	1	13	5	8	0	0
Hope	8,535	88	3	3	4	78	302	66	206	30	0
Hot Springs	38,174	196	5	32	29	130	2,238	363	1,687	188	14
Hoxie	2,710	5	0	1	0	4	22	8	11	3	0
Jacksonville	29,136	327	4	29	40	254	1,350	238	969	143	18
Johnson	3,629	11	0	6	0	5	73	28	30	15	0
Jonesboro	79,865	516	9	83	43	381	2,655	897	1,549	209	11
Judsonia	1,877	5	0	4	0	1	21	3	14	4	0
Kensett	1,396	2	0	2	0	0	18	2	15	1	0
Lake City	2,517	9	0	4	0	5	11	5	4	2	0
Lakeview	784	1	0	0	0	1	11	1	10	0	0
Lake Village	1,984	19	0	3	1	15	57	3	48	6	1
Lamar	1,738	4	0	1	0	3	21	4	17	0	0
Lavaca	2,474	11	0	4	0	7	21	2	16	3	0
Leachville	1,943	6	0	1	1	4	33	12	18	3	0
Lewisville	866	17	0	3	0	14	14	9	5	0	0
Lincoln	2,309	12	0	0	0	12	30	7	19	4	1
Little Flock	3,037	10	0	2	0	8	27	9	13	5	0
Little Rock	201,513	3,694	79	250	429	2,936	10,778	1,926	7,775	1,077	64
Lonoke	4,128	27	0	3	0	24	138	26	101	11	0
Lowell	10,402	22	0	4	0	18	102	49	50	3	0
Luxora	894	3	0	0	0	3	1	1	0	0	0
Magnolia	11,059	60	3	6	6	45	381	140	217	24	2
Malvern	10,824	82	0	8	5	69	399	89	294	16	4
Mansfield	1,061	4	0	0	0	4	15	3	11	1	0
Marianna	3,635	24	1	4	2	17	117	24	87	6	0
Marion	13,602	96	2	8	5	81	378	74	268	36	4
Marked Tree	2,200	9	0	0	0	9	14	1	10	3	0
Marmaduke	1,228	0	0	0	0	0	6	1	5	0	0
Marshall	1,335	4	0	0	0	4	15	5	10	0	0
Maumelle	19,273	37	0	9	3	25	273	41	213	19	4
Mayflower	2,051	11	0	2	1	8	66	12	49	5	0
McCrory	1,502	5	0	1	0	4	27	3	23	1	0
McGehee	3,690	40	0	3	3	34	103	32	62	9	2
Mena	5,652	21	1	5	1	14	185	23	155	7	3
Menifee	281	3	0	2	0	1	2	0	2	0	0
Mineral Springs	1,074	3	0	0	0	3	12	1	11	0	0
Monette	1,557	1	0	0	0	1	22	3	17	2	0
Monticello	8,200	42	1	9	1	31	164	25	124	15	2
Morrilton	7,104	27	1	5	1	20	283	19	255	9	4
Mountain Home	13,180	41	2	10	1	28	380	38	323	19	0
Mountain View	2,905	17	0	1	1	15	74	31	40	3	0
Mulberry	1,553	6	0	5	0	1	33	8	23	2	0
Murfreesboro	1,437	4	0	1	0	3	27	7	18	2	1
Nashville	4,083	16	0	4	2	10	121	26	91	4	1
Norfork	473	0	0	0	0	0	1	0	1	0	0
North Little Rock	63,663	783	18	31	75	659	2,950	476	2,102	372	18
Ola	926	0	0	0	0	0	5	0	3	2	0
Osceola	6,621	142	3	4	9	126	200	82	92	26	5
Ozark	3,575	31	6	1	1	23	48	19	27	2	1
Paragould	30,296	346	0	37	14	295	1,152	168	893	91	4
Paris	3,221	31	1	7	0	23	81	34	39	8	0
Patterson	299	0	0	0	0	0	6	0	5	1	0
Pea Ridge	7,643	20	0	12	0	8	63	16	43	4	0
Perryville	1,383	2	0	2	0	0	51	7	43	1	0
Piggott	3,532	6	0	1	0	5	43	14	28	1	2
Pine Bluff	39,549	644	17	34	62	531	2,025	375	1,330	320	23
Plumerville	736	1	0	0	0	1	12	2	10	0	0
Pocahontas	7,657	28	0	13	0	15	191	26	156	9	1
Pottsville	3,232	4	0	0	0	4	27	5	22	0	0

Table 8. Offenses Known to Law Enforcement, by Selected State and City, 2022—Continued

(Number.)

State/city	Population	Violent crime	Murder and nonnegligent manslaughter	Rape	Robbery	Aggravated assault	Property crime	Burglary	Larceny-theft	Motor vehicle theft	Arson[1]
Prairie Grove	7,714	21	0	1	0	20	93	36	51	6	0
Prescott	2,976	11	0	3	0	8	50	11	34	5	0
Quitman	694	2	0	1	0	1	35	1	32	2	1
Ravenden	428	4	0	1	0	3	5	1	4	0	0
Redfield	1,508	11	0	1	0	10	18	5	10	3	1
Rogers	72,115	285	1	82	14	188	1,539	127	1,303	109	3
Rose Bud	499	0	0	0	0	0	6	1	5	0	0
Russellville	29,533	165	0	17	3	145	842	80	692	70	0
Salem	1,577	3	0	1	0	2	13	2	10	1	0
Searcy	23,175	119	2	31	8	78	856	79	711	66	5
Shannon Hills	4,625	23	4	3	0	16	37	17	14	6	0
Sheridan	5,073	17	0	2	0	15	77	19	55	3	2
Sherwood	33,232	258	1	21	11	225	853	170	593	90	4
Siloam Springs	17,957	102	0	26	5	71	404	83	283	38	2
Springdale	90,892	496	4	120	30	342	2,293	250	1,764	279	4
Stamps	1,191	11	0	1	0	10	24	10	12	2	0
Star City	2,284	27	1	6	3	17	55	9	39	7	0
Stuttgart	7,847	93	3	7	2	81	304	63	226	15	1
Swifton	742	2	0	0	0	2	8	1	6	1	0
Texarkana	29,339	292	7	13	20	252	1,069	187	799	83	3
Tontitown	6,700	17	0	7	0	10	103	14	44	45	0
Trumann	7,283	67	0	14	2	51	292	60	217	15	2
Tuckerman	1,750	9	0	3	0	6	12	2	9	1	0
Turrell	498	0	0	0	0	0	3	1	2	0	0
Van Buren	23,533	106	1	23	4	78	740	224	454	62	2
Vilonia	4,519	3	0	1	0	2	42	10	32	0	0
Waldron	3,313	10	0	3	1	6	118	51	58	9	0
Walnut Ridge	5,495	18	0	2	0	16	52	20	23	9	1
Ward	6,621	46	0	3	2	41	129	35	87	7	1
Warren	5,325	19	0	3	1	15	99	40	53	6	0
Weiner	631	0	0	0	0	0	10	4	5	1	0
West Fork	2,330	5	0	2	0	3	38	3	33	2	0
West Memphis	23,809	628	12	25	44	547	1,131	203	739	189	8
White Hall	5,579	12	0	2	0	10	62	22	32	8	0
Wynne	8,234	87	2	11	1	73	251	48	173	30	1
CALIFORNIA											
Adelanto	38,380	344	0	11	37	296	359	71	193	95	
Agoura Hills	19,397	32	0	5	4	23	255	69	163	23	
Alameda	74,441	232	1	17	100	114	3,200	297	2,302	601	20
Albany	19,011	40	0	5	16	19	564	70	432	62	12
Alhambra	79,703	160	0	12	73	75	2,044	251	1,453	340	6
Aliso Viejo	51,477	44	1	0	8	35	351	41	257	53	1
American Canyon	21,412	75	0	5	16	54	389	29	287	73	
Anaheim	344,795	2,641	12	125	380	2,124	9,548	1,693	6,055	1,800	42
Anderson	11,447	72	0	13	12	47	399	72	268	59	3
Angels Camp	3,846	14	0	1	3	10	90	15	64	11	
Antioch	114,338	702	9	37	159	497	2,528	432	1,456	640	16
Apple Valley	76,520	433	4	26	45	358	1,138	231	717	190	
Arcadia	54,202	141	0	17	47	77	1,653	390	1,147	116	6
Arcata	19,144	120	2	5	24	89	537	58	351	128	13
Arroyo Grande	18,492	92	0	9	5	78	267	67	165	35	2
Artesia	15,608	88	1	4	18	65	413	125	206	82	
Atascadero	29,679	118	0	21	12	85	425	80	312	33	7
Atherton	6,704	6	0	0	0	6	77	18	58	1	
Atwater	32,157	271	5	18	39	209	805	90	635	80	28
Auburn	13,933	58	0	14	4	40	214	34	162	18	4
Avalon	3,303	20	0	1	0	19	47	10	32	5	
Avenal	13,873	43	0	2	4	37	66	24	31	11	0
Azusa	47,754	138	5	11	42	80	991	180	630	181	
Bakersfield	411,873	2,250	38	129	664	1,419	16,361	3,184	8,319	4,858	
Baldwin Park	69,205	317	9	14	64	230	1,102	205	613	284	17
Banning	31,050	180	5	17	18	140	482	118	266	98	
Barstow	25,465	277	6	10	54	207	589	169	238	182	
Bear Valley	120	1	0	1	0	0	10	2	7	1	
Beaumont	57,067	200	2	11	16	171	704	170	426	108	0
Bell	32,140	203	3	15	41	144	415	96	213	106	
Bellflower	75,830	445	4	31	112	298	1,892	342	915	635	
Bell Gardens	37,720	146	5	7	43	91	416	62	179	175	
Belmont	26,277	40	0	9	6	25	371	73	265	33	6
Belvedere	2,089	0	0	0	0	0	15	2	11	2	
Benicia	26,599	43	2	8	13	20	433	67	303	63	
Berkeley	114,872	667	3	90	292	282	6,483	1,036	4,611	836	52
Beverly Hills	31,163	154	0	8	57	89	1,365	269	986	110	
Big Bear	5,085	72	1	7	3	61	78	15	58	5	
Bishop	3,817	31	0	2	3	26	206	34	160	12	
Blythe	17,853	108	2	7	11	88	239	71	127	41	10
Bradbury	878	0	0	0	0	0	9	7	2	0	
Brawley	26,650	95	0	7	12	76	677	107	475	95	
Brea	47,617	91	1	7	26	57	1,543	166	1,254	123	6
Brentwood	65,243	200	2	28	57	113	1,351	226	992	133	
Brisbane	4,503	7	0	0	1	6	141	31	79	31	
Broadmoor	4,136	14	0	1	4	9	78	14	48	16	

Table 8. Offenses Known to Law Enforcement, by Selected State and City, 2022—Continued

(Number.)

State/city	Population	Violent crime	Murder and nonnegligent manslaughter	Rape	Robbery	Aggravated assault	Property crime	Burglary	Larceny-theft	Motor vehicle theft	Arson[1]
Buellton	5,152	6	0	1	3	2	91	10	64	17	
Buena Park	82,065	202	1	22	73	106	2,389	269	1,601	519	
Burbank	103,516	321	1	21	83	216	2,819	278	2,246	295	39
Burlingame	29,003	59	0	9	12	38	1,013	128	781	104	
Calabasas	22,628	33	0	4	8	21	356	87	238	31	
Calexico	38,515	52	2	6	19	25	691	185	267	239	81
California City	15,138	77	1	2	5	69	199	82	78	39	
Calimesa	11,667	26	0	0	6	20	301	53	205	43	
Calistoga	5,151	14	0	3	3	8	71	13	51	7	
Camarillo	70,872	38	2	1	13	22	912	73	779	60	
Campbell	41,605	147	0	25	34	88	1,277	237	819	221	
Canyon Lake	11,238	13	0	1	1	11	76	11	45	20	
Capitola	9,748	26	0	6	5	15	306	24	260	22	
Carlsbad	115,531	241	0	29	48	164	2,047	296	1,565	186	11
Carmel	3,176	8	0	0	2	6	73	18	53	2	1
Carpinteria	12,986	31	0	0	6	25	165	9	140	16	
Carson	92,021	436	7	15	122	292	2,525	372	1,311	842	
Central Marin	35,543	51	0	8	3	40	698	112	503	83	
Ceres	49,282	255	0	21	56	178	1,066	126	761	179	
Cerritos	47,325	139	0	9	58	72	1,836	250	1,301	285	
Chico	102,499	589	1	80	60	448	1,703	224	1,214	265	
Chino	94,611	274	0	31	59	184	2,538	314	1,942	282	8
Chino Hills	78,786	127	1	18	14	94	1,140	258	796	86	
Chowchilla	19,195	119	0	8	5	106	192	35	117	40	
Chula Vista	277,976	975	8	33	295	639	3,550	519	2,035	996	38
Citrus Heights	86,896	353	4	35	69	245	1,771	232	1,248	291	23
Claremont	35,068	104	3	6	20	75	844	221	541	82	
Clayton	10,880	15	0	1	2	12	69	9	56	4	2
Clearlake	16,901	143	1	12	17	113	359	119	162	78	
Cloverdale	8,933	18	0	1	2	15	71	8	57	6	
Clovis	125,348	236	2	34	38	162	2,173	190	1,796	187	7
Coachella	43,065	154	9	1	36	108	718	90	464	164	
Coalinga	17,546	126	0	4	6	116	150	55	85	10	
Colma	1,612	44	0	1	20	23	801	117	649	35	
Colton	54,597	216	7	10	64	135	1,250	200	773	277	8
Colusa	6,444	16	0	8	3	5	76	16	49	11	
Commerce	11,787	183	6	8	70	99	1,634	244	894	496	
Compton	91,625	1,045	19	34	295	697	2,449	279	1,158	1,012	
Concord	122,982	792	4	37	177	574	3,444	514	2,369	561	68
Corcoran	22,609	110	3	8	7	92	289	43	185	61	2
Corning	8,191	50	0	8	1	41	243	33	163	47	3
Corona	161,946	350	4	37	105	204	3,891	642	2,595	654	
Coronado	19,706	56	0	12	6	38	327	42	252	33	0
Costa Mesa	109,785	647	1	66	139	441	3,905	540	2,983	382	
Cotati	7,437	28	0	1	2	25	91	17	57	17	
Covina	49,590	163	2	9	59	93	1,390	557	671	162	12
Crescent City	6,732	82	0	6	9	67	407	41	347	19	
Cudahy	21,807	157	2	10	35	110	290	68	117	105	
Culver City	39,271	289	0	17	118	154	2,160	291	1,603	266	15
Cupertino	56,950	66	1	15	18	32	758	161	535	62	
Cypress	49,588	57	1	7	24	25	983	270	549	164	5
Daly City	98,021	348	1	22	94	231	2,100	145	1,623	332	
Dana Point	32,534	55	1	3	9	42	403	65	261	77	2
Danville	42,945	14	0	1	5	8	291	43	221	27	
Davis	66,939	170	1	31	31	107	1,884	169	1,599	116	9
Delano	52,484	180	3	16	35	126	1,096	120	544	432	31
Del Mar	3,891	6	0	2	2	2	119	25	72	22	1
Del Rey Oaks	1,568	4	0	0	0	4	81	1	77	3	0
Desert Hot Springs	32,923	219	4	17	36	162	507	100	178	229	
Diamond Bar	52,713	92	0	13	25	54	969	256	614	99	
Dinuba	25,650	121	1	8	17	95	584	91	421	72	21
Dixon	19,001	64	0	8	8	48	293	36	224	33	4
Dorris	868	7	0	0	0	7	21	9	9	3	
Dos Palos	5,793	34	0	2	3	29	71	14	37	20	
Downey	109,226	503	10	33	194	266	2,895	282	1,616	997	
Duarte	20,849	67	0	5	16	46	371	67	233	71	
Dunsmuir	1,720	18	0	0	0	18	24	6	16	2	
East Palo Alto	27,800	178	5	14	66	93	643	61	420	162	
Eastvale	72,753	97	2	6	24	65	1,232	146	940	146	
El Cajon	104,693	491	0	29	117	345	1,684	265	1,077	342	23
El Centro	44,076	151	4	15	29	103	919	160	641	118	25
El Cerrito	25,718	111	1	1	60	49	1,039	104	791	144	17
Elk Grove	180,372	364	1	22	72	269	2,366	263	1,912	191	5
El Monte	104,695	402	4	31	153	214	1,957	443	990	524	17
El Segundo	16,550	117	1	8	43	65	897	293	460	144	2
Emeryville	12,781	142	0	3	79	60	1,928	150	1,495	283	5
Encinitas	61,488	112	0	4	17	91	920	147	667	106	1
Escalon	7,552	24	0	2	2	20	106	11	85	10	
Escondido	150,072	518	2	41	146	329	2,694	416	1,702	576	16
Etna	685	4	0	0	0	4	7	1	5	1	
Exeter	10,318	23	3	3	1	16	202	27	159	16	
Fairfax	7,477	11	0	3	0	8	43	4	34	5	
Fairfield	119,583	589	11	60	179	339	3,045	359	2,153	533	

Table 8. Offenses Known to Law Enforcement, by Selected State and City, 2022—Continued

(Number.)

State/city	Population	Violent crime	Murder and nonnegligent manslaughter	Rape	Robbery	Aggravated assault	Property crime	Burglary	Larceny-theft	Motor vehicle theft	Arson[1]
Farmersville	10,351	48	0	1	3	44	117	21	72	24	
Ferndale	1,399	4	0	0	0	4	11	4	7	0	2
Fillmore	16,581	15	0	2	3	10	171	17	114	40	
Firebaugh	8,126	28	0	2	5	21	93	13	58	22	
Folsom	83,011	115	0	20	16	79	1,211	162	945	104	
Fontana	212,730	611	3	75	180	353	2,738	445	1,688	605	17
Fort Bragg	6,968	53	0	5	16	32	224	33	180	11	5
Fort Jones	700	2	0	0	0	2	5	3	2	0	
Fortuna	12,481	41	0	15	7	19	210	25	158	27	7
Foster City	31,389	42	0	6	10	26	385	54	298	33	2
Fountain Valley	55,941	85	0	9	30	46	1,247	182	921	144	
Fowler	7,123	33	0	1	0	32	94	17	59	18	
Fremont	223,430	467	4	38	154	271	6,418	997	4,214	1,207	25
Fresno	546,871	4,732	61	242	963	3,466	18,862	3,980	11,748	3,134	121
Fullerton	140,587	551	1	79	150	321	3,730	749	2,398	583	
Galt	25,463	98	0	15	21	62	389	55	290	44	
Gardena	58,535	376	3	14	125	234	1,845	212	1,014	619	6
Garden Grove	169,157	526	3	56	148	319	3,707	650	2,474	583	30
Gilroy	56,742	273	0	48	77	148	1,237	184	681	372	
Glendale	188,599	283	0	18	130	135	3,444	486	2,545	413	
Glendora	50,650	138	0	16	32	90	1,158	199	869	90	
Goleta	32,929	49	1	4	9	35	535	88	415	32	
Gonzales	8,514	22	0	2	4	16	93	18	61	14	0
Grand Terrace	13,277	72	0	3	7	62	268	52	178	38	
Grass Valley	13,895	173	1	8	13	151	410	61	294	55	7
Greenfield	19,157	82	1	12	11	58	188	34	119	35	8
Gridley	7,349	31	1	9	2	19	138	29	87	22	
Grover Beach	12,728	33	0	4	4	25	286	58	212	16	3
Guadalupe	8,973	5	0	1	0	4	105	25	52	28	
Gustine	6,115	28	0	1	3	24	65	9	46	10	3
Hanford	58,990	253	3	28	26	196	799	113	517	169	13
Hawaiian Gardens	13,510	79	3	3	18	55	324	84	151	89	
Hawthorne	84,283	635	6	53	175	401	1,773	284	902	587	
Hayward	156,458	559	9	55	241	254	4,539	502	2,429	1,608	
Healdsburg	11,229	32	1	6	3	22	230	17	196	17	4
Hemet	91,046	420	6	21	98	295	1,878	563	828	487	11
Hercules	26,157	37	0	7	6	24	218	30	134	54	
Hermosa Beach	18,902	55	0	7	8	40	535	106	363	66	7
Hesperia	101,748	609	3	41	102	463	1,433	323	815	295	
Hidden Hills	1,680	1	0	0	0	1	9	4	4	1	
Highland	57,248	416	6	14	62	334	757	154	442	161	
Hillsborough	10,678	5	0	1	0	4	82	49	30	3	0
Hollister	44,823	137	2	22	21	92	343	34	244	65	9
Holtville	5,561	18	0	0	1	17	59	12	38	9	
Hughson	7,542	2	0	0	1	1	52	8	30	14	
Huntington Beach	194,618	494	3	68	108	315	4,364	494	3,369	501	
Huntington Park	52,507	416	5	20	212	179	1,991	374	866	751	
Huron	6,243	64	0	3	10	51	51	15	24	12	
Imperial	21,626	20	0	1	0	19	78	13	50	15	
Imperial Beach	25,933	103	2	3	25	73	274	35	161	78	0
Indian Wells	4,914	11	0	2	2	7	142	32	97	13	
Indio	91,604	308	7	28	46	227	1,525	220	965	340	
Industry	241	79	1	3	43	32	1,430	332	903	195	
Inglewood	102,879	684	17	54	293	320	2,983	312	1,569	1,102	
Irvine	311,696	234	4	35	41	154	4,611	833	3,488	290	19
Irwindale	1,410	25	2	0	6	17	287	90	143	54	3
Isleton	792	17	0	1	1	15	34	14	18	2	
Jackson	5,196	33	0	5	1	27	104	15	82	7	
Jurupa Valley	108,601	349	4	7	80	258	2,958	314	1,782	862	
Kensington	5,028	2	0	0	0	2	108	22	70	16	0
Kerman	16,304	84	0	3	11	70	245	34	170	41	
King City	13,518	65	2	4	5	54	190	37	86	67	
Kingsburg	12,879	37	1	6	5	25	247	66	140	41	
La Canada Flintridge	19,682	24	0	2	6	16	357	106	245	6	
Lafayette	25,031	25	0	1	11	13	316	41	240	35	
Laguna Beach	22,559	88	1	11	10	66	358	63	254	41	
Laguna Hills	30,610	58	0	1	14	43	420	141	214	65	1
Laguna Niguel	64,119	61	1	3	13	44	670	102	493	75	2
Laguna Woods	17,249	4	1	0	1	2	90	14	58	18	2
La Habra	62,082	262	5	19	54	184	1,234	212	884	138	7
La Habra Heights	5,434	3	0	2	0	1	57	25	30	2	
Lake Elsinore	72,730	139	0	9	34	96	1,805	254	1,214	337	
Lake Forest	85,480	104	0	11	35	58	901	124	652	125	12
Lakeport	5,171	45	0	4	5	36	133	15	101	17	2
Lake Shastina	2,537	3	0	0	0	3	13	2	8	3	
Lakewood	78,858	369	0	19	109	241	1,846	237	1,181	428	
La Mesa	60,333	184	1	10	49	124	1,256	172	883	201	19
La Mirada	45,683	81	1	7	28	45	852	146	578	128	
Lancaster	167,481	1,453	13	83	335	1,022	3,142	756	1,322	1,064	
La Palma	15,236	37	0	3	16	18	305	35	229	41	3
La Puente	36,563	116	1	5	35	75	432	87	232	113	
La Quinta	38,715	70	1	4	19	46	1,004	127	814	63	
La Verne	30,060	57	0	10	17	30	664	123	489	52	1

Table 8. Offenses Known to Law Enforcement, by Selected State and City, 2022—Continued

(Number.)

State/city	Population	Violent crime	Murder and nonnegligent manslaughter	Rape	Robbery	Aggravated assault	Property crime	Burglary	Larceny-theft	Motor vehicle theft	Arson[1]
Lawndale	30,480	133	1	10	28	94	512	79	257	176	
Lemon Grove	27,208	166	3	4	45	114	477	70	262	145	7
Lemoore	27,485	125	0	20	7	98	438	57	293	88	1
Lincoln	51,456	94	1	29	7	57	454	65	334	55	7
Lindsay	12,608	44	0	1	12	31	216	45	121	50	
Livermore	85,151	190	2	36	56	96	1,596	182	1,204	210	
Livingston	14,897	72	3	2	15	52	247	28	188	31	3
Loma Linda	25,350	71	2	7	8	54	554	127	344	83	
Lomita	19,981	93	0	6	23	64	331	45	205	81	
Lompoc	43,363	219	5	19	47	148	845	107	450	288	
Long Beach	447,528	2,455	36	198	707	1,514	11,630	2,137	6,424	3,069	213
Los Alamitos	11,615	34	0	3	9	22	331	148	111	72	0
Los Altos	29,847	20	0	3	8	9	360	100	238	22	3
Los Altos Hills	8,084	2	0	2	0	0	77	54	22	1	
Los Angeles	3,809,182	31,772	387	2,083	9,124	20,178	103,171	15,013	62,665	25,493	1,881
Los Banos	47,398	188	1	18	38	131	1,119	163	777	179	
Los Gatos	31,640	54	0	7	5	42	578	111	417	50	3
Lynwood	64,142	514	8	21	189	296	1,615	143	713	759	
Madera	69,395	320	2	33	54	231	1,122	132	748	242	27
Malibu	10,226	59	0	10	9	40	420	78	317	25	
Mammoth Lakes	7,325	29	0	6	0	23	126	21	101	4	
Manhattan Beach	33,888	65	0	14	17	34	995	138	750	107	
Manteca	87,677	234	3	25	63	143	1,655	186	1,204	265	
Marina	22,651	74	1	11	15	47	421	73	306	42	11
Martinez	36,498	106	0	18	31	57	556	78	349	129	
Marysville	12,711	92	1	13	16	62	269	44	116	109	
Maywood	24,040	135	3	5	45	82	379	95	171	113	
McFarland	14,755	81	3	10	13	55	157	21	66	70	
Mendota	12,819	78	0	6	3	69	171	31	64	76	
Menifee	109,673	318	1	33	32	252	1,505	164	1,066	275	4
Menlo Park	31,332	90	0	8	10	72	554	120	385	49	
Merced	92,191	738	6	107	154	471	2,528	381	1,722	425	133
Mill Valley	14,023	9	0	0	2	7	156	30	113	13	
Milpitas	77,790	197	2	13	71	111	2,845	353	2,123	369	
Mission Viejo	91,382	83	1	8	19	55	1,021	110	808	103	1
Modesto	219,083	1,669	10	111	292	1,256	5,264	582	3,891	791	94
Monrovia	37,104	107	0	9	32	66	904	132	667	105	8
Montague	1,232	19	0	3	0	16	22	6	10	6	
Montclair	38,203	239	3	9	61	166	1,570	306	879	385	45
Montebello	59,909	328	2	18	92	216	1,741	183	951	607	
Monterey	29,709	111	1	12	19	79	673	84	537	52	
Monterey Park	58,352	154	0	7	70	77	1,227	245	709	273	
Monte Sereno	3,307	2	0	0	0	2	37	18	16	3	0
Moorpark	35,692	17	1	1	6	9	215	22	161	32	
Moraga	16,550	30	0	4	4	22	155	42	94	19	0
Moreno Valley	214,014	791	10	22	239	520	4,367	638	2,890	839	
Morgan Hill	45,134	144	1	20	14	109	656	106	424	126	1
Morro Bay	10,807	55	1	3	2	49	150	23	118	9	
Mountain View	80,588	223	1	22	49	151	2,386	400	1,804	182	29
Mount Shasta	3,257	20	0	2	0	18	26	6	14	6	
Murrieta	114,655	314	1	28	44	241	1,428	241	961	226	10
Napa	78,586	255	2	24	44	185	1,162	151	857	154	
National City	55,676	342	7	21	101	213	1,244	184	763	297	11
Needles	4,880	91	0	10	7	74	114	40	60	14	
Newark	46,861	150	4	19	48	79	2,048	389	1,318	341	5
Newman	12,310	26	0	6	3	17	101	14	64	23	
Newport Beach	84,254	158	0	22	46	90	1,749	359	1,248	142	
Norco	26,205	53	0	2	9	42	732	121	528	83	
Norwalk	98,259	379	3	19	111	246	1,838	269	1,011	558	17
Novato	52,412	126	2	12	14	98	850	98	556	196	11
Oakdale	23,284	85	0	14	7	64	325	40	249	36	
Oakland	428,374	6,516	121	330	2,736	3,329	27,737	2,693	17,347	7,697	191
Oakley	44,061	101	2	9	10	80	505	71	323	111	
Oceanside	171,844	826	8	51	173	594	3,448	495	2,469	484	42
Ojai	7,566	4	0	1	0	3	72	15	53	4	
Ontario	180,004	582	7	104	150	321	3,833	653	2,254	926	35
Orange Cove	9,593	34	0	1	2	31	42	5	29	8	
Orinda	19,441	11	0	1	7	3	125	28	83	14	
Orland	8,346	21	0	3	3	15	96	9	61	26	
Oroville	19,868	209	3	37	31	138	712	101	408	203	17
Pacifica	35,742	88	0	15	10	63	532	86	385	61	
Pacific Grove	14,902	13	0	0	1	12	116	13	100	3	0
Palmdale	162,316	904	18	38	198	650	2,516	443	1,441	632	
Palm Desert	51,918	182	2	9	32	139	2,024	303	1,477	244	
Palm Springs	45,463	318	5	33	67	213	2,253	394	1,430	429	
Palo Alto	64,922	134	0	22	45	67	1,945	147	1,688	110	16
Palos Verdes Estates	12,767	4	0	0	1	3	138	48	79	11	0
Paradise	5,860	21	0	4	0	17	80	22	45	13	
Paramount	51,405	309	4	20	111	174	1,406	183	731	492	
Parlier	14,760	110	1	5	12	92	170	24	98	48	
Pasadena	133,312	511	7	28	117	359	3,049	543	2,172	334	33
Paso Robles	31,966	98	0	13	14	71	524	42	433	49	
Patterson	23,836	43	1	5	10	27	349	58	207	84	

Table 8. Offenses Known to Law Enforcement, by Selected State and City, 2022—Continued

(Number.)

State/city	Population	Violent crime	Murder and nonnegligent manslaughter	Rape	Robbery	Aggravated assault	Property crime	Burglary	Larceny-theft	Motor vehicle theft	Arson[1]
Perris	80,784	244	5	6	73	160	2,062	194	1,359	509	
Petaluma	59,129	302	2	37	47	216	714	89	521	104	
Pico Rivera	59,557	293	4	22	79	188	1,423	285	689	449	
Piedmont	10,853	22	0	5	5	12	410	39	322	49	
Pinole	18,651	72	1	9	22	40	539	50	417	72	
Pismo Beach	8,015	95	0	3	8	84	293	31	245	17	
Pittsburg	76,488	456	2	41	112	301	1,673	234	927	512	
Placentia	50,764	118	0	2	14	102	905	301	475	129	3
Placerville	10,951	61	1	4	9	47	212	31	161	20	6
Pleasant Hill	34,060	106	0	5	32	69	1,628	177	1,308	143	
Pleasanton	76,350	84	0	13	18	53	1,350	144	1,108	98	
Pomona	145,600	860	14	81	244	521	4,393	774	2,640	979	
Porterville	62,865	305	6	27	60	212	1,307	178	782	347	5
Port Hueneme	21,545	57	0	8	11	38	392	35	297	60	
Poway	48,011	83	0	3	18	62	459	73	343	43	2
Rancho Cordova	81,041	382	4	23	92	263	1,809	333	1,081	395	
Rancho Cucamonga	175,714	651	1	39	110	501	3,546	721	2,545	280	
Rancho Mirage	17,598	58	1	2	8	47	731	142	496	93	
Rancho Palos Verdes	40,403	52	0	4	6	42	407	87	284	36	
Rancho Santa Margarita	46,889	18	0	1	4	13	220	26	176	18	3
Red Bluff	14,529	133	1	19	29	84	722	81	515	126	43
Redlands	73,554	206	1	31	81	93	2,265	292	1,713	260	7
Redondo Beach	68,332	282	0	11	78	193	1,561	280	1,108	173	
Redwood City	79,182	312	2	41	99	170	1,578	234	1,079	265	
Reedley	25,269	148	3	11	12	122	352	88	199	65	
Rialto	104,589	525	3	61	152	309	3,036	384	2,137	515	
Richmond	115,043	1,005	17	24	240	724	3,117	252	1,830	1,035	33
Ridgecrest	28,290	162	2	16	22	122	390	109	218	63	5
Rio Dell	3,382	20	0	3	2	15	76	9	59	8	1
Rio Vista	10,352	36	0	2	1	33	90	10	68	12	
Ripon	16,789	25	0	6	6	13	196	14	167	15	
Riverbank	24,834	50	1	2	21	26	356	56	268	32	
Riverside	319,889	1,652	17	138	434	1,063	10,366	1,563	7,058	1,745	171
Rocklin	74,168	90	1	15	19	55	942	102	768	72	9
Rohnert Park	44,479	174	0	34	20	120	694	111	479	104	
Rolling Hills	1,667	0	0	0	0	0	8	4	4	0	
Rolling Hills Estates	8,041	9	0	1	4	4	135	48	85	2	
Rosemead	49,368	218	0	21	77	120	1,436	380	779	277	
Roseville	155,448	254	2	38	89	125	2,930	285	2,372	273	
Ross	2,320	0	0	0	0	0	16	2	13	1	
Sacramento	526,671	4,749	54	186	1,243	3,266	16,681	2,769	10,328	3,584	204
Salinas	162,187	845	13	91	245	496	2,720	340	1,695	685	
San Bernardino	222,623	2,640	72	112	675	1,781	6,578	1,244	3,608	1,726	91
San Bruno	40,817	118	1	14	40	63	1,054	128	770	156	
San Clemente	63,449	118	0	7	23	88	778	112	528	138	3
Sand City	335	8	0	1	3	4	74	3	69	2	0
San Diego	1,377,838	5,932	53	410	1,288	4,181	25,044	3,290	15,106	6,648	174
San Dimas	33,339	92	0	16	16	60	776	143	549	84	
San Fernando	23,501	93	1	3	36	53	417	61	260	96	
San Francisco	764,693	5,323	55	308	2,371	2,589	47,759	5,947	35,530	6,282	344
Sanger	26,806	143	1	9	15	118	313	26	250	37	
San Jacinto	56,521	111	2	4	49	56	1,222	194	828	200	
San Jose	956,814	5,046	35	894	1,264	2,853	25,363	3,884	15,010	6,469	176
San Juan Capistrano	34,698	72	1	1	10	60	432	98	253	81	2
San Leandro	86,465	499	4	13	303	179	4,254	480	2,499	1,275	
San Luis Obispo	47,990	267	0	38	40	189	1,745	254	1,372	119	
San Marcos	94,879	206	0	7	62	137	1,007	185	644	178	5
San Marino	12,015	9	0	0	2	7	173	65	88	20	1
San Mateo	99,184	302	1	30	63	208	2,330	536	1,451	343	
San Pablo	31,498	232	0	12	65	155	763	78	331	354	
San Rafael	60,386	323	1	49	78	195	1,822	183	1,085	554	24
San Ramon	87,226	57	0	10	16	31	807	117	621	69	
Santa Barbara	87,817	400	3	45	80	272	1,795	226	1,400	169	
Santa Clara	126,877	396	1	35	86	274	4,564	646	3,394	524	22
Santa Clarita	220,765	360	0	40	89	231	2,409	361	1,687	361	
Santa Cruz	61,650	447	1	38	122	286	2,226	253	1,782	191	40
Santa Fe Springs	18,282	122	3	9	43	67	1,329	175	820	334	
Santa Maria	109,518	712	10	74	209	419	3,039	393	1,504	1,142	33
Santa Monica	89,527	765	3	43	228	491	4,057	665	2,823	569	67
Santa Paula	30,851	102	0	5	19	78	342	68	225	49	9
Santa Rosa	175,999	597	10	130	98	359	2,392	439	1,561	392	35
Santee	59,351	154	1	10	31	112	534	74	387	73	10
Saratoga	29,306	12	0	3	5	4	239	109	123	7	
Sausalito	7,152	8	0	0	0	8	197	32	147	18	
Scotts Valley	12,196	34	0	11	3	20	169	33	125	11	0
Seal Beach	24,665	80	0	6	10	64	603	122	428	53	4
Seaside	31,864	134	0	10	21	103	394	48	293	53	3
Sebastopol	7,393	33	0	2	4	27	126	18	101	7	
Selma	24,595	144	0	7	19	118	629	103	424	102	
Shafter	21,304	84	0	6	10	68	500	86	299	115	
Sierra Madre	10,778	10	0	0	2	8	98	34	57	7	0
Signal Hill	11,312	83	0	1	27	55	699	97	397	205	
Simi Valley	125,585	119	2	22	17	78	1,069	174	791	104	

Table 8. Offenses Known to Law Enforcement, by Selected State and City, 2022—Continued

(Number.)

State/city	Population	Violent crime	Murder and nonnegligent manslaughter	Rape	Robbery	Aggravated assault	Property crime	Burglary	Larceny-theft	Motor vehicle theft	Arson[1]
Solana Beach	12,778	20	0	1	4	15	234	42	166	26	0
Soledad	24,811	75	3	5	18	49	185	32	125	28	1
Solvang	5,985	12	0	2	1	9	70	13	51	6	
Sonora	5,025	41	0	7	2	32	220	31	166	23	
South El Monte	19,523	126	1	5	35	85	868	295	377	196	
South Gate	89,698	493	5	25	200	263	2,943	332	1,710	901	
South Lake Tahoe	21,525	135	0	11	20	104	345	54	233	58	
South Pasadena	25,744	46	1	3	8	34	474	91	317	66	
South San Francisco	62,427	246	2	14	48	182	1,764	223	1,304	237	
Stallion Springs	2,465	3	0	0	0	3	10	4	5	1	
Stanton	38,038	153	2	5	48	98	801	162	521	118	6
St. Helena	5,347	15	0	8	1	6	72	8	57	7	
Stockton	323,501	3,742	48	178	980	2,536	8,878	1,760	5,636	1,482	201
Suisun City	28,917	103	1	21	16	65	476	32	379	65	10
Sunnyvale	148,739	326	0	45	83	198	3,654	621	2,633	400	30
Susanville	16,493	81	2	2	10	67	198	36	140	22	4
Sutter Creek	2,738	3	0	1	0	2	45	2	34	9	
Taft	8,674	68	0	1	11	56	278	30	201	47	
Tehachapi	13,212	61	0	6	13	42	292	44	190	58	
Temecula	111,611	175	1	12	65	97	2,651	438	1,903	310	
Temple City	35,103	70	2	2	23	43	517	185	285	47	
Thousand Oaks	124,862	72	1	9	27	35	1,381	158	1,118	105	
Tiburon	8,997	4	0	2	0	2	67	16	46	5	
Torrance	140,499	372	2	33	141	196	3,709	466	2,519	724	18
Tracy	97,219	289	2	22	58	207	1,474	152	1,112	210	16
Truckee	17,486	102	0	3	5	94	141	34	79	28	4
Tulare	72,303	434	9	41	87	297	1,535	250	809	476	20
Tulelake	903	2	0	2	0	0	2	1	1	0	
Turlock	72,753	418	4	40	106	268	2,087	278	1,560	249	49
Tustin	78,841	252	0	21	65	166	1,960	229	1,493	238	4
Twentynine Palms	27,463	150	0	9	10	131	201	77	88	36	
Ukiah	16,764	99	2	12	20	65	226	68	101	57	
Upland	79,430	275	5	21	73	176	1,626	340	1,050	236	13
Vacaville	103,486	325	1	45	64	215	1,920	221	1,493	206	
Vallejo	123,940	1,207	22	90	361	734	5,245	904	3,213	1,128	49
Ventura	109,439	388	1	29	70	288	2,391	348	1,839	204	
Vernon	212	43	0	1	17	25	738	114	450	174	7
Victorville	137,169	1,290	17	68	218	987	2,486	578	1,366	542	51
Villa Park	5,712	2	0	0	0	2	51	18	30	3	0
Visalia	144,137	716	9	71	130	506	3,421	390	2,421	610	134
Vista	98,802	378	1	16	81	280	1,454	289	852	313	9
Walnut	27,253	35	1	3	10	21	435	152	240	43	
Waterford	9,183	20	0	0	7	13	71	11	48	12	
Watsonville	51,517	302	1	31	56	214	959	137	611	211	
Weed	2,888	29	0	7	3	19	56	17	34	5	
West Covina	104,739	424	3	35	119	267	2,417	343	1,666	408	14
West Hollywood	34,185	324	0	20	124	180	2,257	322	1,757	178	
Westlake Village	7,678	10	0	0	3	7	144	41	93	10	
Westminster	89,490	355	4	18	138	195	2,660	477	1,725	458	
West Sacramento	53,643	93	1	9	28	55	537	58	404	75	
Wheatland	3,804	0	0	0	0	0	39	7	26	6	
Wildomar	37,463	44	0	5	8	31	678	99	451	128	
Williams	5,655	22	0	2	0	20	83	11	60	12	2
Willits	4,963	2	0	0	0	2	2	1	0	1	
Winters	7,531	5	0	1	2	2	73	3	59	11	
Woodlake	7,707	26	0	0	0	26	53	8	36	9	
Woodland	61,883	220	1	26	28	165	1,361	216	949	196	35
Yorba Linda	67,550	36	0	1	9	26	673	158	441	74	0
Yountville	3,349	16	0	2	1	13	38	2	33	3	
Yreka	7,865	118	0	5	0	113	370	35	278	57	
Yuba City	69,122	380	2	46	63	269	1,565	187	1,135	243	9
Yucaipa	54,873	190	1	13	21	155	714	154	447	113	
Yucca Valley	21,890	133	1	6	12	114	265	66	139	60	
COLORADO											
Alamosa	9,874	76	4	13	5	54	609	63	509	37	11
Arvada	122,403	317	1	36	57	223	3,712	436	2,464	812	24
Aspen	6,910	14	0	6	0	8	215	14	195	6	0
Ault	2,913	2	0	0	0	2	6	2	2	2	1
Aurora	392,134	4,225	54	296	827	3,048	16,585	1,821	7,959	6,805	113
Avon	5,968	23	0	3	1	19	87	11	69	7	0
Basalt	4,163	2	0	0	0	2	39	2	36	1	0
Bayfield	2,929	5	0	3	0	2	40	6	25	9	0
Black Hawk	129	8	0	2	4	2	311	5	277	29	0
Boulder	103,099	383	7	51	49	276	3,093	471	2,298	324	25
Breckenridge	4,953	14	0	9	1	4	148	12	129	7	1
Brighton	41,205	170	3	38	5	124	1,209	95	833	281	12
Broomfield	76,137	112	3	31	12	66	1,993	208	1,395	390	3
Buena Vista	3,103	0	0	0	0	0	30	1	27	2	1
Burlington	3,043	3	0	0	0	3	44	11	28	5	0
Canon City	17,582	83	1	7	12	63	498	57	398	43	10
Carbondale	6,528	15	0	4	0	11	35	3	30	2	2
Castle Rock	79,102	25	3	5	3	14	920	63	795	62	6

Table 8. Offenses Known to Law Enforcement, by Selected State and City, 2022—Continued

(Number.)

State/city	Population	Violent crime	Murder and nonnegligent manslaughter	Rape	Robbery	Aggravated assault	Property crime	Burglary	Larceny-theft	Motor vehicle theft	Arson[1]
Centennial	105,849	209	1	14	16	178	2,233	324	1,437	472	14
Center	1,933	8	0	1	0	7	30	3	23	4	0
Cherry Hills Village	6,275	1	0	1	0	0	66	12	37	17	0
Colorado Springs	487,728	3,135	45	446	365	2,279	16,583	2,686	11,164	2,733	207
Commerce City	65,817	467	6	60	61	340	2,502	267	1,389	846	15
Cortez	8,985	46	2	11	5	28	266	29	215	22	8
Craig	8,910	17	0	0	0	17	138	16	106	16	0
Crested Butte	1,696	4	0	0	0	4	8	1	6	1	0
Cripple Creek	1,146	1	0	0	0	1	59	1	56	2	0
Dacono	6,635	5	0	3	1	1	75	7	53	15	0
Del Norte	1,442	0	0	0	0	0	5	3	1	1	0
Delta	9,373	11	0	2	0	9	351	51	256	44	3
Denver	705,264	7,545	90	756	1,301	5,398	45,336	5,171	24,964	15,201	195
Dillon	1,045	6	0	1	0	5	18	3	13	2	0
Eagle	7,614	11	0	2	0	9	60	9	47	4	0
Eaton	5,898	10	0	2	0	8	55	5	39	11	0
Edgewater	4,892	17	0	2	5	10	416	19	318	79	0
Elizabeth	2,344	3	0	1	0	2	14	0	11	3	0
Englewood	33,452	272	4	37	45	186	2,392	323	1,441	628	20
Erie	32,832	15	0	7	0	8	340	52	244	44	2
Estes Park	5,839	8	0	0	0	8	50	10	36	4	1
Evans	22,333	62	0	22	9	31	602	66	340	196	1
Fairplay	732	2	0	1	0	1	24	7	15	2	0
Federal Heights	13,987	118	0	17	20	81	496	61	249	186	6
Florence	3,990	5	0	0	0	5	13	1	8	4	0
Fort Collins	168,045	540	2	56	46	436	4,379	411	3,493	475	25
Fort Lupton	8,539	55	0	16	5	34	258	31	148	79	0
Fort Morgan	11,331	50	0	11	1	38	361	63	270	28	3
Fountain	29,447	101	1	21	23	56	620	96	438	86	10
Frisco	2,858	7	0	1	1	5	51	7	39	5	0
Fruita	13,632	32	0	17	2	13	141	21	114	6	6
Glendale	4,502	84	1	14	9	60	944	105	595	244	6
Glenwood Springs	10,664	37	0	13	4	20	393	53	317	23	0
Golden	19,638	41	0	2	3	36	797	112	584	101	6
Granada	451	3	0	1	0	2	6	2	3	1	0
Granby	2,176	3	0	1	0	2	25	3	22	0	0
Grand Junction	68,126	346	4	55	28	259	2,140	274	1,677	189	13
Greeley	109,258	636	8	59	94	475	3,455	375	2,079	1,001	30
Greenwood Village	15,351	68	0	15	13	40	1,194	152	800	242	5
Gunnison	6,914	22	0	2	0	20	132	15	109	8	1
Gypsum	8,994	9	0	2	0	7	55	5	43	7	0
Hayden	1,993	1	0	0	0	1	38	9	26	3	0
Holyoke	2,319	3	0	1	0	2	3	3	0	0	0
Hudson	1,624	8	0	3	0	5	52	7	36	9	0
Hugo	790	1	0	1	0	0	8	1	7	0	0
Idaho Springs	1,766	7	0	6	0	1	73	11	55	7	0
Ignacio	863	2	0	0	0	2	7	2	4	1	0
Johnstown	19,093	46	0	9	1	36	632	15	541	76	0
Kersey	1,489	2	0	1	0	1	31	1	14	16	0
Kremmling	1,501	4	0	2	0	2	25	16	7	2	0
Lafayette	31,204	64	1	19	7	37	829	98	616	115	3
La Junta	7,264	28	3	10	1	14	365	64	263	38	3
Lakewood	157,068	1,278	12	111	286	869	8,362	1,089	5,159	2,114	66
La Salle	2,326	5	0	4	0	1	49	2	36	11	0
Limon	2,047	1	0	0	0	1	3	0	1	2	0
Littleton	44,821	110	1	31	22	56	1,457	269	881	307	8
Lone Tree	14,204	68	2	8	24	34	1,563	80	1,402	81	9
Longmont	101,159	448	8	125	29	286	2,855	319	2,138	398	35
Louisville	20,587	36	0	7	1	28	496	75	361	60	5
Loveland	77,770	259	5	49	25	180	2,071	228	1,608	235	14
Manitou Springs	4,782	14	0	2	0	12	102	28	62	12	7
Meeker	2,310	2	0	1	0	1	21	4	13	4	0
Milliken	8,948	2	0	1	0	1	37	1	26	10	0
Monte Vista	4,144	15	0	2	1	12	166	30	121	15	0
Montrose	20,944	29	0	2	1	26	555	47	466	42	2
Monument	11,300	32	0	7	14	11	224	20	189	15	0
Mountain View	531	3	0	0	1	2	9	2	4	3	0
Mountain Village	1,269	0	0	0	0	0	16	1	15	0	0
Mount Crested Butte	998	5	0	0	0	5	7	0	7	0	0
Northglenn	36,634	214	7	31	29	147	1,555	152	992	411	26
Palisade	2,600	0	0	0	0	0	35	6	27	2	1
Parker	61,865	139	2	34	5	98	1,060	156	752	152	9
Platteville	3,930	3	0	2	1	0	45	4	31	10	0
Pueblo	112,618	1,825	29	183	362	1,251	7,196	1,336	4,154	1,706	85
Rangely	2,283	2	0	0	0	2	1	0	1	0	0
Rifle	10,612	40	0	15	1	24	208	23	154	31	2
Rocky Ford	3,837	3	0	0	0	3	22	4	15	3	0
Salida	5,912	14	0	1	0	13	46	7	36	3	0
Severance	11,574	12	0	4	0	8	20	1	12	7	1
Sheridan	5,964	54	0	4	16	34	609	59	390	160	5
Silt	3,583	4	0	2	0	2	14	1	12	1	0
Silverthorne	4,870	6	0	1	2	3	92	3	81	8	0
Steamboat Springs	13,593	32	0	15	1	16	208	25	171	12	1

Table 8. Offenses Known to Law Enforcement, by Selected State and City, 2022—Continued
(Number.)

State/city	Population	Violent crime	Murder and nonnegligent manslaughter	Rape	Robbery	Aggravated assault	Property crime	Burglary	Larceny-theft	Motor vehicle theft	Arson[1]
Sterling	13,713	40	0	8	2	30	368	60	284	24	4
Thornton	143,055	408	3	137	92	176	4,982	375	3,407	1,200	33
Timnath	9,063	6	0	2	0	4	113	5	105	3	1
Trinidad	8,350	69	0	6	1	62	304	83	200	21	3
Vail	4,657	16	0	2	3	11	186	13	165	8	0
Westminster	112,844	374	2	48	92	232	5,042	448	3,128	1,466	31
Wheat Ridge	33,104	130	0	17	30	83	1,681	166	1,118	397	15
Windsor	38,498	11	0	0	0	11	221	15	165	41	3
Woodland Park	8,025	15	0	3	0	12	121	7	102	12	3
Wray	2,298	4	0	1	0	3	4	0	4	0	0
CONNECTICUT											
Ansonia	18,750	23	1	5	9	8	371	14	318	39	0
Avon	18,806	1	0	0	0	1	131	9	100	22	0
Berlin	20,109	10	0	2	4	4	385	32	329	24	1
Bethel	20,728	5	0	2	1	2	147	12	123	12	2
Bloomfield	21,461	18	0	1	8	9	647	34	577	36	2
Branford	28,138	24	1	12	6	5	480	18	426	36	1
Bridgeport	148,395	606	15	52	277	262	1,843	303	965	575	9
Bristol	60,657	48	4	7	16	21	796	118	557	121	0
Brookfield	17,492	10	0	0	3	7	151	10	129	12	0
Canton	10,068	2	0	0	1	1	47	6	40	1	0
Cheshire	28,612	3	0	0	1	2	221	11	180	30	0
Clinton	13,566	15	0	4	4	7	249	12	227	10	0
Coventry	12,252	4	0	2	0	2	66	3	53	10	0
Cromwell	14,360	10	0	2	2	6	444	28	382	34	0
Danbury	87,164	120	4	19	23	74	1,138	106	931	101	6
Darien	21,549	6	0	0	2	4	291	30	220	41	0
Derby	12,243	44	0	0	11	33	373	30	267	76	1
East Hampton	12,943	0	0	0	0	0	97	6	84	7	0
East Hartford	50,579	96	3	14	32	47	1,352	89	1,065	198	4
East Haven	27,725	48	1	6	13	28	721	34	631	56	1
East Lyme	18,984	9	0	1	0	8	69	7	57	5	0
Easton	7,613	0	0	0	0	0	56	4	46	6	0
East Windsor	11,148	14	0	0	5	9	239	10	212	17	1
Enfield	41,912	44	1	2	5	36	532	33	453	46	0
Fairfield	62,270	23	1	1	8	13	1,096	76	931	89	2
Farmington	26,618	17	1	4	7	5	485	23	425	37	0
Glastonbury	35,034	13	0	2	4	7	475	29	418	28	1
Granby	11,011	1	0	1	0	0	44	5	38	1	0
Greenwich	63,631	14	0	4	9	1	685	60	489	136	0
Groton Long Point	515	0	0	0	0	0	0	0	0	0	0
Groton Town	28,608	20	0	9	2	9	290	15	263	12	0
Guilford	22,022	10	0	3	3	4	281	19	250	12	2
Hamden	60,831	218	5	4	50	159	1,536	111	1,193	232	3
Hartford	120,196	685	37	22	128	498	2,978	347	2,011	620	36
Ledyard	15,340	6	0	1	2	3	53	6	40	7	0
Madison	17,581	2	0	0	0	2	84	3	74	7	0
Manchester	59,293	97	0	21	26	50	1,533	103	1,308	122	4
Meriden	60,332	176	1	38	36	101	1,415	118	1,042	255	7
Middlebury	7,793	0	0	0	0	0	46	6	30	10	0
Middletown	47,256	48	0	7	9	32	771	46	628	97	1
Milford	52,694	43	2	3	26	12	1,234	74	1,035	125	2
Monroe	18,772	4	0	3	1	0	79	13	58	8	0
Naugatuck	31,356	25	1	5	7	12	376	42	289	45	1
New Britain	73,621	267	3	40	49	175	1,518	178	1,103	237	15
New Canaan	20,924	1	0	1	0	0	172	18	139	15	0
New Haven	136,205	756	15	48	243	450	4,224	395	3,049	780	21
Newington	30,277	41	0	6	20	15	759	67	642	50	2
New London	27,667	66	2	20	25	19	467	63	328	76	8
New Milford	28,252	8	0	1	3	4	184	18	153	13	0
Newtown	27,918	7	0	3	2	2	120	13	98	9	1
North Branford	13,474	2	0	0	2	0	119	7	99	13	0
North Haven	24,119	18	0	2	12	4	709	59	580	70	1
Norwalk	91,414	113	1	10	26	76	1,582	76	1,349	157	1
Norwich	40,096	121	2	33	22	64	667	126	483	58	8
Old Saybrook	10,613	11	1	2	1	7	164	10	142	12	0
Orange	14,239	12	0	0	10	2	589	17	549	23	0
Plainville	17,413	20	0	4	9	7	337	21	280	36	1
Plymouth	11,655	2	0	0	1	1	64	11	43	10	0
Portland	9,499	4	0	0	1	3	40	2	31	7	0
Putnam	9,244	12	0	6	2	4	90	10	78	2	0
Redding	8,732	2	0	0	1	1	18	0	17	1	0
Ridgefield	25,048	0	0	0	0	0	35	2	23	10	0
Rocky Hill	20,692	29	0	2	4	23	380	41	309	30	1
Seymour	16,634	13	1	2	2	8	130	17	96	17	0
Shelton	42,189	21	1	6	5	9	387	61	255	71	0
Simsbury	25,135	7	0	3	2	2	149	9	126	14	0
Southington	43,564	26	1	8	13	4	799	96	637	66	1
South Windsor	26,695	15	0	7	1	7	415	58	332	25	0
Stamford	136,936	264	2	24	74	164	1,601	144	1,285	172	7
Stonington	18,549	13	0	2	2	9	157	15	136	6	0
Stratford	52,320	59	0	10	28	21	973	41	798	134	2

Table 8. Offenses Known to Law Enforcement, by Selected State and City, 2022—Continued

(Number.)

State/city	Population	Violent crime	Murder and nonnegligent manslaughter	Rape	Robbery	Aggravated assault	Property crime	Burglary	Larceny-theft	Motor vehicle theft	Arson[1]
Suffield	15,890	8	0	4	0	4	80	12	56	12	0
Thomaston	7,449	1	0	1	0	0	56	4	50	2	0
Torrington	35,302	19	0	3	6	10	372	31	319	22	2
Trumbull	37,192	22	0	5	11	6	699	40	627	32	0
Vernon	30,584	14	0	2	6	6	381	32	317	32	0
Wallingford	44,099	8	0	0	6	2	281	14	226	41	1
Waterbury	113,464	442	16	46	160	220	3,261	356	2,302	603	13
Waterford	19,565	5	0	1	2	2	212	14	186	12	2
Watertown	22,122	9	0	3	6	0	317	22	257	38	0
West Hartford	63,934	38	0	2	27	9	1,701	105	1,519	77	0
West Haven	55,133	67	0	7	35	25	1,142	62	902	178	2
Weston	10,350	0	0	0	0	0	22	1	12	9	0
Westport	27,484	4	0	0	0	4	444	39	344	61	0
Wethersfield	27,038	26	1	3	15	7	405	43	307	55	0
Willimantic	17,777	11	0	5	3	3	156	6	128	22	1
Wilton	18,469	5	0	0	1	4	122	16	99	7	1
Winchester	10,199	3	0	2	0	1	67	5	50	12	1
Windsor	29,326	18	0	2	7	9	482	9	438	35	3
Windsor Locks	12,497	7	0	0	5	2	161	10	139	12	0
Wolcott	16,180	4	0	0	2	2	190	21	144	25	0
Woodbridge	9,020	1	0	0	1	0	109	14	80	15	1
DELAWARE											
Bethany Beach	1,032	3	0	1	0	2	85	3	82	0	0
Blades	1,270	11	0	0	3	8	35	5	29	1	0
Bridgeville	2,761	14	0	0	0	14	47	6	35	6	0
Camden	4,852	21	1	1	2	17	241	16	212	13	0
Cheswold	1,989	7	0	0	0	7	22	3	16	3	0
Clayton	4,003	3	0	1	0	2	30	5	25	0	0
Dagsboro	939	3	0	0	0	3	24	4	19	1	0
Delaware City	1,881	2	0	0	0	2	18	2	16	0	0
Delmar	2,178	11	0	1	2	8	43	4	36	3	0
Dewey Beach	384	15	0	1	0	14	34	2	29	3	0
Dover	38,438	315	3	24	22	266	1,741	26	1,541	174	2
Ellendale	530	0	0	0	0	0	7	2	5	0	0
Elsmere	6,111	6	0	0	1	5	98	21	59	18	0
Felton	1,331	4	0	0	0	4	24	2	21	1	0
Fenwick Island	366	0	0	0	0	0	23	3	19	1	0
Georgetown	7,667	65	3	2	24	36	277	43	220	14	0
Greenwood	1,062	0	0	0	0	0	13	2	11	0	0
Harrington	3,785	24	0	2	1	21	81	11	65	5	0
Laurel	4,178	69	0	1	7	61	161	12	133	16	0
Lewes	3,533	9	0	2	0	7	37	3	33	1	0
Middletown	25,044	92	0	4	9	79	455	23	411	21	0
Milford	13,326	90	2	14	19	55	479	35	413	31	0
Millsboro	7,386	28	0	3	5	20	180	14	160	6	0
Milton	3,548	4	0	1	0	3	16	0	16	0	0
Newark	31,015	85	0	11	13	61	656	48	569	39	2
New Castle	5,465	27	0	0	4	23	195	13	168	14	0
Newport	885	7	0	0	0	7	35	5	30	0	0
Ocean View	2,851	1	0	0	0	1	18	6	12	0	0
Rehoboth Beach	1,190	13	0	2	1	10	122	5	114	3	0
Seaford	8,526	82	1	2	10	69	533	53	456	24	0
Selbyville	3,104	14	0	0	0	14	52	8	43	1	0
Smyrna	13,361	69	0	4	2	63	287	46	229	12	0
South Bethany	490	1	0	0	0	1	4	0	4	0	0
Wilmington	70,625	848	18	12	216	602	2,382	418	1,566	398	2
Wyoming	1,906	9	1	2	0	6	18	6	10	2	0
DISTRICT OF COLUMBIA											
Washington	671,803	5,003	197	275	2,175	2,356	23,408	1,350	18,265	3,793	0
FLORIDA[2]											
Altamonte Springs	44,833	177	3	19	28	127	1,030	105	854	71	0
Apopka	56,125	313	0	39	82	192	1,579	281	1,178	120	0
Arcadia	7,588	41	1	3	3	34	369	305	54	10	1
Astatula	1,973	5	0	0	0	5	9	7	0	2	0
Atlantic Beach	13,189	22	0	5	1	16	158	16	135	7	1
Auburndale	19,208	60	0	8	12	40	464	91	351	22	1
Aventura	38,484	64	0	2	23	39	1,670	145	1,525	0	0
Bartow	19,634	83	2	5	5	71	357	44	277	36	3
Bay Harbor Islands	5,644	3	0	1	1	1	41	5	30	6	0
Belle Glade	16,723	219	6	19	17	177	400	64	288	48	7
Blountstown	2,253	7	0	0	1	6	48	13	33	2	0
Bonifay	2,804	4	0	0	0	4	10	3	4	3	0
Bowling Green	2,478	9	0	5	0	4	22	4	10	8	0
Bradenton	56,316	255	3	21	38	193	1,020	93	927	0	1
Bradenton Beach	923	0	0	0	0	0	23	6	15	2	0
Brooksville	9,299	57	0	3	8	46	298	13	278	7	1
Casselberry	29,255	92	4	8	19	61	770	60	669	41	3
Chattahoochee	3,324	7	0	0	0	7	46	2	24	20	0
Clearwater	116,303	460	4	84	59	313	2,209	244	1,841	124	8
Clermont	45,785	71	0	16	8	47	572	40	480	52	0

Table 8. Offenses Known to Law Enforcement, by Selected State and City, 2022—Continued

(Number.)

State/city	Population	Violent crime	Murder and nonnegligent manslaughter	Rape	Robbery	Aggravated assault	Property crime	Burglary	Larceny-theft	Motor vehicle theft	Arson[1]
Cocoa	19,618	213	0	5	34	174	941	105	777	59	1
Crescent City	1,681	4	0	0	1	3	34	7	23	4	0
Cross City	1,774	19	1	1	2	15	31	18	12	1	1
Davenport	12,393	6	0	0	0	6	81	26	49	6	0
Daytona Beach	77,130	716	13	55	65	583	2,063	259	1,560	244	1
Daytona Beach Shores	5,251	11	0	0	4	7	128	19	99	10	0
DeFuniak Springs	6,620	35	0	3	2	30	153	18	118	17	2
DeLand	39,924	153	3	3	20	127	719	84	573	62	0
Doral	75,838	121	0	9	18	94	1,302	68	1,234	0	0
Dunnellon	1,991	10	0	0	0	10	69	15	48	6	0
Edgewood	2,641	7	0	2	0	5	65	11	47	7	0
Fellsmere	4,978	11	0	1	3	7	50	8	38	4	0
Flagler Beach	5,361	3	0	2	0	1	33	3	28	2	0
Fort Pierce	48,529	264	8	19	42	195	902	76	717	109	6
Golden Beach	935	0	0	0	0	0	12	6	0	6	0
Greenacres City	43,534	140	5	19	21	95	597	39	515	43	1
Gulf Stream	950	0	0	0	0	0	13	0	10	3	0
Haines City	31,143	41	2	1	8	30	308	41	233	34	0
Hialeah Gardens	22,091	60	0	2	4	54	396	39	283	74	2
Hillsboro Beach	1,937	0	0	0	0	0	12	2	9	1	0
Holly Hill	13,040	40	0	1	2	37	194	27	141	26	0
Holmes Beach	3,058	4	0	0	0	4	33	1	29	3	0
Homestead	80,633	753	5	30	205	513	1,836	180	1,520	136	4
Indian Creek Village	81	0	0	0	0	0	0	0	0	0	0
Indian Harbour Beach	8,950	8	0	1	0	7	68	5	57	6	0
Indian River Shores	4,421	1	0	0	0	1	17	2	14	1	0
Jupiter Island	842	0	0	0	0	0	3	1	2	0	0
Key West	26,169	125	1	20	8	96	601	56	482	63	0
Kissimmee	79,715	326	3	36	55	232	1,351	180	1,171	0	5
Lake Alfred	6,613	6	0	0	0	6	63	13	43	7	0
Lake Hamilton	1,571	3	0	0	0	3	38	10	24	4	0
Lake Helen	2,867	6	0	1	0	5	15	3	12	0	0
Lake Mary	16,469	21	0	2	5	14	199	35	155	9	0
Lake Park	8,908	59	0	2	16	41	540	24	479	37	1
Lake Wales	16,793	101	0	9	10	82	433	74	332	27	0
Lake Worth	39,844	276	2	29	90	155	907	102	702	103	2
Largo	82,167	297	2	50	32	213	1,879	98	1,781	0	7
Lighthouse Point	10,283	8	0	2	0	6	143	9	112	22	0
Longboat Key	7,648	4	0	2	0	2	58	3	54	1	0
Longwood	14,999	50	1	8	12	29	304	35	234	35	1
Loxatachee Groves	3,425	10	0	2	2	6	73	6	55	12	1
Maitland	18,471	32	0	4	3	25	328	50	243	35	0
Manalapan	415	0	0	0	0	0	9	0	7	2	0
Mangonia Park	2,112	39	0	3	7	29	141	13	112	16	1
Marco Island	16,137	14	0	3	0	11	84	1	77	6	0
Marianna	6,253	74	0	6	3	65	167	40	111	16	2
Mascotte	7,972	33	0	6	4	23	90	30	53	7	0
Melbourne Beach	3,231	2	0	0	0	2	25	4	19	2	0
Miami Beach	79,031	849	5	109	243	492	6,763	497	5,848	418	14
Milton	10,755	13	0	2	2	9	186	42	113	31	0
Naples	19,668	21	0	4	1	16	306	22	252	32	0
Neptune Beach	6,971	9	0	0	3	6	83	6	70	7	0
New Port Richey	17,249	121	0	10	13	98	436	85	317	34	5
New Smyrna Beach	31,839	53	0	0	6	47	269	39	202	28	1
North Miami	58,502	438	6	22	100	310	1,658	158	1,297	203	5
North Port	84,459	101	2	24	7	68	797	91	682	24	19
Ocean Ridge	1,824	4	0	1	1	2	18	4	12	2	0
Orange City	14,880	39	0	4	4	31	391	23	340	28	2
Orlando	310,713	2,597	32	226	426	1,913	12,517	1,398	9,861	1,258	22
Ormond Beach	43,860	79	0	11	9	59	814	138	605	71	0
Oviedo	39,027	35	0	12	8	15	237	39	195	3	0
Pahokee	5,356	44	3	2	6	33	120	18	88	14	0
Palatka	10,599	60	1	1	3	55	367	17	328	22	1
Palm Beach Shores	1,320	3	0	0	1	2	35	6	29	0	0
Palmetto	13,621	63	2	6	11	44	352	44	276	32	0
Panama City	35,384	240	1	43	17	179	1,029	168	783	78	3
Parker	5,096	14	0	1	0	13	82	15	66	1	1
Pinellas Park	53,045	153	2	22	36	93	1,650	170	1,350	130	7
Plantation	94,014	249	3	10	63	173	2,355	193	1,881	281	1
Plant City	39,615	214	4	2	19	189	777	116	583	78	3
Ponce Inlet	3,436	2	1	1	0	0	14	3	10	1	0
Port Orange	64,037	29	5	2	4	18	838	79	703	56	2
Port St. Lucie	228,855	267	6	23	30	208	1,743	170	1,487	86	2
Riviera Beach	38,554	345	11	23	47	264	1,147	165	872	110	2
Royal Palm Beach	38,988	82	0	18	6	58	503	19	458	26	5
Sanford	60,602	351	6	42	61	242	1,797	310	1,397	90	1
Sarasota	55,380	365	7	25	75	258	1,741	231	1,327	183	4
Satellite Beach	11,288	12	1	2	2	7	98	17	79	2	0
Sea Ranch Lakes	534	0	0	0	0	0	16	0	15	1	0
Sebastian	26,258	17	0	0	0	17	239	21	214	4	0
Sneads	1,748	3	0	0	0	3	4	3	1	0	0
South Bay	4,453	43	2	7	4	30	64	14	42	8	0
South Daytona	13,712	26	0	0	3	23	185	62	104	19	1

Table 8. Offenses Known to Law Enforcement, by Selected State and City, 2022—Continued

(Number.)

State/city	Population	Violent crime	Murder and nonnegligent manslaughter	Rape	Robbery	Aggravated assault	Property crime	Burglary	Larceny-theft	Motor vehicle theft	Arson[1]
South Miami	11,597	65	0	7	14	44	287	25	262	0	0
South Palm Beach	1,450	0	0	0	0	0	9	0	8	1	0
Springfield	8,044	60	0	14	4	42	202	42	149	11	2
St. Augustine	14,875	50	0	6	5	39	389	27	345	17	0
St. Augustine Beach	7,100	2	0	0	0	2	38	1	37	0	0
St. Cloud	64,799	151	0	20	9	122	651	106	509	36	2
St. Petersburg	257,745	1,622	16	100	202	1,304	6,864	771	5,253	840	18
Sunny Isles Beach	21,908	19	0	5	5	9	262	14	248	0	0
Surfside	5,418	5	0	1	2	2	118	8	101	9	1
Tampa	390,145	1,938	43	133	315	1,447	6,530	756	5,064	710	36
Tavares	20,241	12	1	2	2	7	93	16	72	5	0
Temple Terrace	27,392	81	7	12	9	53	505	89	369	47	2
Titusville	48,979	264	10	40	20	194	879	143	660	76	7
Trenton	2,117	4	0	0	0	4	29	8	20	1	0
Virginia Gardens	2,251	2	0	0	2	0	25	2	20	3	0
Wauchula	4,993	21	0	2	2	17	76	17	58	1	0
Wellington	61,119	79	0	17	4	58	604	34	527	43	1
Westlake	1,075	7	0	0	2	5	39	4	35	0	0
West Melbourne	29,221	68	0	5	9	54	391	44	325	22	1
West Miami	6,911	16	0	0	1	15	71	9	54	8	0
Winter Haven	54,905	174	2	50	7	115	903	125	707	71	5
Winter Park	28,582	87	0	15	17	55	559	77	439	43	0
Zephyrhills	19,106	28	0	3	3	22	614	67	513	34	0
GEORGIA											
Acworth	22,170	25	2	4	5	14	277	10	258	9	0
Adairsville	5,063	10	0	3	1	6	92	5	83	4	0
Alapaha	479	0	0	0	0	0	5	3	2	0	0
Albany	68,613	229	16	15	10	188	519	47	400	72	4
Alma	3,370	11	0	0	2	9	68	15	51	2	0
Alpharetta	66,629	183	0	13	6	164	868	56	771	41	0
Alto	993	2	0	1	0	1	4	0	4	0	0
Americus	15,808	197	2	7	12	176	579	74	473	32	3
Arcade	1,948	2	0	0	0	2	47	10	34	3	0
Athens-Clarke County	128,177	763	4	153	67	539	3,374	424	2,605	345	27
Atlanta	495,707	4,167	168	157	711	3,131	18,579	1,839	13,437	3,303	18
Bainbridge	14,112	94	5	13	11	65	564	129	408	27	7
Ball Ground	2,876	0	0	0	0	0	3	0	3	0	0
Barnesville	6,449	6	0	0	1	5	31	4	24	3	0
Bartow	182	0	0	0	0	0	0	0	0	0	0
Baxley	5,016	39	2	4	4	29	265	41	210	14	1
Blackshear	3,572	4	0	2	1	1	103	19	75	9	0
Blairsville	538	3	0	0	0	3	19	0	19	0	0
Blakely	5,139	80	1	4	4	71	104	20	74	10	1
Bloomingdale	2,849	9	0	0	0	9	43	8	26	9	0
Blythe	747	0	0	0	0	0	0	0	0	0	0
Boston	1,212	2	0	0	0	2	10	0	8	2	0
Braselton	15,203	3	0	0	0	3	148	16	119	13	1
Bremen	7,683	9	0	4	1	4	187	8	173	6	0
Brookhaven	55,614	258	7	28	65	158	1,253	154	974	125	7
Brooklet	2,015	0	0	0	0	0	4	0	4	0	0
Broxton	1,074	2	0	0	0	2	6	1	5	0	0
Brunswick	14,650	204	3	16	58	127	811	108	647	56	0
Byron	5,953	7	1	0	1	5	134	11	112	11	0
Cairo	9,864	35	1	4	5	25	229	28	192	9	0
Calhoun	17,585	54	0	6	2	46	464	33	409	22	0
Camilla	5,001	11	0	0	2	9	100	13	76	11	0
Canon	666	1	0	0	0	1	2	0	1	1	0
Carrollton	27,844	104	0	9	10	85	736	53	651	32	1
Cartersville	23,293	112	1	37	4	70	543	36	469	38	12
Cave Spring	1,195	0	0	0	0	0	25	8	16	1	0
Cecil	287	1	0	0	0	1	6	2	4	0	0
Cedartown	10,397	62	3	13	6	40	237	19	202	16	0
Centerville	8,230	11	0	0	2	9	108	10	88	10	1
Chamblee	29,393	155	1	8	22	124	676	61	535	80	0
Chatsworth	4,775	3	0	0	0	3	33	5	25	3	0
Chickamauga	3,223	1	0	0	0	1	30	6	24	0	1
Clarkston	14,368	69	3	3	30	33	333	60	234	39	1
Claxton	2,549	15	1	2	1	11	113	24	82	7	1
Clayton	2,064	5	0	2	1	2	107	10	67	30	0
Cleveland	3,537	10	0	4	1	5	78	11	63	4	0
Cochran	5,077	11	1	0	1	9	120	25	90	5	0
College Park	13,917	217	11	13	54	139	1,002	115	678	209	1
Columbus	204,986	1,292	19	54	157	1,062	4,819	631	3,602	586	6
Coolidge	534	1	0	0	0	1	7	0	7	0	0
Cordele	9,929	170	3	3	11	153	473	70	377	26	8
Covington	14,549	109	2	8	4	95	535	58	429	48	0
Dallas	14,801	32	1	5	1	25	140	14	113	13	0
Dalton	34,276	127	2	18	23	84	845	79	699	67	8
Danielsville	677	1	0	0	0	1	8	1	6	1	0
Davisboro	1,854	0	0	0	0	0	0	0	0	0	0
Dawson	4,229	17	0	3	2	12	46	10	31	5	0
Decatur	24,259	32	1	8	10	13	659	44	573	42	1

Table 8. Offenses Known to Law Enforcement, by Selected State and City, 2022—Continued

(Number.)

State/city	Population	Violent crime	Murder and nonnegligent manslaughter	Rape	Robbery	Aggravated assault	Property crime	Burglary	Larceny-theft	Motor vehicle theft	Arson[1]
Demorest	1,927	2	0	1	0	1	14	4	9	1	0
Doerun	713	1	0	1	0	0	7	1	4	2	0
Donalsonville	2,834	4	0	0	0	4	24	3	20	1	0
Doraville	11,185	50	1	2	14	33	518	53	395	70	0
Douglas	11,762	11	0	0	0	11	24	0	23	1	0
Douglasville	36,331	239	3	24	21	191	1,835	112	1,615	108	2
Duluth	31,836	39	0	6	2	31	389	41	331	17	0
Dunwoody	50,271	125	3	10	27	85	1,481	133	1,256	92	0
East Ellijay	1,135	2	0	0	0	2	78	0	78	0	0
Eastman	5,538	28	1	0	1	26	259	40	217	2	1
Eatonton	6,568	17	0	2	1	14	124	2	119	3	0
Edison	1,237	2	0	1	0	1	25	6	17	2	0
Elberton	4,719	40	0	7	0	33	140	21	112	7	1
Ellaville	1,521	1	0	1	0	0	11	0	10	1	0
Ellijay	1,861	1	0	0	0	1	42	5	35	2	0
Emerson	1,451	5	0	2	1	2	24	1	18	5	0
Enigma	1,066	1	0	0	0	1	17	5	12	0	0
Eton	825	0	0	0	0	0	7	1	6	0	0
Euharlee	4,345	1	0	1	0	0	24	2	22	0	1
Fairburn	16,710	53	0	1	6	46	221	19	175	27	0
Fayetteville	19,619	32	0	7	8	17	465	23	422	20	0
Fitzgerald	8,960	102	1	4	2	95	358	39	291	28	1
Flowery Branch	10,843	10	0	2	1	7	124	24	95	5	0
Folkston	4,457	6	0	0	0	6	57	16	37	4	0
Forest Park	19,605	176	2	15	45	114	947	121	674	152	2
Fort Oglethorpe	10,626	18	0	2	4	12	336	19	300	17	0
Fort Valley	8,946	107	5	2	12	88	306	49	219	38	0
Franklin	926	1	0	0	1	0	14	0	13	1	0
Franklin Springs	1,125	0	0	0	0	0	0	0	0	0	0
Gainesville	44,314	247	3	33	29	182	1,233	111	1,009	113	9
Garden City	10,248	106	2	8	9	87	381	50	266	65	2
Gordon	1,767	4	2	0	0	2	24	9	14	1	0
Grantville	3,446	35	3	1	0	31	27	2	24	1	0
Gray	3,406	8	0	2	0	6	37	1	36	0	0
Greensboro	3,662	12	0	0	2	10	75	5	59	11	1
Greenville	799	4	0	0	1	3	9	4	5	0	0
Griffin	23,862	319	7	14	9	289	857	117	661	79	0
Grovetown	17,161	23	0	7	2	14	118	11	98	9	1
Guyton	2,826	4	1	1	1	1	7	2	3	2	0
Hagan	939	0	0	0	0	0	0	0	0	0	0
Hahira	3,442	5	1	1	0	3	11	1	9	1	0
Hampton	8,308	12	0	1	0	11	57	4	48	5	0
Harlem	4,130	1	0	0	0	1	8	0	8	0	0
Hartwell	4,567	13	2	0	1	10	163	12	148	3	0
Hazlehurst	4,079	8	1	0	1	6	113	15	90	8	1
Helen	555	7	0	1	0	6	30	5	25	0	0
Hephzibah	3,778	1	0	0	0	1	81	12	54	15	1
Hinesville	35,443	220	1	17	13	189	939	86	786	67	8
Hiram	5,203	15	0	4	1	10	340	13	313	14	2
Hoboken	484	0	0	0	0	0	0	0	0	0	0
Hogansville	3,180	11	1	2	1	7	24	5	18	1	1
Holly Springs	18,511	3	0	1	0	2	63	6	51	6	0
Homerville	2,309	8	0	1	0	7	12	3	9	0	0
Jasper	4,371	2	0	0	1	1	72	9	62	1	0
Jefferson	14,664	8	0	2	0	6	115	12	88	15	0
Johns Creek	81,964	34	1	4	2	27	389	53	315	21	1
Kennesaw	32,974	64	0	12	4	48	329	43	262	24	1
Kingsland	19,650	53	1	8	6	38	252	19	203	30	3
Kingston	750	0	0	0	0	0	0	0	0	0	0
LaGrange	32,146	211	6	34	34	137	1,404	199	1,109	96	8
Lake City	3,042	8	0	0	3	5	73	4	46	23	0
Lake Park	1,406	1	0	1	0	0	17	2	13	2	0
Lavonia	2,170	9	0	0	1	8	88	10	71	7	0
Lawrenceville	30,618	114	1	10	16	87	599	62	488	49	2
Leary	536	0	0	0	0	0	0	0	0	0	0
Leesburg	3,529	1	0	0	0	1	29	3	19	7	0
Lilburn	15,823	35	0	1	3	31	344	34	278	32	0
Lithonia	2,585	11	0	0	1	10	41	3	25	13	0
Locust Grove	10,394	31	1	1	8	21	429	31	373	25	0
Loganville	15,250	37	1	5	5	26	227	23	184	20	0
Lookout Mountain	1,664	0	0	0	0	0	6	0	6	0	0
Louisville	2,336	15	1	0	1	13	27	4	20	3	2
Madison	5,410	11	0	1	1	9	108	9	90	9	0
Manchester	3,563	17	1	3	1	12	65	11	40	14	0
Marietta	62,059	273	3	31	54	185	1,534	168	1,192	174	4
Maysville	2,051	0	0	0	0	0	1	1	0	0	0
McDonough	31,292	113	3	7	13	90	736	58	587	91	6
McIntyre	568	0	0	0	0	0	4	0	2	2	0
McRae-Helena	5,873	18	0	0	0	18	33	18	14	1	0
Metter	4,001	18	0	3	5	10	83	29	40	14	1
Milledgeville	17,102	142	0	9	8	125	783	118	632	33	5
Millen	2,913	10	0	2	2	6	74	13	55	6	1
Milton	41,330	29	0	5	2	22	261	31	224	6	0

Table 8. Offenses Known to Law Enforcement, by Selected State and City, 2022—Continued

(Number.)

State/city	Population	Violent crime	Murder and nonnegligent manslaughter	Rape	Robbery	Aggravated assault	Property crime	Burglary	Larceny-theft	Motor vehicle theft	Arson[1]
Monroe	15,569	51	1	12	2	36	467	42	407	18	2
Montezuma	3,056	8	0	0	0	8	31	11	19	1	1
Morrow	6,493	44	2	2	13	27	577	44	463	70	2
Moultrie	14,454	121	2	6	15	98	667	85	541	41	5
Mount Zion	2,021	2	0	1	0	1	13	0	11	2	0
Nashville	4,830	20	0	1	1	18	197	27	166	4	0
Newington	289	0	0	0	0	0	10	2	7	1	0
Newnan	43,932	533	0	24	15	494	896	90	732	74	6
Norcross	17,731	88	2	10	17	59	617	64	487	66	1
Ocilla	3,714	21	0	0	2	19	63	7	53	3	1
Oglethorpe	1,006	6	0	0	0	6	2	1	1	0	0
Omega	1,289	3	0	0	2	1	24	3	21	0	0
Oxford	2,275	0	0	0	0	0	12	0	11	1	0
Palmetto	5,084	3	0	0	0	3	43	6	35	2	0
Patterson	770	0	0	0	0	0	0	0	0	0	0
Peachtree City	39,301	12	2	1	4	5	401	67	309	25	3
Pelham	3,380	9	0	0	1	8	81	11	61	9	0
Pendergrass	1,779	0	0	0	0	0	12	2	10	0	0
Perry	23,213	57	1	2	6	48	516	32	436	48	1
Pine Mountain	1,282	1	0	0	0	1	17	2	13	2	0
Pooler	28,328	61	0	7	11	43	667	49	561	57	0
Port Wentworth	12,684	19	2	1	0	16	230	22	166	42	1
Quitman	4,097	11	1	1	2	7	59	5	48	6	0
Remerton	1,279	7	0	1	1	5	28	3	23	2	0
Richmond Hill	18,421	29	2	5	3	19	189	17	148	24	0
Rincon	11,050	18	0	2	1	15	151	41	105	5	1
Rockmart	4,877	17	1	3	0	13	185	22	159	4	0
Rome	37,778	319	5	33	25	256	1,479	155	1,195	129	6
Rossville	3,995	18	0	2	1	15	121	18	88	15	1
Roswell	92,550	173	6	29	19	119	1,118	110	915	93	3
Sandersville	5,540	7	0	0	0	7	29	2	23	4	0
Sandy Springs	106,747	148	4	25	29	90	1,597	186	1,258	153	6
Senoia	5,497	3	0	2	0	1	20	3	16	1	0
Smyrna	55,735	190	2	34	26	128	934	109	719	106	0
Snellville	20,988	38	4	7	3	24	469	22	422	25	0
Social Circle	5,252	31	0	0	0	31	71	14	55	2	0
South Fulton	110,102	1,146	22	31	96	997	2,905	284	1,997	624	6
Stapleton	392	0	0	0	0	0	0	0	0	0	0
Statesboro	33,590	102	2	14	21	65	733	101	589	43	4
Stone Mountain	6,541	26	0	2	4	20	140	23	92	25	0
Summerville	4,387	17	0	2	0	15	77	15	59	3	1
Suwanee	22,911	42	0	10	6	26	369	32	323	14	2
Sylvania	2,663	4	0	0	0	4	85	18	64	3	1
Sylvester	5,488	13	0	0	4	9	73	2	67	4	0
Tallapoosa	3,273	3	0	0	1	2	78	11	61	6	0
Temple	6,168	18	0	3	1	14	100	16	78	6	0
Thomaston	9,681	44	3	13	4	24	261	20	222	19	1
Thomasville	18,836	81	1	6	11	63	738	103	584	51	1
Thunderbolt	2,513	12	0	0	4	8	52	6	40	6	0
Toccoa	9,218	34	0	5	3	26	311	31	266	14	1
Tunnel Hill	965	0	0	0	0	0	4	0	2	2	0
Tybee Island	3,075	7	0	0	0	7	81	5	68	8	2
Tyrone	7,917	4	0	0	0	4	38	1	34	3	0
Valdosta	55,666	195	14	16	48	117	1,274	90	1,058	126	2
Vidalia	10,656	80	3	2	8	67	548	86	425	37	3
Wadley	1,606	5	0	1	0	4	33	5	27	1	0
Warner Robins	82,409	591	12	25	78	476	3,015	468	2,291	256	25
Warwick	496	2	0	0	0	2	2	1	1	0	0
Waycross	13,630	121	6	11	23	81	619	85	494	40	4
Waynesboro	5,576	47	1	1	2	43	151	29	113	9	0
Winder	19,401	68	0	3	5	60	317	29	260	28	1
Woodstock	37,325	36	0	8	5	23	406	15	372	19	2
Zebulon	1,289	2	0	0	0	2	10	3	7	0	0
HAWAII											
Honolulu	994,799	2,521	25	297	833	1,366	25,649	2,627	18,400	4,622	260
IDAHO											
American Falls	4,661	14	0	1	1	12	40	1	34	5	0
Ashton	957	0	0	0	0	0	11	1	8	2	0
Bellevue	2,587	5	0	0	0	5	15	8	7	0	0
Blackfoot	12,437	43	1	5	1	36	275	95	159	21	4
Boise	239,074	591	3	186	46	356	2,878	285	2,327	266	26
Bonners Ferry	2,626	16	0	1	0	15	12	3	6	3	1
Buhl	4,744	6	1	0	0	5	31	4	26	1	1
Caldwell	66,940	297	3	48	1	245	875	107	629	139	8
Challis	948	4	0	1	0	3	7	1	5	1	0
Chubbuck	15,970	41	1	4	4	32	405	40	348	17	1
Coeur d'Alene	57,061	176	1	54	14	107	580	72	472	36	9
Cottonwood	875	0	0	0	0	0	1	0	1	0	0
Emmett	8,007	50	0	13	0	37	70	13	51	6	1
Filer	2,888	2	0	0	0	2	26	7	19	0	0
Fruitland	6,823	8	0	2	1	5	48	19	24	5	0

Table 8. Offenses Known to Law Enforcement, by Selected State and City, 2022—Continued

(Number.)

State/city	Population	Violent crime	Murder and nonnegligent manslaughter	Rape	Robbery	Aggravated assault	Property crime	Burglary	Larceny-theft	Motor vehicle theft	Arson[1]
Garden City	12,279	86	0	14	3	69	240	57	169	14	1
Gooding	3,741	9	0	0	1	8	45	5	39	1	2
Grangeville	3,540	4	0	2	0	2	19	5	12	2	0
Hagerman	989	1	0	1	0	0	7	0	7	0	0
Hailey	9,789	21	0	7	0	14	42	14	22	6	0
Heyburn	3,684	17	1	5	1	10	37	1	31	5	0
Homedale	3,095	15	0	1	0	14	42	17	18	7	0
Idaho Falls	68,162	237	2	38	9	188	935	305	529	101	4
Jerome	12,806	48	0	13	1	34	133	11	106	16	1
Kellogg	2,443	10	0	0	0	10	19	4	14	1	0
Ketchum	3,606	10	0	2	0	8	36	3	31	2	0
Kimberly	5,025	6	0	2	0	4	32	17	7	8	1
Lewiston	34,711	63	1	19	2	41	916	171	673	72	5
McCall	4,007	11	0	2	0	9	54	8	39	7	0
Meridian	132,522	186	0	41	12	133	836	85	698	53	10
Middleton	10,845	25	1	8	0	16	84	28	52	4	0
Montpelier	2,720	6	0	0	0	6	34	14	18	2	0
Moscow	26,240	24	4	4	0	16	338	59	270	9	3
Mountain Home	16,357	43	0	10	0	33	159	21	127	11	3
Nampa	111,501	392	5	105	11	271	1,413	140	1,126	147	10
Orofino	3,310	12	0	0	1	11	15	5	10	0	0
Osburn	1,670	2	0	1	0	1	5	4	1	0	0
Payette	8,657	22	0	1	0	21	74	7	60	7	2
Pinehurst	1,784	1	0	1	0	0	5	1	4	0	0
Pocatello	57,914	238	0	24	5	209	781	173	524	84	3
Ponderay	1,653	0	0	0	0	0	23	0	20	3	0
Post Falls	46,306	90	1	9	4	76	485	87	362	36	0
Preston	5,932	8	0	2	1	5	35	0	33	2	0
Priest River	1,810	3	0	0	1	2	12	1	9	2	0
Rexburg	35,711	34	1	10	0	23	151	11	136	4	1
Rigby	5,428	4	0	1	0	3	48	7	38	3	0
Rupert	6,107	16	0	1	2	13	71	9	55	7	0
Salmon	3,274	20	0	0	0	20	13	1	12	0	0
Sandpoint	9,429	7	1	0	0	6	99	27	63	9	2
Shelley	5,232	4	0	1	0	3	42	11	27	4	0
Soda Springs	3,146	11	0	3	0	8	21	3	16	2	0
Spirit Lake	2,578	3	0	1	0	2	20	6	13	1	1
St. Anthony	3,809	5	0	1	0	4	12	2	10	0	0
Sun Valley	1,828	1	0	0	0	1	4	0	4	0	0
Twin Falls	54,648	243	2	36	6	199	793	72	637	84	2
Weiser	5,986	8	0	0	0	8	17	14	3	0	0
Wendell	2,940	10	0	0	0	10	16	4	11	1	0
Wilder	1,720	6	0	2	0	4	18	7	8	3	0
ILLINOIS[2]											
Albers	1,090	0	0	0	0	0	0	0	0	0	0
Aledo	3,602	1	0	0	0	1	24	3	20	1	0
Algonquin	30,212	15	0	7	1	7	293	21	258	14	4
Alsip	18,246	61	0	16	24	21	511	48	366	97	6
Altamont	2,171	3	0	3	0	0	12	1	10	1	1
Alton	25,212	229	1	51	24	153	787	122	509	156	10
Anna	4,096	8	0	1	1	6	87	10	66	11	0
Annawan	874	3	0	2	0	1	5	1	4	0	0
Arcola	2,874	1	0	0	1	0	14	0	14	0	0
Arlington Heights	74,648	54	0	17	7	30	803	80	693	30	7
Arthur	2,227	3	0	1	0	2	14	2	9	3	0
Assumption	1,172	1	0	0	0	1	2	1	0	1	0
Atwood	1,116	3	0	1	0	2	19	12	7	0	0
Auburn	4,463	4	0	2	0	2	25	9	16	0	0
Bannockburn	1,000	2	0	1	0	1	27	8	19	0	0
Barrington	10,614	9	0	4	0	5	54	4	42	8	0
Barrington Hills	4,024	2	0	1	0	1	30	5	20	5	0
Bartonville	5,789	28	0	4	3	21	127	25	93	9	0
Batavia	26,088	26	0	8	2	16	276	32	230	14	0
Beckemeyer	908	0	0	0	0	0	2	0	2	0	0
Beecher	4,675	2	0	1	1	0	20	6	13	1	0
Belleville	41,291	164	2	34	12	116	571	88	392	91	10
Bellwood	17,972	64	1	3	17	43	308	32	174	102	4
Berwyn	54,654	72	0	2	23	47	416	38	287	91	6
Bethalto	9,311	16	0	6	0	10	40	5	30	5	0
Bethany	1,249	2	0	0	0	2	9	3	5	1	0
Blue Island	21,577	126	2	13	28	83	627	87	338	202	7
Bluffs	598	0	0	0	0	0	0	0	0	0	0
Bolingbrook	73,364	162	5	40	24	93	561	60	436	65	3
Braidwood	6,176	8	0	4	0	4	39	8	26	5	0
Breese	4,588	0	0	0	0	0	14	1	12	1	0
Buffalo Grove	42,468	16	4	2	4	6	260	29	216	15	2
Burbank	28,271	49	0	6	19	24	394	39	293	62	4
Calumet Park	6,711	66	4	2	24	36	292	41	153	98	0
Campton Hills	10,802	0	0	0	0	0	1	1	0	0	0
Carbondale	21,612	170	4	33	22	111	680	131	498	51	15
Carlinville	5,500	14	0	1	0	13	159	18	135	6	0
Carlyle	3,200	6	0	2	0	4	46	14	31	1	0

Table 8. Offenses Known to Law Enforcement, by Selected State and City, 2022—Continued

(Number.)

State/city	Population	Violent crime	Murder and nonnegligent manslaughter	Rape	Robbery	Aggravated assault	Property crime	Burglary	Larceny-theft	Motor vehicle theft	Arson[1]
Catlin	1,944	0	0	0	0	0	6	4	2	0	0
Champaign	89,815	580	7	56	50	467	1,547	174	1,339	34	13
Channahon	14,006	16	0	8	0	8	73	8	54	11	0
Chatham	14,420	7	0	2	1	4	106	14	80	12	0
Chenoa	3,121	2	0	1	0	1	3	1	1	1	0
Cherry	422	0	0	0	0	0	0	0	0	0	0
Cherry Valley	2,880	9	1	1	3	4	144	5	128	11	0
Chicago	2,652,124	14,321	604	1,374	8,948	3,395	83,090	7,626	54,273	21,191	152
Chicago Heights	26,393	502	5	20	96	381	704	122	457	125	8
Chicago Ridge	13,867	30	1	7	8	14	293	24	242	27	3
Chillicothe	5,980	22	0	0	2	20	104	27	72	5	3
Cicero	81,492	234	3	8	88	135	1,122	231	633	258	8
Clinton	6,862	10	0	1	1	8	80	19	59	2	0
Coal City	5,800	2	0	1	0	1	27	5	16	6	0
Coal Valley	3,820	4	0	0	1	3	33	3	27	3	0
Colchester	1,058	0	0	0	0	0	9	3	5	1	0
Collinsville	24,131	55	0	23	3	29	463	69	363	31	1
Colona	5,009	10	1	7	0	2	85	21	56	8	4
Cortland	4,404	0	0	0	0	0	32	0	32	0	0
Coulterville	832	1	0	1	0	0	0	0	0	0	0
Countryside	6,159	7	0	2	0	5	179	27	132	20	0
Crest Hill	20,197	53	1	16	7	29	215	23	160	32	1
Crestwood	10,507	13	1	0	6	6	196	10	164	22	0
Crete	8,371	14	0	2	1	11	71	9	59	3	1
Danville	28,480	500	4	42	35	419	1,373	287	1,015	71	16
Decatur	68,789	485	16	54	70	345	1,702	418	1,014	270	38
Deerfield	18,981	7	0	6	1	0	180	17	158	5	0
DeKalb	40,555	222	1	65	31	125	1,046	80	906	60	8
Des Plaines	58,425	69	0	9	14	46	708	120	545	43	6
Dixon	15,396	18	0	5	1	12	90	12	76	2	4
Dupo	3,896	9	0	2	2	5	63	7	43	13	1
Durand	1,387	0	0	0	0	0	7	0	7	0	0
Dwight	3,989	4	0	0	1	3	22	3	19	0	0
East Dundee	3,091	10	0	1	0	9	70	2	54	14	0
East Hazel Crest	1,237	4	1	3	0	0	38	1	29	8	0
East Peoria	22,130	64	0	23	9	32	591	62	497	32	1
Edwardsville	25,117	16	0	3	0	13	196	6	173	17	2
Effingham	12,188	38	0	9	3	26	333	40	281	12	2
Elburn	6,368	3	0	3	0	0	23	0	23	0	0
Eldorado	3,644	8	0	0	0	8	0	0	0	0	0
Elgin	113,205	215	3	87	31	94	851	108	660	83	6
Elk Grove Village	31,479	41	0	12	5	24	541	53	450	38	2
Ellis Grove	319	0	0	0	0	0	0	0	0	0	0
Elmwood Park	23,485	33	0	7	12	14	284	44	203	37	3
Elwood	2,208	5	0	1	1	3	16	2	12	2	0
Evanston	76,259	135	2	29	78	26	1,869	270	1,452	147	10
Evergreen Park	19,103	29	0	5	13	11	899	21	828	50	4
Fairbury	3,585	0	0	0	0	0	2	1	1	0	1
Fairmont City	2,211	7	0	2	2	3	29	5	20	4	0
Fairmount	593	1	0	0	0	1	2	1	1	0	0
Fairview Heights	16,270	50	0	11	4	35	512	60	412	40	0
Farmer City	1,803	2	0	1	0	1	17	1	15	1	0
Findlay	650	0	0	0	0	0	2	2	0	0	0
Fithian	474	0	0	0	0	0	2	1	1	0	0
Flossmoor	9,281	11	0	3	1	7	112	10	89	13	0
Forest Park	13,740	65	0	8	28	29	489	58	339	92	2
Fox Lake	10,876	30	0	4	5	21	179	21	148	10	0
Fox River Grove	4,684	0	0	0	0	0	30	1	29	0	0
Frankfort	20,666	9	0	6	1	2	145	17	121	7	0
Franklin Park	18,230	32	0	4	8	20	238	38	153	47	3
Freeport	23,411	74	2	18	13	41	306	86	194	26	2
Fulton	3,609	6	0	1	0	5	15	2	13	0	0
Geneseo	6,488	15	0	1	1	13	78	2	74	2	0
Geneva	21,152	19	0	7	2	10	133	8	122	3	1
Germantown	1,312	1	0	1	0	0	5	1	3	1	0
Gilberts	8,339	1	0	0	1	0	27	7	20	0	0
Glen Carbon	13,822	10	0	9	0	1	166	7	153	6	0
Glencoe	8,567	3	0	3	0	0	71	12	54	5	0
Glenview	47,092	56	0	8	7	41	619	83	505	31	3
Glenwood	8,317	29	3	5	10	11	168	14	101	53	1
Golf	501	0	0	0	0	0	0	0	0	0	0
Grand Ridge	509	0	0	0	0	0	1	0	1	0	0
Granite City	27,273	178	2	55	15	106	697	145	445	107	21
Grayslake	24,519	45	1	17	1	26	241	27	192	22	2
Grayville	1,512	1	0	0	0	1	22	9	12	1	0
Greenfield	1,028	1	0	1	0	0	4	1	2	1	1
Greenville	6,480	7	0	0	1	6	51	9	38	4	0
Gurnee	30,361	34	1	7	5	21	768	44	645	79	3
Hampshire	7,881	4	0	1	0	3	22	2	17	3	0
Harrisburg	8,020	6	0	1	1	4	10	1	9	0	0
Harvard	9,461	10	0	3	1	6	82	5	69	8	0
Havana	2,868	5	0	2	0	3	71	7	61	3	0
Hazel Crest	12,849	94	3	9	24	58	440	33	250	157	5

Table 8. Offenses Known to Law Enforcement, by Selected State and City, 2022—Continued

(Number.)

State/city	Population	Violent crime	Murder and nonnegligent manslaughter	Rape	Robbery	Aggravated assault	Property crime	Burglary	Larceny-theft	Motor vehicle theft	Arson[1]
Henning	205	0	0	0	0	0	2	0	2	0	0
Henry	2,308	4	0	1	0	3	9	0	7	2	0
Heyworth	2,762	0	0	0	0	0	6	1	5	0	0
Highland	10,026	9	0	5	0	4	71	15	52	4	0
Highland Park	30,173	20	2	5	3	10	352	61	277	14	4
Hillsboro	5,860	6	0	3	1	2	49	14	33	2	1
Hodgkins	1,452	2	0	0	0	2	169	4	152	13	0
Hoffman Estates	50,385	50	0	18	12	20	480	58	376	46	0
Homer Glen	24,524	11	0	3	0	8	92	26	59	7	0
Homewood	18,634	35	1	3	17	14	693	33	599	61	1
Hoopeston	4,782	23	0	1	2	20	77	23	45	9	8
Hopedale	809	0	0	0	0	0	0	0	0	0	0
Hudson	1,733	0	0	0	0	0	0	0	0	0	0
Huntley	28,223	17	0	8	0	9	175	56	116	3	0
Indianola	223	0	0	0	0	0	0	0	0	0	0
Inverness	7,314	2	1	0	0	1	19	12	6	1	0
Jacksonville	17,731	42	0	11	10	21	382	67	283	32	7
Jerseyville	8,271	12	0	8	0	4	111	12	91	8	2
Johnsburg	6,395	6	0	0	0	6	55	0	54	1	0
Joliet	150,545	770	2	81	53	634	1,534	184	1,200	150	7
Kenilworth	2,404	0	0	0	0	0	8	1	7	0	0
Kildeer	4,240	2	0	0	0	2	35	8	27	0	0
Kincaid	1,379	0	0	0	0	0	0	0	0	0	0
Kingston	1,099	0	0	0	0	0	3	0	3	0	0
Lacon	1,857	5	0	1	0	4	1	0	1	0	0
La Grange	15,699	5	0	1	3	1	119	14	100	5	2
La Grange Park	12,992	6	0	4	2	0	97	11	84	2	1
Lake Forest	19,201	3	0	1	0	2	129	36	84	9	1
Lake in the Hills	28,961	16	0	9	0	7	84	17	64	3	0
Lakemoor	6,285	5	0	2	1	2	76	3	69	4	0
Lake Zurich	19,571	11	0	3	1	7	250	22	222	6	1
Lanark	1,592	0	0	0	0	0	7	0	7	0	0
Lansing	27,828	106	1	19	52	34	754	172	406	176	3
La Salle	9,450	6	0	0	1	5	15	3	10	2	0
Leland	927	0	0	0	0	0	1	1	0	0	0
Lemont	17,394	9	0	1	0	8	83	22	46	15	0
Le Roy	3,448	3	0	2	0	1	23	3	20	0	1
Libertyville	20,434	6	0	1	1	4	41	8	26	7	1
Lincoln	13,119	14	0	0	1	13	85	17	63	5	0
Lincolnshire	7,931	3	0	2	0	1	57	11	40	6	1
Lindenhurst	14,242	11	1	2	0	8	44	8	28	8	1
Litchfield	6,705	30	0	4	0	26	300	43	242	15	3
Lockport	26,079	14	0	8	0	6	156	9	134	13	1
Loves Park	23,222	79	3	17	10	49	342	45	256	41	3
Lovington	1,061	1	0	0	0	1	15	5	7	3	0
Machesney Park	22,558	55	0	13	1	41	241	28	197	16	0
Mackinaw	1,851	1	0	1	0	0	28	3	23	2	0
Mahomet	9,709	17	0	1	1	15	53	7	37	9	0
Manhattan	10,569	5	0	3	0	2	33	3	27	3	0
Manito	1,511	1	0	1	0	0	8	1	7	0	0
Maple Park	1,506	0	0	0	0	0	3	1	2	0	0
Marseilles	4,785	9	0	5	2	2	18	2	13	3	0
Marshall	3,867	8	0	0	0	8	38	12	22	4	0
Maryville	8,194	11	1	3	0	7	37	5	29	3	0
Mascoutah	8,622	6	0	1	1	4	34	9	24	1	0
Mason City	2,011	1	0	1	0	0	6	3	2	1	0
McHenry	27,610	18	0	8	1	9	202	13	180	9	2
McLeansboro	2,586	3	0	0	0	3	3	2	1	0	0
McNabb	269	0	0	0	0	0	0	0	0	0	0
Melrose Park	23,739	69	0	16	18	35	405	25	304	76	0
Metropolis	5,849	20	0	4	1	15	178	26	135	17	2
Midlothian	13,721	28	0	4	7	17	262	19	198	45	0
Milan	4,994	13	0	6	1	6	131	17	86	28	1
Milledgeville	1,082	0	0	0	0	0	5	2	3	0	0
Millstadt	3,986	2	0	1	1	0	9	1	8	0	0
Mokena	19,829	11	0	3	3	5	155	22	121	12	0
Moline	42,009	210	1	41	11	157	1,190	183	831	176	11
Monee	5,090	9	0	1	0	8	127	10	107	10	0
Monmouth	8,652	19	1	2	0	16	123	13	93	17	0
Montgomery	22,257	43	3	21	5	14	219	13	189	17	0
Morris	14,511	28	1	13	2	12	202	24	171	7	0
Morrison	4,027	13	0	2	0	11	19	3	14	2	0
Morton	17,169	28	0	11	1	16	182	18	152	12	0
Morton Grove	24,238	25	0	1	2	22	318	79	223	16	2
Mount Carmel	6,733	21	0	5	0	16	24	5	18	1	0
Mount Carroll	1,512	2	0	0	2	0	5	0	5	0	0
Mount Prospect	54,477	38	1	11	6	20	517	50	435	32	2
Mount Pulaski	1,516	1	0	0	1	0	1	0	0	1	0
Mount Zion	5,867	7	0	4	1	2	44	3	38	3	0
Mundelein	31,561	19	0	3	4	12	279	29	223	27	1
Murphysboro	6,973	33	0	8	2	23	199	26	166	7	0
Naperville	148,929	78	3	38	14	23	1,212	95	1,063	54	4
Neoga	1,367	4	0	0	1	3	7	3	4	0	0

Table 8. Offenses Known to Law Enforcement, by Selected State and City, 2022—Continued

(Number.)

State/city	Population	Violent crime	Murder and nonnegligent manslaughter	Rape	Robbery	Aggravated assault	Property crime	Burglary	Larceny-theft	Motor vehicle theft	Arson[1]
New Athens	1,902	0	0	0	0	0	4	0	3	1	0
New Baden	3,362	3	0	2	0	1	12	0	12	0	0
New Lenox	27,699	20	0	13	4	3	246	21	214	11	0
Newman	761	0	0	0	0	0	6	1	4	1	1
Niles	29,784	31	0	6	7	18	718	78	605	35	0
Normal	53,613	122	0	28	16	78	723	46	644	33	3
Northfield	5,534	1	0	1	0	0	66	18	43	5	0
Oak Lawn	55,957	67	0	18	22	27	855	74	659	122	2
Oak Park	52,152	171	3	33	81	54	1,571	168	1,145	258	0
Oakwood	1,296	0	0	0	0	0	17	2	14	1	0
O'Fallon	32,250	50	1	17	3	29	360	33	292	35	0
Oglesby	3,638	2	0	2	0	0	9	1	7	1	0
Olney	8,681	18	1	3	0	14	146	25	118	3	0
Olympia Fields	4,573	5	0	3	1	1	169	15	142	12	0
Onarga	1,308	0	0	0	0	0	0	0	0	0	0
Oswego	35,932	32	0	15	2	15	186	11	161	14	5
Ottawa	18,696	33	0	11	4	18	135	20	104	11	2
Palatine	65,078	71	3	20	8	40	514	55	423	36	5
Palestine	1,224	1	0	0	0	1	6	0	4	2	1
Palos Heights	11,602	8	0	1	2	5	100	7	78	15	1
Palos Hills	17,790	12	0	1	1	10	82	17	54	11	0
Palos Park	4,819	0	0	0	0	0	21	4	17	0	0
Park Forest	20,896	65	4	8	17	36	287	26	171	90	4
Pecatonica	2,044	1	0	0	0	1	11	2	9	0	0
Pekin	31,252	103	5	45	4	49	712	88	586	38	2
Peoria	110,551	1,314	24	103	121	1,066	3,469	679	2,188	602	62
Peoria Heights	5,764	40	0	6	4	30	154	27	109	18	0
Peotone	4,209	1	0	0	1	0	23	3	19	1	0
Peru	9,793	8	0	3	0	5	135	3	127	5	0
Phoenix	1,634	8	0	0	2	6	29	0	17	12	0
Pingree Grove	11,078	5	0	3	0	2	19	0	17	2	0
Pittsfield	4,182	5	0	2	0	3	42	9	32	1	0
Plainfield	46,004	37	1	25	3	8	311	34	246	31	0
Plano	12,474	15	0	6	1	8	76	0	76	0	0
Pleasant Hill	915	0	0	0	0	0	0	0	0	0	0
Polo	2,246	2	0	2	0	0	4	3	1	0	0
Pontiac	11,333	31	0	19	1	11	94	12	79	3	1
Potomac	669	0	0	0	0	0	1	0	1	0	0
Princeton	7,630	5	0	1	0	4	100	2	93	5	1
Prophetstown	1,922	0	0	0	0	0	2	0	2	0	0
Prospect Heights	15,404	22	0	5	3	14	157	12	130	15	2
Rantoul	11,971	73	5	18	3	47	266	57	207	2	4
River Forest	11,403	6	0	0	6	0	170	13	146	11	0
River Grove	10,504	9	0	2	3	4	123	18	88	17	1
Riverwoods	3,744	1	0	1	0	0	17	7	9	1	0
Robinson	7,189	28	0	9	0	19	94	17	70	7	3
Rochester	3,827	7	0	1	0	6	14	2	11	1	0
Rock Falls	8,687	44	0	10	2	32	237	38	182	17	3
Rockford	146,710	2,098	16	128	202	1,752	3,866	626	2,470	770	53
Rock Island	36,235	204	11	3	13	177	939	164	586	189	7
Rockton	7,738	7	0	1	0	6	86	6	78	2	0
Rolling Meadows	23,453	37	0	7	4	26	344	51	267	26	1
Romeoville	41,069	61	0	12	8	41	349	26	275	48	0
Roscoe	10,815	6	1	2	0	3	59	9	46	4	0
Rosemont	3,779	23	3	5	7	8	327	11	281	35	0
Rossville	1,187	2	0	1	0	1	3	1	2	0	0
Round Lake Beach	26,928	29	4	7	3	15	182	20	140	22	1
Roxana	1,438	1	0	0	0	1	12	4	7	1	0
Ruma	308	0	0	0	0	0	0	0	0	0	0
Salem	7,136	36	0	15	1	20	128	19	101	8	0
Sandwich	7,167	1	0	0	0	1	5	2	3	0	0
San Jose	462	0	0	0	0	0	0	0	0	0	0
Schaumburg	75,745	69	0	22	17	30	1,613	77	1,441	95	3
Sherman	4,603	0	0	0	0	0	17	1	16	0	0
Shiloh	14,616	15	0	6	0	9	131	9	75	47	0
Shorewood	18,326	12	0	4	3	5	118	9	99	10	0
Sidell	476	0	0	0	0	0	0	0	0	0	0
Silvis	7,922	28	0	3	1	24	292	52	219	21	1
Skokie	65,185	135	1	23	32	79	1,540	220	1,221	99	3
Sleepy Hollow	3,160	2	0	0	0	2	8	0	6	2	0
Somonauk	1,774	2	0	1	0	1	9	0	9	0	0
South Barrington	4,973	0	0	0	0	0	88	12	73	3	1
South Beloit	7,893	19	1	4	2	12	92	15	56	21	0
South Chicago Heights	3,848	23	0	4	4	15	92	8	60	24	1
South Elgin	23,995	24	0	18	1	5	122	8	98	16	0
Southern View	1,553	6	0	1	1	4	53	15	37	1	0
South Holland	20,626	83	4	21	25	33	416	31	262	123	2
South Roxana	1,884	4	0	1	0	3	11	4	5	2	0
Sparta	4,681	17	0	3	0	14	32	4	28	0	0
Springfield	112,549	867	7	96	147	617	4,777	909	3,361	507	25
Spring Valley	5,415	6	0	4	1	1	56	9	44	3	0
Stanford	590	0	0	0	0	0	10	3	6	1	0
St. Anne	1,111	3	0	0	0	3	18	3	14	1	0

Table 8. Offenses Known to Law Enforcement, by Selected State and City, 2022—Continued

(Number.)

State/city	Population	Violent crime	Murder and nonnegligent manslaughter	Rape	Robbery	Aggravated assault	Property crime	Burglary	Larceny-theft	Motor vehicle theft	Arson[1]
St. Charles	32,973	43	0	15	9	19	397	36	347	14	2
Steger	9,325	34	1	7	8	18	159	13	112	34	0
Sterling	14,681	51	0	25	3	23	226	25	182	19	0
Stickney	6,841	5	0	0	1	4	62	15	44	3	0
Stone Park	4,386	4	0	0	0	4	4	0	4	0	0
Streamwood	37,923	69	2	13	11	43	298	53	215	30	0
Streator	12,303	13	0	2	2	9	84	5	74	5	0
Sullivan	4,385	9	0	0	0	9	8	0	7	1	1
Swansea	14,068	14	0	1	0	13	186	28	129	29	1
Sycamore	18,673	28	0	8	3	17	220	8	208	4	0
Thornton	2,289	1	0	1	0	0	37	8	26	3	0
Tilton	2,584	8	0	2	1	5	109	19	85	5	0
Tinley Park	53,973	41	1	9	14	17	663	44	516	103	1
Tolono	3,489	3	0	1	0	2	46	2	42	2	1
Toluca	1,333	0	0	0	0	0	10	2	8	0	0
Trenton	2,630	0	0	0	0	0	2	0	2	0	0
Troy	11,260	12	1	3	1	7	56	9	40	7	1
Tuscola	4,656	7	0	0	0	7	21	3	17	1	2
Union	552	0	0	0	0	0	3	0	3	0	0
University Park	7,038	24	2	5	5	12	108	6	57	45	0
Valmeyer	1,216	0	0	0	0	0	2	0	2	0	0
Vandalia	6,812	0	0	0	0	0	82	13	61	8	0
Vernon Hills	26,717	28	0	7	6	15	338	27	296	15	1
Villa Park	21,752	25	0	4	6	15	321	34	262	25	0
Virden	3,159	10	0	2	0	8	42	24	15	3	0
Washington	15,910	10	1	6	1	2	147	7	137	3	0
Watseka	4,587	7	0	2	0	5	76	5	66	5	0
Wauconda	13,945	4	0	3	0	1	29	2	20	7	0
Wayne	2,240	0	0	0	0	0	7	6	1	0	0
West Dundee	7,727	8	1	1	0	6	64	8	51	5	0
Western Springs	13,175	0	0	0	0	0	49	6	39	4	1
Westville	3,084	11	0	2	0	9	43	11	31	1	0
Wheeling	37,790	63	1	25	5	32	363	38	303	22	1
Willow Springs	5,628	0	0	0	0	0	24	1	20	3	0
Wilmette	27,144	10	0	5	3	2	340	43	273	24	2
Wilmington	5,602	9	0	2	1	6	47	10	34	3	0
Winfield	10,460	6	0	0	0	6	27	2	23	2	0
Winnebago	2,885	5	0	0	0	5	23	3	19	1	0
Winnetka	12,277	8	0	3	0	5	94	8	69	17	0
Wood River	10,350	37	0	5	2	30	246	24	209	13	3
Woodstock	25,778	15	0	6	2	7	180	3	165	12	1
Worden	1,092	1	0	1	0	0	2	1	1	0	0
Worth	10,507	25	2	7	6	10	135	14	107	14	2
Yorkville	23,635	22	0	13	4	5	105	5	96	4	2
Zion	24,348	123	5	23	10	85	476	60	311	105	2
INDIANA											
Albion	2,232	0	0	0	0	0	28	2	21	5	0
Anderson	54,965	267	7	52	59	149	1,594	242	1,101	251	3
Angola	9,022	7	2	0	0	5	203	9	167	27	0
Auburn	13,645	7	1	2	0	4	169	29	128	12	0
Avon	24,167	40	0	7	9	24	577	27	501	49	0
Bargersville	10,791	4	1	1	0	2	59	5	48	6	0
Bedford	13,824	10	0	0	1	9	132	12	107	13	0
Beech Grove	14,401	45	1	8	8	28	385	86	211	88	2
Bloomington	80,135	407	4	60	59	284	1,874	249	1,508	117	27
Bluffton	10,327	9	0	5	0	4	84	14	63	7	2
Bristol	1,783	1	0	0	0	1	66	13	40	13	1
Brownsburg	31,072	24	0	7	6	11	263	19	212	32	0
Butler	2,646	1	0	0	0	1	25	4	18	3	1
Carmel	101,670	66	2	17	5	42	821	47	704	70	2
Cedar Lake	15,271	16	0	2	0	14	64	9	47	8	0
Charlestown	8,482	21	0	1	1	19	86	11	71	4	0
Chesterton	14,487	28	0	0	1	27	58	3	48	7	0
Cicero	5,537	5	0	0	0	5	6	0	5	1	0
Clarksville	21,890	35	0	3	9	23	923	39	796	88	1
Claypool	396	1	0	0	0	1	7	1	4	2	0
Columbia City	10,027	18	0	1	1	16	84	5	73	6	0
Crawfordsville	16,449	52	0	4	4	44	209	25	175	9	3
Cumberland	6,388	10	1	1	5	3	232	31	185	16	0
Danville	10,925	13	0	4	1	8	93	5	78	10	0
Dayton	1,348	3	0	0	0	3	20	1	18	1	0
Dyer	16,351	4	0	1	2	1	55	6	44	5	0
Edinburgh	4,431	4	0	0	0	4	51	3	40	8	0
Elkhart	53,947	575	8	41	57	469	1,538	300	1,029	209	5
Elwood	8,397	8	0	2	1	5	112	15	80	17	0
Evansville	115,719	832	25	82	70	655	4,359	654	3,250	455	40
Fishers	102,921	80	1	16	7	56	772	39	671	62	1
Fort Wayne	267,791	702	20	120	189	373	6,393	592	5,196	605	54
Frankfort	16,572	6	0	2	0	4	49	6	41	2	1
Franklin	25,714	21	0	7	1	13	323	13	280	30	0
Fremont	2,092	1	0	1	0	0	15	2	9	4	0
Goshen	34,697	87	2	13	7	65	956	140	718	98	6

Table 8. Offenses Known to Law Enforcement, by Selected State and City, 2022—Continued

(Number.)

State/city	Population	Violent crime	Murder and nonnegligent manslaughter	Rape	Robbery	Aggravated assault	Property crime	Burglary	Larceny-theft	Motor vehicle theft	Arson[1]
Greenfield	24,596	36	0	12	1	23	284	67	195	22	0
Greenwood	65,813	48	6	9	13	20	1,182	51	1,046	85	4
Griffith	16,218	17	0	1	4	12	155	17	111	27	0
Hammond	76,366	512	15	28	123	346	2,556	265	2,049	242	20
Hartford City	6,060	23	2	0	0	21	13	8	3	2	0
Highland	23,498	21	0	0	3	18	314	12	276	26	4
Hobart	29,374	29	2	3	5	19	627	31	556	40	1
Huntingburg	6,459	7	0	0	0	7	26	7	17	2	0
Huntington	17,030	12	4	2	2	4	188	17	165	6	2
Indianapolis	886,455	9,109	208	565	1,624	6,712	29,932	4,804	20,451	4,677	248
Jasper	16,699	37	0	6	0	31	88	9	74	5	0
Jeffersonville	51,150	120	0	6	14	100	848	117	578	153	0
Kendallville	10,153	25	0	11	1	13	152	10	136	6	0
Knox	3,583	12	0	0	0	12	26	9	14	3	0
Kokomo	59,776	306	3	28	13	262	921	196	630	95	2
Lafayette	70,861	421	2	66	35	318	1,551	227	1,116	208	18
La Porte	22,371	45	1	10	5	29	372	83	242	47	1
Lawrence	49,421	161	2	26	63	70	979	108	679	192	8
Lebanon	17,042	49	0	2	0	47	161	29	109	23	1
Linton	5,147	3	0	0	0	3	158	6	134	18	0
Logansport	18,195	8	0	6	0	2	337	41	279	17	1
Lowell	11,204	0	0	0	0	0	32	3	29	0	0
Marion	28,108	55	0	15	5	35	646	58	486	102	2
McCordsville	10,193	10	0	2	0	8	106	6	89	11	0
Michigan City	32,051	135	1	5	17	112	1,185	210	865	110	10
Mishawaka	51,022	144	2	35	15	92	1,463	254	1,078	131	3
Mount Vernon	6,380	17	1	4	1	11	106	5	87	14	3
Muncie	65,343	315	11	35	30	239	1,776	315	1,214	247	5
Munster	23,628	13	0	3	3	7	203	13	174	16	0
Nappanee	6,857	9	0	1	0	8	66	7	52	7	1
New Albany	37,198	151	3	10	18	120	1,153	145	859	149	2
New Carlisle	1,901	2	0	0	1	1	11	4	6	1	0
New Haven	15,856	31	0	2	1	28	187	43	124	20	0
New Palestine	2,976	3	0	0	0	3	7	0	6	1	0
New Whiteland	5,597	2	0	1	0	1	19	6	11	2	0
North Vernon	6,455	9	0	2	0	7	145	14	106	25	0
North Webster	993	0	0	0	0	0	37	4	32	1	0
Osceola	2,588	2	0	0	0	2	27	8	15	4	1
Pendleton	4,974	2	0	0	1	1	9	2	7	0	0
Pittsboro	4,145	2	0	1	1	0	14	1	12	1	0
Plainfield	36,189	55	3	15	6	31	643	52	521	70	1
Portage	38,438	61	1	24	5	31	439	28	393	18	1
Porter	5,258	10	0	0	4	6	17	1	14	2	1
Prince's Lakes	1,372	0	0	0	0	0	18	3	15	0	0
Roseland	849	19	0	1	6	12	33	6	20	7	0
Sellersburg	9,784	8	0	0	0	8	48	6	31	11	0
Seymour	21,415	23	0	14	2	7	377	25	309	43	3
Shelbyville	20,074	72	0	4	5	63	306	43	241	22	1
Sheridan	3,079	3	0	1	0	2	3	0	2	1	0
Silver Lake	870	0	0	0	0	0	18	1	15	2	0
Speedway	13,612	43	1	5	18	19	404	31	337	36	2
Syracuse	3,063	10	0	0	0	10	30	4	23	3	0
Tell City	7,587	17	0	0	0	17	148	14	126	8	1
Terre Haute	58,507	340	2	38	67	233	2,776	694	1,667	415	63
Valparaiso	34,708	37	0	13	1	23	289	16	249	24	0
Vincennes	16,487	12	0	3	1	8	438	82	314	42	1
Walkerton	2,080	5	0	0	0	5	45	27	15	3	0
Warsaw	15,952	49	0	9	5	35	317	42	238	37	0
Washington	12,090	7	0	3	1	3	104	13	84	7	0
Westfield	54,552	43	0	9	4	30	411	45	352	14	0
West Lafayette	44,891	46	0	14	2	30	457	43	383	31	1
Whiteland	4,835	0	0	0	0	0	42	2	33	7	0
Whitestown	11,909	16	0	2	2	12	121	7	102	12	0
Whiting	4,532	7	0	0	0	7	89	9	67	13	1
Winona Lake	5,066	14	0	1	0	13	27	2	22	3	0
Zionsville	32,575	5	0	2	1	2	117	3	106	8	0
IOWA											
Adel	6,377	10	0	5	1	4	69	14	50	5	1
Albia	3,717	14	0	2	0	12	35	9	22	4	0
Algona	5,257	18	0	0	0	18	11	1	9	1	1
Altoona	21,830	40	0	2	3	35	270	12	230	28	2
Ames	66,852	146	2	58	11	75	857	79	726	52	6
Ankeny	72,315	142	0	27	6	109	778	50	671	57	3
Asbury	6,005	1	0	0	0	1	16	7	9	0	0
Atlantic	6,726	31	0	5	0	26	119	8	101	10	2
Audubon	2,018	1	0	1	0	0	38	5	31	2	0
Belle Plaine	2,340	8	0	0	1	7	18	6	12	0	0
Bettendorf	39,548	31	0	7	8	16	545	58	431	56	0
Bloomfield	2,694	2	0	0	0	2	6	1	4	1	0
Burlington	23,497	138	0	13	8	117	867	113	659	95	10
Camanche	4,587	19	0	0	0	19	35	4	25	6	0
Carlisle	4,225	14	0	2	0	12	45	4	35	6	0

Table 8. Offenses Known to Law Enforcement, by Selected State and City, 2022—Continued

(Number.)

State/city	Population	Violent crime	Murder and nonnegligent manslaughter	Rape	Robbery	Aggravated assault	Property crime	Burglary	Larceny-theft	Motor vehicle theft	Arson[1]
Carroll	10,195	11	0	2	0	9	145	24	111	10	0
Carter Lake	3,768	47	0	2	1	44	124	18	95	11	2
Cedar Rapids	135,362	433	10	14	55	354	4,124	598	3,108	418	12
Centerville	5,303	15	0	4	0	11	111	34	64	13	0
Charles City	7,211	28	0	8	1	19	75	19	53	3	0
Clarinda	5,499	20	0	3	0	17	55	7	45	3	0
Clear Lake	7,501	53	0	6	3	44	141	28	104	9	1
Clinton	24,443	211	3	23	10	175	913	165	659	89	7
Clive	18,984	51	0	12	3	36	203	25	160	18	2
Colfax	2,246	2	0	0	0	2	15	3	8	4	1
Coralville	23,555	67	0	23	6	38	619	47	532	40	0
Council Bluffs	62,206	262	1	43	54	164	1,867	349	1,200	318	11
Creston	7,438	26	0	4	1	21	88	19	57	12	0
Davenport	100,437	701	4	93	97	507	3,496	659	2,358	479	15
Decorah	7,764	12	0	1	0	11	10	1	9	0	0
Denison	8,048	27	0	4	0	23	67	12	43	12	1
DeWitt	5,528	38	0	2	0	36	107	16	81	10	0
Dubuque	58,676	277	1	56	25	195	1,052	224	765	63	6
Dyersville	4,516	4	0	2	0	2	26	2	21	3	0
Eldora	2,621	64	0	2	0	62	14	4	10	0	0
Eldridge	6,770	3	0	0	0	3	53	10	35	8	0
Emmetsburg	3,612	9	0	0	0	9	21	3	17	1	0
Estherville	5,847	13	0	2	0	11	36	3	31	2	0
Evansdale	4,486	5	0	1	1	3	68	18	43	7	1
Fairfield	9,641	27	0	4	2	21	134	43	83	8	1
Fort Dodge	25,097	130	2	15	17	96	752	103	597	52	13
Fort Madison	10,084	31	0	8	0	23	210	40	156	14	3
Glenwood	5,195	18	0	4	1	13	46	11	25	10	1
Grinnell	9,474	77	0	4	3	70	184	22	153	9	1
Grundy Center	2,804	4	0	2	0	2	6	2	3	1	0
Harlan	4,936	2	0	1	0	1	15	1	10	4	0
Hiawatha	7,109	23	0	1	4	18	147	35	94	18	0
Independence	6,236	9	0	1	0	8	71	10	51	10	0
Indianola	15,817	139	0	25	0	114	270	18	239	13	3
Iowa City	74,749	197	1	18	29	149	1,327	173	1,018	136	1
Iowa Falls	5,023	40	0	6	1	33	80	5	72	3	0
Johnston	24,295	17	1	6	1	9	158	10	130	18	0
Keokuk	9,702	71	0	8	3	60	208	42	135	31	3
Knoxville	7,366	37	0	5	0	32	131	27	92	12	0
Lake City	1,721	4	0	0	0	4	19	6	8	5	0
Lansing	945	2	1	0	0	1	10	1	8	1	0
Le Mars	10,564	29	0	5	0	24	93	8	71	14	0
Manchester	5,134	15	0	2	0	13	83	5	74	4	0
Maquoketa	6,035	20	0	4	1	15	116	24	87	5	1
Marengo	2,411	8	0	1	1	6	36	4	30	2	0
Marion	41,793	102	0	15	6	81	512	53	406	53	2
Mar-Mac	1,152	3	0	0	0	3	10	4	6	0	0
Marshalltown	27,207	179	1	26	6	146	478	86	352	40	6
Mason City	27,032	79	0	14	11	54	723	122	547	54	5
Monroe	2,042	4	0	1	0	3	12	2	8	2	0
Monticello	4,071	9	0	0	0	9	32	4	26	2	0
Mount Pleasant	8,959	38	0	3	0	35	115	19	89	7	2
Mount Vernon-Lisbon	4,435	16	0	6	0	10	29	8	20	1	0
Muscatine	23,237	82	0	13	2	67	378	93	247	38	8
Newton	15,563	69	0	13	3	53	210	35	149	26	0
North Liberty	21,131	24	0	2	1	21	76	14	57	5	0
Norwalk	14,299	8	0	3	1	4	30	6	22	2	0
Oelwein	5,788	23	0	0	0	23	42	8	31	3	0
Osage	3,528	7	0	1	0	6	19	4	15	0	0
Osceola	5,654	25	0	4	1	20	79	16	56	7	1
Oskaloosa	11,479	50	0	21	3	26	135	27	86	22	1
Ottumwa	25,249	196	1	44	7	144	928	138	710	80	8
Pella	10,729	15	0	3	0	12	76	12	57	7	1
Perry	7,986	36	0	6	0	30	57	8	45	4	0
Polk City	5,920	4	0	1	0	3	17	2	13	2	0
Postville	2,434	9	0	2	0	7	19	5	13	1	0
Preston	935	2	0	0	0	2	16	4	12	0	0
Red Oak	5,568	20	0	8	0	12	86	25	49	12	0
Rock Valley	4,106	5	0	2	0	3	15	3	10	2	0
Sabula	491	3	0	0	0	3	15	0	15	0	0
Sheldon	5,385	17	0	6	0	11	43	3	35	5	0
Shenandoah	4,861	31	0	0	0	31	51	10	40	1	1
Sioux Center	8,340	4	0	1	0	3	21	0	16	5	0
Sioux City	85,580	441	1	79	60	301	2,514	342	1,893	279	18
Spencer	11,440	14	0	9	0	5	114	24	85	5	0
Spirit Lake	5,448	15	0	2	1	12	102	17	79	6	0
Storm Lake	11,274	40	0	4	0	36	149	27	114	8	0
Story City	3,443	4	0	0	0	4	46	4	34	8	0
Urbandale	46,284	49	0	3	3	43	320	36	236	48	0
Washington	7,209	30	0	11	2	17	136	29	104	3	1
Waterloo	66,504	385	9	29	43	304	1,658	369	1,078	211	17
Waukee	28,790	40	1	8	2	29	208	25	165	18	0
Waukon	3,706	2	0	0	0	2	41	1	34	6	0

Table 8. Offenses Known to Law Enforcement, by Selected State and City, 2022—Continued

(Number.)

State/city	Population	Violent crime	Murder and nonnegligent manslaughter	Rape	Robbery	Aggravated assault	Property crime	Burglary	Larceny-theft	Motor vehicle theft	Arson[1]
Waverly	10,445	69	0	6	1	62	112	13	94	5	0
Webster City	7,689	19	0	8	1	10	71	16	44	11	0
West Burlington	3,177	19	0	1	0	18	292	20	264	8	1
West Des Moines	70,701	176	1	16	20	139	1,215	86	1,040	89	4
West Liberty	3,796	10	0	2	0	8	16	4	11	1	0
Williamsburg	3,362	10	0	4	1	5	24	3	21	0	0
Windsor Heights	5,108	11	0	0	0	11	171	1	161	9	0
KANSAS											
Abilene	6,489	14	0	4	0	10	80	11	61	8	1
Andover	15,842	21	1	5	0	15	204	20	174	10	2
Anthony	1,993	6	0	3	0	3	19	6	9	4	1
Arkansas City	11,902	59	0	2	2	55	330	64	243	23	2
Arma	1,407	5	0	0	0	5	42	11	25	6	1
Atchison	10,650	34	0	4	2	28	283	38	233	12	1
Atwood	1,279	1	0	0	0	1	14	4	10	0	0
Augusta	9,256	30	0	2	2	26	250	34	204	12	1
Baldwin City	4,955	18	10	1	0	7	35	2	32	1	0
Basehor	7,546	9	0	1	0	8	49	5	37	7	4
Baxter Springs	3,826	7	0	3	0	4	65	13	48	4	0
Bel Aire	8,599	4	0	0	0	4	138	11	110	17	0
Belleville	2,015	1	0	0	0	1	20	5	13	2	0
Beloit	3,396	3	0	1	0	2	24	10	14	0	0
Benton	942	2	0	1	0	1	3	0	3	0	0
Bonner Springs	7,731	38	0	6	3	29	164	7	142	15	4
Burlington	2,637	7	0	0	0	7	38	1	34	3	0
Caney	1,745	2	0	0	0	2	23	1	18	4	1
Carbondale	1,339	3	0	0	0	3	6	2	4	0	0
Cherryvale	2,146	9	0	1	1	7	38	8	24	6	0
Clay Center	4,105	20	0	1	1	18	79	20	54	5	1
Clearwater	2,607	0	0	0	0	0	20	0	18	2	0
Coffeyville	8,788	52	2	2	3	45	305	22	267	16	1
Colby	5,488	22	0	0	0	22	73	13	54	6	0
Columbus	2,857	5	0	0	1	4	60	8	50	2	0
Concordia	5,002	27	0	3	0	24	149	49	90	10	0
Council Grove	2,116	7	0	1	0	6	34	2	30	2	0
Derby	25,907	59	2	10	1	46	566	39	505	22	1
Dodge City	27,641	111	1	15	8	87	447	55	351	41	12
Edwardsville	4,574	13	0	1	1	11	80	3	65	12	1
El Dorado	12,821	37	1	4	3	29	274	24	213	37	2
Elkhart	1,882	2	0	0	0	2	14	0	12	2	0
Ellinwood	1,970	3	0	0	0	3	11	4	6	1	0
Ellsworth	2,997	6	0	0	0	6	20	5	15	0	0
Eudora	6,480	5	0	2	0	3	28	5	22	1	0
Fairway	4,171	2	0	0	0	2	55	10	32	13	0
Fort Scott	7,501	28	0	4	0	24	205	36	159	10	5
Frontenac	3,415	2	0	1	0	1	41	8	28	5	0
Galena	2,737	8	0	0	0	8	38	5	28	5	0
Garden City	27,701	159	2	21	12	124	711	96	530	85	8
Gardner	24,497	38	0	4	0	34	190	7	168	15	5
Garnett	3,150	16	0	2	0	14	24	5	10	9	0
Girard	2,517	14	0	1	0	13	28	5	17	6	1
Goodland	4,459	21	0	2	0	19	145	104	37	4	0
Great Bend	14,456	59	0	13	2	44	336	73	240	23	2
Greensburg	696	0	0	0	0	0	6	1	5	0	0
Halstead	2,159	2	0	0	0	2	13	2	9	2	1
Haysville	11,308	13	0	5	0	8	128	30	93	5	3
Hesston	3,493	3	0	3	0	0	16	2	14	0	1
Hiawatha	3,239	11	0	3	0	8	70	12	57	1	0
Hillsboro	2,724	5	0	1	0	4	45	6	38	1	0
Hoisington	2,629	6	0	2	0	4	14	4	8	2	0
Holton	3,317	3	0	0	0	3	32	4	27	1	0
Horton	1,510	14	0	0	0	14	9	1	7	1	0
Hugoton	3,795	2	0	0	1	1	12	2	8	2	0
Hutchinson	39,424	186	0	36	7	143	882	140	661	81	7
Independence	8,402	47	0	8	3	36	269	51	205	13	3
Iola	5,302	44	0	14	0	30	208	80	115	13	3
Junction City	21,927	218	2	22	6	188	623	96	477	50	6
Kingman	3,021	4	0	1	1	2	11	2	9	0	0
Lansing	11,200	28	0	10	0	18	132	15	102	15	1
Larned	3,607	18	2	1	0	15	52	9	41	2	0
Lawrence	95,580	448	7	68	34	339	2,098	233	1,697	168	7
Leavenworth	37,004	233	9	30	16	178	864	164	595	105	9
Leawood	33,596	43	0	1	6	36	656	31	530	95	0
Lenexa	59,289	131	2	21	9	99	900	99	675	126	0
Liberal	19,557	71	0	7	7	57	211	29	161	21	0
Louisburg	5,023	12	0	1	0	11	71	37	28	6	1
Maize	6,275	23	0	4	1	18	162	79	72	11	1
Marysville	3,405	14	0	2	1	11	57	11	37	9	1
McLouth	858	1	0	0	0	1	0	0	0	0	0
McPherson	13,853	36	0	10	0	26	248	36	192	20	1
Merriam	10,928	75	2	3	10	60	618	21	472	125	1
Minneapolis	1,974	19	0	3	1	15	18	8	8	2	0

Table 8. Offenses Known to Law Enforcement, by Selected State and City, 2022—Continued

(Number.)

State/city	Population	Violent crime	Murder and nonnegligent manslaughter	Rape	Robbery	Aggravated assault	Property crime	Burglary	Larceny-theft	Motor vehicle theft	Arson[1]
Mission	9,787	46	2	2	10	32	482	25	356	101	0
Mission Hills	3,540	3	0	1	0	2	94	14	60	20	0
Mulvane	6,844	7	0	2	2	3	102	10	86	6	0
Neodesha	2,233	8	0	3	0	5	22	5	15	2	0
Newton	18,337	118	0	26	6	86	491	142	321	28	2
Olathe	144,646	324	2	56	27	239	1,747	236	1,276	235	11
Osage City	2,840	27	0	0	0	27	25	3	21	1	0
Ottawa	12,586	49	0	14	4	31	238	32	200	6	3
Overland Park	196,626	437	5	56	43	333	4,708	573	3,559	576	9
Oxford	1,048	5	0	2	0	3	10	2	7	1	1
Paola	5,808	11	0	1	0	10	77	1	72	4	0
Park City	8,565	37	0	9	1	27	297	40	225	32	1
Parsons	9,369	66	0	4	3	59	359	81	245	33	5
Pittsburg	20,774	101	4	15	8	74	887	103	705	79	3
Pleasanton	1,244	3	0	0	0	3	1	0	1	0	0
Prairie Village	22,835	33	0	5	3	25	304	23	218	63	1
Roeland Park	6,762	23	0	2	8	13	267	4	229	34	0
Sabetha	2,517	3	0	0	0	3	8	1	7	0	0
Salina	46,161	203	3	31	28	141	1,499	211	1,165	123	26
Scott City	4,100	9	0	0	0	9	16	2	12	2	0
Shawnee	67,617	169	3	21	10	135	951	73	722	156	4
Spring Hill	9,024	13	0	2	0	11	103	10	78	15	0
Tonganoxie	5,836	6	0	4	0	2	32	3	27	2	0
Topeka	125,658	1,211	13	60	117	1,021	4,659	711	3,243	705	16
Ulysses	5,764	11	0	1	0	10	8	2	5	1	0
Valley Center	7,463	13	0	4	0	9	69	4	56	9	1
Wellington	7,641	33	1	6	3	23	185	26	151	8	6
Wellsville	1,922	4	0	0	2	2	14	2	12	0	0
Westwood	1,729	4	0	0	1	3	94	4	78	12	0
Wichita	394,286	3,670	31	272	302	3,065	13,893	1,689	10,632	1,572	91
Winfield	11,713	47	0	5	1	41	315	47	241	27	3
KENTUCKY											
Adairville	876	0	0	0	0	0	2	0	2	0	0
Albany	1,749	0	0	0	0	0	2	0	2	0	1
Alexandria	10,416	8	0	2	2	4	138	4	129	5	0
Anchorage	2,470	0	0	0	0	0	15	5	10	0	0
Ashland	21,300	40	2	12	6	20	526	76	394	56	4
Auburn	1,625	0	0	0	0	0	1	0	1	0	0
Audubon Park	1,411	1	0	0	0	1	14	6	5	3	0
Augusta	1,104	1	0	0	0	1	5	1	3	1	0
Bancroft	500	0	0	0	0	0	2	0	2	0	0
Barbourville	2,952	3	0	2	0	1	41	14	22	5	0
Bardstown	13,712	19	0	3	7	9	229	33	164	32	0
Bardwell	707	0	0	0	0	0	2	0	2	0	0
Beattyville	2,065	0	0	0	0	0	6	3	0	3	0
Beaver Dam	3,538	1	0	0	0	1	21	1	16	4	0
Bellefonte	902	0	0	0	0	0	1	1	0	0	0
Bellevue	5,534	0	0	0	0	0	71	8	59	4	0
Benton	4,771	2	0	1	0	1	75	11	55	9	0
Berea	16,229	17	0	7	1	9	195	25	126	44	0
Bloomfield	978	0	0	0	0	0	0	0	0	0	0
Booneville	154	0	0	0	0	0	0	0	0	0	0
Bowling Green	74,427	212	4	65	56	87	2,841	356	2,196	289	10
Brandenburg	2,952	1	0	0	0	1	29	4	14	11	0
Brodhead	1,105	0	0	0	0	0	0	0	0	0	1
Brooksville	662	0	0	0	0	0	0	0	0	0	0
Brownsville	943	1	0	0	0	1	5	1	4	0	0
Burgin	1,005	0	0	0	0	0	3	2	1	0	0
Burkesville	1,347	1	0	1	0	0	4	0	2	2	0
Burnside	699	2	0	0	2	0	9	1	6	2	0
Cadiz	2,840	4	0	0	0	4	31	9	21	1	0
Calvert City	2,521	5	0	1	1	3	39	8	31	0	0
Campbellsville	11,548	14	0	4	5	5	178	58	107	13	0
Caneyville	526	0	0	0	0	0	0	0	0	0	0
Carlisle	2,160	1	0	0	0	1	12	7	4	1	0
Carrollton	3,898	1	0	0	0	1	17	4	11	2	1
Catlettsburg	1,724	1	0	0	1	0	22	4	12	6	0
Cave City	2,347	0	0	0	0	0	11	5	1	5	0
Centertown	414	0	0	0	0	0	2	0	1	1	0
Central City	5,884	14	0	3	1	10	130	10	113	7	0
Clarkson	943	0	0	0	0	0	0	0	0	0	0
Clay	998	1	0	0	0	1	6	3	3	0	0
Clay City	1,204	0	0	0	0	0	6	0	5	1	0
Clinton	1,236	0	0	0	0	0	0	0	0	0	0
Coal Run Village	1,627	0	0	0	0	0	12	1	10	1	0
Cold Spring	6,272	4	0	1	1	2	70	10	54	6	0
Columbia	4,995	5	0	0	0	5	13	6	7	0	0
Corbin	7,762	21	0	1	2	18	159	20	120	19	1
Covington	40,657	109	2	18	32	57	712	97	504	111	4
Crab Orchard	742	0	0	0	0	0	0	0	0	0	0
Cumberland	1,856	0	0	0	0	0	3	1	1	1	0
Cynthiana	6,429	5	0	0	0	5	61	8	49	4	2

Table 8. Offenses Known to Law Enforcement, by Selected State and City, 2022—Continued

(Number.)

State/city	Population	Violent crime	Murder and nonnegligent manslaughter	Rape	Robbery	Aggravated assault	Property crime	Burglary	Larceny-theft	Motor vehicle theft	Arson[1]
Danville	17,323	23	0	4	5	14	233	42	171	20	0
Dawson Springs	2,431	2	0	0	1	1	22	8	11	3	0
Dayton	5,685	10	0	3	2	5	47	3	38	6	0
Dry Ridge	2,128	0	0	0	0	0	18	0	16	2	0
Eddyville	2,323	1	0	0	0	1	12	1	10	1	0
Edgewood	8,372	0	0	0	0	0	45	5	38	2	0
Edmonton	1,696	1	0	0	0	1	22	6	7	9	0
Elizabethtown	32,437	40	0	10	16	14	290	63	191	36	2
Elkhorn City	980	0	0	0	0	0	0	0	0	0	0
Elkton	2,072	1	0	0	0	1	39	12	26	1	1
Elsmere	9,157	10	0	4	1	5	108	7	79	22	1
Eminence	2,702	3	0	0	0	3	45	11	33	1	0
Erlanger	24,147	14	0	5	1	8	69	11	43	15	0
Eubank	330	0	0	0	0	0	0	0	0	0	0
Evarts	850	0	0	0	0	0	7	4	1	2	0
Falmouth	2,184	0	0	0	0	0	30	13	17	0	1
Ferguson	885	0	0	0	0	0	7	0	7	0	0
Flatwoods	7,231	5	0	1	1	3	31	11	15	5	1
Fleming-Neon	531	0	0	0	0	0	0	0	0	0	0
Flemingsburg	2,943	3	0	1	0	2	41	18	20	3	1
Florence	32,341	63	0	20	17	26	1,353	73	1,231	49	2
Fort Mitchell	8,643	2	0	1	1	0	73	4	65	4	0
Fort Thomas	17,159	4	0	1	0	3	92	10	74	8	0
Fort Wright	5,819	7	0	1	3	3	33	1	25	7	0
Fountain Run	217	0	0	0	0	0	1	0	1	0	0
Frankfort	28,559	66	3	23	10	30	553	87	390	76	3
Franklin	10,174	19	0	6	7	6	274	38	218	18	2
Fulton	2,387	4	0	0	0	4	114	23	88	3	0
Georgetown	38,213	43	1	9	5	28	534	81	387	66	3
Glasgow	15,194	25	0	6	3	16	288	46	214	28	2
Grayson	3,683	6	0	2	1	3	81	4	64	13	1
Greensburg	2,220	7	0	2	0	5	23	1	17	5	0
Greenup	1,043	1	0	0	1	0	2	0	2	0	0
Greenville	4,424	6	0	0	0	6	27	6	18	3	1
Guthrie	1,334	2	0	0	0	2	8	0	3	5	0
Hardinsburg	2,416	4	0	1	1	2	15	6	7	2	0
Harlan	1,679	3	0	0	1	2	28	12	14	2	0
Harrodsburg	9,200	9	0	3	0	6	90	23	54	13	0
Hartford	2,667	7	0	2	0	5	13	3	8	2	1
Hawesville	1,009	0	0	0	0	0	1	1	0	0	0
Hazard	5,011	9	0	6	0	3	46	7	24	15	0
Henderson	27,503	67	2	19	20	26	560	132	373	55	3
Heritage Creek	1,199	0	0	0	0	0	8	0	8	0	0
Highland Heights	6,784	4	0	2	1	1	41	4	34	3	0
Hillview	8,721	13	0	2	0	11	130	11	83	36	4
Hodgenville	3,365	12	0	3	1	8	36	6	28	2	0
Hopkinsville	30,528	113	5	23	28	57	1,133	170	890	73	4
Horse Cave	2,237	3	0	0	0	3	14	4	7	3	0
Hurstbourne Acres	1,937	0	0	0	0	0	20	1	18	1	0
Hustonville	388	0	0	0	0	0	0	0	0	0	0
Hyden	267	0	0	0	0	0	0	0	0	0	0
Independence	29,211	20	1	10	1	8	106	13	75	18	0
Indian Hills	2,819	0	0	0	0	0	61	4	55	2	0
Irvine	2,317	2	0	1	1	0	24	9	13	2	0
Irvington	1,251	4	0	0	0	4	4	2	0	2	0
Jackson	2,179	3	0	0	0	3	34	10	20	4	0
Jamestown	1,842	1	0	1	0	0	17	1	12	4	0
Jeffersontown	28,519	31	1	4	20	6	724	54	549	121	0
Jenkins	1,855	0	0	0	0	0	2	1	1	0	0
Junction City	2,259	1	0	0	0	1	71	64	5	2	0
La Center	857	0	0	0	0	0	0	0	0	0	0
La Grange	10,348	16	0	5	3	8	136	18	105	13	0
Lakeside Park-Crestview Hills	6,227	1	0	1	0	0	72	2	69	1	0
Lancaster	3,996	7	2	1	0	4	78	18	47	13	0
Lawrenceburg	11,855	10	0	2	1	7	63	7	44	12	0
Lebanon	6,473	11	1	4	0	6	75	17	47	11	0
Lebanon Junction	1,765	0	0	0	0	0	2	0	1	1	0
Leitchfield	6,433	12	0	4	1	7	109	24	74	11	1
Lexington	320,983	868	33	176	225	434	8,717	1,099	6,393	1,225	20
Liberty	1,972	0	0	0	0	0	0	0	0	0	0
Livingston	165	0	0	0	0	0	0	0	0	0	0
London	7,401	13	0	1	4	8	322	52	240	30	0
Louisa	2,639	7	0	0	3	4	31	8	18	5	0
Loyall	606	0	0	0	0	0	1	1	0	0	0
Ludlow	4,339	4	0	3	0	1	53	14	34	5	1
Lyndon	2,831	13	0	1	4	8	265	32	189	44	0
Madisonville	19,292	19	0	6	4	9	177	50	101	26	1
Manchester	1,482	2	0	1	0	1	24	6	8	10	0
Marion	2,832	4	0	1	0	3	31	8	20	3	1
Martin	487	0	0	0	0	0	1	0	1	0	0
Mayfield	9,966	21	0	7	3	11	230	66	151	13	0
Maysville	8,672	10	0	6	1	3	199	25	153	21	0
McKee	804	1	0	0	0	1	7	1	0	6	0

Table 8. Offenses Known to Law Enforcement, by Selected State and City, 2022—Continued

(Number.)

State/city	Population	Violent crime	Murder and nonnegligent manslaughter	Rape	Robbery	Aggravated assault	Property crime	Burglary	Larceny-theft	Motor vehicle theft	Arson[1]
Meadow Vale	716	0	0	0	0	0	8	1	6	1	0
Middlesboro	9,213	27	0	4	4	19	335	23	290	22	3
Middletown	9,600	13	0	1	6	6	294	22	237	35	0
Millersburg	743	0	0	0	0	0	6	2	3	1	0
Monticello	5,685	9	0	0	3	6	71	23	37	11	3
Morehead	7,030	17	0	5	2	10	125	8	111	6	1
Morganfield	3,202	2	0	0	0	2	8	0	5	3	0
Morgantown	2,459	8	0	1	1	6	11	4	4	3	0
Mount Sterling	7,544	7	0	3	0	4	235	15	206	14	0
Mount Vernon	2,409	3	0	0	0	3	9	1	5	3	0
Mount Washington	18,440	9	0	1	2	6	106	19	71	16	0
Muldraugh	1,028	0	0	0	0	0	15	3	5	7	0
Murray	17,506	23	0	4	2	17	288	33	243	12	1
New Haven	808	0	0	0	0	0	0	0	0	0	0
Newport	14,017	41	1	16	5	19	418	37	335	46	1
Nicholasville	31,882	42	1	13	7	21	546	80	417	49	2
Northfield	991	0	0	0	0	0	2	0	1	1	0
Oak Grove	7,810	23	3	7	6	7	218	42	139	37	2
Owensboro	59,839	221	3	49	39	130	2,070	261	1,545	264	14
Owenton	1,587	0	0	0	0	0	1	0	1	0	0
Owingsville	1,587	0	0	0	0	0	10	5	3	2	0
Paducah	26,050	70	6	22	11	31	790	68	650	72	5
Paintsville	4,313	5	0	0	1	4	12	2	5	5	0
Paris	10,174	9	0	2	3	4	121	19	82	20	1
Park Hills	3,158	0	0	0	0	0	21	1	16	4	0
Pembroke	851	0	0	0	0	0	4	0	4	0	0
Perryville	781	0	0	0	0	0	0	0	0	0	0
Pewee Valley	1,633	0	0	0	0	0	4	1	2	1	0
Pikeville	7,190	22	0	2	7	13	156	39	96	21	0
Pineville	1,650	1	0	0	0	1	20	1	16	3	0
Pioneer Village	2,697	1	0	0	0	1	21	6	13	2	0
Pippa Passes	581	0	0	0	0	0	1	0	1	0	0
Powderly	782	0	0	0	0	0	0	0	0	0	0
Prestonsburg	4,034	7	0	1	1	5	41	17	19	5	0
Princeton	6,191	10	1	2	0	7	93	11	73	9	0
Prospect	4,552	1	0	0	1	0	31	6	22	3	0
Providence	2,820	4	0	0	0	4	13	8	4	1	0
Raceland	2,321	1	0	0	0	1	10	4	4	2	0
Radcliff	22,931	47	0	13	6	28	508	99	343	66	3
Ravenna	559	0	0	0	0	0	3	2	1	0	0
Richmond	36,698	66	0	14	17	35	782	94	616	72	2
Russell	3,656	4	0	1	1	2	33	3	28	2	0
Russell Springs	2,784	2	0	0	0	2	12	2	8	2	0
Russellville	7,257	19	0	8	3	8	183	37	127	19	1
Salyersville	1,520	2	0	0	0	2	3	2	0	1	0
Science Hill	657	0	0	0	0	0	4	2	2	0	0
Scottsville	4,368	6	0	1	0	5	75	13	52	10	1
Sebree	1,514	0	0	0	0	0	1	1	0	0	0
Shelbyville	17,481	21	0	0	8	13	205	39	122	44	0
Shepherdsville	14,440	28	0	5	9	14	240	56	146	38	0
Shively	15,438	75	5	9	35	26	478	76	271	131	1
Simpsonville	3,016	5	0	0	2	3	61	1	56	4	0
Smiths Grove	779	0	0	0	0	0	21	2	18	1	0
Somerset	12,170	30	0	8	4	18	226	52	148	26	7
Southgate	3,658	0	0	0	0	0	25	4	15	6	0
South Shore	1,037	0	0	0	0	0	2	2	0	0	0
Springfield	2,854	5	0	0	0	5	18	7	8	3	0
Stamping Ground	807	0	0	0	0	0	3	1	2	0	0
Stanford	3,601	4	0	0	0	4	24	8	15	1	3
Stanton	3,154	6	0	0	1	5	27	5	20	2	2
St. Matthews	17,341	20	0	5	10	5	818	73	680	65	1
Strathmoor Village	673	0	0	0	0	0	0	0	0	0	0
Sturgis	1,579	0	0	0	0	0	2	0	2	0	0
Taylor Mill	6,821	3	0	0	1	2	16	0	14	2	0
Taylorsville	1,287	1	0	0	0	1	18	6	10	2	0
Tompkinsville	2,289	0	0	0	0	0	7	1	3	3	0
Trenton	327	0	0	0	0	0	0	0	0	0	0
Uniontown	847	0	0	0	0	0	0	0	0	0	0
Vanceburg	1,346	1	0	0	0	1	0	0	0	0	0
Versailles	27,242	19	1	4	0	14	247	44	176	27	1
Villa Hills	7,337	2	0	2	0	0	56	2	48	6	1
Vine Grove	6,843	4	0	2	0	2	36	8	21	7	0
Warsaw	1,740	3	0	0	0	3	14	1	12	1	0
Wayland	398	0	0	0	0	0	1	1	0	0	0
West Buechel	1,352	6	0	0	4	2	85	10	58	17	0
West Liberty	3,251	1	0	0	0	1	10	1	8	1	0
West Point	942	0	0	0	0	0	2	0	2	0	0
Wheelwright	481	0	0	0	0	0	0	0	0	0	0
Whitesburg	1,662	0	0	0	0	0	0	0	0	0	0
Wilder	3,125	1	0	0	0	1	29	1	23	5	0
Williamsburg	5,348	10	0	1	1	8	45	11	27	7	0
Williamstown	3,987	3	0	2	0	1	28	5	16	7	1
Wilmore	6,081	2	0	1	1	0	38	4	33	1	0

Table 8. Offenses Known to Law Enforcement, by Selected State and City, 2022—Continued

(Number.)

State/city	Population	Violent crime	Murder and nonnegligent manslaughter	Rape	Robbery	Aggravated assault	Property crime	Burglary	Larceny-theft	Motor vehicle theft	Arson[1]
Winchester	18,989	35	0	6	2	27	642	125	470	47	3
Windy Hills	2,400	0	0	0	0	0	0	0	0	0	0
Woodburn	316	0	0	0	0	0	0	0	0	0	0
Woodlawn Park	931	0	0	0	0	0	0	0	0	0	0
Worthington	1,475	0	0	0	0	0	1	0	1	0	0
LOUISIANA											
Abbeville	10,968	85	2	5	5	73	234	18	195	21	0
Addis	7,438	11	0	4	1	6	37	7	22	8	0
Alexandria	44,349	791	18	56	78	639	2,804	473	2,129	202	9
Baker	12,303	67	3	5	4	55	276	61	188	27	0
Bastrop	9,291	111	1	1	6	103	426	97	312	17	2
Baton Rouge	219,913	2,260	64	134	340	1,722	12,870	3,109	8,168	1,593	18
Bernice	1,328	1	0	0	0	1	2	0	2	0	0
Berwick	4,557	5	0	3	0	2	11	0	10	1	0
Blanchard	3,383	2	0	0	1	1	23	2	17	4	0
Bogalusa	10,461	144	6	8	4	126	465	101	335	29	2
Bossier City	63,078	636	6	46	44	540	2,945	358	2,305	282	4
Broussard	14,103	43	2	1	2	38	319	75	225	19	0
Brusly	2,598	2	0	1	0	1	11	1	8	2	0
Clinton	1,342	5	0	0	0	5	0	0	0	0	0
Covington	11,543	23	2	3	2	16	107	16	80	11	1
De Ridder	9,674	39	1	7	0	31	150	16	127	7	8
Erath	2,002	6	0	0	0	6	11	3	8	0	0
Evergreen	207	0	0	0	0	0	0	0	0	0	0
Ferriday	3,041	50	0	2	1	47	41	11	29	1	0
Golden Meadow	1,735	7	0	0	0	7	38	9	28	1	0
Gonzales	12,869	63	3	10	14	36	880	45	790	45	3
Gramercy	2,801	12	0	0	0	12	75	7	66	2	0
Greenwood	3,077	13	0	0	4	9	108	31	68	9	0
Gretna	17,358	104	1	7	12	84	629	75	500	54	2
Hammond	20,847	256	0	13	18	225	1,373	156	1,150	67	1
Harahan	8,827	15	0	1	2	12	76	4	68	4	1
Haughton	4,457	4	0	0	3	1	17	2	10	5	1
Haynesville	1,884	11	0	1	1	9	24	12	9	3	1
Houma	32,762	272	15	2	26	229	1,337	261	1,006	70	9
Ida	212	0	0	0	0	0	0	0	0	0	0
Iowa	2,972	36	2	1	0	33	66	11	47	8	1
Jennings	9,664	64	1	5	2	56	311	57	227	27	1
Krotz Springs	894	4	0	0	0	4	37	0	37	0	0
Lafayette	121,546	582	22	18	100	442	5,333	797	4,098	438	
Lake Charles	77,054	485	14	32	53	386	2,398	538	1,638	222	3
Lake Providence	3,661	0	0	0	0	0	2	2	0	0	0
Livingston	1,946	1	0	0	0	1	28	4	22	2	0
Mandeville	13,245	24	0	1	1	22	178	16	156	6	0
Mansfield	4,472	20	0	1	0	19	10	6	4	0	0
Marion	619	0	0	0	0	0	0	0	0	0	0
Marksville	4,843	82	1	2	2	77	241	19	215	7	2
Monroe	46,908	1,284	18	18	107	1,141	3,153	662	2,280	211	4
Morgan City	10,909	124	3	9	10	102	358	76	262	20	5
New Orleans	370,128	5,345	266	442	1,039	3,598	17,177	1,837	11,138	4,202	
Norwood	279	0	0	0	0	0	0	0	0	0	0
Opelousas	15,447	337	11	6	26	294	955	256	592	107	6
Patterson	5,681	37	0	0	0	37	37	9	23	5	0
Pearl River	2,680	12	0	1	1	10	35	12	22	1	0
Plaquemine	5,804	47	2	1	1	43	151	26	117	8	2
Ponchatoula	7,977	50	0	1	2	47	295	37	246	12	2
Port Allen	4,984	72	0	2	4	66	132	16	106	10	0
Rayne	7,100	3	0	0	0	3	62	5	54	3	0
Ruston	22,435	180	3	18	18	141	853	130	693	30	2
Shreveport	180,763	1,466	47	137	231	1,051	6,851	1,270	4,894	687	
Slidell	28,686	77	2	12	8	55	813	56	700	57	2
Springhill	4,597	4	0	0	1	3	34	13	20	1	0
Sulphur	19,581	84	1	15	6	62	727	172	517	38	4
Tallulah	5,975	67	1	1	0	65	29	13	12	4	0
Thibodaux	15,166	71	2	4	7	58	456	41	402	13	1
Vidalia	3,771	14	1	2	0	11	132	23	99	10	0
Vinton	2,973	13	0	0	0	13	98	26	64	8	2
Walker	6,450	40	1	8	3	28	236	61	161	14	0
Westlake	4,464	7	0	0	0	7	124	28	91	5	0
West Monroe	12,680	218	0	25	16	177	819	191	589	39	2
Westwego	8,266	40	0	0	2	38	156	27	112	17	3
Wilson	354	0	0	0	0	0	0	0	0	0	0
Zachary	20,344	71	1	10	4	56	396	45	302	49	0
MAINE											
Ashland	1,184	2	0	0	0	2	3	1	2	0	0
Auburn	24,122	40	2	10	4	24	624	31	568	25	3
Augusta	19,013	85	0	14	5	66	737	49	629	59	1
Bangor	32,078	52	0	7	19	26	1,550	100	1,417	33	8
Bar Harbor	7,478	3	0	0	0	3	37	2	33	2	0
Bath	8,834	3	1	0	0	2	77	4	73	0	0
Belfast	7,037	1	0	0	0	1	43	2	40	1	0

Table 8. Offenses Known to Law Enforcement, by Selected State and City, 2022—Continued

(Number.)

State/city	Population	Violent crime	Murder and nonnegligent manslaughter	Rape	Robbery	Aggravated assault	Property crime	Burglary	Larceny-theft	Motor vehicle theft	Arson[1]
Berwick	8,185	9	0	5	0	4	59	9	50	0	0
Biddeford	22,647	76	0	14	7	55	649	37	593	19	7
Boothbay Harbor	2,090	0	0	0	0	0	11	1	10	0	0
Brewer	9,634	3	0	0	2	1	216	6	207	3	0
Bridgton	5,640	5	0	0	0	5	51	9	36	6	0
Brunswick	21,888	16	0	5	2	9	334	14	302	18	3
Bucksport	5,080	2	0	0	0	2	44	2	40	2	1
Buxton	8,528	8	0	4	0	4	74	11	59	4	1
Calais	3,041	3	0	2	0	1	33	4	28	1	0
Camden	5,326	0	0	0	0	0	21	0	20	1	0
Cape Elizabeth	9,535	1	0	0	0	1	25	5	19	1	0
Caribou	7,352	5	0	0	0	5	44	5	37	2	0
Carrabassett Valley	698	1	0	0	0	1	8	0	7	1	0
Clinton	3,380	1	0	0	1	0	10	3	6	1	0
Cumberland	8,616	0	0	0	0	0	18	0	18	0	0
Damariscotta	2,332	1	0	0	0	1	17	3	14	0	0
Dexter	3,793	1	0	1	0	0	30	2	27	1	0
Dover-Foxcroft	4,537	0	0	0	0	0	31	2	26	3	0
East Millinocket	6,823	1	0	0	1	0	80	13	59	8	0
Eastport	1,282	2	0	0	0	2	0	0	0	0	0
Eliot	7,162	1	0	0	0	1	18	2	13	3	0
Ellsworth	8,676	13	0	7	2	4	303	5	293	5	0
Fairfield	6,507	10	0	5	2	3	112	13	90	9	0
Falmouth	12,695	4	0	1	0	3	86	3	76	7	2
Farmington	7,520	7	0	3	0	4	78	6	68	4	0
Fort Fairfield	3,267	3	0	1	1	1	28	5	22	1	0
Fort Kent	4,120	2	0	1	0	1	24	5	16	3	1
Freeport	8,802	2	0	1	0	1	105	5	96	4	0
Fryeburg	3,480	3	0	2	1	0	15	2	13	0	0
Gorham	18,482	8	0	2	0	6	91	6	78	7	1
Gouldsboro	1,768	0	0	0	0	0	0	0	0	0	0
Greenville	1,538	0	0	0	0	0	9	1	8	0	0
Hallowell	2,579	1	0	0	0	1	17	2	12	3	0
Hampden	7,864	1	0	0	0	1	39	7	30	2	0
Holden	3,312	0	0	0	0	0	24	2	20	2	0
Houlton	6,071	5	0	0	0	5	111	8	103	0	0
Islesboro	589	0	0	0	0	0	14	3	11	0	0
Jay	4,706	8	0	1	0	7	41	4	36	1	0
Kennebunk	11,804	3	0	2	0	1	63	11	51	1	0
Kennebunkport	3,716	0	0	0	0	0	18	1	16	1	0
Kittery	10,279	5	0	1	0	4	171	6	159	6	0
Lewiston	36,488	101	3	26	26	46	701	95	570	36	9
Limestone	1,524	0	0	0	0	0	6	3	2	1	0
Lincoln	4,846	5	0	0	1	4	109	16	89	4	0
Lisbon	9,660	7	0	2	3	2	93	8	77	8	1
Livermore Falls	3,074	6	0	3	1	2	34	4	28	2	0
Machias	1,834	4	0	2	0	2	18	4	14	0	0
Madawaska	3,846	6	0	4	0	2	27	5	22	0	0
Mechanic Falls	3,112	4	0	3	0	1	29	4	24	1	0
Mexico	2,787	4	1	0	1	2	90	12	76	2	0
Milbridge	1,358	0	0	0	0	0	0	0	0	0	0
Milo	2,381	4	0	4	0	0	37	6	30	1	0
Newport	3,120	1	0	0	0	1	50	3	45	2	0
North Berwick	5,163	5	0	3	0	2	20	3	17	0	0
Norway	5,201	2	0	1	0	1	101	12	85	4	1
Oakland	6,300	6	0	4	1	1	49	5	33	11	0
Ogunquit	1,603	0	0	0	0	0	20	1	17	2	0
Old Orchard Beach	9,244	15	0	2	1	12	122	15	99	8	0
Old Town	7,372	2	0	0	1	1	61	8	51	2	0
Orono	11,651	5	0	1	0	4	42	2	36	4	1
Paris	5,349	11	0	7	1	3	65	14	45	6	0
Pittsfield	3,904	4	0	2	1	1	31	4	25	2	1
Portland	68,199	126	5	31	17	73	1,149	35	1,018	96	15
Presque Isle	8,746	16	0	4	1	11	213	15	192	6	0
Rangeley	1,253	0	0	0	0	0	2	0	2	0	0
Richmond	3,585	0	0	0	0	0	6	0	5	1	0
Rockland	7,081	6	0	0	0	6	159	25	122	12	0
Rockport	3,719	0	0	0	0	0	22	1	20	1	0
Rumford	5,929	1	0	0	0	1	109	18	89	2	0
Sabattus	5,113	4	0	1	0	3	14	0	13	1	0
Saco	20,936	30	0	6	1	23	317	25	265	27	2
Sanford	22,315	45	1	28	1	15	535	38	469	28	2
Scarborough	22,913	15	0	5	2	8	364	30	328	6	0
Searsport	2,663	0	0	0	0	0	6	0	5	1	0
Skowhegan	8,595	18	1	3	1	13	258	16	229	13	1
South Berwick	7,653	5	0	4	0	1	25	3	21	1	2
South Portland	27,445	43	0	10	9	24	492	26	418	48	3
Southwest Harbor	1,836	0	0	0	0	0	7	2	5	0	0
Thomaston	2,816	1	0	0	0	1	36	2	33	1	0
Topsham	9,680	5	0	1	1	3	109	8	98	3	1
Veazie	1,807	0	0	0	0	0	4	0	3	1	0
Waldoboro	5,314	1	0	0	0	1	34	7	26	1	0
Washburn	1,498	3	0	2	0	1	1	0	1	0	0

Table 8. Offenses Known to Law Enforcement, by Selected State and City, 2022—Continued

(Number.)

State/city	Population	Violent crime	Murder and nonnegligent manslaughter	Rape	Robbery	Aggravated assault	Property crime	Burglary	Larceny-theft	Motor vehicle theft	Arson[1]
Waterville	15,972	33	0	15	3	15	686	45	622	19	1
Wells	11,760	8	1	2	0	5	96	6	84	6	0
Westbrook	20,741	37	0	9	8	20	218	29	167	22	0
Wilton	3,913	2	0	0	1	1	32	4	23	5	0
Windham	19,048	7	0	2	0	5	143	12	125	6	0
Winslow	7,970	8	0	3	1	4	96	5	87	4	1
Winter Harbor	479	1	1	0	0	0	4	0	3	1	0
Winthrop	6,168	5	0	1	0	4	31	3	27	1	1
Wiscasset	3,880	4	0	2	0	2	43	7	35	1	0
Yarmouth	9,009	4	0	2	1	1	49	1	47	1	0
York	13,977	9	0	2	0	7	88	13	67	8	3
MARYLAND[2]											
Aberdeen	17,576	107	1	7	21	78	374	34	317	23	1
Annapolis	40,542	215	1	17	42	155	788	75	644	69	18
Baltimore	570,546	8,861	287	259	3,172	5,143	18,699	3,333	11,940	3,426	76
Baltimore City Sheriff	0	0	0	0	0	0	0	0	0	0	0
Bel Air	10,675	19	0	1	7	11	268	11	254	3	0
Bowie	57,068	62	0	0	19	43	687	40	556	91	1
Brunswick	8,279	16	0	2	5	9	65	15	48	2	0
Chestertown	5,638	18	0	2	5	11	94	13	81	0	0
Cumberland	18,647	114	1	11	24	78	633	115	493	25	4
Denton	4,827	19	0	3	3	13	143	11	125	7	0
Easton	17,237	21	1	5	6	9	211	22	181	8	1
Elkton	15,806	113	4	19	19	71	842	110	671	61	2
Frederick	80,985	301	2	36	40	223	1,259	174	1,024	61	8
Frostburg	7,024	8	0	1	1	6	9	4	5	0	0
Hagerstown	43,548	310	8	31	63	208	894	246	520	128	2
Hampstead	6,342	10	0	0	1	9	54	2	50	2	2
Havre de Grace	14,883	19	0	8	1	10	208	26	174	8	0
Manchester	5,477	23	0	0	0	23	7	1	5	1	0
Mount Rainier	8,112	46	0	2	29	15	226	18	177	31	0
North East	4,100	8	0	0	0	8	90	5	81	4	0
Oakland	1,811	1	0	1	0	0	35	2	33	0	0
Ocean City	6,957	129	0	19	19	91	752	84	646	22	0
Oxford	613	0	0	0	0	0	4	1	1	2	0
Rock Hall	1,195	1	0	0	1	0	8	2	6	0	0
Salisbury	33,063	362	1	14	65	282	854	130	684	40	7
Snow Hill	2,174	10	0	2	0	8	21	3	18	0	0
St. Michaels	1,080	0	0	0	0	0	23	2	19	2	0
Thurmont	6,645	4	0	2	0	2	29	6	23	0	0
Westminster	20,165	93	0	5	2	86	398	37	348	13	1
MASSACHUSETTS											
Abington	17,886	27	0	3	4	20	159	19	120	20	1
Acton	23,833	15	0	2	1	12	127	14	109	4	0
Acushnet	10,612	10	0	5	0	5	33	7	20	6	0
Adams	8,073	29	0	4	5	20	102	31	66	5	0
Agawam	28,536	102	0	12	5	85	444	160	250	34	1
Amesbury	17,276	24	0	2	0	22	130	11	114	5	2
Amherst	39,267	76	0	35	1	40	130	29	97	4	1
Andover	36,631	43	0	5	2	36	183	26	146	11	1
Aquinnah	465	0	0	0	0	0	2	1	1	0	0
Arlington	45,238	27	0	2	2	23	269	46	204	19	1
Ashburnham	6,402	11	0	1	0	10	17	5	12	0	0
Ashby	3,166	3	0	1	2	0	17	5	12	0	0
Ashfield	1,690	0	0	0	0	0	5	1	3	1	1
Ashland	18,373	19	0	1	0	18	42	4	33	5	0
Athol	11,938	69	0	7	1	61	93	7	77	9	0
Attleboro	46,942	118	0	10	10	98	506	58	418	30	4
Auburn	16,878	35	0	2	4	29	269	23	233	13	1
Avon	4,764	11	0	1	1	9	74	12	58	4	0
Ayer	8,368	14	0	3	0	11	41	6	29	6	0
Barnstable	50,501	234	1	26	11	196	401	64	311	26	3
Barre	5,555	23	0	4	0	19	22	3	17	2	1
Becket	1,934	5	0	1	0	4	10	2	4	4	0
Bedford	14,034	2	0	1	0	1	72	10	60	2	0
Belchertown	15,277	19	0	5	0	14	82	17	60	5	2
Bellingham	16,965	29	0	10	2	17	165	15	145	5	0
Belmont	26,557	15	0	0	1	14	182	46	126	10	1
Berkley	6,844	4	0	1	0	3	11	0	7	4	0
Berlin	4,137	3	0	1	0	2	20	0	20	0	0
Bernardston	2,846	2	0	1	1	0	10	2	7	1	0
Beverly	42,441	43	0	5	0	38	206	9	185	12	0
Billerica	41,110	23	0	7	3	13	189	26	147	16	2
Blackstone	9,222	5	0	1	0	4	12	1	8	3	0
Bolton	5,710	5	0	0	0	5	25	3	22	0	0
Boston	638,925	3,955	44	176	770	2,965	11,514	1,213	9,116	1,185	32
Bourne	21,127	44	0	6	1	37	137	24	105	8	1
Boxborough	5,377	4	0	0	0	4	30	8	19	3	0
Boxford	8,134	1	0	0	0	1	4	0	4	0	0
Boylston	4,934	5	0	0	0	5	9	1	6	2	0
Braintree	38,835	94	1	14	5	74	504	42	428	34	0

Table 8. Offenses Known to Law Enforcement, by Selected State and City, 2022—Continued

(Number.)

State/city	Population	Violent crime	Murder and nonnegligent manslaughter	Rape	Robbery	Aggravated assault	Property crime	Burglary	Larceny-theft	Motor vehicle theft	Arson[1]
Brewster	10,647	8	0	0	0	8	50	8	39	3	0
Bridgewater	8,820	32	0	5	2	25	59	10	44	5	0
Brimfield	3,711	3	0	0	0	3	11	1	9	1	0
Brockton	110,084	712	8	78	65	561	1,904	289	1,121	494	9
Brookfield	3,443	6	0	3	0	3	15	2	8	5	0
Brookline	62,825	66	0	4	11	51	563	44	485	34	0
Buckland	1,815	2	0	0	0	2	0	0	0	0	0
Burlington	25,783	35	0	3	5	27	426	19	382	25	3
Cambridge	117,044	475	0	42	96	337	2,622	278	2,205	139	14
Canton	24,717	99	0	7	1	91	170	11	145	14	2
Carlisle	5,149	2	0	1	0	1	4	1	3	0	0
Carver	12,215	18	0	2	1	15	40	3	34	3	3
Charlton	13,394	11	0	1	0	10	57	10	36	11	1
Chatham	6,844	10	0	2	0	8	35	3	32	0	0
Chelmsford	35,630	40	0	5	2	33	260	26	221	13	1
Chelsea	37,590	302	0	26	60	216	678	81	521	76	4
Cheshire	3,226	2	0	1	0	1	2	1	1	0	0
Chester	1,221	0	0	0	0	0	2	0	2	0	0
Chicopee	55,265	301	4	37	31	229	1,032	133	804	95	6
Chilmark	1,292	0	0	0	0	0	2	0	2	0	0
Clinton	15,432	8	0	0	0	8	5	1	4	0	0
Cohasset	8,417	5	0	1	0	4	37	5	30	2	0
Concord	18,040	32	0	9	0	23	84	8	74	2	0
Dalton	6,273	17	0	2	3	12	37	6	26	5	0
Danvers	27,887	54	0	6	3	45	330	20	284	26	0
Dartmouth	34,192	90	0	8	12	70	408	35	364	9	2
Dedham	25,324	47	0	3	3	41	144	3	134	7	0
Deerfield	5,154	6	0	2	0	4	29	4	23	2	0
Dennis	15,200	53	0	8	0	45	159	23	133	3	2
Dighton	8,240	8	0	3	1	4	19	4	11	4	0
Douglas	9,146	4	0	0	0	4	20	6	12	2	0
Dover	5,902	5	0	1	0	4	7	1	6	0	1
Dracut	31,908	53	0	10	3	40	188	21	154	13	4
Dudley	11,914	21	0	6	2	13	25	6	14	5	0
Dunstable	3,333	4	0	0	0	4	4	0	2	2	0
Duxbury	16,861	17	0	2	0	15	34	2	31	1	0
East Bridgewater	15,142	22	0	3	1	18	53	6	44	3	0
East Brookfield	2,208	11	0	4	0	7	8	1	2	5	0
Eastham	5,939	8	0	2	0	6	34	5	29	0	0
Easthampton	15,914	25	0	7	0	18	103	11	86	6	0
East Longmeadow	16,458	34	0	8	4	22	231	29	190	12	0
Easton	25,463	45	0	5	5	35	199	21	169	9	1
Edgartown	5,485	23	0	2	0	21	62	14	46	2	1
Egremont	1,374	2	0	0	0	2	9	1	8	0	0
Erving	1,669	6	0	0	0	6	9	2	7	0	0
Essex	3,678	4	0	0	0	4	14	2	11	1	0
Everett	48,340	169	2	24	19	124	654	94	462	98	2
Fairhaven	15,987	55	1	5	3	46	132	15	109	8	0
Fall River	94,339	935	3	50	103	779	1,162	383	589	190	8
Falmouth	33,873	82	2	6	9	65	273	84	179	10	1
Fitchburg	41,791	186	1	22	19	144	309	60	207	42	5
Foxborough	18,549	46	0	7	3	36	125	11	107	7	1
Framingham	70,716	201	1	17	4	179	990	356	549	85	5
Franklin	33,107	29	0	2	1	26	151	63	87	1	0
Freetown	9,247	24	0	2	0	22	57	11	40	6	2
Gardner	21,231	43	0	5	2	36	181	21	149	11	1
Georgetown	8,409	7	0	0	0	7	29	4	24	1	0
Gill	1,535	0	0	0	0	0	9	0	9	0	0
Gloucester	30,301	73	0	14	5	54	167	29	123	15	4
Goshen	945	0	0	0	0	0	2	0	2	0	0
Grafton	19,965	12	0	1	0	11	30	8	22	0	1
Granby	6,036	4	0	1	0	3	25	6	16	3	0
Granville	1,538	2	0	1	0	1	4	0	3	1	1
Great Barrington	7,143	17	0	3	3	11	41	2	37	2	1
Greenfield	17,203	84	0	21	5	58	289	44	236	9	3
Groton	11,074	9	0	1	0	8	16	4	12	0	1
Hadley	5,244	23	0	5	0	18	184	6	174	4	0
Halifax	8,092	7	0	1	1	5	45	4	38	3	0
Hamilton	7,551	9	0	2	0	7	19	3	14	2	0
Hampden	4,948	5	0	2	0	3	20	1	18	1	0
Hanover	15,578	27	0	3	1	23	69	5	58	6	0
Hanson	11,196	16	0	4	0	12	42	4	36	2	0
Hardwick	2,672	4	0	0	0	4	2	0	2	0	0
Harvard	6,870	10	1	1	0	8	13	4	9	0	0
Harwich	13,891	14	0	1	1	12	97	22	73	2	1
Hatfield	3,301	6	0	0	0	6	17	1	12	4	0
Haverhill	67,359	390	0	3	15	372	537	62	434	41	4
Hingham	25,437	44	0	5	2	37	118	17	94	7	0
Hinsdale	1,905	0	0	0	0	0	0	0	0	0	0
Holbrook	11,350	39	0	4	3	32	134	16	95	23	1
Holden	19,998	21	0	3	1	17	45	8	31	6	1
Holland	2,585	2	0	0	0	2	4	2	1	1	1
Holliston	14,754	4	0	0	0	4	52	9	41	2	0

Table 8. Offenses Known to Law Enforcement, by Selected State and City, 2022—Continued

(Number.)

State/city	Population	Violent crime	Murder and nonnegligent manslaughter	Rape	Robbery	Aggravated assault	Property crime	Burglary	Larceny-theft	Motor vehicle theft	Arson[1]
Holyoke	37,945	364	6	11	57	290	1,411	132	1,161	118	12
Hopedale	6,021	5	0	3	0	2	26	2	21	3	0
Hopkinton	19,180	30	0	3	0	27	47	2	45	0	1
Hudson	19,623	29	0	4	0	25	72	10	56	6	0
Hull	10,676	23	0	8	0	15	64	12	51	1	0
Ipswich	13,735	6	0	1	0	5	35	5	26	4	0
Kingston	14,484	13	1	7	0	5	43	4	38	1	2
Lakeville	12,511	20	0	4	0	16	47	4	41	2	0
Lancaster	8,504	11	0	2	0	9	37	10	27	0	0
Lanesboro	3,021	4	1	0	1	2	31	4	21	6	1
Lawrence	88,422	444	4	28	49	363	799	75	628	96	5
Lee	5,740	11	0	3	0	8	86	13	70	3	0
Leicester	11,084	18	0	2	0	16	91	15	72	4	0
Lenox	5,105	5	0	1	0	4	83	7	72	4	0
Leominster	43,690	187	0	9	17	161	623	75	504	44	4
Leverett	1,861	1	0	0	0	1	8	1	6	1	0
Lexington	33,889	15	0	6	1	8	97	18	71	8	0
Lincoln	6,823	1	0	1	0	0	17	3	14	0	0
Littleton	10,154	4	0	1	1	2	45	3	39	3	0
Longmeadow	15,734	14	0	2	3	9	91	21	61	9	1
Lowell	113,277	455	6	19	72	358	1,979	246	1,536	197	8
Ludlow	20,971	45	0	3	4	38	188	23	147	18	0
Lunenburg	11,903	20	0	5	2	13	75	6	65	4	0
Lynn	101,056	662	7	37	91	527	1,203	157	875	171	6
Lynnfield	12,992	11	0	0	1	10	97	17	77	3	0
Malden	64,356	150	0	3	24	123	803	68	607	128	2
Manchester-by-the-Sea	5,365	0	0	0	0	0	28	1	26	1	0
Mansfield	23,932	29	0	4	4	21	160	11	143	6	1
Marblehead	20,289	14	0	1	1	12	91	16	70	5	1
Marion	5,567	4	0	1	0	3	29	3	26	0	1
Marlborough	40,722	173	0	23	12	138	389	40	309	40	4
Marshfield	27,064	33	0	9	0	24	59	11	42	6	2
Mashpee	15,730	38	0	5	0	33	86	14	68	4	0
Mattapoisett	6,932	12	0	1	0	11	28	3	24	1	1
Maynard	10,464	23	0	4	0	19	63	9	45	9	1
Medfield	13,107	10	0	0	0	10	35	2	30	3	0
Medford	64,122	112	1	14	8	89	605	57	475	73	0
Medway	13,261	9	0	0	0	9	29	3	26	0	0
Melrose	29,013	17	0	1	3	13	144	23	108	13	0
Mendon	6,307	4	0	0	0	4	22	3	17	2	0
Merrimac	6,726	10	0	2	0	8	20	3	16	1	0
Methuen	52,853	76	2	2	9	63	428	80	315	33	0
Middleboro	25,744	107	0	13	4	90	215	39	156	20	2
Middleton	9,790	8	0	5	0	3	37	2	31	4	0
Milford	30,360	45	0	12	4	29	203	26	160	17	1
Millbury	14,008	23	1	2	2	18	140	14	117	9	0
Millis	8,890	7	0	0	0	7	16	2	13	1	0
Millville	3,152	2	0	0	0	2	5	0	5	0	0
Milton	28,454	7	0	0	1	6	140	16	117	7	0
Monson	8,115	25	0	2	0	23	35	6	23	6	0
Montague	8,581	51	0	1	1	49	67	19	40	8	0
Monterey	1,091	0	0	0	0	0	2	1	1	0	0
Nahant	3,315	1	0	0	0	1	7	0	7	0	0
Nantucket	14,814	40	0	8	0	32	253	35	197	21	0
Natick	36,090	53	0	9	6	38	512	34	469	9	2
Needham	32,228	26	0	10	2	14	167	20	139	8	0
New Bedford	101,402	635	4	49	111	471	1,582	198	1,197	187	13
New Braintree	993	2	0	0	0	2	3	0	1	2	0
Newbury	6,717	6	0	1	0	5	24	5	18	1	0
Newburyport	18,366	27	0	10	0	17	93	5	77	11	0
New Marlborough	1,513	3	0	0	0	3	3	3	0	0	0
Newton	86,710	56	1	8	8	39	568	60	497	11	2
Norfolk	11,621	9	0	0	0	9	29	3	24	2	0
North Adams	12,836	129	2	6	7	114	307	50	247	10	2
Northampton	29,150	114	1	23	5	85	363	37	308	18	3
North Andover	30,695	28	0	4	3	21	129	22	92	15	3
North Attleboro	31,071	48	0	4	2	42	329	20	289	20	0
Northborough	15,699	5	0	0	0	5	2	0	0	2	0
Northbridge	16,357	9	0	1	0	8	65	8	50	7	1
Northfield	2,877	7	0	1	0	6	4	1	1	2	0
North Reading	15,197	14	0	0	0	14	55	4	43	8	0
Norton	19,374	21	0	0	1	20	29	2	19	8	0
Norwell	11,866	4	0	1	0	3	57	9	46	2	0
Norwood	31,533	49	0	5	3	41	262	18	222	22	1
Oak Bluffs	5,653	39	0	3	0	36	77	13	60	4	0
Oakham	1,852	1	0	0	0	1	10	2	7	1	0
Orleans	6,546	10	0	4	1	5	49	4	43	2	0
Otis	1,628	0	0	0	0	0	5	2	1	2	0
Oxford	13,316	32	0	9	2	21	99	13	76	10	4
Palmer	12,393	42	0	7	0	35	118	35	71	12	5
Paxton	5,073	10	0	2	0	8	13	1	11	1	0
Pelham	1,257	1	0	0	0	1	0	0	0	0	0
Pembroke	19,289	16	0	5	1	10	45	4	40	1	0

Table 8. Offenses Known to Law Enforcement, by Selected State and City, 2022—Continued

(Number.)

State/city	Population	Violent crime	Murder and nonnegligent manslaughter	Rape	Robbery	Aggravated assault	Property crime	Burglary	Larceny-theft	Motor vehicle theft	Arson[1]
Pepperell	11,600	10	0	0	0	10	62	15	41	6	1
Pittsfield	43,496	326	3	40	32	251	693	231	390	72	9
Plainville	9,921	18	0	1	0	17	98	22	71	5	0
Plymouth	65,779	229	0	30	5	194	550	60	462	28	2
Plympton	3,075	3	0	0	0	3	10	0	6	4	0
Princeton	3,521	5	0	2	0	3	8	2	5	1	0
Provincetown	3,775	6	0	2	1	3	30	10	18	2	0
Quincy	101,434	403	2	34	32	335	1,106	198	816	92	7
Randolph	32,477	84	2	5	9	68	394	49	298	47	0
Raynham	15,404	22	0	6	2	14	161	9	141	11	0
Reading	25,018	4	0	0	0	4	147	23	123	1	0
Rehoboth	12,936	14	0	3	0	11	51	7	40	4	0
Revere	56,961	193	1	23	19	150	696	66	527	103	0
Rochester	6,056	5	0	2	0	3	39	4	32	3	0
Rockland	18,549	53	0	2	0	51	66	12	46	8	0
Rockport	6,961	2	0	1	0	1	8	1	7	0	0
Rowley	6,132	4	0	1	0	3	15	1	12	2	1
Royalston	1,266	1	0	0	1	0	0	0	0	0	0
Rutland	9,316	34	0	5	1	28	22	10	11	1	0
Salem	45,345	85	0	10	11	64	537	57	452	28	7
Salisbury	9,238	26	0	4	0	22	74	13	50	11	1
Sandwich	21,013	24	0	4	1	19	81	11	67	3	0
Saugus	28,880	52	0	7	6	39	338	32	284	22	0
Scituate	20,147	14	0	2	0	12	32	7	25	0	0
Seekonk	15,692	39	0	2	10	27	301	20	253	28	0
Sharon	18,553	7	0	0	0	7	51	4	40	7	0
Shelburne	1,891	0	0	0	0	0	10	3	6	1	1
Sherborn	4,384	4	0	2	0	2	7	0	6	1	0
Shirley	7,228	15	0	2	0	13	18	4	12	2	0
Shrewsbury	39,745	4	0	1	0	3	258	27	207	24	0
Shutesbury	1,734	1	0	0	0	1	1	0	1	0	0
Somerset	18,317	42	0	13	2	27	152	8	136	8	0
Somerville	79,178	200	1	13	42	144	1,095	132	859	104	1
Southampton	6,177	10	0	1	0	9	29	4	25	0	1
Southborough	10,448	5	0	2	0	3	28	7	19	2	0
Southbridge	17,687	67	0	13	4	50	159	28	113	18	1
South Hadley	17,900	26	1	3	2	20	182	21	152	9	2
Southwick	9,229	12	0	1	0	11	74	12	58	4	0
Spencer	11,953	13	0	1	0	12	63	11	47	5	0
Springfield	155,046	1,337	14	82	265	976	3,674	579	2,590	505	37
Sterling	8,372	8	0	4	0	4	24	7	16	1	1
Stockbridge	1,997	5	0	1	0	4	15	2	12	1	0
Stoneham	22,660	48	0	4	5	39	186	41	136	9	1
Stoughton	29,204	76	1	11	7	57	328	31	245	52	3
Stow	6,989	4	0	1	0	3	35	7	27	1	1
Sturbridge	9,892	27	0	3	0	24	73	12	58	3	0
Sudbury	19,314	14	0	5	0	9	45	6	37	2	1
Sunderland	3,655	4	0	0	1	3	26	2	23	1	0
Sutton	9,418	4	0	1	0	3	43	10	30	3	0
Swampscott	15,268	12	0	0	2	10	132	14	116	2	0
Swansea	17,453	26	0	6	0	20	121	7	100	14	0
Taunton	60,062	291	1	22	17	251	549	66	406	77	3
Templeton	8,220	14	0	2	0	12	35	3	32	0	0
Tewksbury	30,656	79	0	14	9	56	345	22	307	16	1
Tisbury	5,079	34	0	1	1	32	41	11	29	1	0
Topsfield	6,581	4	0	0	0	4	24	3	19	2	0
Townsend	8,892	11	0	2	1	8	30	4	24	2	0
Truro	2,536	3	1	0	0	2	12	0	12	0	0
Tyngsboro	12,490	16	0	3	1	12	54	6	36	12	0
Upton	8,137	10	0	2	0	8	15	0	13	2	0
Uxbridge	14,418	23	0	4	0	19	46	14	25	7	1
Wakefield	27,263	41	0	8	4	29	120	11	87	22	1
Wales	1,815	0	0	0	0	0	1	0	1	0	0
Walpole	26,829	41	0	11	1	29	244	25	214	5	0
Waltham	63,525	95	0	14	3	78	349	55	269	25	3
Ware	10,295	64	0	3	0	61	39	3	33	3	1
Wareham	24,389	76	1	12	8	55	243	35	189	19	0
Warren	4,969	9	0	1	1	7	15	3	8	4	0
Watertown	35,088	48	0	4	4	40	359	35	310	14	1
Wayland	13,601	1	0	0	0	1	23	0	21	2	0
Webster	17,651	122	1	16	5	100	209	33	159	17	3
Wellesley	31,354	19	0	5	1	13	118	15	101	2	0
Wellfleet	3,725	3	0	2	0	1	12	3	8	1	0
Wenham	4,998	7	0	0	0	7	12	1	10	1	0
Westborough	21,562	29	0	6	1	22	197	21	169	7	0
West Boylston	7,872	9	0	1	1	7	39	5	25	9	1
West Bridgewater	8,087	10	0	3	2	5	90	23	57	10	0
West Brookfield	3,830	1	0	1	0	0	7	1	4	2	0
Westfield	40,691	92	0	18	5	69	364	30	291	43	2
Westford	24,270	17	0	3	0	14	58	8	44	6	1
Westminster	8,363	19	0	7	0	12	45	5	36	4	2
West Newbury	4,605	1	0	0	0	1	10	0	9	1	0
Weston	11,589	9	0	1	0	8	46	12	33	1	1

Table 8. Offenses Known to Law Enforcement, by Selected State and City, 2022—Continued

(Number.)

State/city	Population	Violent crime	Murder and nonnegligent manslaughter	Rape	Robbery	Aggravated assault	Property crime	Burglary	Larceny-theft	Motor vehicle theft	Arson[1]
Westport	16,475	19	0	4	0	15	78	9	61	8	1
West Springfield	28,655	141	1	25	17	98	1,012	155	782	75	1
West Tisbury	3,757	8	1	0	0	7	10	3	6	1	0
Westwood	16,308	14	0	2	0	12	145	11	127	7	1
Weymouth	58,231	154	0	13	6	135	423	56	339	28	2
Whately	1,639	2	0	1	0	1	7	2	5	0	0
Whitman	16,110	30	0	3	5	22	92	15	58	19	1
Wilbraham	14,600	38	0	4	5	29	155	15	133	7	0
Williamsburg	2,460	3	0	0	0	3	9	1	8	0	0
Williamstown	8,020	6	0	3	0	3	52	3	46	3	0
Wilmington	22,825	34	0	5	4	25	195	19	164	12	0
Winchendon	10,410	29	0	2	1	26	85	22	56	7	0
Winchester	22,496	9	0	0	2	7	61	7	52	2	0
Winthrop	17,954	22	0	1	2	19	83	11	65	7	1
Woburn	41,461	59	0	7	6	46	389	35	312	42	2
Worcester	206,575	1,245	11	42	166	1,026	3,444	696	2,408	340	7
Worthington	1,176	0	0	0	0	0	3	1	2	0	0
Wrentham	12,343	4	0	1	0	3	202	17	183	2	0
Yarmouth	25,705	81	0	16	2	63	227	33	189	5	3
MICHIGAN											
Addison Township	6,223	3	0	1	0	2	9	0	9	0	0
Adrian	20,407	118	0	20	7	91	370	52	283	35	4
Adrian Township	6,325	0	0	0	0	0	5	1	3	1	0
Albion	7,940	87	0	8	2	77	291	57	219	15	2
Allegan	5,155	12	0	5	0	7	38	5	28	5	0
Allen Park	27,917	73	0	9	7	57	441	25	340	76	0
Alma	9,365	35	0	8	1	26	122	13	101	8	0
Almont	2,843	10	1	2	0	7	24	4	19	1	0
Alpena	10,146	48	0	18	0	30	121	14	97	10	2
Ann Arbor	120,549	371	1	49	39	282	2,069	259	1,662	148	10
Argentine Township	7,002	7	0	2	0	5	9	2	6	1	0
Armada	1,658	0	0	0	0	0	6	0	6	0	0
Auburn Hills	25,081	94	0	18	11	65	499	42	389	68	1
Augusta	846	3	0	0	0	3	11	0	8	3	0
Bad Axe	3,014	6	0	3	0	3	47	7	40	0	0
Bancroft	471	0	0	0	0	0	0	0	0	0	0
Bangor	1,988	9	0	1	0	8	40	4	32	4	0
Baroda-Lake Township	4,187	15	0	6	0	9	36	8	28	0	0
Bath Township	13,456	26	0	6	2	18	125	20	93	12	0
Battle Creek	61,347	720	10	97	33	580	1,644	346	1,153	145	15
Bay City	32,249	179	0	29	5	145	384	59	288	37	5
Beaverton	1,150	5	0	0	0	5	2	1	1	0	1
Belding	6,153	22	0	5	0	17	90	9	81	0	0
Belleville	3,928	6	0	3	0	3	59	9	38	12	0
Benton Harbor	8,896	235	4	22	15	194	330	54	176	100	9
Benton Township	14,081	237	6	26	19	186	820	68	613	139	5
Berkley	15,006	4	0	0	1	3	80	10	56	14	0
Berrien Springs-Oronoko Township	9,422	19	0	4	2	13	53	4	46	3	0
Beverly Hills	10,467	9	0	1	1	7	85	7	64	14	0
Birch Run	1,555	4	0	1	0	3	62	5	55	2	0
Birmingham	21,721	7	0	2	0	5	194	18	136	40	0
Blackman Township	38,656	94	2	25	4	63	1,136	129	920	87	7
Blissfield	3,284	5	1	0	0	4	22	9	13	0	1
Bloomfield Hills	4,420	4	0	1	0	3	26	1	24	1	0
Bloomfield Township	43,805	21	0	1	1	19	287	24	232	31	0
Boyne City	3,830	8	0	3	0	5	28	5	23	0	0
Brandon Township	15,284	23	0	4	1	18	25	6	15	4	1
Breckenridge	1,274	2	0	1	0	1	12	0	12	0	0
Bridgeport Township	9,975	40	1	3	2	34	108	17	80	11	0
Bridgman	2,062	4	0	0	0	4	18	6	11	1	0
Brighton	7,483	7	0	1	3	3	104	7	94	3	1
Bronson	2,311	2	0	0	1	1	38	10	25	3	0
Brown City	1,298	2	0	1	0	1	16	0	15	1	0
Brownstown Township	33,033	74	0	10	5	59	336	42	234	60	3
Buchanan	4,179	35	0	10	1	24	101	17	78	6	0
Buena Vista Township	7,588	90	2	6	5	77	142	44	71	27	2
Burton	29,373	242	4	23	11	204	741	99	559	83	1
Cadillac	10,413	55	0	12	3	40	210	36	160	14	2
Cambridge Township	5,681	7	0	1	0	6	21	7	14	0	0
Canton Township	98,582	190	1	19	10	160	1,012	45	860	107	2
Capac	1,972	8	0	0	0	8	15	2	12	1	0
Caro	4,292	14	0	5	0	9	157	23	131	3	0
Carrollton Township	5,669	25	2	3	1	19	61	16	41	4	4
Caseville	646	0	0	0	0	0	8	1	7	0	0
Caspian-Gaastra	1,119	1	0	0	0	1	4	0	2	2	0
Cass City	2,489	10	0	2	0	8	29	2	27	0	0
Cassopolis	1,689	5	0	2	1	2	12	2	8	2	0
Center Line	8,357	33	1	4	3	25	133	19	87	27	1
Charlevoix	2,351	10	0	1	0	9	34	5	29	0	0
Charlotte	9,175	37	0	9	3	25	174	4	164	6	1
Cheboygan	4,849	17	0	9	0	8	90	16	72	2	0

Table 8. Offenses Known to Law Enforcement, by Selected State and City, 2022—Continued

(Number.)

State/city	Population	Violent crime	Murder and nonnegligent manslaughter	Rape	Robbery	Aggravated assault	Property crime	Burglary	Larceny-theft	Motor vehicle theft	Arson[1]
Chelsea	5,322	8	0	3	0	5	36	4	31	1	0
Chesaning	2,440	21	0	0	0	21	28	5	17	6	0
Chesterfield Township	45,519	92	0	17	5	70	437	18	372	47	0
Chikaming Township	2,741	3	0	1	0	2	37	4	32	1	0
Chocolay Township	5,976	7	0	1	0	6	23	0	21	2	1
Clare	3,290	21	0	8	0	13	38	2	35	1	0
Clarkston	909	0	0	0	0	0	14	2	12	0	0
Clawson	11,204	22	0	2	2	18	46	5	36	5	0
Clayton Township	7,274	6	0	2	0	4	19	7	11	1	0
Clay Township	8,430	26	0	7	0	19	37	11	24	2	0
Clinton	2,497	4	0	4	0	0	15	0	14	1	0
Clinton Township	99,274	371	1	51	16	303	1,567	128	1,188	251	2
Clio	2,479	8	0	2	2	4	31	5	26	0	0
Coldwater	13,930	50	0	9	5	36	346	49	283	14	2
Coleman	1,262	0	0	0	0	0	15	1	14	0	0
Colon	1,191	3	0	1	0	2	26	4	20	2	0
Columbia Township	7,470	9	0	3	2	4	52	2	46	4	0
Commerce Township	38,873	23	0	2	2	19	184	13	152	19	1
Constantine	1,968	5	0	4	0	1	19	2	10	7	1
Corunna	3,051	4	0	1	0	3	12	3	8	1	0
Covert Township	2,516	18	0	3	1	14	43	9	27	7	0
Croswell	2,312	5	0	4	0	1	34	4	23	7	0
Davison	5,058	12	1	3	0	8	53	7	37	9	0
Davison Township	20,452	50	1	8	1	40	211	37	150	24	1
Dearborn	107,197	302	2	29	53	218	2,059	149	1,470	440	11
Dearborn Heights	61,789	303	0	20	24	259	937	152	564	221	3
Decatur	1,674	8	0	4	0	4	33	3	29	1	0
Denton Township	5,378	4	0	2	0	2	30	3	24	3	0
Detroit	626,757	12,710	308	712	1,398	10,292	28,068	4,829	13,794	9,445	440
DeWitt	4,813	6	0	3	0	3	17	6	10	1	1
DeWitt Township	15,557	31	0	11	1	19	141	23	106	12	0
Dowagiac	5,591	44	0	9	6	29	202	7	177	18	2
Dryden Township	4,797	6	0	1	0	5	12	4	7	1	0
Durand	4,033	8	0	1	0	7	48	5	40	3	0
East Grand Rapids	11,372	2	0	1	0	1	126	17	91	18	0
East Jordan	2,254	8	0	1	0	7	18	0	18	0	0
East Lansing	46,660	124	0	31	12	81	830	101	623	106	11
Eastpointe	33,829	248	6	18	34	190	840	107	478	255	10
Eaton Rapids	5,184	26	1	6	0	19	87	14	67	6	1
Eau Claire	540	0	0	0	0	0	0	0	0	0	0
Ecorse	9,113	108	4	9	6	89	237	38	146	53	6
Elkton	791	1	0	1	0	0	3	0	3	0	0
Emmett Township	11,607	42	0	6	6	30	672	58	598	16	2
Escanaba	12,404	59	0	29	1	29	204	7	191	6	1
Essexville	3,300	3	0	0	1	2	12	0	10	2	0
Evart	1,774	5	0	2	0	3	14	0	14	0	0
Fair Haven Township	1,087	0	0	0	0	0	5	2	3	0	0
Farmington	11,406	5	0	1	0	4	78	4	65	9	1
Farmington Hills	82,806	119	0	20	7	92	962	78	718	166	4
Fennville	1,733	0	0	0	0	0	1	0	1	0	0
Fenton	11,947	12	0	3	1	8	158	8	134	16	0
Ferndale	19,007	51	0	5	6	40	387	43	302	42	5
Flat Rock	10,369	41	0	6	1	34	136	9	95	32	3
Flint	80,059	985	13	84	28	860	1,047	189	689	169	12
Flint Township	31,097	322	8	24	31	259	1,033	166	767	100	12
Flushing	8,290	6	0	1	1	4	44	5	35	4	1
Flushing Township	10,586	14	0	4	2	8	38	6	25	7	0
Forsyth Township	6,260	14	0	5	0	9	27	0	23	4	1
Fowlerville	2,994	9	0	4	0	5	40	6	34	0	0
Frankenmuth	5,368	17	0	5	0	12	58	9	47	2	0
Frankfort	1,287	3	0	0	0	3	14	1	12	1	0
Franklin	3,113	3	0	0	0	3	26	3	21	2	0
Fraser	14,458	33	2	10	0	21	212	12	167	33	0
Fruitport Township	14,983	25	0	11	5	9	447	9	431	7	2
Garden City	26,696	38	0	8	4	26	232	54	155	23	1
Garfield Township	997	0	0	0	0	0	0	0	0	0	0
Gaylord	4,340	22	0	8	0	14	149	6	140	3	1
Genesee Township	20,336	130	1	13	7	109	237	58	146	33	4
Gerrish Township	2,855	3	0	2	0	1	15	2	13	0	0
Gibraltar	4,899	11	0	5	0	6	37	4	25	8	0
Gladstone	5,246	11	0	6	0	5	23	1	21	1	0
Gladwin	3,101	13	0	0	0	13	58	4	52	2	1
Grand Beach/Michiana	484	0	0	0	0	0	11	2	8	1	0
Grand Blanc	7,970	15	0	1	0	14	64	6	52	6	1
Grand Blanc Township	40,115	93	0	12	6	75	506	49	388	69	1
Grand Haven	10,967	29	0	21	0	8	109	10	94	5	2
Grand Ledge	7,778	6	0	4	0	2	48	3	38	7	0
Grand Rapids	196,662	1,926	19	187	267	1,453	5,912	546	3,894	1,472	58
Grandville	15,847	33	0	8	7	18	487	24	417	46	0
Grayling	1,865	8	0	3	0	5	30	4	25	1	1
Green Oak Township	19,764	4	0	1	0	3	81	7	65	9	1
Greenville	9,303	43	0	13	0	30	204	21	174	9	7
Grosse Ile Township	10,550	4	0	0	0	4	26	3	23	0	1

Table 8. Offenses Known to Law Enforcement, by Selected State and City, 2022—Continued

(Number.)

State/city	Population	Violent crime	Murder and nonnegligent manslaughter	Rape	Robbery	Aggravated assault	Property crime	Burglary	Larceny-theft	Motor vehicle theft	Arson[1]
Grosse Pointe	5,519	10	0	1	0	9	86	5	71	10	0
Grosse Pointe Farms	9,890	6	0	0	0	6	99	6	84	9	0
Grosse Pointe Park	11,287	4	0	0	0	4	164	20	113	31	0
Grosse Pointe Shores	2,584	0	0	0	0	0	9	0	7	2	0
Grosse Pointe Woods	16,079	13	0	2	3	8	161	15	117	29	0
Hamburg Township	21,515	16	0	1	0	15	31	6	23	2	0
Hampton Township	9,564	11	0	1	1	9	80	12	62	6	0
Hamtramck	27,669	182	2	4	45	131	434	95	245	94	5
Hancock	4,515	2	0	0	0	2	23	1	19	3	0
Harbor Beach	1,589	6	0	1	1	4	24	2	21	1	0
Harbor Springs	1,289	2	0	0	0	2	5	0	5	0	0
Harper Woods	15,100	96	6	6	12	72	716	52	354	310	5
Hart	1,988	8	0	1	0	7	112	4	107	1	1
Hartford	2,483	13	0	2	1	10	28	7	17	4	0
Hastings	7,554	31	0	10	0	21	109	17	78	14	2
Hazel Park	14,849	41	3	3	7	28	253	34	173	46	1
Highland Park	8,802	179	3	12	23	141	328	60	171	97	4
Highland Township	19,087	18	0	6	1	11	58	7	40	11	0
Hillsdale	8,157	25	0	13	0	12	86	10	64	12	0
Holland	33,838	109	2	43	5	59	453	18	405	30	1
Holly	5,931	6	0	2	0	4	18	2	15	1	0
Houghton	7,644	6	1	5	0	0	54	3	50	1	0
Howell	10,104	13	0	3	1	9	100	29	69	2	2
Hudson	2,379	9	0	5	0	4	46	3	36	7	0
Huntington Woods	6,286	1	0	0	0	1	35	1	27	7	0
Huron Township	16,837	75	2	18	2	53	100	28	59	13	1
Imlay City	3,707	11	0	5	0	6	32	7	24	1	0
Independence Township	36,584	37	2	9	2	24	222	28	180	14	0
Inkster	25,447	279	11	31	12	225	478	95	250	133	9
Ionia	11,730	22	0	15	0	7	86	18	62	6	1
Iron River	3,001	17	0	3	0	14	17	6	7	4	0
Ironwood	5,021	5	0	1	0	4	66	4	53	9	0
Ishpeming	6,174	15	0	2	0	13	45	5	37	3	0
Ishpeming Township	3,421	0	0	0	0	0	1	1	0	0	0
Jackson	31,206	336	4	44	27	261	1,110	173	787	150	18
Jonesville	2,151	3	0	2	0	1	85	7	72	6	0
Kalamazoo	72,810	1,104	10	106	125	863	3,278	633	2,251	394	43
Kalamazoo Township	24,309	183	3	12	15	153	834	116	603	115	9
Kalkaska	2,122	10	0	1	0	9	66	27	36	3	0
Keego Harbor	2,741	4	0	0	0	4	22	6	15	1	0
Kentwood	53,977	241	2	32	25	182	1,203	114	798	291	3
Kinde	437	0	0	0	0	0	1	0	1	0	0
Kingston	391	0	0	0	0	0	4	0	4	0	0
Kinross Township	5,986	1	0	1	0	0	9	0	7	2	0
Laingsburg	1,408	5	0	1	0	4	12	3	9	0	0
Lake Angelus	290	0	0	0	0	0	2	0	2	0	0
Lake Orion	2,904	2	0	0	1	1	20	0	20	0	0
Lakeview	1,057	4	0	2	0	2	21	1	19	1	0
Lansing	112,567	1,440	15	99	148	1,178	3,029	579	1,797	653	24
Lansing Township	8,037	60	2	10	7	41	353	35	268	50	0
Lapeer	8,924	22	1	3	1	17	118	13	97	8	0
Lapeer Township	4,953	1	0	1	0	0	7	0	7	0	0
Lathrup Village	4,018	3	0	0	1	2	45	2	41	2	0
Laurium	1,942	2	0	1	0	1	8	0	8	0	0
Lawrence	1,013	0	0	0	0	0	2	0	2	0	0
Lawton	1,850	2	0	0	0	2	23	7	15	1	0
Lennon	476	0	0	0	0	0	21	19	0	2	0
Leslie	1,929	3	0	0	0	3	18	3	15	0	0
Lexington	928	2	0	0	1	1	4	0	4	0	0
Lincoln Park	39,189	232	0	22	22	188	752	111	526	115	6
Lincoln Township	14,825	15	0	5	2	8	134	13	115	6	0
Linden	4,168	1	0	0	0	1	15	1	12	2	0
Litchfield	1,379	2	0	1	0	1	8	2	4	2	0
Livonia	93,517	229	0	26	19	184	1,614	111	1,257	246	4
Lowell	4,137	7	0	1	0	6	48	6	37	5	1
Ludington	7,785	25	0	8	0	17	69	13	55	1	1
Lyon Township	24,010	14	0	5	1	8	98	7	83	8	1
Mackinac Island	587	4	0	1	0	3	71	1	70	0	1
Mackinaw City	856	2	0	2	0	0	21	3	17	1	1
Madison Heights	28,079	68	0	7	13	48	535	54	411	70	0
Madison Township	8,404	13	0	8	0	5	199	3	186	10	0
Manistee	6,335	17	1	7	0	9	168	16	145	7	1
Manistique	2,809	24	1	12	0	11	45	13	30	2	0
Marenisco Township	454	0	0	0	0	0	0	0	0	0	0
Marine City	4,029	7	0	0	0	7	29	6	21	2	0
Marlette	1,850	5	0	1	0	4	13	2	10	1	0
Marquette	20,428	40	0	15	2	23	139	7	119	13	1
Marshall	6,754	17	0	3	1	13	76	13	59	4	2
Marysville	9,897	12	0	3	0	9	76	13	62	1	1
Mason	8,195	27	0	5	1	21	48	5	33	10	1
Mattawan	2,663	36	0	2	0	34	36	2	34	0	0
Mayville	909	1	0	0	0	1	0	0	0	0	0
Melvindale	12,524	57	0	3	3	51	182	23	121	38	0

Table 8. Offenses Known to Law Enforcement, by Selected State and City, 2022—Continued

(Number.)

State/city	Population	Violent crime	Murder and nonnegligent manslaughter	Rape	Robbery	Aggravated assault	Property crime	Burglary	Larceny-theft	Motor vehicle theft	Arson[1]
Memphis	1,058	1	1	0	0	0	5	0	5	0	0
Mendon	864	0	0	0	0	0	5	1	4	0	2
Menominee	8,314	36	0	17	0	19	112	20	86	6	0
Meridian Township	44,038	77	0	17	17	43	850	55	723	72	0
Metamora Township	4,438	4	0	0	0	4	17	3	13	1	0
Metro Police Authority of Genesee County	20,995	40	0	9	3	28	206	33	158	15	1
Midland	42,426	49	2	15	0	32	335	81	243	11	3
Milan	5,994	15	0	4	2	9	60	10	46	4	0
Milford	16,972	7	0	0	0	7	63	11	47	5	0
Millington	1,012	0	0	0	0	0	2	0	1	1	0
Montague	2,437	3	0	2	0	1	25	0	25	0	0
Montrose Township	7,662	8	1	4	1	2	51	16	29	6	0
Morenci	2,235	2	0	1	0	1	13	2	10	1	0
Morrice	987	0	0	0	0	0	4	0	4	0	0
Mount Morris	3,113	15	0	3	1	11	61	8	46	7	1
Mount Morris Township	19,713	224	3	9	7	205	340	78	199	63	4
Mount Pleasant	21,363	61	0	14	5	42	393	46	322	25	6
Munising	1,968	3	0	0	0	3	20	4	16	0	0
Muskegon	37,615	320	7	33	27	253	1,007	171	698	138	11
Muskegon Heights	9,944	170	1	20	10	139	326	52	238	36	9
Muskegon Township	17,812	49	1	13	3	32	387	32	318	37	0
Napoleon Township	6,807	4	0	1	0	3	32	5	24	3	0
Negaunee	4,652	7	0	1	2	4	30	1	29	0	0
Newaygo	2,487	7	0	2	0	5	58	8	42	8	0
New Baltimore	11,995	5	0	1	0	4	38	3	30	5	1
New Buffalo	1,680	2	0	0	0	2	13	1	11	1	1
New Era	466	0	0	0	0	0	0	0	0	0	0
New Lothrop	581	0	0	0	0	0	1	0	1	0	0
Niles	11,756	69	1	10	7	51	277	25	209	43	2
Northfield Township	8,438	7	0	2	2	3	59	3	50	6	2
North Muskegon	4,103	5	0	3	0	2	49	0	46	3	0
Northville	6,041	5	0	1	0	4	34	5	28	1	0
Northville Township	31,443	32	0	12	0	20	194	11	153	30	2
Norton Shores	25,226	58	2	14	5	37	583	43	499	41	3
Novi	66,936	49	0	12	6	31	561	18	483	60	0
Oakland Township	20,234	8	0	3	0	5	14	0	12	2	0
Oak Park	29,115	105	3	11	8	83	641	177	325	139	2
Olivet	1,429	4	0	1	0	3	28	1	22	5	1
Ontwa Township-Edwardsburg	6,812	23	1	9	1	12	61	9	44	8	0
Orchard Lake	2,211	1	0	0	0	1	14	3	10	1	0
Orion Township	35,516	18	1	0	0	17	168	12	141	15	0
Oscoda Township	7,210	37	0	8	0	29	51	11	36	4	1
Otisville	812	3	0	0	0	3	2	0	2	0	0
Otsego	4,074	3	0	3	0	0	37	5	29	3	0
Owendale	260	0	0	0	0	0	0	0	0	0	0
Owosso	14,581	115	0	22	1	92	196	36	146	14	6
Oxford	3,440	2	0	0	0	2	10	1	8	1	0
Oxford Township	18,870	9	1	0	0	8	62	5	52	5	0
Paw Paw	3,357	29	0	0	4	25	124	5	116	3	0
Peck	601	0	0	0	0	0	1	0	1	0	0
Pentwater	904	3	0	1	0	2	9	1	7	1	0
Perry	2,110	1	0	1	0	0	20	1	19	0	1
Petoskey	5,922	8	0	3	0	5	27	4	19	4	0
Pigeon	1,205	0	0	0	0	0	0	0	0	0	0
Pinckney	2,451	0	0	0	0	0	14	6	5	3	0
Pittsfield Township	39,298	82	0	10	8	64	801	37	702	62	1
Plainwell	3,738	8	0	4	0	4	63	7	47	9	1
Pleasant Ridge	2,584	1	0	0	0	1	15	1	13	1	0
Plymouth	9,270	14	0	1	0	13	89	7	66	16	0
Plymouth Township	27,426	16	0	3	0	13	236	8	202	26	1
Pontiac	60,581	620	13	34	53	520	1,072	192	718	162	17
Portage	48,811	155	8	34	10	103	1,618	114	1,394	110	1
Port Austin	659	0	0	0	0	0	4	0	4	0	0
Port Huron	28,675	207	1	42	8	156	572	118	418	36	6
Portland	3,954	9	0	1	0	8	39	1	36	2	0
Potterville	3,081	4	0	2	0	2	31	5	25	1	1
Quincy	1,560	1	0	0	0	1	33	6	27	0	0
Raisin Township	7,953	12	1	2	0	9	29	4	22	3	0
Redford Township	48,267	247	1	24	25	197	1,113	140	644	329	10
Reed City	2,518	24	0	5	0	19	31	13	18	0	0
Reese	1,251	0	0	0	0	0	5	0	5	0	0
Richfield Township, Genesee County	8,967	10	0	4	0	6	53	9	32	12	0
Richfield Township, Roscommon County	3,588	1	0	0	0	1	7	2	5	0	0
Richland	941	0	0	0	0	0	12	2	10	0	0
Richland Township, Saginaw County	3,916	5	0	0	0	5	10	3	7	0	0
Richmond	5,784	7	0	1	0	6	20	3	17	0	0
Riverview	12,274	23	1	5	4	13	136	6	112	18	2
Rochester	12,868	4	0	0	0	4	57	5	51	1	0
Rochester Hills	75,921	54	1	10	2	41	510	29	421	60	1

Table 8. Offenses Known to Law Enforcement, by Selected State and City, 2022—Continued

(Number.)

State/city	Population	Violent crime	Murder and nonnegligent manslaughter	Rape	Robbery	Aggravated assault	Property crime	Burglary	Larceny-theft	Motor vehicle theft	Arson[1]
Rockford	6,204	5	0	2	0	3	42	0	41	1	0
Rockwood	3,170	6	0	0	0	6	17	0	14	3	0
Rogers City	2,908	2	0	1	0	1	2	0	2	0	0
Romeo	3,711	3	0	1	0	2	12	0	11	1	0
Romulus	25,071	242	2	17	22	201	623	79	412	132	3
Roosevelt Park	4,186	9	1	2	1	5	230	4	223	3	1
Rose City	561	0	0	0	0	0	3	0	3	0	0
Roseville	46,719	249	4	27	24	194	1,700	119	1,360	221	6
Rothbury	445	0	0	0	0	0	7	0	6	1	0
Royal Oak	57,808	74	0	7	7	60	461	31	378	52	3
Saginaw	43,651	925	20	46	48	811	895	262	498	135	32
Saginaw Township	41,334	87	0	13	10	64	605	46	517	42	1
Saline	8,930	14	0	2	1	11	66	5	56	5	0
Sandusky	2,674	5	0	4	0	1	40	4	33	3	0
Saugatuck-Douglas	2,274	0	0	0	0	0	8	1	7	0	0
Sault Ste. Marie	13,412	23	0	9	0	14	119	8	103	8	0
Schoolcraft	1,443	2	0	0	0	2	14	0	12	2	0
Scottville	1,379	2	0	2	0	0	7	0	7	0	0
Sebewaing	1,717	0	0	0	0	0	13	0	13	0	0
Shelby	2,181	4	0	0	0	4	30	0	27	3	0
Shelby Township	79,391	115	1	24	1	89	476	35	366	75	0
Shepherd	1,525	1	0	0	0	1	24	3	19	2	0
Somerset Township	4,531	2	1	0	0	1	26	4	20	2	0
Southfield	75,432	379	2	40	65	272	1,988	240	1,247	501	2
Southgate	29,769	123	3	4	7	109	570	42	449	79	5
South Haven	4,059	28	0	4	2	22	310	108	192	10	0
South Lyon	11,866	9	0	4	0	5	54	3	50	1	0
Sparta	4,293	10	0	3	0	7	45	5	38	2	0
Spring Arbor Township	8,426	1	0	1	0	0	40	6	32	2	0
Springfield Township	14,663	8	0	2	0	6	81	19	56	6	0
Springport Township	2,154	5	0	1	0	4	16	2	9	5	0
Stanton	1,370	1	0	1	0	0	6	0	6	0	0
St. Charles	1,971	8	0	0	0	8	8	1	7	0	0
St. Clair	5,450	4	0	0	0	4	36	6	28	2	0
St. Clair Shores	57,654	102	0	10	10	82	505	49	357	99	4
Sterling Heights	132,393	272	2	39	22	209	1,547	82	1,209	256	1
St. Ignace	2,300	4	0	3	0	1	27	5	19	3	0
St. Johns	7,640	16	0	7	0	9	47	7	34	6	0
St. Joseph	7,684	21	0	5	1	15	106	6	93	7	0
St. Joseph Township	9,772	14	0	1	2	11	78	9	62	7	0
St. Louis	6,842	10	0	3	1	6	44	2	37	5	2
Stockbridge	1,251	1	0	0	0	1	16	0	14	2	0
Sturgis	10,961	42	1	8	2	31	189	25	128	36	0
Sumpter Township	9,535	13	0	0	0	13	60	12	38	10	0
Sylvan Lake	1,693	4	0	2	0	2	21	0	19	2	0
Tawas City	1,865	0	0	0	0	0	42	0	41	1	0
Taylor	61,901	386	0	44	26	316	1,129	170	774	185	3
Tecumseh	8,638	8	0	3	1	4	37	5	28	4	0
Thomas Township	11,903	31	0	8	0	23	61	12	44	5	1
Three Oaks	1,384	4	0	1	0	3	24	7	15	2	0
Three Rivers	7,911	49	0	6	4	39	326	28	277	21	1
Tittabawassee Township	10,855	8	0	6	0	2	29	7	19	3	1
Traverse City	15,617	44	0	14	0	30	201	24	168	9	1
Trenton	18,108	18	0	2	1	15	107	3	86	18	1
Troy	86,548	102	2	9	20	71	1,304	67	1,104	133	2
Tuscarora Township	3,109	10	0	6	0	4	58	0	58	0	0
Ubly	839	3	0	3	0	0	10	0	10	0	0
Unadilla Township	3,385	1	0	1	0	0	16	2	12	2	0
Union City	1,723	0	0	0	0	0	22	6	15	1	0
Utica	5,129	8	0	0	1	7	135	4	123	8	0
Van Buren Township	30,103	100	0	12	5	83	623	40	504	79	1
Vassar	2,732	9	0	1	1	7	19	8	9	2	0
Vernon	719	0	0	0	0	0	1	0	1	0	0
Vicksburg	3,806	8	0	3	0	5	51	5	41	5	1
Walker	25,067	49	0	7	7	35	709	38	570	101	2
Walled Lake	7,251	10	0	3	1	6	56	9	40	7	1
Warren	137,138	670	5	79	56	530	2,274	295	1,519	460	22
Waterford Township	69,851	162	1	20	13	128	609	116	424	69	6
Watersmeet Township	1,472	0	0	0	0	0	1	0	1	0	0
Watervliet	1,635	4	0	0	0	4	22	2	16	4	0
Wayland	4,421	11	0	3	0	8	54	5	41	8	0
Wayne	17,284	181	2	11	12	156	365	72	217	76	1
West Bloomfield Township	65,271	67	0	18	6	43	325	33	255	37	1
West Branch	2,315	3	0	1	0	2	16	1	14	1	0
Westland	83,763	380	4	42	33	301	1,079	163	750	166	15
Whitehall	2,959	3	0	0	0	3	31	3	28	0	0
White Lake Township	31,001	22	2	2	0	18	174	31	137	6	0
White Pigeon	1,709	4	0	2	0	2	9	0	7	2	0
Williamston	3,780	8	0	4	0	4	30	5	23	2	0
Wixom	17,186	20	1	2	0	17	206	12	156	38	0
Wolverine Lake	4,460	2	0	0	0	2	5	0	4	1	0
Wyandotte	24,414	45	0	4	4	37	229	12	176	41	2
Wyoming	76,726	394	11	80	60	243	1,326	122	868	336	6

Table 8. Offenses Known to Law Enforcement, by Selected State and City, 2022—Continued

(Number.)

State/city	Population	Violent crime	Murder and nonnegligent manslaughter	Rape	Robbery	Aggravated assault	Property crime	Burglary	Larceny-theft	Motor vehicle theft	Arson[1]
Yale	1,903	8	0	0	0	8	8	1	7	0	0
Ypsilanti	19,872	210	2	28	23	157	560	86	420	54	4
Zeeland	5,670	14	0	2	0	12	36	2	30	4	0
Zilwaukee	1,515	1	0	0	0	1	13	2	9	2	0
MINNESOTA											
Ada	1,741	1	0	1	0	0	1	0	1	0	0
Adrian	1,189	3	0	0	0	3	4	0	4	0	0
Aitkin	2,092	3	0	1	0	2	40	4	34	2	0
Akeley	426	0	0	0	0	0	11	2	9	0	0
Albany	2,820	3	0	1	0	2	8	0	8	0	0
Albert Lea	18,338	27	0	3	4	20	325	56	226	43	4
Alexandria	14,564	31	0	6	1	24	244	12	224	8	1
Annandale	3,405	5	0	1	0	4	16	0	14	2	0
Anoka	17,864	45	0	7	8	30	226	16	175	35	2
Appleton	1,360	3	0	0	0	3	7	2	4	1	0
Apple Valley	55,145	134	1	18	9	106	902	57	785	60	2
Arlington	2,284	1	0	0	0	1	8	1	7	0	0
Atwater	1,108	0	0	0	0	0	2	0	2	0	0
Austin	26,275	66	0	11	7	48	538	66	435	37	1
Avon	1,680	2	0	0	0	2	19	8	9	2	0
Babbitt	1,376	7	0	1	0	6	6	2	4	0	0
Barnesville	2,799	0	0	0	0	0	4	1	2	1	0
Baxter	9,024	9	0	3	0	6	201	15	183	3	0
Bayport	3,912	2	0	1	0	1	16	0	11	5	0
Becker	5,033	5	0	0	0	5	39	9	25	5	0
Belgrade/Brooten	1,368	1	0	0	0	1	3	0	3	0	0
Belle Plaine	7,440	9	0	4	0	5	49	2	45	2	0
Bemidji	15,317	100	0	25	13	62	1,209	85	1,076	48	7
Benson	3,359	3	0	0	0	3	2	1	0	1	0
Big Lake	12,625	7	0	4	0	3	32	2	24	6	1
Blackduck	829	0	0	0	0	0	1	1	0	0	0
Blaine	71,368	77	0	19	7	51	1,367	82	1,198	87	5
Blooming Prairie	1,941	3	0	1	0	2	2	1	1	0	0
Bloomington	88,745	259	2	42	52	163	3,321	156	2,878	287	9
Blue Earth	3,251	0	0	0	0	0	6	0	5	1	0
Bovey	808	2	0	0	0	2	2	0	2	0	0
Braham	1,793	0	0	0	0	0	4	0	3	1	0
Brainerd	14,398	73	0	20	1	52	334	41	268	25	0
Breckenridge	3,352	3	0	0	0	3	49	17	30	2	0
Breezy Point	2,741	0	0	0	0	0	6	0	6	0	0
Breitung Township	522	1	0	0	0	1	11	3	7	1	0
Brooklyn Center	32,094	193	1	38	68	86	973	105	677	191	12
Brooklyn Park	82,682	315	2	60	78	175	2,727	245	2,102	380	9
Brownton	717	1	0	0	0	1	5	0	3	2	0
Buffalo	16,531	2	0	0	0	2	123	12	99	12	0
Buffalo Lake	646	0	0	0	0	0	2	0	2	0	0
Burnsville	63,361	177	1	24	26	126	1,567	121	1,263	183	8
Caledonia	2,807	0	0	0	0	0	0	0	0	0	0
Callaway	170	0	0	0	0	0	4	2	2	0	0
Cambridge	10,137	10	0	0	1	9	386	31	343	12	1
Canby	1,682	4	0	1	0	3	5	0	5	0	0
Cannon Falls	4,256	1	0	0	0	1	59	14	44	1	0
Centennial Lakes	11,649	6	0	2	2	2	119	10	90	19	2
Champlin	23,038	25	1	9	1	14	239	20	205	14	3
Chaska	28,204	27	0	5	2	20	222	24	181	17	1
Chatfield	2,994	0	0	0	0	0	3	0	3	0	0
Chisholm	4,686	24	0	5	1	18	157	15	137	5	1
Clearbrook	466	0	0	0	0	0	2	0	2	0	0
Cleveland	769	0	0	0	0	0	1	1	0	0	0
Cloquet	12,747	32	0	2	3	27	182	2	164	16	1
Cold Spring/Richmond	5,730	6	0	1	0	5	32	6	24	2	2
Columbia Heights	22,682	93	0	12	14	67	498	42	387	69	2
Comfrey	379	0	0	0	0	0	0	0	0	0	0
Coon Rapids	63,181	146	2	29	18	97	1,181	151	952	78	7
Corcoran	7,295	2	0	0	0	2	25	5	19	1	0
Cottage Grove	40,871	29	0	8	3	18	384	25	334	25	2
Crookston	7,214	33	0	12	2	19	114	21	83	10	1
Crosby	2,323	3	0	0	0	3	7	0	7	0	0
Crosslake	2,494	1	0	0	0	1	22	5	17	0	0
Crystal	22,175	67	1	10	18	38	537	47	423	67	4
Cuyuna	330	0	0	0	0	0	0	0	0	0	0
Dayton	9,078	2	0	0	1	1	58	4	51	3	0
Deephaven	3,770	1	0	1	0	0	19	2	15	2	0
Deer River	902	4	0	1	0	3	7	0	4	3	0
Deerwood	598	1	0	0	0	1	2	0	1	1	0
Detroit Lakes	9,771	26	0	6	3	17	214	37	168	9	1
Dilworth	4,641	5	0	0	3	2	256	18	229	9	0
Duluth	86,144	249	6	52	28	163	2,509	360	1,984	165	10
Dundas	1,751	1	0	0	0	1	30	5	25	0	0
Eagan	68,518	95	0	29	11	55	1,542	108	1,299	135	1
Eagle Lake	3,275	3	0	1	0	2	21	12	6	3	0
East Grand Forks	9,002	10	0	0	0	10	47	10	30	7	2

Table 8. Offenses Known to Law Enforcement, by Selected State and City, 2022—Continued

(Number.)

State/city	Population	Violent crime	Murder and nonnegligent manslaughter	Rape	Robbery	Aggravated assault	Property crime	Burglary	Larceny-theft	Motor vehicle theft	Arson[1]
East Range	3,650	5	0	0	0	5	9	3	5	1	0
Eden Prairie	62,008	48	0	18	4	26	808	77	676	55	1
Eden Valley	1,023	3	0	0	0	3	6	0	6	0	0
Edina	53,206	49	0	7	16	26	1,052	131	847	74	0
Elko New Market	4,995	1	1	0	0	0	15	0	15	0	0
Elk River	26,519	27	0	7	2	18	452	31	393	28	0
Elmore	542	0	0	0	0	0	0	0	0	0	0
Ely	3,212	6	0	2	0	4	29	3	25	1	0
Emily	872	0	0	0	0	0	0	0	0	0	0
Eveleth	3,434	13	0	3	1	9	120	22	89	9	0
Fairfax	1,235	0	0	0	0	0	5	1	4	0	0
Fairmont	10,369	24	0	5	1	18	136	11	118	7	1
Faribault	24,417	62	0	19	6	37	487	60	409	18	2
Farmington	23,551	21	0	7	0	14	137	19	104	14	0
Fergus Falls	14,017	31	0	7	2	22	324	36	276	12	0
Floodwood	512	0	0	0	0	0	5	0	5	0	0
Foley	2,681	14	0	6	1	7	65	8	56	1	1
Forest Lake	20,512	21	0	7	3	11	404	38	336	30	2
Frazee	1,311	1	0	0	0	1	4	0	4	0	0
Fridley	31,095	146	1	21	28	96	1,289	83	1,069	137	4
Fulda	1,393	2	0	0	0	2	4	0	4	0	0
Gaylord	2,321	1	0	1	0	0	12	3	9	0	0
Gilbert	1,665	4	0	0	0	4	59	1	57	1	0
Glencoe	5,695	10	0	5	0	5	63	6	55	2	0
Glenwood	2,671	4	0	0	0	4	30	3	24	3	0
Glyndon	1,313	0	0	0	0	0	15	3	11	1	0
Golden Valley	21,424	40	0	7	12	21	424	61	320	43	1
Goodhue	1,261	1	0	0	0	1	4	1	3	0	0
Goodview	4,137	0	0	0	0	0	2	0	1	1	0
Grand Rapids	11,388	17	0	5	0	12	102	10	88	4	2
Granite Falls	2,681	5	0	0	1	4	25	0	22	3	0
Hallock	879	0	0	0	0	0	3	1	2	0	1
Hastings	21,772	37	0	7	4	26	288	35	239	14	3
Hawley	2,227	3	0	1	0	2	23	5	18	0	0
Hector	1,004	0	0	0	0	0	6	2	4	0	0
Henderson	975	0	0	0	0	0	0	0	0	0	0
Henning	861	0	0	0	0	0	5	1	4	0	0
Hermantown	10,218	19	0	2	0	17	391	40	342	9	0
Heron Lake	602	0	0	0	0	0	0	0	0	0	0
Hibbing	15,980	5	1	0	0	4	123	0	102	21	0
Hill City	620	0	0	0	0	0	5	1	3	1	0
Hokah	555	0	0	0	0	0	0	0	0	0	0
Hopkins	18,125	36	0	3	2	31	421	56	311	54	0
Houston	976	0	0	0	0	0	4	0	4	0	0
Howard Lake	2,170	2	0	0	0	2	5	2	2	1	0
Hutchinson	14,628	42	0	9	1	32	143	18	122	3	2
International Falls	5,657	18	0	2	1	15	89	20	65	4	0
Inver Grove Heights	35,294	69	1	16	5	47	743	84	559	100	1
Isanti	7,257	7	0	2	0	5	69	7	56	6	0
Isle	836	5	0	0	0	5	37	1	31	5	0
Janesville	2,457	3	0	1	0	2	23	8	14	1	0
Jordan	6,890	7	0	4	0	3	39	2	34	3	0
Kasson	6,997	7	0	0	0	7	50	6	41	3	0
Keewatin	968	0	0	0	0	0	11	1	9	1	0
Kenyon	1,907	0	0	0	0	0	0	0	0	0	0
La Crescent	5,222	2	0	1	0	1	10	1	8	1	0
Lake City	5,318	5	0	4	0	1	46	8	36	2	0
Lake Crystal	2,536	2	0	0	0	2	3	1	2	0	0
Lakefield	1,730	0	0	0	0	0	1	0	1	0	0
Lake Park	721	1	0	1	0	0	3	1	1	1	0
Lakes Area	10,739	13	0	3	1	9	124	17	96	11	1
Lake Shore	1,108	0	0	0	0	0	6	1	5	0	0
Lakeville	75,548	58	0	19	3	36	509	56	399	54	9
Lamberton	792	0	0	0	0	0	0	0	0	0	0
Le Center	2,485	1	0	1	0	0	2	1	1	0	0
Lester Prairie	1,904	1	0	0	0	1	6	0	5	1	0
Le Sueur	4,174	10	0	1	0	9	32	1	30	1	0
Lewiston	1,517	0	0	0	0	0	21	4	15	2	0
Lino Lakes	21,997	16	0	3	0	13	207	15	191	1	2
Litchfield	6,490	3	0	1	0	2	70	4	61	5	0
Little Falls	9,025	6	0	2	0	4	198	22	167	9	0
Long Prairie	3,743	3	0	1	0	2	24	0	24	0	0
Lonsdale	4,908	2	0	1	0	1	13	2	11	0	2
Madelia	2,360	5	0	1	0	4	20	5	13	2	0
Madison Lake	1,264	0	0	0	0	0	7	0	6	1	0
Mankato	44,925	116	0	31	12	73	1,125	141	940	44	1
Maple Grove	70,935	83	1	17	12	53	1,371	103	1,204	64	4
Mapleton	2,193	3	0	1	0	2	12	0	9	3	0
Maplewood	47,144	137	2	12	44	79	1,855	193	1,350	312	4
Marshall	13,658	30	0	9	0	21	62	9	50	3	0
McGregor	379	0	0	0	0	0	0	0	0	0	0
Medina	6,753	3	1	0	0	2	34	3	28	3	0
Melrose	3,604	2	0	1	0	1	12	2	7	3	0

Table 8. Offenses Known to Law Enforcement, by Selected State and City, 2022—Continued

(Number.)

State/city	Population	Violent crime	Murder and nonnegligent manslaughter	Rape	Robbery	Aggravated assault	Property crime	Burglary	Larceny-theft	Motor vehicle theft	Arson[1]
Menahga	1,359	0	0	0	0	0	0	0	0	0	0
Mendota Heights	11,569	15	0	5	2	8	215	35	163	17	0
Milaca	3,092	4	0	0	0	4	102	0	101	1	0
Minneapolis	421,690	5,170	79	330	1,772	2,989	22,191	2,552	13,498	6,141	102
Minneota	1,367	1	0	0	0	1	2	1	1	0	0
Minnesota Lake	644	0	0	0	0	0	0	0	0	0	0
Minnetonka	52,309	47	0	7	13	27	908	102	735	71	2
Minnetrista	10,959	4	1	2	0	1	75	10	63	2	0
Montevideo	5,180	0	0	0	0	0	2	0	2	0	0
Montgomery	3,498	2	0	1	0	1	1	1	0	0	0
Moorhead	44,859	185	1	27	16	141	1,006	190	649	167	9
Moose Lake	2,565	1	0	0	0	1	13	1	12	0	0
Morgan	883	1	0	0	0	1	7	0	7	0	0
Motley	678	1	0	0	0	1	38	1	36	1	0
Mounds View	14,897	27	0	4	3	20	244	20	199	25	0
Mountain Lake	2,009	8	0	4	0	4	5	2	2	1	0
Nashwauk	962	0	0	0	0	0	1	0	1	0	0
New Brighton	26,408	38	0	6	6	26	491	52	376	63	0
New Hope	20,877	47	0	12	9	26	502	46	374	82	3
New Prague	8,354	5	0	1	0	4	59	1	55	3	1
New Richland	1,231	5	0	0	0	5	15	5	10	0	0
New Ulm	14,067	0	0	0	0	0	23	2	21	0	0
Nisswa	2,077	0	0	0	0	0	6	0	6	0	0
North Branch	11,439	18	0	3	1	14	139	8	121	10	0
Northfield	20,746	26	0	7	1	18	154	9	140	5	0
North Mankato	14,403	18	0	7	0	11	134	29	95	10	0
North St. Paul	15,208	16	2	2	2	10	273	23	201	49	2
Oakdale	27,681	43	0	9	6	28	807	40	676	91	1
Oak Park Heights	4,721	2	0	1	0	1	172	14	147	11	0
Olivia	2,327	16	1	4	0	11	28	3	22	3	0
Onamia	806	8	0	0	0	8	22	3	17	2	0
Orono	19,245	23	1	5	1	16	101	23	66	12	0
Osakis	1,729	0	0	0	0	0	6	0	6	0	0
Osseo	2,545	1	0	0	0	1	98	1	84	13	0
Owatonna	26,394	60	0	15	6	39	274	19	237	18	2
Parkers Prairie	1,006	0	0	0	0	0	6	0	6	0	0
Park Rapids	4,186	12	0	4	1	7	121	14	97	10	0
Paynesville	2,497	1	0	0	0	1	4	1	2	1	0
Pelican Rapids	2,571	2	0	1	0	1	6	0	4	2	0
Pequot Lakes	2,449	2	0	0	0	2	10	1	6	3	0
Pierz	1,407	1	0	1	0	0	31	3	26	2	0
Pillager	513	0	0	0	0	0	4	0	4	0	0
Pine River	902	3	0	0	0	3	17	0	17	0	0
Plainview	3,509	2	0	0	0	2	17	0	17	0	0
Plymouth	78,585	46	4	9	10	23	986	175	727	84	0
Preston	1,315	1	0	1	0	0	21	2	18	1	0
Princeton	4,949	7	0	0	0	7	125	1	114	10	0
Prior Lake	28,559	45	0	7	4	34	480	37	427	16	1
Proctor	3,077	6	0	0	0	6	35	1	27	7	0
Ramsey	28,562	20	0	6	0	14	204	35	158	11	0
Red Wing	16,962	48	0	10	1	37	427	49	357	21	1
Redwood Falls	5,090	22	0	5	0	17	62	2	56	4	0
Renville	1,286	2	0	0	0	2	3	1	2	0	0
Rice	2,149	2	0	0	1	1	11	2	9	0	0
Richfield	36,079	122	1	14	28	79	973	84	759	130	4
Robbinsdale	13,907	72	2	14	10	46	290	49	177	64	2
Rochester	121,534	271	1	69	32	169	2,276	277	1,855	144	5
Rogers	13,438	14	0	0	1	13	272	21	231	20	0
Roseau	2,721	16	0	2	0	14	45	2	41	2	0
Rosemount	27,503	13	0	5	2	6	156	21	126	9	2
Roseville	42,031	131	1	21	54	55	2,249	173	1,847	229	6
Royalton	1,266	1	0	0	0	1	55	1	52	2	0
Rushford	1,825	0	0	0	0	0	0	0	0	0	0
Sartell	19,607	24	0	6	0	18	430	23	403	4	0
Sauk Centre	4,641	6	0	1	0	5	80	17	57	6	0
Sauk Rapids	13,860	11	0	2	0	9	239	8	219	12	0
Savage	33,372	25	0	11	2	12	282	25	231	26	1
Sebeka	742	0	0	0	0	0	0	0	0	0	0
Shakopee	45,122	61	0	14	9	38	722	40	607	75	0
Sherburn	1,063	0	0	0	0	0	8	2	6	0	0
Silver Bay	1,865	2	0	0	0	2	4	1	2	1	0
Slayton	1,987	1	0	1	0	0	2	0	2	0	1
Sleepy Eye	3,411	8	0	2	0	6	4	1	2	1	0
South Lake Minnetonka	12,391	5	0	2	0	3	74	10	59	5	2
South St. Paul	20,337	83	0	13	1	69	469	55	315	99	2
Spring Grove	1,228	2	0	0	1	1	8	2	6	0	0
Spring Lake Park	7,163	19	0	4	2	13	155	20	127	8	0
St. Anthony	11,568	14	0	0	9	5	458	70	329	59	1
Staples	2,971	1	0	0	0	1	35	7	23	5	0
Starbuck	1,382	3	0	0	0	3	4	1	2	1	0
St. Charles	4,001	3	0	2	0	1	22	1	20	1	0
St. Cloud	68,925	312	2	48	37	225	2,949	241	2,467	241	11
St. Francis	8,502	13	0	6	0	7	113	9	94	10	0

Table 8. Offenses Known to Law Enforcement, by Selected State and City, 2022—Continued

(Number.)

State/city	Population	Violent crime	Murder and nonnegligent manslaughter	Rape	Robbery	Aggravated assault	Property crime	Burglary	Larceny-theft	Motor vehicle theft	Arson[1]
Stillwater	19,388	19	0	7	1	11	172	14	138	20	0
St. James	4,677	7	0	1	0	6	54	19	30	5	0
St. Joseph	6,937	3	0	1	1	1	33	8	22	3	0
St. Louis Park	48,311	87	0	17	24	46	1,671	110	1,383	178	6
St. Paul	277,533	2,127	34	242	413	1,438	12,900	1,505	8,206	3,189	196
St. Paul Park	5,429	5	0	3	2	0	52	8	31	13	1
St. Peter	11,647	18	0	10	0	8	97	7	88	2	4
Thief River Falls	8,625	5	0	0	0	5	190	20	163	7	2
Tracy	2,069	1	0	1	0	0	6	3	3	0	0
Truman	1,084	1	0	0	0	1	8	1	6	1	0
Twin Valley	720	1	0	0	0	1	0	0	0	0	0
Two Harbors	3,624	3	0	2	0	1	15	2	12	1	0
Tyler	1,109	0	0	0	0	0	0	0	0	0	0
Verndale	508	1	0	0	0	1	0	0	0	0	0
Virginia	8,276	44	0	6	2	36	179	21	140	18	2
Wabasha	2,494	3	0	0	0	3	42	5	34	3	0
Wadena	4,339	18	0	3	0	15	74	6	65	3	0
Waite Park	8,349	43	0	6	1	36	630	36	563	31	6
Walker	958	1	0	0	0	1	6	0	6	0	0
Walnut Grove	741	0	0	0	0	0	4	0	3	1	0
Warroad	1,815	5	0	0	0	5	9	0	8	1	0
Waseca	9,253	13	0	1	0	12	89	18	63	8	0
Waterville	1,740	0	0	0	0	0	4	1	3	0	0
Wayzata	5,986	10	0	4	0	6	129	8	115	6	1
Wells	2,420	1	0	1	0	0	1	0	0	1	0
Westbrook	769	0	0	0	0	0	1	0	0	1	0
West Concord	848	1	0	0	0	1	1	0	1	0	0
West Hennepin	5,311	2	0	2	0	0	36	5	23	8	0
West St. Paul	21,113	78	0	14	17	47	877	68	678	131	4
Wheaton	1,400	4	0	0	0	4	14	5	7	2	0
White Bear Lake	27,700	19	0	3	5	11	482	53	365	64	0
Willmar	21,097	92	0	17	0	75	423	17	365	41	1
Windom	4,850	14	0	4	0	10	46	4	37	5	2
Winnebago	1,379	1	0	0	0	1	3	3	0	0	0
Winona	25,936	43	0	6	3	34	610	56	532	22	1
Winsted	2,197	3	0	0	0	3	13	2	11	0	0
Winthrop	1,329	2	0	0	0	2	0	0	0	0	0
Woodbury	78,531	76	1	27	15	33	1,159	116	943	100	7
Worthington	13,616	35	0	8	1	26	119	10	95	14	0
Wyoming	8,098	9	0	4	1	4	103	14	81	8	0
Zumbrota	3,865	1	0	0	0	1	12	1	11	0	0
MISSISSIPPI											
Ackerman	1,515	3	1	0	1	1	18	7	8	3	0
Amory	6,439	8	0	2	0	6	259	29	174	56	0
Batesville	7,238	25	0	0	4	21	205	31	151	23	1
Bay Springs	1,569	5	0	3	0	2	15	5	10	0	0
Bay St. Louis	10,591	18	2	2	6	8	360	82	252	26	2
Blue Springs	439	0	0	0	0	0	2	0	2	0	0
Booneville	8,676	23	0	6	1	16	381	53	296	32	2
Brandon	25,636	29	0	9	3	17	123	20	88	15	1
Brookhaven	11,901	67	4	2	8	53	446	235	172	39	1
Bruce	1,616	7	0	0	0	7	12	6	6	0	0
Byhalia	1,350	3	0	0	2	1	39	5	27	7	0
Byram	12,299	29	0	2	7	20	145	16	95	34	1
Calhoun City	1,432	1	0	0	0	1	11	2	6	3	0
Charleston	1,713	26	3	1	2	20	33	12	18	3	0
Cleveland	10,687	111	3	2	9	97	505	77	387	41	2
Clinton	27,001	25	1	8	2	14	297	15	266	16	3
Collins	2,232	12	0	2	3	7	60	14	37	9	0
Corinth	14,216	69	4	6	5	54	728	187	494	47	1
Derma	938	5	1	3	0	1	1	0	1	0	0
Ellisville	4,468	8	0	0	2	6	65	14	44	7	0
Eupora	1,956	5	1	1	0	3	26	2	20	4	0
Florence	4,680	4	0	1	0	3	7	1	5	1	0
Flowood	10,518	22	0	6	1	15	166	5	155	6	0
Forest	5,262	40	1	0	12	27	135	74	51	10	0
Fulton	4,005	2	0	0	0	2	130	8	113	9	0
Gautier	18,992	62	3	6	4	49	416	76	293	47	2
Guntown	2,416	0	0	0	0	0	10	1	8	1	0
Hattiesburg	46,862	161	3	29	24	105	2,099	259	1,673	167	3
Heidelberg	630	3	1	0	0	2	12	3	9	0	0
Hernando	17,622	16	0	4	1	11	113	25	81	7	0
Holly Springs	6,488	23	2	3	2	16	21	2	13	6	0
Horn Lake	26,729	40	6	1	11	22	560	64	433	63	3
Iuka	3,051	8	0	3	0	5	69	7	53	9	1
Kosciusko	6,955	11	1	2	2	6	106	32	66	8	0
Laurel	17,066	105	5	14	6	80	780	141	573	66	5
Long Beach	16,944	8	1	0	3	4	263	54	189	20	0
Louisville	5,963	59	0	0	4	55	147	16	116	15	1
Lucedale	2,981	31	0	4	2	25	126	27	83	16	0
Madison	27,674	13	0	0	0	13	161	11	149	1	0
Mathiston	860	1	0	0	0	1	2	1	1	0	0

Table 8. Offenses Known to Law Enforcement, by Selected State and City, 2022—Continued

(Number.)

State/city	Population	Violent crime	Murder and nonnegligent manslaughter	Rape	Robbery	Aggravated assault	Property crime	Burglary	Larceny-theft	Motor vehicle theft	Arson[1]
Mendenhall	2,159	5	0	1	1	3	14	3	8	3	0
Morton	3,558	22	2	0	1	19	37	10	21	6	0
Myrtle	483	0	0	0	0	0	4	2	2	0	0
New Albany	7,645	2	0	0	1	1	178	57	119	2	0
Oakland	463	1	0	0	0	1	8	1	6	1	0
Ocean Springs	18,361	18	1	3	5	9	416	35	352	29	7
Olive Branch	40,651	128	2	11	10	105	755	60	602	93	1
Oxford	26,975	35	2	12	5	16	441	52	377	12	0
Pascagoula	21,736	88	2	11	8	67	989	141	794	54	3
Pass Christian	6,032	1	0	0	1	0	138	10	123	5	0
Petal	11,580	8	0	3	0	5	49	24	24	1	0
Picayune	11,710	76	0	6	11	59	346	38	282	26	0
Pontotoc	5,771	26	0	0	1	25	190	20	160	10	1
Poplarville	2,808	5	0	1	1	3	28	6	20	2	1
Port Gibson	1,150	4	0	0	2	2	26	3	19	4	0
Purvis	1,951	4	0	0	1	3	20	6	13	1	0
Quitman	1,938	3	0	0	0	3	30	3	25	2	0
Raymond	1,838	2	0	0	0	2	7	4	2	1	0
Richland	7,245	10	0	2	2	6	101	19	75	7	1
Ridgeland	23,896	86	1	6	7	72	463	76	350	37	0
Sandersville	628	0	0	0	0	0	17	2	10	5	0
Seminary	297	0	0	0	0	0	4	0	3	1	0
Senatobia	8,104	43	0	4	3	36	141	11	122	8	0
Smithville	523	0	0	0	0	0	4	2	2	0	0
Southaven	56,092	128	0	28	25	75	1,832	145	1,444	243	3
Starkville	24,720	38	0	2	3	33	617	266	313	38	4
Sumner	251	0	0	0	0	0	0	0	0	0	0
Sumrall	1,929	3	0	0	0	3	15	4	11	0	0
Tunica	958	1	0	0	1	0	41	20	18	3	0
Tupelo	37,534	145	3	35	27	80	1,545	395	1,026	124	8
Union	1,952	7	0	1	0	6	28	5	23	0	0
Vardaman	1,089	1	0	0	0	1	0	0	0	0	0
Vicksburg	20,381	103	3	4	20	76	915	123	688	104	6
Walnut	699	2	0	0	1	1	19	8	9	2	0
Water Valley	3,296	14	0	2	2	10	75	8	61	6	0
Waveland	6,920	5	0	2	0	3	101	14	81	6	0
Waynesboro	4,530	47	3	1	1	42	84	27	46	11	1
West Point	9,893	86	1	6	6	73	253	26	199	28	5
Wiggins	4,324	4	1	1	0	2	151	38	106	7	0
MISSOURI											
Adrian	1,734	3	0	0	0	3	15	1	12	2	0
Alma	394	0	0	0	0	0	0	0	0	0	0
Arcadia	606	0	0	0	0	0	0	0	0	0	0
Arnold	20,794	13	0	1	0	12	313	8	263	42	2
Ash Grove	1,506	15	0	1	0	14	32	12	17	3	1
Ashland	4,948	10	0	1	0	9	37	5	32	0	1
Aurora	7,329	71	1	11	1	58	154	30	106	18	0
Auxvasse	1,011	3	0	1	1	1	20	6	11	3	0
Ava	2,924	5	0	4	0	1	42	5	36	1	1
Ballwin	30,630	9	0	1	0	8	198	18	153	27	3
Battlefield	6,078	10	0	1	0	9	39	9	26	4	0
Bellefontaine Neighbors	10,524	130	2	1	16	111	363	49	168	146	2
Bel-Nor	1,371	5	0	1	0	4	34	9	14	11	0
Belton	24,395	97	0	24	9	64	594	41	488	65	1
Berkeley	8,078	227	6	2	18	201	626	143	229	254	4
Bernie	1,837	1	0	0	0	1	13	4	7	2	0
Bertrand	719	2	0	0	0	2	25	6	14	5	0
Bethany	2,894	9	0	1	0	8	86	20	55	11	0
Bismarck	1,263	7	0	1	0	6	18	5	11	2	1
Bloomfield	1,753	2	0	0	0	2	22	13	9	0	0
Blue Springs	60,093	125	3	25	6	91	1,305	80	1,052	173	5
Bolivar	11,129	14	0	2	1	11	290	29	248	13	1
Bonne Terre	6,757	10	0	2	0	8	67	8	37	22	0
Boonville	7,882	20	0	3	0	17	176	20	142	14	2
Bourbon	1,543	1	0	0	0	1	16	1	14	1	0
Branson	13,021	59	0	18	7	34	813	53	698	62	3
Branson West	480	0	0	0	0	0	32	2	28	2	0
Breckenridge Hills	4,378	43	1	1	4	37	149	21	81	47	0
Brentwood	8,101	16	0	2	8	6	408	30	333	45	1
Bridgeton	11,342	79	0	11	12	56	673	66	483	124	2
Brookfield	4,068	13	0	6	0	7	34	12	21	1	1
Buckner	2,896	14	0	1	0	13	37	7	24	6	0
Buffalo	3,370	6	0	1	0	5	45	5	38	2	0
Butler	4,189	58	0	5	0	53	111	42	69	0	0
Byrnes Mill	3,160	23	0	0	0	23	10	3	4	3	1
Cabool	2,024	2	0	0	0	2	1	1	0	0	0
Calverton Park	1,129	0	0	0	0	0	0	0	0	0	0
Camdenton	4,074	20	0	4	0	16	168	22	139	7	0
Cameron	8,429	11	0	2	0	9	96	9	82	5	0
Campbell	1,535	4	0	0	0	4	15	1	13	1	1
Canton	2,640	4	0	1	0	3	28	2	25	1	0
Cape Girardeau	40,067	241	4	32	11	194	984	151	732	101	7

Table 8. Offenses Known to Law Enforcement, by Selected State and City, 2022—Continued

(Number.)

State/city	Population	Violent crime	Murder and nonnegligent manslaughter	Rape	Robbery	Aggravated assault	Property crime	Burglary	Larceny-theft	Motor vehicle theft	Arson[1]
Carl Junction	8,355	15	0	2	0	13	85	13	64	8	2
Carrollton	3,389	6	0	3	0	3	22	2	17	3	0
Carterville	1,839	2	0	0	0	2	33	3	23	7	1
Carthage	15,510	41	0	15	1	25	328	37	265	26	2
Cassville	3,201	7	0	1	0	6	241	21	202	18	11
Centralia	4,729	7	0	0	3	4	61	5	52	4	0
Charleston	4,987	34	3	3	1	27	94	10	72	12	0
Chesterfield	49,451	35	0	4	5	26	749	49	630	70	2
Chillicothe	9,177	9	0	2	0	7	101	27	63	11	1
Claycomo	1,374	2	0	0	0	2	62	5	33	24	0
Clayton	16,851	12	0	2	2	8	235	31	138	66	0
Cleveland	643	0	0	0	0	0	1	1	0	0	0
Clever	3,101	18	0	1	0	17	16	5	11	0	0
Cole Camp	1,141	0	0	0	0	0	0	0	0	0	0
Columbia	127,862	603	11	91	65	436	3,343	397	2,487	459	23
Cottleville	5,828	1	0	0	0	1	16	0	15	1	1
Country Club Hills	1,004	6	0	0	1	5	44	1	21	22	0
Crestwood	12,267	14	0	0	0	14	216	22	163	31	0
Creve Coeur	18,527	12	0	2	3	7	371	31	259	81	1
Crocker	915	0	0	0	0	0	11	0	8	3	0
Crystal City	4,698	7	0	1	1	5	38	1	30	7	0
Cuba	3,153	14	0	8	0	6	180	28	140	12	0
Desloge	4,964	20	0	10	3	7	175	9	145	21	1
Des Peres	9,135	13	0	2	6	5	312	10	284	18	0
Dexter	7,854	16	0	2	1	13	166	25	125	16	0
Dixon	1,217	3	0	2	0	1	37	21	11	5	0
Doniphan	1,703	2	0	0	0	2	45	4	40	1	0
Duquesne	2,565	7	0	2	0	5	71	14	51	6	0
East Prairie	2,955	11	1	0	1	9	42	5	33	4	2
Edgar Springs	202	0	0	0	0	0	0	0	0	0	0
Edmundson	851	0	0	0	0	0	42	3	22	17	2
Eldon	4,470	12	0	7	0	5	49	6	41	2	0
Ellisville	9,890	19	0	1	0	18	116	6	99	11	0
Ellsinore	432	0	0	0	0	0	3	0	3	0	0
Eureka	12,589	11	0	0	2	9	148	11	115	22	1
Excelsior Springs	10,608	40	1	9	5	25	235	18	202	15	1
Fair Play	430	0	0	0	0	0	1	0	0	1	0
Farmington	18,565	56	0	11	5	40	739	18	673	48	2
Ferguson	18,178	146	9	1	25	111	724	61	371	292	3
Festus	13,036	38	1	5	0	32	188	6	141	41	0
Florissant	51,565	142	2	21	28	91	1,197	86	684	427	4
Foristell	585	0	0	0	0	0	29	1	26	2	0
Forsyth	2,710	6	0	1	0	5	45	2	39	4	0
Fredericktown	4,353	14	0	3	1	10	128	8	108	12	2
Frontenac	4,067	4	0	1	0	3	86	3	65	18	0
Fulton	12,792	26	1	2	1	22	245	32	193	20	1
Gerald	1,355	3	0	0	0	3	12	1	8	3	0
Gideon	749	0	0	0	0	0	0	0	0	0	0
Gladstone	26,953	85	0	12	10	63	737	74	526	137	1
Glendale	6,104	0	0	0	0	0	38	4	19	15	0
Gower	1,511	0	0	0	0	0	4	0	3	1	0
Grain Valley	16,320	22	1	10	0	11	230	20	168	42	0
Grandview	25,542	183	5	22	35	121	907	68	654	185	7
Greenfield	1,200	13	1	1	0	11	20	4	16	0	0
Greenwood	6,077	7	0	0	0	7	22	3	15	4	0
Hannibal	17,028	80	2	6	6	66	569	64	444	61	7
Harrisonville	9,956	35	0	5	1	29	213	58	146	9	1
Hartville	598	2	0	1	0	1	7	0	7	0	0
Hayti	2,367	31	0	5	1	25	134	37	84	13	2
Hazelwood	25,029	189	12	19	25	133	770	78	401	291	2
Herculaneum	5,118	11	0	3	1	7	93	4	72	17	3
Hermann	2,190	8	0	0	0	8	21	0	20	1	0
Higginsville	4,642	0	0	0	0	0	35	1	33	1	0
Hillsboro	3,497	37	0	0	0	37	36	2	31	3	1
Holden	2,206	6	0	4	0	2	22	6	12	4	0
Hollister	4,684	5	0	0	2	3	44	4	36	4	0
Holts Summit	5,431	4	0	0	0	4	34	8	23	3	1
Houston	2,187	18	2	3	0	13	119	9	105	5	0
Iberia	717	0	0	0	0	0	8	2	6	0	0
Independence	121,255	640	12	112	91	425	4,012	446	2,655	911	10
Ironton	1,440	0	0	0	0	0	3	0	3	0	0
Jackson	15,561	18	0	3	0	15	150	14	123	13	0
Jefferson City	42,653	152	2	50	7	93	728	65	542	121	3
Joplin	51,989	253	8	45	35	165	3,172	495	2,323	354	36
Kansas City	508,856	7,538	166	379	1,118	5,875	23,995	2,886	15,023	6,086	134
Kearney	11,041	19	0	7	0	12	147	6	126	15	0
Kennett	10,139	44	0	5	3	36	391	96	274	21	1
Kimberling City	2,385	0	0	0	0	0	0	0	0	0	0
Kirksville	17,515	88	1	18	8	61	812	125	644	43	7
Kirkwood	29,276	41	2	0	3	36	511	30	419	62	1
Ladue	8,948	5	0	1	1	3	108	18	76	14	0
Lake Lafayette	286	0	0	0	0	0	6	3	1	2	0
Lake Lotawana	2,350	3	0	0	0	3	27	1	17	9	0

Table 8. Offenses Known to Law Enforcement, by Selected State and City, 2022—Continued

(Number.)

State/city	Population	Violent crime	Murder and nonnegligent manslaughter	Rape	Robbery	Aggravated assault	Property crime	Burglary	Larceny-theft	Motor vehicle theft	Arson[1]
Lake Ozark	2,161	6	0	2	0	4	3	0	3	0	0
Lakeshire	1,529	2	0	0	0	2	10	1	7	2	0
Lake St. Louis	17,846	20	0	3	0	17	166	10	145	11	0
Lake Tapawingo	783	0	0	0	0	0	1	0	0	1	0
Lamar	4,318	6	0	1	1	4	191	41	146	4	0
Laurie	1,027	3	0	2	0	1	20	2	13	5	0
Lawson	2,511	3	0	1	0	2	30	8	19	3	1
Lebanon	15,143	58	1	17	4	36	417	46	331	40	6
Lee's Summit	103,976	144	6	24	11	103	2,181	155	1,719	307	3
Licking	2,749	2	0	1	0	1	7	0	7	0	0
Lincoln	1,170	5	0	2	1	2	7	1	5	1	0
Linn Creek	226	0	0	0	0	0	0	0	0	0	0
Lone Jack	1,578	5	0	0	0	5	19	0	16	3	0
Macon	5,480	7	0	1	1	5	82	7	65	10	4
Malden	3,568	19	0	1	1	17	96	24	64	8	0
Manchester	18,142	9	1	1	0	7	264	12	229	23	1
Mansfield	1,259	4	0	1	0	3	12	0	12	0	1
Maplewood	8,117	24	1	2	2	19	429	30	310	89	0
Marble Hill	1,336	9	0	0	0	9	38	6	31	1	0
Marceline	2,124	0	0	0	0	0	8	2	6	0	0
Marionville	2,079	3	0	1	0	2	19	10	5	4	0
Marquand	193	0	0	0	0	0	0	0	0	0	0
Marshall	13,490	51	0	17	3	31	188	18	151	19	1
Marshfield	7,605	26	1	4	0	21	192	36	139	17	0
Maryland Heights	27,795	85	0	7	12	66	743	45	511	187	1
Maryville	10,791	27	0	11	0	16	202	43	146	13	4
Milan	1,787	5	0	0	0	5	12	1	11	0	0
Miner	896	5	0	2	0	3	25	5	18	2	0
Moberly	13,998	36	1	2	2	31	216	34	165	17	4
Moline Acres	2,118	11	0	0	1	10	40	6	8	26	0
Monett	9,782	20	0	1	1	18	228	35	165	28	0
Moscow Mills	3,911	3	0	0	0	3	11	1	9	1	0
Mountain Grove	4,530	24	0	5	0	19	87	15	64	8	1
Mountain View	2,578	14	1	5	0	8	55	8	41	6	1
Mount Vernon	4,555	3	0	1	1	1	67	7	55	5	0
Napoleon	209	0	0	0	0	0	0	0	0	0	0
Neosho	12,864	19	1	10	2	6	355	48	271	36	6
Nevada	8,182	75	0	22	1	52	442	39	371	32	2
New Haven	2,361	3	0	2	0	1	17	6	11	0	0
New Madrid	2,654	7	0	1	0	6	53	14	36	3	1
Niangua	398	0	0	0	0	0	0	0	0	0	0
Nixa	24,860	18	0	6	0	12	209	17	182	10	0
Normandy	8,653	133	6	5	5	117	302	36	145	121	2
North Kansas City	4,534	49	0	6	6	37	573	15	437	121	1
Northmoor	292	1	0	0	0	1	4	2	2	0	0
Northwoods	3,877	14	0	0	1	13	30	4	18	8	0
Oak Grove	8,388	11	0	6	2	3	101	9	72	20	0
Oakview Village	363	0	0	0	0	0	4	0	1	3	0
Odessa	5,546	7	0	1	0	6	46	7	35	4	0
O'Fallon	95,689	90	2	24	8	56	688	44	581	63	3
Olivette	8,387	14	0	0	2	12	169	10	114	45	0
Oronogo	2,654	2	0	2	0	0	14	1	11	2	0
Osage Beach	4,741	15	0	6	0	9	179	9	161	9	0
Overland	15,632	71	3	4	9	55	555	41	355	159	0
Owensville	2,750	3	0	0	0	3	24	2	21	1	0
Ozark	22,447	24	1	8	1	14	291	20	242	29	0
Pacific	7,398	23	0	2	0	21	101	12	78	11	0
Pagedale	2,527	57	2	0	6	49	129	28	53	48	0
Palmyra	3,629	1	0	0	0	1	55	7	41	7	0
Park Hills	8,764	24	0	12	1	11	196	19	139	38	1
Parkville	8,412	8	0	1	3	4	123	9	93	21	1
Peculiar	6,037	12	0	2	0	10	105	10	85	10	0
Perry	673	0	0	0	0	0	2	0	2	0	0
Perryville	8,458	27	2	7	2	16	117	7	99	11	0
Pevely	5,998	14	0	4	0	10	141	13	107	21	0
Piedmont	1,859	7	0	0	0	7	36	10	23	3	0
Pilot Knob	648	0	0	0	0	0	3	1	2	0	0
Platte City	4,775	12	0	4	0	8	63	7	49	7	0
Pleasant Hill	8,811	6	0	1	0	5	42	5	31	6	0
Pleasant Valley	2,733	9	0	1	1	7	25	4	15	6	0
Poplar Bluff	16,181	7	0	0	0	7	70	7	47	16	1
Portageville	2,832	8	0	2	0	6	38	5	31	2	0
Potosi	2,519	23	0	5	0	18	189	13	166	10	1
Prairie Home	267	0	0	0	0	0	0	0	0	0	0
Puxico	865	0	0	0	0	0	0	0	0	0	0
Raymore	25,351	30	0	3	4	23	367	31	296	40	0
Raytown	29,224	163	5	9	34	115	1,089	135	700	254	2
Republic	19,481	13	1	3	0	9	148	15	126	7	1
Rich Hill	1,246	2	0	1	0	1	19	8	10	1	0
Richland	1,726	2	0	0	0	2	23	1	17	5	0
Richmond Heights	9,120	53	0	1	12	40	608	13	490	105	1
Riverside	4,063	17	0	2	1	14	236	3	191	42	1
Riverview	2,352	66	2	3	6	55	91	15	23	53	0

Table 8. Offenses Known to Law Enforcement, by Selected State and City, 2022—Continued

(Number.)

State/city	Population	Violent crime	Murder and nonnegligent manslaughter	Rape	Robbery	Aggravated assault	Property crime	Burglary	Larceny-theft	Motor vehicle theft	Arson[1]
Rock Hill	4,689	8	0	0	1	7	65	6	41	18	0
Rock Port	1,251	2	0	0	0	2	3	1	2	0	0
Rogersville	4,972	11	0	4	0	7	42	11	27	4	1
Rolla	20,321	112	0	13	6	93	681	130	508	43	4
Rosebud	397	1	0	0	0	1	8	0	6	2	0
Salem	4,571	15	0	5	0	10	98	8	82	8	2
Savannah	5,032	5	0	0	0	5	19	2	12	5	0
Scott City	4,373	11	0	3	1	7	69	9	51	9	0
Sedalia	21,924	108	0	28	7	73	617	131	429	57	2
Seligman	843	1	0	0	0	1	15	1	13	1	0
Seneca	2,290	2	0	0	0	2	63	15	43	5	0
Seymour	1,854	9	0	0	0	9	22	4	15	3	1
Shelbina	1,551	6	0	2	0	4	24	5	17	2	0
Shrewsbury	6,280	19	0	1	5	13	296	11	242	43	0
Sikeston	16,024	237	2	12	10	213	568	61	454	53	21
Smithville	10,654	13	0	3	1	9	60	5	47	8	0
Sparta	1,965	7	0	1	0	6	13	0	11	2	0
Springfield	169,822	2,408	17	190	309	1,892	8,336	1,368	5,819	1,149	21
St. Ann	12,788	39	1	2	5	31	263	18	174	71	0
St. Charles	71,079	151	1	16	20	114	1,242	197	877	168	3
St. Clair	4,746	48	0	7	1	40	199	20	154	25	0
Steelville	1,373	24	0	5	0	19	62	13	45	4	1
Ste. Genevieve	4,686	12	0	4	0	8	59	4	52	3	0
St. James	4,010	7	0	2	1	4	129	14	106	9	2
St. John	6,538	39	0	4	5	30	162	16	91	55	4
St. Joseph	70,918	536	4	150	60	322	3,068	362	2,251	455	17
St. Louis	286,053	4,212	200	151	803	3,058	20,750	2,306	11,150	7,294	139
St. Peters	58,584	133	1	19	4	109	908	67	779	62	3
Strafford	2,633	4	0	1	0	3	68	5	51	12	0
Sugar Creek	3,177	9	0	2	1	6	84	11	54	19	0
Sullivan	6,811	35	0	7	2	26	359	43	291	25	2
Sunrise Beach	480	2	0	1	0	1	16	0	11	5	0
Sunset Hills	9,053	11	0	1	3	7	196	12	148	36	1
Thayer	1,861	4	0	0	0	4	15	5	7	3	0
Town and Country	11,479	3	0	0	0	3	187	15	155	17	0
Trenton	5,581	8	1	1	0	6	82	9	60	13	0
Troy	14,027	37	0	1	4	32	268	26	227	15	1
Truesdale	963	4	0	1	0	3	9	0	8	1	0
Union	12,575	60	0	15	1	44	466	38	372	56	3
University City	34,326	75	2	11	19	43	742	46	489	207	5
Van Buren	761	4	0	0	0	4	4	0	3	1	0
Velda City	1,165	56	1	2	3	50	78	11	42	25	1
Versailles	2,571	6	0	1	0	5	26	5	20	1	1
Vinita Park	8,852	106	9	5	12	80	491	85	234	172	1
Warrensburg	19,703	40	0	16	1	23	527	37	461	29	1
Warrenton	9,215	26	0	3	0	23	239	18	195	26	0
Warsaw	2,282	5	0	1	0	4	46	3	34	9	0
Warson Woods	1,997	1	0	0	0	1	13	1	11	1	0
Washburn	407	0	0	0	0	0	0	0	0	0	0
Washington	15,175	24	0	3	0	21	347	25	300	22	0
Waynesville	5,419	17	0	5	1	11	73	8	56	9	1
Webb City	13,433	35	0	7	2	26	510	44	411	55	2
Webster Groves	23,598	27	1	1	3	22	240	35	124	81	0
Wentzville	46,018	137	0	17	5	115	568	34	496	38	0
Weston	1,772	4	0	1	1	2	18	1	16	1	0
West Plains	12,252	51	1	9	1	40	399	54	309	36	0
Willard	6,430	20	0	0	0	20	39	1	30	8	0
Willow Springs	2,173	8	0	0	0	8	36	3	31	2	1
Winfield	1,574	9	0	1	1	7	5	0	4	1	0
Woodson Terrace	3,900	17	2	2	4	9	106	8	48	50	0
Wright City	5,360	18	0	2	0	16	27	2	22	3	1
MONTANA											
Baker	1,823	2	0	0	0	2	11	0	10	1	0
Belgrade	12,529	64	0	9	0	55	214	12	183	19	0
Billings	117,866	1,095	13	89	144	849	5,088	674	3,613	801	28
Bozeman	55,997	166	2	40	2	122	996	76	848	72	6
Colstrip	2,009	2	0	0	0	2	1	0	1	0	0
Columbia Falls	5,734	15	0	3	1	11	120	11	99	10	2
Columbus	1,863	7	0	0	0	7	28	2	21	5	0
Conrad	2,398	6	0	0	0	6	35	5	27	3	0
Cut Bank	3,053	29	0	2	1	26	75	14	55	6	0
Deer Lodge	2,949	16	1	0	0	15	31	1	25	5	0
Dillon	4,075	10	0	1	0	9	29	5	24	0	0
Ennis	1,008	0	0	0	0	0	8	0	8	0	0
Fairview	858	3	0	0	0	3	12	3	7	2	0
Fort Benton	1,510	7	0	0	0	7	5	0	5	0	0
Glasgow	3,183	17	0	8	0	9	45	2	39	4	1
Glendive	4,860	17	0	3	0	14	34	4	27	3	1
Great Falls	60,386	300	2	48	19	231	2,708	236	2,290	182	12
Hamilton	5,138	7	0	1	0	6	69	1	65	3	0
Hardin	3,656	11	0	0	2	9	39	2	28	9	0
Havre	9,270	92	0	22	6	64	367	22	318	27	1

Table 8. Offenses Known to Law Enforcement, by Selected State and City, 2022—Continued

(Number.)

State/city	Population	Violent crime	Murder and nonnegligent manslaughter	Rape	Robbery	Aggravated assault	Property crime	Burglary	Larceny-theft	Motor vehicle theft	Arson[1]
Helena	33,896	256	1	54	9	192	1,088	93	899	96	10
Hot Springs	610	1	0	1	0	0	5	2	3	0	0
Kalispell	27,710	138	1	22	5	110	723	43	620	60	4
Laurel	7,139	32	0	2	2	28	235	7	216	12	0
Lewistown	6,135	25	0	9	0	16	3	1	1	1	1
Libby	3,055	11	0	2	1	8	37	0	37	0	0
Livingston	8,552	31	0	7	1	23	188	21	153	14	8
Manhattan	2,154	2	0	0	0	2	30	0	29	1	0
Miles City	8,437	31	0	0	1	30	55	7	44	4	1
Missoula	75,705	480	2	62	31	385	2,683	259	2,260	164	10
Plains	1,203	1	0	0	0	1	3	0	3	0	0
Polson	5,495	58	0	4	6	48	249	19	198	32	3
Ronan City	2,255	14	0	0	0	14	92	4	81	7	0
Sidney	6,066	29	1	4	0	24	62	14	46	2	0
St. Ignatius	803	1	0	0	0	1	33	2	24	7	1
Thompson Falls	1,447	8	0	3	0	5	23	5	16	2	0
Troy	865	4	0	0	0	4	15	2	13	0	0
West Yellowstone	1,268	2	0	0	0	2	12	1	11	0	0
Whitefish	9,189	25	0	3	0	22	172	12	149	11	0
Wolf Point	2,620	22	0	0	1	21	33	5	26	2	0
NEBRASKA											
Alliance	7,807	37	0	4	1	32	131	17	105	9	1
Ashland	3,279	0	0	0	0	0	4	0	2	2	0
Aurora	4,631	5	0	3	0	2	21	4	17	0	0
Beatrice	12,164	33	0	11	1	21	122	19	92	11	0
Bellevue	63,178	115	1	68	14	32	883	73	682	128	4
Blair	7,855	6	0	3	0	3	69	8	58	3	0
Boys Town	413	6	0	1	0	5	11	2	9	0	1
Broken Bow	3,448	1	0	0	0	1	4	0	4	0	0
Central City	3,038	2	0	0	0	2	12	0	8	4	0
Columbus	24,158	17	1	12	0	4	286	21	239	26	2
Cozad	3,857	3	0	1	1	1	40	4	33	3	1
Creighton	1,152	0	0	0	0	0	0	0	0	0	0
Crete	7,200	24	0	12	1	11	125	23	93	9	3
Emerson	814	0	0	0	0	0	1	0	1	0	0
Falls City	4,032	7	0	1	1	5	36	2	32	2	0
Franklin	934	0	0	0	0	0	3	1	2	0	0
Gordon	1,493	3	0	3	0	0	22	3	18	1	0
Gothenburg	3,372	4	0	0	0	4	20	2	15	3	0
Grand Island	51,733	210	1	49	20	140	1,333	191	992	150	9
Hastings	24,930	93	0	17	2	74	588	36	499	53	8
Holdrege	5,469	7	0	4	1	2	17	1	15	1	0
Kearney	34,186	117	1	40	7	69	550	70	444	36	2
Laurel	962	0	0	0	0	0	0	0	0	0	0
La Vista	16,515	19	0	7	1	11	246	30	187	29	2
Lexington	10,382	14	0	4	1	9	193	10	174	9	0
Lincoln	293,937	1,123	11	239	145	728	8,354	879	6,633	842	85
Madison	2,174	0	0	0	0	0	3	0	3	0	0
Milford	2,142	2	0	1	0	1	7	5	1	1	0
Minatare	715	0	0	0	0	0	23	3	18	2	0
Norfolk	25,048	16	0	7	1	8	201	19	163	19	0
North Platte	22,684	43	0	11	3	29	647	97	505	45	9
Ogallala	4,788	6	0	2	0	4	98	14	75	9	0
Omaha	483,462	2,713	29	298	336	2,050	16,768	1,255	12,156	3,357	
O'Neill	3,536	2	0	1	0	1	4	0	3	1	0
Ord	2,114	4	0	0	0	4	9	3	6	0	0
Papillion	23,874	22	0	12	3	7	273	17	244	12	3
Pierce	1,823	0	0	0	0	0	7	1	6	0	0
Plattsmouth	6,710	9	0	5	1	3	82	15	60	7	0
Ralston	6,448	7	0	1	3	3	112	10	78	24	0
Schuyler	6,476	1	0	0	0	1	7	0	6	1	0
Scottsbluff	15,224	64	1	13	2	48	447	42	367	38	5
Seward	7,695	6	0	3	0	3	44	1	40	3	1
Sidney	6,469	33	0	1	0	32	106	13	88	5	1
South Sioux City	13,652	25	0	8	2	15	371	18	313	40	0
St. Paul	2,407	1	0	0	0	1	14	2	12	0	0
Tilden	972	0	0	0	0	0	0	0	0	0	0
Valentine	2,605	17	0	10	0	7	33	5	20	8	0
Waterloo	911	0	0	0	0	0	11	1	7	3	0
Wayne	6,056	7	0	5	0	2	44	3	40	1	0
West Point	3,445	4	0	3	0	1	5	1	4	0	0
York	8,214	17	1	4	2	10	80	7	63	10	1
NEVADA											
Boulder City	14,848	9	0	2	0	7	159	31	106	22	0
Carlin	2,048	4	0	0	0	4	27	13	10	4	1
Elko	20,664	96	1	16	10	69	398	71	264	63	2
Fallon	9,359	16	1	1	0	14	135	10	110	15	0
Henderson	325,332	985	3	97	234	651	6,242	950	4,421	871	44
Las Vegas Metropolitan Police Department	1,667,961	8,605	147	1,041	1,622	5,795	48,669	9,338	28,710	10,621	150
Mesquite	21,732	34	0	5	2	27	282	45	206	31	3

Table 8. Offenses Known to Law Enforcement, by Selected State and City, 2022—Continued

(Number.)

State/city	Population	Violent crime	Murder and nonnegligent manslaughter	Rape	Robbery	Aggravated assault	Property crime	Burglary	Larceny-theft	Motor vehicle theft	Arson[1]
North Las Vegas	284,422	1,199	26	132	363	678	5,046	827	2,381	1,838	29
Reno	273,671	1,565	11	277	300	977	6,994	1,113	4,790	1,091	36
Sparks	110,475	461	6	85	103	267	2,222	281	1,586	355	14
West Wendover	4,473	17	0	4	1	12	107	13	84	10	1
Winnemucca	8,775	47	2	7	3	35	234	60	135	39	3
NEW HAMPSHIRE											
Alexandria	1,789	1	0	0	0	1	4	0	4	0	0
Allenstown	4,788	7	0	4	0	3	21	1	20	0	1
Alstead	1,909	0	0	0	0	0	1	0	1	0	0
Alton	6,054	7	0	6	0	1	32	7	22	3	0
Amherst	11,876	4	0	2	1	1	98	5	93	0	1
Andover	2,434	1	0	1	0	0	6	0	6	0	0
Antrim	2,683	4	0	2	1	1	21	4	17	0	0
Ashland	1,969	1	0	0	1	0	46	0	43	3	0
Atkinson	7,343	7	0	2	1	4	10	4	3	3	0
Auburn	6,090	1	0	0	0	1	26	0	24	2	1
Barnstead	5,024	9	0	4	2	3	48	8	37	3	2
Barrington	9,531	6	0	4	0	2	40	7	25	8	0
Bartlett	3,363	3	0	1	0	2	19	1	18	0	0
Bedford	23,845	8	0	3	1	4	123	6	111	6	1
Belmont	7,425	6	0	4	0	2	114	7	98	9	0
Bennington	1,506	2	0	1	0	1	10	2	7	1	0
Berlin	9,717	18	0	3	2	13	172	13	150	9	4
Bethlehem	2,543	1	0	0	0	1	55	11	38	6	0
Bow	8,429	1	0	0	0	1	46	0	44	2	0
Bradford	1,726	1	0	1	0	0	9	1	7	1	0
Brentwood	4,610	2	0	0	1	1	10	0	10	0	0
Bridgewater	1,184	0	0	0	0	0	1	0	1	0	0
Bristol	3,303	3	0	1	0	2	31	1	28	2	0
Brookline	5,774	3	0	2	0	1	23	5	15	3	0
Campton	3,418	11	0	7	0	4	32	2	28	2	1
Canaan	3,818	1	0	1	0	0	22	3	18	1	0
Candia	4,162	2	0	0	0	2	15	1	14	0	0
Canterbury	2,483	1	0	0	0	1	13	1	11	1	0
Carroll	812	0	0	0	0	0	7	0	7	0	0
Charlestown	4,950	4	0	1	0	3	19	3	15	1	1
Chester	5,279	3	0	1	0	2	16	0	15	1	0
Chesterfield	3,638	7	0	3	3	1	26	10	12	4	0
Chichester	2,777	5	0	1	0	4	36	3	31	2	0
Claremont	13,153	22	0	5	7	10	297	20	255	22	3
Colebrook	2,051	1	0	1	0	0	28	3	22	3	0
Concord	44,305	61	3	16	14	28	600	22	538	40	8
Conway	10,334	17	0	6	0	11	214	8	197	9	0
Cornish	1,659	0	0	0	0	0	7	0	7	0	0
Danbury	1,277	0	0	0	0	0	4	1	3	0	0
Danville	4,596	0	0	0	0	0	4	0	3	1	0
Deerfield	4,934	3	0	2	0	1	20	0	20	0	0
Deering	1,912	3	0	0	0	3	15	2	13	0	0
Derry	34,290	41	0	13	3	25	283	20	243	20	5
Dover	33,453	13	0	3	3	7	340	15	308	17	2
Dublin	1,586	2	0	1	0	1	4	0	4	0	0
Dunbarton	3,112	0	0	0	0	0	14	1	12	1	0
Durham	15,550	9	0	6	1	2	49	3	44	2	0
East Kingston	2,427	0	0	0	0	0	4	0	4	0	0
Effingham	1,781	1	0	0	0	1	4	1	2	1	0
Enfield	4,540	0	0	0	0	0	14	1	11	2	0
Epping	7,274	7	0	2	0	5	86	1	83	2	2
Epsom	4,957	4	0	2	0	2	26	1	21	4	0
Exeter	16,155	13	0	5	1	7	94	4	80	10	0
Farmington	6,872	25	0	10	0	15	78	9	60	9	3
Fitzwilliam	2,437	1	0	1	0	0	8	3	5	0	1
Francestown	1,640	0	0	0	0	0	0	0	0	0	0
Franconia	1,101	1	0	1	0	0	7	1	6	0	0
Franklin	8,850	8	0	3	1	4	95	3	89	3	0
Freedom	1,767	6	0	0	0	6	8	1	7	0	0
Fremont	4,797	3	0	1	0	2	13	1	11	1	1
Gilford	7,880	4	0	3	0	1	113	8	104	1	0
Gilmanton	4,022	3	0	3	0	0	19	3	10	6	0
Goffstown	18,375	17	0	6	1	10	118	6	106	6	2
Gorham	2,641	5	2	0	2	1	79	3	75	1	0
Grantham	3,497	2	0	1	0	1	6	1	3	2	0
Greenfield	1,719	2	0	2	0	0	4	0	3	1	0
Greenland	4,091	3	0	0	0	3	24	2	21	1	0
Greenville	1,970	0	0	0	0	0	0	0	0	0	0
Groton	577	0	0	0	0	0	1	0	1	0	0
Hampstead	9,058	6	0	2	1	3	27	1	22	4	0
Hampton	16,384	19	0	4	3	12	122	6	110	6	0
Hampton Falls	2,408	1	0	0	0	1	13	1	11	1	0
Hanover	11,778	10	0	7	0	3	61	4	55	2	0
Harrisville	1,008	0	0	0	0	0	0	0	0	0	0
Haverhill	4,622	6	1	2	0	3	65	5	55	5	0
Hebron	649	0	0	0	0	0	1	0	1	0	0

Table 8. Offenses Known to Law Enforcement, by Selected State and City, 2022—Continued

(Number.)

State/city	Population	Violent crime	Murder and nonnegligent manslaughter	Rape	Robbery	Aggravated assault	Property crime	Burglary	Larceny-theft	Motor vehicle theft	Arson[1]
Henniker	5,870	9	0	2	1	6	26	4	18	4	1
Hinsdale	4,033	1	0	0	0	1	120	7	113	0	0
Holderness	2,037	4	0	0	0	4	14	1	10	3	0
Hollis	8,661	3	0	1	0	2	34	1	32	1	0
Hooksett	15,313	21	1	10	4	6	139	5	120	14	2
Hopkinton	6,079	1	0	1	0	0	15	0	14	1	0
Hudson	25,530	16	1	10	2	3	203	14	177	12	1
Jaffrey	5,495	17	0	11	1	5	25	3	22	0	2
Keene	23,271	40	1	18	11	10	498	26	452	20	3
Kensington	2,090	1	0	1	0	0	3	0	2	1	0
Kingston	6,231	2	0	2	0	0	17	3	12	2	0
Laconia	17,109	25	0	15	2	8	470	17	435	18	4
Lancaster	3,209	2	0	0	0	2	14	1	12	1	0
Langdon	661	0	0	0	0	0	0	0	0	0	0
Lebanon	15,702	25	0	14	4	7	271	16	247	8	2
Lee	4,634	2	0	1	1	0	26	0	24	2	0
Lincoln	1,652	1	0	1	0	0	34	3	29	2	0
Lisbon	1,651	2	0	0	0	2	23	3	20	0	0
Litchfield	8,556	2	0	1	0	1	15	4	9	2	0
Littleton	6,058	2	0	1	0	1	40	1	35	4	0
Londonderry	26,340	32	0	24	3	5	182	9	157	16	3
Loudon	5,781	2	0	0	0	2	29	3	21	5	0
Lyme	1,758	0	0	0	0	0	3	0	3	0	0
Lyndeborough	1,705	0	0	0	0	0	2	0	2	0	0
Madbury	1,938	0	0	0	0	0	4	1	3	0	0
Manchester	114,650	472	5	50	87	330	2,854	226	2,381	247	17
Marlborough	2,163	2	0	1	0	1	12	0	12	0	0
Mason	1,450	1	0	0	0	1	5	3	2	0	0
Meredith	6,786	6	0	1	0	5	72	8	57	7	0
Merrimack	27,403	6	0	1	1	4	117	2	115	0	0
Milford	16,331	7	0	2	0	5	57	6	47	4	2
Milton	4,530	5	0	3	0	2	41	0	35	6	0
Nashua	91,027	143	4	50	21	68	973	63	845	65	9
New Boston	6,216	4	0	3	0	1	12	0	11	1	0
Newbury	2,236	0	0	0	0	0	10	1	9	0	0
New Castle	999	0	0	0	0	0	2	0	2	0	0
New Durham	2,765	0	0	0	0	0	37	5	31	1	0
Newfields	1,761	0	0	0	0	0	4	2	2	0	0
New Hampton	2,433	2	0	1	0	1	22	1	19	2	0
Newington	817	1	0	0	1	0	56	3	51	2	0
New Ipswich	5,333	1	0	1	0	0	34	2	26	6	0
New London	4,354	5	1	4	0	0	16	3	13	0	0
Newmarket	9,417	8	0	1	1	6	47	2	43	2	3
Newport	6,411	13	0	2	2	9	80	6	71	3	1
Northfield	4,998	2	0	0	0	2	51	4	43	4	0
Northwood	4,670	3	0	1	0	2	22	4	17	1	0
Orford	1,253	0	0	0	0	0	8	0	8	0	0
Ossipee	4,565	13	0	5	0	8	60	3	50	7	2
Pelham	14,364	4	0	1	0	3	80	2	71	7	0
Pembroke	7,684	17	0	11	0	6	41	2	35	4	0
Peterborough	6,479	5	0	1	1	3	27	3	23	1	1
Piermont	778	1	0	0	0	1	5	0	5	0	0
Pittsburg	806	0	0	0	0	0	1	0	1	0	0
Pittsfield	4,155	14	0	5	0	9	23	3	17	3	0
Plainfield	2,505	0	0	0	0	0	13	1	12	0	0
Plaistow	7,856	4	0	1	1	2	60	6	48	6	1
Plymouth	6,658	13	0	4	2	7	91	4	84	3	0
Portsmouth	22,513	40	0	10	2	28	282	12	252	18	2
Raymond	10,996	16	0	10	1	5	64	2	57	5	1
Rindge	6,633	2	0	1	0	1	32	5	26	1	13
Rochester	33,098	63	0	19	4	40	574	91	450	33	2
Rollinsford	2,646	5	0	1	1	3	18	2	13	3	0
Roxbury	226	0	0	0	0	0	0	0	0	0	0
Rumney	1,513	0	0	0	0	0	1	0	1	0	0
Rye	5,550	0	0	0	0	0	15	1	13	1	0
Salem	30,712	29	0	9	11	9	436	16	400	20	1
Sanbornton	3,072	1	0	0	0	1	10	2	8	0	0
Sandown	6,575	2	0	2	0	0	20	2	17	1	0
Somersworth	12,160	11	0	7	1	3	245	10	218	17	2
South Hampton	896	0	0	0	0	0	1	0	1	0	0
Springfield	1,316	0	0	0	0	0	9	1	8	0	0
Stoddard	1,422	0	0	0	0	0	0	0	0	0	0
Strafford	4,324	1	0	0	0	1	2	0	2	0	0
Stratham	7,844	1	0	0	0	1	18	1	16	1	0
Sugar Hill	662	0	0	0	0	0	1	0	1	0	0
Sunapee	3,457	1	0	1	0	0	17	2	15	0	1
Sutton	2,038	1	0	1	0	0	0	0	0	0	0
Swanzey	7,468	17	0	9	1	7	37	18	19	0	0
Tamworth	2,949	1	0	0	0	1	25	2	23	0	0
Thornton	2,785	0	0	0	0	0	8	0	5	3	0
Tilton	4,106	5	0	1	1	3	167	4	154	9	0
Tuftonboro	2,614	2	0	2	0	0	16	2	14	0	0
Wakefield	6,315	10	0	1	0	9	34	4	28	2	0

Table 8. Offenses Known to Law Enforcement, by Selected State and City, 2022—Continued

(Number.)

State/city	Population	Violent crime	Murder and nonnegligent manslaughter	Rape	Robbery	Aggravated assault	Property crime	Burglary	Larceny-theft	Motor vehicle theft	Arson[1]
Warner	2,969	1	0	0	0	1	20	0	19	1	0
Warren	840	0	0	0	0	0	0	0	0	0	0
Washington	1,221	0	0	0	0	0	2	0	2	0	0
Waterville Valley	510	1	0	1	0	0	17	0	17	0	0
Weare	9,213	7	0	6	0	1	25	1	20	4	0
Webster	1,976	3	0	2	0	1	5	0	4	1	1
Wentworth	856	0	0	0	0	0	3	0	3	0	0
Whitefield	2,563	1	0	0	0	1	8	0	8	0	0
Wilmot	1,444	0	0	0	0	0	0	0	0	0	0
Wilton	3,994	11	0	2	0	9	25	3	20	2	2
Winchester	4,246	3	1	0	1	1	34	7	23	4	3
Windham	15,994	6	1	3	0	2	60	9	45	6	0
Wolfeboro	6,710	5	0	2	0	3	42	2	37	3	0
Woodstock	1,454	3	0	2	0	1	29	8	19	2	0
NEW JERSEY											
Aberdeen Township	19,345	24	0	0	2	22	113	16	84	13	0
Absecon	9,153	30	0	7	4	19	302	31	257	14	0
Allenhurst	470	0	0	0	0	0	9	1	7	1	0
Allentown	1,737	0	0	0	0	0	5	0	5	0	0
Alpha	2,348	2	0	1	0	1	24	2	21	1	0
Alpine	1,743	0	0	0	0	0	34	10	11	13	0
Andover Township	6,227	3	0	0	0	3	11	1	9	1	0
Asbury Park	15,209	164	3	9	32	120	551	89	438	24	1
Atlantic City	38,502	651	7	56	205	383	3,093	738	2,103	252	6
Atlantic Highlands	4,416	3	1	0	0	2	20	3	17	0	0
Audubon	8,665	10	0	0	5	5	261	16	238	7	0
Avalon	1,209	1	0	0	0	1	95	15	75	5	0
Avon-by-the-Sea	1,899	0	0	0	0	0	34	7	27	0	0
Barnegat Township	25,142	18	0	4	1	13	108	11	93	4	0
Barrington	7,013	9	0	0	1	8	101	6	86	9	0
Bayonne	66,990	201	2	13	46	140	876	98	692	86	0
Beach Haven	1,082	0	0	0	0	0	112	0	112	0	1
Beachwood	11,188	10	0	0	1	9	102	17	79	6	0
Bedminster Township	8,123	0	0	0	0	0	35	6	24	5	0
Belleville	37,348	66	0	5	11	50	700	39	524	137	0
Bellmawr	11,645	20	0	0	4	16	211	25	178	8	2
Belmar	5,868	4	0	1	0	3	118	12	103	3	0
Belvidere	2,531	3	0	1	1	1	38	6	31	1	0
Bergenfield	28,082	12	0	1	2	9	89	9	62	18	0
Berkeley Heights Township	13,096	2	0	0	0	2	68	10	48	10	1
Berkeley Township	45,006	65	0	15	4	46	291	39	242	10	1
Berlin	7,522	6	0	0	0	6	127	19	100	8	0
Bernards Township	27,682	1	0	0	1	0	66	8	45	13	0
Bernardsville	7,786	0	0	0	0	0	27	1	20	6	0
Beverly	2,487	20	1	0	1	18	31	2	26	3	0
Blairstown Township	5,766	3	0	1	0	2	16	3	9	4	0
Bloomfield	52,663	46	1	0	9	36	640	30	494	116	0
Bloomingdale	7,616	5	0	2	0	3	23	5	17	1	0
Boonton	8,805	6	0	1	1	4	81	10	64	7	0
Boonton Township	4,387	3	0	2	0	1	9	0	9	0	0
Bound Brook	11,948	13	0	0	6	7	123	9	106	8	0
Bradley Beach	4,267	2	0	0	0	2	63	2	58	3	0
Branchburg Township	14,690	10	0	5	0	5	101	11	83	7	1
Brick Township	76,287	106	0	17	6	83	801	112	672	17	3
Bridgeton	26,524	187	1	22	78	86	845	111	689	45	3
Brielle	4,985	4	0	0	0	4	19	1	16	2	0
Brigantine	7,642	6	0	0	0	6	74	10	62	2	1
Brooklawn	1,802	17	0	1	3	13	184	18	149	17	0
Burlington Township	23,927	23	0	4	3	16	232	35	179	18	1
Butler	8,203	1	0	0	0	1	40	6	32	2	0
Caldwell	8,734	4	0	0	0	4	37	1	33	3	0
Califon	1,016	0	0	0	0	0	0	0	0	0	0
Camden County Police Department	71,616	1,125	28	52	244	801	1,970	316	1,222	432	32
Cape May	2,845	6	0	0	0	6	108	3	100	5	0
Carlstadt	6,316	3	0	0	1	2	128	3	108	17	0
Carney's Point Township	8,763	22	0	5	4	13	79	9	62	8	1
Cedar Grove Township	13,822	4	0	0	1	3	78	7	55	16	0
Chatham	9,307	1	0	0	0	1	67	9	36	22	0
Chatham Township	10,897	0	0	0	0	0	26	4	19	3	0
Cherry Hill Township	76,401	112	1	0	60	51	2,416	99	2,199	118	0
Chesilhurst	1,543	2	0	0	0	2	14	5	7	2	0
Chester	1,676	0	0	0	0	0	20	1	19	0	0
Chester Township	7,711	0	0	0	0	0	31	3	27	1	0
Clark Township	15,308	8	0	1	2	5	276	13	243	20	0
Clayton	9,017	12	0	1	0	11	40	9	27	4	0
Clementon	5,318	14	0	0	9	5	125	32	92	1	0
Cliffside Park	25,531	7	0	3	3	1	107	3	101	3	0
Clifton	88,768	93	2	7	41	43	1,714	104	1,420	190	0
Clinton	2,795	3	0	0	0	3	9	1	7	1	0
Clinton Township	13,759	3	0	0	0	3	57	21	34	2	0
Closter	8,474	0	0	0	0	0	61	6	45	10	0

Table 8. Offenses Known to Law Enforcement, by Selected State and City, 2022—Continued

(Number.)

State/city	Population	Violent crime	Murder and nonnegligent manslaughter	Rape	Robbery	Aggravated assault	Property crime	Burglary	Larceny-theft	Motor vehicle theft	Arson[1]
Collingswood	14,108	31	0	0	6	25	427	91	315	21	0
Colts Neck Township	9,967	1	0	1	0	0	77	17	38	22	0
Cranbury Township	3,989	1	0	0	0	1	39	4	32	3	0
Cranford Township	24,133	9	0	3	0	6	244	71	144	29	3
Cresskill	9,069	1	0	0	1	0	32	4	13	15	0
Deal	892	1	0	0	0	1	35	3	19	13	0
Delanco Township	4,805	8	0	1	1	6	41	10	29	2	0
Delaware Township	4,589	0	0	0	0	0	9	4	4	1	0
Delran Township	17,822	12	0	3	2	7	216	7	190	19	1
Demarest	4,812	1	0	1	0	0	31	4	17	10	0
Denville Township	17,119	0	0	0	0	0	94	12	66	16	0
Deptford Township	32,429	77	1	11	24	41	1,316	89	1,185	42	0
Dumont	18,533	7	1	0	0	6	62	2	57	3	0
Dunellen	7,525	3	0	0	0	3	62	7	53	2	0
Eastampton Township	6,319	11	0	2	3	6	67	2	61	4	1
East Brunswick Township	49,038	45	1	8	8	28	640	75	526	39	4
East Hanover Township	11,103	1	0	0	1	0	170	14	148	8	0
East Newark	2,383	5	0	0	1	4	13	0	11	2	0
East Rutherford	9,904	8	0	1	2	5	167	8	138	21	0
East Windsor Township	29,788	12	0	1	2	9	236	20	199	17	0
Eatontown	13,607	28	0	3	9	16	242	21	204	17	1
Edgewater	14,793	8	0	2	1	5	182	18	140	24	1
Edison Township	108,050	177	0	8	41	128	1,827	192	1,476	159	4
Egg Harbor City	4,402	11	0	0	3	8	120	14	99	7	4
Egg Harbor Township	47,747	37	1	5	11	20	1,032	165	826	41	4
Elizabeth	134,065	644	2	50	228	364	3,421	300	2,426	695	5
Elmwood Park	21,154	40	0	6	6	28	283	35	215	33	6
Englewood	28,975	105	0	7	23	75	338	37	247	54	2
Englewood Cliffs	5,352	0	0	0	0	0	86	8	42	36	0
Englishtown	2,362	1	0	0	1	0	17	3	12	2	0
Essex Fells	2,144	2	0	1	0	1	33	4	26	3	0
Evesham Township	49,166	33	1	6	2	24	515	34	454	27	3
Ewing Township	37,408	76	2	13	20	41	955	55	826	74	7
Fairfield Township, Essex County	7,777	2	1	0	0	1	83	7	64	12	0
Fair Haven	6,156	0	0	0	0	0	29	4	20	5	0
Fair Lawn	35,424	18	0	1	5	12	255	26	207	22	3
Fairview	14,850	12	0	0	2	10	149	19	125	5	0
Flemington	4,923	6	0	0	1	5	112	12	92	8	1
Florence Township	12,747	7	1	0	0	6	15	5	8	2	0
Florham Park	13,685	4	0	2	0	2	53	4	39	10	0
Fort Lee	39,636	61	0	0	17	44	538	77	391	70	2
Franklin	4,983	3	0	0	0	3	59	5	54	0	0
Franklin Lakes	10,899	2	0	0	0	2	115	20	72	23	0
Franklin Township, Gloucester County	16,579	26	1	1	3	21	206	62	119	25	1
Franklin Township, Hunterdon County	3,303	1	0	0	0	1	26	1	23	2	0
Franklin Township, Somerset County	68,782	67	1	7	19	40	598	51	472	75	0
Freehold Township	35,791	31	0	4	4	23	550	36	477	37	0
Frenchtown	1,387	2	0	0	0	2	20	2	17	1	1
Galloway Township	37,961	62	0	7	5	50	520	106	376	38	2
Garfield	32,351	36	0	3	9	24	499	32	431	36	1
Garwood	4,358	2	0	0	0	2	19	1	18	0	0
Gibbsboro	2,208	1	0	0	0	1	50	4	44	2	0
Glassboro	21,115	49	0	6	7	36	318	65	229	24	1
Glen Ridge	7,620	4	0	1	1	2	106	9	82	15	0
Glen Rock	12,017	4	0	0	3	1	57	7	42	8	0
Gloucester City	11,430	27	0	0	4	23	297	23	271	3	0
Gloucester Township	65,848	82	2	5	8	67	737	60	602	75	1
Green Brook Township	7,314	2	0	0	0	2	44	13	25	6	0
Greenwich Township, Gloucester County	5,018	0	0	0	0	0	52	4	47	1	0
Greenwich Township, Warren County	5,490	0	0	0	0	0	75	2	72	1	0
Hackensack	45,413	94	0	10	14	70	1,097	75	943	79	1
Hackettstown	10,389	3	0	0	2	1	45	6	36	3	0
Haddonfield	12,467	4	0	0	3	1	151	29	113	9	0
Haddon Heights	7,461	3	0	0	1	2	58	9	46	3	0
Haledon	8,848	2	0	1	1	0	166	15	140	11	0
Hamburg	3,311	1	0	1	0	0	8	1	6	1	0
Hamilton Township, Atlantic County	28,658	44	0	5	8	31	508	37	454	17	0
Hamilton Township, Mercer County	91,408	203	1	20	54	128	1,647	169	1,369	109	4
Hammonton	14,861	44	0	1	4	39	104	13	78	13	1
Hanover Township	14,630	9	0	0	2	7	195	7	178	10	0
Harding Township	3,883	0	0	0	0	0	28	3	24	1	0
Hardyston Township	8,351	3	0	3	0	0	41	8	30	3	0
Harrison	18,999	57	0	5	18	34	395	16	333	46	0
Harrison Township	13,886	14	0	0	1	13	65	11	48	6	1
Hasbrouck Heights	12,005	3	0	0	2	1	76	1	74	1	1

Table 8. Offenses Known to Law Enforcement, by Selected State and City, 2022—Continued

(Number.)

State/city	Population	Violent crime	Murder and nonnegligent manslaughter	Rape	Robbery	Aggravated assault	Property crime	Burglary	Larceny-theft	Motor vehicle theft	Arson[1]
Hawthorne	19,163	4	0	0	2	2	156	8	128	20	0
Hazlet Township	20,547	13	1	1	1	10	174	19	148	7	0
Helmetta	2,426	0	0	0	0	0	1	1	0	0	0
High Bridge	3,641	2	0	0	0	2	23	5	16	2	0
Highland Park	14,914	20	0	2	5	13	129	10	105	14	1
Highlands	4,654	8	0	0	0	8	12	0	12	0	0
Hightstown	5,859	7	0	0	2	5	40	7	30	3	0
Hillsborough Township	42,893	6	0	0	0	6	129	19	97	13	1
Hillsdale	10,011	1	0	0	0	1	33	1	28	4	0
Hillside Township	22,026	53	0	5	19	29	635	45	464	126	1
Hi-Nella	923	3	0	0	0	3	14	6	8	0	0
Hoboken	56,882	88	1	4	16	67	880	81	741	58	0
Holmdel Township	17,421	1	0	0	0	1	185	11	149	25	0
Hopatcong	14,561	14	0	4	1	9	28	5	20	3	0
Hopewell Township	17,339	9	2	2	1	4	99	18	77	4	1
Howell Township	54,073	42	0	3	3	36	442	49	378	15	1
Independence Township	5,510	2	0	0	1	1	7	1	4	2	0
Jackson Township	60,762	21	1	8	0	12	263	26	217	20	1
Jamesburg	5,703	5	1	0	0	4	8	0	8	0	0
Jefferson Township	20,498	4	0	0	0	4	38	2	35	1	0
Jersey City	276,300	609	12	39	89	469	3,825	61	3,125	639	3
Keansburg	9,757	35	1	0	2	32	131	21	102	8	2
Kearny	38,906	47	1	0	33	13	867	30	724	113	0
Kenilworth	8,280	1	0	0	0	1	96	8	81	7	0
Kinnelon	9,983	0	0	0	0	0	31	2	23	6	0
Lacey Township	29,903	45	1	2	3	39	220	23	191	6	0
Lakehurst	2,708	6	0	1	0	5	24	5	19	0	1
Lakewood Township	141,190	123	0	14	25	84	914	151	661	102	17
Lambertville	4,173	0	0	0	0	0	20	0	20	0	0
Laurel Springs	1,971	4	0	0	1	3	15	2	12	1	0
Lavallette	1,852	0	0	0	0	0	10	0	9	1	0
Lawnside	3,343	4	0	0	1	3	163	5	156	2	0
Lawrence Township, Mercer County	32,949	14	0	4	10	0	524	51	450	23	1
Lebanon Township	6,243	2	0	1	0	1	18	2	15	1	0
Leonia	9,198	4	1	0	0	3	80	19	57	4	0
Lincoln Park	10,904	4	0	3	0	1	74	9	59	6	0
Linden	43,652	141	0	16	35	90	1,307	89	1,098	120	1
Lindenwold	21,524	83	2	6	15	60	408	97	259	52	3
Linwood	6,950	2	0	2	0	0	54	5	46	3	0
Little Falls Township	13,220	14	1	1	1	11	109	12	84	13	0
Little Silver	6,050	0	0	0	0	0	41	7	27	7	0
Livingston Township	30,844	7	0	1	4	2	313	21	251	41	0
Lodi	25,788	34	2	3	4	25	334	24	272	38	1
Logan Township	6,103	5	0	0	0	5	95	1	80	14	1
Long Branch	33,094	62	0	11	7	44	421	54	339	28	1
Long Hill Township	8,610	1	0	0	0	1	50	5	41	4	0
Longport	879	0	0	0	0	0	3	0	2	1	0
Lopatcong Township	10,057	3	0	0	2	1	45	8	35	2	0
Lower Township	22,238	34	0	4	4	26	164	20	139	5	3
Lyndhurst Township	22,183	12	0	0	4	8	211	11	182	18	1
Mahwah Township	25,150	6	0	0	4	2	102	9	78	15	0
Manalapan Township	40,897	10	0	3	3	4	225	44	145	36	0
Manasquan	5,949	1	0	1	0	0	80	9	68	3	1
Manchester Township	46,265	24	0	6	4	14	196	31	145	20	6
Mansfield Township, Warren County	7,846	0	0	0	0	0	95	3	88	4	0
Manville	10,763	9	1	4	0	4	128	12	106	10	0
Maple Shade Township	19,911	60	3	7	14	36	444	62	324	58	1
Maplewood Township	25,088	26	0	1	17	8	353	24	235	94	1
Margate City	5,202	3	0	0	1	2	78	11	60	7	0
Marlboro Township	41,576	24	1	2	3	18	474	50	326	98	0
Matawan	9,734	0	0	0	0	0	4	2	1	1	0
Maywood	9,966	7	0	0	1	6	108	9	87	12	0
Medford Township	24,447	26	0	10	2	14	197	20	167	10	2
Mendham	4,975	0	0	0	0	0	15	7	7	1	0
Middlesex Borough	14,423	7	0	2	3	2	86	12	72	2	0
Middle Township	20,845	64	1	10	4	49	379	28	337	14	0
Midland Park	6,930	4	0	0	1	3	32	2	29	1	0
Millburn Township	22,417	4	0	0	4	0	550	23	487	40	0
Milltown	6,947	2	0	0	1	1	134	5	125	4	0
Millville	27,550	139	1	12	26	100	1,063	104	921	38	2
Monmouth Beach	3,242	0	0	0	0	0	22	1	13	8	0
Monroe Township, Gloucester County	38,222	31	0	3	3	25	358	70	260	28	0
Monroe Township, Middlesex County	48,097	5	0	0	0	5	106	12	75	19	0
Montclair	41,117	44	1	6	9	28	440	59	293	88	0
Montgomery Township	23,441	1	0	0	0	1	66	27	29	10	0
Montvale	8,436	2	0	0	1	1	46	4	38	4	0
Moonachie	3,093	1	0	0	0	1	52	5	43	4	1
Morris Plains	6,138	2	0	0	0	2	78	9	66	3	0
Morristown	20,418	39	0	7	9	23	195	9	167	19	0

Table 8. Offenses Known to Law Enforcement, by Selected State and City, 2022—Continued

(Number.)

State/city	Population	Violent crime	Murder and nonnegligent manslaughter	Rape	Robbery	Aggravated assault	Property crime	Burglary	Larceny-theft	Motor vehicle theft	Arson[1]
Morris Township	23,455	12	0	0	2	10	134	31	90	13	0
Mount Arlington	5,908	6	0	0	1	5	27	5	22	0	0
Mount Ephraim	4,615	11	0	3	2	6	288	13	267	8	1
Mount Olive Township	28,970	13	0	5	4	4	129	12	111	6	0
Mullica Township	5,798	9	1	1	0	7	61	22	38	1	0
Neptune City	4,620	15	0	1	2	12	88	5	80	3	1
Neptune Township	28,491	111	6	6	15	84	829	117	678	34	1
Netcong	3,973	4	0	0	0	4	29	8	20	1	0
Newark	304,311	1,582	53	86	469	974	5,539	537	2,869	2,133	29
New Brunswick	55,971	480	4	47	217	212	1,211	152	959	100	3
New Milford	16,897	1	1	0	0	0	59	2	53	4	0
New Providence	13,548	1	0	1	0	0	57	1	47	9	0
Newton	8,593	7	0	1	0	6	44	1	43	0	1
North Bergen Township	58,378	80	0	14	16	50	377	39	284	54	1
North Brunswick Township	43,419	94	0	6	14	74	557	33	476	48	2
Northfield	8,435	3	0	0	0	3	50	3	44	3	0
North Haledon	8,788	3	0	0	0	3	36	11	21	4	0
North Plainfield	22,394	36	1	7	12	16	314	25	261	28	1
Northvale	4,759	2	0	1	0	1	8	0	8	0	0
North Wildwood	3,602	9	0	0	1	8	149	10	136	3	0
Norwood	5,565	0	0	0	0	0	26	6	18	2	0
Oakland	12,616	4	0	0	0	4	56	4	41	11	0
Oaklyn	3,908	9	0	0	3	6	185	40	137	8	0
Ocean City	11,258	14	0	0	0	14	672	22	637	13	0
Ocean Gate	2,000	2	0	0	0	2	30	9	20	1	0
Oceanport	6,119	6	1	0	2	3	40	12	25	3	0
Ocean Township, Monmouth County	28,119	35	0	1	7	27	726	63	612	51	3
Ocean Township, Ocean County	9,031	2	0	1	1	0	38	10	27	1	0
Old Bridge Township	67,876	41	2	0	4	35	564	61	425	78	0
Old Tappan	5,799	0	0	0	0	0	28	4	17	7	0
Oradell	8,139	1	0	0	1	0	43	12	25	6	1
Orange City	33,615	123	2	11	31	79	610	99	383	128	1
Oxford Township	2,456	0	0	0	0	0	5	2	3	0	0
Palisades Park	19,991	14	0	1	2	11	146	33	101	12	0
Palmyra	7,418	15	1	2	3	9	134	18	99	17	0
Paramus	26,242	10	0	0	7	3	1,095	47	962	86	0
Park Ridge	10,040	1	0	0	0	1	27	1	26	0	0
Parsippany-Troy Hills Township	56,193	17	0	6	5	6	568	80	445	43	1
Passaic	69,003	375	2	23	85	265	1,386	148	1,043	195	3
Paulsboro	6,292	24	1	0	5	18	106	26	73	7	0
Peapack-Gladstone	2,588	0	0	0	0	0	37	15	21	1	0
Pennsauken Township	37,198	106	1	3	41	61	1,282	186	948	148	11
Penns Grove	4,821	50	0	3	12	35	78	16	55	7	0
Pennsville Township	12,651	19	0	3	3	13	381	17	351	13	0
Pequannock Township	15,560	9	0	0	3	6	70	8	54	8	0
Perth Amboy	55,229	182	4	6	28	144	808	94	626	88	9
Phillipsburg	15,374	47	0	26	8	13	263	35	213	15	3
Piscataway Township	61,170	94	2	0	20	72	473	32	397	44	3
Plainfield	55,494	251	4	3	104	140	731	110	564	57	2
Plainsboro Township	23,798	6	0	0	1	5	151	7	136	8	0
Pleasantville	20,603	45	2	0	7	36	207	49	126	32	1
Plumsted Township	8,582	2	0	1	0	1	40	7	31	2	0
Pohatcong Township	3,270	3	0	0	1	2	150	5	143	2	0
Point Pleasant	19,501	21	0	3	0	18	123	10	108	5	0
Point Pleasant Beach	4,903	11	0	1	0	10	110	9	99	2	0
Pompton Lakes	10,875	9	0	3	0	6	66	5	59	2	0
Princeton	30,797	9	0	1	3	5	226	23	193	10	0
Prospect Park	6,225	2	0	0	2	0	78	16	57	5	1
Rahway	30,149	42	1	8	12	21	294	26	227	41	5
Ramsey	14,621	5	0	0	2	3	105	6	86	13	0
Randolph Township	26,500	7	0	0	1	6	88	14	64	10	0
Raritan	10,609	1	0	0	0	1	81	4	71	6	0
Raritan Township	24,202	4	0	0	0	4	42	8	29	5	0
Readington Township	16,348	8	1	1	1	5	54	7	43	4	1
Red Bank	12,927	20	0	11	5	4	123	15	93	15	3
Ridgefield	11,368	3	0	0	0	3	83	8	64	11	0
Ridgefield Park	13,067	14	0	0	2	12	178	11	159	8	0
Ridgewood	26,485	8	0	1	1	6	202	21	128	53	1
Ringwood	11,456	0	0	0	0	0	21	7	14	0	0
Riverdale	4,105	1	0	1	0	0	77	2	66	9	0
River Edge	11,950	1	1	0	0	0	100	5	85	10	0
River Vale Township	9,789	2	0	0	0	2	36	4	26	6	2
Rochelle Park Township	5,841	9	1	0	5	3	68	10	53	5	1
Rockaway	6,589	0	0	0	0	0	17	1	16	0	0
Rockaway Township	26,377	18	0	2	4	12	223	13	200	10	0
Rockleigh	395	0	0	0	0	0	0	0	0	0	0
Roseland	6,149	0	0	0	0	0	57	3	46	8	0
Roselle	22,257	28	0	1	8	19	254	27	168	59	0
Roselle Park	13,825	6	0	2	1	3	133	11	114	8	0
Roxbury Township	23,293	2	0	0	0	2	196	15	170	11	1

Table 8. Offenses Known to Law Enforcement, by Selected State and City, 2022—Continued

(Number.)

State/city	Population	Violent crime	Murder and nonnegligent manslaughter	Rape	Robbery	Aggravated assault	Property crime	Burglary	Larceny-theft	Motor vehicle theft	Arson[1]
Rumson	7,228	1	0	0	0	1	41	4	22	15	0
Rutherford	18,592	7	0	0	1	6	218	21	166	31	1
Saddle Brook Township	14,408	4	0	0	2	2	208	3	193	12	0
Saddle River	3,338	1	0	0	0	1	50	29	13	8	0
Salem	5,319	79	3	5	8	63	91	18	55	18	1
Sayreville	44,981	39	1	1	6	31	430	46	328	56	2
Scotch Plains Township	24,490	15	0	3	3	9	199	22	125	52	0
Sea Bright	1,453	4	0	0	0	4	4	1	2	1	0
Sea Girt	1,885	1	0	0	0	1	3	1	1	1	0
Sea Isle City	2,135	11	0	2	1	8	114	17	95	2	0
Seaside Heights	2,507	23	0	0	2	21	88	12	76	0	0
Seaside Park	1,486	1	0	0	0	1	19	4	13	2	0
Secaucus	20,519	48	0	8	22	18	600	29	547	24	0
Shrewsbury	4,188	4	0	1	1	2	83	7	64	12	0
Somerdale	5,531	15	0	2	3	10	306	7	284	15	1
Somers Point	10,467	27	1	2	5	19	214	16	192	6	1
Somerville	12,759	10	0	0	3	7	141	13	118	10	0
South Amboy	9,277	12	0	1	1	10	113	21	65	27	0
South Bound Brook	4,784	1	0	0	0	1	43	4	32	7	0
South Brunswick Township	46,442	56	0	12	6	38	416	115	269	32	4
South Hackensack Township	2,668	16	0	1	5	10	89	3	74	12	0
South Harrison Township	3,459	0	0	0	0	0	7	0	6	1	0
South Orange Village	18,029	7	0	0	1	6	227	12	186	29	0
South Plainfield	24,211	29	0	2	8	19	367	40	302	25	0
South River	15,877	10	0	1	2	7	101	12	79	10	1
Sparta Township	20,348	5	0	1	1	3	89	19	68	2	0
Springfield Township, Burlington County	3,222	0	0	0	0	0	11	0	10	1	0
Springfield Township, Union County	16,860	10	0	1	1	8	234	18	186	30	2
Spring Lake	2,807	1	0	0	0	1	53	8	33	12	0
Spring Lake Heights	4,888	0	0	0	0	0	9	2	7	0	0
Stafford Township	30,365	13	0	1	0	12	249	7	226	16	0
Stanhope	3,572	3	0	0	1	2	12	3	8	1	0
Stone Harbor	792	3	0	1	0	2	56	2	53	1	0
Stratford	6,954	7	0	0	0	7	87	24	61	2	0
Summit	22,414	7	0	3	1	3	200	21	153	26	0
Surf City	1,302	1	0	1	0	0	10	0	9	1	0
Swedesboro	2,749	2	0	0	0	2	29	2	21	6	0
Teaneck Township	42,128	39	0	7	13	19	444	35	381	28	0
Tenafly	15,109	4	0	0	1	3	96	12	56	28	0
Teterboro	69	1	0	0	1	0	148	0	142	6	0
Tewksbury Township	5,918	1	0	0	0	1	4	3	1	0	0
Tinton Falls	19,556	19	0	3	2	14	185	14	160	11	0
Toms River Township	99,239	82	1	21	5	55	1,038	104	871	63	4
Totowa	10,813	9	1	0	2	6	225	15	178	32	0
Trenton	90,313	960	23	66	282	589	1,690	245	1,130	315	13
Tuckerton	3,682	7	0	0	0	7	36	3	31	2	0
Union Beach	5,732	2	0	0	0	2	8	2	4	2	0
Union City	63,312	212	1	0	51	160	1,101	69	950	82	2
Upper Saddle River	8,248	1	0	0	0	1	58	9	33	16	0
Ventnor City	9,226	6	0	0	1	5	265	22	238	5	0
Vernon Township	22,623	0	0	0	0	0	35	2	33	0	0
Verona	14,272	3	0	0	0	3	137	7	122	8	0
Vineland	61,110	280	7	28	31	214	1,566	226	1,282	58	8
Waldwick	10,055	2	0	0	0	2	31	3	24	4	0
Wallington	11,749	6	0	1	0	5	151	9	134	8	4
Wall Township	26,458	27	0	1	1	25	287	24	236	27	0
Wanaque	11,089	4	0	0	0	4	28	1	26	1	1
Warren Township	15,747	3	0	0	0	3	79	30	30	19	1
Washington	7,349	4	0	0	0	4	43	14	28	1	0
Washington Township, Gloucester County	49,625	60	2	2	11	45	838	76	726	36	1
Washington Township, Morris County	18,172	4	0	2	0	2	44	4	36	4	0
Washington Township, Warren County	6,539	0	0	0	0	0	67	6	60	1	0
Watchung	6,468	4	0	0	0	4	289	22	253	14	0
Waterford Township	10,393	2	0	1	0	1	72	7	61	4	0
Wayne Township	53,828	52	0	1	3	48	1,087	81	966	40	1
Weehawken Township	17,499	13	0	0	3	10	260	23	216	21	0
Westampton Township	9,099	23	0	3	5	15	218	23	182	13	0
West Amwell Township	3,033	0	0	0	0	0	26	5	20	1	0
West Caldwell Township	10,756	1	0	0	0	1	77	8	62	7	0
Westfield	30,628	5	0	1	2	2	233	13	193	27	0
West Long Branch	8,525	6	0	0	0	6	96	13	69	14	0
West Milford Township	24,373	5	0	2	0	3	70	6	58	6	0
West New York	52,021	129	1	11	36	81	603	61	501	41	0
West Orange	47,722	85	1	13	18	53	733	180	464	89	0
Westville	4,337	14	0	0	1	13	112	15	87	10	1
West Windsor Township	29,452	9	0	0	1	8	457	21	424	12	2
Wharton	7,225	9	0	0	0	9	70	8	61	1	0
Wildwood	5,105	55	0	0	7	48	339	28	305	6	0

Table 8. Offenses Known to Law Enforcement, by Selected State and City, 2022—Continued

(Number.)

State/city	Population	Violent crime	Murder and nonnegligent manslaughter	Rape	Robbery	Aggravated assault	Property crime	Burglary	Larceny-theft	Motor vehicle theft	Arson[1]
Wildwood Crest	3,079	11	0	0	0	11	70	11	56	3	0
Winfield Township	1,395	0	0	0	0	0	20	4	14	2	0
Winslow Township	39,881	105	1	3	15	86	445	92	331	22	2
Woodbridge Township	102,980	194	1	11	46	136	1,817	138	1,506	173	5
Woodbury	10,108	36	0	3	16	17	354	22	306	26	1
Woodbury Heights	3,122	0	0	0	0	0	25	1	24	0	0
Woodcliff Lake	6,058	6	0	0	2	4	47	2	40	5	0
Woodland Park	13,171	7	0	0	1	6	143	8	127	8	0
Woodlynne	2,888	6	0	0	3	3	83	20	55	8	0
Woodstown	3,692	4	0	0	1	3	22	7	13	2	0
Woolwich Township	13,625	1	0	0	0	1	49	3	39	7	0
NEW MEXICO											
Albuquerque	560,557	7,737	125	344	1,651	5,617	26,883	4,555	16,431	5,897	74
Angel Fire	1,215	5	0	0	0	5	14	1	13	0	0
Anthony	8,631	16	0	0	1	15	55	21	25	9	0
Artesia	12,084	44	0	14	1	29	312	64	215	33	2
Aztec	6,130	29	0	1	2	26	84	12	64	8	1
Bayard	2,070	12	0	1	0	11	12	5	4	3	1
Belen	7,460	82	1	4	3	74	333	128	166	39	3
Bloomfield	7,335	38	1	7	1	29	115	26	80	9	1
Bosque Farms	4,099	13	0	0	1	12	54	11	40	3	0
Capitan	1,414	5	0	0	0	5	20	2	16	2	1
Carlsbad	31,532	176	1	10	13	152	895	100	650	145	8
Cimarron	814	2	0	0	0	2	5	0	4	1	0
Clayton	2,779	4	0	0	0	4	3	1	2	0	0
Cloudcroft	786	2	0	1	0	1	7	1	6	0	0
Clovis	37,734	260	1	26	11	222	907	302	510	95	29
Corrales	8,652	13	0	1	1	11	48	12	30	6	0
Dexter	1,065	0	0	0	0	0	0	0	0	0	0
Edgewood	6,125	16	1	3	1	11	111	13	87	11	0
Farmington	46,249	495	4	78	29	384	1,103	164	818	121	12
Gallup	21,228	330	2	16	59	253	1,019	132	736	151	12
Grants	9,199	26	3	0	2	21	48	4	34	10	1
Hobbs	38,912	371	3	56	35	277	1,881	453	1,178	250	15
Hope	106	0	0	0	0	0	1	0	1	0	0
Jal	2,099	5	0	1	0	4	28	9	16	3	0
Las Cruces	114,102	704	10	75	60	559	6,093	1,270	3,927	896	8
Las Vegas	13,151	134	1	12	8	113	342	70	231	41	2
Logan	966	2	0	2	0	0	11	8	2	1	0
Lordsburg	2,229	14	1	1	0	12	21	9	9	3	0
Los Alamos	19,227	9	0	4	0	5	62	4	53	5	0
Los Lunas	18,366	94	0	6	12	76	725	257	377	91	1
Magdalena	795	7	0	0	0	7	15	3	9	3	0
Mesilla	1,788	2	0	0	1	1	25	7	8	10	0
Milan	2,567	24	0	0	0	24	24	4	12	8	0
Moriarty	1,973	6	0	0	2	4	87	19	47	21	0
Peralta	3,432	12	0	0	1	11	36	19	14	3	0
Portales	11,975	78	1	9	4	64	297	142	136	19	2
Raton	6,063	15	0	3	2	10	87	32	40	15	2
Rio Rancho	107,435	491	3	51	41	396	1,796	205	1,383	208	10
Roswell	47,625	420	9	38	28	345	1,421	223	1,036	162	30
Santa Clara	1,588	8	0	0	0	8	19	5	12	2	0
Santa Fe	88,705	819	5	42	100	672	4,333	955	2,713	665	34
Santa Rosa	2,846	2	0	0	0	2	44	5	27	12	0
San Ysidro	166	0	0	0	0	0	0	0	0	0	0
Springer	945	3	0	0	0	3	6	2	4	0	0
Sunland Park	17,441	80	1	3	1	75	118	27	71	20	2
Taos	6,613	46	0	3	7	36	422	129	256	37	3
Truth or Consequences	6,060	13	0	1	0	12	114	30	73	11	1
Tucumcari	5,162	0	0	0	0	0	50	16	31	3	1
NEW YORK											
Adams Village	1,703	0	0	0	0	0	3	1	2	0	0
Addison Town and Village	2,349	1	0	0	0	1	10	1	7	2	0
Afton Village	787	0	0	0	0	0	0	0	0	0	0
Akron Village	2,889	0	0	0	0	0	6	1	5	0	0
Albany	98,104	912	11	60	230	611	3,710	529	2,626	555	24
Albion Village	5,620	19	0	5	2	12	136	17	115	4	1
Alexandria Bay Village	965	0	0	0	0	0	1	0	1	0	0
Alfred Village	3,777	4	0	0	0	4	12	1	11	0	0
Allegany Village	1,571	1	0	0	0	1	16	0	16	0	0
Altamont Village	1,652	0	0	0	0	0	1	0	1	0	1
Amherst Town	123,527	193	2	21	44	126	2,125	168	1,784	173	4
Amityville Village	9,542	3	0	0	2	1	64	3	56	5	0
Amsterdam	18,199	24	0	1	5	18	255	38	199	18	1
Angelica Village	713	0	0	0	0	0	3	1	2	0	0
Arcade Village	1,975	2	0	1	0	1	9	3	5	1	0
Ardsley Village	4,944	1	0	0	0	1	32	5	24	3	0
Asharoken Village	619	0	0	0	0	0	0	0	0	0	0
Attica Village	2,497	1	0	1	0	0	3	0	3	0	0
Auburn	26,531	65	3	16	8	38	566	60	471	35	8
Baldwinsville Village	7,712	7	0	0	0	7	43	2	38	3	0

Table 8. Offenses Known to Law Enforcement, by Selected State and City, 2022—Continued

(Number.)

State/city	Population	Violent crime	Murder and nonnegligent manslaughter	Rape	Robbery	Aggravated assault	Property crime	Burglary	Larceny-theft	Motor vehicle theft	Arson[1]
Ballston Spa Village	5,088	7	0	0	2	5	25	4	21	0	0
Batavia	15,438	64	0	10	8	46	388	44	334	10	6
Beacon	13,729	14	0	0	2	12	133	15	114	4	0
Bedford Town	16,989	0	0	0	0	0	16	0	15	1	0
Belmont Village	846	0	0	0	0	0	0	0	0	0	0
Bethlehem Town	34,872	20	0	6	5	9	385	22	350	13	4
Binghamton	47,259	318	0	21	49	248	1,746	294	1,343	109	21
Black River	1,268	0	0	0	0	0	0	0	0	0	0
Blasdell Village	2,546	5	0	0	1	4	33	5	26	2	0
Blooming Grove Town	13,073	15	0	2	1	12	101	15	77	9	1
Boonville Village	1,997	0	0	0	0	0	58	1	57	0	0
Brewster	2,512	1	0	0	0	1	15	1	12	2	1
Briarcliff Manor Village	7,391	1	0	0	0	1	31	6	23	2	0
Brighton Town	36,380	29	0	9	3	17	723	55	607	61	2
Brockport Village	6,924	1	0	0	0	1	37	1	35	1	0
Brookville	2,844	1	0	0	1	0	27	4	16	7	0
Brownville Village	955	0	0	0	0	0	2	0	2	0	0
Buchanan Village	2,227	1	0	1	0	0	4	0	4	0	0
Buffalo	275,710	2,030	67	110	533	1,320	8,852	1,324	6,005	1,523	77
Cairo Town	6,853	0	0	0	0	0	19	0	18	1	0
Cambridge Village	1,799	2	1	0	0	1	9	2	7	0	0
Camden Village	2,148	2	0	0	0	2	16	3	12	1	0
Camillus Town and Village	25,268	15	0	1	6	8	301	17	275	9	2
Canajoharie Village	2,085	2	0	0	0	2	12	2	10	0	0
Canandaigua	10,479	46	0	15	2	29	216	24	181	11	1
Canastota Village	4,541	24	0	2	1	21	56	12	40	4	0
Canisteo Village	2,179	13	0	2	0	11	13	3	6	4	0
Canton Village	7,046	1	0	0	0	1	43	7	34	2	0
Cape Vincent Village	739	0	0	0	0	0	0	0	0	0	0
Carmel Town	33,868	22	0	1	3	18	150	5	132	13	2
Carthage Village	3,328	2	0	0	0	2	24	7	17	0	0
Catskill Village	3,884	6	0	1	0	5	78	10	68	0	0
Cattaraugus Village	978	0	0	0	0	0	0	0	0	0	0
Cayuga Heights Village	3,977	1	0	0	0	1	22	2	19	1	0
Cazenovia Village	2,697	3	0	1	0	2	25	4	17	4	0
Central Square Village	1,843	0	0	0	0	0	43	2	41	0	0
Centre Island Village	394	0	0	0	0	0	0	0	0	0	0
Cheektowaga Town	79,606	220	1	12	63	144	2,610	242	2,151	217	7
Chester Town	8,571	0	0	0	0	0	9	1	4	4	0
Chester Village	4,079	2	0	1	0	1	24	1	21	2	0
Cicero Town	29,252	10	0	0	0	10	367	32	311	24	1
Clarkstown Town	80,487	72	0	6	5	61	1,155	44	1,065	46	5
Clayton Village	1,735	0	0	0	0	0	1	0	1	0	0
Clyde Village	2,144	0	0	0	0	0	6	3	3	0	0
Cobleskill Village	4,206	7	0	0	2	5	88	6	78	4	0
Coeymans Town	7,161	8	0	0	3	5	32	5	26	1	1
Cohoes	17,890	48	0	7	6	35	264	25	214	25	1
Colchester Town	1,809	2	0	0	0	2	8	1	5	2	0
Cold Spring Village	1,999	0	0	0	0	0	2	0	2	0	0
Colonie Town	81,035	107	2	1	44	60	2,632	168	2,363	101	6
Corning	10,900	53	1	13	9	30	276	62	197	17	0
Cornwall-on-Hudson Village	3,056	1	0	0	0	1	5	0	5	0	0
Cornwall Town	9,840	2	0	0	1	1	17	2	15	0	0
Cortland	17,061	45	0	10	4	31	633	70	549	14	4
Coxsackie Village	2,821	1	0	0	0	1	5	1	4	0	0
Crawford Town	9,179	4	0	0	0	4	29	3	25	1	0
Croton-on-Hudson Village	8,114	3	0	2	0	1	59	3	53	3	0
Cuba Town	3,115	9	0	3	0	6	25	3	21	1	0
Dansville Village	4,332	1	0	0	1	0	81	5	75	1	0
Deerpark Town	7,531	3	0	0	0	3	33	7	22	4	0
Delhi Village	2,912	2	0	0	0	2	23	3	18	2	0
Depew Village	14,974	23	0	3	7	13	213	19	175	19	1
DeWitt Town	25,623	55	0	4	21	30	831	95	682	54	6
Dexter Village	1,014	0	0	0	0	0	0	0	0	0	0
Dobbs Ferry Village	11,361	5	0	1	1	3	107	7	96	4	7
Dolgeville Village	2,028	0	0	0	0	0	6	0	6	0	0
Dryden Village	1,930	1	0	0	1	0	32	0	32	0	0
Dunkirk	12,530	21	0	3	2	16	208	23	175	10	0
Durham Town	2,699	0	0	0	0	0	5	1	4	0	0
East Aurora-Aurora Town	13,936	11	0	2	3	6	121	11	97	13	0
Eastchester Town	20,277	4	0	0	2	2	135	8	104	23	1
East Fishkill Town	29,769	7	0	3	0	4	151	5	142	4	0
East Greenbush Town	16,558	21	0	3	3	15	363	40	303	20	0
East Hampton Town	25,765	4	0	0	0	4	96	2	89	5	0
East Hampton Village	1,531	1	0	0	0	1	33	1	30	2	0
East Rochester Village	6,212	6	0	1	2	3	71	7	57	7	0
Eden Town	7,504	3	0	1	0	2	35	4	31	0	0
Ellicott Town	5,350	7	0	1	0	6	167	29	133	5	0
Ellicottville	1,306	1	0	0	0	1	20	1	16	3	0
Elmira Town	5,645	1	0	1	0	0	35	0	35	0	0
Elmsford Village	5,114	5	0	0	0	5	9	0	6	3	0
Endicott Village	13,397	67	0	13	6	48	347	60	274	13	7
Evans Town	15,117	11	0	5	1	5	128	17	100	11	0

Table 8. Offenses Known to Law Enforcement, by Selected State and City, 2022—Continued

(Number.)

State/city	Population	Violent crime	Murder and nonnegligent manslaughter	Rape	Robbery	Aggravated assault	Property crime	Burglary	Larceny-theft	Motor vehicle theft	Arson[1]
Fairport Village	5,378	4	0	1	0	3	15	4	11	0	0
Fishkill Village	2,153	4	0	0	1	3	36	1	32	3	0
Floral Park Village	16,000	10	0	0	2	8	136	12	117	7	0
Florida Village	2,931	1	0	0	0	1	3	1	2	0	0
Fort Plain Village	2,028	5	0	0	0	5	52	10	38	4	1
Frankfort Town	4,614	3	0	0	0	3	16	3	13	0	0
Frankfort Village	2,307	1	0	0	0	1	6	1	5	0	0
Franklinville Village	1,674	0	0	0	0	0	3	0	3	0	0
Fredonia Village	9,763	5	0	1	0	4	177	19	158	0	0
Freeport Village	44,003	79	0	0	19	60	407	22	345	40	0
Friendship Town	1,936	0	0	0	0	0	4	1	2	1	0
Garden City Village	22,929	6	0	0	2	4	193	3	174	16	1
Geddes Town	10,323	6	0	0	2	4	155	18	123	14	0
Geneseo Village	8,123	6	0	0	0	6	86	6	75	5	0
Geneva	12,365	56	2	11	5	38	259	49	197	13	3
Glen Cove	28,004	14	0	3	2	9	186	13	164	9	0
Glen Park Village	452	0	0	0	0	0	0	0	0	0	0
Glens Falls	14,639	22	0	9	0	13	121	6	107	8	3
Glenville Town	22,061	17	0	0	1	16	334	19	311	4	3
Goshen Town	8,679	1	0	0	0	1	66	8	55	3	0
Goshen Village	5,777	4	0	1	0	3	28	1	27	0	0
Gouverneur Village	3,587	5	1	2	0	2	138	20	110	8	1
Gowanda Village	2,469	3	0	0	1	2	26	3	21	2	0
Granville Village	2,413	0	0	0	0	0	25	0	25	0	0
Great Neck Estates Village	2,919	0	0	0	0	0	32	5	14	13	0
Greece Town	95,525	132	1	11	47	73	1,973	167	1,661	145	5
Greenburgh Town	45,094	31	0	5	14	12	707	25	660	22	0
Greene Village	1,448	0	0	0	0	0	0	0	0	0	0
Greenwich Village	1,666	1	0	0	0	1	3	0	2	1	0
Groton Village	2,183	0	0	0	0	0	14	2	12	0	0
Guilderland Town	35,488	27	0	11	2	14	718	44	659	15	0
Hamburg Town	47,939	41	1	0	7	33	728	79	608	41	4
Hamburg Village	9,787	13	0	0	2	11	93	12	76	5	0
Hamilton Village	3,726	0	0	0	0	0	8	2	6	0	0
Hammondsport Village	590	0	0	0	0	0	9	0	9	0	0
Hancock Village	914	1	0	0	0	1	4	1	3	0	0
Harriman Village	2,680	1	0	0	0	1	12	0	12	0	0
Harrison Town	28,928	5	0	1	0	4	219	26	182	11	0
Hastings-on-Hudson Village	8,381	1	0	0	1	0	46	2	40	4	0
Hempstead Village	58,469	303	3	3	84	213	629	82	422	125	5
Herkimer Village	7,289	64	0	6	2	56	434	42	389	3	0
Highland Falls Village	3,728	0	0	0	0	0	0	0	0	0	0
Highlands Town	8,412	0	0	0	0	0	0	0	0	0	0
Hoosick Falls Village	3,191	4	0	0	0	3	17	3	12	2	0
Hudson Falls Village	7,370	9	0	2	1	6	21	2	19	0	1
Hunter Town	3,083	0	0	0	0	0	20	2	18	0	0
Huntington Bay Village	1,433	0	0	0	0	0	8	0	5	3	0
Hyde Park Town	21,071	9	0	1	1	7	94	11	76	7	0
Ilion Village	7,629	11	0	1	0	10	210	19	189	2	2
Independence Town	1,083	0	0	0	0	0	2	1	1	0	0
Inlet Town	369	0	0	0	0	0	0	0	0	0	0
Interlaken Village	626	0	0	0	0	0	1	0	1	0	0
Irondequoit Town	50,090	64	0	4	12	48	810	147	528	135	1
Irvington Village	6,449	1	0	0	0	1	30	1	23	6	0
Ithaca	31,576	96	2	8	16	70	1,191	185	983	23	3
Jamestown	28,208	223	2	32	26	163	822	179	580	63	11
Johnson City Village	15,107	61	0	13	7	41	608	72	517	19	4
Jordan Village	1,225	0	0	0	0	0	2	0	2	0	0
Kensington Village	1,221	0	0	0	0	0	7	0	2	5	0
Kent Town	12,943	4	0	3	0	1	40	5	35	0	0
Kings Point Village	5,530	2	0	0	0	2	46	8	24	14	0
Kingston	24,203	62	0	6	13	43	497	35	433	29	1
Lackawanna	19,692	79	1	12	8	58	344	43	260	41	3
Lake Placid Village	2,235	5	0	5	0	0	26	7	17	2	0
Lakewood-Busti	7,434	2	0	0	1	1	297	37	256	4	0
Lancaster Town	39,305	16	0	2	2	12	425	28	380	17	0
Larchmont Village	6,448	1	0	0	1	0	80	10	60	10	0
Le Roy Village	4,263	9	0	2	0	7	79	7	68	4	1
Lewisboro Town	11,912	0	0	0	0	0	2	0	2	0	0
Lewiston Town and Village	15,781	4	1	1	0	2	116	6	93	17	3
Liberty Village	5,367	31	1	5	3	22	83	10	69	4	0
Little Falls	4,558	12	0	1	0	11	32	5	25	2	1
Liverpool Village	2,280	1	0	0	0	1	25	11	10	4	0
Lloyd Harbor Village	3,569	2	0	0	0	2	18	1	12	5	0
Lloyd Town	11,372	3	0	0	0	3	74	1	65	8	0
Long Beach	34,651	31	0	1	8	22	50	11	32	7	0
Lowville Village	3,332	2	0	1	0	1	16	2	14	0	0
Lynbrook Village	20,200	16	0	0	3	13	121	16	94	11	0
Macedon Town and Village	9,247	6	0	4	0	2	182	17	162	3	0
Malone Village	5,274	25	1	8	2	14	194	22	168	4	1
Malverne Village	8,477	0	0	0	0	0	18	1	11	6	0
Mamaroneck Town	12,479	0	0	0	0	0	104	12	81	11	0
Mamaroneck Village	19,674	24	0	6	4	14	258	29	212	17	0

Table 8. Offenses Known to Law Enforcement, by Selected State and City, 2022—Continued

(Number.)

State/city	Population	Violent crime	Murder and nonnegligent manslaughter	Rape	Robbery	Aggravated assault	Property crime	Burglary	Larceny-theft	Motor vehicle theft	Arson[1]
Marcellus Village	1,776	0	0	0	0	0	7	1	6	0	
Marlborough Town	8,900	3	0	0	0	3	17	2	14	1	0
Massena Village	10,165	18	1	0	5	12	103	13	87	3	0
Maybrook Village	3,184	0	0	0	0	0	7	1	5	1	0
Mechanicville	5,158	22	0	2	0	20	59	5	51	3	0
Medina Village	5,978	16	0	0	2	14	78	8	67	3	2
Menands Village	4,478	8	0	1	2	5	106	8	88	10	0
Middleport Village	1,710	3	0	0	0	3	8	0	7	1	0
Middletown	30,538	109	2	8	22	77	438	42	373	23	5
Millerton Village	2,966	1	0	0	0	1	8	0	7	1	0
Mohawk Village	2,397	2	0	0	2	0	36	4	30	2	0
Monroe Village	9,552	7	0	1	4	2	64	7	55	2	0
Montgomery Town	9,563	6	0	1	0	5	30	1	23	6	0
Montgomery Village	3,816	0	0	0	0	0	4	0	4	0	0
Monticello Village	7,386	22	0	2	8	12	144	44	90	10	0
Moravia Village	1,264	0	0	0	0	0	9	0	9	0	0
Moriah Town	4,672	0	0	0	0	0	0	0	0	0	0
Mount Hope Town	6,405	2	0	0	0	2	17	0	17	0	0
Mount Pleasant Town	25,892	27	0	0	2	25	235	14	210	11	0
Mount Vernon	71,690	331	4	17	96	214	1,119	103	864	152	1
Muttontown	3,512	1	0	1	0	0	17	5	6	6	0
Nassau Village	1,094	0	0	0	0	0	2	1	1	0	0
Newark Village	8,939	18	0	3	4	11	326	30	280	16	0
New Berlin Town	1,588	0	0	0	0	0	3	1	2	0	0
Newburgh	28,819	318	3	21	70	224	714	97	550	67	7
Newburgh Town	32,207	23	0	2	8	13	655	30	603	22	1
New Castle Town	17,777	1	0	0	0	1	76	2	66	8	1
New Hartford Town and Village	20,415	11	0	2	5	4	716	22	681	13	3
New Paltz Town and Village	14,732	5	0	1	0	4	88	0	88	0	0
New Rochelle	82,628	63	0	2	25	36	572	39	499	34	0
New Windsor Town	28,008	23	0	5	2	16	352	29	309	14	0
New York	8,236,567	61,293	438	2,619	17,433	40,803	176,361	14,553	147,831	13,977	
New York Mills Village	3,197	7	0	0	0	7	53	2	44	7	0
Niagara Falls	48,129	388	5	10	69	304	1,374	266	948	160	14
Niagara Town	7,808	9	0	2	2	5	188	20	144	24	1
Niskayuna Town	23,403	11	0	1	3	7	476	36	424	16	0
Nissequogue Village	1,610	0	0	0	0	0	2	1	1	0	0
Norfolk Town	4,344	0	0	0	0	0	3	1	2	0	1
North Castle Town	12,124	7	0	0	0	7	91	10	71	10	0
North Greenbush Town	13,323	6	0	1	0	5	316	15	295	6	2
Northport Village	7,352	1	0	0	0	1	60	1	59	0	0
North Tonawanda	30,358	48	0	9	2	37	323	29	268	26	5
Northville Village	1,009	0	0	0	0	0	3	0	3	0	0
Ocean Beach Village	171	0	0	0	0	0	28	0	28	0	0
Ogdensburg	9,933	30	1	3	4	22	352	43	297	12	5
Ogden Town	20,293	18	0	5	3	10	154	10	133	11	2
Old Brookville Village	2,070	0	0	0	0	0	25	7	6	12	0
Old Westbury Village	4,229	2	0	0	1	1	37	12	13	12	0
Olean	13,671	57	0	6	5	46	431	42	368	21	3
Oneida	10,268	62	0	8	4	50	422	48	355	19	2
Oneonta City	12,447	10	0	2	3	5	116	14	91	11	2
Orangetown Town	39,317	22	0	0	7	15	289	26	250	13	1
Orchard Park Town	29,775	15	0	2	2	11	374	34	303	37	1
Oriskany Village	1,314	0	0	0	0	0	5	1	4	0	0
Ossining Village	26,980	18	0	0	5	13	183	9	171	3	0
Oswego City	17,299	69	0	7	4	58	595	34	536	25	1
Oxford Village	1,327	0	0	0	0	0	2	0	2	0	0
Oyster Bay Cove Village	4,192	0	0	0	0	0	27	5	10	12	1
Peekskill	26,178	68	1	2	11	54	276	17	250	9	3
Pelham Manor Village	5,587	6	0	0	3	3	162	5	143	14	0
Pelham Village	7,115	6	0	0	4	2	40	1	39	0	0
Perry Village	3,664	6	0	3	0	3	46	3	40	3	0
Philmont Village	1,527	0	0	0	0	0	7	1	5	1	0
Phoenix Village	2,208	1	0	1	0	0	12	2	6	4	0
Pine Plains Town	2,215	0	0	0	0	0	1	0	1	0	0
Plattekill Town	10,534	2	0	0	1	1	25	1	23	1	0
Plattsburgh City	19,904	25	1	6	3	15	294	23	251	20	2
Pleasantville Village	7,324	1	0	0	0	1	51	2	46	3	0
Port Byron Village	1,093	0	0	0	0	0	1	0	1	0	0
Port Chester Village	30,804	19	0	0	8	11	329	15	295	19	0
Port Dickinson Village	1,697	0	0	0	0	0	2	1	1	0	0
Port Jervis	8,738	45	0	5	7	33	148	16	127	5	1
Portville Village	900	0	0	0	0	0	10	0	10	0	0
Port Washington	20,071	6	0	0	2	4	138	12	118	8	0
Potsdam Village	8,279	4	0	1	0	3	70	8	59	3	0
Poughkeepsie	32,202	198	5	16	36	141	594	71	473	50	4
Poughkeepsie Town	40,966	68	1	12	17	38	908	51	833	24	3
Pound Ridge Town	4,929	3	0	0	0	3	31	2	28	1	0
Pulaski Village	2,411	0	0	0	0	0	10	0	10	0	0
Quogue Village	1,687	0	0	0	0	0	22	1	17	4	0
Red Hook Village	1,956	1	0	0	0	1	51	1	48	2	0
Rensselaer City	9,292	10	0	3	2	5	95	7	76	12	2
Rhinebeck Village	2,692	1	0	0	0	1	23	0	23	0	0

Table 8. Offenses Known to Law Enforcement, by Selected State and City, 2022—Continued

(Number.)

State/city	Population	Violent crime	Murder and nonnegligent manslaughter	Rape	Robbery	Aggravated assault	Property crime	Burglary	Larceny-theft	Motor vehicle theft	Arson[1]
Riverhead Town	36,064	42	0	3	18	21	744	48	683	13	
Rochester	210,270	1,538	66	69	478	925	7,529	932	5,233	1,364	126
Rockville Centre Village	25,703	15	0	0	8	7	131	9	105	17	0
Rome	31,834	77	0	11	18	48	481	57	399	25	3
Rosendale Town	5,813	0	0	0	0	0	23	1	21	1	0
Rotterdam Town	30,569	18	0	2	3	13	673	30	620	23	1
Rye	16,243	0	0	0	0	0	25	3	14	8	0
Rye Brook Village	9,863	1	0	0	0	1	82	14	56	12	0
Sackets Harbor Village	1,387	0	0	0	0	0	1	0	1	0	0
Sag Harbor Village	2,792	0	0	0	0	0	0	0	0	0	0
Salamanca	5,837	35	0	3	5	27	105	10	86	9	1
Sands Point Village	2,716	1	0	0	0	1	7	0	6	1	0
Saratoga Springs	28,436	95	0	18	11	66	519	75	434	10	2
Saugerties Town	19,323	20	0	7	4	9	153	24	120	9	1
Schenectady	67,101	508	8	29	118	353	2,296	315	1,773	208	26
Schodack Town	11,424	9	0	0	0	9	57	4	49	4	0
Schoharie Village	954	0	0	0	0	0	5	0	5	0	0
Scotia Village	7,253	15	0	4	1	10	95	7	81	7	1
Seneca Falls Town	8,894	25	0	6	3	16	154	4	137	13	0
Shandaken Town	2,896	1	0	0	0	1	16	2	14	0	0
Shawangunk Town	13,680	1	0	0	0	1	25	6	19	0	0
Shelter Island Town	3,293	1	0	1	0	0	19	3	16	0	0
Sherburne Village	1,366	1	0	0	0	1	9	1	8	0	
Sherrill	3,001	1	0	0	0	1	14	2	9	3	0
Sidney Village	3,707	8	0	2	0	6	68	21	47	0	1
Skaneateles Village	2,546	0	0	0	0	0	7	0	7	0	0
Sleepy Hollow Village	12,088	0	0	0	0	0	1	0	1	0	1
Solvay Village	6,574	15	0	0	3	12	65	15	43	7	1
Southampton Town	59,691	28	0	4	5	19	558	31	477	50	1
Southampton Village	4,636	2	0	1	0	1	61	5	48	8	0
South Glens Falls Village	3,781	11	0	2	3	6	52	9	41	2	0
Southold Town	21,347	13	0	1	0	12	310	22	275	13	0
Spring Valley Village	33,044	111	2	9	37	63	545	33	503	9	5
Stillwater Town	7,405	2	0	0	0	2	22	3	19	0	0
St. Johnsville Village	1,701	1	0	0	1	0	22	1	20	1	0
Stony Point Town	14,749	9	2	0	2	5	51	3	45	3	0
Syracuse	145,179	1,294	17	80	287	910	4,430	1,171	2,636	623	24
Tarrytown Village	11,587	5	0	1	1	3	60	11	45	4	0
Theresa Village	766	0	0	0	0	0	0	0	0	0	0
Tonawanda	14,988	25	0	5	4	16	199	15	171	13	1
Tonawanda Town	56,698	113	4	11	16	82	898	101	658	139	4
Troy	50,106	337	5	18	82	232	1,679	248	1,319	112	8
Trumansburg Village	1,745	0	0	0	0	0	11	0	11	0	0
Tuckahoe Village	6,887	1	0	0	1	0	3	0	2	1	0
Tuxedo Park Village	639	0	0	0	0	0	0	0	0	0	0
Ulster Town	12,803	8	0	2	1	5	145	9	127	9	1
Utica	63,906	363	1	40	82	240	2,178	274	1,749	155	10
Vernon Village	1,164	0	0	0	0	0	0	0	0	0	0
Vestal Town	29,553	26	1	3	4	18	667	32	626	9	0
Walden Village	6,819	3	0	0	1	2	77	10	65	2	0
Wappingers Falls Village	6,077	1	0	0	0	1	68	2	66	0	0
Warsaw Village	3,632	3	0	1	0	2	18	2	14	2	0
Warwick Town	19,419	7	0	1	1	5	64	7	56	1	1
Washingtonville Village	5,804	1	0	1	0	0	35	1	34	0	0
Waterford Town and Village	8,228	4	0	0	2	2	39	12	21	6	1
Waterloo Village	4,841	13	0	1	0	12	44	4	34	6	1
Watertown	24,558	156	0	33	11	112	1,009	103	883	23	7
Wayland Village	1,716	1	0	1	0	0	0	0	0	0	0
Webb Town	1,804	1	0	0	0	1	4	0	4	0	0
Webster Town and Village	45,230	25	0	9	2	14	353	32	304	17	1
Weedsport Village	1,790	0	0	0	0	0	9	0	9	0	0
Wellsville Village	4,595	16	0	3	4	9	69	7	57	5	0
West Carthage Village	1,782	0	0	0	0	0	9	2	7	0	0
Westfield Village	2,951	1	0	1	0	0	19	2	16	1	0
Westhampton Beach Village	2,190	4	0	0	2	2	40	5	31	4	1
West Seneca Town	45,119	63	1	11	14	37	795	87	672	36	4
Whitehall Village	2,478	9	0	7	0	2	36	8	26	2	0
White Plains	59,488	68	0	7	14	47	757	37	701	19	4
Whitesboro Village	3,599	0	0	0	0	0	42	3	36	3	0
Windham Town	1,769	0	0	0	0	0	0	0	0	0	0
Wolcott Village	1,581	0	0	0	0	0	0	0	0	0	0
Woodbury Town	11,705	4	0	2	1	1	408	6	398	4	0
Woodridge Village	722	1	0	0	0	1	7	1	6	0	0
Woodstock Town	6,322	0	0	0	0	0	33	1	32	0	0
Yonkers	208,100	645	2	18	207	418	1,907	238	1,412	257	6
Yorktown Town	35,529	12	0	1	3	8	249	20	221	8	0
Yorkville Village	2,590	8	0	1	2	5	118	11	103	4	0
NORTH CAROLINA											
Aberdeen	9,528	28	0	2	6	20	259	26	217	16	2
Ahoskie	4,830	29	1	3	3	22	111	21	83	7	1
Albemarle	16,819	98	1	10	7	80	594	85	474	35	9
Andrews	1,707	6	0	4	0	2	31	1	29	1	1

Table 8. Offenses Known to Law Enforcement, by Selected State and City, 2022—Continued

(Number.)

State/city	Population	Violent crime	Murder and nonnegligent manslaughter	Rape	Robbery	Aggravated assault	Property crime	Burglary	Larceny-theft	Motor vehicle theft	Arson[1]
Angier	6,127	18	0	5	1	12	162	98	63	1	1
Apex	66,024	36	0	11	9	16	755	66	650	39	6
Archdale	12,002	20	0	1	5	14	198	31	137	30	1
Asheboro	27,275	112	2	15	13	82	1,047	214	761	72	5
Asheville	93,729	879	12	61	136	670	4,811	676	3,717	418	29
Atlantic Beach	1,420	2	1	0	0	1	72	20	46	6	1
Ayden	5,068	22	2	3	2	15	75	12	59	4	1
Beaufort	4,678	28	0	2	0	26	89	15	71	3	0
Beech Mountain	678	6	0	1	0	5	9	3	5	1	0
Belhaven	1,405	6	0	3	0	3	19	3	14	2	0
Belmont	15,297	30	0	1	7	22	544	48	472	24	1
Benson	4,246	47	0	6	4	37	184	38	131	15	1
Bessemer City	5,569	17	2	2	1	12	76	18	46	12	0
Beulaville	1,109	0	0	0	0	0	38	1	36	1	0
Biltmore Forest	1,433	0	0	0	0	0	13	6	5	2	1
Biscoe	1,868	6	0	0	0	6	96	1	95	0	0
Blowing Rock	1,399	2	0	0	0	2	31	8	22	1	0
Boiling Spring Lakes	6,349	11	0	3	1	7	86	26	58	2	0
Boone	18,007	20	0	5	2	13	275	50	212	13	2
Boonville	1,190	0	0	0	0	0	16	4	11	1	0
Brevard	7,778	14	0	3	0	11	110	18	88	4	1
Broadway	1,300	2	0	0	2	0	17	5	12	0	0
Bryson City	1,445	9	0	2	0	7	12	0	12	0	0
Bunn	353	0	0	0	0	0	13	1	11	1	0
Burgaw	3,138	22	0	3	0	19	53	3	45	5	0
Burlington	60,069	500	4	33	64	399	2,270	342	1,703	225	6
Butner	8,618	18	0	2	6	10	153	16	126	11	1
Candor	813	1	0	0	1	0	12	3	8	1	1
Canton	4,433	16	0	3	4	9	136	47	78	11	0
Carolina Beach	6,652	31	0	7	0	24	148	37	107	4	1
Carrboro	21,190	58	1	6	5	46	367	59	275	33	1
Carthage	2,839	5	0	2	0	3	64	12	46	6	0
Cary	178,600	142	0	12	29	101	1,975	300	1,534	141	6
Chadbourn	1,534	29	3	1	0	25	87	20	58	9	0
Chapel Hill	60,984	113	2	9	26	76	1,213	190	951	72	6
Charlotte-Mecklenburg	955,466	7,132	108	271	1,381	5,372	32,246	4,095	24,356	3,795	148
Cherryville	6,194	12	0	4	2	6	113	32	70	11	0
China Grove	4,477	6	1	0	0	5	71	14	46	11	1
Clayton	30,036	34	2	3	5	24	371	30	312	29	7
Cleveland	862	1	0	0	0	1	11	2	7	2	0
Clinton	8,004	79	2	9	6	62	290	52	225	13	4
Columbus	1,020	0	0	0	0	0	14	0	14	0	0
Concord	109,660	116	6	15	31	64	1,079	82	863	134	5
Conover	8,525	33	2	6	2	23	340	40	266	34	2
Cornelius	31,781	42	1	3	5	33	320	48	245	27	3
Creedmoor	5,095	20	0	6	2	12	58	19	38	1	0
Dallas	6,086	13	0	2	3	8	115	20	81	14	1
Davidson	15,189	5	0	1	1	3	71	10	58	3	0
Dobson	1,386	3	0	1	0	2	20	3	17	0	0
Drexel	1,757	0	0	0	0	0	2	0	1	1	0
Duck	770	0	0	0	0	0	20	3	16	1	0
Dunn	8,426	72	3	10	12	47	386	114	250	22	0
Durham	286,377	1,968	42	146	587	1,193	9,498	1,462	7,166	870	40
East Spencer	1,581	18	1	3	1	13	25	4	16	5	0
Eden	15,253	82	1	4	4	73	379	79	290	10	2
Edenton	4,400	16	1	3	2	10	82	14	62	6	0
Elizabeth City	18,751	101	8	9	7	77	528	151	333	44	2
Elkin	4,045	14	1	2	2	9	214	34	171	9	0
Elon	11,369	10	0	0	2	8	71	46	21	4	0
Emerald Isle	3,940	13	0	1	1	11	82	21	57	4	0
Erwin	4,662	23	3	4	3	13	120	27	84	9	1
Fair Bluff	720	0	0	0	0	0	14	5	9	0	0
Fairmont	2,169	27	2	0	2	23	143	38	96	9	1
Farmville	4,495	39	0	5	3	31	86	17	65	4	1
Fayetteville	208,980	2,044	35	90	242	1,677	7,224	1,298	5,381	545	82
Fletcher	8,059	13	0	5	2	6	138	43	83	12	0
Forest City	7,353	50	0	8	6	36	499	137	332	30	2
Franklin	4,289	11	0	2	0	9	125	10	108	7	0
Franklinton	2,664	5	0	0	2	3	49	17	29	3	0
Fuquay-Varina	39,037	27	0	4	7	16	332	37	278	17	1
Garner	32,577	149	0	12	29	108	1,131	91	979	61	3
Gastonia	81,937	645	8	27	99	511	3,227	474	2,411	342	22
Gibsonville	9,049	18	0	5	1	12	85	24	51	10	0
Goldsboro	32,464	366	6	15	38	307	1,660	241	1,302	117	2
Graham	17,377	73	0	12	10	51	358	53	257	48	6
Granite Falls	4,920	7	0	2	3	2	219	63	140	16	1
Granite Quarry	3,023	6	0	0	0	6	28	3	20	5	0
Greensboro	298,719	2,447	40	79	465	1,863	11,308	1,662	8,415	1,231	75
Greenville	89,363	508	12	22	67	407	2,438	273	2,017	148	13
Grifton	2,495	6	0	0	0	6	17	4	10	3	0
Havelock	17,108	34	3	1	3	27	343	61	273	9	1
Haw River	2,271	3	0	2	1	0	55	8	40	7	0
Henderson	14,806	262	7	10	31	214	618	100	478	40	3

Table 8. Offenses Known to Law Enforcement, by Selected State and City, 2022—Continued

(Number.)

State/city	Population	Violent crime	Murder and nonnegligent manslaughter	Rape	Robbery	Aggravated assault	Property crime	Burglary	Larceny-theft	Motor vehicle theft	Arson[1]
Hendersonville	15,122	37	0	8	3	26	594	125	431	38	5
Hickory	43,756	232	8	17	22	185	1,532	267	1,142	123	9
Highlands	1,102	0	0	0	0	0	44	7	36	1	1
High Point	114,280	626	15	24	108	479	3,076	525	2,239	312	12
Hillsborough	9,732	50	2	3	9	36	546	34	489	23	0
Holly Ridge	4,639	4	0	0	0	4	28	18	10	0	0
Holly Springs	45,406	30	0	7	5	18	456	59	386	11	1
Hope Mills	17,843	79	4	6	12	57	665	97	515	53	5
Hudson	3,769	10	0	4	0	6	84	14	63	7	2
Huntersville	62,105	84	0	12	13	59	753	100	576	77	4
Indian Beach	227	1	0	0	0	1	11	7	4	0	0
Jacksonville	72,570	226	5	26	24	171	1,505	247	1,194	64	5
Jefferson	1,523	1	0	0	0	1	23	2	19	2	0
Jonesville	2,310	9	0	1	0	8	72	15	48	9	0
Kannapolis	55,480	109	4	16	27	62	1,135	161	822	152	2
Kernersville	27,076	75	0	7	8	60	971	93	819	59	6
Kill Devil Hills	7,911	18	1	0	3	14	215	37	170	8	1
King	7,213	5	0	2	0	3	132	6	120	6	0
Kings Mountain	11,624	56	1	1	8	46	262	32	200	30	2
Kinston	19,342	137	9	7	7	114	627	164	399	64	13
Knightdale	19,659	41	0	4	4	33	503	37	430	36	1
Laurinburg	15,199	237	7	11	20	199	679	209	410	60	6
Lenoir	18,160	38	0	13	5	20	668	172	426	70	0
Lexington	19,544	95	3	5	12	75	615	116	438	61	3
Lillington	4,603	14	0	4	2	8	97	32	49	16	0
Lincolnton	11,651	44	1	7	4	32	424	64	327	33	4
Long View	5,148	20	1	4	6	9	127	21	79	27	2
Louisburg	3,098	24	1	5	1	17	107	10	97	0	1
Lowell	3,740	4	1	0	0	3	51	10	37	4	1
Lumberton	18,583	446	8	16	61	361	2,087	558	1,378	151	11
Madison	2,112	6	0	0	0	6	66	12	49	5	1
Maggie Valley	1,702	8	3	1	0	4	168	107	54	7	0
Magnolia	833	8	0	0	0	8	19	3	15	1	0
Manteo	1,647	2	0	1	1	0	42	3	38	1	0
Marion	7,633	19	2	1	3	13	313	92	190	31	3
Marshville	2,603	17	0	4	1	12	56	16	39	1	0
Matthews	29,739	49	1	4	18	26	886	111	726	49	0
Maxton	2,110	18	3	2	1	12	91	20	59	12	3
Mayodan	2,419	1	0	0	0	1	163	9	148	6	0
Maysville	838	0	0	0	0	0	8	0	8	0	0
Mebane	18,956	45	0	8	3	34	568	35	506	27	0
Middlesex	913	1	0	0	0	1	16	2	10	4	0
Mint Hill	26,728	23	1	1	7	14	259	40	199	20	4
Monroe	35,204	277	6	36	27	208	1,387	258	1,024	105	12
Mooresville	52,762	95	0	24	12	59	1,125	84	952	89	3
Morehead City	9,810	29	0	5	0	24	251	45	193	13	1
Morganton	17,568	72	0	9	5	58	585	164	386	35	1
Morrisville	32,600	39	0	3	18	18	699	87	558	54	3
Mount Airy	10,511	40	1	4	5	30	283	67	187	29	3
Mount Gilead	1,176	8	0	1	0	7	40	10	25	5	0
Mount Holly	18,177	38	0	7	3	28	265	50	180	35	1
Mount Olive	4,027	9	0	1	2	6	104	22	76	6	0
Murfreesboro	2,490	8	0	3	2	3	32	5	25	2	0
Nags Head	3,218	11	0	2	0	9	74	12	60	2	0
New Bern	31,614	160	3	11	12	134	645	146	466	33	2
Newland	719	1	0	0	0	1	11	1	10	0	0
Newport	4,564	12	0	6	1	5	81	10	64	7	1
Newton	13,252	31	1	1	3	26	275	57	192	26	2
North Topsail Beach	1,001	1	0	1	0	0	23	5	17	1	0
North Wilkesboro	4,215	15	0	3	2	10	114	33	72	9	0
Oxford	8,895	65	3	2	9	51	188	23	150	15	1
Pembroke	2,803	19	0	2	1	16	187	16	160	11	1
Pinehurst	18,426	6	0	5	1	0	69	15	51	3	3
Pine Knoll Shores	1,397	1	0	0	0	1	17	7	9	1	0
Pineville	10,718	55	0	2	13	40	967	86	814	67	0
Pittsboro	4,662	17	0	1	1	15	88	4	75	9	2
Plymouth	3,204	45	2	2	2	39	93	33	56	4	2
Raeford	4,725	17	3	0	3	11	90	14	75	1	0
Raleigh	470,829	2,353	44	174	439	1,696	10,992	1,207	8,584	1,201	44
Ranlo	4,621	11	0	2	0	9	35	12	19	4	0
Red Springs	3,102	26	0	1	7	18	198	52	135	11	3
Reidsville	14,481	143	2	5	8	128	555	77	425	53	4
Richlands	2,325	1	0	1	0	0	24	5	17	2	0
Roanoke Rapids	15,025	111	1	13	28	69	690	161	480	49	5
Robbins	1,220	0	0	0	0	0	3	2	1	0	1
Rockingham	8,865	68	0	4	9	44	394	93	272	29	3
Rocky Mount	53,668	473	19	17	89	348	1,486	312	1,026	148	18
Rolesville	10,549	9	0	1	0	8	69	9	58	2	0
Rowland	884	0	0	0	0	0	15	0	11	4	0
Roxboro	8,079	104	5	7	5	87	357	54	287	16	0
Rutherfordton	3,622	14	0	2	1	11	87	27	56	4	0
Salisbury	35,938	318	7	5	41	265	1,314	169	1,005	140	7
Selma	6,843	43	2	5	5	31	111	26	67	18	1

Table 8. Offenses Known to Law Enforcement, by Selected State and City, 2022—Continued

(Number.)

State/city	Population	Violent crime	Murder and nonnegligent manslaughter	Rape	Robbery	Aggravated assault	Property crime	Burglary	Larceny-theft	Motor vehicle theft	Arson[1]
Shallotte	4,453	7	0	1	1	5	169	10	157	2	1
Shelby	21,989	199	2	13	24	160	558	113	395	50	11
Siler City	7,969	58	0	4	4	49	253	62	169	22	1
Smithfield	12,042	75	0	3	6	66	620	132	453	35	3
Snow Hill	1,532	4	0	2	1	1	38	15	22	1	0
Southern Pines	16,388	40	1	5	7	27	326	71	221	34	3
Southern Shores	3,237	0	0	0	0	0	10	3	6	1	0
Southport	4,253	10	0	1	0	9	64	7	57	0	1
Spencer	3,327	10	1	1	1	7	67	14	39	14	0
Spring Lake	11,603	65	0	6	10	49	356	61	275	20	4
Spruce Pine	2,227	0	0	0	0	0	3	0	3	0	0
Stallings	16,758	16	1	1	2	12	158	40	101	17	1
Stantonsburg	743	4	0	0	0	4	10	2	8	0	0
Star	812	2	1	0	0	1	13	4	7	2	0
Stoneville	1,318	0	0	0	0	0	15	6	9	0	0
St. Pauls	2,050	10	0	0	0	10	77	6	67	4	1
Sugar Mountain	376	0	0	0	0	0	1	0	1	0	0
Surf City	4,338	13	1	6	1	5	84	13	70	1	1
Swansboro	3,920	5	0	2	0	3	59	5	53	1	0
Sylva	2,633	13	0	4	2	7	135	37	88	10	0
Tabor City	3,646	12	1	5	1	5	93	29	57	7	0
Taylorsville	2,328	2	0	1	0	1	36	6	27	3	0
Troutman	3,889	15	0	3	1	11	95	17	76	2	0
Troy	2,915	9	0	5	0	4	53	10	41	2	0
Tryon	1,584	0	0	0	0	0	36	13	20	3	0
Valdese	4,663	10	0	1	1	8	69	21	43	5	0
Vass	1,003	0	0	0	0	0	22	7	15	0	0
Wadesboro	5,036	132	2	4	9	117	391	108	247	36	6
Wake Forest	51,385	59	1	6	5	47	536	53	451	32	3
Wallace	3,296	17	0	3	2	12	167	25	135	7	0
Warrenton	861	19	2	0	2	15	58	3	52	3	1
Warsaw	2,668	11	0	3	3	5	97	24	68	5	0
Washington	9,614	41	0	2	5	34	271	37	214	20	1
Waxhaw	22,613	19	0	7	1	11	166	16	143	7	0
Waynesville	10,225	44	0	5	2	37	352	39	300	13	5
Weaverville	4,689	1	0	0	0	1	159	5	153	1	0
Weldon	1,414	7	0	0	0	7	55	15	34	6	0
Wendell	13,408	23	0	2	3	18	106	20	76	10	1
West Jefferson	1,237	6	0	2	0	4	102	15	86	1	0
Whispering Pines	5,235	3	1	1	1	0	17	3	14	0	0
Whiteville	4,630	47	1	3	2	41	420	76	325	19	1
Wilkesboro	3,567	17	0	1	2	14	187	29	145	13	3
Williamston	5,047	83	1	7	8	67	208	37	157	14	2
Wilmington	119,159	634	12	77	111	434	3,415	470	2,675	270	16
Wilson	47,518	245	5	6	41	193	1,171	187	907	77	16
Windsor	3,304	4	1	1	0	2	31	6	23	2	0
Winston-Salem	251,295	2,954	30	87	282	2,555	9,785	1,796	7,070	919	51
Winterville	10,725	17	1	4	1	11	52	15	35	2	0
Woodfin	8,097	15	0	3	0	12	87	31	44	12	0
Woodland	534	1	0	0	0	1	3	1	2	0	1
Wrightsville Beach	2,396	9	0	2	1	6	88	16	71	1	0
Youngsville	2,197	3	0	0	1	2	47	3	38	6	0
Zebulon	9,003	53	1	1	11	40	278	39	227	12	3
NORTH DAKOTA											
Berthold	463	0	0	0	0	0	1	0	1	0	0
Beulah	3,032	6	0	0	1	5	24	4	17	3	0
Bismarck	74,604	231	6	32	43	150	2,509	383	1,870	256	7
Bowman	1,394	3	0	2	0	1	14	2	11	1	0
Burlington	1,255	0	0	0	0	0	0	0	0	0	0
Carrington	2,029	2	1	1	0	0	4	2	1	1	1
Cavalier	1,228	0	0	0	0	0	6	1	4	1	0
Devils Lake	7,212	35	0	15	2	18	293	37	204	52	1
Dickinson	24,577	61	0	10	2	49	426	63	318	45	0
Drayton	737	0	0	0	0	0	4	1	2	1	0
Dunseith	624	0	0	0	0	0	6	1	3	2	0
Ellendale	1,067	0	0	0	0	0	5	1	4	0	0
Emerado	449	1	0	0	0	1	13	2	10	1	1
Fargo	127,649	787	5	144	116	522	5,294	1,075	3,534	685	36
Garrison	1,435	3	0	0	0	3	8	2	6	0	0
Grafton	4,117	10	0	1	0	9	53	6	40	7	0
Grand Forks	58,620	172	2	30	19	121	1,751	365	1,263	123	3
Harvey	1,586	1	0	0	0	1	5	0	4	1	1
Hazen	2,271	0	0	0	0	0	3	0	3	0	0
Jamestown	15,772	36	0	11	0	25	328	68	243	17	0
Kenmare	912	0	0	0	0	0	5	0	4	1	0
Killdeer	892	2	0	0	0	2	17	2	13	2	0
Lincoln	4,387	6	0	1	0	5	23	2	20	1	1
Lisbon	2,177	0	0	0	0	0	13	1	10	2	0
Mandan	24,666	58	1	12	2	43	858	132	599	127	8
Medora	119	0	0	0	0	0	0	0	0	0	0
Minot	47,278	141	3	45	8	85	495	94	270	131	7
Napoleon	752	0	0	0	0	0	0	0	0	0	1

Table 8. Offenses Known to Law Enforcement, by Selected State and City, 2022—Continued

(Number.)

State/city	Population	Violent crime	Murder and nonnegligent manslaughter	Rape	Robbery	Aggravated assault	Property crime	Burglary	Larceny-theft	Motor vehicle theft	Arson[1]
New Town	2,713	5	0	1	0	4	5	1	4	0	0
Northwood	946	0	0	0	0	0	1	0	1	0	0
Oakes	1,778	0	0	0	0	0	5	3	2	0	0
Powers Lake	377	0	0	0	0	0	3	0	3	0	0
Ray	666	0	0	0	0	0	2	1	1	0	0
Rolette	478	2	0	0	0	2	8	0	7	1	0
Rolla	1,173	1	0	0	0	1	14	0	9	5	0
Rugby	2,505	5	0	0	0	5	21	7	9	5	0
Stanley	2,327	1	0	0	0	1	6	1	5	0	0
Steele	657	0	0	0	0	0	9	2	5	2	1
Surrey	1,343	0	0	0	0	0	2	0	0	2	0
Thompson	1,086	1	0	0	0	1	0	0	0	0	0
Tioga	1,922	1	0	0	0	1	14	1	12	1	0
Valley City	6,547	10	0	2	0	8	115	14	93	8	2
Wahpeton	7,956	15	0	3	2	10	182	39	117	26	0
Watford City	5,513	28	0	6	0	22	123	7	103	13	0
West Fargo	39,987	73	0	16	3	54	515	92	373	50	4
Williston	25,513	127	1	17	7	102	549	80	414	55	1
Wishek	852	1	0	0	0	1	2	0	1	1	0
OHIO											
Ada	5,238	0	0	0	0	0	10	1	9	0	0
Akron	188,534	1,548	38	206	156	1,148	6,464	1,030	4,525	909	89
Alliance	21,817	68	0	3	1	64	535	56	452	27	3
Amberley Village	3,801	2	0	0	0	2	25	5	20	0	0
American Township	12,355	16	0	2	0	14	167	22	143	2	0
Amherst	12,993	1	0	0	0	1	99	5	93	1	1
Archbold	4,484	8	0	2	0	6	52	8	44	0	0
Ashland	19,193	23	0	10	4	9	260	24	230	6	1
Ashville	4,696	10	0	3	0	7	51	4	46	1	0
Athens	24,220	41	0	8	5	28	544	68	430	46	3
Aurora	17,486	6	0	1	2	3	99	2	91	6	0
Austintown	35,462	36	2	4	6	24	640	54	538	48	0
Avon Lake	25,846	18	0	1	1	16	112	10	94	8	1
Barberton	24,840	85	0	22	7	56	630	91	506	33	2
Barnesville	3,955	1	0	1	0	0	9	2	7	0	0
Batavia	1,906	1	0	0	0	1	27	1	25	1	1
Bath Township, Summit County	9,922	0	0	0	0	0	178	6	171	1	0
Bay Village	15,826	7	0	0	0	7	51	3	40	8	0
Bazetta Township	5,916	4	0	0	3	1	135	4	130	1	0
Beachwood	13,797	22	0	5	1	16	448	14	388	46	0
Beavercreek	46,749	44	0	16	9	19	743	35	664	44	2
Beaver Township	6,716	7	0	0	0	7	76	21	53	2	0
Bedford Heights	10,736	39	1	0	7	31	273	12	170	91	0
Bellaire	3,808	11	0	1	0	10	19	5	12	2	0
Bellbrook	7,345	5	0	3	0	2	43	5	37	1	0
Bellefontaine	14,065	17	0	7	0	10	109	8	101	0	1
Bellville	1,976	1	0	0	0	1	20	4	13	3	0
Belpre	6,649	9	0	3	0	6	62	5	54	3	0
Berea	18,736	7	0	0	1	6	94	8	68	18	0
Bethel	2,646	4	0	1	0	3	19	4	15	0	0
Beverly	1,225	2	0	2	0	0	15	3	12	0	1
Blanchester	4,234	5	0	1	0	4	117	30	79	8	1
Blendon Township	7,926	11	0	0	4	7	112	10	69	33	1
Blue Ash	13,314	14	0	7	1	6	276	8	255	13	1
Bluffton	4,256	2	0	1	0	1	21	7	11	3	0
Boardman	39,490	90	1	21	30	38	1,440	143	1,238	59	6
Bowling Green	30,730	16	0	8	1	7	412	25	377	10	1
Bratenahl	1,399	1	0	0	0	1	8	3	2	3	0
Brecksville	13,466	4	0	0	1	3	48	1	47	0	0
Brewster	2,107	4	0	0	0	4	26	9	17	0	1
Bridgeport	1,559	0	0	0	0	0	5	1	4	0	0
Brimfield Township	11,450	7	0	1	2	4	220	7	204	9	0
Broadview Heights	19,490	2	0	0	0	2	28	2	26	0	0
Brooklyn	11,043	8	0	2	1	5	521	14	459	48	0
Brookville	5,945	11	0	1	1	9	25	2	21	2	0
Brunswick	35,235	38	1	1	0	36	182	8	157	17	0
Buckeye Lake	2,575	7	0	1	0	6	39	8	29	2	2
Bucyrus	11,571	34	1	9	5	19	212	26	178	8	1
Butler Township	8,219	13	0	5	4	4	439	26	387	26	0
Byesville	2,352	9	0	0	1	8	24	1	22	1	0
Cambridge	9,978	10	0	5	0	5	78	6	71	1	0
Canal Fulton	5,321	6	0	2	1	3	42	10	31	1	0
Canfield	7,551	1	0	1	0	0	32	3	25	4	0
Canton	70,070	827	10	154	92	571	3,887	602	2,711	574	15
Carrollton	3,101	9	0	2	0	7	27	3	23	1	0
Centerville	25,249	10	0	4	1	5	259	23	221	15	2
Chagrin Falls	4,084	2	0	1	0	1	40	2	32	6	0
Cheviot	8,579	18	0	4	0	14	225	41	151	33	0
Cincinnati	307,761	2,591	73	259	640	1,619	11,543	1,877	7,655	2,011	1
Circleville	14,274	34	1	15	4	14	401	56	330	15	6
Clayton	13,228	17	0	6	2	9	123	15	86	22	0

Table 8. Offenses Known to Law Enforcement, by Selected State and City, 2022—Continued

(Number.)

State/city	Population	Violent crime	Murder and nonnegligent manslaughter	Rape	Robbery	Aggravated assault	Property crime	Burglary	Larceny-theft	Motor vehicle theft	Arson[1]
Clearcreek Township	19,152	9	0	2	0	7	67	5	59	3	0
Cleveland	363,764	5,870	145	453	1,549	3,723	15,704	3,004	8,728	3,972	124
Cleveland Heights	44,105	98	1	15	32	50	503	68	353	82	11
Clinton Township	4,353	2	0	0	0	2	61	1	59	1	0
Coldwater	4,676	3	0	3	0	0	24	0	24	0	0
Colerain Township	58,548	96	0	17	19	60	1,263	119	1,058	86	6
Columbiana	6,806	0	0	0	0	0	21	2	18	1	0
Columbus	907,196	4,082	127	1,005	1,275	1,675	31,609	4,288	20,028	7,293	14
Commercial Point	3,168	5	0	0	0	5	33	9	22	2	0
Copley Township	18,244	21	0	5	4	12	185	15	164	6	2
Cortland	7,090	4	0	0	0	4	35	5	30	0	0
Covington	2,576	0	0	0	0	0	1	0	1	0	0
Crestline	4,466	7	0	2	0	5	30	4	25	1	0
Cuyahoga Falls	50,607	70	2	13	5	50	921	91	764	66	4
Dayton	137,084	1,605	34	203	259	1,109	5,875	1,339	3,096	1,440	42
Defiance	16,923	44	0	16	2	26	203	18	175	10	0
Delaware	44,042	62	0	26	1	35	412	27	369	16	5
Delhi Township	28,476	25	0	8	6	11	368	25	315	28	1
Delphos	7,007	12	0	7	0	5	44	3	37	4	1
Delta	3,374	6	0	0	1	5	17	1	16	0	0
Dennison	2,658	1	0	0	0	1	1	0	1	0	0
Dover	12,936	17	0	8	1	8	57	11	40	6	0
Dublin	48,799	33	0	15	11	7	549	35	439	75	1
East Canton	1,509	2	0	1	0	1	48	8	35	5	0
East Cleveland	13,418	142	5	5	25	107	303	59	140	104	2
East Palestine	4,697	3	1	1	0	1	56	8	46	2	1
Eaton	8,347	9	1	6	0	2	118	2	103	13	0
Elida	1,859	0	0	0	0	0	8	0	8	0	0
Elyria	52,902	105	8	24	22	51	1,007	158	766	83	1
Englewood	13,338	33	0	11	7	15	326	16	293	17	1
Euclid	48,344	131	4	17	28	82	921	84	604	233	11
Evendale	2,624	2	0	0	0	2	148	8	134	6	0
Fairborn	34,725	95	1	36	7	51	421	74	304	43	11
Fairfax	1,738	3	0	0	2	1	226	4	222	0	0
Fairlawn	7,665	2	1	0	0	1	316	2	308	6	0
Fairview Park	16,821	12	0	4	1	7	93	4	73	16	0
Findlay	39,881	70	1	27	10	32	707	94	589	24	3
Forest Park	19,824	72	1	7	22	42	383	41	269	73	2
Franklin	11,604	41	0	11	2	28	391	38	331	22	1
Franklin Township	10,484	0	0	0	0	0	12	1	9	2	0
Fredericktown	2,643	0	0	0	0	0	24	3	21	0	0
Fremont	15,757	8	0	2	1	5	358	47	290	21	0
Gahanna	35,167	84	0	20	9	55	835	54	679	102	1
Galion	10,338	16	0	4	1	11	99	14	81	4	1
Gallipolis	3,296	19	0	3	1	15	135	11	117	7	0
Garfield Heights	29,022	140	8	23	13	96	511	79	403	29	2
Gates Mills	2,231	0	0	0	0	0	2	1	1	0	0
Georgetown	4,453	3	1	2	0	0	28	5	22	1	0
Germantown	5,798	17	0	5	0	12	33	3	28	2	0
Goshen Township, Clermont County	16,296	23	0	3	1	19	109	24	82	3	2
Goshen Township, Mahoning County	3,046	9	0	2	0	7	68	12	53	3	0
Grafton	5,621	0	0	0	0	0	16	0	16	0	0
Grandview Heights	8,254	8	0	0	1	7	191	13	166	12	1
Granville	5,741	4	0	4	0	0	30	3	26	1	0
Greenfield	4,334	9	0	5	0	4	21	4	13	4	0
Greenhills	3,658	8	0	1	0	7	41	6	35	0	0
Green Township	59,568	65	2	10	12	41	984	124	792	68	4
Grove City	42,248	59	0	16	7	36	1,026	51	902	73	0
Groveport	5,820	12	1	2	2	7	107	9	84	14	0
Hamilton	62,536	240	4	34	40	162	1,376	243	986	147	22
Hamilton Township, Warren County	27,421	7	0	1	0	6	78	3	70	5	1
Hartville	3,331	3	0	0	1	2	39	6	32	1	1
Heath	10,641	17	0	5	2	10	472	92	363	17	2
Hebron	2,376	4	0	1	1	2	39	6	29	4	0
Highland Heights	8,536	2	0	1	0	1	67	1	65	1	1
Hilliard	36,644	52	0	7	5	40	352	35	287	30	1
Hillsboro	6,482	6	0	2	0	4	151	20	124	7	1
Hinckley Township	8,119	1	0	0	0	1	9	2	7	0	0
Holland	1,797	6	0	1	3	2	376	7	365	4	0
Howland Township	17,177	16	0	1	1	14	227	30	175	22	0
Hubbard	7,607	15	0	3	1	11	65	6	58	1	0
Hubbard Township	5,319	6	0	0	0	6	58	9	43	6	1
Huber Heights	43,233	69	0	28	10	31	806	75	631	100	4
Hudson	22,902	6	0	2	0	4	96	10	84	2	0
Independence	7,474	17	0	4	6	7	116	0	105	11	0
Ironton	10,312	15	0	2	4	9	61	16	39	6	1
Jackson	6,168	21	0	5	0	16	108	10	93	5	0
Jackson Township, Mahoning County	2,096	1	0	1	0	0	17	3	13	1	0

Table 8. Offenses Known to Law Enforcement, by Selected State and City, 2022—Continued

(Number.)

State/city	Population	Violent crime	Murder and nonnegligent manslaughter	Rape	Robbery	Aggravated assault	Property crime	Burglary	Larceny-theft	Motor vehicle theft	Arson[1]
Jackson Township, Stark County	42,745	65	1	24	13	27	984	101	838	45	1
Jamestown	2,056	0	0	0	0	0	15	3	11	1	0
Kent	27,723	39	0	0	4	35	327	47	258	22	1
Kenton	7,938	27	0	8	0	19	213	21	184	8	0
Kettering	57,107	29	0	11	6	12	804	85	633	86	6
Kirtland	6,899	0	0	0	0	0	4	0	4	0	0
Lakemore	2,894	15	0	3	0	12	76	12	63	1	0
Lakewood	49,490	62	0	4	25	33	670	71	493	106	3
Lancaster	40,937	109	0	22	19	68	881	107	717	57	10
Lawrence Township	8,179	10	0	3	0	7	42	7	31	4	1
Lebanon	21,547	32	0	10	0	22	303	13	267	23	2
Lexington	4,863	1	0	0	0	1	1	0	1	0	0
Liberty Township	11,925	36	0	9	7	20	186	17	151	18	0
Lima	35,633	230	3	23	30	174	1,290	301	954	35	1
Lisbon	2,566	0	0	0	0	0	8	1	7	0	0
Lockland	3,467	30	1	3	5	21	85	12	59	14	0
Lodi	2,765	5	0	1	0	4	14	1	13	0	0
London	10,646	15	0	1	1	13	72	7	63	2	0
Lorain	65,536	308	1	26	51	230	1,191	222	873	96	19
Lordstown	3,341	5	0	1	0	4	38	6	32	0	0
Loudonville	2,774	5	0	3	0	2	19	3	16	0	0
Louisville	9,497	4	0	1	1	2	120	15	100	5	1
Loveland	13,095	6	0	2	0	4	79	8	66	5	2
Lyndhurst	13,682	16	0	1	2	13	138	9	124	5	1
Macedonia	12,248	7	0	2	0	5	218	2	211	5	0
Madison	3,410	5	0	1	0	4	15	1	14	0	0
Madison Township, Franklin County	18,785	29	0	4	3	22	142	24	97	21	1
Mansfield	47,845	229	6	43	28	152	1,529	287	1,131	111	15
Mariemont	3,446	0	0	0	0	0	10	1	9	0	0
Marietta	13,366	10	0	6	0	4	233	9	221	3	1
Marion	35,775	81	4	35	5	37	635	146	468	21	6
Martins Ferry	6,171	18	0	6	0	12	39	10	29	0	0
Marysville	27,026	17	0	11	1	5	331	19	304	8	0
Mason	35,344	5	0	2	0	3	236	11	221	4	0
Maumee	13,725	27	0	3	7	17	381	20	332	29	1
Mayfield Heights	19,813	15	0	4	4	7	223	8	197	18	0
McArthur	1,754	3	0	0	1	2	30	12	18	0	0
McConnelsville	1,631	4	0	0	0	4	40	6	31	3	0
Mechanicsburg	1,702	6	0	1	0	5	15	2	12	1	0
Medina	25,921	22	0	10	3	9	184	20	159	5	0
Mentor	47,063	75	0	10	1	64	667	38	614	15	4
Mentor-on-the-Lake	7,072	6	0	2	0	4	37	2	34	1	0
Miamisburg	19,723	28	1	7	7	13	327	31	263	33	1
Miami Township, Clermont County	44,356	32	1	14	1	16	359	21	313	25	0
Middleport	2,171	2	0	0	0	2	16	9	7	0	0
Middletown	50,970	124	0	5	22	97	1,112	186	838	88	8
Mifflin Township	2,563	0	0	0	0	0	5	0	3	2	0
Milford	6,456	18	0	12	0	6	144	9	130	5	1
Mogadore	3,785	5	0	1	0	4	40	5	31	4	0
Monroe	17,817	17	0	4	1	12	298	8	270	20	0
Monroeville	1,287	2	0	0	0	2	9	0	8	1	0
Montgomery	10,766	8	0	2	0	6	121	3	110	8	1
Montpelier	3,865	17	0	10	0	7	119	22	87	10	2
Montville Township	13,304	3	0	0	1	2	45	6	37	2	0
Moraine	6,540	53	1	13	7	32	429	29	362	38	2
Mount Gilead	3,514	5	0	1	2	2	41	16	25	0	0
Munroe Falls	5,007	7	0	1	0	6	16	1	15	0	0
Napoleon	8,744	21	0	4	0	17	128	11	115	2	0
Nelsonville	4,542	11	1	1	1	8	72	20	48	4	0
New Albany	10,851	10	0	4	1	5	149	14	127	8	0
Newark	50,818	118	0	19	27	72	1,381	220	1,020	141	30
New Boston	2,267	9	0	0	0	9	87	6	79	2	2
New Franklin	13,744	8	0	2	1	5	77	12	63	2	0
New Lebanon	3,781	16	0	3	1	12	36	5	30	1	1
New Lexington	4,437	14	0	2	0	12	67	13	51	3	0
New Philadelphia	17,508	4	0	1	0	3	19	6	13	0	0
New Richmond	2,761	10	0	1	0	9	12	1	9	2	0
New Waterford	1,175	0	0	0	0	0	2	0	2	0	0
Niles	18,344	52	0	9	16	27	499	69	401	29	3
North Canton	17,855	16	0	1	0	15	224	8	212	4	0
Northfield	3,511	1	0	0	1	0	36	0	33	3	0
North Olmsted	31,641	28	0	3	3	22	446	22	393	31	3
North Ridgeville	36,968	15	0	5	0	10	145	29	107	9	1
North Royalton	30,687	12	0	5	0	7	162	10	141	11	0
Northwood	5,190	11	0	1	2	8	127	6	107	14	0
Norton	11,507	16	0	2	4	10	187	25	148	14	0
Norwalk	16,986	20	1	8	3	8	179	21	156	2	0
Norwood	18,602	54	2	9	8	35	531	61	439	31	4
Oak Harbor	2,798	5	0	2	0	3	26	1	24	1	0
Oberlin	8,238	11	0	8	0	3	109	6	100	3	1

Table 8. Offenses Known to Law Enforcement, by Selected State and City, 2022—Continued

(Number.)

State/city	Population	Violent crime	Murder and nonnegligent manslaughter	Rape	Robbery	Aggravated assault	Property crime	Burglary	Larceny-theft	Motor vehicle theft	Arson[1]
Obetz	6,074	6	0	1	2	3	113	12	80	21	0
Olmsted Falls	8,614	2	0	0	0	2	48	3	37	8	0
Olmsted Township	14,486	3	0	0	0	3	46	6	27	13	0
Oregon	19,800	33	0	11	3	19	858	52	774	32	0
Orrville	8,453	16	0	9	0	7	56	8	47	1	0
Ottawa Hills	4,816	0	0	0	0	0	42	4	26	12	0
Parma	79,098	114	2	18	15	79	711	80	490	141	5
Parma Heights	20,306	5	0	0	1	4	79	5	61	13	0
Pataskala	18,283	14	0	1	3	10	118	8	99	11	0
Paulding	3,578	10	0	3	0	7	13	3	8	2	0
Pepper Pike	6,834	2	0	0	0	2	42	4	30	8	0
Perrysburg	25,165	4	0	4	0	0	155	8	147	0	0
Perrysburg Township	13,666	10	0	0	1	9	109	7	95	7	0
Perry Township, Franklin County	3,786	0	0	0	0	0	16	3	12	1	0
Perry Township, Stark County	28,143	71	0	14	9	48	420	99	285	36	1
Pickerington	24,647	24	1	5	9	9	231	18	201	12	2
Pierce Township	15,277	16	0	2	4	9	146	14	124	8	1
Pioneer	1,412	1	0	0	0	1	16	1	15	0	0
Piqua	20,516	74	0	27	8	39	617	75	506	36	1
Plain City	4,651	3	0	0	0	3	4	0	4	0	0
Port Clinton	5,951	11	0	4	0	7	83	18	61	4	0
Portsmouth	17,896	71	3	12	10	46	465	97	340	28	0
Powell	14,407	6	0	2	0	4	88	5	80	3	0
Ravenna	11,299	20	1	2	2	15	260	25	218	17	1
Reading	11,177	28	0	5	2	21	282	32	229	21	1
Richmond Heights	10,546	24	0	3	1	20	179	16	127	36	1
Richwood	2,398	4	0	2	0	2	40	4	35	1	0
Riverside	24,322	51	1	15	11	24	387	46	286	55	5
Rocky River	21,309	17	0	4	3	10	151	5	135	11	0
Ross Township	8,776	5	0	0	0	5	55	11	42	2	0
Rutland	422	1	0	0	1	0	12	1	11	0	0
Sabina	2,495	8	1	3	0	4	43	13	27	3	0
Sagamore Hills	10,759	0	0	0	0	0	12	6	6	0	0
Salem	11,776	16	0	2	0	14	196	21	164	11	0
Salineville	1,183	1	0	0	0	1	13	2	11	0	0
Sandusky	24,531	23	1	1	7	14	443	71	339	33	2
Sebring	4,154	8	2	1	0	5	35	16	18	1	3
Seven Hills	11,516	11	4	0	0	7	77	4	67	6	0
Shaker Heights	28,615	16	1	0	10	5	167	11	137	19	0
Shawnee Township	12,314	7	0	5	0	2	91	15	74	2	0
Sheffield Village	4,444	2	1	0	0	1	23	1	22	0	1
Shelby	9,303	13	0	3	0	10	124	15	106	3	2
Sidney	20,309	61	0	23	7	31	466	115	331	20	5
Solon	23,680	15	0	2	4	9	195	14	168	13	0
South Bloomfield	2,181	1	0	0	0	1	23	2	19	2	0
South Euclid	21,360	37	1	6	6	24	540	22	499	19	0
South Zanesville	1,905	2	0	0	0	2	11	0	10	1	0
Spencerville	2,153	1	0	1	0	0	18	0	16	2	0
Springboro	19,431	6	0	2	1	3	93	6	82	5	1
Springfield	58,725	707	6	58	136	507	2,651	531	1,765	355	46
Springfield Township, Hamilton County	35,363	43	1	1	10	31	525	59	405	61	1
Springfield Township, Mahoning County	6,703	8	0	2	0	6	65	21	44	0	0
Springfield Township, Summit County	14,025	36	0	8	6	22	548	36	491	21	2
St. Bernard	3,941	15	0	1	2	12	116	6	96	14	0
St. Clairsville	5,021	3	0	0	1	2	2	0	2	0	0
Steubenville	17,869	29	2	1	6	20	616	57	544	15	2
Stow	34,244	36	0	12	2	22	481	34	434	13	1
Strasburg	2,696	1	0	0	0	1	7	0	7	0	0
Streetsboro	17,908	23	0	2	3	18	261	19	231	11	1
Strongsville	45,703	31	3	4	0	24	390	20	352	18	0
Sugarcreek Township	9,579	9	0	2	2	5	174	9	158	7	0
Swanton	3,853	3	0	0	0	3	29	4	25	0	0
Sylvania	19,055	8	0	1	0	6	151	18	122	11	0
Sylvania Township	31,833	34	1	3	10	20	641	41	539	61	2
Tallmadge	18,240	21	0	4	1	16	180	21	144	15	2
Tiffin	17,773	37	0	23	3	11	309	30	275	14	1
Toledo	266,984	3,105	61	227	494	2,323	8,225	1,505	5,564	1,156	161
Toronto	5,264	7	1	3	0	3	7	0	7	0	0
Trotwood	22,930	134	6	25	12	91	752	153	434	165	13
Troy	26,544	31	0	3	5	23	324	94	218	12	2
Twinsburg	19,402	15	0	2	1	12	127	7	111	9	0
Uhrichsville	5,177	27	1	4	1	21	97	21	63	13	0
Union	6,865	3	0	2	0	1	37	5	27	5	0
Uniontown	3,304	4	1	1	0	2	91	8	82	1	0
Union Township, Clermont County	50,164	31	0	18	3	10	541	32	495	14	1
University Heights	13,701	19	0	2	3	14	109	6	92	11	0
Upper Arlington	35,831	12	0	4	3	8	363	22	305	36	0
Upper Sandusky	6,577	9	0	4	1	4	83	10	67	6	2

Table 8. Offenses Known to Law Enforcement, by Selected State and City, 2022—Continued

(Number.)

State/city	Population	Violent crime	Murder and nonnegligent manslaughter	Rape	Robbery	Aggravated assault	Property crime	Burglary	Larceny-theft	Motor vehicle theft	Arson[1]
Urbana	11,119	19	0	10	1	8	227	20	199	8	3
Utica	2,114	2	0	0	0	2	8	2	6	0	0
Van Wert	11,005	35	0	12	3	20	258	46	204	8	1
Village of Leesburg	1,269	2	0	2	0	0	16	1	14	1	0
Wadsworth	24,546	37	0	19	4	14	244	23	217	4	1
Wapakoneta	9,742	10	0	2	0	8	170	9	157	4	0
Warren	38,943	171	2	14	38	117	1,115	282	746	87	20
Washington Court House	14,494	22	1	7	3	11	267	22	228	17	6
Waterville	6,022	8	0	1	1	6	31	7	24	0	0
Wauseon	7,492	16	0	8	0	8	100	5	90	5	1
Waverly	4,139	3	0	3	0	0	18	2	16	0	0
Weathersfield	8,043	9	0	1	0	8	125	17	103	5	3
Wellston	5,400	16	2	1	0	13	116	16	88	12	1
West Carrollton	12,951	30	0	6	1	23	235	30	138	67	0
West Chester Township	62,374	57	2	9	14	32	1,046	97	902	47	3
Westerville	38,528	56	0	13	6	37	764	65	635	64	3
West Jefferson	4,293	10	0	1	0	9	53	8	37	8	0
Westlake	33,734	14	0	2	2	10	141	20	101	20	0
Whitehall	20,094	171	1	25	47	98	1,212	117	964	131	8
Whitehouse	5,042	2	0	0	1	1	15	0	15	0	0
Wickliffe	12,622	10	0	0	0	10	132	2	119	11	0
Williamsburg	2,590	3	0	2	0	1	16	1	15	0	0
Willoughby	23,853	24	1	5	5	13	231	15	204	12	0
Willoughby Hills	9,943	10	0	4	0	6	116	18	82	16	1
Willowick	14,103	7	0	0	1	6	38	5	32	1	1
Wintersville	3,724	9	0	2	0	7	38	1	35	2	1
Woodville	1,988	2	0	0	0	2	4	1	3	0	0
Wooster	26,750	73	2	25	10	36	633	63	542	28	8
Worthington	14,346	14	0	1	3	10	229	13	197	19	0
Wyoming	8,646	2	0	0	0	2	50	6	37	7	0
Xenia	25,513	48	0	24	1	23	488	57	386	45	4
Yellow Springs	3,710	2	0	0	0	2	54	6	43	5	0
Youngstown	59,944	411	18	36	61	296	1,721	447	1,004	270	15
Zanesville	24,703	74	0	16	14	44	872	77	770	25	1
OKLAHOMA											
Achille	411	0	0	0	0	0	3	0	2	1	0
Ada	16,946	30	1	3	3	23	412	72	287	53	0
Adair	732	0	0	0	0	0	9	4	3	2	0
Alex	494	0	0	0	0	0	4	1	3	0	0
Allen	788	0	0	0	0	0	16	2	12	2	1
Altus	18,757	50	0	3	5	42	276	74	181	21	1
Alva	4,991	8	0	3	0	5	43	12	27	4	0
Amber	429	0	0	0	0	0	1	1	0	0	0
Anadarko	5,865	55	0	4	3	48	230	55	160	15	3
Antlers	2,179	4	0	0	0	4	41	9	29	3	2
Apache	1,071	4	0	0	0	4	23	6	14	3	0
Ardmore	24,999	220	4	20	12	184	722	173	457	92	5
Arkoma	1,831	1	1	0	0	0	6	2	3	1	0
Atoka	3,210	29	0	0	1	28	120	33	74	13	1
Avant	298	0	0	0	0	0	1	0	1	0	0
Barnsdall	1,016	1	0	1	0	0	14	3	11	0	0
Bartlesville	37,479	113	2	26	12	73	996	234	648	114	3
Beaver	1,225	1	0	1	0	0	12	3	8	1	0
Beggs	1,178	8	0	0	3	5	13	6	5	2	0
Bennington	290	0	0	0	0	0	0	0	0	0	0
Bernice	436	0	0	0	0	0	12	2	10	0	0
Bethany	20,322	54	1	3	8	42	400	184	172	44	6
Big Cabin	171	0	0	0	0	0	1	0	1	0	0
Binger	436	1	0	0	0	1	11	1	8	2	0
Bixby	29,690	31	2	8	3	18	327	49	229	49	0
Blackwell	6,089	27	0	8	0	19	105	23	74	8	1
Blair	730	0	0	0	0	0	1	0	1	0	0
Blanchard	9,488	4	0	1	0	3	66	13	46	7	1
Boise City	1,119	5	1	1	2	1	19	4	7	8	0
Bokchito	594	2	0	0	0	2	14	2	11	1	0
Boley	950	2	0	0	0	2	3	3	0	0	0
Boswell	593	1	0	0	0	1	2	0	0	2	0
Bristow	4,262	17	0	3	1	13	109	24	68	17	0
Broken Arrow	118,683	185	6	34	12	133	1,910	268	1,419	223	2
Broken Bow	4,270	30	1	3	3	23	289	67	187	35	3
Burns Flat	1,953	0	0	0	0	0	13	4	6	3	0
Butler	202	0	0	0	0	0	0	0	0	0	0
Cache	3,073	5	0	0	1	4	36	9	22	5	0
Caddo	1,048	1	0	0	0	1	5	1	3	1	0
Calera	2,998	2	0	1	0	1	52	7	38	7	1
Calumet	472	0	0	0	0	0	4	1	2	1	0
Calvin	321	0	0	0	0	0	2	0	1	1	0
Caney	204	0	0	0	0	0	4	1	2	1	0
Canton	448	0	0	0	0	0	0	0	0	0	0
Carnegie	1,428	5	0	2	0	3	21	7	11	3	1
Carney	558	0	0	0	0	0	4	0	3	1	0
Cashion	889	0	0	0	0	0	4	1	3	0	0

Table 8. Offenses Known to Law Enforcement, by Selected State and City, 2022—Continued

(Number.)

State/city	Population	Violent crime	Murder and nonnegligent manslaughter	Rape	Robbery	Aggravated assault	Property crime	Burglary	Larceny-theft	Motor vehicle theft	Arson[1]
Catoosa	7,402	42	0	4	2	36	200	35	117	48	0
Cement	455	0	0	0	0	0	0	0	0	0	0
Chandler	2,913	7	0	1	0	6	59	14	37	8	0
Chattanooga	409	0	0	0	0	0	0	0	0	0	0
Checotah	3,077	10	0	1	1	8	51	12	30	9	0
Chelsea	1,991	10	0	4	0	6	32	7	22	3	2
Cherokee	1,507	4	0	1	0	3	27	12	13	2	0
Chickasha	16,031	64	0	21	1	42	549	182	296	71	2
Choctaw	12,228	23	0	8	0	15	153	38	101	14	0
Chouteau	2,095	4	0	0	0	4	57	13	32	12	1
Claremore	19,659	49	0	14	2	33	437	106	296	35	0
Cleveland	3,243	4	0	1	1	2	52	13	30	9	0
Clinton	8,280	37	0	6	4	27	164	42	103	19	2
Coalgate	1,648	2	0	0	1	1	8	2	3	3	0
Colbert	1,066	1	0	0	0	1	5	0	3	2	0
Colcord	759	2	0	0	0	2	5	0	5	0	1
Collinsville	8,740	11	0	4	1	6	79	16	51	12	0
Comanche	1,396	4	0	0	0	4	28	9	16	3	0
Commerce	2,285	9	0	1	0	8	42	19	18	5	1
Cordell	2,770	1	0	1	0	0	16	4	9	3	0
Covington	460	1	0	1	0	0	4	1	3	0	0
Coweta	10,623	18	0	5	1	12	109	20	68	21	0
Crescent	1,355	1	0	0	0	1	5	2	3	0	0
Cushing	8,195	19	0	1	2	16	205	47	137	21	2
Cyril	855	1	0	0	0	1	4	0	3	1	0
Davenport	849	2	0	0	0	2	16	2	12	2	0
Davis	2,773	17	0	3	0	14	92	25	56	11	1
Del City	21,382	125	1	15	12	97	722	86	561	75	2
Depew	406	2	0	1	0	1	16	7	8	1	0
Dewar	761	0	0	0	0	0	3	0	1	2	0
Dewey	3,387	4	0	1	0	3	115	35	69	11	1
Dibble	943	1	0	0	0	1	7	3	4	0	0
Dickson	1,350	2	0	1	0	1	16	8	7	1	0
Disney	223	0	0	0	0	0	0	0	0	0	0
Drumright	2,539	9	0	0	1	8	98	24	57	17	1
Duke	395	0	0	0	0	0	0	0	0	0	0
Duncan	22,915	34	1	5	3	25	503	138	324	41	4
Durant	19,481	58	1	16	2	39	573	100	410	63	4
Earlsboro	608	2	0	0	2	0	6	3	1	2	0
Edmond	95,946	153	0	34	14	105	1,557	207	1,279	71	4
Eldorado	315	0	0	0	0	0	1	1	0	0	0
Elgin	3,782	0	0	0	0	0	1	0	1	0	0
Elk City	11,417	24	0	5	2	17	165	30	112	23	4
Elmore City	749	0	0	0	0	0	7	1	5	1	0
El Reno	18,385	32	1	9	1	21	245	40	173	32	3
Enid	49,990	204	0	45	13	146	1,424	360	980	84	7
Erick	978	0	0	0	0	0	1	0	1	0	0
Eufaula	2,777	13	0	4	2	7	57	8	31	18	0
Fairfax	1,109	3	0	1	0	2	13	4	8	1	0
Fairland	1,112	1	0	0	0	1	6	0	5	1	1
Fairview	2,658	2	0	0	0	2	36	9	23	4	1
Forest Park	1,042	0	0	0	0	0	6	3	2	1	0
Fort Cobb	537	0	0	0	0	0	0	0	0	0	0
Fort Gibson	3,818	8	0	1	0	7	48	8	36	4	0
Fort Towson	502	0	0	0	0	0	0	0	0	0	0
Foyil	388	2	0	1	0	1	3	0	3	0	0
Frederick	3,560	9	0	0	0	9	81	33	44	4	1
Gans	250	0	0	0	0	0	1	0	0	1	0
Garber	710	0	0	0	0	0	1	1	0	0	0
Geary	969	2	0	0	0	2	27	8	18	1	1
Geronimo	1,171	2	0	1	0	1	8	3	5	0	0
Glenpool	13,983	37	1	10	1	25	344	76	234	34	1
Goodwell	1,059	0	0	0	0	0	3	0	2	1	0
Gore	941	1	0	0	1	0	10	0	9	1	0
Grandfield	934	5	0	0	0	5	14	3	10	1	1
Granite	1,753	4	0	2	0	2	5	1	2	2	4
Grove	7,179	24	0	2	1	21	218	23	180	15	1
Guthrie	11,255	32	0	3	3	26	173	46	119	8	2
Guymon	12,292	24	0	5	3	16	132	39	82	11	1
Hammon	465	0	0	0	0	0	1	0	0	1	0
Harrah	6,425	8	1	3	0	4	122	40	72	10	0
Hartshorne	1,904	3	0	0	0	3	30	10	16	4	0
Haskell	1,702	11	0	0	1	10	54	17	30	7	0
Haworth	283	0	0	0	0	0	0	0	0	0	0
Healdton	2,335	3	0	0	1	2	35	12	16	7	0
Heavener	3,009	13	0	1	0	12	33	6	17	10	0
Hennessey	2,154	0	0	0	0	0	14	7	7	0	0
Henryetta	5,619	10	0	1	0	9	109	45	47	17	1
Hinton	3,144	5	0	0	1	4	38	4	24	10	0
Hobart	3,344	5	0	1	1	3	36	10	21	5	1
Holdenville	5,788	9	0	0	0	9	68	26	37	5	3
Hollis	1,714	7	1	0	0	6	15	6	7	2	2
Hominy	3,244	8	0	1	0	7	22	10	10	2	1

Table 8. Offenses Known to Law Enforcement, by Selected State and City, 2022—Continued

(Number.)

State/city	Population	Violent crime	Murder and nonnegligent manslaughter	Rape	Robbery	Aggravated assault	Property crime	Burglary	Larceny-theft	Motor vehicle theft	Arson[1]
Hooker	1,705	5	0	0	0	5	4	1	2	1	0
Howe	630	1	0	0	0	1	5	1	3	1	0
Hugo	5,215	25	0	1	3	21	131	36	80	15	2
Hulbert	516	2	0	0	0	2	12	1	7	4	0
Hydro	929	0	0	0	0	0	7	3	3	1	0
Idabel	7,043	12	0	1	2	9	293	39	241	13	3
Inola	1,884	2	0	1	0	1	17	2	13	2	0
Jay	2,410	16	0	6	0	10	72	19	37	16	4
Jenks	27,208	35	0	6	2	27	303	50	213	40	1
Jennings	290	1	0	0	0	1	2	0	1	1	1
Jones	2,991	11	0	1	0	10	35	13	18	4	0
Kansas	732	0	0	0	0	0	9	3	5	1	2
Kellyville	1,010	0	0	0	0	0	7	0	5	2	0
Kiefer	2,220	2	0	0	0	2	30	7	21	2	0
Kingfisher	4,832	8	0	1	0	7	79	15	59	5	1
Kingston	1,466	1	0	0	0	1	30	11	13	6	0
Kiowa	589	2	0	0	0	2	10	2	3	5	1
Konawa	1,299	3	0	1	0	2	13	3	5	5	4
Krebs	2,085	7	0	0	0	7	57	17	35	5	1
Lahoma	515	0	0	0	0	0	3	1	1	1	0
Lamont	291	0	0	0	0	0	0	0	0	0	0
Langley	608	0	0	0	0	0	2	1	0	1	0
Langston	1,756	1	0	0	0	1	9	1	7	1	0
Laverne	1,170	0	0	0	0	0	2	0	1	1	0
Lawton	91,596	767	22	98	54	593	1,898	884	786	228	57
Lexington	1,989	11	0	1	0	10	43	7	29	7	1
Lindsay	2,895	11	0	1	1	9	51	15	33	3	1
Locust Grove	1,373	8	0	1	1	6	91	18	50	23	2
Lone Grove	5,109	14	0	3	0	11	53	15	30	8	0
Luther	1,491	0	0	0	0	0	9	4	5	0	0
Madill	4,031	6	0	1	0	5	113	10	95	8	0
Mangum	2,674	10	0	0	0	10	25	7	14	4	1
Mannford	3,279	5	0	2	0	3	27	2	20	5	0
Marble City	186	0	0	0	0	0	0	0	0	0	0
Marietta	2,847	11	0	6	0	5	54	16	31	7	0
Marlow	4,435	8	0	4	0	4	50	18	29	3	0
Maud	867	1	0	0	0	1	12	6	4	2	0
Maysville	1,091	2	0	0	0	2	22	5	15	2	0
McAlester	18,219	50	0	17	8	25	478	73	376	29	3
McCurtain	363	0	0	0	0	0	0	0	0	0	0
McLoud	4,265	12	0	0	0	12	51	14	31	6	0
Medford	882	0	0	0	0	0	6	2	2	2	0
Medicine Park	449	0	0	0	0	0	3	1	2	0	0
Meeker	1,017	1	0	0	0	1	17	2	13	2	0
Miami	12,904	65	0	5	4	56	449	85	301	63	9
Midwest City	57,826	195	0	23	9	163	1,540	186	1,212	142	3
Minco	1,523	0	0	0	0	0	6	1	3	2	0
Moore	63,421	152	1	19	12	120	1,297	254	927	116	2
Mooreland	1,143	1	0	0	0	1	6	1	5	0	0
Morris	1,304	2	0	0	0	2	4	2	2	0	0
Mounds	957	6	0	0	0	6	13	0	10	3	0
Mountain Park	312	0	0	0	0	0	0	0	0	0	0
Mountain View	729	2	0	0	0	2	4	2	0	2	0
Muldrow	3,350	29	0	5	1	23	72	18	42	12	1
Muskogee	36,713	408	2	37	30	339	1,239	293	832	114	12
Mustang	22,026	36	0	8	3	25	205	26	158	21	1
Nash	189	0	0	0	0	0	0	0	0	0	0
Newcastle	13,290	9	0	5	0	4	191	27	143	21	0
Newkirk	2,201	2	0	0	0	2	39	8	26	5	0
Nichols Hills	3,827	0	0	0	0	0	68	11	47	10	0
Nicoma Park	2,283	6	0	1	0	5	44	15	20	9	0
Ninnekah	800	0	0	0	0	0	4	0	3	1	0
Noble	7,746	9	0	2	0	7	109	26	71	12	0
Norman	128,878	391	2	78	38	273	3,547	455	2,729	363	9
North Enid	976	0	0	0	0	0	11	3	6	2	0
Nowata	3,480	5	0	0	0	5	85	17	61	7	3
Oilton	875	3	0	1	0	2	11	3	6	2	1
Okeene	1,032	0	0	0	0	0	5	0	4	1	0
Okemah	3,045	10	0	0	1	9	109	34	57	18	2
Oklahoma City	692,726	4,448	65	506	642	3,235	21,191	3,831	14,398	2,962	130
Okmulgee	11,408	42	0	6	11	25	349	82	229	38	1
Olustee	466	0	0	0	0	0	1	1	0	0	0
Oologah	1,316	10	1	1	0	8	27	12	12	3	0
Owasso	38,998	57	0	14	3	40	615	66	481	68	0
Panama	1,293	1	0	0	0	1	5	3	0	2	0
Paoli	586	0	0	0	0	0	3	2	1	0	0
Pauls Valley	6,066	33	0	6	0	27	258	63	177	18	0
Pawhuska	2,924	7	0	1	0	6	54	13	34	7	3
Pawnee	1,935	7	0	1	1	5	15	5	7	3	0
Perkins	3,318	5	0	1	0	4	40	7	29	4	1
Perry	4,537	13	0	3	1	9	85	20	53	12	1
Piedmont	8,318	3	0	1	0	2	42	10	31	1	0
Pocola	4,402	4	0	0	0	4	32	11	13	8	1

Table 8. Offenses Known to Law Enforcement, by Selected State and City, 2022—Continued

(Number.)

State/city	Population	Violent crime	Murder and nonnegligent manslaughter	Rape	Robbery	Aggravated assault	Property crime	Burglary	Larceny-theft	Motor vehicle theft	Arson[1]
Ponca City	24,487	139	1	17	7	114	766	176	501	89	10
Pond Creek	893	2	0	0	0	2	7	4	2	1	0
Porum	608	8	0	0	0	8	8	4	4	0	0
Poteau	8,871	56	2	8	3	43	332	95	198	39	0
Prague	2,379	8	0	0	0	8	64	14	46	4	0
Pryor Creek	9,467	53	2	11	2	38	252	32	180	40	0
Purcell	6,647	31	1	3	1	26	178	46	109	23	1
Quinton	849	4	0	1	0	3	41	3	16	22	1
Ramona	540	0	0	0	0	0	7	2	4	1	1
Ratliff City	64	1	0	0	0	1	5	0	4	1	0
Rattan	280	0	0	0	0	0	1	0	1	0	0
Roland	3,645	12	1	2	0	9	73	18	44	11	0
Rush Springs	1,008	5	0	1	0	4	20	4	13	3	0
Salina	1,078	5	0	0	1	4	44	14	28	2	1
Sallisaw	8,505	37	0	5	3	29	346	42	284	20	5
Sand Springs	20,006	39	0	7	4	28	788	89	632	67	1
Sapulpa	22,447	55	4	15	5	31	366	84	234	48	3
Savanna	619	0	0	0	0	0	17	6	10	1	0
Sawyer	344	0	0	0	0	0	3	0	1	2	0
Sayre	4,363	4	0	0	0	4	36	8	23	5	0
Seiling	827	0	0	0	0	0	1	0	0	1	0
Seminole	7,063	20	0	2	0	18	152	36	89	27	2
Shady Point	990	0	0	0	0	0	5	3	1	1	0
Shattuck	1,248	0	0	0	0	0	1	0	1	0	0
Shawnee	31,865	182	0	30	17	135	1,114	210	761	143	6
Skiatook	8,651	22	0	12	2	8	162	36	117	9	1
Snyder	1,241	2	0	1	1	0	17	6	8	3	0
South Coffeyville	680	1	0	1	0	0	12	1	10	1	0
Sparks	123	0	0	0	0	0	0	0	0	0	0
Spavinaw	352	1	0	0	0	1	10	5	5	0	0
Spencer	3,890	24	0	0	2	22	62	8	38	16	1
Sperry	1,123	7	0	0	0	7	32	6	17	9	1
Spiro	2,135	8	0	1	0	7	25	3	18	4	3
Sterling	674	1	0	0	0	1	2	0	1	1	0
Stigler	2,699	1	0	0	1	0	39	6	31	2	0
Stillwater	48,384	150	5	25	9	111	928	213	646	69	6
Stilwell	3,651	26	0	1	1	23	188	51	111	26	8
Stratford	1,414	4	0	0	0	4	19	5	9	5	0
Stringtown	460	0	0	0	0	0	0	0	0	0	0
Stroud	2,772	10	0	2	1	7	76	21	42	13	1
Sulphur	4,841	15	0	2	3	10	67	17	46	4	0
Tahlequah	16,757	26	0	0	2	24	244	21	217	6	1
Talala	260	0	0	0	0	0	2	0	2	0	0
Talihina	919	2	0	1	0	1	18	8	9	1	2
Tecumseh	6,365	12	1	2	2	7	126	38	72	16	0
Texhoma	817	0	0	0	0	0	3	0	2	1	0
Thackerville	412	0	0	0	0	0	10	1	8	1	0
The Village	9,402	24	0	6	4	14	181	19	148	14	0
Thomas	1,126	2	0	0	1	1	7	1	3	3	1
Tipton	911	0	0	0	0	0	6	3	1	2	0
Tishomingo	2,974	4	0	0	0	4	34	14	13	7	0
Tonkawa	3,051	8	0	2	0	6	50	10	35	5	1
Tryon	389	0	0	0	0	0	0	0	0	0	0
Tulsa	410,135	3,810	57	369	470	2,914	17,522	3,590	10,793	3,139	56
Tupelo	322	0	0	0	0	0	2	1	1	0	0
Tushka	452	3	0	2	0	1	5	1	3	1	0
Tuttle	7,981	5	0	1	0	4	60	9	43	8	0
Tyrone	698	1	0	0	0	1	5	5	0	0	0
Union City	1,941	2	0	1	0	1	9	1	8	0	1
Valley Brook	650	8	0	1	1	6	17	4	13	0	0
Valliant	811	2	0	0	0	2	31	4	21	6	0
Velma	567	0	0	0	0	0	5	4	0	1	0
Verden	519	1	0	0	0	1	4	3	1	0	0
Verdigris	5,605	3	0	0	0	3	23	11	11	1	0
Vian	1,368	5	0	0	1	4	38	9	27	2	0
Vici	590	0	0	0	0	0	1	0	1	0	0
Vinita	5,170	8	0	2	0	6	119	32	67	20	1
Wagoner	8,071	26	0	4	2	20	228	43	167	18	1
Wakita	289	0	0	0	0	0	0	0	0	0	0
Walters	2,361	6	0	0	0	6	47	15	28	4	0
Warner	1,554	7	0	0	0	7	23	6	16	1	0
Warr Acres	10,439	37	1	3	8	25	413	63	322	28	3
Washington	695	0	0	0	0	0	2	1	1	0	0
Watonga	2,579	6	0	1	0	5	40	16	23	1	0
Watts	278	2	1	0	0	1	2	0	1	1	1
Waukomis	1,303	0	0	0	0	0	12	4	6	2	0
Waurika	1,921	15	0	1	0	14	32	12	16	4	1
Waynoka	716	2	0	1	0	1	6	1	5	0	0
Weatherford	11,891	9	0	1	1	7	149	16	120	13	0
Webbers Falls	340	1	0	1	0	0	13	1	4	8	0
Weleetka	794	1	0	0	0	1	12	1	7	4	0
Wellston	686	1	0	0	0	1	10	1	5	4	0
West Siloam Springs	989	2	0	0	0	2	42	7	28	7	0

Table 8. Offenses Known to Law Enforcement, by Selected State and City, 2022—Continued

(Number.)

State/city	Population	Violent crime	Murder and nonnegligent manslaughter	Rape	Robbery	Aggravated assault	Property crime	Burglary	Larceny-theft	Motor vehicle theft	Arson[1]
Westville	1,361	4	0	1	0	3	43	10	23	10	0
Wetumka	1,152	8	0	0	0	8	42	5	25	12	1
Wewoka	3,077	11	2	0	1	8	41	7	28	6	0
Wilburton	2,321	1	0	0	0	1	61	16	42	3	0
Wilson	1,429	5	0	0	1	4	37	13	20	4	1
Wister	1,054	0	0	0	0	0	11	3	8	0	0
Woodward	11,876	49	0	17	0	32	358	124	219	15	7
Wyandotte	497	0	0	0	0	0	4	1	3	0	0
Wynnewood	1,939	4	0	0	0	4	24	6	13	5	0
Wynona	369	0	0	0	0	0	3	2	1	0	0
Yale	1,089	6	0	0	0	6	29	8	20	1	0
Yukon	25,514	50	0	4	3	43	581	73	490	18	0
OREGON											
Albany	57,058	107	2	12	33	60	1,577	148	1,246	183	23
Ashland	21,797	36	0	5	13	18	531	61	414	56	7
Astoria	10,448	47	0	14	8	25	345	48	266	31	8
Baker City	10,259	27	1	9	5	12	241	44	179	18	1
Bandon	3,342	1	0	0	0	1	57	9	44	4	0
Banks	1,821	1	0	0	0	1	28	9	18	1	0
Beaverton	98,991	303	3	37	46	217	2,707	317	2,019	371	16
Bend	104,649	158	2	30	27	99	1,660	169	1,327	164	18
Boardman	4,005	18	0	3	1	14	48	12	28	8	0
Brookings	6,880	19	1	4	1	13	120	13	93	14	1
Canby	18,101	22	1	5	4	12	210	17	165	28	6
Carlton	2,243	1	0	0	0	1	30	4	23	3	0
Central Point	19,670	27	0	5	5	17	286	33	234	19	5
Columbia City	1,958	1	0	0	0	1	18	3	13	2	0
Coos Bay	15,871	98	1	13	12	72	928	213	643	72	11
Coquille	4,042	12	0	1	0	11	59	9	41	9	2
Cornelius	14,107	61	1	6	6	48	297	23	250	24	2
Corvallis	60,031	124	0	22	29	73	2,197	249	1,829	119	19
Cottage Grove	10,622	31	0	1	1	29	100	9	86	5	3
Dallas	17,622	49	0	6	2	41	346	33	281	32	10
Eagle Point	10,035	16	0	6	4	6	164	19	138	7	1
Eugene	175,390	662	3	124	132	403	5,989	803	4,416	770	97
Florence	9,514	13	1	2	0	10	261	14	241	6	5
Forest Grove	26,016	89	1	17	11	60	484	58	382	44	9
Gaston	673	0	0	0	0	0	16	4	12	0	0
Gervais	2,597	2	0	1	0	1	29	3	25	1	0
Gladstone	11,946	24	0	7	1	16	340	32	227	81	4
Grants Pass	39,519	146	1	20	39	86	1,563	128	1,280	155	20
Gresham	111,590	485	10	55	132	288	3,287	448	1,690	1,149	26
Hermiston	19,438	57	0	10	9	38	605	43	506	56	5
Hillsboro	106,345	315	4	58	63	190	2,730	318	2,077	335	35
Hood River	8,396	7	0	0	0	7	329	18	274	37	0
Hubbard	3,437	2	0	0	0	2	24	2	15	7	1
Independence	10,368	17	0	0	1	16	150	14	119	17	1
Jacksonville	3,011	4	0	1	1	2	35	6	27	2	0
Junction City	7,442	12	1	2	3	6	112	14	87	11	1
Keizer	38,958	76	1	3	13	59	1,001	81	798	122	8
King City	5,043	4	0	0	1	3	45	15	24	6	0
Klamath Falls	23,078	118	0	8	22	88	596	95	378	123	11
La Grande	13,174	37	0	8	3	26	326	56	236	34	13
Lake Oswego	40,044	32	0	10	3	19	633	92	471	70	2
Lebanon	19,456	35	0	1	4	30	244	20	184	40	2
Lincoln City	10,110	38	2	3	6	27	247	58	164	25	1
McMinnville	34,912	104	0	24	11	69	803	91	648	64	10
Medford	86,876	323	2	46	76	199	3,566	337	2,866	363	62
Milton-Freewater	7,119	30	0	4	7	19	154	29	91	34	4
Milwaukie	20,784	27	0	4	2	21	278	29	172	77	4
Molalla	10,179	22	0	6	0	16	119	18	83	18	5
Monmouth	11,123	20	0	0	0	20	164	10	139	15	2
Mount Angel	3,403	7	1	2	0	4	23	1	20	2	3
Myrtle Creek	3,522	7	0	1	0	6	98	12	72	14	3
Newberg-Dundee	25,503	34	0	12	3	19	408	37	331	40	16
Newport	10,667	40	0	6	2	32	313	36	258	19	6
North Bend	10,256	13	0	1	2	10	421	88	300	33	11
North Plains	3,406	3	0	2	0	1	45	12	25	8	0
Nyssa	3,218	10	1	5	0	4	44	8	21	15	1
Ontario	11,638	98	0	15	14	69	699	79	568	52	4
Oregon City	37,192	136	0	20	23	93	824	84	621	119	18
Pendleton	16,780	42	0	5	7	30	643	91	484	68	2
Philomath	5,881	8	0	2	1	5	61	7	49	5	0
Phoenix	4,051	8	0	1	0	7	136	18	102	16	2
Pilot Rock	1,332	6	0	1	0	5	16	7	8	1	0
Portland	630,129	4,733	94	354	1,279	3,006	39,852	4,790	24,206	10,856	252
Prineville	11,586	29	0	9	1	19	140	32	94	14	0
Rainier	1,912	3	0	0	3	0	102	20	71	11	1
Redmond	37,472	62	0	8	7	47	801	54	661	86	7
Reedsport	4,346	7	0	3	1	3	104	15	85	4	1
Rogue River	2,427	2	0	0	1	1	160	82	77	1	1
Roseburg	23,973	85	0	19	14	52	1,138	115	920	103	16

Table 8. Offenses Known to Law Enforcement, by Selected State and City, 2022—Continued

(Number.)

State/city	Population	Violent crime	Murder and nonnegligent manslaughter	Rape	Robbery	Aggravated assault	Property crime	Burglary	Larceny-theft	Motor vehicle theft	Arson[1]
Salem	179,661	866	7	44	175	640	6,506	749	4,568	1,189	145
Scappoose	8,102	12	0	1	1	10	109	14	70	25	1
Sherwood	20,102	40	0	11	3	26	447	25	384	38	0
Silverton	10,622	16	0	4	1	11	139	12	107	20	0
Springfield	62,217	201	4	24	40	133	2,041	229	1,593	219	23
Stanfield	2,153	3	0	0	0	3	30	6	20	4	0
Stayton	8,162	20	0	2	0	18	184	11	140	33	1
St. Helens	14,356	40	0	3	1	36	164	46	81	37	5
Sunriver	1,390	0	0	0	0	0	32	7	23	2	0
Sutherlin	8,662	24	0	3	4	17	198	30	140	28	4
Sweet Home	10,055	22	0	6	3	13	375	48	308	19	4
The Dalles	16,100	58	0	5	19	34	610	81	451	78	8
Tigard	56,550	202	3	17	67	115	2,080	249	1,564	267	15
Tillamook	5,314	12	0	3	2	7	186	17	160	9	3
Tualatin	27,195	71	0	7	17	47	1,072	92	830	150	7
Umatilla	7,513	8	0	1	0	7	77	8	56	13	0
Warrenton	6,537	19	0	4	5	10	380	12	356	12	0
West Linn	26,842	22	0	5	3	14	288	41	205	42	4
Winston	5,701	6	0	0	1	5	105	10	79	16	2
Woodburn	26,117	100	0	11	30	59	939	48	717	174	7
Yamhill	1,165	0	0	0	0	0	11	1	10	0	0
PENNSYLVANIA[2]											
Allegheny Valley Regional	4,565	3	0	0	0	3	16	1	13	2	1
Avoca	2,516	1	0	0	0	1	11	1	10	0	0
Baldwin Borough	20,941	31	0	1	1	29	78	12	54	12	1
Bellevue	8,091	13	1	1	6	5	90	9	75	6	0
Bentleyville	2,325	2	0	0	1	1	10	0	10	0	0
Berwick	10,360	17	2	5	1	9	135	10	121	4	1
Brentwood	9,819	9	0	1	2	6	64	10	42	12	1
Butler Township, Luzerne County	9,819	12	1	0	1	10	59	9	48	2	0
California	5,852	12	0	0	1	11	42	6	32	4	0
Camp Hill	8,203	4	0	0	1	3	73	0	73	0	1
Carlisle	20,237	45	2	9	4	30	284	12	265	7	2
Carroll Valley	4,485	3	0	2	0	1	22	1	21	0	0
Conemaugh Township, Cambria County	1,913	1	0	0	0	1	7	3	3	1	0
Coraopolis	5,405	16	0	0	1	15	54	3	49	2	0
Cranberry Township	34,468	6	0	2	1	3	305	8	293	4	0
Crescent Township	2,438	1	0	0	0	1	8	0	8	0	0
Danville	4,185	5	1	0	0	4	32	1	28	3	0
Derry Township, Dauphin County	24,896	32	0	7	4	21	253	16	225	12	1
Donora	4,504	2	0	1	0	1	23	5	18	0	0
East Earl Township	8,142	3	0	1	0	2	52	3	45	4	0
Eastern Pike Regional	5,160	12	0	2	1	9	160	6	149	5	0
East Lampeter Township	26,642	44	0	5	2	37	477	20	444	13	1
East Pennsboro Township	21,146	15	0	8	1	6	111	7	99	5	0
Elizabeth Township	12,643	12	0	5	2	5	75	13	58	4	2
Erie	93,363	567	5	49	86	427	2,114	280	1,719	115	20
Etna	3,345	2	0	0	0	2	23	4	15	4	0
Fairview Township, York County	17,772	22	0	3	0	19	148	8	133	7	0
Forest Hills	6,257	2	0	0	0	2	47	3	36	8	0
Foster Township, Schuylkill County	247	0	0	0	0	0	2	0	2	0	0
Green Tree	4,809	1	0	0	0	1	27	1	23	3	0
Hampden Township	34,244	16	0	10	0	6	98	6	84	8	2
Hatboro	8,228	4	0	2	1	1	55	9	43	3	0
Hawley	1,226	0	0	0	0	0	7	0	7	0	0
Hellam Township	10,910	17	0	5	0	12	76	7	61	8	0
Hooversville	616	0	0	0	0	0	1	1	0	0	0
Jamestown	572	0	0	0	0	0	5	0	5	0	0
Jeannette	8,636	65	1	1	4	59	30	5	25	0	0
Jenkins Township	4,389	1	0	1	0	0	40	1	37	2	0
Kingston	14,232	12	1	0	2	9	207	16	182	9	0
Kingston Township	7,110	2	0	0	0	2	22	0	21	1	0
Kline Township	1,486	0	0	0	0	0	22	2	19	1	0
Latrobe	7,934	39	0	3	1	35	64	8	55	1	1
Lehigh Township	1,878	0	0	0	0	0	14	0	13	1	0
Ligonier Valley Regional	7,635	3	0	0	0	3	61	6	55	0	0
Limerick Township	20,764	13	0	7	0	6	267	16	249	2	0
Mahanoy Township	3,047	0	0	0	0	0	11	3	8	0	0
Mahoning Township, Montour County	4,588	7	1	0	0	6	13	1	8	4	0
Marlborough Township	3,522	0	0	0	0	0	11	0	11	0	0
McDonald Borough	7,527	5	0	1	0	4	30	4	23	3	0
Mifflinburg	3,394	2	0	0	0	2	26	6	20	0	0
Montgomery Township	26,158	14	0	1	3	10	370	15	345	10	0
Mount Lebanon	33,188	14	0	4	3	7	112	11	97	4	0
Narberth	4,492	6	0	0	1	5	60	4	54	2	0
New Cumberland	7,588	5	1	1	1	2	58	1	55	2	0

Table 8. Offenses Known to Law Enforcement, by Selected State and City, 2022—Continued

(Number.)

State/city	Population	Violent crime	Murder and nonnegligent manslaughter	Rape	Robbery	Aggravated assault	Property crime	Burglary	Larceny-theft	Motor vehicle theft	Arson[1]
Norristown	35,888	162	9	6	66	81	722	69	474	179	2
North Strabane Township	16,162	19	0	6	1	12	38	5	30	3	1
Osceola Township	583	0	0	0	0	0	0	0	0	0	0
Palmyra	7,714	6	0	0	0	6	64	2	61	1	0
Penbrook	3,254	11	0	2	3	6	49	9	29	11	0
Penn	430	0	0	0	0	0	0	0	0	0	0
Philadelphia	1,555,812	16,202	514	785	5,763	9,140	67,233	6,485	48,067	12,681	528
Plymouth	5,747	59	0	2	5	52	116	14	88	14	0
Plymouth Township, Montgomery County	18,329	29	0	1	13	15	973	54	876	43	1
Point Marion	1,122	1	0	0	0	1	1	1	0	0	0
Ralpho Township	4,184	1	0	0	0	1	36	6	30	0	0
Rockledge	2,619	5	0	0	4	1	54	2	41	11	0
Rockwood	837	0	0	0	0	0	0	0	0	0	0
Ross Township	32,854	15	0	6	4	5	551	18	524	9	3
Rostraver Township	11,368	17	2	3	2	10	234	8	223	3	0
Saxton	716	2	0	1	0	1	27	5	21	1	0
Scottdale	4,349	8	0	0	0	8	42	5	35	2	0
Scranton	75,798	310	1	111	34	164	1,281	134	1,059	88	13
Shaler Township	27,427	8	0	1	3	4	174	17	150	7	0
Shamokin	6,874	13	1	2	3	7	56	15	41	0	2
Shamokin Dam	1,626	9	0	1	0	8	8	0	8	0	0
Sharpsburg	3,099	3	0	0	1	2	27	1	22	4	0
Shippensburg	5,521	7	0	1	0	6	71	4	65	2	1
Silver Spring Township	20,806	12	0	3	0	9	154	11	137	6	0
South Londonderry Township	8,833	2	0	0	0	2	31	1	28	2	1
South Pymatuning Township	2,619	2	0	0	0	2	9	1	7	1	0
Springfield Township, Montgomery County	20,839	10	0	0	5	5	204	15	180	9	0
St. Marys City	12,602	14	3	9	0	2	102	13	89	0	1
Sunbury	9,624	16	5	5	1	5	54	17	37	0	1
Trafford	3,259	2	0	0	0	2	44	2	35	7	0
Tunkhannock	1,757	6	0	2	0	4	9	0	8	1	0
Upper Allen Township	23,290	12	0	4	3	5	90	5	77	8	0
Upper Providence Township, Montgomery County	24,741	17	0	6	3	8	353	8	333	12	0
Washington Township, Franklin County	15,104	4	0	0	0	4	199	12	182	5	1
Washington Township, Westmoreland County	6,818	5	0	0	0	5	12	0	12	0	0
Waynesboro	10,925	27	3	5	3	16	134	19	108	7	0
West Conshohocken	1,502	4	0	1	1	2	41	2	36	3	0
Westfield	1,108	0	0	0	0	0	33	1	32	0	0
West Mifflin	19,122	8	0	0	4	4	63	4	57	2	0
West Pike Run	1,914	1	0	0	0	1	2	0	2	0	0
West Shore Regional	7,783	7	0	2	1	4	57	13	42	2	0
Wilkes-Barre	44,497	177	1	17	27	132	717	85	580	52	10
Wilson	8,192	12	0	2	6	4	117	8	101	8	0
York	44,901	319	15	22	78	204	1,149	134	820	195	10
York County Regional	12,612	118	0	11	9	98	467	39	383	45	1
RHODE ISLAND											
Barrington	17,364	8	0	4	0	4	97	13	78	6	1
Bristol	22,220	12	0	0	0	12	67	6	57	4	1
Burrillville	16,246	10	0	7	0	3	55	12	41	2	0
Central Falls	22,340	90	0	15	10	65	266	22	192	52	1
Charlestown	8,117	6	1	3	0	2	38	4	34	0	0
Coventry	35,730	26	0	14	1	11	355	33	301	21	0
Cranston	82,205	98	0	27	12	59	950	189	695	66	3
Cumberland	36,345	21	1	14	0	6	202	50	133	19	2
East Greenwich	14,260	9	0	4	0	5	80	8	68	4	0
East Providence	46,655	31	0	10	4	17	391	50	295	46	4
Foster	4,454	7	0	1	0	6	15	2	12	1	1
Glocester	10,147	4	0	0	0	4	20	1	11	8	0
Hopkinton	8,486	4	0	1	0	3	26	4	20	2	0
Jamestown	5,545	1	0	0	0	1	23	5	16	2	0
Johnston	29,430	31	0	7	3	21	368	47	276	45	4
Lincoln	22,400	29	0	9	7	13	233	21	184	28	2
Little Compton	3,599	0	0	0	0	0	9	4	5	0	0
Middletown	16,898	22	0	10	1	11	119	11	104	4	0
Narragansett	14,653	9	0	5	0	4	64	9	49	6	0
Newport	25,039	57	1	22	4	30	394	57	317	20	9
New Shoreham	1,423	1	0	0	1	0	10	1	9	0	0
North Kingstown	28,008	32	0	14	4	14	168	18	143	7	1
North Providence	33,809	39	1	5	4	29	320	30	230	60	2
North Smithfield	12,538	10	0	6	0	4	117	8	103	6	1
Pawtucket	74,967	215	3	36	35	141	1,689	152	1,304	233	9
Portsmouth	17,716	3	0	2	0	1	62	12	47	3	1
Providence	189,064	643	7	65	136	435	4,786	385	3,687	714	7
Richmond	8,243	3	0	2	0	1	22	2	18	2	1
Scituate	10,385	1	0	1	0	0	17	3	14	0	1
Smithfield	21,762	9	0	8	0	1	113	7	98	8	0
South Kingstown	32,046	15	0	12	0	3	138	11	117	10	2

Table 8. Offenses Known to Law Enforcement, by Selected State and City, 2022—Continued

(Number.)

State/city	Population	Violent crime	Murder and nonnegligent manslaughter	Rape	Robbery	Aggravated assault	Property crime	Burglary	Larceny-theft	Motor vehicle theft	Arson[1]
Tiverton	16,244	11	0	5	0	6	139	11	109	19	2
Warren	11,243	24	0	2	2	20	86	20	59	7	0
Warwick	82,966	63	0	19	6	38	1,167	82	990	95	8
Westerly	23,563	16	0	7	1	8	209	32	158	19	0
West Greenwich	6,727	2	0	0	0	2	34	3	28	3	0
West Warwick	31,227	49	0	15	7	27	217	39	144	34	4
Woonsocket	42,925	193	0	24	26	143	767	128	518	121	9
SOUTH CAROLINA											
Abbeville	4,868	28	3	2	0	23	94	11	76	7	1
Aiken	31,985	190	2	19	13	156	1,113	80	971	62	2
Allendale	2,626	33	2	2	0	29	69	18	47	4	0
Anderson	29,398	181	2	11	14	154	1,728	242	1,353	133	15
Aynor	1,048	2	0	0	1	1	14	2	10	2	0
Bamberg	3,019	34	1	2	4	27	84	5	70	9	0
Barnwell	4,468	55	3	8	2	42	169	34	119	16	1
Batesburg-Leesville	5,249	38	0	4	1	33	190	21	158	11	0
Beaufort	13,003	43	0	3	6	34	396	39	344	13	2
Belton	4,463	10	0	1	0	9	250	150	91	9	0
Bennettsville	6,891	88	2	3	5	78	221	32	177	12	1
Bishopville	2,899	23	2	0	0	21	112	36	73	3	2
Blacksburg	1,886	7	0	1	1	5	46	13	30	3	0
Blackville	1,952	10	0	1	2	7	27	9	15	3	1
Bluffton	36,064	25	1	3	4	17	211	30	160	21	2
Bowman	766	9	2	0	1	6	9	2	6	1	0
Branchville	966	1	0	0	0	1	17	3	13	1	0
Burnettown	3,181	6	0	0	0	6	17	4	11	2	0
Calhoun Falls	1,726	11	0	0	1	10	40	10	25	5	2
Camden	8,044	88	1	3	1	83	394	38	338	18	1
Cameron	371	0	0	0	0	0	4	2	2	0	0
Cayce	13,710	138	3	4	6	125	549	87	399	63	3
Central	5,335	1	0	0	1	0	95	3	83	9	0
Chapin	1,876	7	1	1	1	4	32	2	30	0	0
Charleston	152,324	571	8	54	73	436	2,878	229	2,146	503	8
Cheraw	4,920	57	1	2	6	48	301	49	236	16	2
Chesnee	866	0	0	0	0	0	37	6	25	6	0
Chester	5,222	134	2	5	2	125	154	37	107	10	1
Chesterfield	1,326	11	0	1	0	10	33	2	30	1	0
Clemson	18,174	41	0	10	5	26	354	20	295	39	0
Clinton	7,663	92	0	5	12	75	303	52	233	18	3
Clio	600	5	0	1	0	4	9	4	3	2	0
Clover	7,153	8	0	2	2	4	88	6	78	4	0
Columbia	137,768	825	13	45	100	667	3,934	495	3,011	428	15
Conway	23,664	162	5	11	11	135	643	35	548	60	2
Cottageville	700	1	0	0	0	1	26	4	21	1	0
Coward	746	0	0	0	0	0	0	0	0	0	0
Cowpens	2,104	4	0	1	1	2	60	9	44	7	0
Darlington	6,051	85	7	3	8	67	422	62	322	38	0
Dillon	6,213	159	2	3	8	146	498	81	386	31	4
Due West	1,197	1	0	1	0	0	3	0	3	0	0
Duncan	4,241	11	0	0	1	10	67	4	52	11	0
Easley	23,786	85	1	5	6	73	634	50	553	31	1
Edgefield	2,416	2	1	0	0	1	18	5	11	2	1
Edisto Beach	1,024	1	0	0	0	1	31	2	29	0	0
Elgin	1,603	5	0	1	0	4	77	3	73	1	0
Elloree	553	2	0	0	1	1	11	2	8	1	0
Estill	1,790	44	0	0	2	42	54	8	38	8	0
Eutawville	235	2	0	0	0	2	26	3	22	1	0
Florence	39,997	520	21	19	49	431	2,227	203	1,900	124	8
Forest Acres	10,514	35	1	5	3	26	381	41	310	30	0
Fort Mill	31,023	21	0	2	1	18	230	23	186	21	2
Fountain Inn	11,523	52	1	2	3	46	206	46	146	14	0
Gaffney	12,291	44	1	9	3	31	519	60	407	52	2
Gaston	1,629	4	0	2	0	2	67	8	51	8	0
Georgetown	8,323	147	1	7	8	131	407	49	335	23	3
Goose Creek	46,665	130	2	14	11	103	835	121	621	93	5
Great Falls	1,935	14	0	0	2	12	73	15	52	6	0
Greenville	73,311	397	4	24	55	314	2,696	274	2,156	266	5
Greenwood	22,145	182	58	18	19	87	898	169	689	40	8
Greer	42,196	107	0	9	12	86	850	93	688	69	1
Hampton	2,727	13	0	2	2	9	110	29	71	10	1
Hanahan	22,320	88	0	18	9	61	323	39	250	34	2
Hardeeville	9,995	24	0	2	6	16	253	32	206	15	0
Hartsville	7,614	133	1	4	15	113	528	73	435	20	1
Hemingway	489	3	0	0	2	1	33	3	30	0	0
Holly Hill	1,254	14	0	0	0	14	44	4	33	7	0
Honea Path	3,793	10	0	1	0	9	63	3	50	10	0
Inman	3,111	11	0	0	2	9	45	2	38	5	0
Irmo	11,937	55	1	6	8	40	396	59	317	20	2
Isle of Palms	4,284	12	0	1	0	11	55	6	45	4	0
Iva	1,154	9	0	0	0	9	66	13	45	8	0
Jamestown	71	1	0	0	1	0	3	1	2	0	0
Johnsonville	1,358	2	0	1	0	1	18	5	11	2	0

Table 8. Offenses Known to Law Enforcement, by Selected State and City, 2022—Continued

(Number.)

State/city	Population	Violent crime	Murder and nonnegligent manslaughter	Rape	Robbery	Aggravated assault	Property crime	Burglary	Larceny-theft	Motor vehicle theft	Arson[1]
Johnston	2,081	5	0	1	1	3	45	9	32	4	0
Jonesville	832	6	0	2	1	3	17	5	10	2	0
Kingstree	3,122	24	0	1	1	22	118	13	92	13	0
Lake City	5,946	123	2	7	6	108	223	52	150	21	2
Landrum	2,587	9	0	1	2	6	47	8	34	5	0
Lane	473	0	0	0	0	0	1	0	1	0	0
Latta	1,270	7	0	0	0	7	45	5	36	4	0
Laurens	9,307	58	0	5	2	51	285	32	238	15	0
Lexington	24,880	60	3	6	3	48	409	34	351	24	0
Liberty	3,310	8	0	3	0	5	76	7	56	13	2
Loris	2,676	14	0	0	0	14	64	5	56	3	0
Lyman	6,437	17	0	0	1	16	53	6	43	4	0
Manning	3,830	48	0	2	2	44	278	46	225	7	0
Marion	6,232	63	5	0	6	52	337	63	260	14	0
Mauldin	26,576	78	1	15	12	50	498	67	375	56	3
McBee	760	0	0	0	0	0	0	0	0	0	0
McColl	2,051	32	0	2	1	29	70	23	43	4	2
McCormick	2,252	1	0	0	0	1	47	8	35	4	0
Moncks Corner	13,906	86	1	4	6	75	392	49	309	34	1
Mount Pleasant	93,951	119	0	17	12	90	1,332	129	1,016	187	3
Mullins	3,884	36	2	3	5	26	160	53	97	10	3
Myrtle Beach	38,117	386	6	68	65	247	2,553	218	2,138	197	7
Newberry	10,507	68	5	8	3	52	291	38	241	12	4
Ninety Six	2,074	5	0	1	0	4	25	2	23	0	0
North	680	0	0	0	0	0	36	6	28	2	0
North Augusta	24,957	42	4	8	13	17	570	61	476	33	1
North Charleston	119,198	1,123	33	83	228	779	5,728	565	4,455	708	24
North Myrtle Beach	19,888	89	2	11	12	64	864	75	733	56	1
Olanta	538	0	0	0	0	0	0	0	0	0	0
Orangeburg	12,307	209	10	12	28	159	755	203	522	30	10
Pacolet	2,375	10	0	1	1	8	25	4	19	2	0
Pageland	2,436	50	0	1	2	47	112	21	84	7	0
Pamplico	1,046	14	1	4	3	6	35	10	23	2	0
Pelion	622	4	0	1	0	3	26	4	21	1	0
Pendleton	3,608	15	0	2	0	13	96	19	66	11	0
Pickens	3,365	20	0	2	0	18	120	3	113	4	0
Pine Ridge	2,267	1	0	0	1	0	16	4	10	2	0
Port Royal	13,430	35	0	5	5	25	168	16	136	16	0
Quinby	904	0	0	0	0	0	1	0	1	0	0
Ridgeland	3,680	3	1	0	0	2	47	9	38	0	0
Ridge Spring	577	11	0	2	0	9	5	0	3	2	0
Ridgeville	1,539	0	0	0	0	0	0	0	0	0	0
Rock Hill	74,047	355	8	25	22	300	1,984	194	1,627	163	8
Salem	121	0	0	0	0	0	3	0	3	0	0
Saluda	3,025	13	0	4	0	9	31	5	25	1	0
Santee	780	17	0	1	2	14	73	14	54	5	0
Seneca	8,964	59	0	8	4	47	192	30	144	18	0
Simpsonville	25,847	81	0	10	8	63	949	87	820	42	3
South Congaree	2,391	17	0	3	0	14	89	16	66	7	1
Spartanburg	38,271	457	2	39	42	374	2,247	391	1,665	191	19
Springdale	2,749	28	1	1	1	25	66	9	41	16	1
Springfield	438	1	0	0	0	1	16	7	8	1	0
St. George	1,774	12	0	1	0	11	76	17	48	11	0
St. Stephen	1,533	11	0	1	1	9	77	12	58	7	0
Sullivan's Island	1,870	0	0	0	0	0	18	4	14	0	0
Summerton	793	6	0	0	1	5	47	5	39	3	0
Summerville	51,423	188	2	28	23	135	1,378	118	1,106	154	7
Sumter	42,613	376	6	10	24	336	1,372	181	1,076	115	5
Surfside Beach	4,301	10	0	2	2	6	152	12	125	15	0
Swansea	737	8	0	0	1	7	84	4	78	2	0
Tega Cay	13,607	6	0	1	0	5	141	11	129	1	0
Timmonsville	2,085	41	0	0	3	38	77	13	53	11	1
Travelers Rest	7,836	1	0	0	0	1	219	16	194	9	0
Union	7,977	87	0	6	8	73	431	66	333	32	0
Walhalla	4,121	11	1	1	2	7	61	8	48	5	1
Walterboro	5,432	52	1	2	5	44	397	30	348	19	3
Wellford	3,478	3	0	3	0	0	30	0	22	8	0
West Columbia	17,581	129	2	5	19	103	971	93	799	79	1
Westminster	2,374	13	0	1	1	11	95	23	68	4	3
Whitmire	1,418	5	0	0	0	5	52	3	48	1	0
Williamston	4,172	26	0	0	3	23	116	9	95	12	0
Williston	2,882	16	4	1	2	9	130	26	96	8	0
Winnsboro	3,126	12	1	0	0	11	73	19	49	5	0
Woodruff	4,372	21	0	0	4	17	138	63	64	11	2
Yemassee	1,149	13	0	0	2	11	37	3	25	9	0
York	8,699	60	1	3	7	49	342	44	281	17	0
SOUTH DAKOTA											
Aberdeen	28,206	103	0	27	2	74	441	83	325	33	5
Belle Fourche	5,799	7	0	0	0	7	74	5	66	3	0
Beresford	2,112	2	0	0	0	2	34	9	21	4	0
Box Elder	12,710	51	1	15	2	33	184	23	132	29	1
Brandon	10,914	6	0	0	0	6	67	11	49	7	1

Table 8. Offenses Known to Law Enforcement, by Selected State and City, 2022—Continued

(Number.)

State/city	Population	Violent crime	Murder and nonnegligent manslaughter	Rape	Robbery	Aggravated assault	Property crime	Burglary	Larceny-theft	Motor vehicle theft	Arson[1]
Brookings	23,725	42	0	12	1	29	311	29	270	12	0
Canton	3,033	12	0	7	0	5	34	5	27	2	0
Chamberlain	2,451	12	0	0	0	12	78	10	63	5	0
Deadwood	1,255	11	0	0	0	11	40	1	38	1	0
Flandreau	2,338	6	0	0	0	6	34	10	22	2	0
Hot Springs	3,605	10	0	0	0	10	6	0	6	0	0
Madison	5,967	8	0	4	0	4	40	5	33	2	0
Martin	957	9	0	3	0	6	42	6	32	4	0
Mitchell	15,579	51	0	14	1	36	387	24	318	45	4
Mobridge	3,154	4	0	0	0	4	20	2	16	2	1
North Sioux City	2,987	9	0	0	0	9	51	2	44	5	0
Pierre	13,977	69	1	20	5	43	248	30	200	18	0
Rapid City	78,063	532	5	97	65	365	2,799	475	1,921	403	3
Sioux Falls	199,879	1,092	7	75	140	870	6,162	738	4,345	1,079	35
Sisseton	2,389	10	0	1	0	9	2	0	2	0	0
Spearfish	12,517	31	1	16	1	13	296	26	252	18	0
Sturgis	7,121	31	0	4	1	26	187	59	113	15	0
Tea	6,894	14	0	1	0	13	96	13	64	19	0
Wagner	1,425	1	1	0	0	0	1	1	0	0	0
Watertown	22,832	50	0	21	1	28	356	68	257	31	0
Yankton	15,507	62	1	15	0	46	402	29	353	20	1
TENNESSEE											
Adamsville	2,244	15	0	2	1	12	30	10	18	2	0
Alamo	2,335	7	0	0	1	6	25	5	17	3	1
Alcoa	11,689	47	1	8	3	35	246	23	189	34	0
Algood	4,012	11	0	0	0	11	60	3	50	7	0
Ashland City	5,152	23	0	0	1	22	130	16	100	14	1
Athens	14,409	114	0	9	7	98	803	125	602	76	2
Atoka	10,345	21	0	1	1	19	50	9	38	3	0
Bartlett	56,928	137	1	17	16	103	1,111	86	900	125	6
Baxter	1,677	1	0	0	0	1	25	4	17	4	0
Belle Meade	2,593	0	0	0	0	0	24	5	17	2	0
Bells	2,501	15	0	3	0	12	21	4	15	2	2
Benton	1,506	4	0	1	0	3	35	1	32	2	0
Berry Hill	1,865	3	0	0	1	2	85	9	73	3	0
Big Sandy	484	0	0	0	0	0	2	1	1	0	0
Blaine	2,103	6	0	1	0	5	21	1	15	5	0
Bluff City	1,820	7	0	0	0	7	21	3	11	7	0
Bolivar	5,127	98	3	2	1	92	88	29	50	9	0
Brentwood	45,581	31	2	10	2	17	384	43	320	21	0
Brighton	2,858	10	0	1	0	9	17	3	11	3	0
Bristol	27,862	140	0	16	4	120	640	85	479	76	2
Brownsville	9,578	120	2	4	5	109	228	45	159	24	0
Bruceton	1,496	2	0	0	0	2	21	1	16	4	0
Camden	3,711	10	0	0	1	9	59	6	51	2	0
Carthage	2,276	5	0	0	0	5	112	8	103	1	0
Caryville	2,179	12	0	1	0	11	38	5	27	6	0
Centerville	3,569	7	0	0	0	7	45	10	30	5	1
Chapel Hill	1,780	5	0	1	1	3	16	0	15	1	0
Charleston	678	1	0	0	1	0	6	3	3	0	0
Chattanooga	182,603	2,077	24	166	218	1,669	9,534	1,066	7,108	1,360	23
Church Hill	7,105	21	0	1	0	20	25	4	19	2	4
Clarksville	174,738	871	11	93	68	699	3,493	514	2,537	442	9
Cleveland	48,579	352	1	17	26	308	1,650	172	1,336	142	5
Clinton	10,050	48	0	3	4	41	232	25	182	25	3
Collegedale	12,032	12	0	2	1	9	184	5	170	9	0
Collierville	51,439	76	0	9	9	58	611	50	533	28	1
Columbia	44,852	306	2	17	24	263	940	121	708	111	6
Cookeville	35,771	88	2	7	8	71	834	96	652	86	2
Coopertown	4,702	3	0	0	0	3	37	9	26	2	0
Cornersville	1,267	2	0	0	0	2	11	7	3	1	0
Covington	8,582	92	2	4	7	79	169	29	116	24	0
Cowan	1,779	10	0	1	0	9	22	1	19	2	0
Crossville	12,487	87	1	10	3	73	438	73	345	20	3
Dandridge	3,475	17	0	1	1	15	60	6	52	2	0
Dayton	7,170	17	0	1	0	16	153	23	114	16	0
Decatur	1,646	24	0	3	0	21	44	2	38	4	0
Decherd	2,369	13	0	1	0	12	40	4	28	8	0
Dickson	16,154	118	1	11	1	105	384	26	316	42	0
Dover	1,768	1	0	0	0	1	4	0	2	2	0
Dresden	3,026	4	0	1	0	3	37	8	28	1	0
Dunlap	5,644	20	0	0	1	19	100	11	69	20	0
Dyer	2,312	4	1	0	0	3	24	2	22	0	0
Dyersburg	15,988	183	4	14	6	159	801	176	572	53	3
East Ridge	21,790	132	1	11	8	112	477	63	341	73	4
Elizabethton	13,868	42	1	0	0	41	269	26	229	14	1
Englewood	1,519	3	0	0	0	3	18	3	12	3	0
Erin	1,209	2	0	0	0	2	5	1	4	0	0
Erwin	5,931	3	0	0	0	3	33	5	22	6	0
Estill Springs	2,266	13	0	0	1	12	25	6	17	2	0
Etowah	3,668	15	0	2	0	13	50	1	43	6	0
Fairview	9,844	18	1	3	1	13	50	7	37	6	0

Table 8. Offenses Known to Law Enforcement, by Selected State and City, 2022—Continued

(Number.)

State/city	Population	Violent crime	Murder and nonnegligent manslaughter	Rape	Robbery	Aggravated assault	Property crime	Burglary	Larceny-theft	Motor vehicle theft	Arson[1]
Fayetteville	6,942	85	3	4	3	75	202	25	161	16	0
Franklin	87,081	170	0	19	9	142	899	101	733	65	0
Gallatin	49,220	125	0	12	10	103	331	35	267	29	1
Gallaway	502	4	0	0	0	4	11	0	10	1	0
Gatlinburg	3,873	18	1	4	2	11	127	20	94	13	0
Germantown	40,859	69	0	4	6	59	625	28	527	70	2
Gleason	1,407	2	0	0	0	2	24	6	17	1	0
Goodlettsville	16,963	43	0	3	10	30	317	35	232	50	0
Greenbrier	6,963	38	1	3	1	33	36	13	16	7	1
Greeneville	15,556	55	2	7	2	44	481	57	365	59	1
Greenfield	2,083	8	0	0	0	8	21	7	11	3	0
Halls	2,076	12	0	1	1	10	47	8	33	6	0
Harriman	5,984	6	0	1	0	5	99	12	76	11	0
Henderson	6,372	29	0	1	1	27	67	11	48	8	0
Hendersonville	62,475	85	3	2	3	77	522	38	446	38	3
Hohenwald	3,882	8	0	0	0	8	71	4	61	6	0
Humboldt	7,831	74	0	7	3	64	143	36	96	11	3
Huntingdon	4,432	9	0	0	0	9	51	1	47	3	1
Jacksboro	2,313	2	0	0	0	2	53	2	48	3	1
Jackson	68,059	612	9	28	55	520	1,973	249	1,525	199	7
Jamestown	1,920	11	0	2	0	9	51	11	39	1	0
Jasper	3,626	9	0	0	1	8	38	4	24	10	0
Jefferson City	8,319	23	0	0	2	21	153	31	111	11	1
Jellico	2,131	8	0	0	0	8	33	4	20	9	1
Johnson City	71,987	270	3	55	24	188	2,461	229	2,048	184	18
Jonesborough	6,081	5	0	1	0	4	90	7	70	13	2
Kenton	1,184	6	1	1	0	4	14	1	11	2	0
Kimball	1,578	13	0	0	1	12	60	4	52	4	0
Kingsport	55,799	439	2	42	28	367	2,271	255	1,706	310	11
Kingston	6,067	3	0	0	0	3	47	5	37	5	0
Knoxville	194,724	1,640	32	151	179	1,278	7,609	874	5,780	955	4
Lafayette	5,650	19	0	3	0	16	160	12	139	9	0
La Follette	7,271	24	0	0	0	24	110	22	69	19	1
La Vergne	39,424	150	1	12	16	121	557	35	435	87	1
Lawrenceburg	11,874	48	0	3	3	42	272	50	205	17	0
Lebanon	43,321	196	1	23	14	158	712	105	536	71	2
Lenoir City	10,597	41	0	1	2	38	254	17	224	13	0
Lewisburg	12,659	67	1	8	2	56	255	39	191	25	4
Lexington	7,944	24	1	2	0	21	184	29	134	21	1
Livingston	4,047	12	0	1	0	11	55	4	43	8	0
Loretto	1,783	2	0	0	0	2	15	6	6	3	0
Loudon	6,479	1	0	1	0	0	32	9	22	1	0
Madisonville	5,118	26	0	1	0	25	160	17	133	10	1
Manchester	13,045	71	0	5	5	61	327	67	236	24	1
Martin	10,562	48	1	0	5	42	241	39	193	9	0
Maryville	32,717	60	1	12	0	47	291	40	229	22	2
Maynardville	2,507	6	0	0	0	6	21	0	20	1	0
McEwen	1,735	1	0	0	0	1	12	6	6	0	0
McKenzie	5,451	21	0	2	0	19	99	30	63	6	0
McMinnville	13,952	70	0	16	4	50	307	35	253	19	1
Medina	5,338	6	0	1	0	5	28	5	19	4	0
Memphis	624,944	15,129	269	397	2,324	12,139	44,783	6,022	27,837	10,924	329
Metropolitan Nashville Police Department	679,562	7,491	83	385	1,224	5,799	25,991	3,470	19,534	2,987	88
Milan	8,167	41	0	2	0	39	184	49	121	14	1
Millersville	6,239	18	0	2	0	16	33	3	25	5	1
Millington	10,461	78	0	2	8	68	429	96	295	38	0
Monteagle	1,375	4	0	0	0	4	36	11	22	3	0
Monterey	2,750	3	0	0	0	3	35	9	17	9	0
Morristown	30,988	223	0	15	14	194	1,141	132	851	158	6
Mosheim	2,488	8	0	1	0	7	59	10	39	10	0
Mountain City	2,467	15	0	0	0	15	41	7	30	4	0
Mount Carmel	5,522	11	0	1	0	10	58	11	37	10	0
Mount Pleasant	4,871	30	0	4	1	25	68	12	44	12	1
Munford	6,466	10	0	3	0	7	73	13	51	9	1
Murfreesboro	161,810	827	9	114	59	645	3,415	291	2,762	362	6
Newbern	3,296	14	0	2	1	11	61	6	53	2	1
New Johnsonville	1,851	5	0	1	0	4	7	0	6	1	0
New Market	1,369	2	0	0	0	2	2	0	2	0	0
Newport	6,972	31	0	4	1	26	397	26	342	29	0
New Tazewell	2,802	6	1	0	0	5	39	6	31	2	0
Nolensville	16,990	15	0	2	1	12	56	8	45	3	0
Oakland	10,004	10	2	0	0	8	23	3	17	3	0
Oak Ridge	32,243	102	1	14	3	84	572	52	481	39	2
Oliver Springs	3,305	7	1	0	0	6	34	9	19	6	0
Oneida	3,793	23	0	2	0	21	111	8	95	8	0
Paris	10,371	37	1	0	1	35	272	35	224	13	0
Parsons	2,074	3	0	0	0	3	29	6	21	2	0
Pigeon Forge	6,340	52	0	10	5	37	250	29	191	30	2
Pikeville	1,889	4	0	0	0	4	28	5	22	1	0
Pleasant View	5,379	15	0	0	4	11	55	2	44	9	0
Portland	13,460	35	0	4	2	29	103	24	68	11	3
Pulaski	8,240	37	1	7	1	28	249	29	196	24	5

Table 8. Offenses Known to Law Enforcement, by Selected State and City, 2022—Continued

(Number.)

State/city	Population	Violent crime	Murder and nonnegligent manslaughter	Rape	Robbery	Aggravated assault	Property crime	Burglary	Larceny-theft	Motor vehicle theft	Arson[1]
Red Bank	11,862	48	1	1	4	42	96	21	60	15	0
Ripley	7,772	158	4	2	5	147	211	53	143	15	2
Rockwood	5,571	41	0	4	3	34	257	37	198	22	3
Rocky Top	3,594	14	0	1	0	13	66	8	48	10	3
Rogersville	4,665	16	0	2	1	13	127	24	94	9	0
Savannah	7,207	39	0	1	0	38	273	50	203	20	0
Selmer	4,419	25	0	1	1	23	110	10	86	14	1
Sevierville	19,021	125	2	15	3	105	706	40	620	46	0
Shelbyville	24,160	136	2	24	4	106	484	81	334	69	1
Signal Mountain	8,824	1	0	0	0	1	27	1	24	2	0
Smithville	5,242	20	1	1	0	18	114	18	87	9	0
Smyrna	57,595	153	2	17	12	122	1,092	69	888	135	2
Soddy-Daisy	13,112	27	1	1	0	25	199	30	153	16	0
Somerville	3,470	22	0	1	1	20	46	10	32	4	0
South Fulton	2,178	13	0	0	0	13	30	8	19	3	0
South Pittsburg	3,065	6	0	0	0	5	14	4	8	2	0
Sparta	4,993	5	1	0	0	4	116	18	88	10	0
Spencer	1,592	0	0	0	0	0	1	0	1	0	0
Springfield	19,330	97	1	4	3	89	231	16	182	33	0
Spring Hill	56,232	59	2	10	3	44	460	32	402	26	2
Sweetwater	6,345	33	1	1	2	29	145	15	111	19	2
Tazewell	2,360	14	0	1	0	13	54	9	39	6	0
Tiptonville	4,071	17	0	0	1	16	37	10	23	4	1
Townsend	598	0	0	0	0	0	8	2	6	0	0
Tracy City	1,424	6	0	1	1	4	32	0	24	8	2
Tullahoma	20,948	105	2	8	1	94	462	48	379	35	5
Unicoi	3,763	10	0	0	0	10	14	2	11	1	0
Union City	10,996	95	0	9	1	85	446	52	355	39	1
Vonore	1,600	16	0	0	1	15	50	8	40	2	0
Wartburg	897	1	0	0	0	1	14	1	11	2	0
Watertown	1,556	5	0	0	0	5	7	2	5	0	0
Waynesboro	2,353	14	0	1	1	12	24	1	19	4	0
Westmoreland	2,740	8	0	1	0	7	4	0	2	2	0
White Bluff	4,065	12	0	1	0	11	22	2	13	7	0
White House	14,290	23	0	5	0	18	205	23	169	13	0
White Pine	2,583	9	3	0	0	6	42	3	36	3	0
Whitwell	1,612	4	0	0	0	4	21	5	10	6	0
Winchester	9,703	56	0	3	2	51	255	37	203	15	3
Woodbury	2,713	2	0	0	0	2	18	1	17	0	1
TEXAS											
Abernathy	2,783	5	0	0	0	5	12	8	0	4	0
Abilene	125,186	587	7	107	82	391	2,498	446	1,854	198	10
Addison	17,531	83	1	15	12	55	1,424	115	1,074	235	2
Alamo	20,383	116	1	20	14	81	839	153	638	48	1
Alamo Heights	7,412	11	0	3	3	5	240	25	202	13	0
Alba	493	0	0	0	0	0	7	5	2	0	0
Alice	17,727	175	5	11	5	154	668	145	474	49	10
Alma	407	0	0	0	0	0	0	0	0	0	0
Alpine	5,757	8	0	1	0	7	10	3	7	0	2
Alton	19,391	95	0	1	6	88	210	32	157	21	1
Alvarado	5,504	31	0	5	2	24	75	3	59	13	1
Alvin	27,974	73	0	12	8	53	481	67	368	46	1
Amarillo	201,572	1,537	23	197	199	1,118	6,997	1,166	4,899	932	53
Andrews	13,233	65	1	4	0	60	192	22	154	16	1
Angleton	19,369	52	1	14	4	33	279	57	175	47	2
Anna	23,541	29	0	8	7	14	211	35	159	17	2
Anthony	3,662	9	0	2	3	4	40	0	30	10	0
Aransas Pass	8,056	45	3	7	4	31	244	53	166	25	0
Archer City	1,593	1	0	1	0	0	8	4	2	2	0
Arcola	2,260	11	0	2	3	6	24	7	12	5	0
Argyle	4,986	1	0	1	0	0	22	2	19	1	0
Arlington	391,591	2,272	16	336	276	1,644	9,886	1,024	7,625	1,237	18
Arp	953	0	0	0	0	0	12	4	7	1	0
Athens	12,986	44	1	7	2	34	225	36	160	29	1
Atlanta	5,443	13	1	4	1	7	80	14	56	10	0
Aubrey	7,873	15	0	4	2	9	84	23	54	7	0
Austin	965,234	5,215	69	528	939	3,679	34,650	4,816	24,481	5,353	149
Azle	13,615	39	1	12	5	21	310	35	246	29	0
Baird	1,529	0	0	0	0	0	12	6	5	1	0
Balch Springs	26,973	129	3	14	26	86	810	92	472	246	1
Balcones Heights	2,709	43	0	0	8	35	282	38	195	49	3
Ballinger	3,577	10	0	0	0	10	68	49	17	2	0
Bangs	1,541	3	0	0	0	3	2	1	0	1	0
Bastrop	11,101	51	0	5	5	41	331	16	277	38	5
Bay City	17,796	66	1	8	11	46	594	92	478	24	1
Baytown	81,477	358	2	58	68	230	3,182	438	2,225	519	1
Beaumont	110,898	1,198	18	105	257	818	4,305	971	2,973	361	25
Bedford	48,579	102	1	21	18	62	1,072	115	856	101	2
Bee Cave	8,870	12	0	2	0	10	158	20	123	15	0
Beeville	13,592	57	0	6	7	44	709	426	252	31	3
Bellaire	16,783	27	0	4	16	7	368	47	259	62	0
Bellmead	10,589	41	1	11	5	24	292	50	199	43	4

Table 8. Offenses Known to Law Enforcement, by Selected State and City, 2022—Continued

(Number.)

State/city	Population	Violent crime	Murder and nonnegligent manslaughter	Rape	Robbery	Aggravated assault	Property crime	Burglary	Larceny-theft	Motor vehicle theft	Arson[1]
Bells	1,557	1	0	0	0	1	2	1	0	1	0
Bellville	4,066	25	0	8	0	17	38	5	25	8	0
Belton	24,188	39	3	14	6	16	506	42	445	19	2
Benbrook	24,739	54	2	12	9	31	278	20	236	22	2
Bertram	1,913	3	0	0	0	3	10	3	5	2	0
Beverly Hills	1,867	14	0	3	0	11	57	16	33	8	1
Big Sandy	1,295	9	0	2	1	6	13	5	6	2	0
Big Spring	25,254	172	5	15	15	137	543	118	378	47	3
Blanco	1,870	9	0	2	0	7	19	3	13	3	0
Blue Mound	2,325	3	0	0	0	3	7	2	2	3	0
Boerne	20,488	22	0	6	1	15	311	89	177	45	0
Bogata	1,098	3	0	2	1	0	18	3	14	1	0
Borger	12,366	54	0	14	1	39	213	97	93	23	0
Bovina	1,706	3	0	0	0	3	5	2	3	0	0
Bowie	5,659	7	0	0	2	5	163	91	60	12	2
Brady	4,998	4	1	1	0	2	71	25	36	10	0
Brazoria	2,823	5	0	1	0	4	54	5	40	9	0
Breckenridge	5,294	15	0	1	2	12	69	17	43	9	2
Bremond	862	1	0	0	0	1	77	77	0	0	0
Brenham	18,785	69	0	9	0	60	277	42	203	32	0
Bridge City	9,495	7	0	2	1	4	68	10	48	10	0
Bridgeport	6,186	13	0	1	1	11	84	27	50	7	0
Brookshire	5,739	24	1	2	4	17	54	7	39	8	0
Brownfield	8,877	46	0	8	1	37	111	31	66	14	2
Brownsville	188,906	817	4	71	127	615	3,467	398	2,880	189	18
Brownwood	18,751	72	2	14	4	52	440	78	327	35	2
Bruceville-Eddy	1,428	3	0	1	0	2	18	10	6	2	0
Buda	16,000	33	0	2	3	28	353	28	279	46	2
Buffalo	1,812	5	1	0	0	4	30	10	19	1	0
Bullard	4,062	4	0	0	0	4	26	8	17	1	0
Bulverde	6,268	12	0	0	1	11	140	10	124	6	0
Burkburnett	11,057	21	1	11	0	9	52	14	32	6	1
Burleson	55,356	138	1	39	7	91	659	53	553	53	1
Burnet	6,861	23	1	2	0	20	62	11	44	7	0
Cactus	3,058	10	0	2	1	7	28	4	17	7	0
Caddo Mills	3,568	8	0	2	2	4	21	9	9	3	0
Caldwell	4,249	2	0	0	1	1	35	10	22	3	0
Calvert	965	4	0	2	0	2	19	9	9	1	0
Cameron	5,415	14	0	0	1	13	32	12	15	5	0
Canton	4,408	11	1	1	2	7	147	49	84	14	2
Canyon	15,680	26	0	2	2	22	125	23	97	5	3
Carrollton	133,610	276	3	44	49	180	2,219	271	1,734	214	2
Carthage	6,558	29	0	3	4	22	231	20	197	14	1
Castle Hills	3,921	20	3	0	5	12	249	44	163	42	1
Castroville	3,052	1	0	0	0	1	73	20	48	5	0
Cedar Hill	48,483	81	3	13	10	55	913	68	728	117	2
Cedar Park	79,353	85	1	33	7	44	1,049	86	886	77	0
Celina	24,190	19	0	4	1	14	214	21	190	3	3
Center	5,111	23	0	3	1	19	112	26	81	5	1
Chandler	3,529	2	0	1	0	1	21	4	16	1	0
Childress	5,915	11	0	3	0	8	38	22	11	5	2
China Grove	1,128	3	0	0	1	2	15	2	8	5	0
Cibolo	34,159	45	0	14	3	28	500	108	353	39	0
Cisco	3,902	7	0	3	0	4	55	21	29	5	0
Cleburne	32,728	60	2	22	4	32	345	61	265	19	2
Clifton	3,526	7	0	0	1	6	10	2	6	2	0
Clute	10,557	44	0	12	6	26	327	123	175	29	0
Clyde	4,038	5	0	1	1	3	33	15	16	2	0
Cockrell Hill	3,687	7	0	0	1	6	86	18	43	25	0
Coffee City	246	3	0	0	0	3	4	1	0	3	0
Coleman	3,943	6	0	2	1	3	20	6	9	5	0
College Station	121,618	248	1	89	16	142	2,342	251	1,905	186	0
Colleyville	25,897	15	0	9	0	6	113	10	100	3	0
Collinsville	1,993	4	0	0	0	4	0	0	0	0	0
Columbus	3,598	7	1	3	0	3	52	3	44	5	1
Comanche	4,276	10	0	2	0	8	80	13	59	8	4
Combes	3,071	8	0	2	0	6	38	7	22	9	0
Commerce	8,876	35	0	5	0	30	168	25	124	19	1
Conroe	98,623	314	3	59	35	217	2,001	225	1,561	215	3
Converse	29,503	111	1	6	5	99	492	122	323	47	1
Coppell	42,021	40	1	13	2	24	580	50	502	28	0
Copperas Cove	37,841	120	2	35	8	75	654	89	506	59	9
Corinth	22,719	19	0	4	1	14	179	9	148	22	0
Corpus Christi	317,694	2,512	41	240	355	1,876	9,915	1,593	7,478	844	84
Corrigan	1,487	0	0	0	0	0	24	4	13	7	0
Corsicana	25,585	157	6	26	11	114	536	64	422	50	7
Crandall	4,671	32	0	5	6	21	139	37	86	16	0
Crane	3,485	2	0	1	0	1	9	7	2	0	0
Crockett	6,428	28	0	6	7	15	205	31	153	21	0
Crowley	20,362	47	1	11	2	33	300	42	238	20	0
Cuero	8,271	54	1	0	2	51	114	14	91	9	0
Cuney	115	1	0	0	0	1	0	0	0	0	0
Daingerfield	2,520	11	1	0	1	9	41	7	30	4	0

Table 8. Offenses Known to Law Enforcement, by Selected State and City, 2022—Continued

(Number.)

State/city	Population	Violent crime	Murder and nonnegligent manslaughter	Rape	Robbery	Aggravated assault	Property crime	Burglary	Larceny-theft	Motor vehicle theft	Arson[1]
Dalhart	8,410	21	0	2	3	16	55	12	29	14	1
Dallas	1,286,121	10,009	157	492	2,134	7,226	49,037	6,787	28,878	13,372	186
Dayton	9,451	27	2	2	5	18	147	31	89	27	2
Decatur	7,147	31	0	5	5	21	204	5	188	11	1
Deer Park	33,022	37	0	10	3	24	512	62	409	41	0
De Leon	2,310	9	0	0	1	8	30	12	13	5	0
Del Rio	34,495	75	1	16	13	45	488	147	310	31	7
Denison	25,828	73	0	12	1	60	323	60	201	62	4
Denton	154,230	445	7	117	45	276	3,672	450	2,780	442	8
Denver City	4,346	7	0	0	0	7	20	11	9	0	1
DeSoto	55,956	168	4	19	32	113	1,130	119	772	239	3
Devine	4,483	3	0	0	1	2	84	6	70	8	1
Diboll	4,466	13	0	3	0	10	31	8	18	5	0
Dickinson	21,936	58	4	12	12	30	355	57	248	50	0
Dilley	3,318	3	0	0	1	2	17	9	3	5	0
Dimmitt	4,183	7	0	2	1	4	19	7	8	4	0
Donna	16,842	193	2	11	6	174	447	54	347	46	4
Double Oak	3,052	1	0	0	0	1	14	4	10	0	0
Driscoll	668	0	0	0	0	0	1	0	0	1	0
Dublin	3,469	2	1	0	0	1	17	13	2	2	0
Dumas	14,140	32	1	5	1	25	267	31	217	19	0
Duncanville	39,474	126	3	11	47	65	1,003	132	633	238	2
Eagle Pass	28,811	66	0	1	10	55	771	167	520	84	2
Early	3,161	14	1	0	0	13	21	4	16	1	0
Eastland	3,630	3	0	1	0	2	48	5	40	3	0
Edgewood	1,649	2	2	0	0	0	0	0	0	0	0
Edinburg	104,987	352	3	68	59	222	2,323	229	2,008	86	6
Edna	5,976	25	0	3	1	21	33	7	18	8	0
El Campo	12,235	74	1	12	0	61	477	49	403	25	4
Electra	2,286	3	0	2	0	1	25	0	21	4	0
Elgin	11,245	18	3	2	0	13	141	18	116	7	0
Elmendorf	2,202	3	0	0	0	3	23	4	12	7	0
El Paso	678,232	2,123	22	294	267	1,540	9,353	970	6,973	1,410	61
Elsa	5,683	29	1	2	2	24	254	45	200	9	0
Emory	1,359	0	0	0	0	0	8	1	6	1	0
Ennis	22,254	27	0	4	1	22	449	49	352	48	1
Euless	59,901	175	1	35	35	104	1,336	145	1,058	133	2
Everman	5,993	9	0	1	2	6	53	8	40	5	0
Fairfield	2,939	17	0	1	1	15	225	192	27	6	0
Fair Oaks Ranch	11,119	9	0	5	0	4	124	38	74	12	0
Fairview	10,917	5	0	0	0	5	68	3	61	4	0
Falfurrias	4,754	12	0	1	1	10	10	4	4	2	0
Farmers Branch	36,595	90	3	14	19	54	1,456	172	1,066	218	1
Farmersville	4,024	5	0	0	0	5	38	11	26	1	0
Farwell	1,383	0	0	0	0	0	4	0	3	1	0
Fate	23,955	16	0	10	0	6	101	6	89	6	1
Ferris	2,893	6	0	0	1	5	41	7	29	5	0
Flatonia	1,348	5	1	0	0	4	8	3	2	3	1
Florence	1,218	1	0	0	0	1	6	2	3	1	0
Floresville	7,971	16	0	3	1	12	134	38	73	23	1
Flower Mound	78,167	37	0	12	5	20	607	63	513	31	0
Floydada	2,638	12	0	1	1	10	30	7	14	9	0
Forest Hill	13,685	50	5	9	14	22	246	42	152	52	1
Forney	31,105	62	0	5	3	54	361	32	286	43	1
Fort Stockton	8,411	7	0	2	0	5	37	12	17	8	1
Fort Worth	948,605	4,765	100	591	689	3,385	25,989	3,993	18,439	3,557	112
Franklin	1,781	1	0	0	0	1	9	3	4	2	0
Frankston	1,117	6	0	1	0	5	19	2	16	1	0
Fredericksburg	11,348	18	0	7	0	11	112	13	95	4	0
Freeport	10,500	64	0	4	2	58	150	26	124	0	1
Freer	2,454	7	0	0	0	7	10	6	2	2	0
Friendswood	40,851	34	1	15	6	12	233	33	174	26	0
Friona	4,121	2	0	1	0	1	18	9	5	4	0
Frisco	218,962	225	0	43	25	157	2,928	210	2,592	126	4
Fulshear	18,058	5	0	1	0	4	103	10	80	13	0
Gainesville	17,789	41	1	4	5	31	431	55	320	56	0
Galena Park	10,240	32	0	5	4	23	136	23	82	31	0
Galveston	52,920	248	6	64	38	140	1,548	202	1,137	209	1
Ganado	1,998	1	0	0	0	1	14	3	6	5	0
Garden Ridge	4,442	4	0	1	0	3	68	12	46	10	0
Garland	241,095	593	5	73	198	317	6,178	914	4,207	1,057	11
Garrison	791	1	0	0	0	1	3	1	2	0	0
Gatesville	17,154	23	0	5	3	15	130	20	90	20	3
Georgetown	83,371	133	2	44	11	76	1,048	128	865	55	14
George West	2,194	3	0	0	0	3	32	5	17	10	0
Giddings	5,144	17	0	4	1	12	97	19	69	9	2
Gilmer	4,997	19	0	4	1	14	145	13	122	10	0
Gladewater	6,174	7	0	0	1	6	65	9	50	6	0
Glenn Heights	18,398	51	1	6	3	41	205	25	143	37	1
Godley	2,245	6	0	1	0	5	24	3	17	4	0
Gonzales	7,089	105	1	7	1	96	124	32	75	17	0
Graham	8,823	14	0	4	1	9	101	6	84	11	0
Granbury	12,132	15	3	3	2	7	436	38	390	8	2

Table 8. Offenses Known to Law Enforcement, by Selected State and City, 2022—Continued

(Number.)

State/city	Population	Violent crime	Murder and nonnegligent manslaughter	Rape	Robbery	Aggravated assault	Property crime	Burglary	Larceny-theft	Motor vehicle theft	Arson[1]
Grand Prairie	199,663	405	8	42	67	288	3,770	304	2,971	495	6
Grand Saline	3,236	2	0	1	0	1	23	7	11	5	1
Grapeland	1,504	2	0	1	0	1	4	1	3	0	0
Grapevine	50,988	72	0	25	4	43	1,500	101	1,200	199	2
Greenville	30,890	95	2	19	14	60	468	74	351	43	6
Groesbeck	3,638	18	1	5	1	11	79	18	54	7	0
Groves	16,682	54	1	6	5	42	193	43	128	22	2
Gun Barrel City	6,551	10	0	1	1	8	52	9	33	10	0
Gunter	2,449	0	0	0	0	0	11	5	6	0	0
Hallettsville	2,762	15	1	3	1	10	38	6	31	1	3
Hallsville	4,707	5	0	0	1	4	21	12	6	3	0
Haltom City	45,488	74	8	8	13	45	464	77	295	92	0
Hamilton	2,860	9	0	2	0	7	31	11	19	1	0
Hamlin	1,899	3	0	1	0	2	11	2	8	1	0
Harker Heights	34,001	76	3	20	8	45	454	68	342	44	1
Harlingen	72,047	233	3	11	52	167	2,034	260	1,646	128	11
Haskell	3,033	3	0	0	0	3	21	2	12	7	1
Hawkins	1,353	3	1	0	0	2	9	5	4	0	0
Hawley	575	0	0	0	0	0	0	0	0	0	0
Hearne	4,517	28	1	2	1	24	36	12	12	12	1
Heath	10,661	9	0	6	0	3	67	18	49	0	0
Hedwig Village	2,295	7	0	0	6	1	127	8	114	5	0
Helotes	9,263	3	0	1	0	2	169	29	135	5	0
Hempstead	6,388	35	1	5	4	25	120	13	85	22	2
Hereford	14,626	44	1	5	6	32	272	55	170	47	6
Hewitt	16,291	27	0	9	2	16	146	13	120	13	0
Hickory Creek	5,786	5	0	2	0	3	93	5	79	9	0
Hico	1,360	0	0	0	0	0	0	0	0	0	0
Hidalgo	14,468	9	1	3	3	2	195	16	160	19	1
Highland Park	8,732	7	0	1	4	2	189	23	156	10	0
Highland Village	15,988	11	0	3	1	7	134	8	122	4	0
Hill Country Village	939	2	0	0	1	1	35	3	30	2	0
Hillsboro	8,407	17	0	0	3	14	150	11	123	16	0
Hitchcock	7,502	26	0	9	2	15	151	29	100	22	5
Hollywood Park	3,091	3	0	0	0	3	69	3	55	11	0
Hondo	8,522	24	0	2	1	21	178	49	104	25	2
Honey Grove	1,789	8	0	2	0	6	10	0	10	0	1
Hooks	2,510	8	0	0	1	7	34	6	21	7	0
Horizon City	23,726	33	0	4	1	28	198	24	142	32	0
Horseshoe Bay	4,693	7	0	3	0	4	49	12	35	2	0
Houston	2,276,533	25,987	433	1,140	6,955	17,459	104,304	14,939	72,021	17,344	454
Howe	3,659	7	0	3	0	4	23	7	11	5	0
Hudson Oaks	2,547	8	0	1	0	7	103	8	87	8	0
Hughes Springs	1,542	1	0	0	0	1	0	0	0	0	0
Humble	16,085	177	2	33	45	97	1,739	146	1,388	205	6
Huntington	2,020	2	0	1	0	1	27	14	8	5	0
Huntsville	46,780	222	1	35	16	170	853	101	657	95	3
Hurst	39,796	98	0	29	18	51	938	63	809	66	2
Hutchins	5,594	41	0	4	8	29	325	35	185	105	0
Hutto	33,891	39	0	8	4	27	216	31	171	14	2
Idalou	2,118	5	0	1	0	4	15	5	10	0	1
Ingleside	10,207	36	0	10	1	25	183	54	107	22	0
Ingram	1,834	4	0	1	0	3	40	17	22	1	1
Iowa Colony	11,056	18	0	3	1	14	78	30	39	9	0
Iowa Park	6,595	3	0	1	0	2	27	7	17	3	0
Irving	254,141	853	12	144	164	533	6,433	748	4,698	987	8
Italy	2,038	3	0	0	0	3	25	9	13	3	0
Itasca	1,682	3	0	1	1	1	0	0	0	0	0
Jacinto City	9,190	7	0	0	2	5	334	17	278	39	0
Jacksboro	4,292	7	0	2	0	5	26	6	19	1	1
Jacksonville	14,196	78	0	6	2	70	360	72	245	43	1
Jamaica Beach	1,065	2	0	1	0	1	5	0	5	0	0
Jarrell	2,469	3	0	0	1	2	19	1	15	3	0
Jasper	7,706	36	1	0	8	27	284	43	229	12	2
Jefferson	1,830	6	0	1	1	4	10	2	5	3	2
Jersey Village	7,575	28	1	2	6	19	308	49	170	89	0
Jonestown	2,506	8	0	3	0	5	31	11	14	6	0
Josephine	4,711	1	1	0	0	0	25	12	13	0	0
Joshua	8,256	23	0	6	3	14	72	12	53	7	1
Jourdanton	4,179	14	0	0	0	14	23	5	11	7	1
Junction	2,536	1	0	0	0	1	6	3	2	1	0
Karnes City	3,271	5	0	2	0	3	33	9	19	5	0
Katy	25,511	56	0	13	15	28	844	57	713	74	2
Kaufman	7,829	24	0	1	3	20	71	6	58	7	0
Keene	6,355	18	1	7	1	9	61	15	42	4	0
Keller	45,080	44	0	10	2	32	301	43	249	9	3
Kemah	1,794	8	0	2	2	4	76	8	61	7	0
Kemp	1,237	6	0	3	0	3	27	7	17	3	0
Kempner	1,211	0	0	0	0	0	0	0	0	0	0
Kenedy	3,589	13	0	2	4	7	89	30	53	6	2
Kennedale	8,417	17	3	5	3	6	102	25	62	15	0
Kerens	1,518	7	0	0	1	6	13	4	6	3	0
Kermit	5,749	4	0	0	0	4	27	7	14	6	0

Table 8. Offenses Known to Law Enforcement, by Selected State and City, 2022—Continued

(Number.)

State/city	Population	Violent crime	Murder and nonnegligent manslaughter	Rape	Robbery	Aggravated assault	Property crime	Burglary	Larceny-theft	Motor vehicle theft	Arson[1]
Kerrville	24,696	45	0	9	3	33	225	25	178	22	1
Kilgore	13,419	54	1	12	2	39	285	61	192	32	0
Killeen	159,546	864	19	79	85	681	2,787	560	1,808	419	6
Kingsville	24,802	73	0	15	10	48	726	145	533	48	0
Kirby	8,069	102	0	4	3	95	136	11	80	45	1
Knox City	1,047	4	0	1	0	3	19	12	7	0	0
Kountze	2,371	1	0	0	0	1	19	4	9	6	0
Kyle	57,724	139	2	19	13	105	747	61	610	76	2
Lacy-Lakeview	7,143	29	1	2	2	24	183	36	126	21	0
La Feria	6,791	34	0	8	2	24	165	23	135	7	0
Lago Vista	9,637	9	0	3	0	6	51	8	40	3	1
La Grange	4,455	17	0	3	0	14	100	17	78	5	0
La Grulla	1,208	4	0	0	2	2	8	1	4	3	1
Laguna Vista	3,673	1	0	1	0	0	15	5	10	0	0
La Joya	4,666	22	0	5	0	17	24	8	16	0	0
Lake Dallas	7,738	12	0	6	3	3	53	6	34	13	0
Lake Jackson	27,595	69	1	18	5	45	458	36	384	38	1
Lakeport	970	0	0	0	0	0	2	0	0	2	0
Lakeside	1,603	6	0	2	1	3	21	1	19	1	0
Lakeview, Harrison County	6,490	4	0	0	0	4	47	10	30	7	0
Lakeway	19,267	11	0	4	0	7	208	26	168	14	0
Lake Worth	4,652	29	0	7	2	20	341	22	292	27	0
La Marque	19,068	84	5	23	5	51	695	122	513	60	3
Lamesa	8,726	43	1	6	2	34	211	44	150	17	3
Lampasas	7,737	20	0	4	0	16	185	15	158	12	0
Lancaster	40,615	255	3	14	45	193	1,252	197	841	214	6
La Porte	36,646	84	1	7	6	70	525	89	375	61	1
Laredo	256,973	814	12	67	130	605	3,303	404	2,621	278	35
La Vernia	1,224	0	0	0	0	0	44	12	16	16	0
Lavon	6,277	5	0	2	0	3	37	5	30	2	1
League City	116,511	126	2	36	13	75	1,497	187	1,181	129	2
Leonard	2,085	1	0	0	0	1	6	2	3	1	0
Leon Valley	11,402	64	2	7	15	40	732	55	526	151	1
Levelland	12,579	134	0	5	5	124	278	80	174	24	0
Lewisville	113,568	334	7	69	43	215	2,505	232	1,915	358	9
Lexington	1,246	1	0	0	0	1	2	0	2	0	0
Liberty	8,790	32	0	6	2	24	196	24	149	23	0
Liberty Hill	6,909	4	0	1	0	3	51	7	39	5	0
Lindale	6,509	10	0	2	1	7	94	9	67	18	0
Linden	1,788	4	0	0	0	4	10	2	7	1	0
Little Elm	55,340	89	1	24	6	58	264	26	197	41	2
Littlefield	5,814	9	0	1	0	8	87	18	61	8	0
Live Oak	15,884	36	0	5	13	18	604	45	485	74	3
Livingston	5,937	45	0	4	2	39	348	13	305	30	1
Llano	3,406	3	0	1	0	2	30	13	11	6	0
Lockhart	15,068	19	1	4	3	11	122	19	79	24	2
Lockney	1,474	3	0	0	0	3	5	3	1	1	0
Log Cabin	820	0	0	0	0	0	2	0	2	0	0
Lone Star	1,412	5	0	0	0	5	9	2	5	2	0
Longview	81,811	360	13	54	71	222	2,350	477	1,659	214	2
Lorena	1,787	3	0	0	0	3	21	3	14	4	1
Los Fresnos	8,164	35	0	2	0	33	114	4	106	4	0
Lubbock	264,142	2,809	25	301	349	2,134	10,922	2,260	7,445	1,217	82
Lufkin	34,063	161	2	33	21	105	1,258	199	960	99	4
Luling	5,511	16	0	3	2	11	68	8	51	9	0
Lumberton	14,004	17	1	9	0	7	119	14	96	9	0
Lytle	3,037	4	0	0	2	2	202	91	92	19	1
Madisonville	4,670	16	0	4	1	11	65	12	42	11	0
Magnolia	2,906	3	0	1	0	2	40	11	25	4	0
Manor	23,497	48	1	8	7	32	251	28	200	23	3
Mansfield	75,993	61	0	17	10	34	1,077	99	905	73	1
Manvel	14,821	15	0	2	0	13	130	24	94	12	0
Marble Falls	7,408	28	2	8	0	18	160	46	102	12	0
Marfa	1,749	2	0	0	0	2	4	0	3	1	0
Marlin	5,631	14	0	1	1	12	56	34	12	10	2
Marshall	22,628	102	4	13	12	73	419	137	251	31	1
Mathis	4,379	14	1	0	3	10	105	40	56	9	6
Maud	969	1	0	0	0	1	13	4	6	3	0
Maypearl	945	2	0	0	0	2	3	1	2	0	0
McAllen	145,510	285	5	58	42	180	2,840	159	2,618	63	13
McKinney	208,415	238	3	49	24	162	2,163	210	1,767	186	7
Meadows Place	4,591	5	0	1	3	1	143	4	108	31	0
Melissa	20,071	5	0	1	0	4	64	4	55	5	0
Memorial Villages	10,987	4	0	0	2	2	82	9	69	4	0
Memphis	2,086	1	0	0	0	1	6	3	2	1	0
Mercedes	16,365	131	0	12	7	112	474	47	387	40	4
Meridian	1,424	2	0	0	0	2	9	4	5	0	0
Merkel	2,431	6	0	1	0	5	19	6	7	6	0
Mesquite	147,226	687	9	57	134	487	5,372	718	3,618	1,036	9
Mexia	6,865	23	0	2	6	15	129	19	98	12	0
Midland	129,945	639	13	70	42	514	2,482	289	1,906	287	6
Midlothian	38,587	41	2	9	2	28	382	29	299	54	1
Miles	927	0	0	0	0	0	1	1	0	0	0

Table 8. Offenses Known to Law Enforcement, by Selected State and City, 2022—Continued

(Number.)

State/city	Population	Violent crime	Murder and nonnegligent manslaughter	Rape	Robbery	Aggravated assault	Property crime	Burglary	Larceny-theft	Motor vehicle theft	Arson[1]
Milford	736	4	0	2	0	2	5	2	2	1	0
Mineola	5,031	17	0	6	1	10	75	10	64	1	1
Mineral Wells	15,010	27	0	7	3	17	511	145	319	47	2
Mission	86,577	294	1	74	30	189	1,451	160	1,174	117	6
Missouri City	75,323	119	3	17	23	76	895	141	679	75	3
Monahans	7,185	28	2	3	3	20	49	7	33	9	0
Mont Belvieu	8,902	22	1	5	3	13	148	15	110	23	0
Montgomery	2,679	6	0	0	0	6	36	2	31	3	0
Morgans Point Resort	4,789	2	0	1	0	1	22	0	19	3	0
Moulton	869	0	0	0	0	0	1	0	1	0	0
Mount Pleasant	16,044	79	0	19	5	55	274	46	200	28	2
Mount Vernon	2,500	9	0	5	0	4	122	104	15	3	0
Muleshoe	5,066	2	0	0	0	2	28	6	19	3	0
Murphy	21,297	9	0	0	2	7	148	11	137	0	0
Mustang Ridge	991	6	0	1	0	5	30	4	17	9	0
Nacogdoches	32,055	73	2	16	8	47	647	90	522	35	2
Nassau Bay	5,105	7	0	3	0	4	99	20	73	6	0
Natalia	1,342	3	0	0	2	1	22	15	3	4	0
Navasota	8,459	60	1	4	3	52	201	51	132	18	2
Nederland	18,034	34	0	6	3	25	282	28	222	32	1
Needville	3,040	4	0	0	0	4	31	2	26	3	0
New Boston	4,557	36	0	0	5	31	132	15	107	10	2
New Braunfels	107,017	201	0	30	20	151	1,513	179	1,157	177	1
Newton	1,997	4	0	0	0	4	17	6	11	0	1
Nolanville	6,560	10	0	5	0	5	39	8	22	9	1
Northeast	3,962	1	0	0	0	1	3	2	1	0	0
Northlake	8,513	7	0	0	1	6	102	7	76	19	0
North Richland Hills	70,108	159	4	35	23	97	1,393	139	1,108	146	2
Oak Ridge, Kaufman County	979	0	0	0	0	0	6	5	1	0	0
Oak Ridge North	3,011	7	0	1	1	5	65	1	57	7	0
Odem	2,277	6	0	0	0	6	27	6	13	8	0
Odessa	110,163	573	8	65	64	436	2,278	357	1,632	289	16
Olmos Park	2,151	2	0	0	1	1	40	17	20	3	0
Olney	3,033	8	0	1	1	6	21	7	14	0	0
Onalaska	3,225	22	0	11	0	11	43	6	23	14	0
Orange	19,056	93	3	14	10	66	317	67	204	46	0
Overton	2,294	4	0	0	0	4	30	6	24	0	1
Ovilla	4,365	3	0	0	1	2	18	3	13	2	0
Oyster Creek	1,196	2	0	0	0	2	23	8	12	3	0
Palacios	4,425	20	0	1	1	18	43	12	30	1	3
Palestine	19,113	133	1	31	7	94	493	122	340	31	3
Palmer	2,510	6	0	0	0	6	25	10	6	9	0
Palmhurst	2,600	6	0	1	1	4	177	4	172	1	0
Palmview	15,919	70	0	5	7	58	227	70	144	13	0
Pampa	16,343	70	0	10	4	56	388	79	292	17	1
Panhandle	2,310	0	0	0	0	0	1	0	1	0	0
Pantego	2,497	6	0	3	0	3	46	5	29	12	0
Paris	24,392	189	2	27	9	151	650	159	433	58	5
Parker	6,144	5	0	0	0	5	20	3	14	3	0
Pasadena	145,954	915	11	116	126	662	4,090	594	2,858	638	11
Patton Village	1,799	10	0	0	0	10	16	3	12	1	0
Payne Springs	755	0	0	0	0	0	0	0	0	0	0
Pearland	125,894	117	1	14	33	69	2,152	164	1,822	166	0
Pearsall	7,661	34	0	1	1	32	109	42	50	17	2
Pecos	12,483	68	1	4	3	60	99	30	58	11	0
Penitas	6,348	6	0	2	1	3	32	5	25	2	0
Perryton	8,143	33	1	5	1	26	95	20	71	4	0
Petersburg	972	1	0	0	0	1	2	1	0	1	0
Pflugerville	67,817	116	2	23	22	69	1,079	61	923	95	1
Pharr	79,558	207	0	54	27	126	1,213	164	938	111	0
Pilot Point	4,892	4	0	2	0	2	25	6	15	4	0
Pinehurst	2,209	10	0	0	0	10	54	20	29	5	1
Pineland	910	3	0	1	0	2	2	1	1	0	0
Pittsburg	4,433	16	1	2	1	12	78	22	43	13	1
Plainview	19,554	72	0	7	5	60	413	85	285	43	1
Plano	289,847	458	1	91	86	280	5,496	682	4,293	521	12
Pleasanton	10,951	20	0	5	2	13	255	27	205	23	0
Point Comfort	565	1	0	0	0	1	0	0	0	0	0
Ponder	2,417	4	0	2	0	2	8	0	8	0	0
Port Aransas	3,286	21	0	5	1	15	183	16	136	31	3
Port Arthur	55,899	417	8	40	48	321	1,008	273	620	115	1
Port Isabel	5,165	28	0	4	0	24	110	13	88	9	0
Portland	20,742	28	0	7	4	17	273	18	243	12	1
Port Lavaca	11,048	22	0	3	0	19	207	39	153	15	0
Port Neches	13,293	38	1	5	0	32	129	24	81	24	0
Poteet	2,970	9	1	0	0	8	39	15	19	5	0
Prairie View	7,059	17	0	1	2	14	79	29	38	12	0
Primera	5,319	5	0	1	0	4	9	1	7	1	0
Princeton	22,867	33	0	7	3	23	186	15	152	19	0
Prosper	37,752	29	0	8	3	18	331	34	275	22	1
Queen City	1,410	4	0	2	0	2	16	10	5	1	0
Quitman	2,021	1	0	0	0	1	2	0	2	0	0
Rancho Viejo	2,867	0	0	0	0	0	19	4	14	1	0

Table 8. Offenses Known to Law Enforcement, by Selected State and City, 2022—Continued

(Number.)

State/city	Population	Violent crime	Murder and nonnegligent manslaughter	Rape	Robbery	Aggravated assault	Property crime	Burglary	Larceny-theft	Motor vehicle theft	Arson[1]
Ranger	2,287	3	0	2	0	1	26	7	15	4	1
Raymondville	10,552	62	1	5	7	49	209	57	144	8	4
Red Oak	16,396	39	0	9	5	25	205	22	137	46	0
Refugio	2,866	2	0	0	0	2	27	6	18	3	0
Reno, Lamar County	3,457	3	0	0	0	3	27	4	22	1	0
Reno, Parker County	3,457	7	0	0	0	7	40	13	21	6	1
Rhome	1,839	2	0	0	0	2	9	2	2	5	0
Rice	1,259	4	0	0	0	4	8	2	2	5	0
Richardson	115,771	183	2	31	60	90	2,630	281	2,004	345	1
Richland Hills	8,385	34	0	3	5	26	206	25	165	16	1
Richmond	12,936	39	0	6	12	21	288	38	234	16	0
Richwood	4,730	6	0	3	0	3	52	3	44	5	1
Rio Grande City	15,705	23	1	0	2	20	272	71	179	22	1
Rio Hondo	2,012	8	0	1	1	6	34	4	27	3	0
River Oaks	7,420	26	0	9	2	15	113	17	80	16	0
Roanoke	10,024	7	0	3	1	3	132	17	102	13	0
Robinson	12,954	32	0	8	4	20	142	29	102	11	3
Robstown	10,155	55	0	8	3	44	300	88	199	13	3
Rockdale	5,473	38	0	0	6	32	111	43	52	16	0
Rockport	10,759	47	0	6	2	39	324	71	236	17	0
Rockwall	51,724	53	0	8	10	35	794	44	685	65	0
Rogers	1,107	0	0	0	0	0	1	1	0	0	0
Rollingwood	1,398	1	0	0	0	1	32	3	23	6	0
Roma	11,547	39	0	2	2	35	85	11	65	9	0
Roman Forest	1,963	8	0	1	0	7	69	15	48	6	0
Roscoe	1,231	0	0	0	0	0	4	1	3	0	0
Rosenberg	40,472	114	1	18	20	75	695	83	546	66	0
Round Rock	127,349	215	2	47	42	124	2,934	166	2,597	171	5
Rowlett	65,196	154	3	13	15	123	968	96	780	92	0
Royse City	18,613	43	1	6	5	31	316	43	253	20	0
Runaway Bay	1,764	3	0	0	0	3	14	1	13	0	0
Rusk	5,583	23	1	3	0	19	67	6	54	7	0
Sabinal	1,410	3	0	0	0	3	4	4	0	0	0
Sachse	31,317	11	0	8	2	1	218	30	164	24	1
Saginaw	23,993	59	2	16	8	33	301	21	244	36	0
Salado	2,395	1	0	1	0	0	20	2	15	3	0
San Angelo	99,243	334	6	64	26	238	2,802	428	2,174	200	15
San Antonio	1,465,608	12,935	230	1,555	1,700	9,450	74,288	9,338	52,586	12,364	255
San Augustine	1,844	12	1	0	2	9	40	18	20	2	1
San Benito	24,712	128	0	0	10	118	426	65	327	34	2
San Elizario	10,080	4	0	0	1	3	30	6	19	5	0
Sanger	9,877	21	0	0	1	20	152	11	122	19	0
San Juan	35,806	97	0	12	14	71	691	79	560	52	2
San Marcos	69,470	445	0	106	47	292	1,811	211	1,380	220	9
San Saba	3,197	2	0	0	0	2	22	9	13	0	1
Sansom Park Village	5,336	35	0	7	3	25	115	24	61	30	1
Santa Anna	1,029	1	0	0	0	1	2	0	0	2	0
Santa Fe	12,802	21	0	9	4	8	120	30	73	17	0
Schertz	43,162	62	0	8	10	44	502	64	345	93	1
Schulenburg	2,742	13	0	1	0	12	41	5	31	5	1
Seabrook	13,544	31	0	13	6	12	187	27	141	19	0
Seadrift	997	3	0	0	0	3	4	0	4	0	0
Seagoville	19,389	29	1	6	6	16	389	99	178	112	1
Sealy	6,720	4	0	0	1	3	99	15	67	17	0
Seguin	32,452	135	3	11	17	104	676	80	528	68	3
Selma	11,824	26	0	5	4	17	323	22	268	33	0
Seminole	7,066	18	0	0	2	16	63	9	46	8	1
Seven Points	1,430	9	1	1	0	7	34	6	21	7	0
Seymour	2,590	1	0	0	0	1	6	4	0	2	0
Shallowater	2,917	6	0	1	0	5	34	8	20	6	0
Shavano Park	3,609	4	0	0	1	3	73	5	57	11	0
Shenandoah	3,682	10	0	0	4	6	355	13	301	41	0
Sherman	45,881	161	3	25	15	118	866	272	496	98	5
Shiner	2,183	6	0	0	0	6	8	3	4	1	0
Silsbee	6,831	20	0	5	0	15	69	7	57	5	0
Sinton	5,602	23	1	8	1	13	104	10	90	4	0
Slaton	5,752	9	0	1	1	7	111	34	61	16	0
Smithville	4,150	7	0	2	0	5	44	2	41	1	1
Snyder	11,179	161	0	15	3	143	150	33	109	8	1
Socorro	37,952	85	3	22	9	51	281	42	182	57	1
Somerset	1,777	2	0	1	0	1	11	3	2	6	1
Somerville	1,346	4	0	1	0	3	15	5	9	1	0
Sonora	2,432	2	0	1	0	1	11	5	3	3	0
Sour Lake	1,807	0	0	0	0	0	24	2	20	2	0
South Houston	15,613	97	3	8	32	54	500	80	297	123	0
Southlake	30,949	16	1	6	3	6	376	28	335	13	0
South Padre Island	2,048	32	0	12	5	15	288	12	257	19	0
Southside Place	1,820	0	0	0	0	0	46	1	38	7	0
Spearman	3,034	0	0	0	0	0	0	0	0	0	0
Splendora	1,860	7	0	0	1	6	31	6	19	6	0
Springtown	3,638	13	0	0	0	13	19	2	17	0	0
Spring Valley	4,209	3	0	0	1	2	82	2	72	8	0
Stafford	17,110	88	2	11	19	56	884	44	743	97	0

Table 8. Offenses Known to Law Enforcement, by Selected State and City, 2022—Continued

(Number.)

State/city	Population	Violent crime	Murder and nonnegligent manslaughter	Rape	Robbery	Aggravated assault	Property crime	Burglary	Larceny-theft	Motor vehicle theft	Arson[1]
Stamford	3,005	3	0	1	0	2	33	9	17	7	1
Stanton	2,630	3	0	0	2	1	33	14	14	5	2
Stephenville	21,505	49	0	26	2	21	239	36	189	14	0
Stratford	1,973	0	0	0	0	0	0	0	0	0	0
Sudan	934	1	0	1	0	0	0	0	0	0	0
Sugar Land	107,989	97	0	12	33	52	1,745	133	1,497	115	0
Sullivan City	3,896	11	0	0	1	10	40	12	26	2	0
Sulphur Springs	16,128	29	0	7	4	18	105	16	81	8	0
Sunnyvale	8,381	7	0	0	1	6	122	6	94	22	0
Sunray	1,701	1	0	1	0	0	13	3	2	8	0
Sunrise Beach Village	787	1	0	1	0	0	2	0	2	0	0
Sunset Valley	637	4	0	0	1	3	172	8	138	26	0
Surfside Beach	669	2	0	0	0	2	8	2	6	0	0
Sweeny	3,566	16	0	5	1	10	44	5	37	2	0
Sweetwater	10,420	61	0	1	7	53	146	60	70	16	1
Taft	2,835	0	0	0	0	0	30	20	7	3	0
Tahoka	2,419	8	0	0	1	7	29	9	19	1	1
Tatum	1,357	0	0	0	0	0	9	1	8	0	0
Taylor	17,259	26	1	8	1	16	274	82	175	17	3
Teague	3,497	6	1	1	1	3	42	15	20	7	0
Temple	88,484	312	5	81	34	192	1,549	191	1,220	138	8
Tenaha	995	0	0	0	0	0	0	0	0	0	0
Terrell	19,670	52	0	4	4	44	535	69	392	74	0
Terrell Hills	5,036	2	1	1	0	0	64	22	34	8	0
Texarkana	35,859	150	2	13	28	107	1,045	105	821	119	4
Texas City	56,311	156	7	38	24	87	1,304	173	1,022	109	2
The Colony	45,357	132	0	36	8	88	1,278	57	1,146	75	2
Thorndale	1,312	1	0	0	0	1	1	0	1	0	0
Tioga	1,220	1	0	1	0	0	0	0	0	0	0
Todd Mission	126	0	0	0	0	0	2	0	2	0	0
Tomball	13,322	68	1	15	9	43	335	17	276	42	1
Tom Bean	934	0	0	0	0	0	0	0	0	0	0
Tool	2,243	3	0	0	0	3	21	4	14	3	0
Trophy Club	13,794	6	0	2	0	4	79	4	66	9	0
Tulia	4,501	24	2	4	2	16	98	29	61	8	1
Tye	1,192	2	0	1	0	1	4	1	2	1	0
Tyler	108,422	575	11	87	43	434	2,523	274	2,038	211	1
Universal City	19,903	62	0	18	14	30	527	73	398	56	3
University Park	24,918	10	0	2	8	0	330	145	157	28	0
Uvalde	15,410	118	22	18	4	74	380	65	293	22	3
Valley Mills	1,256	0	0	0	0	0	9	2	7	0	0
Van	2,825	2	0	0	0	2	19	5	5	9	0
Van Alstyne	6,023	13	0	5	0	8	31	4	24	3	0
Venus	7,843	8	0	2	0	6	27	1	22	4	0
Vernon	9,945	39	2	10	1	26	90	25	54	11	2
Victoria	65,165	247	7	35	36	169	1,452	269	1,107	76	14
Vidor	9,671	20	0	4	1	15	193	75	92	26	0
Waco	140,911	906	14	117	106	669	4,550	750	3,420	380	22
Wake Village	5,861	2	0	0	0	2	73	15	50	8	1
Waller	2,846	6	0	1	0	5	34	3	15	16	1
Wallis	1,302	1	0	0	0	1	10	4	6	0	0
Watauga	23,027	40	2	3	4	31	285	73	179	33	1
Waxahachie	45,422	113	0	24	8	81	739	55	625	59	1
Weatherford	36,796	72	0	29	3	40	630	111	448	71	2
Webster	11,952	57	0	7	13	37	1,003	125	754	124	1
Weimar	2,083	3	0	0	2	1	15	5	7	3	0
Weslaco	41,478	147	1	25	26	95	1,247	126	1,088	33	0
West	2,587	2	0	0	1	1	21	9	9	3	0
West Columbia	3,587	12	0	1	0	11	57	6	45	6	0
West Lake Hills	3,220	1	0	0	0	1	84	2	79	3	0
West Orange	3,418	20	0	2	2	16	89	13	71	5	0
Westover Hills	638	5	0	0	0	5	7	3	3	1	0
West University Place	14,524	7	0	1	3	3	144	21	94	29	0
Westworth	2,614	18	0	0	1	17	91	8	78	5	1
Wharton	8,627	26	0	1	4	21	268	30	223	15	3
Whitehouse	9,175	11	0	4	0	7	80	13	58	9	0
White Oak	6,147	16	0	10	1	5	58	10	41	7	0
White Settlement	17,954	56	1	7	13	35	433	75	264	94	0
Wichita Falls	103,337	486	14	110	53	309	2,964	516	2,147	301	0
Willis	6,986	28	1	4	6	17	204	29	145	30	1
Willow Park	5,427	15	0	2	0	13	90	17	60	13	0
Wills Point	3,977	4	0	0	0	4	24	10	9	5	0
Wilmer	5,590	15	0	4	3	8	71	13	34	24	0
Windcrest	5,793	17	0	0	3	14	388	21	322	45	2
Wink	844	3	0	1	0	2	7	3	4	0	0
Winnsboro	3,581	6	0	0	1	5	29	9	18	2	0
Winters	2,363	5	0	1	1	3	23	12	9	2	1
Wolfforth	6,482	6	0	1	0	5	32	6	21	5	0
Woodbranch	1,497	0	0	0	0	0	0	0	0	0	0
Woodsboro	1,275	1	0	0	0	1	5	1	3	1	0
Woodville	2,471	4	0	0	1	3	27	5	15	7	0
Woodway	9,514	5	0	0	0	5	101	1	93	7	0
Wortham	1,015	7	0	0	2	5	17	9	4	4	0

Table 8. Offenses Known to Law Enforcement, by Selected State and City, 2022—Continued

(Number.)

State/city	Population	Violent crime	Murder and nonnegligent manslaughter	Rape	Robbery	Aggravated assault	Property crime	Burglary	Larceny-theft	Motor vehicle theft	Arson[1]
Wylie	60,910	36	0	7	4	25	352	36	288	28	2
Yoakum	5,958	3	0	0	0	3	22	6	11	5	1
Zavalla	610	1	0	0	0	1	12	0	10	2	0
UTAH											
American Fork/Cedar Hills	45,310	46	0	20	8	18	767	64	649	54	4
Blanding	3,295	3	0	1	0	2	32	5	26	1	0
Bluffdale	20,386	18	0	7	0	11	154	19	108	27	0
Bountiful	45,098	50	0	23	2	25	540	43	448	49	1
Brian Head	159	1	0	1	0	0	13	0	13	0	0
Cedar City	39,266	31	0	14	2	15	517	54	420	43	3
Centerville	16,719	26	0	11	1	14	298	32	246	20	7
Clearfield	32,586	77	2	18	6	51	500	67	396	37	3
Clinton	23,784	24	0	6	1	17	287	15	251	21	0
Cottonwood Heights	32,191	40	0	8	7	25	637	57	525	55	0
Draper	53,049	51	0	14	1	36	878	136	663	79	6
Enoch	8,518	7	0	2	0	5	23	4	18	1	0
Ephraim	5,834	8	0	7	0	1	42	4	38	0	0
Grantsville	14,431	23	1	3	0	19	119	8	93	18	0
Harrisville	6,948	5	0	2	0	3	225	6	215	4	1
Heber	17,659	17	1	5	0	11	143	13	123	7	1
Helper	2,082	2	0	0	0	2	27	4	22	1	0
Herriman	60,138	46	0	13	6	27	469	40	373	56	4
Hurricane	23,607	47	0	11	0	36	326	57	224	45	0
Kanab	5,324	10	0	1	0	9	36	2	32	2	0
Kaysville	33,004	21	0	12	1	8	261	25	218	18	1
La Verkin	4,582	8	0	3	0	5	73	5	64	4	0
Layton	84,636	138	0	38	8	92	1,410	152	1,155	103	12
Lindon	11,922	9	1	3	1	4	366	31	321	14	0
Logan	56,267	100	0	40	2	58	716	82	588	46	1
Lone Peak	30,258	7	0	2	1	4	116	11	94	11	0
Mantua	1,336	1	0	0	0	1	7	4	3	0	0
Mapleton	13,415	16	0	8	0	8	45	6	35	4	0
Moab	5,263	39	0	12	0	27	106	6	91	9	0
Mount Pleasant	3,836	5	0	3	0	2	21	0	19	2	0
Murray	48,884	175	1	31	33	110	2,470	233	1,876	361	17
Naples	2,383	4	0	3	0	1	23	4	16	3	0
Nephi	6,739	6	0	3	0	3	51	9	35	7	0
North Ogden	21,977	19	0	4	2	13	171	42	109	20	0
North Park	16,904	16	0	6	1	9	132	52	73	7	0
North Salt Lake	22,679	28	0	13	1	14	401	54	289	58	0
Ogden	86,870	482	3	98	44	337	2,204	272	1,661	271	9
Orem	97,430	182	6	90	10	76	1,642	129	1,363	150	4
Park City	8,516	42	0	23	2	17	204	18	182	4	0
Payson	22,989	20	0	6	2	12	193	27	162	4	0
Perry	5,921	3	0	1	1	1	121	7	105	9	1
Pleasant Grove	38,095	32	1	16	4	11	362	62	265	35	0
Pleasant View	11,234	9	0	1	0	8	80	18	48	14	0
Price	8,230	24	0	6	0	18	99	19	78	2	1
Provo	114,120	168	0	46	14	108	1,597	159	1,301	137	27
Richfield	8,379	15	0	1	0	14	254	15	227	12	1
Riverdale	9,408	30	0	7	2	21	443	29	398	16	1
Riverton	44,920	36	0	10	5	21	491	33	420	38	0
Roosevelt	7,004	22	0	4	1	17	179	21	145	13	2
Roy	39,305	66	0	14	8	44	406	81	288	37	0
Salem	10,308	2	0	1	0	1	46	4	38	4	0
Salt Lake City	201,373	1,970	13	380	413	1,164	12,934	1,316	9,887	1,731	65
Santaquin/Genola	18,616	7	0	2	2	3	62	8	50	4	0
Saratoga Springs	50,850	51	0	19	1	31	329	27	286	16	0
Smithfield	14,455	3	0	0	1	2	47	11	35	1	1
South Jordan	82,250	54	0	21	10	23	1,117	101	908	108	2
South Ogden	17,585	36	0	12	7	17	205	35	142	28	1
Spanish Fork	45,005	40	2	20	4	14	451	20	394	37	1
Springdale	589	1	0	0	0	1	15	1	13	1	0
Springville	36,907	40	3	13	6	18	385	27	326	32	1
St. George	104,158	170	3	38	8	121	1,139	95	918	126	6
Sunset	5,557	15	0	2	0	13	84	13	61	10	0
Syracuse	34,354	22	0	10	0	12	297	26	256	15	4
Taylorsville City	58,059	126	2	17	28	79	1,535	109	1,226	200	4
Tooele	38,318	177	3	38	12	124	692	98	534	60	3
Tremonton Garland	13,682	13	0	5	0	8	210	62	141	7	2
Washington	33,535	62	0	19	1	42	426	39	342	45	1
West Jordan	115,900	386	5	107	34	240	2,498	202	2,023	273	4
West Valley	138,020	609	8	82	97	422	3,960	420	2,908	632	16
Woods Cross	11,846	16	0	1	2	13	210	21	145	44	0
VERMONT											
Barre	8,447	45	0	17	2	26	219	17	201	1	1
Barre Town	7,970	5	0	1	0	4	81	7	73	1	0
Bellows Falls	2,820	5	0	0	0	5	52	4	44	4	0
Bennington	15,301	93	2	2	7	82	475	34	435	6	1
Berlin	2,936	26	0	8	1	17	174	6	165	3	0
Bradford	2,822	1	0	0	0	1	12	6	5	1	0

Table 8. Offenses Known to Law Enforcement, by Selected State and City, 2022—Continued

(Number.)

State/city	Population	Violent crime	Murder and nonnegligent manslaughter	Rape	Robbery	Aggravated assault	Property crime	Burglary	Larceny-theft	Motor vehicle theft	Arson[1]
Brandon	4,112	15	0	0	0	15	45	8	37	0	0
Brattleboro	12,256	60	1	8	5	46	747	134	610	3	0
Bristol	3,730	2	0	0	0	2	4	0	4	0	0
Burlington	44,689	183	5	14	12	152	2,291	175	1,804	312	5
Castleton	4,599	1	0	0	0	1	5	0	5	0	0
Colchester	17,710	45	0	12	2	31	334	19	304	11	0
Dover	1,859	3	0	1	0	2	33	0	30	3	0
Essex	22,481	36	0	8	2	26	326	24	293	9	0
Hardwick	2,997	4	0	0	0	4	49	3	46	0	0
Hartford	10,863	38	0	13	0	25	163	15	133	15	1
Hinesburg	4,699	1	0	1	0	0	6	3	3	0	0
Killington	1,414	4	0	0	0	4	4	0	3	1	0
Ludlow	2,204	3	0	0	0	3	30	1	29	0	0
Lyndonville	1,200	4	0	0	0	4	41	1	36	4	0
Manchester	4,499	8	0	2	0	6	37	10	27	0	0
Middlebury	9,037	14	0	3	0	11	80	9	67	4	0
Milton	10,656	17	0	7	0	10	69	5	62	2	1
Montpelier	7,995	26	0	6	1	19	147	13	131	3	1
Morristown	5,610	7	0	2	0	5	88	2	86	0	2
Newport	4,433	41	0	5	3	33	106	9	96	1	0
Northfield	6,291	18	0	5	2	11	10	0	10	0	0
Norwich	3,681	1	0	0	0	1	25	5	17	3	0
Pittsford	2,879	0	0	0	0	0	30	2	28	0	0
Royalton	2,794	1	0	1	0	0	21	2	19	0	0
Rutland	15,858	76	1	5	13	57	770	39	711	20	3
Rutland Town	3,929	7	0	0	1	6	244	6	233	5	0
Shelburne	7,903	5	0	1	1	3	131	8	117	6	1
South Burlington	20,307	60	1	9	4	46	810	31	740	39	0
Springfield	9,180	25	0	7	5	13	198	47	133	18	0
St. Albans	7,022	40	0	4	2	34	257	16	236	5	2
St. Johnsbury	7,404	26	0	2	3	21	272	29	240	3	0
Stowe	5,359	3	0	1	0	2	80	8	69	3	1
Swanton	6,813	9	0	1	0	6	30	2	28	0	0
Vergennes	2,565	2	0	1	0	1	33	0	33	0	1
Weathersfield	2,887	8	0	6	0	2	10	0	8	2	0
Williston	10,067	6	0	0	0	6	329	12	304	13	0
Wilmington	2,310	7	0	2	0	5	9	0	8	1	0
Windsor	3,595	4	0	2	1	1	39	3	34	2	0
Winooski	8,647	47	1	3	7	36	343	33	284	26	1
Woodstock	3,064	2	0	1	0	1	28	1	27	0	0
VIRGINIA											
Abingdon	8,265	16	0	5	0	11	127	13	105	9	0
Alexandria	150,957	281	6	7	103	165	2,946	155	2,459	332	4
Altavista	3,348	10	0	1	1	8	77	5	68	4	0
Ashland	7,661	44	0	3	3	38	168	9	147	12	0
Bedford	6,681	15	0	8	1	6	201	10	181	10	1
Berryville	4,588	2	0	2	0	0	29	2	24	3	0
Big Stone Gap	5,155	8	0	1	1	6	92	5	81	6	0
Blacksburg	45,749	20	1	11	3	5	266	21	235	10	2
Blackstone	3,347	7	0	0	0	7	111	5	105	1	1
Bluefield	4,957	16	0	5	4	7	246	8	233	5	0
Bridgewater	6,215	5	0	0	0	5	42	7	34	1	0
Bristol	16,909	63	2	14	5	42	456	49	361	46	0
Broadway	4,269	3	0	1	0	2	26	3	20	3	0
Buena Vista	6,605	10	0	2	0	8	50	2	42	6	1
Charlottesville	45,089	244	2	36	35	171	1,538	126	1,249	163	2
Chase City	2,037	7	1	0	1	5	24	5	17	2	0
Chatham	1,182	0	0	0	0	0	1	0	1	0	0
Chesapeake	253,745	1,059	25	72	104	858	5,102	409	4,287	406	15
Chilhowie	1,652	8	0	1	1	6	18	1	13	4	0
Chincoteague	3,284	4	0	1	0	3	34	3	27	4	1
Christiansburg	21,746	40	0	10	2	28	514	22	473	19	0
Clifton Forge	3,433	16	0	3	0	13	53	10	43	0	1
Colonial Beach	3,980	15	0	3	1	11	49	3	42	4	0
Colonial Heights	18,419	56	1	8	14	33	630	25	593	12	2
Covington	5,733	16	0	10	0	6	55	6	47	2	3
Crewe	2,257	6	0	2	0	4	52	9	37	6	0
Culpeper	20,836	43	1	7	5	30	339	8	315	16	2
Damascus	782	0	0	0	0	0	51	8	41	2	0
Danville	42,111	137	8	20	25	84	1,345	75	1,172	98	8
Dublin	2,636	6	1	3	2	0	43	6	34	3	0
Dumfries	5,659	15	3	1	4	7	93	4	65	24	1
Eastville	295	0	0	0	0	0	0	0	0	0	0
Elkton	3,008	3	0	1	0	2	37	1	32	4	0
Emporia	5,637	25	3	2	10	10	199	24	162	13	0
Exmore	1,432	3	0	0	1	2	42	4	34	4	1
Fairfax City	24,509	27	1	7	12	7	566	17	507	42	2
Falls Church	14,384	8	0	2	6	0	249	12	216	21	1
Farmville	7,216	33	1	5	1	26	212	8	203	1	1
Franklin	8,292	43	3	3	11	26	259	26	217	16	1
Fredericksburg	28,844	119	0	7	14	98	1,146	57	1,039	50	5
Front Royal	15,201	32	0	16	2	14	230	20	191	19	0

Table 8. Offenses Known to Law Enforcement, by Selected State and City, 2022—Continued

(Number.)

State/city	Population	Violent crime	Murder and nonnegligent manslaughter	Rape	Robbery	Aggravated assault	Property crime	Burglary	Larceny-theft	Motor vehicle theft	Arson[1]
Galax	6,652	17	0	2	1	14	254	22	202	30	0
Gate City	2,015	7	0	1	0	6	16	1	13	2	1
Glade Spring	1,355	2	0	0	0	2	10	0	9	1	0
Gordonsville	1,466	4	0	0	0	4	8	1	7	0	0
Gretna	1,274	1	0	0	0	1	13	0	10	3	0
Grottoes	2,965	3	0	0	1	2	12	1	11	0	0
Grundy	805	1	0	0	0	1	38	0	36	2	0
Halifax	1,098	4	0	1	0	3	14	3	10	1	0
Hampton	138,843	375	21	45	86	223	4,035	274	3,387	374	23
Harrisonburg	51,363	129	1	26	8	94	929	65	812	52	1
Herndon	24,070	61	1	8	26	26	411	13	378	20	0
Hillsville	2,856	7	2	2	0	3	40	4	33	3	0
Hopewell	23,395	126	9	10	30	77	459	61	349	49	2
Jonesville	862	0	0	0	0	0	6	0	6	0	0
Kenbridge	1,110	5	0	1	0	4	16	2	13	1	0
Kilmarnock	1,419	1	0	0	0	1	47	0	46	1	0
Lawrenceville	1,025	2	0	0	0	2	10	4	6	0	0
Lebanon	3,098	3	0	1	0	2	91	2	83	6	1
Leesburg	49,395	148	2	22	16	108	697	21	645	31	5
Lexington	7,628	8	0	3	1	4	50	5	44	1	0
Louisa	2,118	5	0	1	0	4	33	0	32	1	0
Luray	4,813	7	0	3	0	4	101	8	92	1	1
Lynchburg	79,421	284	8	24	52	200	1,955	214	1,436	305	6
Manassas	42,836	126	0	21	38	67	948	50	823	75	4
Marion	5,711	18	0	2	3	13	131	11	104	16	1
Martinsville	13,660	52	0	7	10	35	289	30	234	25	1
Middletown	1,413	1	0	1	0	0	9	1	8	0	0
Mount Jackson	2,010	1	0	1	0	0	26	1	25	0	0
New Market	2,180	2	0	0	1	1	21	2	18	1	0
Newport News	183,903	1,121	31	58	177	855	4,233	337	3,434	462	30
Norfolk	233,419	1,640	63	98	301	1,178	11,372	546	8,962	1,864	9
Norton	3,666	14	3	2	2	7	248	6	227	15	2
Onancock	1,156	0	0	0	0	0	28	9	19	0	0
Orange	5,254	24	0	3	2	19	82	7	71	4	0
Pearisburg	2,812	1	0	1	0	0	64	5	57	2	2
Pembroke	1,124	0	0	0	0	0	17	0	17	0	0
Pennington Gap	1,595	3	0	0	0	3	43	5	38	0	1
Petersburg	33,546	273	21	17	45	190	857	88	682	87	3
Pocahontas	259	0	0	0	0	0	2	0	2	0	0
Poquoson	12,738	21	0	4	3	14	61	9	48	4	7
Portsmouth	98,003	858	47	48	209	554	4,784	421	3,940	423	10
Pulaski	8,944	30	0	7	1	22	310	63	227	20	0
Purcellville	9,103	6	0	2	0	4	56	4	50	2	0
Radford	16,978	54	0	4	4	46	185	9	153	23	1
Rich Creek	719	1	0	0	0	1	15	1	12	2	0
Richlands	5,158	20	1	8	0	11	67	11	51	5	0
Richmond	227,323	818	59	10	221	528	7,803	785	6,253	765	37
Roanoke	98,204	594	18	114	98	364	4,212	508	3,295	409	24
Rocky Mount	4,929	10	1	2	3	4	181	5	169	7	0
Rural Retreat	1,527	0	0	0	0	0	14	1	13	0	0
Salem	25,460	32	0	9	7	16	441	52	349	40	3
Saltville	1,774	3	0	0	0	3	26	5	14	7	0
Shenandoah	2,510	1	0	1	0	0	25	5	19	1	0
Smithfield	8,827	20	0	0	7	13	96	2	89	5	1
South Boston	7,884	26	3	3	2	18	184	17	157	10	0
South Hill	4,737	27	3	1	3	20	194	14	169	11	0
Stanley	1,721	4	0	3	0	1	28	3	24	1	0
Staunton	25,611	36	1	6	3	26	478	33	425	20	7
Stephens City	2,109	0	0	0	0	0	25	0	25	0	0
St. Paul	838	1	0	0	0	1	16	2	13	1	1
Strasburg	7,270	12	0	3	2	7	56	5	50	1	0
Suffolk	98,065	467	12	35	60	360	1,757	102	1,487	168	11
Tappahannock	2,236	12	0	2	0	10	55	4	48	3	1
Tazewell	4,374	6	0	3	1	2	63	16	38	9	0
Timberville	3,013	5	0	0	1	4	6	3	3	0	0
Vienna	16,194	9	0	3	2	4	167	5	153	9	0
Vinton	7,996	16	0	2	3	11	158	6	132	20	0
Virginia Beach	457,556	400	21	54	139	186	7,369	352	6,216	801	24
Warrenton	10,218	16	0	5	2	9	110	5	96	9	0
Waynesboro	22,903	52	0	10	7	35	429	39	350	40	4
Weber City	1,228	3	0	0	0	3	14	1	13	0	0
West Point	3,424	4	0	1	1	2	12	1	10	1	0
White Stone	388	0	0	0	0	0	0	0	0	0	0
Williamsburg	15,790	33	0	4	3	26	243	10	226	7	0
Winchester	28,363	76	1	28	11	36	787	75	683	29	5
Windsor	2,876	11	0	1	0	10	28	1	24	3	0
Wintergreen	166	1	0	0	0	1	21	1	20	0	0
Wise	2,884	3	0	0	1	2	45	4	37	4	0
Woodstock	5,929	15	0	6	0	9	83	3	79	1	2
Wytheville	8,199	10	0	7	1	2	303	33	252	18	0
WASHINGTON											
Aberdeen	17,338	76	0	15	17	44	723	148	480	95	6

Table 8. Offenses Known to Law Enforcement, by Selected State and City, 2022—Continued

(Number.)

State/city	Population	Violent crime	Murder and nonnegligent manslaughter	Rape	Robbery	Aggravated assault	Property crime	Burglary	Larceny-theft	Motor vehicle theft	Arson[1]
Airway Heights	10,803	35	1	3	8	23	437	44	296	97	3
Algona	3,194	15	0	0	1	14	62	15	32	15	0
Anacortes	17,990	16	1	6	4	5	591	82	458	51	1
Arlington	20,176	67	0	7	16	44	574	114	354	106	1
Auburn	84,279	421	13	42	125	241	4,334	882	2,186	1,266	32
Bainbridge Island	24,336	23	0	12	0	11	340	55	256	29	1
Battle Ground	21,385	33	0	13	3	17	333	25	267	41	2
Beaux Arts	304	1	0	1	0	0	2	0	2	0	0
Bellevue	147,079	230	2	17	103	108	5,569	786	4,299	484	12
Bellingham	93,014	378	2	22	135	219	6,058	801	4,764	493	20
Bingen	737	1	0	1	0	0	13	4	8	1	1
Black Diamond	7,021	0	0	0	0	0	72	24	43	5	0
Blaine	6,050	15	1	0	1	13	122	34	71	17	0
Bonney Lake	22,898	50	0	5	13	32	711	96	537	78	2
Bothell	47,407	37	1	10	10	16	985	120	752	113	3
Bremerton	44,256	210	1	40	44	125	1,859	316	1,191	352	13
Brewster	2,027	2	0	1	0	1	19	4	13	2	0
Brier	6,448	10	0	0	0	10	63	15	30	18	0
Buckley	5,982	17	1	1	0	15	66	14	37	15	1
Burien	50,159	249	2	30	78	139	2,063	416	1,037	610	17
Burlington	10,187	34	2	5	22	5	1,166	130	933	103	1
Camas	27,653	8	0	5	0	3	313	40	231	42	1
Carnation	2,170	0	0	0	0	0	27	6	19	2	0
Castle Rock	2,442	3	0	2	0	1	74	25	41	8	1
Centralia	18,993	63	2	13	12	36	974	125	730	119	5
Chehalis	7,870	24	0	1	7	16	538	54	434	50	0
Cheney	13,092	26	0	10	3	13	241	42	178	21	3
Clarkston	7,267	42	0	9	1	32	344	69	256	19	4
Cle Elum	3,198	8	0	2	1	5	107	14	77	16	0
College Place	9,907	7	0	0	2	5	221	49	163	9	0
Colville	5,026	2	0	0	0	2	20	6	8	6	0
Connell	4,945	6	0	3	1	2	46	11	26	9	0
Coulee Dam	1,241	3	0	2	0	1	13	5	7	1	0
Covington	20,686	67	0	11	28	28	852	153	577	122	0
Darrington	1,468	6	0	1	0	5	10	4	3	3	0
Des Moines	32,541	99	3	9	33	54	1,136	132	740	264	9
Dupont	10,024	9	0	2	3	4	214	33	136	45	1
Duvall	8,778	5	0	0	1	4	49	3	43	3	0
East Wenatchee	14,243	20	0	3	4	13	294	47	223	24	0
Eatonville	2,849	8	0	0	1	7	21	2	11	8	2
Edgewood	12,900	22	0	8	4	10	434	109	253	72	3
Edmonds	42,714	104	1	7	32	64	1,119	171	838	110	5
Ellensburg	19,822	50	2	9	9	30	533	71	425	37	1
Elma	3,509	6	0	2	0	4	72	21	43	8	0
Enumclaw	12,833	7	0	2	3	2	264	33	174	57	0
Ephrata	8,465	20	0	5	2	13	430	115	279	36	1
Everett	110,694	490	12	54	110	314	4,816	738	3,082	996	20
Everson	4,653	4	1	1	0	2	26	2	23	1	0
Federal Way	97,094	534	8	56	154	316	5,099	724	2,904	1,471	27
Ferndale	15,816	28	3	5	8	12	442	40	373	29	5
Fife	10,900	170	1	14	49	106	1,324	180	699	445	10
Fircrest	7,047	12	0	1	4	7	153	21	86	46	2
Gig Harbor	12,301	30	0	2	12	16	746	90	537	119	1
Gold Bar	2,384	3	0	1	1	1	23	10	12	1	0
Goldendale	3,551	3	0	0	0	3	162	22	139	1	0
Grand Coulee	1,919	4	1	0	0	3	65	11	39	15	1
Grandview	10,901	33	0	5	6	22	384	110	221	53	4
Granite Falls	4,842	8	0	2	1	5	54	22	29	3	0
Hoquiam	8,918	11	2	0	0	9	205	45	141	19	1
Ilwaco	1,132	0	0	0	0	0	15	3	8	4	0
Index	157	0	0	0	0	0	2	0	2	0	0
Issaquah	38,917	19	0	2	12	5	1,692	133	1,422	137	1
Kalama	3,061	4	0	0	0	4	80	32	39	9	1
Kelso	12,723	52	2	9	10	31	594	124	402	68	6
Kenmore	23,107	14	0	4	2	8	296	54	198	44	4
Kennewick	85,058	406	8	68	61	269	3,961	505	2,720	736	18
Kent	133,066	611	9	73	209	320	7,356	1,545	3,802	2,009	24
Kettle Falls	1,665	7	0	1	1	5	26	1	22	3	0
Kirkland	91,464	106	0	19	28	59	2,161	247	1,678	236	4
La Center	4,142	7	0	0	0	7	60	13	45	2	0
Lacey	55,101	121	2	16	32	71	1,896	257	1,362	277	10
Lake Forest Park	13,096	13	0	3	2	8	263	29	206	28	2
Lake Stevens	36,828	62	0	13	10	39	366	56	249	61	2
Lakewood	63,044	529	4	34	112	379	3,282	537	1,749	996	17
Langley	1,155	2	0	0	1	1	29	7	21	1	1
Liberty Lake	12,897	26	0	5	3	18	246	20	201	25	0
Long Beach	1,752	11	0	6	0	5	37	14	20	3	0
Longview	37,768	132	0	26	35	71	1,694	292	1,188	214	10
Lynden	16,275	18	0	7	2	9	340	30	299	11	2
Lynnwood	42,764	141	5	18	54	64	2,528	310	1,949	269	4
Maple Valley	28,175	31	0	5	11	15	497	91	332	74	2
Marysville	71,395	181	0	38	36	107	1,240	180	847	213	7

Table 8. Offenses Known to Law Enforcement, by Selected State and City, 2022—Continued

(Number.)

State/city	Population	Violent crime	Murder and nonnegligent manslaughter	Rape	Robbery	Aggravated assault	Property crime	Burglary	Larceny-theft	Motor vehicle theft	Arson[1]
Medina	2,849	1	0	0	0	1	33	8	19	6	0
Mercer Island	25,121	25	2	3	5	15	425	54	328	43	0
Mill Creek	20,925	36	1	3	9	23	527	95	373	59	3
Milton	9,113	40	0	1	17	22	359	48	210	101	0
Monroe	20,309	54	0	10	11	33	549	63	446	40	4
Montesano	4,196	1	0	0	0	1	53	8	44	1	0
Moses Lake	25,709	134	2	9	25	98	1,399	193	1,103	103	13
Mountlake Terrace	21,589	34	1	6	9	18	613	88	419	106	4
Mount Vernon	35,511	96	1	9	20	66	1,047	155	737	155	15
Moxee	4,408	10	1	1	0	8	34	6	21	7	0
Mukilteo	21,009	25	0	3	4	18	510	93	370	47	1
Napavine	1,999	2	0	0	0	2	38	14	20	4	0
Newcastle	12,782	11	0	2	3	6	300	53	186	61	1
Newport	2,182	4	1	0	0	3	37	4	30	3	1
Normandy Park	6,519	6	0	1	2	3	127	25	86	16	0
North Bend	7,889	7	0	1	2	4	341	40	267	34	0
Oak Harbor	24,858	15	0	4	2	9	220	33	151	36	0
Oakville	733	2	0	0	0	2	37	3	27	7	0
Olympia	56,214	293	2	31	84	176	2,363	344	1,661	358	12
Orting	8,877	15	0	0	1	14	108	19	71	18	2
Othello	8,876	13	0	7	1	5	257	24	192	41	1
Pacific	6,966	16	0	2	5	9	201	52	102	47	1
Pasco	79,899	254	2	28	58	166	2,255	313	1,414	528	17
Port Angeles	20,290	136	1	29	18	88	768	157	531	80	7
Port Orchard	16,351	72	0	15	17	40	955	136	596	223	2
Port Townsend	10,452	19	0	0	1	18	145	24	106	15	2
Poulsbo	11,814	38	0	6	8	24	442	63	317	62	1
Prosser	6,136	7	0	0	1	6	138	13	96	29	1
Pullman	32,848	30	0	15	1	14	309	50	248	11	0
Puyallup	42,580	162	1	21	70	70	3,095	384	1,929	782	39
Quincy	8,413	14	1	4	3	6	210	46	126	38	3
Raymond	3,201	4	1	1	1	1	44	12	25	7	0
Reardan	685	0	0	0	0	0	10	4	4	2	0
Redmond	79,403	94	0	16	41	37	2,520	265	2,036	219	16
Renton	103,619	382	7	22	141	212	4,796	669	2,773	1,354	20
Richland	63,081	197	5	43	25	124	2,341	282	1,742	317	5
Ridgefield	14,465	15	0	6	1	8	165	29	113	23	1
Ritzville	1,704	4	0	2	0	2	96	5	86	5	0
Roy	805	3	0	1	0	2	13	7	4	2	1
Royal City	1,828	2	0	1	0	1	27	5	9	13	0
Ruston	1,053	4	0	0	0	4	63	9	31	23	2
Sammamish	65,738	39	1	13	3	22	603	102	460	41	0
SeaTac	30,203	191	2	33	53	103	1,573	140	900	533	4
Seattle	729,691	6,115	54	311	1,748	4,002	41,745	8,765	26,038	6,942	180
Sedro Woolley	12,565	16	0	0	0	16	269	66	171	32	0
Selah	8,258	10	0	7	1	2	182	25	141	16	2
Sequim	8,439	20	0	4	2	14	310	58	216	36	0
Shelton	11,102	66	2	18	14	32	377	72	249	56	3
Shoreline	57,147	156	2	24	48	82	1,629	335	993	301	23
Skykomish	156	0	0	0	0	0	7	5	2	0	0
Snohomish	10,125	21	0	0	8	13	275	59	180	36	2
Snoqualmie	13,523	1	0	0	1	0	326	27	258	41	1
Soap Lake	1,708	9	0	2	0	7	62	12	39	11	0
South Bend	1,784	1	0	0	0	1	24	3	19	2	0
Spokane	229,292	1,541	18	194	309	1,020	13,153	1,771	9,579	1,803	75
Spokane Valley	108,076	360	3	49	71	237	4,390	593	3,230	567	8
Stanwood	9,132	7	0	1	1	5	123	22	93	8	0
Steilacoom	6,690	5	1	1	0	3	91	11	61	19	0
Sultan	6,102	14	0	0	3	11	76	16	55	5	0
Sumas	1,647	3	0	2	0	1	7	1	5	1	0
Sumner	10,681	24	1	6	4	13	619	126	367	126	7
Sunnyside	16,300	78	1	4	17	56	607	83	422	102	2
Tacoma	219,027	3,526	41	147	746	2,592	18,704	2,381	10,422	5,901	243
Toppenish	8,717	76	2	7	13	54	649	124	420	105	5
Tukwila	21,473	166	3	12	88	63	4,293	321	3,077	895	4
Tumwater	26,227	60	0	8	13	39	881	143	600	138	3
Union Gap	6,514	24	3	4	10	7	513	67	399	47	1
University Place	34,846	87	1	9	20	57	1,025	123	639	263	9
Vancouver	193,273	1,229	14	132	293	790	10,777	1,351	6,625	2,801	53
Walla Walla	33,899	126	2	27	10	87	1,037	206	741	90	18
Warden	2,574	2	0	0	0	2	103	21	65	17	0
Washougal	16,902	47	0	10	8	29	304	40	211	53	7
Wenatchee	35,462	85	2	17	9	57	982	154	733	95	16
Westport	2,280	6	0	2	1	3	113	27	79	7	0
West Richland	17,557	16	0	4	2	10	199	30	141	28	0
White Salmon	2,663	0	0	0	0	0	22	5	15	2	0
Winlock	1,704	2	0	1	0	1	32	4	24	4	0
Woodinville	13,357	25	0	6	12	7	528	69	403	56	2
Woodland	6,544	12	0	3	3	6	206	23	147	36	1
Woodway	1,302	0	0	0	0	0	17	6	11	0	0
Yakima	96,267	589	12	51	121	405	3,026	545	1,975	506	23
Yelm	10,749	29	0	7	6	16	301	51	219	31	2

Table 8. Offenses Known to Law Enforcement, by Selected State and City, 2022—Continued

(Number.)

State/city	Population	Violent crime	Murder and nonnegligent manslaughter	Rape	Robbery	Aggravated assault	Property crime	Burglary	Larceny-theft	Motor vehicle theft	Arson[1]
WEST VIRGINIA											
Barboursville	4,264	0	0	0	0	0	91	0	91	0	0
Beckley	16,843	125	1	15	8	101	1,297	134	1,114	49	0
Bluefield	9,411	131	2	2	0	127	8	0	8	0	0
Bridgeport	9,206	25	0	3	0	22	104	4	94	6	0
Buckhannon	5,243	3	0	1	0	2	86	0	86	0	0
Ceredo	1,372	4	0	1	0	3	13	2	10	1	1
Chapmanville	980	0	0	0	0	0	16	3	10	3	0
Charleston	47,350	302	10	44	35	213	1,943	423	1,375	145	29
Clearview	455	0	0	0	0	0	1	0	1	0	0
Fairmont	18,121	71	1	9	5	56	251	54	179	18	5
Fayetteville	2,815	2	0	0	0	2	143	2	141	0	0
Follansbee	2,760	0	0	0	0	0	15	2	10	3	0
Glen Dale	1,467	0	0	0	0	0	13	1	11	1	0
Grafton	4,578	0	0	0	0	0	31	14	15	2	1
Huntington	45,547	288	6	31	36	215	1,274	236	871	167	19
Kenova	2,940	0	0	0	0	0	28	3	18	7	0
Madison	2,779	9	0	1	0	8	22	6	15	1	1
Moorefield	2,459	25	0	1	0	24	48	4	43	1	0
Morgantown	29,279	84	6	19	8	51	715	41	648	26	0
Nitro	6,444	11	0	2	0	9	259	38	210	11	0
Parkersburg	29,190	129	5	26	9	89	1,011	110	825	76	23
Ripley	3,061	8	0	0	0	8	30	3	27	0	0
Romney	1,718	14	0	1	0	13	6	0	5	1	0
Shepherdstown	1,504	0	0	0	0	0	8	0	7	1	0
South Charleston	13,138	82	1	6	3	72	610	39	547	24	3
Spencer	2,022	3	0	2	0	1	49	2	47	0	0
Summersville	3,371	7	0	0	0	7	85	9	75	1	0
Vienna	10,521	19	0	6	2	11	381	12	362	7	2
Weirton	18,544	17	0	7	0	10	70	0	70	0	4
Wheeling	26,244	323	5	25	14	279	633	187	405	41	1
Williamstown	2,971	4	0	0	0	4	1	0	1	0	0
WISCONSIN											
Adams	1,776	6	0	3	0	3	60	6	52	2	1
Algoma	3,205	5	0	2	0	3	15	4	10	1	1
Altoona	9,320	8	1	4	0	3	178	14	156	8	0
Amery	2,942	8	0	2	0	6	32	3	28	1	0
Antigo	7,947	17	0	2	0	15	133	12	112	9	0
Appleton	74,411	200	1	31	8	160	1,115	115	949	51	4
Arcadia	3,654	2	0	0	0	2	6	1	5	0	0
Ashland	7,975	13	0	6	1	6	264	23	223	18	2
Ashwaubenon	16,833	25	0	12	1	12	359	24	318	17	0
Augusta	1,534	3	0	2	0	1	27	5	21	1	0
Bangor	1,420	2	0	2	0	0	6	0	5	1	0
Baraboo	12,312	31	0	7	2	22	193	8	170	15	0
Barneveld	1,318	0	0	0	0	0	1	0	1	0	0
Barron	3,644	8	0	0	0	8	17	4	10	3	0
Bayfield	590	0	0	0	0	0	0	0	0	0	1
Bayside	4,365	0	0	0	0	0	25	1	21	3	0
Beaver Dam	16,656	26	1	10	1	14	114	6	104	4	1
Belleville	2,614	2	0	0	0	2	15	5	10	0	1
Beloit	36,784	225	3	22	26	174	773	98	568	107	10
Beloit Town	7,895	9	0	1	1	7	83	19	56	8	1
Berlin	5,665	21	0	1	0	20	60	6	51	3	0
Birchwood	408	0	0	0	0	0	0	0	0	0	0
Black River Falls	3,495	2	0	1	0	1	89	5	79	5	2
Bloomer	3,742	4	0	1	0	3	23	1	19	3	0
Boscobel	3,291	7	0	0	0	7	15	0	12	3	1
Boyceville	1,094	5	0	5	0	0	10	0	9	1	0
Brillion	3,395	4	0	2	0	2	17	0	15	2	0
Brodhead	3,241	2	0	1	1	0	29	0	27	2	0
Brookfield	41,489	17	0	5	7	5	541	29	469	43	0
Brookfield Township	6,429	4	0	1	1	2	95	3	86	6	0
Brown Deer	12,817	33	2	3	9	19	653	11	528	114	3
Burlington	10,991	7	0	1	0	6	64	7	56	1	0
Butler	1,765	3	0	1	1	1	58	2	50	6	0
Caledonia	25,165	9	0	1	1	7	115	25	79	11	0
Campbell Township	4,198	3	0	1	0	2	46	3	42	1	0
Cashton	1,150	1	0	0	0	1	6	0	6	0	0
Cedarburg	12,636	4	0	0	0	4	82	1	78	3	0
Chetek	2,160	1	0	0	0	1	11	3	6	2	0
Chilton	3,898	8	1	4	0	3	15	2	12	1	0
Chippewa Falls	14,832	41	3	7	1	30	79	9	59	11	2
Cleveland	1,599	0	0	0	0	0	4	1	3	0	0
Clinton	2,178	2	0	0	0	2	20	2	15	3	0
Colby-Abbotsford	4,312	4	0	0	0	4	43	1	38	4	0
Columbus	5,478	0	0	0	0	0	35	0	30	5	0
Cornell	1,448	3	0	2	0	1	10	1	9	0	0
Cottage Grove	7,328	3	0	0	0	3	11	1	7	3	0
Crandon	1,764	2	0	0	0	2	7	1	6	0	0
Cross Plains	4,011	2	0	0	0	2	14	1	8	5	0
Cudahy	17,702	23	0	5	0	18	200	14	134	52	2

Table 8. Offenses Known to Law Enforcement, by Selected State and City, 2022—Continued

(Number.)

State/city	Population	Violent crime	Murder and nonnegligent manslaughter	Rape	Robbery	Aggravated assault	Property crime	Burglary	Larceny-theft	Motor vehicle theft	Arson[1]
Cumberland	2,269	1	0	0	0	1	0	0	0	0	0
Darlington	2,458	1	0	0	0	1	7	1	6	0	0
Deforest	10,869	8	4	0	0	4	126	6	107	13	0
Delafield	7,192	3	0	1	0	2	101	2	99	0	0
Delavan	10,193	11	0	2	0	9	155	5	136	14	0
Delavan Town	5,347	2	0	0	0	2	11	3	8	0	0
De Pere	25,382	20	0	3	1	16	148	12	125	11	0
Eagle Village	2,119	0	0	0	0	0	6	0	6	0	0
East Troy	4,748	4	0	0	0	4	14	0	13	1	0
Eau Claire	69,569	96	1	38	5	52	1,549	217	1,250	82	8
Edgar	1,456	0	0	0	0	0	5	1	4	0	0
Edgerton	5,954	3	0	0	0	3	38	3	32	3	0
Elkhorn	10,359	9	0	2	0	7	69	3	64	2	0
Elk Mound	979	4	0	2	0	2	22	1	21	0	0
Ellsworth	3,318	5	0	2	0	3	19	2	13	4	0
Elm Grove	6,512	1	0	0	1	0	41	5	34	2	0
Everest Metropolitan	17,819	41	0	14	2	25	154	28	106	20	1
Fall River	1,802	2	0	1	0	1	0	0	0	0	0
Fennimore	2,783	0	0	0	0	0	8	3	5	0	0
Fitchburg	31,796	98	0	13	12	73	421	45	306	70	1
Fond du Lac	44,613	129	4	28	5	92	732	42	653	37	1
Fort Atkinson	12,432	38	0	3	2	33	112	10	98	4	0
Fox Crossing	18,866	9	0	5	0	4	174	24	135	15	1
Fox Point	6,749	1	0	0	0	1	51	1	43	7	0
Franklin	36,396	16	0	3	2	11	487	23	436	28	0
Fulton	3,660	0	0	0	0	0	3	0	3	0	0
Geneva Town	5,484	0	0	0	0	0	9	0	7	2	0
Genoa City	2,997	2	0	0	0	2	11	0	10	1	0
Germantown	20,956	11	0	1	1	9	347	11	318	18	0
Gillett	1,282	1	0	1	0	0	14	1	11	2	0
Glendale	13,004	35	0	4	14	17	641	22	516	103	0
Grafton	12,471	6	0	3	1	2	115	4	108	3	0
Grand Chute	23,871	72	0	28	2	42	1,020	83	902	35	1
Green Bay	106,916	456	6	67	30	353	1,844	251	1,419	174	8
Greendale	14,459	18	0	4	3	11	231	4	200	27	0
Greenfield	36,924	61	1	7	13	40	956	46	788	122	0
Hales Corners	7,516	2	0	1	0	1	64	4	59	1	0
Hartford	15,803	42	0	4	0	38	60	1	57	2	0
Hartford Township	3,399	0	0	0	0	0	0	0	0	0	0
Hartland	9,644	9	3	0	1	5	27	3	23	1	1
Hayward	2,566	12	0	3	0	9	98	6	91	1	1
Hobart-Lawrence	16,948	1	0	1	0	0	23	5	17	1	0
Holmen	11,058	2	0	1	0	1	67	8	57	2	0
Horicon	3,827	7	0	4	0	3	17	0	16	1	0
Hortonville	3,111	2	0	1	0	1	16	1	14	1	1
Hudson	15,571	27	1	3	2	21	361	14	311	36	0
Hurley	1,564	3	0	1	0	2	12	0	11	1	0
Janesville	66,242	112	1	28	17	66	1,299	112	1,086	101	9
Jefferson	7,709	17	0	2	0	15	130	2	123	5	0
Juneau	2,656	2	0	0	0	2	2	0	2	0	0
Kaukauna	17,288	14	1	5	1	7	160	51	101	8	0
Kenosha	98,841	393	7	62	46	278	1,078	117	837	124	10
Kewaskum	4,429	7	0	3	0	4	20	1	18	1	0
Kewaunee	2,774	2	0	2	0	0	12	0	11	1	0
Kiel	3,969	2	0	0	0	2	18	0	18	0	0
Kohler	2,184	1	0	1	0	0	68	0	68	0	0
Kronenwetter	8,530	9	2	4	0	3	23	4	18	1	0
La Crosse	51,727	158	3	44	16	95	1,601	114	1,394	93	5
La Farge	720	0	0	0	0	0	5	2	3	0	0
Lake Delton	3,447	23	0	4	3	16	314	11	291	12	0
Lake Geneva	8,631	12	1	4	0	7	147	2	140	5	0
Lake Hallie	7,352	11	0	0	1	10	98	2	92	4	0
Lake Mills	6,662	15	0	4	2	9	47	3	42	2	0
Lancaster	3,911	33	0	12	0	21	49	1	47	1	0
Linden	505	0	0	0	0	0	0	0	0	0	0
Linn Township	2,734	0	0	0	0	0	13	2	11	0	0
Lodi	3,213	5	0	0	0	5	17	2	13	2	0
Lomira	2,680	3	0	2	0	1	15	1	13	1	0
Luxemburg	2,699	4	0	3	0	1	4	0	3	1	0
Madison	269,546	810	6	85	113	606	6,459	921	4,866	672	21
Manitowoc	34,688	68	0	9	5	54	523	85	415	23	2
Maple Bluff	1,326	11	0	0	0	11	6	0	3	3	0
Marinette	11,015	44	1	6	0	37	211	13	185	13	1
Markesan	1,386	0	0	0	0	0	5	0	4	1	0
Marshall Village	3,833	14	0	0	0	14	22	4	16	2	0
Mauston	4,294	11	0	1	1	9	84	2	80	2	0
Mayville	5,124	4	0	2	0	2	45	0	45	0	1
McFarland	9,555	10	0	0	0	10	81	11	66	4	0
Medford	4,298	7	0	5	0	2	78	20	55	3	0
Menasha	17,971	25	0	10	1	14	187	20	162	5	0
Menomonee Falls	39,312	28	1	7	2	18	357	18	303	36	1
Menomonie	16,781	31	0	1	0	30	218	12	196	10	0
Mequon	25,347	16	0	0	3	13	199	20	166	13	2

Table 8. Offenses Known to Law Enforcement, by Selected State and City, 2022—Continued
(Number.)

State/city	Population	Violent crime	Murder and nonnegligent manslaughter	Rape	Robbery	Aggravated assault	Property crime	Burglary	Larceny-theft	Motor vehicle theft	Arson[1]
Merrill	9,341	16	1	0	2	13	262	18	234	10	1
Middleton	23,346	19	0	3	1	15	221	13	185	23	0
Milton	5,683	2	0	0	0	2	27	3	22	2	0
Milton Town	3,106	0	0	0	0	0	0	0	0	0	0
Milwaukee	561,743	8,474	214	425	1,577	6,258	19,702	2,232	8,027	9,443	249
Minocqua	5,186	3	0	2	0	1	39	4	35	0	0
Monona	8,920	13	0	3	4	6	297	14	267	16	0
Monroe	10,461	10	1	2	1	6	176	1	167	8	0
Montello	1,444	0	0	0	0	0	13	0	13	0	0
Mount Horeb	7,687	5	0	0	0	5	12	1	11	0	0
Mount Pleasant	27,625	31	0	4	2	25	488	26	438	24	1
Mukwonago	8,477	6	0	0	2	4	96	1	93	2	0
Mukwonago Town	7,792	4	0	0	0	4	10	0	9	1	0
Muscoda	1,301	2	0	1	0	1	11	4	7	0	0
Muskego	25,406	12	0	0	2	10	116	4	105	7	0
Neenah	27,706	64	0	15	5	44	352	57	254	41	1
Nekoosa	2,434	7	0	2	0	5	10	1	8	1	0
New Berlin	40,358	18	0	3	3	12	311	33	264	14	2
New Glarus	2,221	0	0	0	0	0	22	1	21	0	0
New Holstein	3,033	4	0	2	0	2	28	2	23	3	0
New London	7,286	8	0	5	0	3	39	1	38	0	0
New Richmond	10,610	13	2	3	0	8	112	4	98	10	0
Niagara	1,582	4	0	0	0	4	9	0	7	2	0
North Fond du Lac	5,423	5	0	4	0	1	47	4	38	5	1
North Hudson	3,953	3	0	2	0	1	18	0	12	6	0
Norwalk	594	0	0	0	0	0	1	1	0	0	0
Oak Creek	35,995	45	0	11	5	29	744	22	643	79	0
Oconomowoc	18,531	3	0	2	1	0	95	4	89	2	0
Oconomowoc Town	8,853	0	0	0	0	0	15	4	10	1	0
Oconto	4,589	2	0	0	0	2	33	5	28	0	0
Oconto Falls	2,961	3	0	3	0	0	27	2	25	0	0
Omro	3,662	3	0	3	0	0	16	0	16	0	2
Onalaska	18,807	7	0	3	1	3	399	20	368	11	1
Oregon	11,538	10	0	5	1	4	72	11	57	4	0
Osceola	2,849	3	1	1	0	1	20	6	12	2	0
Oshkosh	66,521	224	1	56	14	153	1,080	147	862	71	2
Palmyra	1,686	2	0	1	0	1	13	3	10	0	0
Park Falls	2,379	7	0	0	0	7	14	1	13	0	0
Pewaukee Village	8,177	4	0	0	4	0	166	5	160	1	0
Phillips	1,512	2	0	2	0	0	9	0	9	0	0
Pittsville	835	3	0	1	0	2	8	0	8	0	0
Platteville	11,771	31	1	7	0	23	250	5	238	7	2
Pleasant Prairie	21,421	56	0	6	2	48	207	13	179	15	1
Plover	13,850	21	0	11	0	10	206	9	192	5	2
Plymouth	8,885	0	0	0	0	0	68	0	65	3	0
Portage	10,251	16	0	4	0	12	202	15	176	11	1
Port Washington	12,867	5	0	2	0	3	66	6	59	1	0
Poynette	2,580	3	0	0	0	3	6	3	3	0	0
Prairie du Chien	5,461	10	0	6	0	4	77	9	65	3	0
Prescott	4,340	4	0	0	0	4	15	4	9	2	1
Princeton	1,280	0	0	0	0	0	2	0	2	0	0
Racine	76,679	333	5	30	68	230	1,154	339	647	168	7
Reedsburg	10,113	13	0	5	0	8	162	3	157	2	0
Rhinelander	8,341	11	0	4	0	7	111	6	98	7	0
Rice Lake	8,941	44	0	6	0	38	145	4	128	13	1
Richland Center	4,997	5	0	2	0	3	54	6	43	5	0
Ripon	7,793	14	0	6	0	8	51	5	41	5	1
River Falls	17,169	10	0	2	0	8	103	4	94	5	0
Roberts	2,050	2	0	0	0	2	9	0	9	0	0
Rome Town	3,158	3	0	2	0	1	19	4	15	0	0
Rosendale	1,052	0	0	0	0	0	0	0	0	0	0
Rothschild	5,522	2	0	0	0	2	35	1	30	4	0
Sauk Prairie	4,572	8	0	2	0	6	87	2	79	6	0
Saukville	4,283	5	0	0	0	5	51	2	48	1	0
Seymour	3,512	7	0	2	0	5	7	0	6	1	0
Sharon	1,590	0	0	0	0	0	2	1	0	1	0
Shawano	9,240	13	0	3	3	7	147	9	126	12	0
Sheboygan	49,917	166	0	45	11	110	696	66	601	29	10
Sheboygan Falls	8,140	5	1	1	0	3	37	5	30	2	0
Shorewood	13,453	15	0	0	8	7	231	11	172	48	1
Siren	835	4	0	1	0	3	12	1	10	1	0
South Milwaukee	20,247	28	2	3	5	18	235	16	199	20	0
Sparta	9,901	57	1	21	0	35	315	40	268	7	1
Stanley	3,800	10	0	1	0	9	24	0	23	1	0
St. Croix Falls	2,242	13	0	1	0	12	140	6	128	6	0
Stevens Point	25,777	43	0	13	2	28	245	25	202	18	2
St. Francis	9,758	20	0	3	1	16	97	2	79	16	1
Stoughton	12,948	14	0	1	0	13	177	18	148	11	1
Strum	1,056	0	0	0	0	0	1	0	1	0	0
Sturgeon Bay	9,758	8	0	0	0	8	67	4	61	2	0
Sturtevant	6,970	5	0	0	0	5	49	1	40	8	0
Summit	5,201	4	0	0	0	4	26	4	21	1	0
Sun Prairie	36,153	99	0	9	5	85	555	38	463	54	2

Table 8. Offenses Known to Law Enforcement, by Selected State and City, 2022—Continued

(Number.)

State/city	Population	Violent crime	Murder and nonnegligent manslaughter	Rape	Robbery	Aggravated assault	Property crime	Burglary	Larceny-theft	Motor vehicle theft	Arson[1]
Superior	26,429	56	0	19	3	34	630	56	514	60	3
Thiensville	3,302	0	0	0	0	0	6	0	6	0	0
Thorp	1,767	2	0	1	0	1	21	0	21	0	0
Tomahawk	3,432	4	0	2	0	2	41	4	34	3	0
Town of East Troy	4,068	1	0	0	0	1	8	1	6	1	0
Two Rivers	11,273	21	0	5	1	15	56	2	51	3	1
Verona	14,413	8	0	5	1	2	119	16	100	3	0
Viroqua	4,421	4	0	3	0	1	92	6	80	6	0
Walworth	2,778	0	0	0	0	0	29	0	29	0	0
Washburn	2,060	8	0	0	0	8	7	0	6	1	0
Waterford Town	6,455	2	0	0	0	2	15	3	12	0	0
Waterloo	3,475	9	0	3	0	6	12	1	11	0	0
Watertown	22,885	56	0	13	1	42	309	32	269	8	0
Waukesha	71,147	71	1	20	1	49	564	50	473	41	1
Waunakee	14,914	9	0	2	0	7	44	7	34	3	0
Waupaca	6,436	13	0	4	0	9	117	4	111	2	0
Waupun	11,530	19	0	5	1	13	32	2	28	2	0
Wausau	39,349	153	0	40	7	106	504	59	409	36	3
Wautoma	2,252	2	0	0	0	2	21	1	18	2	0
Wauwatosa	47,149	94	0	5	42	47	1,201	62	893	246	1
West Allis	58,681	168	1	15	60	92	1,530	127	1,122	281	3
West Bend	31,773	68	0	14	1	53	677	23	631	23	3
Westby	2,360	3	0	3	0	0	32	8	21	3	0
West Milwaukee	3,997	52	0	3	27	22	579	17	442	120	2
West Salem	5,271	7	0	2	0	5	43	5	34	4	0
Whitefish Bay	14,549	13	1	0	3	9	117	3	97	17	0
Whitehall	1,616	0	0	0	0	0	4	0	3	1	0
Whitewater	14,327	33	0	10	2	21	184	11	166	7	1
Williams Bay	3,017	2	0	1	0	1	10	1	8	1	0
Wilton	520	0	0	0	0	0	0	0	0	0	0
Winneconne	2,515	0	0	0	0	0	5	0	4	1	0
Wisconsin Dells	3,448	28	0	8	2	18	129	14	110	5	3
Wisconsin Rapids	18,693	80	0	32	1	47	391	38	324	29	2
Woodruff	2,105	1	0	0	0	1	15	0	15	0	0
WYOMING											
Buffalo	4,567	4	0	2	0	2	43	8	31	4	0
Cheyenne	64,941	181	0	63	16	102	2,361	272	1,821	268	9
Cody	10,281	22	0	8	1	13	90	17	69	4	0
Diamondville	530	1	0	1	0	0	7	6	1	0	0
Douglas	6,336	12	0	0	0	12	58	6	50	2	0
Evanston	11,886	47	0	31	0	16	186	28	144	14	1
Gillette	32,320	105	0	30	3	72	636	41	571	24	1
Glenrock	2,396	3	0	1	0	2	18	2	13	3	0
Green River	11,435	22	2	5	0	15	91	8	78	5	2
Hanna	687	1	0	1	0	0	7	4	2	1	0
Jackson	10,932	8	0	6	0	2	84	9	70	5	1
Laramie	32,009	34	1	12	2	19	401	66	329	6	4
Lingle	401	0	0	0	0	0	7	7	0	0	0
Lusk	1,496	8	0	0	0	8	14	3	10	1	0
Medicine Bow	249	0	0	0	0	0	0	0	0	0	0
Mills	4,239	7	0	1	0	6	72	3	61	8	0
Moorcroft	981	0	0	0	0	0	10	1	9	0	0
Newcastle	3,176	2	0	2	0	0	29	0	27	2	0
Pine Bluffs	1,146	1	0	0	0	1	2	0	1	1	0
Powell	6,484	21	0	4	0	17	80	16	57	7	3
Riverton	10,623	65	1	11	4	49	362	13	296	53	0
Rock Springs	22,914	39	0	9	1	29	288	32	236	20	1
Sheridan	19,373	27	0	0	2	25	336	29	294	13	2
Thermopolis	2,691	1	0	1	0	0	29	2	25	2	1
Torrington	6,145	9	0	6	0	3	138	40	88	10	0
Upton	904	5	0	2	0	3	16	0	15	1	0
Worland	4,817	3	0	3	0	0	26	5	18	3	0

1 The FBI does not publish arson data unless it receives data from either the agency or the state for all 12 months of the calendar year.   2 Limited data for 2022 were available for Florida, Illinois, Maryland, and Pennsylvania.

Table 9. Offenses Known to Law Enforcement, by Selected State and University and College, 2022

(Number.)

State and university/college	Student enrollment[1]	Violent crime	Murder and nonnegligent manslaughter	Rape	Robbery	Aggravated assault	Property crime	Burglary	Larceny-theft	Motor vehicle theft	Arson[2]
ALABAMA											
Alabama State University	4,478	0	0	0	0	0	0	0	0	0	0
Jacksonville State University	10,752	9	0	4	0	5	27	1	24	2	0
Samford University	6,160	3	0	2	0	1	20	2	17	1	0
Southern Union State Community College	5,789	0	0	0	0	0	0	0	0	0	0
Troy University	20,866	6	0	3	1	2	38	2	30	6	0
University of Alabama											
Birmingham	26,327	55	0	5	2	48	298	12	260	26	2
Huntsville	11,318	1	0	1	0	0	42	4	38	0	0
Tuscaloosa	41,992	26	0	4	6	16	227	27	198	2	1
University of Montevallo	2,960	0	0	0	0	0	0	0	0	0	0
University of North Alabama	10,003	7	0	2	1	4	32	3	28	1	0
University of South Alabama	16,311	23	1	4	1	17	74	11	60	3	1
University of West Alabama	8,711	1	0	1	0	0	20	2	18	0	0
Wallace State Community College	6,298	0	0	0	0	0	10	2	8	0	0
ALASKA											
University of Alaska, Fairbanks	10,725	2	0	0	0	2	40	1	36	3	0
ARIZONA											
Arizona State University, Main Campus	161,117	44	0	9	7	28	1,121	57	1,032	32	4
Central Arizona College	6,317	0	0	0	0	0	3	1	2	0	0
Northern Arizona University	33,349	19	0	16	1	2	191	15	173	3	1
Pima Community College	32,802	1	0	0	0	1	51	3	42	6	1
University of Arizona	52,329	54	1	12	5	36	718	31	656	31	2
ARKANSAS											
Arkansas State University											
Beebe	3,939	0	0	0	0	0	0	0	0	0	0
Jonesboro	18,451	2	0	0	0	2	32	2	28	2	0
Arkansas Tech University	12,257	6	0	4	0	2	52	2	50	0	0
Henderson State University	3,610	1	0	0	0	1	13	2	11	0	0
Southern Arkansas University	5,209	2	0	2	0	0	13	1	9	3	0
Southern Arkansas University Tech	1,588	0	0	0	0	0	1	0	1	0	0
University of Arkansas											
Fayetteville	30,349	10	0	6	0	4	171	17	137	17	0
Little Rock	10,955	1	0	0	0	1	30	8	21	1	0
Medical Sciences	3,241	7	0	0	0	7	94	1	90	3	0
Monticello	3,293	1	0	1	0	0	6	0	6	0	0
Pine Bluff	2,898	3	0	1	0	2	43	9	34	0	0
Pulaski Technical College	6,967	0	0	0	0	0	12	0	12	0	0
University of Arkansas Community College at											
Morrilton	2,400	0	0	0	0	0	2	0	2	0	0
University of Central Arkansas	11,834	5	0	1	0	4	71	8	62	1	1
CALIFORNIA											
Allan Hancock College	14,876	0	0	0	0	0	13	3	10	0	
California State Polytechnic University											
Humboldt	7,184	2	0	1	1	0	89	12	74	3	
Pomona	31,745	7	0	4	1	2	131	10	113	8	
San Luis Obispo	23,319	3	0	3	0	0	223	19	174	30	1
California State University											
Bakersfield	13,088	5	0	0	5	0	38	2	33	3	
Channel Islands	8,370	8	0	7	0	1	44	4	37	3	
Chico	18,141	4	0	2	1	1	90	4	82	4	
Dominguez Hills	20,180	2	0	1	0	1	32	12	18	2	
East Bay	18,567	4	0	3	1	0	44	3	40	1	1
Fresno	27,235	10	0	2	2	6	183	9	170	4	
Fullerton	47,482	3	0	1	0	2	158	5	143	10	
Long Beach	43,455	8	0	0	1	7	54	5	33	16	1
Los Angeles	29,167	7	0	1	3	3	106	9	79	18	
Monterey Bay	8,273	7	0	1	0	6	23	4	18	1	1
Northridge	43,286	7	0	5	1	1	133	5	123	5	
Sacramento	36,476	8	0	3	2	3	215	15	185	15	
San Bernardino	21,793	7	0	1	2	4	79	3	67	9	
San Jose	39,940	34	0	7	4	23	259	36	215	8	2
San Marcos	17,565	3	0	2	1	0	48	7	40	1	2
Stanislaus	12,470	3	0	2	0	1	11	0	10	1	0
Chaffey College	27,808	0	0	0	0	0	10	0	8	2	
College of the Sequoias	15,729	0	0	0	0	0	14	2	11	1	
Contra Costa Community College	49,068	3	0	1	0	2	75	24	49	2	
Cuesta College	13,912	0	0	0	0	0	4	0	4	0	
El Camino College	30,759	3	0	0	1	2	29	1	25	3	0
Foothill-De Anza College	56,506	2	0	0	0	2	17	3	12	2	0
Irvine Valley College	18,155	0	0	0	0	0	8	0	8	0	
Marin Community College	6,494	1	0	0	0	1	4	0	4	0	
Mt. San Jacinto College	19,172	0	0	0	0	0	12	4	6	2	
Pasadena Community College	35,760	0	0	0	0	0	36	1	32	3	
Riverside Community College	59,448	2	0	0	0	2	40	12	19	9	
San Bernardino Community College	25,704	0	0	0	0	0	38	13	23	2	
San Diego State University	38,811	27	0	12	6	9	358	63	283	12	
San Francisco State University	31,072	13	0	1	2	10	120	9	95	16	4
San Joaquin Delta College	25,009	1	0	1	0	0	28	3	24	1	4

Table 9. Offenses Known to Law Enforcement, by Selected State and University and College, 2022—Continued

(Number.)

State and university/college	Student enrollment[1]	Violent crime	Murder and nonnegligent manslaughter	Rape	Robbery	Aggravated assault	Property crime	Burglary	Larceny-theft	Motor vehicle theft	Arson[2]
San Jose/Evergreen Community College	26,623	0	0	0	0	0	44	20	23	1	
Sonoma County Junior College	24,673	2	0	0	0	2	15	2	12	1	
Sonoma State University	8,775	7	0	4	0	3	56	6	47	3	
State Center Community College District	61,021	0	0	0	0	0	96	12	79	5	
University of California											
Berkeley	45,584	95	0	14	18	63	920	50	519	351	19
Davis	41,743	24	0	10	4	10	936	119	674	143	5
Irvine	38,479	23	1	9	0	13	490	23	459	8	
Los Angeles	47,499	64	0	9	8	47	723	131	442	150	7
Medical Center, Sacramento[3]		5	0	3	0	2	87	11	73	3	0
Merced	9,488	7	0	2	0	5	63	1	60	2	
Riverside	28,597	6	0	3	1	2	534	64	409	61	
San Diego	41,682	14	0	3	3	8	909	31	564	314	
San Francisco	3,313	21	0	2	6	13	380	43	298	39	3
Santa Barbara	28,222	21	0	13	3	5	456	20	419	17	5
Santa Cruz	20,781	18	0	12	2	4	186	12	166	8	2
Ventura County Community College District	50,633	0	0	0	0	0	12	4	8	0	
West Valley-Mission College	23,203	0	0	0	0	0	22	12	9	1	
COLORADO											
Adams State University	3,863	8	0	1	0	7	39	2	37	0	0
Colorado School of Mines	7,281	0	0	0	0	0	107	2	97	8	0
Colorado State University, Fort Collins	36,626	12	0	3	0	9	488	22	456	10	2
Fort Lewis College	3,899	4	0	4	0	0	19	3	16	0	0
Red Rocks Community College	9,871	0	0	0	0	0	15	1	9	5	0
University of Colorado											
Boulder	41,927	20	0	12	1	7	472	28	431	13	4
Colorado Springs	15,955	7	0	7	0	0	85	4	79	2	0
Denver	30,432	3	0	0	1	2	231	2	64	165	0
University of Northern Colorado	13,818	1	0	1	0	0	113	7	83	23	0
CONNECTICUT											
Central Connecticut State University	12,467	1	0	1	0	0	9	0	9	0	0
University of Connecticut, all campuses[3]		4	0	2	0	2	126	5	102	19	1
Western Connecticut State University	6,001	0	0	0	0	0	13	0	12	1	0
Yale University	13,555	4	0	0	0	4	179	13	150	16	0
DELAWARE											
Delaware State University	5,230	10	0	7	1	2	41	1	39	1	0
University of Delaware	25,695	5	0	4	1	0	166	4	161	1	3
FLORIDA[4]											
Florida A&M University	10,221	5	0	4	0	1	29	6	21	2	0
Florida Atlantic University	37,656	5	0	4	0	1	45	2	30	13	0
Florida Polytechnic University	1,498	1	0	1	0	0	6	1	5	0	0
Florida State University, Panama City[3]		0	0	0	0	0	5	0	5	0	0
New College of Florida	706	4	0	3	0	1	20	1	17	2	0
Santa Fe College	17,486	0	0	0	0	0	6	1	5	0	0
University of Central Florida	83,889	10	0	5	3	2	186	13	165	8	0
University of Florida	60,790	9	0	4	1	4	184	10	174	0	0
University of North Florida	20,138	12	0	10	0	2	64	3	60	1	0
University of South Florida, St. Petersburg[3]		0	0	0	0	0	18	0	17	1	0
University of West Florida	16,584	0	0	0	0	0	20	1	19	0	0
GEORGIA											
Abraham Baldwin Agricultural College	4,735	1	0	1	0	0	32	0	31	1	0
Agnes Scott College	1,130	0	0	0	0	0	15	0	13	2	0
Athens Technical College	5,778	0	0	0	0	0	0	0	0	0	0
Atlanta Technical College	4,973	0	0	0	0	0	1	0	1	0	0
Augusta Technical College	5,549	0	0	0	0	0	3	0	3	0	0
Augusta University	9,979	4	0	0	4	0	116	8	104	4	1
Berry College	2,308	0	0	0	0	0	19	0	19	0	0
Clayton State University	8,659	4	0	2	0	2	21	1	19	1	0
College of Coastal Georgia	4,303	2	0	1	0	1	20	0	18	2	0
Columbus State University	10,094	0	0	0	0	0	54	5	47	2	0
Dalton State College	5,513	0	0	0	0	0	0	0	0	0	0
Emory University	15,201	18	0	11	3	4	274	32	240	2	1
Fort Valley State University	3,202	4	0	0	1	3	14	1	7	6	0
Georgia College and State University	7,914	4	0	2	0	2	28	1	24	3	0
Georgia Gwinnett College	14,559	0	0	0	0	0	24	0	24	0	0
Georgia Highlands College	7,367	0	0	0	0	0	5	0	5	0	0
Georgia Institute of Technology	47,787	10	0	0	4	6	332	18	246	68	3
Georgia Military College	12,823	0	0	0	0	0	0	0	0	0	0
Georgia Northwestern Technical College	8,768	0	0	0	0	0	4	1	3	0	0
Georgia Piedmont Technical College	3,920	0	0	0	0	0	12	2	7	3	0
Georgia Southern University	31,082	12	0	9	2	1	136	4	127	5	0
Georgia Southwestern State University	3,926	0	0	0	0	0	6	0	5	1	0
Gordon State College	3,908	6	0	4	1	1	5	2	3	0	0
Gwinnett Technical College	11,675	0	0	0	0	0	0	0	0	0	0
Kennesaw State University	48,071	7	0	6	0	1	92	7	82	3	0
Mercer University	10,403	1	0	0	1	0	45	1	37	7	0
Middle Georgia State University	10,346	3	0	1	1	1	27	3	22	2	0
Morehouse College	2,482	2	0	1	0	1	20	1	16	3	0

Table 9. Offenses Known to Law Enforcement, by Selected State and University and College, 2022—Continued

(Number.)

State and university/college	Student enrollment[1]	Violent crime	Murder and nonnegligent manslaughter	Rape	Robbery	Aggravated assault	Property crime	Burglary	Larceny-theft	Motor vehicle theft	Arson[2]
Piedmont College	3,055	0	0	0	0	0	0	0	0	0	0
Savannah Technical College	5,536	1	0	0	0	1	3	1	2	0	0
Southern Regional Technical College	5,685	0	0	0	0	0	0	0	0	0	0
South Georgia State College	2,649	0	0	0	0	0	2	1	1	0	0
Spelman College	2,286	0	0	0	0	0	4	1	3	0	0
University of Georgia	43,314	26	0	20	2	4	369	12	352	5	1
University of North Georgia	23,080	3	0	3	0	0	12	2	10	0	0
University of West Georgia	16,100	4	0	1	1	2	27	0	27	0	0
West Georgia Technical College	8,932	0	0	0	0	0	1	0	1	0	0
Young Harris College	1,620	1	0	1	0	0	25	0	25	0	0
ILLINOIS[4]											
Bradley University[3]		0	0	0	0	0	0	0	0	0	0
Chicago State University	3,246	1	1	0	0	0	3	1	1	1	0
College of DuPage	36,245	0	0	0	0	0	9	0	9	0	0
Eastern Illinois University	10,562	5	0	5	0	0	41	3	38	0	0
Elgin Community College	11,788	0	0	0	0	0	2	0	1	1	0
Eureka College	551	0	0	0	0	0	0	0	0	0	0
Harper College	22,623	0	0	0	0	0	0	0	0	0	0
Illinois Central College	11,132	1	0	1	0	0	21	2	19	0	0
Illinois State University	22,580	17	0	8	0	9	90	1	88	1	1
John Wood Community College	2,724	0	0	0	0	0	0	0	0	0	0
Joliet Junior College	20,745	0	0	0	0	0	3	0	3	0	0
Lewis University	7,703	0	0	0	0	0	12	1	11	0	0
Loyola University of Chicago	19,223	2	0	1	1	0	33	0	33	0	0
McHenry County College	11,883	0	0	0	0	0	5	0	5	0	0
Millikin University	2,147	3	0	2	1	0	17	0	16	1	0
Moraine Valley Community College	17,693	0	0	0	0	0	1	0	1	0	0
Morton College	5,387	0	0	0	0	0	5	2	3	0	0
Northeastern Illinois University	8,778	0	0	0	0	0	6	0	5	1	0
Northern Illinois University	18,759	15	0	13	0	2	72	1	69	2	0
Oakton Community College	14,960	0	0	0	0	0	4	0	4	0	0
Parkland College	9,133	0	0	0	0	0	9	0	9	0	0
Rock Valley College	8,551	0	0	0	0	0	4	0	4	0	0
Southern Illinois University											
Carbondale	12,905	0	0	0	0	0	123	5	113	5	0
School of Medicine[3]		0	0	0	0	0	2	0	2	0	0
South Suburban College	7,210	0	0	0	0	0	5	0	5	0	0
Southwestern Illinois College	13,299	0	0	0	0	0	17	4	13	0	0
University of Chicago, Cook County	19,996	4	0	0	4	0	32	0	27	5	0
University of Illinois											
Chicago	36,710	10	0	1	3	6	216	5	207	4	0
Urbana	59,691	32	0	10	6	16	388	11	346	31	3
Waubonsee Community College	13,452	0	0	0	0	0	0	0	0	0	0
INDIANA											
Indiana State University	12,410	6	0	4	1	1	60	3	54	3	1
Purdue University	51,304	12	1	5	0	6	346	13	332	1	1
University of Indianapolis	6,075	2	0	0	2	0	44	3	37	4	0
IOWA											
Iowa State University	33,336	8	0	7	0	1	136	3	129	4	1
University of Iowa	33,345	39	0	5	2	32	187	11	161	15	1
University of Northern Iowa	10,888	5	0	0	1	4	44	1	41	2	0
KANSAS											
Emporia State University	7,245	0	0	0	0	0	14	0	14	0	0
Kansas State University	22,693	4	0	3	0	1	71	3	64	4	0
Pittsburg State University	8,034	1	0	1	0	0	37	0	35	2	0
University of Kansas											
Main Campus	30,068	4	0	0	1	3	152	8	139	5	0
Medical Center[3]		21	0	1	3	17	199	1	174	24	0
Washburn University	6,743	1	0	0	0	1	25	3	21	1	0
KENTUCKY											
Eastern Kentucky University	16,847	5	0	5	0	0	59	5	53	1	0
Morehead State University	10,581	1	0	1	0	0	19	0	16	3	0
Murray State University	10,570	2	0	2	0	0	32	3	29	0	0
Northern Kentucky University	19,162	1	0	1	0	0	22	2	20	0	0
University of Kentucky	32,446	31	0	12	3	16	481	14	453	14	0
University of Louisville	26,237	7	0	0	6	1	271	26	227	18	0
Western Kentucky University	20,304	2	0	1	1	0	111	5	103	3	0
LOUISIANA											
Louisiana State University											
Baton Rouge	37,306	22	0	8	4	10	390	65	309	16	1
Health Sciences Center, Shreveport	1,150	5	0	0	0	5	39	2	34	3	0
Southern University and A&M College, New Orleans	2,688	0	0	0	0	0	0	0	0	0	0
University of Louisiana, Monroe	10,197	2	0	1	0	1	30	2	28	0	0
University of New Orleans	9,867	3	0	0	1	2	22	4	17	1	0

Table 9. Offenses Known to Law Enforcement, by Selected State and University and College, 2022—Continued

(Number.)

State and university/college	Student enrollment[1]	Violent crime	Murder and nonnegligent manslaughter	Rape	Robbery	Aggravated assault	Property crime	Burglary	Larceny-theft	Motor vehicle theft	Arson[2]
MAINE										
University of Maine										
Farmington	2,292	1	0	1	0	0	15	2	12	1	0
Orono	14,808	1	0	0	0	1	32	0	32	0	0
University of Southern Maine	10,662	2	0	2	0	0	12	0	11	1	0
MARYLAND[4]										
Bowie State University	6,994	7	0	0	0	7	29	10	19	0	0
Morgan State University	8,294	16	0	2	1	13	33	1	31	1	0
Prince George's County Community College	16,951	1	0	0	0	1	20	4	15	1	0
Towson University	24,486	8	0	5	1	2	48	5	42	1	0
MASSACHUSETTS										
Amherst College	1,863	0	0	0	0	0	0	0	0	0	0
Assumption College	2,670	0	0	0	0	0	14	2	12	0	0
Babson College	3,877	0	0	0	0	0	33	1	31	1	0
Bentley University	5,541	2	0	1	0	1	15	1	13	1	0
Boston College	16,198	2	0	1	0	1	70	2	62	6	0
Boston University	40,492	13	0	7	2	4	370	8	361	1	0
Bridgewater State University	12,652	10	0	5	1	4	8	0	7	1	0
Bristol Community College	8,925	0	0	0	0	0	1	0	1	0	0
Bunker Hill Community College	14,143	0	0	0	0	0	4	0	4	0	0
Cape Cod Community College	4,216	0	0	0	0	0	2	0	2	0	0
Clark University	3,766	3	0	1	0	2	23	3	20	0	0
College of the Holy Cross	3,051	1	0	0	0	1	18	4	14	0	0
Curry College	2,825	0	0	0	0	0	5	1	4	0	0
Dean College	1,401	0	0	0	0	0	17	8	9	0	0
Emerson College	5,883	0	0	0	0	0	13	0	13	0	0
Endicott College	5,081	5	0	1	0	4	6	0	6	0	0
Fisher College	2,299	0	0	0	0	0	5	3	2	0	0
Fitchburg State University	10,165	3	0	1	0	2	21	7	14	0	0
Framingham State University	7,568	1	0	1	0	0	19	0	19	0	0
Gordon College	2,263	0	0	0	0	0	11	0	11	0	0
Greenfield Community College	2,268	0	0	0	0	0	0	0	0	0	0
Harvard University	39,981	6	0	1	0	5	534	41	420	73	0
Holyoke Community College	5,496	0	0	0	0	0	2	1	0	1	0
Lasell College	2,416	2	0	1	0	1	11	0	11	0	0
Massachusetts Bay Community College	6,236	0	0	0	0	0	1	0	1	0	0
Massachusetts College of Art	2,117	0	0	0	0	0	9	0	9	0	0
Massachusetts College of Liberal Arts	1,765	1	0	0	0	1	4	0	4	0	0
Massachusetts Institute of Technology	12,217	3	0	2	0	1	232	14	218	0	0
Massasoit Community College	8,472	0	0	0	0	0	4	1	3	0	0
MCPHS University	9,543	0	0	0	0	0	18	1	17	0	0
Merrimack College	6,233	3	0	1	0	2	27	11	16	0	0
Mount Holyoke College	2,303	0	0	0	0	0	38	0	38	0	0
Mount Wachusett Community College	4,343	0	0	0	0	0	4	0	4	0	0
Northeastern University	31,124	8	0	5	1	2	309	13	287	9	0
North Shore Community College	6,919	0	0	0	0	0	0	0	0	0	0
Quinsigamond Community College	9,370	3	0	0	0	3	3	0	3	0	1
Salem State University	8,742	3	0	3	0	0	11	3	8	0	0
Simmons College	7,362	0	0	0	0	0	25	5	20	0	0
Smith College	2,979	0	0	0	0	0	1	1	0	0	1
Springfield College	3,250	0	0	0	0	0	2	2	0	0	0
Springfield Technical Community College	5,743	1	0	0	0	1	2	1	1	0	0
Stonehill College	2,574	1	0	1	0	0	11	0	11	0	0
Tufts University											
Medford	13,878	2	0	1	1	0	27	3	22	2	0
Suffolk[3]		1	0	1	0	0	14	0	14	0	0
Worcester[3]		0	0	0	0	0	3	0	3	0	0
University of Massachusetts											
Amherst	36,827	12	0	5	0	7	171	17	154	0	0
Dartmouth	9,244	5	0	0	0	5	49	6	42	1	3
Harbor Campus, Boston	19,398	1	0	0	0	1	21	0	21	0	0
Lowell	22,559	9	0	5	2	2	64	5	56	3	0
Medical Center, Worcester	1,339	15	0	0	0	15	33	1	30	2	0
Wellesley College	2,405	0	0	0	0	0	22	1	21	0	0
Wentworth Institute of Technology	5,319	0	0	0	0	0	29	1	28	0	0
Western New England University	3,951	1	0	1	0	0	19	3	16	0	1
Westfield State University	6,391	5	0	2	0	3	12	0	12	0	0
Wheaton College	1,748	0	0	0	0	0	14	3	11	0	0
Worcester Polytechnic Institute	7,876	13	0	0	0	13	28	2	26	0	0
Worcester State University	7,737	0	0	0	0	0	11	0	10	1	0
MICHIGAN										
Central Michigan University	20,057	6	0	1	0	5	37	1	35	1	0
Delta College	9,738	0	0	0	0	0	5	1	4	0	0
Eastern Michigan University	19,451	12	0	4	1	7	66	6	57	3	3
Grand Valley State University	26,320	7	0	5	1	1	98	5	91	2	0
Kalamazoo Valley Community College	10,128	0	0	0	0	0	9	0	9	0	0
Kellogg Community College	5,335	0	0	0	0	0	3	0	3	0	0
Kirtland Community College	1,982	0	0	0	0	0	0	0	0	0	0
Lansing Community College	14,739	1	0	0	0	1	19	0	18	1	0
Macomb Community College	24,180	0	0	0	0	0	15	0	15	0	0

Table 9. Offenses Known to Law Enforcement, by Selected State and University and College, 2022—Continued

(Number.)

State and university/college	Student enrollment[1]	Violent crime	Murder and nonnegligent manslaughter	Rape	Robbery	Aggravated assault	Property crime	Burglary	Larceny-theft	Motor vehicle theft	Arson[2]
Michigan State University	54,245	18	0	10	3	5	524	21	469	34	5
Michigan Technological University	7,241	0	0	0	0	0	28	0	27	1	0
Mott Community College	7,479	0	0	0	0	0	3	0	3	0	0
Northern Michigan University	8,365	7	0	5	0	2	34	1	30	3	0
Oakland Community College	23,708	0	0	0	0	0	11	2	9	0	0
Oakland University	21,329	2	0	1	0	1	25	1	24	0	0
Saginaw Valley State University	8,827	6	0	4	0	2	13	2	11	0	0
Schoolcraft College	13,994	0	0	0	0	0	7	0	7	0	0
University of Michigan											
Ann Arbor	50,002	24	0	7	1	16	453	13	430	10	2
Dearborn	10,105	0	0	0	0	0	3	0	3	0	0
Flint	8,032	1	0	1	0	0	35	3	31	1	0
Washtenaw Community College	18,734	0	0	0	0	0	10	0	10	0	0
Western Michigan University	22,035	6	0	2	1	3	131	2	124	5	0
MINNESOTA											
University of Minnesota											
Duluth	11,024	0	0	0	0	0	36	4	32	0	0
Morris	1,441	0	0	0	0	0	6	0	5	1	0
Twin Cities	62,309	14	0	4	4	6	451	22	376	53	1
MISSISSIPPI											
East Mississippi Community College											
Communiversity[3]		0	0	0	0	0	1	0	1	0	0
Golden Triangle[3]		0	0	0	0	0	2	0	2	0	0
West Point[3]		0	0	0	0	0	0	0	0	0	0
Scooba	4,644	0	0	0	0	0	2	0	2	0	0
Holmes Community College											
Goodman	7,549	0	0	0	0	0	2	0	2	0	0
Grenada[3]		0	0	0	0	0	1	0	1	0	0
Ridgeland[3]		0	0	0	0	0	0	0	0	0	0
Jones County Junior College	6,213	0	0	0	0	0	8	2	6	0	0
Mississippi Delta Community College	5,205	0	0	0	0	0	2	0	2	0	0
Mississippi State University	25,760	3	0	1	0	2	4	0	4	0	0
Northeast Mississippi Community College	5,809	0	0	0	0	0	11	0	11	0	0
Northwest Mississippi Community College											
Desoto[3]		0	0	0	0	0	1	0	1	0	0
Senatobia	9,427	0	0	0	0	0	6	0	6	0	0
Pearl River Community College											
Forrest	7,068	0	0	0	0	0	1	0	1	0	0
Poplarville[3]		1	0	0	0	1	7	4	3	0	0
University of Mississippi, Oxford	23,683	3	0	2	0	1	56	12	43	1	0
MISSOURI											
Metropolitan Community College	18,231	0	0	0	0	0	24	0	20	4	0
Missouri Southern State University	5,858	1	0	0	0	1	16	0	16	0	0
Missouri University of Science and Technology	8,165	0	0	0	0	0	47	1	45	1	0
Missouri Western State University	5,390	2	0	1	0	1	14	1	10	3	0
Northwest Missouri State University	8,872	2	0	0	0	2	7	0	7	0	0
Southeast Missouri State University	11,387	1	0	0	0	1	35	2	33	0	0
St. Charles Community College	8,648	0	0	0	0	0	0	0	0	0	0
St. Louis Community College, Meramec	23,466	1	0	1	0	0	26	1	22	3	0
University of Central Missouri	14,187	4	0	4	0	0	63	5	51	7	0
University of Missouri											
Columbia	33,987	12	0	4	0	8	235	5	219	11	2
Kansas City	18,650	4	0	0	0	4	77	9	60	8	0
Washington University	17,889	0	0	0	0	0	73	2	69	2	0
MONTANA											
Montana State University	18,344	6	0	3	0	3	104	3	99	2	1
Montana State University, Billings	5,402	3	0	1	0	2	9	1	6	2	0
University of Montana	11,821	0	0	0	0	0	0	0	0	0	0
NEBRASKA											
University of Nebraska											
Lincoln	27,390	18	0	6	1	11	166	8	153	5	1
Omaha	18,632	2	0	1	0	1	105	1	102	2	0
NEVADA											
University of Nevada, Reno	22,982	6	0	3	1	2	191	12	172	7	0
NEW HAMPSHIRE											
Plymouth State University	5,079	3	0	3	0	0	58	1	56	1	0
University of New Hampshire	15,585	3	0	2	0	1	49	3	46	0	0
NEW JERSEY											
Brookdale Community College	14,796	0	0	0	0	0	2	0	2	0	0
Kean University	16,448	0	0	0	0	0	21	0	18	3	2
Monmouth University	6,166	0	0	0	0	0	14	0	14	0	0
New Jersey Institute of Technology	13,687	3	0	1	1	1	59	3	54	2	0
Princeton University	7,942	0	0	0	0	0	185	4	135	46	0
Rowan University	22,640	9	0	4	2	3	113	15	96	2	0

Table 9. Offenses Known to Law Enforcement, by Selected State and University and College, 2022—Continued

(Number.)

State and university/college	Student enrollment[1]	Violent crime	Murder and nonnegligent manslaughter	Rape	Robbery	Aggravated assault	Property crime	Burglary	Larceny-theft	Motor vehicle theft	Arson[2]
Rutgers University											
Newark	15,444	12	0	2	2	8	172	13	144	15	0
New Brunswick	56,771	31	0	4	5	22	330	42	281	7	0
Stevens Institute of Technology	8,436	0	0	0	0	0	24	0	24	0	0
Stockton University	11,788	5	0	4	0	1	43	1	42	0	0
The College of New Jersey	8,773	2	0	1	0	1	25	1	18	6	0
William Paterson University	11,681	2	0	1	0	1	21	2	17	2	0
NEW MEXICO											
Eastern New Mexico University	6,620	1	0	1	0	0	37	2	31	4	0
New Mexico Institute of Mining and Technology	1,882	1	0	0	1	0	28	5	22	1	0
New Mexico Military Institute	570	0	0	0	0	0	5	0	5	0	0
New Mexico State University	16,089	8	0	3	2	3	178	32	135	11	0
University of New Mexico	24,776	47	0	10	6	31	544	46	417	81	1
Western New Mexico University	3,717	0	0	0	0	0	13	0	13	0	0
NEW YORK											
Cornell University	24,486	8	0	3	1	4	264	16	246	2	1
Ithaca College	6,034	9	0	9	0	0	94	7	87	0	0
State University of New York Police											
Alfred	3,977	2	0	1	0	1	25	1	24	0	0
Binghamton	19,919	3	0	3	0	0	114	5	109	0	1
Brockport	8,882	0	0	0	0	0	28	1	26	1	0
Buffalo	35,847	6	0	3	2	1	187	21	161	5	0
Buffalo State College	9,509	4	0	3	0	1	75	3	66	6	3
Canton	4,611	1	0	1	0	0	6	0	6	0	0
Cobleskill	2,372	0	0	0	0	0	12	2	7	3	0
Delhi	3,438	1	0	1	0	0	19	0	19	0	0
Downstate Medical	2,415	1	0	0	0	1	20	0	20	0	0
Environmental Science	2,318	0	0	0	0	0	11	3	8	0	0
Maritime	1,832	0	0	0	0	0	9	4	5	0	0
New Paltz	8,597	2	0	1	0	1	24	0	24	0	0
Old Westbury	5,954	3	0	2	0	1	10	0	10	0	0
Oneonta	7,123	1	0	1	0	0	31	0	30	1	0
Oswego	8,882	1	0	1	0	0	40	5	35	0	0
Plattsburgh	5,906	1	0	0	0	1	20	0	20	0	0
Potsdam	3,442	1	0	1	0	0	10	0	10	0	0
Purchase	4,243	1	0	1	0	0	17	3	12	2	0
Upstate Medical	1,623	17	0	0	2	15	89	3	83	3	0
NORTH CAROLINA											
Appalachian State University	21,706	6	0	5	0	1	59	1	57	1	0
Duke University	18,120	8	0	0	0	8	347	13	322	12	1
East Carolina University	32,009	13	0	9	1	3	100	5	94	1	0
Elizabeth City State University	2,351	4	0	1	0	3	18	1	17	0	0
Elon University	7,461	1	0	1	0	0	33	3	28	2	1
Fayetteville State University	8,658	3	0	2	0	1	29	8	19	2	1
Methodist University	2,075	1	0	1	0	0	24	5	19	0	0
North Carolina Agricultural and Technical State University	14,121	8	0	4	0	4	87	22	57	8	0
North Carolina Central University	9,000	10	0	3	1	6	54	9	41	4	0
North Carolina State University, Raleigh	40,482	6	0	2	1	3	245	49	189	7	0
University of North Carolina											
Chapel Hill	32,943	18	0	7	2	9	206	27	155	24	0
Charlotte	34,188	10	0	1	0	9	155	4	147	4	0
Greensboro	21,720	12	0	6	1	5	95	7	87	1	0
Pembroke	10,152	5	0	2	1	2	19	1	18	0	0
Wake Forest University	9,572	2	0	0	0	2	83	8	69	6	0
Western Carolina University	13,820	18	0	17	0	1	58	10	47	1	0
NORTH DAKOTA											
Bismarck State College	4,825	1	0	1	0	0	7	1	6	0	1
North Dakota State College of Science	3,485	1	0	1	0	0	19	3	15	1	0
North Dakota State University	14,102	2	0	1	1	0	93	0	89	4	0
University of North Dakota	16,791	5	0	2	0	3	89	8	79	2	0
OHIO											
Bowling Green State University	21,239	1	0	1	0	0	96	4	92	0	0
Capital University	4,447	1	0	1	0	0	28	3	22	3	0
Hocking College	3,411	2	0	0	0	2	27	6	21	0	0
Kent State University	31,555	9	0	6	0	3	116	1	115	0	0
Miami University	20,330	0	0	0	0	0	28	0	26	2	0
Ohio State University, Columbus	66,749	35	0	12	9	14	684	32	621	31	3
Ohio University	30,163	16	0	14	0	2	88	13	74	1	1
University of Cincinnati	48,219	5	0	2	2	1	166	6	147	13	1
University of Toledo	18,929	6	0	2	2	2	63	10	50	3	0
OKLAHOMA											
Cameron University	4,745	1	0	1	0	0	7	1	6	0	0
East Central University	4,326	0	0	0	0	0	19	1	16	2	0
Eastern Oklahoma State College	1,699	0	0	0	0	0	3	0	3	0	0
Langston University	2,207	5	0	2	1	2	28	5	22	1	0
Mid-America Christian University	2,617	0	0	0	0	0	2	0	2	0	0

Table 9. Offenses Known to Law Enforcement, by Selected State and University and College, 2022—Continued

(Number.)

State and university/college	Student enrollment[1]	Violent crime	Murder and nonnegligent manslaughter	Rape	Robbery	Aggravated assault	Property crime	Burglary	Larceny-theft	Motor vehicle theft	Arson[2]
Northeastern Oklahoma A&M College	2,148	0	0	0	0	0	2	2	0	0	0
Northeastern State University, Tahlequah	8,756	0	0	0	0	0	29	1	27	1	0
Oklahoma City Community College	17,029	0	0	0	0	0	5	0	5	0	1
Oklahoma City University	2,960	2	0	1	0	1	40	1	39	0	0
Oklahoma Panhandle State University	1,617	0	0	0	0	0	4	2	2	0	0
Oklahoma State University											
Main Campus	26,947	11	0	10	0	1	131	17	114	0	0
Okmulgee	3,017	0	0	0	0	0	10	0	10	0	0
Tulsa	1,442	0	0	0	0	0	3	0	3	0	0
Rogers State University	4,106	0	0	0	0	0	2	0	2	0	0
Southeastern Oklahoma State University	7,208	1	0	0	0	1	11	4	7	0	0
Southern Nazarene University	2,883	0	0	0	0	0	20	4	15	1	1
Southwestern Oklahoma State University	5,664	2	0	1	0	1	7	0	7	0	0
Tulsa Community College	21,523	0	0	0	0	0	34	2	31	1	0
University of Central Oklahoma	16,527	2	0	1	0	1	45	5	39	1	0
University of Oklahoma											
Health Sciences Center	3,668	3	0	2	0	1	107	6	95	6	0
Norman	31,285	17	0	5	0	12	266	3	242	21	0
OREGON											
Oregon State University	38,654	2	0	1	1	0	343	17	318	8	1
Portland State University	29,053	7	0	0	6	1	267	43	212	12	6
PENNSYLVANIA[4]											
Albright University	1,695	2	0	1	0	1	21	5	16	0	1
Bucknell University	3,815	4	0	4	0	0	58	1	55	2	0
Dickinson College	2,088	6	0	1	0	5	48	3	44	1	0
Drexel University	27,010	52	1	8	28	15	401	13	350	38	0
Franklin and Marshall College	2,365	9	0	9	0	0	16	3	13	0	0
Juniata College	1,440	0	0	0	0	0	14	2	11	1	0
Lafayette College	2,619	3	0	2	0	1	57	6	51	0	0
Luzerne County Community College	6,303	0	0	0	0	0	0	0	0	0	0
Mansfield University	2,110	0	0	0	0	0	4	0	4	0	0
Pennsylvania State University, Abington[3]		8	0	6	0	2	7	0	7	0	0
RHODE ISLAND											
University of Rhode Island	20,720	11	0	5	0	6	46	1	43	2	2
SOUTH CAROLINA											
Bob Jones University	3,654	0	0	0	0	0	0	0	0	0	0
Clemson University	29,483	5	0	3	0	2	117	4	92	21	0
Coastal Carolina University	11,421	6	0	3	1	2	61	0	60	1	1
Francis Marion University	4,743	1	0	1	0	0	13	0	13	0	0
Lander University	3,857	10	0	5	0	5	21	2	17	2	0
Medical University of South Carolina	3,638	8	0	0	2	6	88	3	79	6	0
Orangeburg-Calhoun Technical College	3,219	0	0	0	0	0	2	0	1	1	0
Presbyterian College	1,337	0	0	0	0	0	27	10	15	2	0
South Carolina State University	2,625	11	0	4	1	6	45	13	29	3	0
Spartanburg Methodist College	1,116	4	0	2	0	2	9	4	5	0	0
University of South Carolina											
Aiken	4,870	0	0	0	0	0	5	0	5	0	1
Columbia	38,770	5	0	2	1	2	168	14	133	21	0
Upstate	7,107	1	0	1	0	0	12	4	7	1	0
Winthrop University	6,589	2	0	1	0	1	32	3	28	1	0
York Technical College	5,556	0	0	0	0	0	0	0	0	0	0
SOUTH DAKOTA											
South Dakota State University	13,678	1	0	0	0	1	21	0	21	0	0
University of South Dakota	12,018	1	0	1	0	0	49	3	45	1	0
TENNESSEE											
Austin Peay State University	12,108	4	0	2	0	2	28	9	17	2	0
East Tennessee State University	15,797	8	0	3	0	5	64	12	49	3	0
Middle Tennessee State University	25,626	2	1	1	0	0	65	1	62	2	0
Tennessee State University	8,424	4	0	1	0	3	33	1	32	0	1
Tennessee Technological University	11,296	1	0	0	0	1	72	3	65	4	0
University of Memphis	25,700	5	0	1	2	2	170	14	110	46	0
University of Tennessee											
Chattanooga	12,675	5	0	3	2	0	110	13	91	6	0
Health Science Center	3,387	0	0	0	0	0	37	4	29	4	0
Knoxville	33,245	13	0	4	3	6	149	10	133	6	0
Martin	8,151	2	0	0	0	2	16	0	15	1	0
University of the South	1,940	2	0	2	0	0	34	6	27	1	0
Vanderbilt University	14,356	24	0	2	1	21	447	6	388	53	0
TEXAS											
Alvin Community College	7,481	0	0	0	0	0	0	0	0	0	0
Amarillo College	11,769	0	0	0	0	0	8	5	3	0	0
Angelo State University	12,391	6	0	4	1	1	37	0	37	0	0
Austin College	1,324	0	0	0	0	0	0	0	0	0	0
Austin Community College District	61,370	2	0	0	0	2	64	5	55	4	0
Baylor Health Care System[3]		2	0	0	0	2	355	3	318	34	0
Brazosport College	5,501	0	0	0	0	0	2	0	2	0	0

Table 9. Offenses Known to Law Enforcement, by Selected State and University and College, 2022—Continued

(Number.)

State and university/college	Student enrollment[1]	Violent crime	Murder and nonnegligent manslaughter	Rape	Robbery	Aggravated assault	Property crime	Burglary	Larceny-theft	Motor vehicle theft	Arson[2]
Central Texas College	18,388	0	0	0	0	0	7	3	4	0	0
Cisco College	4,445	3	0	0	0	3	2	1	1	0	0
Concordia University	2,763	0	0	0	0	0	0	0	0	0	0
Dallas County Community College District	110,694	0	0	0	0	0	11	3	6	2	1
El Paso Community College	33,704	0	0	0	0	0	9	0	9	0	0
Grayson College	4,101	0	0	0	0	0	0	0	0	0	0
Hardin-Simmons University	2,279	1	0	1	0	0	19	1	18	0	0
Houston Community College	72,749	0	0	0	0	0	79	11	63	5	0
Kilgore College	6,886	0	0	0	0	0	3	0	3	0	0
Lamar University, Beaumont	22,837	7	0	6	0	1	47	7	39	1	0
Lone Star College System District	107,768	1	0	0	0	1	63	10	49	4	0
Lubbock Christian University	1,858	0	0	0	0	0	8	3	5	0	0
McLennan Community College	12,405	0	0	0	0	0	0	0	0	0	0
Midwestern State University	6,837	0	0	0	0	0	11	0	11	0	0
Odessa College	9,971	0	0	0	0	0	8	3	5	0	0
Panola College	3,277	0	0	0	0	0	0	0	0	0	0
Paris Junior College	6,148	1	0	1	0	0	2	0	2	0	0
Prairie View A&M University	10,303	16	0	7	0	9	117	39	72	6	0
Rice University	8,270	1	0	1	0	0	131	6	109	16	0
Sam Houston State University	24,652	7	0	3	0	4	94	12	76	6	2
San Jacinto College, Central Campus	41,796	3	0	1	0	2	48	1	44	3	1
Southern Methodist University	13,602	1	0	1	0	0	178	18	139	21	0
South Plains College	12,259	3	0	0	0	3	3	0	3	0	0
St. Edwards University	4,006	0	0	0	0	0	26	1	25	0	0
Stephen F. Austin State University	14,155	1	0	0	1	0	22	1	21	0	0
St. Mary's University	3,683	2	0	1	0	1	48	0	43	5	0
St. Thomas University	4,297	0	0	0	0	0	23	2	19	2	0
Sul Ross State University	2,879	0	0	0	0	0	6	3	3	0	0
Tarleton State University	16,109	6	0	5	0	1	48	0	45	3	0
Texas A&M International University	9,961	1	0	1	0	0	14	0	14	0	0
Texas A&M University											
College Station	75,001	8	0	5	0	3	450	19	366	65	3
Commerce	14,782	3	0	1	0	2	31	2	28	1	0
San Antonio	8,124	1	0	0	0	1	21	1	20	0	0
Texas Christian University	11,957	0	0	0	0	0	73	8	65	0	0
Texas State Technical College											
Harlingen[3]		0	0	0	0	0	1	0	1	0	0
Waco	12,577	2	0	0	0	2	79	7	71	1	0
West Texas[3]		0	0	0	0	0	3	2	1	0	0
Texas State University, San Marcos	42,111	21	0	13	2	6	55	6	45	4	0
Texas Tech University, Lubbock	43,379	12	0	3	0	9	282	14	256	12	1
Texas Woman's University	20,404	0	0	0	0	0	27	1	25	1	0
Trinity Valley Community College	6,696	3	0	1	0	2	10	3	7	0	0
Tyler Junior College	15,918	1	0	1	0	0	14	2	12	0	0
University of Houston											
Central Campus	52,440	22	0	10	8	4	384	31	339	14	1
Clearlake	11,255	0	0	0	0	0	18	0	18	0	0
Downtown Campus	18,860	0	0	0	0	0	0	0	0	0	0
University of North Texas, Denton	47,297	9	0	5	1	3	191	14	163	14	0
University of Texas											
Arlington	60,276	9	0	8	0	1	136	8	127	1	0
Austin	53,502	13	0	0	3	10	456	22	414	20	4
Dallas	31,508	3	0	3	0	0	104	4	96	4	0
El Paso	29,288	6	0	0	0	6	97	3	91	3	1
Health Science Center, San Antonio	4,104	1	0	0	0	1	12	0	10	2	0
Health Science Center, Tyler[3]		2	0	0	0	2	9	1	8	0	0
Houston	7,375	6	0	1	4	1	265	20	233	12	0
Medical Branch	3,940	1	0	0	0	1	83	1	80	2	0
Permian Basin	7,561	1	0	1	0	0	13	2	11	0	0
Rio Grande Valley	44,634	3	0	2	0	1	58	2	55	1	0
San Antonio	38,737	10	0	5	1	4	149	11	129	9	0
Southwestern Medical School	2,538	0	0	0	0	0	208	12	180	16	1
Tyler	12,027	2	0	2	0	0	13	0	12	1	0
West Texas A&M University	11,481	1	0	1	0	0	22	1	21	0	0
UTAH											
Dixie State University	14,051	3	0	0	0	3	15	1	14	0	0
Snow College	7,064	2	0	2	0	0	10	0	10	0	0
Southern Utah University	17,896	1	0	1	0	0	19	0	19	0	0
University of Utah	38,804	15	0	6	1	8	308	26	265	17	0
Utah State University, Logan	32,967	4	0	2	0	2	32	1	30	1	0
Utah Valley University	43,749	0	0	0	0	0	27	3	23	1	0
Weber State University	36,680	3	0	1	0	2	37	5	32	0	0
VERMONT											
University of Vermont	15,499	5	0	4	0	1	184	14	164	6	3
VIRGINIA											
Christopher Newport University	5,034	4	0	2	0	2	87	4	80	3	0
College of William and Mary	9,959	2	0	0	0	2	74	2	72	0	0
Eastern Virginia Medical School	1,450	4	0	0	0	4	32	0	31	1	0
Emory and Henry College	1,414	1	0	1	0	0	0	0	0	0	1
George Mason University	46,687	8	0	5	1	2	82	1	77	4	1

Table 9. Offenses Known to Law Enforcement, by Selected State and University and College, 2022—Continued

(Number.)

State and university/college	Student enrollment[1]	Violent crime	Murder and nonnegligent manslaughter	Rape	Robbery	Aggravated assault	Property crime	Burglary	Larceny-theft	Motor vehicle theft	Arson[2]
Hampton University	3,807	1	0	1	0	0	34	5	28	1	0
James Madison University	23,827	5	0	2	2	1	108	3	102	3	1
Norfolk State University	6,041	2	0	0	0	2	52	4	45	3	0
Old Dominion University	28,478	48	0	7	2	39	210	7	193	10	0
Radford University	13,511	6	0	3	1	2	48	5	43	0	0
University of Mary Washington	4,728	0	0	0	0	0	36	0	35	1	0
University of Richmond	4,357	3	0	3	0	0	66	10	53	3	1
University of Virginia	28,322	30	3	8	1	18	344	5	248	91	1
Virginia Commonwealth University	32,089	18	0	0	4	14	346	4	329	13	0
Virginia Highlands Community College	2,729	0	0	0	0	0	1	0	1	0	0
Virginia Polytechnic Institute and State University	39,078	11	0	8	1	2	236	5	228	3	3
Virginia State University	8,654	13	0	4	1	8	43	0	42	1	1
WASHINGTON											
Eastern Washington University	16,129	4	0	1	0	3	30	8	21	1	0
Evergreen State College	2,856	0	0	0	0	0	0	0	0	0	0
University of Washington	56,931	12	0	5	1	6	732	68	576	88	5
Washington State University											
Pullman	34,825	6	0	4	1	1	79	8	68	3	0
Vancouver[3]		0	0	0	0	0	0	0	0	0	0
Western Washington University	16,881	2	0	1	1	0	130	4	110	16	0
WISCONSIN											
University of Wisconsin											
Eau Claire	11,937	2	0	2	0	0	57	1	56	0	1
Green Bay	11,192	0	0	0	0	0	14	0	14	0	0
Madison	48,646	6	0	5	1	0	260	23	227	10	1
Oshkosh	17,570	4	0	3	0	1	12	0	11	1	0
Parkside	5,299	3	0	3	0	0	6	0	6	0	0
River Falls	6,531	0	0	0	0	0	25	1	23	1	0
Stout	9,006	5	0	0	0	5	69	0	69	0	0
Whitewater	14,126	6	0	5	1	0	13	0	13	0	0
WYOMING											
University of Wyoming	13,300	4	0	1	0	3	51	3	47	1	0

NOTE: Caution should be exercised in making any intercampus comparisons or ranking schools because university/college crime statistics are affected by a variety of factors. These include demographic characteristics of the surrounding community, ratio of male to female students, number of on-campus residents, accessibility of the campus to outside visitors, size of enrollment, etc.   1 The student enrollment figures provided by the United States Department of Education are for the 2021 school year, the most recent available. The enrollment figures include full-time and part-time students.   2 The FBI does not publish arson data unless it receives data from either the agency or the state for all 12 months of the calendar year.   3 Student enrollment figures were not available.   4 Limited data for 2022 were available for Florida, Illinois, Maryland, and Pennsylvania.

Table 10. Offenses Known to Law Enforcement, by Selected State Metropolitan and Nonmetropolitan Counties, 2022

(Number.)

State/county	Violent crime	Murder and nonnegligent manslaughter	Rape	Robbery	Aggravated assault	Property crime	Burglary	Larceny-theft	Motor vehicle theft	Arson[1]
ALABAMA										
Metropolitan Counties										
Autauga	62	2	4	2	54	228	52	152	24	4
Bibb	26	0	1	0	25	94	25	54	15	1
Blount	103	2	18	4	79	571	220	258	93	2
Calhoun	253	0	7	1	245	308	75	232	1	0
Chilton	108	1	10	3	94	374	97	218	59	2
Colbert	58	5	8	1	44	195	60	110	25	2
Elmore	31	2	1	0	28	237	37	169	31	0
Etowah	6	0	1	0	5	47	9	30	8	3
Geneva	5	0	1	0	4	76	20	40	16	1
Greene	5	0	0	0	5	24	6	15	3	0
Henry	34	5	5	1	23	100	22	65	13	0
Houston	128	2	19	6	101	528	150	299	79	10
Jefferson	791	13	49	64	665	2,701	589	1,708	404	17
Lauderdale	104	0	10	1	93	431	67	280	84	4
Lawrence	21	1	3	0	17	75	20	35	20	0
Lee	162	5	27	4	126	667	130	431	106	4
Lowndes	7	1	0	1	5	50	11	29	10	2
Mobile	328	9	11	14	294	1,284	284	753	247	8
Montgomery	101	0	4	13	84	367	68	242	57	2
Pickens	22	0	1	2	19	57	26	20	11	0
Russell	51	0	7	3	41	135	26	90	19	2
Shelby	1	0	0	0	1	11	3	7	1	0
St. Clair	87	6	19	4	58	276	83	146	47	7
Washington	18	0	1	0	17	57	12	32	13	2
Nonmetropolitan Counties										
Barbour	13	0	1	1	11	24	4	14	6	0
Chambers	26	0	2	0	24	111	8	98	5	0
Cherokee	52	1	4	2	45	280	77	159	44	6
Choctaw	11	2	1	0	8	74	28	34	12	2
Clarke	35	0	3	2	30	95	24	58	13	0
Clay	15	0	2	0	13	48	17	30	1	0
Cleburne	13	0	1	0	12	164	37	111	16	0
Coffee	35	3	8	2	22	148	45	77	26	2
Coosa	31	1	1	0	29	90	17	55	18	1
Covington	0	0	0	0	0	0	0	0	0	0
Crenshaw	27	0	5	0	22	84	18	42	24	1
Cullman	92	2	17	5	68	730	154	475	101	4
Dale	15	0	5	0	10	108	19	76	13	0
Dallas	61	3	4	4	50	264	78	157	29	10
DeKalb	16	1	5	1	9	109	26	60	23	3
Fayette	10	1	1	0	8	31	5	13	13	1
Franklin	41	2	7	2	30	178	39	106	33	3
Macon	14	2	0	1	11	20	5	10	5	0
Marengo	13	1	0	1	11	52	13	31	8	1
Marion	3	0	0	0	3	15	6	8	1	0
Marshall	40	1	9	0	30	320	89	168	63	2
Monroe	16	2	0	1	13	38	11	21	6	1
Perry	0	0	0	0	0	0	0	0	0	0
Pike	11	0	2	1	8	48	1	7	40	0
Randolph	28	0	4	0	24	177	40	132	5	3
Sumter	9	1	0	0	8	2	0	1	1	0
Talladega	95	2	5	4	84	421	81	262	78	3
Tallapoosa	35	6	1	4	24	88	15	59	14	0
Walker	27	1	2	0	24	224	42	152	30	3
Winston	9	0	2	1	6	66	16	44	6	0
ARIZONA										
Metropolitan Counties										
Cochise	99	5	3	1	90	385	122	219	44	3
Coconino	99	1	16	6	76	298	102	166	30	14
Mohave	263	10	76	11	166	1,599	361	1,046	192	7
Pima	796	22	62	100	612	7,459	1,199	5,647	613	53
Pinal	274	6	12	11	245	1,429	226	991	212	9
Yavapai	304	4	20	1	279	600	120	396	84	5
Yuma	177	6	26	6	139	834	225	475	134	19
Nonmetropolitan Counties										
Apache	61	0	9	0	52	151	67	69	15	1
Graham	19	0	0	0	19	59	7	41	11	7
La Paz	40	2	6	0	32	178	36	107	35	2
Navajo	83	3	17	0	63	203	56	115	32	0
ARKANSAS										
Metropolitan Counties										
Benton	143	3	24	0	116	337	114	177	46	3
Cleveland	23	1	1	1	20	138	50	71	17	1
Craighead	75	1	16	2	56	267	88	146	33	3

Table 10. Offenses Known to Law Enforcement, by Selected State Metropolitan and Nonmetropolitan Counties, 2022—Continued

(Number.)

State/county	Violent crime	Murder and nonnegligent manslaughter	Rape	Robbery	Aggravated assault	Property crime	Burglary	Larceny-theft	Motor vehicle theft	Arson[1]
Crawford	58	0	3	0	55	255	37	170	48	2
Crittenden	159	3	22	2	132	268	80	143	45	4
Faulkner	133	3	17	2	111	617	130	387	100	10
Franklin	53	0	6	0	47	94	31	45	18	1
Garland	353	1	47	9	296	1,164	460	566	138	0
Grant	19	0	4	0	15	149	46	82	21	3
Jefferson	100	4	18	5	73	429	96	254	79	14
Lincoln	29	1	5	0	23	90	30	45	15	0
Little River	17	1	2	1	13	62	17	32	13	1
Lonoke	97	3	15	2	77	371	56	224	91	0
Madison	53	1	12	0	40	110	40	55	15	4
Miller	42	0	6	0	36	160	38	90	32	2
Perry	43	0	1	0	42	109	22	87	0	0
Poinsett	56	1	13	0	42	180	41	106	33	4
Pulaski	512	5	19	19	469	1,674	252	1,165	257	19
Saline	145	0	29	2	114	635	237	299	99	5
Sebastian	16	0	2	0	14	149	43	94	12	0
Washington	140	2	13	2	123	453	80	296	77	4
Nonmetropolitan Counties										
Arkansas	16	0	3	0	13	62	25	35	2	0
Ashley	12	0	0	0	12	112	20	80	12	4
Baxter	43	0	8	0	35	350	66	251	33	0
Boone	93	2	27	1	63	143	19	115	9	3
Calhoun	16	0	6	1	9	53	18	30	5	5
Carroll	34	0	2	0	32	112	26	53	33	2
Chicot	1	0	0	0	1	63	14	47	2	0
Clark	21	0	2	0	19	68	11	48	9	1
Clay	13	1	3	0	9	73	12	54	7	1
Cleburne	186	0	16	2	168	281	74	179	28	7
Columbia	43	0	0	3	40	86	18	56	12	0
Conway	73	0	6	1	66	239	36	166	37	6
Cross	37	0	2	4	31	146	49	81	16	0
Desha	4	1	0	0	3	2	1	1	0	0
Drew	32	0	7	1	24	74	15	44	15	3
Fulton	47	1	9	0	37	84	0	72	12	1
Greene	65	0	15	2	48	251	45	158	48	2
Hempstead	43	0	7	0	36	138	22	91	25	1
Hot Spring	10	0	2	0	8	87	33	30	24	1
Howard	23	0	5	1	17	41	13	24	4	0
Independence	131	1	35	3	92	407	88	260	59	13
Izard	105	1	6	0	98	94	33	49	12	0
Jackson	33	2	8	1	22	101	5	80	16	1
Johnson	51	1	15	1	34	81	42	35	4	4
Lafayette	9	0	2	0	7	33	0	28	5	0
Lawrence	26	0	5	0	21	112	35	66	11	2
Lee	7	0	1	0	6	57	19	30	8	3
Logan	60	2	7	0	51	222	81	97	44	0
Marion	57	5	10	2	40	132	40	81	11	0
Mississippi	29	0	4	0	25	245	44	162	39	0
Nevada	9	0	0	0	9	29	8	11	10	0
Newton	22	0	5	0	17	39	9	28	2	0
Pike	8	0	1	0	7	34	14	16	4	0
Polk	75	0	2	0	73	65	22	40	3	0
Pope	79	0	7	2	70	253	71	144	38	4
Prairie	12	1	3	0	8	67	20	42	5	2
Randolph	40	0	13	0	27	132	39	80	13	3
Scott	18	0	0	0	18	59	19	33	7	1
Searcy	15	0	0	0	15	31	11	14	6	0
Sevier	33	0	8	1	24	22	6	14	2	0
St. Francis	67	3	6	4	54	72	69	3	0	2
Union	84	1	1	0	82	215	56	139	20	2
Van Buren	32	1	1	0	30	155	25	85	45	2
White	263	0	79	3	181	530	108	332	90	5
Woodruff	2	0	0	0	2	27	5	14	8	0
Yell	98	0	8	3	87	118	28	77	13	4
CALIFORNIA										
Metropolitan Counties										
Alameda	766	4	36	182	544	2,577	412	1,355	810	
Butte	431	6	51	27	347	972	267	666	39	
Contra Costa	397	6	37	67	287	1,780	336	1,406	38	17
El Dorado	324	9	106	23	186	1,283	318	933	32	5
Fresno	1,166	14	21	154	977	3,754	1,182	1,710	862	
Imperial	186	4	20	8	154	496	139	309	48	31
Kern	3,537	45	107	480	2,905	9,396	2,663	3,650	3,083	334
Kings	110	5	10	16	79	414	97	287	30	3
Los Angeles	6,382	91	292	1,374	4,625	17,070	2,822	9,225	5,023	246
Madera	376	3	48	26	299	941	206	692	43	7
Marin	68	2	8	9	49	420	98	318	4	

Table 10. Offenses Known to Law Enforcement, by Selected State Metropolitan and Nonmetropolitan Counties, 2022—Continued

(Number.)

State/county	Violent crime	Murder and nonnegligent manslaughter	Rape	Robbery	Aggravated assault	Property crime	Burglary	Larceny-theft	Motor vehicle theft	Arson[1]
Merced	479	20	40	53	366	1,564	345	963	256	37
Monterey	376	2	38	40	296	938	259	634	45	8
Napa	56	0	11	7	38	234	84	143	7	
Orange	310	0	4	29	277	1,194	208	779	207	10
Riverside	1,034	19	50	163	802	7,415	1,264	4,483	1,668	
Sacramento	2,721	39	112	660	1,910	9,043	1,853	7,025	165	69
San Benito	72	1	10	5	56	149	47	77	25	3
San Bernardino	2,004	40	108	163	1,693	3,752	912	1,798	1,042	66
San Diego	1,902	21	68	239	1,574	5,802	1,021	3,390	1,391	52
San Joaquin	873	6	26	119	722	2,321	525	1,693	103	
San Luis Obispo	435	2	26	20	387	974	346	605	23	
San Mateo	376	1	45	54	276	1,912	324	1,396	192	17
Santa Barbara	243	2	29	26	186	1,401	283	1,086	32	
Santa Clara	276	0	37	24	215	1,479	180	940	359	
Santa Cruz	371	0	45	37	289	1,013	204	791	18	18
Solano	115	0	13	17	85	337	93	152	92	
Sonoma	336	6	74	38	218	820	198	597	25	27
Stanislaus	438	11	28	88	311	1,332	389	914	29	
Tulare	337	16	30	73	218	1,905	493	1,307	105	
Ventura	71	4	12	9	46	735	170	486	79	
Yolo	81	1	5	6	69	380	70	278	32	
Yuba	187	4	20	24	139	914	251	647	16	
Nonmetropolitan Counties										
Alpine	11	0	4	0	7	25	12	13	0	
Amador	95	0	12	12	71	278	53	224	1	
Calaveras	243	1	30	11	201	510	165	330	15	3
Colusa	21	0	9	1	11	190	74	109	7	
Del Norte	85	3	20	7	55	154	79	62	13	
Glenn	97	0	2	1	94	180	41	125	14	7
Humboldt	237	5	27	29	176	760	260	481	19	21
Inyo	93	1	12	7	73	105	32	71	2	
Lake	292	0	41	18	233	471	163	302	6	9
Lassen	59	1	12	2	44	215	128	78	9	3
Mariposa	71	1	12	3	55	207	53	149	5	0
Modoc	29	0	1	0	28	50	12	31	7	0
Mono	21	0	4	2	15	27	10	16	1	
Nevada	213	1	38	15	159	366	145	218	3	
Plumas	152	0	4	4	144	272	69	194	9	
Sierra	10	0	0	0	10	19	8	10	1	
Siskiyou	84	0	13	5	66	104	56	44	4	
Tehama	142	3	25	10	104	350	129	205	16	6
Trinity	85	0	5	2	78	167	74	91	2	9
Tuolumne	330	0	63	12	255	478	168	302	8	
COLORADO										
Metropolitan Counties										
Adams	493	8	37	58	390	2,559	264	1,203	1,092	39
Arapahoe	220	0	8	14	198	2,360	404	1,222	734	20
Boulder	96	3	17	3	73	740	151	508	81	5
Clear Creek	1	0	0	0	1	48	6	37	5	1
Douglas	260	1	71	23	165	1,420	163	959	298	7
Elbert	1	1	0	0	0	31	4	17	10	0
El Paso	560	15	116	30	399	2,415	432	1,583	400	36
Gilpin	9	0	0	0	9	75	22	45	8	0
Jefferson	421	2	81	33	305	3,371	500	2,288	583	25
Larimer	205	2	32	11	160	1,083	192	702	189	14
Mesa	144	1	27	7	109	1,038	183	718	137	12
Park	32	0	2	0	30	40	21	14	5	0
Pueblo	61	4	0	15	42	1,190	219	738	233	4
Teller	37	3	3	1	30	49	14	25	10	1
Nonmetropolitan Counties										
Alamosa	15	0	4	0	11	109	45	57	7	4
Archuleta	20	0	4	1	15	46	7	33	6	0
Baca	1	0	0	0	1	0	0	0	0	0
Bent	9	0	1	2	6	96	27	50	19	0
Chaffee	4	0	3	0	1	61	13	40	8	2
Crowley	11	0	0	0	11	42	11	20	11	0
Custer	17	1	3	1	12	40	8	24	8	4
Delta	3	0	1	0	2	168	39	101	28	2
Dolores	1	0	0	0	1	24	3	19	2	0
Eagle	33	0	5	0	28	135	16	106	13	0
Fremont	25	3	6	1	15	173	30	109	34	7
Garfield	70	4	24	0	42	158	31	110	17	1
Kiowa	2	0	1	0	1	24	6	16	2	0
Kit Carson	3	0	0	0	3	25	3	16	6	0
Las Animas	15	0	4	0	11	99	41	40	18	0
Lincoln	2	0	1	0	1	29	4	21	4	0
Logan	28	0	4	0	24	84	34	40	10	0

Table 10. Offenses Known to Law Enforcement, by Selected State Metropolitan and Nonmetropolitan Counties, 2022—Continued

(Number.)

State/county	Violent crime	Murder and nonnegligent manslaughter	Rape	Robbery	Aggravated assault	Property crime	Burglary	Larceny-theft	Motor vehicle theft	Arson[1]
Moffat	9	0	3	0	6	33	5	19	9	0
Montezuma	45	2	6	1	36	133	38	65	30	3
Montrose	18	1	0	1	16	177	37	120	20	2
Morgan	12	0	3	0	9	50	17	24	9	1
Otero	6	2	0	0	4	53	10	23	20	0
Ouray	2	0	2	0	0	21	5	16	0	0
Phillips	0	0	0	0	0	1	0	1	0	0
Pitkin	4	0	0	0	4	29	1	23	5	0
Prowers	11	1	0	0	10	39	12	23	4	2
Rio Blanco	1	0	1	0	0	4	2	2	0	0
Routt	11	0	2	1	8	51	4	41	6	0
Saguache	6	3	0	0	3	60	13	41	6	2
San Juan	1	0	1	0	0	5	2	2	1	0
San Miguel	4	0	1	0	3	5	2	2	1	0
Summit	30	0	15	0	15	203	24	165	14	1
Washington	1	0	0	0	1	64	12	43	9	1
Yuma	4	0	1	0	3	37	5	26	6	0
DELAWARE										
Metropolitan Counties										
New Castle County Police Department	763	3	68	71	621	3,444	462	2,557	425	0
FLORIDA[2]										
Metropolitan Counties										
Bay	304	2	52	13	237	1,284	259	929	96	7
Brevard	484	6	29	28	421	2,479	370	1,878	231	6
Charlotte	152	2	9	4	137	1,068	125	857	86	6
Citrus	319	6	20	24	269	1,469	281	1,065	123	8
Collier	774	8	61	107	598	2,686	230	2,249	207	4
Flagler	196	3	41	5	147	681	73	560	48	4
Hernando	449	8	42	39	360	1,938	264	1,544	130	17
Indian River	168	2	2	17	147	1,308	150	1,051	107	5
Jacksonville Sheriff's Office	5,927	127	394	622	4,784	23,703	2,478	19,224	2,001	72
Lee	1,379	18	157	202	1,002	4,533	669	3,341	523	30
Leon	348	4	46	18	280	1,220	238	883	99	3
Marion	637	1	81	4	551	1,600	169	1,399	32	2
Miami-Dade	5,606	98	524	933	4,051	26,220	1,980	20,520	3,720	43
Nassau	157	1	26	5	125	643	146	416	81	5
Orange	4,730	63	438	913	3,316	16,400	2,260	12,115	2,025	0
Palm Beach	1,452	27	179	193	1,053	7,499	757	5,946	796	37
Pinellas	108	2	10	15	81	550	47	451	52	2
Polk	1,329	17	46	95	1,171	3,677	685	2,570	422	3
Sarasota	403	5	23	35	340	3,197	310	2,523	364	4
Seminole	335	7	57	42	229	1,793	225	1,436	132	2
St. Johns	118	0	10	4	104	552	77	469	6	3
St. Lucie	376	2	52	31	291	1,101	130	863	108	6
Volusia	769	8	110	146	505	1,270	244	874	152	9
Walton	110	0	28	7	75	199	23	176	0	0
Nonmetropolitan Counties										
Dixie	33	2	4	1	26	78	42	22	14	0
Hamilton	33	0	1	2	30	157	28	112	17	2
Hardee	58	0	10	3	45	218	52	143	23	0
Holmes	78	1	12	1	64	135	21	101	13	1
Monroe	162	3	8	10	141	416	28	358	30	0
Okeechobee	111	1	11	6	93	540	96	387	57	2
Putnam	74	1	6	1	66	459	109	263	87	1
Union	24	3	4	1	16	56	28	21	7	0
GEORGIA										
Metropolitan Counties										
Augusta-Richmond	105	1	16	12	76	608	94	428	86	3
Barrow	76	1	9	3	63	663	50	554	59	3
Bartow	10	0	0	0	10	439	79	331	29	11
Bibb	2,294	65	95	240	1,894	5,833	1,252	3,669	912	54
Brantley	21	2	1	2	16	206	49	131	26	1
Brooks	41	0	3	1	37	120	25	73	22	0
Bryan	44	0	5	3	36	238	29	133	76	1
Burke	26	3	8	2	13	242	49	150	43	1
Butts	41	1	8	2	30	139	15	91	33	5
Carroll	145	1	27	8	109	963	174	634	155	3
Catoosa	66	1	12	6	47	457	73	310	74	1
Cherokee	180	4	37	12	127	1,028	125	818	85	5
Clarke	0	0	0	0	0	0	0	0	0	0
Cobb	30	0	3	0	27	219	0	212	7	0
Cobb County Police Department	1,186	24	151	157	854	7,744	830	6,128	786	25
Columbia	33	1	7	5	20	434	57	344	33	0
Coweta	672	0	63	9	600	742	116	535	91	0
Crawford	23	2	6	1	14	152	35	93	24	1
Dawson	59	0	9	1	49	239	23	216	0	2

Table 10. Offenses Known to Law Enforcement, by Selected State Metropolitan and Nonmetropolitan Counties, 2022—Continued

(Number.)

State/county	Violent crime	Murder and nonnegligent manslaughter	Rape	Robbery	Aggravated assault	Property crime	Burglary	Larceny-theft	Motor vehicle theft	Arson[1]
DeKalb	23	0	0	0	23	1	0	1	0	1
DeKalb County Police Department	4,618	128	229	789	3,472	17,815	2,475	12,016	3,324	74
Dougherty	2	0	0	0	2	16	0	16	0	0
Dougherty County Police Department	17	0	1	1	15	74	34	28	12	1
Douglas	209	3	11	20	175	862	140	600	122	1
Effingham	23	1	5	3	14	189	53	115	21	2
Fayette	44	1	3	1	39	309	52	229	28	1
Floyd County Police Department	176	0	41	9	126	623	116	420	87	2
Forsyth	129	3	22	8	96	1,009	100	848	61	0
Fulton	14	0	0	1	13	21	2	18	1	0
Fulton County Police Department	31	0	2	11	18	46	4	28	14	0
Glynn County Police Department	211	1	30	21	159	1,156	198	827	131	6
Gwinnett	10	0	0	0	10	11	0	11	0	0
Gwinnett County Police Department	2,618	27	306	287	1,998	8,016	1,027	5,899	1,090	34
Hall	296	10	52	23	211	1,434	258	1,009	167	5
Haralson	46	0	11	2	33	323	75	197	51	5
Harris	5	0	0	1	4	125	23	98	4	0
Heard	8	1	0	1	6	92	22	51	19	1
Henry	2	0	0	1	1	0	0	0	0	0
Henry County Police Department	530	8	87	50	385	2,582	266	1,941	375	2
Jasper	31	0	6	0	25	118	22	80	16	5
Jones	35	0	6	7	22	187	36	123	28	2
Lanier	18	2	2	0	14	65	14	47	4	0
Lee	63	0	16	4	43	329	51	244	34	1
Long	7	0	2	0	5	69	22	35	12	0
Lowndes	155	1	49	16	89	943	146	704	93	3
Madison	54	3	10	4	37	269	49	188	32	4
Marion	8	1	2	0	5	54	17	31	6	1
McDuffie	36	1	2	3	30	129	30	78	21	1
McIntosh	24	1	2	2	19	175	37	120	18	0
Meriwether	37	1	2	1	33	127	15	85	27	0
Monroe	20	1	4	1	14	168	23	127	18	1
Murray	53	0	4	2	47	98	11	69	18	0
Newton	345	5	38	33	269	1,158	191	801	166	5
Oconee	28	0	9	4	15	597	44	526	27	1
Oglethorpe	52	0	2	0	50	127	22	79	26	0
Paulding	575	7	277	21	270	1,108	164	813	131	10
Peach	41	1	4	3	33	90	22	62	6	1
Pickens	40	0	8	2	30	136	19	98	19	0
Pike	19	1	0	0	18	141	26	88	27	1
Spalding	156	2	13	9	132	539	68	375	96	3
Twiggs	16	0	3	1	12	54	10	36	8	0
Walton	52	1	9	2	40	352	35	287	30	4
Whitfield	334	1	45	4	284	848	135	616	97	6
Nonmetropolitan Counties										
Baldwin	103	5	15	7	76	479	67	373	39	2
Banks	40	0	6	2	32	373	23	323	27	0
Ben Hill	36	0	6	2	28	152	39	85	28	0
Berrien	27	1	11	0	15	108	20	79	9	1
Bleckley	11	0	3	0	8	80	16	47	17	0
Bulloch	5	0	0	1	4	271	62	182	27	1
Camden	50	1	9	5	35	119	17	80	22	1
Candler	16	0	4	0	12	66	9	51	6	1
Chattooga	29	0	3	2	24	225	34	170	21	0
Clay	16	0	5	0	11	16	3	12	1	0
Clinch	3	0	0	0	3	36	13	23	0	0
Coffee	110	1	11	3	95	373	65	278	30	6
Cook	10	0	2	0	8	84	18	53	13	2
Crisp	11	0	2	1	8	134	21	100	13	0
Decatur	40	1	6	6	27	201	61	120	20	1
Dodge	22	1	4	1	16	125	40	71	14	2
Early	5	0	2	0	3	42	11	26	5	0
Elbert	4	0	0	0	4	43	11	30	2	0
Fannin	42	2	8	2	30	216	64	134	18	0
Franklin	33	0	6	3	24	127	27	85	15	0
Gilmer	76	2	11	4	59	304	100	163	41	2
Glascock	3	0	0	1	2	19	2	12	5	0
Gordon	64	0	9	1	54	355	84	226	45	2
Greene	42	0	1	3	38	72	13	57	2	1
Habersham	43	0	14	3	26	330	78	209	43	2
Hancock	15	0	3	0	12	47	6	32	9	0
Hart	51	3	4	3	41	191	48	128	15	1
Irwin	11	1	2	0	8	53	4	44	5	1
Jackson	58	1	17	3	37	548	72	411	65	2
Jeff Davis	12	0	0	0	12	47	6	28	13	0
Jefferson	19	1	1	1	16	101	24	62	15	2
Jenkins	4	0	2	0	2	40	7	23	10	0
Laurens	103	4	12	3	84	367	64	252	51	0
Lumpkin	53	0	8	1	44	184	34	132	18	2

Table 10. Offenses Known to Law Enforcement, by Selected State Metropolitan and Nonmetropolitan Counties, 2022—Continued

(Number.)

State/county	Violent crime	Murder and nonnegligent manslaughter	Rape	Robbery	Aggravated assault	Property crime	Burglary	Larceny-theft	Motor vehicle theft	Arson[1]
Mitchell	14	0	0	2	12	174	34	113	27	1
Pierce	51	0	8	1	42	183	48	111	24	4
Polk	4	0	0	0	4	2	0	2	0	0
Pulaski	38	0	4	3	31	172	32	120	20	3
Putnam	33	0	6	2	25	139	18	111	10	1
Rabun	14	0	7	0	7	154	39	109	6	0
Randolph	10	0	0	1	9	26	7	19	0	0
Schley	4	3	0	0	1	11	2	9	0	0
Sumter	10	0	1	3	6	84	31	45	8	0
Tattnall	19	0	4	0	15	185	61	100	24	1
Thomas	86	1	7	4	74	372	81	249	42	1
Tift	171	1	7	9	154	509	106	351	52	1
Towns	11	0	1	0	10	44	7	29	8	0
Treutlen	15	0	4	2	9	44	10	26	8	2
Troup	103	2	27	3	71	528	91	373	64	2
Turner	9	0	1	0	8	37	9	21	7	0
Union	15	0	3	0	12	152	29	109	14	1
Ware	28	2	2	2	22	101	31	58	12	0
Wayne	57	1	16	3	37	383	72	272	39	1
Webster	0	0	0	0	0	0	0	0	0	0
Wheeler	9	0	0	1	8	54	20	31	3	1
White	21	0	2	1	18	140	45	79	16	0
Wilcox	10	0	3	0	7	49	10	37	2	0
Wilkes	52	2	3	4	43	103	21	70	12	0
Wilkinson	12	0	2	1	9	14	2	7	5	1
HAWAII										
Metropolitan Counties										
Kauai Police Department	188	0	51	18	119	1,264	167	978	119	54
IDAHO										
Metropolitan Counties										
Ada	284	0	61	11	212	556	104	414	38	7
Bannock	16	0	5	0	11	98	25	63	10	0
Boise	28	1	3	0	24	29	17	6	6	0
Bonneville	111	1	14	1	95	686	249	369	68	3
Butte	4	0	0	0	4	13	3	9	1	0
Canyon	134	2	25	0	107	354	94	195	65	1
Franklin	2	0	0	0	2	11	0	10	1	0
Gem	9	0	5	0	4	20	9	8	3	1
Jefferson	9	0	2	0	7	128	28	88	12	0
Jerome	31	0	6	1	24	123	30	66	27	1
Kootenai	119	4	12	3	100	499	88	364	47	8
Nez Perce	5	0	0	0	5	35	12	21	2	0
Power	4	0	1	0	3	29	3	19	7	0
Twin Falls	50	0	4	1	45	119	70	40	9	0
Nonmetropolitan Counties										
Adams	14	2	0	0	12	40	3	32	5	0
Bear Lake	0	0	0	0	0	3	0	3	0	1
Benewah	24	2	2	0	20	63	7	46	10	0
Bingham	21	0	4	0	17	139	38	80	21	1
Blaine	15	0	4	0	11	29	2	19	8	0
Bonner	33	1	8	3	21	255	70	158	27	7
Boundary	22	0	14	0	8	39	8	29	2	1
Camas	1	0	1	0	0	4	0	4	0	0
Caribou	4	0	1	0	3	10	5	4	1	0
Cassia	29	0	0	0	29	264	19	221	24	0
Clearwater	10	1	1	0	8	8	2	6	0	1
Custer	8	1	3	0	4	19	5	11	3	0
Elmore	30	0	0	0	30	23	5	12	6	0
Fremont	6	0	2	0	4	43	5	32	6	0
Gooding	15	0	3	0	12	36	3	26	7	0
Idaho	41	0	1	0	40	26	11	12	3	1
Latah	28	0	11	0	17	80	25	51	4	0
Lemhi	6	0	0	0	6	27	7	17	3	2
Lewis	0	0	0	0	0	30	5	23	2	0
Lincoln	17	1	4	0	12	30	3	23	4	0
Madison	13	0	4	0	9	25	3	18	4	0
Minidoka	16	1	2	1	12	100	27	57	16	0
Oneida	11	0	4	1	6	28	10	14	4	0
Payette	28	0	5	1	22	65	11	43	11	1
Shoshone	37	1	6	1	29	79	12	59	8	0
Teton	17	0	9	0	8	37	5	31	1	0
Valley	27	0	5	0	22	63	13	44	6	1
Washington	10	0	1	0	9	9	1	6	2	1
ILLINOIS[1]										
Metropolitan Counties										
Bond	5	0	5	0	0	34	17	9	8	0
Calhoun	3	0	3	0	0	10	2	7	1	0

Table 10. Offenses Known to Law Enforcement, by Selected State Metropolitan and Nonmetropolitan Counties, 2022—Continued

(Number.)

State/county	Violent crime	Murder and nonnegligent manslaughter	Rape	Robbery	Aggravated assault	Property crime	Burglary	Larceny- theft	Motor vehicle theft	Arson[1]
Clinton	5	1	1	0	3	57	20	33	4	2
DeKalb	26	0	10	2	14	105	22	71	12	1
Grundy	26	2	10	0	14	83	15	62	6	1
Henry	14	0	7	0	7	133	21	95	17	0
Jackson	24	1	7	0	16	180	43	106	31	2
Jersey	12	0	2	0	10	12	3	8	1	0
Kendall	55	2	30	2	21	126	12	95	19	2
Macon	20	5	9	1	5	221	32	172	17	2
Madison	99	4	33	6	56	829	186	563	80	7
Marshall	1	0	1	0	0	44	22	16	6	1
McLean	18	0	3	1	14	90	23	50	17	1
Monroe	5	0	0	0	5	21	4	16	1	0
Peoria	157	0	19	7	131	563	116	383	64	1
Piatt	17	0	5	0	12	79	23	51	5	0
Rock Island	22	0	6	1	15	230	40	146	44	1
Sangamon	200	3	31	16	150	622	154	387	81	6
St. Clair	106	0	8	9	89	330	75	203	52	2
Tazewell	33	0	12	1	20	255	55	159	41	2
Vermilion	63	1	26	3	33	453	147	277	29	3
Will	208	4	41	11	152	568	108	364	96	3
Winnebago	147	1	34	4	108	359	106	210	43	9
Nonmetropolitan Counties										
Adams	29	1	18	0	10	180	68	108	4	2
Cass	0	0	0	0	0	1	0	0	1	0
Crawford	14	0	3	0	11	54	24	23	7	0
DeWitt	6	0	1	0	5	37	15	15	7	0
Effingham	18	0	7	0	11	105	30	63	12	1
Fayette	7	0	0	0	7	68	22	31	15	0
Ford	2	0	0	0	2	27	5	19	3	1
Hancock	15	1	1	0	13	32	20	7	5	0
Iroquois	11	0	4	0	7	129	12	107	10	1
Jefferson	16	0	11	0	5	180	50	120	10	0
La Salle	50	1	27	0	22	114	28	62	24	0
Livingston	17	0	10	0	7	59	16	41	2	1
Logan	5	0	1	1	3	55	16	36	3	1
Marion	34	0	16	1	17	131	54	62	15	0
Mason	0	0	0	0	0	0	0	0	0	0
Massac	7	0	1	0	6	38	7	25	6	1
Montgomery	10	0	6	0	4	38	10	18	10	2
Morgan	10	0	1	0	9	28	8	19	1	0
Pike	4	0	3	0	1	26	2	20	4	6
Pulaski	12	0	2	0	10	31	12	15	4	1
Putnam	0	0	0	0	0	25	0	21	4	0
Scott	3	0	0	0	3	8	2	5	1	0
Shelby	6	0	2	0	4	22	7	14	1	2
Stephenson	11	0	5	0	6	92	26	61	5	1
Warren	10	0	4	1	5	56	22	30	4	0
Whiteside	26	1	13	0	12	83	40	33	10	0
INDIANA										
Metropolitan Counties										
Bartholomew	0	0	0	0	0	30	30	0	0	2
Clark	49	3	6	2	38	231	46	144	41	2
Delaware	55	7	8	3	37	266	60	172	34	0
Elkhart	58	0	8	3	47	297	52	195	50	2
Floyd	36	0	3	2	31	175	17	119	39	1
Franklin	11	0	5	0	6	104	23	71	10	0
Hamilton	29	0	6	0	23	121	14	91	16	4
Hancock	46	0	2	2	42	204	41	121	42	1
Harrison	62	0	5	0	57	191	27	131	33	0
Hendricks	49	1	12	5	31	440	45	326	69	6
Howard	34	2	2	1	29	81	27	40	14	0
Johnson	12	0	7	0	5	221	15	180	26	1
La Porte	24	2	2	4	16	443	191	197	55	2
Madison	27	0	5	2	20	253	42	183	28	0
Monroe	24	1	10	3	10	399	39	315	45	3
Porter	75	0	7	1	67	208	32	146	30	0
Posey	17	0	6	0	11	98	20	66	12	2
Shelby	39	0	3	2	34	157	30	83	44	1
St. Joseph	117	2	15	14	86	894	220	553	121	5
Sullivan	22	0	0	1	21	104	22	55	27	2
Tippecanoe	86	0	15	5	66	327	71	186	70	1
Vanderburgh	168	1	18	2	147	411	68	299	44	1
Vigo	95	1	13	5	76	688	183	403	102	6
Warrick	169	3	15	2	149	417	31	350	36	4
Washington	47	0	3	0	44	84	13	57	14	0
Nonmetropolitan Counties										
Jackson	14	0	2	1	11	20	5	10	5	0
Jennings	13	0	4	0	9	92	24	46	22	1

Table 10. Offenses Known to Law Enforcement, by Selected State Metropolitan and Nonmetropolitan Counties, 2022—Continued

(Number.)

State/county	Violent crime	Murder and nonnegligent manslaughter	Rape	Robbery	Aggravated assault	Property crime	Burglary	Larceny-theft	Motor vehicle theft	Arson[1]
Kosciusko	84	0	9	2	73	360	52	240	68	3
Montgomery	21	0	7	0	14	124	32	73	19	1
Noble	22	1	7	0	14	141	32	78	31	0
Starke	29	0	1	1	27	107	38	49	20	2
Steuben	7	0	4	0	3	233	72	115	46	1
Wells	7	0	1	0	6	26	5	16	5	0
IOWA										
Metropolitan Counties										
Benton	35	1	10	0	24	64	23	34	7	0
Black Hawk	17	0	9	0	8	62	20	34	8	1
Bremer	7	0	1	0	6	30	15	13	2	0
Dallas	52	0	9	1	42	58	6	44	8	1
Dubuque	32	0	10	0	22	150	48	94	8	1
Jasper	18	0	5	1	12	45	13	20	12	0
Johnson	68	0	23	4	41	170	50	101	19	8
Jones	16	0	3	0	13	16	9	4	3	1
Linn	36	0	13	2	21	177	54	103	20	1
Madison	16	0	1	0	15	24	7	10	7	1
Mills	7	0	3	0	4	85	12	55	18	0
Polk	84	1	9	8	66	655	79	479	97	6
Pottawattamie	86	0	13	2	71	171	31	117	23	1
Scott	46	0	4	4	38	130	8	100	22	0
Story	15	2	7	0	6	111	31	57	23	4
Washington	41	0	1	1	39	91	31	51	9	0
Woodbury	24	1	5	1	17	87	18	58	11	2
Nonmetropolitan Counties										
Adair	2	0	0	0	2	16	2	7	7	0
Adams	3	0	0	0	3	6	1	5	0	0
Allamakee	10	0	4	0	6	28	7	20	1	0
Appanoose	15	0	4	0	11	54	18	26	10	1
Buchanan	14	0	2	0	12	37	9	21	7	0
Buena Vista	9	0	2	0	7	23	8	13	2	1
Butler	3	0	0	0	3	15	9	6	0	0
Carroll	0	0	0	0	0	11	2	6	3	1
Cass	18	0	3	0	15	57	23	25	9	0
Cedar	12	0	5	1	6	36	4	31	1	0
Cerro Gordo	6	0	2	0	4	38	10	16	12	1
Cherokee	1	0	0	0	1	21	3	15	3	0
Chickasaw	15	0	1	0	14	22	8	13	1	0
Clarke	4	0	1	0	3	37	14	13	10	1
Clay	7	0	1	0	6	8	1	5	2	0
Clayton	11	0	3	0	8	28	7	18	3	0
Clinton	30	0	4	1	25	101	40	46	15	0
Crawford	2	0	1	0	1	2	0	1	1	1
Davis	4	0	0	0	4	7	3	4	0	0
Delaware	26	0	1	0	25	19	6	11	2	0
Des Moines	14	0	0	0	14	138	40	77	21	0
Emmet	8	0	0	0	8	4	1	1	2	0
Fayette	20	0	5	0	15	18	3	9	6	0
Floyd	10	0	2	0	8	22	6	13	3	1
Franklin	3	0	0	0	3	9	3	6	0	0
Fremont	15	0	1	0	14	55	16	32	7	1
Hamilton	11	0	0	1	10	25	12	11	2	1
Hancock	14	0	2	0	12	43	17	23	3	0
Hardin	29	0	1	1	27	87	25	51	11	0
Henry	25	0	3	0	22	43	7	29	7	1
Howard	6	1	0	0	5	27	3	20	4	2
Humboldt	6	0	1	0	5	51	16	34	1	0
Ida	4	0	1	0	3	20	4	15	1	0
Iowa	17	0	1	2	14	67	21	38	8	0
Jackson	11	5	0	0	6	62	24	30	8	2
Jefferson	5	0	0	0	5	13	4	7	2	0
Keokuk	15	0	3	0	12	62	30	18	14	1
Lee	33	0	1	1	31	87	42	36	9	0
Louisa	28	0	5	0	23	26	6	15	5	0
Lucas	23	0	7	1	15	62	13	43	6	0
Lyon	15	0	1	0	14	66	22	32	12	1
Mahaska	11	0	0	0	11	33	17	9	7	0
Marion	26	0	11	0	15	40	13	18	9	0
Monona	11	0	2	1	8	72	22	43	7	0
Muscatine	14	1	4	1	8	45	12	22	11	0
O'Brien	18	0	7	0	11	52	17	34	1	1
Osceola	5	0	3	0	2	15	2	12	1	0
Page	6	0	0	1	5	25	9	13	3	0
Palo Alto	14	0	1	0	13	16	3	12	1	0
Plymouth	11	0	3	0	8	19	2	15	2	0
Pocahontas	4	0	1	0	3	17	4	11	2	0
Poweshiek	9	0	3	0	6	66	12	48	6	0

Table 10. Offenses Known to Law Enforcement, by Selected State Metropolitan and Nonmetropolitan Counties, 2022—Continued

(Number.)

State/county	Violent crime	Murder and nonnegligent manslaughter	Rape	Robbery	Aggravated assault	Property crime	Burglary	Larceny-theft	Motor vehicle theft	Arson[1]
Ringgold	3	0	0	0	3	16	5	8	3	0
Sac	18	0	5	0	13	55	25	29	1	1
Sioux	9	0	9	0	0	48	16	26	6	0
Tama	24	0	0	1	23	40	13	16	11	0
Union	6	0	1	0	5	31	2	11	18	0
Van Buren	4	0	0	0	4	26	8	17	1	0
Wapello	16	0	0	0	16	76	18	49	9	4
Wayne	4	0	2	0	2	24	4	20	0	2
Webster	41	0	3	0	38	89	25	56	8	1
Winneshiek	17	1	1	0	15	16	4	5	7	0
Worth	5	0	2	0	3	20	8	10	2	0
Wright	5	0	0	0	5	22	10	10	2	0
KANSAS										
Metropolitan Counties										
Butler	35	1	2	4	28	218	72	115	31	5
Doniphan	3	0	0	0	3	17	4	8	5	0
Geary	12	0	4	0	8	41	10	26	5	0
Harvey	12	0	0	0	12	63	12	39	12	0
Jackson	18	0	3	0	15	68	13	47	8	2
Jefferson	41	0	5	0	36	154	17	119	18	0
Johnson	42	0	9	1	32	233	19	192	22	3
Leavenworth	46	1	1	1	43	138	41	68	29	7
Miami	26	0	2	0	24	102	20	64	18	1
Osage	9	0	1	0	8	36	6	27	3	1
Pottawatomie	20	0	4	0	16	129	41	82	6	2
Riley County Police Department	179	1	30	5	143	883	99	713	71	14
Sedgwick	63	1	1	1	60	225	27	161	37	3
Shawnee	88	0	6	5	77	593	103	419	71	2
Sumner	44	1	5	4	34	139	39	94	6	1
Wabaunsee	21	0	1	1	19	103	32	58	13	0
Wyandotte	65	2	5	11	47	43	5	35	3	2
Nonmetropolitan Counties										
Allen	11	2	2	0	7	51	15	33	3	1
Anderson	10	0	2	1	7	14	3	7	4	1
Barber	0	0	0	0	0	25	4	17	4	2
Barton	14	0	5	0	9	53	19	32	2	0
Bourbon	24	0	4	1	19	39	10	21	8	2
Brown	2	0	0	0	2	16	1	12	3	2
Chautauqua	1	0	1	0	0	11	7	4	0	0
Cherokee	46	0	6	0	40	148	39	83	26	3
Cheyenne	7	0	2	1	4	19	3	12	4	1
Clark	2	0	0	1	1	26	5	19	2	0
Clay	13	0	7	0	6	7	0	6	1	0
Cowley	13	0	3	0	10	99	25	64	10	2
Crawford	19	0	4	0	15	123	1	111	11	3
Decatur	1	0	0	0	1	7	1	6	0	0
Dickinson	12	0	4	0	8	64	17	38	9	0
Edwards	20	0	1	0	19	10	2	7	1	0
Ellsworth	2	0	1	0	1	29	6	17	6	1
Finney	39	0	8	0	31	140	55	46	39	1
Ford	11	2	0	0	9	139	100	29	10	0
Franklin	41	0	5	3	33	73	19	43	11	3
Gove	1	0	0	0	1	6	0	4	2	0
Grant	2	0	0	0	2	9	3	2	4	0
Greenwood	14	0	1	1	12	65	13	42	10	1
Harper	1	0	0	0	1	23	5	15	3	1
Haskell	12	0	3	0	9	14	1	12	1	0
Kingman	7	0	0	0	7	29	9	14	6	0
Kiowa	0	0	0	0	0	8	2	3	3	1
Labette	11	0	4	1	6	87	49	32	6	2
Lane	5	0	0	0	5	10	3	7	0	0
Marion	11	0	0	0	11	37	12	13	12	0
Marshall	7	1	1	0	5	20	6	11	3	0
Mitchell	10	0	0	0	10	8	0	8	0	1
Montgomery	28	0	3	3	22	117	40	64	13	0
Morris	8	0	3	1	4	26	4	20	2	2
Nemaha	1	0	1	0	0	17	2	12	3	0
Neosho	12	0	1	1	10	326	283	36	7	4
Norton	2	0	1	0	1	7	2	1	4	0
Phillips	12	0	0	0	12	4	2	1	1	0
Pratt	6	0	0	0	6	19	6	6	7	0
Reno	39	0	5	1	33	151	48	76	27	3
Republic	6	0	0	0	6	16	4	10	2	0
Rice	9	0	0	0	9	27	4	17	6	1
Rooks	6	0	3	0	3	39	10	27	2	0
Rush	8	1	2	0	5	40	17	20	3	1
Russell	5	0	0	0	5	48	17	30	1	0
Saline	30	1	7	2	20	105	27	66	12	2

Table 10. Offenses Known to Law Enforcement, by Selected State Metropolitan and Nonmetropolitan Counties, 2022—Continued

(Number.)

State/county	Violent crime	Murder and nonnegligent manslaughter	Rape	Robbery	Aggravated assault	Property crime	Burglary	Larceny-theft	Motor vehicle theft	Arson[1]
Seward	4	0	0	0	4	6	1	4	1	0
Smith	4	0	1	0	3	14	7	5	2	0
Thomas	9	0	1	0	8	10	0	9	1	1
Washington	11	0	2	0	9	17	4	11	2	0
Woodson	4	0	0	0	4	14	2	10	2	0
KENTUCKY										
Metropolitan Counties										
Allen	2	0	0	0	2	55	20	22	13	2
Boone	74	2	28	7	37	692	79	542	71	3
Bourbon	4	0	1	0	3	64	28	28	8	0
Boyd	29	0	5	0	24	151	46	76	29	0
Bracken	4	0	0	0	4	14	4	3	7	0
Bullitt	23	3	2	4	14	240	45	146	49	0
Butler	5	0	0	0	5	21	3	12	6	0
Campbell	0	0	0	0	0	0	0	0	0	0
Campbell County Police Department	10	0	6	0	4	75	7	59	9	0
Carter	4	0	0	1	3	45	11	14	20	1
Christian	22	0	4	2	16	176	63	86	27	1
Clark	8	0	2	2	4	177	61	107	9	0
Daviess	12	0	2	2	8	273	61	172	40	1
Edmonson	0	0	0	0	0	31	6	19	6	0
Fayette	0	0	0	0	0	0	0	0	0	1
Gallatin	1	0	0	0	1	18	4	12	2	1
Grant	12	0	0	0	12	94	20	57	17	0
Greenup	2	0	0	0	2	16	4	9	3	0
Hancock	3	0	2	1	0	15	4	7	4	0
Hardin	13	0	5	1	7	153	48	76	29	1
Henderson	18	0	8	3	7	128	41	70	17	1
Henry	3	0	0	0	3	32	11	14	7	1
Jefferson	0	0	0	0	0	9	0	4	5	0
Jessamine	11	0	2	1	8	159	30	108	21	3
Kenton	5	0	0	0	5	4	0	4	0	1
Kenton County Police Department	12	0	4	1	7	67	11	48	8	0
Larue	1	0	0	0	1	19	5	9	5	0
McLean	5	0	2	0	3	23	6	13	4	0
Meade	19	1	2	2	14	88	21	38	29	2
Oldham	0	0	0	0	0	3	0	3	0	0
Oldham County Police Department	27	0	7	3	17	364	62	249	53	2
Pendleton	6	1	2	1	2	43	8	30	5	1
Scott	15	0	5	2	8	123	25	76	22	1
Shelby	18	0	6	2	10	148	21	103	24	0
Spencer	3	0	0	0	3	47	13	27	7	1
Trigg	6	0	1	1	4	45	14	26	5	0
Warren	52	2	14	5	31	462	97	315	50	1
Woodford	0	0	0	0	0	13	1	11	1	0
Nonmetropolitan Counties										
Adair	6	0	0	1	5	16	5	8	3	0
Anderson	3	0	0	0	3	16	3	11	2	0
Ballard	6	0	1	0	5	44	11	27	6	0
Barren	10	0	3	0	7	124	33	63	28	0
Bath	2	0	0	0	2	55	17	30	8	0
Bell	16	0	3	1	12	88	30	43	15	1
Boyle	3	0	1	0	2	12	4	3	5	0
Breathitt	1	0	0	1	0	9	2	6	1	0
Breckinridge	6	0	0	2	4	48	11	23	14	0
Caldwell	0	0	0	0	0	19	6	12	1	0
Calloway	13	0	4	0	9	138	43	82	13	2
Carlisle	0	0	0	0	0	13	6	4	3	0
Carroll	6	0	1	0	5	47	8	28	11	0
Casey	1	0	0	1	0	16	6	5	5	0
Clay	5	1	1	2	1	86	11	52	23	1
Clinton	0	0	0	0	0	10	1	7	2	0
Crittenden	1	0	1	0	0	14	5	6	3	1
Cumberland	2	0	2	0	0	5	3	2	0	0
Elliott	4	0	1	0	3	16	3	8	5	0
Estill	1	0	0	0	1	19	9	9	1	0
Fleming	2	0	0	0	2	18	2	8	8	2
Floyd	3	0	2	1	0	33	9	17	7	0
Franklin	17	1	7	0	9	119	24	71	24	3
Fulton	0	0	0	0	0	13	3	6	4	0
Garrard	11	0	7	0	4	63	17	29	17	1
Graves	14	0	3	2	9	147	45	85	17	3
Grayson	8	0	1	1	6	46	13	20	13	0
Green	1	0	0	0	1	10	3	6	1	0
Harlan	4	0	1	0	3	28	7	18	3	0
Harrison	0	0	0	0	0	36	10	20	6	0
Hart	5	0	0	0	5	30	10	13	7	0
Hickman	0	0	0	0	0	13	6	6	1	0

Table 10. Offenses Known to Law Enforcement, by Selected State Metropolitan and Nonmetropolitan Counties, 2022—Continued

(Number.)

State/county	Violent crime	Murder and nonnegligent manslaughter	Rape	Robbery	Aggravated assault	Property crime	Burglary	Larceny-theft	Motor vehicle theft	Arson[1]
Hopkins	21	1	9	0	11	132	27	85	20	3
Jackson	2	0	0	0	2	43	20	16	7	0
Johnson	7	1	0	0	6	27	5	11	11	1
Knott	0	0	0	0	0	26	1	16	9	0
Knox	23	0	4	1	18	66	22	16	28	1
Laurel	24	2	9	4	9	326	56	186	84	1
Lawrence	9	2	0	1	6	43	18	15	10	1
Lee	1	0	0	0	1	18	5	10	3	0
Leslie	1	0	0	0	1	11	2	6	3	0
Letcher	2	0	0	0	2	15	4	6	5	0
Lewis	0	0	0	0	0	18	8	3	7	0
Lincoln	4	0	1	1	2	47	17	15	15	0
Livingston	5	0	0	0	5	64	16	38	10	1
Logan	11	1	7	0	3	53	13	27	13	1
Lyon	3	0	1	1	1	22	7	13	2	2
Madison	19	0	9	0	10	191	38	112	41	1
Magoffin	1	0	0	0	1	5	0	4	1	0
Marion	3	0	3	0	0	43	11	22	10	1
Marshall	24	1	11	1	11	149	22	113	14	2
Martin	3	0	0	0	3	10	6	3	1	0
Mason	15	2	4	0	9	68	16	42	10	0
McCracken	31	0	11	4	16	201	51	130	20	2
McCreary	0	0	0	0	0	18	3	8	7	0
Menifee	5	0	0	0	5	11	1	8	2	0
Mercer	2	0	0	0	2	22	6	14	2	1
Metcalfe	0	0	0	0	0	28	12	10	6	0
Monroe	2	0	0	0	2	10	2	5	3	0
Montgomery	12	0	3	2	7	229	86	119	24	1
Morgan	3	0	0	0	3	34	10	19	5	1
Muhlenberg	6	0	0	0	6	60	29	24	7	2
Nicholas	5	0	3	0	2	8	3	3	2	0
Ohio	22	1	10	0	11	107	31	46	30	2
Owen	3	0	0	1	2	44	23	17	4	0
Owsley	0	0	0	0	0	0	0	0	0	0
Perry	3	1	1	1	0	24	5	9	10	1
Pike	0	0	0	0	0	29	5	20	4	0
Powell	1	0	0	0	1	6	4	1	1	0
Pulaski	23	1	5	2	15	178	67	74	37	2
Robertson	0	0	0	0	0	0	0	0	0	0
Rockcastle	2	0	0	0	2	25	6	6	13	0
Rowan	5	0	1	0	4	46	13	30	3	1
Russell	6	0	0	0	6	36	17	16	3	2
Simpson	7	1	2	0	4	40	22	13	5	0
Taylor	8	0	3	0	5	107	33	65	9	0
Todd	5	0	1	0	4	37	10	23	4	1
Trimble	3	0	0	0	3	10	4	4	2	0
Union	6	0	3	0	3	67	19	36	12	1
Washington	2	0	0	0	2	5	1	1	3	0
Wayne	9	0	2	1	6	44	13	15	16	0
Webster	1	0	0	0	1	35	11	20	4	0
Whitley	9	0	0	1	8	66	24	22	20	3
Wolfe	0	0	0	0	0	18	2	11	5	0
LOUISIANA										
Metropolitan Counties										
Acadia	123	2	7	6	108	484	133	301	50	0
Ascension	385	10	26	31	318	1,901	337	1,384	180	7
Bossier	158	0	41	4	113	425	75	312	38	3
Caddo	35	0	1	2	32	546	108	390	48	0
Calcasieu	804	2	72	18	712	4,005	614	3,034	357	11
De Soto	34	2	4	1	27	210	32	145	33	0
East Baton Rouge	657	7	31	100	519	5,637	981	4,168	488	3
East Feliciana	29	0	3	2	24	125	21	78	26	2
Grant	57	0	12	1	44	231	59	146	26	1
Iberville	64	2	5	1	56	232	36	177	19	0
Jefferson	1,357	42	71	229	1,015	8,737	1,790	6,040	907	44
Lafayette	267	9	22	19	217	991	223	646	122	1
Lafourche	250	7	27	10	206	1,455	228	1,107	120	1
Livingston	511	1	78	25	407	2,339	552	1,562	225	6
Morehouse	98	4	5	6	83	307	62	208	37	4
Ouachita	745	4	38	41	662	2,519	576	1,688	255	6
Plaquemines	75	1	1	1	72	109	21	83	5	1
Rapides	405	12	29	10	354	1,475	542	776	157	10
St. Bernard	204	2	17	10	175	862	150	613	99	11
St. Charles	163	4	7	17	135	669	119	484	66	9
St. Helena	96	6	1	5	84	151	20	104	27	2
St. James	72	2	1	7	62	240	52	169	19	2
St. John the Baptist	123	4	3	15	101	747	192	497	58	3
St. Martin	175	5	11	9	150	597	156	369	72	2
St. Tammany	250	9	31	18	192	1,302	278	852	172	8

Table 10. Offenses Known to Law Enforcement, by Selected State Metropolitan and Nonmetropolitan Counties, 2022—Continued

(Number.)

State/county	Violent crime	Murder and nonnegligent manslaughter	Rape	Robbery	Aggravated assault	Property crime	Burglary	Larceny-theft	Motor vehicle theft	Arson[1]
Tangipahoa	586	10	40	28	508	1,609	356	1,030	223	12
Terrebonne	307	3	2	20	282	2,038	308	1,622	108	8
Vermilion	86	0	9	1	76	349	157	155	37	1
West Baton Rouge	74	1	1	7	65	447	58	336	53	1
Nonmetropolitan Counties										
Allen	24	1	4	0	19	95	17	67	11	1
Beauregard	85	2	13	2	68	234	55	156	23	2
Bienville	42	1	3	3	35	136	34	86	16	0
Caldwell	80	0	2	0	78	92	21	65	6	1
Catahoula	35	0	1	1	33	70	14	51	5	1
Claiborne	22	0	0	0	22	34	8	21	5	0
Concordia	83	0	9	1	73	123	39	70	14	0
East Carroll	45	4	0	1	40	28	12	16	0	1
Evangeline	78	1	3	6	68	340	69	235	36	2
Franklin	94	0	5	0	89	291	52	209	30	3
Jefferson Davis	45	0	3	1	41	202	36	139	27	3
La Salle	15	0	1	1	13	21	8	8	5	0
Lincoln	55	1	3	1	50	169	48	108	13	1
St. Landry	143	4	5	5	129	611	154	382	75	1
St. Mary	90	2	11	1	76	393	89	274	30	1
Tensas	19	0	1	0	18	23	4	18	1	0
Washington	172	1	15	5	151	332	78	203	51	6
Webster	54	1	8	1	44	192	41	123	28	0
West Carroll	5	0	1	0	4	43	12	23	8	0
Winn	23	0	0	0	23	37	11	16	10	1
MAINE										
Metropolitan Counties										
Androscoggin	23	0	10	0	13	144	24	109	11	3
Cumberland	31	0	11	2	18	303	58	220	25	0
Penobscot	13	0	0	0	13	332	47	253	32	0
Sagadahoc	8	0	1	1	6	42	2	37	3	0
York	29	0	14	0	15	194	28	147	19	2
Nonmetropolitan Counties										
Aroostook	16	0	3	1	12	104	36	62	6	0
Franklin	4	0	3	0	1	81	7	67	7	0
Hancock	14	0	10	0	4	110	14	91	5	0
Kennebec	33	0	16	1	16	254	48	186	20	0
Knox	10	0	1	0	9	137	16	105	16	0
Lincoln	25	0	16	0	9	81	17	60	4	0
Oxford	12	0	6	0	6	197	38	143	16	2
Piscataquis	3	0	0	0	3	75	11	57	7	0
Somerset	21	0	10	0	11	313	54	237	22	1
Waldo	3	0	0	0	3	52	9	36	7	0
Washington	20	0	11	0	9	79	19	50	10	1
MARYLAND[2]										
Metropolitan Counties										
Allegany	22	1	10	2	9	76	32	40	4	0
Baltimore County	0	0	0	0	0	0	0	0	0	0
Baltimore County Police Department	3,008	34	320	749	1,905	16,471	1,608	13,343	1,520	110
Calvert	102	2	6	8	86	477	37	412	28	2
Cecil	80	4	30	6	40	416	87	275	54	0
Charles	486	11	47	102	326	1,705	164	1,348	193	7
Frederick	241	3	27	15	196	1,162	101	1,028	33	3
Howard County Police Department	460	4	64	117	275	4,114	383	3,304	427	25
Montgomery County Police Department	1,494	16	297	426	755	13,056	1,050	10,670	1,336	25
Prince George's County Police Department	2,611	79	149	1,250	1,133	13,684	1,185	8,690	3,809	0
Somerset	7	0	2	1	4	35	8	26	1	0
St. Mary's	277	4	30	24	219	1,127	236	824	67	3
Washington	205	4	10	14	177	846	138	652	56	1
Nonmetropolitan Counties										
Dorchester	16	0	0	0	16	99	19	69	11	0
Garrett	8	0	1	0	7	137	53	81	3	0
Kent	15	1	3	5	6	55	14	38	3	0
Talbot	25	0	6	0	19	79	16	61	2	0
MICHIGAN										
Metropolitan Counties										
Bay	62	1	13	5	43	401	42	331	28	5
Berrien	125	2	26	3	94	686	152	471	63	7
Calhoun	132	0	25	3	104	670	139	482	49	0
Cass	63	0	17	4	42	431	99	264	68	2
Clinton	20	0	5	0	15	134	32	81	21	2
Eaton	132	0	37	10	85	756	86	594	76	6
Genesee	113	0	32	5	76	426	53	230	143	1
Ingham	140	0	33	4	103	531	89	371	71	1

Table 10. Offenses Known to Law Enforcement, by Selected State Metropolitan and Nonmetropolitan Counties, 2022—Continued

(Number.)

State/county	Violent crime	Murder and nonnegligent manslaughter	Rape	Robbery	Aggravated assault	Property crime	Burglary	Larceny-theft	Motor vehicle theft	Arson[1]
Jackson	166	0	40	4	122	494	73	362	59	2
Kalamazoo	313	1	42	32	238	2,205	261	1,607	337	6
Kent	521	1	158	31	331	3,021	353	2,323	345	10
Lapeer	65	1	26	0	38	174	53	105	16	2
Livingston	64	0	26	1	37	371	67	276	28	2
Macomb	197	2	36	14	145	902	72	685	145	3
Midland	40	0	21	0	19	218	34	169	15	0
Montcalm	85	0	36	1	48	265	57	189	19	2
Oakland	16	0	0	2	14	23	3	18	2	1
Ottawa	598	2	195	10	391	1,953	219	1,600	134	6
Saginaw	116	0	15	5	96	354	44	286	24	4
St. Clair	164	0	36	0	128	538	87	382	69	3
Washtenaw	693	9	60	39	585	1,248	218	856	174	17
Wayne	10	0	1	0	9	0	0	0	0	0
Nonmetropolitan Counties										
Alcona	13	0	3	0	10	67	5	56	6	0
Alger	1	0	0	0	1	19	2	16	1	0
Allegan	103	0	14	2	87	571	92	420	59	9
Alpena	5	0	3	0	2	24	1	20	3	0
Antrim	41	0	13	0	28	105	22	79	4	0
Arenac	31	0	6	0	25	92	59	30	3	1
Baraga	3	0	0	0	3	16	6	9	1	0
Benzie	13	0	1	0	12	91	13	64	14	0
Branch	23	0	6	1	16	174	54	113	7	2
Charlevoix	23	0	9	0	14	58	9	43	6	0
Cheboygan	26	0	9	0	17	31	9	21	1	0
Chippewa	12	0	3	0	9	16	1	14	1	0
Clare	41	0	11	0	30	95	23	63	9	1
Crawford	29	0	13	0	16	57	11	39	7	2
Delta	4	0	1	0	3	39	8	30	1	0
Emmet	60	1	25	0	34	79	15	64	0	0
Gladwin	37	0	6	1	30	130	32	84	14	0
Gogebic	9	0	3	0	6	8	1	5	2	0
Grand Traverse	180	0	65	3	112	419	57	331	31	8
Gratiot	34	2	9	2	21	293	16	250	27	1
Hillsdale	67	0	30	0	37	204	37	152	15	4
Houghton	18	0	7	0	11	55	14	39	2	1
Huron	17	0	4	0	13	85	14	67	4	0
Iosco	0	0	0	0	0	0	0	0	0	0
Isabella	74	0	24	3	47	411	76	293	42	3
Kalkaska	69	1	16	0	52	128	40	77	11	1
Keweenaw	1	0	0	0	1	10	2	8	0	1
Leelanau	22	0	9	0	13	62	13	46	3	1
Lenawee	52	0	21	1	30	216	53	139	24	1
Luce	16	0	1	1	14	48	8	34	6	1
Mackinac	6	0	4	0	2	58	6	52	0	0
Manistee	23	0	9	0	14	123	30	88	5	0
Marquette	8	0	2	0	6	102	10	84	8	0
Mason	32	1	8	1	22	101	17	81	3	1
Missaukee	26	0	14	0	12	93	18	71	4	2
Montmorency	17	0	4	0	13	27	11	13	3	0
Oceana	48	2	8	1	37	209	41	153	15	4
Ogemaw	29	0	4	0	25	142	42	98	2	0
Ontonagon	1	0	0	0	1	10	0	9	1	0
Oscoda	16	0	2	0	14	48	13	25	10	2
Otsego	5	0	2	0	3	8	0	8	0	0
Presque Isle	10	0	0	0	10	13	2	10	1	0
Roscommon	37	3	23	0	11	99	37	58	4	0
Sanilac	34	1	6	0	27	113	28	61	24	1
Schoolcraft	1	0	0	0	1	2	0	2	0	0
St. Joseph	88	0	18	0	70	245	69	137	39	6
Tuscola	49	0	12	0	37	185	60	104	21	3
MINNESOTA										
Metropolitan Counties										
Anoka	48	0	16	0	32	599	70	506	23	3
Benton	11	0	4	0	7	107	30	70	7	0
Blue Earth	19	0	4	0	15	102	23	63	16	1
Carlton	26	0	7	0	19	135	33	87	15	0
Carver	44	0	18	2	24	445	41	377	27	0
Chisago	29	0	8	0	21	195	39	140	16	2
Clay	4	0	2	0	2	30	10	14	6	0
Dakota	27	0	0	1	26	28	10	16	2	0
Dodge	5	0	1	0	4	42	11	28	3	0
Fillmore	8	0	2	0	6	53	11	42	0	0
Hennepin	30	0	0	0	30	18	0	18	0	0
Houston	5	0	0	0	5	28	10	15	3	0
Isanti	18	0	3	0	15	187	32	138	17	2
Lake	7	0	4	0	3	23	3	20	0	0

Table 10. Offenses Known to Law Enforcement, by Selected State Metropolitan and Nonmetropolitan Counties, 2022—Continued

(Number.)

State/county	Violent crime	Murder and nonnegligent manslaughter	Rape	Robbery	Aggravated assault	Property crime	Burglary	Larceny-theft	Motor vehicle theft	Arson[1]
Le Sueur	10	0	2	0	8	77	15	55	7	0
Mille Lacs	33	0	7	0	26	197	44	123	30	3
Nicollet	1	0	1	0	0	43	13	28	2	0
Olmsted	30	1	14	3	12	240	55	155	30	2
Polk	23	0	6	0	17	83	21	55	7	2
Ramsey	193	4	27	17	145	1,440	118	1,159	163	2
Scott	10	2	0	0	8	90	7	80	3	1
Sherburne	31	0	13	1	17	218	39	160	19	0
Stearns	33	0	13	0	20	169	47	103	19	0
St. Louis	92	0	18	0	74	502	124	331	47	2
Wabasha	4	0	2	0	2	26	6	16	4	0
Washington	84	0	25	7	52	562	56	437	69	3
Wright	77	0	18	2	57	527	31	455	41	2
Nonmetropolitan Counties										
Aitkin	22	2	6	0	14	201	104	87	10	0
Becker	47	0	13	0	34	108	17	72	19	1
Beltrami	52	1	24	0	27	203	51	130	22	3
Big Stone	8	0	5	0	3	32	5	22	5	0
Brown	1	0	0	0	1	17	0	14	3	0
Cass	48	1	3	2	42	111	30	73	8	2
Chippewa	0	0	0	0	0	1	1	0	0	0
Clearwater	9	0	0	0	9	7	0	6	1	0
Cook	15	0	1	0	14	61	8	49	4	0
Cottonwood	2	0	0	0	2	15	1	12	2	0
Crow Wing	27	2	7	0	18	152	36	100	16	0
Douglas	6	0	0	0	6	32	4	24	4	0
Faribault	3	0	0	0	3	20	6	5	9	0
Freeborn	10	1	4	0	5	82	15	51	16	1
Goodhue	13	0	7	0	6	178	32	131	15	2
Grant	3	0	0	0	3	1	0	1	0	0
Hubbard	28	0	11	0	17	111	42	63	6	0
Itasca	50	1	9	1	39	111	19	74	18	4
Jackson	5	0	0	0	5	20	10	7	3	1
Kanabec	17	2	2	0	13	84	20	55	9	5
Kandiyohi	36	0	11	0	25	149	15	116	18	0
Kittson	2	0	0	0	2	9	1	5	3	0
Koochiching	18	0	1	0	17	28	11	15	2	0
Lac qui Parle	1	0	0	1	0	4	0	4	0	0
Lincoln	1	0	0	0	1	4	1	2	1	0
Lyon	8	0	1	0	7	31	6	20	5	0
Mahnomen	26	0	2	0	24	56	10	39	7	0
Marshall	18	1	3	1	13	13	5	8	0	0
Martin	2	0	0	0	2	5	2	2	1	0
McLeod	19	0	3	0	16	41	8	25	8	0
Meeker	18	0	10	1	7	114	22	85	7	0
Morrison	22	1	4	0	17	219	37	167	15	0
Mower	17	0	1	1	15	99	21	64	14	2
Murray	3	0	1	0	2	9	2	5	2	0
Nobles	15	0	3	0	12	18	5	13	0	0
Norman	2	0	0	0	2	13	2	9	2	0
Otter Tail	16	2	2	0	12	77	18	54	5	0
Pennington	5	0	0	0	5	47	5	37	5	0
Pine	78	0	10	1	67	352	82	222	48	6
Pipestone	4	0	1	0	3	20	0	20	0	0
Pope	4	0	1	0	3	25	3	19	3	0
Red Lake	4	0	0	0	4	4	1	3	0	0
Redwood	9	0	4	0	5	39	5	30	4	1
Renville	12	0	5	0	7	92	26	57	9	0
Rice	17	1	3	1	12	111	16	82	13	0
Rock	4	0	2	0	2	42	4	31	7	1
Roseau	15	0	2	0	13	35	10	23	2	0
Sibley	5	0	0	0	5	13	1	9	3	0
Steele	16	1	5	0	10	64	19	38	7	0
Stevens	6	0	1	0	5	42	5	33	4	0
Swift	1	0	0	0	1	2	1	1	0	0
Todd	29	0	16	0	13	111	29	72	10	1
Traverse	4	0	1	0	3	8	0	7	1	0
Wadena	0	0	0	0	0	2	0	2	0	0
Waseca	10	0	3	0	7	47	9	35	3	0
Watonwan	7	0	1	0	6	27	9	14	4	0
Wilkin	2	0	0	0	2	10	1	8	1	0
Winona	9	0	5	0	4	72	13	52	7	1
Yellow Medicine	4	0	0	0	4	26	6	19	1	0
MISSISSIPPI										
Metropolitan Counties										
Covington	10	1	2	2	5	135	29	82	24	4
DeSoto	43	1	17	2	23	215	22	154	39	2
Forrest	58	0	17	3	38	308	81	180	47	1

Table 10. Offenses Known to Law Enforcement, by Selected State Metropolitan and Nonmetropolitan Counties, 2022—Continued

(Number.)

State/county	Violent crime	Murder and nonnegligent manslaughter	Rape	Robbery	Aggravated assault	Property crime	Burglary	Larceny-theft	Motor vehicle theft	Arson[1]
Hancock	32	0	7	3	22	492	90	350	52	1
Harrison	66	4	9	8	45	849	117	606	126	8
Lamar	60	3	10	5	42	500	270	153	77	6
Madison	84	1	1	4	78	175	45	115	15	0
Stone	28	0	10	2	16	184	45	110	29	1
Tate	28	1	13	2	12	125	44	58	23	2
Tunica	65	2	7	8	48	454	61	302	91	5
Nonmetropolitan Counties										
Alcorn	11	0	3	0	8	245	50	169	26	1
Amite	17	1	3	0	13	31	13	9	9	1
Attala	18	0	2	0	16	72	24	31	17	1
Bolivar	60	6	4	7	43	245	61	151	33	0
Calhoun	21	0	1	1	19	26	10	13	3	1
Chickasaw	7	0	0	0	7	10	4	6	0	0
Choctaw	10	0	1	0	9	45	13	26	6	4
Claiborne	18	2	1	1	14	17	5	6	6	0
Clay	18	3	2	2	11	44	22	16	6	0
Coahoma	9	0	1	0	8	16	3	9	4	0
George	60	0	6	3	51	368	92	231	45	3
Greene	13	0	2	0	11	35	13	12	10	0
Grenada	56	0	5	1	50	211	69	128	14	0
Jasper	27	1	1	1	24	66	16	45	5	1
Kemper	15	0	4	0	11	23	0	20	3	0
Lafayette	19	0	4	3	12	157	39	109	9	0
Leake	33	0	3	4	26	132	33	79	20	2
Lee	74	2	19	4	49	503	135	303	65	5
Lincoln	33	1	11	0	21	219	39	149	31	1
Lowndes	76	4	12	12	48	373	109	230	34	5
Marion	67	0	9	3	55	116	31	60	25	7
Monroe	35	0	9	1	25	118	46	50	22	3
Neshoba	39	0	13	5	21	112	37	56	19	1
Noxubee	19	0	1	1	17	34	13	16	5	1
Oktibbeha	63	2	7	7	47	321	86	207	28	0
Pike	95	3	9	6	77	298	109	141	48	11
Pontotoc	61	3	24	2	32	203	61	110	32	5
Prentiss	23	1	3	0	19	138	33	93	12	1
Smith	5	0	2	0	3	46	8	16	22	0
Sunflower	16	2	1	3	10	93	25	56	12	1
Tallahatchie	36	2	4	2	28	119	28	63	28	3
Tishomingo	22	2	2	1	17	94	27	53	14	5
Union	50	9	6	0	35	146	40	97	9	3
Walthall	24	0	2	3	19	93	14	56	23	0
Wayne	25	0	2	1	22	96	33	53	10	0
Winston	28	1	6	1	20	67	24	38	5	0
MISSOURI										
Metropolitan Counties										
Andrew	24	0	6	0	18	93	11	63	19	3
Bates	60	0	2	0	58	117	36	63	18	4
Bollinger	55	1	2	0	52	42	12	23	7	1
Boone	120	1	18	6	95	611	86	435	90	3
Buchanan	19	0	8	0	11	148	24	100	24	2
Caldwell	4	0	1	0	3	19	3	12	4	0
Callaway	69	0	10	0	59	285	63	200	22	2
Cape Girardeau	56	1	9	0	46	156	38	83	35	2
Clay	35	0	2	2	31	126	31	75	20	0
Clinton	12	1	2	0	9	75	32	33	10	0
Cole	49	0	2	2	45	200	21	144	35	3
Dallas	35	1	6	0	28	81	26	46	9	5
DeKalb	15	0	5	0	10	46	14	27	5	0
Franklin	32	0	3	1	28	292	53	194	45	2
Greene	117	1	15	8	93	758	193	467	98	3
Howard	22	0	1	0	21	32	13	14	5	0
Jackson	118	2	12	3	101	387	95	223	69	4
Jasper	62	0	14	3	45	499	96	278	125	2
Jefferson	469	4	21	8	436	1,930	382	1,160	388	24
Lafayette	2	0	0	0	2	68	13	36	19	0
Lincoln	125	3	12	3	107	265	67	152	46	2
Newton	98	0	34	0	64	572	109	350	113	4
Osage	7	0	1	0	6	81	14	56	11	0
Platte	58	1	9	2	46	283	49	182	52	1
Polk	44	2	11	4	27	205	52	121	32	7
Ray	92	1	7	1	83	123	31	73	19	3
St. Charles	0	0	0	0	0	0	0	0	0	0
St. Charles County Police Department	101	0	20	1	80	297	38	214	45	5
St. Louis County Police Department	1,808	31	104	238	1,435	8,679	1,001	4,767	2,911	57
Warren	23	0	7	0	16	141	17	102	22	3
Webster	152	1	11	0	140	115	37	54	24	2

Table 10. Offenses Known to Law Enforcement, by Selected State Metropolitan and Nonmetropolitan Counties, 2022—Continued

(Number.)

State/county	Violent crime	Murder and nonnegligent manslaughter	Rape	Robbery	Aggravated assault	Property crime	Burglary	Larceny-theft	Motor vehicle theft	Arson[1]
Nonmetropolitan Counties										
Audrain	32	0	2	1	29	82	21	56	5	2
Barry	29	0	4	0	25	185	36	92	57	1
Barton	21	0	3	0	18	80	11	49	20	13
Benton	26	0	3	0	23	132	34	71	27	1
Butler	71	1	14	2	54	496	100	306	90	5
Camden	71	1	15	0	55	195	31	124	40	1
Carter	27	0	1	0	26	26	4	17	5	1
Cedar	50	1	8	0	41	73	23	41	9	0
Chariton	25	0	1	1	23	44	6	34	4	0
Clark	2	0	0	0	2	67	14	44	9	0
Crawford	31	0	1	0	30	97	14	65	18	4
Dade	41	2	4	0	35	97	26	60	11	4
Daviess	27	0	3	2	22	61	7	47	7	1
Dent	20	0	4	0	16	55	10	38	7	1
Douglas	20	0	3	0	17	43	9	27	7	1
Dunklin	3	0	0	0	3	45	11	24	10	0
Henry	105	3	23	1	78	256	80	128	48	0
Hickory	16	0	5	0	11	46	9	29	8	0
Holt	10	0	1	0	9	23	5	17	1	0
Howell	45	0	5	1	39	185	33	110	42	1
Iron	16	0	4	0	12	16	4	10	2	1
Johnson	31	2	12	0	17	216	48	130	38	4
Laclede	19	0	3	1	15	212	26	155	31	0
Lawrence	31	0	8	3	20	219	48	124	47	1
Lewis	1	0	0	0	1	11	6	5	0	0
Linn	14	0	3	1	10	12	3	7	2	0
Livingston	10	0	0	1	9	32	9	21	2	0
Macon	9	0	2	0	7	65	10	45	10	0
Madison	6	0	3	0	3	19	6	11	2	1
Maries	26	0	4	0	22	139	5	22	112	0
Marion	0	0	0	0	0	44	7	34	3	0
McDonald	153	0	24	1	128	225	28	152	45	3
Mercer	1	0	0	0	1	7	3	3	1	1
Miller	69	0	9	0	60	153	30	86	37	3
Mississippi	13	1	5	0	7	99	12	79	8	0
Monroe	47	0	4	0	43	46	10	31	5	1
Montgomery	13	0	4	0	9	55	11	32	12	0
New Madrid	38	0	4	2	32	132	31	72	29	2
Nodaway	15	0	7	0	8	53	14	33	6	0
Oregon	12	0	1	0	11	24	11	9	4	0
Ozark	28	1	4	1	22	43	10	27	6	1
Pemiscot	10	1	1	0	8	78	13	51	14	1
Perry	22	0	0	0	22	28	3	21	4	0
Pettis	8	1	3	0	4	27	5	19	3	1
Phelps	35	1	15	2	17	202	44	127	31	2
Pike	20	1	7	1	11	84	22	50	12	0
Ralls	5	0	1	0	4	36	9	26	1	0
Randolph	44	0	0	0	44	28	3	22	3	0
Reynolds	5	0	1	0	4	3	0	1	2	0
Ripley	4	1	1	0	2	72	30	32	10	0
Saline	108	0	9	0	99	105	28	60	17	2
Schuyler	6	0	3	0	3	60	12	43	5	3
Shannon	17	1	2	0	14	37	7	12	18	0
Shelby	0	0	0	0	0	6	2	4	0	0
St. Clair	8	0	3	0	5	35	5	24	6	3
Ste. Genevieve	63	0	8	0	55	97	13	59	25	0
St. Francois	55	1	19	1	34	351	71	189	91	2
Stoddard	41	0	14	0	27	165	31	105	29	1
Stone	42	0	15	0	27	376	96	221	59	0
Taney	60	1	10	1	48	194	30	130	34	1
Texas	53	1	13	0	39	95	16	63	16	1
Vernon	29	0	10	1	18	114	9	91	14	1
Washington	45	0	14	2	29	85	36	32	17	1
Wayne	60	0	3	0	57	111	41	60	10	1
Wright	37	2	13	0	22	51	6	28	17	2
MONTANA										
Metropolitan Counties										
Carbon	4	0	1	0	3	6	1	5	0	0
Cascade	56	0	4	1	51	200	47	140	13	2
Missoula	128	0	19	6	103	369	104	223	42	2
Stillwater	27	0	5	0	22	38	5	31	2	1
Yellowstone	128	1	11	4	112	622	60	439	123	7
Nonmetropolitan Counties										
Big Horn	35	1	5	0	29	131	13	72	46	1
Broadwater	20	0	0	0	20	31	3	24	4	0
Butte-Silver Bow	117	0	7	12	98	1,569	137	1,206	226	9
Carter	0	0	0	0	0	0	0	0	0	0

Table 10. Offenses Known to Law Enforcement, by Selected State Metropolitan and Nonmetropolitan Counties, 2022—Continued

(Number.)

State/county	Violent crime	Murder and nonnegligent manslaughter	Rape	Robbery	Aggravated assault	Property crime	Burglary	Larceny-theft	Motor vehicle theft	Arson[1]
Chouteau	3	0	0	0	3	0	0	0	0	0
Custer	12	0	3	0	9	21	4	15	2	1
Dawson	10	0	1	0	9	26	6	15	5	0
Deer Lodge	24	1	0	1	22	160	34	109	17	0
Fallon	3	0	0	0	3	1	1	0	0	0
Fergus	5	0	2	0	3	1	0	1	0	0
Flathead	222	7	31	2	182	786	129	540	117	5
Gallatin	130	3	26	0	101	386	25	308	53	1
Garfield	0	0	0	0	0	1	0	1	0	0
Glacier	9	2	1	0	6	24	1	17	6	0
Golden Valley	0	0	0	0	0	4	3	1	0	0
Granite	5	0	0	0	5	37	10	25	2	1
Hill	15	0	1	0	14	138	9	113	16	2
Jefferson	19	0	1	0	18	79	21	52	6	1
Judith Basin	3	0	0	0	3	0	0	0	0	0
Lake	116	2	15	1	98	257	33	161	63	3
Lewis and Clark	91	1	19	1	70	267	63	156	48	3
Liberty	1	0	0	0	1	6	1	5	0	0
Lincoln	16	3	1	0	12	22	4	16	2	0
Madison	5	0	2	0	3	19	2	17	0	0
McCone	1	0	1	0	0	1	0	1	0	0
Mineral	18	0	0	1	17	40	10	23	7	2
Musselshell	21	0	5	0	16	34	2	27	5	0
Park	15	2	2	0	11	45	7	31	7	3
Petroleum	0	0	0	0	0	0	0	0	0	0
Phillips	31	1	2	0	28	23	1	19	3	0
Pondera	0	0	0	0	0	23	2	18	3	0
Powder River	1	0	0	0	1	0	0	0	0	0
Powell	21	1	4	0	16	13	1	9	3	0
Prairie	3	0	0	0	3	1	0	1	0	0
Ravalli	21	0	2	0	19	42	3	29	10	2
Richland	9	0	0	0	9	15	1	11	3	0
Roosevelt	35	0	2	1	32	28	11	10	7	0
Rosebud	6	0	0	0	6	4	1	2	1	0
Sanders	18	0	6	0	12	27	0	13	14	0
Sheridan	21	0	4	0	17	48	5	34	9	1
Sweet Grass	23	0	6	0	17	19	4	13	2	1
Teton	11	0	2	0	9	26	5	18	3	0
Toole	10	0	4	0	6	66	8	54	4	1
Treasure	0	0	0	0	0	0	0	0	0	0
Valley	8	0	0	0	8	5	2	3	0	0
Wheatland	6	0	1	0	5	3	0	2	1	1
Wibaux	0	0	0	0	0	0	0	0	0	0
NEBRASKA										
Metropolitan Counties										
Cass	13	1	6	0	6	113	12	87	14	2
Dakota	14	0	2	1	11	73	9	53	11	0
Dixon	10	0	2	0	8	11	3	7	1	0
Douglas	79	3	37	3	36	646	113	456	77	0
Hall	7	1	1	1	4	125	11	99	15	0
Lancaster	22	0	14	2	6	208	42	143	23	3
Sarpy	52	0	21	3	28	691	38	588	65	3
Saunders	4	0	1	0	3	58	15	38	5	0
Seward	8	0	0	0	8	10	2	3	5	0
Nonmetropolitan Counties										
Adams	3	0	3	0	0	24	3	21	0	0
Box Butte	3	0	2	0	1	27	13	12	2	0
Buffalo	25	0	8	0	17	116	22	83	11	1
Burt	1	0	1	0	0	4	0	4	0	1
Butler	1	0	1	0	0	8	1	4	3	0
Cedar	5	0	1	0	4	26	10	14	2	0
Chase	0	0	0	0	0	2	0	1	1	0
Cherry	2	0	1	0	1	6	2	3	1	0
Cheyenne	15	0	1	1	13	7	0	5	2	0
Colfax	2	0	0	0	2	20	4	9	7	0
Custer	4	1	0	0	3	37	8	27	2	0
Furnas	4	0	2	0	2	42	13	26	3	0
Gage	22	0	4	1	17	47	7	34	6	1
Gosper	0	0	0	0	0	1	1	0	0	0
Hamilton	2	0	1	0	1	18	6	8	4	1
Jefferson	3	0	0	0	3	56	8	47	1	0
Johnson	4	0	0	0	4	13	1	9	3	0
Kearney	3	0	2	0	1	19	6	9	4	0
Keith	1	0	0	0	1	12	2	8	2	0
Lincoln	5	0	1	0	4	43	15	24	4	0
Logan	0	0	0	0	0	0	0	0	0	0
Madison	6	0	0	0	6	19	1	15	3	0
McPherson	0	0	0	0	0	1	1	0	0	0

Table 10. Offenses Known to Law Enforcement, by Selected State Metropolitan and Nonmetropolitan Counties, 2022—Continued

(Number.)

State/county	Violent crime	Murder and nonnegligent manslaughter	Rape	Robbery	Aggravated assault	Property crime	Burglary	Larceny-theft	Motor vehicle theft	Arson[1]
Morrill	2	0	0	0	2	22	1	20	1	0
Nemaha	13	0	5	0	8	43	7	33	3	0
Otoe	7	0	5	0	2	41	3	31	7	0
Perkins	1	0	0	0	1	19	3	12	4	0
Pierce	1	0	0	0	1	13	2	9	2	0
Platte	15	0	3	0	12	75	9	60	6	1
Richardson	5	0	1	0	4	19	3	13	3	0
Scotts Bluff	10	0	3	0	7	78	15	52	11	0
Sheridan	7	1	2	0	4	10	1	6	3	1
Stanton	1	0	1	0	0	0	0	0	0	0
Thayer	9	0	2	0	7	16	2	12	2	0
Valley	3	0	3	0	0	4	3	1	0	0
Wayne	1	0	0	0	1	10	3	4	3	0
NEVADA										
Metropolitan Counties										
Carson City	187	1	36	14	136	570	128	360	82	7
Storey	18	0	2	0	16	58	20	31	7	0
Washoe	323	1	32	19	271	773	164	512	97	7
Nonmetropolitan Counties										
Churchill	22	0	0	2	20	94	23	62	9	3
Douglas	79	1	36	3	39	444	54	365	25	2
Elko	48	1	7	2	38	198	36	110	52	1
Eureka	6	1	1	0	4	41	15	17	9	1
Humboldt	21	0	3	1	17	134	84	40	10	3
Lander	40	1	8	1	30	99	47	36	16	4
Lyon	159	4	22	15	118	491	102	311	78	10
Mineral	8	0	1	0	7	39	7	16	16	1
Nye	174	3	18	18	135	860	253	498	109	21
White Pine	37	2	11	0	24	49	16	25	8	0
NEW HAMPSHIRE										
Metropolitan Counties										
Hillsborough	2	0	0	0	2	0	0	0	0	0
Rockingham	4	0	2	1	1	1	0	0	1	0
Strafford	3	0	1	0	2	1	0	1	0	0
Nonmetropolitan Counties										
Belknap	1	0	1	0	0	14	1	13	0	0
Carroll	3	0	0	0	3	42	9	31	2	0
Cheshire	6	0	4	0	2	12	2	8	2	0
Grafton	0	0	0	0	0	0	0	0	0	0
Merrimack	0	0	0	0	0	1	0	1	0	0
Sullivan	1	0	0	0	1	6	1	4	1	0
NEW JERSEY										
Metropolitan Counties										
Atlantic	0	0	0	0	0	0	0	0	0	0
Bergen	0	0	0	0	0	0	0	0	0	0
Burlington	0	0	0	0	0	0	0	0	0	0
Camden	3	0	0	1	2	38	0	30	8	0
Cape May	0	0	0	0	0	0	0	0	0	0
Cumberland	0	0	0	0	0	0	0	0	0	0
Essex	81	1	2	26	52	140	23	86	31	1
Gloucester	0	0	0	0	0	2	1	1	0	0
Hudson	0	0	0	0	0	0	0	0	0	0
Hunterdon	0	0	0	0	0	0	0	0	0	0
Middlesex	0	0	0	0	0	0	0	0	0	0
Monmouth	3	1	0	0	2	0	0	0	0	0
Morris	0	0	0	0	0	0	0	0	0	0
Ocean	0	0	0	0	0	5	1	3	1	0
Salem	0	0	0	0	0	0	0	0	0	0
Somerset	3	0	0	0	3	0	0	0	0	0
Sussex	0	0	0	0	0	0	0	0	0	0
Union	0	0	0	0	0	0	0	0	0	0
Warren	0	0	0	0	0	0	0	0	0	0
NEW MEXICO										
Metropolitan Counties										
Bernalillo	777	19	58	90	610	2,243	485	1,239	519	13
Dona Ana	339	3	28	17	291	1,209	281	597	331	12
San Juan	240	1	45	5	189	413	103	244	66	9
Santa Fe	134	0	14	3	117	465	196	190	79	3
Torrance	58	1	2	2	53	198	96	65	37	2
Valencia	224	0	14	7	203	768	307	315	146	4
Nonmetropolitan Counties										
Chaves	57	1	3	2	51	215	63	107	45	2
Curry	20	1	1	0	18	191	111	58	22	4

Table 10. Offenses Known to Law Enforcement, by Selected State Metropolitan and Nonmetropolitan Counties, 2022—Continued

(Number.)

State/county	Violent crime	Murder and nonnegligent manslaughter	Rape	Robbery	Aggravated assault	Property crime	Burglary	Larceny-theft	Motor vehicle theft	Arson[1]
De Baca	9	3	1	0	5	20	4	14	2	0
Eddy	69	2	10	7	50	393	87	236	70	2
Guadalupe	0	0	0	0	0	6	1	4	1	0
Hidalgo	6	0	0	0	6	20	6	9	5	1
Lea	75	3	11	2	59	557	169	334	54	2
McKinley	58	0	2	6	50	147	39	90	18	2
Mora	13	0	1	0	12	22	7	12	3	1
Quay	4	0	2	0	2	22	4	12	6	0
San Miguel	0	0	0	0	0	1	1	0	0	0
Sierra	12	0	2	0	10	27	11	13	3	2
Socorro	18	1	2	1	14	68	14	35	19	1
Union	5	0	1	1	3	7	4	2	1	0
NEW YORK										
Metropolitan Counties										
Albany	10	0	2	1	7	116	10	97	9	0
Broome	41	1	15	2	23	609	71	488	50	2
Dutchess	44	1	14	1	28	344	29	299	16	5
Erie	111	3	24	5	79	617	52	505	60	2
Herkimer	0	0	0	0	0	19	0	19	0	0
Jefferson	12	0	1	0	11	182	21	156	5	0
Livingston	18	1	2	0	15	255	37	206	12	0
Madison	10	2	2	2	4	109	34	69	6	1
Monroe	189	0	24	50	115	2,360	198	1,980	182	5
Nassau	1,748	14	92	489	1,153	13,870	888	12,356	626	
Niagara	32	1	8	3	20	540	69	421	50	6
Oneida	47	0	39	0	8	263	51	194	18	4
Onondaga	198	2	39	33	124	1,330	213	978	139	13
Ontario	47	0	14	2	31	563	59	487	17	0
Orange	2	0	0	0	2	5	3	2	0	0
Orleans	9	0	1	0	8	141	26	103	12	0
Oswego	44	2	10	1	31	365	140	205	20	0
Rensselaer	23	1	6	2	14	172	17	146	9	0
Saratoga	84	0	24	2	58	1,200	105	1,077	18	8
Schenectady	0	0	0	0	0	29	0	28	1	0
Schoharie	3	0	0	0	3	12	2	10	0	1
Suffolk County Police Department	1,201	27	108	257	809	17,089	880	14,856	1,353	31
Tompkins	29	0	3	6	20	288	43	235	10	0
Ulster	14	0	2	3	9	121	11	101	9	1
Warren	24	0	13	5	6	488	46	435	7	0
Washington	34	0	13	3	18	109	14	88	7	
Westchester Public Safety	6	0	0	3	3	140	11	127	2	2
Yates	12	0	9	1	2	88	20	59	9	0
Nonmetropolitan Counties										
Allegany	10	0	0	0	10	0	0	0	0	0
Cattaraugus	41	0	3	6	32	212	40	153	19	3
Cayuga	10	0	6	1	3	96	15	76	5	1
Chautauqua	42	1	10	1	30	381	92	256	33	6
Columbia	9	0	2	0	7	318	28	279	11	0
Cortland	26	0	3	1	22	289	42	240	7	1
Delaware	12	0	4	0	8	106	38	66	2	2
Essex	4	0	0	0	4	6	1	5	0	0
Genesee	23	2	6	4	11	286	34	241	11	5
Greene	17	0	1	1	15	30	3	23	4	0
Hamilton	0	0	0	0	0	6	0	6	0	0
Lewis	4	0	0	0	4	73	19	52	2	2
Montgomery	3	0	2	0	1	173	14	156	3	0
Otsego	4	0	3	0	1	8	0	8	0	0
Schuyler	6	0	2	1	3	34	6	27	1	1
Seneca	12	1	0	0	11	86	8	74	4	0
Steuben	10	0	1	1	8	112	26	74	12	1
St. Lawrence	10	0	1	1	8	33	5	23	5	0
Wyoming	11	0	1	0	10	100	15	84	1	1
NORTH CAROLINA										
Metropolitan Counties										
Alamance	164	1	16	2	145	608	114	418	76	5
Alexander	70	1	10	1	58	352	111	210	31	0
Brunswick	185	3	31	7	144	790	288	448	54	11
Buncombe	142	2	15	8	117	1,482	531	738	213	24
Burke	142	5	33	6	98	747	215	450	82	5
Cabarrus	52	0	3	7	42	561	86	402	73	3
Caldwell	56	4	9	5	38	825	208	499	118	8
Catawba	125	5	44	4	72	863	201	534	128	7
Chatham	84	2	11	8	63	530	147	324	59	3
Craven	94	0	5	4	85	499	134	284	81	2
Currituck	64	0	12	0	52	267	55	198	14	1
Davidson	73	3	7	14	49	1,276	324	778	174	9
Durham	88	2	2	14	70	421	133	237	51	3

Table 10. Offenses Known to Law Enforcement, by Selected State Metropolitan and Nonmetropolitan Counties, 2022—Continued

(Number.)

State/county	Violent crime	Murder and nonnegligent manslaughter	Rape	Robbery	Aggravated assault	Property crime	Burglary	Larceny-theft	Motor vehicle theft	Arson[1]
Edgecombe	102	7	8	4	83	300	116	162	22	2
Forsyth	264	9	14	21	220	1,509	332	1,057	120	34
Gaston	21	0	0	0	21	2	0	2	0	0
Gaston County Police Department	137	5	12	13	107	783	236	405	142	13
Gates	11	1	2	0	8	81	13	58	10	0
Granville	62	2	11	2	47	397	178	186	33	4
Guilford	265	5	27	32	201	1,047	224	703	120	12
Harnett	266	6	17	19	224	1,539	404	944	191	31
Haywood	66	0	20	1	45	536	153	312	71	3
Henderson	105	1	27	2	75	839	246	499	94	2
Iredell	148	3	6	6	133	632	210	330	92	4
Johnston	124	2	17	12	93	1,597	239	1,208	150	6
Lincoln	112	0	14	7	91	910	210	587	113	6
Madison	10	0	2	0	8	120	34	67	19	2
Nash	49	1	5	2	41	290	73	199	18	0
New Hanover	112	1	22	15	74	1,210	165	971	74	17
Orange	119	5	8	12	94	467	99	311	57	4
Pamlico	35	0	4	1	30	144	35	90	19	1
Pender	89	2	29	3	55	549	86	411	52	4
Person	56	2	9	4	41	248	92	141	15	3
Pitt	170	5	5	16	144	632	191	398	43	2
Randolph	102	1	22	7	72	851	225	553	73	17
Rockingham	45	1	20	1	23	590	160	370	60	0
Rowan	150	7	9	6	128	825	183	517	125	12
Union	155	2	31	10	112	1,512	235	1,155	122	7
Wake	222	3	15	23	181	1,272	234	850	188	14
Wayne	201	6	8	6	181	1,074	336	567	171	4
Yadkin	41	1	12	1	27	286	64	190	32	2
Nonmetropolitan Counties										
Alleghany	6	1	2	0	3	102	32	61	9	2
Ashe	26	0	6	1	19	169	55	98	16	3
Avery	18	0	3	0	15	104	36	52	16	1
Bertie	69	2	5	1	61	165	51	84	30	1
Cherokee	63	2	13	1	47	524	95	373	56	6
Chowan	3	0	3	0	0	90	31	46	13	2
Clay	19	1	6	0	12	154	39	103	12	1
Cleveland	182	2	34	8	138	627	172	375	80	1
Dare	18	1	4	2	11	191	39	145	7	0
Duplin	79	9	10	6	54	691	250	350	91	8
Greene	47	1	15	2	29	240	83	132	25	1
Halifax	104	6	12	11	75	401	127	218	56	1
Hertford	20	1	1	3	15	112	31	70	11	1
Jackson	73	1	23	1	48	313	131	155	27	1
Lee	41	5	2	4	30	208	41	126	41	1
Macon	33	2	10	4	17	374	124	217	33	4
Martin	44	4	7	5	28	199	43	131	25	3
McDowell	69	1	9	7	52	676	205	366	105	7
Montgomery	43	2	7	2	32	212	56	125	31	4
Moore	59	2	11	5	41	461	125	307	29	4
Pasquotank	51	0	10	2	39	256	73	157	26	3
Perquimans	33	1	10	2	20	113	30	76	7	0
Polk	13	1	6	0	6	138	50	76	12	3
Richmond	241	11	12	15	203	1,043	339	584	120	5
Robeson	974	26	13	63	872	2,382	881	1,171	330	45
Rutherford	130	1	21	3	105	543	202	310	31	6
Scotland	123	4	6	7	106	405	165	189	51	12
Surry	87	3	38	2	44	524	130	284	110	12
Swain	38	0	9	0	29	158	51	98	9	4
Transylvania	24	0	10	1	13	190	61	109	20	3
Tyrrell	16	0	2	1	13	38	11	25	2	1
Vance	105	3	11	12	79	465	138	267	60	7
Warren	50	2	7	6	35	325	111	161	53	5
Watauga	15	2	2	1	10	198	49	130	19	4
Wilkes	130	3	15	6	106	576	180	317	79	7
Wilson	46	2	0	4	40	180	25	123	32	2
Yancey	15	3	1	0	11	56	21	33	2	2
NORTH DAKOTA										
Metropolitan Counties										
Burleigh	20	0	3	1	16	112	26	71	15	0
Cass	27	0	10	1	16	114	36	59	19	2
Grand Forks	21	0	4	1	16	70	19	43	8	0
Morton	8	2	1	0	5	78	22	46	10	2
Oliver	1	0	0	0	1	2	0	2	0	0
Nonmetropolitan Counties										
Adams	3	0	0	0	3	10	1	7	2	0
Barnes	2	0	1	0	1	9	1	3	5	1
Benson	2	0	0	0	2	13	8	1	4	0

Table 10. Offenses Known to Law Enforcement, by Selected State Metropolitan and Nonmetropolitan Counties, 2022—Continued

(Number.)

State/county	Violent crime	Murder and nonnegligent manslaughter	Rape	Robbery	Aggravated assault	Property crime	Burglary	Larceny- theft	Motor vehicle theft	Arson[1]
Billings	0	0	0	0	0	1	0	1	0	0
Bottineau	8	0	2	0	6	54	4	41	9	7
Bowman	0	0	0	0	0	3	2	1	0	0
Burke	1	0	0	0	1	6	2	3	1	0
Cavalier	4	0	3	0	1	12	2	7	3	0
Dickey	0	0	0	0	0	1	1	0	0	0
Divide	1	0	0	0	1	7	0	4	3	0
Dunn	1	0	0	0	1	21	4	14	3	0
Eddy	2	0	0	0	2	16	3	7	6	1
Emmons	2	0	0	0	2	41	9	26	6	0
Foster	1	1	0	0	0	3	1	2	0	0
Golden Valley	4	0	2	0	2	8	0	7	1	0
Griggs	1	0	1	0	0	9	2	4	3	0
Hettinger	4	0	2	0	2	7	4	3	0	0
Kidder	0	0	0	0	0	4	0	3	1	0
Lamoure	1	0	0	0	1	4	0	1	3	0
Logan	0	0	0	0	0	3	0	3	0	0
McHenry	9	0	3	0	6	36	14	16	6	1
McIntosh	1	0	0	0	1	18	3	14	1	0
McKenzie	16	0	2	0	14	87	5	61	21	1
McLean	9	0	0	1	8	72	13	47	12	0
Mercer	1	0	0	0	1	13	1	11	1	0
Mountrail	7	0	2	0	5	67	6	43	18	1
Nelson	1	0	0	0	1	16	5	7	4	0
Pembina	4	0	0	0	4	26	6	15	5	0
Pierce	0	0	0	0	0	12	0	10	2	0
Ramsey	9	0	5	0	4	17	4	7	6	0
Ransom	2	0	1	0	1	12	4	7	1	0
Renville	3	0	2	0	1	12	3	8	1	0
Richland	2	0	1	1	0	52	10	38	4	1
Rolette	6	0	1	0	5	17	7	4	6	0
Sargent	2	0	1	0	1	15	2	4	9	0
Sheridan	1	0	1	0	0	16	4	8	4	0
Sioux	0	0	0	0	0	1	0	1	0	0
Slope	0	0	0	0	0	1	1	0	0	0
Stark	5	0	0	1	4	76	6	63	7	0
Steele	0	0	0	0	0	0	0	0	0	0
Stutsman	5	0	3	0	2	28	3	22	3	1
Towner	4	3	1	0	0	18	3	6	9	0
Traill	2	0	2	0	0	40	7	25	8	0
Walsh	9	0	5	0	4	31	5	25	1	1
Ward	26	0	9	1	16	103	36	49	18	0
Wells	4	0	1	0	3	4	1	1	2	1
Williams	23	2	3	1	17	138	40	64	34	0
OHIO										
Metropolitan Counties										
Allen	78	1	10	11	56	614	126	459	29	4
Belmont	77	0	7	1	69	115	23	85	7	0
Butler	38	1	16	4	17	615	81	506	28	4
Carroll	9	0	1	0	8	65	9	52	4	0
Clark	35	0	8	2	25	570	105	435	30	2
Clermont	90	4	14	1	71	611	111	473	27	2
Delaware	67	1	36	2	28	889	75	783	31	3
Fairfield	84	5	26	6	47	971	92	793	86	2
Franklin	118	5	39	27	47	539	101	366	72	2
Fulton	17	0	5	0	12	159	20	126	13	1
Geauga	10	0	4	0	6	64	18	39	7	0
Greene	32	0	9	1	22	287	58	205	24	1
Hamilton	188	5	41	17	125	1,883	129	1,627	127	6
Hocking	64	1	19	2	42	210	51	129	30	1
Jefferson	38	1	9	0	28	71	21	46	4	0
Lawrence	47	1	15	1	30	382	77	268	37	3
Licking	71	0	12	11	48	826	232	510	84	2
Lorain	69	0	10	7	52	438	155	271	12	2
Lucas	63	0	6	5	52	785	60	565	160	0
Madison	43	1	10	3	29	180	25	140	15	0
Miami	43	1	2	0	40	283	63	188	32	2
Montgomery	253	4	48	45	156	1,200	249	640	311	12
Morrow	53	2	9	0	42	91	28	48	15	0
Perry	25	0	4	2	19	65	32	25	8	1
Pickaway	23	0	7	0	16	492	67	398	27	3
Portage	74	1	10	3	60	641	120	467	54	1
Richland	64	0	32	2	30	565	63	452	50	6
Stark	106	0	28	9	69	1,231	324	783	124	5
Summit	99	0	33	4	62	1,069	85	904	80	0
Trumbull	9	0	0	1	8	156	41	99	16	0
Union	33	0	13	2	18	213	20	174	19	2
Warren	43	0	14	10	19	834	55	727	52	3
Wood	29	0	15	0	14	310	36	235	39	3

Table 10. Offenses Known to Law Enforcement, by Selected State Metropolitan and Nonmetropolitan Counties, 2022—Continued

(Number.)

State/county	Violent crime	Murder and nonnegligent manslaughter	Rape	Robbery	Aggravated assault	Property crime	Burglary	Larceny-theft	Motor vehicle theft	Arson[1]
Nonmetropolitan Counties										
Adams	7	0	1	0	6	64	33	24	7	0
Ashland	37	5	16	0	16	71	24	35	12	0
Ashtabula	48	1	10	2	35	495	86	353	56	1
Athens	16	3	8	0	5	279	54	191	34	0
Auglaize	7	0	5	0	2	36	5	30	1	0
Champaign	37	0	8	0	29	145	31	102	12	1
Clinton	8	0	3	0	5	63	11	42	10	0
Columbiana	17	1	2	0	14	120	41	67	12	1
Coshocton	53	0	10	1	42	366	41	295	30	2
Crawford	6	0	3	0	3	53	14	33	6	0
Darke	9	0	9	0	0	167	32	134	1	2
Defiance	18	0	2	0	16	96	12	81	3	1
Erie	3	0	0	0	3	61	6	51	4	0
Fayette	22	0	7	1	14	277	67	188	22	2
Gallia	24	0	3	1	20	116	46	64	6	0
Hancock	28	0	10	2	16	216	60	138	18	1
Harrison	6	0	3	0	3	55	15	37	3	0
Henry	16	0	5	0	11	133	22	104	7	0
Highland	23	1	7	1	14	205	34	143	28	1
Jackson	29	1	12	0	16	123	24	85	14	0
Knox	22	0	5	0	17	234	45	175	14	1
Logan	21	0	8	1	12	116	29	76	11	0
Meigs	32	0	6	3	23	118	27	80	11	2
Mercer	2	0	1	0	1	19	3	16	0	0
Monroe	1	0	0	0	1	20	12	8	0	0
Morgan	32	0	2	0	30	94	32	56	6	1
Pike	31	0	5	1	25	195	50	101	44	5
Preble	21	0	6	1	14	98	21	69	8	1
Ross	79	1	37	9	32	787	152	530	105	22
Scioto	101	1	32	4	64	517	126	309	82	4
Seneca	18	0	13	2	3	200	13	185	2	0
Shelby	13	0	9	0	4	86	19	59	8	0
Tuscarawas	47	1	13	3	30	294	63	203	28	1
Van Wert	24	0	8	1	15	75	25	47	3	0
Vinton	24	2	7	0	15	116	26	67	23	1
Washington	21	0	12	2	7	248	64	161	23	1
Wayne	49	0	12	0	37	549	172	332	45	3
OKLAHOMA										
Metropolitan Counties										
Canadian	13	0	2	2	9	127	18	75	34	3
Cleveland	39	1	12	0	26	159	33	94	32	2
Comanche	20	0	2	0	18	147	44	85	18	1
Cotton	11	0	1	0	10	49	15	30	4	0
Creek	29	1	6	0	22	292	78	138	76	3
Garfield	14	0	5	0	9	78	25	34	19	8
Grady	28	1	6	0	21	223	52	120	51	3
Lincoln	84	1	29	2	52	234	81	118	35	7
Logan	35	1	12	3	19	333	87	204	42	4
McClain	21	0	5	1	15	185	52	97	36	0
Oklahoma	29	3	7	2	17	148	50	75	23	1
Okmulgee	24	0	5	1	18	174	57	74	43	0
Osage	45	5	8	3	29	408	114	213	81	6
Pawnee	12	2	3	0	7	78	22	42	14	2
Rogers	61	1	21	1	38	410	137	230	43	1
Sequoyah	63	3	8	3	49	218	61	114	43	7
Tulsa	178	2	20	24	132	726	175	404	147	18
Wagoner	98	1	17	5	75	386	103	220	63	11
Nonmetropolitan Counties										
Adair	36	0	1	2	33	141	46	51	44	2
Alfalfa	5	0	1	0	4	39	7	31	1	1
Atoka	8	0	0	0	8	77	15	47	15	2
Beaver	0	0	0	0	0	28	2	24	2	1
Beckham	5	0	1	0	4	46	17	21	8	0
Blaine	17	2	1	0	14	74	24	42	8	1
Bryan	55	0	4	1	50	353	127	146	80	0
Caddo	16	0	3	0	13	140	41	82	17	2
Carter	13	0	2	0	11	134	25	93	16	6
Cherokee	49	3	12	1	33	371	121	167	83	12
Choctaw	29	2	7	0	20	107	39	47	21	9
Cimarron	0	0	0	0	0	10	5	4	1	0
Coal	4	0	0	0	4	8	2	5	1	0
Craig	21	1	4	1	15	126	40	67	19	4
Custer	10	0	3	0	7	70	12	42	16	4
Delaware	56	1	12	0	43	264	52	137	75	8
Dewey	8	0	0	0	8	48	15	25	8	0
Ellis	3	0	0	0	3	32	7	24	1	2
Garvin	40	2	4	2	32	165	40	112	13	6

Table 10. Offenses Known to Law Enforcement, by Selected State Metropolitan and Nonmetropolitan Counties, 2022—Continued

(Number.)

State/county	Violent crime	Murder and nonnegligent manslaughter	Rape	Robbery	Aggravated assault	Property crime	Burglary	Larceny-theft	Motor vehicle theft	Arson[1]
Grant	1	0	0	0	1	38	13	20	5	0
Greer	5	0	1	0	4	8	3	4	1	0
Harmon	1	0	0	0	1	4	3	1	0	0
Harper	1	0	0	0	1	12	1	8	3	2
Haskell	7	1	0	0	6	71	23	36	12	2
Hughes	13	1	0	0	12	121	23	76	22	3
Jackson	7	0	1	1	5	24	7	14	3	0
Jefferson	7	0	1	0	6	17	3	10	4	1
Johnston	23	1	3	1	18	53	29	16	8	2
Kay	28	2	7	0	19	102	26	60	16	1
Kingfisher	2	0	1	0	1	63	13	46	4	2
Kiowa	2	0	2	0	0	7	1	4	2	1
Latimer	15	2	2	0	11	62	21	31	10	3
Le Flore	41	1	3	2	35	216	50	110	56	3
Love	11	0	2	0	9	73	21	43	9	0
Major	9	0	5	0	4	34	12	18	4	6
Marshall	32	0	4	0	28	161	56	79	26	0
Mayes	48	0	14	1	33	431	123	226	82	16
McCurtain	45	0	7	2	36	263	75	120	68	9
McIntosh	23	1	3	0	19	156	53	77	26	4
Murray	4	0	0	0	4	34	9	19	6	1
Muskogee	69	2	7	0	60	204	52	127	25	1
Noble	13	0	7	1	5	101	20	63	18	0
Nowata	7	0	1	1	5	73	13	53	7	1
Okfuskee	5	0	2	0	3	73	23	40	10	0
Ottawa	49	0	4	1	44	235	45	139	51	13
Payne	34	0	5	1	28	265	62	159	44	2
Pittsburg	41	3	6	2	30	317	141	128	48	2
Pontotoc	13	1	2	1	9	74	15	46	13	0
Pottawatomie	79	2	13	0	64	406	117	212	77	6
Pushmataha	14	0	0	0	14	60	24	24	12	2
Roger Mills	3	0	2	0	1	31	7	22	2	4
Seminole	22	2	3	1	16	239	69	124	46	6
Stephens	40	0	4	0	36	95	21	59	15	4
Texas	8	0	2	0	6	79	32	44	3	1
Tillman	15	0	3	0	12	15	5	8	2	0
Washington	27	0	3	0	24	87	19	57	11	1
Washita	6	0	0	0	6	45	14	23	8	0
Woods	5	0	1	0	4	30	12	13	5	0
Woodward	7	0	1	0	6	59	21	31	7	0
OREGON										
Metropolitan Counties										
Benton	24	0	3	1	20	177	40	121	16	2
Clackamas	549	5	50	132	362	5,966	700	4,109	1,157	25
Columbia	46	0	8	1	37	99	28	42	29	3
Deschutes	77	1	9	7	60	549	68	422	59	9
Jackson	161	3	12	16	130	1,101	235	736	130	20
Josephine	170	2	18	8	142	380	61	155	164	8
Linn	79	0	11	13	55	950	159	630	161	7
Marion	152	3	60	39	50	2,134	302	1,387	445	6
Multnomah	240	2	23	38	177	1,670	141	1,110	419	6
Polk	54	0	9	2	43	280	69	181	30	2
Washington	504	6	113	56	329	2,811	402	1,908	501	25
Yamhill	49	2	7	1	39	326	63	215	48	4
Nonmetropolitan Counties										
Baker	3	0	0	0	3	56	14	35	7	1
Clatsop	21	0	3	0	18	171	40	112	19	6
Crook	35	0	5	0	30	59	9	48	2	0
Douglas	129	0	16	10	103	846	191	487	168	10
Gilliam	0	0	0	0	0	47	5	37	5	0
Hood River	27	0	3	4	20	182	37	135	10	1
Jefferson	13	0	2	2	9	117	20	68	29	0
Klamath	113	5	21	5	82	538	143	242	153	5
Lincoln	57	0	6	5	46	233	79	137	17	4
Malheur	20	0	4	2	14	149	44	86	19	0
Morrow	23	1	4	2	16	140	23	94	23	1
Sherman	2	0	0	0	2	32	1	17	14	0
Tillamook	36	2	5	2	27	240	57	156	27	3
Umatilla	41	1	8	3	29	482	162	222	98	7
Union	18	0	2	1	15	163	22	122	19	1
Wallowa	0	0	0	0	0	32	3	29	0	0
Wasco	36	0	4	1	31	92	14	73	5	2
PENNSYLVANIA[1]										
Metropolitan Counties										
Allegheny County Police Department	370	46	127	20	177	147	22	118	7	9
Franklin	0	0	0	0	0	0	0	0	0	0

Table 10. Offenses Known to Law Enforcement, by Selected State Metropolitan and Nonmetropolitan Counties, 2022—Continued

(Number.)

State/county	Violent crime	Murder and nonnegligent manslaughter	Rape	Robbery	Aggravated assault	Property crime	Burglary	Larceny-theft	Motor vehicle theft	Arson[1]
Nonmetropolitan Counties										
Northumberland	0	0	0	0	0	0	0	0	0	0
SOUTH CAROLINA										
Metropolitan Counties										
Anderson	691	7	64	38	582	3,963	691	2,786	486	21
Beaufort	590	8	41	38	503	1,952	329	1,435	188	10
Berkeley	475	12	37	31	395	2,228	321	1,572	335	5
Calhoun	48	0	6	4	38	289	50	187	52	3
Charleston	258	8	9	26	215	1,178	146	824	208	5
Chester	111	4	11	4	92	359	75	242	42	0
Clarendon	117	3	17	9	88	741	290	390	61	8
Darlington	406	8	19	28	351	1,528	493	842	193	10
Dorchester	201	3	29	23	146	1,288	194	890	204	6
Edgefield	13	0	2	2	9	111	25	68	18	4
Fairfield	193	5	6	3	179	347	93	214	40	1
Florence	511	17	53	33	408	2,236	441	1,552	243	19
Greenville	1,693	23	170	156	1,344	6,628	1,162	4,626	840	38
Horry	1	0	0	0	1	1	0	1	0	1
Horry County Police Department	809	16	85	55	653	4,533	487	3,541	505	22
Jasper	146	1	12	10	123	456	59	320	77	6
Kershaw	217	6	25	4	182	947	211	641	95	16
Lancaster	322	4	56	21	241	1,406	319	1,005	82	9
Laurens	185	3	22	3	157	932	188	589	155	8
Lexington	721	7	60	66	588	4,746	812	3,278	656	18
Pickens	171	2	22	6	141	876	233	509	134	13
Richland	2,041	32	76	166	1,767	7,451	1,207	5,283	961	27
Saluda	26	2	6	1	17	102	17	73	12	2
Spartanburg	1,213	25	110	60	1,018	4,307	845	2,948	514	28
Sumter	513	9	19	26	459	1,423	282	933	208	10
York	345	6	20	25	294	2,149	357	1,619	173	25
Nonmetropolitan Counties										
Abbeville	84	1	11	3	69	322	192	107	23	2
Bamberg	32	1	3	1	27	109	25	76	8	0
Barnwell	72	0	0	2	70	230	47	146	37	3
Cherokee	153	2	12	10	129	784	197	478	109	8
Chesterfield	202	3	15	7	177	707	160	457	90	7
Colleton	196	15	3	10	168	614	117	400	97	5
Dillon	280	11	11	9	249	473	130	285	58	6
Georgetown	168	5	10	4	149	724	136	488	100	8
Greenwood	113	29	16	6	62	775	145	613	17	1
Hampton	81	0	5	3	73	194	48	123	23	2
Lee	84	4	4	5	71	291	61	173	57	2
Marion	92	1	3	3	85	308	60	213	35	2
Marlboro	129	6	8	4	111	424	94	285	45	4
McCormick	9	0	1	0	8	20	1	16	3	1
Newberry	75	0	6	2	67	276	92	161	23	1
Oconee	195	3	32	5	155	1,434	268	1,006	160	9
Orangeburg	895	19	3	44	829	2,031	518	1,245	268	12
Union	56	1	5	1	49	424	57	322	45	4
Williamsburg	100	3	5	3	89	206	44	131	31	2
SOUTH DAKOTA										
Metropolitan Counties										
Lincoln	20	1	5	1	13	224	57	141	26	0
McCook	5	0	0	0	5	22	5	13	4	0
Meade	17	0	1	2	14	152	70	61	21	0
Minnehaha	56	1	4	1	50	260	74	139	47	3
Pennington	114	1	37	1	75	316	49	224	43	0
Turner	9	0	3	0	6	23	4	17	2	0
Union	3	0	1	1	1	45	11	30	4	0
Nonmetropolitan Counties										
Bennett	2	0	0	0	2	4	2	1	1	0
Bon Homme	1	0	1	0	0	2	0	2	0	0
Brookings	8	0	2	0	6	18	3	14	1	0
Brown	17	0	0	0	17	32	2	27	3	0
Charles Mix	8	0	1	0	7	30	7	18	5	0
Clay	3	1	0	0	2	35	11	18	6	0
Codington	5	0	1	0	4	29	7	18	4	0
Corson	12	0	0	0	12	19	6	9	4	0
Davison	2	0	0	0	2	10	1	5	4	0
Day	7	0	0	0	7	13	4	3	6	0
Hamlin	3	0	2	0	1	24	9	12	3	0
Hughes	4	0	2	0	2	13	3	9	1	0
Hutchinson	0	0	0	0	0	5	1	2	2	0
Lake	5	0	2	0	3	31	15	16	0	0
Lawrence	7	0	2	0	5	30	6	22	2	0

Table 10. Offenses Known to Law Enforcement, by Selected State Metropolitan and Nonmetropolitan Counties, 2022—Continued

(Number.)

State/county	Violent crime	Murder and nonnegligent manslaughter	Rape	Robbery	Aggravated assault	Property crime	Burglary	Larceny-theft	Motor vehicle theft	Arson[1]
Lyman	3	0	0	0	3	20	5	13	2	0
McPherson	0	0	0	0	0	17	3	13	1	0
Moody	6	0	0	0	6	5	2	2	1	0
Spink	4	0	1	0	3	21	2	17	2	1
Yankton	17	0	6	0	11	60	8	45	7	0
TENNESSEE										
Metropolitan Counties										
Anderson	141	0	15	2	124	345	85	191	69	11
Blount	283	0	39	6	238	676	189	407	80	4
Bradley	167	1	10	4	152	568	108	387	73	1
Campbell	53	0	4	0	49	224	60	109	55	6
Cannon	1	0	0	0	1	22	4	11	7	0
Carter	53	1	11	0	41	374	84	234	56	5
Cheatham	74	0	5	1	68	229	33	155	41	3
Chester	19	0	1	0	18	40	8	29	3	0
Crockett	15	0	2	0	13	89	20	50	19	1
Dickson	110	0	15	3	92	216	52	116	48	3
Fayette	70	5	2	0	63	148	24	100	24	0
Gibson	40	1	2	4	33	141	29	85	27	0
Grainger	25	1	4	0	20	136	21	95	20	4
Hamblen	123	1	10	4	108	345	72	203	70	7
Hamilton	243	2	35	7	199	849	150	589	110	4
Hartsville/Trousdale	29	1	3	0	25	123	30	79	14	3
Hawkins	48	0	3	1	44	385	74	233	78	1
Jefferson	92	0	9	3	80	353	64	225	64	5
Knox	633	5	65	18	545	2,695	323	1,995	377	13
Loudon	62	1	5	1	55	268	50	189	29	1
Macon	72	1	5	0	66	37	10	20	7	2
Madison	81	0	6	3	72	173	40	103	30	1
Marion	55	0	3	0	52	175	27	99	49	0
Maury	119	0	11	3	105	357	57	238	62	3
Montgomery	67	0	5	0	62	418	90	281	47	3
Morgan	11	0	1	0	10	140	14	101	25	2
Polk	33	2	4	1	26	268	53	157	58	2
Roane	50	4	8	0	38	240	63	134	43	0
Robertson	55	3	1	0	51	200	28	130	42	3
Rutherford	286	1	28	11	246	595	62	428	105	5
Sequatchie	35	0	5	0	30	116	12	77	27	1
Shelby	684	9	46	50	579	2,476	404	1,575	497	6
Smith	25	0	1	0	24	108	29	67	12	0
Stewart	22	0	3	0	19	72	24	38	10	1
Sullivan	313	2	35	4	272	751	160	455	136	19
Sumner	127	1	15	2	109	294	71	182	41	1
Tipton	84	0	8	3	73	292	41	198	53	5
Unicoi	38	2	3	0	33	47	11	31	5	2
Union	39	0	5	0	34	196	52	112	32	5
Washington	150	1	13	3	133	639	131	407	101	3
Williamson	135	1	16	3	115	283	54	219	10	6
Wilson	68	2	0	1	65	402	108	244	50	1
Nonmetropolitan Counties										
Bedford	73	0	9	1	63	213	48	133	32	0
Benton	41	2	6	1	32	138	41	73	24	2
Bledsoe	14	0	1	0	13	102	17	67	18	0
Carroll	30	0	2	1	27	82	27	39	16	1
Clay	3	0	0	0	3	22	3	18	1	0
Cocke	117	0	8	4	105	410	82	230	98	8
Coffee	94	0	4	2	88	330	86	214	30	0
Cumberland	62	3	0	0	59	450	139	253	58	2
Decatur	17	0	0	0	17	101	43	47	11	1
DeKalb	28	0	2	0	26	57	21	29	7	1
Dyer	24	2	0	0	22	163	31	108	24	0
Fentress	54	0	4	1	49	188	46	110	32	2
Franklin	81	3	8	3	67	199	39	133	27	0
Giles	20	1	0	0	19	81	20	53	8	1
Greene	183	3	11	3	166	589	147	346	96	9
Grundy	65	1	7	1	56	228	41	130	57	6
Hancock	22	0	2	1	19	83	21	60	2	1
Hardeman	108	1	6	0	101	164	56	84	24	0
Hardin	52	1	5	0	46	291	77	164	50	4
Haywood	20	0	2	2	16	118	31	63	24	0
Henderson	51	0	11	0	40	171	62	89	20	0
Henry	31	0	1	0	30	184	55	99	30	0
Hickman	93	0	11	2	80	356	72	199	85	1
Houston	16	0	0	0	16	54	34	12	8	0
Humphreys	63	1	8	1	53	108	44	42	22	4
Jackson	19	5	2	0	12	52	4	39	9	0
Johnson	40	0	8	0	32	125	25	68	32	0
Lake	3	0	0	0	3	30	6	21	3	0

Table 10. Offenses Known to Law Enforcement, by Selected State Metropolitan and Nonmetropolitan Counties, 2022—Continued

(Number.)

State/county	Violent crime	Murder and nonnegligent manslaughter	Rape	Robbery	Aggravated assault	Property crime	Burglary	Larceny-theft	Motor vehicle theft	Arson[1]
Lauderdale	63	0	6	1	56	144	44	78	22	3
Lawrence	23	1	3	1	18	174	54	97	23	0
Lewis	15	0	4	0	11	77	23	39	15	0
Lincoln	51	1	3	3	44	199	41	125	33	4
Marshall	46	0	5	0	41	65	13	42	10	1
McMinn	83	0	4	4	75	390	88	200	102	1
McNairy	54	1	3	1	49	299	48	214	37	4
Meigs	57	0	4	0	53	140	28	77	35	8
Monroe	121	4	8	3	106	502	119	307	76	7
Moore	6	0	2	0	4	44	8	32	4	1
Obion	38	0	4	0	34	159	48	92	19	0
Overton	86	0	2	0	84	160	41	98	21	1
Putnam	63	1	6	0	56	293	71	194	28	1
Rhea	27	0	1	1	25	96	15	66	15	0
Scott	8	0	1	0	7	145	39	87	19	0
Sevier	163	3	18	5	137	546	146	321	79	2
Van Buren	5	1	0	0	4	12	0	9	3	1
Warren	96	0	13	3	80	310	73	185	52	14
Wayne	21	0	2	0	19	58	7	36	15	1
Weakley	38	3	2	0	33	133	58	60	15	0
White	21	0	2	1	18	83	18	51	14	2
TEXAS										
Metropolitan Counties										
Armstrong	1	0	0	0	1	25	4	13	8	0
Atascosa	111	2	0	1	108	454	69	293	92	18
Austin	23	1	4	0	18	108	32	60	16	1
Bandera	31	0	3	0	28	145	52	70	23	2
Bastrop	349	7	45	18	279	867	206	500	161	5
Bell	97	1	19	3	74	517	106	368	43	0
Bexar	912	11	82	100	719	6,082	1,081	4,105	896	13
Bowie	43	2	13	3	25	233	48	137	48	2
Brazoria	231	4	50	34	143	1,468	213	1,092	163	3
Brazos	74	2	21	0	51	362	82	241	39	3
Burleson	28	0	8	2	18	97	36	44	17	0
Caldwell	44	1	9	2	32	82	24	29	29	0
Callahan	12	0	1	1	10	44	18	16	10	0
Cameron	283	4	52	17	210	714	156	462	96	7
Carson	18	0	2	0	16	17	0	13	4	0
Chambers	136	10	24	8	94	827	140	556	131	1
Clay	15	0	3	0	12	61	27	21	13	1
Collin	64	1	20	0	43	424	80	282	62	0
Comal	115	1	31	3	80	766	222	450	94	1
Coryell	17	0	1	0	16	85	24	54	7	2
Crosby	4	0	0	0	4	21	10	7	4	0
Dallas	39	2	16	2	19	184	33	84	67	1
Denton	56	1	14	1	40	386	61	271	54	0
Ector	98	4	6	5	83	254	38	88	128	3
Ellis	86	2	26	2	56	384	79	257	48	0
El Paso	360	10	41	31	278	973	135	645	193	12
Fort Bend	938	10	120	129	679	5,577	815	4,329	433	0
Galveston	146	5	38	7	96	620	134	392	94	9
Goliad	15	0	5	0	10	87	25	55	7	1
Grayson	73	5	25	2	41	436	132	265	39	2
Gregg	78	1	9	2	66	243	76	113	54	1
Hardin	53	3	19	2	29	238	65	136	37	2
Harris	9,199	141	1,069	1,716	6,273	50,747	6,826	36,516	7,405	309
Harrison	67	4	17	2	44	426	146	211	69	1
Hays	191	4	55	11	121	894	174	604	116	2
Hidalgo	564	14	101	100	349	2,842	559	1,886	397	14
Hudspeth	0	0	0	0	0	2	1	0	1	0
Hunt	341	0	18	5	318	527	114	302	111	1
Irion	5	1	0	0	4	10	2	6	2	1
Jefferson	73	1	9	4	59	374	65	265	44	3
Johnson	149	4	38	3	104	616	140	387	89	4
Jones	10	0	2	0	8	42	12	24	6	0
Kaufman	125	1	30	8	86	562	130	341	91	0
Kendall	11	0	2	1	8	107	22	71	14	2
Lampasas	9	0	0	0	9	21	5	15	1	0
Liberty	194	10	44	14	126	817	205	417	195	8
Lubbock	131	2	26	18	85	628	161	334	133	3
Lynn	2	0	1	0	1	11	2	6	3	1
Martin	9	0	2	0	7	107	4	103	0	0
McLennan	99	0	37	5	57	520	96	359	65	6
Medina	57	2	8	4	43	285	51	139	95	2
Midland	129	1	13	3	112	637	89	386	162	3
Montgomery	1,092	14	117	72	889	5,336	915	3,826	595	6
Nueces	42	1	6	0	35	158	49	103	6	2
Oldham	0	0	0	0	0	2	1	1	0	0
Orange	80	0	16	3	61	370	113	177	80	5

Table 10. Offenses Known to Law Enforcement, by Selected State Metropolitan and Nonmetropolitan Counties, 2022—Continued

(Number.)

State/county	Violent crime	Murder and nonnegligent manslaughter	Rape	Robbery	Aggravated assault	Property crime	Burglary	Larceny-theft	Motor vehicle theft	Arson[1]
Parker	131	2	15	5	109	902	187	591	124	5
Potter	63	1	18	3	41	203	40	130	33	2
Randall	59	1	15	1	42	151	30	86	35	4
Robertson	25	0	2	1	22	117	34	66	17	1
Rockwall	16	0	3	0	13	65	10	50	5	1
Rusk	61	1	13	4	43	353	106	193	54	2
Smith	310	3	26	9	272	865	237	477	151	1
Sterling	1	0	0	0	1	9	3	4	2	0
Tarrant	139	1	31	10	97	750	150	455	145	1
Taylor	20	1	6	0	13	84	27	53	4	0
Tom Green	49	0	16	1	32	166	44	102	20	3
Travis	860	10	116	75	659	3,538	647	2,382	509	22
Upshur	63	0	14	2	47	162	63	84	15	4
Victoria	78	0	13	5	60	213	58	126	29	0
Waller	84	0	27	6	51	325	68	208	49	0
Webb	44	0	10	3	31	134	26	80	28	2
Wichita	20	0	3	2	15	79	28	48	3	1
Williamson	175	6	51	8	110	1,709	294	1,290	125	4
Wilson	56	1	19	1	35	349	55	258	36	1
Wise	94	2	25	5	62	357	100	219	38	0
Nonmetropolitan Counties										
Andrews	1	0	1	0	0	56	11	39	6	0
Angelina	148	4	41	5	98	552	188	288	76	11
Aransas	73	0	6	3	64	160	27	121	12	0
Bailey	2	0	2	0	0	12	0	12	0	0
Baylor	1	0	1	0	0	10	3	4	3	0
Bee	32	1	1	1	29	135	46	70	19	2
Blanco	13	1	2	0	10	68	17	46	5	3
Borden	1	0	0	0	1	8	2	6	0	0
Bosque	8	0	2	0	6	44	23	19	2	2
Brewster	3	0	0	1	2	10	2	5	3	0
Briscoe	0	0	0	0	0	12	5	5	2	0
Brooks	0	0	0	0	0	0	0	0	0	0
Brown	34	0	9	2	23	175	61	97	17	3
Burnet	66	0	16	2	48	227	52	144	31	1
Calhoun	19	1	7	0	11	59	10	42	7	0
Camp	8	0	3	0	5	54	21	28	5	0
Cass	18	1	1	2	14	103	41	53	9	2
Castro	5	2	0	0	3	16	4	10	2	0
Cherokee	111	3	3	2	103	338	65	213	60	2
Childress	1	0	1	0	0	23	6	16	1	0
Cochran	1	0	0	0	1	36	9	21	6	1
Coke	1	0	1	0	0	154	129	20	5	0
Coleman	2	0	1	0	1	17	4	12	1	0
Collingsworth	0	0	0	0	0	3	0	3	0	0
Colorado	20	0	2	2	16	121	33	67	21	0
Comanche	11	0	3	0	8	62	9	49	4	1
Concho	3	0	1	0	2	10	3	7	0	0
Cooke	28	0	10	2	16	124	37	80	7	1
Crane	2	0	0	0	2	3	1	2	0	0
Crockett	3	0	1	0	2	21	8	10	3	0
Dallam	3	0	2	0	1	6	2	3	1	0
Dawson	1	0	0	0	1	42	15	24	3	1
Deaf Smith	8	0	0	0	8	26	9	15	2	0
Delta	13	0	3	1	9	48	20	21	7	2
DeWitt	16	0	2	1	13	68	25	38	5	2
Donley	12	0	0	1	11	19	6	9	4	0
Duval	32	0	4	1	27	90	24	42	24	3
Eastland	10	0	1	0	9	41	12	23	6	1
Edwards	5	1	0	1	3	20	7	10	3	1
Erath	9	1	2	0	6	67	16	46	5	1
Fannin	39	0	2	0	37	165	31	116	18	2
Fayette	17	0	9	1	7	101	29	60	12	0
Fisher	17	1	3	1	12	36	17	16	3	1
Floyd	4	0	2	0	2	25	13	9	3	0
Foard	0	0	0	0	0	0	0	0	0	0
Franklin	12	0	1	1	10	36	10	24	2	0
Freestone	19	0	5	0	14	81	27	44	10	0
Gaines	7	0	0	1	6	72	15	47	10	1
Garza	9	0	3	0	6	36	13	23	0	1
Gillespie	15	0	11	0	4	34	11	21	2	0
Glasscock	0	0	0	0	0	42	15	24	3	0
Gonzales	40	1	4	1	34	118	43	61	14	1
Gray	7	0	1	1	5	29	9	15	5	0
Grimes	62	0	17	1	44	187	95	70	22	3
Hall	3	0	0	0	3	8	4	2	2	0
Hamilton	4	0	0	0	4	10	5	5	0	0
Hansford	0	0	0	0	0	12	3	7	2	0
Hardeman	4	0	1	0	3	17	8	9	0	0

Table 10. Offenses Known to Law Enforcement, by Selected State Metropolitan and Nonmetropolitan Counties, 2022—Continued

(Number.)

State/county	Violent crime	Murder and nonnegligent manslaughter	Rape	Robbery	Aggravated assault	Property crime	Burglary	Larceny-theft	Motor vehicle theft	Arson[1]
Hartley	2	0	0	0	2	4	0	4	0	1
Haskell	2	0	0	0	2	18	2	9	7	0
Hemphill	6	0	1	0	5	29	20	9	0	0
Henderson	162	7	37	3	115	550	181	263	106	3
Hill	54	1	25	2	26	253	58	159	36	2
Hockley	20	0	1	1	18	125	34	72	19	1
Hood	46	2	7	4	33	313	67	196	50	3
Hopkins	26	0	3	0	23	40	13	12	15	0
Houston	13	0	5	0	8	98	28	59	11	0
Howard	36	0	1	1	34	269	51	190	28	0
Hutchinson	16	0	2	0	14	53	22	26	5	0
Jack	4	0	1	0	3	17	4	10	3	0
Jackson	10	2	1	0	7	59	6	32	21	0
Jasper	31	0	6	4	21	198	38	146	14	4
Jeff Davis	1	0	0	0	1	5	1	2	2	0
Jim Hogg	7	0	0	1	6	39	19	14	6	0
Jim Wells	81	1	14	0	66	221	86	105	30	3
Karnes	5	0	0	0	5	81	32	37	12	1
Kenedy	1	0	1	0	0	2	0	0	2	0
Kerr	40	1	14	2	23	166	57	91	18	0
Kimble	1	0	0	0	1	3	1	0	2	0
King	0	0	0	0	0	0	0	0	0	0
Kleberg	10	0	1	0	9	29	12	14	3	0
Lamar	46	0	5	0	41	187	51	101	35	2
Lamb	9	0	0	2	7	29	13	13	3	0
La Salle	1	0	1	0	0	8	4	4	0	0
Lavaca	11	0	6	1	4	48	13	29	6	2
Lee	23	1	9	2	11	69	23	38	8	2
Leon	21	2	2	0	17	147	46	87	14	1
Limestone	40	0	6	6	28	164	71	79	14	4
Lipscomb	3	0	0	0	3	5	3	2	0	0
Llano	23	1	2	4	16	161	43	102	16	2
Loving	0	0	0	0	0	23	2	18	3	0
Madison	11	1	1	0	9	37	15	16	6	0
Marion	32	0	5	0	27	111	42	57	12	1
Mason	0	0	0	0	0	3	0	3	0	0
Matagorda	98	2	11	2	83	301	75	195	31	2
Maverick	90	0	15	6	69	481	175	253	53	1
McCulloch	9	0	0	0	9	25	11	11	3	0
Milam	5	0	0	0	5	61	13	32	16	0
Mills	4	0	1	0	3	15	7	7	1	1
Montague	24	0	4	0	20	101	42	52	7	1
Moore	12	0	4	0	8	30	11	14	5	2
Morris	23	1	1	4	17	29	11	15	3	1
Motley	6	0	0	0	6	3	2	1	0	4
Nacogdoches	33	0	3	3	27	222	53	140	29	3
Navarro	54	4	11	1	38	202	67	118	17	6
Newton	19	1	3	0	15	68	27	35	6	1
Nolan	8	0	3	1	4	23	2	21	0	0
Ochiltree	5	0	4	0	1	22	5	14	3	0
Palo Pinto	25	0	8	0	17	114	28	63	23	3
Panola	41	0	8	0	33	164	38	113	13	2
Parmer	1	0	0	0	1	50	27	18	5	1
Polk	79	5	22	1	51	464	134	252	78	4
Presidio	0	0	0	0	0	1	1	0	0	0
Reagan	4	2	1	0	1	23	6	13	4	0
Real	4	0	3	0	1	55	19	31	5	1
Red River	12	1	2	0	9	29	7	15	7	1
Refugio	7	0	1	0	6	35	8	10	17	0
Roberts	0	0	0	0	0	1	1	0	0	0
Runnels	5	0	3	0	2	13	6	6	1	0
Sabine	12	0	5	1	6	39	17	18	4	2
San Augustine	16	1	3	0	12	69	25	38	6	0
Schleicher	4	0	0	0	4	15	9	6	0	1
Scurry	7	0	1	0	6	47	13	30	4	0
Shackelford	6	0	2	0	4	12	4	7	1	0
Shelby	33	1	9	0	23	204	77	103	24	5
Somervell	1	0	0	0	1	76	22	54	0	1
Starr	45	0	8	3	34	133	50	55	28	2
Stephens	8	0	2	0	6	32	10	17	5	0
Sutton	1	0	0	0	1	3	1	1	1	0
Swisher	3	0	0	0	3	16	4	4	8	0
Terrell	0	0	0	0	0	0	0	0	0	0
Terry	1	0	0	0	1	57	26	31	0	0
Throckmorton	1	0	0	0	1	5	2	3	0	0
Titus	33	1	5	3	24	131	40	74	17	5
Trinity	20	0	3	0	17	78	30	38	10	2
Tyler	24	0	7	1	16	140	57	59	24	1
Upton	3	0	0	0	3	21	4	16	1	0
Uvalde	18	0	10	0	8	74	21	28	25	0

Table 10. Offenses Known to Law Enforcement, by Selected State Metropolitan and Nonmetropolitan Counties, 2022—Continued

(Number.)

State/county	Violent crime	Murder and nonnegligent manslaughter	Rape	Robbery	Aggravated assault	Property crime	Burglary	Larceny-theft	Motor vehicle theft	Arson[1]
Val Verde	57	1	11	11	34	134	44	82	8	3
Van Zandt	44	0	16	4	24	270	85	165	20	1
Walker	67	0	18	3	46	309	96	155	58	1
Ward	13	0	1	1	11	136	26	85	25	0
Washington	30	1	9	0	20	99	27	56	16	0
Wharton	82	1	2	4	75	289	57	177	55	1
Wheeler	5	0	1	0	4	8	1	4	3	0
Wilbarger	2	0	0	0	2	18	9	7	2	2
Willacy	19	0	0	0	19	71	21	38	12	2
Winkler	3	0	1	0	2	53	13	27	13	0
Wood	61	0	6	9	46	268	79	156	33	4
Yoakum	10	0	0	0	10	33	0	25	8	0
Young	9	0	0	0	9	20	10	5	5	0
Zapata	5	0	0	0	5	33	12	21	0	0
Zavala	14	0	2	0	12	44	9	23	12	1
UTAH										
Metropolitan Counties										
Box Elder	10	1	8	0	1	91	23	62	6	0
Cache	72	0	13	1	58	254	44	194	16	3
Davis	17	0	9	1	7	190	25	146	19	1
Morgan	12	0	5	0	7	80	55	23	2	1
Salt Lake County Unified Police Department	513	6	96	83	328	5,215	579	3,958	678	7
Tooele	51	1	16	3	31	252	34	192	26	3
Utah	75	0	32	1	42	290	28	239	23	1
Washington	29	0	14	3	12	81	15	51	15	1
Weber	88	0	30	5	53	685	148	478	59	6
Nonmetropolitan Counties										
Beaver	13	0	7	0	6	55	12	37	6	0
Carbon	19	0	3	0	16	59	10	45	4	0
Duchesne	51	0	18	1	32	216	65	123	28	3
Garfield	6	0	3	0	3	39	2	31	6	0
Grand	10	0	3	0	7	52	5	40	7	0
Iron	21	0	10	0	11	91	23	56	12	2
Kane	16	0	1	0	15	23	4	15	4	0
Millard	28	0	6	0	22	137	20	98	19	0
San Juan	4	0	0	0	4	7	0	6	1	0
Sanpete	29	0	18	0	11	56	6	47	3	0
Sevier	9	0	2	0	7	67	13	47	7	0
Summit	63	0	42	2	19	359	46	267	46	0
Wasatch	30	0	6	0	24	83	14	59	10	0
VERMONT										
Metropolitan Counties										
Franklin	26	0	4	2	20	163	7	149	7	1
Nonmetropolitan Counties										
Lamoille	11	0	3	0	8	69	10	59	0	0
Orange	8	0	5	1	2	25	1	24	0	0
Orleans	11	0	7	0	4	85	9	74	2	0
Rutland	3	0	1	0	2	11	1	9	1	0
Windham	1	0	0	0	1	9	2	5	2	0
VIRGINIA										
Metropolitan Counties										
Albemarle County Police Department	120	3	37	15	65	1,800	101	1,592	107	3
Amelia	16	1	4	0	11	127	13	109	5	0
Amherst	65	1	18	1	45	350	18	281	51	1
Appomattox	32	1	3	0	28	100	3	97	0	0
Arlington County Police Department	600	1	59	166	374	4,096	170	3,525	401	4
Augusta	79	1	36	3	39	739	148	527	64	5
Bedford	78	4	12	5	57	530	94	391	45	3
Botetourt	40	2	10	3	25	205	24	161	20	3
Campbell	90	4	18	0	68	580	61	455	64	6
Charles City	10	0	2	0	8	56	11	38	7	0
Chesterfield County Police Department	741	17	96	105	523	5,205	442	4,294	469	21
Clarke	4	0	3	0	1	43	7	31	5	0
Craig	8	0	1	0	7	30	8	20	2	0
Culpeper	51	0	9	2	40	121	9	96	16	1
Dinwiddie	121	3	9	6	103	318	31	268	19	1
Fairfax County Police Department	1,212	23	179	438	572	16,752	662	14,731	1,359	13
Fauquier	49	1	13	3	32	260	17	225	18	1
Fluvanna	34	0	10	3	21	152	19	120	13	3
Franklin	62	1	22	1	38	403	42	300	61	2
Frederick	55	2	13	7	33	891	67	765	59	0
Giles	18	0	3	0	15	89	13	68	8	0
Gloucester	44	3	26	4	11	348	11	311	26	3
Goochland	23	1	1	0	21	199	13	163	23	2
Greene	13	1	2	1	9	235	20	199	16	1

Table 10. Offenses Known to Law Enforcement, by Selected State Metropolitan and Nonmetropolitan Counties, 2022—Continued

(Number.)

State/county	Violent crime	Murder and nonnegligent manslaughter	Rape	Robbery	Aggravated assault	Property crime	Burglary	Larceny-theft	Motor vehicle theft	Arson[1]
Hanover	190	2	32	3	153	977	33	892	52	6
Henrico County Police Department	667	31	47	114	475	8,087	543	6,948	596	30
Isle of Wight	53	1	1	5	46	232	30	183	19	0
James City County Police Department	91	1	15	14	61	825	51	748	26	5
King and Queen	6	0	2	1	3	17	3	13	1	0
King William	16	0	5	0	11	79	4	73	2	1
Loudoun	295	4	89	33	169	2,362	103	2,085	174	29
Madison	5	1	1	0	3	88	5	77	6	0
Mathews	12	2	6	0	4	53	8	42	3	0
Montgomery	116	2	24	1	89	288	55	199	34	6
Nelson	23	0	4	0	19	167	23	130	14	0
New Kent	48	1	5	2	40	146	8	136	2	2
Powhatan	55	0	12	1	42	348	9	337	2	3
Prince George County Police Department	131	3	10	16	102	457	51	363	43	5
Prince William County Police Department	1,300	20	108	219	953	6,387	408	5,418	561	30
Pulaski	32	0	10	1	21	543	51	470	22	2
Rappahannock	10	0	2	0	8	50	3	46	1	0
Roanoke County Police Department	226	5	24	21	176	1,090	152	878	60	4
Rockingham	86	1	30	4	51	315	86	215	14	0
Scott	48	2	14	4	28	258	56	170	32	4
Southampton	24	2	5	0	17	199	36	140	23	0
Spotsylvania	237	1	30	14	192	655	64	509	82	6
Stafford	307	4	63	30	210	1,374	101	1,171	102	8
Sussex	40	4	4	5	27	126	31	89	6	2
Warren	23	0	15	1	7	203	12	180	11	0
Washington	43	1	15	4	23	587	101	419	67	4
York	117	1	13	22	81	1,070	40	1,002	28	6
Nonmetropolitan Counties										
Accomack	96	3	18	12	63	221	36	174	11	0
Alleghany	17	1	1	0	15	232	181	48	3	2
Bath	5	0	0	0	5	10	5	5	0	0
Bland	2	0	0	0	2	50	14	32	4	0
Brunswick	18	3	7	3	5	117	21	76	20	1
Buchanan	62	1	37	2	22	262	41	176	45	4
Buckingham	14	0	5	1	8	164	21	117	26	3
Caroline	68	0	12	3	53	232	36	194	2	1
Carroll	28	1	21	0	6	210	46	138	26	2
Charlotte	13	0	5	0	8	101	14	75	12	0
Cumberland	10	0	0	0	10	33	7	23	3	0
Dickenson	11	0	3	0	8	50	7	33	10	2
Essex	19	1	0	0	18	47	7	34	6	1
Floyd	14	1	8	0	5	72	18	40	14	0
Grayson	7	0	4	2	1	128	4	100	24	3
Halifax	33	2	3	0	28	148	33	95	20	1
Henry	118	9	24	15	70	759	133	503	123	6
King George	37	1	6	5	25	272	25	227	20	3
Lancaster	17	0	3	0	14	35	5	28	2	0
Lee	44	2	9	1	32	218	39	164	15	5
Louisa	35	1	16	1	17	321	18	271	32	1
Lunenburg	12	0	0	0	12	58	17	38	3	1
Mecklenburg	31	5	3	2	21	134	12	111	11	1
Middlesex	9	0	3	1	5	90	13	72	5	0
Northampton	21	0	0	3	18	61	11	49	1	0
Nottoway	11	1	0	0	10	75	16	49	10	2
Orange	56	3	13	1	39	164	19	135	10	0
Page	17	0	9	0	8	140	22	114	4	2
Patrick	47	0	11	2	34	215	37	152	26	4
Pittsylvania	59	4	10	2	43	372	79	278	15	3
Prince Edward	30	1	4	1	24	100	9	78	13	1
Richmond	17	0	3	0	14	20	4	14	2	1
Rockbridge	28	0	3	0	25	279	58	199	22	3
Russell	43	1	13	2	27	145	26	96	23	5
Shenandoah	31	0	13	0	18	183	11	165	7	0
Smyth	19	1	6	0	12	157	28	110	19	4
Surry	5	0	3	0	2	43	6	36	1	2
Tazewell	50	1	24	1	24	226	37	169	20	2
Westmoreland	34	2	7	1	24	84	9	70	5	2
Wise	60	1	9	1	49	359	32	284	43	4
Wythe	16	1	11	0	4	148	8	109	31	0
WASHINGTON										
Metropolitan Counties										
Asotin	15	1	5	0	9	168	51	103	14	1
Benton	73	8	13	5	47	610	149	360	101	6
Chelan	25	1	7	0	17	317	150	143	24	1
Clark	348	5	96	72	175	3,904	509	2,420	975	20
Cowlitz	67	2	20	6	39	472	180	211	81	5
Douglas	24	0	9	0	15	302	78	174	50	0
Franklin	33	1	3	3	26	243	66	145	32	4

Table 10. Offenses Known to Law Enforcement, by Selected State Metropolitan and Nonmetropolitan Counties, 2022—Continued

(Number.)

State/county	Violent crime	Murder and nonnegligent manslaughter	Rape	Robbery	Aggravated assault	Property crime	Burglary	Larceny-theft	Motor vehicle theft	Arson[1]
King	656	15	78	164	399	3,973	741	2,242	990	64
Kitsap	595	4	88	58	445	3,974	805	2,520	649	23
Pierce	1,541	20	128	253	1,140	9,473	1,819	5,052	2,602	63
Skagit	78	1	2	12	63	878	211	552	115	6
Skamania	8	0	0	2	6	76	20	48	8	0
Snohomish	481	3	41	77	360	3,922	757	2,266	899	17
Spokane	220	6	32	20	162	2,637	458	1,851	328	13
Stevens	27	1	6	1	19	224	64	124	36	3
Thurston	248	4	25	37	182	1,607	446	919	242	10
Walla Walla	44	1	4	1	38	246	77	114	55	3
Whatcom	141	1	28	15	97	910	237	562	111	9
Yakima	175	2	13	23	137	1,339	390	669	280	9
Nonmetropolitan Counties										
Adams	48	2	7	3	36	376	84	246	46	3
Clallam	69	2	15	5	47	512	143	328	41	1
Columbia	4	0	1	0	3	93	27	59	7	0
Ferry	7	0	3	0	4	34	11	21	2	0
Garfield	30	0	0	0	30	39	6	29	4	0
Grant	116	0	28	13	75	1,085	235	636	214	4
Grays Harbor	37	0	17	4	16	297	110	149	38	9
Island	41	0	3	3	35	609	211	345	53	2
Jefferson	32	1	4	1	26	361	144	193	24	2
Kittitas	30	0	10	3	17	228	62	134	32	0
Lewis	85	0	18	3	64	592	220	312	60	10
Lincoln	19	1	9	4	5	108	32	57	19	0
Mason	90	2	9	12	67	782	255	378	149	4
Pend Oreille	18	0	3	0	15	145	31	101	13	3
San Juan	6	1	1	0	4	125	30	92	3	0
Wahkiakum	2	0	2	0	0	17	7	8	2	1
WEST VIRGINIA										
Berkeley	98	2	28	4	64	326	53	263	10	3
Cabell	54	0	13	3	38	506	74	407	25	0
Fayette	29	2	4	0	23	162	35	106	21	0
Jackson	56	1	2	0	53	27	9	14	4	0
Jefferson	32	0	10	1	21	167	23	131	13	1
Marshall	11	0	0	1	10	55	13	36	6	1
Mineral	7	0	3	0	4	43	7	34	2	0
Preston	4	0	0	1	3	78	1	66	11	0
Raleigh	103	1	29	6	67	562	154	374	34	6
Wirt	6	0	2	0	4	16	6	7	3	2
Nonmetropolitan Counties										
Doddridge	14	0	0	0	14	37	13	21	3	1
Grant	9	1	0	0	8	1	0	1	0	0
Hardy	2	0	1	0	1	10	1	8	1	0
Logan	81	1	2	0	78	3	0	3	0	3
Marion	41	4	4	1	32	166	37	112	17	2
McDowell	6	0	0	0	6	1	0	1	0	0
Mingo	35	0	0	0	35	18	7	5	6	0
Monroe	0	0	0	0	0	16	9	7	0	0
Nicholas	79	0	1	0	78	6	0	6	0	0
Pleasants	0	0	0	0	0	0	0	0	0	0
Randolph	52	1	1	0	50	89	20	64	5	0
Summers	11	0	0	0	11	20	6	11	3	1
Upshur	3	0	0	0	3	4	0	4	0	1
Wetzel	45	0	3	0	42	37	24	12	1	0
Wyoming	59	0	0	0	59	46	7	32	7	0
WISCONSIN										
Metropolitan Counties										
Brown	98	0	34	2	62	819	117	659	43	1
Calumet	9	0	2	0	7	88	18	62	8	0
Chippewa	35	0	11	0	24	191	32	152	7	0
Columbia	35	0	6	1	28	134	19	104	11	1
Dane	99	1	19	8	71	544	107	390	47	3
Douglas	14	0	1	0	13	164	59	82	23	1
Eau Claire	15	1	8	0	6	188	55	122	11	0
Fond du Lac	36	0	8	1	27	137	35	93	9	3
Green	6	0	2	0	4	69	2	63	4	0
Iowa	14	0	0	0	14	36	16	15	5	0
Kenosha	75	0	19	2	54	477	44	409	24	1
Kewaunee	15	0	8	0	7	45	7	35	3	0
La Crosse	11	0	2	0	9	112	31	71	10	0
Lincoln	128	1	4	0	123	77	27	39	11	1
Marathon	56	0	19	0	37	307	43	250	14	1
Milwaukee	54	0	4	5	45	46	2	25	19	0
Oconto	31	2	14	0	15	191	61	117	13	0

Table 10. Offenses Known to Law Enforcement, by Selected State Metropolitan and Nonmetropolitan Counties, 2022—Continued

(Number.)

State/county	Violent crime	Murder and nonnegligent manslaughter	Rape	Robbery	Aggravated assault	Property crime	Burglary	Larceny-theft	Motor vehicle theft	Arson[1]
Outagamie	35	1	13	1	20	421	59	353	9	1
Ozaukee	14	0	7	0	7	95	46	45	4	0
Pierce	10	0	1	0	9	62	14	39	9	0
Racine	34	0	6	2	26	99	14	71	14	2
Rock	45	0	6	4	35	193	40	134	19	0
Sheboygan	36	0	15	1	20	328	56	261	11	2
St. Croix	56	1	3	0	52	297	23	250	24	0
Washington	22	0	7	0	15	136	20	105	11	1
Waukesha	42	1	15	0	26	296	23	252	21	0
Winnebago	15	0	1	0	14	250	56	173	21	0
Nonmetropolitan Counties										
Adams	33	0	2	1	30	116	32	74	10	1
Ashland	17	0	11	0	6	47	8	34	5	0
Barron	18	0	4	0	14	102	25	70	7	0
Bayfield	17	2	1	0	14	124	43	74	7	0
Buffalo	12	0	2	0	10	27	8	18	1	0
Burnett	31	0	7	2	22	199	55	117	27	1
Clark	17	2	0	0	15	88	14	69	5	1
Crawford	24	1	10	0	13	250	14	232	4	0
Dodge	45	1	9	2	33	152	29	109	14	2
Door	2	0	0	0	2	21	8	13	0	0
Florence	12	0	0	0	12	7	1	4	2	0
Forest	10	0	1	0	9	45	2	36	7	0
Grant	26	0	3	0	23	142	42	88	12	3
Green Lake	2	2	0	0	0	35	4	30	1	0
Iron	6	0	4	0	2	12	2	10	0	0
Jefferson	23	1	5	1	16	128	26	93	9	0
Juneau	37	2	10	1	24	150	42	90	18	2
Lafayette	15	1	3	0	11	51	11	34	6	0
Manitowoc	21	0	1	1	19	114	29	79	6	0
Marinette	31	0	18	0	13	139	33	100	6	0
Marquette	3	0	0	0	3	77	46	30	1	0
Monroe	22	1	7	0	14	38	9	25	4	0
Oneida	25	0	5	0	20	105	23	73	9	0
Polk	50	0	13	0	37	135	47	70	18	1
Portage	47	1	22	0	24	123	23	89	11	0
Price	3	0	2	0	1	56	14	40	2	0
Richland	8	0	1	0	7	41	7	33	1	0
Rusk	33	0	6	0	27	41	9	27	5	0
Sauk	36	0	13	1	22	212	32	173	7	0
Sawyer	44	0	6	0	38	97	29	61	7	1
Shawano	24	1	4	0	19	148	33	103	12	0
Taylor	10	0	3	1	6	96	35	59	2	0
Trempealeau	8	0	2	0	6	36	10	15	11	0
Vernon	14	1	4	0	9	107	24	78	5	0
Vilas	0	0	0	0	0	68	6	53	9	0
Walworth	19	0	6	1	12	75	11	50	14	0
Washburn	13	0	4	0	9	45	8	30	7	0
Waupaca	16	0	4	1	11	35	7	27	1	0
Waushara	18	0	5	0	13	132	17	104	11	2
Wood	45	1	18	0	26	98	15	74	9	0
WYOMING										
Metropolitan Counties										
Laramie	52	1	4	3	44	324	66	210	48	2
Natrona	16	2	4	0	10	112	15	77	20	1
Nonmetropolitan Counties										
Albany	10	0	3	0	7	49	15	32	2	0
Campbell	23	2	11	0	10	106	21	75	10	1
Converse	3	0	0	0	3	43	6	30	7	0
Crook	3	0	0	0	3	27	1	25	1	0
Goshen	2	0	0	0	2	49	22	26	1	1
Hot Springs	0	0	0	0	0	10	2	5	3	0
Johnson	3	0	2	0	1	39	3	33	3	0
Lincoln	18	0	3	0	15	76	5	67	4	1
Niobrara	0	0	0	0	0	6	0	6	0	0
Park	20	0	12	0	8	69	13	53	3	0
Sheridan	7	0	6	0	1	38	6	30	2	0
Sublette	6	0	2	0	4	34	4	29	1	1
Sweetwater	15	0	6	0	9	82	12	55	15	2
Teton	5	0	2	0	3	39	3	33	3	0
Uinta	8	0	4	0	4	48	7	35	6	1
Washakie	5	1	1	0	3	7	1	6	0	0
Weston	2	0	0	0	2	20	4	15	1	0

1 The FBI does not publish arson data unless it receives data from either the agency or the state for all 12 months of the calendar year.   2 Limited data for 2022 were available for Florida, Illinois, Maryland, and Pennsylvania.

Table 11. Offenses Known to Law Enforcement, by Selected State, Tribal, and Other Agencies, 2022

(Number.)

State/other agency unit/office	Violent crime	Murder and nonnegligent manslaughter	Rape	Robbery	Aggravated assault	Property crime	Burglary	Larceny-theft	Motor vehicle theft	Arson[1]
ALABAMA										
State Agencies										
Alabama Department of Mental Health	0	0	0	0	0	0	0	0	0	0
Alabama Drug Enforcement Task Force	1	1	0	0	0	6	0	6	0	0
Alabama Highway Patrol Department of Public Safety Headquarters	2	0	0	0	2	2	0	0	2	0
Alabama Law Enforcement Agency	0	0	0	0	0	11	2	3	6	0
Alabama Law Enforcement Agency, State Bureau of Investigation Headquarters	10	4	2	0	4	6	1	3	2	0
Department of Conservation, Montgomery	0	0	0	0	0	0	0	0	0	0
Department of Corrections Investigations and Intelligence Division	303	8	95	1	199	3	1	2	0	1
Other Agencies										
22nd Judicial Circuit Drug Task Force	0	0	0	0	0	0	0	0	0	0
District Attorney										
25th Circuit	3	1	2	0	0	4	0	4	0	1
31st Circuit	0	0	0	0	0	0	0	0	0	0
Dothan-Houston County Airport Authority	0	0	0	0	0	9	0	1	8	0
Etowah County Drug Enforcement Unit	0	0	0	0	0	0	0	0	0	0
Huntsville International Airport	0	0	0	0	0	0	0	0	0	0
Marshall County Drug Enforcement Unit	0	0	0	0	0	0	0	0	0	0
ALASKA										
State Agencies										
Alaska State Troopers	1,340	24	311	42	963	1,941	498	1,102	341	24
ARIZONA										
Cocopah Tribal	9	1	0	0	8	21	1	17	3	0
Fort McDowell Tribal	1	0	0	0	1	16	0	12	4	1
Gila River Indian Community	331	9	40	13	269	600	58	415	127	16
Hopi Resource Enforcement Agency	35	0	1	1	33	43	31	10	2	0
Hualapai Tribal	2	0	1	0	1	16	3	7	6	0
Navajo Nation	243	2	11	0	230	91	21	30	40	12
San Carlos Apache	388	10	33	7	338	248	128	101	19	33
Truxton Canon Agency	3	0	0	0	3	0	0	0	0	0
Yavapai-Apache Nation	2	0	0	0	2	9	2	4	3	0
Yavapai-Prescott Tribal	5	0	1	0	4	35	1	33	1	0
Other Agencies										
Tucson Airport Authority	2	1	0	0	1	47	3	28	16	0
ARKANSAS										
State Agencies										
Camp Robinson	0	0	0	0	0	2	0	2	0	0
State Capitol Police	1	0	0	0	1	12	1	9	2	0
Other Agencies										
Fort Smith Public Schools	10	0	4	0	6	9	2	7	0	0
Northwest Arkansas Regional Airport	1	0	1	0	0	37	2	25	10	0
Pottsville School District	3	0	2	0	1	1	0	1	0	0
CALIFORNIA										
State Agencies										
California State Fair	3	0	0	0	3	54	1	46	7	0
California State Parks										
Angeles	6	0	0	0	6	54	38	14	2	0
Bay Area	1	0	0	1	0	20	11	9	0	0
Capital	4	0	0	0	4	13	8	4	1	1
Central Valley	3	0	0	0	3	11	3	8	0	0
Channel Coast	6	0	1	0	5	58	13	43	2	1
Colorado Desert	0	0	0	0	0	12	6	5	1	0
Diablo Range	1	0	0	0	1	19	11	6	2	0
Gold Fields	15	0	1	0	14	74	41	32	1	3
Great Basin	0	0	0	0	0	4	1	1	2	0
Inland Empire	5	0	2	0	3	21	12	9	0	0
Monterey	3	0	0	1	2	45	26	18	1	0
North Coast Redwoods	3	0	0	0	3	48	25	21	2	3
Northern Buttes	5	0	0	0	5	39	16	23	0	0
Oceano Dunes	6	0	1	0	5	78	8	69	1	0
Ocotillo Wells	2	0	0	0	2	2	0	2	0	1
Orange Coast	19	0	0	0	19	150	78	61	11	0
San Diego Coast	9	0	1	0	8	140	12	124	4	1
San Simeon	0	0	0	0	0	48	19	29	0	0
Santa Cruz	4	0	0	0	4	144	91	51	2	1
Sierra	2	0	0	0	2	11	6	5	0	0
Sonoma-Mendocino	6	0	0	0	6	31	5	24	2	0
Coalinga State Hospital	46	0	3	0	43	4	0	4	0	0
Highway Patrol										
Altadena Area Office	0	0	0	0	0	7	0	0	7	0
Alturas Area Office	0	0	0	0	0	4	0	1	3	0
Amador Area Office	0	0	0	0	0	41	0	10	31	0
Antelope Valley Area Office	0	0	0	0	0	1	0	0	1	0
Arrowhead Area Office	0	0	0	0	0	3	0	0	3	0
Auburn Area Office	8	0	0	0	8	158	0	45	113	0
Bakersfield Area Office	10	3	0	0	7	180	0	13	167	0
Baldwin Park Area Office	47	0	0	0	47	39	4	5	30	0

Table 11. Offenses Known to Law Enforcement, by Selected State, Tribal, and Other Agencies, 2022—Continued

(Number.)

State/other agency unit/office	Violent crime	Murder and nonnegligent manslaughter	Rape	Robbery	Aggravated assault	Property crime	Burglary	Larceny-theft	Motor vehicle theft	Arson[1]
Barstow Area Office	1	0	0	0	1	9	3	6	0	0
Bishop Area Office	5	0	0	0	5	29	0	10	19	0
Blythe Area Office	0	0	0	0	0	1	0	1	0	0
Border Division Area Office	0	0	0	0	0	8	0	1	7	0
Border Investigative Services Unit	0	0	0	0	0	9	0	0	9	0
Bridgeport Area Office	1	0	0	0	1	0	0	0	0	0
Buellton Area Office	2	0	0	0	2	42	0	10	32	0
Buttonwillow Area Office	0	0	0	0	0	35	0	0	35	0
Calexico Commercial Vehicle Enforcement Facility	0	0	0	0	0	1	0	0	1	0
Capistrano Area Office	3	0	0	0	3	4	0	3	1	0
Capitol Protection Section	4	0	0	1	3	33	18	15	0	3
Castaic Commercial Vehicle Enforcement Facility	0	0	0	0	0	0	0	0	0	0
Castro Valley Area Office	0	0	0	0	0	251	0	25	226	0
Central Division	1	0	0	0	1	6	0	0	6	0
Central Investigative Services Unit	0	0	0	0	0	0	0	0	0	0
Central Los Angeles Area Office	2	0	0	0	2	15	0	0	15	0
Chico Area Office	0	0	0	0	0	58	0	0	58	0
Chowchilla River Commercial Vehicle Enforcement Facility	0	0	0	0	0	0	0	0	0	0
Clear Lake Area Office	0	0	0	0	0	207	0	52	155	0
Coalinga Area Office	6	0	0	0	6	22	2	1	19	0
Conejo Commercial Vehicle Enforcement Facility	0	0	0	0	0	0	0	0	0	0
Contra Costa Area Office	14	1	0	0	13	420	0	44	376	0
Cordelia Commercial Vehicle Enforcement Facility	0	0	0	0	0	0	0	0	0	0
Costal Division	0	0	0	0	0	2	0	1	1	0
Costal Investigative Services Unit, Ventura	0	0	0	0	0	0	0	0	0	0
Costal Investigative Service Unit, Monterey	0	0	0	0	0	0	0	0	0	0
Cottonwood Commercial Vehicle Enforcement Facility	0	0	0	0	0	0	0	0	0	0
Crescent City Area Office	8	0	0	0	8	82	6	30	46	0
Delta Regional Auto Theft Team	0	0	0	0	0	0	0	0	0	0
Desert Hills Commercial Vehicle Enforcement Facility	0	0	0	0	0	0	0	0	0	0
Dignitary Protection Section, North	0	0	0	0	0	0	0	0	0	0
Dignitary Protection Section, South	0	0	0	0	0	0	0	0	0	0
Donner Pass Commercial Vehicle Enforcement Facility	0	0	0	0	0	1	0	1	0	0
Dublin Area Office	4	0	0	0	4	14	0	5	9	0
Dunsmuir Grade Commercial Vehicle Enforcement Facility	0	0	0	0	0	0	0	0	0	0
East Los Angeles Area Office	22	1	0	0	21	90	9	15	66	2
East Sacramento Area Office	1	0	0	0	1	290	2	77	211	0
El Cajon Area Office	0	0	0	0	0	23	0	11	12	0
El Centro Area Office	4	1	0	0	3	51	0	5	46	0
Fort Tejon Area Office	8	5	0	0	3	13	1	6	6	0
Fresno Area Office	3	0	1	1	1	227	3	28	196	1
Garberville Area Office	0	0	0	0	0	55	0	14	41	0
Gilroy Commercial Vehicle Enforcement Facility	0	0	0	0	0	0	0	0	0	0
Golden Gate Division	0	0	0	0	0	0	0	0	0	0
Golden Gate Investigative Services Unit	0	0	0	0	0	0	0	0	0	0
Gold Run Area Office	8	0	0	0	8	5	0	1	4	0
Governor's Protective Detail Section	0	0	0	0	0	0	0	0	0	0
Grapevine Commercial Vehicle Enforcement Facility	0	0	0	0	0	0	0	0	0	0
Grass Valley Area Office	4	0	0	0	4	87	0	23	64	0
Hanford Area Office	6	5	0	0	1	101	0	11	90	0
Hayward Area Office	18	0	0	0	18	19	3	6	10	0
Help Eliminate Auto Theft (Fresno HEAT)	0	0	0	0	0	8	0	1	7	0
Hollister-Gilroy Area Office	0	0	0	0	0	3	0	1	2	0
Humboldt Area Office	6	0	0	0	6	170	2	47	121	1
Indio Area Office	7	0	0	0	7	5	0	0	5	0
Inland Division	0	0	0	0	0	1	0	1	0	0
Inland Investigative Services Unit	0	0	0	0	0	0	0	0	0	0
Judicial Protection Section, North	0	0	0	0	0	0	0	0	0	0
Kern County Auto Theft Task Force	0	0	0	0	0	0	0	0	0	0
King City Area Office	1	0	0	0	1	8	0	1	7	0
Los Banos Area Office	2	0	0	1	1	46	4	11	31	0
Madera Area Office	7	1	0	0	6	30	0	7	23	0
Marin Area Office	9	0	0	0	9	153	87	15	51	0
Mariposa Area Office	0	0	0	0	0	18	0	5	13	0
Merced Area Office	1	0	0	1	0	82	0	13	69	0
Mission Grade Commercial Vehicle Enforcement Facility	0	0	0	0	0	0	0	0	0	0
Modesto Area Office	2	0	0	0	2	404	0	88	316	0
Mojave Area Office	0	0	0	0	0	1	0	1	0	0
Monterey Area Office	2	0	0	0	2	154	0	58	96	0

Table 11. Offenses Known to Law Enforcement, by Selected State, Tribal, and Other Agencies, 2022—Continued

(Number.)

State/other agency unit/office	Violent crime	Murder and nonnegligent manslaughter	Rape	Robbery	Aggravated assault	Property crime	Burglary	Larceny-theft	Motor vehicle theft	Arson[1]
Moorpark Area Office	6	0	1	0	5	1	0	0	1	0
Morongo Basin Area Office	0	0	0	0	0	1	0	1	0	0
Mountain Pass Port of Entry Commercial Vehicle Enforcement Facility	0	0	0	0	0	0	0	0	0	0
Mount Shasta Area Office	3	0	0	0	3	19	3	6	10	0
Napa Area Office	1	0	0	0	1	71	0	14	57	0
Needles Area Office	2	0	0	0	2	7	1	1	5	0
Newhall Area Office	25	0	0	2	23	33	4	8	21	0
Nimitz Commercial Vehicle Enforcement Facility	0	0	0	0	0	0	0	0	0	0
Northern Division	0	0	0	0	0	7	0	4	3	0
Northern Investigative Services Unit	0	0	0	0	0	0	0	0	0	0
North Sacramento Area Office	2	0	0	0	2	2,068	0	600	1,468	0
Oakhurst Area Office	0	0	0	0	0	19	0	3	16	0
Oakland Area Office	0	0	0	0	0	105	0	13	92	0
Oceanside Area Office	4	1	0	0	3	21	0	0	21	0
Office of Internal Affairs	0	0	0	0	0	0	0	0	0	0
Oroville Area Office	1	0	0	0	1	157	0	22	135	0
Otay Mesa Commercial Vehicle Enforcement Facility	0	0	0	0	0	0	0	0	0	0
Placerville Area Office	3	0	0	0	3	214	0	102	112	0
Porterville Area Office	0	0	0	0	0	167	0	17	150	0
Quincy Area Office	0	0	0	0	0	15	0	6	9	0
Rainbow Commercial Vehicle Enforcement Facility	0	0	0	0	0	0	0	0	0	0
Rancho Cucamonga Area Office	0	0	0	0	0	1	0	0	1	0
Red Bluff Area Office	3	0	0	1	2	172	0	19	153	2
Redding Area Office	0	0	0	0	0	212	0	29	183	0
Redwood City Area Office	2	0	0	0	2	10	2	4	4	0
Riverside Area Office	0	0	0	0	0	0	0	0	0	0
Sacramento Area Vehicle Theft Reduction Unit	0	0	0	0	0	1	0	0	1	0
Sacramento County	4	0	0	0	4	306	2	101	203	0
San Andreas Area Office	0	0	0	0	0	66	0	28	38	0
San Bernardino Area Office	4	0	0	0	4	4	0	1	3	0
San Diego Area Office	1	0	0	0	1	12	0	0	12	0
San Francisco Area Office	7	0	0	0	7	26	0	4	22	0
San Gorgonio Pass Area Office	8	1	0	0	7	8	2	0	6	0
San Jose Area Office	0	0	0	0	0	43	0	11	32	0
San Luis Obispo Area Office	8	0	0	0	8	94	1	15	78	0
San Onofre Commercial Vehicle Enforcement Facility	0	0	0	0	0	0	0	0	0	0
Santa Ana Area Office	3	1	0	0	2	27	3	21	3	1
Santa Barbara Area Office	2	0	0	0	2	54	0	11	43	0
Santa Cruz Area Office	0	0	0	0	0	235	0	95	140	0
Santa Fe Springs Area Office	1	0	0	0	1	5	1	0	4	0
Santa Maria Area Office	2	0	0	0	2	59	0	6	53	0
Santa Rosa Area Office	5	0	0	0	5	173	0	43	130	0
Solano Area Office	27	0	0	2	25	27	2	8	17	0
Sonora Area Office	2	0	0	0	2	31	0	1	30	0
Southern Division	4	0	0	0	4	28	3	6	19	0
Southern Investigative Services Unit	0	0	0	0	0	28	0	0	28	0
South Lake Tahoe Area Office	1	1	0	0	0	3	0	2	1	0
South Los Angeles Area Office	7	0	0	0	7	56	0	5	51	0
South Sacramento Area Office	0	0	0	0	0	652	0	140	512	0
Stanislaus County Auto Theft Task Force	0	0	0	0	0	0	0	0	0	0
Stockton Area Office	17	0	0	0	17	90	0	14	76	0
Susanville Area Office	3	0	0	0	3	35	0	13	22	0
Temecula Area Office	11	0	0	0	11	24	1	5	18	0
Templeton Area Office	13	0	0	0	13	29	1	2	26	0
Tracy Area Office	0	0	0	0	0	24	1	1	22	0
Trinity River Area Office	2	0	0	0	2	71	0	39	32	0
Truckee Area Office	0	0	0	0	0	9	0	5	4	0
Ukiah Area Office	17	0	0	1	16	96	0	17	79	1
Valley Division	0	0	0	0	0	6	1	2	3	0
Valley Investigative Services Unit	0	0	0	0	0	2	0	0	2	0
Ventura Area Office	0	0	0	0	0	29	0	3	26	0
Victorville Area Office	24	2	0	0	22	74	1	38	35	0
Visalia Area Office	11	0	0	0	11	344	4	64	276	0
West Los Angeles Area Office	0	0	0	0	0	23	1	0	22	0
Westminster Area Office	4	0	0	1	3	45	0	8	37	1
West Valley Area Office	0	0	0	0	0	17	0	1	16	0
Williams Area Office	6	0	0	0	6	12	0	1	11	0
Willows Area Office	0	0	0	0	0	24	0	2	22	0
Winterhaven Area Office	1	0	0	0	1	10	0	0	10	0
Woodland Area Office	3	0	0	0	3	47	4	14	29	0
Yreka Area Office	10	1	0	0	9	67	1	19	47	0
Yuba-Sutter Area Office	3	0	0	0	3	307	0	40	267	0
Metropolitan State Hospital	44	0	10	0	34	4	0	4	0	0
Napa State Hospital	22	0	6	0	16	5	0	5	0	0
Patton State Hospital	16	0	5	0	11	1	0	1	0	0
Porterville Developmental Center	21	0	2	0	19	7	1	6	0	2

Table 11. Offenses Known to Law Enforcement, by Selected State, Tribal, and Other Agencies, 2022—Continued

(Number.)

State/other agency unit/office	Violent crime	Murder and nonnegligent manslaughter	Rape	Robbery	Aggravated assault	Property crime	Burglary	Larceny-theft	Motor vehicle theft	Arson[1]
Tribal Agencies										
Bear River Band	4	0	0	0	4	5	1	3	1	0
San Pasqual Band of Mission Indians Tribal	9	0	0	2	7	59	5	38	16	0
Sycuan Tribal	10	0	1	2	7	64	13	25	26	0
Table Mountain Rancheria	2	0	0	0	2	51	6	35	10	0
Yurok Tribal	7	0	3	0	4	39	11	27	1	3
Other Agencies										
Clovis Unified School District	5	0	0	0	5	6	2	4	0	
East Bay Regional Park District	27	0	2	12	13	291	21	252	18	
Fontana Unified School District	18	0	1	4	13	46	7	38	1	
Kern High School District	60	0	0	11	49	202	32	149	21	
Los Angeles County Metropolitan Transportation Authority	5	0	0	0	5	15	0	15	0	
Los Angeles Transportation Services Bureau	272	1	5	110	156	158	7	134	17	
Port of San Diego Harbor	124	0	4	5	115	590	75	459	56	6
San Bernardino Unified School District	110	0	1	43	66	173	56	105	12	10
San Francisco Bay Area Rapid Transit										
Alameda County	189	0	3	123	63	773	10	593	170	
Contra Costa County	48	0	4	23	21	381	4	328	49	
San Francisco County	91	1	0	65	25	124	7	117	0	
San Mateo County	18	0	1	14	3	103	1	90	12	
Santa Clara County	2	0	0	0	2	0	0	0	0	
Santa Clara Transit District	76	0	1	31	44	88	8	67	13	
Shasta County Marshal	0	0	0	0	0	0	0	0	0	
Stockton Unified School District	45	0	4	16	25	97	16	76	5	2
Twin Rivers Unified School District	46	0	6	6	34	109	33	63	13	
Union Pacific Railroad										
Alameda County	1	0	0	0	1	18	5	13	0	
Amador County	0	0	0	0	0	0	0	0	0	
Butte County	0	0	0	0	0	0	0	0	0	
Calaveras County	0	0	0	0	0	0	0	0	0	
Colusa County	0	0	0	0	0	0	0	0	0	
Contra Costa County	0	0	0	0	0	3	0	3	0	
El Dorado County	0	0	0	0	0	2	1	1	0	
Fresno County	0	0	0	0	0	6	2	4	0	
Glenn County	0	0	0	0	0	0	0	0	0	
Humboldt County	0	0	0	0	0	0	0	0	0	
Imperial County	0	0	0	0	0	0	0	0	0	
Inyo County	0	0	0	0	0	0	0	0	0	
Kern County	0	0	0	0	0	175	31	144	0	
Kings County	0	0	0	0	0	3	0	3	0	
Lassen County	0	0	0	0	0	0	0	0	0	
Los Angeles County	1	0	0	0	1	1,635	1,024	611	0	
Madera County	0	0	0	0	0	0	0	0	0	
Marin County	0	0	0	0	0	0	0	0	0	
Mendocino County	0	0	0	0	0	0	0	0	0	
Merced County	0	0	0	0	0	3	1	2	0	
Modoc County	0	0	0	0	0	0	0	0	0	
Monterey County	0	0	0	0	0	2	0	2	0	
Napa County	0	0	0	0	0	0	0	0	0	
Nevada County	0	0	0	0	0	1	0	1	0	
Orange County	0	0	0	0	0	2	1	1	0	
Placer County	0	0	0	0	0	7	1	6	0	
Plumas County	0	0	0	0	0	1	0	1	0	
Riverside County	0	0	0	0	0	25	20	5	0	
Sacramento County	1	0	0	0	1	8	2	6	0	
San Benito County	0	0	0	0	0	0	0	0	0	
San Bernardino County	0	0	0	0	0	90	69	21	0	
San Francisco County	0	0	0	0	0	2	0	2	0	
San Joaquin County	1	0	0	0	1	318	173	145	0	
San Luis Obispo County	0	0	0	0	0	1	0	1	0	
San Mateo County	0	0	0	0	0	0	0	0	0	
Santa Barbara County	0	0	0	0	0	0	0	0	0	
Santa Clara County	0	0	0	0	0	5	0	5	0	
Santa Cruz County	0	0	0	0	0	0	0	0	0	
Shasta County	0	0	0	0	0	4	2	2	0	
Sierra County	0	0	0	0	0	0	0	0	0	
Siskiyou County	0	0	0	0	0	1	1	0	0	
Solano County	0	0	0	0	0	1	0	1	0	
Sonoma County	0	0	0	0	0	0	0	0	0	
Stanislaus County	0	0	0	0	0	9	1	8	0	
Sutter County	0	0	0	0	0	1	0	1	0	
Tehama County	0	0	0	0	0	2	0	2	0	
Trinity County	0	0	0	0	0	0	0	0	0	
Tulare County	0	0	0	0	0	6	2	4	0	
Ventura County	0	0	0	0	0	3	0	3	0	
Yolo County	0	0	0	0	0	0	0	0	0	
Yuba County	0	0	0	0	0	5	0	5	0	
COLORADO										
State Agencies										
Colorado Bureau of Investigation	0	0	0	0	0	0	0	0	0	0
Colorado Mental Health Institute	0	0	0	0	0	1	0	1	0	0

Table 11. Offenses Known to Law Enforcement, by Selected State, Tribal, and Other Agencies, 2022—Continued

(Number.)

State/other agency unit/office	Violent crime	Murder and nonnegligent manslaughter	Rape	Robbery	Aggravated assault	Property crime	Burglary	Larceny-theft	Motor vehicle theft	Arson[1]
Division of Gaming Criminal Enforcement and Investigations Section, Golden	0	0	0	0	0	0	0	0	0	0
State Patrol	18	0	0	0	18	10	0	0	10	0
Tribal Agencies										
Southern Ute Tribal	45	0	4	0	41	28	4	19	5	2
Ute Mountain Tribal	2	0	1	0	1	8	0	5	3	0
Other Agencies										
Southwest Drug Task Force	0	0	0	0	0	0	0	0	0	0
CONNECTICUT										
State Agencies										
Connecticut State Police	207	12	52	28	115	1,585	190	1,137	258	7
Department of Energy and Environmental Protection	0	0	0	0	0	57	6	48	3	1
State Capitol Police	0	0	0	0	0	1	0	1	0	0
Tribal Agencies										
Mashantucket Pequot Tribal	2	0	0	0	2	104	3	94	7	0
Mohegan Tribal	3	0	0	2	1	156	1	151	4	0
Other Agencies										
Metropolitan Transportation Authority	2	0	0	1	1	37	0	37	0	0
DELAWARE										
State Agencies										
Alcohol and Tobacco Enforcement	0	0	0	0	0	0	0	0	0	0
Animal Welfare										
Kent County	0	0	0	0	0	0	0	0	0	0
New Castle County	0	0	0	0	0	0	0	0	0	0
Sussex County	0	0	0	0	0	0	0	0	0	0
Environmental Control	0	0	0	0	0	1	0	1	0	0
Fish and Wildlife	1	0	0	0	1	13	0	13	0	0
Park Rangers	3	0	0	0	3	103	37	61	5	0
River and Bay Authority	3	0	0	0	3	22	0	22	0	0
State Capitol Police	0	0	0	0	0	10	0	10	0	0
State Fire Marshal	2	0	0	0	2	2	2	0	0	93
State Police										
Headquarters	1	0	1	0	0	5	0	5	0	0
Kent County	272	5	18	14	235	886	136	637	113	0
New Castle County	466	7	24	130	305	4,887	228	4,420	239	1
Sussex County	402	5	9	20	368	1,851	330	1,392	129	1
DISTRICT OF COLUMBIA										
State Agencies										
Metro Transit Police	454	0	4	227	223	518	2	431	85	6
FLORIDA[2]										
State Agencies										
Capitol Police	0	0	0	0	0	11	2	9	0	0
Department of Corrections, Office of the Inspector General										
Alachua County	0	0	0	0	0	0	0	0	0	0
Baker County	0	0	0	0	0	0	0	0	0	0
Bay County	0	0	0	0	0	0	0	0	0	0
Bradford County	0	0	0	0	0	0	0	0	0	0
Brevard County	0	0	0	0	0	0	0	0	0	0
Broward County	0	0	0	0	0	0	0	0	0	0
Calhoun County	0	0	0	0	0	0	0	0	0	0
Charlotte County	0	0	0	0	0	0	0	0	0	0
Citrus County	0	0	0	0	0	0	0	0	0	0
Clay County	0	0	0	0	0	0	0	0	0	0
Collier County	0	0	0	0	0	0	0	0	0	0
Columbia County	0	0	0	0	0	0	0	0	0	0
DeSoto County	0	0	0	0	0	0	0	0	0	0
Dixie County	0	0	0	0	0	0	0	0	0	0
Duval County	0	0	0	0	0	0	0	0	0	0
Escambia County	0	0	0	0	0	0	0	0	0	0
Flagler County	0	0	0	0	0	0	0	0	0	0
Franklin County	0	0	0	0	0	0	0	0	0	0
Gadsden County	0	0	0	0	0	0	0	0	0	0
Gilchrist County	0	0	0	0	0	0	0	0	0	0
Glades County	0	0	0	0	0	0	0	0	0	0
Gulf County	0	0	0	0	0	0	0	0	0	0
Hamilton County	0	0	0	0	0	0	0	0	0	0
Hardee County	0	0	0	0	0	0	0	0	0	0
Hendry County	0	0	0	0	0	0	0	0	0	0
Hernando County	0	0	0	0	0	0	0	0	0	0
Highlands County	0	0	0	0	0	0	0	0	0	0
Hillsborough County	0	0	0	0	0	0	0	0	0	0
Holmes County	0	0	0	0	0	0	0	0	0	0
Indian River County	0	0	0	0	0	0	0	0	0	0
Jackson County	0	0	0	0	0	0	0	0	0	0
Jefferson County	0	0	0	0	0	0	0	0	0	0
Lafayette County	0	0	0	0	0	0	0	0	0	0
Lake County	0	0	0	0	0	0	0	0	0	0
Lee County	0	0	0	0	0	0	0	0	0	0

Table 11. Offenses Known to Law Enforcement, by Selected State, Tribal, and Other Agencies, 2022—Continued
(Number.)

State/other agency unit/office	Violent crime	Murder and nonnegligent manslaughter	Rape	Robbery	Aggravated assault	Property crime	Burglary	Larceny-theft	Motor vehicle theft	Arson[1]
Leon County	0	0	0	0	0	0	0	0	0	0
Levy County	0	0	0	0	0	0	0	0	0	0
Liberty County	0	0	0	0	0	0	0	0	0	0
Madison County	0	0	0	0	0	0	0	0	0	0
Manatee County	0	0	0	0	0	0	0	0	0	0
Marion County	0	0	0	0	0	0	0	0	0	0
Martin County	0	0	0	0	0	0	0	0	0	0
Miami-Dade County	0	0	0	0	0	0	0	0	0	0
Monroe County	0	0	0	0	0	0	0	0	0	0
Nassau County	0	0	0	0	0	0	0	0	0	0
Okaloosa County	0	0	0	0	0	0	0	0	0	0
Okeechobee County	0	0	0	0	0	0	0	0	0	0
Orange County	0	0	0	0	0	0	0	0	0	0
Osceola County	0	0	0	0	0	0	0	0	0	0
Palm Beach County	0	0	0	0	0	0	0	0	0	0
Pasco County	0	0	0	0	0	0	0	0	0	0
Pinellas County	0	0	0	0	0	0	0	0	0	0
Polk County	0	0	0	0	0	0	0	0	0	0
Putnam County	0	0	0	0	0	0	0	0	0	0
Santa Rosa County	0	0	0	0	0	0	0	0	0	0
Sarasota County	0	0	0	0	0	0	0	0	0	0
Seminole County	0	0	0	0	0	0	0	0	0	0
St. Johns County	0	0	0	0	0	0	0	0	0	0
St. Lucie County	0	0	0	0	0	0	0	0	0	0
Sumter County	0	0	0	0	0	0	0	0	0	0
Suwannee County	0	0	0	0	0	0	0	0	0	0
Taylor County	0	0	0	0	0	0	0	0	0	0
Union County	0	0	0	0	0	0	0	0	0	0
Volusia County	0	0	0	0	0	0	0	0	0	0
Wakulla County	0	0	0	0	0	0	0	0	0	0
Walton County	0	0	0	0	0	0	0	0	0	0
Washington County	0	0	0	0	0	0	0	0	0	0
Department of Law Enforcement										
Escambia County, Pensacola	0	0	0	0	0	0	0	0	0	0
Hillsborough County, Tampa	0	0	0	0	0	0	0	0	0	0
Lee County, Fort Myers	0	0	0	0	0	0	0	0	0	0
Leon County, Tallahassee	0	0	0	0	0	0	0	0	0	0
Miami-Dade County, Miami	0	0	0	0	0	0	0	0	0	0
Division of Investigative and Forensic Services										
Broward County	0	0	0	0	0	0	0	0	0	0
Duval County	0	0	0	0	0	0	0	0	0	0
Escambia County	0	0	0	0	0	0	0	0	0	0
Hillsborough County	0	0	0	0	0	0	0	0	0	0
Lee County	0	0	0	0	0	0	0	0	0	0
Leon County	0	0	0	0	0	0	0	0	0	0
Miami-Dade County	0	0	0	0	0	0	0	0	0	0
Orange County	0	0	0	0	0	0	0	0	0	0
Palm Beach County	0	0	0	0	0	0	0	0	0	0
Pinellas County	0	0	0	0	0	0	0	0	0	0
Fish and Wildlife Conservation Commission										
Alachua County	0	0	0	0	0	0	0	0	0	0
Baker County	0	0	0	0	0	0	0	0	0	0
Bay County	0	0	0	0	0	0	0	0	0	0
Bradford County	0	0	0	0	0	0	0	0	0	0
Brevard County	0	0	0	0	0	0	0	0	0	0
Broward County	0	0	0	0	0	0	0	0	0	0
Calhoun County	0	0	0	0	0	0	0	0	0	0
Charlotte County	0	0	0	0	0	0	0	0	0	0
Citrus County	0	0	0	0	0	0	0	0	0	0
Clay County	0	0	0	0	0	0	0	0	0	0
Collier County	0	0	0	0	0	0	0	0	0	0
Columbia County	0	0	0	0	0	0	0	0	0	0
DeSoto County	0	0	0	0	0	0	0	0	0	0
Dixie County	0	0	0	0	0	0	0	0	0	0
Duval County	0	0	0	0	0	0	0	0	0	0
Escambia County	0	0	0	0	0	0	0	0	0	0
Flagler County	0	0	0	0	0	0	0	0	0	0
Franklin County	0	0	0	0	0	0	0	0	0	0
Gadsden County	0	0	0	0	0	0	0	0	0	0
Gilchrist County	0	0	0	0	0	0	0	0	0	0
Glades County	0	0	0	0	0	0	0	0	0	0
Gulf County	0	0	0	0	0	0	0	0	0	0
Hamilton County	0	0	0	0	0	0	0	0	0	0
Hardee County	0	0	0	0	0	0	0	0	0	0
Hendry County	0	0	0	0	0	0	0	0	0	0
Hernando County	0	0	0	0	0	0	0	0	0	0
Highlands County	0	0	0	0	0	0	0	0	0	0
Hillsborough County	0	0	0	0	0	0	0	0	0	0
Holmes County	0	0	0	0	0	0	0	0	0	0
Indian River County	0	0	0	0	0	0	0	0	0	0
Jackson County	0	0	0	0	0	0	0	0	0	0
Jefferson County	0	0	0	0	0	0	0	0	0	0
Lafayette County	0	0	0	0	0	0	0	0	0	0

Table 11. Offenses Known to Law Enforcement, by Selected State, Tribal, and Other Agencies, 2022—Continued

(Number.)

State/other agency unit/office	Violent crime	Murder and nonnegligent manslaughter	Rape	Robbery	Aggravated assault	Property crime	Burglary	Larceny-theft	Motor vehicle theft	Arson[1]
Lake County	0	0	0	0	0	0	0	0	0	0
Lee County	0	0	0	0	0	0	0	0	0	0
Leon County	0	0	0	0	0	0	0	0	0	0
Levy County	0	0	0	0	0	0	0	0	0	0
Liberty County	0	0	0	0	0	0	0	0	0	0
Madison County	0	0	0	0	0	0	0	0	0	0
Manatee County	0	0	0	0	0	0	0	0	0	0
Marion County	0	0	0	0	0	0	0	0	0	0
Martin County	0	0	0	0	0	0	0	0	0	0
Miami-Dade County	0	0	0	0	0	0	0	0	0	0
Monroe County	0	0	0	0	0	0	0	0	0	0
Nassau County	0	0	0	0	0	0	0	0	0	0
Okaloosa County	0	0	0	0	0	0	0	0	0	0
Okeechobee County	0	0	0	0	0	0	0	0	0	0
Orange County	0	0	0	0	0	0	0	0	0	0
Osceola County	0	0	0	0	0	0	0	0	0	0
Palm Beach County	0	0	0	0	0	0	0	0	0	0
Pasco County	0	0	0	0	0	0	0	0	0	0
Pinellas County	0	0	0	0	0	0	0	0	0	0
Polk County	0	0	0	0	0	0	0	0	0	0
Putnam County	0	0	0	0	0	0	0	0	0	0
Santa Rosa County	0	0	0	0	0	0	0	0	0	0
Sarasota County	0	0	0	0	0	0	0	0	0	0
Seminole County	0	0	0	0	0	0	0	0	0	0
St. Johns County	0	0	0	0	0	0	0	0	0	0
St. Lucie County	0	0	0	0	0	0	0	0	0	0
Sumter County	0	0	0	0	0	0	0	0	0	0
Suwannee County	0	0	0	0	0	0	0	0	0	0
Taylor County	0	0	0	0	0	0	0	0	0	0
Union County	0	0	0	0	0	0	0	0	0	0
Volusia County	0	0	0	0	0	0	0	0	0	0
Wakulla County	0	0	0	0	0	0	0	0	0	0
Walton County	0	0	0	0	0	0	0	0	0	0
Washington County	0	0	0	0	0	0	0	0	0	0
Tribal Agencies										
Miccosukee Tribal	5	0	0	2	3	37	5	28	4	0
Seminole Tribal	70	1	10	30	29	722	24	652	46	3
Other Agencies										
Duval County Schools	134	0	0	4	130	119	15	104	0	3
Jacksonville Aviation Authority	6	0	0	0	6	91	0	54	37	0
Melbourne International Airport	1	0	0	0	1	10	1	8	1	0
Northwest Florida Beaches International Airport	0	0	0	0	0	2	0	1	1	0
Sarasota County Schools	7	0	0	0	7	37	3	34	0	0
Sarasota-Manatee Airport Authority	0	0	0	0	0	11	0	2	9	0
Tampa International Airport	7	0	0	1	6	1,165	16	1,022	127	0
Volusia County Beach Safety	12	0	0	0	12	53	1	51	1	0
GEORGIA										
State Agencies										
Georgia Department of Transportation, Office of Investigations	0	0	0	0	0	0	0	0	0	0
Georgia Forestry Commission	0	0	0	0	0	5	0	3	2	36
Georgia Public Safety Training Center	0	0	0	0	0	0	0	0	0	0
Georgia World Congress	2	0	0	1	1	104	2	96	6	0
Ports Authority, Savannag	0	0	0	0	0	14	0	14	0	0
State Board of Workers Compensation Fraud Investigation Division	0	0	0	0	0	0	0	0	0	0
Other Agencies										
Atlanta Public Schools	46	0	38	2	6	172	21	146	5	15
Augusta Board of Education	12	0	4	1	7	33	12	21	0	0
Chatham County Board of Education	10	0	2	1	7	14	4	10	0	1
Cherokee County Board of Education	2	0	2	0	0	35	4	31	0	0
Cherokee County Marshal	0	0	0	0	0	0	0	0	0	0
Cobb County Board of Education	21	0	9	1	11	91	6	85	0	1
Decatur County Schools	1	0	1	0	0	0	0	0	0	0
Dougherty County Board of Education	7	0	1	0	6	25	3	22	0	2
Fayette County Marshal	0	0	0	0	0	0	0	0	0	0
Forsyth County Fire Investigation Unit	0	0	0	0	0	0	0	0	0	0
Fulton County Marshal	0	0	0	0	0	5	0	4	1	0
Fulton County School System	24	0	2	0	22	75	6	65	4	3
Glynn County School System	7	0	2	1	4	12	2	9	1	0
Gwinnett County Public Schools	65	0	37	8	20	116	4	109	3	6
Hall County Marshal	0	0	0	0	0	0	0	0	0	0
Hartsfield-Jackson Atlanta International Airport	5	0	0	0	5	384	2	282	100	0
Metropolitan Atlanta Rapid Transit Authority	86	2	4	22	58	113	1	95	17	1
Muscogee County Schools	9	0	2	0	7	484	9	474	1	0
Paulding County Marshal	0	0	0	0	0	0	0	0	0	0
IDAHO										
State Agencies										
Attorney General	0	0	0	0	0	0	0	0	0	0

Table 11. Offenses Known to Law Enforcement, by Selected State, Tribal, and Other Agencies, 2022—Continued

(Number.)

State/other agency unit/office	Violent crime	Murder and nonnegligent manslaughter	Rape	Robbery	Aggravated assault	Property crime	Burglary	Larceny-theft	Motor vehicle theft	Arson[1]
Idaho State Lottery Security Division	0	0	0	0	0	34	0	34	0	0
Idaho State Police	57	5	6	1	45	6	2	4	0	2
Tribal Agencies										
Fort Hall Tribal	50	1	10	6	33	133	5	96	32	4
Nez Perce Tribal	4	0	1	0	3	51	4	34	13	1
ILLINOIS[2]										
State Agencies										
Illinois Department of Revenue	0	0	0	0	0	0	0	0	0	0
Illinois Liquor Control Commission	0	0	0	0	0	0	0	0	0	0
Illinois State Police	337	20	70	10	237	126	3	117	6	1
Other Agencies										
Belt Railway	0	0	0	0	0	0	0	0	0	0
Canton Park District	0	0	0	0	0	0	0	0	0	0
Fox Valley Park District	0	0	0	0	0	3	0	3	0	2
Naperville Park District	1	0	0	1	0	6	0	6	0	3
Pekin Park District	3	0	3	0	0	4	0	4	0	0
Rockford Park District	16	2	3	3	8	37	4	32	1	1
Terminal Railroad Association	0	0	0	0	0	0	0	0	0	0
Tri-County Drug Enforcement Narcotics Team	0	0	0	0	0	0	0	0	0	0
Will County Forest Preserve	2	0	1	1	0	24	0	24	0	0
INDIANA										
State Agencies										
Indiana Gaming Commission	16	0	0	3	13	213	1	210	2	0
Indiana State Excise Police	0	0	0	0	0	3	0	3	0	0
Indiana State Police	379	26	95	9	249	691	67	416	208	7
Other Agencies										
Indiana Harbor Belt Railroad	0	0	0	0	0	0	0	0	0	0
Indianapolis International Airport	2	0	0	0	2	90	7	60	23	0
Indianapolis Public Schools	16	0	7	3	6	20	0	14	6	0
KANSAS										
State Agencies										
Highway Patrol										
Capitol	1	0	0	0	1	15	0	14	1	1
Troop A	14	0	0	0	14	1	0	0	1	0
Troop B	7	0	0	0	7	3	0	1	2	0
Troop C	4	0	0	0	4	1	0	1	0	0
Troop D	6	0	0	0	6	7	0	4	3	2
Troop E	5	0	0	0	5	0	0	0	0	0
Troop F	4	0	0	0	4	12	2	10	0	0
Troop G	10	0	0	0	10	18	1	12	5	0
Troop H	1	0	0	0	1	2	0	1	1	0
Troop N	2	0	0	0	2	0	0	0	0	0
Tribal Agencies										
Potawatomi Tribal	5	0	0	0	5	23	2	19	2	1
Other Agencies										
Johnson County Park	4	0	0	1	3	48	2	46	0	2
Unified School District, Kansas City	10	0	2	1	7	65	3	60	2	2
KENTUCKY										
State Agencies										
Alcohol Beverage Control										
Enforcement Division	0	0	0	0	0	0	0	0	0	0
Investigative Division	0	0	0	0	0	0	0	0	0	0
Department of Agriculture Animal Health										
Enforcement Division	0	0	0	0	0	0	0	0	0	0
Fish and Wildlife Enforcement	0	0	0	0	0	5	0	5	0	0
Kentucky Horse Park	0	0	0	0	0	22	0	22	0	0
Kentucky State Park Rangers Division	0	0	0	0	0	32	8	24	0	0
Motor Vehicle Enforcement	1	0	0	0	1	9	0	7	2	0
State Police										
Ashland	39	2	14	0	23	93	13	64	16	3
Bowling Green	37	6	16	0	15	78	20	42	16	1
Campbellsburg	60	1	21	0	38	103	35	51	17	0
Cannabis Suppression Section	0	0	0	0	0	0	0	0	0	0
Columbia	61	1	40	2	18	81	32	40	9	4
Dry Ridge	20	0	11	1	8	59	14	37	8	0
East Drug Enforcement Branch	0	0	0	0	0	4	0	4	0	0
Electronic Crimes	3	0	3	0	0	0	0	0	0	0
Elizabethtown	30	4	9	0	17	101	28	34	39	2
Frankfort	16	2	5	1	8	41	8	20	13	0
Harlan	46	1	26	6	13	187	57	81	49	4
Hazard	38	1	10	0	27	126	36	52	38	2
Headquarters	0	0	0	0	0	0	0	0	0	0
Henderson	25	2	10	0	13	73	21	41	11	0
London	72	1	29	5	37	129	37	50	42	5
Madisonville	31	4	14	0	13	23	5	13	5	1
Mayfield	41	1	22	1	17	87	17	57	13	1
Morehead	41	2	21	1	17	77	16	42	19	4
Pikeville	96	8	36	4	48	291	85	115	91	1

Table 11. Offenses Known to Law Enforcement, by Selected State, Tribal, and Other Agencies, 2022—Continued

(Number.)

State/other agency unit/office	Violent crime	Murder and nonnegligent manslaughter	Rape	Robbery	Aggravated assault	Property crime	Burglary	Larceny-theft	Motor vehicle theft	Arson[1]
Richmond	51	3	30	4	14	176	56	82	38	1
Special Operations	0	0	0	0	0	0	0	0	0	3
Vehicle Investigations	0	0	0	0	0	19	0	4	15	0
West Drug Enforcement Branch	3	0	0	0	3	3	0	3	0	0
Unlawful Narcotics Investigation Treatment and Education	0	0	0	0	0	0	0	0	0	0
Other Agencies										
Barren County Drug Task Force	0	0	0	0	0	0	0	0	0	0
Bluegrass Narcotics Task Force	0	0	0	0	0	0	0	0	0	0
Bourbon County Constable District 7	0	0	0	0	0	0	0	0	0	0
Bourbon County Schools	2	0	0	0	2	3	1	2	0	0
Campbellsville Independent Public Schools	0	0	0	0	0	1	0	1	0	0
Casey County Constable District 2	0	0	0	0	0	0	0	0	0	0
Cincinnati-Northern Kentucky International Airport	2	0	0	0	2	42	0	25	17	0
Clark County Constable	0	0	0	0	0	0	0	0	0	0
Clark County School System	1	0	0	0	1	4	1	3	0	0
Fayette County Schools	10	0	0	0	10	44	6	38	0	4
FIVCO Area Drug Task Force	0	0	0	0	0	0	0	0	0	0
Garrard County Constable District 2	0	0	0	0	0	0	0	0	0	0
Gateway Area Drug Task Force	0	0	0	0	0	0	0	0	0	0
Graves County Schools	0	0	0	0	0	0	0	0	0	0
Greater Hardin County Narcotics Task Force	3	3	0	0	0	6	0	6	0	0
Jefferson County Constable District 1	0	0	0	0	0	0	0	0	0	0
Jefferson County Constable District 2	0	0	0	0	0	0	0	0	0	0
Jefferson County School District	47	0	0	4	43	72	32	39	1	1
Jenkins Independent School	0	0	0	0	0	0	0	0	0	0
Johnson County Constable District 2	0	0	0	0	0	0	0	0	0	0
Lake Cumberland Area Drug Enforcement Task Force	0	0	0	0	0	0	0	0	0	0
Lawrence County Constable District 3	0	0	0	0	0	0	0	0	0	0
Lexington Bluegrass Airport	0	0	0	0	0	4	0	4	0	0
Louisville Regional Airport Authority	1	0	0	0	1	64	0	23	41	0
McCracken County Public Schools	1	0	0	0	1	2	0	2	0	0
McCreary County Constable District 3	0	0	0	0	0	0	0	0	0	0
Montgomery County Constable District 2	0	0	0	0	0	0	0	0	0	0
Montgomery County School District	0	0	0	0	0	3	0	3	0	0
Northeast Kentucky Drug Task Force	0	0	0	0	0	0	0	0	0	0
Northern Kentucky Drug Strike Force	3	0	0	0	3	0	0	0	0	0
Pennyrile Narcotics Task Force	1	0	0	0	1	1	0	0	1	0
Pulaski County Constable District 4	0	0	0	0	0	0	0	0	0	0
Russell County Constable District 3	0	0	0	0	0	0	0	0	0	0
South Central Kentucky Drug Task Force	0	0	0	0	0	0	0	0	0	0
Taylor County Schools	0	0	0	0	0	0	0	0	0	0
Woodford County Public Schools	0	0	0	0	0	2	1	1	0	0
LOUISIANA										
Tribal Agencies										
Chitimacha Tribal	2	0	0	0	2	16	0	16	0	0
Coushatta Tribal	0	0	0	0	0	88	1	84	3	0
Tunica-Biloxi Tribal	7	0	0	1	6	66	1	63	2	0
MAINE										
State Agencies										
Bureau of Capitol Police	0	0	0	0	0	8	0	8	0	0
Drug Enforcement Agency	0	0	0	0	0	0	0	0	0	0
State Fire Marshal	1	0	0	0	1	3	2	0	1	78
State Police	102	13	32	2	55	725	141	504	80	0
Tribal Agencies										
Passamaquoddy Indian Township	14	0	3	0	11	8	1	6	1	0
MARYLAND[2]										
State Agencies										
Department of Public Safety and Correctional Services, Internal Investigation Division	226	3	20	0	203	1	0	1	0	0
General Services										
Annapolis, Anne Arundel County	0	0	0	0	0	0	0	0	0	0
Baltimore City	0	0	0	0	0	0	0	0	0	0
Maryland State Police Statewide	49	8	27	2	12	33	1	27	5	0
Natural Resources Police	8	0	2	0	6	111	17	91	3	2
State Police										
Allegany County	43	0	7	2	34	132	23	101	8	0
Anne Arundel County	16	0	1	0	15	55	1	40	14	0
Baltimore City	0	0	0	0	0	2	0	2	0	0
Baltimore County	18	0	2	1	15	46	3	25	18	0
Calvert County	28	0	2	0	26	78	3	63	12	1
Caroline County	27	0	0	0	27	41	13	21	7	0
Carroll County	38	1	7	3	27	161	10	143	8	1
Cecil County	120	2	13	7	98	509	72	375	62	2
Charles County	3	0	0	1	2	10	0	8	2	0
Dorchester County	15	0	1	0	14	35	7	25	3	0
Frederick County	60	0	2	3	55	113	11	90	12	1

Table 11. Offenses Known to Law Enforcement, by Selected State, Tribal, and Other Agencies, 2022—Continued

(Number.)

State/other agency unit/office	Violent crime	Murder and nonnegligent manslaughter	Rape	Robbery	Aggravated assault	Property crime	Burglary	Larceny-theft	Motor vehicle theft	Arson[1]
Garrett County	11	0	1	1	9	74	22	49	3	0
Harford County	32	1	2	2	27	155	7	134	14	0
Howard County	9	0	0	0	9	23	1	15	7	0
Kent County	2	0	0	0	2	12	2	9	1	0
Montgomery County	15	0	1	2	12	11	1	4	6	0
Prince Georges County	38	0	0	1	37	76	0	21	55	0
Queen Annes's County	22	0	3	2	17	74	8	61	5	0
Somerset County	27	0	1	1	25	68	16	43	9	0
St. Mary's County	49	0	9	3	37	160	26	121	13	0
Talbot County	4	0	1	0	3	26	3	20	3	0
Washington County	40	0	3	3	34	202	11	180	11	0
Wicomico County	92	0	3	3	86	78	24	41	13	0
Worcester County	23	1	1	2	19	95	15	71	9	0
Transit Administration	54	0	0	18	36	63	2	57	4	4
Transportation Authority	97	1	0	3	93	275	0	187	88	0
MASSACHUSETTS										
State Agencies										
State Police										
Barnstable County	1	0	0	0	1	1	0	0	1	0
Berkshire County	2	0	0	1	1	7	3	3	1	0
Bristol County	2	0	0	0	2	1	0	0	1	0
Essex County	12	0	0	0	12	7	0	1	6	0
Franklin County	9	0	0	0	9	3	1	1	1	0
Hampden County	8	0	0	0	8	7	2	4	1	0
Hampshire County	7	0	0	0	7	5	2	3	0	0
Middlesex County	22	0	2	0	20	14	5	4	5	1
Nantucket County	1	0	0	0	1	1	0	0	1	0
Norfolk County	8	0	0	0	8	4	1	0	3	0
Plymouth County	1	0	0	0	1	1	0	0	1	0
Suffolk County	36	0	2	3	31	99	23	59	17	0
Worcester County	26	0	0	0	26	10	0	1	9	0
Tribal Agencies										
Wampanoag Tribe of Gay Head	0	0	0	0	0	0	0	0	0	0
MICHIGAN										
State Agencies										
State Police										
Alcona County	3	1	1	0	1	2	0	2	0	0
Alger County	14	0	3	0	11	19	6	10	3	1
Allegan County	64	0	45	0	19	234	59	150	25	2
Alpena County	21	0	10	1	10	109	22	81	6	2
Antrim County	14	0	10	0	4	48	29	16	3	0
Arenac County	10	0	7	0	3	1	1	0	0	1
Baraga County	22	0	4	0	18	19	2	15	2	2
Barry County	39	0	14	0	25	171	78	89	4	1
Bay County	41	2	17	2	20	82	19	49	14	0
Benzie County	8	1	4	0	3	16	0	12	4	0
Berrien County	57	0	27	0	30	99	35	53	11	2
Branch County	37	0	8	1	28	70	34	18	18	2
Calhoun County	29	0	12	0	17	119	27	72	20	2
Cass County	17	1	6	1	9	32	14	10	8	0
Charlevoix County	8	0	6	0	2	8	3	3	2	1
Cheboygan County	7	0	4	0	3	49	35	13	1	0
Chippewa County	46	2	7	0	37	19	4	12	3	0
Clare County	34	0	21	0	13	21	3	16	2	1
Clinton County	15	0	5	0	10	17	2	13	2	0
Crawford County	8	0	2	0	6	16	9	7	0	0
Delta County	20	0	8	0	12	43	11	30	2	0
Dickinson County	15	0	5	0	10	40	18	16	6	0
Eaton County	61	0	20	0	41	97	23	66	8	3
Emmet County	9	0	4	0	5	18	3	12	3	1
Genesee County	158	19	43	6	90	226	137	62	27	2
Gladwin County	2	0	2	0	0	1	0	1	0	0
Gogebic County	7	0	2	0	5	13	2	10	1	0
Grand Traverse County	20	0	15	0	5	40	4	35	1	0
Gratiot County	10	0	5	0	5	19	3	16	0	1
Hillsdale County	69	2	25	0	42	146	54	67	25	1
Houghton County	11	1	3	0	7	50	14	32	4	0
Huron County	13	0	10	0	3	14	1	13	0	0
Ingham County	24	1	12	1	10	40	10	26	4	0
Ionia County	47	0	25	0	22	92	14	66	12	1
Iosco County	38	0	14	0	24	63	20	38	5	2
Iron County	13	0	7	0	6	20	7	9	4	0
Isabella County	33	1	17	1	14	70	32	37	1	1
Jackson County	82	0	19	0	63	133	40	74	19	0
Kalamazoo County	50	0	6	1	43	112	20	76	16	1
Kalkaska County	15	0	10	0	5	25	17	7	1	0
Kent County	30	1	11	2	16	60	0	52	8	0
Lake County	6	0	5	0	1	22	12	10	0	1
Lapeer County	41	0	17	0	24	44	20	20	4	0
Lenawee County	31	0	17	0	14	56	11	30	15	0
Livingston County	59	0	24	1	34	145	28	99	18	1

Table 11. Offenses Known to Law Enforcement, by Selected State, Tribal, and Other Agencies, 2022—Continued

(Number.)

State/other agency unit/office	Violent crime	Murder and nonnegligent manslaughter	Rape	Robbery	Aggravated assault	Property crime	Burglary	Larceny-theft	Motor vehicle theft	Arson[1]
Luce County	12	3	2	0	7	12	2	8	2	0
Mackinac County	8	0	4	0	4	12	8	1	3	0
Macomb County	63	5	10	0	48	39	7	22	10	0
Manistee County	15	0	6	0	9	50	19	28	3	0
Marquette County	65	0	16	0	49	116	28	81	7	4
Mason County	5	0	3	0	2	28	6	20	2	1
Mecosta County	15	0	12	0	3	20	2	16	2	0
Menominee County	12	0	7	0	5	12	4	6	2	0
Midland County	14	0	11	0	3	29	9	17	3	0
Missaukee County	15	0	12	0	3	27	14	11	2	1
Monroe County	54	0	14	2	38	178	128	42	8	0
Montcalm County	85	0	35	0	50	378	194	152	32	3
Muskegon County	86	1	37	0	48	165	26	124	15	3
Newaygo County	66	0	24	0	42	107	30	68	9	0
Oakland County	105	4	24	6	71	200	41	116	43	2
Oceana County	26	0	11	0	15	65	15	41	9	0
Ogemaw County	33	0	15	0	18	25	6	14	5	0
Ontonagon County	5	0	4	0	1	9	0	8	1	0
Osceola County	14	0	10	0	4	17	3	11	3	0
Otsego County	37	0	15	0	22	46	11	28	7	2
Ottawa County	7	0	3	0	4	0	0	0	0	0
Presque Isle County	1	0	0	0	1	4	2	2	0	0
Roscommon County	10	0	3	1	6	64	42	19	3	0
Saginaw County	61	5	18	0	38	91	30	40	21	2
Sanilac County	6	0	5	0	1	18	7	11	0	0
Schoolcraft County	16	0	7	0	9	38	11	23	4	2
Shiawassee County	55	0	16	0	39	123	33	72	18	3
St. Clair County	25	0	9	0	16	39	11	24	4	1
St. Joseph County	40	0	16	0	24	104	33	54	17	4
Tuscola County	46	0	11	0	35	83	43	29	11	0
Van Buren County	90	1	16	2	71	129	27	81	21	4
Washtenaw County	73	0	23	0	50	150	59	70	21	1
Wayne County	166	11	20	4	131	150	0	100	50	1
Wexford County	40	1	15	1	23	85	16	65	4	2
Tribal Agencies										
Bay Mills Tribal	11	0	3	0	8	11	0	10	1	0
Gun Lake Tribal	0	0	0	0	0	104	1	103	0	0
Hannahville Tribal	20	0	4	0	16	53	6	42	5	0
Keweenaw Bay Tribal	1	0	0	0	1	0	0	0	0	0
Little River Band of Ottawa Indians	3	0	3	0	0	27	0	26	1	1
Little Traverse Bay Bands of Odawa Indians	0	0	0	0	0	38	0	38	0	0
Nottawaseppi Huron Band of Potawatomi	9	0	1	0	8	57	2	52	3	0
Pokagon Tribal	1	0	0	1	0	160	0	154	6	0
Saginaw Chippewa Tribal	47	3	14	1	29	163	9	137	17	0
Other Agencies										
Bishop International Airport	0	0	0	0	0	4	0	0	4	0
Capitol Region Airport Authority	0	0	0	0	0	1	0	1	0	0
Genesee County Parks and Recreation	2	0	2	0	0	14	1	12	1	0
Gerald R. Ford International Airport	0	0	0	0	0	32	0	15	17	0
Huron-Clinton Metropolitan Authority										
Hudson Mills Metropark	0	0	0	0	0	1	0	1	0	0
Kensington Metropark	0	0	0	0	0	4	0	4	0	0
Lower Huron Metropark	0	0	0	0	0	10	0	10	0	0
Stony Creek Metropark	0	0	0	0	0	13	0	13	0	0
Wayne County Airport	6	0	0	2	4	302	0	175	127	0
MINNESOTA										
State Agencies										
Bureau of Criminal Apprehension	1	0	0	0	1	0	0	0	0	0
Capitol Security, St. Paul	0	0	0	0	0	1	0	1	0	0
Department of Natural Resources										
Enforcement Division	0	0	0	0	0	1	0	1	0	0
Minnesota Department of Public Safety										
Alcohol and Gambling Enforcement	0	0	0	0	0	1	0	1	0	0
Minnesota State Fair Police	0	0	0	0	0	19	1	18	0	0
Minnesota State Patrol	0	0	0	0	0	0	0	0	0	0
Brainerd	0	0	0	0	0	0	0	0	0	0
Detroit Lakes	0	0	0	0	0	0	0	0	0	0
Duluth	0	0	0	0	0	0	0	0	0	0
Golden Valley	0	0	0	0	0	4	0	4	0	0
Mankato	0	0	0	0	0	0	0	0	0	0
Marshall	0	0	0	0	0	0	0	0	0	0
Oakdale	0	0	0	0	0	5	0	5	0	0
Rochester	0	0	0	0	0	3	0	3	0	0
St. Cloud	0	0	0	0	0	1	0	1	0	0
Thief River Falls	0	0	0	0	0	0	0	0	0	0
Virginia	0	0	0	0	0	2	0	2	0	0
Tribal Agencies										
Fond du Lac Tribal	13	0	2	0	11	45	3	37	5	0
Lower Sioux Tribal	3	0	3	0	0	11	1	6	4	0
Mille Lacs Tribal	21	0	1	1	19	81	13	57	11	0
White Earth Tribal	37	0	5	1	31	128	24	91	13	0

Table 11. Offenses Known to Law Enforcement, by Selected State, Tribal, and Other Agencies, 2022—Continued

(Number.)

State/other agency unit/office	Violent crime	Murder and nonnegligent manslaughter	Rape	Robbery	Aggravated assault	Property crime	Burglary	Larceny-theft	Motor vehicle theft	Arson[1]
Other Agencies										
Metropolitan Transit Commission	319	3	10	136	170	350	6	329	15	31
Minneapolis-St. Paul International Airport	3	0	0	0	3	274	2	234	38	0
Three Rivers Park District	1	0	0	0	1	93	0	93	0	0
MISSISSIPPI										
State Agencies										
Reservoir Police Department	2	0	0	0	2	2	0	1	1	0
Other Agencies										
Forrest General Hospital	0	0	0	0	0	8	1	6	1	0
MISSOURI										
State Agencies										
Department of Revenue, Compliance and Investigation Bureau	0	0	0	0	0	5	0	3	2	0
Department of Social Services, State Technical Assistance Team	21	0	20	0	1	0	0	0	0	0
Division of Alcohol and Tobacco Control	0	0	0	0	0	0	0	0	0	0
Missouri State Highway Patrol	45	1	0	1	43	408	2	172	234	2
State Park Rangers	1	0	0	0	1	16	1	15	0	1
Other Agencies										
Blue Spring Public Schools	0	0	0	0	0	0	0	0	0	0
Jackson County Drug Task Force	0	0	0	0	0	0	0	0	0	0
Jackson County Park Rangers	0	0	0	0	0	0	0	0	0	0
Kansas City International Airport	5	0	0	0	5	529	0	396	133	0
Lambert-St. Louis International Airport	20	0	0	2	18	146	2	131	13	0
St. Louis County Park Rangers	0	0	0	0	0	2	0	2	0	1
Terminal Railroad	0	0	0	0	0	0	0	0	0	0
MONTANA										
Tribal Agencies										
Blackfeet Agency	25	0	1	0	24	50	12	23	15	0
Fort Peck Assiniboine and Sioux Tribes	10	0	0	0	10	6	2	0	4	0
Rocky Boy's Tribal	36	0	1	0	35	36	12	14	10	0
NEBRASKA										
State Agencies										
State Patrol										
Box Butte County	2	1	0	0	1	0	0	0	0	0
Buffalo County	2	0	0	0	2	0	0	0	0	0
Cheyenne County	1	0	0	0	1	0	0	0	0	0
Custer County	1	0	0	0	1	0	0	0	0	0
Dakota County	0	0	0	0	0	0	0	0	0	0
Dawson County	3	0	0	0	3	0	0	0	0	0
Douglas County	4	0	0	0	4	1	0	1	0	0
Hall County	0	0	0	0	0	1	0	0	1	0
Hamilton County	0	0	0	0	0	0	0	0	0	0
Keith County	1	0	0	0	1	0	0	0	0	0
Kimball County	0	0	0	0	0	0	0	0	0	0
Lancaster County	2	0	0	0	2	1	0	1	0	0
Lincoln County	4	0	0	0	4	0	0	0	0	0
Madison County	0	0	0	0	0	1	0	1	0	0
Otoe County	0	0	0	0	0	0	0	0	0	0
Platte County	0	0	0	0	0	0	0	0	0	0
Sarpy County	3	0	0	0	3	0	0	0	0	0
Saunders County	1	0	0	0	1	1	1	0	0	0
York County	2	1	0	0	1	0	0	0	0	0
Tribal Agencies										
Omaha Tribal	20	0	2	0	18	2	2	0	0	2
Santee Tribal	3	0	1	0	2	8	2	1	5	0
Winnebago Tribal	5	0	2	0	3	0	0	0	0	0
NEVADA										
State Agencies										
Attorney General Investigations Division	0	0	0	0	0	0	0	0	0	0
Capitol Police	8	0	0	0	8	45	13	28	4	0
Department of Public Safety, Investigative Division	14	1	6	1	6	6	3	3	0	0
Department of Wildlife, Law Enforcement Division	0	0	0	0	0	2	0	2	0	0
Highway Patrol										
Northwestern Division	29	1	0	0	28	7	0	1	6	0
Southern Division	37	0	1	0	36	10	0	2	8	1
Nevada Gaming Control Board										
Carson City County	0	0	0	0	0	5	0	5	0	0
Clark County	1	0	0	1	0	165	13	152	0	0
Elko County	0	0	0	0	0	8	3	5	0	0
Washoe County	1	0	0	1	0	32	1	31	0	0
State Fire Marshal	0	0	0	0	0	0	0	0	0	10
Tribal Agencies										
Eastern Nevada Agency	3	0	0	0	3	12	2	4	6	0
Lovelock Paiute Tribal	0	0	0	0	0	0	0	0	0	0
Moapa Tribal	1	0	0	1	0	121	0	120	1	0

Table 11. Offenses Known to Law Enforcement, by Selected State, Tribal, and Other Agencies, 2022—Continued

(Number.)

State/other agency unit/office	Violent crime	Murder and nonnegligent manslaughter	Rape	Robbery	Aggravated assault	Property crime	Burglary	Larceny-theft	Motor vehicle theft	Arson[1]
Pyramid Lake Tribal	11	0	1	0	10	15	4	3	8	1
Western Nevada Agency	1	0	0	0	1	4	2	2	0	0
Western Shoshone Tribal	2	0	0	0	2	10	1	6	3	0
Yomba Shoshone Tribal	0	0	0	0	0	0	0	0	0	0
Other Agencies										
City of Las Vegas Department of Public Safety	56	0	0	10	46	276	12	246	18	7
Las Vegas Fire and Rescue, Arson Bomb Unit	0	0	0	0	0	0	0	0	0	33
Reno Municipal Court Marshal	0	0	0	0	0	0	0	0	0	0
Reno Tahoe Airport Authority	0	0	0	0	0	39	0	27	12	0
Washoe County School District	27	0	1	4	22	37	10	27	0	2
NEW HAMPSHIRE										
State Agencies										
Liquor Commission	0	0	0	0	0	6	0	6	0	0
State Police										
Cheshire County	2	0	1	0	1	5	1	3	1	0
Coos County	6	0	3	0	3	25	3	18	4	0
Grafton County	2	0	1	0	1	20	4	15	1	0
Hillsborough County	5	0	0	0	5	1	1	0	0	0
Merrimack County	9	3	4	0	2	11	3	7	1	0
Rockingham County	2	0	0	0	2	1	0	0	1	0
NEW JERSEY										
State Agencies										
Department of Corrections	105	1	0	0	104	0	0	0	0	0
Department of Human Services	2	0	0	0	2	4	0	4	0	0
Division of Fish and Wildlife	0	0	0	0	0	4	0	4	0	0
New Jersey Transit Police	185	1	2	27	155	880	17	858	5	6
Port Authority of New York and New Jersey	72	0	0	16	56	734	18	658	58	1
State Park Police	7	0	1	2	4	64	5	57	2	4
Other Agencies										
Delaware River Port Authority Police Department	15	0	1	2	12	60	1	57	2	0
Park Police, Union County	5	0	0	1	4	49	0	42	7	0
Prosecutor										
Atlantic County	0	0	0	0	0	0	0	0	0	0
Bergen County	0	0	0	0	0	0	0	0	0	0
Burlington County	0	0	0	0	0	0	0	0	0	0
Camden County	0	0	0	0	0	0	0	0	0	0
Cape May County	0	0	0	0	0	0	0	0	0	0
Cumberland County	0	0	0	0	0	0	0	0	0	0
Essex County	0	0	0	0	0	0	0	0	0	0
Gloucester County	0	0	0	0	0	0	0	0	0	0
Hudson County	0	0	0	0	0	0	0	0	0	0
Hunterdon County	1	0	0	0	1	0	0	0	0	0
Mercer County	0	0	0	0	0	0	0	0	0	0
Middlesex County	0	0	0	0	0	0	0	0	0	0
Monmouth County	0	0	0	0	0	0	0	0	0	0
Morris County	0	0	0	0	0	0	0	0	0	0
Ocean County	0	0	0	0	0	0	0	0	0	0
Passaic County	0	0	0	0	0	0	0	0	0	0
Salem County	0	0	0	0	0	0	0	0	0	0
Somerset County	0	0	0	0	0	0	0	0	0	0
Union County	0	0	0	0	0	0	0	0	0	0
Warren County	0	0	0	0	0	0	0	0	0	0
NEW MEXICO										
State Agencies										
New Mexico State Police	546	27	29	22	468	312	9	107	196	7
Tribal Agencies										
Acoma Tribal	10	0	0	0	10	21	1	17	3	0
Isleta Tribal	20	0	0	0	20	56	9	28	19	0
Jemez Pueblo	4	0	1	0	3	2	1	0	1	0
Laguna Tribal	1	0	0	0	1	53	2	36	15	0
Mescalero Tribal	2	0	0	0	2	1	0	1	0	1
Pojoaque Tribal	15	0	2	1	12	61	5	52	4	0
Ramah Navajo Tribal	6	0	0	1	5	1	0	1	0	2
Santa Ana Tribal	3	0	1	1	1	67	3	59	5	0
Santa Clara Pueblo	8	0	2	3	3	38	6	25	7	1
Southern Pueblos Agency	11	0	1	0	10	8	4	1	3	1
Taos Pueblo	0	0	0	0	0	0	0	0	0	0
NEW YORK										
State Agencies										
State Police										
Albany County	42	0	26	5	11	89	7	77	5	1
Allegany County	57	0	28	3	26	161	46	103	12	
Broome County	85	0	30	3	52	385	71	286	28	6
Cattaraugus County	46	0	21	2	23	298	43	234	21	
Cayuga County	39	0	16	3	20	163	25	124	14	2
Chautauqua County	23	0	11	0	12	187	30	147	10	3

Table 11. Offenses Known to Law Enforcement, by Selected State, Tribal, and Other Agencies, 2022—Continued
(Number.)

State/other agency unit/office	Violent crime	Murder and nonnegligent manslaughter	Rape	Robbery	Aggravated assault	Property crime	Burglary	Larceny-theft	Motor vehicle theft	Arson[1]
Chemung County	71	0	27	1	43	232	30	190	12	2
Chenango County	35	0	24	0	11	168	47	116	5	0
Clinton County	115	1	65	5	44	657	74	554	29	7
Columbia County	33	1	12	1	19	230	35	186	9	0
Cortland County	12	0	7	0	5	132	13	115	4	0
Delaware County	41	1	19	1	20	175	39	125	11	
Dutchess County	216	3	39	8	166	441	24	402	15	2
Erie County	55	0	27	0	28	325	18	285	22	1
Essex County	34	0	18	2	14	173	38	127	8	3
Franklin County	75	1	59	1	14	407	84	302	21	5
Fulton County	17	2	11	1	3	67	15	51	1	0
Genesee County	11	0	7	0	4	119	11	106	2	0
Greene County	180	0	8	2	170	205	37	156	12	7
Hamilton County	5	0	5	0	0	19	5	14	0	
Herkimer County	54	0	33	0	21	167	39	113	15	1
Jefferson County	83	1	50	4	28	496	106	373	17	2
Lewis County	17	0	11	0	6	70	17	50	3	0
Livingston County	16	0	14	0	2	18	5	13	0	1
Madison County	33	0	25	1	7	134	18	107	9	0
Monroe County	43	1	32	0	10	49	1	40	8	0
Montgomery County	17	0	12	0	5	83	8	73	2	
Nassau County	15	0	2	6	7	18	2	11	5	0
Niagara County	35	0	13	4	18	206	24	162	20	1
Oneida County	95	0	34	4	57	378	66	265	47	4
Onondaga County	81	1	48	8	24	475	49	382	44	6
Ontario County	53	0	29	3	21	265	36	213	16	
Orange County	102	1	74	2	25	374	22	325	27	
Orleans County	22	0	9	1	12	71	12	54	5	1
Otsego County	41	0	22	0	19	383	62	301	20	2
Putnam County	15	0	8	0	7	70	10	52	8	1
Rensselaer County	38	1	27	4	6	240	24	201	15	
Rockland County	13	0	9	0	4	13	0	12	1	3
Saratoga County	64	0	39	3	22	534	29	486	19	4
Schenectady County	5	0	2	0	3	40	7	33	0	1
Schoharie County	20	1	7	1	11	99	11	83	5	0
Schuyler County	5	0	3	0	2	46	13	26	7	0
Seneca County	28	1	10	0	17	126	13	107	6	0
Steuben County	65	1	45	1	18	378	83	256	39	
St. Lawrence County	65	1	37	3	24	394	93	274	27	
Suffolk County	20	0	8	5	7	23	2	19	2	0
Sullivan County	66	2	32	3	29	234	31	181	22	5
Tioga County	20	0	10	0	10	77	17	55	5	2
Tompkins County	32	0	13	3	16	242	52	177	13	2
Ulster County	71	2	22	0	47	264	32	219	13	0
Warren County	39	0	27	2	10	275	25	242	8	0
Washington County	30	0	16	0	14	134	25	97	12	3
Wayne County	80	2	29	10	39	426	69	337	20	
Westchester County	149	0	22	3	124	518	20	477	21	4
Wyoming County	20	0	3	0	17	42	7	33	2	
Yates County	10	0	9	0	1	17	2	15	0	0
Tribal Agencies										
Oneida Indian Nation	6	0	0	0	6	91	4	83	4	0
St. Regis Tribal	2	0	1	0	1	7	1	5	1	0
Other Agencies										
New York City Department of Environmental Protection Police										
Ashokan Precinct	0	0	0	0	0	0	0	0	0	0
Beerston Precinct	0	0	0	0	0	0	0	0	0	0
Eastview Precinct	0	0	0	0	0	4	0	4	0	0
Gilboa Precinct	0	0	0	0	0	0	0	0	0	0
Grahamsville Precinct	0	0	0	0	0	0	0	0	0	0
Hillview Precinct	0	0	0	0	0	0	0	0	0	0
New York City Metropolitan Transportation Authority	0	0	0	0	0	0	0	0	0	0
Niagara Frontier Transportation Authority	42	1	0	18	23	86	2	73	11	0
Onondaga County Parks	0	0	0	0	0	26	4	22	0	0
NORTH CAROLINA										
State Agencies										
State Capitol Police	8	1	3	1	3	24	11	11	2	2
State Park Rangers										
Elk Knob	0	0	0	0	0	0	0	0	0	0
Eno River	0	0	0	0	0	21	12	9	0	0
Merchants Millpond	0	0	0	0	0	0	0	0	0	0
Raven Rock	0	0	0	0	0	0	0	0	0	0
Tribal Agencies										
Cherokee Tribal	245	2	21	5	217	295	45	223	27	2
Other Agencies										
Moore County Schools	6	0	1	0	5	7	0	7	0	0
North Carolina State Port Authority, Division 1	0	0	0	0	0	0	0	0	0	0
Raleigh-Durham International Airport	6	0	0	2	4	157	1	104	52	0
University of North Carolina Hospitals	1	0	0	0	1	50	1	49	0	0

Table 11. Offenses Known to Law Enforcement, by Selected State, Tribal, and Other Agencies, 2022—Continued

(Number.)

State/other agency unit/office	Violent crime	Murder and nonnegligent manslaughter	Rape	Robbery	Aggravated assault	Property crime	Burglary	Larceny-theft	Motor vehicle theft	Arson[1]
WakeMed Campus Police	20	0	2	2	16	79	9	68	2	0
NORTH DAKOTA										
State Agencies										
North Dakota Bureau of Criminal Investigation	0	0	0	0	0	0	0	0	0	0
North Dakota Highway Patrol	11	0	0	0	11	26	1	5	20	0
Tribal Agencies										
Three Affiliated Tribes	24	0	7	0	17	58	8	22	28	0
OHIO										
State Agencies										
Ohio Department of Natural Resources	35	1	5	2	27	274	7	260	7	7
Ohio Investigative Unit	0	0	0	0	0	0	0	0	0	0
Ohio State Highway Patrol	292	8	46	5	233	178	7	131	40	3
Other Agencies										
Akron Metro Regional Transit Authority	0	0	0	0	0	3	0	3	0	0
Cleveland Metropolitan Park District	20	0	0	3	17	123	2	113	8	1
Hamilton County Park District	3	0	1	0	2	101	10	90	1	0
Mill Creek Metropark	5	0	0	4	1	18	2	15	1	0
OKLAHOMA										
State Agencies										
Capitol Park Police	0	0	0	0	0	0	0	0	0	0
Grand River Dam Authority Lake Patrol	4	0	1	0	3	28	1	25	2	1
Oklahoma Department of Corrections	218	11	77	0	130	0	0	0	0	0
Oklahoma Highway Patrol	0	0	0	0	0	0	0	0	0	0
State Bureau of Investigation	0	0	0	0	0	0	0	0	0	0
State Park Rangers	11	0	3	0	8	73	9	53	11	5
Tribal Agencies										
Absentee Shawnee Tribal	3	0	0	0	3	14	1	11	2	1
Anadarko Agency	2	0	0	2	0	34	5	23	6	0
Cherokee Nation	16	1	3	2	10	23	7	14	2	2
Chickasaw Nation	154	2	24	14	114	1,117	118	997	2	3
Choctaw Nation	59	0	11	0	48	420	46	322	52	8
Citizen Potawatomi Nation	7	0	0	1	6	128	3	120	5	0
Comanche Nation	3	0	0	0	3	87	7	74	6	0
Concho Agency	1	0	0	0	1	16	1	14	1	2
Eastern Shawnee Tribal	1	0	0	0	1	67	1	61	5	0
Iowa Tribal	0	0	0	0	0	15	1	14	0	1
Kaw Tribal	0	0	0	0	0	1	0	1	0	0
Keetoowah Tribal	1	0	0	0	1	5	3	1	1	0
Kickapoo Tribal	3	0	0	0	3	26	3	19	4	0
Miami Agency	3	0	0	1	2	43	0	36	7	0
Miami Tribal	1	0	0	0	1	31	15	15	1	0
Osage Nation	18	2	4	2	10	365	19	229	117	6
Otoe-Missouria Tribal	1	0	0	0	1	5	0	5	0	0
Pawnee Tribal	0	0	0	0	0	4	0	4	0	0
Ponca Tribal	0	0	0	0	0	3	0	2	1	0
Quapaw Tribal	25	1	2	3	19	249	32	201	16	7
Sac and Fox Tribal	1	0	0	0	1	21	2	14	5	0
Seminole Nation Lighthorse	17	3	1	0	13	64	11	35	18	7
Tonkawa Tribal	2	0	0	0	2	15	3	10	2	0
Wyandotte Nation	4	0	1	0	3	22	6	16	0	0
Other Agencies										
Beggs Public Schools	0	0	0	0	0	1	0	1	0	0
District 1 Narcotics Task Force	0	0	0	0	0	0	0	0	0	0
District 8 Narcotics Task Force	1	0	0	0	1	1	0	1	0	0
Jenks Public Schools	0	0	0	0	0	1	0	1	0	1
Lawton Public Schools	12	0	2	0	10	22	0	22	0	0
Muskogee City Schools	9	0	1	0	8	2	0	1	1	1
Okmulgee County Criminal Justice Authority	3	0	0	0	3	0	0	0	0	0
Putnam City Campus	2	0	0	0	2	31	1	30	0	0
Victory Life	0	0	0	0	0	0	0	0	0	0
OREGON										
State Agencies										
Liquor Commission										
Baker County	0	0	0	0	0	0	0	0	0	0
Benton County	0	0	0	0	0	0	0	0	0	0
Clatsop County	0	0	0	0	0	0	0	0	0	0
Columbia County	0	0	0	0	0	0	0	0	0	0
Coos County	0	0	0	0	0	0	0	0	0	0
Crook County	0	0	0	0	0	0	0	0	0	0
Deschutes County	0	0	0	0	0	0	0	0	0	0
Douglas County	0	0	0	0	0	0	0	0	0	0
Gilliam County	0	0	0	0	0	0	0	0	0	0
Grant County	0	0	0	0	0	0	0	0	0	0
Hood River County	0	0	0	0	0	0	0	0	0	0
Klamath County	0	0	0	0	0	0	0	0	0	0
Lane County	0	0	0	0	0	0	0	0	0	0
Lincoln County	0	0	0	0	0	0	0	0	0	0
Marion County	0	0	0	0	0	0	0	0	0	0

Table 11. Offenses Known to Law Enforcement, by Selected State, Tribal, and Other Agencies, 2022—Continued

(Number.)

State/other agency unit/office	Violent crime	Murder and nonnegligent manslaughter	Rape	Robbery	Aggravated assault	Property crime	Burglary	Larceny-theft	Motor vehicle theft	Arson[1]
Multnomah County	0	0	0	0	0	0	0	0	0	0
Polk County	0	0	0	0	0	0	0	0	0	0
Sherman County	0	0	0	0	0	0	0	0	0	0
Umatilla County	0	0	0	0	0	0	0	0	0	0
Washington County	0	0	0	0	0	0	0	0	0	0
Wheeler County	0	0	0	0	0	0	0	0	0	0
Yamhill County	0	0	0	0	0	0	0	0	0	0
State Police										
Baker County	3	0	0	0	3	6	1	4	1	1
Clackamas County	27	0	1	0	26	22	1	13	8	0
Clatsop County	4	0	0	0	4	11	0	9	2	0
Columbia County	9	0	0	0	9	9	0	6	3	0
Coos County	4	0	0	0	4	55	5	47	3	0
Curry County	4	0	1	0	3	27	1	26	0	0
Deschutes County	6	0	3	0	3	10	1	5	4	2
Douglas County	32	0	1	1	30	38	1	28	9	0
Grant County	1	0	0	0	1	5	1	2	2	0
Harney County	7	0	0	0	7	5	1	4	0	0
Hood River County	2	0	0	0	2	6	1	4	1	0
Jackson County	9	0	0	3	6	32	1	26	5	1
Jefferson County	6	0	0	0	6	1	1	0	0	0
Josephine County	28	3	6	0	19	13	1	7	5	1
Klamath County	27	0	1	0	26	22	0	15	7	3
Lane County	32	0	2	1	29	67	2	56	9	2
Lincoln County	3	0	0	0	3	42	1	39	2	2
Linn County	14	0	0	0	14	24	0	19	5	0
Malheur County	18	0	0	0	18	8	0	8	0	2
Marion County	56	0	5	3	48	93	10	67	16	7
Multnomah County	0	0	0	0	0	16	0	13	3	0
Polk County	2	0	0	0	2	8	0	6	2	1
Tillamook County	4	0	0	0	4	35	2	31	2	0
Umatilla County	25	0	1	0	24	12	2	7	3	0
Union County	4	1	0	1	2	3	0	2	1	0
Wasco County	21	0	0	1	20	10	2	5	3	0
Washington County	9	0	0	0	9	6	0	2	4	0
Yamhill County	1	0	0	0	1	3	0	2	1	0
Tribal Agencies										
Burns Paiute Tribal	2	0	0	0	2	1	0	0	1	0
Columbia River Inter-Tribal Fisheries Enforcement	3	0	0	0	3	1	1	0	0	0
Coos, Lower Umpqua, and Siuslaw Tribal	0	0	0	0	0	21	2	19	0	0
Coquille Tribal	0	0	0	0	0	2	0	2	0	0
Cow Creek Tribal	2	0	1	1	0	42	1	41	0	0
Grand Ronde Tribal	11	0	2	0	9	74	2	64	8	0
Umatilla Tribal	4	1	0	2	1	13	13	0	0	0
Other Agencies										
Hillsboro School District	0	0	0	0	0	0	0	0	0	0
Port of Portland	15	1	1	4	9	868	2	684	182	3
PENNSYLVANIA[2]										
State Agencies										
Bureau of Forestry										
Adams County	0	0	0	0	0	0	0	0	0	2
Allegheny County	0	0	0	0	0	0	0	0	0	0
Armstrong County	0	0	0	0	0	0	0	0	0	0
Beaver County	0	0	0	0	0	0	0	0	0	0
Bedford County	0	0	0	0	0	0	0	0	0	0
Berks County	0	0	0	0	0	0	0	0	0	3
Blair County	0	0	0	0	0	0	0	0	0	2
Bradford County	0	0	0	0	0	0	0	0	0	1
Bucks County	0	0	0	0	0	0	0	0	0	2
Butler County	0	0	0	0	0	0	0	0	0	0
Cambria County	0	0	0	0	0	0	0	0	0	2
Cameron County	0	0	0	0	0	0	0	0	0	0
Carbon County	0	0	0	0	0	0	0	0	0	7
Centre County	0	0	0	0	0	0	0	0	0	8
Chester County	0	0	0	0	0	0	0	0	0	2
Clarion County	0	0	0	0	0	0	0	0	0	0
Clearfield County	0	0	0	0	0	0	0	0	0	1
Clinton County	0	0	0	0	0	0	0	0	0	1
Columbia County	0	0	0	0	0	0	0	0	0	0
Crawford County	0	0	0	0	0	0	0	0	0	0
Cumberland County	0	0	0	0	0	0	0	0	0	1
Dauphin County	0	0	0	0	0	0	0	0	0	2
Delaware County	0	0	0	0	0	0	0	0	0	0
Elk County	0	0	0	0	0	0	0	0	0	0
Erie County	0	0	0	0	0	0	0	0	0	2
Fayette County	0	0	0	0	0	0	0	0	0	1
Forest County	0	0	0	0	0	0	0	0	0	0
Franklin County	0	0	0	0	0	0	0	0	0	1
Fulton County	0	0	0	0	0	0	0	0	0	0
Greene County	0	0	0	0	0	0	0	0	0	0
Huntingdon County	0	0	0	0	0	0	0	0	0	0

Table 11. Offenses Known to Law Enforcement, by Selected State, Tribal, and Other Agencies, 2022—Continued

(Number.)

State/other agency unit/office	Violent crime	Murder and nonnegligent manslaughter	Rape	Robbery	Aggravated assault	Property crime	Burglary	Larceny-theft	Motor vehicle theft	Arson[1]
Indiana County	0	0	0	0	0	0	0	0	0	7
Jefferson County	0	0	0	0	0	0	0	0	0	0
Juniata County	0	0	0	0	0	0	0	0	0	1
Lackawanna County	0	0	0	0	0	0	0	0	0	3
Lancaster County	0	0	0	0	0	0	0	0	0	8
Lawrence County	0	0	0	0	0	0	0	0	0	1
Lebanon County	0	0	0	0	0	0	0	0	0	0
Lehigh County	0	0	0	0	0	0	0	0	0	0
Luzerne County	0	0	0	0	0	0	0	0	0	13
Lycoming County	0	0	0	0	0	0	0	0	0	0
McKean County	0	0	0	0	0	0	0	0	0	0
Mercer County	0	0	0	0	0	0	0	0	0	0
Mifflin County	0	0	0	0	0	0	0	0	0	0
Monroe County	0	0	0	0	0	0	0	0	0	4
Montgomery	0	0	0	0	0	0	0	0	0	0
Montour County	0	0	0	0	0	0	0	0	0	0
Northampton County	0	0	0	0	0	0	0	0	0	4
Northumberland County	0	0	0	0	0	0	0	0	0	0
Perry County	0	0	0	0	0	0	0	0	0	1
Philadelphia County	0	0	0	0	0	0	0	0	0	0
Pike County	0	0	0	0	0	0	0	0	0	1
Potter County	0	0	0	0	0	0	0	0	0	0
Schuylkill County	0	0	0	0	0	0	0	0	0	42
Snyder County	0	0	0	0	0	0	0	0	0	1
Somerset County	0	0	0	0	0	0	0	0	0	0
Sullivan County	0	0	0	0	0	0	0	0	0	0
Susquehanna County	0	0	0	0	0	0	0	0	0	0
Tioga County	0	0	0	0	0	0	0	0	0	0
Union County	0	0	0	0	0	0	0	0	0	0
Venango County	0	0	0	0	0	0	0	0	0	0
Warren County	0	0	0	0	0	0	0	0	0	3
Washington County	0	0	0	0	0	0	0	0	0	0
Wayne County	0	0	0	0	0	0	0	0	0	0
Westmoreland County	0	0	0	0	0	0	0	0	0	0
Wyoming County	0	0	0	0	0	0	0	0	0	0
York County	0	0	0	0	0	0	0	0	0	0
State Park Rangers										
Hills Creek	0	0	0	0	0	0	0	0	0	0
Jacobsburg Environmental Education Center	0	0	0	0	0	0	0	0	0	0
Leonard Harrison	0	0	0	0	0	0	0	0	0	0
Little Pine	0	0	0	0	0	0	0	0	0	0
Lyman Run	0	0	0	0	0	3	1	2	0	0
Maurice K. Goddard	0	0	0	0	0	0	0	0	0	0
Oil Creek	0	0	0	0	0	0	0	0	0	0
Ole Bull	0	0	0	0	0	0	0	0	0	0
Samuel S. Lewis	0	0	0	0	0	1	0	1	0	0
Shikellamy	0	0	0	0	0	0	0	0	0	0
Tuscarora	0	0	0	0	0	7	0	7	0	0
Worlds End	0	0	0	0	0	0	0	0	0	0
State Police										
Adams County	54	0	19	0	35	299	43	241	15	3
Allegheny County	43	1	5	5	32	179	20	120	39	2
Armstrong County	61	2	21	2	36	256	52	190	14	0
Beaver County	31	2	8	3	18	41	8	31	2	0
Bedford County	61	3	21	2	35	368	73	270	25	2
Berks County	68	2	20	6	40	345	65	227	53	4
Blair County	19	1	13	0	5	178	38	123	17	0
Bradford County	39	0	18	1	20	185	51	122	12	1
Bucks County	27	0	9	1	17	280	26	230	24	0
Butler County	55	1	26	3	25	248	26	196	26	2
Cambria County	30	0	8	3	19	120	44	62	14	14
Cameron County	4	0	0	1	3	19	6	12	1	0
Carbon County	26	2	7	1	16	163	28	122	13	2
Centre County	37	1	19	1	16	279	49	211	19	2
Chester County	135	0	54	14	67	769	106	626	37	1
Clarion County	26	0	5	1	20	221	52	155	14	1
Clearfield County	44	0	15	3	26	330	88	220	22	2
Clinton County	17	0	6	2	9	122	19	100	3	1
Columbia County	17	3	6	1	7	81	21	56	4	1
Crawford County	65	0	27	0	38	456	100	320	36	6
Cumberland County	82	5	21	3	53	385	48	320	17	8
Delaware County	70	2	11	8	49	609	33	523	53	8
Elizabethville	102	0	42	6	54	520	70	420	30	2
Elk County	13	0	6	1	6	83	14	66	3	1
Erie County	98	0	39	4	55	1,253	128	1,073	52	1
Fayette County	175	3	46	12	114	1,136	180	897	59	23
Franklin County	120	2	35	9	74	621	76	524	21	3
Fulton County	21	0	6	0	15	160	25	125	10	1
Greene County	30	0	10	2	18	176	30	113	33	1
Huntingdon County	63	0	21	0	42	272	54	188	30	2
Indiana County	47	1	25	1	20	499	72	403	24	2
Jefferson County	29	0	12	0	17	155	43	101	11	2
Juniata County	35	0	18	0	17	127	40	81	6	0

Table 11. Offenses Known to Law Enforcement, by Selected State, Tribal, and Other Agencies, 2022—Continued

(Number.)

State/other agency unit/office	Violent crime	Murder and nonnegligent manslaughter	Rape	Robbery	Aggravated assault	Property crime	Burglary	Larceny-theft	Motor vehicle theft	Arson[1]
Lackawanna County	26	1	6	1	18	80	19	58	3	7
Lancaster County	98	4	43	4	47	452	78	340	34	5
Lawrence County	14	2	4	0	8	92	20	67	5	0
Lebanon County	25	0	16	2	7	184	33	125	26	3
Lehigh County	55	0	19	6	30	671	57	568	46	2
Luzerne County	52	3	19	3	27	681	178	487	16	11
Lycoming County	69	3	25	3	38	408	45	346	17	0
McKean County	18	0	10	0	8	73	13	54	6	2
Mercer County	42	0	13	2	27	203	29	161	13	0
Mifflin County	21	1	4	1	15	70	23	43	4	1
Monroe County	84	1	23	13	47	570	135	397	38	3
Montour County	15	1	4	0	10	52	9	40	3	0
Northampton County	15	0	5	1	9	267	16	236	15	2
Northumberland County	33	1	15	2	15	176	52	107	17	2
Perry County	62	0	21	2	39	262	48	197	17	3
Philadelphia County	36	1	10	0	25	196	38	144	14	1
Pike County	13	0	3	0	10	69	16	50	3	0
Potter County	72	0	19	4	49	490	98	353	39	6
Schuylkill County	24	1	10	4	9	215	25	172	18	7
Skippack	61	1	11	4	45	247	35	193	19	7
Snyder County	60	1	20	3	36	372	88	254	30	0
Somerset County	5	0	2	1	2	38	17	20	1	0
Sullivan County	31	0	19	1	11	236	65	139	32	6
Susquehanna County	26	2	8	1	15	226	75	126	25	1
Tioga County	23	0	9	0	14	150	28	110	12	0
Tionesta	19	0	6	0	13	40	10	28	2	2
Union County	28	1	17	2	8	201	33	155	13	3
Venango County	22	1	10	0	11	155	40	100	15	2
Warren County	54	1	16	3	34	311	53	224	34	8
Washington County	38	0	18	1	19	277	55	204	18	1
Wayne County	175	0	58	11	106	761	106	610	45	14
Westmoreland County	9	0	3	0	6	75	17	56	2	0
Wyoming County	86	7	30	7	42	369	54	293	22	3
York County	52	3	3	9	37	237	1	219	17	0
County Detective										
Montgomery County	11	0	0	0	11	8	0	8	0	0
Wayne County	9	0	3	0	6	5	0	5	0	0
Westmoreland County	3	0	0	0	3	71	0	71	0	0
Franklin County Drug Task Force	0	0	0	0	0	0	0	0	0	0
RHODE ISLAND										
State Agencies										
Department of Environmental Management	2	0	0	1	1	4	1	3	0	3
Rhode Island State Police Headquarters	29	1	23	0	5	42	0	38	4	0
State Police										
Hope Valley	2	1	1	0	0	23	1	15	7	0
Lincoln	25	0	6	2	17	44	1	24	19	3
Scituate	6	0	2	1	3	21	0	11	10	0
Wickford	5	0	2	1	2	12	0	9	3	0
Tribal Agencies										
Narragansett Tribal	0	0	0	0	0	0	0	0	0	0
Other Agencies										
T.F. Green International Airport	0	0	0	0	0	35	0	29	6	0
SOUTH CAROLINA										
State Agencies										
Department of Health and Environmental Control Drug Control, Horry County	0	0	0	0	0	5	1	4	0	0
Department of Mental Health	5	0	0	1	4	4	0	4	0	0
Department of Natural Resources										
Abbeville County	0	0	0	0	0	0	0	0	0	0
Aiken County	0	0	0	0	0	0	0	0	0	0
Allendale County	0	0	0	0	0	0	0	0	0	0
Anderson County	0	0	0	0	0	0	0	0	0	0
Bamberg County	0	0	0	0	0	0	0	0	0	0
Barnwell County	0	0	0	0	0	0	0	0	0	0
Beaufort County	0	0	0	0	0	0	0	0	0	0
Berkeley County	0	0	0	0	0	0	0	0	0	0
Calhoun County	0	0	0	0	0	0	0	0	0	0
Charleston County	0	0	0	0	0	0	0	0	0	0
Cherokee County	0	0	0	0	0	0	0	0	0	0
Chester County	0	0	0	0	0	0	0	0	0	0
Chesterfield County	0	0	0	0	0	0	0	0	0	0
Clarendon County	0	0	0	0	0	0	0	0	0	0
Colleton County	0	0	0	0	0	0	0	0	0	0
Darlington County	0	0	0	0	0	0	0	0	0	0
Dillon County	0	0	0	0	0	0	0	0	0	0
Dorchester County	0	0	0	0	0	0	0	0	0	0
Edgefield County	0	0	0	0	0	0	0	0	0	0
Fairfield County	0	0	0	0	0	0	0	0	0	0
Florence County	0	0	0	0	0	0	0	0	0	0
Georgetown County	0	0	0	0	0	0	0	0	0	0
Greenville County	0	0	0	0	0	0	0	0	0	0

Table 11. Offenses Known to Law Enforcement, by Selected State, Tribal, and Other Agencies, 2022—Continued

(Number.)

State/other agency unit/office	Violent crime	Murder and nonnegligent manslaughter	Rape	Robbery	Aggravated assault	Property crime	Burglary	Larceny-theft	Motor vehicle theft	Arson[1]
Greenwood County	0	0	0	0	0	0	0	0	0	0
Hampton County	0	0	0	0	0	0	0	0	0	0
Horry County	0	0	0	0	0	0	0	0	0	0
Jasper County	0	0	0	0	0	0	0	0	0	0
Kershaw County	0	0	0	0	0	0	0	0	0	0
Lancaster County	0	0	0	0	0	0	0	0	0	0
Laurens County	0	0	0	0	0	0	0	0	0	0
Lee County	0	0	0	0	0	0	0	0	0	0
Lexington County	0	0	0	0	0	0	0	0	0	0
Marion County	0	0	0	0	0	0	0	0	0	0
Marlboro County	0	0	0	0	0	0	0	0	0	0
McCormick County	0	0	0	0	0	0	0	0	0	0
Newberry County	0	0	0	0	0	0	0	0	0	0
Oconee County	0	0	0	0	0	0	0	0	0	0
Orangeburg County	0	0	0	0	0	0	0	0	0	0
Pickens County	0	0	0	0	0	0	0	0	0	0
Richland County	0	0	0	0	0	0	0	0	0	0
Saluda County	0	0	0	0	0	0	0	0	0	0
Spartanburg County	0	0	0	0	0	0	0	0	0	0
Sumter County	0	0	0	0	0	0	0	0	0	0
Union County	0	0	0	0	0	0	0	0	0	0
Williamsburg County	0	0	0	0	0	0	0	0	0	0
York County	0	0	0	0	0	0	0	0	0	0
Forestry Commission										
Abbeville County	0	0	0	0	0	0	0	0	0	0
Aiken County	0	0	0	0	0	0	0	0	0	0
Allendale County	0	0	0	0	0	0	0	0	0	0
Anderson County	0	0	0	0	0	0	0	0	0	0
Bamberg County	0	0	0	0	0	0	0	0	0	0
Barnwell County	0	0	0	0	0	0	0	0	0	0
Beaufort County	0	0	0	0	0	0	0	0	0	0
Berkeley County	0	0	0	0	0	0	0	0	0	0
Calhoun County	0	0	0	0	0	0	0	0	0	0
Charleston County	0	0	0	0	0	0	0	0	0	0
Cherokee County	0	0	0	0	0	0	0	0	0	0
Chester County	0	0	0	0	0	0	0	0	0	0
Chesterfield County	0	0	0	0	0	0	0	0	0	0
Clarendon County	0	0	0	0	0	0	0	0	0	0
Colleton County	0	0	0	0	0	0	0	0	0	0
Darlington County	0	0	0	0	0	0	0	0	0	0
Dillon County	0	0	0	0	0	0	0	0	0	0
Dorchester County	0	0	0	0	0	0	0	0	0	0
Edgefield County	0	0	0	0	0	0	0	0	0	0
Fairfield County	0	0	0	0	0	0	0	0	0	0
Florence County	0	0	0	0	0	0	0	0	0	0
Georgetown County	0	0	0	0	0	0	0	0	0	0
Greenville County	0	0	0	0	0	0	0	0	0	0
Greenwood County	0	0	0	0	0	0	0	0	0	0
Hampton County	0	0	0	0	0	0	0	0	0	0
Horry County	0	0	0	0	0	0	0	0	0	0
Jasper County	0	0	0	0	0	0	0	0	0	0
Kershaw County	0	0	0	0	0	0	0	0	0	0
Lancaster County	0	0	0	0	0	0	0	0	0	0
Laurens County	0	0	0	0	0	0	0	0	0	0
Lee County	0	0	0	0	0	0	0	0	0	0
Lexington County	0	0	0	0	0	0	0	0	0	0
Marion County	0	0	0	0	0	0	0	0	0	0
Marlboro County	0	0	0	0	0	0	0	0	0	0
McCormick County	0	0	0	0	0	0	0	0	0	0
Newberry County	0	0	0	0	0	0	0	0	0	0
Oconee County	0	0	0	0	0	0	0	0	0	0
Orangeburg County	0	0	0	0	0	0	0	0	0	0
Pickens County	0	0	0	0	0	0	0	0	0	0
Richland County	0	0	0	0	0	0	0	0	0	0
Saluda County	0	0	0	0	0	0	0	0	0	0
Spartanburg County	0	0	0	0	0	0	0	0	0	0
Sumter County	0	0	0	0	0	0	0	0	0	0
Union County	0	0	0	0	0	0	0	0	0	0
Williamsburg County	0	0	0	0	0	0	0	0	0	0
York County	0	0	0	0	0	0	0	0	0	0
Highway Patrol										
Abbeville County	0	0	0	0	0	0	0	0	0	0
Aiken County	0	0	0	0	0	0	0	0	0	0
Allendale County	0	0	0	0	0	0	0	0	0	0
Anderson County	0	0	0	0	0	0	0	0	0	0
Bamberg County	0	0	0	0	0	0	0	0	0	0
Barnwell County	0	0	0	0	0	0	0	0	0	0
Beaufort County	0	0	0	0	0	0	0	0	0	0
Berkeley County	0	0	0	0	0	0	0	0	0	0
Calhoun County	0	0	0	0	0	0	0	0	0	0
Charleston County	0	0	0	0	0	0	0	0	0	0
Cherokee County	0	0	0	0	0	0	0	0	0	0
Chester County	0	0	0	0	0	0	0	0	0	0

Table 11. Offenses Known to Law Enforcement, by Selected State, Tribal, and Other Agencies, 2022—Continued

(Number.)

State/other agency unit/office	Violent crime	Murder and nonnegligent manslaughter	Rape	Robbery	Aggravated assault	Property crime	Burglary	Larceny-theft	Motor vehicle theft	Arson[1]
Chesterfield County	0	0	0	0	0	0	0	0	0	0
Clarendon County	0	0	0	0	0	0	0	0	0	0
Colleton County	0	0	0	0	0	0	0	0	0	0
Darlington County	0	0	0	0	0	0	0	0	0	0
Dillon County	0	0	0	0	0	0	0	0	0	0
Dorchester County	0	0	0	0	0	0	0	0	0	0
Edgefield County	0	0	0	0	0	0	0	0	0	0
Fairfield County	0	0	0	0	0	0	0	0	0	0
Florence County	0	0	0	0	0	0	0	0	0	0
Georgetown County	0	0	0	0	0	0	0	0	0	0
Greenville County	0	0	0	0	0	0	0	0	0	0
Greenwood County	0	0	0	0	0	0	0	0	0	0
Hampton County	0	0	0	0	0	0	0	0	0	0
Horry County	0	0	0	0	0	0	0	0	0	0
Jasper County	0	0	0	0	0	0	0	0	0	0
Kershaw County	0	0	0	0	0	0	0	0	0	0
Lancaster County	0	0	0	0	0	0	0	0	0	0
Laurens County	0	0	0	0	0	0	0	0	0	0
Lee County	0	0	0	0	0	0	0	0	0	0
Lexington County	0	0	0	0	0	0	0	0	0	0
Marion County	0	0	0	0	0	0	0	0	0	0
Marlboro County	0	0	0	0	0	0	0	0	0	0
McCormick County	0	0	0	0	0	0	0	0	0	0
Newberry County	0	0	0	0	0	0	0	0	0	0
Oconee County	0	0	0	0	0	0	0	0	0	0
Orangeburg County	0	0	0	0	0	0	0	0	0	0
Pickens County	0	0	0	0	0	0	0	0	0	0
Richland County	0	0	0	0	0	0	0	0	0	0
Saluda County	0	0	0	0	0	0	0	0	0	0
Spartanburg County	0	0	0	0	0	0	0	0	0	0
Sumter County	0	0	0	0	0	0	0	0	0	0
Union County	0	0	0	0	0	0	0	0	0	0
Williamsburg County	0	0	0	0	0	0	0	0	0	0
York County	0	0	0	0	0	0	0	0	0	0
Santee Cooper	0	0	0	0	0	0	0	0	0	0
South Carolina School for the Deaf and Blind	0	0	0	0	0	0	0	0	0	0
State Museum	0	0	0	0	0	0	0	0	0	0
State Ports Authority	0	0	0	0	0	0	0	0	0	0
Other Agencies										
Atlantic Railways	0	0	0	0	0	1	0	1	0	0
Charleston County Aviation Authority	2	0	0	0	2	55	0	19	36	0
Columbia Metropolitan Airport	0	0	0	0	0	13	1	10	2	0
Florence Regional Airport	0	0	0	0	0	4	1	3	0	0
Greenville Hospital, Greenville	1	0	0	0	1	57	1	55	1	0
Greenville-Spartanburg International Airport	0	0	0	0	0	40	0	20	20	0
Lexington County Medical Center	1	0	0	1	0	45	2	43	0	0
SOUTH DAKOTA										
State Agencies										
Highway Patrol	12	0	0	0	12	11	0	8	3	0
Tribal Agencies										
Cheyenne River Tribal	82	3	10	0	69	23	5	13	5	2
Crow Creek Tribal	38	0	1	1	36	21	5	5	11	1
Flandreau Santee Sioux Tribal	4	0	0	0	4	7	1	6	0	0
Lower Brule Tribal	15	0	1	0	14	21	4	8	9	0
Pine Ridge Sioux Tribal	77	13	8	1	55	40	4	24	12	1
Rosebud Tribal	273	2	38	1	232	273	86	129	58	4
Sisseton-Wahpeton Tribal	29	0	4	0	25	58	20	26	12	1
TENNESSEE										
State Agencies										
Alcoholic Beverage Commission	0	0	0	0	0	0	0	0	0	0
Department of Safety	114	0	0	0	114	97	2	21	74	1
TennCare Office of Inspector General	0	0	0	0	0	0	0	0	0	0
Tennessee Bureau of Investigation	10	0	0	0	10	4	0	4	0	11
Other Agencies										
Drug Task Force										
2nd Judicial District	0	0	0	0	0	0	0	0	0	0
3rd Judicial District	0	0	0	0	0	0	0	0	0	0
4th Judicial District	0	0	0	0	0	0	0	0	0	0
5th Judicial District	0	0	0	0	0	0	0	0	0	0
9th Judicial District	0	0	0	0	0	1	0	1	0	0
10th Judicial District	0	0	0	0	0	0	0	0	0	0
12th Judicial District	3	0	0	0	3	1	0	0	1	0
18th Judicial District	0	0	0	0	0	0	0	0	0	0
19th Judicial District	0	0	0	0	0	1	0	1	0	0
23rd Judicial District	0	0	0	0	0	0	0	0	0	0
24th Judicial District	0	0	0	0	0	0	0	0	0	0
Knoxville Metropolitan Airport	0	0	0	0	0	14	0	14	0	0
Memphis-Shelby County Airport Authority	3	0	0	1	2	523	2	336	185	0
Metropolitan Nashville Park Police	5	0	0	1	4	74	5	68	1	0
Nashville International Airport	2	0	1	0	1	130	3	94	33	0

Table 11. Offenses Known to Law Enforcement, by Selected State, Tribal, and Other Agencies, 2022—Continued
(Number.)

State/other agency unit/office	Violent crime	Murder and nonnegligent manslaughter	Rape	Robbery	Aggravated assault	Property crime	Burglary	Larceny-theft	Motor vehicle theft	Arson[1]
West Tennessee Violent Crime Task Force	0	0	0	0	0	0	0	0	0	0
TEXAS										
Tribal Agencies										
Ysleta del Sur Pueblo Tribal	2	0	2	0	0	13	2	11	0	0
Other Agencies										
Amarillo International Airport	1	0	0	0	1	6	0	6	0	0
Dallas-Fort Worth International Airport	26	0	1	5	20	769	6	648	115	1
Ector County Hospital District	0	0	0	0	0	14	2	12	0	0
Elm Ridge	9	0	2	0	7	72	5	58	9	0
Hidalgo County Constable, Precinct 1	1	0	0	0	1	0	0	0	0	0
Hospital District, Tarrant County	4	0	0	1	3	67	0	62	5	0
Houston Metropolitan Transit Authority	8	0	1	1	6	103	1	95	7	0
Independent School District										
Aldine	34	0	2	4	28	168	8	148	12	5
Alief	1	0	0	0	1	55	9	32	14	0
Alvin	4	0	1	1	2	53	2	50	1	0
Angleton	3	0	0	0	3	4	1	3	0	0
Anna	1	0	1	0	0	1	0	1	0	0
Aubrey	0	0	0	0	0	0	0	0	0	0
Austin	15	0	4	3	8	108	24	78	6	0
Barbers Hill	1	0	1	0	0	13	1	12	0	0
Bastrop	64	0	23	0	41	10	3	6	1	0
Bay City	22	0	0	0	22	11	0	11	0	0
Blooming Grove	0	0	0	0	0	0	0	0	0	0
Brazosport	4	0	0	0	4	11	0	11	0	0
Brownsboro	2	0	0	0	2	2	1	1	0	0
Brownsville	17	0	0	0	17	87	3	84	0	0
Burkburnett	0	0	0	0	0	5	0	5	0	0
Calhoun County	0	0	0	0	0	1	0	1	0	0
Castleberry	0	0	0	0	0	0	0	0	0	0
Centerpoint	0	0	0	0	0	0	0	0	0	0
Columbia-Brazoria	4	0	2	0	2	3	1	2	0	0
Conroe	10	0	3	0	7	98	3	95	0	2
Corsicana	0	0	0	0	0	1	0	1	0	0
Crowley	4	0	1	0	3	22	2	20	0	1
Dumas	2	0	0	1	1	5	2	3	0	0
Ector County	21	0	0	2	19	31	4	26	1	2
Edinburg	2	0	2	0	0	9	0	9	0	0
El Paso	17	0	4	2	11	78	14	63	1	1
Floresville	2	0	0	0	2	8	0	8	0	1
Fort Bend	54	0	15	5	34	128	8	119	1	3
Gonzales	0	0	0	0	0	0	0	0	0	0
Hallsville	0	0	0	0	0	0	0	0	0	0
Houston	94	0	45	9	40	352	54	277	21	13
Hudson	0	0	0	0	0	0	0	0	0	0
Humble	5	0	1	1	3	54	1	48	5	0
Huntington	0	0	0	0	0	0	0	0	0	0
Hutto	0	0	0	0	0	8	2	5	1	1
Idalou	0	0	0	0	0	0	0	0	0	0
Jonesboro	0	0	0	0	0	0	0	0	0	0
Judson	20	0	4	0	16	81	2	79	0	1
Katy	62	0	0	2	60	213	3	210	0	2
Killeen	6	0	1	1	4	17	6	10	1	0
Klein	28	0	13	6	9	148	3	139	6	3
Lamar Consolidated	8	0	1	0	7	14	3	11	0	0
Lancaster	1	0	1	0	0	16	1	15	0	0
Laredo	6	0	0	0	6	3	0	3	0	1
Lufkin	1	0	0	0	1	12	0	12	0	1
Lyford	0	0	0	0	0	0	0	0	0	0
Malakoff	0	0	0	0	0	0	0	0	0	0
Mansfield	4	0	0	1	3	22	2	20	0	0
Marlin	1	0	1	0	0	0	0	0	0	0
McAllen	4	0	0	0	4	44	0	43	1	0
Midland	7	0	1	0	6	5	2	2	1	1
Montgomery County	1	0	1	0	0	4	0	4	0	0
Nacogdoches	0	0	0	0	0	15	2	12	1	0
Northside	12	0	4	0	8	0	0	0	0	0
Pasadena	3	0	0	0	3	78	7	65	6	0
Pecos Barstow Toyah	0	0	0	0	0	3	0	2	1	0
Pflugerville	3	0	1	0	2	7	1	6	0	1
Pleasanton	0	0	0	0	0	1	1	0	0	0
Rio Grande City	0	0	0	0	0	6	0	6	0	0
Roma	0	0	0	0	0	1	0	1	0	0
Round Rock	4	0	1	0	3	54	11	42	1	0
Royal	0	0	0	0	0	7	0	7	0	0
San Antonio	10	0	1	7	2	164	36	120	8	4
Santa Fe	1	0	1	0	0	6	0	6	0	0
Santa Rosa	0	0	0	0	0	0	0	0	0	0
Sealy	0	0	0	0	0	2	0	2	0	0
Socorro	24	0	5	1	18	20	2	16	2	1
Spring	8	0	1	2	5	27	1	26	0	1
Spring Branch	2	0	0	0	2	35	1	34	0	0

Table 11. Offenses Known to Law Enforcement, by Selected State, Tribal, and Other Agencies, 2022—Continued
(Number.)

State/other agency unit/office	Violent crime	Murder and nonnegligent manslaughter	Rape	Robbery	Aggravated assault	Property crime	Burglary	Larceny-theft	Motor vehicle theft	Arson[1]
Taft	0	0	0	0	0	0	0	0	0	0
Terrell	2	0	0	0	2	6	1	5	0	0
Trinity	0	0	0	0	0	0	0	0	0	0
United	0	0	0	0	0	0	0	0	0	0
Van Vleck	0	0	0	0	0	0	0	0	0	0
Vensus	2	0	1	0	1	3	0	3	0	0
Warren	1	0	0	0	1	0	0	0	0	0
Wharton	0	0	0	0	0	0	0	0	0	0
Whitesboro	1	0	0	0	1	1	0	1	0	0
Wichita Falls	8	0	1	1	6	30	0	30	0	0
Kaufman County Constable, Precinct 2	32	0	0	5	27	240	63	143	34	0
Montgomery County Constable										
Precinct 1	7	0	1	0	6	1	1	0	0	0
Precinct 3	52	0	6	3	43	155	31	108	16	0
Montgomery County Constable's Office	5	0	0	0	5	1	0	1	0	0
Pewitt Consolidated Independent School District	1	0	0	0	1	0	0	0	0	0
Port of Brownsville	0	0	0	0	0	4	4	0	0	0
Port of Houston Authority	0	0	0	0	0	11	0	9	2	0
Sabine County Constable, Precinct 2	4	0	0	0	4	1	1	0	0	0
University Medical Center	4	0	0	0	4	12	0	9	3	0
UTAH										
State Agencies										
Parks and Recreation	6	0	0	2	4	22	0	20	2	0
Utah Highway Patrol	113	3	10	2	98	71	2	53	16	0
Utah Tax Commission Motor Vehicle Division, Vehicle Investigation Section	0	0	0	0	0	1	1	0	0	0
Wildlife Resources	1	0	0	0	1	10	2	7	1	0
Tribal Agencies										
Goshute Tribal	2	0	0	0	2	0	0	0	0	0
Other Agencies										
Cache-Rich Drug Task Force	0	0	0	0	0	3	0	3	0	0
Davis Metropolitan Narcotics Strike Force	0	0	0	0	0	0	0	0	0	0
Granite School District	11	0	4	2	5	72	5	64	3	2
Iron, Garfield, Beaver Task Force	0	0	0	0	0	2	0	2	0	0
Utah County Attorney, Investigations Division	0	0	0	0	0	1	0	1	0	0
Utah County Major Crimes Task Force	0	0	0	0	0	2	0	1	1	0
Utah Transit Authority	52	0	1	14	37	1,502	0	1,473	29	6
Weber Morgan Narcotics Strike Force	8	0	0	1	7	3	1	2	0	0
VERMONT										
State Agencies										
Attorney General	0	0	0	0	0	0	0	0	0	0
Fish and Wildlife Department, Law Enforcement Division	1	0	0	0	1	0	0	0	0	0
State Police										
Berlin	24	0	6	1	17	78	13	64	1	0
Derby	42	0	7	1	34	76	18	54	4	1
New Haven	21	0	0	0	21	77	18	55	4	2
Royalton	22	0	3	0	19	101	38	58	5	0
Rutland	46	2	5	2	37	165	28	122	15	2
Shaftsbury	21	0	3	0	18	39	13	25	1	1
St. Albans	44	2	11	0	31	89	13	74	2	2
St. Johnsbury	33	1	2	0	30	32	4	25	3	1
Westminster	42	3	2	2	35	136	34	91	11	0
Williston	29	3	6	0	20	52	3	47	2	3
Vermont State Police Headquarters Bureau of Criminal Investigations	0	0	0	0	0	0	0	0	0	0
VIRGINIA										
State Agencies										
Alcoholic Beverage Control Commission	0	0	0	0	0	21	1	20	0	0
Department of Conservation and Recreation	2	0	0	0	2	40	3	37	0	1
Department of Game and Inland Fisheries, Enforcement Division	4	0	0	0	4	30	0	30	0	0
Department of Motor Vehicles	0	0	0	0	0	39	0	1	38	0
State Police										
Accomack County	11	1	2	0	8	17	3	9	5	1
Albemarle County	7	6	0	0	1	1	0	1	0	0
Alexandria	1	0	0	0	1	3	0	1	2	0
Alleghany County	7	3	0	0	4	4	1	1	2	0
Amherst County	3	0	0	0	3	1	0	1	0	0
Arlington County	3	0	0	0	3	1	0	0	1	0
Augusta County	16	0	0	1	15	9	0	8	1	1
Bedford County	4	0	1	0	3	5	1	4	0	0
Botetourt County	5	0	0	0	5	5	0	3	2	0
Buchanan County	2	1	0	0	1	14	1	10	3	0
Campbell County	2	0	0	0	2	1	0	1	0	0
Caroline County	5	0	0	0	5	23	0	14	9	2
Carroll County	3	0	2	0	1	5	0	3	2	0
Chesapeake	6	0	0	0	6	165	0	6	159	1

Table 11. Offenses Known to Law Enforcement, by Selected State, Tribal, and Other Agencies, 2022—Continued

(Number.)

State/other agency unit/office	Violent crime	Murder and nonnegligent manslaughter	Rape	Robbery	Aggravated assault	Property crime	Burglary	Larceny-theft	Motor vehicle theft	Arson[1]
Chesterfield County	12	1	0	1	10	6	0	2	4	0
Colonial Heights	2	0	0	0	2	1	0	0	1	0
Culpeper County	4	0	0	0	4	2	0	1	1	1
Danville	0	0	0	0	0	1	0	1	0	0
Dinwiddie County	7	0	1	0	6	4	0	2	2	0
Essex County	1	1	0	0	0	3	0	2	1	1
Fairfax County	34	0	0	0	34	41	0	16	25	0
Fauquier County	0	0	0	0	0	2	0	1	1	1
Franklin County	2	0	0	0	2	2	0	2	0	0
Frederick County	2	0	0	0	2	8	0	2	6	0
Fredericksburg	1	0	0	0	1	3	0	3	0	0
Giles County	2	0	1	0	1	4	1	3	0	0
Gloucester County	0	0	0	0	0	5	1	3	1	0
Greensville County	5	0	0	0	5	1	0	1	0	0
Halifax County	2	0	0	0	2	2	0	2	0	0
Hampton	17	0	0	0	17	6	0	1	5	1
Hanover County	8	0	0	0	8	7	0	3	4	0
Harrisonburg	2	2	0	0	0	1	0	1	0	0
Henrico County	4	0	0	0	4	12	0	5	7	0
Henry County	3	1	0	0	2	9	0	5	4	0
Hopewell	1	0	0	0	1	0	0	0	0	0
Isle of Wight County	2	0	0	0	2	0	0	0	0	0
James City County	3	0	2	0	1	3	0	3	0	0
Lee County	3	2	0	1	0	11	1	4	6	2
Loudoun County	5	1	1	0	3	5	0	5	0	2
Lunenburg County	5	1	1	0	3	2	0	2	0	0
Lynchburg	1	0	0	0	1	0	0	0	0	0
Mecklenburg County	9	0	0	0	9	6	0	5	1	0
Montgomery County	2	0	0	0	2	3	1	1	1	0
New Kent County	5	0	0	0	5	5	0	3	2	0
Newport News	9	0	0	1	8	3	0	1	2	0
Norfolk	10	1	0	0	9	15	0	1	14	1
Northampton County	0	0	0	0	0	1	0	1	0	0
Northumberland County	1	1	0	0	0	0	0	0	0	0
Nottoway County	1	0	1	0	0	3	0	3	0	0
Orange County	5	1	1	0	3	5	0	5	0	0
Page County	5	0	1	0	4	0	0	0	0	0
Petersburg	5	1	0	0	4	5	0	3	2	0
Pittsylvania County	4	0	0	0	4	31	0	6	25	0
Portsmouth	4	0	0	0	4	7	0	1	6	1
Prince Edward County	1	0	0	0	1	2	0	2	0	0
Prince William County	14	0	1	0	13	7	0	4	3	0
Pulaski County	4	0	1	0	3	9	0	7	2	0
Richmond	21	0	0	1	20	14	1	3	10	0
Richmond County	0	0	0	0	0	2	0	2	0	0
Roanoke	4	0	0	0	4	2	0	2	0	0
Roanoke County	4	0	1	0	3	4	1	3	0	0
Rockbridge County	7	0	0	1	6	2	0	0	2	0
Rockingham County	9	2	1	0	6	16	1	5	10	0
Russell County	6	0	2	0	4	6	0	5	1	1
Salem	0	0	0	0	0	1	0	1	0	0
Scott County	0	0	0	0	0	4	0	2	2	5
Shenandoah County	5	0	0	0	5	1	0	0	1	0
Smyth County	2	0	2	0	0	29	0	19	10	0
Spotsylvania County	3	0	0	0	3	3	0	0	3	0
Stafford County	4	0	0	0	4	5	0	5	0	0
Staunton	0	0	0	0	0	0	0	0	0	0
Suffolk	1	0	0	0	1	4	0	1	3	0
Tazewell County	2	0	0	0	2	9	1	7	1	1
Virginia Beach	6	0	0	0	6	11	0	1	10	0
Warren County	2	0	0	0	2	2	1	1	0	0
Washington County	10	0	1	0	9	5	0	2	3	3
Waynesboro	1	0	0	0	1	0	0	0	0	0
Westmoreland County	4	0	1	0	3	0	0	0	0	0
Winchester	0	0	0	0	0	2	0	0	2	1
Wise County	1	0	0	0	1	5	0	3	2	2
Wythe County	14	0	4	0	10	24	2	14	8	0
York County	5	0	0	0	5	0	0	0	0	0
Virginia Marine Resources Commission Law Enforcement Division	0	0	0	0	0	0	0	0	0	0
Virginia State Capitol	4	0	0	0	4	26	5	20	1	0
Other Agencies										
Norfolk Airport Authority	0	0	0	0	0	58	0	47	11	0
Port Authority, Norfolk	0	0	0	0	0	4	0	3	1	0
Reagan National Airport	4	0	0	1	3	376	0	293	83	0
Richmond International Airport	1	0	0	0	1	71	0	50	21	0
WASHINGTON										
State Agencies										
State Insurance Commissioner, Special Investigations Unit	0	0	0	0	0	0	0	0	0	0
Washington State Parks and Recreation Law Enforcement	3	0	0	1	2	276	102	169	5	1
Washington State Patrol	0	0	0	0	0	0	0	0	0	0

Table 11. Offenses Known to Law Enforcement, by Selected State, Tribal, and Other Agencies, 2022—Continued

(Number.)

State/other agency unit/office	Violent crime	Murder and nonnegligent manslaughter	Rape	Robbery	Aggravated assault	Property crime	Burglary	Larceny-theft	Motor vehicle theft	Arson[1]
Tribal Agencies										
Chehalis Tribal	15	0	2	3	10	90	4	64	22	1
Hoh Tribal	0	0	0	0	0	0	0	0	0	0
Jamestown S'Klallam Tribal	0	0	0	0	0	2	0	2	0	0
Kalispel Tribal	8	0	1	6	1	268	7	238	23	0
La Push Tribal	1	0	1	0	0	5	2	2	1	0
Lummi Tribal	26	0	8	3	15	264	97	132	35	0
Muckleshoot Tribal	7	0	1	0	6	25	6	15	4	2
Nooksack Tribal	0	0	0	0	0	11	1	10	0	0
Puyallup Tribal	21	0	3	5	13	770	145	169	456	1
Shoalwater Bay Tribal	0	0	0	0	0	7	1	4	2	0
Skokomish Tribal	1	0	0	0	1	23	5	17	1	0
Snoqualmie Tribal	0	0	0	0	0	0	0	0	0	0
Squaxin Island Tribal	4	0	0	2	2	67	6	40	21	0
Suquamish Tribal	6	0	5	0	1	75	11	59	5	3
Swinomish Tribal	0	0	0	0	0	34	6	25	3	0
Tulalip Tribal	51	1	3	5	42	583	59	461	63	3
Upper Skagit Tribal	0	0	0	0	0	0	0	0	0	0
Yakama Nation	22	4	8	0	10	2	0	2	0	0
WEST VIRGINIA										
State Agencies										
State Police										
Beckley	25	0	9	0	16	199	23	163	13	1
Berkeley Springs	18	0	9	1	8	54	10	42	2	0
Buckhannon	6	0	2	0	4	51	12	35	4	2
Clay	7	1	1	0	5	44	16	20	8	0
Elkins	13	0	7	0	6	53	5	40	8	0
Franklin	10	0	1	0	9	11	3	7	1	0
Glenville	7	0	7	0	0	20	3	14	3	1
Grafton	5	1	2	0	2	17	4	11	2	0
Grantsville	9	0	2	0	7	30	7	19	4	1
Hamlin	25	3	5	0	17	101	19	62	20	1
Harrisville	18	0	5	0	13	23	7	14	2	0
Hinton	6	1	4	0	1	19	5	10	4	0
Huntington	34	0	27	0	7	186	8	163	15	0
Internet Crimes Against Children Unit	50	0	48	0	2	1	0	1	0	0
Jesse	3	0	2	0	1	24	7	13	4	0
Kearneysville	9	0	3	0	6	54	4	49	1	0
Keyser	6	0	4	0	2	59	9	48	2	0
Kingwood	11	1	5	0	5	54	12	34	8	1
Lewisburg	5	0	3	0	2	87	13	68	6	0
Logan	11	0	4	0	7	73	12	51	10	0
Madison	15	1	4	1	9	45	7	32	6	0
Martinsburg	29	1	11	1	16	144	22	113	9	3
Morgantown	19	2	12	0	5	200	55	129	16	0
Moundsville	3	0	1	0	2	14	5	6	3	0
Oak Hill	6	0	4	0	2	28	4	20	4	0
Paden City	13	0	3	0	10	34	10	23	1	1
Parkersburg	8	0	5	0	3	42	10	29	3	0
Parsons	1	0	1	0	0	17	6	10	1	0
Princeton	26	0	8	0	18	149	21	113	15	2
Rainelle	5	0	0	0	5	51	13	37	1	0
Richwood	8	0	3	0	5	19	5	11	3	0
Ripley	8	0	6	0	2	29	3	24	2	2
South Charleston	25	0	17	0	8	194	9	166	19	0
Spencer	2	0	2	0	0	21	7	10	4	0
St. Marys	4	0	2	0	2	5	2	3	0	0
Summersville	3	0	0	0	3	29	6	21	2	1
Sutton	14	0	8	0	6	71	16	47	8	2
Union	3	0	2	0	1	21	5	13	3	0
Wayne	16	1	4	0	11	171	42	101	28	4
Welch	19	1	4	1	13	38	14	23	1	1
Wellsburg	6	0	6	0	0	3	1	2	0	0
Weston	10	0	5	0	5	43	7	33	3	1
West Union	7	0	4	0	3	6	1	5	0	0
Wheeling	4	0	1	0	3	9	0	6	3	0
Whitesville	3	0	1	0	2	9	1	7	1	0
Williamson	9	0	3	0	6	39	3	24	12	0
Winfield	6	0	1	1	4	83	12	64	7	0
Other Agencies										
Ohio Valley Drug and Violent Crime Task Force	0	0	0	0	0	0	0	0	0	0
Three Rivers Drug and Violent Crime Task Force	0	0	0	0	0	0	0	0	0	0
WISCONSIN										
State Agencies										
Department of Natural Resources	0	0	0	0	0	0	0	0	0	0
State Fair Park Police	0	0	0	0	0	14	0	12	2	0
Wisconsin State Patrol	0	0	0	0	0	0	0	0	0	0
Tribal Agencies										
Lac Courte Oreilles Tribal	26	1	16	0	9	22	3	14	5	0

Table 11. Offenses Known to Law Enforcement, by Selected State, Tribal, and Other Agencies, 2022—Continued

(Number.)

State/other agency unit/office	Violent crime	Murder and nonnegligent manslaughter	Rape	Robbery	Aggravated assault	Property crime	Burglary	Larceny-theft	Motor vehicle theft	Arson[1]
Oneida Tribal	29	0	8	0	21	145	8	123	14	1
Red Cliff Tribal	3	0	2	0	1	18	3	11	4	0
St. Croix Tribal	10	0	0	0	10	25	2	19	4	0
Stockbridge Munsee Tribal	1	0	0	0	1	30	4	22	4	0
WYOMING										
State Agencies										
Wyoming Division of Criminal Investigation	112	4	9	0	99	10	0	5	5	1
Tribal Agencies										
Wind River Agency	41	0	3	0	38	117	20	38	59	0
PUERTO RICO AND OTHER OUTLYING AREAS										
Guam Police Department	425	3	50	91	281	2,693	735	1,648	310	8
Puerto Rico	5,528	572	230	1,188	3,538	15,106	2,529	10,128	2,449	
U.S. Virgin Islands										
St. Croix	179	26	11	34	108	318	158	118	42	2
St. Thomas	199	11	23	26	139	174	76	70	28	0

1 The FBI does not publish arson data unless it receives data from either the agency or the state for all 12 months of the calendar year.   2 Limited data for 2022 were available for Florida, Illinois, Maryland, and Pennsylvania.

Table 12. Crime Trends, by Population Group, 2021–2022

(Number, percent change.)

Population group	Violent crime	Murder and nonnegligent manslaughter	Rape	Robbery	Aggravated assault	Property crime	Burglary	Larceny-theft	Motor vehicle theft	Arson	Number of agencies	Estimated population, 2022
Total, All Agencies												
2021	869,174	15,747	102,135	126,604	624,688	4,254,010	641,698	3,027,333	584,979	28,639		
2022	849,318	14,801	94,659	125,515	614,343	4,457,811	630,520	3,181,017	646,274	26,994	11,596	228,266,062
Percent change	-2.3	-6.0	-7.3	-0.9	-1.7	4.8	-1.7	5.1	10.5	-5.7		
Total, Cities												
2021	687,502	12,129	73,882	111,574	489,917	3,398,516	481,757	2,444,890	471,869	21,631		
2022	670,870	11,519	68,698	109,996	480,657	3,594,762	478,314	2,586,510	529,938	20,641	8,404	148,873,755
Percent change	-2.4	-5.0	-7.0	-1.4	-1.9	5.8	-0.7	5.8	12.3	-4.6		
Group I (250,000 and over)												
2021	312,779	6,200	23,513	63,058	220,008	1,234,772	186,592	823,408	224,772	8,335		
2022	298,879	5,812	21,583	60,798	210,686	1,310,695	183,515	864,794	262,386	7,365	67	37,942,034
Percent change	-4.4	-6.3	-8.2	-3.6	-4.2	6.1	-1.6	5.0	16.7	-11.6		
1,000,000 and over (Group I subset)												
2021	76,944	1,524	5,480	18,184	51,756	315,714	45,657	211,091	58,966	1,804		
2022	75,871	1,410	5,217	18,090	51,154	354,816	48,703	235,813	70,300	1,635	6	9,629,873
Percent change	-1.4	-7.5	-4.8	-0.5	-1.2	12.4	6.7	11.7	19.2	-9.4		
500,000 to 999,999 (Group I subset)												
2021	145,023	2,781	10,097	27,665	104,480	554,208	88,492	360,514	105,202	3,888		
2022	136,415	2,538	9,085	25,744	99,048	574,078	83,259	368,815	122,004	3,367	22	15,603,228
Percent change	-5.9	-8.7	-10.0	-6.9	-5.2	3.6	-5.9	2.3	16.0	-13.4		
250,000 to 499,999 (Group I subset)												
2021	90,812	1,895	7,936	17,209	63,772	364,850	52,443	251,803	60,604	2,643		
2022	86,593	1,864	7,281	16,964	60,484	381,801	51,553	260,166	70,082	2,363	39	12,708,933
Percent change	-4.6	-1.6	-8.3	-1.4	-5.2	4.6	-1.7	3.3	15.6	-10.6		
Group II (100,000 to 249,999)												
2021	115,095	2,037	12,054	17,843	83,161	580,364	80,936	415,590	83,838	3,646		
2022	114,825	1,863	11,328	18,454	83,180	614,639	81,770	439,148	93,721	3,474	160	22,881,624
Percent change	-0.2	-8.5	-6.0	3.4	*	5.9	1.0	5.7	11.8	-4.7		
Group III (50,000 to 99,999)												
2021	83,734	1,226	11,031	12,316	59,161	490,460	65,167	369,127	56,166	2,799		
2022	84,100	1,214	10,431	12,699	59,756	519,693	67,066	391,583	61,044	2,860	365	25,241,903
Percent change	0.4	-1.0	-5.4	3.1	1.0	6.0	2.9	6.1	8.7	2.2		
Group IV (25,000 to 49,999)												
2021	67,021	1,012	9,515	8,390	48,104	412,568	54,264	315,692	42,612	2,337		
2022	66,493	959	9,096	8,352	48,086	436,559	52,821	338,900	44,838	2,525	673	23,393,069
Percent change	-0.8	-5.2	-4.4	-0.5	*	5.8	-2.7	7.4	5.2	8.0		
Group V (10,000 to 24,999)												
2021	58,168	889	9,311	6,199	41,769	385,282	52,037	296,725	36,520	2,055		
2022	56,495	883	8,608	5,951	41,053	402,316	51,974	311,769	38,573	2,091	1,420	22,680,998
Percent change	-2.9	-0.7	-7.6	-4.0	-1.7	4.4	-0.1	5.1	5.6	1.8		
Group VI (under 10,000)												
2021	50,705	765	8,458	3,768	37,714	295,070	42,761	224,348	27,961	2,459		
2022	50,078	788	7,652	3,742	37,896	310,860	41,168	240,316	29,376	2,326	5,719	16,734,127
Percent change	-1.2	3.0	-9.5	-0.7	0.5	5.4	-3.7	7.1	5.1	-5.4		
Metropolitan Counties												
2021	135,668	2,549	19,286	13,482	100,351	663,043	111,626	464,235	87,182	4,784		
2022	134,685	2,296	17,799	14,069	100,521	684,329	109,416	482,208	92,705	4,323	1,301	57,390,620
Percent change	-0.7	-9.9	-7.7	4.4	0.2	3.2	-2.0	3.9	6.3	-9.6		
Nonmetropolitan Counties[1]												
2021	46,004	1,069	8,967	1,548	34,420	192,451	48,315	118,208	25,928	2,224		
2022	43,763	986	8,162	1,450	33,165	178,720	42,790	112,299	23,631	2,030	1,891	22,001,687
Percent change	-4.9	-7.8	-9.0	-6.3	-3.6	-7.1	-11.4	-5.0	-8.9	-8.7		
Suburban Areas[2]												
2021	233,765	3,957	34,960	25,595	169,253	1,342,286	193,664	990,449	158,173	8,243		
2022	232,407	3,636	32,487	26,173	170,111	1,413,870	191,663	1,051,274	170,933	7,970	5,908	101,565,981
Percent change	-0.6	-8.1	-7.1	2.3	0.5	5.3	-1.0	6.1	8.1	-3.3		

* = Less than one-tenth of one percent.
1 Includes state police agencies that report aggregately for the entire state.   2 Suburban areas include law enforcement agencies in cities with less than 50,000 inhabitants and county law enforcement agencies that are within a Metropolitan Statistical Area. Suburban areas exclude all metropolitan agencies associated with a principal city. The agencies associated with suburban areas also appear in other groups within this table.

Table 13. Crime Trends, by Suburban and Nonsuburban Cities,[1] by Population Group, 2021–2022

(Number, percent change.)

Population group	Violent crime	Murder and nonnegligent manslaughter	Rape	Robbery	Aggravated assault	Property crime	Burglary	Larceny-theft	Motor vehicle theft	Arson	Number of agencies	Estimated population, 2022
Suburban Cities												
2021	97,793	1,406	15,633	12,043	68,711	676,014	81,691	523,672	70,651	3,451		
2022	97,358	1,332	14,627	12,040	69,359	725,505	81,884	565,784	77,837	3,636	4,602	43,941,909
Percent change	-0.4	-5.3	-6.4	*	0.9	7.3	0.2	8.0	10.2	5.4		
Group IV (25,000 to 49,999)												
2021	37,096	532	5,706	5,159	25,699	258,658	29,830	200,467	28,361	1,236		
2022	37,187	485	5,379	5,353	25,970	278,889	29,749	218,413	30,727	1,354	509	17,425,547
Percent change	0.2	-8.8	-5.7	3.8	1.1	7.8	-0.3	9.0	8.3	9.5		
Group V (10,000 to 24,999)												
2021	34,720	509	5,537	4,353	24,321	246,545	30,122	191,124	25,299	1,115		
2022	33,891	470	5,262	4,123	24,036	261,197	30,578	202,734	27,885	1,178	1,045	16,846,220
Percent change	-2.4	-7.7	-5.0	-5.3	-1.2	5.9	1.5	6.1	10.2	5.7		
Group VI (under 10,000)												
2021	25,977	365	4,390	2,531	18,691	170,811	21,739	132,081	16,991	1,100		
2022	26,280	377	3,986	2,564	19,353	185,419	21,557	144,637	19,225	1,104	3,048	9,670,142
Percent change	1.2	3.3	-9.2	1.3	3.5	8.6	-0.8	9.5	13.1	0.4		
Nonsuburban Cities												
2021	54,244	879	8,889	3,581	40,895	292,350	48,587	218,650	25,113	2,550		
2022	52,306	901	8,051	3,527	39,827	294,360	45,950	224,875	23,535	2,460	3,202	18,490,747
Percent change	-3.6	2.5	-9.4	-1.5	-2.6	0.7	-5.4	2.8	-6.3	-3.5		
Group IV (25,000 to 49,999)												
2021	8,159	141	1,353	712	5,953	46,796	7,806	34,796	4,194	322		
2022	8,081	112	1,329	726	5,914	46,667	7,083	35,585	3,999	386	156	5,591,984
Percent change	-1.0	-20.6	-1.8	2.0	-0.7	-0.3	-9.3	2.3	-4.6	19.9		
Group V (10,000 to 24,999)												
2021	21,357	338	3,468	1,632	15,919	121,295	19,759	91,587	9,949	869		
2022	20,427	378	3,056	1,623	15,370	122,252	19,256	93,611	9,385	852	375	5,834,778
Percent change	-4.4	11.8	-11.9	-0.6	-3.4	0.8	-2.5	2.2	-5.7	-2.0		
Group VI (under 10,000)												
2021	24,728	400	4,068	1,237	19,023	124,259	21,022	92,267	10,970	1,359		
2022	23,798	411	3,666	1,178	18,543	125,441	19,611	95,679	10,151	1,222	2,671	7,063,985
Percent change	-3.8	2.8	-9.9	-4.8	-2.5	1.0	-6.7	3.7	-7.5	-10.1		

* = Less than one-tenth of one percent.

1 Suburban cities include law enforcement agencies in cities with less than 50,000 inhabitants that are within a Metropolitan Statistical Area. Suburban cities exclude all metropolitan agencies associated with a principal city. Nonsuburban cities include law enforcement agencies in cities with less than 50,000 inhabitants that are not associated with a Metropolitan Statistical Area.

Table 14. Crime Trends, by Metropolitan and Nonmetropolitan Counties,[1] by Population Group, 2021–2022

(Number, percent change.)

Population group and range	Violent crime	Murder and nonnegligent manslaughter	Rape	Robbery	Aggravated assault	Property crime	Burglary	Larceny-theft	Motor vehicle theft	Arson	Number of agencies	Estimated population, 2022
Metropolitan Counties												
100,000 and over												
2021	79,256	1,407	9,696	10,675	57,478	405,634	58,017	292,828	54,789	2,320		
2022	80,914	1,322	8,961	11,422	59,209	435,228	59,964	313,483	61,781	2,187	132	31,967,248
Percent change	2.1	-6.0	-7.6	7.0	3.0	7.3	3.4	7.1	12.8	-5.7		
25,000 to 99,999												
2021	41,921	763	6,985	2,157	32,016	202,447	41,936	135,572	24,939	1,650		
2022	40,205	632	6,433	2,035	31,105	196,854	38,983	133,602	24,269	1,456	400	20,785,901
Percent change	-4.1	-17.2	-7.9	-5.7	-2.8	-2.8	-7.0	-1.5	-2.7	-11.8		
Under 25,000												
2021	14,491	379	2,605	650	10,857	54,962	11,673	35,835	7,454	814		
2022	13,566	342	2,405	612	10,207	52,247	10,469	35,123	6,655	680	769	4,637,471
Percent change	-6.4	-9.8	-7.7	-5.8	-6.0	-4.9	-10.3	-2.0	-10.7	-16.5		
Nonmetropolitan Counties												
25,000 and over												
2021	19,321	434	3,640	856	14,391	87,998	21,498	55,217	11,283	957		
2022	18,033	409	3,241	818	13,565	82,775	19,336	52,946	10,493	828	241	9,776,300
Percent change	-6.7	-5.8	-11.0	-4.4	-5.7	-5.9	-10.1	-4.1	-7.0	-13.5		
10,000 to 24,999												
2021	15,346	346	2,754	451	11,795	65,783	16,617	40,432	8,734	743		
2022	15,050	295	2,592	422	11,741	61,394	14,893	38,635	7,866	673	516	8,331,111
Percent change	-1.9	-14.7	-5.9	-6.4	-0.5	-6.7	-10.4	-4.4	-9.9	-9.4		
Under 10,000												
2021	11,337	289	2,573	241	8,234	38,670	10,200	22,559	5,911	524		
2022	10,680	282	2,329	210	7,859	34,551	8,561	20,718	5,272	529	1,134	3,894,276
Percent change	-5.8	-2.4	-9.5	-12.9	-4.6	-10.7	-16.1	-8.2	-10.8	1.0		

1 Metropolitan counties include sheriffs and county law enforcement agencies associated with a Metropolitan Statistical Area. Nonmetropolitan counties include sheriffs and county law enforcement agencies that are not associated with a Metropolitan Statistical Area.

Table 15. Crime Trends, Additional Information About Selected Offenses, by Population Group, 2021–2022

(Number, percent change.)

Population group	Rape	Assault to rape-attempts	Firearm (Robbery)	Knife or cutting instrument (Robbery)	Other weapon (Robbery)	Strong-arm	Firearm (Aggravated assault)	Knife or cutting instrument (Aggravated assault)	Other weapon (Aggravated assault)	Hands, fists, feet, etc.
Total, All Agencies										
2021	98,958	3,177	56,063	10,210	14,152	46,179	255,653	92,779	170,005	106,251
2022	91,792	2,867	55,215	10,030	14,189	46,081	250,482	90,826	164,323	108,712
Percent change	-7.2	-9.8	-1.5	-1.8	0.3	-0.2	-2.0	-2.1	-3.3	2.3
Total, Cities										
2021	71,535	2,347	48,878	9,056	12,401	41,239	207,597	75,173	129,190	77,957
2022	66,629	2,069	47,525	8,927	12,465	41,079	201,203	73,844	125,277	80,333
Percent change	-6.9	-11.8	-2.8	-1.4	0.5	-0.4	-3.1	-1.8	-3.0	3.0
Group I (250,000 and over)										
2021	22,571	942	30,114	4,622	6,370	21,952	113,029	31,292	53,226	22,461
2022	20,796	787	28,999	4,483	6,160	21,156	108,220	30,845	50,036	21,585
Percent change	-7.9	-16.5	-3.7	-3.0	-3.3	-3.6	-4.3	-1.4	-6.0	-3.9
1,000,000 and over (Group I subset)										
2021	5,233	247	9,177	1,345	1,862	5,800	24,779	8,505	13,668	4,804
2022	5,001	216	9,081	1,360	1,851	5,798	24,903	8,145	13,425	4,681
Percent change	-4.4	-12.6	-1.0	1.1	-0.6	*	0.5	-4.2	-1.8	-2.6
500,000 to 999,999 (Group I subset)										
2021	9,693	404	13,345	2,173	3,059	9,088	55,476	13,592	25,064	10,348
2022	8,718	367	12,425	1,957	2,890	8,472	52,287	13,692	23,256	9,813
Percent change	-10.1	-9.2	-6.9	-9.9	-5.5	-6.8	-5.7	0.7	-7.2	-5.2
250,000 to 499,999 (Group I subset)										
2021	7,645	291	7,592	1,104	1,449	7,064	32,774	9,195	14,494	7,309
2022	7,077	204	7,493	1,166	1,419	6,886	31,030	9,008	13,355	7,091
Percent change	-7.4	-29.9	-1.3	5.6	-2.1	-2.5	-5.3	-2.0	-7.9	-3.0
Group II (100,000 to 249,999)										
2021	11,745	309	7,288	1,686	2,197	6,672	35,047	13,479	21,630	13,005
2022	11,005	323	7,468	1,704	2,305	6,977	34,638	13,556	21,205	13,781
Percent change	-6.3	4.5	2.5	1.1	4.9	4.6	-1.2	0.6	-2.0	6.0
Group III (50,000 to 99,999)										
2021	10,756	275	4,384	1,167	1,502	5,263	20,078	10,143	16,413	12,527
2022	10,219	212	4,367	1,243	1,578	5,511	19,378	9,972	16,694	13,712
Percent change	-5.0	-22.9	-0.4	6.5	5.1	4.7	-3.5	-1.7	1.7	9.5
Group IV (25,000 to 49,999)										
2021	9,273	242	3,181	749	1,068	3,392	16,121	7,973	13,783	10,227
2022	8,871	225	3,024	757	1,124	3,447	15,973	7,680	13,864	10,569
Percent change	-4.3	-7.0	-4.9	1.1	5.2	1.6	-0.9	-3.7	0.6	3.3
Group V (10,000 to 24,999)										
2021	9,065	246	2,567	502	784	2,346	13,359	6,445	12,336	9,629
2022	8,391	217	2,346	456	810	2,339	13,035	6,197	11,872	9,949
Percent change	-7.4	-11.8	-8.6	-9.2	3.3	-0.3	-2.4	-3.8	-3.8	3.3
Group VI (under 10,000)										
2021	8,125	333	1,344	330	480	1,614	9,963	5,841	11,802	10,108
2022	7,347	305	1,321	284	488	1,649	9,959	5,594	11,606	10,737
Percent change	-9.6	-8.4	-1.7	-13.9	1.7	2.2	*	-4.2	-1.7	6.2
Metropolitan Counties										
2021	18,727	559	6,480	1,028	1,534	4,440	37,399	13,605	29,747	19,600
2022	17,273	526	7,001	1,002	1,544	4,522	38,807	13,093	28,681	19,940
Percent change	-7.8	-5.9	8.0	-2.5	0.7	1.8	3.8	-3.8	-3.6	1.7
Nonmetropolitan Counties										
2021	8,696	271	705	126	217	500	10,657	4,001	11,068	8,694
2022	7,890	272	689	101	180	480	10,472	3,889	10,365	8,439
Percent change	-9.3	0.4	-2.3	-19.8	-17.1	-4.0	-1.7	-2.8	-6.4	-2.9
Suburban Areas[1]										
2021	33,925	1,035	11,250	2,033	3,089	9,223	57,881	24,329	51,027	36,016
2022	31,542	945	11,603	1,986	3,123	9,461	59,462	23,689	50,050	36,910
Percent change	-7.0	-8.7	3.1	-2.3	1.1	2.6	2.7	-2.6	-1.9	2.5

Table 15. Crime Trends, Additional Information About Selected Offenses, by Population Group, 2021–2022—Continued

(Number, percent change.)

Population group	Burglary			Motor vehicle theft			Arson			Number of agencies	Estimated population, 2022
	Forcible entry	Unlawful entry	Attempted forcible entry	Autos	Trucks and buses	Other vehicles	Structure	Mobile	Other		
Total, All Agencies											
2021	345,574	253,997	42,127	456,543	81,094	47,342	10,260	6,282	10,664		
2022	347,837	242,164	40,519	510,366	86,409	49,499	9,614	5,271	10,809	11,596	228,266,062
Percent change	0.7	-4.7	-3.8	11.8	6.6	4.6	-6.3	-16.1	1.4		
Total, Cities											
2021	261,213	186,698	33,846	372,972	64,656	34,241	7,701	4,661	8,186		
2022	266,362	179,181	32,771	424,430	69,143	36,365	7,271	3,998	8,398	8,404	148,873,755
Percent change	2.0	-4.0	-3.2	13.8	6.9	6.2	-5.6	-14.2	2.6		
Group I (250,000 and over)											
2021	108,958	62,791	14,843	172,024	38,874	13,874	3,004	2,274	2,705		
2022	110,295	59,063	14,157	205,866	41,680	14,840	2,497	1,755	2,853	67	37,942,034
Percent change	1.2	-5.9	-4.6	19.7	7.2	7.0	-16.9	-22.8	5.5		
1,000,000 and over (Group I subset)											
2021	27,388	14,522	3,747	37,415	17,985	3,566	667	556	511		
2022	29,804	15,163	3,736	45,838	20,743	3,719	449	468	679	6	9,629,873
Percent change	8.8	4.4	-0.3	22.5	15.3	4.3	-32.7	-15.8	32.9		
500,000 to 999,999 (Group I subset)											
2021	51,863	29,477	7,152	83,634	15,024	6,544	1,444	1,103	1,161		
2022	50,588	26,219	6,452	99,240	15,654	7,110	1,303	815	1,100	22	15,603,228
Percent change	-2.5	-11.1	-9.8	18.7	4.2	8.6	-9.8	-26.1	-5.3		
250,000 to 499,999 (Group I subset)											
2021	29,707	18,792	3,944	50,975	5,865	3,764	893	615	1,033		
2022	29,903	17,681	3,969	60,788	5,283	4,011	745	472	1,074	39	12,708,933
Percent change	0.7	-5.9	0.6	19.3	-9.9	6.6	-16.6	-23.3	4.0		
Group II (100,000 to 249,999)											
2021	44,025	31,089	5,822	67,846	9,599	6,393	1,078	782	1,624		
2022	45,837	30,473	5,460	76,154	10,450	7,117	1,090	643	1,557	160	22,881,624
Percent change	4.1	-2.0	-6.2	12.2	8.9	11.3	1.1	-17.8	-4.1		
Group III (50,000 to 99,999)											
2021	33,500	27,583	4,084	45,608	5,712	4,846	930	503	1,225		
2022	36,141	26,769	4,156	49,943	6,226	4,875	915	541	1,264	365	25,241,903
Percent change	7.9	-3.0	1.8	9.5	9.0	0.6	-1.6	7.6	3.2		
Group IV (25,000 to 49,999)											
2021	27,144	23,582	3,538	35,257	3,953	3,402	820	386	1,000		
2022	26,733	22,643	3,445	37,293	4,104	3,441	887	408	1,077	673	23,393,069
Percent change	-1.5	-4.0	-2.6	5.8	3.8	1.1	8.2	5.7	7.7		
Group V (10,000 to 24,999)											
2021	26,306	22,755	2,976	29,986	3,559	2,975	770	334	824		
2022	26,570	22,339	3,065	31,847	3,771	2,955	791	326	857	1,420	22,680,998
Percent change	1.0	-1.8	3.0	6.2	6.0	-0.7	2.7	-2.4	4.0		
Group VI (under 10,000)											
2021	21,280	18,898	2,583	22,251	2,959	2,751	1,099	382	808		
2022	20,786	17,894	2,488	23,327	2,912	3,137	1,091	325	790	5,719	16,734,127
Percent change	-2.3	-5.3	-3.7	4.8	-1.6	14.0	-0.7	-14.9	-2.2		
Metropolitan Counties											
2021	57,600	47,349	6,677	65,622	11,760	9,800	1,619	1,075	1,842		
2022	57,617	45,531	6,268	69,983	12,775	9,947	1,495	833	1,775	1,301	57,390,620
Percent change	*	-3.8	-6.1	6.6	8.6	1.5	-7.7	-22.5	-3.6		
Nonmetropolitan Counties											
2021	26,761	19,950	1,604	17,949	4,678	3,301	940	546	636		
2022	23,858	17,452	1,480	15,953	4,491	3,187	848	440	636	1,891	22,001,687
Percent change	-10.8	-12.5	-7.7	-11.1	-4.0	-3.5	-9.8	-19.4	0.0		
Suburban Areas[1]											
2021	99,080	82,010	12,574	124,226	18,552	15,395	2,777	1,679	3,321		
2022	100,145	79,308	12,210	134,936	19,984	16,013	2,759	1,396	3,360	5,908	101,565,981
Percent change	1.1	-3.3	-2.9	8.6	7.7	4.0	-0.6	-16.9	1.2		

* = Less than one-tenth of one percent.
1 Suburban areas include law enforcement agencies in cities with less than 50,000 inhabitants and county law enforcement agencies that are within a Metropolitan Statistical Area. Suburban areas exclude all metropolitan agencies associated with a principal city. The agencies associated with suburban areas also appear in other groups within this table.

Table 16. Rate: Number of Crimes Per 100,000 Population, by Population Group, 2022

(Number, rate.)

Population group	Violent crime		Murder and nonnegligent manslaughter		Rape		Robbery		Aggravated assault	
	Number of offenses known	Rate	Number of offenses known	Rate	Number of offenses known	Rate	Number of offenses known	Rate	Number of offenses known	Rate
Total, All Agencies	1,177,359	408.8	19,243	6.7	120,508	41.8	210,134	73.0	827,474	287.3
Total, Cities	940,367	485.5	15,066	7.8	88,927	45.9	186,021	96.0	650,353	335.8
Group I (250,000 and over)	471,924	781.7	8,297	13.7	32,845	54.4	115,388	191.1	315,394	522.4
1,000,000 and over (Group I subset)	200,571	772.4	3,180	12.2	12,604	48.5	58,174	224.0	126,613	487.6
500,000 to 999,999 (Group I subset)	156,729	878.2	2,887	16.2	10,705	60.0	33,539	187.9	109,598	614.1
250,000 to 499,999 (Group I subset)	114,624	692.1	2,230	13.5	9,536	57.6	23,675	143.0	79,183	478.1
Group II (100,000 to 249,999)	148,585	493.7	2,255	7.5	14,227	47.3	26,462	87.9	105,641	351.0
Group III (50,000 to 99,999)	113,646	358.4	1,483	4.7	13,016	41.0	20,037	63.2	79,110	249.5
Group IV (25,000 to 49,999)	82,895	292.9	1,175	4.2	10,758	38.0	11,719	41.4	59,243	209.3
Group V (10,000 to 24,999)	66,581	261.6	1,011	4.0	9,670	38.0	7,585	29.8	48,315	189.8
Group VI (under 10,000)	56,736	319.8	845	4.8	8,411	47.4	4,830	27.2	42,650	240.4
Metropolitan Counties	189,170	261.9	3,127	4.3	22,569	31.2	22,462	31.1	141,012	195.2
Nonmetropolitan Counties[1]	47,822	216.5	1,050	4.8	9,012	40.8	1,651	7.5	36,109	163.5
Suburban Areas[2]	313,307	252.4	4,785	3.9	39,923	32.2	39,677	32.0	228,922	184.4

Table 16. Rate: Number of Crimes Per 100,000 Population, by Population Group, 2022—Continued

(Number, rate.)

Population group	Property crime Number of offenses known	Rate	Burglary Number of offenses known	Rate	Larceny-theft Number of offenses known	Rate	Motor vehicle theft Number of offenses known	Rate	Number of agencies	Estimated population, 2022
Total, All Agencies	5,908,587	2,051.7	823,502	285.9	4,202,362	1,459.2	882,723	306.5	12,454	287,991,222
Total, Cities	4,812,443	2,484.8	634,934	327.8	3,440,148	1,776.2	737,361	380.7	9,085	193,674,996
Group I (250,000 and over)	1,974,429	3,270.4	258,908	428.9	1,335,366	2,211.9	380,155	629.7	85	60,372,598
1,000,000 and over (Group I subset)	778,727	2,999.1	93,635	360.6	543,768	2,094.2	141,324	544.3	10	25,965,648
500,000 to 999,999 (Group I subset)	678,341	3,801.2	95,718	536.4	442,235	2,478.1	140,388	786.7	25	17,845,655
250,000 to 499,999 (Group I subset)	517,361	3,123.9	69,555	420.0	349,363	2,109.5	98,443	594.4	50	16,561,295
Group II (100,000 to 249,999)	788,301	2,619.1	108,111	359.2	556,431	1,848.7	123,759	411.2	210	30,097,924
Group III (50,000 to 99,999)	685,372	2,161.5	89,536	282.4	507,622	1,600.9	88,214	278.2	456	31,707,788
Group IV (25,000 to 49,999)	538,855	1,904.1	68,491	242.0	412,876	1,459.0	57,488	203.1	815	28,299,282
Group V (10,000 to 24,999)	460,354	1,808.5	61,473	241.5	352,685	1,385.5	46,196	181.5	1,587	25,455,623
Group VI (under 10,000)	365,132	2,058.0	48,415	272.9	275,168	1,551.0	41,549	234.2	5,932	17,741,781
Metropolitan Counties	906,697	1,255.4	142,574	197.4	643,172	890.5	120,951	167.5	1,500	72,226,528
Nonmetropolitan Counties[1]	189,447	857.6	45,994	208.2	119,042	538.9	24,411	110.5	1,869	22,089,698
Suburban Areas[2]	1,816,877	1,463.8	250,817	202.1	1,338,616	1,078.4	227,444	183.2	6,686	124,124,203

1 Includes state police agencies that report aggregately for the entire state.   2 Suburban areas include law enforcement agencies in cities with less than 50,000 inhabitants and county law enforcement agencies that are within a Metropolitan Statistical Area. Suburban areas exclude all metropolitan agencies associated with a principal city. The agencies associated with suburban areas also appear in other groups within this table.

Table 17. Rate: Number of Crimes Per 100,000 Inhabitants, by Suburban and Nonsuburban Cities,[1] by Population Group, 2022

(Number, rate.)

Population group	Violent crime		Murder and nonnegligent manslaughter		Rape		Robbery		Aggravated assault	
	Number of offenses known	Rate	Number of offenses known	Rate	Number of offenses known	Rate	Number of offenses known	Rate	Number of offenses known	Rate
Total, Suburban Cities	124,137	239.2	1,658	3.2	17,354	33.4	17,215	33.2	87,910	169.4
Group IV (25,000 to 49,999)	50,411	230.0	659	3.0	6,685	30.5	8,164	37.2	34,903	159.2
Group V (10,000 to 24,999)	42,077	218.2	568	2.9	6,080	31.5	5,501	28.5	29,928	155.2
Group VI (under 10,000)	31,649	296.0	431	4.0	4,589	42.9	3,550	33.2	23,079	215.8
Total, Nonsuburban Cities	55,465	379.7	931	6.4	8,519	58.3	3,836	26.3	42,179	288.7
Group IV (25,000 to 49,999)	8,644	401.0	121	5.6	1,471	68.2	780	36.2	6,272	291.0
Group V (10,000 to 24,999)	21,734	402.3	396	7.3	3,226	59.7	1,776	32.9	16,336	302.4
Group VI (under 10,000)	25,087	355.9	414	5.9	3,822	54.2	1,280	18.2	19,571	277.6

Population group	Property crime		Burglary		Larceny-theft		Motor vehicle theft		Number of agencies	Estimated population, 2022
	Number of offenses known	Rate	Number of offenses known	Rate	Number of offenses known	Rate	Number of offenses known	Rate		
Total, Suburban Cities	910,180	1,753.8	108,243	208.6	695,444	1,340.0	106,493	205.2	5,186	51,897,675
Group IV (25,000 to 49,999)	368,354	1,680.3	42,952	195.9	283,025	1,291.1	42,377	193.3	638	21,921,926
Group V (10,000 to 24,999)	309,983	1,607.5	38,043	197.3	237,462	1,231.4	34,478	178.8	1,192	19,283,266
Group VI (under 10,000)	231,843	2,168.3	27,248	254.8	174,957	1,636.3	29,638	277.2	3,356	10,692,483
Total, Nonsuburban Cities	311,014	2,129.1	49,582	339.4	235,081	1,609.3	26,351	180.4	2,995	14,607,471
Group IV (25,000 to 49,999)	49,522	2,297.4	7,601	352.6	37,652	1,746.7	4,269	198.0	66	2,155,582
Group V (10,000 to 24,999)	128,203	2,373.0	20,814	385.3	97,218	1,799.5	10,171	188.3	353	5,402,591
Group VI (under 10,000)	133,289	1,890.8	21,167	300.3	100,211	1,421.6	11,911	169.0	2,576	7,049,298

[1] Suburban cities include law enforcement agencies in cities with less than 50,000 inhabitants that are within a Metropolitan Statistical Area. Suburban cities exclude all metropolitan agencies associated with a principal city. Nonsuburban cities include law enforcement agencies in cities with less than 50,000 inhabitants that are not associated with a Metropolitan Statistical Area.

Table 18. Rate: Number of Crimes Per 100,000 Inhabitants, by Metropolitan and Nonmetropolitan Counties,[1] by Population Group, 2022

(Number, rate.)

Population group	Violent crime		Murder and nonnegligent manslaughter		Rape		Robbery		Aggravated assault	
	Number of offenses known	Rate	Number of offenses known	Rate	Number of offenses known	Rate	Number of offenses known	Rate	Number of offenses known	Rate
Metropolitan Counties										
100,000 and over	130,452	286.0	2,072	4.5	12,501	27.4	19,349	42.4	96,530	211.6
25,000 to 99,999	42,803	194.1	685	3.1	6,837	31.0	2,288	10.4	32,993	149.6
Under 25,000	15,915	349.2	370	8.1	3,231	70.9	825	18.1	11,489	252.1
Nonmetropolitan Counties										
25,000 and over	19,536	196.3	422	4.2	3,440	34.6	915	9.2	14,759	148.3
10,000 to 24,999	16,057	189.4	310	3.7	2,774	32.7	472	5.6	12,501	147.5
Under 10,000	12,229	334.1	318	8.7	2,798	76.4	264	7.2	8,849	241.8

Table 18. Rate: Number of Crimes Per 100,000 Inhabitants, by Metropolitan and Nonmetropolitan Counties,[1] by Population Group, 2022—Continued

(Number, rate.)

Population group	Property crime		Burglary		Larceny-theft		Motor vehicle theft		Number of agencies	Estimated population, 2022
	Number of offenses known	Rate	Number of offenses known	Rate	Number of offenses known	Rate	Number of offenses known	Rate		
Metropolitan Counties										
100,000 and over	633,060	1,387.9	87,448	191.7	457,880	1,003.8	87,732	192.3	168	45,613,085
25,000 to 99,999	210,461	954.2	41,986	190.4	142,670	646.8	25,805	117.0	419	22,056,320
Under 25,000	63,176	1,386.3	13,140	288.3	42,622	935.3	7,414	162.7	913	4,557,123
Nonmetropolitan Counties										
25,000 and over	85,623	860.3	20,139	202.3	54,875	551.3	10,609	106.6	241	9,953,246
10,000 to 24,999	64,162	757.0	16,068	189.6	39,968	471.5	8,126	95.9	523	8,476,290
Under 10,000	39,662	1,083.6	9,787	267.4	24,199	661.1	5,676	155.1	1,105	3,660,162

1 Metropolitan counties include sheriffs and county law enforcement agencies associated with a Metropolitan Statistical Area. Nonmetropolitan counties include sheriffs and county law enforcement agencies that are not associated with a Metropolitan Statistical Area. The offenses from state police agencies are not included in this table.

Table 19. Rate: Number of Crimes Per 100,000 Inhabitants, Additional Information About Selected Offenses, by Population Group, 2022

(Number, rate.)

Population group	Rape		Robbery				Aggravated assault		
	Rape	Assault to rape-attempts	Firearm	Knife or cutting instrument	Other weapon	Strong-arm	Firearm	Knife or cutting instrument	Other weapon
Total, All Agencies									
Number of offenses known	116,506	4,002	78,051	17,941	24,831	89,311	302,781	129,765	231,032
Rate	40.5	1.4	27.1	6.2	8.6	31.0	105.1	45.1	80.2
Total, Cities									
Number of offenses known	85,893	3,034	67,615	16,138	21,992	80,276	241,879	106,200	178,423
Rate	44.3	1.6	34.9	8.3	11.4	41.4	124.9	54.8	92.1
Group I (250,000 and over)									
Number of offenses known	31,493	1,352	43,122	9,834	12,306	50,126	133,504	53,117	82,799
Rate	52.2	2.2	71.4	16.3	20.4	83.0	221.1	88.0	137.1
1,000,000 and over (Group I subset)									
Number of offenses known	11,978	626	17,999	5,653	6,622	27,900	42,439	25,367	34,852
Rate	46.1	2.4	69.3	21.8	25.5	107.4	163.4	97.7	134.2
500,000 to 999,999 (Group I subset)									
Number of offenses known	10,295	410	14,976	2,544	3,702	12,317	54,169	15,854	27,824
Rate	57.7	2.3	83.9	14.3	20.7	69.0	303.5	88.8	155.9
250,000 to 499,999 (Group I subset)									
Number of offenses known	9,220	316	10,147	1,637	1,982	9,909	36,896	11,896	20,123
Rate	55.7	1.9	61.3	9.9	12.0	59.8	222.8	71.8	121.5
Group II (100,000 to 249,999)									
Number of offenses known	13,739	488	9,859	2,382	3,637	10,584	40,497	17,085	28,351
Rate	45.6	1.6	32.8	7.9	12.1	35.2	134.6	56.8	94.2
Group III (50,000 to 99,999)									
Number of offenses known	12,695	321	6,348	1,901	2,807	8,981	24,227	12,982	22,761
Rate	40.0	1.0	20.0	6.0	8.9	28.3	76.4	40.9	71.8
Group IV (25,000 to 49,999)									
Number of offenses known	10,465	293	3,943	1,056	1,589	5,131	18,492	9,522	17,348
Rate	37.0	1.0	13.9	3.7	5.6	18.1	65.3	33.6	61.3
Group V (10,000 to 24,999)									
Number of offenses known	9,416	254	2,785	600	1,044	3,156	14,610	7,213	14,057
Rate	37.0	1.0	10.9	2.4	4.1	12.4	57.4	28.3	55.2
Group VI (under 10,000)									
Number of offenses known	8,085	326	1,558	365	609	2,298	10,549	6,281	13,107
Rate	45.6	1.8	8.8	2.1	3.4	13.0	59.5	35.4	73.9
Metropolitan Counties									
Number of offenses known	21,882	687	9,687	1,675	2,632	8,468	50,093	19,313	41,310
Rate	30.3	1.0	13.4	2.3	3.6	11.7	69.4	26.7	57.2
Nonmetropolitan Counties									
Number of offenses known	8,731	281	749	128	207	567	10,809	4,252	11,299
Rate	39.5	1.3	3.4	0.6	0.9	2.6	48.9	19.2	51.2
Suburban Areas[1]									
Number of offenses known	38,716	1,207	15,663	3,077	4,918	16,019	74,522	32,510	68,466
Rate	31.2	1.0	12.6	2.5	4.0	12.9	60.0	26.2	55.2

Table 19. Rate: Number of Crimes Per 100,000 Inhabitants, Additional Information About Selected Offenses, by Population Group, 2022—Continued

(Number, rate.)

Population group	Hands, fists, feet, etc.	Burglary			Motor vehicle theft			Number of agencies	Estimated population, 2022
		Forcible entry	Unlawful entry	Attempted forcible entry	Autos	Trucks and buses	Other vehicles		
Total, All Agencies									
Number of offenses known	163,896	468,325	303,824	51,353	676,584	134,238	71,901	12,454	287,991,222
Rate	56.9	162.6	105.5	17.8	234.9	46.6	25.0		
Total, Cities									
Number of offenses known	123,851	363,408	228,999	42,527	571,592	111,392	54,377	9,085	193,674,996
Rate	63.9	187.6	118.2	22.0	295.1	57.5	28.1		
Group I (250,000 and over)									
Number of offenses known	45,974	160,512	79,534	18,862	291,639	64,626	23,890	85	60,372,598
Rate	76.2	265.9	131.7	31.2	483.1	107.0	39.6		
1,000,000 and over (Group I subset)									
Number of offenses known	23,955	61,201	26,082	6,352	96,136	35,755	9,433	10	25,965,648
Rate	92.3	235.7	100.4	24.5	370.2	137.7	36.3		
500,000 to 999,999 (Group I subset)									
Number of offenses known	11,751	58,137	30,308	7,273	112,280	19,307	8,801	25	17,845,655
Rate	65.8	325.8	169.8	40.8	629.2	108.2	49.3		
250,000 to 499,999 (Group I subset)									
Number of offenses known	10,268	41,174	23,144	5,237	83,223	9,564	5,656	50	16,561,295
Rate	62.0	248.6	139.7	31.6	502.5	57.7	34.2		
Group II (100,000 to 249,999)									
Number of offenses known	19,708	62,221	38,673	7,217	97,208	17,105	9,446	210	30,097,924
Rate	65.5	206.7	128.5	24.0	323.0	56.8	31.4		
Group III (50,000 to 99,999)									
Number of offenses known	19,140	48,838	35,166	5,532	69,160	11,639	7,415	456	31,707,788
Rate	60.4	154.0	110.9	17.4	218.1	36.7	23.4		
Group IV (25,000 to 49,999)									
Number of offenses known	13,881	35,267	28,668	4,556	46,799	5,987	4,702	815	28,299,282
Rate	49.1	124.6	101.3	16.1	165.4	21.2	16.6		
Group V (10,000 to 24,999)									
Number of offenses known	12,435	31,856	26,039	3,578	37,536	5,053	3,607	1,587	25,455,623
Rate	48.8	125.1	102.3	14.1	147.5	19.9	14.2		
Group VI (under 10,000)									
Number of offenses known	12,713	24,714	20,919	2,782	29,250	6,982	5,317	5,932	17,741,781
Rate	71.7	139.3	117.9	15.7	164.9	39.4	30.0		
Metropolitan Counties									
Number of offenses known	30,296	79,445	55,830	7,299	88,523	18,220	14,208	1,500	72,226,528
Rate	41.9	110.0	77.3	10.1	122.6	25.2	19.7		
Nonmetropolitan Counties									
Number of offenses known	9,749	25,472	18,995	1,527	16,469	4,626	3,316	1,869	22,089,698
Rate	44.1	115.3	86.0	6.9	74.6	20.9	15.0		
Suburban Areas[1]									
Number of offenses known	53,424	136,434	99,491	14,892	171,951	31,688	23,805	6,686	124,124,203
Rate	43.0	109.9	80.2	12.0	138.5	25.5	19.2		

1 Suburban areas include law enforcement agencies in cities with less than 50,000 inhabitants and county law enforcement agencies that are within a Metropolitan Statistical Area. Suburban areas exclude all metropolitan agencies associated with a principal city. The agencies associated with suburban areas also appear in other groups within this table.

Table 20. Murder, by Selected State and Type of Weapon, 2022

(Number.)

State	Total murders[1]	Total firearms	Handguns	Rifles	Shotguns	Firearms (type unknown)	Knives or cutting instruments	Other weapons	Hands, fists, feet, etc.[2]
Alabama	478	374	174	21	13	166	19	70	15
Alaska	70	38	20	3	7	8	13	8	11
Arizona	456	345	229	26	1	89	40	62	9
Arkansas	306	242	102	13	7	120	12	49	3
California	2,197	1,566	962	39	13	552	270	275	86
Colorado	375	297	229	5	7	56	35	31	12
Connecticut	136	107	14	1	0	92	12	13	4
Delaware	49	37	21	1	0	15	7	2	3
District of Columbia	197	171	135	5	0	31	15	7	4
Florida[3]	344	288	111	18	2	157	19	25	12
Georgia	830	690	417	31	2	240	43	71	26
Hawaii	28	10	8	0	1	1	9	7	2
Idaho	53	37	25	3	0	9	8	5	3
Illinois[3]	881	738	372	16	3	347	51	76	16
Indiana	405	323	201	10	1	111	25	40	17
Iowa	53	37	26	0	2	9	5	6	5
Kansas	126	85	54	4	3	24	12	25	4
Kentucky	291	239	154	10	2	73	20	27	5
Louisiana	408	315	135	17	6	157	16	70	7
Maine	30	15	10	0	1	4	7	4	4
Maryland[3]	511	429	212	3	1	213	38	38	6
Massachusetts	148	100	52	1	1	46	30	15	3
Michigan	692	544	215	20	6	303	38	92	18
Minnesota	182	130	44	2	2	82	21	18	13
Mississippi	131	104	50	13	2	39	7	19	1
Missouri	623	537	262	26	3	246	26	43	17
Montana	49	32	16	1	3	12	11	4	2
Nebraska	32	15	12	0	1	2	8	7	2
Nevada	214	139	53	6	0	80	32	30	13
New Hampshire	25	17	11	0	0	6	5	2	1
New Jersey	254	166	98	1	0	67	42	25	21
New Mexico	209	152	77	6	4	65	13	38	6
New York	762	473	326	16	9	122	169	73	47
North Carolina	821	665	333	38	17	277	51	77	28
North Dakota	27	18	13	0	0	5	2	4	3
Ohio	701	541	227	7	3	304	38	103	19
Oklahoma	270	163	104	8	2	49	44	47	16
Oregon	188	130	74	3	1	52	19	34	5
Pennsylvania[3]	857	722	601	14	6	101	51	58	26
Rhode Island	16	10	5	0	0	5	4	2	0
South Carolina	585	505	266	21	5	213	26	44	10
South Dakota	39	20	15	0	0	5	5	9	5
Tennessee	608	494	187	12	10	285	41	57	16
Texas	2,020	1,539	692	88	14	745	166	236	79
Utah	67	42	28	0	2	12	6	10	9
Vermont	22	19	16	1	0	2	3	0	0
Virginia	637	536	262	20	13	241	34	46	21
Washington	385	267	145	6	6	110	36	59	23
West Virginia	77	51	33	2	2	14	7	19	0
Wisconsin	314	264	101	3	1	159	15	28	7
Wyoming	14	9	7	0	1	1	3	2	0
Guam	3	2	0	0	0	2	1	0	0

1 Total number of murders for which supplemental homicide data were received.   2 Pushed is included in hands, fists, feet, etc.   3 Limited data for 2022 were available for Florida, Illinois, Maryland, and Pennsylvania.

Table 21. Robbery, by State and Type of Weapon, 2022

(Number.)

State	Total robberies[1]	Firearms	Knives or cutting instruments	Other weapons	Strong-arm	Agency count	Population
Alabama	1,477	772	55	244	406	333	4,116,187
Alaska	551	97	40	85	329	28	728,061
Arizona	4,609	1,567	534	532	1,976	91	5,979,879
Arkansas	1,193	557	61	124	451	270	2,939,335
California	46,933	13,551	4,190	6,905	22,287	795	37,411,021
Colorado	4,288	1,773	357	710	1,448	175	5,568,117
Connecticut	1,625	555	228	188	654	102	3,601,911
Delaware	578	220	54	62	242	52	1,013,255
District of Columbia	2,402	1,243	156	207	796	2	671,803
Florida[2]	6,396	2,094	419	703	3,180	329	12,372,295
Georgia	4,188	2,400	189	318	1,281	389	9,353,344
Hawaii	851	147	113	128	463	2	1,068,961
Idaho	159	25	18	17	99	105	1,914,857
Illinois[2]	11,144	1,451	224	1,403	8,066	423	8,783,930
Indiana	2,713	1,482	158	281	792	144	4,755,647
Iowa	572	183	47	85	257	189	2,634,203
Kansas	781	288	54	85	354	194	2,455,385
Kentucky	834	356	65	100	313	417	3,790,569
Louisiana	2,891	1,704	121	245	821	125	3,955,436
Maine	138	29	24	29	56	125	1,367,258
Maryland[2]	6,326	3,059	552	721	1,994	81	4,951,587
Massachusetts	2,619	617	466	330	1,206	378	6,885,869
Michigan	3,637	1,667	220	302	1,448	582	9,386,427
Minnesota	3,260	1,518	220	311	1,211	397	5,698,146
Mississippi	387	232	14	48	93	143	1,644,720
Missouri	3,363	1,912	207	341	903	389	5,728,888
Montana	262	48	27	60	127	98	1,097,777
Nebraska	562	205	40	62	255	120	1,713,028
Nevada	2,732	1,237	253	292	950	49	3,162,409
New Hampshire	220	47	23	28	122	191	1,328,560
New Jersey	3,703	972	432	314	1,985	448	7,742,608
New Mexico	2,258	1,088	227	369	574	86	1,806,455
New York	21,776	5,000	3,319	2,331	11,126	481	18,666,708
North Carolina	5,624	2,960	438	488	1,738	328	9,600,572
North Dakota	214	33	20	35	126	106	776,111
Ohio	6,017	1,837	212	452	3,516	417	9,899,619
Oklahoma	1,632	650	160	172	650	445	4,012,441
Oregon	2,842	907	281	540	1,114	180	3,996,089
Pennsylvania[2]	6,410	3,191	459	538	2,222	262	5,434,864
Rhode Island	269	75	42	24	128	47	1,093,734
South Carolina	2,089	1,187	155	169	578	337	5,128,795
South Dakota	228	79	28	30	91	63	704,986
Tennessee	4,718	3,063	211	259	1,185	305	6,886,897
Texas	21,102	10,747	1,582	2,332	6,441	1,018	29,301,660
Utah	925	248	107	126	444	112	3,025,029
Vermont	85	22	16	15	32	66	618,683
Virginia	3,327	1,524	317	339	1,147	322	8,610,603
Washington	6,745	2,188	667	1,115	2,775	226	7,647,856
West Virginia	142	45	21	29	47	105	921,582
Wisconsin	2,305	1,193	110	203	799	333	5,585,872
Wyoming	47	20	4	11	12	44	427,908

1 The number of robberies from agencies that submitted 12 months of data in 2022 for which breakdowns by type of weapon were included.   2 Limited data for 2022 were available for Florida, Illinois, Maryland, and Pennsylvania.

Table 22. Aggravated Assault, by State and Type of Weapon, 2022

(Number.)

State	Total aggravated assaults[1]	Firearms	Knives or cutting instruments	Other weapons	Personal weapons	Agency count	Population
Alabama	14,454	6,448	1,204	2,453	4,349	333	4,116,187
Alaska	3,953	864	765	1,458	866	28	728,061
Arizona	19,304	7,357	3,216	4,741	3,990	91	5,979,879
Arkansas	15,418	5,597	1,478	3,260	5,083	270	2,939,335
California	126,474	27,609	19,045	42,496	37,324	795	37,411,021
Colorado	20,190	8,629	3,394	4,989	3,178	175	5,568,117
Connecticut	3,006	791	674	870	671	102	3,601,911
Delaware	3,031	1,142	590	984	315	52	1,013,255
District of Columbia	2,579	1,097	536	715	231	2	671,803
Florida[2]	33,971	12,569	6,028	11,249	4,125	329	12,372,295
Georgia	27,262	14,830	2,524	4,462	5,446	389	9,353,344
Hawaii	1,485	227	440	490	328	2	1,068,961
Idaho	3,470	831	528	1,079	1,032	105	1,914,857
Illinois[2]	14,907	6,727	1,666	3,022	3,492	423	8,783,930
Indiana	13,250	5,870	1,231	2,906	3,243	144	4,755,647
Iowa	5,910	1,061	873	1,375	2,601	189	2,634,203
Kansas	8,746	3,013	1,247	2,297	2,189	194	2,455,385
Kentucky	2,663	461	357	1,394	451	417	3,790,569
Louisiana	20,081	9,321	2,341	6,558	1,861	125	3,955,436
Maine	809	117	135	334	223	125	1,367,258
Maryland[2]	12,768	3,411	2,401	4,577	2,379	81	4,951,587
Massachusetts	17,508	2,455	3,825	8,067	3,161	378	6,885,869
Michigan	34,638	13,090	5,722	9,695	6,131	582	9,386,427
Minnesota	10,229	3,516	2,047	2,247	2,419	397	5,698,146
Mississippi	2,871	1,397	263	815	396	143	1,644,720
Missouri	22,332	10,054	2,117	7,697	2,464	389	5,728,888
Montana	3,689	847	485	1,199	1,158	98	1,097,777
Nebraska	3,684	1,029	749	1,278	628	120	1,713,028
Nevada	9,555	3,649	2,043	2,004	1,859	49	3,162,409
New Hampshire	929	223	202	243	261	191	1,328,560
New Jersey	10,300	1,727	1,842	3,418	3,313	448	7,742,608
New Mexico	11,912	4,868	1,854	2,940	2,250	86	1,806,455
New York	54,825	8,095	15,303	16,220	15,207	481	18,666,708
North Carolina	30,415	17,053	3,661	5,273	4,428	328	9,600,572
North Dakota	1,460	69	206	615	570	106	776,111
Ohio	20,302	9,904	3,312	5,387	1,699	417	9,899,619
Oklahoma	12,635	4,070	2,168	3,917	2,480	445	4,012,441
Oregon	9,347	1,999	1,490	3,226	2,632	180	3,996,089
Pennsylvania[2]	12,958	5,116	1,883	3,301	2,658	262	5,434,864
Rhode Island	1,184	257	323	395	209	47	1,093,734
South Carolina	20,858	11,572	2,458	3,868	2,960	337	5,128,795
South Dakota	2,372	421	547	700	704	63	704,986
Tennessee	35,571	20,147	4,750	8,797	1,877	305	6,886,897
Texas	90,561	44,150	15,186	23,637	7,588	1,018	29,301,660
Utah	4,624	925	914	1,402	1,383	112	3,025,029
Vermont	1,087	176	150	205	556	66	618,683
Virginia	13,700	6,055	1,623	3,493	2,529	322	8,610,603
Washington	18,904	6,192	2,587	5,576	4,549	226	7,647,856
West Virginia	2,295	737	234	430	894	105	921,582
Wisconsin	12,333	4,738	1,017	3,135	3,443	333	5,585,872
Wyoming	665	278	131	143	113	49	451,193

1 The number of aggravated assaults from agencies that submitted 12 months of data in 2022 for which breakdowns by type of weapon were included.   2 Limited data for 2022 were available for Florida, Illinois, Maryland, and Pennsylvania.

Table 23. Offense Analysis, Number and Percent Distritbution, 2021–2022

(Number, percent, dollars; 14,643 agencies; 2022 estimated population 304,768,145; 11,794 agencies in 2021; 2021 estimated population 212,416,063.)

Classification	Number of offenses, 2022	Percent change from 2021	Percent distribution[1]	Average value[2] (dollars)
Murder	19,863	-6.3	1.0	X
Rape[2]	123,512	-7.2	1.0	X
Robbery for which location is known	214,535	-0.4	100.0	32,606
By location				
Street/highway	68,142	-1.5	31.8	46,797
Commercial house	41,589	2.2	19.4	2,270
Gas or service station	8,321	1.5	3.9	2,650
Convenience store	14,078	0.3	6.6	2,028
Residence	33,395	-5.2	15.6	105,356
Bank	3,093	6.5	1.4	4,137
Miscellaneous	45,917	2.1	21.4	2,834
Burglary for which location is known	844,460	-1.6	100.0	50,026
By location				
Residence (dwelling)	447,464	-4.5	53.0	63,470
Residence, night	184,162	-6.5	21.8	81,240
Residence, day	238,352	-2.5	28.2	55,744
Residence, unknown	24,950	-14.1	3.0	6,114
Nonresidence (store, office, etc.)	396,996	2.2	47.0	34,873
Nonresidence, night	197,588	5.6	23.4	24,955
Nonresidence, day	173,840	-0.4	20.6	50,287
Nonresidence, unknown	25,568	-14.9	3.0	6,715
Larceny-theft (except motor vehicle theft)	4,318,039	5.4	100.0	19,559
By type				
Pocket-picking	30,582	14.5	0.7	3,915
Purse-snatching	13,423	5.6	0.3	224,422
Shoplifting	915,375	15.7	21.2	12,590
From motor vehicles (except accessories)	1,025,356	-1.1	23.7	23,076
Motor vehicle accessories	530,801	2.1	12.3	1,381
Bicycles	117,533	1.9	2.7	17,843
From buildings	348,855	3.5	8.1	45,027
From coin-operated machines	6,018	-2.5	0.1	5,971
All others	1,330,096	6.2	30.8	20,726
By value				
Over $200	2,393,073	7.6	55.4	35,260
$50 to $200	760,238	3.9	17.6	100
Under $50	1,164,724	2.2	27.0	12
Motor Vehicle Theft	897,822	11.4	100.0	25,337

X = Not applicable.
1 Because of rounding, the percentages may not add to 100.0.   2 Due to technical system changes and data quality issues, some average values may be inflated.

Table 24. Property Stolen and Recovered, by Type and Value, 2022

(Dollars, percent; 14,643 agencies; 2022 estimated population 304,768,145.)

Type of property	Value of property (dollars)		Percent recovered
	Stolen	Recovered	
Total	$69,488,653,231	$9,969,928,361	14.3
Currency, notes, etc.	13,565,406,934	50,734,697	0.4
Jewelry and precious metals	2,386,607,507	44,524,152	1.9
Clothing and furs	6,575,587,637	30,224,648	0.5
Locally stolen motor vehicles	11,122,512,140	5,128,961,719	46.1
Office equipment	2,422,352,077	19,089,607	0.8
Televisions, radios, stereos, etc.	334,644,651	10,112,522	3.0
Firearms	174,758,913	14,016,105	8.0
Household goods	359,949,064	10,319,580	2.9
Consumable goods	2,273,888,413	14,621,018	0.6
Livestock	11,005,391	560,583	5.1
Miscellaneous	30,261,940,504	4,646,763,730	15.4

NOTE: Due to technical system changes and data quality issues, some property stolen and recovered data may be inflated.

SECTION III

OFFENSES CLEARED

OFFENSES CLEARED

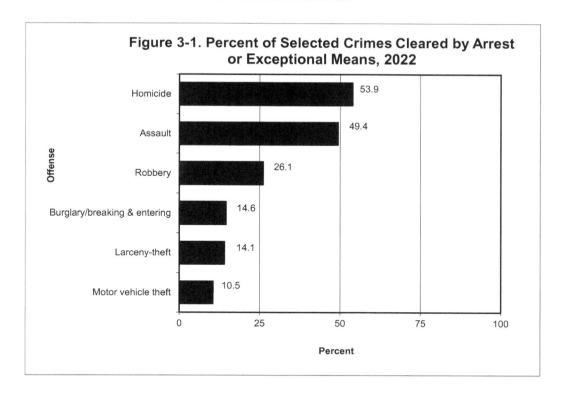

Figure 3-1. Percent of Selected Crimes Cleared by Arrest or Exceptional Means, 2022

Law enforcement agencies that report crime to the Federal Bureau of Investigation (FBI) can clear, or "close," offenses in one of two ways: by arrest or by exceptional means. However, the administrative closing of a case by a local law enforcement agency does not necessarily mean that the agency can clear an offense for Uniform Crime Reporting (UCR) purposes. To clear an offense within the program's guidelines, the reporting agency must adhere to certain criteria, which are outlined in this section. *(The UCR program does not distinguish between offenses cleared by arrest and those cleared by exceptional means in its data presentations. The distinction is made solely for the purpose of a definition and not for data collection and publication.)* *See Appendix I for information on the UCR program's statistical methodology.*

Important Note: Transition to NIBRS

As of January 1, 2021, the FBI's National Incident-Based Reporting System (NIBRS) became the national standard for law enforcement crime data reporting in the United States. The 2021 data year will mark the first time that the FBI and BJS estimate reported crime in the United States based solely on NIBRS data.

Section III—clearances—has been impacted by this limited release. New data for 2021 is included in Table 25. Data from 2020 is included in Table 25A through Table 28. However, given the alterations to the categories present in the 2021

data, year-over-year comparison is not provided between 2020 and 2021.

As of June 2022, all 50 U.S. states and the District of Columbia were certified to report crime data to NIBRS. Just under two-thirds of the U.S. population is covered by NIBRS-reporting law enforcement agencies, and 62 NIBRS-certified agencies serve cities with a population of 250,000 or more; these agencies cover a total population of more than 37 million.

CLEARED BY ARREST

In the UCR program, a law enforcement agency reports that an offense is cleared by arrest, or solved for crime reporting purposes, when at least one person is arrested, charged with the commission of the offense, and turned over to the court for prosecution (whether following arrest, court summons, or police notice). To qualify as a clearance, all of these conditions must be met.

In its calculations, the UCR program counts the number of offenses that are cleared, not the number of arrestees. Therefore, the arrest of one person may clear several crimes, and the arrest of many persons may clear only one offense. In addition, some clearances recorded by an agency during a particular calendar year, such as 2022, may pertain to offenses that occurred in previous years.

CLEARED BY EXCEPTIONAL MEANS

In certain situations, elements beyond law enforcement's control prevent the agency from arresting and formally charging the offender. When this occurs, the agency can clear the offense exceptionally. There are four UCR program requirements that law enforcement must meet in order to clear an offense by exceptional means. The agency must have:

- Identified the offender

- Gathered enough evidence to support an arrest, make a charge, and turn over the offender to the court for prosecution

- Identified the offender's exact location so that the suspect could be taken into custody immediately

- Encountered a circumstance outside the control of law enforcement that prohibits the agency from arresting, charging, and prosecuting the offender

Examples of exceptional clearances include, but are not limited to, the death of the offender (e.g., suicide or justifiably killed by a law enforcement officer or a citizen), the victim's refusal to cooperate with the prosecution after the offender has been identified, or the denial of extradition because the offender committed a crime in another jurisdiction and is being prosecuted for that offense. In the UCR program, the recovery of property does not clear an offense.

NATIONAL CLEARANCES

A review of the data for 2022 revealed law enforcement agencies in the United States cleared 41.1 percent of crimes against persons (murder, assault, human trafficking, kidnapping/abduction, and sexual offenses); 13.9 percent of crimes against property (arson, bribery, burglary/breaking and entering, counterfeiting/forgery, destruction/damage/vandalism, embezzlement, extortion/blackmail, fraud, robbery, stolen property, larceny-theft, and motor vehicle theft); and 72.1 percent of crimes against society (animal cruelty, drug/narcotic offenses, gambling offenses, pornography/obscene material, weapon law violations, and prostitution offenses) brought to their attention. (Table 25)

As in most years, law enforcement agencies cleared a higher percentage of crimes against persons and society than crimes against property in 2022. As a rule, clearance rates generally rise due to the more vigorous investigative efforts put forth for these crimes. In addition, these crimes more often involve victims and/or witnesses who are able to identify the perpetrators.

A further breakdown of the clearances for 2022 revealed that the nation's law enforcement agencies cleared 49.4 percent of homicide offenses, 42.2 percent of assault offenses, and 24.1 percent of robbery offenses. (Table 25)

For property crime offenses in 2022, law enforcement agencies throughout the nation collectively 13.5 percent of burglary/breaking and entering offenses, 12.9 percent of larceny-theft offenses, and 9.2 percent of motor vehicle theft offenses. (Table 25)

Table 25. Incidents Cleared, by Offense Category, 2022

(Number; percent.)

Population group	Total incidents[2]	Incidents cleared[1]					
		Total incidents cleared	Percent of incidents cleared	Cleared by arrest[3]	Percent cleared by arrest[3]	Cleared by exceptional means	Percent cleared by exceptional means
Total	11,195,659	3,656,630	32.7	3,295,013	29.4	361,617	3.2
Crimes Against Persons	2,988,454	1,226,806	41.1	1,011,584	33.8	215,222	7.2
Assault offenses	2,737,786	1,154,467	42.2	956,577	34.9	197,890	7.2
Homicide offenses	17,189	8,489	49.4	7,713	44.9	776	4.5
Human trafficking offenses	2,234	731	32.7	686	30.7	45	2.0
Kidnapping/abduction	39,098	20,925	53.5	19,342	49.5	1,583	4.0
Sex offenses	192,147	42,194	22.0	27,266	14.2	14,928	7.8
Crimes Against Property	7,849,624	1,087,397	13.9	976,362	12.4	111,035	1.4
Arson	30,166	7,686	25.5	7,123	23.6	563	1.9
Bribery	652	365	56.0	357	54.8	8	1.2
Burglary/breaking & entering	672,139	90,619	13.5	82,772	12.3	7,847	1.2
Counterfeiting/forgery	147,573	25,859	17.5	23,934	16.2	1,925	1.3
Destruction/damage/vandalism	1,497,908	221,268	14.8	189,347	12.6	31,921	2.1
Embezzlement	32,481	9,363	28.8	7,950	24.5	1,413	4.4
Extortion/blackmail	20,298	846	4.2	604	3.0	242	1.2
Fraud offenses	843,491	89,383	10.6	78,615	9.3	10,768	1.3
Larceny/theft offenses	3,618,452	465,841	12.9	422,976	11.7	42,865	1.2
Motor vehicle theft	721,157	66,484	9.2	57,248	7.9	9,236	1.3
Robbery	149,862	36,067	24.1	33,039	22.0	3,028	2.0
Stolen property offenses	115,445	73,616	63.8	72,397	62.7	1,219	1.1
Crimes Against Society	1,860,969	1,342,427	72.1	1,307,067	70.2	35,360	1.9
Animal cruelty	20,512	5,067	24.7	4,704	22.9	363	1.8
Drug/narcotic offenses	1,459,460	1,117,586	76.6	1,090,285	74.7	27,301	1.9
Gambling offenses	2,121	820	38.7	677	31.9	143	6.7
Pornography/obscene material	39,871	7,969	20.0	6,066	15.2	1,903	4.8
Prostitution offenses	13,007	9,271	71.3	9,149	70.3	122	0.9
Weapon law violations	325,998	201,714	61.9	196,186	60.2	5,528	1.7

1 Clearance figures in this table represent the total number of incidents cleared and a breakdown of the clearance method for each offense category.   2 The total number of incidents is 11,195,659. However, the column figures will not add to the total because incidents may include more than one offense type, and one incident was counted for each offense type within each offense category in this table.   3 In the National Incident-Based Reporting System, the submission of arrestee data in connection with an incident automatically clears all offenses within the incident.

Table 25A. Number and Percent of Offenses Cleared by Arrest or Exceptional Means, by Population Group, 2022

(Number, percent.)

Population group	Violent crime	Murder and nonnegligent manslaughter	Rape	Robbery	Aggravated assault	Property crime	Burglary	Larceny-theft	Motor vehicle theft	Arson[1]	Number of agencies	Estimated population, 2022
Total, All Agencies												
Offenses known	1,208,688	19,897	123,850	215,051	849,890	6,120,810	846,437	4,335,066	901,206	38,101	14,719	305,490,930
Percent cleared by arrest	36.7	52.3	26.1	23.2	41.4	12.1	13.0	12.4	9.3	25.2		
Total Cities												
Offenses known	964,978	15,623	91,310	190,475	667,570	4,988,159	652,901	3,552,645	752,767	29,846	10,807	206,650,600
Percent cleared by arrest	35.2	50.6	24.1	22.7	39.9	11.9	12.6	12.4	8.4	24.7		
Group I (250,000 and over)												
Offenses known	479,308	8,541	33,259	117,005	320,503	2,019,123	263,789	1,358,285	385,486	11,563	89	62,100,184
Percent cleared by arrest	27.1	46.2	20.3	18.1	30.6	6.7	9.3	6.1	6.6	19.0		
1,000,000 and over (Group I subset)												
Offenses known	200,571	3,180	12,604	58,174	126,613	782,764	93,635	543,768	141,324	4,037	10	25,965,648
Percent cleared by arrest	20.3	40.6	17.4	13.1	23.4	4.5	6.9	3.8	5.0	12.4		
500,000 to 999,999 (Group I subset)												
Offenses known	160,983	3,033	10,890	34,342	112,718	699,740	98,868	453,094	143,638	4,140	26	18,523,209
Percent cleared by arrest	32.4	46.2	24.1	23.6	35.5	6.9	9.9	6.1	7.0	22.4		
250,000 to 499,999 (Group I subset)												
Offenses known	117,754	2,328	9,765	24,489	81,172	536,619	71,286	361,423	100,524	3,386	53	17,611,327
Percent cleared by arrest	31.5	54.0	19.9	22.2	35.0	9.5	11.8	9.4	8.0	22.7		
Group II (100,000 to 249,999)												
Offenses known	152,205	2,302	14,581	27,154	108,168	813,115	110,888	571,345	125,736	5,146	220	31,698,148
Percent cleared by arrest	38.5	53.7	24.3	27.3	42.9	10.7	12.1	10.8	8.2	26.9		
Group III (50,000 to 99,999)												
Offenses known	117,452	1,559	13,402	20,894	81,597	714,515	92,441	526,753	91,050	4,271	485	33,734,495
Percent cleared by arrest	43.9	61.0	27.0	29.7	49.9	14.1	14.0	14.8	9.3	26.2		
Group IV (25,000 to 49,999)												
Offenses known	85,186	1,235	11,028	12,131	60,792	560,609	70,104	428,077	59,055	3,373	868	29,992,048
Percent cleared by arrest	43.9	57.8	26.6	32.6	49.0	17.4	15.6	18.4	11.7	28.7		
Group V (10,000 to 24,999)												
Offenses known	69,652	1,063	10,028	8,066	50,495	485,993	63,911	371,461	47,968	2,653	1,763	28,167,125
Percent cleared by arrest	47.0	52.4	27.0	33.2	53.0	20.0	16.6	21.4	13.5	33.0		
Group VI (under 10,000)												
Offenses known	61,175	923	9,012	5,225	46,015	394,804	51,768	296,724	43,472	2,840	7,382	20,958,600
Percent cleared by arrest	47.9	54.2	27.0	35.8	53.3	19.1	18.2	19.9	13.9	28.7		
Metropolitan Counties												
Offenses known	194,255	3,179	23,206	22,878	144,992	933,137	145,693	658,315	123,164	5,965	1,726	75,026,703
Percent cleared by arrest	41.5	58.4	31.6	25.8	45.2	12.8	13.9	12.6	12.4	27.0		
Nonmetropolitan Counties												
Offenses known	49,455	1,095	9,334	1,698	37,328	199,514	47,843	124,106	25,275	2,290	2,186	23,813,627
Percent cleared by arrest	48.3	57.9	32.5	36.0	52.6	14.8	16.2	13.1	19.4	27.1		
Suburban Areas[2]												
Offenses known	325,490	4,975	41,397	41,143	237,975	1,901,395	259,263	1,397,249	233,762	11,121	7,970	133,070,428
Percent cleared by arrest	43.4	57.0	29.5	29.0	48.0	15.2	14.7	15.8	11.7	28.4		

1 Not all agencies submit reports for arson to the FBI. As a result, the number of reports the FBI uses to compute the percent of offenses cleared for arson is less than the number it uses to compute the percent of offenses cleared for all other offenses.
2 Suburban area includes law enforcement agencies in cities with less than 50,000 inhabitants and county law enforcement agencies that are within a Metropolitan Statistical Area. Suburban area excludes all metropolitan agencies associated with a principal city. The agencies associated with suburban areas also appear in other groups within this table.

Table 26. Number and Percent of Offenses Cleared by Arrest or Exceptional Means, by Region and Geographic Division, 2022

(Number, percent.)

Geographic region/division	Violent crime	Murder and nonnegligent manslaughter	Rape	Robbery	Aggravated assault	Property crime	Burglary	Larceny-theft	Motor vehicle theft	Arson[1]	Number of agencies	Estimated population, 2022
Total, All Agencies												
Offenses known	1,208,688	19,897	123,850	215,051	849,890	6,120,810	846,437	4,335,066	901,206	38,101	14,719	305,490,930
Percent cleared by arrest	36.7	52.3	26.1	23.2	41.4	12.1	13.0	12.4	9.3	25.2		
Northeast												
Offenses known	163,685	2,269	14,393	38,536	108,487	785,521	78,552	627,587	75,986	3,396	2,929	53,154,501
Percent cleared by arrest	28.6	41.7	21.7	15.2	34.0	12.4	15.0	12.4	9.4	29.4		
New England												
Offenses known	34,326	377	4,316	4,971	24,662	185,363	19,884	146,232	18,275	972	962	15,056,132
Percent cleared by arrest	48.7	52.5	25.0	26.8	57.2	14.5	18.3	14.2	11.6	33.0		
Middle Atlantic												
Offenses known	129,359	1,892	10,077	33,565	83,825	600,158	58,668	481,355	57,711	2,424	1,967	38,098,369
Percent cleared by arrest	23.3	39.6	20.2	13.5	27.2	11.8	14.0	11.8	8.7	27.9		
Midwest												
Offenses known	221,094	4,100	29,866	35,005	152,123	1,106,185	144,234	777,989	176,927	7,035	3,977	61,046,278
Percent cleared by arrest	38.6	49.7	25.7	20.9	44.9	13.5	13.5	14.5	8.8	21.1		
East North Central												
Offenses known	145,797	2,989	20,206	25,989	96,613	690,045	91,579	483,727	110,429	4,310	2,184	40,489,419
Percent cleared by arrest	36.3	43.0	25.0	19.0	43.2	12.5	12.7	13.5	7.7	19.4		
West North Central												
Offenses known	75,297	1,111	9,660	9,016	55,510	416,140	52,655	294,262	66,498	2,725	1,793	20,556,859
Percent cleared by arrest	43.0	68.0	27.4	26.7	47.9	15.0	14.9	16.0	10.6	23.8		
South												
Offenses known	474,506	9,206	45,953	67,440	351,907	2,329,843	338,272	1,693,299	287,078	11,194	5,664	115,092,040
Percent cleared by arrest	34.9	52.2	27.9	23.1	37.6	13.2	13.7	13.3	11.8	25.6		
South Atlantic												
Offenses known	208,676	4,408	18,665	32,274	153,329	1,020,038	130,384	777,029	107,977	4,648	2,383	56,633,914
Percent cleared by arrest	34.3	53.0	33.2	24.1	36.1	14.7	17.1	14.4	13.1	28.3		
East South Central												
Offenses known	75,054	1,506	6,083	8,285	59,180	337,135	53,645	234,618	46,805	2,067	1,345	17,777,076
Percent cleared by arrest	38.9	50.7	36.7	23.9	40.9	16.4	15.5	16.8	14.9	23.7		
West South Central												
Offenses known	190,776	3,292	21,205	26,881	139,398	972,670	154,243	681,652	132,296	4,479	1,936	40,681,050
Percent cleared by arrest	33.9	51.8	20.8	21.6	37.9	10.5	10.2	10.7	9.6	23.8		
West												
Offenses known	349,403	4,322	33,638	74,070	237,373	1,899,261	285,379	1,236,191	361,215	16,476	2,149	76,198,111
Percent cleared by arrest	41.9	60.3	25.9	28.4	48.0	9.9	11.4	10.0	7.5	25.7		
Mountain												
Offenses known	104,853	1,454	13,211	15,405	74,783	561,027	78,823	378,919	99,797	3,488	865	23,859,656
Percent cleared by arrest	42.5	64.2	23.7	29.5	48.1	13.7	13.2	14.8	9.4	30.8		
Pacific												
Offenses known	244,550	2,868	20,427	58,665	162,590	1,338,234	206,556	857,272	261,418	12,988	1,284	52,338,455
Percent cleared by arrest	41.6	58.4	27.4	28.2	47.9	8.2	10.6	7.9	6.8	24.3		

1 Not all agencies submit reports for arson to the FBI. As a result, the number of reports the FBI uses to compute the percent of offenses cleared for arson is less than the number it uses to compute the percent of offenses cleared for all other offenses.

Table 27. Number and Percent of Offenses Cleared by Arrest or Exceptional Means, Additional Information About Selected Offenses, by Population Group, 2022

(Number, percent.)

Population group	Rape by force		Robbery				Aggravated assault			
	Rape by force	Assault to rape-attempts	Firearm	Knife or cutting instrument	Other weapon	Strong-arm	Firearm	Knife or cutting instrument	Other weapon	Hands, fists, feet, etc.
Total, All Agencies										
Offenses known	119,668	4,182	79,959	18,311	25,277	91,504	309,814	132,737	236,824	170,515
Percent cleared by arrest	26.0	29.3	20.0	27.4	25.1	24.5	28.8	50.8	45.0	51.7
Total Cities										
Offenses known	88,148	3,162	69,328	16,472	22,390	82,285	247,544	108,525	182,831	128,670
Percent cleared by arrest	23.9	28.8	19.7	27.0	24.8	23.8	27.3	49.5	43.5	50.8
Group I (250,000 and over)										
Offenses known	31,889	1,370	43,883	9,935	12,407	50,780	136,058	53,629	84,352	46,464
Percent cleared by arrest	20.1	26.1	17.5	21.0	19.8	17.6	22.9	41.0	34.1	34.9
1,000,000 and over (Group I subset)										
Offenses known	11,978	626	17,999	5,653	6,622	27,900	42,439	25,367	34,852	23,955
Percent cleared by arrest	17.3	20.4	13.5	14.2	15.1	12.1	20.1	29.4	24.3	22.0
500,000 to 999,999 (Group I subset)										
Offenses known	10,465	425	15,462	2,579	3,756	12,545	55,909	16,022	28,847	11,940
Percent cleared by arrest	23.6	37.9	20.4	30.5	26.0	25.4	24.1	51.9	43.0	48.7
250,000 to 499,999 (Group I subset)										
Offenses known	9,446	319	10,422	1,703	2,029	10,335	37,710	12,240	20,653	10,569
Percent cleared by arrest	19.8	21.6	19.9	29.3	23.5	23.0	24.3	50.8	38.3	48.8
Group II (100,000 to 249,999)										
Offenses known	14,080	501	10,071	2,455	3,710	10,918	41,440	17,612	28,917	20,199
Percent cleared by arrest	24.0	32.3	21.3	32.1	28.3	31.3	27.6	54.8	48.1	56.5
Group III (50,000 to 99,999)										
Offenses known	13,067	335	6,629	1,961	2,888	9,416	24,942	13,361	23,465	19,829
Percent cleared by arrest	26.7	37.0	22.6	36.4	31.6	32.9	34.0	58.5	52.5	61.1
Group IV (25,000 to 49,999)										
Offenses known	10,728	300	4,055	1,091	1,637	5,348	18,915	9,743	17,742	14,392
Percent cleared by arrest	26.5	27.3	28.1	37.5	32.8	35.0	33.7	58.5	52.0	59.0
Group V (10,000 to 24,999)										
Offenses known	9,753	275	2,978	629	1,102	3,357	15,029	7,524	14,470	13,472
Percent cleared by arrest	26.9	30.2	25.4	42.3	33.2	38.4	37.0	61.6	55.1	63.8
Group VI (under 10,000)										
Offenses known	8,631	381	1,712	401	646	2,466	11,160	6,656	13,885	14,314
Percent cleared by arrest	27.0	27.0	27.2	45.6	37.0	40.0	40.6	59.7	53.6	59.9
Metropolitan Counties										
Offenses known	22,490	716	9,863	1,707	2,674	8,634	51,107	19,800	42,374	31,711
Percent cleared by arrest	31.6	30.6	21.1	30.9	26.1	30.2	32.9	55.5	48.7	53.9
Nonmetropolitan Counties										
Offenses known	9,030	304	768	132	213	585	11,163	4,412	11,619	10,134
Percent cleared by arrest	32.5	31.6	31.0	34.1	42.7	40.7	43.4	62.1	54.7	56.0
Suburban Areas[2]										
Offenses known	40,112	1,285	16,233	3,188	5,078	16,644	76,623	33,630	70,568	57,154
Percent cleared by arrest	29.5	29.3	22.9	35.9	29.8	33.4	34.2	57.5	50.6	57.7

Table 27. Number and Percent of Offenses Cleared by Arrest or Exceptional Means, Additional Information About Selected Offenses, by Population Group, 2022—Continued

(Number, percent.)

Population group	Burglary			Motor vehicle theft			Arson[1]			Number of agencies	Estimated population, 2022
	Forcible entry	Unlawful entry	Attempted forcible entry	Autos	Trucks and buses	Other vehicles	Structure	Mobile	Other		
Total, All Agencies											
Offenses known	480,090	313,493	52,854	690,379	136,943	73,884	13,298	7,160	16,165	14,719	305,490,930
Percent cleared by arrest	11.5	15.2	13.8	9.7	8.1	7.6	27.0	12.3	28.4		
Total Cities											
Offenses known	372,555	236,628	43,718	583,180	113,670	55,917	10,279	5,349	13,083	10,807	206,650,600
Percent cleared by arrest	11.0	14.9	13.3	8.8	7.2	6.9	25.9	12.0	28.0		
Group I (250,000 and over)											
Offenses known	163,000	81,651	19,138	295,153	65,964	24,369	3,765	2,337	5,146	89	62,100,184
Percent cleared by arrest	8.2	11.1	11.0	6.7	6.3	5.1	21.5	8.6	21.3		
1,000,000 and over (Group I subset)											
Offenses known	61,201	26,082	6,352	96,136	35,755	9,433	1,004	633	2,313	10	25,965,648
Percent cleared by arrest	5.7	9.4	8.2	5.1	5.1	4.4	19.0	7.3	10.8		
500,000 to 999,999 (Group I subset)											
Offenses known	59,723	31,671	7,474	114,284	20,315	9,039	1,669	1,029	1,287	26	18,523,209
Percent cleared by arrest	8.7	11.6	11.3	7.4	6.3	4.5	21.6	10.0	32.0		
250,000 to 499,999 (Group I subset)											
Offenses known	42,076	23,898	5,312	84,733	9,894	5,897	1,092	675	1,546	53	17,611,327
Percent cleared by arrest	11.2	12.4	13.9	7.8	10.6	7.2	23.5	7.6	28.1		
Group II (100,000 to 249,999)											
Offenses known	63,650	39,917	7,321	98,685	17,317	9,734	1,645	906	2,381	220	31,698,148
Percent cleared by arrest	10.8	13.9	13.7	8.5	7.4	6.3	25.6	12.9	32.4		
Group III (50,000 to 99,999)											
Offenses known	50,342	36,409	5,690	71,463	11,973	7,614	1,317	809	1,979	485	33,734,495
Percent cleared by arrest	12.5	15.9	15.0	9.8	7.4	7.5	27.5	12.6	30.5		
Group IV (25,000 to 49,999)											
Offenses known	36,071	29,349	4,684	48,055	6,155	4,845	1,192	507	1,494	868	29,992,048
Percent cleared by arrest	14.0	17.5	16.1	12.2	10.5	8.8	28.9	17.6	31.3		
Group V (10,000 to 24,999)											
Offenses known	33,160	26,972	3,779	39,042	5,133	3,793	1,042	416	1,071	1,763	28,167,125
Percent cleared by arrest	15.1	18.5	15.4	14.0	11.7	10.8	33.5	15.6	38.1		
Group VI (under 10,000)											
Offenses known	26,332	22,330	3,106	30,782	7,128	5,562	1,318	374	1,012	7,382	20,958,600
Percent cleared by arrest	16.5	20.5	16.5	15.8	8.7	10.5	29.0	17.9	31.0		
Metropolitan Counties											
Offenses known	81,021	57,156	7,516	90,137	18,492	14,535	2,088	1,336	2,313	1,726	75,026,703
Percent cleared by arrest	12.2	16.1	16.0	13.1	11.5	8.9	30.9	12.4	30.7		
Nonmetropolitan Counties											
Offenses known	26,514	19,709	1,620	17,062	4,781	3,432	931	475	769	2,186	23,813,627
Percent cleared by arrest	15.8	16.7	18.6	21.8	15.0	13.5	29.5	16.4	29.0		
Suburban Areas[2]											
Offenses known	140,739	102,925	15,599	176,987	32,183	24,592	3,964	2,103	4,553	7,970	133,070,428
Percent cleared by arrest	12.9	17.0	15.8	12.3	10.2	8.9	31.4	13.7	31.4		

1 Not all agencies submit reports for arson to the FBI. As a result, the number of reports the FBI uses to compute the percent of offenses cleared for arson is less than the number it uses to compute the percent of offenses cleared for all other offenses. Agencies must report arson clearances by detailed property classification as specified on the *Monthly Return of Arson Offenses Known to Law Enforcement* to be included in this table; therefore, clearances in this table may differ from other clearance tables.   2 Suburban area includes law enforcement agencies in cities with less than 50,000 inhabitants and county law enforcement agencies that are within a Metropolitan Statistical Area. Suburban area excludes all metropolitan agencies associated with a principal city. The agencies associated with suburban areas also appear in other groups within this table.

Table 28. Number of Offenses Cleared by Arrest or Exceptional Means and Percent Involving Persons Under 18 Years of Age, by Population Group, 2022

(Number, percent.)

Population group	Violent crime	Murder and nonnegligent manslaughter	Rape	Robbery	Aggravated assault	Property crime	Burglary	Larceny-theft	Motor vehicle theft	Arson[1]	Number of agencies	Estimated population, 2022
Total, All Agencies												
Total clearances	443,994	10,397	32,353	49,798	351,446	740,756	109,990	538,083	83,618	9,065	14,719	305,490,930
Percent under 18 years	7.8	5.9	17.0	11.6	6.5	7.3	6.2	6.6	12.4	12.2		
Total Cities												
Total clearances	339,494	7,907	21,991	43,274	266,322	591,590	81,987	439,144	63,491	6,968	10,807	206,650,600
Percent under 18 years	7.7	6.2	15.0	11.4	6.5	7.1	6.0	6.4	12.7	11.4		
Group I (250,000 and over)												
Total clearances	129,990	3,949	6,766	21,146	98,129	134,231	24,599	82,214	25,314	2,104	89	62,100,184
Percent under 18 years	6.4	6.6	12.0	12.0	4.8	6.7	4.1	5.4	13.7	6.7		
1,000,000 and over (Group I subset)												
Total clearances	40,781	1,291	2,196	7,605	29,689	34,840	6,453	20,773	7,128	486	10	25,965,648
Percent under 18 years	5.8	5.6	9.7	11.5	4.1	4.7	2.1	3.8	9.4	6.0		
500,000 to 999,999 (Group I subset)												
Total clearances	52,134	1,401	2,628	8,112	39,993	48,254	9,740	27,519	10,120	875	26	18,523,209
Percent under 18 years	6.2	7.3	12.5	12.0	4.6	6.4	3.7	4.3	14.8	6.4		
250,000 to 499,999 (Group I subset)												
Total clearances	37,075	1,257	1,942	5,429	28,447	51,137	8,406	33,922	8,066	743	53	17,611,327
Percent under 18 years	7.3	6.9	13.9	12.8	5.8	8.4	6.1	7.2	16.0	7.5		
Group II (100,000 to 249,999)												
Total clearances	58,584	1,236	3,541	7,402	46,405	86,572	13,445	61,552	10,265	1,310	220	31,698,148
Percent under 18 years	7.1	6.1	14.2	9.4	6.2	7.1	5.5	6.7	11.3	9.2		
Group III (50,000 to 99,999)												
Total clearances	51,507	951	3,613	6,214	40,729	100,479	12,946	78,025	8,440	1,068	485	33,734,495
Percent under 18 years	7.9	6.2	15.9	10.9	6.8	7.4	6.2	7.0	12.4	13.4		
Group IV (25,000 to 49,999)												
Total clearances	37,392	714	2,928	3,960	29,790	97,669	10,966	78,868	6,934	901	868	29,992,048
Percent under 18 years	8.8	4.9	16.9	11.2	7.7	7.0	6.9	6.3	13.7	14.9		
Group V (10,000 to 24,999)												
Total clearances	32,706	557	2,711	2,679	26,759	97,310	10,591	79,421	6,476	822	1,763	28,167,125
Percent under 18 years	9.7	8.1	18.5	11.5	8.7	7.1	7.5	6.6	12.4	14.0		
Group VI (under 10,000)												
Total clearances	29,315	500	2,432	1,873	24,510	75,329	9,440	59,064	6,062	763	7,382	20,958,600
Percent under 18 years	10.6	3.0	17.4	15.1	9.7	7.3	8.5	6.5	11.0	18.7		
Metropolitan Counties												
Total clearances	80,604	1,856	7,332	5,912	65,504	119,706	20,240	82,722	15,223	1,521	1,726	75,026,703
Percent under 18 years	8.7	4.5	21.2	13.5	6.9	8.5	7.7	7.8	12.4	16.9		
Nonmetropolitan Counties												
Total clearances	23,896	634	3,030	612	19,620	29,460	7,763	16,217	4,904	576	2,186	23,813,627
Percent under 18 years	7.4	5.8	20.7	6.5	5.4	6.2	4.9	6.2	8.0	9.0		
Suburban Areas[2]												
Total clearances	141,245	2,837	12,208	11,935	114,265	288,590	38,075	220,284	27,268	2,963	7,970	133,070,428
Percent under 18 years	9.2	4.6	20.0	13.2	7.8	7.6	7.8	6.9	12.3	16.2		

1 Not all agencies submit reports for arson to the FBI. As a result, the number of reports the FBI uses to compute the percent of offenses cleared for arson is less than the number it uses to compute the percent of offenses cleared for all other offenses.
2 Suburban area includes law enforcement agencies in cities with less than 50,000 inhabitants and county law enforcement agencies that are within a Metropolitan Statistical Area. Suburban area excludes all metropolitan agencies associated with a principal city. The agencies associated with suburban areas also appear in other groups within this table.

SECTION IV

PERSONS ARRESTED

PERSONS ARRESTED

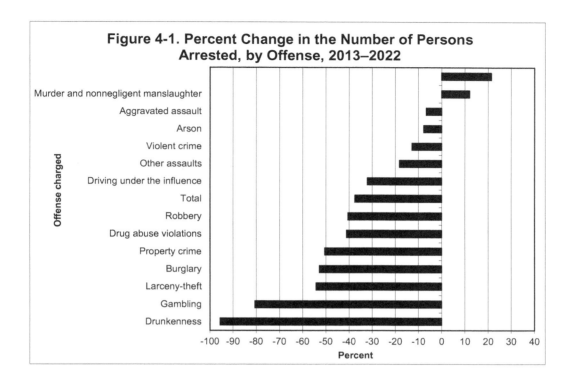

Figure 4-1. Percent Change in the Number of Persons Arrested, by Offense, 2013–2022

In the Uniform Crime Reporting (UCR) program, one arrest is counted for each separate instance in which an individual is arrested, cited, or summoned for criminal acts in Part I and Part II crimes. (See Appendix I for additional information concerning Part I and Part II crimes.) One person may be arrested multiple times during the year; as a result, the arrest figures in this section should not be taken as the total number of individuals arrested. Instead, it provides the number of arrest occurrences reported by law enforcement. Information regarding the UCR program's statistical methodology and table construction can be found in Appendix I.

Important Note: Rape Data

In 2013, the UCR Program initiated the collection of rape data under a revised definition and removed the term "forcible" from the offense name. The UCR Program now defines rape as follows:

Rape (revised definition): Penetration, no matter how slight, of the vagina or anus with any body part or object, or oral penetration by a sex organ of another person, without the consent of the victim. (This includes the offenses of rape, sodomy, and sexual assault with an object as converted from data submitted via the National Incident-Based Reporting System.)

Rape (legacy definition): The carnal knowledge of a female forcibly and against her will. For tables within this publication that present data for 2019 only or provide a 2-year trend,

the rape figures are an aggregate total of the data submitted based on both the legacy and revised UCR definitions. For 5- and 10-year trend tables, the rape figures for the previous year (2014 or 2009) are based on the legacy definition and the 2019 rape figures are an aggregate total based on both the legacy and revised definitions. For this reason, a percent change is not provided.

Data Collection: Juveniles

The UCR Program considers a juvenile to be an individual under 18 years of age regardless of state definition. The program does not collect data regarding police contact with a juvenile who has not committed an offense, nor does it collect data on situations in which police take a juvenile into custody for his or her protection, e.g., neglect cases.

National Volume, Trends, and Rates

Volume

The FBI reported an estimated 7,364,553 arrests occurred in 2022 for all offenses. Of these arrests, 429,593 were for violent crimes (murder, rape, robbery, and aggravated assault) and 791,013 were for property crimes (arson, burglary, larceny-theft, and motor vehicle theft). Outside of these categories, the most frequent identifiable arrests made in 2022 were for other assault offenses (estimated at 947,552 arrests).

These arrests comprised 12.9 percent of the total number of all arrests. (Table 29)

A comparison of arrest figures from 2021 to 2022 revealed a 0.3 percent increase. This number should be interpreted with caution, given switch to NBIRS for reporting data. Arrests for violent crimes increased 1.1 percent and arrests for property crimes increased 10.5 percent over this time period. An examination of the 5-year and 10-year arrest trends showed that the total number of arrests in 2022 fell 29.1 percent from the 2018 total. Arrests for violent crimes showed a 15.7 percent decrease from 2018 to 2022 and property crimes showed a 32.3 percent decrease. In the 10-year trend data (2013 to 2022), the number of arrests decreased 37.5 percent. For violent crimes, the number of arrests fell 12.9 percent, while arrests for property crimes decreased 50.5 percent. (Tables 32, 34, and 36)

Trends

The number of adults arrested for violent crime (arrestees age 18 years and over) decreased 0.2 percent from 2021 to 2022, decreased 15.0 percent from 2018 to 2022, and decreased 10.5 percent from 2013 to 2022. The number of juveniles arrested for violent crime (arrestees under 18 years of age) increased 13.9 percent from 2021 to 2022, decreased 22.2 percent from 2018 to 2022, and decreased 31.9 percent from 2013 to 2022. (Tables 32, 34, and 36)

The trend data for murder and nonnegligent manslaughter showed that the number of arrests for this offense decreased 4.9 percent from 2021 to 2022, increased 1.7 percent from 2018 to 2022, and increased 12.0 percent from 2013 to 2022. The number of adults arrested for murder decreased 6.8 percent from 2021 to 2022, decreased 1.0 percent from 2018 to 2022, and rose 9.0 percent from 2013 to 2022. The number of juveniles arrested for murder increased 14.5 percent from 2021 to 2022, increased 33.5 percent from 2018 to 2022, and rose 50.8 percent from 2013 to 2022. (Tables 32, 34, and 36)

For rape, the trend data showed that arrests decreased 2.3 percent from 2021 to 2022, with adult arrests decreasing 2.0 percent and juvenile arrests falling 3.9 percent. The five-year data (2018 to 2022) shows arrests decreasing 21.9 percent overall, with adult arrests falling 20.7 percent and juvenile arrests decreasing 27.6 percent. The 10-year trend data percentages were not calculated due to the program changes in the classification of rape data. (Tables 32, 34, and 36)

For robbery, the data showed that arrests increased 3.1 percent from 2021 to 2022, with adult arrests increasing percent and juvenile arrests rising 10.1 percent. The 5-year trend data showed that total robbery arrests fell 31.5 percent from 2018 to 2022; adult arrests decreased 30.3 percent and juvenile arrests dropped 36.8 percent during this period. The 10-year trend data showed that arrests fell 30.5 percent from 2013 to 2022, with adult arrests dropping 38.5 percent and juvenile arrests falling by 48.6 percent. (Tables 32, 34, and 36)

The aggravated assault trend data showed that the number of arrests for this offense rose 1.2 percent from 2021 to 2022, decreased 12.1 percent from 2018 to 2022, and fell 6.7 percent from 2013 to 2022. The number of adults arrested for aggravated assault remained nearly the same from 2021 to 2022, decreased 12.1 percent from 2018 to 2022, and fell 5.0 percent from 2013 to 2022. The number of juveniles arrested for aggravated assault increased 29.6 percent from 2021 to 2022, fell 13.8 percent from 2018 to 2022, and dropped 15.9 percent from 2013 to 2022. (Tables 32, 34, and 36)

The 2-year, 5-year, and 10-year trend data showed that the number of arrests for property crime increased 10.5 percent from 2021 to 2022, decreased 32.3 percent from 2018 to 2022, and decreased 50.5 percent from 2013 to 2022. The number of adults arrested for property crime offenses (arrestees age 18 years and over) increased 9.1 percent from 2021 to 2022, decreased 30.3 percent from 2018 to 2022, and decreased 46.4 percent from 2013 to 2022. The number of juveniles arrested for property crime (arrestees under 18 years of age) increased 26.3 percent from 2021 to 2022, decreased 47.5 percent from 2018 to 2022, and decreased 72.6 percent from 2013 to 2022. (Tables 32, 34, and 36)

The trend data for burglary showed that the number of arrests for this offense increased 3.0 percent from 2021 to 2022, decreased 31.8 percent from 2018 to 2022, and decreased 52.8 percent from 2013 to 2022. The number of adults arrested for burglary rose 1.9 percent from 2021 to 2022, fell 29.1 percent from 2018 to 2022, and decreased 48.2 percent from 2013 to 2022. The number of juveniles arrested for burglary increased 14.3 percent from 2021 to 2022, decreased 50.5 percent from 2018 to 2022, and fell 75.3 percent from 2013 to 2022. (Tables 32, 34, and 36)

For larceny-theft, the 2-year trend data showed that arrests rose 13.1 percent from 2021 to 2022, with adult arrests increasing 11.5 percent and juvenile arrests increasing 34.8 percent. The 5-year trend data showed that total larceny-theft arrests decreased 35.0 percent from 2018 to 2022; adult arrests fell 33.1 percent and juvenile arrests dropped by 50.9 percent during this period. The 10-year trend data showed that larceny-theft arrests fell 54.2 percent from 2013 to 2022, with adult arrests decreasing by 50.2 percent and juvenile arrests falling by 76.3 percent. (Tables 32, 34, and 36)

For motor vehicle theft, the 2-year trend data showed that arrests rose 2.5 percent from 2021 to 2022, with adult arrests increasing 1.3 percent and juvenile arrests increasing 9.3 percent. The 5-year trend data showed that total motor vehicle theft arrests dropped 10.8 percent from 2018 to 2022; juvenile arrests fell 24.4 percent and adult arrests dropped 8.1 percent during this period. The 10-year trend data showed that arrests rose 21.4 percent from 2011 to 2020, with adult arrests rising 27.8 percent and juvenile arrests dropping 7.1 percent. (Tables 32, 34, and 36)

The arson trend data showed that the number of arrests for this offense increased 1.8 percent from 2021 to 2022, rose 11.8 percent from 2018 to 2022, and fell 7.8 percent from 2013 to 2022. The number of adults arrested for arson rose 0.2 percent from 2021 to 2022, increased 20.4 percent from 2018 to 2022, and increased 20.8 percent from 2013 to 2022. The number of juveniles arrested for arson increased 11.2 percent from 2021 to 2022, dropped 24.4 percent from 2018 to 2022, and dropped 63.6 percent from 2013 to 2022. (Tables 32, 34, and 36)

Rates

The rate of arrests was estimated at 2,181.7 arrests per 100,000 inhabitants in 2022. The arrest rate for violent crime was 129.1 arrests per 100,000 inhabitants, and the arrest rate for property crime was 235.8 arrests per 100,000 inhabitants. Law enforcement agencies throughout the nation reported arrest rates of 3.7 for murder, 5.9 for rape, 17.7 for robbery, and 101.9 for aggravated assault per 100,000 inhabitants in 2022. Law enforcement agencies throughout the nation reported arrest rates of 36.2 for burglary, 173.3 for larceny-theft, 23.4 for motor vehicle theft, and 2.9 for arson per 100,000 inhabitants in 2022. (Table 30)

By Age, Sex, and Race

Law enforcement agencies that contributed arrest data to the UCR program reported information on the age, sex, and race of the persons they arrested. According to the data for 2022, adults accounted for 93.5 percent of arrestees nationally. (Table 38)

A review of arrest data by age from 2021 to 2022 showed that arrests of adults increased 1.1 percent during this period, with a 0.2 percent decrease in arrests for violent crime and a 9.1 percent increase in arrests for property crimes. The arrest total for juveniles (those under 18 years of age) rose 17.7 percent from 2021 to 2022. Over the 2-year period, arrests of juveniles for violent crimes increased 13.9 percent; juvenile arrests for property crimes increased 26.3 percent. (Table 36)

By sex, males accounted for 73.1 percent of all persons arrested in 2022. Males represented 79.1 percent of arrestees for violent crime, 88.6 percent of arrestees for murder, 97.1 percent of arrestees for rape, 84.5 percent for robbery, and 76.8 percent for aggravated assault. Females accounted for 20.9 percent of violent crime arrestees, 11.4 percent of murder arrestees, 2.9 percent of rape arrestees, 15.5 percent of robbery arrestees, and 23.2 percent of aggravated assault arrestees. (Table 42)

Most arrestees for property crime in 2022 (91.2 percent) were over 18 years of age. By sex, males accounted for 66.3 percent

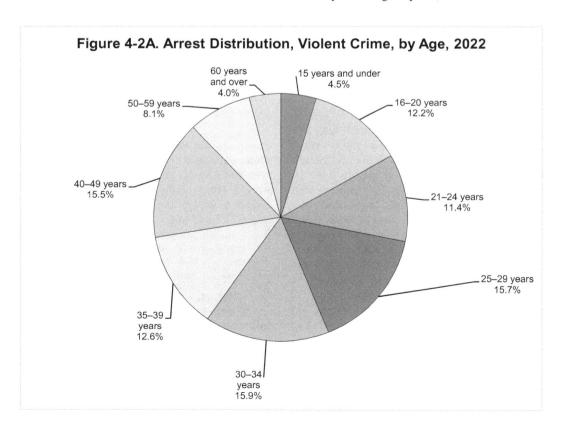

Figure 4-2A. Arrest Distribution, Violent Crime, by Age, 2022

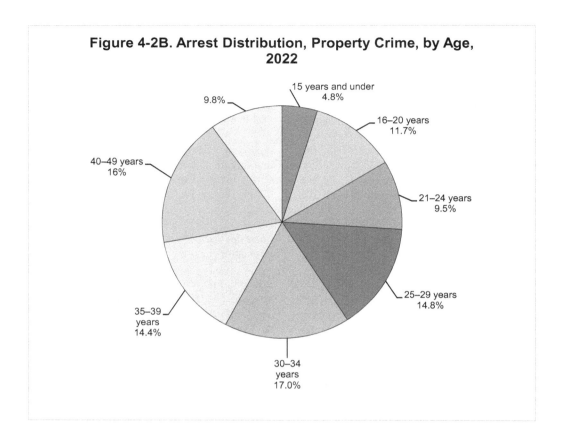

Figure 4-2B. Arrest Distribution, Property Crime, by Age, 2022

- 15 years and under 4.8%
- 16–20 years 11.7%
- 21–24 years 9.5%
- 25–29 years 14.8%
- 30–34 years 17.0%
- 35–39 years 14.4%
- 40–49 years 16%
- 9.8%

of arrestees for property crime, 81.0 percent of arrestees for burglary, 61.5 percent of arrestees for larceny-theft, 78.1 percent of arrestees for motor vehicle theft, and 76.6 percent of arrestees for arson. Females accounted for 33.7 percent of property crime arrestees. Of the four property crimes, larceny-theft had the highest proportion of female arrestees at 38.5 percent. (Tables 38 and 42)

In 2020, 67.9 percent of all persons arrested were White, 28.1 percent were Black, and the remaining 4.0 percent were of other races (American Indian or Alaskan Native, Asian, and Native Hawaiian or Pacific Islander). Of all arrestees for violent crimes, 57.1 percent were White, 39.1 percent were Black, and 3.9 percent were of other races. For murder, 40.6 percent of arrestees were White, 56.5 percent were Black, and 2.8 percent were of other races. For rape, 69.5 percent of arrestees were White, 26.5 percent were Black, and 4.0 percent of arrestees were of other races. For robbery, 44.4 percent of arrestees were White, 52.8 percent of arrestees were Black, and 2.8 percent were of other races. For aggravated assault, 59.2 percent of arrestees were White, 36.8 percent of arrestees were Black, and 4.0 percent were of other races. (Table 43)

Of all arrestees for property crimes in 2022, 66.1 percent were White, 30.5 percent were Black, and 3.4 percent were of other races. For burglary, 67.9 percent of arrestees were

White, 29.1 percent were Black, and 3.0 percent were of other races. For larceny-theft, 65.8 percent of arrestees were White, 30.7 percent were Black, and 3.5 percent were of other races. For motor vehicle theft, 65.3 percent of arrestees were White, 31.6 percent of arrestees were Black, and 3.1 percent were of other races. For arson, 72.3 percent of arrestees were White, 23.6 percent of arrestees were Black, and 4.1 percent were of other races. (Table 43)

Outside of the scope of violent and property crimes, White adults were most commonly arrested for drug abuse violations (499,860 arrests) and driving under the influence (478,958 arrests). Black adults were most frequently arrested for other assaults (244,435 arrests) and drug abuse violations (194,750 arrests). (Table 43)

Regional Arrest Rates

The UCR program divides the United States into four regions: the Northeast, the Midwest, the South, and the West. (Appendix III provides more information about the regions.) Law enforcement agencies in the Northeast had an overall arrest rate of 1,678.5 arrests per 100,000 inhabitants in 2022, below the national rate (2,181.7 arrests per 100,000 inhabitants). In this region, the arrest rate for violent crimes was 98.4 arrests per 100,000 inhabitants, and for property crime, the arrest rate was 230.8 arrests per 100,000 inhabitants. In the Midwest, law enforcement agencies reported an arrest rate of 2,129.1 arrests per 100,000 inhabitants. The arrest rate for violent crimes was 107.4 and the arrest rate for property crime was 227.2. Law enforcement agencies in the South, the nation's most populous region, reported an arrest rate of 2,331.5 per 100,000 inhabitants. Arrests for violent crime occurred at a rate of 113.1 arrests per 100,000 residents, and for property crime, the arrest rate was 240.3 arrests per 100,000 inhabitants. In the West, law enforcement agencies reported an overall arrest rate of 2,272.1 arrests per 100,000 inhabitants. The region's violent crime arrest rate was 184.0, the highest of the regions, while its property crime arrest rate was 238.8. (Table 30)

The regional murder arrest rates (per 100,000 inhabitants) were 2.5 in the Northeast, 3.3 in the Midwest, 4.4 in the South, and 3.7 in the West. For rape, the regional arrest rates were 5.7 in the Northeast, 6.8 in the Midwest, 5.3 in the South, and 6.0 in the West. Regional arrest rates for robbery were 15.6 in the Northeast, 11.7 in the Midwest, 14.9 in the South, and 27.3 in the West. For aggravated assault, the regional arrest rates were 74.6 in the Northeast, 85.6 in the Midwest, 88.5 in the South, and 147.0 in the West. (Table 30)

The regional burglary arrest rates (per 100,000 inhabitants) were 30.1 in the Northeast, 27.0 in the Midwest, 35.3 in the South, and 47.6 in the West. For larceny-theft, the regional arrest rates were 182.6 in the Northeast, 179.2 in the Midwest, 181.6 in the South, and 152.6 in the West. Regional arrest rates for motor vehicle theft were 16.0 in the Northeast, 19.0 in the Midwest, 21.4 in the South, and 33.4 in the West. For arson, the regional arrest rates were 2.1 in the Northeast, 2.0 in the Midwest, 2.0 in the South, and 5.1 in the West. (Table 30)

Population Groups: Trends and Rates

The national UCR program aggregates data by various population groups, which include cities, metropolitan counties, and nonmetropolitan counties. Definitions of these groups can be found in Appendix III. The total number of arrests in U.S. cities rose 3.0 percent from 2021 to 2022. The number of arrests for violent crimes increased 1.5 percent and arrests for property crimes increased 11.0 percent during the 2-year time frame. (Table 44)

In 2022, law enforcement agencies in cities collectively recorded an arrest rate of 2,342.9 arrests per 100,000 inhabitants. The nation's smallest cities, those with fewer than 10,000 inhabitants, had the highest arrest rate among the city population groups with 3,903.3 arrests per 100,000 inhabitants. Law enforcement agencies in cities with 250,000 or more inhabitants recorded the lowest rate, 1,910.3. In the nation's metropolitan counties, law enforcement agencies reported an arrest rate of 1,698.2 per 100,000 inhabitants. Agencies in nonmetropolitan counties reported an arrest rate

of 2,355.0, and agencies in suburban areas reported an arrest rate of 1,954.3. (Table 31)

By population group, law enforcement agencies in the nation's cities collectively reported 149.2 violent crime arrests per 100,000 inhabitants in 2022. In the city population groups, cities with 250,000 or more inhabitants reported the highest violent crime arrest rate (203.2) and cities with 10,000 to 24,999 inhabitants reported the lowest violent crime arrest rate (102.2). Cities reported an overall murder arrest rate of 4.2 per 100,000 inhabitants; cities with less than 10,000 inhabitants had the highest murder arrest rate (7.4) and cities with 10,000 to 24,999 inhabitants had the lowest murder arrest rate (2.4). The collective city rape arrest rate was 6.1 per 100,000 inhabitants, with the highest rate in cities with less than 10,000 inhabitants (7.4) and the lowest rate in cities with 50,000 to 99,999 inhabitants and 100,000 to 249,999 inhabitants (5.6 each). The overall robbery arrest rate for cities was 22.7 per 100,000 inhabitants; cities with 250,000 or more inhabitants had the highest robbery arrest rate (38.1) and cities with 10,000 to 24,999 inhabitants had the lowest robbery arrest rate (10.5). For aggravated assault, the collective city arrest rate was 116.2 per 100,000 inhabitants, with the greatest arrest rate in cities with 250,000 or more inhabitants (151.3) and the lowest arrest rate in cities with 10,000 to 24,999 inhabitants (83.4). (Table 31)

Agencies in metropolitan counties reported a violent crime arrest rate of 92.5 per 100,000 inhabitants, with arrest rates of 2.8 for murder, 4.9 for rape, 9.2 for robbery, and 75.6 for aggravated assault. Agencies in nonmetropolitan counties reported arrest rates of 78.1 for violent crime, 2.6 for murder, 7.0 for rape, 3.0 for robbery, and 65.5 for aggravated assault. Agencies in suburban areas reported arrest rates of 93.2 for violent crime, 2.4 for murder, 5.0 for rape, 10.3 for robbery, and 75.5 for aggravated assault. (Table 31)

By population group, law enforcement agencies in the nation's cities collectively reported 285.5 property crime arrests per 100,000 inhabitants in 2022. In the city population groups, cities with less than 10,000 inhabitants reported the highest property crime arrest rate (359.4) and cities with 250,000 or more inhabitants reported the lowest property crime arrest rate (222.5). Cities reported an overall burglary arrest rate of 41.1 per 100,000 inhabitants; cities with less than 10,000 inhabitants had the highest burglary arrest rate (45.2) and cities with 25,000 to 49,999 inhabitants had the lowest burglary arrest rate (36.0). The collective city larceny-theft arrest rate was 213.8 per 100,000 inhabitants, with the highest rate in cities with 10,000 to 24,999 inhabitants (292.8) and the lowest rate in cities with 250,000 or more inhabitants (135.0). The overall motor vehicle theft arrest rate for cities was 27.2 per 100,000 inhabitants; cities with 250,000 or more inhabitants had the highest motor vehicle theft arrest rate (39.4), and cities with 10,000 to 24,999 inhabitants had the lowest motor vehicle theft arrest rate (19.3). For arson, the collective city arrest rate was 3.4 per 100,000 inhabitants, with the greatest arrest rate in cities with 100,000 to 249,999 inhabitants (3.9) and the lowest arrest rate in cities with 10,000 to 24,999 inhabitants (2.8). (Table 31)

Agencies in metropolitan counties reported a property crime arrest rate of 143.5 per 100,000 inhabitants, with arrest rates of 25.0 for burglary, 101.0 for larceny-theft, 15.7 for motor vehicle theft, and 1.7 for arson. Agencies in nonmetropolitan counties reported arrest rates of 112.7 for property crime, 30.1 for burglary, 64.6 for larceny-theft, 15.8 for motor vehicle theft, and 2.2 for arson. Agencies in suburban areas reported arrest rates of 205.9 for property crime, 27.7 for burglary, 259.4 for larceny-theft, 16.6 for motor vehicle theft, and 2.1 for arson. (Table 31)

Community Types

In 2022, law enforcement agencies in the nation's cities reported that 93.0 percent of arrests in their jurisdictions were of adults and 7.0 percent of arrests were of juveniles. Adults accounted for 91.0 percent of arrestees for violent crimes, while juveniles accounted for 9.0 percent of these arrests. Adults made up 91.1 percent of the arrestees for property crimes, and juveniles accounted for the remaining 8.9 percent. Of all arrests in the nation's cities in 2022, 24.6 percent were of individuals under 25 years of age. In metropolitan counties, 22.3 percent of arrests were of individuals under 25 years of age. In nonmetropolitan counties, 19.6 percent of persons arrested were of individuals under 25 years of age, and in suburban areas, 24.0 percent of arrestees were under 25 years old. (Tables 46, 47, 53, 59, and 65)

Males accounted for 72.8 percent and females accounted for 27.2 percent of arrestees in the nation's cities in 2022. In metropolitan counties, males comprised 73.9 percent of arrestees; in nonmetropolitan counties, males represented 73.2 percent of all arrestees; and in suburban areas, males comprised 73.0 percent of arrestees. (Tables 48, 54, 60, and 66)

By race, 65.6 percent of arrestees in the nation's cities in 2022 were White, 30.0 percent were Black, and 4.4 percent were of other races (American Indian or Alaska Native, Asian, and Native Hawaiian or Pacific Islander). Whites accounted for 70.5 percent of arrestees in metropolitan counties in 2022, Blacks made up 27.4 percent of arrestees, and persons of other races made up 2.1 percent of the total. In nonmetropolitan counties, Whites made up 82.1 percent of arrestees, Blacks accounted for 13.9 percent of arrestees, and other races made up 4.0 percent of the total. In suburban areas, Whites made up 70.6 percent of arrestees, Blacks accounted for 27.1 percent of arrestees, and other races made up 2.4 percent of the total. (Tables 49, 55, 61, and 67)

Table 29. Estimated Number of Arrests, 2022

(Number.)

Offense	Arrests
Total[1]	7,364,553
Violent Crime[2]	429,593
Murder and nonnegligent manslaughter	12,317
Rape	19,660
Robbery	58,410
Aggravated assault	339,206
Property Crime[2]	791,013
Burglary	120,840
Larceny-theft	582,456
Motor vehicle theft	78,179
Arson	9,538
Other Crimes	
Other assaults	947,552
Forgery and counterfeiting	29,166
Fraud	77,942
Embezzlement	9,587
Stolen property; buying, receiving, possessing	83,352
Vandalism	163,329
Weapons; carrying, possessing, etc.	181,267
Prostitution and commercialized vice	15,250
Sex offenses (except rape and prostitution)	24,535
Drug abuse violations	907,958
Gambling	1,418
Offenses against the family and children	47,340
Driving under the influence	788,402
Liquor laws	98,507
Drunkenness[3]	17,465
Disorderly conduct	242,611
Vagrancy	16,051
All other offenses	2,485,165
Suspicion[4]	85
Curfew and loitering law violations	7,050

1 Does not include suspicion.   2 Violent crimes are offenses of murder and nonnegligent manslaughter, rape, robbery, and aggravated assault. Property crimes are offenses of burglary, larceny-theft, motor vehicle theft, and arson.   3 Drunkenness figures were submitted by Summary reporting agencies only. As of 2021 drunkenness is no longer a separate offense in the National Incident-Based Reporting System (NIBRS), but it is included with All Other Offenses (except traffic) category.   4 Figures for suspicion include only data submitted by Summary reporting agencies because suspicion is not collected as a crime via NIBRS.

Table 30. Number and Rate of Arrests, by Geographic Region, 2022

(Number, rate per 100,000 inhabitants.)

Offense charged	United States total (11,933 agencies; population 270,485,978)		Northeast (1,887 agencies; population 37,491,967)		Midwest (3,356 agencies; population 57,638,780)		South (4,705 agencies; population 101,728,212)		West (1,985 agencies; population 73,627,019)	
	Total	Rate	Total	Rate	Total	Rate	Total	Rate	Total	Rate
Total[1]	5,901,221	2,181.7	629,313	1,678.5	1,227,184	2,129.1	2,371,843	2,331.5	1,672,881	2,272.1
Violent crime[2]	349,283	129.1	36,891	98.4	61,909	107.4	115,039	113.1	135,444	184.0
Murder and nonnegligent manslaughter	10,047	3.7	921	2.5	1,928	3.3	4,478	4.4	2,720	3.7
Rape	15,930	5.9	2,152	5.7	3,914	6.8	5,442	5.3	4,422	6.0
Robbery	47,807	17.7	5,848	15.6	6,746	11.7	15,108	14.9	20,105	27.3
Aggravated assault	275,499	101.9	27,970	74.6	49,321	85.6	90,011	88.5	108,197	147.0
Property crime[2]	637,682	235.8	86,548	230.8	130,943	227.2	244,404	240.3	175,787	238.8
Burglary	97,790	36.2	11,289	30.1	15,557	27.0	35,880	35.3	35,064	47.6
Larceny-theft	468,839	173.3	68,448	182.6	103,273	179.2	184,728	181.6	112,390	152.6
Motor vehicle theft	63,342	23.4	6,017	16.0	10,975	19.0	21,759	21.4	24,591	33.4
Arson	7,711	2.9	794	2.1	1,138	2.0	2,037	2.0	3,742	5.1
Other assaults	765,816	283.1	101,592	271.0	171,782	298.0	293,491	288.5	198,951	270.2
Forgery and counterfeiting	23,315	8.6	3,685	9.8	4,148	7.2	10,854	10.7	4,628	6.3
Fraud	62,135	23.0	5,358	14.3	13,972	24.2	29,402	28.9	13,403	18.2
Embezzlement	7,780	2.9	592	1.6	1,920	3.3	3,594	3.5	1,674	2.3
Stolen property; buying, receiving, possessing	67,827	25.1	6,481	17.3	12,416	21.5	20,657	20.3	28,273	38.4
Vandalism	131,854	48.7	21,174	56.5	26,688	46.3	36,790	36.2	47,202	64.1
Weapons; carrying, possessing, etc.	146,785	54.3	15,089	40.2	31,299	54.3	55,045	54.1	45,352	61.6
Prostitution and commercialized vice	12,455	4.6	988	2.6	964	1.7	3,423	3.4	7,080	9.6
Sex offenses (except forcible rape and prostitution)	19,821	7.3	3,159	8.4	3,359	5.8	4,878	4.8	8,425	11.4
Drug abuse violations	726,746	268.7	57,192	152.5	151,370	262.6	329,528	323.9	188,656	256.2
Gambling	1,103	0.4	165	0.4	74	0.1	473	0.5	391	0.5
Offenses against the family and children	38,065	14.1	4,962	13.2	7,459	12.9	17,505	17.2	8,139	11.1
Driving under the influence	622,344	230.1	79,099	211.0	145,382	252.2	192,992	189.7	204,871	278.3
Liquor laws	76,369	28.2	4,263	11.4	28,867	50.1	25,312	24.9	17,927	24.3
Drunkenness[3]	14,324	5.3	735	2.0	0	*	67	0.1	13,522	18.4
Disorderly conduct	193,449	71.5	27,197	72.5	55,787	96.8	53,238	52.3	57,227	77.7
Vagrancy	12,673	4.7	1,530	4.1	1,765	3.1	3,970	3.9	5,408	7.3
All other offenses (except traffic)	1,985,747	734.1	172,470	460.0	374,738	650.1	929,479	913.7	509,060	691.4
Suspicion[4]	62	*	38	0.1	0	*	24	*	0	*
Curfew and loitering law violations	5,648	2.1	143	0.4	2,342	4.1	1,702	1.7	1,461	2.0

* = Less than one-tenth of 1 percent.
1 Does not include suspicion.   2 Violent crimes are offenses of murder and nonnegligent manslaughter, rape, robbery, and aggravated assault. Property crimes are offenses of burglary, larceny-theft, motor vehicle theft, and arson.   3 Drunkenness figures were submitted by Summary reporting agencies only. As of 2021 drunkenness is no longer a separate offense in the National Incident-Based Reporting System (NIBRS), but it is included with All Other Offenses (except traffic) category.   4 Figures for suspicion include only data submitted by Summary reporting agencies because suspicion is not collected as a crime via NIBRS.

Table 31. Number and Rate of Arrests, by Population Group, 2022

(Number, rate per 100,000 inhabitants.)

Offense charged	Total (11,933 agencies; population 270,485,978)		Total cities (8,754 cities; population 180,514,188)		Group I (81 cities, 250,000 and over; population 51,084,111)		Group II (205 cities, 100,000 to 249,999; population 29,335,585)		Group III (441 cities, 50,000 to 99,999; population 30,676,781)	
	Total	Rate	Total	Rate	Total	Rate	Total	Rate	Total	Rate
Total[2]	5,901,221	2,181.7	4,229,293	2,342.9	975,844	1,910.3	643,083	2,192.2	686,621	2,238.2
Violent crime[3]	349,283	129.1	269,242	149.2	103,820	203.2	47,477	161.8	41,111	134.0
Murder and nonnegligent manslaughter	10,047	3.7	7,584	4.2	3,720	7.3	1,206	4.1	932	3.0
Rape	15,930	5.9	11,044	6.1	3,344	6.5	1,651	5.6	1,709	5.6
Robbery	47,807	17.7	40,904	22.7	19,470	38.1	6,796	23.2	6,167	20.1
Aggravated assault	275,499	101.9	209,710	116.2	77,286	151.3	37,824	128.9	32,303	105.3
Property crime[3]	637,682	235.8	515,295	285.5	113,658	222.5	76,821	261.9	88,558	288.7
Burglary	97,790	36.2	74,149	41.1	22,779	44.6	12,507	42.6	11,840	38.6
Larceny-theft	468,839	173.3	385,938	213.8	68,948	135.0	55,213	188.2	69,193	225.6
Motor vehicle theft	63,342	23.4	49,159	27.2	20,102	39.4	7,969	27.2	6,611	21.6
Arson	7,711	2.9	6,049	3.4	1,829	3.6	1,132	3.9	914	3.0
Other assaults	765,816	283.1	572,016	316.9	160,318	313.8	95,140	324.3	96,938	316.0
Forgery and counterfeiting	23,315	8.6	16,854	9.3	2,683	5.3	2,360	8.0	3,184	10.4
Fraud	62,135	23.0	46,609	25.8	7,715	15.1	6,532	22.3	8,292	27.0
Embezzlement	7,780	2.9	6,180	3.4	1,448	2.8	805	2.7	1,151	3.8
Stolen property; buying, receiving, possessing	67,827	25.1	50,140	27.8	14,307	28.0	9,767	33.3	9,128	29.8
Vandalism	131,854	48.7	101,356	56.1	26,513	51.9	17,104	58.3	16,657	54.3
Weapons; carrying, possessing, etc.	146,785	54.3	111,168	61.6	43,100	84.4	18,543	63.2	15,875	51.7
Prostitution and commercialized vice	12,455	4.6	11,089	6.1	8,303	16.3	1,022	3.5	719	2.3
Sex offenses (except forcible rape and prostitution)	19,821	7.3	13,817	7.7	4,118	8.1	2,323	7.9	2,181	7.1
Drug abuse violations	726,746	268.7	496,019	274.8	98,442	192.7	79,444	270.8	84,202	274.5
Gambling	1,103	0.4	756	0.4	427	0.8	78	0.3	90	0.3
Offenses against the family and children	38,065	14.1	23,991	13.3	4,409	8.6	3,856	13.1	3,683	12.0
Driving under the influence	622,344	230.1	404,342	224.0	66,088	129.4	50,810	173.2	59,080	192.6
Liquor laws	76,369	28.2	58,516	32.4	7,623	14.9	6,185	21.1	7,167	23.4
Drunkenness[4]	14,324	5.3	12,244	6.8	849	1.7	4,478	15.3	3,193	10.4
Disorderly conduct	193,449	71.5	156,994	87.0	23,032	45.1	23,522	80.2	29,561	96.4
Vagrancy	12,673	4.7	10,000	5.5	2,686	5.3	2,353	8.0	884	2.9
All other offenses (except traffic)	1,985,747	734.1	1,347,617	746.5	285,507	558.9	193,771	660.5	214,107	697.9
Suspicion[5]	62	*	62	*	0	0.0	0	0.0	11	*
Curfew and loitering law violations	5,648	2.1	5,048	2.8	798	1.6	692	2.4	860	2.8

286 CRIME IN THE UNITED STATES

Table 31. Number and Rate of Arrests, by Population Group, 2022—Continued

(Number, rate per 100,000 inhabitants.)

Offense charged	Group IV (791 cities, 25,000 to 49,999; population 27,441,589)		Group V (1,553 cities, 10,000 to 24,999; population 24,918,364)		Group VI (5,683 cities, under 10,000; population 17,057,758)		Metropolitan counties (1,370 agencies; population 68,043,758)		Nonmetropolitan counties (1,809 agencies; population 21,928,032)		Suburban areas[1] (6,320 agencies; population 118,233,444)	
	Total	Rate	Total	Rate	Total	Rate	Total	Rate	Total	Rate	Total	Rate
Total[2]	622,236	2,267.5	635,691	2,551.1	665,818	3,903.3	1,155,515	1,698.2	516,413	2,355.0	2,310,584	1,954.3
Violent crime[3]	30,152	109.9	25,478	102.2	21,204	124.3	62,918	92.5	17,123	78.1	110,203	93.2
Murder and nonnegligent manslaughter	699	2.5	600	2.4	427	2.5	1,886	2.8	577	2.6	2,815	2.4
Rape	1,603	5.8	1,482	5.9	1,255	7.4	3,352	4.9	1,534	7.0	5,941	5.0
Robbery	4,039	14.7	2,624	10.5	1,808	10.6	6,254	9.2	649	3.0	12,222	10.3
Aggravated assault	23,811	86.8	20,772	83.4	17,714	103.8	51,426	75.6	14,363	65.5	89,225	75.5
Property crime[3]	87,069	317.3	87,889	352.7	61,300	359.4	97,668	143.5	24,719	112.7	243,419	205.9
Burglary	9,883	36.0	9,426	37.8	7,714	45.2	17,031	25.0	6,610	30.1	32,758	27.7
Larceny-theft	70,996	258.7	72,960	292.8	48,628	285.1	68,735	101.0	14,166	64.6	188,503	159.4
Motor vehicle theft	5,367	19.6	4,806	19.3	4,304	25.2	10,712	15.7	3,471	15.8	19,685	16.6
Arson	823	3.0	697	2.8	654	3.8	1,190	1.7	472	2.2	2,473	2.1
Other assaults	80,645	293.9	74,655	299.6	64,320	377.1	145,749	214.2	48,051	219.1	277,433	234.6
Forgery and counterfeiting	2,720	9.9	2,965	11.9	2,942	17.2	5,292	7.8	1,169	5.3	10,686	9.0
Fraud	8,048	29.3	7,145	28.7	8,877	52.0	11,865	17.4	3,661	16.7	28,537	24.1
Embezzlement	1,266	4.6	814	3.3	696	4.1	1,370	2.0	230	1.0	3,105	2.6
Stolen property; buying, receiving, possessing	7,182	26.2	5,486	22.0	4,270	25.0	14,355	21.1	3,332	15.2	26,744	22.6
Vandalism	15,365	56.0	13,720	55.1	11,997	70.3	23,368	34.3	7,130	32.5	47,337	40.0
Weapons; carrying, possessing, etc.	12,026	43.8	10,993	44.1	10,631	62.3	27,729	40.8	7,888	36.0	50,559	42.8
Prostitution and commercialized vice	591	2.2	259	1.0	195	1.1	1,271	1.9	95	0.4	1,985	1.7
Sex offenses (except forcible rape and prostitution)	1,907	6.9	1,782	7.2	1,506	8.8	4,534	6.7	1,470	6.7	7,926	6.7
Drug abuse violations	73,295	267.1	76,276	306.1	84,360	494.6	152,392	224.0	78,335	357.2	292,404	247.3
Gambling	50	0.2	68	0.3	43	0.3	308	0.5	39	0.2	413	0.3
Offenses against the family and children	4,470	16.3	3,784	15.2	3,789	22.2	9,335	13.7	4,739	21.6	15,972	13.5
Driving under the influence	58,595	213.5	68,328	274.2	101,441	594.7	130,447	191.7	87,555	399.3	289,029	244.5
Liquor laws	8,368	30.5	11,180	44.9	17,993	105.5	9,986	14.7	7,867	35.9	29,271	24.8
Drunkenness[4]	1,841	6.7	888	3.6	995	5.8	1,835	2.7	245	1.1	4,590	3.9
Disorderly conduct	26,291	95.8	27,268	109.4	27,320	160.2	24,169	35.5	12,286	56.0	69,099	58.4
Vagrancy	902	3.3	802	3.2	2,373	13.9	2,139	3.1	534	2.4	3,640	3.1
All other offenses (except traffic)	200,585	731.0	214,668	861.5	238,979	1,401.0	428,360	629.5	209,770	956.6	796,261	673.5
Suspicion[5]	24	0.1	0	0.0	27	0.2	0	0.0	0	0.0	51	*
Curfew and loitering law violations	868	3.2	1,243	5.0	587	3.4	425	0.6	175	0.8	1,971	1.7

* = Less than one-tenth of one percent.
1 Suburban areas include law enforcement agencies in cities with less than 50,000 inhabitants and county law enforcement agencies that are within a Metropolitan Statistical Area. Suburban areas exclude all metropolitan agencies associated with a principal city. The agencies associated with suburban areas also appear in other groups within this table.   2 Does not include suspicion.   3 Violent crimes are offenses of murder and nonnegligent manslaughter, forcible rape, robbery, and aggravated assault. Property crimes are offenses of burglary, larceny-theft, motor vehicle theft, and arson.   4 Drunkenness figures were submitted by Summary reporting agencies only. As of 2021 drunkenness is no longer a separate offense in the National Incident-Based Reporting System (NIBRS), but it is included with All Other Offenses (except traffic) category.   5 Figures for suspicion include only data submitted by Summary reporting agencies because suspicion is not collected as a crime via NIBRS.

Table 32. Ten-Year Arrest Trends, 2013 and 2022

(Number, percent change; 8,794 agencies; 2022 estimated population 234,749,315; 2013 estimated population 222,464,508.)

| Offense charged | Number of persons arrested | | | | | | | | |
| | Total, all ages | | | Under 18 years of age | | | 18 years of age and over | | |
	2013	2022	Percent change	2013	2022	Percent change	2013	2022	Percent change
Total[1]	8,052,844	5,034,462	-37.5	780,450	333,089	-57.3	7,272,394	4,701,373	-35.4
Violent crime[2]	359,543	313,329	-12.9	39,766	27,064	-31.9	319,777	286,265	-10.5
Murder and nonnegligent manslaughter	7,760	8,694	+12.0	571	861	+50.8	7,189	7,833	+9.0
Rape[3]	14,296	14,206	NA	2,280	2,171	NA	12,016	12,035	NA
Robbery	72,077	42,879	-40.5	14,624	7,518	-48.6	57,453	35,361	-38.5
Aggravated assault	265,410	247,550	-6.7	22,291	16,514	-25.9	243,119	231,036	-5.0
Property crime[2]	1,135,208	561,566	-50.5	179,413	49,098	-72.6	955,795	512,468	-46.4
Burglary	184,704	87,174	-52.8	31,397	7,763	-75.3	153,307	79,411	-48.2
Larceny-theft	896,113	410,550	-54.2	136,826	32,360	-76.3	759,287	378,190	-50.2
Motor vehicle theft	46,961	56,988	+21.4	8,678	8,061	-7.1	38,283	48,927	+27.8
Arson	7,430	6,854	-7.8	2,512	914	-63.6	4,918	5,940	+20.8
Other assaults	806,695	660,110	-18.2	105,961	73,572	-30.6	700,734	586,538	-16.3
Forgery and counterfeiting	43,636	20,763	-52.4	738	322	-56.4	42,898	20,441	-52.3
Fraud	101,803	54,535	-46.4	3,249	1,661	-48.9	98,554	52,874	-46.4
Embezzlement	11,932	6,996	-41.4	300	300	+0.0	11,632	6,696	-42.4
Stolen property; buying, receiving, possessing	66,953	60,497	-9.6	7,468	5,532	-25.9	59,485	54,965	-7.6
Vandalism	143,474	116,056	-19.1	32,994	16,592	-49.7	110,480	99,464	-10.0
Weapons; carrying, possessing, etc.	102,486	126,397	+23.3	14,822	13,081	-11.7	87,664	113,316	+29.3
Prostitution and commercialized vice	39,463	11,803	-70.1	603	63	-89.6	38,860	11,740	-69.8
Sex offenses (except forcible rape and prostitution)	41,244	17,999	-56.4	7,303	2,721	-62.7	33,941	15,278	-55.0
Drug abuse violations	1,076,547	633,576	-41.1	83,717	32,010	-61.8	992,830	601,566	-39.4
Gambling	4,469	868	-80.6	527	18	-96.6	3,942	850	-78.4
Offenses against the family and children	68,843	33,128	-51.9	1,740	1,457	-16.3	67,103	31,671	-52.8
Driving under the influence	730,825	496,878	-32.0	4,928	3,196	-35.1	725,897	493,682	-32.0
Liquor laws	245,673	61,277	-75.1	41,877	10,009	-76.1	203,796	51,268	-74.8
Drunkenness[4]	319,392	14,185	-95.6	5,417	90	-98.3	313,975	14,095	-95.5
Disorderly conduct	313,780	168,316	-46.4	64,048	23,090	-63.9	249,732	145,226	-41.8
Vagrancy	20,216	9,469	-53.2	617	20	-96.8	19,599	9,449	-51.8
All other offenses (except traffic)	2,376,053	1,661,611	-30.1	140,353	68,090	-51.5	2,235,700	1,593,521	-28.7
Suspicion[5]	518	62	-88.0	53	0	-100.0	465	62	-86.7
Curfew and loitering law violations	44,609	5,103	-88.6	44,609	5,103	-88.6	NA	NA	NA

NA = Not available.

1 Does not include suspicion.   2 Violent crimes are offenses of murder and nonnegligent manslaughter, rape, robbery, and aggravated assault. Property crimes are offenses of burglary, larceny-theft, motor vehicle theft, and arson.   3 The 2013 rape figures are based on the legacy definition, and the 2022 rape figures are aggregate totals based on both the legacy and revised Uniform Crime Reporting definitions. For this reason, a percent change is not provided.   4 The 2013 drunkenness figures were submitted by agencies that reported via Summary and National Incident Based Reporting System (NIBRS). As of 2021, drunkenness is no longer a separate offense in NIBRS, but it is included with All Other Offenses (except traffic) category.   5 Figures for suspicion include only data submitted by Summary reporting agencies because suspicion is not collected as a crime via NIBRS.

Table 33. Ten-Year Arrest Trends, by Age and Sex, 2013 and 2022

(Number, percent change; 8,794 agencies; 2022 estimated population 234,749,315; 2013 estimated population 222,464,508.)

Offense charged	Male						Female					
	Total			Under 18			Total			Under 18		
	2013	2022	Percent change	2013	2022	Percent change	2013	2022	Percent change	2013	2022	Percent change
Total[1]	5,926,157	3,676,172	-38.0	555,728	228,977	-58.8	2,126,687	1,358,290	-36.1	224,722	104,112	-53.7
Violent crime[2]	287,738	247,610	-13.9	32,466	21,612	-33.4	71,805	65,719	-8.5	7,300	5,452	-25.3
Murder and nonnegligent manslaughter	6,844	7,704	+12.6	503	808	+60.6	916	990	+8.1	68	53	-22.1
Rape[3]	13,999	13,800		2,176	2,070		297	406		104	101	
Robbery	62,466	36,176	-42.1	13,204	6,572	-50.2	9,611	6,703	-30.3	1,420	946	-33.4
Aggravated assault	204,429	189,930	-7.1	16,583	12,162	-26.7	60,981	57,620	-5.5	5,708	4,352	-23.8
Property crime[2]	706,533	372,614	-47.3	117,885	34,580	-70.7	428,675	188,952	-55.9	61,528	14,518	-76.4
Burglary	153,140	70,441	-54.0	27,753	6,644	-76.1	31,564	16,733	-47.0	3,644	1,119	-69.3
Larceny-theft	509,783	252,436	-50.5	80,835	20,524	-74.6	386,330	158,114	-59.1	55,991	11,836	-78.9
Motor vehicle theft	37,659	44,481	+18.1	7,168	6,660	-7.1	9,302	12,507	+34.5	1,510	1,401	-7.2
Arson	5,951	5,256	-11.7	2,129	752	-64.7	1,479	1,598	+8.0	383	162	-57.7
Other assaults	583,252	460,063	-21.1	67,404	43,554	-35.4	223,443	200,047	-10.5	38,557	30,018	-22.1
Forgery and counterfeiting	27,318	14,331	-47.5	527	264	-49.9	16,318	6,432	-60.6	211	58	-72.5
Fraud	61,213	35,917	-41.3	2,205	1,104	-49.9	40,590	18,618	-54.1	1,044	557	-46.6
Embezzlement	6,171	3,661	-40.7	195	163	-16.4	5,761	3,335	-42.1	105	137	+30.5
Stolen property; buying, receiving, possessing	52,616	47,848	-9.1	6,256	4,711	-24.7	14,337	12,649	-11.8	1,212	821	-32.3
Vandalism	114,701	89,390	-22.1	27,885	13,342	-52.2	28,773	26,666	-7.3	5,109	3,250	-36.4
Weapons; carrying, possessing, etc.	93,863	114,267	+21.7	13,325	11,896	-10.7	8,623	12,130	+40.7	1,497	1,185	-20.8
Prostitution and commercialized vice	12,861	4,964	-61.4	112	29	-74.1	26,602	6,839	-74.3	491	34	-93.1
Sex offenses (except forcible rape and prostitution)	38,154	17,006	-55.4	6,493	2,438	-62.5	3,090	993	-67.9	810	283	-65.1
Drug abuse violations	851,458	470,558	-44.7	68,540	22,531	-67.1	225,089	163,018	-27.6	15,177	9,479	-37.5
Gambling	3,955	620	-84.3	520	16	-96.9	514	248	-51.8	7	2	-71.4
Offenses against the family and children	50,586	21,608	-57.3	1,060	754	-28.9	18,257	11,520	-36.9	680	703	+3.4
Driving under the influence	550,192	369,776	-32.8	3,713	2,408	-35.1	180,633	127,102	-29.6	1,215	788	-35.1
Liquor laws	175,632	41,181	-76.6	25,518	5,780	-77.3	70,041	20,096	-71.3	16,359	4,229	-74.1
Drunkenness[4]	259,986	11,357	-95.6	3,967	62	-98.4	59,406	2,828	-95.2	1,450	28	-98.1
Disorderly conduct	227,302	119,465	-47.4	41,979	14,153	-66.3	86,478	48,851	-43.5	22,069	8,937	-59.5
Vagrancy	15,956	7,229	-54.7	478	18	-96.2	4,260	2,240	-47.4	139	2	-98.6
All other offenses (except traffic)	1,774,577	1,223,254	-31.1	103,107	46,109	-55.3	601,476	438,357	-27.1	37,246	21,981	-41.0
Suspicion[5]	414	52	-87.4	46	0	-100.0	104	10	-90.4	7	0	-100.0
Curfew and loitering law violations	32,093	3,453	-89.2	32,093	3,453	-89.2	12,516	1,650	-86.8	12,516	1,650	-86.8

NA = Not available.
1 Does not include suspicion.   2 Violent crimes are offenses of murder and nonnegligent manslaughter, rape, robbery, and aggravated assault. Property crimes are offenses of burglary, larceny-theft, motor vehicle theft, and arson.   3 The 2013 rape figures are based on the legacy definition, and the 2022 rape figures are aggregate totals based on both the legacy and revised Uniform Crime Reporting definitions. For this reason, a percent change is not provided.   4 The 2013 drunkenness figures were submitted by agencies that reported via Summary and National Incident Based Reporting System (NIBRS). As of 2021, drunkenness is no longer a separate offense in NIBRS, but it is included with All Other Offenses (except traffic) category.   5 Figures for suspicion include only data submitted by Summary reporting agencies because suspicion is not collected as a crime via NIBRS.

Table 34. Five-Year Arrest Trends, by Age, 2018 and 2022

(Number, percent change; 9,465 agencies; 2022 estimated population 243,370,086; 2018 estimated population 238,789,696.)

Offense charged	Number of persons arrested								
	Total, all ages			Under 18 years of age			18 years of age and over		
	2018	2022	Percent change	2018	2022	Percent change	2018	2022	Percent change
Total¹	7,431,663	5,267,602	-29.1	521,472	346,118	-33.6	6,910,191	4,921,484	-28.8
Violent crime²	386,240	325,756	-15.7	36,606	28,496	-22.2	349,634	297,260	-15.0
Murder and nonnegligent manslaughter	8,970	9,120	+1.7	695	928	+33.5	8,275	8,192	-1.0
Rape	18,859	14,735	-21.9	3,120	2,258	-27.6	15,739	12,477	-20.7
Robbery	66,060	45,224	-31.5	12,865	8,125	-36.8	53,195	37,099	-30.3
Aggravated assault	292,351	256,677	-12.2	19,926	17,185	-13.8	272,425	239,492	-12.1
Property crime²	866,591	587,021	-32.3	97,234	51,010	-47.5	769,357	536,011	-30.3
Burglary	133,136	90,828	-31.8	16,445	8,136	-50.5	116,691	82,692	-29.1
Larceny-theft	660,186	429,347	-35.0	68,591	33,652	-50.9	591,595	395,695	-33.1
Motor vehicle theft	66,730	59,538	-10.8	10,934	8,267	-24.4	55,796	51,271	-8.1
Arson	6,539	7,308	+11.8	1,264	955	-24.4	5,275	6,353	+20.4
Other assaults	785,861	691,786	-12.0	90,764	77,723	-14.4	695,097	614,063	-11.7
Forgery and counterfeiting	36,723	21,623	-41.1	711	339	-52.3	36,012	21,284	-40.9
Fraud	87,888	56,273	-36.0	3,540	1,727	-51.2	84,348	54,546	-35.3
Embezzlement	11,404	7,118	-37.6	443	302	-31.8	10,961	6,816	-37.8
Stolen property; buying, receiving, possessing	69,134	63,502	-8.1	6,909	5,855	-15.3	62,225	57,647	-7.4
Vandalism	131,895	120,520	-8.6	22,242	17,148	-22.9	109,653	103,372	-5.7
Weapons; carrying, possessing, etc.	123,144	132,892	+7.9	12,221	13,923	+13.9	110,923	118,969	+7.3
Prostitution and commercialized vice	23,143	11,892	-48.6	179	64	-64.2	22,964	11,828	-48.5
Sex offenses (except forcible rape and prostitution)	32,771	18,606	-43.2	5,123	2,787	-45.6	27,648	15,819	-42.8
Drug abuse violations	1,177,688	649,128	-44.9	64,616	33,180	-48.7	1,113,072	615,948	-44.7
Gambling	2,290	1,027	-55.2	130	21	-83.8	2,160	1,006	-53.4
Offenses against the family and children	63,207	34,247	-45.8	2,366	1,480	-37.4	60,841	32,767	-46.1
Driving under the influence	623,974	521,214	-16.5	3,531	3,341	-5.4	620,443	517,873	-16.5
Liquor laws	123,482	65,974	-46.6	18,380	10,302	-43.9	105,102	55,672	-47.0
Drunkenness³	239,709	14,122	-94.1	2,333	91	-96.1	237,376	14,031	-94.1
Disorderly conduct	215,855	175,166	-18.9	36,427	23,582	-35.3	179,428	151,584	-15.5
Vagrancy	17,532	10,861	-38.1	453	20	-95.6	17,079	10,841	-36.5
All other offenses (except traffic)	2,397,189	1,753,766	-26.8	101,321	69,619	-31.3	2,295,868	1,684,147	-26.6
Suspicion⁴	373	62	-83.4	34	0	-100.0	339	62	-81.7
Curfew and loitering law violations	15,943	5,108	-68.0	15,943	5,108	-68.0	NA	NA	NA

NA = Not available.
1 Does not include suspicion.   2 Violent crimes are offenses of murder and nonnegligent manslaughter, rape, robbery, and aggravated assault. Property crimes are offenses of burglary, larceny-theft, motor vehicle theft, and arson.   3 The 2018 figures for drunkenness were submitted by agencies that reported via Summary and those that reported via National Incident Based Reporting System (NIBRS). As of 2021, drunkenness is no longer a separate offense in NIBRS, but it is included with All Other Offenses (except traffic) category.   4 Figures for suspicion include only data submitted by Summary reporting agencies because suspicion is not collected as a crime via NIBRS.

Table 35. Five-Year Arrest Trends, by Age and Sex, 2018 and 2022

(Number, percent change; 9,465 agencies; 2022 estimated population 243,370,086; 2018 estimated population 238,789,696.)

Offense charged	Male						Female					
	Total			Under 18			Total			Under 18		
	2018	2022	Percent change	2018	2022	Percent change	2018	2022	Percent change	2018	2022	Percent change
Total[1]	5,406,979	3,852,810	-28.7	366,871	238,176	-35.1	2,024,684	1,414,792	-30.1	154,601	107,942	-30.2
Violent crime[2]	305,783	257,674	-15.7	29,530	22,762	-22.9	80,457	68,082	-15.4	7,076	5,734	-19.0
Murder and nonnegligent manslaughter	7,887	8,100	+2.7	626	868	+38.7	1,083	1,020	-5.8	69	60	-13.0
Rape[3]	18,283	14,315	-21.7	2,999	2,153	-28.2	576	420	-27.1	121	105	-13.2
Robbery	56,075	38,096	-32.1	11,405	7,113	-37.6	9,985	7,128	-28.6	1,460	1,012	-30.7
Aggravated assault	223,538	197,163	-11.8	14,500	12,628	-12.9	68,813	59,514	-13.5	5,426	4,557	-16.0
Property crime[2]	546,356	389,657	-28.7	65,668	35,909	-45.3	320,235	197,364	-38.4	31,566	15,101	-52.2
Burglary	106,941	73,431	-31.3	14,349	6,965	-51.5	26,195	17,397	-33.6	2,096	1,171	-44.1
Larceny-theft	382,922	264,157	-31.0	41,424	21,341	-48.5	277,264	165,190	-40.4	27,167	12,311	-54.7
Motor vehicle theft	51,437	46,489	-9.6	8,848	6,827	-22.8	15,293	13,049	-14.7	2,086	1,440	-31.0
Arson	5,056	5,580	+10.4	1,047	776	-25.9	1,483	1,728	+16.5	217	179	-17.5
Other assaults	559,132	482,535	-13.7	57,203	45,907	-19.7	226,729	209,251	-7.7	33,561	31,816	-5.2
Forgery and counterfeiting	24,251	14,916	-38.5	558	276	-50.5	12,472	6,707	-46.2	153	63	-58.8
Fraud	55,845	37,111	-33.5	2,414	1,142	-52.7	32,043	19,162	-40.2	1,126	585	-48.0
Embezzlement	5,703	3,720	-34.8	256	163	-36.3	5,701	3,398	-40.4	187	139	-25.7
Stolen property; buying, receiving, possessing	54,017	50,347	-6.8	5,785	4,993	-13.7	15,117	13,155	-13.0	1,124	862	-23.3
Vandalism	101,524	92,847	-8.5	18,039	13,817	-23.4	30,371	27,673	-8.9	4,203	3,331	-20.7
Weapons; carrying, possessing, etc.	111,738	120,430	+7.8	10,897	12,670	+16.3	11,406	12,462	+9.3	1,324	1,253	-5.4
Prostitution and commercialized vice	8,331	5,025	-39.7	70	28	-60.0	14,812	6,867	-53.6	109	36	-67.0
Sex offenses (except forcible rape and prostitution)	30,600	17,577	-42.6	4,624	2,497	-46.0	2,171	1,029	-52.6	499	290	-41.9
Drug abuse violations	888,002	481,912	-45.7	48,330	23,383	-51.6	289,686	167,216	-42.3	16,286	9,797	-39.8
Gambling	1,902	749	-60.6	119	19	-84.0	388	278	-28.4	11	2	-81.8
Offenses against the family and children	44,392	22,240	-49.9	1,432	767	-46.4	18,815	12,007	-36.2	934	713	-23.7
Driving under the influence	464,687	388,064	-16.5	2,646	2,522	-4.7	159,287	133,150	-16.4	885	819	-7.5
Liquor laws	86,420	44,894	-48.1	10,591	5,975	-43.6	37,062	21,080	-43.1	7,789	4,327	-44.4
Drunkenness[3]	189,721	11,318	-94.0	1,619	62	-96.2	49,988	2,804	-94.4	714	29	-95.9
Disorderly conduct	152,932	124,382	-18.7	23,246	14,456	-37.8	62,923	50,784	-19.3	13,181	9,126	-30.8
Vagrancy	13,264	8,335	-37.2	348	18	-94.8	4,268	2,526	-40.8	105	2	-98.1
All other offenses (except traffic)	1,751,210	1,295,606	-26.0	72,327	47,339	-34.5	645,979	458,160	-29.1	28,994	22,280	-23.2
Suspicion[4]	276	52	-81.2	22	0	-100.0	97	10	-89.7	12	0	-100.0
Curfew and loitering law violations	11,169	3,471	-68.9	11,169	3,471	-68.9	4,774	1,637	-65.7	4,774	1,637	-65.7

1 Does not include suspicion.   2 Violent crimes are offenses of murder and nonnegligent manslaughter, rape, robbery, and aggravated assault. Property crimes are offenses of burglary, larceny-theft, motor vehicle theft, and arson.   3 Drunkenness figures were submitted by Summary reporting agencies only. As of 2021 drunkenness is no longer a separate offense in the National Incident-Based Reporting System (NIBRS), but it is included with All Other Offenses (except traffic) category.   4 Figures for suspicion include only data submitted by Summary reporting agencies because suspicion is not collected as a crime via NIBRS.

SECTION IV: PERSONS ARRESTED 291

Table 36. Year Over Previous Year Arrest Trends, 2021–2022

(Number, percent change; 9,364 agencies; 2022 estimated population 207,160,630; 2021 estimated population 205,917,933.)

Offense charged	Total, all ages			Under 15 years of age			Under 18 years of age			18 years of age and over		
	2021	2022	Percent change	2021	2022	Percent change	2021	2022	Percent change	2021	2022	Percent change
Total[1]	4,606,486	4,702,683	+2.1	93,761	114,412	+22.0	280,300	329,901	+17.7	4,326,186	4,372,782	+1.1
Violent crime[2]	233,753	236,210	+1.1	6,057	7,360	+21.5	20,122	22,911	+13.9	213,631	213,299	-0.2
Murder and nonnegligent manslaughter	7,853	7,471	-4.9	79	110	+39.2	705	807	+14.5	7,148	6,664	-6.8
Rape[3]	12,789	12,492	-2.3	935	841	-10.1	2,112	2,030	-3.9	10,677	10,462	-2.0
Robbery	29,315	30,238	+3.1	1,128	1,334	+18.3	5,328	5,866	+10.1	23,987	24,372	+1.6
Aggravated assault	183,796	186,009	+1.2	3,915	5,075	+29.6	11,977	14,208	+18.6	171,819	171,801	*
Property crime[2]	464,637	513,221	+10.5	12,065	15,217	+26.1	37,598	47,483	+26.3	427,039	465,738	+9.1
Burglary	69,899	72,009	+3.0	2,488	2,835	13.9	6,327	7,231	+14.3	63,572	64,778	+1.9
Larceny-theft	344,542	389,791	+13.1	7,144	9,618	+34.6	23,747	32,015	+34.8	320,795	357,776	+11.5
Motor vehicle theft	45,070	46,202	+2.5	2,003	2,265	+13.1	6,768	7,396	+9.3	38,302	38,806	+1.3
Arson	5,126	5,219	+1.8	430	499	+16.0	756	841	+11.2	4,370	4,378	+0.2
Other assaults	601,930	625,832	+4.0	25,793	33,914	+31.5	59,309	75,282	+26.9	542,621	550,550	+1.5
Forgery and counterfeiting	16,178	18,674	+15.4	32	34	+6.3	297	325	+9.4	15,881	18,349	+15.5
Fraud	48,348	52,016	+7.6	367	398	+8.4	1,591	1,680	+5.6	46,757	50,336	+7.7
Embezzlement	5,242	6,311	+20.4	9	8	-11.1	265	290	+9.4	4,977	6,021	+21.0
Stolen property; buying, receiving, possessing	46,255	48,752	+5.4	990	1,166	+17.8	4,568	5,159	+12.9	41,687	43,593	+4.6
Vandalism	100,755	98,366	-2.4	6,537	6,958	+6.4	14,919	15,451	+3.6	85,836	82,915	-3.4
Weapons; carrying, possessing, etc.	100,981	102,352	+1.4	2,019	2,810	+39.2	8,242	11,062	+34.2	92,739	91,290	-1.6
Prostitution and commercialized vice	7,947	7,612	-4.2	11	7	-36.4	68	50	-26.5	7,879	7,562	-4.0
Sex offenses (except forcible rape and prostitution)	12,104	12,229	+1.0	1,060	1,163	+9.7	2,175	2,292	+5.4	9,929	9,937	+0.1
Drug abuse violations	602,966	562,839	-6.7	5,417	8,286	+53.0	27,097	34,020	+25.5	575,869	528,819	-8.2
Gambling	769	771	+0.3	1	3	+200.0	12	18	+50.0	757	753	-0.5
Offenses against the family and children	34,823	34,816	*	589	592	+0.5	1,463	1,509	+3.1	33,360	33,307	-0.2
Driving under the influence	487,351	480,648	-1.4	58	53	-8.6	3,357	3,243	-3.4	483,994	477,405	-1.4
Liquor laws	70,008	68,650	-1.9	1,266	1,585	+25.2	9,837	10,460	+6.3	60,171	58,190	-3.3
Drunkenness[3]	51	61	+19.6	0	0	NA	0	0	NA	51	61	+19.6
Disorderly conduct	158,436	160,440	+1.3	9,146	10,961	+19.8	20,453	24,322	+18.9	137,983	136,118	-1.4
Vagrancy	7,706	9,600	+24.6	0	0	NA	0	0	NA	7,706	9,600	+24.6
All other offenses (except traffic)	1,600,591	1,658,107	+3.6	20,436	22,245	+8.9	63,272	69,168	+9.3	1,537,319	1,588,939	+3.4
Suspicion[4]	0	0	NA	0	0	NA	0	0	NA	0	0	NA
Curfew and loitering law violations	5,655	5,176	-8.5	1,908	1,652	-13.4	5,655	5,176	-8.5	NA	NA	NA

NA = Not available.

* = Less than one-tenth of one percent.
1 Does not include suspicion.   2 Violent crimes are offenses of murder and nonnegligent manslaughter, rape, robbery, and aggravated assault. Property crimes are offenses of burglary, larceny-theft, motor vehicle theft, and arson.   3 The 2018 figures for drunkenness were submitted by agencies that reported via Summary and those that reported via National Incident Based Reporting System (NIBRS). As of 2021, drunkenness is no longer a separate offense in NIBRS, but it is included with All Other Offenses (except traffic) category.   4 Figures for suspicion include only data submitted by Summary reporting agencies because suspicion is not collected as a crime via NIBRS.

Table 37. Year Over Previous Year Arrest Trends, by Age and Sex, 2021–2022

(Number, percent change; 9,364 agencies; 2022 estimated population 207,160,630; 2021 estimated population 205,917,933.)

Offense charged	Male Total			Male Under 18			Female Total			Female Under 18		
	2021	2022	Percent change	2021	2022	Percent change	2021	2022	Percent change	2019	2020	Percent change
Total[1]	3,352,104	3,397,932	+1.4	193,194	224,708	+16.3	1,254,382	1,304,751	+4.0	87,106	105,193	+20.8
Violent crime[2]	187,410	188,097	+0.4	16,240	18,282	+12.6	46,343	48,113	+3.8	3,882	4,629	+19.2
Murder and nonnegligent manslaughter	6,895	6,585	-4.5	643	749	+16.5	958	886	-7.5	62	58	-6.5
Rape[3]	12,455	12,117	-2.7	2,022	1,937	-4.2	334	375	+12.3	90	93	+3.3
Robbery	25,145	25,681	+2.1	4,792	5,186	+8.2	4,170	4,557	+9.3	536	680	+26.9
Aggravated assault	142,915	143,714	0.6	8,783	10,410	+18.5	40,881	42,295	+3.5	3,194	3,798	+18.9
Property crime[2]	306,949	335,270	+9.2	27,572	33,623	+21.9	157,688	177,951	+12.9	10,026	13,860	+38.2
Burglary	56,974	58,669	+3.0	5,518	6,310	+14.4	12,925	13,340	+3.2	809	921	+13.8
Larceny-theft	210,853	236,540	+12.2	15,883	20,560	+29.4	133,689	153,251	+14.6	7,864	11,455	+45.7
Motor vehicle theft	35,177	36,069	+2.5	5,574	6,067	+8.8	9,893	10,133	+2.4	1,194	1,329	+11.3
Arson	3,945	3,992	+1.2	597	686	+14.9	1,181	1,227	+3.9	159	155	-2.5
Other assaults	425,190	433,951	+2.1	35,503	44,280	+24.7	176,740	191,881	+8.6	23,806	31,002	+30.2
Forgery and counterfeiting	10,935	12,749	+16.6	217	268	+23.5	5,243	5,925	+13.0	80	57	-28.8
Fraud	31,188	33,756	+8.2	1,062	1,101	+3.7	17,160	18,260	+6.4	529	579	+9.5
Embezzlement	2,710	3,186	+17.6	141	154	+9.2	2,532	3,125	+23.4	124	136	+9.7
Stolen property; buying, receiving, possessing	36,878	38,893	+5.5	3,931	4,440	+12.9	9,377	9,859	+5.1	637	719	+12.9
Vandalism	76,966	75,200	-2.3	11,874	12,385	+4.3	23,789	23,166	-2.6	3,045	3,066	+0.7
Weapons; carrying, possessing, etc.	91,085	92,469	+1.5	7,433	10,040	+35.1	9,896	9,883	-0.1	809	1,022	+26.3
Prostitution and commercialized vice	3,950	3,406	-13.8	16	21	+31.3	3,997	4,206	+5.2	52	29	-44.2
Sex offenses (except forcible rape and prostitution)	11,499	11,583	+0.7	1,991	2,065	+3.7	605	646	+6.8	184	227	+23.4
Drug abuse violations	438,599	409,705	-6.6	19,353	23,803	+23.0	164,367	153,134	-6.8	7,744	10,217	+31.9
Gambling	586	579	-1.2	12	17	+41.7	183	192	+4.9	0	1	NA
Offenses against the family and children	22,778	22,592	-0.8	807	781	-3.2	12,045	12,224	+1.5	656	728	+11.0
Driving under the influence	360,385	355,445	-1.4	2,499	2,443	-2.2	126,966	125,203	-1.4	858	800	-6.8
Liquor laws	48,271	46,718	-3.2	5,642	6,006	+6.5	21,737	21,932	+0.9	4,195	4,454	+6.2
Drunkenness[3]	36	54	+50.0	0	0	NA	15	7	-53.3	0	0	NA
Disorderly conduct	111,686	112,330	+0.6	12,802	14,911	+16.5	46,750	48,110	+2.9	7,651	9,411	+23.0
Vagrancy	5,965	7,444	+24.8	0	0		1,741	2,156	+23.8	0	0	NA
All other offenses (except traffic)	1,175,394	1,210,998	+3.0	42,455	46,581	+9.7	425,197	447,109	+5.2	20,817	22,587	+8.5
Suspicion[4]	0	0	NA	0	0	NA	0	0	NA	0	0	NA
Curfew and loitering law violations	3,644	3,507	-3.8	3,644	3,507	-3.8	2,011	1,669	-17.0	2,011	1,669	-17.0

NA = Not available.

1 Does not include suspicion.   2 Violent crimes are offenses of murder and nonnegligent manslaughter, rape, robbery, and aggravated assault. Property crimes are offenses of burglary, larceny-theft, motor vehicle theft, and arson.   3 The 2018 figures for drunkenness were submitted by agencies that reported via Summary and those that reported via National Incident Based Reporting System (NIBRS). As of 2021, drunkenness is no longer a separate offense in NIBRS, but it is included with All Other Offenses (except traffic) category.   4 Figures for suspicion include only data submitted by Summary reporting agencies because suspicion is not collected as a crime via NIBRS.

Table 38. Arrests, Distribution by Age, by Arrest Offense Category, 2022

(Number; percent; 11,933 agencies; 2022 estimated population 270,485,978.)

Offense charged	Total, all ages	Under 15 years	Under 18 years	Age 18 years and over	Under 10 years	10–12 years	13–14 years	15 years	16 years
Total	5,901,283	131,213	384687	5,516,596.0	1,294	29,594	100,325	77,759	85,276
Total, percent distribution[1]	100.0	2.2	6.5	93.5	*	0.5	1.7	1.3	1.4
Violent crime[2]	349,283	9,693	30896	318,387.0	99	2,118	7,476	6,329	7,263
Violent crime, percent distribution[1]	100.0	2.8	8.8	91.2	*	0.6	2.1	1.8	2.1
Murder and nonnegligent manslaughter	10,047	134	1014	9,033.0	0	6	128	184	298
Rape	15,930	972	2408	13,522.0	20	279	673	469	469
Robbery	47,807	2,083	8789	39,018.0	1	251	1,831	2,057	2,297
Aggravated assault	275,499	6,504	18685	256,814.0	78	1,582	4,844	3,619	4,199
Property crime[2]	637,682	17,681	55953	581,729.0	120	3,368	14,193	11,854	13,218
Property crime, percent distribution[1]	100.0	2.8	8.8	91.2	*	0.5	2.2	1.9	2.1
Burglary	97,790	3,401	8899	88,891.0	41	732	2,628	1,930	1,811
Larceny-theft	468,839	11,034	36961	431,878.0	59	2,185	8,790	7,508	9,010
Motor vehicle theft	63,342	2,633	9065	54,277.0	3	266	2,364	2,238	2,247
Arson	7,711	613	1028	6,683.0	17	185	411	178	150
Other assaults	765,816	38,044	85958	679,858.0	370	10,334	27,340	17,229	16,472
Forgery and counterfeiting	23,315	38	371	22,944.0	0	5	33	37	93
Fraud	62,135	462	1944	60,191.0	1	79	382	327	477
Embezzlement	7,780	11	322	7,458.0	0	1	10	16	99
Stolen property; buying, receiving, possessing	67,827	1,381	6210	61,617.0	4	129	1,248	1,458	1,659
Vandalism	131,854	8,224	18715	113,139.0	166	2,320	5,738	3,584	3,512
Weapons; carrying, possessing, etc.	146,785	3,762	15485	131,300.0	42	834	2,886	2,892	3,864
Prostitution and commercialized vice	12,455	10	67	12,388.0	0	2	8	11	13
Sex offenses (except forcible rape and prostitution)	19,821	1,468	2978	16,843.0	25	371	1,072	534	499
Drug abuse violations	726,746	9,045	37394	689,352.0	17	1,286	7,742	7,434	9,358
Gambling	1,103	3	22	1,081.0	0	0	3	5	3
Offenses against the family and children	38,065	613	1570	36,495.0	14	154	445	331	335
Driving under the influence	622,344	68	3925	618,419.0	9	4	55	201	998
Liquor laws	76,369	1,738	11429	64,940.0	4	210	1,524	1,891	3,040
Drunkenness[3]	14,324	17	96	14,228.0	0	0	17	21	23
Disorderly conduct	193,449	11,803	26719	166,730.0	103	3,031	8,669	5,560	5,080
Vagrancy	12,673	2	20	12,653.0	0	2	0	5	6
All other offenses (except traffic)	1,985,747	25,343	78965	1,906,782.0	314	5,088	19,941	16,607	17,829
Suspicion[4]	62	0	0	62.0	0	0	0	0	0
Curfew and loitering law violations	5,648	1,807	5648	NA	6	258	1,543	1,433	1,435

Table 38. Arrests, Distribution by Age, by Arrest Offense Category, 2022—Continued

(Number; percent; 11,933 agencies; 2022 estimated population 270,485,978.)

Offense charged	17 years	18 years	19 years	20 years	21 years	22 years	23 years	24 years
Total	90,439	121,149	134,113	138,735	149,066	154,175	156,871	160,180
Total, percent distribution[1]	1.5	2.1	2.3	2.4	2.5	2.6	2.7	2.7
Violent crime[2]	7,611	9,118	9,349	9,213	9,978	9,949	9,892	10,300
Violent crime, percent distribution[1]	2.2	2.6	2.7	2.6	2.9	2.8	2.8	2.9
Murder and nonnegligent manslaughter	398	544	495	468	439	416	401	359
Rape	498	598	533	541	481	474	396	371
Robbery	2,352	2,426	2,122	1,732	1,677	1,489	1,373	1,420
Aggravated assault	4,363	5,550	6,199	6,472	7,381	7,570	7,722	8,150
Property crime[2]	13,200	16,114	15,149	13,858	13,917	14,359	14,817	15,293
Property crime, percent distribution[1]	2.1	2.5	2.4	2.2	2.2	2.3	2.3	2.4
Burglary	1,757	2,193	2,047	1,960	2,070	2,076	2,238	2,415
Larceny-theft	9,409	11,852	11,450	10,335	10,318	10,697	10,895	11,144
Motor vehicle theft	1,947	1,950	1,549	1,456	1,437	1,484	1,550	1,588
Arson	87	119	103	107	92	102	134	146
Other assaults	14,213	14,038	14,808	16,099	18,154	19,330	19,879	20,594
Forgery and counterfeiting	203	655	1,048	1,045	595	626	606	625
Fraud	678	1,212	1,519	1,571	1,509	1,606	1,532	1,609
Embezzlement	196	380	375	357	356	300	280	240
Stolen property; buying, receiving, possessing	1,712	2,053	1,925	1,790	1,612	1,570	1,764	1,745
Vandalism	3,395	3,455	3,266	3,234	3,491	3,458	3,515	3,508
Weapons; carrying, possessing, etc.	4,967	6,039	6,253	5,858	6,237	6,114	5,672	5,306
Prostitution and commercialized vice	33	332	459	516	625	592	509	515
Sex offenses (except forcible rape and prostitution)	477	512	475	413	497	438	390	366
Drug abuse violations	11,557	18,212	19,905	19,786	20,052	20,349	20,408	20,409
Gambling	11	29	43	52	24	22	19	26
Offenses against the family and children	291	345	447	518	648	734	778	940
Driving under the influence	2,658	7,438	10,460	12,656	19,448	20,586	21,228	21,024
Liquor laws	4,760	9,205	10,023	8,243	2,026	1,514	1,216	1,109
Drunkenness[3]	35	118	165	191	326	331	359	392
Disorderly conduct	4,276	4,023	3,799	3,987	4,779	4,736	4,676	4,573
Vagrancy	7	237	204	221	208	227	234	248
All other offenses (except traffic)	19,186	27,633	34,441	39,127	44,579	47,331	49,095	51,354
Suspicion[4]	0	1	0	0	5	3	2	4
Curfew and loitering law violations	973	NA	NA	NA	NA	NA	NA	NA

Table 38. Arrests, Distribution by Age, by Arrest Offense Category, 2022—Continued

(Number; percent; 11,933 agencies; 2022 estimated population 270,485,978.)

Offense charged	25–29 years	30–34 years	35–39 years	40–44 years	45–49 years	50–54 years	55–59 years	60–64 years	65 years and over
Total	884,882	956,799	807,352	634,932	405,676	321,301	237,181	148,506	105,678
Total, percent distribution[1]	15.0	16.2	13.7	10.8	6.9	5.4	4.0	2.5	1.8
Violent crime[2]	54,702	55,453	43,927	33,229	20,827	15,997	12,273	7,843	6,337
Violent crime, percent distribution[1]	15.7	15.9	12.6	9.5	6.0	4.6	3.5	2.2	1.8
Murder and nonnegligent manslaughter	1,619	1,361	907	724	416	334	227	170	153
Rape	1,812	1,986	1,862	1,402	933	769	526	408	430
Robbery	7,215	6,862	4,802	3,286	1,767	1,239	943	483	182
Aggravated assault	44,056	45,244	36,356	27,817	17,711	13,655	10,577	6,782	5,572
Property crime[2]	90,916	104,586	88,611	68,150	42,324	34,798	25,400	14,465	8,972
Property crime, percent distribution[1]	14.3	16.4	13.9	10.7	6.6	5.5	4.0	2.3	1.4
Burglary	15,075	17,192	14,475	10,682	6,094	4,689	3,225	1,590	870
Larceny-theft	65,136	75,146	64,491	50,426	32,366	27,423	20,477	12,012	7,710
Motor vehicle theft	9,769	11,020	8,598	6,112	3,313	2,258	1,329	632	232
Arson	936	1,228	1,047	930	551	428	369	231	160
Other assaults	111,842	118,673	98,629	76,701	49,761	38,972	28,740	18,496	15,142
Forgery and counterfeiting	3,546	3,859	3,418	2,597	1,639	1,203	804	428	250
Fraud	9,581	10,943	9,410	7,364	4,370	3,423	2,314	1,339	889
Embezzlement	1,091	1,073	951	742	496	376	235	134	72
Stolen property; buying, receiving, possessing	10,594	11,914	9,700	7,136	4,096	2,781	1,770	810	357
Vandalism	19,550	20,808	16,746	12,064	7,010	5,226	3,799	2,321	1,688
Weapons; carrying, possessing, etc.	24,951	21,470	15,299	11,059	6,403	4,519	2,986	1,796	1,338
Prostitution and commercialized vice	2,311	1,829	1,282	1,021	723	598	516	306	254
Sex offenses (except forcible rape and prostitution)	2,116	2,344	2,207	1,779	1,305	1,129	1,034	797	1,041
Drug abuse violations	112,382	121,461	103,101	81,852	49,248	37,032	24,890	13,982	6,283
Gambling	131	155	94	132	95	76	74	48	61
Offenses against the family and children	5,966	7,506	6,753	4,966	2,821	1,792	1,202	611	468
Driving under the influence	105,683	98,859	80,066	64,247	45,991	38,589	31,110	22,201	18,833
Liquor laws	5,495	5,407	4,690	4,122	3,109	2,877	2,596	1,964	1,344
Drunkenness[3]	2,215	2,397	2,056	1,605	1,168	1,073	860	594	378
Disorderly conduct	24,470	27,116	23,169	18,723	12,756	10,598	8,804	5,836	4,685
Vagrancy	1,458	2,003	1,922	1,602	1,171	1,069	819	633	397
All other offenses (except traffic)	295,872	338,934	295,313	235,838	150,351	119,171	86,953	53,902	36,888
Suspicion[4]	10	9	8	3	12	2	2	0	1
Curfew and loitering law violations	NA	NA	NA	NA	NA	NA	NA	NA	NA

NA = Not available.
* = Less than one-tenth of one percent.
1 Because of rounding, the percentages may not add to 100.0.   2 Violent crimes are offenses of murder and nonnegligent manslaughter, rape, robbery, and aggravated assault. Property crimes are offenses of burglary, larceny-theft, motor vehicle theft, and arson.   3 Drunkenness figures were submitted by Summary reporting agencies only. As of 2021 drunkenness is no longer a separate offense in National Incident Based Reporting System (NIBRS), but it is included with All Other Offenses (except traffic) category.   4 Figures for suspicion include only data submitted by Summary reporting agencies because suspicion is not collected as a crime via NIBRS.

Table 39. Male Arrests, Distribution by Age, 2022

(Number, percent; 11,933 agencies; 2022 estimated population 270,485,978.)

Offense charged	Total, all ages	Under 15 years	Under 18 years	Age 18 years and over	Under 10 years	10–12 years	13–14 years	15 years	16 years
Total	4,312,398	85,163	265086	4,047,312.0	1,002	19,168	64,993	53,192	60,485
Total, percent distribution[1]	100.0	2.0	6.1	93.9	*	0.4	1.5	1.2	1.4
Violent crime[2]	276,308	7,336	24705	251,603.0	85	1,586	5,665	5,080	5,928
Violent crime, percent distribution[1]	100.0	2.7	8.9	91.1	*	0.6	2.1	1.8	2.1
Murder and nonnegligent manslaughter	8,901	120	945	7,956.0	0	6	114	171	279
Rape	15,470	905	2297	13,173.0	17	254	634	454	452
Robbery	40,378	1,802	7720	32,658.0	1	205	1,596	1,807	2,029
Aggravated assault	211,559	4,509	13743	197,816.0	67	1,121	3,321	2,648	3,168
Property crime[2]	422,706	12,542	39555	383,151.0	103	2,375	10,064	8,552	9,393
Property crime, percent distribution[1]	100.0	3.0	9.4	90.6	*	0.6	2.4	2.0	2.2
Burglary	79,225	2,856	7650	71,575.0	38	619	2,199	1,667	1,562
Larceny-theft	288,105	7,079	23597	264,508.0	46	1,398	5,635	4,913	5,826
Motor vehicle theft	49,466	2,115	7474	41,992.0	2	211	1,902	1,825	1,880
Arson	5,910	492	834	5,076.0	17	147	328	147	125
Other assaults	533,132	21,837	50865	482,267.0	290	6,167	15,380	10,202	9,944
Forgery and counterfeiting	16,117	35	306	15,811.0	0	5	30	32	77
Fraud	40,834	299	1286	39,548.0	0	57	242	200	330
Embezzlement	4,060	6	176	3,884.0	0	1	5	12	59
Stolen property; buying, receiving, possessing	53,807	1,134	5307	48,500.0	3	109	1,022	1,241	1,444
Vandalism	101,371	6,637	15060	86,311.0	135	1,867	4,635	2,893	2,810
Weapons; carrying, possessing, etc.	132,860	3,209	14100	118,760.0	34	683	2,492	2,619	3,579
Prostitution and commercialized vice	5,349	7	30	5,319.0	0	2	5	4	5
Sex offenses (except forcible rape and prostitution)	18,742	1,286	2674	16,068.0	22	308	956	483	456
Drug abuse violations	538,712	5,511	26350	512,362.0	12	710	4,789	5,093	6,922
Gambling	811	2	20	791.0	0	0	2	5	3
Offenses against the family and children	24,644	323	822	23,822.0	9	98	216	165	167
Driving under the influence	463,775	47	2954	460,821.0	8	2	37	140	743
Liquor laws	52,026	724	6618	45,408.0	3	88	633	1,010	1,844
Drunkenness[3]	11,475	12	67	11,408.0	0	0	12	11	16
Disorderly conduct	137,093	7,015	16438	120,655.0	85	1,893	5,037	3,395	3,243
Vagrancy	9,722	2	18	9,704.0	0	2	0	3	6
All other offenses (except traffic)	1,464,947	16,031	53880	1,411,067.0	208	3,071	12,752	11,063	12,537
Suspicion[4]	52	0	0	52.0	0	0	0	0	0
Curfew and loitering law violations	3,855	1,168	3855	NA	5	144	1,019	989	979

Table 39. Male Arrests, Distribution by Age, 2022—Continued

(Number, percent; 11,933 agencies; 2022 estimated population 270,485,978.)

Offense charged	17 years	18 years	19 years	20 years	21 years	22 years	23 years	24 years	25–29 years
Total	66,246	89,318	97,832	100,264	108,258	111,782	113,548	116,105	646,221
Total, percent distribution[1]	1.5	2.1	2.3	2.3	2.5	2.6	2.6	2.7	15.0
Violent crime[2]	6,361	7,599	7,601	7,311	7,839	7,800	7,678	7,999	42,630
Violent crime, percent distribution[1]	2.3	2.8	2.8	2.6	2.8	2.8	2.8	2.9	15.4
Murder and nonnegligent manslaughter	375	511	460	423	390	377	368	301	1,388
Rape	486	575	522	525	468	451	389	355	1,753
Robbery	2,082	2,188	1,836	1,475	1,386	1,225	1,140	1,182	5,993
Aggravated assault	3,418	4,325	4,783	4,888	5,595	5,747	5,781	6,161	33,496
Property crime[2]	9,068	10,742	9,540	8,648	8,816	9,081	9,417	9,902	60,542
Property crime, percent distribution[1]	2.1	2.5	2.3	2.0	2.1	2.1	2.2	2.3	14.3
Burglary	1,565	1,887	1,708	1,578	1,636	1,649	1,798	1,952	12,151
Larceny-theft	5,779	7,097	6,503	5,845	5,993	6,235	6,334	6,632	40,268
Motor vehicle theft	1,654	1,666	1,245	1,140	1,118	1,125	1,179	1,210	7,387
Arson	70	92	84	85	69	72	106	108	736
Other assaults	8,882	8,906	9,337	10,377	11,818	12,788	13,452	13,923	78,687
Forgery and counterfeiting	162	450	755	683	421	443	425	435	2,478
Fraud	457	816	988	1,029	1,033	1,035	998	1,051	6,207
Embezzlement	99	224	208	185	189	159	178	138	600
Stolen property; buying, receiving, possessing	1,488	1,786	1,632	1,467	1,287	1,211	1,365	1,347	8,117
Vandalism	2,720	2,679	2,462	2,366	2,585	2,567	2,579	2,589	14,834
Weapons; carrying, possessing, etc.	4,693	5,674	5,878	5,470	5,791	5,625	5,172	4,806	22,466
Prostitution and commercialized vice	14	43	66	85	126	118	125	130	878
Sex offenses (except forcible rape and prostitution)	449	484	455	387	467	417	370	341	1,982
Drug abuse violations	8,824	13,954	15,213	14,968	14,966	15,171	15,200	15,320	83,460
Gambling	10	22	33	38	19	16	17	21	100
Offenses against the family and children	167	229	266	298	401	421	417	501	3,504
Driving under the influence	2,024	5,695	7,983	9,606	14,347	15,258	15,600	15,414	78,430
Liquor laws	3,040	5,849	6,503	5,286	1,409	1,039	868	816	3,962
Drunkenness[3]	28	83	130	145	255	249	286	294	1,767
Disorderly conduct	2,785	2,712	2,555	2,656	3,341	3,290	3,199	3,193	17,587
Vagrancy	7	177	149	159	171	172	193	194	1,137
All other offenses (except traffic)	14,249	21,193	26,078	29,100	32,973	34,919	36,007	37,688	216,846
Suspicion[4]	0	1	0	0	4	3	2	3	7
Curfew and loitering law violations	719	NA	NA	NA	NA	NA	NA	NA	NA

298 CRIME IN THE UNITED STATES

Table 39. Male Arrests, Distribution by Age, 2022—Continued

(Number, percent; 11,933 agencies; 2022 estimated population 270,485,978.)

Offense charged	30–34 years	35–39 years	40–44 years	45–49 years	50–54 years	55–59 years	60–64 years	65 years and over
Total	692,722	581,840	463,509	300,399	241,524	183,458	117,045	83,487
Total, percent distribution[1]	16.1	13.5	10.7	7.0	5.6	4.3	2.7	1.9
Violent crime[2]	43,373	34,363	26,312	16,523	12,727	9,969	6,522	5,357
Violent crime, percent distribution[1]	15.7	12.4	9.5	6.0	4.6	3.6	2.4	1.9
Murder and nonnegligent manslaughter	1,193	786	621	362	284	205	149	138
Rape	1,925	1,819	1,375	912	753	520	402	429
Robbery	5,624	3,934	2,724	1,483	1,054	817	436	161
Aggravated assault	34,631	27,824	21,592	13,766	10,636	8,427	5,535	4,629
Property crime[2]	69,115	58,052	44,754	27,734	23,345	17,546	10,006	5,911
Property crime, percent distribution[1]	16.4	13.7	10.6	6.6	5.5	4.2	2.4	1.4
Burglary	13,712	11,442	8,523	4,914	3,829	2,717	1,353	726
Larceny-theft	46,220	39,292	30,784	19,772	17,329	13,434	7,924	4,846
Motor vehicle theft	8,247	6,560	4,743	2,644	1,861	1,124	541	202
Arson	936	758	704	404	326	271	188	137
Other assaults	84,375	70,404	55,801	36,593	28,586	21,391	14,173	11,656
Forgery and counterfeiting	2,594	2,249	1,760	1,098	874	603	349	194
Fraud	7,119	5,964	4,749	2,890	2,343	1,662	1,003	661
Embezzlement	571	457	320	241	187	111	72	44
Stolen property; buying, receiving, possessing	9,094	7,511	5,587	3,338	2,259	1,499	696	304
Vandalism	15,860	12,882	9,284	5,491	4,000	2,953	1,852	1,328
Weapons; carrying, possessing, etc.	19,062	13,493	9,884	5,756	4,084	2,705	1,663	1,231
Prostitution and commercialized vice	836	752	619	443	347	303	220	228
Sex offenses (except forcible rape and prostitution)	2,232	2,103	1,691	1,256	1,079	1,000	779	1,025
Drug abuse violations	88,101	74,055	59,844	36,910	28,473	19,864	11,472	5,391
Gambling	122	74	98	63	48	52	29	39
Offenses against the family and children	4,581	4,389	3,579	2,174	1,350	931	450	331
Driving under the influence	73,406	59,481	47,675	34,267	28,723	23,351	16,984	14,601
Liquor laws	3,893	3,411	3,046	2,290	2,218	2,083	1,621	1,114
Drunkenness[3]	1,943	1,675	1,289	925	845	723	483	316
Disorderly conduct	19,656	16,668	13,491	9,296	7,913	6,781	4,603	3,714
Vagrancy	1,537	1,457	1,199	880	808	611	519	341
All other offenses (except traffic)	245,244	212,394	172,524	112,221	91,313	69,318	43,549	29,700
Suspicion[4]	8	6	3	10	2	2	0	1
Curfew and loitering law violations	NA	NA	NA	NA	NA	NA	NA	NA

NA = Not available.
* = Less than one-tenth of one percent.
1 Because of rounding, the percentages may not add to 100.0. 2 Violent crimes are offenses of murder and nonnegligent manslaughter, rape, robbery, and aggravated assault. Property crimes are offenses of burglary, larceny-theft, motor vehicle theft, and arson. 3 Drunkenness figures were submitted by Summary reporting agencies only. As of 2021 drunkenness is no longer a separate offense in National Incident Based Reporting System (NIBRS), but it is included with All Other Offenses (except traffic) category. 4 Figures for suspicion include only data submitted by Summary reporting agencies because suspicion is not collected as a crime via NIBRS.

Table 40. Female Arrests, Distribution by Age, 2022

(Number, percent; 11,933 agencies; 2022 estimated population 270,485,978.)

Offense charged	Total, all ages	Under 15 years	Under 18 years	Age 18 years and over	Under 10 years	10–12 years	13–14 years	15 years	16 years
Total	1,588,885	46,050	119601	1,469,284.0	292	10,426	35,332	24,567	24,791
Total, percent distribution[1]	100.0	2.9	7.5	92.5	*	0.7	2.2	1.5	1.6
Violent crime[2]	72,975	2,357	6191	66,784.0	14	532	1,811	1,249	1,335
Violent crime, percent distribution[1]	100.0	3.2	8.5	91.5	*	0.7	2.5	1.7	1.8
Murder and nonnegligent manslaughter	1,146	14	69	1,077.0	0	0	14	13	19
Rape	460	67	111	349.0	3	25	39	15	17
Robbery	7,429	281	1069	6,360.0	0	46	235	250	268
Aggravated assault	63,940	1,995	4942	58,998.0	11	461	1,523	971	1,031
Property crime[2]	214,976	5,139	16398	198,578.0	17	993	4,129	3,302	3,825
Property crime, percent distribution[1]	100.0	2.4	7.6	92.4	*	0.5	1.9	1.5	1.8
Burglary	18,565	545	1249	17,316.0	3	113	429	263	249
Larceny-theft	180,734	3,955	13364	167,370.0	13	787	3,155	2,595	3,184
Motor vehicle theft	13,876	518	1591	12,285.0	1	55	462	413	367
Arson	1,801	121	194	1,607.0	0	38	83	31	25
Other assaults	232,684	16,207	35093	197,591.0	80	4,167	11,960	7,027	6,528
Forgery and counterfeiting	7,198	3	65	7,133.0	0	0	3	5	16
Fraud	21,301	163	658	20,643.0	1	22	140	127	147
Embezzlement	3,720	5	146	3,574.0	0	0	5	4	40
Stolen property; buying, receiving, possessing	14,020	247	903	13,117.0	1	20	226	217	215
Vandalism	30,483	1,587	3655	26,828.0	31	453	1,103	691	702
Weapons; carrying, possessing, etc.	13,925	553	1385	12,540.0	8	151	394	273	285
Prostitution and commercialized vice	7,106	3	37	7,069.0	0	0	3	7	8
Sex offenses (except forcible rape and prostitution)	1,079	182	304	775.0	3	63	116	51	43
Drug abuse violations	188,034	3,534	11044	176,990.0	5	576	2,953	2,341	2,436
Gambling	292	1	2	290.0	0	0	1	0	0
Offenses against the family and children	13,421	290	748	12,673.0	5	56	229	166	168
Driving under the influence	158,569	21	971	157,598.0	1	2	18	61	255
Liquor laws	24,343	1,014	4811	19,532.0	1	122	891	881	1,196
Drunkenness[3]	2,849	5	29	2,820.0	0	0	5	10	7
Disorderly conduct	56,356	4,788	10281	46,075.0	18	1,138	3,632	2,165	1,837
Vagrancy	2,951	0	2	2,949.0	0	0	0	2	0
All other offenses (except traffic)	520,800	9,312	25085	495,715.0	106	2,017	7,189	5,544	5,292
Suspicion[4]	10	0	0	10.0	0	0	0	0	0
Curfew and loitering law violations	1,793	639	1793	NA	1	114	524	444	456

Table 40. Female Arrests, Distribution by Age, 2022—Continued

(Number, percent; 11,933 agencies; 2022 estimated population 270,485,978.)

Offense charged	17 years	18 years	19 years	20 years	21 years	22 years	23 years	24 years	25–29 years
Total	24,193	31,831	36,281	38,471	40,808	42,393	43,323	44,075	238,661
Total, percent distribution[1]	1.5	2.0	2.3	2.4	2.6	2.7	2.7	2.8	15.0
Violent crime[2]	1,250	1,519	1,748	1,902	2,139	2,149	2,214	2,301	12,072
Violent crime, percent distribution[1]	1.7	2.1	2.4	2.6	2.9	2.9	3.0	3.2	16.5
Murder and nonnegligent manslaughter	23	33	35	45	49	39	33	58	231
Rape	12	23	11	16	13	23	7	16	59
Robbery	270	238	286	257	291	264	233	238	1,222
Aggravated assault	945	1,225	1,416	1,584	1,786	1,823	1,941	1,989	10,560
Property crime[2]	4,132	5,372	5,609	5,210	5,101	5,278	5,400	5,391	30,374
Property crime, percent distribution[1]	1.9	2.5	2.6	2.4	2.4	2.5	2.5	2.5	14.1
Burglary	192	306	339	382	434	427	440	463	2,924
Larceny-theft	3,630	4,755	4,947	4,490	4,325	4,462	4,561	4,512	24,868
Motor vehicle theft	293	284	304	316	319	359	371	378	2,382
Arson	17	27	19	22	23	30	28	38	200
Other assaults	5,331	5,132	5,471	5,722	6,336	6,542	6,427	6,671	33,155
Forgery and counterfeiting	41	205	293	362	174	183	181	190	1,068
Fraud	221	396	531	542	476	571	534	558	3,374
Embezzlement	97	156	167	172	167	141	102	102	491
Stolen property; buying, receiving, possessing	224	267	293	323	325	359	399	398	2,477
Vandalism	675	776	804	868	906	891	936	919	4,716
Weapons; carrying, possessing, etc.	274	365	375	388	446	489	500	500	2,485
Prostitution and commercialized vice	19	289	393	431	499	474	384	385	1,433
Sex offenses (except forcible rape and prostitution)	28	28	20	26	30	21	20	25	134
Drug abuse violations	2,733	4,258	4,692	4,818	5,086	5,178	5,208	5,089	28,922
Gambling	1	7	10	14	5	6	2	5	31
Offenses against the family and children	124	116	181	220	247	313	361	439	2,462
Driving under the influence	634	1,743	2,477	3,050	5,101	5,328	5,628	5,610	27,253
Liquor laws	1,720	3,356	3,520	2,957	617	475	348	293	1,533
Drunkenness[3]	7	35	35	46	71	82	73	98	448
Disorderly conduct	1,491	1,311	1,244	1,331	1,438	1,446	1,477	1,380	6,883
Vagrancy	0	60	55	62	37	55	41	54	321
All other offenses (except traffic)	4,937	6,440	8,363	10,027	11,606	12,412	13,088	13,666	79,026
Suspicion[4]	0	0	0	0	1	0	0	1	3
Curfew and loitering law violations	254	NA	NA	NA	NA	NA	NA	NA	NA

Table 40. Female Arrests, Distribution by Age, 2022—Continued

(Number, percent; 11,933 agencies; 2022 estimated population 270,485,978.)

Offense charged	30–34 years	35–39 years	40–44 years	45–49 years	50–54 years	55–59 years	60–64 years	65 years and over
Total	264,077	225,512	171,423	105,277	79,777	53,723	31,461	22,191
Total, percent distribution[1]	16.6	14.2	10.8	6.6	5.0	3.4	2.0	1.4
Violent crime[2]	12,080	9,564	6,917	4,304	3,270	2,304	1,321	980
Violent crime, percent distribution[1]	16.6	13.1	9.5	5.9	4.5	3.2	1.8	1.3
Murder and nonnegligent manslaughter	168	121	103	54	50	22	21	15
Rape	61	43	27	21	16	6	6	1
Robbery	1,238	868	562	284	185	126	47	21
Aggravated assault	10,613	8,532	6,225	3,945	3,019	2,150	1,247	943
Property crime[2]	35,471	30,559	23,396	14,590	11,453	7,854	4,459	3,061
Property crime, percent distribution[1]	16.5	14.2	10.9	6.8	5.3	3.7	2.1	1.4
Burglary	3,480	3,033	2,159	1,180	860	508	237	144
Larceny-theft	28,926	25,199	19,642	12,594	10,094	7,043	4,088	2,864
Motor vehicle theft	2,773	2,038	1,369	669	397	205	91	30
Arson	292	289	226	147	102	98	43	23
Other assaults	34,298	28,225	20,900	13,168	10,386	7,349	4,323	3,486
Forgery and counterfeiting	1,265	1,169	837	541	329	201	79	56
Fraud	3,824	3,446	2,615	1,480	1,080	652	336	228
Embezzlement	502	494	422	255	189	124	62	28
Stolen property; buying, receiving, possessing	2,820	2,189	1,549	758	522	271	114	53
Vandalism	4,948	3,864	2,780	1,519	1,226	846	469	360
Weapons; carrying, possessing, etc.	2,408	1,806	1,175	647	435	281	133	107
Prostitution and commercialized vice	993	530	402	280	251	213	86	26
Sex offenses (except forcible rape and prostitution)	112	104	88	49	50	34	18	16
Drug abuse violations	33,360	29,046	22,008	12,338	8,559	5,026	2,510	892
Gambling	33	20	34	32	28	22	19	22
Offenses against the family and children	2,925	2,364	1,387	647	442	271	161	137
Driving under the influence	25,453	20,585	16,572	11,724	9,866	7,759	5,217	4,232
Liquor laws	1,514	1,279	1,076	819	659	513	343	230
Drunkenness[3]	454	381	316	243	228	137	111	62
Disorderly conduct	7,460	6,501	5,232	3,460	2,685	2,023	1,233	971
Vagrancy	466	465	403	291	261	208	114	56
All other offenses (except traffic)	93,690	82,919	63,314	38,130	27,858	17,635	10,353	7,188
Suspicion[4]	1	2	0	2	0	0	0	0
Curfew and loitering law violations	NA	NA	NA	NA	NA	NA	NA	NA

NA = Not available.
* = Less than one-tenth of one percent.
1 Because of rounding, the percentages may not add to 100.0.   2 Violent crimes are offenses of murder and nonnegligent manslaughter, rape, robbery, and aggravated assault. Property crimes are offenses of burglary, larceny-theft, motor vehicle theft, and arson.   3 Drunkenness figures were submitted by Summary reporting agencies only. As of 2021 drunkenness is no longer a separate offense in National Incident Based Reporting System (NIBRS), but it is included with All Other Offenses (except traffic) category.   4 Figures for suspicion include only data submitted by Summary reporting agencies because suspicion is not collected as a crime via NIBRS.

Table 41. Arrests of Persons Under 15, 18, 21, and 25 Years of Age, 2022

(Number, percent; 11,933 agencies; 2022 estimated population 270,485,978.)

Offense charged	Total, all ages	Number of persons arrested				Percent of total all ages			
		Under 15	Under 18	Under 21	Under 25	Under 15	Under 18	Under 21	Under 25
Total	5,901,283	131,213	384,687	778,684	1,398,976	2.2	6.5	13.2	23.7
Violent crime[1]	349,283	9,693	30,896	58,576	98,695	2.8	8.8	16.8	28.3
Murder and nonnegligent manslaughter	10,047	134	1,014	2,521	4,136	1.3	10.1	25.1	41.2
Rape	15,930	972	2,408	4,080	5,802	6.1	15.1	25.6	36.4
Robbery	47,807	2,083	8,789	15,069	21,028	4.4	18.4	31.5	44.0
Aggravated assault	275,499	6,504	18,685	36,906	67,729	2.4	6.8	13.4	24.6
Property crime[1]	637,682	17,681	55,953	101,074	159,460	2.8	8.8	15.9	25.0
Burglary	97,790	3,401	8,899	15,099	23,898	3.5	9.1	15.4	24.4
Larceny-theft	468,839	11,034	36,961	70,598	113,652	2.4	7.9	15.1	24.2
Motor vehicle theft	63,342	2,633	9,065	14,020	20,079	4.2	14.3	22.1	31.7
Arson	7,711	613	1,028	1,357	1,831	7.9	13.3	17.6	23.7
Other assaults	765,816	38,044	85,958	130,903	208,860	5.0	11.2	17.1	27.3
Forgery and counterfeiting	23,315	38	371	3,119	5,571	0.2	1.6	13.4	23.9
Fraud	62,135	462	1,944	6,246	12,502	0.7	3.1	10.1	20.1
Embezzlement	7,780	11	322	1,434	2,610	0.1	4.1	18.4	33.5
Stolen property; buying, receiving, possessing	67,827	1,381	6,210	11,978	18,669	2.0	9.2	17.7	27.5
Vandalism	131,854	8,224	18,715	28,670	42,642	6.2	14.2	21.7	32.3
Weapons; carrying, possessing, etc.	146,785	3,762	15,485	33,635	56,964	2.6	10.5	22.9	38.8
Prostitution and commercialized vice	12,455	10	67	1,374	3,615	0.1	0.5	11.0	29.0
Sex offenses (except forcible rape and prostitution)	19,821	1,468	2,978	4,378	6,069	7.4	15.0	22.1	30.6
Drug abuse violations	726,746	9,045	37,394	95,297	176,515	1.2	5.1	13.1	24.3
Gambling	1,103	3	22	146	237	0.3	2.0	13.2	21.5
Offenses against the family and children	38,065	613	1,570	2,880	5,980	1.6	4.1	7.6	15.7
Driving under the influence	622,344	68	3,925	34,479	116,765	*	0.6	5.5	18.8
Liquor laws	76,369	1,738	11,429	38,900	44,765	2.3	15.0	50.9	58.6
Drunkenness[2]	14,324	17	96	570	1,978	0.1	0.7	4.0	13.8
Disorderly conduct	193,449	11,803	26,719	38,528	57,292	6.1	13.8	19.9	29.6
Vagrancy	12,673	2	20	682	1,599	*	0.2	5.4	12.6
All other offenses (except traffic)	1,985,747	25,343	78,965	180,166	372,525	1.3	4.0	9.1	18.8
Suspicion[3]	62	0	0	1	15	0.0	0.0	1.6	24.2
Curfew and loitering law violations	5,648	1,807	5,648	5,648	5,648	32.0	100.0	100.0	100.0

* = Less than one-tenth of one percent.
1 Violent crimes in this table are offenses of murder and nonnegligent manslaughter, rape, robbery, and aggravated assault. Property crimes are offenses of burglary, larceny-theft, motor vehicle theft, and arson.   2 Drunkenness figures were submitted by Summary reporting agencies only. As of 2021 drunkenness is no longer a separate offense in the National Incident-Based Reporting System (NIBRS), but it is included with All Other Offenses (except traffic) category.   3 Figures for suspicion include only data submitted by Summary reporting agencies because suspicion is not collected as a crime via NIBRS.

Table 42. Arrests, Distribution by Sex, 2022

(Number, percent; 11,933 agencies; 2022 estimated population 270,485,978.)

Offense charged	Number of persons arrested			Percent male	Percent female	Percent distribution[1]		
	Total	Male	Female			Total	Male	Female
Total	5,901,283	4,312,398	1,588,885	73.1	26.9	100.0	100.0	100.0
Violent crime[2]	349,283	276,308	72,975	79.1	20.9	5.9	6.4	4.6
Murder and nonnegligent manslaughter	10,047	8,901	1,146	88.6	11.4	0.2	0.2	0.1
Rape	15,930	15,470	460	97.1	2.9	0.3	0.4	*
Robbery	47,807	40,378	7,429	84.5	15.5	0.8	0.9	0.5
Aggravated assault	275,499	211,559	63,940	76.8	23.2	4.7	4.9	4.0
Property crime[2]	637,682	422,706	214,976	66.3	33.7	10.8	9.8	13.5
Burglary	97,790	79,225	18,565	81.0	19.0	1.7	1.8	1.2
Larceny-theft	468,839	288,105	180,734	61.5	38.5	7.9	6.7	11.4
Motor vehicle theft	63,342	49,466	13,876	78.1	21.9	1.1	1.1	0.9
Arson	7,711	5,910	1,801	76.6	23.4	0.1	0.1	0.1
Other assaults	765,816	533,132	232,684	69.6	30.4	13.0	12.4	14.6
Forgery and counterfeiting	23,315	16,117	7,198	69.1	30.9	0.4	0.4	0.5
Fraud	62,135	40,834	21,301	65.7	34.3	1.1	0.9	1.3
Embezzlement	7,780	4,060	3,720	52.2	47.8	0.1	0.1	0.2
Stolen property; buying, receiving, possessing	67,827	53,807	14,020	79.3	20.7	1.1	1.2	0.9
Vandalism	131,854	101,371	30,483	76.9	23.1	2.2	2.4	1.9
Weapons; carrying, possessing, etc.	146,785	132,860	13,925	90.5	9.5	2.5	3.1	0.9
Prostitution and commercialized vice	12,455	5,349	7,106	42.9	57.1	0.2	0.1	0.4
Sex offenses (except forcible rape and prostitution)	19,821	18,742	1,079	94.6	5.4	0.3	0.4	0.1
Drug abuse violations	726,746	538,712	188,034	74.1	25.9	12.3	12.5	11.8
Gambling	1,103	811	292	73.5	26.5	*	*	*
Offenses against the family and children	38,065	24,644	13,421	64.7	35.3	0.6	0.6	0.8
Driving under the influence	622,344	463,775	158,569	74.5	25.5	10.5	10.8	10.0
Liquor laws	76,369	52,026	24,343	68.1	31.9	1.3	1.2	1.5
Drunkenness[3]	14,324	11,475	2,849	80.1	19.9	0.2	0.3	0.2
Disorderly conduct	193,449	137,093	56,356	70.9	29.1	3.3	3.2	3.5
Vagrancy	12,673	9,722	2,951	76.7	23.3	0.2	0.2	0.2
All other offenses (except traffic)	1,985,747	1,464,947	520,800	73.8	26.2	33.6	34.0	32.8
Suspicion[4]	62	52	10	83.9	16.1	*	*	*
Curfew and loitering law violations	5,648	3,855	1,793	68.3	31.7	0.1	0.1	0.1

* = Less than one-tenth of 1 percent.
1 Because of rounding, the percentages may not sum to 100.   2 Violent crimes in this table are offenses of murder and nonnegligent manslaughter, rape, robbery, and aggravated assault. Property crimes are offenses of burglary, larceny-theft, motor vehicle theft, and arson.   3 Drunkenness figures were submitted by Summary reporting agencies only. As of 2021 drunkenness is no longer a separate offense in the National Incident-Based Reporting System (NIBRS), but it is included with All Other Offenses (except traffic) category.   4 Figures for suspicion include only data submitted by Summary reporting agencies because suspicion is not collected as a crime via NIBRS.

Table 43. Arrests, Distribution by Race, by Offense Category, 2022

(Number, percent; 11,933 agencies; 2022 estimated population 270,485,978.)

Offense charged	Total arrests						Percent distribution[1]					
	Total	White	Black or African American	American Indian or Alaskan Native	Asian	Native Hawaiian or Other Pacific Islander	Total	White	Black or African American	American Indian or Alaskan Native	Asian	Native Hawaiian or Other Pacific Islander
Total	5,780,699	3,927,541	1,623,876	130,540	76,416	22,326	100.0	67.9	28.1	2.3	1.3	0.4
Violent crime[2]	344,113	196,479	134,573	6,385	5,347	1,329	100.0	57.1	39.1	1.9	1.6	0.4
Murder and nonnegligent manslaughter	9,941	4,035	5,626	133	113	34	100.0	40.6	56.6	1.3	1.1	0.3
Rape	15,502	10,769	4,107	274	299	53	100.0	69.5	26.5	1.8	1.9	0.3
Robbery	47,252	20,965	24,935	566	531	255	100.0	44.4	52.8	1.2	1.1	0.5
Aggravated assault	271,418	160,710	99,905	5,412	4,404	987	100.0	59.2	36.8	2.0	1.6	0.4
Property crime[2]	626,674	414,514	191,074	11,474	7,680	1,932	100.0	66.1	30.5	1.8	1.2	0.3
Burglary	96,412	65,438	28,082	1,537	1,058	297	100.0	67.9	29.1	1.6	1.1	0.3
Larceny-theft	460,139	302,743	141,468	8,677	5,847	1,404	100.0	65.8	30.7	1.9	1.3	0.3
Motor vehicle theft	62,525	40,840	19,731	1,113	627	214	100.0	65.3	31.6	1.8	1.0	0.3
Arson	7,598	5,493	1,793	147	148	17	100.0	72.3	23.6	1.9	1.9	0.2
Other assaults	751,509	476,052	244,435	16,056	11,490	3,476	100.0	63.3	32.5	2.1	1.5	0.5
Forgery and counterfeiting	22,842	15,063	7,098	216	391	74	100.0	65.9	31.1	0.9	1.7	0.3
Fraud	60,830	38,454	20,291	1,041	863	181	100.0	63.2	33.4	1.7	1.4	0.3
Embezzlement	7,609	4,476	2,929	80	110	14	100.0	58.8	38.5	1.1	1.4	0.2
Stolen property; buying, receiving, possessing	66,628	40,330	23,849	926	1,045	478	100.0	60.5	35.8	1.4	1.6	0.7
Vandalism	129,439	85,957	38,279	3,096	1,696	411	100.0	66.4	29.6	2.4	1.3	0.3
Weapons; carrying, possessing, etc.	144,681	68,344	73,085	1,313	1,571	368	100.0	47.2	50.5	0.9	1.1	0.3
Prostitution and commercialized vice	12,333	6,376	5,006	57	858	36	100.0	51.7	40.6	0.5	7.0	0.3
Sex offenses (except forcible rape and prostitution)	19,382	14,049	4,400	378	452	103	100.0	72.5	22.7	2.0	2.3	0.5
Drug abuse violations	714,442	499,860	194,750	11,275	6,972	1,585	100.0	70.0	27.3	1.6	1.0	0.2
Gambling	1,071	590	342	5	120	14	100.0	55.1	31.9	0.5	11.2	1.3
Offenses against the family and children	37,250	25,466	9,416	1,908	357	103	100.0	68.4	25.3	5.1	1.0	0.3
Driving under the influence	598,932	478,958	92,249	12,990	12,396	2,339	100.0	80.0	15.4	2.2	2.1	0.4
Liquor laws	73,191	56,721	11,226	3,582	1,191	471	100.0	77.5	15.3	4.9	1.6	0.6
Drunkenness[3]	14,324	12,474	1,459	120	229	42	100.0	87.1	10.2	0.8	1.6	0.3
Disorderly conduct	189,364	125,784	52,859	8,067	2,066	588	100.0	66.4	27.9	4.3	1.1	0.3
Vagrancy	12,524	7,378	2,992	1,921	150	83	100.0	58.9	23.9	15.3	1.2	0.7
All other offenses (except traffic)	1,948,006	1,356,584	511,902	49,475	21,393	8,652	100.0	69.6	26.3	2.5	1.1	0.4
Suspicion[4]	62	30	32	0	0	0	100.0	48.4	51.6	0.0	0.0	0.0
Curfew and loitering law violations	5,493	3,602	1,630	175	39	47	100.0	65.6	29.7	3.2	0.7	0.9

Table 43. Arrests, Distribution by Race, by Offense Category, 2022—Continued

(Number, percent; 11,933 agencies; 2022 estimated population 270,485,978.)

Offense charged	Arrests under 18						Percent distribution[1]					
	Total	White	Black or African American	American Indian or Alaskan Native	Asian	Native Hawaiian or Other Pacific Islander	Total	White	Black or African American	American Indian or Alaskan Native	Asian	Native Hawaiian or Other Pacific Islander
Total	375,608	226,285	135,105	8,793	3,851	1,574	100.0	60.2	36.0	2.3	1.0	0.4
Violent crime[2]	30,307	14,765	14,656	462	310	114	100.0	48.7	48.4	1.5	1.0	0.4
Murder and nonnegligent manslaughter	1,004	335	654	10	4	1	100.0	33.4	65.1	1.0	0.4	*
Rape	2,311	1,653	586	35	29	8	100.0	71.5	25.4	1.5	1.3	0.3
Robbery	8,698	2,869	5,634	63	84	48	100.0	33.0	64.8	0.7	1.0	0.6
Aggravated assault	18,294	9,908	7,782	354	193	57	100.0	54.2	42.5	1.9	1.1	0.3
Property crime[2]	54,781	30,043	22,724	1,009	770	235	100.0	54.8	41.5	1.8	1.4	0.4
Burglary	8,746	4,969	3,511	158	78	30	100.0	56.8	40.1	1.8	0.9	0.3
Larceny-theft	36,084	20,976	13,615	695	620	178	100.0	58.1	37.7	1.9	1.7	0.5
Motor vehicle theft	8,944	3,396	5,325	139	58	26	100.0	38.0	59.5	1.6	0.6	0.3
Arson	1,007	702	273	17	14	1	100.0	69.7	27.1	1.7	1.4	*
Other assaults	84,151	48,128	33,208	1,608	785	422	100.0	57.2	39.5	1.9	0.9	0.5
Forgery and counterfeiting	361	210	137	4	8	2	100.0	58.2	38.0	1.1	2.2	0.6
Fraud	1,896	969	853	40	30	4	100.0	51.1	45.0	2.1	1.6	0.2
Embezzlement	306	136	165	2	3	0	100.0	44.4	53.9	0.7	1.0	0.0
Stolen property; buying, receiving, possessing	6,103	1,527	4,412	77	51	36	100.0	25.0	72.3	1.3	0.8	0.6
Vandalism	18,215	12,721	4,892	412	153	37	100.0	69.8	26.9	2.3	0.8	0.2
Weapons; carrying, possessing, etc.	15,275	6,891	7,974	170	191	49	100.0	45.1	52.2	1.1	1.3	0.3
Prostitution and commercialized vice	66	30	36	0	0	0	100.0	45.5	54.5	0.0	0.0	0.0
Sex offenses (except forcible rape and prostitution)	2,877	2,114	670	49	35	9	100.0	73.5	23.3	1.7	1.2	0.3
Drug abuse violations	36,484	26,391	8,757	854	337	145	100.0	72.3	24.0	2.3	0.9	0.4
Gambling	22	15	7	0	0	0	100.0	68.2	31.8	0.0	0.0	0.0
Offenses against the family and children	1,547	1,059	300	177	6	5	100.0	68.5	19.4	11.4	0.4	0.3
Driving under the influence	3,724	3,276	242	151	40	15	100.0	88.0	6.5	4.1	1.1	0.4
Liquor laws	10,903	9,217	742	770	121	53	100.0	84.5	6.8	7.1	1.1	0.5
Drunkenness[3]	96	84	6	4	2	0	100.0	87.5	6.3	4.2	2.1	0.0
Disorderly conduct	26,008	14,424	10,474	866	192	52	100.0	55.5	40.3	3.3	0.7	0.2
Vagrancy	20	12	8	0	0	0	100.0	60.0	40.0	0.0	0.0	0.0
All other offenses (except traffic)	76,973	50,671	23,212	1,963	778	349	100.0	65.8	30.2	2.6	1.0	0.5
Suspicion[4]	0	0	0	0	0	0	NA	NA	NA	NA	NA	NA
Curfew and loitering law violations	5,493	3,602	1,630	175	39	47	100.0	65.6	29.7	3.2	0.7	0.9

Table 43. Arrests, Distribution by Race, by Offense Category, 2022—Continued

(Number, percent; 11,933 agencies; 2022 estimated population 270,485,978.)

Offense charged	Arrests 18 and over						Percent distribution[1]					
	Total	White	Black or African American	American Indian or Alaskan Native	Asian	Native Hawaiian or Other Pacific Islander	Total	White	Black or African American	American Indian or Alaskan Native	Asian	Native Hawaiian or Other Pacific Islander
Total	5,405,091	3,701,256	1,488,771	121,747	72,565	20,752	100.0	68.5	27.5	2.3	1.3	0.4
Violent crime[2]	313,806	181,714	119,917	5,923	5,037	1,215	100.0	57.9	38.2	1.9	1.6	0.4
Murder and nonnegligent manslaughter	8,937	3,700	4,972	123	109	33	100.0	41.4	55.6	1.4	1.2	0.4
Rape	13,191	9,116	3,521	239	270	45	100.0	69.1	26.7	1.8	2.0	0.3
Robbery	38,554	18,096	19,301	503	447	207	100.0	46.9	50.1	1.3	1.2	0.5
Aggravated assault	253,124	150,802	92,123	5,058	4,211	930	100.0	59.6	36.4	2.0	1.7	0.4
Property crime[2]	571,893	384,471	168,350	10,465	6,910	1,697	100.0	67.2	29.4	1.8	1.2	0.3
Burglary	87,666	60,469	24,571	1,379	980	267	100.0	69.0	28.0	1.6	1.1	0.3
Larceny-theft	424,055	281,767	127,853	7,982	5,227	1,226	100.0	66.4	30.2	1.9	1.2	0.3
Motor vehicle theft	53,581	37,444	14,406	974	569	188	100.0	69.9	26.9	1.8	1.1	0.4
Arson	6,591	4,791	1,520	130	134	16	100.0	72.7	23.1	2.0	2.0	0.2
Other assaults	667,358	427,924	211,227	14,448	10,705	3,054	100.0	64.1	31.7	2.2	1.6	0.5
Forgery and counterfeiting	22,481	14,853	6,961	212	383	72	100.0	66.1	31.0	0.9	1.7	0.3
Fraud	58,934	37,485	19,438	1,001	833	177	100.0	63.6	33.0	1.7	1.4	0.3
Embezzlement	7,303	4,340	2,764	78	107	14	100.0	59.4	37.8	1.1	1.5	0.2
Stolen property; buying, receiving, possessing	60,525	38,803	19,437	849	994	442	100.0	64.1	32.1	1.4	1.6	0.7
Vandalism	111,224	73,236	33,387	2,684	1,543	374	100.0	65.8	30.0	2.4	1.4	0.3
Weapons; carrying, possessing, etc.	129,406	61,453	65,111	1,143	1,380	319	100.0	47.5	50.3	0.9	1.1	0.2
Prostitution and commercialized vice	12,267	6,346	4,970	57	858	36	100.0	51.7	40.5	0.5	7.0	0.3
Sex offenses (except forcible rape and prostitution)	16,505	11,935	3,730	329	417	94	100.0	72.3	22.6	2.0	2.5	0.6
Drug abuse violations	677,958	473,469	185,993	10,421	6,635	1,440	100.0	69.8	27.4	1.5	1.0	0.2
Gambling	1,049	575	335	5	120	14	100.0	54.8	31.9	0.5	11.4	1.3
Offenses against the family and children	35,703	24,407	9,116	1,731	351	98	100.0	68.4	25.5	4.8	1.0	0.3
Driving under the influence	595,208	475,682	92,007	12,839	12,356	2,324	100.0	79.9	15.5	2.2	2.1	0.4
Liquor laws	62,288	47,504	10,484	2,812	1,070	418	100.0	76.3	16.8	4.5	1.7	0.7
Drunkenness[3]	14,228	12,390	1,453	116	227	42	100.0	87.1	10.2	0.8	1.6	0.3
Disorderly conduct	163,356	111,360	42,385	7,201	1,874	536	100.0	68.2	25.9	4.4	1.1	0.3
Vagrancy	12,504	7,366	2,984	1,921	150	83	100.0	58.9	23.9	15.4	1.2	0.7
All other offenses (except traffic)	1,871,033	1,305,913	488,690	47,512	20,615	8,303	100.0	69.8	26.1	2.5	1.1	0.4
Suspicion[4]	62	30	32	0	0	0	100.0	48.4	51.6	0.0	0.0	0.0
Curfew and loitering law violations	NA	NA	NA	NA	NA	NA	NA	NA	NA	NA	NA	NA

NA = Not available.
1 Because of rounding, the percentages may not sum to 100. 2 Violent crimes in this table are offenses of murder and nonnegligent manslaughter, rape, robbery, and aggravated assault. Property crimes are offenses of burglary, larceny-theft, motor vehicle theft, and arson. 3 Drunkenness figures were submitted by Summary reporting agencies only. As of 2021 drunkenness is no longer a separate offense in the National Incident-Based Reporting System (NIBRS), but it is included with All Other Offenses (except traffic) category. 4 Figures for suspicion include only data submitted by Summary reporting agencies because suspicion is not collected as a crime via NIBRS.

Table 43A. Arrests, Distribution by Ethnicity, 2022

(Number, percent; 11,933 agencies; 2022 estimated population 270,485,978.)

Offense charged	Total arrests			Percent distribution[1]			Arrests under 18		
	Total[2]	Hispanic or Latino	Not Hispanic or Latino	Total[2]	Hispanic or Latino	Not Hispanic or Latino	Total[2]	Hispanic or Latino	Not Hispanic or Latino
Total	4,936,217	1,022,717	3,913,500	100.0	20.7	79.3	313,519	73,276	240,243
Violent crime[3]	300,106	76,585	223,521	100.0	25.5	74.5	25,840	6,636	19,204
Murder and nonnegligent manslaughter	8,377	1,786	6,591	100.0	21.3	78.7	816	219	597
Rape	13,067	3,731	9,336	100.0	28.6	71.4	1,880	427	1,453
Robbery	41,264	10,274	30,990	100.0	24.9	75.1	7,457	1,876	5,581
Aggravated assault	237,398	60,794	176,604	100.0	25.6	74.4	15,687	4,114	11,573
Property crime[3]	532,540	94,252	438,288	100.0	17.7	82.3	45,725	9,079	36,646
Burglary	83,213	16,725	66,488	100.0	20.1	79.9	7,373	1,466	5,907
Larceny-theft	389,177	61,569	327,608	100.0	15.8	84.2	29,978	5,932	24,046
Motor vehicle theft	53,705	14,454	39,251	100.0	26.9	73.1	7,548	1,490	6,058
Arson	6,445	1,504	4,941	100.0	23.3	76.7	826	191	635
Other assaults	642,657	134,476	508,181	100.0	20.9	79.1	71,616	15,259	56,357
Forgery and counterfeiting	20,320	4,265	16,055	100.0	21.0	79.0	313	73	240
Fraud	52,559	8,222	44,337	100.0	15.6	84.4	1,594	293	1,301
Embezzlement	6,418	957	5,461	100.0	14.9	85.1	274	35	239
Stolen property; buying, receiving, possessing	56,837	12,124	44,713	100.0	21.3	78.7	4,939	774	4,165
Vandalism	111,575	22,989	88,586	100.0	20.6	79.4	15,238	3,336	11,902
Weapons; carrying, possessing, etc.	121,657	29,416	92,241	100.0	24.2	75.8	13,146	4,056	9,090
Prostitution and commercialized vice	11,638	3,000	8,638	100.0	25.8	74.2	57	18	39
Sex offenses (except forcible rape and prostitution)	16,927	5,153	11,774	100.0	30.4	69.6	2,410	586	1,824
Drug abuse violations	630,635	129,207	501,428	100.0	20.5	79.5	31,764	10,454	21,310
Gambling	900	334	566	100.0	37.1	62.9	21	7	14
Offenses against the family and children	31,657	4,805	26,852	100.0	15.2	84.8	1,409	282	1,127
Driving under the influence	503,985	151,443	352,542	100.0	30.0	70.0	3,080	1,073	2,007
Liquor laws	57,728	10,436	47,292	100.0	18.1	81.9	8,646	1,656	6,990
Drunkenness[4]	14,257	6,323	7,934	100.0	44.4	55.6	96	46	50
Disorderly conduct	155,365	28,269	127,096	100.0	18.2	81.8	20,814	4,060	16,754
Vagrancy	10,082	1,477	8,605	100.0	14.6	85.4	18	5	13
All other offenses (except traffic)	1,654,021	298,074	1,355,947	100.0	18.0	82.0	62,228	14,645	47,583
Suspicion[5]	62	7	55	100.0	11.3	88.7	0	0	0
Curfew and loitering law violations	4,291	903	3,388	100.0	21.0	79.0	4,291	903	3,388

Table 43A. Arrests, Distribution by Ethnicity, 2022—Continued

(Number, percent; 11,933 agencies; 2022 estimated population 270,485,978.)

Offense charged	Percent distribution[1]			Arrests 18 and over			Percent distribution[1]		
	Total[2]	Hispanic or Latino	Not Hispanic or Latino	Total[2]	Hispanic or Latino	Not Hispanic or Latino	Total[2]	Hispanic or Latino	Not Hispanic or Latino
Total	100.0	23.4	76.6	4,622,698	949,441	3,673,257	100.0	20.5	79.5
Violent crime[3]	100.0	25.7	74.3	274,266	69,949	204,317	100.0	25.5	74.5
Murder and nonnegligent manslaughter	100.0	26.8	73.2	7,561	1,567	5,994	100.0	20.7	79.3
Rape	100.0	22.7	77.3	11,187	3,304	7,883	100.0	29.5	70.5
Robbery	100.0	25.2	74.8	33,807	8,398	25,409	100.0	24.8	75.2
Aggravated assault	100.0	26.2	73.8	221,711	56,680	165,031	100.0	25.6	74.4
Property crime[3]	100.0	19.9	80.1	486,815	85,173	401,642	100.0	17.5	82.5
Burglary	100.0	19.9	80.1	75,840	15,259	60,581	100.0	20.1	79.9
Larceny-theft	100.0	19.8	80.2	359,199	55,637	303,562	100.0	15.5	84.5
Motor vehicle theft	100.0	19.7	80.3	46,157	12,964	33,193	100.0	28.1	71.9
Arson	100.0	23.1	76.9	5,619	1,313	4,306	100.0	23.4	76.6
Other assaults	100.0	21.3	78.7	571,041	119,217	451,824	100.0	20.9	79.1
Forgery and counterfeiting	100.0	23.3	76.7	20,007	4,192	15,815	100.0	21.0	79.0
Fraud	100.0	18.4	81.6	50,965	7,929	43,036	100.0	15.6	84.4
Embezzlement	100.0	12.8	87.2	6,144	922	5,222	100.0	15.0	85.0
Stolen property; buying, receiving, possessing	100.0	15.7	84.3	51,898	11,350	40,548	100.0	21.9	78.1
Vandalism	100.0	21.9	78.1	96,337	19,653	76,684	100.0	20.4	79.6
Weapons; carrying, possessing, etc.	100.0	30.9	69.1	108,511	25,360	83,151	100.0	23.4	76.6
Prostitution and commercialized vice	100.0	31.6	68.4	11,581	2,982	8,599	100.0	25.7	74.3
Sex offenses (except forcible rape and prostitution)	100.0	24.3	75.7	14,517	4,567	9,950	100.0	31.5	68.5
Drug abuse violations	100.0	32.9	67.1	598,871	118,753	480,118	100.0	19.8	80.2
Gambling	100.0	33.3	66.7	879	327	552	100.0	37.2	62.8
Offenses against the family and children	100.0	20.0	80.0	30,248	4,523	25,725	100.0	15.0	85.0
Driving under the influence	100.0	34.8	65.2	500,905	150,370	350,535	100.0	30.0	70.0
Liquor laws	100.0	19.2	80.8	49,082	8,780	40,302	100.0	17.9	82.1
Drunkenness[4]	100.0	47.9	52.1	14,161	6,277	7,884	100.0	44.3	55.7
Disorderly conduct	100.0	19.5	80.5	134,551	24,209	110,342	100.0	18.0	82.0
Vagrancy	100.0	27.8	72.2	10,064	1,472	8,592	100.0	14.6	85.4
All other offenses (except traffic)	100.0	23.5	76.5	1,591,793	283,429	1,308,364	100.0	17.8	82.2
Suspicion[5]	NA	NA	NA	62	7	55	100.0	11.3	88.7
Curfew and loitering law violations	100.0	21.0	79.0	NA	NA	NA	NA	NA	NA

NA = Not available.

1 Because of rounding, the percentages may not sum to 100.   2 The ethnicity totals are representative of those agencies that provided ethnicity breakdowns. Not all agencies provide ethnicity data; therefore, the race and ethnicity totals will not equal.
3 Violent crimes are offenses of murder and nonnegligent manslaughter, rape, robbery, and aggravated assault. Property crimes are offenses of burglary, larceny-theft, motor vehicle theft, and arson.   4 Drunkenness figures were submitted by Summary reporting agencies only. As of 2021 drunkenness is no longer a separate offense in the National Incident-Based Reporting System (NIBRS), but it is included with All Other Offenses (except traffic) category.   5 Figures for suspicion include only data submitted by Summary reporting agencies because suspicion is not collected as a crime via NIBRS.

Table 44. Arrest Trends, Cities, 2021–2022

(Number, percent change; 6,783 agencies; 2022 estimated population 132,414,831; 2021 estimated population 132,070,624].)

Offense charged	Number of persons arrested								
	Total, all ages			Under 18 years of age			18 years of age and over		
	2021	2022	Percent change	2021	2022	Percent change	2021	2022	Percent change
Total[1]	3,207,541	3,303,364	+3.0	211,857	251,323	+18.6	2,995,684	3,052,041	+1.9
Violent crime[2]	176,029	178,591	+1.5	15,697	17,604	+12.1	160,332	160,987	+0.4
Murder and nonnegligent manslaughter	5,823	5,569	-4.4	572	646	+12.9	5,251	4,923	-6.2
Rape	8,765	8,595	-1.9	1,408	1,341	-4.8	7,357	7,254	-1.4
Robbery	25,001	25,681	+2.7	4,573	4,947	+8.2	20,428	20,734	+1.5
Aggravated assault	136,440	138,746	+1.7	9,144	10,670	+16.7	127,296	128,076	+0.6
Property crime[2]	373,430	414,570	+11.0	30,459	38,620	+26.8	342,971	375,950	+9.6
Burglary	50,359	53,113	+5.5	4,733	5,391	+13.9	45,626	47,722	+4.6
Larceny-theft	285,230	322,094	+12.9	19,765	26,593	+34.5	265,465	295,501	+11.3
Motor vehicle theft	34,021	35,381	+4.0	5,378	6,004	+11.6	28,643	29,377	+2.6
Arson	3,820	3,982	+4.2	583	632	+8.4	3,237	3,350	+3.5
Other assaults	442078	459858	+4.0	42854	54066	+26.2	399224	405792	+1.6
Forgery and counterfeiting	12,160	13,904	+14.3	225	226	+0.4	11,935	13,678	+14.6
Fraud	35,425	38,576	+8.9	1,265	1,311	+3.6	34,160	37,265	+9.1
Embezzlement	4,054	4,982	+22.9	224	240	+7.1	3,830	4,742	+23.8
Stolen property; buying, receiving, possessing	33,314	35,655	+7.0	3,647	4,009	+9.9	29,667	31,646	+6.7
Vandalism	76,522	74,935	-2.1	11,281	11,927	+5.7	65,241	63,008	-3.4
Weapons; carrying, possessing, etc.	75,199	76,154	+1.3	6,421	8,633	+34.4	68,778	67,521	-1.8
Prostitution and commercialized vice	6,749	6,619	-1.9	61	46	-24.6	6,688	6,573	-1.7
Sex offenses (except forcible rape and prostitution)	8,285	8,295	+0.1	1,431	1,489	+4.1	6,854	6,806	-0.7
Drug abuse violations	391,331	374,497	-4.3	20,177	25,860	+28.2	371,154	348,637	-6.1
Gambling	560	539	-3.8	11	12	+9.1	549	527	-4.0
Offenses against the family and children	22,085	21,846	-1.1	1,222	1,265	+3.5	20,863	20,581	-1.4
Driving under the influence	293,443	289,917	-1.2	2,060	1,985	-3.6	291,383	287,932	-1.2
Liquor laws	53,977	52,324	-3.1	6,670	7,083	+6.2	47,307	45,241	-4.4
Drunkenness[3]	51	61	+19.6	0	0	NA	51	61	+19.6
Disorderly conduct	125,682	127,492	+1.4	15,738	19,519	+24.0	109,944	107,973	-1.8
Vagrancy	5,978	7,881	+31.8	0	0	NA	5,978	7,881	+31.8
All other offenses (except traffic)	1,066,291	1,112,073	+4.3	47,516	52,833	+11.2	1,018,775	1,059,240	+4.0
Suspicion[4]	0	0	NA	0	0	NA	NA	NA	NA
Curfew and loitering law violations	4,898	4,595	-6.2	4,898	4,595	-6.2	NA	NA	NA

NA = Not available.
1 Does not include suspicion.   2 Violent crimes in this table are offenses of murder and nonnegligent manslaughter, rape, robbery, and aggravated assault. Property crimes are offenses of burglary, larceny-theft, motor vehicle theft, and arson.
3 Drunkenness figures were submitted by Summary reporting agencies only. As of 2021 drunkenness is no longer a separate offense in the National Incident-Based Reporting System (NIBRS), but it is included with All Other Offenses (except traffic) category.   4 Figures for suspicion include only data submitted by Summary reporting agencies because suspicion is not collected as a crime via NIBRS.

Table 45. Arrest Trends, Cities, by Age and Sex, 2021–2022

(Number, percent change; 6,783 agencies; 2022 estimated population 132,414,831; 2021 estimated population 132,070,624.)

Offense charged	Male						Female					
	Total			Under 18			Total			Under 18		
	2021	2022	Percent change	2021	2022	Percent change	2021	2022	Percent change	2021	2022	Percent change
Total[1]	2,323,977	2,374,246	+2.2	145,508	170,194	+17.0	883,564	929,118	+5.2	66,349	81,129	+22.3
Violent crime[2]	140,416	141,650	+0.9	12,709	14,131	+11.2	35,613	36,941	3.7	2,988	3,473	+16.2
Murder and nonnegligent manslaughter	5,146	4,926	-4.3	525	600	+14.3	677	643	-5.0	47	46	-2.1
Rape	8,567	8,351	-2.5	1,353	1,274	-5.8	198	244	+23.2	55	67	+21.8
Robbery	21,423	21,770	+1.6	4,119	4,368	+6.0	3,578	3,911	+9.3	454	579	+27.5
Aggravated assault	105,280	106,603	+1.3	6,712	7,889	+17.5	31,160	32,143	+3.2	2,432	2,781	+14.4
Property crime[2]	243,142	267,593	+10.1	22,035	26,980	+22.4	130,288	146,977	+12.8	8,424	11,640	+38.2
Burglary	41,218	43,388	+5.3	4,109	4,694	+14.2	9,141	9,725	+6.4	624	697	+11.7
Larceny-theft	172,427	193,612	+12.3	12,988	16,848	+29.7	112,803	128,482	+13.9	6,777	9,745	+43.8
Motor vehicle theft	26,547	27,568	+3.8	4,475	4,928	+10.1	7,474	7,813	+4.5	903	1,076	+19.2
Arson	2,950	3,025	+2.5	463	510	+10.2	870	957	+10.0	120	122	+1.7
Other assaults	311,354	317,861	+2.1	25,331	31,373	+23.9	130,724	141,997	+8.6	17,523	22,693	+29.5
Forgery and counterfeiting	8,196	9,405	+14.8	163	182	+11.7	3,964	4,499	+13.5	62	44	-29.0
Fraud	22,820	24,956	+9.4	851	852	+0.1	12,605	13,620	+8.1	414	459	+10.9
Embezzlement	2,062	2,466	+19.6	120	127	+5.8	1,992	2,516	+26.3	104	113	+8.7
Stolen property; buying, receiving, possessing	26,462	28,368	+7.2	3,149	3,437	+9.1	6,852	7,287	+6.3	498	572	+14.9
Vandalism	57,951	56,947	-1.7	8,902	9,536	+7.1	18,571	17,988	-3.1	2,379	2,391	+0.5
Weapons; carrying, possessing, etc.	67,872	68,890	+1.5	5,861	7,952	+35.7	7,327	7,264	-0.9	560	681	+21.6
Prostitution and commercialized vice	3,108	2,809	-9.6	13	18	+38.5	3,641	3,810	+4.6	48	28	-41.7
Sex offenses (except forcible rape and prostitution)	7,865	7,872	+0.1	1,302	1,340	+2.9	420	423	+0.7	129	149	+15.5
Drug abuse violations	286,940	274,598	-4.3	14,438	17,980	+24.5	104,391	99,899	-4.3	5,739	7,880	+37.3
Gambling	429	398	-7.2	11	11	+0.0	131	141	+7.6	0	1	NA
Offenses against the family and children	13,784	13,351	-3.1	686	645	-6.0	8,301	8,495	+2.3	536	620	+15.7
Driving under the influence	215,191	212,661	-1.2	1,529	1,496	-2.2	78,252	77,256	-1.3	531	489	-7.9
Liquor laws	37,507	35,752	-4.7	3,837	3,999	+4.2	16,470	16,572	+0.6	2,833	3,084	+8.9
Drunkenness[3]	36	54	+50.0	0	0	NA	15	7	-53.3	0	0	NA
Disorderly conduct	88,636	89,144	+0.6	9,772	11,853	+21.3	37,046	38,348	+3.5	5,966	7,666	+28.5
Vagrancy	4,600	6,009	+30.6	0	0	NA	1,378	1,872	+35.8	0	0	NA
All other offenses (except traffic)	782,407	810,339	+3.6	31,600	35,159	+11.3	283,884	301,734	+6.3	15,916	17,674	+11.0
Suspicion[4]	0	0	NA	0	0	NA	0	0	NA	0	0	NA
Curfew and loitering law violations	3,199	3,123	-2.4	3,199	3,123	-2.4	1,699	1,472	-13.4	1,699	1,472	-13.4

NA = Not available.
1 Does not include suspicion.   2 Violent crimes in this table are offenses of murder and nonnegligent manslaughter, rape, robbery, and aggravated assault. Property crimes are offenses of burglary, larceny-theft, motor vehicle theft, and arson.
3 Drunkenness figures were submitted by Summary reporting agencies only. As of 2021 drunkenness is no longer a separate offense in the National Incident-Based Reporting System (NIBRS), but it is included with All Other Offenses (except traffic) category.   4 Figures for suspicion include only data submitted by Summary reporting agencies because suspicion is not collected as a crime via NIBRS.

Table 46. Arrests, Cities, Distribution by Age, 2022

(Number, percent; 8,754 agencies; 2022 estimated population 180,514,188.)

Offense charged	Total, all ages	Under 15 years	Under 18 years	Age 18 years and over	Under 10 years	10–12 years	13–14 years	15 years	16 years	17 years	18 years	19 years
Total	4,229,355	102,040	296,369	3,932,986	915	22,900	78,225	60,229	65,622	68,478	90,527	99,677
Total, percent distribution[1]	100.0	2.4	7.0	93.0	*	0.5	1.8	1.4	1.6	1.6	2.1	2.4
Violent crime[2]	269,242	7,476	24,319	244,923	56	1,588	5,832	5,030	5,765	6,048	7,215	7,428
Violent crime, percent distribution[1]	100.0	2.8	9.0	91.0	*	0.6	2.2	1.9	2.1	2.2	2.7	2.8
Murder and nonnegligent manslaughter	7,584	110	823	6,761	0	4	106	157	242	314	420	404
Rape	11,044	634	1,594	9,450	7	184	443	312	322	326	380	363
Robbery	40,904	1,773	7,572	33,332	1	211	1,561	1,781	1,971	2,047	2,075	1,804
Aggravated assault	209,710	4,959	14,330	195,380	48	1,189	3,722	2,780	3,230	3,361	4,340	4,857
Property crime[2]	515,295	14,493	45,722	469,573	101	2,779	11,613	9,627	10,786	10,816	13,083	12,354
Property crime, percent distribution[1]	100.0	2.8	8.9	91.1	*	0.5	2.3	1.9	2.1	2.1	2.5	2.4
Burglary	74,149	2,621	6,719	67,430	33	547	2,041	1,448	1,326	1,324	1,653	1,551
Larceny-theft	385,938	9,221	30,806	355,132	51	1,859	7,311	6,199	7,502	7,884	9,768	9,495
Motor vehicle theft	49,159	2,166	7,409	41,750	3	227	1,936	1,849	1,843	1,551	1,572	1,234
Arson	6,049	485	788	5,261	14	146	325	131	115	57	90	74
Other assaults	572,016	28,011	62,673	509,343	250	7,685	20,076	12,480	11,984	10,198	10,492	11,435
Forgery and counterfeiting	16,854	27	263	16,591	0	3	24	22	68	146	479	751
Fraud	46,609	365	1,540	45,069	1	58	306	259	382	534	952	1,180
Embezzlement	6,180	10	268	5,912	0	0	10	14	83	161	329	306
Stolen property; buying, receiving, possessing	50,140	1,143	4,871	45,269	2	111	1,030	1,140	1,255	1,333	1,572	1,448
Vandalism	101,356	6,598	14,510	86,846	139	1,875	4,584	2,706	2,644	2,562	2,648	2,492
Weapons; carrying, possessing, etc.	111,168	2,832	12,467	98,701	29	601	2,202	2,389	3,166	4,080	4,874	5,040
Prostitution and commercialized vice	11,089	9	60	11,029	0	2	7	11	10	30	319	447
Sex offenses (except forcible rape and prostitution)	13,817	991	2,003	11,814	13	238	740	361	332	319	332	309
Drug abuse violations	496,019	7,111	28,637	467,382	12	998	6,101	5,845	7,112	8,569	12,943	13,892
Gambling	756	3	15	741	0	0	3	4	3	5	19	30
Offenses against the family and children	23,991	536	1,322	22,669	11	142	383	275	280	231	266	340
Driving under the influence	404,342	50	2,555	401,787	7	3	40	138	643	1,724	4,662	6,749
Liquor laws	58,516	1,292	7,800	50,716	0	144	1,148	1,322	2,034	3,152	6,976	7,727
Drunkenness[3]	12,244	13	76	12,168	0	0	13	18	21	24	104	136
Disorderly conduct	156,994	9,607	21,594	135,400	70	2,480	7,057	4,457	4,118	3,412	3,314	3,191
Vagrancy	10,000	2	19	9,981	0	2	0	5	6	6	204	159
All other offenses (except traffic)	1,347,617	19,852	60,607	1,287,010	221	3,959	15,672	12,857	13,631	14,267	19,743	24,263
Suspicion[4]	62	0	0	62	0	0	0	0	0	0	1	0
Curfew and loitering law violations	5,048	1,619	5,048	NA	3	232	1,384	1,269	1,299	861	NA	NA

Table 46. Arrests, Cities, Distribution by Age, 2022—Continued

(Number, percent; 8,754 agencies; 2022 estimated population 180,514,188.)

Offense charged	20 years	21 years	22 years	23 years	24 years	25–29 years	30–34 years	35–39 years	40–44 years	45–49 years	50–54 years	55–59 years	60–64 years	65 years and over
Total	101,987	109,261	112,632	113,993	116,303	641,510	685,664	566,987	442,887	281,268	224,166	167,143	105,067	73,914
Total, percent distribution[1]	2.4	2.6	2.7	2.7	2.7	15.2	16.2	13.4	10.5	6.7	5.3	4.0	2.5	1.7
Violent crime[2]	7,219	7,842	7,817	7,748	8,093	43,088	43,139	33,476	25,006	15,559	11,939	9,138	5,820	4,396
Violent crime, percent distribution[1]	2.7	2.9	2.9	2.9	3.0	16.0	16.0	12.4	9.3	5.8	4.4	3.4	2.2	1.6
Murder and nonnegligent manslaughter	370	334	311	303	282	1,239	1,021	658	529	302	232	146	116	94
Rape	372	333	332	288	264	1,334	1,435	1,299	969	636	555	369	269	252
Robbery	1,460	1,413	1,255	1,165	1,207	6,175	5,915	4,132	2,776	1,520	1,064	804	417	150
Aggravated assault	5,017	5,762	5,919	5,992	6,340	34,340	34,768	27,387	20,732	13,101	10,088	7,819	5,018	3,900
Property crime[2]	11,280	11,329	11,621	12,027	12,436	73,833	84,679	71,113	54,771	33,790	27,936	20,435	11,679	7,207
Property crime, percent distribution[1]	2.2	2.2	2.3	2.3	2.4	14.3	16.4	13.8	10.6	6.6	5.4	4.0	2.3	1.4
Burglary	1,493	1,596	1,563	1,722	1,902	11,665	13,120	10,926	8,006	4,450	3,508	2,420	1,190	665
Larceny-theft	8,536	8,575	8,832	9,017	9,217	53,766	62,113	52,845	41,356	26,387	22,403	16,729	9,850	6,243
Motor vehicle theft	1,174	1,091	1,146	1,190	1,212	7,637	8,463	6,536	4,654	2,510	1,712	997	449	173
Arson	77	67	80	98	105	765	983	806	755	443	313	289	190	126
Other assaults	12,494	14,164	14,995	15,469	15,956	86,456	90,119	73,101	56,325	36,029	27,917	20,573	13,246	10,572
Forgery and counterfeiting	717	431	444	406	459	2,559	2,859	2,470	1,870	1,186	894	586	297	183
Fraud	1,182	1,144	1,221	1,179	1,220	7,268	8,158	7,019	5,483	3,210	2,484	1,697	1,021	651
Embezzlement	294	294	256	221	203	875	832	727	575	371	289	181	108	51
Stolen property; buying, receiving, possessing	1,337	1,173	1,183	1,312	1,288	7,854	8,854	7,040	5,129	2,945	2,000	1,266	609	259
Vandalism	2,503	2,722	2,697	2,786	2,733	15,215	16,044	12,849	9,173	5,335	3,888	2,843	1,701	1,217
Weapons; carrying, possessing, etc.	4,637	4,872	4,754	4,382	4,098	19,127	16,157	11,134	7,957	4,475	3,114	2,039	1,151	890
Prostitution and commercialized vice	490	595	566	480	482	2,101	1,613	1,106	853	579	494	418	275	211
Sex offenses (except forcible rape and prostitution)	286	363	325	270	268	1,518	1,710	1,522	1,280	919	776	712	551	673
Drug abuse violations	13,568	13,681	13,927	14,037	13,944	77,305	83,672	69,162	54,833	32,290	24,430	16,455	9,180	4,063
Gambling	31	18	19	17	21	97	103	68	92	54	48	45	36	43
Offenses against the family and children	386	502	536	574	695	3,985	4,658	3,939	2,770	1,586	1,005	730	391	306
Driving under the influence	8,331	13,151	13,906	14,342	14,113	70,751	65,060	51,722	40,996	29,075	24,047	19,385	13,603	11,894
Liquor laws	6,379	1,589	1,213	934	857	4,283	4,204	3,662	3,243	2,460	2,308	2,140	1,642	1,099
Drunkenness[3]	169	280	275	318	343	1,918	2,041	1,731	1,358	983	932	752	503	325
Disorderly conduct	3,350	4,060	3,970	3,945	3,850	20,368	22,178	18,632	14,971	10,072	8,354	6,940	4,615	3,590
Vagrancy	182	169	183	185	181	1,161	1,574	1,475	1,234	947	841	646	532	308
All other offenses (except traffic)	27,152	30,877	32,721	33,359	35,059	201,738	228,001	195,031	154,965	99,391	80,468	60,160	38,107	25,975
Suspicion[4]	0	5	3	2	4	10	9	8	3	12	2	2	0	1
Curfew and loitering law violations	NA	NA	NA	NA	NA	NA	NA	NA	NA	NA	NA	NA	NA	NA

NA = Not available.
* = Less than one-tenth of one percent.
1 Because of rounding, the percentages may not add to 100.0.   2 Violent crimes are offenses of murder and nonnegligent manslaughter, rape, robbery, and aggravated assault. Property crimes are offenses of burglary, larceny-theft, motor vehicle theft, and arson.   3 Drunkenness figures were submitted by Summary reporting agencies only. As of 2021 drunkenness is no longer a separate offense in National Incident Based Reporting System (NIBRS), but it is included with All Other Offenses (except traffic) category.   4 Figures for suspicion include only data submitted by Summary reporting agencies because suspicion is not collected as a crime via NIBRS.

Table 47. Arrests, Cities, Persons Under 15, 18, 21, and 25 Years of Age, 2022

(Number; percent; 8,754 agencies; 2022 estimated population 180,514,188.)

Offense charged	Total, all ages	Number of persons arrested				Percent of total of all ages			
		Under 15	Under 18	Under 21	Under 25	Under 15	Under 18	Under 21	Under 25
Total	4,229,355	102,040	296,369	588,560	1,040,749	2.4	7.0	13.9	24.6
Violent crime[1]	269,242	7,476	24,319	46,181	77,681	2.8	9.0	17.2	28.9
Murder and nonnegligent manslaughter	7,584	110	823	2,017	3,247	1.5	10.9	26.6	42.8
Rape	11,044	634	1,594	2,709	3,926	5.7	14.4	24.5	35.5
Robbery	40,904	1,773	7,572	12,911	17,951	4.3	18.5	31.6	43.9
Aggravated assault	209,710	4,959	14,330	28,544	52,557	2.4	6.8	13.6	25.1
Property crime[1]	515,295	14,493	45,722	82,439	129,852	2.8	8.9	16.0	25.2
Burglary	74,149	2,621	6,719	11,416	18,199	3.5	9.1	15.4	24.5
Larceny-theft	385,938	9,221	30,806	58,605	94,246	2.4	8.0	15.2	24.4
Motor vehicle theft	49,159	2,166	7,409	11,389	16,028	4.4	15.1	23.2	32.6
Arson	6,049	485	788	1,029	1,379	8.0	13.0	17.0	22.8
Other assaults	572,016	28,011	62,673	97,094	157,678	4.9	11.0	17.0	27.6
Forgery and counterfeiting	16,854	27	263	2,210	3,950	0.2	1.6	13.1	23.4
Fraud	46,609	365	1,540	4,854	9,618	0.8	3.3	10.4	20.6
Embezzlement	6,180	10	268	1,197	2,171	0.2	4.3	19.4	35.1
Stolen property; buying, receiving, possessing	50,140	1,143	4,871	9,228	14,184	2.3	9.7	18.4	28.3
Vandalism	101,356	6,598	14,510	22,153	33,091	6.5	14.3	21.9	32.6
Weapons; carrying, possessing, etc.	111,168	2,832	12,467	27,018	45,124	2.5	11.2	24.3	40.6
Prostitution and commercialized vice	11,089	9	60	1,316	3,439	0.1	0.5	11.9	31.0
Sex offenses (except forcible rape and prostitution)	13,817	991	2,003	2,930	4,156	7.2	14.5	21.2	30.1
Drug abuse violations	496,019	7,111	28,637	69,040	124,629	1.4	5.8	13.9	25.1
Gambling	756	3	15	95	170	0.4	2.0	12.6	22.5
Offenses against the family and children	23,991	536	1,322	2,314	4,621	2.2	5.5	9.6	19.3
Driving under the influence	404,342	50	2,555	22,297	77,809	*	0.6	5.5	19.2
Liquor laws	58,516	1,292	7,800	28,882	33,475	2.2	13.3	49.4	57.2
Drunkenness[2]	12,244	13	76	485	1,701	0.1	0.6	4.0	13.9
Disorderly conduct	156,994	9,607	21,594	31,449	47,274	6.1	13.8	20.0	30.1
Vagrancy	10,000	2	19	564	1,282	*	0.2	5.6	12.8
All other offenses (except traffic)	1,347,617	19,852	60,607	131,765	263,781	1.5	4.5	9.8	19.6
Suspicion[3]	62	0	0	1	15	0.0	0.0	1.6	24.2
Curfew and loitering law violations	5,048	1,619	5,048	5,048	5,048	32.1	100.0	100.0	100.0

* = Less than one-tenth of one percent.
1 Violent crimes in this table are offenses of murder and nonnegligent manslaughter, rape, robbery, and aggravated assault. Property crimes are offenses of burglary, larceny-theft, motor vehicle theft, and arson. 2 Drunkenness figures were submitted by Summary reporting agencies only. As of 2021 drunkenness is no longer a separate offense in the National Incident-Based Reporting System (NIBRS), but it is included with All Other Offenses (except traffic) category. 3 Figures for suspicion include only data submitted by Summary reporting agencies because suspicion is not collected as a crime via NIBRS.

Table 48. Arrests, Cities, Distribution by Sex, 2022

(Number, percent; 8,754 agencies; 2022 estimated population 180,514,188.)

Offense charged	Number of persons arrested			Percent male	Percent female	Percent distribution[1]		
	Total	Male	Female			Total	Male	Female
Total	4,229,355	3,080,310	1,149,045	72.8	27.2	100.0	100.0	100.0
Violent crime[2]	269,242	212,160	57,082	78.8	21.2	6.4	6.9	5.0
Murder and nonnegligent manslaughter	7,584	6,734	850	88.8	11.2	0.2	0.2	0.1
Rape	11,044	10,747	297	97.3	2.7	0.3	0.3	*
Robbery	40,904	34,505	6,399	84.4	15.6	1.0	1.1	0.6
Aggravated assault	209,710	160,174	49,536	76.4	23.6	5.0	5.2	4.3
Property crime[2]	515,295	338,822	176,473	65.8	34.2	12.2	11.0	15.4
Burglary	74,149	60,163	13,986	81.1	18.9	1.8	2.0	1.2
Larceny-theft	385,938	235,702	150,236	61.1	38.9	9.1	7.7	13.1
Motor vehicle theft	49,159	38,322	10,837	78.0	22.0	1.2	1.2	0.9
Arson	6,049	4,635	1,414	76.6	23.4	0.1	0.2	0.1
Other assaults	572,016	397,066	174,950	69.4	30.6	13.5	12.9	15.2
Forgery and counterfeiting	16,854	11,523	5,331	68.4	31.6	0.4	0.4	0.5
Fraud	46,609	30,593	16,016	65.6	34.4	1.1	1.0	1.4
Embezzlement	6,180	3,187	2,993	51.6	48.4	0.1	0.1	0.3
Stolen property; buying, receiving, possessing	50,140	39,658	10,482	79.1	20.9	1.2	1.3	0.9
Vandalism	101,356	77,556	23,800	76.5	23.5	2.4	2.5	2.1
Weapons; carrying, possessing, etc.	111,168	100,806	10,362	90.7	9.3	2.6	3.3	0.9
Prostitution and commercialized vice	11,089	4,561	6,528	41.1	58.9	0.3	0.1	0.6
Sex offenses (except forcible rape and prostitution)	13,817	13,055	762	94.5	5.5	0.3	0.4	0.1
Drug abuse violations	496,019	370,922	125,097	74.8	25.2	11.7	12.0	10.9
Gambling	756	556	200	73.5	26.5	*	*	*
Offenses against the family and children	23,991	14,573	9,418	60.7	39.3	0.6	0.5	0.8
Driving under the influence	404,342	300,146	104,196	74.2	25.8	9.6	9.7	9.1
Liquor laws	58,516	39,955	18,561	68.3	31.7	1.4	1.3	1.6
Drunkenness[3]	12,244	9,844	2,400	80.4	19.6	0.3	0.3	0.2
Disorderly conduct	156,994	111,307	45,687	70.9	29.1	3.7	3.6	4.0
Vagrancy	10,000	7,579	2,421	75.8	24.2	0.2	0.2	0.2
All other offenses (except traffic)	1,347,617	992,935	354,682	73.7	26.3	31.9	32.2	30.9
Suspicion[4]	62	52	10	83.9	16.1	*	*	*
Curfew and loitering law violations	5,048	3,454	1,594	68.4	31.6	0.1	0.1	0.1

* = Less than one-tenth of 1 percent.
1 Because of rounding, the percentages may not sum to 100. 2 Violent crimes in this table are offenses of murder and nonnegligent manslaughter, rape, robbery, and aggravated assault. Property crimes are offenses of burglary, larceny-theft, motor vehicle theft, and arson. 3 Drunkenness figures were submitted by Summary reporting agencies only. As of 2021 drunkenness is no longer a separate offense in the National Incident-Based Reporting System (NIBRS), but it is included with All Other Offenses (except traffic) category. 4 Figures for suspicion include only data submitted by Summary reporting agencies because suspicion is not collected as a crime via NIBRS.

Table 49. Arrests, Cities, Distribution by Race, 2022

(Number, percent; 8,754 agencies; 2022 estimated population 180,514,188.)

Offense charged	Total	White	Black or African American	American Indian or Alaskan Native	Asian	Native Hawaiian or Other Pacific Islander	Total	White	Black or African American	American Indian or Alaskan Native	Asian	Native Hawaiian or Other Pacific Islander
Total	4,150,461	2,720,868	1,244,094	106,207	60,671	18,621	100.0	65.6	30.0	2.6	1.5	0.4
Violent crime[2]	265,217	143,215	111,395	5,093	4,387	1,127	100.0	54.0	42.0	1.9	1.7	0.4
Murder and nonnegligent manslaughter	7,495	2,678	4,603	88	94	32	100.0	35.7	61.4	1.2	1.3	0.4
Rape	10,746	6,978	3,280	192	249	47	100.0	64.9	30.5	1.8	2.3	0.4
Robbery	40,401	17,674	21,530	499	457	241	100.0	43.7	53.3	1.2	1.1	0.6
Aggravated assault	206,575	115,885	81,982	4,314	3,587	807	100.0	56.1	39.7	2.1	1.7	0.4
Property crime[2]	506,262	329,283	158,660	10,184	6,440	1,695	100.0	65.0	31.3	2.0	1.3	0.3
Burglary	73,128	47,144	23,609	1,211	906	258	100.0	64.5	32.3	1.7	1.2	0.4
Larceny-theft	378,642	247,641	116,935	7,942	4,876	1,248	100.0	65.4	30.9	2.1	1.3	0.3
Motor vehicle theft	48,535	30,297	16,614	917	531	176	100.0	62.4	34.2	1.9	1.1	0.4
Arson	5,957	4,201	1,502	114	127	13	100.0	70.5	25.2	1.9	2.1	0.2
Other assaults	561,423	338,608	197,134	13,269	9,523	2,889	100.0	60.3	35.1	2.4	1.7	0.5
Forgery and counterfeiting	16,507	10,781	5,215	178	270	63	100.0	65.3	31.6	1.1	1.6	0.4
Fraud	45,769	28,067	15,961	870	707	164	100.0	61.3	34.9	1.9	1.5	0.4
Embezzlement	6,033	3,511	2,349	67	95	11	100.0	58.2	38.9	1.1	1.6	0.2
Stolen property; buying, receiving, possessing	49,337	28,797	18,506	714	870	450	100.0	58.4	37.5	1.4	1.8	0.9
Vandalism	99,447	64,198	30,911	2,608	1,381	349	100.0	64.6	31.1	2.6	1.4	0.4
Weapons; carrying, possessing, etc.	109,584	49,425	57,563	1,023	1,280	293	100.0	45.1	52.5	0.9	1.2	0.3
Prostitution and commercialized vice	10,985	5,651	4,600	47	655	32	100.0	51.4	41.9	0.4	6.0	0.3
Sex offenses (except forcible rape and prostitution)	13,501	9,356	3,410	296	352	87	100.0	69.3	25.3	2.2	2.6	0.6
Drug abuse violations	489,764	335,153	139,951	8,369	5,013	1,278	100.0	68.4	28.6	1.7	1.0	0.3
Gambling	732	392	242	4	82	12	100.0	53.6	33.1	0.5	11.2	1.6
Offenses against the family and children	23,346	15,284	6,115	1,582	283	82	100.0	65.5	26.2	6.8	1.2	0.4
Driving under the influence	393,934	312,049	60,692	9,839	9,419	1,935	100.0	79.2	15.4	2.5	2.4	0.5
Liquor laws	56,481	42,741	9,309	3,044	958	429	100.0	75.7	16.5	5.4	1.7	0.8
Drunkenness[3]	12,244	10,616	1,326	65	204	33	100.0	86.7	10.8	0.5	1.7	0.3
Disorderly conduct	153,795	99,242	45,136	7,157	1,758	502	100.0	64.5	29.3	4.7	1.1	0.3
Vagrancy	9,861	5,503	2,241	1,917	131	69	100.0	55.8	22.7	19.4	1.3	0.7
All other offenses (except traffic)	1,321,270	885,803	371,841	39,721	16,828	7,077	100.0	67.0	28.1	3.0	1.3	0.5
Suspicion[4]	62	30	32	0	0	0	100.0	48.4	51.6	0.0	0.0	0.0
Curfew and loitering law violations	4,907	3,163	1,505	160	35	44	100.0	64.5	30.7	3.3	0.7	0.9

Table 49. Arrests, Cities, Distribution by Race, 2022—Continued

(Number, percent; 8,754 agencies; 2022 estimated population 180,514,188.)

Offense charged	Arrests under 18						Percent distribution[1]					
	Total	White	Black or African American	American Indian or Alaskan Native	Asian	Native Hawaiian or Other Pacific Islander	Total	White	Black or African American	American Indian or Alaskan Native	Asian	Native Hawaiian or Other Pacific Islander
Total	289,643	172,188	105,709	7,324	3,141	1,281	100.0	59.4	36.5	2.5	1.1	0.4
Violent crime[2]	23,853	11,286	11,834	375	258	100	100.0	47.3	49.6	1.6	1.1	0.4
Murder and nonnegligent manslaughter	815	264	538	9	3	1	100.0	32.4	66.0	1.1	0.4	0.1
Rape	1,532	1,026	451	22	27	6	100.0	67.0	29.4	1.4	1.8	0.4
Robbery	7,492	2,470	4,846	55	74	47	100.0	33.0	64.7	0.7	1.0	0.6
Aggravated assault	14,014	7,526	5,999	289	154	46	100.0	53.7	42.8	2.1	1.1	0.3
Property crime[2]	44,734	24,049	18,957	890	632	206	100.0	53.8	42.4	2.0	1.4	0.5
Burglary	6,612	3,566	2,835	120	61	30	100.0	53.9	42.9	1.8	0.9	0.5
Larceny-theft	30,036	17,422	11,308	642	510	154	100.0	58.0	37.6	2.1	1.7	0.5
Motor vehicle theft	7,316	2,526	4,602	115	51	22	100.0	34.5	62.9	1.6	0.7	0.3
Arson	770	535	212	13	10	0	100.0	69.5	27.5	1.7	1.3	0.0
Other assaults	61,324	35,210	23,865	1,298	627	324	100.0	57.4	38.9	2.1	1.0	0.5
Forgery and counterfeiting	257	143	105	3	4	2	100.0	55.6	40.9	1.2	1.6	0.8
Fraud	1,503	748	691	35	25	4	100.0	49.8	46.0	2.3	1.7	0.3
Embezzlement	255	118	132	2	3	0	100.0	46.3	51.8	0.8	1.2	0.0
Stolen property; buying, receiving, possessing	4,808	1,174	3,505	57	37	35	100.0	24.4	72.9	1.2	0.8	0.7
Vandalism	14,127	9,796	3,850	328	123	30	100.0	69.3	27.3	2.3	0.9	0.2
Weapons; carrying, possessing, etc.	12,295	5,567	6,377	141	166	44	100.0	45.3	51.9	1.1	1.4	0.4
Prostitution and commercialized vice	59	26	33	0	0	0	100.0	44.1	55.9	0.0	0.0	0.0
Sex offenses (except forcible rape and prostitution)	1,934	1,390	479	28	28	9	100.0	71.9	24.8	1.4	1.4	0.5
Drug abuse violations	28,013	20,408	6,525	694	267	119	100.0	72.9	23.3	2.5	1.0	0.4
Gambling	15	11	4	0	0	0	100.0	73.3	26.7	0.0	0.0	0.0
Offenses against the family and children	1,303	860	264	171	4	4	100.0	66.0	20.3	13.1	0.3	0.3
Driving under the influence	2,467	2,136	161	122	34	14	100.0	86.6	6.5	4.9	1.4	0.6
Liquor laws	7,500	6,155	560	653	95	37	100.0	82.1	7.5	8.7	1.3	0.5
Drunkenness[3]	76	65	5	4	2	0	100.0	85.5	6.6	5.3	2.6	0.0
Disorderly conduct	21,040	11,492	8,613	728	163	44	100.0	54.6	40.9	3.5	0.8	0.2
Vagrancy	19	11	8	0	0	0	100.0	57.9	42.1	0.0	0.0	0.0
All other offenses (except traffic)	59,154	38,380	18,236	1,635	638	265	100.0	64.9	30.8	2.8	1.1	0.4
Suspicion[4]	0	0	0	0	0	0	NA	NA	NA	NA	NA	NA
Curfew and loitering law violations	4,907	3,163	1,505	160	35	44	100.0	64.5	30.7	3.3	0.7	0.9

Table 49. Arrests, Cities, Distribution by Race, 2022—Continued

(Number, percent; 8,754 agencies; 2022 estimated population 180,514,188.)

Offense charged	Arrests 18 and over						Percent distribution[1]					
	Total	White	Black or African American	American Indian or Alaskan Native	Asian	Native Hawaiian or Other Pacific Islander	Total	White	Black or African American	American Indian or Alaskan Native	Asian	Native Hawaiian or Other Pacific Islander
Total	3,860,818	2,548,680	1,138,385	98,883	57,530	17,340	100.0	66.0	29.5	2.6	1.5	0.4
Violent crime[2]	241,364	131,929	99,561	4,718	4,129	1,027	100.0	54.7	41.2	2.0	1.7	0.4
Murder and nonnegligent manslaughter	6,680	2,414	4,065	79	91	31	100.0	36.1	60.9	1.2	1.4	0.5
Rape	9,214	5,952	2,829	170	222	41	100.0	64.6	30.7	1.8	2.4	0.4
Robbery	32,909	15,204	16,684	444	383	194	100.0	46.2	50.7	1.3	1.2	0.6
Aggravated assault	192,561	108,359	75,983	4,025	3,433	761	100.0	56.3	39.5	2.1	1.8	0.4
Property crime[2]	461,528	305,234	139,703	9,294	5,808	1,489	100.0	66.1	30.3	2.0	1.3	0.3
Burglary	66,516	43,578	20,774	1,091	845	228	100.0	65.5	31.2	1.6	1.3	0.3
Larceny-theft	348,606	230,219	105,627	7,300	4,366	1,094	100.0	66.0	30.3	2.1	1.3	0.3
Motor vehicle theft	41,219	27,771	12,012	802	480	154	100.0	67.4	29.1	1.9	1.2	0.4
Arson	5,187	3,666	1,290	101	117	13	100.0	70.7	24.9	1.9	2.3	0.3
Other assaults	500,099	303,398	173,269	11,971	8,896	2,565	100.0	60.7	34.6	2.4	1.8	0.5
Forgery and counterfeiting	16,250	10,638	5,110	175	266	61	100.0	65.5	31.4	1.1	1.6	0.4
Fraud	44,266	27,319	15,270	835	682	160	100.0	61.7	34.5	1.9	1.5	0.4
Embezzlement	5,778	3,393	2,217	65	92	11	100.0	58.7	38.4	1.1	1.6	0.2
Stolen property; buying, receiving, possessing	44,529	27,623	15,001	657	833	415	100.0	62.0	33.7	1.5	1.9	0.9
Vandalism	85,320	54,402	27,061	2,280	1,258	319	100.0	63.8	31.7	2.7	1.5	0.4
Weapons; carrying, possessing, etc.	97,289	43,858	51,186	882	1,114	249	100.0	45.1	52.6	0.9	1.1	0.3
Prostitution and commercialized vice	10,926	5,625	4,567	47	655	32	100.0	51.5	41.8	0.4	6.0	0.3
Sex offenses (except forcible rape and prostitution)	11,567	7,966	2,931	268	324	78	100.0	68.9	25.3	2.3	2.8	0.7
Drug abuse violations	461,751	314,745	133,426	7,675	4,746	1,159	100.0	68.2	28.9	1.7	1.0	0.3
Gambling	717	381	238	4	82	12	100.0	53.1	33.2	0.6	11.4	1.7
Offenses against the family and children	22,043	14,424	5,851	1,411	279	78	100.0	65.4	26.5	6.4	1.3	0.4
Driving under the influence	391,467	309,913	60,531	9,717	9,385	1,921	100.0	79.2	15.5	2.5	2.4	0.5
Liquor laws	48,981	36,586	8,749	2,391	863	392	100.0	74.7	17.9	4.9	1.8	0.8
Drunkenness[3]	12,168	10,551	1,321	61	202	33	100.0	86.7	10.9	0.5	1.7	0.3
Disorderly conduct	132,755	87,750	36,523	6,429	1,595	458	100.0	66.1	27.5	4.8	1.2	0.3
Vagrancy	9,842	5,492	2,233	1,917	131	69	100.0	55.8	22.7	19.5	1.3	0.7
All other offenses (except traffic)	1,262,116	847,423	353,605	38,086	16,190	6,812	100.0	67.1	28.0	3.0	1.3	0.5
Suspicion[4]	62	30	32	0	0	0	100.0	48.4	51.6	0.0	0.0	0.0
Curfew and loitering law violations	NA	NA	NA	NA	NA	NA	NA	NA	NA	NA	NA	NA

NA = Not available.
1 Because of rounding, the percentages may not sum to 100.   2 Violent crimes in this table are offenses of murder and nonnegligent manslaughter, rape, robbery, and aggravated assault. Property crimes are offenses of burglary, larceny-theft, motor vehicle theft, and arson.   3 Drunkenness figures were submitted by Summary reporting agencies only. As of 2021 drunkenness is no longer a separate offense in the National Incident-Based Reporting System (NIBRS), but it is included with All Other Offenses (except traffic) category.   4 Figures for suspicion include only data submitted by Summary reporting agencies because suspicion is not collected as a crime via NIBRS.

Table 49A. Arrests, Cities, Distribution by Ethnicity, 2022

(Number, percent; 8,754 agencies; 2022 estimated population 180,514,188.)

Offense charged	Total arrests			Percent distribution[1]			Arrests under 18		
	Total[2]	Hispanic or Latino	Not Hispanic or Latino	Total[2]	Hispanic or Latino	Not Hispanic or Latino	Total[2]	Hispanic or Latino	Not Hispanic or Latino
Total	3,546,914	813,812	2,733,102	100.0	22.9	77.1	240,676	61,397	179,279
Violent crime[3]	230,614	62,430	168,184	100.0	27.1	72.9	20,277	5,634	14,643
Murder and nonnegligent manslaughter	6,233	1,393	4,840	100.0	22.3	77.7	648	187	461
Rape	9,138	2,891	6,247	100.0	31.6	68.4	1,274	332	942
Robbery	35,133	9,031	26,102	100.0	25.7	74.3	6,396	1,671	4,725
Aggravated assault	180,110	49,115	130,995	100.0	27.3	72.7	11,959	3,444	8,515
Property crime[3]	427,772	79,844	347,928	100.0	18.7	81.3	37,229	7,605	29,624
Burglary	62,913	14,029	48,884	100.0	22.3	77.7	5,612	1,227	4,385
Larceny-theft	318,325	52,814	265,511	100.0	16.6	83.4	24,791	4,991	19,800
Motor vehicle theft	41,500	11,721	29,779	100.0	28.2	71.8	6,202	1,221	4,981
Arson	5,034	1,280	3,754	100.0	25.4	74.6	624	166	458
Other assaults	479,222	111,055	368,167	100.0	23.2	76.8	52,081	12,640	39,441
Forgery and counterfeiting	14,503	2,935	11,568	100.0	20.2	79.8	222	47	175
Fraud	39,510	6,368	33,142	100.0	16.1	83.9	1,249	228	1,021
Embezzlement	5,071	821	4,250	100.0	16.2	83.8	227	31	196
Stolen property; buying, receiving, possessing	41,583	9,367	32,216	100.0	22.5	77.5	3,823	629	3,194
Vandalism	85,401	19,095	66,306	100.0	22.4	77.6	11,811	2,865	8,946
Weapons; carrying, possessing, etc.	92,365	23,959	68,406	100.0	25.9	74.1	10,529	3,522	7,007
Prostitution and commercialized vice	10,393	2,762	7,631	100.0	26.6	73.4	53	17	36
Sex offenses (except forcible rape and prostitution)	11,755	3,873	7,882	100.0	32.9	67.1	1,630	471	1,159
Drug abuse violations	433,692	99,782	333,910	100.0	23.0	77.0	24,369	8,976	15,393
Gambling	590	229	361	100.0	38.8	61.2	14	6	8
Offenses against the family and children	19,552	3,726	15,826	100.0	19.1	80.9	1,193	249	944
Driving under the influence	341,123	117,324	223,799	100.0	34.4	65.6	2,091	837	1,254
Liquor laws	44,484	8,261	36,223	100.0	18.6	81.4	5,948	1,240	4,708
Drunkenness[4]	12,177	5,318	6,859	100.0	43.7	56.3	76	36	40
Disorderly conduct	125,624	24,847	100,777	100.0	19.8	80.2	16,595	3,584	13,011
Vagrancy	7,586	1,264	6,322	100.0	16.7	83.3	17	5	12
All other offenses (except traffic)	1,120,064	229,700	890,364	100.0	20.5	79.5	47,471	11,930	35,541
Suspicion[5]	62	7	55	100.0	11.3	88.7	0	0	0
Curfew and loitering law violations	3,771	845	2,926	100.0	22.4	77.6	3,771	845	2,926

Table 49A. Arrests, Cities, Distribution by Ethnicity, 2022—Continued

(Number, percent; 8,754 agencies; 2022 estimated population 180,514,188.)

Offense charged	Percent distribution[1]				Arrests 18 and over			Percent distribution[1]	
	Total[2]	Hispanic or Latino	Not Hispanic or Latino	Total[2]	Hispanic or Latino	Not Hispanic or Latino	Total[2]	Hispanic or Latino	Not Hispanic or Latino
Total	100.0	25.5	74.5	3,306,238	752,415	2,553,823	100.0	22.8	77.2
Violent crime[3]	100.0	27.8	72.2	210,337	56,796	153,541	100.0	27.0	73.0
Murder and nonnegligent manslaughter	100.0	28.9	71.1	5,585	1,206	4,379	100.0	21.6	78.4
Rape	100.0	26.1	73.9	7,864	2,559	5,305	100.0	32.5	67.5
Robbery	100.0	26.1	73.9	28,737	7,360	21,377	100.0	25.6	74.4
Aggravated assault	100.0	28.8	71.2	168,151	45,671	122,480	100.0	27.2	72.8
Property crime[3]	100.0	20.4	79.6	390,543	72,239	318,304	100.0	18.5	81.5
Burglary	100.0	21.9	78.1	57,301	12,802	44,499	100.0	22.3	77.7
Larceny-theft	100.0	20.1	79.9	293,534	47,823	245,711	100.0	16.3	83.7
Motor vehicle theft	100.0	19.7	80.3	35,298	10,500	24,798	100.0	29.7	70.3
Arson	100.0	26.6	73.4	4,410	1,114	3,296	100.0	25.3	74.7
Other assaults	100.0	24.3	75.7	427,141	98,415	328,726	100.0	23.0	77.0
Forgery and counterfeiting	100.0	21.2	78.8	14,281	2,888	11,393	100.0	20.2	79.8
Fraud	100.0	18.3	81.7	38,261	6,140	32,121	100.0	16.0	84.0
Embezzlement	100.0	13.7	86.3	4,844	790	4,054	100.0	16.3	83.7
Stolen property; buying, receiving, possessing	100.0	16.5	83.5	37,760	8,738	29,022	100.0	23.1	76.9
Vandalism	100.0	24.3	75.7	73,590	16,230	57,360	100.0	22.1	77.9
Weapons; carrying, possessing, etc.	100.0	33.5	66.5	81,836	20,437	61,399	100.0	25.0	75.0
Prostitution and commercialized vice	100.0	32.1	67.9	10,340	2,745	7,595	100.0	26.5	73.5
Sex offenses (except forcible rape and prostitution)	100.0	28.9	71.1	10,125	3,402	6,723	100.0	33.6	66.4
Drug abuse violations	100.0	36.8	63.2	409,323	90,806	318,517	100.0	22.2	77.8
Gambling	100.0	42.9	57.1	576	223	353	100.0	38.7	61.3
Offenses against the family and children	100.0	20.9	79.1	18,359	3,477	14,882	100.0	18.9	81.1
Driving under the influence	100.0	40.0	60.0	339,032	116,487	222,545	100.0	34.4	65.6
Liquor laws	100.0	20.8	79.2	38,536	7,021	31,515	100.0	18.2	81.8
Drunkenness[4]	100.0	47.4	52.6	12,101	5,282	6,819	100.0	43.6	56.4
Disorderly conduct	100.0	21.6	78.4	109,029	21,263	87,766	100.0	19.5	80.5
Vagrancy	100.0	29.4	70.6	7,569	1,259	6,310	100.0	16.6	83.4
All other offenses (except traffic)	100.0	25.1	74.9	1,072,593	217,770	854,823	100.0	20.3	79.7
Suspicion[5]	NA	NA	NA	62	7	55	100.0	11.3	88.7
Curfew and loitering law violations	100.0	22.4	77.6	NA	NA	NA	NA	NA	NA

NA = Not available.
1 Because of rounding, the percentages may not sum to 100.   2 The ethnicity totals are representative of those agencies that provided ethnicity breakdowns. Not all agencies provide ethnicity data; therefore, the race and ethnicity totals will not equal.
3 Violent crimes are offenses of murder and nonnegligent manslaughter, rape, robbery, and aggravated assault. Property crimes are offenses of burglary, larceny-theft, motor vehicle theft, and arson.   4 Drunkenness figures were submitted by Summary reporting agencies only. As of 2021 drunkenness is no longer a separate offense in the National Incident-Based Reporting System (NIBRS), but it is included with All Other Offenses (except traffic) category.   5 Figures for suspicion include only data submitted by Summary reporting agencies because suspicion is not collected as a crime via NIBRS.

Table 50. Arrest Trends, Metropolitan Counties, 2021–2022

(Number, percent change; 1,043 agencies; 2022 estimated population 54,768,063; 2021 estimated population 53,843,750.)

Offense charged	Number of persons arrested								
	Total, all ages			Under 18 years of age			18 years of age and over		
	2021	2022	Percent change	2021	2022	Percent change	2021	2022	Percent change
Total[1]	919,623	928,290	+0.9	51,939	60,944	+17.3	867,684	867,346	*
Violent crime[2]	42,416	42,665	+0.6	3,551	4,296	+21.0	38,865	38,369	-1.3
Murder and nonnegligent manslaughter	1,417	1,382	-2.5	103	128	+24.3	1,314	1,254	-4.6
Rape	2,587	2,512	-2.9	451	457	+1.3	2,136	2,055	-3.8
Robbery	3,823	4,020	+5.2	717	869	+21.2	3,106	3,151	+1.4
Aggravated assault	34,589	34,751	+0.5	2,280	2,842	+24.6	32,309	31,909	-1.2
Property crime[2]	69,434	76,923	+10.8	5,659	7,353	+29.9	63,775	69,570	+9.1
Burglary	13,225	12,947	-2.1	1,149	1,433	+24.7	12,076	11,514	-4.7
Larceny-theft	47,805	55,557	+16.2	3,339	4,689	+40.4	44,466	50,868	+14.4
Motor vehicle theft	7,538	7,578	+0.5	1,042	1,073	+3.0	6,496	6,505	+0.1
Arson	866	841	-2.9	129	158	+22.5	737	683	-7.3
Other assaults	115,885	121,916	+5.2	12,943	17,145	+32.5	102,942	104,771	+1.8
Forgery and counterfeiting	3,051	3,797	+24.5	62	88	+41.9	2,989	3,709	+24.1
Fraud	9,420	10,064	+6.8	252	309	+22.6	9,168	9,755	+6.4
Embezzlement	973	1,118	+14.9	39	46	+17.9	934	1,072	+14.8
Stolen property; buying, receiving, possessing	9,709	10,192	+5.0	765	1,000	+30.7	8,944	9,192	+2.8
Vandalism	17,883	17,317	-3.2	2,784	2,719	-2.3	15,099	14,598	-3.3
Weapons; carrying, possessing, etc.	18,725	19,384	+3.5	1,588	2,099	+32.2	17,137	17,285	+0.9
Prostitution and commercialized vice	1,129	909	-19.5	2	2	+0.0	1,127	907	-19.5
Sex offenses (except forcible rape and prostitution)	2,513	2,659	+5.8	519	555	+6.9	1,994	2,104	+5.5
Drug abuse violations	130,845	117,798	-10.0	4,989	6,235	+25.0	125,856	111,563	-11.4
Gambling	161	199	+23.6	1	6	+500.0	160	193	+20.6
Offenses against the family and children	8,107	8,367	+3.2	138	163	+18.1	7,969	8,204	+2.9
Driving under the influence	112,473	109,611	-2.5	705	651	-7.7	111,768	108,960	-2.5
Liquor laws	8,455	8,872	+4.9	1,785	2,019	+13.1	6,670	6,853	+2.7
Drunkenness[3]	0	0	NA	0	0	NA	0	0	NA
Disorderly conduct	21,253	21,665	+1.9	3,460	3,562	+2.9	17,793	18,103	+1.7
Vagrancy	1,027	1,206	+17.4	0	0		1,027	1,206	+17.4
All other offenses (except traffic)	345,619	353,220	+2.2	12,152	12,288	+1.1	333,467	340,932	+2.2
Suspicion[4]	0	0	NA	0	0	NA	0	0	NA
Curfew and loitering law violations	545	408	-25.1	545	408	-25.1	NA	NA	NA

NA = Not available.
* = Less than one-tenth of one percent.
1 Does not include suspicion.   2 Violent crimes in this table are offenses of murder and nonnegligent manslaughter, rape, robbery, and aggravated assault. Property crimes are offenses of burglary, larceny-theft, motor vehicle theft, and arson.
3 Drunkenness figures were submitted by Summary reporting agencies only. As of 2021 drunkenness is no longer a separate offense in the National Incident-Based Reporting System (NIBRS), but it is included with All Other Offenses (except traffic) category.   4 Figures for suspicion include only data submitted by Summary reporting agencies because suspicion is not collected as a crime via NIBRS.

Table 51. Arrest Trends, Metropolitan Counties, by Age and Sex, 2021–2022

(Number, percent change; 1,043 agencies; 2022 estimated population 54,768,063; 2021 estimated population 53,843,750.)

Offense charged	Male						Female					
	Total			Under 18			Total			Under 18		
	2021	2022	Percent change	2021	2022	Percent change	2021	2022	Percent change	2021	2022	Percent change
Total[1]	677,016	679,251	+0.3	36,106	42,115	+16.6	242,607	249,039	+2.7	15,833	18,829	+18.9
Violent crime[2]	34,320	34,049	-0.8	2,801	3,338	+19.2	8,096	8,616	+6.4	750	958	+27.7
Murder and nonnegligent manslaughter	1,223	1,218	-0.4	90	122	+35.6	194	164	-15.5	13	6	-53.8
Rape	2,504	2,440	-2.6	425	442	+4.0	83	72	-13.3	26	15	-42.3
Robbery	3,300	3,450	+4.5	642	774	+20.6	523	570	+9.0	75	95	+26.7
Aggravated assault	27,293	26,941	-1.3	1,644	2,000	+21.7	7,296	7,810	+7.0	636	842	+32.4
Property crime[2]	48,017	52,077	+8.5	4,373	5,485	+25.4	21,417	24,846	+16.0	1,286	1,868	+45.3
Burglary	10,757	10,563	-1.8	1,027	1,268	+23.5	2,468	2,384	-3.4	122	165	+35.2
Larceny-theft	30,672	34,855	+13.6	2,416	3,194	+32.2	17,133	20,702	+20.8	923	1,495	+62.0
Motor vehicle theft	5,930	6,005	+1.3	832	891	+7.1	1,608	1,573	-2.2	210	182	-13.3
Arson	658	654	-0.6	98	132	+34.7	208	187	-10.1	31	26	-16.1
Other assaults	81,940	84,501	+3.1	7,939	10,292	+29.6	33,945	37,415	+10.2	5,004	6,853	+37.0
Forgery and counterfeiting	2,093	2,721	+30.0	49	76	+55.1	958	1,076	+12.3	13	12	-7.7
Fraud	6,096	6,630	+8.8	170	206	+21.2	3,324	3,434	+3.3	82	103	+25.6
Embezzlement	547	619	+13.2	19	24	+26.3	426	499	+17.1	20	22	+10.0
Stolen property; buying, receiving, possessing	7,871	8,221	+4.4	654	875	+33.8	1,838	1,971	+7.2	111	125	+12.6
Vandalism	14,035	13,392	-4.6	2,282	2,176	-4.6	3,848	3,925	+2.0	502	543	+8.2
Weapons; carrying, possessing, etc.	16,950	17,540	+3.5	1,365	1,808	+32.5	1,775	1,844	+3.9	223	291	+30.5
Prostitution and commercialized vice	788	537	-31.9	1	2	+100.0	341	372	+9.1	1	0	-100.0
Sex offenses (except forcible rape and prostitution)	2,379	2,505	+5.3	476	494	+3.8	134	154	+14.9	43	61	+41.9
Drug abuse violations	95,089	85,902	-9.7	3,568	4,459	+25.0	35,756	31,896	-10.8	1,421	1,776	+25.0
Gambling	118	158	+33.9	1	6	+500.0	43	41	-4.7	0	0	NA
Offenses against the family and children	5,611	5,927	+5.6	72	88	+22.2	2,496	2,440	-2.2	66	75	+13.6
Driving under the influence	83,968	81,879	-2.5	521	480	-7.9	28,505	27,732	-2.7	184	171	-7.1
Liquor laws	5,648	5,832	+3.3	1,004	1,149	+14.4	2,807	3,040	+8.3	781	870	+11.4
Drunkenness[3]	0	0	NA	0	0	NA	0	0	NA	0	0	NA
Disorderly conduct	15,009	15,277	+1.8	2,205	2,245	+1.8	6,244	6,388	+2.3	1,255	1,317	+4.9
Vagrancy	859	1,008	+17.3	0	0	NA	168	198	+17.9	0	0	NA
All other offenses (except traffic)	255,343	260,189	+1.9	8,271	8,625	+4.3	90,276	93,031	+3.1	3,881	3,663	-5.6
Suspicion[4]	0	0	NA	0	0	NA	0	0	NA	0	0	NA
Curfew and loitering law violations	335	287	-14.3	335	287	-14.3	210	121	-42.4	210	121	-42.4

NA = Not available.
1 Does not include suspicion.   2 Violent crimes in this table are offenses of murder and nonnegligent manslaughter, rape, robbery, and aggravated assault. Property crimes are offenses of burglary, larceny-theft, motor vehicle theft, and arson.
3 Drunkenness figures were submitted by Summary reporting agencies only. As of 2021 drunkenness is no longer a separate offense in the National Incident-Based Reporting System (NIBRS), but it is included with All Other Offenses (except traffic) category.   4 Figures for suspicion include only data submitted by Summary reporting agencies because suspicion is not collected as a crime via NIBRS.

Table 52. Arrests, Metropolitan Counties, Distribution by Age, 2022

(Number, percent; 1,370 agencies; 2022 estimated population 68,043,758.)

Offense charged	Total, all ages	Under 15 years	Under 18 years	Age 18 years and over	Under 10 years	10–12 years	13–14 years	15 years	16 years	17 years	18 years	19 years	20 years
Total	1,155,515	23,118	69,351	1,086,164	266	5,243	17,609	14,039	15,503	16,691	21,441	23,739	25,506
Total, percent distribution[1]	100.0	2.0	6.0	94.0	*	0.5	1.5	1.2	1.3	1.4	1.9	2.1	2.2
Violent crime[2]	62,918	1,790	5,428	57,490	31	419	1,340	1,082	1,248	1,308	1,556	1,555	1,616
Violent crime, percent distribution[1]	100.0	2.8	8.6	91.4	*	0.7	2.1	1.7	2.0	2.1	2.5	2.5	2.6
Murder and nonnegligent manslaughter	1,886	16	153	1,733	0	2	14	21	44	72	104	78	85
Rape	3,352	231	554	2,798	11	63	157	102	101	120	142	114	107
Robbery	6,254	298	1,160	5,094	0	38	260	269	306	287	323	296	244
Aggravated assault	51,426	1,245	3,561	47,865	20	316	909	690	797	829	987	1,067	1,180
Property crime[2]	97,668	2,584	8,561	89,107	14	428	2,142	1,890	2,092	1,995	2,469	2,276	2,128
Property crime, percent distribution[1]	100.0	2.6	8.8	91.2	*	0.4	2.2	1.9	2.1	2.0	2.5	2.3	2.2
Burglary	17,031	593	1,726	15,305	6	118	469	398	399	336	413	364	338
Larceny-theft	68,735	1,530	5,338	63,397	6	248	1,276	1,159	1,323	1,326	1,749	1,662	1,553
Motor vehicle theft	10,712	356	1,310	9,402	0	31	325	300	343	311	290	232	216
Arson	1,190	105	187	1,003	2	31	72	33	27	22	17	18	21
Other assaults	145,749	8,195	18,974	126,775	83	2,177	5,935	3,862	3,676	3,241	2,754	2,585	2,775
Forgery and counterfeiting	5,292	9	96	5,196	0	1	8	12	23	52	155	250	282
Fraud	11,865	81	342	11,523	0	18	63	55	85	121	210	248	265
Embezzlement	1,370	1	50	1,320	0	1	0	1	14	34	47	65	60
Stolen property; buying, receiving, possessing	14,355	205	1,174	13,181	1	12	192	284	356	329	401	404	372
Vandalism	23,368	1,214	3,263	20,105	19	317	878	705	678	666	612	569	569
Weapons; carrying, possessing, etc.	27,729	799	2,660	25,069	10	208	581	449	618	794	988	1,034	1,025
Prostitution and commercialized vice	1,271	1	4	1,267	0	0	1	0	2	1	12	12	23
Sex offenses (except forcible rape and prostitution)	4,534	350	699	3,835	9	109	232	126	111	112	115	120	90
Drug abuse violations	152,392	1,561	6,682	145,710	3	239	1,319	1,263	1,715	2,143	3,438	3,866	4,011
Gambling	308	0	6	302	0	0	0	1	0	5	8	11	19
Offenses against the family and children	9,335	52	167	9,168	2	10	40	35	36	44	58	76	97
Driving under the influence	130,447	14	725	129,722	2	1	11	37	194	480	1,439	2,076	2,487
Liquor laws	9,986	298	2,213	7,773	2	43	253	354	607	954	1,239	1,267	1,045
Drunkenness[3]	1,835	1	6	1,829	0	0	1	1	0	4	13	26	21
Disorderly conduct	24,169	1,655	3,826	20,343	25	405	1,225	823	717	631	486	404	451
Vagrancy	2,139	0	1	2,138	0	0	0	0	0	1	31	42	37
All other offenses (except traffic)	428,360	4,186	14,049	414,311	65	834	3,287	2,956	3,215	3,692	5,410	6,853	8,133
Suspicion[4]	0	0	0	0	0	0	0	0	0	0	0	0	0
Curfew and loitering law violations	425	122	425	NA	0	21	101	103	116	84	NA	NA	NA

Table 52. Arrests, Metropolitan Counties, Distribution by Age, 2022—Continued

(Number, percent; 1,370 agencies; 2022 estimated population 68,043,758.)

Offense charged	21 years	22 years	23 years	24 years	25–29 years	30–34 years	35–39 years	40–44 years	45–49 years	50–54 years	55–59 years	60–64 years	65 years and over
Total	27,547	29,046	29,875	30,708	170,229	189,036	163,927	129,494	83,259	65,362	47,311	28,967	20,717
Total, percent distribution[1]	2.4	2.5	2.6	2.7	14.7	16.4	14.2	11.2	7.2	5.7	4.1	2.5	1.8
Violent crime[2]	1,717	1,750	1,740	1,797	9,359	9,677	8,109	6,260	3,965	3,072	2,353	1,518	1,446
Violent crime, percent distribution[1]	2.7	2.8	2.8	2.9	14.9	15.4	12.9	9.9	6.3	4.9	3.7	2.4	2.3
Murder and nonnegligent manslaughter	84	87	79	64	299	260	172	147	81	68	51	35	39
Rape	98	94	74	82	343	379	389	301	201	147	112	98	117
Robbery	240	219	193	189	944	844	591	442	219	148	119	58	25
Aggravated assault	1,295	1,350	1,394	1,462	7,773	8,194	6,957	5,370	3,464	2,709	2,071	1,327	1,265
Property crime[2]	2,121	2,208	2,283	2,328	13,664	15,794	13,612	10,439	6,672	5,456	4,011	2,251	1,395
Property crime, percent distribution[1]	2.2	2.3	2.3	2.4	14.0	16.2	13.9	10.7	6.8	5.6	4.1	2.3	1.4
Burglary	365	378	390	373	2,441	2,916	2,485	1,885	1,132	825	588	276	136
Larceny-theft	1,483	1,557	1,600	1,630	9,476	10,727	9,437	7,357	4,882	4,154	3,112	1,823	1,195
Motor vehicle theft	260	255	268	293	1,623	1,969	1,525	1,074	578	397	252	125	45
Arson	13	18	25	32	124	182	165	123	80	80	59	27	19
Other assaults	3,072	3,388	3,453	3,559	19,380	21,475	18,758	14,789	9,994	7,882	5,892	3,805	3,214
Forgery and counterfeiting	138	159	179	145	823	810	729	589	357	252	178	102	48
Fraud	283	300	281	297	1,824	2,154	1,809	1,396	864	699	468	244	181
Embezzlement	56	40	55	32	187	195	187	144	99	75	43	19	16
Stolen property; buying, receiving, possessing	363	323	381	389	2,223	2,482	2,123	1,591	899	617	385	158	70
Vandalism	571	599	557	619	3,417	3,673	2,988	2,146	1,243	1,020	724	461	337
Weapons; carrying, possessing, etc.	1,121	1,098	1,029	970	4,650	4,136	3,135	2,252	1,333	948	652	423	275
Prostitution and commercialized vice	28	26	26	30	190	201	164	159	138	102	90	30	36
Sex offenses (except forcible rape and prostitution)	104	85	89	74	487	499	534	390	300	263	236	193	256
Drug abuse violations	4,080	4,181	4,103	4,194	23,458	25,410	22,403	17,670	10,940	8,144	5,444	3,012	1,356
Gambling	5	2	2	4	31	45	25	36	38	22	26	11	17
Offenses against the family and children	106	131	126	182	1,388	1,904	1,829	1,430	799	508	306	128	100
Driving under the influence	3,674	3,924	4,093	4,196	21,143	20,921	17,286	14,158	10,136	8,658	6,800	4,898	3,833
Liquor laws	222	165	153	129	613	647	545	481	357	322	265	184	139
Drunkenness[3]	43	49	39	44	277	320	280	224	160	122	102	68	41
Disorderly conduct	501	511	481	484	2,681	3,252	2,895	2,366	1,702	1,439	1,211	795	684
Vagrancy	31	36	35	50	240	351	342	272	178	187	139	88	79
All other offenses (except traffic)	9,311	10,071	10,770	11,185	64,194	75,090	66,174	52,702	33,085	25,574	17,986	10,579	7,194
Suspicion[4]	0	0	0	0	0	0	0	0	0	0	0	0	0
Curfew and loitering law violations	NA	NA	NA	NA	NA	NA	NA	NA	NA	NA	NA	NA	NA

NA = Not available.
* = Less than one-tenth of one percent.
1 Because of rounding, the percentages may not add to 100.0.   2 Violent crimes are offenses of murder and nonnegligent manslaughter, rape, robbery, and aggravated assault. Property crimes are offenses of burglary, larceny-theft, motor vehicle theft, and arson.   3 Drunkenness figures were submitted by Summary reporting agencies only. As of 2021 drunkenness is no longer a separate offense in National Incident Based Reporting System (NIBRS), but it is included with All Other Offenses (except traffic) category.   4 Figures for suspicion include only data submitted by Summary reporting agencies because suspicion is not collected as a crime via NIBRS.

Table 53. Arrests, Metropolitan Counties, Persons Under 15, 18, 21, and 25 Years of Age, 2022

(Number, percent; 1,370 agencies; 2022 estimated population 68,043,758.)

Offense charged	Total, all ages	Number of persons arrested				Percent of total all ages			
		Under 15	Under 18	Under 21	Under 25	Under 15	Under 18	Under 21	Under 25
Total	1,155,515	23,118	69,351	140,037	257,213	2.0	6.0	12.1	22.3
Violent crime[1]	62,918	1,790	5,428	10,155	17,159	2.8	8.6	16.1	27.3
Murder and nonnegligent manslaughter	1,886	16	153	420	734	0.8	8.1	22.3	38.9
Rape	3,352	231	554	917	1,265	6.9	16.5	27.4	37.7
Robbery	6,254	298	1,160	2,023	2,864	4.8	18.5	32.3	45.8
Aggravated assault	51,426	1,245	3,561	6,795	12,296	2.4	6.9	13.2	23.9
Property crime[1]	97,668	2,584	8,561	15,434	24,374	2.6	8.8	15.8	25.0
Burglary	17,031	593	1,726	2,841	4,347	3.5	10.1	16.7	25.5
Larceny-theft	68,735	1,530	5,338	10,302	16,572	2.2	7.8	15.0	24.1
Motor vehicle theft	10,712	356	1,310	2,048	3,124	3.3	12.2	19.1	29.2
Arson	1,190	105	187	243	331	8.8	15.7	20.4	27.8
Other assaults	145,749	8,195	18,974	27,088	40,560	5.6	13.0	18.6	27.8
Forgery and counterfeiting	5,292	9	96	783	1,404	0.2	1.8	14.8	26.5
Fraud	11,865	81	342	1,065	2,226	0.7	2.9	9.0	18.8
Embezzlement	1,370	1	50	222	405	0.1	3.6	16.2	29.6
Stolen property; buying, receiving, possessing	14,355	205	1,174	2,351	3,807	1.4	8.2	16.4	26.5
Vandalism	23,368	1,214	3,263	5,013	7,359	5.2	14.0	21.5	31.5
Weapons; carrying, possessing, etc.	27,729	799	2,660	5,707	9,925	2.9	9.6	20.6	35.8
Prostitution and commercialized vice	1,271	1	4	51	161	0.1	0.3	4.0	12.7
Sex offenses (except forcible rape and prostitution)	4,534	350	699	1,024	1,376	7.7	15.4	22.6	30.3
Drug abuse violations	152,392	1,561	6,682	17,997	34,555	1.0	4.4	11.8	22.7
Gambling	308	0	6	44	57	0.0	1.9	14.3	18.5
Offenses against the family and children	9,335	52	167	398	943	0.6	1.8	4.3	10.1
Driving under the influence	130,447	14	725	6,727	22,614	*	0.6	5.2	17.3
Liquor laws	9,986	298	2,213	5,764	6,433	3.0	22.2	57.7	64.4
Drunkenness[2]	1,835	1	6	66	241	0.1	0.3	3.6	13.1
Disorderly conduct	24,169	1,655	3,826	5,167	7,144	6.8	15.8	21.4	29.6
Vagrancy	2,139	0	1	111	263	0.0	*	5.2	12.3
All other offenses (except traffic)	428,360	4,186	14,049	34,445	75,782	1.0	3.3	8.0	17.7
Suspicion[3]	0	0	0	0	0	NA	NA	NA	NA
Curfew and loitering law violations	425	122	425	425	425	28.7	100.0	100.0	100.0

NA = Not available.
* = Less than one-tenth of one percent.
1 Violent crimes in this table are offenses of murder and nonnegligent manslaughter, rape, robbery, and aggravated assault. Property crimes are offenses of burglary, larceny-theft, motor vehicle theft, and arson.   2 Drunkenness figures were submitted by Summary reporting agencies only. As of 2021 drunkenness is no longer a separate offense in the National Incident-Based Reporting System (NIBRS), but it is included with All Other Offenses (except traffic) category.   3 Figures for suspicion include only data submitted by Summary reporting agencies because suspicion is not collected as a crime via NIBRS.

Table 54. Arrests, Metropolitan Counties, Distribution by Sex, 2022

(Number, percent; 1,370 agencies; 2022 estimated population 68,043,758.)

Offense charged	Number of persons arrested			Percent male	Percent female	Percent distribution[1]		
	Total	Male	Female			Total	Male	Female
Total	1,155,515	854,127	301,388	73.9	26.1	100.0	100.0	100.0
Violent crime[2]	62,918	50,085	12,833	79.6	20.4	5.4	5.9	4.3
Murder and nonnegligent manslaughter	1,886	1,675	211	88.8	11.2	0.2	0.2	0.1
Rape[3]	3,352	3,256	96	97.1	2.9	0.3	0.4	*
Robbery	6,254	5,321	933	85.1	14.9	0.5	0.6	0.3
Aggravated assault	51,426	39,833	11,593	77.5	22.5	4.5	4.7	3.8
Property crime[2]	97,668	66,266	31,402	67.8	32.2	8.5	7.8	10.4
Burglary	17,031	13,828	3,203	81.2	18.8	1.5	1.6	1.1
Larceny-theft	68,735	43,054	25,681	62.6	37.4	5.9	5.0	8.5
Motor vehicle theft	10,712	8,476	2,236	79.1	20.9	0.9	1.0	0.7
Arson	1,190	908	282	76.3	23.7	0.1	0.1	0.1
Other assaults	145,749	101,624	44,125	69.7	30.3	12.6	11.9	14.6
Forgery and counterfeiting	5,292	3,842	1,450	72.6	27.4	0.5	0.4	0.5
Fraud	11,865	7,866	3,999	66.3	33.7	1.0	0.9	1.3
Embezzlement	1,370	761	609	55.5	44.5	0.1	0.1	0.2
Stolen property; buying, receiving, possessing	14,355	11,516	2,839	80.2	19.8	1.2	1.3	0.9
Vandalism	23,368	18,140	5,228	77.6	22.4	2.0	2.1	1.7
Weapons; carrying, possessing, etc.	27,729	25,084	2,645	90.5	9.5	2.4	2.9	0.9
Prostitution and commercialized vice	1,271	721	550	56.7	43.3	0.1	0.1	0.2
Sex offenses (except forcible rape and prostitution)	4,534	4,297	237	94.8	5.2	0.4	0.5	0.1
Drug abuse violations	152,392	113,129	39,263	74.2	25.8	13.2	13.2	13.0
Gambling	308	229	79	74.4	25.6	*	*	*
Offenses against the family and children	9,335	6,669	2,666	71.4	28.6	0.8	0.8	0.9
Driving under the influence	130,447	97,936	32,511	75.1	24.9	11.3	11.5	10.8
Liquor laws	9,986	6,641	3,345	66.5	33.5	0.9	0.8	1.1
Drunkenness[3]	1,835	1,454	381	79.2	20.8	0.2	0.2	0.1
Disorderly conduct	24,169	17,145	7,024	70.9	29.1	2.1	2.0	2.3
Vagrancy	2,139	1,702	437	79.6	20.4	0.2	0.2	0.1
All other offenses (except traffic)	428,360	318,718	109,642	74.4	25.6	37.1	37.3	36.4
Suspicion[4]	0	0	0	NA	NA	NA	NA	NA
Curfew and loitering law violations	425	302	123	71.1	28.9	*	*	*

NA = Not available.
* = Less than one-tenth of one percent.

[1] Because of rounding, the percentages may not sum to 100.   [2] Violent crimes in this table are offenses of murder and nonnegligent manslaughter, rape, robbery, and aggravated assault. Property crimes are offenses of burglary, larceny-theft, motor vehicle theft, and arson.   [3] Drunkenness figures were submitted by Summary reporting agencies only. As of 2021 drunkenness is no longer a separate offense in the National Incident-Based Reporting System (NIBRS), but it is included with All Other Offenses (except traffic) category.   [4] Figures for suspicion include only data submitted by Summary reporting agencies because suspicion is not collected as a crime via NIBRS.

Table 55. Arrests, Metropolitan Counties, Distribution by Race, 2022

(Number, percent; 1,370 agencies; 2022 estimated population 68,043,758.)

Offense charged	Total arrests						Percent distribution[1]					
	Total	White	Black or African American	American Indian or Alaskan Native	Asian	Native Hawaiian or Other Pacific Islander	Total	White	Black or African American	American Indian or Alaskan Native	Asian	Native Hawaiian or Other Pacific Islander
Total	1,133,024	798,297	310,635	10,016	12,154	1,922	100.0	70.5	27.4	0.9	1.1	0.2
Violent crime[2]	62,171	40,084	20,580	475	894	138	100.0	64.5	33.1	0.8	1.4	0.2
Murder and nonnegligent manslaughter	1,874	990	853	12	18	1	100.0	52.8	45.5	0.6	1.0	*
Rape	3,274	2,518	694	17	44	1	100.0	76.9	21.2	0.5	1.3	*
Robbery	6,208	2,892	3,202	37	68	9	100.0	46.6	51.6	0.6	1.1	0.1
Aggravated assault	50,815	33,684	15,831	409	764	127	100.0	66.3	31.2	0.8	1.5	0.2
Property crime[2]	96,191	64,491	29,810	648	1,125	117	100.0	67.0	31.0	0.7	1.2	0.1
Burglary	16,799	12,615	3,936	101	127	20	100.0	75.1	23.4	0.6	0.8	0.1
Larceny-theft	67,615	43,275	22,902	468	900	70	100.0	64.0	33.9	0.7	1.3	0.1
Motor vehicle theft	10,603	7,704	2,720	70	84	25	100.0	72.7	25.7	0.7	0.8	0.2
Arson	1,174	897	252	9	14	2	100.0	76.4	21.5	0.8	1.2	0.2
Other assaults	143,487	98,344	41,920	1,186	1,716	321	100.0	68.5	29.2	0.8	1.2	0.2
Forgery and counterfeiting	5,215	3,381	1,692	21	114	7	100.0	64.8	32.4	0.4	2.2	0.1
Fraud	11,590	7,687	3,698	55	139	11	100.0	66.3	31.9	0.5	1.2	*
Embezzlement	1,352	765	558	12	14	3	100.0	56.6	41.3	0.9	1.0	0.2
Stolen property; buying, receiving, possessing	14,078	9,043	4,747	106	159	23	100.0	64.2	33.7	0.8	1.1	0.2
Vandalism	23,028	15,940	6,523	227	293	45	100.0	69.2	28.3	1.0	1.3	0.2
Weapons; carrying, possessing, etc.	27,433	13,682	13,334	121	244	52	100.0	49.9	48.6	0.4	0.9	0.2
Prostitution and commercialized vice	1,257	653	394	6	200	4	100.0	51.9	31.3	0.5	15.9	0.3
Sex offenses (except forcible rape and prostitution)	4,464	3,471	863	22	93	15	100.0	77.8	19.3	0.5	2.1	0.3
Drug abuse violations	150,284	106,129	41,655	922	1,405	173	100.0	70.6	27.7	0.6	0.9	0.1
Gambling	303	179	89	1	33	1	100.0	59.1	29.4	0.3	10.9	0.3
Offenses against the family and children	9,247	6,499	2,625	47	59	17	100.0	70.3	28.4	0.5	0.6	0.2
Driving under the influence	123,004	97,213	22,682	1,017	1,847	245	100.0	79.0	18.4	0.8	1.5	0.2
Liquor laws	9,567	7,955	1,297	136	153	26	100.0	83.2	13.6	1.4	1.6	0.3
Drunkenness[3]	1,835	1,655	132	19	21	8	100.0	90.2	7.2	1.0	1.1	0.4
Disorderly conduct	23,699	16,707	6,301	411	236	44	100.0	70.5	26.6	1.7	1.0	0.2
Vagrancy	2,133	1,397	703	4	16	13	100.0	65.5	33.0	0.2	0.8	0.6
All other offenses (except traffic)	422,269	302,731	110,911	4,578	3,391	658	100.0	71.7	26.3	1.1	0.8	0.2
Suspicion[4]	0	0	0	0	0	0	NA	NA	NA	NA	NA	NA
Curfew and loitering law violations	417	291	121	2	2	1	100.0	69.8	29.0	0.5	0.5	0.2

Table 55. Arrests, Metropolitan Counties, Distribution by Race, 2022—Continued

(Number, percent; 1,370 agencies; 2022 estimated population 68,043,758.)

Offense charged	Arrests under 18						Percent distribution[1]					
	Total	White	Black or African American	American Indian or Alaskan Native	Asian	Native Hawaiian or Other Pacific Islander	Total	White	Black or African American	American Indian or Alaskan Native	Asian	Native Hawaiian or Other Pacific Islander
Total	67,906	39,989	26,488	729	575	125	100.0	58.9	39.0	1.1	0.8	0.2
Violent crime[2]	5,335	2,654	2,587	33	52	9	100.0	49.7	48.5	0.6	1.0	0.2
Murder and nonnegligent manslaughter	151	50	100	0	1	0	100.0	33.1	66.2	0.0	0.7	0.0
Rape	528	401	120	4	2	1	100.0	75.9	22.7	0.8	0.4	0.2
Robbery	1,152	373	762	6	10	1	100.0	32.4	66.1	0.5	0.9	*
Aggravated assault	3,504	1,830	1,605	23	39	7	100.0	52.2	45.8	0.7	1.1	0.2
Property crime[2]	8,417	4,725	3,504	55	122	11	100.0	56.1	41.6	0.7	1.4	0.1
Burglary	1,689	1,037	626	11	15	0	100.0	61.4	37.1	0.7	0.9	0.0
Larceny-theft	5,251	2,953	2,158	33	99	8	100.0	56.2	41.1	0.6	1.9	0.2
Motor vehicle theft	1,292	609	665	9	6	3	100.0	47.1	51.5	0.7	0.5	0.2
Arson	185	126	55	2	2	0	100.0	68.1	29.7	1.1	1.1	0.0
Other assaults	18,662	9,884	8,437	177	125	39	100.0	53.0	45.2	0.9	0.7	0.2
Forgery and counterfeiting	93	61	28	1	3	0	100.0	65.6	30.1	1.1	3.2	0.0
Fraud	332	181	145	3	3	0	100.0	54.5	43.7	0.9	0.9	0.0
Embezzlement	48	16	32	0	0	0	100.0	33.3	66.7	0.0	0.0	0.0
Stolen property; buying, receiving, possessing	1,143	280	840	9	13	1	100.0	24.5	73.5	0.8	1.1	*
Vandalism	3,191	2,174	940	45	26	6	100.0	68.1	29.5	1.4	0.8	0.2
Weapons; carrying, possessing, etc.	2,631	1,116	1,459	26	25	5	100.0	42.4	55.5	1.0	1.0	0.2
Prostitution and commercialized vice	4	2	2	0	0	0	100.0	50.0	50.0	0.0	0.0	0.0
Sex offenses (except forcible rape and prostitution)	684	496	174	7	7	0	100.0	72.5	25.4	1.0	1.0	0.0
Drug abuse violations	6,510	4,442	1,925	78	53	12	100.0	68.2	29.6	1.2	0.8	0.2
Gambling	6	3	3	0	0	0	100.0	50.0	50.0	0.0	0.0	0.0
Offenses against the family and children	165	126	31	5	2	1	100.0	76.4	18.8	3.0	1.2	0.6
Driving under the influence	683	621	50	8	3	1	100.0	90.9	7.3	1.2	0.4	0.1
Liquor laws	2,107	1,903	139	35	21	9	100.0	90.3	6.6	1.7	1.0	0.4
Drunkenness[3]	6	5	1	0	0	0	100.0	83.3	16.7	0.0	0.0	0.0
Disorderly conduct	3,726	1,956	1,686	62	17	5	100.0	52.5	45.2	1.7	0.5	0.1
Vagrancy	1	1	0	0	0	0	100.0	100.0	0.0	0.0	0.0	0.0
All other offenses (except traffic)	13,745	9,052	4,384	183	101	25	100.0	65.9	31.9	1.3	0.7	0.2
Suspicion[4]	0	0	0	0	0	0	NA	NA	NA	NA	NA	NA
Curfew and loitering law violations	417	291	121	2	2	1	100.0	69.8	29.0	0.5	0.5	0.2

Table 55. Arrests, Metropolitan Counties, Distribution by Race, 2022—Continued

(Number, percent; 1,370 agencies; 2022 estimated population 68,043,758.)

Offense charged	Arrests 18 and over						Percent distribution[1]					
	Total	White	Black or African American	American Indian or Alaskan Native	Asian	Native Hawaiian or Other Pacific Islander	Total	White	Black or African American	American Indian or Alaskan Native	Asian	Native Hawaiian or Other Pacific Islander
Total	1,065,118	758,308	284,147	9,287	11,579	1,797	100.0	71.2	26.7	0.9	1.1	0.2
Violent crime[2]	56,836	37,430	17,993	442	842	129	100.0	65.9	31.7	0.8	1.5	0.2
Murder and nonnegligent manslaughter	1,723	940	753	12	17	1	100.0	54.6	43.7	0.7	1.0	*
Rape	2,746	2,117	574	13	42	0	100.0	77.1	20.9	0.5	1.5	0.0
Robbery	5,056	2,519	2,440	31	58	8	100.0	49.8	48.3	0.6	1.1	0.2
Aggravated assault	47,311	31,854	14,226	386	725	120	100.0	67.3	30.1	0.8	1.5	0.3
Property crime[2]	87,774	59,766	26,306	593	1,003	106	100.0	68.1	30.0	0.7	1.1	0.1
Burglary	15,110	11,578	3,310	90	112	20	100.0	76.6	21.9	0.6	0.7	0.1
Larceny-theft	62,364	40,322	20,744	435	801	62	100.0	64.7	33.3	0.7	1.3	*
Motor vehicle theft	9,311	7,095	2,055	61	78	22	100.0	76.2	22.1	0.7	0.8	0.2
Arson	989	771	197	7	12	2	100.0	78.0	19.9	0.7	1.2	0.2
Other assaults	124,825	88,460	33,483	1,009	1,591	282	100.0	70.9	26.8	0.8	1.3	0.2
Forgery and counterfeiting	5,122	3,320	1,664	20	111	7	100.0	64.8	32.5	0.4	2.2	0.1
Fraud	11,258	7,506	3,553	52	136	11	100.0	66.7	31.6	0.5	1.2	*
Embezzlement	1,304	749	526	12	14	3	100.0	57.4	40.3	0.9	1.1	0.2
Stolen property; buying, receiving, possessing	12,935	8,763	3,907	97	146	22	100.0	67.7	30.2	0.7	1.1	0.2
Vandalism	19,837	13,766	5,583	182	267	39	100.0	69.4	28.1	0.9	1.3	0.2
Weapons; carrying, possessing, etc.	24,802	12,566	11,875	95	219	47	100.0	50.7	47.9	0.4	0.9	0.2
Prostitution and commercialized vice	1,253	651	392	6	200	4	100.0	52.0	31.3	0.5	16.0	0.3
Sex offenses (except forcible rape and prostitution)	3,780	2,975	689	15	86	15	100.0	78.7	18.2	0.4	2.3	0.4
Drug abuse violations	143,774	101,687	39,730	844	1,352	161	100.0	70.7	27.6	0.6	0.9	0.1
Gambling	297	176	86	1	33	1	100.0	59.3	29.0	0.3	11.1	0.3
Offenses against the family and children	9,082	6,373	2,594	42	57	16	100.0	70.2	28.6	0.5	0.6	0.2
Driving under the influence	122,321	96,592	22,632	1,009	1,844	244	100.0	79.0	18.5	0.8	1.5	0.2
Liquor laws	7,460	6,052	1,158	101	132	17	100.0	81.1	15.5	1.4	1.8	0.2
Drunkenness[3]	1,829	1,650	131	19	21	8	100.0	90.2	7.2	1.0	1.1	0.4
Disorderly conduct	19,973	14,751	4,615	349	219	39	100.0	73.9	23.1	1.7	1.1	0.2
Vagrancy	2,132	1,396	703	4	16	13	100.0	65.5	33.0	0.2	0.8	0.6
All other offenses (except traffic)	408,524	293,679	106,527	4,395	3,290	633	100.0	71.9	26.1	1.1	0.8	0.2
Suspicion[4]	0	0	0	0	0	0	NA	NA	NA	NA	NA	NA
Curfew and loitering law violations	NA	NA	NA	NA	NA	NA	NA	NA	NA	NA	NA	NA

NA = Not available.
* = Less than one-tenth of one percent.
1 Because of rounding, the percentages may not sum to 100. 2 Violent crimes in this table are offenses of murder and nonnegligent manslaughter, rape, robbery, and aggravated assault. Property crimes are offenses of burglary, larceny-theft, motor vehicle theft, and arson. 3 Drunkenness figures were submitted by Summary reporting agencies only. As of 2021 drunkenness is no longer a separate offense in the National Incident-Based Reporting System (NIBRS), but it is included with All Other Offenses (except traffic) category. 4 Figures for suspicion include only data submitted by Summary reporting agencies because suspicion is not collected as a crime via NIBRS.

Table 55A. Arrests, Metropolitan Counties, Distribution by Ethnicity, 2022

(Number, percent; 1,370 agencies; 2022 estimated population 68,043,758.)

Offense charged	Total arrests			Percent distribution[1]			Arrests under 18		
	Total[2]	Hispanic or Latino	Not Hispanic or Latino	Total[2]	Hispanic or Latino	Not Hispanic or Latino	Total[2]	Hispanic or Latino	Not Hispanic or Latino
Total	984,444	172,126	812,318	100.0	17.5	82.5	58,412	10,305	48,107
Violent crime[3]	55,860	12,930	42,930	100.0	23.1	76.9	4,673	918	3,755
Murder and nonnegligent manslaughter	1,672	356	1,316	100.0	21.3	78.7	137	26	111
Rape	2,832	730	2,102	100.0	25.8	74.2	434	84	350
Robbery	5,572	1,198	4,374	100.0	21.5	78.5	1,016	202	814
Aggravated assault	45,784	10,646	35,138	100.0	23.3	76.7	3,086	606	2,480
Property crime[3]	84,225	13,147	71,078	100.0	15.6	84.4	7,212	1,340	5,872
Burglary	14,826	2,362	12,464	100.0	15.9	84.1	1,405	199	1,206
Larceny-theft	59,017	8,129	50,888	100.0	13.8	86.2	4,561	891	3,670
Motor vehicle theft	9,354	2,458	6,896	100.0	26.3	73.7	1,086	227	859
Arson	1,028	198	830	100.0	19.3	80.7	160	23	137
Other assaults	125,366	20,627	104,739	100.0	16.5	83.5	16,217	2,373	13,844
Forgery and counterfeiting	4,874	1,215	3,659	100.0	24.9	75.1	83	25	58
Fraud	10,193	1,596	8,597	100.0	15.7	84.3	291	57	234
Embezzlement	1,184	125	1,059	100.0	10.6	89.4	44	4	40
Stolen property; buying, receiving, possessing	12,496	2,538	9,958	100.0	20.3	79.7	991	131	860
Vandalism	20,385	3,458	16,927	100.0	17.0	83.0	2,737	413	2,324
Weapons; carrying, possessing, etc.	23,296	4,920	18,376	100.0	21.1	78.9	2,310	501	1,809
Prostitution and commercialized vice	1,184	227	957	100.0	19.2	80.8	3	0	3
Sex offenses (except forcible rape and prostitution)	4,039	1,172	2,867	100.0	29.0	71.0	577	97	480
Drug abuse violations	134,467	24,128	110,339	100.0	17.9	82.1	5,776	1,242	4,534
Gambling	280	102	178	100.0	36.4	63.6	6	1	5
Offenses against the family and children	7,943	787	7,156	100.0	9.9	90.1	141	22	119
Driving under the influence	105,577	25,038	80,539	100.0	23.7	76.3	554	146	408
Liquor laws	7,578	1,518	6,060	100.0	20.0	80.0	1,667	307	1,360
Drunkenness[4]	1,835	972	863	100.0	53.0	47.0	6	5	1
Disorderly conduct	19,884	2,737	17,147	100.0	13.8	86.2	3,206	401	2,805
Vagrancy	1,985	203	1,782	100.0	10.2	89.8	1	0	1
All other offenses (except traffic)	361,418	54,636	306,782	100.0	15.1	84.9	11,542	2,272	9,270
Suspicion[5]	0	0	0	NA	NA	NA	0	0	0
Curfew and loitering law violations	375	50	325	100.0	13.3	86.7	375	50	325

Table 55A. Arrests, Metropolitan Counties, Distribution by Ethnicity, 2022—Continued

(Number, percent; 1,370 agencies; 2022 estimated population 68,043,758.)

Offense charged	Percent distribution[1]				Arrests 18 and over			Percent distribution[1]	
	Total[2]	Hispanic or Latino	Not Hispanic or Latino	Total[2]	Hispanic or Latino	Not Hispanic or Latino	Total[2]	Hispanic or Latino	Not Hispanic or Latino
Total	100.0	17.6	82.4	926,032	161,821	764,211	100.0	17.5	82.5
Violent crime[3]	100.0	19.6	80.4	51,187	12,012	39,175	100.0	23.5	76.5
Murder and nonnegligent manslaughter	100.0	19.0	81.0	1,535	330	1,205	100.0	21.5	78.5
Rape	100.0	19.4	80.6	2,398	646	1,752	100.0	26.9	73.1
Robbery	100.0	19.9	80.1	4,556	996	3,560	100.0	21.9	78.1
Aggravated assault	100.0	19.6	80.4	42,698	10,040	32,658	100.0	23.5	76.5
Property crime[3]	100.0	18.6	81.4	77,013	11,807	65,206	100.0	15.3	84.7
Burglary	100.0	14.2	85.8	13,421	2,163	11,258	100.0	16.1	83.9
Larceny-theft	100.0	19.5	80.5	54,456	7,238	47,218	100.0	13.3	86.7
Motor vehicle theft	100.0	20.9	79.1	8,268	2,231	6,037	100.0	27.0	73.0
Arson	100.0	14.4	85.6	868	175	693	100.0	20.2	79.8
Other assaults	100.0	14.6	85.4	109,149	18,254	90,895	100.0	16.7	83.3
Forgery and counterfeiting	100.0	30.1	69.9	4,791	1,190	3,601	100.0	24.8	75.2
Fraud	100.0	19.6	80.4	9,902	1,539	8,363	100.0	15.5	84.5
Embezzlement	100.0	9.1	90.9	1,140	121	1,019	100.0	10.6	89.4
Stolen property; buying, receiving, possessing	100.0	13.2	86.8	11,505	2,407	9,098	100.0	20.9	79.1
Vandalism	100.0	15.1	84.9	17,648	3,045	14,603	100.0	17.3	82.7
Weapons; carrying, possessing, etc.	100.0	21.7	78.3	20,986	4,419	16,567	100.0	21.1	78.9
Prostitution and commercialized vice	100.0	0.0	100.0	1,181	227	954	100.0	19.2	80.8
Sex offenses (except forcible rape and prostitution)	100.0	16.8	83.2	3,462	1,075	2,387	100.0	31.1	68.9
Drug abuse violations	100.0	21.5	78.5	128,691	22,886	105,805	100.0	17.8	82.2
Gambling	100.0	16.7	83.3	274	101	173	100.0	36.9	63.1
Offenses against the family and children	100.0	15.6	84.4	7,802	765	7,037	100.0	9.8	90.2
Driving under the influence	100.0	26.4	73.6	105,023	24,892	80,131	100.0	23.7	76.3
Liquor laws	100.0	18.4	81.6	5,911	1,211	4,700	100.0	20.5	79.5
Drunkenness[4]	100.0	83.3	16.7	1,829	967	862	100.0	52.9	47.1
Disorderly conduct	100.0	12.5	87.5	16,678	2,336	14,342	100.0	14.0	86.0
Vagrancy	100.0	0.0	100.0	1,984	203	1,781	100.0	10.2	89.8
All other offenses (except traffic)	100.0	19.7	80.3	349,876	52,364	297,512	100.0	15.0	85.0
Suspicion[5]	NA	NA	NA	0	0	0	NA	NA	NA
Curfew and loitering law violations	100.0	13.3	86.7	NA	NA	NA	NA	NA	NA

NA = Not available.
1 Because of rounding, the percentages may not sum to 100.   2 The ethnicity totals are representative of those agencies that provided ethnicity breakdowns. Not all agencies provide ethnicity data; therefore, the race and ethnicity totals will not equal.
3 Violent crimes are offenses of murder and nonnegligent manslaughter, rape, robbery, and aggravated assault. Property crimes are offenses of burglary, larceny-theft, motor vehicle theft, and arson.   4 Drunkenness figures were submitted by Summary reporting agencies only. As of 2021 drunkenness is no longer a separate offense in the National Incident-Based Reporting System (NIBRS), but it is included with All Other Offenses (except traffic) category.   5 Figures for suspicion include only data submitted by Summary reporting agencies because suspicion is not collected as a crime via NIBRS.

Table 56. Arrest Trends, Nonmetropolitan Counties, 2021–2022

(Number, percent change; 1,538 agencies; 2022 estimated population 19,977,736; 2021 estimated population 20,003,559.)

	Number of persons arrested								
	Total, all ages			Under 18 years of age			18 years of age and over		
Offense charged	2021	2022	Percent change	2021	2022	Percent change	2021	2022	Percent change
Total[1]	479,322	471,029	-1.7	16,504	17,634	+6.8	462,818	453,395	-2.0
Violent crime[2]	15,308	14,954	-2.3	874	1,011	+15.7	14,434	13,943	-3.4
Murder and nonnegligent manslaughter	613	520	-15.2	30	33	+10.0	583	487	-16.5
Rape	1,437	1,385	-3.6	253	232	(8.3)	1,184	1,153	-2.6
Robbery	491	537	+9.4	38	50	+31.6	453	487	+7.5
Aggravated assault	12,767	12,512	-2.0	553	696	+25.9	12,214	11,816	-3.3
Property crime[2]	21,773	21,728	-0.2	1,480	1,510	+2.0	20,293	20,218	-0.4
Burglary	6,315	5,949	-5.8	445	407	-8.5	5,870	5,542	-5.6
Larceny-theft	11,507	12,140	+5.5	643	733	+14.0	10,864	11,407	+5.0
Motor vehicle theft	3,511	3,243	-7.6	348	319	-8.3	3,163	2,924	-7.6
Arson	440	396	-10.0	44	51	+15.9	396	345	-12.9
Other assaults	43,967	44,058	+0.2	3,512	4,071	+15.9	40,455	39,987	-1.2
Forgery and counterfeiting	967	973	+0.6	10	11	+10.0	957	962	+0.5
Fraud	3,503	3,376	-3.6	74	60	-18.9	3,429	3,316	-3.3
Embezzlement	215	211	-1.9	2	4	+100.0	213	207	-2.8
Stolen property; buying, receiving, possessing	3,232	2,905	-10.1	156	150	-3.8	3,076	2,755	-10.4
Vandalism	6,350	6,114	-3.7	854	805	-5.7	5,496	5,309	-3.4
Weapons; carrying, possessing, etc.	7,057	6,814	-3.4	233	330	+41.6	6,824	6,484	-5.0
Prostitution and commercialized vice	69	84	+21.7	5	2	(60.0)	64	82	+28.1
Sex offenses (except forcible rape and prostitution)	1,306	1,275	-2.4	225	248	+10.2	1,081	1,027	-5.0
Drug abuse violations	80,790	70,544	-12.7	1,931	1,925	-0.3	78,859	68,619	-13.0
Gambling	48	33	-31.3	0	0	NA	48	33	-31.3
Offenses against the family and children	4,631	4,603	-0.6	103	81	-21.4	4,528	4,522	-0.1
Driving under the influence	81,435	81,120	-0.4	592	607	+2.5	80,843	80,513	-0.4
Liquor laws	7,576	7,454	-1.6	1,382	1,358	-1.7	6,194	6,096	-1.6
Drunkenness[3]	0	0	NA	0	0	NA	0	0	NA
Disorderly conduct	11,501	11,283	-1.9	1,255	1,241	-1.1	10,246	10,042	-2.0
Vagrancy	701	513	-26.8	0	0	NA	701	513	-26.8
All other offenses (except traffic)	188,681	192,814	+2.2	3,604	4,047	+12.3	185,077	188,767	+2.0
Suspicion[4]	0	0	NA	0	0	NA	0	0	NA
Curfew and loitering law violations	212	173	-18.4	212	173	-18.4	NA	NA	NA

NA = Not available.

1 Does not include suspicion.   2 Violent crimes in this table are offenses of murder and nonnegligent manslaughter, rape, robbery, and aggravated assault. Property crimes are offenses of burglary, larceny-theft, motor vehicle theft, and arson.
3 Drunkenness figures were submitted by Summary reporting agencies only. As of 2021 drunkenness is no longer a separate offense in the National Incident-Based Reporting System (NIBRS), but it is included with All Other Offenses (except traffic) category.   4 Figures for suspicion include only data submitted by Summary reporting agencies because suspicion is not collected as a crime via NIBRS.

Table 57. Arrest Trends, Nonmetropolitan Counties, by Age and Sex, 2021–2022

(Number, percent; 1,538 agencies; 2022 estimated population 19,977,736; 2021 estimated population 20,003,559.)

Offense charged	Male Total			Male Under 18			Female Total			Female Under 18		
	2021	2022	Percent change	2021	2022	Percent change	2021	2022	Percent change	2021	2022	Percent change
Total[1]	351,111	344,435	-1.9	11,580	12,399	+7.1	128,211	126,594	-1.3	4,924	5,235	+6.3
Violent crime[2]	12,674	12,398	-2.2	730	813	+11.4	2,634	2,556	-3.0	144	198	+37.5
Murder and nonnegligent manslaughter	526	441	-16.2	28	27	-3.6	87	79	-9.2	2	6	+200.0
Rape	1,384	1,326	-4.2	244	221	-9.4	53	59	+11.3	9	11	+22.2
Robbery	422	461	+9.2	31	44	+41.9	69	76	+10.1	7	6	-14.3
Aggravated assault	10,342	10,170	-1.7	427	521	+22.0	2,425	2,342	-3.4	126	175	38.9
Property crime[2]	15,790	15,600	-1.2	1,164	1,158	-0.5	5,983	6,128	+2.4	316	352	+11.4
Burglary	4,999	4,718	-5.6	382	348	-8.9	1,316	1,231	-6.5	63	59	-6.3
Larceny-theft	7,754	8,073	+4.1	479	518	+8.1	3,753	4,067	+8.4	164	215	+31.1
Motor vehicle theft	2,700	2,496	-7.6	267	248	-7.1	811	747	-7.9	81	71	-12.3
Arson	337	313	-7.1	36	44	+22.2	103	83	-19.4	8	7	-12.5
Other assaults	31,896	31,589	-1.0	2,233	2,615	+17.1	12,071	12,469	+3.3	1,279	1,456	+13.8
Forgery and counterfeiting	646	623	-3.6	5	10	+100.0	321	350	+9.0	5	1	-80.0
Fraud	2,272	2,170	-4.5	41	43	+4.9	1,231	1,206	-2.0	33	17	-48.5
Embezzlement	101	101	+0.0	2	3	+50.0	114	110	-3.5	0	1	
Stolen property; buying, receiving, possessing	2,545	2,304	-9.5	128	128	+0.0	687	601	-12.5	28	22	-21.4
Vandalism	4,980	4,861	-2.4	690	673	-2.5	1,370	1,253	-8.5	164	132	-19.5
Weapons; carrying, possessing, etc.	6,263	6,039	-3.6	207	280	+35.3	794	775	-2.4	26	50	+92.3
Prostitution and commercialized vice	54	60	+11.1	2	1	-50.0	15	24	+60.0	3	1	-66.7
Sex offenses (except forcible rape and prostitution)	1,255	1,206	-3.9	213	231	+8.5	51	69	+35.3	12	17	+41.7
Drug abuse violations	56,570	49,205	-13.0	1,347	1,364	+1.3	24,220	21,339	-11.9	584	561	-3.9
Gambling	39	23	-41.0	0	0	NA	9	10	+11.1	0	0	NA
Offenses against the family and children	3,383	3,314	-2.0	49	48	-2.0	1,248	1,289	+3.3	54	33	-38.9
Driving under the influence	61,226	60,905	-0.5	449	467	4.0	20,209	20,215	*	143	140	-2.1
Liquor laws	5,116	5,134	+0.4	801	858	+7.1	2,460	2,320	-5.7	581	500	-13.9
Drunkenness[3]	0	0	NA	0	0	NA	0	0	NA	0	0	NA
Disorderly conduct	8,041	7,909	-1.6	825	813	-1.5	3,460	3,374	-2.5	430	428	-0.5
Vagrancy	506	427	-15.6	0	0	NA	195	86	-55.9	0	0	NA
All other offenses (except traffic)	137,644	140,470	+2.1	2,584	2,797	+8.2	51,037	52,344	+2.6	1,020	1,250	+22.5
Suspicion[4]	0	0	NA	0	0	NA	0	0	NA	0	0	NA
Curfew and loitering law violations	110	97	-11.8	110	97	-11.8	102	76	-25.5	102	76	-25.5

NA = Not available.
* = Less than one-tenth of one percent.
1 Does not include suspicion.   2 Violent crimes in this table are offenses of murder and nonnegligent manslaughter, rape, robbery, and aggravated assault. Property crimes are offenses of burglary, larceny-theft, motor vehicle theft, and arson.
3 Drunkenness figures were submitted by Summary reporting agencies only. As of 2021 drunkenness is no longer a separate offense in the National Incident-Based Reporting System (NIBRS), but it is included with All Other Offenses (except traffic) category.   4 Figures for suspicion include only data submitted by Summary reporting agencies because suspicion is not collected as a crime via NIBRS.

Table 58. Arrests, Nonmetropolitan Counties, Distribution by Age, 2022

(Number, percent; 1,809 agencies; 2022 estimated population 21,928,032.)

Offense charged	Total, all ages	Under 15 years	Under 18 years	Age 18 years and over	Under 10 years	10–12 years	13–14 years	15 years	16 years	17 years	18 years	19 years	20 years
Total	516,413	6,055	18,967	497,446	113	1,451	4,491	3,491	4,151	5,270	9,181	10,697	11,242
Total, percent distribution[1]	100.0	1.2	3.7	96.3	*	0.3	0.9	0.7	0.8	1.0	1.8	2.1	2.2
Violent crime[2]	17,123	427	1,149	15,974	12	111	304	217	250	255	347	366	378
Violent crime, percent distribution[1]	100.0	2.5	6.7	93.3	0.1	0.6	1.8	1.3	1.5	1.5	2.0	2.1	2.2
Murder and nonnegligent manslaughter	577	8	38	539	0	0	8	6	12	12	20	13	13
Rape	1,534	107	260	1,274	2	32	73	55	46	52	76	56	62
Robbery	649	12	57	592	0	2	10	7	20	18	28	22	28
Aggravated assault	14,363	300	794	13,569	10	77	213	149	172	173	223	275	275
Property crime[2]	24,719	604	1,670	23,049	5	161	438	337	340	389	562	519	450
Property crime, percent distribution[1]	100.0	2.4	6.8	93.2	*	0.7	1.8	1.4	1.4	1.6	2.3	2.1	1.8
Burglary	6,610	187	454	6,156	2	67	118	84	86	97	127	132	129
Larceny-theft	14,166	283	817	13,349	2	78	203	150	185	199	335	293	246
Motor vehicle theft	3,471	111	346	3,125	0	8	103	89	61	85	88	83	66
Arson	472	23	53	419	1	8	14	14	8	8	12	11	9
Other assaults	48,051	1,838	4,311	43,740	37	472	1,329	887	812	774	792	788	830
Forgery and counterfeiting	1,169	2	12	1,157	0	1	1	3	2	5	21	47	46
Fraud	3,661	16	62	3,599	0	3	13	13	10	23	50	91	124
Embezzlement	230	0	4	226	0	0	0	1	2	1	4	4	3
Stolen property; buying, receiving, possessing	3,332	33	165	3,167	1	6	26	34	48	50	80	73	81
Vandalism	7,130	412	942	6,188	8	128	276	173	190	167	195	205	162
Weapons; carrying, possessing, etc.	7,888	131	358	7,530	3	25	103	54	80	93	177	179	196
Prostitution and commercialized vice	95	0	3	92	0	0	0	0	1	2	1	0	3
Sex offenses (except forcible rape and prostitution)	1,470	127	276	1,194	3	24	100	47	56	46	65	46	37
Drug abuse violations	78,335	373	2,075	76,260	2	49	322	326	531	845	1,831	2,147	2,207
Gambling	39	0	1	38	0	0	0	0	0	1	2	2	2
Offenses against the family and children	4,739	25	81	4,658	1	2	22	21	19	16	21	31	35
Driving under the influence	87,555	4	645	86,910	0	0	4	26	161	454	1,337	1,635	1,838
Liquor laws	7,867	148	1,416	6,451	2	23	123	215	399	654	990	1,029	819
Drunkenness[3]	245	3	14	231	0	0	3	2	2	7	1	3	1
Disorderly conduct	12,286	541	1,299	10,987	8	146	387	280	245	233	223	204	186
Vagrancy	534	0	0	534	0	0	0	0	0	0	2	3	2
All other offenses (except traffic)	209,770	1,305	4,309	205,461	28	295	982	794	983	1,227	2,480	3,325	3,842
Suspicion[4]	0	0	0	0	0	0	0	0	0	0	0	0	0
Curfew and loitering law violations	175	66	175	NA	3	5	58	61	20	28	NA	NA	NA

Table 58. Arrests, Nonmetropolitan Counties, Distribution by Age, 2022—Continued

(Number, percent; 1,809 agencies; 2022 estimated population 21,928,032.)

Offense charged	21 years	22 years	23 years	24 years	25–29 years	30–34 years	35–39 years	40–44 years	45–49 years	50–54 years	55–59 years	60–64 years	65 years and over
Total	12,258	12,497	13,003	13,169	73,143	82,099	76,438	62,551	41,149	31,773	22,727	14,472	11,047
Total, percent distribution[1]	2.4	2.4	2.5	2.6	14.2	15.9	14.8	12.1	8.0	6.2	4.4	2.8	2.1
Violent crime[2]	419	382	404	410	2,255	2,637	2,342	1,963	1,303	986	782	505	495
Violent crime, percent distribution[1]	2.4	2.2	2.4	2.4	13.2	15.4	13.7	11.5	7.6	5.8	4.6	2.9	2.9
Murder and nonnegligent manslaughter	21	18	19	13	81	80	77	48	33	34	30	19	20
Rape	50	48	34	25	135	172	174	132	96	67	45	41	61
Robbery	24	15	15	24	96	103	79	68	28	27	20	8	7
Aggravated assault	324	301	336	348	1,943	2,282	2,012	1,715	1,146	858	687	437	407
Property crime[2]	467	530	507	529	3,419	4,113	3,886	2,940	1,862	1,406	954	535	370
Property crime, percent distribution[1]	1.9	2.1	2.1	2.1	13.8	16.6	15.7	11.9	7.5	5.7	3.9	2.2	1.5
Burglary	109	135	126	140	969	1,156	1,064	791	512	356	217	124	69
Larceny-theft	260	308	278	297	1,894	2,306	2,209	1,713	1,097	866	636	339	272
Motor vehicle theft	86	83	92	83	509	588	537	384	225	149	80	58	14
Arson	12	4	11	9	47	63	76	52	28	35	21	14	15
Other assaults	918	947	957	1,079	6,006	7,079	6,770	5,587	3,738	3,173	2,275	1,445	1,356
Forgery and counterfeiting	26	23	21	21	164	190	219	138	96	57	40	29	19
Fraud	82	85	72	92	489	631	582	485	296	240	149	74	57
Embezzlement	6	4	4	5	29	46	37	23	26	12	11	7	5
Stolen property; buying, receiving, possessing	76	64	71	68	517	578	537	416	252	164	119	43	28
Vandalism	198	162	172	156	918	1,091	909	745	432	318	232	159	134
Weapons; carrying, possessing, etc.	244	262	261	238	1,174	1,177	1,030	850	595	457	295	222	173
Prostitution and commercialized vice	2	0	3	3	20	15	12	9	6	2	8	1	7
Sex offenses (except forcible rape and prostitution)	30	28	31	24	111	135	151	109	86	90	86	53	112
Drug abuse violations	2,291	2,241	2,268	2,271	11,619	12,379	11,536	9,349	6,018	4,458	2,991	1,790	864
Gambling	1	1	0	1	3	7	1	4	3	6	3	1	1
Offenses against the family and children	40	67	78	63	593	944	985	766	436	279	166	92	62
Driving under the influence	2,623	2,756	2,793	2,715	13,789	12,878	11,058	9,093	6,780	5,884	4,925	3,700	3,106
Liquor laws	215	136	129	123	599	556	483	398	292	247	191	138	106
Drunkenness[3]	3	7	2	5	20	36	45	23	25	19	6	23	12
Disorderly conduct	218	255	250	239	1,421	1,686	1,642	1,386	982	805	653	426	411
Vagrancy	8	8	14	17	57	78	105	96	46	41	34	13	10
All other offenses (except traffic)	4,391	4,539	4,966	5,110	29,940	35,843	34,108	28,171	17,875	13,129	8,807	5,216	3,719
Suspicion[4]	0	0	0	0	0	0	0	0	0	0	0	0	0
Curfew and loitering law violations	NA	NA	NA	NA	NA	NA	NA	NA	NA	NA	NA	NA	NA

NA = Not available.
* = Less than one-tenth of one percent.
1 Because of rounding, the percentages may not add to 100.0.   2 Violent crimes are offenses of murder and nonnegligent manslaughter, rape, robbery, and aggravated assault. Property crimes are offenses of burglary, larceny-theft, motor vehicle theft, and arson.   3 Drunkenness figures were submitted by Summary reporting agencies only. As of 2021 drunkenness is no longer a separate offense in National Incident Based Reporting System (NIBRS), but it is included with All Other Offenses (except traffic) category.   4 Figures for suspicion include only data submitted by Summary reporting agencies because suspicion is not collected as a crime via NIBRS.

Table 59. Arrests, Nonmetropolitan Counties, Persons Under 15, 18, 21, and 25 Years of Age, 2022

(Number, percent; 1,809 agencies; 2022 estimated population 21,928,032.)

Offense charged	Total, all ages	Number of persons arrested				Percent of total all ages			
		Under 15	Under 18	Under 21	Under 25	Under 15	Under 18	Under 21	Under 25
Total	516,413	6,055	18,967	50,087	101,014	1.2	3.7	9.7	19.6
Violent crime[1]	17,123	427	1,149	2,240	3,855	2.5	6.7	13.1	22.5
Murder and nonnegligent manslaughter	577	8	38	84	155	1.4	6.6	14.6	26.9
Rape	1,534	107	260	454	611	7.0	16.9	29.6	39.8
Robbery	649	12	57	135	213	1.8	8.8	20.8	32.8
Aggravated assault	14,363	300	794	1,567	2,876	2.1	5.5	10.9	20.0
Property crime[1]	24,719	604	1,670	3,201	5,234	2.4	6.8	12.9	21.2
Burglary	6,610	187	454	842	1,352	2.8	6.9	12.7	20.5
Larceny-theft	14,166	283	817	1,691	2,834	2.0	5.8	11.9	20.0
Motor vehicle theft	3,471	111	346	583	927	3.2	10.0	16.8	26.7
Arson	472	23	53	85	121	4.9	11.2	18.0	25.6
Other assaults	48,051	1,838	4,311	6,721	10,622	3.8	9.0	14.0	22.1
Forgery and counterfeiting	1,169	2	12	126	217	0.2	1.0	10.8	18.6
Fraud	3,661	16	62	327	658	0.4	1.7	8.9	18.0
Embezzlement	230	0	4	15	34	0.0	1.7	6.5	14.8
Stolen property; buying, receiving, possessing	3,332	33	165	399	678	1.0	5.0	12.0	20.3
Vandalism	7,130	412	942	1,504	2,192	5.8	13.2	21.1	30.7
Weapons; carrying, possessing, etc.	7,888	131	358	910	1,915	1.7	4.5	11.5	24.3
Prostitution and commercialized vice	95	0	3	7	15	0.0	3.2	7.4	15.8
Sex offenses (except forcible rape and prostitution)	1,470	127	276	424	537	8.6	18.8	28.8	36.5
Drug abuse violations	78,335	373	2,075	8,260	17,331	0.5	2.6	10.5	22.1
Gambling	39	0	1	7	10	0.0	2.6	17.9	25.6
Offenses against the family and children	4,739	25	81	168	416	0.5	1.7	3.5	8.8
Driving under the influence	87,555	4	645	5,455	16,342	*	0.7	6.2	18.7
Liquor laws	7,867	148	1,416	4,254	4,857	1.9	18.0	54.1	61.7
Drunkenness[2]	245	3	14	19	36	1.2	5.7	7.8	14.7
Disorderly conduct	12,286	541	1,299	1,912	2,874	4.4	10.6	15.6	23.4
Vagrancy	534	0	0	7	54	0.0	0.0	1.3	10.1
All other offenses (except traffic)	209,770	1,305	4,309	13,956	32,962	0.6	2.1	6.7	15.7
Suspicion[3]	0	0	0	0	0	NA	NA	NA	NA
Curfew and loitering law violations	175	66	175	175	175	37.7	100.0	100.0	100.0

NA = Not available.
* = Less than one-tenth of one percent.
1 Violent crimes in this table are offenses of murder and nonnegligent manslaughter, rape, robbery, and aggravated assault. Property crimes are offenses of burglary, larceny-theft, motor vehicle theft, and arson.   2 Drunkenness figures were submitted by Summary reporting agencies only. As of 2021 drunkenness is no longer a separate offense in the National Incident-Based Reporting System (NIBRS), but it is included with All Other Offenses (except traffic) category.   3 Figures for suspicion include only data submitted by Summary reporting agencies because suspicion is not collected as a crime via NIBRS.

Table 60. Arrests, Nonmetropolitan Counties, Distribution by Sex, 2022

(Number, percent; 1,809 agencies; 2022 estimated population 21,928,032.)

Offense charged	Number of persons arrested			Percent male	Percent female	Percent distribution[1]		
	Total	Male	Female			Total	Male	Female
Total	516,413	377,961	138,452	73.2	26.8	100.0	100.0	100.0
Violent crime[2]	17,123	14,063	3,060	82.1	17.9	3.3	3.7	2.2
Murder and nonnegligent manslaughter	577	492	85	85.3	14.7	0.1	0.1	0.1
Rape	1,534	1,467	67	95.6	4.4	0.3	0.4	*
Robbery	649	552	97	85.1	14.9	0.1	0.1	0.1
Aggravated assault	14,363	11,552	2,811	80.4	19.6	2.8	3.1	2.0
Property crime[2]	24,719	17,618	7,101	71.3	28.7	4.8	4.7	5.1
Burglary	6,610	5,234	1,376	79.2	20.8	1.3	1.4	1.0
Larceny-theft	14,166	9,349	4,817	66.0	34.0	2.7	2.5	3.5
Motor vehicle theft	3,471	2,668	803	76.9	23.1	0.7	0.7	0.6
Arson	472	367	105	77.8	22.2	0.1	0.1	0.1
Other assaults	48,051	34,442	13,609	71.7	28.3	9.3	9.1	9.8
Forgery and counterfeiting	1,169	752	417	64.3	35.7	0.2	0.2	0.3
Fraud	3,661	2,375	1,286	64.9	35.1	0.7	0.6	0.9
Embezzlement	230	112	118	48.7	51.3	*	*	0.1
Stolen property; buying, receiving, possessing	3,332	2,633	699	79.0	21.0	0.6	0.7	0.5
Vandalism	7,130	5,675	1,455	79.6	20.4	1.4	1.5	1.1
Weapons; carrying, possessing, etc.	7,888	6,970	918	88.4	11.6	1.5	1.8	0.7
Prostitution and commercialized vice	95	67	28	70.5	29.5	*	*	*
Sex offenses (except forcible rape and prostitution)	1,470	1,390	80	94.6	5.4	0.3	0.4	0.1
Drug abuse violations	78,335	54,661	23,674	69.8	30.2	15.2	14.5	17.1
Gambling	39	26	13	66.7	33.3	*	*	*
Offenses against the family and children	4,739	3,402	1,337	71.8	28.2	0.9	0.9	1.0
Driving under the influence	87,555	65,693	21,862	75.0	25.0	17.0	17.4	15.8
Liquor laws	7,867	5,430	2,437	69.0	31.0	1.5	1.4	1.8
Drunkenness[3]	245	177	68	72.2	27.8	*	*	*
Disorderly conduct	12,286	8,641	3,645	70.3	29.7	2.4	2.3	2.6
Vagrancy	534	441	93	82.6	17.4	0.1	0.1	0.1
All other offenses (except traffic)	209,770	153,294	56,476	73.1	26.9	40.6	40.6	40.8
Suspicion[4]	0	0	0	NA	NA	NA	NA	NA
Curfew and loitering law violations	175	99	76	56.6	43.4	*	*	0.1

NA = Not available.

* = Less than one-tenth of 1 percent.

1 Because of rounding, the percentages may not sum to 100.   2 Violent crimes in this table are offenses of murder and nonnegligent manslaughter, rape, robbery, and aggravated assault. Property crimes are offenses of burglary, larceny-theft, motor vehicle theft, and arson.   3 Drunkenness figures were submitted by Summary reporting agencies only. As of 2021 drunkenness is no longer a separate offense in the National Incident-Based Reporting System (NIBRS), but it is included with All Other Offenses (except traffic) category.   4 Figures for suspicion include only data submitted by Summary reporting agencies because suspicion is not collected as a crime via NIBRS.

Table 61A. Arrests, Nonmetropolitan Counties, Distribution by Ethnicity, 2022

(Number, percent; 1,809 agencies; 2022 estimated population 21,928,032.)

Offense charged	Total arrests			Percent distribution[1]			Arrests under 18		
	Total[2]	Hispanic or Latino	Not Hispanic or Latino	Total[2]	Hispanic or Latino	Not Hispanic or Latino	Total[2]	Hispanic or Latino	Not Hispanic or Latino
Total	404,859	36,779	368,080	100.0	9.1	90.9	14,431	1,574	12,857
Violent crime[3]	13,632	1,225	12,407	100.0	9.0	91.0	890	84	806
Murder and nonnegligent manslaughter	472	37	435	100.0	7.8	92.2	31	6	25
Rape	1,097	110	987	100.0	10.0	90.0	172	11	161
Robbery	559	45	514	100.0	8.1	91.9	45	3	42
Aggravated assault	11,504	1,033	10,471	100.0	9.0	91.0	642	64	578
Property crime[3]	20,543	1,261	19,282	100.0	6.1	93.9	1,284	134	1,150
Burglary	5,474	334	5,140	100.0	6.1	93.9	356	40	316
Larceny-theft	11,835	626	11,209	100.0	5.3	94.7	626	50	576
Motor vehicle theft	2,851	275	2,576	100.0	9.6	90.4	260	42	218
Arson	383	26	357	100.0	6.8	93.2	42	2	40
Other assaults	38,069	2,794	35,275	100.0	7.3	92.7	3,318	246	3,072
Forgery and counterfeiting	943	115	828	100.0	12.2	87.8	8	1	7
Fraud	2,856	258	2,598	100.0	9.0	91.0	54	8	46
Embezzlement	163	11	152	100.0	6.7	93.3	3	0	3
Stolen property; buying, receiving, possessing	2,758	219	2,539	100.0	7.9	92.1	125	14	111
Vandalism	5,789	436	5,353	100.0	7.5	92.5	690	58	632
Weapons; carrying, possessing, etc.	5,996	537	5,459	100.0	9.0	91.0	307	33	274
Prostitution and commercialized vice	61	11	50	100.0	18.0	82.0	1	1	0
Sex offenses (except forcible rape and prostitution)	1,133	108	1,025	100.0	9.5	90.5	203	18	185
Drug abuse violations	62,476	5,297	57,179	100.0	8.5	91.5	1,619	236	1,383
Gambling	30	3	27	100.0	10.0	90.0	1	0	1
Offenses against the family and children	4,162	292	3,870	100.0	7.0	93.0	75	11	64
Driving under the influence	57,285	9,081	48,204	100.0	15.9	84.1	435	90	345
Liquor laws	5,666	657	5,009	100.0	11.6	88.4	1,031	109	922
Drunkenness[4]	245	33	212	100.0	13.5	86.5	14	5	9
Disorderly conduct	9,857	685	9,172	100.0	6.9	93.1	1,013	75	938
Vagrancy	511	10	501	100.0	2.0	98.0	0	0	0
All other offenses (except traffic)	172,539	13,738	158,801	100.0	8.0	92.0	3,215	443	2,772
Suspicion[5]	0	0	0	NA	NA	NA	0	0	0
Curfew and loitering law violations	145	8	137	100.0	5.5	94.5	145	8	137

Table 61A. Arrests, Nonmetropolitan Counties, Distribution by Ethnicity, 2022—Continued

(Number, percent; 1,809 agencies; 2022 estimated population 21,928,032.)

Offense charged	Percent distribution[1]				Arrests 18 and over			Percent distribution[1]	
	Total[2]	Hispanic or Latino	Not Hispanic or Latino	Total[2]	Hispanic or Latino	Not Hispanic or Latino	Total[2]	Hispanic or Latino	Not Hispanic or Latino
Total	100.0	10.9	89.1	390,428	35,205	355,223	100.0	9.0	91.0
Violent crime[3]	100.0	9.4	90.6	12,742	1,141	11,601	100.0	9.0	91.0
Murder and nonnegligent manslaughter	100.0	19.4	80.6	441	31	410	100.0	7.0	93.0
Rape	100.0	6.4	93.6	925	99	826	100.0	10.7	89.3
Robbery	100.0	6.7	93.3	514	42	472	100.0	8.2	91.8
Aggravated assault	100.0	10.0	90.0	10,862	969	9,893	100.0	8.9	91.1
Property crime[3]	100.0	10.4	89.6	19,259	1,127	18,132	100.0	5.9	94.1
Burglary	100.0	11.2	88.8	5,118	294	4,824	100.0	5.7	94.3
Larceny-theft	100.0	8.0	92.0	11,209	576	10,633	100.0	5.1	94.9
Motor vehicle theft	100.0	16.2	83.8	2,591	233	2,358	100.0	9.0	91.0
Arson	100.0	4.8	95.2	341	24	317	100.0	7.0	93.0
Other assaults	100.0	7.4	92.6	34,751	2,548	32,203	100.0	7.3	92.7
Forgery and counterfeiting	100.0	12.5	87.5	935	114	821	100.0	12.2	87.8
Fraud	100.0	14.8	85.2	2,802	250	2,552	100.0	8.9	91.1
Embezzlement	100.0	0.0	100.0	160	11	149	100.0	6.9	93.1
Stolen property; buying, receiving, possessing	100.0	11.2	88.8	2,633	205	2,428	100.0	7.8	92.2
Vandalism	100.0	8.4	91.6	5,099	378	4,721	100.0	7.4	92.6
Weapons; carrying, possessing, etc.	100.0	10.7	89.3	5,689	504	5,185	100.0	8.9	91.1
Prostitution and commercialized vice	100.0	100.0	0.0	60	10	50	100.0	16.7	83.3
Sex offenses (except forcible rape and prostitution)	100.0	8.9	91.1	930	90	840	100.0	9.7	90.3
Drug abuse violations	100.0	14.6	85.4	60,857	5,061	55,796	100.0	8.3	91.7
Gambling	100.0	0.0	100.0	29	3	26	100.0	10.3	89.7
Offenses against the family and children	100.0	14.7	85.3	4,087	281	3,806	100.0	6.9	93.1
Driving under the influence	100.0	20.7	79.3	56,850	8,991	47,859	100.0	15.8	84.2
Liquor laws	100.0	10.6	89.4	4,635	548	4,087	100.0	11.8	88.2
Drunkenness[4]	100.0	35.7	64.3	231	28	203	100.0	12.1	87.9
Disorderly conduct	100.0	7.4	92.6	8,844	610	8,234	100.0	6.9	93.1
Vagrancy	NA	NA	NA	511	10	501	100.0	2.0	98.0
All other offenses (except traffic)	100.0	13.8	86.2	169,324	13,295	156,029	100.0	7.9	92.1
Suspicion[5]	NA	NA	NA	0	0	0	NA	NA	NA
Curfew and loitering law violations	100.0	5.5	94.5	NA	NA	NA	NA	NA	NA

NA = Not available.
1 Because of rounding, the percentages may not sum to 100.   2 The ethnicity totals are representative of those agencies that provided ethnicity breakdowns. Not all agencies provide ethnicity data; therefore, the race and ethnicity totals will not equal.
3 Violent crimes are offenses of murder and nonnegligent manslaughter, rape, robbery, and aggravated assault. Property crimes are offenses of burglary, larceny-theft, motor vehicle theft, and arson.   4 Drunkenness figures were submitted by Summary reporting agencies only. As of 2021 drunkenness is no longer a separate offense in the National Incident-Based Reporting System (NIBRS), but it is included with All Other Offenses (except traffic) category.   5 Figures for suspicion include only data submitted by Summary reporting agencies because suspicion is not collected as a crime via NIBRS.

Table 61. Arrests, Nonmetropolitan Counties, Distribution by Race, 2022

(Number, percent; 1,809 agencies; 2022 estimated population 21,928,032.)

Offense charged	Total arrests						Percent distribution[1]					
	Total	White	Black or African American	American Indian or Alaskan Native	Asian	Native Hawaiian or Other Pacific Islander	Total	White	Black or African American	American Indian or Alaskan Native	Asian	Native Hawaiian or Other Pacific Islander
Total	497,214	408,376	69,147	14,317	3,591	1,783	100.0	82.1	13.9	2.9	0.7	0.4
Violent crime[2]	16,725	13,180	2,598	817	66	64	100.0	78.8	15.5	4.9	0.4	0.4
Murder and nonnegligent manslaughter	572	367	170	33	1	1	100.0	64.2	29.7	5.8	0.2	0.2
Rape	1,482	1,273	133	65	6	5	100.0	85.9	9.0	4.4	0.4	0.3
Robbery	643	399	203	30	6	5	100.0	62.1	31.6	4.7	0.9	0.8
Aggravated assault	14,028	11,141	2,092	689	53	53	100.0	79.4	14.9	4.9	0.4	0.4
Property crime[2]	24,221	20,740	2,604	642	115	120	100.0	85.6	10.8	2.7	0.5	0.5
Burglary	6,485	5,679	537	225	25	19	100.0	87.6	8.3	3.5	0.4	0.3
Larceny-theft	13,882	11,827	1,631	267	71	86	100.0	85.2	11.7	1.9	0.5	0.6
Motor vehicle theft	3,387	2,839	397	126	12	13	100.0	83.8	11.7	3.7	0.4	0.4
Arson	467	395	39	24	7	2	100.0	84.6	8.4	5.1	1.5	0.4
Other assaults	46,599	39,100	5,381	1,601	251	266	100.0	83.9	11.5	3.4	0.5	0.6
Forgery and counterfeiting	1,120	901	191	17	7	4	100.0	80.4	17.1	1.5	0.6	0.4
Fraud	3,471	2,700	632	116	17	6	100.0	77.8	18.2	3.3	0.5	0.2
Embezzlement	224	200	22	1	1	0	100.0	89.3	9.8	0.4	0.4	0.0
Stolen property; buying, receiving, possessing	3,213	2,490	596	106	16	5	100.0	77.5	18.5	3.3	0.5	0.2
Vandalism	6,964	5,819	845	261	22	17	100.0	83.6	12.1	3.7	0.3	0.2
Weapons; carrying, possessing, etc.	7,664	5,237	2,188	169	47	23	100.0	68.3	28.5	2.2	0.6	0.3
Prostitution and commercialized vice	91	72	12	4	3	0	100.0	79.1	13.2	4.4	3.3	0.0
Sex offenses (except forcible rape and prostitution)	1,417	1,222	127	60	7	1	100.0	86.2	9.0	4.2	0.5	*
Drug abuse violations	74,394	58,578	13,144	1,984	554	134	100.0	78.7	17.7	2.7	0.7	0.2
Gambling	36	19	11	0	5	1	100.0	52.8	30.6	0.0	13.9	2.8
Offenses against the family and children	4,657	3,683	676	279	15	4	100.0	79.1	14.5	6.0	0.3	*
Driving under the influence	81,994	69,696	8,875	2,134	1,130	159	100.0	85.0	10.8	2.6	1.4	0.2
Liquor laws	7,143	6,025	620	402	80	16	100.0	84.3	8.7	5.6	1.1	0.2
Drunkenness[3]	245	203	1	36	4	1	100.0	82.9	0.4	14.7	1.6	0.4
Disorderly conduct	11,870	9,835	1,422	499	72	42	100.0	82.9	12.0	4.2	0.6	0.4
Vagrancy	530	478	48	0	3	1	100.0	90.2	9.1	0.0	0.6	0.2
All other offenses (except traffic)	204,467	168,050	29,150	5,176	1,174	917	100.0	82.2	14.3	2.5	0.6	0.4
Suspicion[4]	0	0	0	0	0	0	NA	NA	NA	NA	NA	NA
Curfew and loitering law violations	169	148	4	13	2	2	100.0	87.6	2.4	7.7	1.2	1.2

Table 61. Arrests, Nonmetropolitan Counties, Distribution by Race, 2022—Continued

(Number, percent; 1,809 agencies; 2022 estimated population 21,928,032.)

Offense charged	Arrests under 18						Percent distribution[1]					
	Total	White	Black or African American	American Indian or Alaskan Native	Asian	Native Hawaiian or Other Pacific Islander	Total	White	Black or African American	American Indian or Alaskan Native	Asian	Native Hawaiian or Other Pacific Islander
Total	18,059	14,108	2,908	740	135	168	100.0	78.1	16.1	4.1	0.7	0.9
Violent crime[2]	1,119	825	235	54	0	5	100.0	73.7	21.0	4.8	0.0	0.4
Murder and nonnegligent manslaughter	38	21	16	1	0	0	100.0	55.3	42.1	2.6	0.0	0.0
Rape	251	226	15	9	0	1	100.0	90.0	6.0	3.6	0.0	0.4
Robbery	54	26	26	2	0	0	100.0	48.1	48.1	3.7	0.0	0.0
Aggravated assault	776	552	178	42	0	4	100.0	71.1	22.9	5.4	0.0	0.5
Property crime[2]	1,630	1,269	263	64	16	18	100.0	77.9	16.1	3.9	1.0	1.1
Burglary	445	366	50	27	2	0	100.0	82.2	11.2	6.1	0.4	0.0
Larceny-theft	797	601	149	20	11	16	100.0	75.4	18.7	2.5	1.4	2.0
Motor vehicle theft	336	261	58	15	1	1	100.0	77.7	17.3	4.5	0.3	0.3
Arson	52	41	6	2	2	1	100.0	78.8	11.5	3.8	3.8	1.9
Other assaults	4,165	3,034	906	133	33	59	100.0	72.8	21.8	3.2	0.8	1.4
Forgery and counterfeiting	11	6	4	0	1	0	100.0	54.5	36.4	0.0	9.1	0.0
Fraud	61	40	17	2	2	0	100.0	65.6	27.9	3.3	3.3	0.0
Embezzlement	3	2	1	0	0	0	100.0	66.7	33.3	0.0	0.0	0.0
Stolen property; buying, receiving, possessing	152	73	67	11	1	0	100.0	48.0	44.1	7.2	0.7	0.0
Vandalism	897	751	102	39	4	1	100.0	83.7	11.4	4.3	0.4	0.1
Weapons; carrying, possessing, etc.	349	208	138	3	0	0	100.0	59.6	39.5	0.9	0.0	0.0
Prostitution and commercialized vice	3	2	1	0	0	0	100.0	66.7	33.3	0.0	0.0	0.0
Sex offenses (except forcible rape and prostitution)	259	228	17	14	0	0	100.0	88.0	6.6	5.4	0.0	0.0
Drug abuse violations	1,961	1,541	307	82	17	14	100.0	78.6	15.7	4.2	0.9	0.7
Gambling	1	1	0	0	0	0	100.0	100.0	0.0	0.0	0.0	0.0
Offenses against the family and children	79	73	5	1	0	0	100.0	92.4	6.3	1.3	0.0	0.0
Driving under the influence	574	519	31	21	3	0	100.0	90.4	5.4	3.7	0.5	0.0
Liquor laws	1,296	1,159	43	82	5	7	100.0	89.4	3.3	6.3	0.4	0.5
Drunkenness[3]	14	14	0	0	0	0	100.0	100.0	0.0	0.0	0.0	0.0
Disorderly conduct	1,242	976	175	76	12	3	100.0	78.6	14.1	6.1	1.0	0.2
Vagrancy	0	0	0	0	0	0	NA	NA	NA	NA	NA	NA
All other offenses (except traffic)	4,074	3,239	592	145	39	59	100.0	79.5	14.5	3.6	1.0	1.4
Suspicion[4]	0	0	0	0	0	0	NA	NA	NA	NA	NA	NA
Curfew and loitering law violations	169	148	4	13	2	2	100.0	87.6	2.4	7.7	1.2	1.2

Table 61. Arrests, Nonmetropolitan Counties, Distribution by Race, 2022—Continued

(Number, percent; 1,809 agencies; 2022 estimated population 21,928,032.)

Offense charged	Arrests 18 and over						Percent distribution[1]					
	Total	White	Black or African American	American Indian or Alaskan Native	Asian	Native Hawaiian or Other Pacific Islander	Total	White	Black or African American	American Indian or Alaskan Native	Asian	Native Hawaiian or Other Pacific Islander
Total	479,155	394,268	66,239	13,577	3,456	1,615	100.0	82.3	13.8	2.8	0.7	0.3
Violent crime[2]	15,606	12,355	2,363	763	66	59	100.0	79.2	15.1	4.9	0.4	0.4
Murder and nonnegligent manslaughter	534	346	154	32	1	1	100.0	64.8	28.8	6.0	0.2	0.2
Rape	1,231	1,047	118	56	6	4	100.0	85.1	9.6	4.5	0.5	0.3
Robbery	589	373	177	28	6	5	100.0	63.3	30.1	4.8	1.0	0.8
Aggravated assault	13,252	10,589	1,914	647	53	49	100.0	79.9	14.4	4.9	0.4	0.4
Property crime[2]	22,591	19,471	2,341	578	99	102	100.0	86.2	10.4	2.6	0.4	0.5
Burglary	6,040	5,313	487	198	23	19	100.0	88.0	8.1	3.3	0.4	0.3
Larceny-theft	13,085	11,226	1,482	247	60	70	100.0	85.8	11.3	1.9	0.5	0.5
Motor vehicle theft	3,051	2,578	339	111	11	12	100.0	84.5	11.1	3.6	0.4	0.4
Arson	415	354	33	22	5	1	100.0	85.3	8.0	5.3	1.2	0.2
Other assaults	42,434	36,066	4,475	1,468	218	207	100.0	85.0	10.5	3.5	0.5	0.5
Forgery and counterfeiting	1,109	895	187	17	6	4	100.0	80.7	16.9	1.5	0.5	0.4
Fraud	3,410	2,660	615	114	15	6	100.0	78.0	18.0	3.3	0.4	0.2
Embezzlement	221	198	21	1	1	0	100.0	89.6	9.5	0.5	0.5	0.0
Stolen property; buying, receiving, possessing	3,061	2,417	529	95	15	5	100.0	79.0	17.3	3.1	0.5	0.2
Vandalism	6,067	5,068	743	222	18	16	100.0	83.5	12.2	3.7	0.3	0.3
Weapons; carrying, possessing, etc.	7,315	5,029	2,050	166	47	23	100.0	68.7	28.0	2.3	0.6	0.3
Prostitution and commercialized vice	88	70	11	4	3	0	100.0	79.5	12.5	4.5	3.4	0.0
Sex offenses (except forcible rape and prostitution)	1,158	994	110	46	7	1	100.0	85.8	9.5	4.0	0.6	*
Drug abuse violations	72,433	57,037	12,837	1,902	537	120	100.0	78.7	17.7	2.6	0.7	0.2
Gambling	35	18	11	0	5	1	100.0	51.4	31.4	0.0	14.3	2.9
Offenses against the family and children	4,578	3,610	671	278	15	4	100.0	78.9	14.7	6.1	0.3	*
Driving under the influence	81,420	69,177	8,844	2,113	1,127	159	100.0	85.0	10.9	2.6	1.4	0.2
Liquor laws	5,847	4,866	577	320	75	9	100.0	83.2	9.9	5.5	1.3	0.2
Drunkenness[3]	231	189	1	36	4	1	100.0	81.8	0.4	15.6	1.7	0.4
Disorderly conduct	10,628	8,859	1,247	423	60	39	100.0	83.4	11.7	4.0	0.6	0.4
Vagrancy	530	478	48	0	3	1	100.0	90.2	9.1	0.0	0.6	0.2
All other offenses (except traffic)	200,393	164,811	28,558	5,031	1,135	858	100.0	82.2	14.3	2.5	0.6	0.4
Suspicion[4]	0	0	0	0	0	0	NA	NA	NA	NA	NA	NA
Curfew and loitering law violations	NA	NA	NA	NA	NA	NA	NA	NA	NA	NA	NA	NA

NA = Not available.
* = Less than one-tenth of one percent.
1 Because of rounding, the percentages may not sum to 100.   2 Violent crimes in this table are offenses of murder and nonnegligent manslaughter, rape, robbery, and aggravated assault. Property crimes are offenses of burglary, larceny-theft, motor vehicle theft, and arson.   3 Drunkenness figures were submitted by Summary reporting agencies only. As of 2021 drunkenness is no longer a separate offense in the National Incident-Based Reporting System (NIBRS), but it is included with All Other Offenses (except traffic) category.   4 Figures for suspicion include only data submitted by Summary reporting agencies because suspicion is not collected as a crime via NIBRS.

Table 62. Arrest Trends, Suburban Areas,[1] 2021–2022

(Number, percent change; 4,726 agencies; 2022 estimated population 92,695,163; 2021 estimated population 91,211,609.)

Offense charged	Number of persons arrested								
	Total, all ages			Under 18 years of age			18 years of age and over		
	2021	2022	Percent change	2021	2022	Percent change	2021	2022	Percent change
Total[2]	1,766,307	1,816,273	+2.8	111,084	133,977	+20.6	1,655,223	1,682,296	+1.6
Violent crime[3]	73,916	75,251	+1.8	6,671	8,157	+22.3	67,245	67,094	-0.2
Murder and nonnegligent manslaughter	2,172	2,074	-4.5	169	195	+15.4	2,003	1,879	-6.2
Rape	4,676	4,626	-1.1	834	867	+4.0	3,842	3,759	-2.2
Robbery	7,510	7,989	+6.4	1,396	1,733	+24.1	6,114	6,256	+2.3
Aggravated assault	59,558	60,562	+1.7	4,272	5,362	+25.5	55,286	55,200	-0.2
Property crime[3]	171,914	194,243	+13.0	13,690	17,647	+28.9	158,224	176,596	+11.6
Burglary	23,701	23,982	+1.2	2,487	2,835	+14.0	21,214	21,147	-0.3
Larceny-theft	132,706	154,649	+16.5	8,865	12,370	+39.5	123,841	142,279	+14.9
Motor vehicle theft	13,946	13,959	+0.1	2,026	2,115	+4.4	11,920	11,844	-0.6
Arson	1,561	1,653	+5.9	312	327	+4.8	1,249	1,326	+6.2
Other assaults	215,024	226,568	+5.4	24,224	32,257	+33.2	190,800	194,311	+1.8
Forgery and counterfeiting	6,993	8,221	+17.6	142	164	+15.5	6,851	8,057	+17.6
Fraud	21,559	24,200	+12.3	643	748	+16.3	20,916	23,452	+12.1
Embezzlement	2,138	2,614	+22.3	103	122	+18.4	2,035	2,492	+22.5
Stolen property; buying, receiving, possessing	18,448	19,147	+3.8	1,588	2,008	+26.4	16,860	17,139	+1.7
Vandalism	36,096	35,470	-1.7	6,141	6,518	+6.1	29,955	28,952	-3.3
Weapons; carrying, possessing, etc.	34,133	35,421	+3.8	2,899	3,983	+37.4	31,234	31,438	+0.7
Prostitution and commercialized vice	1,719	1,414	-17.7	7	8	+14.3	1,712	1,406	-17.9
Sex offenses (except forcible rape and prostitution)	4,712	4,849	+2.9	963	1,025	+6.4	3,749	3,824	+2.0
Drug abuse violations	245,335	227,707	-7.2	11,958	15,714	+31.4	233,377	211,993	-9.2
Gambling	231	253	+9.5	8	9	+12.5	223	244	+9.4
Offenses against the family and children	13,700	14,139	+3.2	444	465	+4.7	13,256	13,674	+3.2
Driving under the influence	207,834	206,655	-0.6	1,322	1,252	-5.3	206,512	205,403	-0.5
Liquor laws	25,988	25,731	-1.0	4,158	4,457	+7.2	21,830	21,274	-2.5
Drunkenness[4]	0	0	NA	0	0	NA	0	0	NA
Disorderly conduct	55,539	56,823	+2.3	8,175	9,484	+16.0	47,364	47,339	-0.1
Vagrancy	1,923	2,316	+20.4	0	0	NA	1,923	2,316	+20.4
All other offenses (except traffic)	627,023	653,482	+4.2	25,866	28,190	+9.0	601,157	625,292	+4.0
Suspicion[5]	0	0	NA	0	0	NA	NA	NA	NA
Curfew and loitering law violations	2,082	1,769	-15.0	2,082	1,769	-15.0	NA	NA	NA

NA = Not available.
1 Suburban areas include law enforcement agencies in cities with less than 50,000 inhabitants and county law enforcement agencies that are within a Metropolitan Statistical Area. Suburban areas exclude all metropolitan agencies associated with a principal city.   2 Does not include suspicion.   3 Violent crimes in this table are offenses of murder and nonnegligent manslaughter, rape, robbery, and aggravated assault. Property crimes are offenses of burglary, larceny-theft, motor vehicle theft, and arson.   4 Drunkenness figures were submitted by Summary reporting agencies only. As of 2021 drunkenness is no longer a separate offense in the National Incident-Based Reporting System (NIBRS), but it is included with All Other Offenses (except traffic) category.   5 Figures for suspicion include only data submitted by Summary reporting agencies because suspicion is not collected as a crime via NIBRS.

Table 63. Arrest Trends, Suburban Areas[1], by Age and Sex, 2021–2022

(Number, percent change; 4,726 agencies; 2022 estimated population 92,695,163; 2021 estimated population 91,211,609.)

| | Male | | | | | | Female | | | | | |
| | Total | | | Under 18 | | | Total | | | Under 18 | | |
Offense charged	2021	2022	Percent change	2021	2022	Percent change	2021	2022	Percent change	2021	2022	Percent change
Total[2]	1,282,696	1,311,044	+2.2	77,112	91,692	+18.9	483,611	505,229	+4.5	33,972	42,285	+24.5
Violent crime[3]	59,572	60,072	+0.8	5,303	6,431	+21.3	14,344	15,179	+5.8	1,368	1,726	+26.2
Murder and nonnegligent manslaughter	1,883	1,829	-2.9	150	185	+23.3	289	245	-15.2	19	10	-47.4
Rape	4,548	4,500	-1.1	797	837	+5.0	128	126	-1.6	37	30	-18.9
Robbery	6,458	6,816	+5.5	1,264	1,553	+22.9	1,052	1,173	+11.5	132	180	+36.4
Aggravated assault	46,683	46,927	+0.5	3,092	3,856	+24.7	12,875	13,635	+5.9	1,180	1,506	+27.6
Property crime[3]	112,463	125,292	+11.4	10,169	12,600	+23.9	59,451	68,951	+16.0	3,521	5,047	+43.3
Burglary	19,423	19,675	+1.3	2,215	2,486	+12.2	4,278	4,307	+0.7	272	349	+28.3
Larceny-theft	80,896	93,384	+15.4	6,044	8,109	+34.2	51,810	61,265	+18.2	2,821	4,261	+51.0
Motor vehicle theft	10,921	10,946	+0.2	1,655	1,734	+4.8	3,025	3,013	-0.4	371	381	+2.7
Arson	1,223	1,287	+5.2	255	271	+6.3	338	366	+8.3	57	56	-1.8
Other assaults	152,062	157,049	+3.3	14,858	19,250	+29.6	62,962	69,519	+10.4	9,366	13,007	+38.9
Forgery and counterfeiting	4,744	5,773	+21.7	108	136	+25.9	2,249	2,448	+8.8	34	28	-17.6
Fraud	14,162	16,024	+13.1	439	479	+9.1	7,397	8,176	+10.5	204	269	+31.9
Embezzlement	1,134	1,301	+14.7	58	55	-5.2	1,004	1,313	+30.8	45	67	+48.9
Stolen property; buying, receiving, possessing	14,669	15,249	+4.0	1,367	1,732	+26.7	3,779	3,898	+3.1	221	276	+24.9
Vandalism	28,112	27,536	-2.0	4,990	5,292	+6.1	7,984	7,934	-0.6	1,151	1,226	+6.5
Weapons; carrying, possessing, etc.	30,590	31,716	+3.7	2,527	3,480	+37.7	3,543	3,705	+4.6	372	503	+35.2
Prostitution and commercialized vice	1,129	807	-28.5	3	7	+133.3	590	607	+2.9	4	1	-75.0
Sex offenses (except forcible rape and prostitution)	4,454	4,576	+2.7	861	915	+6.3	258	273	+5.8	102	110	+7.8
Drug abuse violations	176,396	164,274	-6.9	8,465	10,925	+29.1	68,939	63,433	-8.0	3,493	4,789	+37.1
Gambling	176	200	+13.6	8	9	+12.5	55	53	-3.6	0	0	NA
Offenses against the family and children	9,213	9,552	+3.7	254	231	-9.1	4,487	4,587	+2.2	190	234	+23.2
Driving under the influence	153,492	152,576	-0.6	1,012	932	-7.9	54,342	54,079	-0.5	310	320	+3.2
Liquor laws	17,447	17,236	-1.2	2,384	2,583	+8.3	8,541	8,495	-0.5	1,774	1,874	+5.6
Drunkenness[4]	0	0	NA	0	0	NA	0	0	NA	0	0	NA
Disorderly conduct	39,459	40,043	+1.5	5,262	6,017	+14.3	16,080	16,780	+4.4	2,913	3,467	+19.0
Vagrancy	1,567	1,878	+19.8	0	0	NA	356	438	+23.0	0	0	NA
All other offenses (except traffic)	460,475	478,671	+4.0	17,664	19,399	+9.8	166,548	174,811	+5.0	8,202	8,791	+7.2
Suspicion[5]	0	0	NA	0	0	NA	0	0	NA	0	0	NA
Curfew and loitering law violations	1,380	1,219	-11.7	1,380	1,219	-11.7	702	550	-21.7	702	550	-21.7

NA = Not available.
1 Suburban areas include law enforcement agencies in cities with less than 50,000 inhabitants and county law enforcement agencies that are within a Metropolitan Statistical Area. Suburban areas exclude all metropolitan agencies associated with a principal city.   2 Does not include suspicion.   3 Violent crimes in this table are offenses of murder and nonnegligent manslaughter, rape, robbery, and aggravated assault. Property crimes are offenses of burglary, larceny-theft, motor vehicle theft, and arson.   4 Drunkenness figures were submitted by Summary reporting agencies only. As of 2021 drunkenness is no longer a separate offense in the National Incident-Based Reporting System (NIBRS), but it is included with All Other Offenses (except traffic) category.   5 Figures for suspicion include only data submitted by Summary reporting agencies because suspicion is not collected as a crime via NIBRS.

Table 64. Arrests, Suburban Areas,[1] Distribution by Age, 2022

(Number, percent; 6,320 agencies; 2022 estimated population 118,233,444.)

Offense charged	Total, all ages	Under 15 years	Under 18 years	Age 18 years and over	Under 10 years	10–12 years	13–14 years	15 years	16 years	17 years	18 years	19 years	20 years
Total	2,310,635	53,719	157,682	2,152,953	537	12,136	41,046	31,872	35,029	37,062	49,305	52,888	54,753
Total, percent distribution[2]	100.0	2.3	6.8	93.2	*	0.5	1.8	1.4	1.5	1.6	2.1	2.3	2.4
Violent crime[3]	110,203	3,627	10,710	99,493	48	810	2,769	2,159	2,407	2,517	2,879	2,872	2,820
Violent crime, percent distribution[2]	100.0	3.3	9.7	90.3	*	0.7	2.5	2.0	2.2	2.3	2.6	2.6	2.6
Murder and nonnegligent manslaughter	2,815	24	234	2,581	0	2	22	37	67	106	143	127	147
Rape	5,941	418	1,022	4,919	14	108	296	194	191	219	264	209	187
Robbery	12,222	587	2,330	9,892	1	63	523	542	596	605	637	589	443
Aggravated assault	89,225	2,598	7,124	82,101	33	637	1,928	1,386	1,553	1,587	1,835	1,947	2,043
Property crime[3]	243,419	6,359	20,919	222,500	44	1,142	5,173	4,467	4,974	5,119	6,423	5,908	5,362
Property crime, percent distribution[2]	100.0	2.6	8.6	91.4	*	0.5	2.1	1.8	2.0	2.1	2.6	2.4	2.2
Burglary	32,758	1,294	3,533	29,225	16	263	1,015	780	757	702	832	730	659
Larceny-theft	188,503	4,117	14,370	174,133	25	747	3,345	3,002	3,490	3,761	4,928	4,669	4,234
Motor vehicle theft	19,685	703	2,597	17,088	0	62	641	620	665	609	618	469	433
Arson	2,473	245	419	2,054	3	70	172	65	62	47	45	40	36
Other assaults	277,433	16,626	37,247	240,186	162	4,522	11,942	7,398	7,225	5,998	5,453	5,349	5,549
Forgery and counterfeiting	10,686	13	183	10,503	0	1	12	19	47	104	358	579	525
Fraud	28,537	194	848	27,689	1	38	155	135	202	317	604	708	712
Embezzlement	3,105	9	136	2,969	0	1	8	8	37	82	155	162	157
Stolen property; buying, receiving, possessing	26,744	469	2,390	24,354	2	34	433	586	659	676	804	753	703
Vandalism	47,337	3,404	7,965	39,372	54	939	2,411	1,575	1,520	1,466	1,458	1,224	1,183
Weapons; carrying, possessing, etc.	50,559	1,670	5,561	44,998	21	422	1,227	1,025	1,301	1,565	1,889	1,864	1,871
Prostitution and commercialized vice	1,985	6	17	1,968	0	1	5	2	4	5	15	26	35
Sex offenses (except forcible rape and prostitution)	7,926	634	1,302	6,624	12	169	453	246	207	215	236	205	173
Drug abuse violations	292,404	4,308	17,408	274,996	8	646	3,654	3,514	4,363	5,223	8,071	8,524	8,368
Gambling	413	2	12	401	0	0	2	3	2	5	15	26	28
Offenses against the family and children	15,972	162	490	15,482	11	32	119	111	98	119	131	151	188
Driving under the influence	289,029	30	1,637	287,392	7	1	22	78	403	1,126	3,143	4,518	5,709
Liquor laws	29,271	687	5,057	24,214	2	83	602	816	1,363	2,191	4,136	4,121	3,240
Drunkenness[4]	4,590	8	33	4,557	0	0	8	7	8	10	34	49	56
Disorderly conduct	69,099	4,572	10,815	58,284	40	1,120	3,412	2,306	2,111	1,826	1,680	1,419	1,474
Vagrancy	3,640	2	5	3,635	0	2	0	0	1	2	60	69	71
All other offenses (except traffic)	796,261	10,326	32,976	763,285	124	2,090	8,112	6,911	7,572	8,167	11,760	14,361	16,529
Suspicion[5]	51	0	0	51	0	0	0	0	0	0	1	0	0
Curfew and loitering law violations	1,971	611	1,971	NA	1	83	527	506	525	329	NA	NA	NA

Table 64. Arrests, Suburban Areas,[1] Distribution by Age, 2022—Continued

(Number, percent; 6,320 agencies; 2022 estimated population 118,233,444.)

Offense charged	21 years	22 years	23 years	24 years	25–29 years	30–34 years	35–39 years	40–44 years	45–49 years	50–54 years	55–59 years	60–64 years	65 years and over
Total	57,823	59,599	60,810	62,093	338,972	369,126	315,255	250,131	160,306	127,432	93,166	58,781	42,513
Total, percent distribution[2]	2.5	2.6	2.6	2.7	14.7	16.0	13.6	10.8	6.9	5.5	4.0	2.5	1.8
Violent crime[3]	3,063	3,079	3,018	3,120	16,415	16,923	13,768	10,669	6,858	5,214	3,928	2,576	2,291
Violent crime, percent distribution[2]	2.8	2.8	2.7	2.8	14.9	15.4	12.5	9.7	6.2	4.7	3.6	2.3	2.1
Murder and nonnegligent manslaughter	124	135	113	98	432	368	262	213	130	106	68	60	55
Rape	184	173	129	145	646	690	673	477	351	273	190	159	169
Robbery	445	402	350	353	1,830	1,688	1,163	832	456	311	224	117	52
Aggravated assault	2,310	2,369	2,426	2,524	13,507	14,177	11,670	9,147	5,921	4,524	3,446	2,240	2,015
Property crime[3]	5,362	5,493	5,643	5,797	33,455	38,617	33,791	26,271	16,465	13,873	10,230	5,992	3,818
Property crime, percent distribution[2]	2.2	2.3	2.3	2.4	13.7	15.9	13.9	10.8	6.8	5.7	4.2	2.5	1.6
Burglary	704	716	756	727	4,656	5,487	4,863	3,591	2,035	1,530	1,078	535	326
Larceny-theft	4,177	4,280	4,340	4,484	25,522	29,356	25,835	20,451	13,246	11,490	8,611	5,160	3,350
Motor vehicle theft	451	460	503	530	3,000	3,406	2,781	1,953	1,022	706	431	234	91
Arson	30	37	44	56	277	368	312	276	162	147	110	63	51
Other assaults	6,095	6,446	6,664	6,883	37,464	40,838	35,123	27,853	18,244	14,443	10,745	7,088	5,949
Forgery and counterfeiting	288	296	306	296	1,574	1,679	1,486	1,136	730	548	373	212	117
Fraud	709	788	713	744	4,351	4,961	4,098	3,282	1,989	1,680	1,169	714	467
Embezzlement	133	116	105	93	413	389	389	300	214	156	98	55	34
Stolen property; buying, receiving, possessing	663	635	693	700	4,061	4,637	3,865	2,847	1,672	1,138	727	320	136
Vandalism	1,285	1,201	1,187	1,230	6,647	7,060	5,626	4,063	2,353	1,932	1,383	870	670
Weapons; carrying, possessing, etc.	2,079	1,986	1,859	1,757	8,225	7,363	5,473	3,987	2,414	1,759	1,173	748	551
Prostitution and commercialized vice	46	47	45	58	284	296	259	243	207	157	136	61	53
Sex offenses (except forcible rape and prostitution)	187	150	164	152	822	859	867	683	523	452	403	322	426
Drug abuse violations	8,197	8,293	8,179	8,158	44,455	47,657	40,797	32,553	19,613	14,627	9,793	5,365	2,346
Gambling	5	6	3	6	38	57	35	46	49	26	29	13	19
Offenses against the family and children	228	258	270	338	2,440	3,143	2,909	2,237	1,336	831	553	265	204
Driving under the influence	8,581	9,138	9,566	9,640	48,502	46,228	37,502	30,603	21,862	18,427	14,771	10,439	8,763
Liquor laws	688	538	428	387	1,940	1,852	1,587	1,420	1,045	959	858	577	438
Drunkenness[4]	97	105	102	113	674	737	684	551	409	345	278	200	123
Disorderly conduct	1,718	1,634	1,557	1,535	7,948	9,169	8,015	6,460	4,559	3,872	3,146	2,248	1,850
Vagrancy	60	63	67	82	404	586	560	453	295	322	232	166	145
All other offenses (except traffic)	18,337	19,324	20,239	21,001	118,851	136,068	118,414	94,472	59,458	46,670	33,139	20,550	14,112
Suspicion[5]	2	3	2	3	9	7	7	2	11	1	2	0	1
Curfew and loitering law violations	NA	NA	NA	NA	NA	NA	NA	NA	NA	NA	NA	NA	NA

NA = Not available.
* = Less than one-tenth of one percent.
1 Suburban areas include law enforcement agencies in cities with less than 50,000 inhabitants and county law enforcement agencies that are within a Metropolitan Statistical Area. Suburban areas exclude all metropolitan agencies associated with a principal city.   2 Because of rounding, the percentages may not add to 100.0.   3 Violent crimes are offenses of murder and nonnegligent manslaughter, rape, robbery, and aggravated assault. Property crimes are offenses of burglary, larceny-theft, motor vehicle theft, and arson.   4 Drunkenness figures were submitted by Summary reporting agencies only. As of 2021 drunkenness is no longer a separate offense in National Incident Based Reporting System (NIBRS), but it is included with All Other Offenses (except traffic) category.   5 Figures for suspicion include only data submitted by Summary reporting agencies because suspicion is not collected as a crime via NIBRS.

Table 65. Arrests, Suburban Areas,[1] Persons Under 15, 18, 21, and 25 Years of Age, 2022

(Number, percent; 6,320 agencies; 2022 estimated population 118,233,444.)

Offense charged	Total, all ages	Number of persons arrested				Percent of total all ages			
		Under 15	Under 18	Under 21	Under 25	Under 15	Under 18	Under 21	Under 25
Total	2,310,635	53,719	157,682	314,628	554,953	2.3	6.8	13.6	24.0
Violent crime[2]	110,203	3,627	10,710	19,281	31,561	3.3	9.7	17.5	28.6
Murder and nonnegligent manslaughter	2,815	24	234	651	1,121	0.9	8.3	23.1	39.8
Rape	5,941	418	1,022	1,682	2,313	7.0	17.2	28.3	38.9
Robbery	12,222	587	2,330	3,999	5,549	4.8	19.1	32.7	45.4
Aggravated assault	89,225	2,598	7,124	12,949	22,578	2.9	8.0	14.5	25.3
Property crime[2]	243,419	6,359	20,919	38,612	60,907	2.6	8.6	15.9	25.0
Burglary	32,758	1,294	3,533	5,754	8,657	4.0	10.8	17.6	26.4
Larceny-theft	188,503	4,117	14,370	28,201	45,482	2.2	7.6	15.0	24.1
Motor vehicle theft	19,685	703	2,597	4,117	6,061	3.6	13.2	20.9	30.8
Arson	2,473	245	419	540	707	9.9	16.9	21.8	28.6
Other assaults	277,433	16,626	37,247	53,598	79,686	6.0	13.4	19.3	28.7
Forgery and counterfeiting	10,686	13	183	1,645	2,831	0.1	1.7	15.4	26.5
Fraud	28,537	194	848	2,872	5,826	0.7	3.0	10.1	20.4
Embezzlement	3,105	9	136	610	1,057	0.3	4.4	19.6	34.0
Stolen property; buying, receiving, possessing	26,744	469	2,390	4,650	7,341	1.8	8.9	17.4	27.4
Vandalism	47,337	3,404	7,965	11,830	16,733	7.2	16.8	25.0	35.3
Weapons; carrying, possessing, etc.	50,559	1,670	5,561	11,185	18,866	3.3	11.0	22.1	37.3
Prostitution and commercialized vice	1,985	6	17	93	289	0.3	0.9	4.7	14.6
Sex offenses (except forcible rape and prostitution)	7,926	634	1,302	1,916	2,569	8.0	16.4	24.2	32.4
Drug abuse violations	292,404	4,308	17,408	42,371	75,198	1.5	6.0	14.5	25.7
Gambling	413	2	12	81	101	0.5	2.9	19.6	24.5
Offenses against the family and children	15,972	162	490	960	2,054	1.0	3.1	6.0	12.9
Driving under the influence	289,029	30	1,637	15,007	51,932	*	0.6	5.2	18.0
Liquor laws	29,271	687	5,057	16,554	18,595	2.3	17.3	56.6	63.5
Drunkenness[3]	4,590	8	33	172	589	0.2	0.7	3.7	12.8
Disorderly conduct	69,099	4,572	10,815	15,388	21,832	6.6	15.7	22.3	31.6
Vagrancy	3,640	2	5	205	477	0.1	0.1	5.6	13.1
All other offenses (except traffic)	796,261	10,326	32,976	75,626	154,527	1.3	4.1	9.5	19.4
Suspicion[4]	51	0	0	1	11	0.0	0.0	2.0	21.6
Curfew and loitering law violations	1,971	611	1,971	1,971	1,971	31.0	100.0	100.0	100.0

* = Less than one-tenth of one percent.
1 Suburban areas include law enforcement agencies in cities with less than 50,000 inhabitants and county law enforcement agencies that are within a Metropolitan Statistical Area. Suburban areas exclude all metropolitan agencies associated with a principal city.   2 Violent crimes in this table are offenses of murder and nonnegligent manslaughter, rape, robbery, and aggravated assault. Property crimes are offenses of burglary, larceny-theft, motor vehicle theft, and arson.   3 Drunkenness figures were submitted by Summary reporting agencies only. As of 2021 drunkenness is no longer a separate offense in the National Incident-Based Reporting System (NIBRS), but it is included with All Other Offenses (except traffic) category.   4 Figures for suspicion include only data submitted by Summary reporting agencies because suspicion is not collected as a crime via NIBRS.

Table 66. Arrests, Suburban Areas,[1] Distribution by Sex, 2022

(Number, percent; 6,320 agencies; 2022 estimated population 118,233,444.)

Offense charged	Number of persons arrested			Percent male	Percent female	Percent distribution[2]		
	Total	Male	Female			Total	Male	Female
Total	2,310,635	1,686,775	623,860	73.0	27.0	100.0	100.0	100.0
Violent crime[3]	110,203	87,578	22,625	79.5	20.5	4.8	5.2	3.6
Murder and nonnegligent manslaughter	2,815	2,489	326	88.4	11.6	0.1	0.1	0.1
Rape	5,941	5,777	164	97.2	2.8	0.3	0.3	*
Robbery	12,222	10,376	1,846	84.9	15.1	0.5	0.6	0.3
Aggravated assault	89,225	68,936	20,289	77.3	22.7	3.9	4.1	3.3
Property crime[3]	243,419	158,773	84,646	65.2	34.8	10.5	9.4	13.6
Burglary	32,758	26,750	6,008	81.7	18.3	1.4	1.6	1.0
Larceny-theft	188,503	114,699	73,804	60.8	39.2	8.2	6.8	11.8
Motor vehicle theft	19,685	15,413	4,272	78.3	21.7	0.9	0.9	0.7
Arson	2,473	1,911	562	77.3	22.7	0.1	0.1	0.1
Other assaults	277,433	193,148	84,285	69.6	30.4	12.0	11.5	13.5
Forgery and counterfeiting	10,686	7,594	3,092	71.1	28.9	0.5	0.5	0.5
Fraud	28,537	19,054	9,483	66.8	33.2	1.2	1.1	1.5
Embezzlement	3,105	1,575	1,530	50.7	49.3	0.1	0.1	0.2
Stolen property; buying, receiving, possessing	26,744	21,197	5,547	79.3	20.7	1.2	1.3	0.9
Vandalism	47,337	36,926	10,411	78.0	22.0	2.0	2.2	1.7
Weapons; carrying, possessing, etc.	50,559	45,335	5,224	89.7	10.3	2.2	2.7	0.8
Prostitution and commercialized vice	1,985	1,095	890	55.2	44.8	0.1	0.1	0.1
Sex offenses (except forcible rape and prostitution)	7,926	7,487	439	94.5	5.5	0.3	0.4	0.1
Drug abuse violations	292,404	214,820	77,584	73.5	26.5	12.7	12.7	12.4
Gambling	413	311	102	75.3	24.7	*	*	*
Offenses against the family and children	15,972	10,831	5,141	67.8	32.2	0.7	0.6	0.8
Driving under the influence	289,029	215,490	73,539	74.6	25.4	12.5	12.8	11.8
Liquor laws	29,271	19,611	9,660	67.0	33.0	1.3	1.2	1.5
Drunkenness[4]	4,590	3,689	901	80.4	19.6	0.2	0.2	0.1
Disorderly conduct	69,099	49,077	20,022	71.0	29.0	3.0	2.9	3.2
Vagrancy	3,640	2,870	770	78.8	21.2	0.2	0.2	0.1
All other offenses (except traffic)	796,261	588,910	207,351	74.0	26.0	34.5	34.9	33.2
Suspicion[5]	51	43	8	84.3	15.7	*	*	*
Curfew and loitering law violations	1,971	1,361	610	69.1	30.9	0.1	0.1	0.1

* = Less than one-tenth of one percent.
1 Suburban areas include law enforcement agencies in cities with less than 50,000 inhabitants and county law enforcement agencies that are within a Metropolitan Statistical Area. Suburban areas exclude all metropolitan agencies associated with a principal city.   2 Because of rounding, the percentages may not sum to 100.   3 Violent crimes in this table are offenses of murder and nonnegligent manslaughter, rape, robbery, and aggravated assault. Property crimes are offenses of burglary, larceny-theft, motor vehicle theft, and arson.   4 Drunkenness figures were submitted by Summary reporting agencies only. As of 2021 drunkenness is no longer a separate offense in the National Incident-Based Reporting System (NIBRS), but it is included with All Other Offenses (except traffic) category.   5 Figures for suspicion include only data submitted by Summary reporting agencies because suspicion is not collected as a crime via NIBRS.

Table 67. Arrests, Suburban Areas,[1] Distribution by Race, 2022

(Number, percent; 6,320 agencies; 2022 estimated population 118,233,444.)

Offense charged	Total arrests						Percent distribution[2]					
	Total	White	Black or African American	American Indian or Alaskan Native	Asian	Native Hawaiian or Other Pacific Islander	Total	White	Black or African American	American Indian or Alaskan Native	Asian	Native Hawaiian or Other Pacific Islander
Total	2,263,764	1,597,897	613,174	22,298	26,449	3,946	100.0	70.6	27.1	1.0	1.2	0.2
Violent crime[3]	108,577	68,962	36,953	929	1,476	257	100.0	63.5	34.0	0.9	1.4	0.2
Murder and nonnegligent manslaughter	2,796	1,419	1,329	20	26	2	100.0	50.8	47.5	0.7	0.9	*
Rape	5,767	4,289	1,328	42	101	7	100.0	74.4	23.0	0.7	1.8	0.1
Robbery	12,060	5,666	6,174	76	120	24	100.0	47.0	51.2	0.6	1.0	0.2
Aggravated assault	87,954	57,588	28,122	791	1,229	224	100.0	65.5	32.0	0.9	1.4	0.3
Property crime[3]	239,029	158,711	75,096	2,300	2,607	315	100.0	66.4	31.4	1.0	1.1	0.1
Burglary	32,294	23,630	8,093	251	265	55	100.0	73.2	25.1	0.8	0.8	0.2
Larceny-theft	184,871	119,478	61,180	1,861	2,138	214	100.0	64.6	33.1	1.0	1.2	0.1
Motor vehicle theft	19,431	13,734	5,311	172	170	44	100.0	70.7	27.3	0.9	0.9	0.2
Arson	2,433	1,869	512	16	34	2	100.0	76.8	21.0	0.7	1.4	*
Other assaults	272,571	185,744	80,099	2,644	3,501	583	100.0	68.1	29.4	1.0	1.3	0.2
Forgery and counterfeiting	10,486	6,906	3,326	55	182	17	100.0	65.9	31.7	0.5	1.7	0.2
Fraud	27,936	16,625	10,751	181	330	49	100.0	59.5	38.5	0.6	1.2	0.2
Embezzlement	3,035	1,720	1,256	17	36	6	100.0	56.7	41.4	0.6	1.2	0.2
Stolen property; buying, receiving, possessing	26,226	16,273	9,347	219	325	62	100.0	62.0	35.6	0.8	1.2	0.2
Vandalism	46,326	32,533	12,618	512	569	94	100.0	70.2	27.2	1.1	1.2	0.2
Weapons; carrying, possessing, etc.	49,893	25,901	23,153	276	461	102	100.0	51.9	46.4	0.6	0.9	0.2
Prostitution and commercialized vice	1,953	1,045	594	9	297	8	100.0	53.5	30.4	0.5	15.2	0.4
Sex offenses (except forcible rape and prostitution)	7,752	5,936	1,593	41	155	27	100.0	76.6	20.5	0.5	2.0	0.3
Drug abuse violations	288,198	204,488	78,760	2,042	2,547	361	100.0	71.0	27.3	0.7	0.9	0.1
Gambling	402	254	103	2	40	3	100.0	63.2	25.6	0.5	10.0	0.7
Offenses against the family and children	15,664	11,382	3,983	131	135	33	100.0	72.7	25.4	0.8	0.9	0.2
Driving under the influence	276,850	223,194	45,169	2,348	5,541	598	100.0	80.6	16.3	0.8	2.0	0.2
Liquor laws	28,285	22,996	4,275	437	515	62	100.0	81.3	15.1	1.5	1.8	0.2
Drunkenness[4]	4,590	4,069	414	29	64	14	100.0	88.6	9.0	0.6	1.4	0.3
Disorderly conduct	67,653	46,789	18,824	1,249	683	108	100.0	69.2	27.8	1.8	1.0	0.2
Vagrancy	3,618	2,218	1,323	21	36	20	100.0	61.3	36.6	0.6	1.0	0.6
All other offenses (except traffic)	782,761	560,818	204,953	8,831	6,936	1,223	100.0	71.6	26.2	1.1	0.9	0.2
Suspicion[5]	51	25	26	0	0	0	100.0	49.0	51.0	0.0	0.0	0.0
Curfew and loitering law violations	1,908	1,308	558	25	13	4	100.0	68.6	29.2	1.3	0.7	0.2

Table 67. Arrests, Suburban Areas,[1] Distribution by Race, 2022—Continued

(Number, percent; 6,320 agencies; 2022 estimated population 118,233,444.)

Offense charged	Arrests under 18						Percent distribution[2]					
	Total	White	Black or African American	American Indian or Alaskan Native	Asian	Native Hawaiian or Other Pacific Islander	Total	White	Black or African American	American Indian or Alaskan Native	Asian	Native Hawaiian or Other Pacific Islander
Total	153,904	96,779	53,730	1,689	1,430	276	100.0	62.9	34.9	1.1	0.9	0.2
Violent crime[3]	10,476	5,495	4,781	83	95	22	100.0	52.5	45.6	0.8	0.9	0.2
Murder and nonnegligent manslaughter	232	83	147	0	1	1	100.0	35.8	63.4	0.0	0.4	0.4
Rape	969	728	224	7	8	2	100.0	75.1	23.1	0.7	0.8	0.2
Robbery	2,306	791	1,479	13	18	5	100.0	34.3	64.1	0.6	0.8	0.2
Aggravated assault	6,969	3,893	2,931	63	68	14	100.0	55.9	42.1	0.9	1.0	0.2
Property crime[3]	20,446	11,700	8,258	191	262	35	100.0	57.2	40.4	0.9	1.3	0.2
Burglary	3,459	2,144	1,255	29	25	6	100.0	62.0	36.3	0.8	0.7	0.2
Larceny-theft	14,022	8,121	5,520	138	219	24	100.0	57.9	39.4	1.0	1.6	0.2
Motor vehicle theft	2,551	1,142	1,368	21	15	5	100.0	44.8	53.6	0.8	0.6	0.2
Arson	414	293	115	3	3	0	100.0	70.8	27.8	0.7	0.7	0.0
Other assaults	36,515	20,949	14,871	343	280	72	100.0	57.4	40.7	0.9	0.8	0.2
Forgery and counterfeiting	177	111	61	1	3	1	100.0	62.7	34.5	0.6	1.7	0.6
Fraud	824	432	372	5	13	2	100.0	52.4	45.1	0.6	1.6	0.2
Embezzlement	130	48	80	0	2	0	100.0	36.9	61.5	0.0	1.5	0.0
Stolen property; buying, receiving, possessing	2,333	592	1,693	19	27	2	100.0	25.4	72.6	0.8	1.2	*
Vandalism	7,725	5,569	1,985	100	63	8	100.0	72.1	25.7	1.3	0.8	0.1
Weapons; carrying, possessing, etc.	5,482	2,669	2,685	52	64	12	100.0	48.7	49.0	0.9	1.2	0.2
Prostitution and commercialized vice	16	9	7	0	0	0	100.0	56.3	43.8	0.0	0.0	0.0
Sex offenses (except forcible rape and prostitution)	1,259	941	297	10	11	0	100.0	74.7	23.6	0.8	0.9	0.0
Drug abuse violations	16,982	12,612	4,004	172	157	37	100.0	74.3	23.6	1.0	0.9	0.2
Gambling	12	9	3	0	0	0	100.0	75.0	25.0	0.0	0.0	0.0
Offenses against the family and children	482	376	82	20	3	1	100.0	78.0	17.0	4.1	0.6	0.2
Driving under the influence	1,560	1,414	110	21	13	2	100.0	90.6	7.1	1.3	0.8	0.1
Liquor laws	4,836	4,293	362	103	64	14	100.0	88.8	7.5	2.1	1.3	0.3
Drunkenness[4]	33	30	2	1	0	0	100.0	90.9	6.1	3.0	0.0	0.0
Disorderly conduct	10,509	5,891	4,395	145	66	12	100.0	56.1	41.8	1.4	0.6	0.1
Vagrancy	5	4	1	0	0	0	100.0	80.0	20.0	0.0	0.0	0.0
All other offenses (except traffic)	32,194	22,327	9,123	398	294	52	100.0	69.4	28.3	1.2	0.9	0.2
Suspicion[5]	0	0	0	0	0	0	NA	NA	NA	NA	NA	NA
Curfew and loitering law violations	1,908	1,308	558	25	13	4	100.0	68.6	29.2	1.3	0.7	0.2

Table 67. Arrests, Suburban Areas,[1] Distribution by Race, 2022—Continued

(Number, percent; 6,320 agencies; 2022 estimated population 118,233,444.)

Offense charged	Arrests 18 and over						Percent distribution[2]					
	Total	White	Black or African American	American Indian or Alaskan Native	Asian	Native Hawaiian or Other Pacific Islander	Total	White	Black or African American	American Indian or Alaskan Native	Asian	Native Hawaiian or Other Pacific Islander
Total	2,109,860	1,501,118	559,444	20,609	25,019	3,670	100.0	71.1	26.5	1.0	1.2	0.2
Violent crime[3]	98,101	63,467	32,172	846	1,381	235	100.0	64.7	32.8	0.9	1.4	0.2
Murder and nonnegligent manslaughter	2,564	1,336	1,182	20	25	1	100.0	52.1	46.1	0.8	1.0	*
Rape	4,798	3,561	1,104	35	93	5	100.0	74.2	23.0	0.7	1.9	0.1
Robbery	9,754	4,875	4,695	63	102	19	100.0	50.0	48.1	0.6	1.0	0.2
Aggravated assault	80,985	53,695	25,191	728	1,161	210	100.0	66.3	31.1	0.9	1.4	0.3
Property crime[3]	218,583	147,011	66,838	2,109	2,345	280	100.0	67.3	30.6	1.0	1.1	0.1
Burglary	28,835	21,486	6,838	222	240	49	100.0	74.5	23.7	0.8	0.8	0.2
Larceny-theft	170,849	111,357	55,660	1,723	1,919	190	100.0	65.2	32.6	1.0	1.1	0.1
Motor vehicle theft	16,880	12,592	3,943	151	155	39	100.0	74.6	23.4	0.9	0.9	0.2
Arson	2,019	1,576	397	13	31	2	100.0	78.1	19.7	0.6	1.5	*
Other assaults	236,056	164,795	65,228	2,301	3,221	511	100.0	69.8	27.6	1.0	1.4	0.2
Forgery and counterfeiting	10,309	6,795	3,265	54	179	16	100.0	65.9	31.7	0.5	1.7	0.2
Fraud	27,112	16,193	10,379	176	317	47	100.0	59.7	38.3	0.6	1.2	0.2
Embezzlement	2,905	1,672	1,176	17	34	6	100.0	57.6	40.5	0.6	1.2	0.2
Stolen property; buying, receiving, possessing	23,893	15,681	7,654	200	298	60	100.0	65.6	32.0	0.8	1.2	0.3
Vandalism	38,601	26,964	10,633	412	506	86	100.0	69.9	27.5	1.1	1.3	0.2
Weapons; carrying, possessing, etc.	44,411	23,232	20,468	224	397	90	100.0	52.3	46.1	0.5	0.9	0.2
Prostitution and commercialized vice	1,937	1,036	587	9	297	8	100.0	53.5	30.3	0.5	15.3	0.4
Sex offenses (except forcible rape and prostitution)	6,493	4,995	1,296	31	144	27	100.0	76.9	20.0	0.5	2.2	0.4
Drug abuse violations	271,216	191,876	74,756	1,870	2,390	324	100.0	70.7	27.6	0.7	0.9	0.1
Gambling	390	245	100	2	40	3	100.0	62.8	25.6	0.5	10.3	0.8
Offenses against the family and children	15,182	11,006	3,901	111	132	32	100.0	72.5	25.7	0.7	0.9	0.2
Driving under the influence	275,290	221,780	45,059	2,327	5,528	596	100.0	80.6	16.4	0.8	2.0	0.2
Liquor laws	23,449	18,703	3,913	334	451	48	100.0	79.8	16.7	1.4	1.9	0.2
Drunkenness[4]	4,557	4,039	412	28	64	14	100.0	88.6	9.0	0.6	1.4	0.3
Disorderly conduct	57,144	40,898	14,429	1,104	617	96	100.0	71.6	25.3	1.9	1.1	0.2
Vagrancy	3,613	2,214	1,322	21	36	20	100.0	61.3	36.6	0.6	1.0	0.6
All other offenses (except traffic)	750,567	538,491	195,830	8,433	6,642	1,171	100.0	71.7	26.1	1.1	0.9	0.2
Suspicion[5]	51	25	26	0	0	0	100.0	49.0	51.0	0.0	0.0	0.0
Curfew and loitering law violations	NA	NA	NA	NA	NA	NA	NA	NA	NA	NA	NA	NA

NA = Not available.
* = Less than one-tenth of one percent.
1 Suburban areas include law enforcement agencies in cities with less than 50,000 inhabitants and county law enforcement agencies that are within a Metropolitan Statistical Area. Suburban areas exclude all metropolitan agencies associated with a principal city.   2 Because of rounding, the percentages may not sum to 100.   3 Violent crimes in this table are offenses of murder and nonnegligent manslaughter, rape, robbery, and aggravated assault. Property crimes are offenses of burglary, larceny-theft, motor vehicle theft, and arson.   4 Drunkenness figures were submitted by Summary reporting agencies only. As of 2021 drunkenness is no longer a separate offense in the National Incident-Based Reporting System (NIBRS), but it is included with All Other Offenses (except traffic) category.   5 Figures for suspicion include only data submitted by Summary reporting agencies because suspicion is not collected as a crime via NIBRS.

Table 67A. Arrests, Suburban Areas,[1] Distribution by Ethnicity, 2022

(Number, percent; 6,320 agencies; 2022 estimated population 118,233,444.)

Offense charged	Total arrests			Percent distribution[2]			Arrests under 18		
	Total[3]	Hispanic or Latino	Not Hispanic or Latino	Total[3]	Hispanic or Latino	Not Hispanic or Latino	Total[3]	Hispanic or Latino	Not Hispanic or Latino
Total	1,926,239	366,266	1,559,973	100.0	19.0	81.0	126,606	26,920	99,686
Violent crime[4]	95,057	22,168	72,889	100.0	23.3	76.7	8,880	1,963	6,917
Murder and nonnegligent manslaughter	2,434	512	1,922	100.0	21.0	79.0	199	36	163
Rape	4,862	1,212	3,650	100.0	24.9	75.1	777	141	636
Robbery	10,504	2,331	8,173	100.0	22.2	77.8	1,987	433	1,554
Aggravated assault	77,257	18,113	59,144	100.0	23.4	76.6	5,917	1,353	4,564
Property crime[4]	199,937	30,413	169,524	100.0	15.2	84.8	16,659	2,965	13,694
Burglary	28,004	4,851	23,153	100.0	17.3	82.7	2,871	440	2,431
Larceny-theft	152,921	20,844	132,077	100.0	13.6	86.4	11,300	2,022	9,278
Motor vehicle theft	16,912	4,259	12,653	100.0	25.2	74.8	2,136	436	1,700
Arson	2,100	459	1,641	100.0	21.9	78.1	352	67	285
Other assaults	230,203	40,505	189,698	100.0	17.6	82.4	30,691	5,795	24,896
Forgery and counterfeiting	9,518	2,081	7,437	100.0	21.9	78.1	151	38	113
Fraud	24,082	3,175	20,907	100.0	13.2	86.8	667	103	564
Embezzlement	2,496	296	2,200	100.0	11.9	88.1	112	14	98
Stolen property; buying, receiving, possessing	22,319	4,314	18,005	100.0	19.3	80.7	1,841	259	1,582
Vandalism	39,853	7,109	32,744	100.0	17.8	82.2	6,383	1,222	5,161
Weapons; carrying, possessing, etc.	41,437	9,199	32,238	100.0	22.2	77.8	4,659	1,254	3,405
Prostitution and commercialized vice	1,724	374	1,350	100.0	21.7	78.3	16	5	11
Sex offenses (except forcible rape and prostitution)	6,833	1,986	4,847	100.0	29.1	70.9	1,028	196	832
Drug abuse violations	250,771	47,006	203,765	100.0	18.7	81.3	14,638	4,589	10,049
Gambling	378	151	227	100.0	39.9	60.1	12	4	8
Offenses against the family and children	13,432	1,556	11,876	100.0	11.6	88.4	437	52	385
Driving under the influence	235,782	70,763	165,019	100.0	30.0	70.0	1,283	417	866
Liquor laws	22,320	4,062	18,258	100.0	18.2	81.8	3,801	689	3,112
Drunkenness[5]	4,590	2,174	2,416	100.0	47.4	52.6	33	18	15
Disorderly conduct	54,225	8,371	45,854	100.0	15.4	84.6	8,123	1,315	6,808
Vagrancy	3,295	364	2,931	100.0	11.0	89.0	5	0	5
All other offenses (except traffic)	666,522	109,945	556,577	100.0	16.5	83.5	25,773	5,775	19,998
Suspicion[6]	51	7	44	100.0	13.7	86.3	0	0	0
Curfew and loitering law violations	1,414	247	1,167	100.0	17.5	82.5	1,414	247	1,167

Table 67A. Arrests, Suburban Areas,[1] Distribution by Ethnicity, 2022—Continued

(Number, percent; 6,320 agencies; 2022 estimated population 118,233,444.)

Offense charged	Percent distribution[2]			Arrests 18 and over			Percent distribution[2]		
	Total[3]	Hispanic or Latino	Not Hispanic or Latino	Total[3]	Hispanic or Latino	Not Hispanic or Latino	Total[3]	Hispanic or Latino	Not Hispanic or Latino
Total	100.0	21.3	78.7	1,799,633	339,346	1,460,287	100.0	18.9	81.1
Violent crime[4]	100.0	22.1	77.9	86,177	20,205	65,972	100.0	23.4	76.6
Murder and nonnegligent manslaughter	100.0	18.1	81.9	2,235	476	1,759	100.0	21.3	78.7
Rape	100.0	18.1	81.9	4,085	1,071	3,014	100.0	26.2	73.8
Robbery	100.0	21.8	78.2	8,517	1,898	6,619	100.0	22.3	77.7
Aggravated assault	100.0	22.9	77.1	71,340	16,760	54,580	100.0	23.5	76.5
Property crime[4]	100.0	17.8	82.2	183,278	27,448	155,830	100.0	15.0	85.0
Burglary	100.0	15.3	84.7	25,133	4,411	20,722	100.0	17.6	82.4
Larceny-theft	100.0	17.9	82.1	141,621	18,822	122,799	100.0	13.3	86.7
Motor vehicle theft	100.0	20.4	79.6	14,776	3,823	10,953	100.0	25.9	74.1
Arson	100.0	19.0	81.0	1,748	392	1,356	100.0	22.4	77.6
Other assaults	100.0	18.9	81.1	199,512	34,710	164,802	100.0	17.4	82.6
Forgery and counterfeiting	100.0	25.2	74.8	9,367	2,043	7,324	100.0	21.8	78.2
Fraud	100.0	15.4	84.6	23,415	3,072	20,343	100.0	13.1	86.9
Embezzlement	100.0	12.5	87.5	2,384	282	2,102	100.0	11.8	88.2
Stolen property; buying, receiving, possessing	100.0	14.1	85.9	20,478	4,055	16,423	100.0	19.8	80.2
Vandalism	100.0	19.1	80.9	33,470	5,887	27,583	100.0	17.6	82.4
Weapons; carrying, possessing, etc.	100.0	26.9	73.1	36,778	7,945	28,833	100.0	21.6	78.4
Prostitution and commercialized vice	100.0	31.3	68.8	1,708	369	1,339	100.0	21.6	78.4
Sex offenses (except forcible rape and prostitution)	100.0	19.1	80.9	5,805	1,790	4,015	100.0	30.8	69.2
Drug abuse violations	100.0	31.3	68.7	236,133	42,417	193,716	100.0	18.0	82.0
Gambling	100.0	33.3	66.7	366	147	219	100.0	40.2	59.8
Offenses against the family and children	100.0	11.9	88.1	12,995	1,504	11,491	100.0	11.6	88.4
Driving under the influence	100.0	32.5	67.5	234,499	70,346	164,153	100.0	30.0	70.0
Liquor laws	100.0	18.1	81.9	18,519	3,373	15,146	100.0	18.2	81.8
Drunkenness[5]	100.0	54.5	45.5	4,557	2,156	2,401	100.0	47.3	52.7
Disorderly conduct	100.0	16.2	83.8	46,102	7,056	39,046	100.0	15.3	84.7
Vagrancy	100.0	0.0	100.0	3,290	364	2,926	100.0	11.1	88.9
All other offenses (except traffic)	100.0	22.4	77.6	640,749	104,170	536,579	100.0	16.3	83.7
Suspicion[6]	NA	NA	NA	51	7	44	100.0	13.7	86.3
Curfew and loitering law violations	100.0	17.5	82.5	NA	NA	NA	NA	NA	NA

NA = Not available.
1 Suburban areas include law enforcement agencies in cities with less than 50,000 inhabitants and county law enforcement agencies that are within a Metropolitan Statistical Area. Suburban areas exclude all metropolitan agencies associated with a principal city.   2 Because of rounding, the percentages may not sum to 100.   3 The ethnicity totals are representative of those agencies that provided ethnicity breakdowns. Not all agencies provide ethnicity data; therefore, the race and ethnicity totals will not equal.   4 Violent crimes are offenses of murder and nonnegligent manslaughter, rape, robbery, and aggravated assault. Property crimes are offenses of burglary, larceny-theft, motor vehicle theft, and arson.   5 Drunkenness figures were submitted by Summary reporting agencies only. As of 2021 drunkenness is no longer a separate offense in the National Incident-Based Reporting System (NIBRS), but it is included with All Other Offenses (except traffic) category.   6 Figures for suspicion include only data submitted by Summary reporting agencies because suspicion is not collected as a crime via NIBRS.

Table 68. Police Disposition of Juvenile Offenders Taken into Custody, 2022

(Number, percent.)

Population group	Total[1]	Handled within department and released	Referred to juvenile court jurisdiction[2]	Referred to welfare agency[2]	Referred to other police agency[2]	Referred to criminal or adult court[2]	Referred to other authorities not specified	Number of agencies	Estimated population, 2022
Total Agencies									
Number	360,803	117,649	15,216	18	280	100	246,470	12,177	277,723,523
Percent[3]	100.0	32.6	4.2	*	0.1	*	68.3		
Total Cities									
Number	276,364	88,905	12,462	16	233	66	190,065	8,873	183,669,345
Percent[3]	100.0	32.2	4.5	*	0.1	*	68.8		
Group I (250,000 and over)									
Number	48,441	16,547	2,973	0	148	1	32,231	83	51,652,569
Percent[3]	100.0	34.2	6.1	0.0	0.3	*	66.5		
Group II (100,000 to 249,999)									
Number	42,787	12,915	3,146	0	7	0	30,105	207	29,680,743
Percent[3]	100.0	30.2	7.4	0.0	*	0.0	70.4		
Group III (50,000 to 99,999)									
Number	47,743	14,522	2,577	10	34	10	34,100	455	31,620,562
Percent[3]	100.0	30.4	5.4	*	0.1	*	71.4		
Group IV (25,000 to 49,999)									
Number	46,691	14,887	1,245	1	17	11	32,032	812	28,218,304
Percent[3]	100.0	31.9	2.7	*	*	*	68.6		
Group V (10,000 to 24,999)									
Number	47,530	15,624	1,406	4	9	17	32,405	1,574	25,258,606
Percent[3]	100.0	32.9	3.0	*	*	*	68.2		
Group VI (under 10,000)									
Number	43,172	14,410	1,115	1	18	27	29,192	5,742	17,238,561
Percent[3]	100.0	33.4	2.6	*	*	0.1	67.6		
Metropolitan Counties									
Number	65,906	22,518	2,527	2	47	33	44,098	1,453	72,021,962
Percent[3]	100.0	34.2	3.8	*	0.1	0.1	66.9		
Nonmetropolitan Counties									
Number	18,533	6,226	227	0	0	1	12,307	1,851	22,032,216
Percent[3]	100.0	33.6	1.2	0.0	0.0	*	66.4		
Suburban Areas[4]									
Number	148,674	49,576	5,846	8	91	78	100,632	6,489	123,239,275
Percent[3]	100.0	33.3	3.9	*	0.1	0.1	67.7		

* = Less than one-tenth of one percent.
1 Includes all offenses except traffic and neglect cases.   2 Because National Incident Based Reporting System (NIBRS) only collects juvenile disposition in the categories Handled within department and released, and Referred to other authorities not specified, the other categories are lower than previous years since the majority of reporting agencies are NIBRS.   3 Because of rounding, the percentages may not sum to 100.   4 Suburban areas include law enforcement agencies in cities with less than 50,000 inhabitants and county law enforcement agencies that are within a Metropolitan Statistical Area. Suburban areas exclude all metropolitan agencies associated with a principal city. The agencies associated with suburban areas also appear in other groups within this table.

Table 69. Arrests, by State, 2022

(Number.)

State	Total, all classes[1]	Violent crime[2]	Property crime[2]	Murder and nonnegligent manslaughter	Rape	Robbery	Aggravated assault	Burglary	Larceny-theft	Motor vehicle theft	Arson	Other assaults	Forgery and counterfeiting	Fraud	Embezzlement	Stolen property; buying, receiving, possessing	Vandalism
Alabama																	
Under 18	2,977	282	514	22	21	81	158	128	308	74	4	464	10	28	0	102	127
Total, all ages	121,188	3,726	10,324	262	213	421	2,830	1,425	8,224	597	78	9,512	492	1,200	32	1,443	1,458
Alaska																	
Under 18	1,179	172	175	6	25	16	125	60	95	17	3	356	0	7	2	2	114
Total, all ages	21,107	2,273	1,853	55	129	197	1,892	428	1,060	323	42	3,841	44	104	30	70	987
Arizona																	
Under 18	11,738	875	1,504	29	42	216	588	199	1,130	161	14	2,936	2	35	5	69	820
Total, all ages	165,478	9,575	19,571	324	278	1,334	7,639	2,505	15,622	1,268	176	20,956	374	1,325	418	970	6,221
Arkansas																	
Under 18	7,308	548	914	30	46	56	416	224	603	77	10	1,779	6	17	0	182	219
Total, all ages	101,026	5,400	10,295	193	291	336	4,580	1,651	7,976	604	64	11,412	535	507	15	1,688	1,461
California																	
Under 18	25,513	4,909	3,236	92	161	1,780	2,876	805	1,736	594	101	4,647	27	117	12	534	1,539
Total, all ages	744,620	84,193	62,588	1,415	1,891	12,626	68,261	18,005	29,246	13,173	2,164	72,260	2,237	6,013	713	15,928	17,658
Colorado																	
Under 18	11,095	668	1,578	45	45	151	427	160	1,098	277	43	1,988	3	34	5	17	620
Total, all ages	157,869	8,768	19,149	275	403	1,058	7,032	2,472	12,399	3,974	304	16,335	372	1,393	73	1,103	5,130
Connecticut																	
Under 18	4,464	255	675	7	23	106	119	97	343	210	25	1,198	4	28	4	56	233
Total, all ages	73,456	2,395	8,053	77	170	573	1,575	909	6,374	699	71	14,966	225	435	67	237	1,550
Delaware																	
Under 18	2,040	221	298	3	11	58	149	79	155	59	5	609	1	39	4	101	119
Total, all ages	25,020	1,761	3,592	36	72	255	1,398	501	2,863	211	17	5,452	128	1,026	69	375	811
District of Columbia[5]																	
Under 18	1,326	342	50	8	5	273	56	5	25	20	0	220	1	1	0	8	39
Total, all ages	16,594	1,299	928	89	73	483	654	112	747	63	6	5,216	112	33	0	84	641
Florida[6,7]																	
Under 18	18,823	1,363	3,791	16	87	353	907	871	2,038	852	30	4,351	17	107	9	45	409
Total, all ages	285,349	15,847	29,072	340	689	1,974	12,844	5,003	21,032	2,876	161	41,391	528	3,380	334	473	3,171
Georgia																	
Under 18	13,015	1,013	2,037	41	74	231	667	277	1,395	324	41	3,131	32	101	0	280	457
Total, all ages	178,284	9,734	17,294	432	399	931	7,972	1,798	14,112	1,221	163	20,283	1,085	4,386	33	2,006	3,566
Hawaii																	
Under 18	1,318	92	143	0	9	47	36	10	123	4	6	461	2	2	0	26	11
Total, all ages	25,015	769	1,830	33	66	220	450	187	1,528	84	31	4,101	66	198	7	468	82
Idaho																	
Under 18	5,498	172	665	0	14	25	133	133	484	41	7	697	3	29	3	28	250
Total, all ages	51,174	1,869	3,333	25	149	74	1,621	682	2,445	156	50	3,712	70	404	27	188	766
Illinois[6]																	
Under 18	9,493	748	1,478	25	15	289	419	176	983	301	18	2,432	5	87	5	73	555
Total, all ages	121,752	5,773	11,773	276	176	864	4,457	1,541	9,424	712	96	24,740	261	1,872	79	304	3,984
Indiana																	
Under 18	8,217	549	980	12	36	162	339	134	648	185	13	1,849	10	36	7	85	130
Total, all ages	107,123	4,817	10,019	141	178	696	3,802	1,195	7,671	1,088	65	13,643	270	888	173	569	493
Iowa																	
Under 18	7,246	608	1,488	2	72	54	480	115	1,142	200	31	1,793	3	46	7	86	558
Total, all ages	66,043	4,192	7,668	26	260	235	3,671	920	5,972	687	89	7,993	282	779	106	339	1,812
Kansas																	
Under 18	5,057	291	783	14	31	43	203	72	612	74	25	1,118	0	16	4	29	318
Total, all ages	65,112	3,222	5,443	86	157	244	2,735	553	4,440	372	78	9,306	136	336	59	543	2,247
Kentucky																	
Under 18	2,013	183	397	10	31	52	90	120	177	84	16	749	1	4	6	108	100
Total, all ages	164,192	1,928	7,455	98	281	312	1,237	1,507	5,285	592	71	8,771	364	630	217	1,304	962
Louisiana																	
Under 18	10,795	1,020	1,819	66	46	305	603	420	1,127	259	13	2,678	9	18	2	346	401
Total, all ages	97,201	8,068	17,880	272	280	874	6,642	3,244	13,389	1,123	124	16,787	357	667	144	2,688	3,129
Maine																	
Under 18	1,787	67	389	2	9	11	45	67	244	53	25	422	4	11	0	3	179
Total, all ages	30,476	624	4,522	19	50	88	467	362	3,885	219	56	4,360	93	255	14	79	854
Maryland[6]																	
Under 18	6,733	896	1,275	27	44	455	370	274	712	264	25	2,021	2	30	5	55	361
Total, all ages	78,184	6,734	7,581	184	265	1,675	4,610	1,573	5,081	860	67	9,023	79	369	89	259	1,250
Massachusetts																	
Under 18	4,799	680	639	2	29	61	588	172	369	86	12	1,381	4	25	2	108	311
Total, all ages	83,027	7,589	6,992	47	302	459	6,781	1,305	5,078	524	85	16,850	338	672	61	678	2,043
Michigan																	
Under 18	8,143	829	1,398	26	130	101	572	279	802	284	33	2,273	10	74	20	272	407
Total, all ages	161,250	12,430	15,046	375	806	917	10,332	2,153	11,083	1,624	186	26,978	421	1,997	685	2,155	2,822
Minnesota																	
Under 18	10,491	753	1,712	21	83	248	401	179	1,327	197	9	1,826	13	89	13	299	422
Total, all ages	117,367	5,464	17,194	176	498	857	3,933	1,618	14,520	947	109	12,805	667	2,460	136	2,178	2,007
Mississippi																	
Under 18	1,977	81	363	7	3	29	42	88	234	39	2	417	0	12	10	33	56
Total, all ages	45,860	1,054	4,576	65	78	118	793	627	3,671	251	27	3,984	104	424	229	408	368
Missouri																	
Under 18	9,345	861	1,489	28	62	148	623	277	869	332	11	1,885	11	38	24	397	411
Total, all ages	140,708	8,493	16,750	327	410	797	6,959	2,632	12,009	1,976	133	15,577	946	1,524	271	2,411	3,059
Montana																	
Under 18	3,777	184	587	0	15	30	139	46	496	35	10	606	3	6	0	12	198
Total, all ages	26,928	1,737	4,324	17	72	127	1,521	336	3,642	296	50	4,740	89	140	21	245	822

Table 69. Arrests, by State, 2022—Continued

(Number.)

State	Weapons; carrying, possessing, etc.	Prostitution and commercialized vice	Sex offenses (except rape and prostitution)	Drug abuse violations	Gambling	Offenses against the family and children	Driving under the influence	Liquor laws	Drunk-enness[3]	Disorderly conduct	Vagrancy	All other offenses (except traffic)	Suspi-cion[4]	Curfew and loitering law violations	Number of agencies	Estimated population, 2022
Alabama																
Under 18	145	0	0	450	0	8	35	157	0	208	0	447	0	0	333	4,116,187
Total, all ages	1,896	46	88	16,805	9	305	6,189	6,150	0	2,436	0	59,077	0	0		
Alaska																
Under 18	16	0	26	116	0	0	41	25	2	16	0	108	0	1	28	728,061
Total, all ages	291	9	204	827	0	120	3,195	131	4	513	4	6,606	0	1		
Arizona																
Under 18	335	1	124	973	0	22	166	525	20	907	1	2,217	0	201	90	5,976,919
Total, all ages	3,265	573	685	19,656	0	626	15,406	2,796	31	10,059	1,832	50,938	0	201		
Arkansas																
Under 18	169	0	22	1,029	0	6	46	119	0	621	0	1,513	0	118	270	2,939,335
Total, all ages	1,008	26	106	14,462	5	243	5,947	976	0	2,481	207	44,134	0	118		
California																
Under 18	2,779	15	404	944	2	1	460	458	60	629	16	4,542	0	182	786	37,183,296
Total, all ages	30,542	3,797	5,045	113,418	288	254	96,048	2,297	13,487	25,239	2,247	190,186	0	182		
Colorado																
Under 18	325	0	87	1,304	0	17	186	589	0	1,102	0	2,450	0	122	175	5,568,117
Total, all ages	2,254	147	395	10,731	0	2,235	15,698	2,148	0	4,191	167	67,458	0	122		
Connecticut																
Under 18	244	0	46	112	0	22	22	6	0	959	0	596	0	4	102	3,601,911
Total, all ages	1,472	32	294	3,025	17	1,732	6,177	31	0	8,884	13	23,847	0	4		
Delaware																
Under 18	91	0	9	147	3	1	1	24	0	116	0	243	0	13	52	1,013,255
Total, all ages	451	13	83	3,633	17	136	309	420	0	776	76	5,879	0	13		
District of Columbia[5]																
Under 18	184	0	3	22	0	0	1	2	0	13	0	440	0	0	2	671,803
Total, all ages	1,437	14	131	750	7	5	577	130	0	366	29	4,835	0	0		
Florida[6,7]																
Under 18	630	2	97	1,127	0	1	57	172	0	78	0	6,523	0	44	279	12,369,280
Total, all ages	4,689	805	1,442	33,713	25	487	15,107	5,079	0	565	895	128,302	0	44		
Georgia																
Under 18	596	2	117	1,125	0	114	125	109	0	962	0	2,608	0	206	389	9,353,344
Total, all ages	2,947	215	583	27,425	12	1,064	18,566	1,627	6	8,070	1,208	57,968	0	206		
Hawaii																
Under 18	10	0	22	121	0	0	11	12	0	16	0	349	0	40	2	1,068,961
Total, all ages	128	1	124	933	43	17	2,623	840	0	676	210	11,859	0	40		
Idaho																
Under 18	120	0	39	843	0	5	96	197	0	304	0	1,926	0	121	105	1,914,857
Total, all ages	420	11	200	10,266	0	490	7,544	1,049	0	1,500	4	19,200	0	121		
Illinois[6]																
Under 18	504	0	5	830	0	2	48	208	0	883	0	1,418	0	212	423	8,783,930
Total, all ages	4,288	81	111	12,003	3	429	13,534	1,502	0	3,565	3	37,235	0	212		
Indiana																
Under 18	391	0	60	829	0	7	32	248	0	330	0	2,577	0	97	144	4,755,647
Total, all ages	2,671	50	340	17,080	5	351	12,207	1,879	0	2,165	0	39,406	0	97		
Iowa																
Under 18	85	1	16	920	0	2	85	377	0	211	0	946	0	14	189	2,634,203
Total, all ages	694	24	80	8,327	9	441	8,197	1,499	0	706	3	22,878	0	14		
Kansas																
Under 18	86	0	28	879	0	12	83	256	0	241	0	913	0	0	194	2,455,385
Total, all ages	799	94	164	10,354	0	236	7,289	1,537	0	1,654	0	21,693	0	0		
Kentucky																
Under 18	50	0	28	348	0	0	0	0	0	0	0	39	0	0	417	3,790,569
Total, all ages	460	10	237	16,068	0	3,402	10,355	19	0	2,906	8	109,096	0	0		
Louisiana																
Under 18	577	1	51	984	2	7	6	78	0	1,269	0	1,476	0	51	123	3,653,127
Total, all ages	3,658	105	542	18,913	124	609	2,749	930	61	3,299	4	16,436	0	51		
Maine																
Under 18	5	0	17	107	0	0	34	191	0	70	0	284	0	4	125	1,367,258
Total, all ages	118	26	80	2,535	1	113	4,437	626	0	746	2	10,987	0	4		
Maryland[6]																
Under 18	375	0	74	431	0	5	21	104	0	196	0	876	0	6	81	4,951,587
Total, all ages	2,985	73	247	7,050	0	805	8,804	642	0	1,300	35	30,829	24	6		
Massachusetts																
Under 18	214	1	37	79	3	9	30	157	0	134	0	985	0	0	378	6,885,869
Total, all ages	1,430	226	279	4,420	8	960	7,591	756	0	2,200	3	29,931	0	0		
Michigan																
Under 18	386	0	78	287	0	3	100	144	0	179	0	1,579	0	104	582	9,386,427
Total, all ages	7,864	101	561	11,389	27	1,102	20,952	2,685	0	3,042	50	50,839	0	104		
Minnesota																
Under 18	318	0	74	725	0	1	184	809	0	1,063	0	1,940	0	250	397	5,698,146
Total, all ages	2,638	88	437	12,467	8	134	20,415	3,192	0	4,246	59	30,522	0	250		
Mississippi																
Under 18	117	0	3	173	0	35	42	20	0	306	0	277	0	32	143	1,644,720
Total, all ages	782	3	61	7,427	2	452	6,915	328	0	3,462	3	15,246	0	32		
Missouri																
Under 18	157	6	37	881	2	20	150	345	0	733	0	1,663	0	235	389	5,728,888
Total, all ages	2,567	65	188	22,655	19	773	17,295	2,022	0	4,470	129	41,259	0	235		
Montana																
Under 18	10	0	47	98	0	48	60	483	0	379	0	862	0	194	98	1,097,777
Total, all ages	51	2	186	1,462	0	396	3,811	945	0	2,204	6	5,553	0	194		

Table 69. Arrests, by State, 2022—Continued

(Number.)

State	Total, all classes[1]	Violent crime[2]	Property crime[2]	Murder and nonnegligent manslaughter	Rape	Robbery	Aggravated assault	Burglary	Larceny-theft	Motor vehicle theft	Arson	Other assaults	Forgery and counterfeiting	Fraud	Embezzlement	Stolen property; buying, receiving, possessing	Vandalism
Nebraska																	
Under 18	4,991	125	758	1	26	15	83	33	562	126	37	1,182	2	42	5	27	453
Total, all ages	37,222	1,571	3,409	28	115	62	1,366	229	2,887	236	57	4,208	144	445	13	297	1,295
Nevada																	
Under 18	6,142	601	581	7	39	315	240	91	360	115	15	1,926	0	13	4	138	251
Total, all ages	106,085	6,187	8,322	161	286	1,296	4,444	2,210	5,122	835	155	19,874	212	1,006	208	2,092	2,166
New Hampshire																	
Under 18	2,295	48	132	1	10	13	24	16	101	10	5	466	2	6	2	15	151
Total, all ages	35,638	544	2,121	9	70	112	353	149	1,846	109	17	4,272	107	303	52	276	940
New Jersey																	
Under 18	5,202	567	1,410	7	13	187	360	187	1,045	157	21	617	6	22	4	378	203
Total, all ages	109,956	7,134	15,212	145	226	1,191	5,572	1,920	12,577	591	124	16,347	543	827	123	1,835	1,999
New Mexico																	
Under 18	1,691	154	148	2	3	30	119	30	93	24	1	535	0	3	1	18	84
Total, all ages	44,787	2,873	5,090	43	26	203	2,601	803	3,906	343	38	9,123	58	174	90	1,065	1,561
New York																	
Under 18	6,411	886	1,821	22	129	252	483	404	1,052	324	41	1,197	9	20	0	218	951
Total, all ages	148,658	9,802	32,247	260	727	1,836	6,979	4,108	25,880	2,015	244	20,519	1,565	1,218	42	2,272	10,536
North Carolina																	
Under 18	9,145	649	1,570	60	20	219	350	383	822	338	27	2,528	1	55	16	359	297
Total, all ages	222,527	9,374	22,678	489	229	1,521	7,135	5,102	16,080	1,298	198	22,581	492	2,376	699	3,393	2,623
North Dakota																	
Under 18	4,333	97	554	1	12	17	67	49	427	68	10	724	7	21	10	29	162
Total, all ages	30,158	834	3,103	18	45	82	689	364	2,407	294	38	3,210	117	538	34	271	492
Ohio																	
Under 18	18,186	862	2,043	33	72	272	485	310	1,287	407	39	4,505	1	100	0	537	747
Total, all ages	155,418	6,961	20,964	258	356	1,192	5,155	2,717	16,845	1,249	153	32,851	220	1,124	17	2,146	3,361
Oklahoma																	
Under 18	5,703	309	859	20	8	62	219	181	540	125	13	938	1	15	13	82	255
Total, all ages	79,441	4,253	11,372	150	139	393	3,571	2,141	7,783	1,288	160	8,947	297	736	193	1,260	1,585
Oregon																	
Under 18	4,495	307	801	8	29	62	208	112	558	120	11	908	7	22	2	15	494
Total, all ages	96,183	5,217	15,914	99	186	902	4,030	2,071	11,154	2,302	387	9,968	436	1,199	42	984	3,617
Pennsylvania[6]																	
Under 18	8,380	900	1,237	43	92	360	405	216	615	378	28	2,133	20	40	6	127	425
Total, all ages	113,932	7,167	13,931	336	434	1,442	4,955	1,909	10,299	1,575	148	19,130	646	1,184	137	804	2,088
Rhode Island																	
Under 18	1,949	95	202	1	17	15	62	48	110	29	15	377	3	10	2	33	149
Total, all ages	22,084	756	1,829	17	86	92	561	417	1,196	182	34	3,632	117	293	61	216	811
South Carolina																	
Under 18	9,273	620	1,244	59	52	120	389	272	843	111	18	2,927	11	45	15	148	366
Total, all ages	138,141	7,089	17,127	408	396	667	5,618	2,510	13,454	1,018	145	16,274	732	2,091	232	1,929	2,937
South Dakota																	
Under 18	4,222	135	355	1	3	20	111	68	197	80	10	679	4	30	2	38	129
Total, all ages	43,619	1,331	1,739	27	48	92	1,164	292	1,076	341	30	4,637	99	488	25	192	486
Tennessee																	
Under 18	13,390	721	1,576	13	44	123	541	249	973	328	26	3,563	32	76	19	84	552
Total, all ages	250,586	11,967	23,967	342	325	912	10,388	3,484	17,064	3,269	150	25,709	1,538	3,070	486	1,666	3,682
Texas																	
Under 18	44,794	3,468	6,072	126	287	921	2,134	779	4,183	1,014	96	11,403	66	249	13	95	1,082
Total, all ages	549,897	31,390	58,541	1,021	1,734	4,628	24,007	7,467	42,867	7,646	561	86,134	3,245	6,468	232	1,029	7,648
Utah																	
Under 18	8,768	333	1,707	7	78	53	195	101	1,522	74	10	1,263	5	29	0	38	749
Total, all ages	88,426	2,774	11,338	67	349	323	2,035	776	10,098	382	82	9,046	353	737	12	849	3,035
Vermont																	
Under 18	549	68	50	0	20	9	39	18	29	3	0	136	0	4	1	5	54
Total, all ages	12,124	880	1,641	11	87	55	727	210	1,313	103	15	1,516	51	171	35	84	353
Virginia																	
Under 18	8,340	601	1,567	27	65	183	326	158	1,270	116	23	1,828	13	70	21	127	230
Total, all ages	194,308	7,020	20,575	338	477	1,166	5,039	1,708	17,547	1,166	154	27,870	1,011	4,297	677	870	3,147
Washington																	
Under 18	6,122	767	889	20	79	254	414	186	553	116	34	2,179	2	15	0	117	556
Total, all ages	130,926	8,932	21,436	201	554	1,737	6,440	4,497	15,315	1,367	257	23,462	314	682	27	4,300	4,864
West Virginia																	
Under 18	387	17	37	0	2	1	14	12	23	1	1	143	0	1	0	1	13
Total, all ages	21,226	914	2,838	37	47	39	791	377	2,350	89	22	2,633	86	140	16	156	287
Wisconsin																	
Under 18	25,200	918	2,835	24	201	180	513	258	1,932	605	40	2,323	8	86	40	269	1,206
Total, all ages	181,412	6,821	17,835	190	865	708	5,058	1,343	14,939	1,449	104	15,834	585	1,521	322	1,011	4,630
Wyoming																	
Under 18	2,152	16	173	1	2	1	12	16	145	11	1	330	0	4	1	0	82
Total, all ages	14,283	277	1,039	5	33	8	231	92	853	88	6	1,533	3	28	6	11	293

Table 69. Arrests, by State, 2022—Continued

(Number.)

State	Weapons; carrying, possessing, etc.	Prostitution and commercialized vice	Sex offenses (except rape and prostitution)	Drug abuse violations	Gambling	Offenses against the family and children	Driving under the influence	Liquor laws	Drunkenness[3]	Disorderly conduct	Vagrancy	All other offenses (except traffic)	Suspicion[4]	Curfew and loitering law violations	Number of agencies	Estimated population, 2022
Nebraska																
Under 18	52	0	24	722	0	337	68	325	0	107	0	710	0	52	119	1,229,566
Total, all ages	510	5	92	6,544	0	649	4,306	1,888	0	1,491	752	9,551	0	52		
Nevada																
Under 18	194	22	60	657	4	0	61	434	0	252	0	688	0	256	49	3,162,409
Total, all ages	2,882	2,280	434	7,833	55	545	11,260	1,378	0	2,055	469	36,571	0	256		
New Hampshire																
Under 18	4	0	10	163	0	14	23	152	0	55	0	1,045	0	7	191	1,328,560
Total, all ages	232	2	98	3,235	3	292	3,435	1,023	0	757	92	17,847	0	7		
New Jersey																
Under 18	495	1	47	134	0	14	41	9	1	324	0	840	0	89	448	7,742,608
Total, all ages	3,594	288	566	9,609	7	984	11,549	242	14	4,579	222	34,155	38	89		
New Mexico																
Under 18	77	0	11	197	0	8	36	31	0	167	0	219	0	2	85	1,806,455
Total, all ages	590	16	43	2,730	0	905	5,131	764	0	1,349	121	13,102	0	2		
New York																
Under 18	319	1	157	83	0	3	59	28	0	50	0	609	0	0	278	9,462,066
Total, all ages	3,838	128	1,205	14,213	26	321	19,475	366	0	1,826	66	28,993	0	0		
North Carolina																
Under 18	476	2	26	738	0	2	97	83	0	614	0	1,625	0	7	328	9,600,572
Total, all ages	5,013	96	386	32,150	29	3,221	13,377	1,361	0	2,971	145	99,555	0	7		
North Dakota																
Under 18	27	1	28	476	0	191	40	330	0	613	0	920	0	103	106	776,111
Total, all ages	260	3	100	3,820	0	318	4,391	2,224	0	1,320	0	9,020	0	103		
Ohio																
Under 18	453	0	62	841	0	5	65	382	0	1,617	0	5,776	0	190	417	9,899,619
Total, all ages	4,725	245	317	18,146	2	492	11,387	3,419	0	7,492	1	41,358	0	190		
Oklahoma																
Under 18	258	0	12	857	0	2	75	56	0	779	0	911	0	281	445	4,012,441
Total, all ages	2,797	167	162	12,182	0	302	8,566	762	0	2,340	105	23,134	0	281		
Oregon																
Under 18	106	1	47	512	0	2	105	207	0	351	0	549	0	59	180	3,996,089
Total, all ages	2,055	105	311	3,205	0	207	11,961	1,079	0	4,710	52	35,062	0	59		
Pennsylvania[6]																
Under 18	402	0	121	640	1	13	113	214	13	1,030	1	908	0	36	252	5,391,278
Total, all ages	3,886	283	529	18,166	98	488	21,589	863	721	5,793	1,131	15,262	0	36		
Rhode Island																
Under 18	112	0	16	84	0	11	2	36	0	535	0	279	0	3	47	1,093,734
Total, all ages	493	2	69	1,293	5	57	2,656	314	0	1,991	1	7,485	0	3		
South Carolina																
Under 18	721	0	37	1,270	1	19	39	204	0	290	0	1,311	0	5	337	5,128,795
Total, all ages	4,344	66	271	27,910	48	907	10,901	3,382	0	6,736	638	34,522	0	5		
South Dakota																
Under 18	97	0	11	525	0	183	97	333	0	632	0	915	0	57	63	704,986
Total, all ages	352	5	58	5,143	0	865	5,618	1,380	0	3,312	497	17,335	0	57		
Tennessee																
Under 18	395	0	67	1,919	0	12	82	232	0	818	0	2,907	0	335	305	6,886,897
Total, all ages	2,996	425	401	36,196	21	2,134	17,436	1,954	0	3,909	8	112,686	0	335		
Texas																
Under 18	1,531	7	178	7,593	2	125	343	499	0	925	0	10,725	0	418	1,018	29,301,660
Total, all ages	17,390	1,646	879	84,859	181	2,351	58,260	4,378	0	5,636	569	178,643	0	418		
Utah																
Under 18	138	0	141	1,600	0	24	103	408	0	244	0	1,787	0	199	112	3,025,029
Total, all ages	1,005	33	429	13,991	2	2,078	7,912	2,936	0	1,768	14	29,915	0	199		
Vermont																
Under 18	6	0	6	27	0	0	20	30	0	31	0	111	0	0	66	618,683
Total, all ages	26	1	39	696	0	15	2,190	42	0	421	0	3,963	0	0		
Virginia																
Under 18	386	0	72	548	2	58	71	204	0	95	0	2,269	0	178	322	8,610,603
Total, all ages	5,054	222	567	13,252	12	1,037	17,011	1,667	0	5,507	17	84,317	0	178		
Washington																
Under 18	226	1	31	157	0	11	114	164	0	136	0	757	0	0	226	7,647,856
Total, all ages	1,815	101	347	1,334	3	179	22,075	559	0	1,999	277	38,220	0	0		
West Virginia																
Under 18	4	0	4	39	0	0	5	4	0	16	0	95	0	8	105	921,582
Total, all ages	241	81	36	4,295	0	45	1,629	166	0	478	23	7,154	0	8		
Wisconsin																
Under 18	468	3	335	2,278	0	183	155	996	0	4,963	2	7,104	0	1,028	333	5,585,872
Total, all ages	3,931	203	911	23,442	1	1,669	19,791	5,640	0	22,324	271	53,642	0	1,028		
Wyoming																
Under 18	19	0	3	287	0	5	35	308	0	150	0	655	0	84	49	451,193
Total, all ages	54	5	22	2,270	0	87	2,207	1,005	0	964	5	4,390	0	84		

NOTE: Because the number of agencies submitting arrest data varies from year to year, users are cautioned about making direct comparisons between 2022 arrest totals and those published in previous years' editions of *Crime in the United States*. Further, arrest figures may vary widely from state to state because some Part II crimes are not considered crimes in some states.
1 Does not include traffic arrests.   2 Violent crimes in this table are offenses of murder and nonnegligent manslaughter, rape, robbery, and aggravated assault. Property crimes are offenses of burglary, larceny-theft, motor vehicle theft, and arson.
3 Drunkenness figures were submitted by Summary reporting agencies only. As of 2021 drunkenness is no longer a separate offense in National Incident Based Reporting System (NIBRS), but it is included with All Other Offenses (except traffic) category.   4 Figures for suspicion include only data submitted by Summary reporting agencies because suspicion is not collected as a crime via NIBRS.   5 Includes arrests reported by the Metro Transit Police. This agency has no population associated with it.   6 Limited data for 2022 were available for Florida, Illinois, Maryland, and Pennsylvania.   7 The Florida arrest counts for offenses against the family and children, drunkenness, disorderly conduct, vagrancy, suspicion, and curfew and loitering law violations are included under the category All other offenses (except for the data submitted by NIBRS agencies using those specific breakdowns).

SECTION V

LAW ENFORCEMENT PERSONNEL

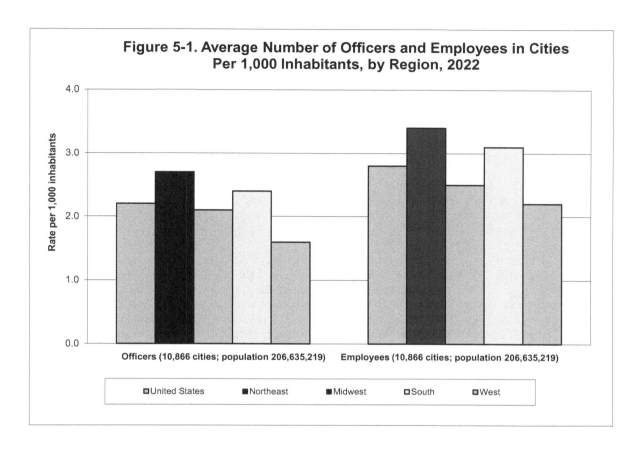

Figure 5-1. Average Number of Officers and Employees in Cities Per 1,000 Inhabitants, by Region, 2022

The Uniform Crime Reporting (UCR) program defines law enforcement officers as individuals who ordinarily carry a firearm and a badge, have full arrest powers, and are paid from government funds set aside specifically for sworn law enforcement representatives. Because of law enforcement's varied service requirements and functions, as well as the distinct demographic traits and characteristics of jurisdictions, readers should use caution when comparing staffing levels between agencies based on police employment data from the UCR program. In addition, the data presented here reflect existing staff levels and should not be interpreted as preferred officer strengths recommended by the Federal Bureau of Investigation (FBI). Also, readers should note that the totals given for sworn officers for any particular agency reflect both patrol officers on the street and officers assigned to various other duties, such as administrative and investigative positions and assignments to special teams.

Each year, law enforcement agencies across the United States report the total number of sworn law enforcement officers and civilians in their agencies as of October 31 to the UCR program. Civilian employees include personnel such as clerks, radio dispatchers, meter attendants, stenographers, jailers, correctional officers, and mechanics, (provided that they are full-time employees of the agency).

Due to the varied service requirements and functions of law enforcement and the distinctive demographic traits and characteristics of each jurisdiction, caution should be exercised when comparing agencies' staffing levels based on the UCR Program's police employment data. The data presented here reflect existing staffing levels in locations reporting data and should not be interpreted as FBI-preferred or FBI-recommended officer strengths. The total number of sworn officers for any particular agency reflects patrol officers on the street and officers assigned to other duties, such as those in administrative, investigative, and special-teams roles. Care should also be taken with year-over-year and other timeline comparisons, as different numbers of agencies report data each year, and this has been compounded for 2021 by the FBI's data migration to its Crime Data Explorer.

This section of *Crime in the United States* presents those data as the number and rate of law enforcement officers and civilian employees throughout the United States. In 2022, among agencies reporting data, 708,001 sworn officers and 310,344 civilians provided law enforcement services to more than 305 million people nationwide. These law enforcement personnel were employed by 14,009 state, city, university/college, metropolitan/nonmetropolitan county, and other designated law enforcement agencies. Of the slightly more than 1 million law enforcement employees, 72.2 percent were male. (Table 74)

The data in this section are broken down by geographic region and division, population group, state, city, university/college, metropolitan/nonmetropolitan county, and other law enforcement agency groups. (Information about geographic regions and divisions and population groups can be found in Appendix III.) UCR program staff compute the rate of sworn officers and law enforcement employees by taking the number of employees (sworn officers only or in combination with civilians), dividing by the population for which the agency provides law enforcement service, and multiplying by 1,000.

- Tables 70 and 71 present the number and rate of law enforcement personnel per 1,000 inhabitants collectively employed by agencies, broken down by geographic region and division by population group

- Tables 72 and 73 provide a count of law enforcement agencies by population group, based on the employment rate ranges for sworn officer and civilian employees per 1,000 inhabitants

- Table 74 provides the number of total officers, the percentage of male and female sworn officers, and the civilian employees by population group

- Table 75 lists the percentage of full-time civilian law enforcement employees by population group

- Table 76 breaks down by state the number of sworn law enforcement officers and civilians employed by state law enforcement agencies

- Table 77 provides the number of total officers, the percentage of male and female sworn officers, and the civilian employees by state

- Tables 78 to 80 list the number of law enforcement employees for cities, universities and colleges, and metropolitan and nonmetropolitan counties

- Table 81 supplies employee data for those law enforcement agencies that serve selected transit systems, parks and forests, schools and school districts, hospitals, etc., in the nation

The demographic traits and characteristics of a jurisdiction affect its requirements for law enforcement service. For instance, a village between two large cities may require more law enforcement than a community of the same size with no urban center nearby. A town with legal gambling may have different law enforcement needs than a town near a military base. A city largely made up of college students may have different law enforcement needs than a city whose residents are mainly retirees.

Similarly, the functions of law enforcement agencies are diverse. Employees of these agencies patrol local streets and major highways, protect citizens in the nation's smallest towns and largest cities, and conduct investigations on offenses at the local and state levels. State police in one area may enforce traffic laws on state highways and interstates; in another area, they may be responsible for investigating violent crimes. Sheriff's departments may collect tax monies, serve as the enforcement authority for local and state courts, administer jail facilities, or carry out some combination of these duties. This has an impact on an agency's staffing levels.

Because of the differing service requirements and functions, care should be taken when drawing comparisons between and among the staffing levels of law enforcement agencies. The data in this section are not intended as recommended or preferred officer strength; they should be used merely as guides. Adequate staffing levels can be determined only after careful study of the conditions that affect the service requirements in a particular jurisdiction.

RATE

The UCR program computes these rates by taking the number of employees, dividing by the population of the agency's jurisdiction, and multiplying by 1,000.

An examination of the 2022 law enforcement employee data by population group showed that the nation's participating cities (10,866 cities; population 206,635,219) had a collective rate of 2.8 law enforcement employees per 1,000 inhabitants. Cities with fewer than 10,000 inhabitants had the highest rate of law enforcement employees, with a rate of 5.6 per 1,000 inhabitants. Cities with 50,000 to 99,999 inhabitants and 100,000 to 249,999 inhabitants had the lowest rates of law enforcement employees (2.0 per 1,000 in population). The nation's largest cities, those with 250,000 or more inhabitants, averaged 3.2 law enforcement employees for every 1,000 inhabitants. (Table 70)

SWORN PERSONNEL

An analysis of the 2022 data showed that participating law enforcement agencies (10,866 cities; population 206,635,219) in the cities in the Northeast had the highest rate of sworn officers—2.8 per 1,000 inhabitants, followed by the South (2.4), the Midwest (1.9), and the West (1.6). (Table 71)

By population group in 2022, there were 2.2 sworn officers for each 1,000 resident population. Cities with fewer than 10,000 inhabitants had the highest rate at 4.3 sworn officers per 1,000 inhabitants. The nation's largest cities, those with 250,000 or more inhabitants, averaged 2.4 officers per 1,000 inhabitants. The lowest rates were in cities with 50,000 to 99,999 inhabitants and 100,000 to 249,999 inhabitants (1.6 per 1,000 resident population for each). (Table 71)

Males accounted for 86.5 percent of all full-time sworn law enforcement officers in 2022. Cities with populations of 1 million and over employed the highest percentage (19.5 percent) of full-time female officers. Of the city population groups and subsets, cities with populations of 10,000 to 24,999 inhabitants employed the highest percentage (89.4 percent) of male officers. In metropolitan counties, 85.7 percent of officers were male; in nonmetropolitan counties, 91.3 percent of officers were male; and in suburban areas, 86.9 percent of officers were male. (Table 74) Among states, the District of Columbia and Louisiana had female sworn officer proportions of over 15 percent, while less than 5 percent of Idaho's sworn officers and less than 4 percent of West Virginia's sworn officers were female. (Table 77)

CIVILIAN EMPLOYEES

Civilian employees provide a myriad of services to the nation's law enforcement and criminal justice agencies. Among other duties, they dispatch officers, provide administrative and record keeping support, and query local, state, and national databases.

In 2021, 30.8 percent of all law enforcement employees in the nation were civilians. Male employees accounted for 39.7 percent of all full-time civilian law enforcement employees in 2021. In cities, civilians made up 22.7 percent of law enforcement agency employees. Civilians made up 40.7 percent of law enforcement employees in metropolitan counties, 41.1 percent of law enforcement employees in nonmetropolitan counties, and 34.2 percent of law enforcement employees in suburban areas. (Table 75) More than half of the civilian employees in Illinois, the District of Columbia, and Indiana were male, while less than 30 percent of the civilian employees in Idaho, Virginia, and Nevada were male. (Table 77)

Table 70. Full-Time Law Enforcement Employees,[1] by Region and Geographic Division and Population Group, 2022

(Number, rate per 1,000 inhabitants.)

Region/geographic division	Total (10,866 cities; population 206,635,219)	Group I (89 cities, 250,000 and over; population 62,404,976)	Group II (225 cities, 100,000 to 249,999; population 32,519,393)	Group III (467 cities, 50,000 to 99,999; population 32,508,467)	Group IV (860 cities, 25,000 to 49,999; population 29,659,777)	Group V (1,750 cities, 10,000 to 24,999; population 27,868,454)	Group VI (7,475 cities, under 10,000; population 21,674,152)	Total city agencies	2022 estimated city population	County[2] (3,233 agencies; population 99,335,178)	Total city and county agencies	2022 estimated total agency population	Suburban areas[3] (7,540 agencies; population 132,833,931)
Total, United States													
Number of employees	577,776	198,558	66,575	65,474	62,195	63,847	121,127	10,866	206,635,219	440,569	14,099	305,970,397	478,074
Average number of employees per 1,000 inhabitants	2.8	3.2	2.0	2.0	2.1	2.3	5.6			4.4			3.6
Northeast													
Number of employees	155,826	62,842	9,226	15,592	19,074	18,414	30,678	2,525	45,608,673				
Average number of employees per 1,000 inhabitants	3.4	5.4	2.6	2.3	2.1	2.1	5.0						
New England													
Number of employees	34,540	2,782	5,157	5,585	7,394	7,193	6,429	838	13,591,511				
Average number of employees per 1,000 inhabitants	2.5	4.4	2.6	2.2	2.2	2.2	3.4						
Middle Atlantic													
Number of employees	121,286	60,060	4,069	10,007	11,680	11,221	24,249	1,687	32,017,162				
Average number of employees per 1,000 inhabitants	3.8	5.5	2.6	2.4	2.1	2.0	5.7						
Midwest													
Number of employees	105,610	32,730	8,401	13,190	14,099	15,735	21,455	2,744	42,252,276				
Average number of employees per 1,000 inhabitants	2.5	3.3	2.0	1.8	1.9	2.1	3.7						
East North Central													
Number of employees	73,548	25,958	4,799	9,238	10,719	10,774	12,060	1,633	28,570,590				
Average number of employees per 1,000 inhabitants	2.6	3.7	2.1	1.9	1.9	2.1	3.5						
West North Central													
Number of employees	32,062	6,772	3,602	3,952	3,380	4,961	9,395	1,111	13,681,686				
Average number of employees per 1,000 inhabitants	2.3	2.5	1.9	1.6	1.8	2.1	4.0						
South													
Number of employees	198,164	51,810	28,159	21,716	19,930	22,449	54,100	4,177	64,125,322				
Average number of employees per 1,000 inhabitants	3.1	2.7	2.3	2.4	2.5	2.8	7.2						
South Atlantic													
Number of employees	86,987	19,974	12,416	11,682	10,213	9,592	23,110	1,683	26,318,280				
Average number of employees per 1,000 inhabitants	3.3	3.3	2.3	2.5	2.6	2.9	7.9						
East South Central													
Number of employees	34,850	5,643	4,893	2,865	4,347	5,080	12,022	941	10,224,511				
Average number of employees per 1,000 inhabitants	3.4	2.8	2.7	2.4	2.6	2.9	6.7						
West South Central													
Number of employees	76,327	26,193	10,850	7,169	5,370	7,777	18,968	1,553	27,582,531				
Average number of employees per 1,000 inhabitants	2.8	2.4	2.1	2.2	2.2	2.6	6.7						
West													
Number of employees	118,176	51,176	20,789	14,976	9,092	7,249	14,894	1,420	54,648,948				
Average number of employees per 1,000 inhabitants	2.2	2.3	1.7	1.6	1.8	2.0	7.0						
Mountain													
Number of employees	46,119	19,902	7,383	4,421	3,493	2,750	8,170	647	18,717,694				
Average number of employees per 1,000 inhabitants	2.5	2.4	2.0	1.8	1.9	2.2	7.2						
Pacific													
Number of employees	72,057	31,274	13,406	10,555	5,599	4,499	6,724	773	35,931,254				
Average number of employees per 1,000 inhabitants	2.0	2.3	1.5	1.5	1.7	1.9	6.7						

1 Full-time law enforcement employees include civilians.   2 The designation *county* is a combination of both metropolitan and nonmetropolitan counties.   3 Suburban areas include law enforcement agencies in cities with less than 50,000 inhabitants and county law enforcement agencies that are within a Metropolitan Statistical Area. Suburban areas exclude all metropolitan agencies associated with a principal city. The agencies associated with suburban areas also appear in other groups within this table.

Table 71. Full-Time Law Enforcement Officers, by Region, Geographic Division, and Population Group, 2022

(Number, rate per 1,000 inhabitants.)

Region/geographic division	Total (10,866 cities; population 206,635,219)	Group I (89 cities, 250,000 and over; population 62,404,976)	Group II (225 cities, 100,000 to 249,999; population 32,519,393)	Group III (467 cities, 50,000 to 99,999; population 32,508,467)	Group IV (860 cities, 25,000 to 49,999; population 29,659,777)	Group V (1,750 cities, 10,000 to 24,999; population 27,868,454)	Group VI (7,475 cities, under 10,000; population 21,674,152)	Total city agencies	2022 estimated city population	County[1] (3,233 agencies; population 99,335,178)	Total city and county agencies	2022 estimated total agency population	Suburban areas[2] (7,540 agencies; population 132,833,931)
Total, United States													
Number of officers	448,911	152,730	51,020	50,878	49,648	51,804	92,831	10,866	206,635,219	259,090	14,099	305,970,397	314,322
Average number of officers per 1,000 inhabitants	2.2	2.4	1.6	1.6	1.7	1.9	4.3			2.6			2.4
Northeast													
Number of officers	123,378	45,559	7,904	13,055	16,098	15,707	25,055	2,525	45,608,673				
Average number of officers per 1,000 inhabitants	2.7	3.9	2.2	2.0	1.8	1.8	4.1						
New England													
Number of officers	28,136	2,112	4,465	4,695	6,093	5,759	5,012	838	13,591,511				
Average number of officers per 1,000 inhabitants	2.1	3.3	2.3	1.9	1.8	1.8	2.6						
Middle Atlantic													
Number of officers	95,242	43,447	3,439	8,360	10,005	9,948	20,043	1,687	32,017,162				
Average number of officers per 1,000 inhabitants	3.0	4.0	2.2	2.0	1.8	1.8	4.7						
Midwest													
Number of officers	87,457	28,382	6,843	10,618	11,332	12,951	17,331	2,744	42,252,276				
Average number of officers per 1,000 inhabitants	2.1	2.9	1.6	1.5	1.5	1.7	3.0						
East North Central													
Number of officers	62,246	23,254	3,988	7,451	8,621	8,912	10,020	1,633	28,570,590				
Average number of officers per 1,000 inhabitants	2.2	3.3	1.7	1.5	1.5	1.7	2.9						
West North Central													
Number of officers	25,211	5,128	2,855	3,167	2,711	4,039	7,311	1,111	13,681,686				
Average number of officers per 1,000 inhabitants	1.8	1.9	1.5	1.3	1.4	1.7	3.1						
South													
Number of officers	153,226	40,963	21,525	16,718	15,702	17,726	40,592	4,177	64,125,322				
Average number of officers per 1,000 inhabitants	2.4	2.2	1.7	1.8	2.0	2.2	5.4						
South Atlantic													
Number of officers	68,017	15,896	9,534	8,956	8,158	7,725	17,748	1,683	26,318,280				
Average number of officers per 1,000 inhabitants	2.6	2.6	1.8	1.9	2.1	2.4	6.1						
East South Central													
Number of officers	26,970	4,343	3,853	2,307	3,461	4,097	8,909	941	10,224,511				
Average number of officers per 1,000 inhabitants	2.6	2.2	2.1	1.9	2.1	2.3	4.9						
West South Central													
Number of officers	58,239	20,724	8,138	5,455	4,083	5,904	13,935	1,553	27,582,531				
Average number of officers per 1,000 inhabitants	2.1	1.9	1.6	1.6	1.7	2.0	4.9						
West													
Number of officers	84,850	37,826	14,748	10,487	6,516	5,420	9,853	1,420	54,648,948				
Average number of officers per 1,000 inhabitants	1.6	1.7	1.2	1.1	1.3	1.5	4.6						
Mountain													
Number of officers	32,885	14,321	5,319	3,186	2,597	2,102	5,360	647	18,717,694				
Average number of officers per 1,000 inhabitants	1.8	1.7	1.4	1.3	1.4	1.7	4.8						
Pacific													
Number of officers	51,965	23,505	9,429	7,301	3,919	3,318	4,493	773	35,931,254				
Average number of officers per 1,000 inhabitants	1.4	1.7	1.1	1.1	1.2	1.4	4.5						

1 The designation *county* is a combination of both metropolitan and nonmetropolitan counties.   2 Suburban areas include law enforcement agencies in cities with less than 50,000 inhabitants and county law enforcement agencies that are within a Metropolitan Statistical Area. Suburban areas exclude all metropolitan agencies associated with a principal city. The agencies associated with suburban areas also appear in other groups within this table.

Table 72. Full-Time Law Enforcement Employees,[1] Range in Rate, by Population Group, 2022

(Number; percent.)

Rate range	Total cities[2] (9,452 cities; population 206,635,219)	Group I (89 cities, 250,000 and over; population 62,404,976)	Group II (225 cities, 100,000 to 249,999; population 32,519,393)	Group III (467 cities, 50,000 to 99,999; population 32,508,467)	Group IV (860 cities, 25,000 to 49,999; population 29,659,777)	Group V (1,750 cities, 10,000 to 24,999; population 27,868,454)	Group VI (6,061 cities, under 10,000; population 21,674,152)
Total Cities							
Number	9,452	89	225	467	860	1,750	6,061
Percent[3]	100.0	100.0	100.0	100.0	100.0	100.0	100.0
0.1–0.5							
Number	76	0	0	0	2	5	69
Percent	0.8	0.0	0.0	0.0	0.2	0.3	1.1
0.6–1.0							
Number	392	0	3	12	23	46	308
Percent	4.1	0.0	1.3	2.6	2.7	2.6	5.1
1.1–1.5							
Number	1,230	4	51	109	172	235	659
Percent	13.0	4.5	22.7	23.3	20.0	13.4	10.9
1.6–2.0							
Number	1,860	23	72	145	250	436	934
Percent	19.7	25.8	32.0	31.0	29.1	24.9	15.4
2.1–2.5							
Number	1,812	30	54	116	232	444	936
Percent	19.2	33.7	24.0	24.8	27.0	25.4	15.4
2.6–3.0							
Number	1,266	9	28	52	96	301	780
Percent	13.4	10.1	12.4	11.1	11.2	17.2	12.9
3.1–3.5							
Number	810	8	14	19	59	145	565
Percent	8.6	9.0	6.2	4.1	6.9	8.3	9.3
3.6–4.0							
Number	531	3	2	7	15	75	429
Percent	5.6	3.4	0.9	1.5	1.7	4.3	7.1
4.1–4.5							
Number	380	5	1	3	5	29	337
Percent	4.0	5.6	0.4	0.6	0.6	1.7	5.6
4.6–5.0							
Number	279	5	0	1	2	17	254
Percent	3.0	5.6	0.0	0.2	0.2	1.0	4.2
5.1 and over							
Number	816.0	2.0	0.0	3.0	4.0	17.0	790.0
Percent	8.6	2.2	0.0	0.6	0.5	1.0	13.0

1 Full-time law enforcement employees include civilians.   2 The number of agencies used to compile these figures differs from other tables that include data about law enforcement employees because agencies with no resident population are excluded from this table. Agencies not included in this table are associated with universities and colleges (see Table 79) and other agencies (see Table 81), as well as some state agencies that have concurrent jurisdiction with other local law enforcement.   3 Because of rounding, the percentages may not sum to 100.

Table 73. Full-Time Law Enforcement Officers, Range in Rate, by Population Group, 2022

(Number, rate per 1,000 inhabitants.)

Rate range	Total cities[1] (9,452 cities; population 206,635,219)	Group I (89 cities, 250,000 and over; population 62,404,976)	Group II (225 cities, 100,000 to 249,999; population 32,519,393)	Group III (467 cities, 50,000 to 99,999; population 32,508,467)	Group IV (860 cities, 25,000 to 49,999; population 29,659,777)	Group V (1,750 cities, 10,000 to 24,999; population 27,868,454)	Group VI (6,061 cities, under 10,000; population 21,674,152)
Total Cities							
Number	9,452	89	225	467	860	1,750	6,061
Percent[2]	100.0	100.0	100.0	100.0	100.0	100.0	100.0
0.1–0.5							
Number	91	0	1	3	3	6	78
Percent	1.0	0.0	0.4	0.6	0.3	0.3	1.3
0.6–1.0							
Number	660	3	38	85	84	89	361
Percent	7.0	3.4	16.9	18.2	9.8	5.1	6.0
1.1–1.5							
Number	1,879	26	85	156	294	467	851
Percent	19.9	29.2	37.8	33.4	34.2	26.7	14.0
1.6–2.0							
Number	2,328	29	59	144	305	600	1,191
Percent	24.6	32.6	26.2	30.8	35.5	34.3	19.7
2.1–2.5							
Number	1,600	12	27	55	112	355	1,039
Percent	16.9	13.5	12.0	11.8	13.0	20.3	17.1
2.6–3.0							
Number	999	6	11	16	48	157	761
Percent	10.6	6.7	4.9	3.4	5.6	9.0	12.6
3.1–3.5							
Number	580	5	4	5	8	41	517
Percent	6.1	5.6	1.8	1.1	0.9	2.3	8.5
3.6–4.0							
Number	353	4	0	0	3	21	325
Percent	3.7	4.5	0.0	0.0	0.3	1.2	5.4
4.1–4.5							
Number	245	3	0	1	1	9	231
Percent	2.6	3.4	0.0	0.2	0.1	0.5	3.8
4.6–5.0							
Number	173	0	0	0	0	2	171
Percent	1.8	0.0	0.0	0.0	0.0	0.1	2.8
5.1 and over							
Number	544	1	0	2	2	3	536
Percent	5.8	1.1	0.0	0.4	0.2	0.2	8.8

1 The number of agencies used to compile these figures differs from other tables that include data about law enforcement officers because agencies with no resident population are excluded from this table. Agencies not included in this table are associated with universities and colleges (see Table 79) and other agencies (see Table 81), as well as some state agencies that have concurrent jurisdiction with other local law enforcement.   2 Because of rounding, the percentages may not sum to 100.

Table 74. Full-Time Law Enforcement Employees, by Population Group, Percent Male and Female, 2022

(Number, percent.)

Population group	Total law enforcement employees (number)	Law enforcement employees (percent)		Total officers (number)	Officers (percent)		Civilians (number) Total civilians	Civilians (percent)		Agencies (number)	Population, 2022, estimated
		Male	Female		Male	Female		Male	Female		
Total Agencies	1,018,345	72.2	27.8	708,001	86.5	13.5	310,344	39.7	60.3	14,099	305,970,397
Total Cities	577,776	74.2	25.8	448,911	86.0	14.0	128,865	33.0	67.0	10,866	206,635,219
Group I (250,000 and over)	198,558	70.9	29.1	152,730	82.1	17.9	45,828	33.8	66.2	89	62,404,976
1,000,000 and over (Group I subset)	104,588	69.6	30.4	79,862	80.5	19.5	24,726	34.6	65.4	10	25,965,648
500,000 to 999,999 (Group I subset)	52,309	73.1	26.9	40,463	84.2	15.8	11,846	35.2	64.8	27	19,067,838
250,000 to 499,999 (Group I subset)	41,661	71.3	28.7	32,405	83.3	16.7	9,256	29.6	70.4	52	17,371,490
Group II (100,000 to 249,999)	66,575	73.3	26.7	51,020	86.9	13.1	15,555	28.9	71.1	225	32,519,393
Group III (50,000 to 99,999)	65,474	74.2	25.8	50,878	87.2	12.8	14,596	29.0	71.0	467	32,508,467
Group IV (25,000 to 49,999)	62,195	76.6	23.4	49,648	88.6	11.4	12,547	29.0	71.0	860	29,659,777
Group V (10,000 to 24,999)	63,847	77.7	22.3	51,804	89.4	10.6	12,043	27.2	72.8	1,750	27,868,454
Group VI (under 10,000)	121,127	76.8	23.2	92,831	88.0	12.0	28,296	40.1	59.9	7,475	21,674,152
Metropolitan Counties	309,025	69.0	31.0	181,183	85.7	14.3	127,842	45.3	54.7	1,320	75,347,529
Nonmetropolitan Counties	131,544	71.3	28.7	77,907	91.3	8.7	53,637	42.4	57.6	1,913	23,987,649
Suburban Areas[1]	478,074	72.0	28.0	314,322	86.9	13.1	163,752	43.4	56.6	7,540	132,833,931

1 Suburban areas include law enforcement agencies in cities with less than 50,000 inhabitants and county law enforcement agencies that are within a Metropolitan Statistical Area. Suburban areas exclude all metropolitan agencies associated with a principal city. The agencies associated with suburban areas also appear in other groups within this table.

Table 75. Full-Time Civilian Law Enforcement Employees, by Population Group, 2022

(Percent; number.)

Population group	Civilian employees (percent)	Agencies (number)	Population, 2022, estimated
Total Agencies	30.5	14,099	305,970,397
Total Cities	22.3	10,866	206,635,219
Group I (250,000 and over)	23.1	89	62,404,976
1,000,000 and over (Group I subset)	23.6	10	25,965,648
500,000 to 999,999 (Group I subset)	22.6	27	19,067,838
250,000 to 499,999 (Group I subset)	22.2	52	17,371,490
Group II (100,000 to 249,999)	23.4	225	32,519,393
Group III (50,000 to 99,999)	22.3	467	32,508,467
Group IV (25,000 to 49,999)	20.2	860	29,659,777
Group V (10,000 to 24,999)	18.9	1,750	27,868,454
Group VI (under 10,000)	23.4	7,475	21,674,152
Metropolitan Counties	41.4	1,320	75,347,529
Nonmetropolitan Counties	40.8	1,913	23,987,649
Suburban Areas[1]	34.3	7,540	132,833,931

1 Suburban areas include law enforcement agencies in cities with less than 50,000 inhabitants and county law enforcement agencies that are within a Metropolitan Statistical Area. Suburban areas exclude all metropolitan agencies associated with a principal city. The agencies associated with suburban areas also appear in other groups within this table.

Table 76. Full-Time State Law Enforcement Employees, by Selected State, 2022

(Number.)

State/agency	Law enforcement employees	Officers		Civilians	
		Male	Female	Male	Female
Alabama					
Other state agencies	1,516	856	34	163	463
Alaska					
State Troopers	581	343	22	93	123
Arizona					
Department of Public Safety	1,909	1,045	40	370	454
Arkansas					
State Patrol	910	486	27	121	276
Other state agencies	63	36	3	12	12
California					
Highway Patrol	9,774	6,231	420	1,346	1,777
Other state agencies	1,410	1,091	207	32	80
Colorado					
State Patrol	1,079	647	62	160	210
Other state agencies	356	68	11	66	211
Connecticut					
State Police	1,293	773	115	171	234
Other state agencies	135	98	19	12	6
Delaware					
State Police	938	626	94	74	144
Other state agencies	820	236	36	163	385
Florida					
Highway Patrol	2,147	1,593	167	122	265
Other state agencies	3,077	1,294	214	565	1,004
Georgia					
Department of Public Safety	1,539	1,022	35	212	270
Other state agencies	1,409	434	114	217	644
Idaho					
State Police	532	283	16	68	165
Other state agencies	35	19	4	0	12
Illinois					
State Police	2,919	1,580	176	542	621
Other state agencies	354	168	24	120	42
Indiana					
State Police	1,592	1,058	55	194	285
Other state agencies	75	57	11	0	7
Iowa					
Department of Public Safety	861	526	36	123	176
Kansas					
Highway Patrol	480	337	22	52	69
Other state agencies	285	227	20	10	28
Kentucky					
State Police	1,809	982	27	353	447
Other state agencies	218	195	9	1	13
Louisiana[1]					
Other state agencies	3	2	0	0	1
Maine					
State Police	507	258	25	93	131
Other state agencies	58	28	1	21	8
Maryland					
State Police	2,186	1,344	110	370	362
Other state agencies	1,566	928	151	233	254
Massachusetts					
State Police	2,870	2,098	142	250	380
Other state agencies	129	90	4	12	23
Michigan					
State Police	3,045	1,719	169	448	709
Other state agencies	245	193	22	9	21
Minnesota					
State Police	716	518	56	59	83
Other state agencies	699	266	46	133	254

Table 76. Full-Time State Law Enforcement Employees, by Selected State, 2022—Continued

(Number.)

State/agency	Law enforcement employees	Officers		Civilians	
		Male	Female	Male	Female
Mississippi					
Highway Safety Patrol	493	391	11	31	60
Other state agencies	132	101	18	2	11
Missouri					
State Highway Patrol	2,200	1,093	58	510	539
Other state agencies	178	135	11	3	29
Montana					
Highway Patrol	315	232	20	26	37
Other state agencies	34	13	1	10	10
Nebraska					
State Patrol	683	382	27	87	187
Other state agencies	9	8	0	1	0
Nevada					
Highway Patrol	717	532	51	49	85
Other state agencies	541	168	39	111	223
New Hampshire					
State Police	474	284	29	52	109
Other state agencies	33	15	5	3	10
New Jersey					
State Police	4,365	2,975	174	567	649
Other state agencies	7,403	4,752	951	837	863
Port Authority of New York and New Jersey[2]	1,917	1,521	215	82	99
New Mexico					
State Police	825	574	46	94	111
New York					
State Police	5,581	4,165	558	324	534
Other state agencies	351	280	40	11	20
North Carolina					
Highway Patrol	2,058	1,501	49	276	232
Other state agencies	1,182	722	142	137	181
North Dakota					
Highway Patrol	188	149	7	10	22
Other state agencies	57	50	7	0	0
Ohio					
State Highway Patrol	2,223	1,256	109	413	445
Oklahoma					
Highway Patrol	1,109	735	14	168	192
Other state agencies	566	217	32	127	190
Oregon					
State Police	1,316	636	54	218	408
Other state agencies	83	54	23	2	4
Pennsylvania					
State Police	6,450	4,393	344	760	953
Other state agencies	397	272	41	52	32
Rhode Island					
State Police	304	227	26	28	23
Other state agencies	40	27	3	4	6
South Carolina					
Highway Patrol	1,181	895	61	83	142
Other State Agency	862	593	93	78	98
South Dakota					
Highway Patrol	266	166	13	51	36
Other state agencies	183	43	6	50	84
Tennessee					
Department of Safety	1,725	872	54	207	592
Other state agencies	1,057	555	184	107	211
Texas					
Department of Public Safety	10,176	3,727	319	2,009	4,121
Utah					
Highway Patrol	769	567	33	30	139
Other state agencies	196	153	13	12	18

Table 76. Full-Time State Law Enforcement Employees, by Selected State, 2022—Continued

(Number.)

State/agency	Law enforcement employees	Officers		Civilians	
		Male	Female	Male	Female
Vermont					
State Police	359	242	36	30	51
Other state agencies	107	72	10	18	7
Virginia					
State Police	2,647	1,742	134	264	507
Other state agencies	749	452	65	113	119
Washington					
State Patrol	2,051	841	89	532	589
Other state agencies	300	114	28	89	69
West Virginia					
State Police	613	481	20	23	89
Other state agencies	213	162	3	19	29
Wisconsin					
State Patrol	602	421	29	80	72
Other state agencies	436	293	43	30	70
Wyoming					
Highway Patrol	292	155	4	65	68
Other state agencies	86	36	1	13	36

NOTE: Caution should be used when comparing data from one state to that of another. The responsibilities of the various state police, highway patrol, and department of public safety agencies range from full law enforcement duties to only traffic patrol, which can impact both the level of employment for agencies as well as the ratio of sworn officers to civilians employed. Any valid comparison must take these factors and the other identified variables affecting crime into consideration.
1 Police employee data were not received from the State Police/Highway Patrol for the state.   2 Data reported are the number of law enforcement employees for the state of New Jersey.

Table 77. Full-Time Law Enforcement Employees, by State, 2022

(Number.)

State	Total law enforcement employees	Total officers		Total civilians		Total agencies	Population, 2022, estimated
		Male	Female	Male	Female		
Alabama	17,411	10,727	959	2,117	3,608	412	5,066,976
Alaska	1,918	1,162	109	228	419	38	733,583
Arizona	21,628	11,202	1,454	3,866	5,106	122	7,352,208
Arkansas	10,635	6,163	881	1,405	2,186	303	3,044,780
California	116,036	65,393	10,758	15,146	24,739	470	33,466,112
Colorado	17,319	9,687	1,752	2,220	3,660	188	5,328,802
Connecticut	9,109	6,452	949	681	1,027	105	3,615,592
Delaware	3,368	1,988	292	379	709	55	1,017,183
District of Columbia	4,627	2,973	841	325	488	2	671,803
Florida	68,356	36,479	6,745	9,103	16,029	340	19,145,158
Georgia	36,062	20,756	4,148	3,679	7,479	485	10,523,414
Hawaii	3,378	2,377	322	197	482	4	1,440,196
Idaho	5,748	2,845	275	1,119	1,509	110	1,938,085
Illinois	40,201	24,278	5,023	5,773	5,127	493	10,400,263
Indiana	12,138	7,807	788	1,673	1,870	115	4,333,039
Iowa	8,487	4,852	531	1,258	1,846	226	3,018,738
Kansas	8,810	5,581	780	896	1,553	294	2,519,618
Kentucky	8,923	6,258	446	835	1,384	266	3,425,295
Louisiana	15,721	9,221	2,569	1,075	2,856	175	3,875,098
Maine	3,035	2,120	202	289	424	132	1,385,340
Maryland	19,995	13,066	2,123	1,816	2,990	124	5,978,008
Massachusetts	20,920	15,142	1,815	1,561	2,402	340	6,810,065
Michigan	24,299	14,858	2,380	3,265	3,796	492	9,351,610
Minnesota	15,695	8,732	1,240	2,562	3,161	404	5,713,322
Mississippi	8,618	5,060	671	1,066	1,821	196	2,628,070
Missouri	17,196	10,495	1,359	2,218	3,124	350	5,015,121
Montana	3,499	2,016	214	601	668	112	1,122,092
Nebraska	5,410	3,281	410	634	1,085	173	1,933,010
Nevada	11,184	6,694	1,059	949	2,482	58	3,115,468
New Hampshire	3,772	2,545	309	299	619	192	1,358,245
New Jersey	48,546	33,639	4,382	4,234	6,291	537	8,967,566
New Mexico	6,640	4,121	551	703	1,265	126	2,099,452
New York	81,699	51,127	10,057	7,644	12,871	439	19,288,024
North Carolina	33,205	20,340	3,085	4,274	5,506	515	10,690,849
North Dakota	2,421	1,620	224	182	395	106	759,214
Ohio	26,416	16,503	2,210	3,267	4,436	433	8,917,388
Oklahoma	13,321	8,330	916	1,602	2,473	446	4,014,882
Oregon	10,645	5,572	731	1,956	2,386	194	4,199,523
Pennsylvania	29,794	22,066	2,759	1,639	3,330	883	9,217,287
Rhode Island	3,085	2,287	216	243	339	48	1,093,734
South Carolina	16,554	10,572	1,779	1,413	2,790	419	5,275,004
South Dakota	3,302	1,694	197	633	778	138	897,287
Tennessee	27,250	15,578	2,004	4,382	5,286	398	7,046,409
Texas	98,256	51,491	8,340	16,251	22,174	1,064	29,613,658
Utah	8,281	5,354	515	1,029	1,383	138	3,373,253
Vermont	1,419	945	125	133	216	82	641,454
Virginia	24,060	16,008	2,795	1,502	3,755	280	8,681,374
Washington	15,221	9,222	1,171	1,949	2,879	255	7,755,215
West Virginia	4,079	3,248	130	272	429	338	1,763,446
Wisconsin	17,924	11,047	1,802	2,210	2,865	421	5,773,643
Wyoming	2,729	1,426	208	411	684	63	575,441

Table 78. Full-Time Law Enforcement Employees, by Selected State and City, 2022

(Number.)

State/city	Population	Total law enforcement employees	Total officers	Total civilians
ALABAMA				
Abbeville	2,390	9	8	1
Adamsville	4,233	23	13	10
Addison	672	4	4	0
Alabaster	33,974	82	68	14
Albertville	22,660	64	41	23
Alexander City	14,476	64	49	15
Aliceville	2,081	2	2	0
Altoona	949	2	2	0
Andalusia	8,699	36	26	10
Anniston	21,007	86	79	7
Arab	8,550	35	28	7
Ardmore	1,406	10	7	3
Argo	4,421	8	8	0
Arley	332	2	2	0
Ashford	2,255	8	6	2
Ashland	1,962	13	8	5
Ashville	2,376	5	5	0
Athens	28,438	55	44	11
Atmore	8,536	34	24	10
Attalla	5,840	27	22	5
Auburn	80,759	140	131	9
Autaugaville	787	3	3	0
Baker Hill	204	4	4	0
Bay Minette	8,000	32	24	8
Bayou La Batre	2,166	16	12	4
Bear Creek	1,047	4	4	0
Berry	1,193	4	4	0
Bessemer	25,265	122	85	37
Birmingham	195,050	873	687	186
Blountsville	1,825	5	3	2
Boaz	10,222	38	28	10
Brantley	798	4	4	0
Brent	2,995	6	6	0
Brewton	5,251	33	23	10
Bridgeport	2,256	10	7	3
Brighton	2,270	10	6	4
Brilliant	831	1	1	0
Brookside	1,218	12	6	6
Brookwood	2,448	8	8	0
Brundidge	2,053	6	5	1
Butler	1,846	9	8	1
Calera	18,189	44	36	8
Camden	1,808	9	8	1
Camp Hill	977	3	3	0
Carbon Hill	1,714	9	4	5
Carrollton	981	3	3	0
Castleberry	469	1	1	0
Cedar Bluff	1,879	5	5	0
Centre	3,546	14	13	1
Centreville	2,803	5	5	0
Chatom	1,034	3	3	0
Cherokee	958	4	4	0
Chickasaw	6,333	20	20	0
Childersburg	4,631	16	14	2
Citronelle	3,916	24	12	12
Clanton	8,799	31	30	1
Clayhatchee	473	2	2	0
Clayton	2,258	2	2	0
Cleveland	1,242	5	5	0
Clio	1,193	5	5	0
Coaling	1,987	4	4	0
Collinsville	2,029	8	4	4
Columbia	691	2	2	0
Columbiana	4,347	16	12	4
Coosada	1,276	5	5	0
Cordova	1,663	8	5	3
Cottonwood	1,046	3	3	0
Courtland	584	2	2	0
Creola	1,936	12	7	5
Crossville	1,810	5	5	0
Cuba	301	3	3	0
Cullman	19,065	56	47	9
Dadeville	2,962	10	9	1
Daleville	4,876	18	12	6
Daphne	29,871	95	62	33
Dauphin Island	1,843	19	13	6
Decatur	57,831	131	112	19
Demopolis	6,885	27	23	4
Dora	2,281	11	7	4
Dothan	71,196	255	179	76
Double Springs	1,083	9	8	1
Douglas	765	4	4	0
East Brewton	2,261	7	4	3
Eclectic	1,234	9	8	1

Table 78. Full-Time Law Enforcement Employees, by Selected State and City, 2022—Continued

(Number.)

State/city	Population	Total law enforcement employees	Total officers	Total civilians
Elba	3,398	21	12	9
Elberta	2,036	9	8	1
Enterprise	29,936	65	48	17
Eufaula	12,528	49	29	20
Eutaw	2,823	15	13	2
Evergreen	3,309	21	16	5
Excel	546	2	2	0
Fairfield	9,691	9	5	4
Fairhope	23,747	67	46	21
Falkville	1,143	7	7	0
Fayette	4,132	10	10	0
Flomaton	1,455	11	6	5
Florala	1,904	4	4	0
Florence	40,063	143	111	32
Foley	23,629	86	58	28
Forkland	442	1	1	0
Fort Deposit	1,154	2	2	0
Fort Payne	14,845	58	38	20
Franklin	566	1	1	0
Frisco City	1,156	2	2	0
Fultondale	9,699	40	32	8
Fyffe	963	5	5	0
Gadsden	33,521	110	80	30
Gantt	199	1	1	0
Gardendale	16,861	41	31	10
Geneva	4,169	15	12	3
Georgiana	1,303	9	6	3
Geraldine	910	5	5	0
Gilbertown	721	1	1	0
Glencoe	5,406	10	10	0
Goodwater	1,281	8	4	4
Gordo	1,590	4	4	0
Gordon	293	1	1	0
Grant	1,042	2	2	0
Graysville	1,889	2	2	0
Greensboro	2,179	8	8	0
Greenville	7,177	30	28	2
Grove Hill	1,732	8	8	0
Guin	2,158	6	5	1
Gulf Shores	16,274	72	52	20
Guntersville	8,858	44	32	12
Gurley	826	5	5	0
Hackleburg	1,430	5	5	0
Haleyville	4,366	20	15	5
Hamilton	6,970	17	15	2
Hanceville	3,261	22	14	8
Harpersville	1,752	6	6	0
Hartford	2,666	14	10	4
Hartselle	15,626	33	32	1
Hayden	1,328	3	3	0
Hayneville	751	3	3	0
Headland	5,320	26	11	15
Heflin	3,402	13	12	1
Helena	22,035	34	28	6
Henagar	2,293	11	7	4
Hillsboro	408	2	2	0
Hokes Bluff	4,451	8	8	0
Hollywood	921	3	3	0
Homewood	25,788	106	79	27
Hoover	92,491	206	170	36
Hueytown	16,313	48	31	17
Huntsville	218,897	537	429	108
Ider	743	7	3	4
Irondale	13,528	42	35	7
Jackson	4,576	26	20	6
Jacksons Gap	757	1	1	0
Jacksonville	13,025	48	35	13
Jasper	14,312	60	42	18
Jemison	2,662	13	13	0
Killen	1,043	5	5	0
Kimberly	4,036	7	7	0
Kinsey	2,290	2	2	0
Kinston	589	1	1	0
LaFayette	2,579	8	7	1
Lake View	3,709	5	4	1
Lanett	6,716	23	21	2
Leeds	12,206	31	30	1
Leesburg	914	5	5	0
Leighton	662	2	2	0
Level Plains	1,823	5	5	0
Lexington	739	1	1	0
Lincoln	7,256	18	16	2
Linden	1,856	7	7	0
Lineville	2,469	11	7	4
Lipscomb	2,018	8	4	4

Table 78. Full-Time Law Enforcement Employees, by Selected State and City, 2022—Continued

(Number.)

State/city	Population	Total law enforcement employees	Total officers	Total civilians
Littleville	1,041	3	3	0
Livingston	3,112	10	5	5
Louisville	387	2	2	0
Loxley	4,510	27	18	9
Luverne	2,658	12	11	1
Lynn	622	1	1	0
Madison	59,341	114	87	27
Maplesville	643	3	3	0
Margaret	5,685	9	7	2
Marion	3,138	6	4	2
McIntosh	198	8	8	0
Mentone	322	2	2	0
Midfield	5,036	12	8	4
Midland City	2,285	6	6	0
Millbrook	17,567	47	35	12
Millport	960	1	1	0
Millry	439	1	1	0
Mobile	239,323	557	422	135
Monroeville	5,797	26	20	6
Montevallo	7,517	18	16	2
Montgomery	197,333	467	390	77
Moody	13,862	27	26	1
Morris	2,246	6	6	0
Moulton	3,353	9	9	0
Moundville	3,114	12	11	1
Mountain Brook	21,910	66	62	4
Mount Vernon	1,371	11	5	6
Munford	1,323	1	1	0
Muscle Shoals	16,917	51	41	10
Napier Field	410	2	2	0
New Brockton	1,453	2	2	0
New Hope	2,884	4	4	0
New Site	770	2	2	0
Newton	1,615	5	4	1
Newville	555	1	1	0
North Courtland	486	2	2	0
Northport	30,901	81	62	19
Notasulga	894	9	4	5
Odenville	5,026	14	14	0
Ohatchee	1,203	5	5	0
Oneonta	6,798	29	28	1
Opelika	32,010	109	86	23
Opp	6,641	26	18	8
Orange Beach	8,530	86	53	33
Owens Crossroads	2,648	5	5	0
Oxford	22,318	82	67	15
Ozark	14,299	35	26	9
Parrish	977	3	3	0
Pelham	24,920	82	67	15
Pell City	13,607	38	35	3
Pennington	329	2	2	0
Phenix City	38,076	93	72	21
Phil Campbell	988	4	2	2
Pickensville	545	1	1	0
Piedmont	4,779	21	14	7
Pinckard	593	1	1	0
Pine Hill	751	1	1	0
Pleasant Grove	9,454	20	15	5
Powell	885	4	4	0
Prattville	38,679	85	80	5
Priceville	3,822	8	8	0
Prichard	18,936	47	31	16
Ragland	1,715	6	5	1
Rainbow City	10,150	27	25	2
Rainsville	5,685	18	14	4
Ranburne	420	3	3	0
Red Bay	3,177	11	7	4
Red Level	431	2	2	0
Reform	1,472	3	3	0
Repton	230	2	1	1
River Falls	487	2	2	0
Riverside	2,265	5	5	0
Roanoke	5,266	28	23	5
Robertsdale	7,116	32	21	11
Rockford	353	1	1	0
Rogersville	1,370	6	6	0
Russellville	10,768	22	18	4
Samson	1,856	8	8	0
Saraland	16,459	54	43	11
Sardis City	1,787	5	5	0
Satsuma	6,811	18	13	5
Scottsboro	15,730	66	39	27
Section	768	3	2	1
Selma	17,296	51	32	19
Semmes	5,431	16	15	1

Table 78. Full-Time Law Enforcement Employees, by Selected State and City, 2022—Continued

(Number.)

State/city	Population	Total law enforcement employees	Total officers	Total civilians
Sheffield	9,287	35	29	6
Shorter	366	12	5	7
Silverhill	1,341	10	9	1
Skyline	843	1	1	0
Slocomb	2,099	7	7	0
Snead	1,023	4	4	0
Somerville	802	2	2	0
Southside	9,524	16	13	3
Spanish Fort	10,689	32	28	4
Springville	5,048	13	12	1
Steele	1,007	2	2	0
Stevenson	1,963	10	5	5
St. Florian	704	6	6	0
Sulligent	1,806	10	10	0
Sumiton	2,405	14	6	8
Summerdale	1,587	10	9	1
Susan Moore	790	1	1	0
Sylacauga	12,205	32	30	2
Sylvania	1,805	3	3	0
Talladega	15,448	44	40	4
Tallassee	4,816	30	21	9
Tarrant	5,913	25	18	7
Taylor	2,280	3	3	0
Thomaston	321	1	1	0
Thomasville	3,518	28	21	7
Thorsby	2,117	6	6	0
Town Creek	1,052	3	3	0
Trafford	598	9	5	4
Triana	3,829	3	3	0
Trinity	2,553	9	9	0
Troy	17,639	63	52	11
Trussville	26,561	88	70	18
Tuscaloosa	101,280	325	261	64
Tuscumbia	9,081	28	21	7
Tuskegee	8,600	19	10	9
Union Springs	3,301	17	8	9
Uniontown	2,010	6	5	1
Valley	10,475	25	24	1
Valley Head	585	2	2	0
Vance	2,163	6	6	0
Vernon	1,833	9	9	0
Vestavia Hills	38,515	104	101	3
Wadley	596	3	3	0
Warrior	3,189	23	15	8
Weaver	3,394	12	9	3
Webb	1,291	3	3	0
Wedowee	719	9	9	0
West Blocton	1,236	2	2	0
Wetumpka	7,317	34	31	3
Winfield	4,805	14	13	1
Woodstock	1,691	5	5	0
York	2,387	5	2	3
ALASKA				
Anchorage	285,821	563	406	157
Bethel	6,267	26	16	10
Bristol Bay Borough	846	11	5	6
Cordova	2,160	9	3	6
Craig	1,028	11	4	7
Dillingham	2,172	12	6	6
Fairbanks	32,785	39	33	6
Haines	2,058	8	5	3
Homer	5,894	22	13	9
Hoonah	953	9	4	5
Juneau	31,775	80	46	34
Kenai	7,713	28	18	10
Ketchikan	7,953	35	25	10
Klawock	717	2	2	0
Kodiak	5,357	33	14	19
Kotzebue	3,041	18	15	3
Nome	3,546	22	11	11
North Pole	2,335	15	13	2
North Slope Borough	10,959	69	40	29
Palmer	6,305	23	15	8
Petersburg	3,314	10	8	2
Sand Point	768	5	3	2
Seldovia	241	1	1	0
Seward	2,667	22	9	13
Sitka	8,392	26	13	13
Skagway	1,035	9	4	5
Soldotna	4,527	17	14	3
St. Paul	468	7	3	4
Unalaska	3,908	21	10	11
Valdez	3,839	11	11	0
Wasilla	9,809	28	24	4

Table 78. Full-Time Law Enforcement Employees, by Selected State and City, 2022—Continued

(Number.)

State/city	Population	Total law enforcement employees	Total officers	Total civilians
Whittier	203	7	7	0
Wrangell	1,984	11	5	6
ARIZONA				
Apache Junction	41,099	103	67	36
Avondale	91,467	220	152	68
Benson	5,368	22	14	8
Bisbee	4,909	12	8	4
Buckeye	110,002	144	107	37
Bullhead City	42,953	112	75	37
Camp Verde	12,362	37	23	14
Casa Grande	61,271	105	81	24
Chandler	281,373	485	329	156
Chino Valley	13,875	34	26	8
Clarkdale	4,815	11	10	1
Clifton	3,774	9	3	6
Colorado City	2,560	22	9	13
Coolidge	16,027	47	33	14
Cottonwood	12,680	63	36	27
Douglas	16,529	44	30	14
Eagar	4,448	7	6	1
El Mirage	36,039	77	57	20
Eloy	15,717	39	29	10
Flagstaff	77,018	139	94	45
Florence	26,814	30	20	10
Fredonia	1,330	1	1	0
Gilbert	277,123	466	319	147
Glendale	250,466	550	418	132
Globe	7,155	33	28	5
Goodyear	107,212	184	129	55
Hayden	811	11	9	2
Holbrook	4,872	9	8	1
Huachuca City	1,622	6	4	2
Jerome	471	4	4	0
Kearny	1,824	12	7	5
Kingman	34,803	72	56	16
Lake Havasu City	59,166	116	74	42
Mammoth	1,135	5	4	1
Marana	57,119	127	97	30
Maricopa	66,525	81	63	18
Mesa	513,116	1,308	834	474
Miami	1,540	5	4	1
Nogales	19,725	63	44	19
Oro Valley	48,441	118	93	25
Page	7,328	36	17	19
Paradise Valley	12,663	49	33	16
Parker	3,263	14	11	3
Payson	16,638	43	28	15
Peoria	197,894	309	216	93
Phoenix	1,637,902	3,614	2,599	1,015
Pima	2,960	6	6	0
Pinetop-Lakeside	4,179	20	15	5
Prescott	47,878	89	72	17
Prescott Valley	49,422	108	81	27
Quartzsite	2,302	11	8	3
Queen Creek	72,229	76	67	9
Safford	10,404	24	18	6
Sahuarita	36,229	61	47	14
San Luis	38,528	61	39	22
Scottsdale	243,576	591	351	240
Sedona	9,829	37	24	13
Show Low	12,157	49	27	22
Sierra Vista	45,611	79	61	18
Snowflake-Taylor	10,834	17	14	3
Somerton	14,480	27	16	11
South Tucson	4,537	13	12	1
Springerville	1,706	6	5	1
St. Johns	3,365	9	6	3
Superior	2,528	10	9	1
Surprise	154,128	216	159	57
Tempe	187,473	467	343	124
Thatcher	5,369	13	12	1
Tolleson	7,308	54	31	23
Tombstone	1,308	9	7	2
Tucson	544,629	1,090	777	313
Wellton	2,528	8	7	1
Wickenburg	7,868	26	16	10
Willcox	3,202	17	10	7
Williams	3,316	20	10	10
Winslow	8,985	34	19	15
Yuma	98,164	246	147	99
ARKANSAS				
Alexander	3,798	10	10	0
Alma	5,874	19	16	3

Table 78. Full-Time Law Enforcement Employees, by Selected State and City, 2022—Continued

(Number.)

State/city	Population	Total law enforcement employees	Total officers	Total civilians
Amity	680	1	1	0
Arkadelphia	10,233	27	21	6
Ashdown	4,150	14	12	2
Ash Flat	1,128	5	5	0
Atkins	2,864	9	8	1
Augusta	1,928	6	6	0
Austin	4,547	4	4	0
Bald Knob	2,534	11	8	3
Barling	4,894	10	10	0
Batesville	11,129	23	22	1
Bay	1,825	5	5	0
Beebe	8,683	25	20	5
Bella Vista	31,316	56	39	17
Benton	36,282	84	75	9
Bentonville	58,871	130	92	38
Berryville	5,727	15	14	1
Blytheville	12,732	49	32	17
Bono	2,738	4	4	0
Booneville	3,826	13	9	4
Bradford	681	3	3	0
Brinkley	2,616	15	8	7
Brookland	4,355	6	6	0
Bryant	21,407	62	51	11
Bull Shoals	1,948	3	3	0
Cabot	26,750	61	50	11
Caddo Valley	589	4	4	0
Camden	10,223	34	16	18
Cammack Village	756	2	2	0
Caraway	1,106	3	3	0
Carlisle	1,991	9	5	4
Cave Springs	6,218	12	12	0
Cedarville	1,444	2	2	0
Centerton	21,927	25	23	2
Charleston	2,642	4	4	0
Cherokee Village	4,944	8	7	1
Cherry Valley	562	1	1	0
Clarendon	1,476	4	4	0
Clarksville	9,559	21	18	3
Clinton	2,489	8	7	1
Conway	66,487	161	123	38
Corning	3,124	10	6	4
Cotter	924	3	3	0
Crossett	4,619	23	14	9
Danville	2,001	6	5	1
Dardanelle	4,485	21	15	6
Decatur	1,733	7	7	0
De Queen	6,069	18	16	2
Des Arc	1,844	6	6	0
DeWitt	2,832	12	7	5
Diamond City	789	1	1	0
Diaz	1,266	3	3	0
Dover	1,335	6	6	0
Dumas	3,796	24	11	13
Dyer	772	1	1	0
Earle	1,758	3	3	0
El Dorado	17,037	64	48	16
Elkins	3,828	10	10	0
England	2,427	11	7	4
Etowah	243	1	1	0
Eudora	1,664	6	4	2
Eureka Springs	2,195	18	14	4
Fairfield Bay	2,111	7	7	0
Farmington	8,862	20	20	0
Fayetteville	96,456	170	123	47
Flippin	1,344	7	7	0
Fordyce	3,254	10	7	3
Forrest City	12,807	34	30	4
Fort Smith	90,013	205	162	43
Gassville	2,208	4	4	0
Gentry	4,156	13	11	2
Gillett	586	1	1	0
Glenwood	2,016	4	4	0
Goshen	2,250	5	5	0
Gosnell	2,761	6	6	0
Gravette	3,721	13	12	1
Greenbrier	5,954	14	10	4
Green Forest	3,081	13	10	3
Greenland	1,215	4	4	0
Greenwood	9,705	22	21	1
Greers Ferry	833	5	4	1
Gurdon	1,847	7	5	2
Guy	743	2	2	0
Hackett	842	2	2	0
Hamburg	2,425	7	6	1
Hampton	1,191	3	3	0

Table 78. Full-Time Law Enforcement Employees, by Selected State and City, 2022—Continued

(Number.)

State/city	Population	Total law enforcement employees	Total officers	Total civilians
Hardy	766	4	4	0
Harrisburg	2,199	6	5	1
Harrison	13,350	37	31	6
Hartford	501	1	1	0
Haskell	4,061	7	7	0
Hazen	1,418	6	6	0
Heber Springs	7,353	20	18	2
Helena-West Helena	8,874	28	14	14
Higginson	799	1	1	0
Highfill	2,099	5	5	0
Highland	1,041	4	4	0
Hope	8,535	33	23	10
Hot Springs	38,174	146	106	40
Hoxie	2,710	4	4	0
Hughes	999	2	2	0
Huntington	494	1	1	0
Huntsville	3,156	11	9	2
Jacksonville	29,136	60	47	13
Johnson	3,629	7	7	0
Jonesboro	79,865	183	165	18
Judsonia	1,877	6	5	1
Kensett	1,396	5	4	1
Kibler	1,019	2	2	0
Lake City	2,517	4	4	0
Lakeview	784	2	2	0
Lake Village	1,984	14	9	5
Lamar	1,738	3	3	0
Lavaca	2,474	3	3	0
Leachville	1,943	4	4	0
Lead Hill	286	1	1	0
Lewisville	866	2	2	0
Lincoln	2,309	9	9	0
Little Flock	3,037	9	8	1
Little Rock	201,513	631	514	117
Lonoke	4,128	14	13	1
Lowell	10,402	31	24	7
Luxora	894	1	1	0
Madison	721	6	3	3
Magnolia	11,059	25	22	3
Malvern	10,824	23	21	2
Mammoth Spring	939	2	2	0
Mansfield	1,061	4	4	0
Marianna	3,635	22	10	12
Marion	13,602	32	30	2
Marked Tree	2,200	12	8	4
Marmaduke	1,228	4	4	0
Marshall	1,335	3	3	0
Maumelle	19,273	47	37	10
Mayflower	2,051	12	9	3
McCrory	1,502	6	5	1
McGehee	3,690	24	11	13
McRae	614	2	2	0
Mena	5,652	13	12	1
Menifee	281	2	2	0
Mineral Springs	1,074	3	3	0
Monette	1,557	3	3	0
Monticello	8,200	23	21	2
Morrilton	7,104	28	25	3
Mountainburg	527	1	1	0
Mountain Home	13,180	40	32	8
Mountain View	2,905	11	10	1
Mulberry	1,553	4	4	0
Murfreesboro	1,437	4	4	0
Nashville	4,083	18	17	1
Newport	7,878	26	19	7
North Little Rock	63,663	206	172	34
Ola	926	4	3	1
Osceola	6,621	33	20	13
Ozark	3,575	12	10	2
Paragould	30,296	54	48	6
Paris	3,221	9	9	0
Parkin	775	2	1	1
Patterson	299	1	1	0
Pea Ridge	7,643	17	15	2
Perryville	1,383	6	6	0
Piggott	3,532	8	8	0
Pine Bluff	39,549	105	86	19
Plumerville	736	1	1	0
Pocahontas	7,657	18	17	1
Pottsville	3,232	9	7	2
Prairie Grove	7,714	16	16	0
Prescott	2,976	12	10	2
Quitman	694	4	4	0
Ravenden	428	1	1	0
Redfield	1,508	8	7	1

Table 78. Full-Time Law Enforcement Employees, by Selected State and City, 2022—Continued

(Number.)

State/city	Population	Total law enforcement employees	Total officers	Total civilians
Rogers	72,115	146	108	38
Rose Bud	499	4	3	1
Russellville	29,533	65	59	6
Salem	1,577	4	3	1
Searcy	23,175	71	53	18
Shannon Hills	4,625	5	5	0
Sheridan	5,073	30	17	13
Sherwood	33,232	94	71	23
Siloam Springs	17,957	61	48	13
Smackover	1,593	8	7	1
Springdale	90,892	196	140	56
Stamps	1,191	2	2	0
Star City	2,284	7	6	1
St. Charles	196	1	1	0
Stuttgart	7,847	30	22	8
Sulphur Springs	471	3	3	0
Swifton	742	2	2	0
Texarkana	29,339	85	73	12
Trumann	7,283	26	18	8
Tuckerman	1,750	5	5	0
Turrell	498	1	1	0
Tyronza	689	2	1	1
Van Buren	23,533	56	52	4
Vilonia	4,519	9	9	0
Waldron	3,313	10	9	1
Walnut Ridge	5,495	10	10	0
Ward	6,621	14	13	1
Warren	5,325	23	16	7
Weiner	631	2	1	1
West Fork	2,330	7	6	1
West Memphis	23,809	92	73	19
White Hall	5,579	20	18	2
Wilson	728	1	1	0
Wynne	8,234	18	16	2
CALIFORNIA				
Alameda	74,441	105	71	34
Albany	19,011	33	22	11
Alhambra	79,703	118	77	41
Alturas	2,692	6	5	1
Anaheim	344,795	551	396	155
Anderson	11,447	32	23	9
Angels Camp	3,846	8	7	1
Antioch	114,338	132	101	31
Arcadia	54,202	87	62	25
Arcata	19,144	35	22	13
Arroyo Grande	18,492	28	25	3
Arvin	19,841	29	20	9
Atascadero	29,679	41	31	10
Atherton	6,704	29	20	9
Atwater	32,157	33	23	10
Auburn	13,933	31	22	9
Avenal	13,873	18	16	2
Azusa	47,754	79	51	28
Bakersfield	411,873	678	469	209
Baldwin Park	69,205	81	59	22
Banning	31,050	49	36	13
Barstow	25,465	62	40	22
Bear Valley	120	7	6	1
Beaumont	57,067	75	54	21
Bell	32,140	42	33	9
Bell Gardens	37,720	68	47	21
Belmont	26,277	42	31	11
Belvedere	2,089	6	6	0
Benicia	26,599	46	29	17
Berkeley	114,872	258	150	108
Beverly Hills	31,163	224	138	86
Bishop	3,817	20	11	9
Blythe	17,853	30	21	9
Brawley	26,650	38	25	13
Brea	47,617	86	54	32
Brentwood	65,243	97	66	31
Brisbane	4,503	17	13	4
Broadmoor	4,136	10	9	1
Buena Park	82,065	119	81	38
Burbank	103,516	223	150	73
Burlingame	29,003	59	39	20
Calexico	38,515	40	23	17
California City	15,138	27	14	13
Calipatria	6,415	4	4	0
Calistoga	5,151	18	12	6
Campbell	41,605	68	44	24
Capitola	9,748	29	21	8
Carlsbad	115,531	188	129	59
Carmel	3,176	20	12	8

Table 78. Full-Time Law Enforcement Employees, by Selected State and City, 2022—Continued

(Number.)

State/city	Population	Total law enforcement employees	Total officers	Total civilians
Cathedral City	52,871	73	50	23
Central Marin	35,543	48	42	6
Ceres	49,282	74	53	21
Chico	102,499	140	90	50
Chino	94,611	171	116	55
Chowchilla	19,195	31	20	11
Chula Vista	277,976	348	252	96
Citrus Heights	86,896	132	78	54
Claremont	35,068	63	36	27
Clayton	10,880	13	11	2
Clearlake	16,901	35	21	14
Cloverdale	8,933	21	13	8
Clovis	125,348	171	105	66
Coalinga	17,546	29	21	8
Colma	1,612	25	19	6
Colton	54,597	76	53	23
Colusa	6,444	9	8	1
Concord	122,982	171	128	43
Corcoran	22,609	33	19	14
Corning	8,191	17	11	6
Corona	161,946	228	154	74
Coronado	19,706	71	46	25
Costa Mesa	109,785	200	133	67
Cotati	7,437	16	11	5
Covina	49,590	90	59	31
Crescent City	6,732	12	12	0
Culver City	39,271	161	109	52
Cypress	49,588	66	54	12
Daly City	98,021	112	85	27
Davis	66,939	80	52	28
Delano	52,484	65	45	20
Del Rey Oaks	1,568	9	9	0
Desert Hot Springs	32,923	48	27	21
Dinuba	25,650	45	35	10
Dixon	19,001	32	27	5
Dos Palos	5,793	15	10	5
Downey	109,226	158	114	44
East Palo Alto	27,800	44	28	16
El Cajon	104,693	178	124	54
El Centro	44,076	73	43	30
El Cerrito	25,718	32	23	9
Elk Grove	180,372	230	135	95
El Monte	104,695	152	111	41
El Segundo	16,550	76	60	16
Emeryville	12,781	49	33	16
Escalon	7,552	14	12	2
Escondido	150,072	198	144	54
Etna	685	4	4	0
Eureka	26,465	62	37	25
Exeter	10,318	16	13	3
Fairfax	7,477	16	10	6
Fairfield	119,583	198	126	72
Farmersville	10,351	18	16	2
Ferndale	1,399	5	5	0
Firebaugh	8,126	18	13	5
Folsom	83,011	106	73	33
Fontana	212,730	295	189	106
Fort Bragg	6,968	22	15	7
Fortuna	12,481	26	19	7
Foster City	31,389	48	34	14
Fountain Valley	55,941	79	58	21
Fowler	7,123	12	11	1
Fremont	223,430	265	177	88
Fresno	546,871	1,150	825	325
Fullerton	140,587	166	116	50
Galt	25,463	50	34	16
Gardena	58,535	107	84	23
Garden Grove	169,157	236	171	65
Gilroy	56,742	88	59	29
Glendale	188,599	338	233	105
Glendora	50,650	78	47	31
Gonzales	8,514	15	12	3
Grass Valley	13,895	35	28	7
Greenfield	19,157	24	17	7
Gridley	7,349	22	13	9
Grover Beach	12,728	23	19	4
Guadalupe	8,973	14	12	2
Gustine	6,115	9	7	2
Hanford	58,990	88	61	27
Hawthorne	84,283	136	89	47
Hayward	156,458	270	159	111
Healdsburg	11,229	26	15	11
Hemet	91,046	97	65	32
Hercules	26,157	32	26	6
Hermosa Beach	18,902	60	32	28

Table 78. Full-Time Law Enforcement Employees, by Selected State and City, 2022—Continued

(Number.)

State/city	Population	Total law enforcement employees	Total officers	Total civilians
Hillsborough	10,678	37	28	9
Hollister	44,823	50	32	18
Huntington Beach	194,618	308	205	103
Huntington Park	52,507	84	51	33
Huron	6,243	11	8	3
Imperial	21,626	22	18	4
Indio	91,604	104	62	42
Inglewood	102,879	222	170	52
Ione	5,478	8	8	0
Irvine	311,696	335	228	107
Irwindale	1,410	35	28	7
Jackson	5,196	9	8	1
Kensington	5,028	7	7	0
Kerman	16,304	28	23	5
King City	13,518	20	17	3
Kingsburg	12,879	28	23	5
Laguna Beach	22,559	87	51	36
La Habra	62,082	99	70	29
Lakeport	5,171	13	9	4
Lake Shastina	2,537	4	4	0
La Mesa	60,333	94	66	28
La Palma	15,236	28	22	6
La Verne	30,060	56	39	17
Lemoore	27,485	41	33	8
Lincoln	51,456	40	28	12
Lindsay	12,608	22	19	3
Livermore	85,151	133	92	41
Livingston	14,897	23	17	6
Lodi	67,576	105	73	32
Lompoc	43,363	67	46	21
Long Beach	447,528	986	699	287
Los Alamitos	11,615	26	21	5
Los Altos	29,847	44	30	14
Los Angeles	3,809,182	11,894	9,226	2,668
Los Banos	47,398	68	42	26
Los Gatos	31,640	48	36	12
Madera	69,395	88	57	31
Mammoth Lakes	7,325	18	14	4
Manhattan Beach	33,888	96	61	35
Manteca	87,677	104	75	29
Marina	22,651	37	29	8
Martinez	36,498	40	28	12
Marysville	12,711	28	18	10
McFarland	14,755	22	15	7
Mendota	12,819	23	17	6
Menifee	109,673	103	78	25
Merced	92,191	136	95	41
Mill Valley	14,023	24	19	5
Milpitas	77,790	120	88	32
Modesto	219,083	256	172	84
Monrovia	37,104	80	48	32
Montclair	38,203	68	45	23
Montebello	59,909	83	63	20
Monterey	29,709	61	47	14
Monterey Park	58,352	108	71	37
Moraga	16,550	15	13	2
Morgan Hill	45,134	61	39	22
Morro Bay	10,807	18	16	2
Mountain View	80,588	116	83	33
Mount Shasta	3,257	17	9	8
Murrieta	114,655	156	103	53
Napa	78,586	114	68	46
National City	55,676	115	84	31
Nevada City	3,147	13	10	3
Newark	46,861	72	47	25
Newman	12,310	15	12	3
Newport Beach	84,254	220	135	85
Novato	52,412	76	57	19
Oakdale	23,284	36	23	13
Oakland	428,374	954	700	254
Oceanside	171,844	282	203	79
Ontario	180,004	360	278	82
Orange	135,862	228	147	81
Orange Cove	9,593	14	14	0
Orland	8,346	14	11	3
Oroville	19,868	36	19	17
Oxnard	201,517	354	232	122
Pacifica	35,742	35	30	5
Pacific Grove	14,902	33	21	12
Palm Springs	45,463	146	103	43
Palo Alto	64,922	123	78	45
Palos Verdes Estates	12,767	29	20	9
Paradise	5,860	24	18	6
Parlier	14,760	22	18	4
Pasadena	133,312	326	219	107

Table 78. Full-Time Law Enforcement Employees, by Selected State and City, 2022—Continued

(Number.)

State/city	Population	Total law enforcement employees	Total officers	Total civilians
Paso Robles	31,966	62	41	21
Petaluma	59,129	100	67	33
Piedmont	10,853	26	17	9
Pinole	18,651	43	24	19
Pismo Beach	8,015	38	24	14
Pittsburg	76,488	102	80	22
Placentia	50,764	62	44	18
Placerville	10,951	25	18	7
Pleasant Hill	34,060	55	37	18
Pleasanton	76,350	115	80	35
Pomona	145,600	239	147	92
Porterville	62,865	92	65	27
Port Hueneme	21,545	34	22	12
Red Bluff	14,529	40	23	17
Redding	93,531	153	110	43
Redlands	73,554	117	77	40
Redondo Beach	68,332	145	90	55
Redwood City	79,182	116	87	29
Reedley	25,269	47	32	15
Rialto	104,589	153	110	43
Richmond	115,043	153	106	47
Ridgecrest	28,290	45	28	17
Rio Dell	3,382	6	5	1
Rio Vista	10,352	14	12	2
Ripon	16,789	39	25	14
Riverside	319,889	496	345	151
Rocklin	74,168	78	55	23
Rohnert Park	44,479	98	72	26
Roseville	155,448	194	130	64
Ross	2,320	5	5	0
Sacramento	526,671	973	680	293
Salinas	162,187	186	145	41
San Bernardino	222,623	361	248	113
San Bruno	40,817	60	45	15
Sand City	335	11	10	1
San Diego	1,377,838	2,233	1,769	464
San Fernando	23,501	43	29	14
San Francisco	764,693	2,686	1,942	744
San Gabriel	37,891	62	47	15
Sanger	26,806	44	38	6
San Jose	956,814	1,567	1,109	458
San Leandro	86,465	101	65	36
San Luis Obispo	47,990	83	56	27
San Marino	12,015	35	28	7
San Mateo	99,184	146	104	42
San Pablo	31,498	84	58	26
San Rafael	60,386	83	64	19
San Ramon	87,226	82	63	19
Santa Ana	308,995	574	355	219
Santa Barbara	87,817	168	114	54
Santa Clara	126,877	201	137	64
Santa Cruz	61,650	111	79	32
Santa Maria	109,518	164	106	58
Santa Monica	89,527	394	200	194
Santa Paula	30,851	41	31	10
Santa Rosa	175,999	236	157	79
Sausalito	7,152	24	18	6
Scotts Valley	12,196	25	16	9
Seal Beach	24,665	60	39	21
Seaside	31,864	40	26	14
Sebastopol	7,393	18	11	7
Selma	24,595	42	29	13
Shafter	21,304	38	29	9
Sierra Madre	10,778	22	17	5
Signal Hill	11,312	40	28	12
Simi Valley	125,585	168	111	57
Soledad	24,811	24	18	6
Sonora	5,025	16	10	6
South Gate	89,698	115	73	42
South Lake Tahoe	21,525	57	39	18
South Pasadena	25,744	45	30	15
South San Francisco	62,427	107	76	31
Stallion Springs	2,465	4	4	0
St. Helena	5,347	17	11	6
Stockton	323,501	566	379	187
Suisun City	28,917	37	26	11
Sunnyvale	148,739	287	208	79
Susanville	16,493	19	17	2
Sutter Creek	2,738	5	5	0
Taft	8,674	21	13	8
Tehachapi	13,212	27	19	8
Tiburon	8,997	18	14	4
Torrance	140,499	276	180	96
Tracy	97,219	164	104	60
Truckee	17,486	32	22	10

Table 78. Full-Time Law Enforcement Employees, by Selected State and City, 2022—Continued

(Number.)

State/city	Population	Total law enforcement employees	Total officers	Total civilians
Tulare	72,303	101	69	32
Tulelake	903	3	3	0
Turlock	72,753	112	75	37
Tustin	78,841	146	97	49
Ukiah	16,764	44	27	17
Union City	66,947	93	66	27
Upland	79,430	122	65	57
Vacaville	103,486	168	105	63
Vallejo	123,940	123	86	37
Ventura	109,439	180	131	49
Vernon	212	55	42	13
Visalia	144,137	218	147	71
Walnut Creek	69,417	110	75	35
Watsonville	51,517	91	71	20
Weed	2,888	14	8	6
West Covina	104,739	143	97	46
Westminster	89,490	127	91	36
Westmorland	1,996	4	4	0
West Sacramento	53,643	96	68	28
Wheatland	3,804	8	8	0
Whittier	83,612	166	118	48
Williams	5,655	13	11	2
Willits	4,963	13	9	4
Winters	7,531	13	11	2
Woodlake	7,707	13	12	1
Woodland	61,883	84	69	15
Yreka	7,865	29	17	12
Yuba City	69,122	86	60	26
COLORADO				
Alamosa	9,874	31	25	6
Arvada	122,403	211	150	61
Aspen	6,910	36	25	11
Ault	2,913	9	8	1
Aurora	392,134	866	701	165
Avon	5,968	25	21	4
Basalt	4,163	11	8	3
Bayfield	2,929	8	7	1
Black Hawk	129	33	24	9
Boulder	103,099	254	165	89
Breckenridge	4,953	20	16	4
Brighton	41,205	106	69	37
Broomfield	76,137	228	122	106
Brush	5,262	13	10	3
Buena Vista	3,103	14	11	3
Burlington	3,043	8	6	2
Castle Rock	79,102	119	86	33
Center	1,933	14	7	7
Collbran	366	2	2	0
Colorado Springs	487,728	1,042	732	310
Columbine Valley	1,603	6	6	0
Commerce City	65,817	145	101	44
Craig	8,910	23	17	6
Cripple Creek	1,146	14	6	8
Dacono	6,635	17	13	4
De Beque	485	4	4	0
Del Norte	1,442	4	3	1
Delta	9,373	30	24	6
Denver	705,264	1,831	1,512	319
Dillon	1,045	12	11	1
Durango	19,402	71	52	19
Eagle	7,614	14	12	2
Eaton	5,898	14	12	2
Edgewater	4,892	23	18	5
Elizabeth	2,344	10	9	1
Englewood	33,452	113	74	39
Erie	32,832	53	41	12
Estes Park	5,839	33	19	14
Evans	22,333	39	33	6
Fairplay	732	4	4	0
Florence	3,990	8	6	2
Fort Collins	168,045	322	212	110
Fort Lupton	8,539	29	23	6
Fort Morgan	11,331	33	28	5
Fountain	29,447	67	60	7
Fowler	1,240	4	4	0
Fraser/Winter Park	2,472	12	9	3
Frederick	16,900	36	32	4
Frisco	2,858	15	13	2
Fruita	13,632	21	18	3
Garden City	256	5	5	0
Georgetown	1,303	3	3	0
Glendale	4,502	44	27	17
Glenwood Springs	10,664	26	21	5
Golden	19,638	65	51	14

Table 78. Full-Time Law Enforcement Employees, by Selected State and City, 2022—Continued

(Number.)

State/city	Population	Total law enforcement employees	Total officers	Total civilians
Granada	451	2	1	1
Granby	2,176	11	8	3
Grand Junction	68,126	184	101	83
Greeley	109,258	209	151	58
Greenwood Village	15,351	90	66	24
Gunnison	6,914	20	14	6
Gypsum	8,994	3	3	0
Haxtun	968	3	3	0
Hayden	1,993	3	3	0
Holyoke	2,319	4	4	0
Hotchkiss	922	5	5	0
Hudson	1,624	13	10	3
Hugo	790	3	3	0
Idaho Springs	1,766	10	7	3
Ignacio	863	8	8	0
Johnstown	19,093	29	24	5
Kremmling	1,501	3	2	1
Lafayette	31,204	52	36	16
La Junta	7,264	21	11	10
Lakeside	17	16	14	2
Lakewood	157,068	385	269	116
Lamar	7,657	29	15	14
La Salle	2,326	7	7	0
Littleton	44,821	107	77	30
Lochbuie	8,083	11	9	2
Lone Tree	14,204	65	53	12
Longmont	101,159	250	151	99
Louisville	20,587	41	33	8
Loveland	77,770	165	106	59
Manitou Springs	4,782	17	16	1
Mead	5,957	14	13	1
Meeker	2,310	8	6	2
Milliken	8,948	13	9	4
Monte Vista	4,144	13	11	2
Montrose	20,944	59	40	19
Monument	11,300	30	24	6
Mountain View	531	11	10	1
Mountain Village	1,269	7	5	2
Mount Crested Butte	998	8	8	0
New Castle	4,852	11	9	2
Northglenn	36,634	82	67	15
Nunn	529	4	4	0
Oak Creek	848	3	3	0
Pagosa Springs	1,693	9	8	1
Palisade	2,600	11	10	1
Parachute	1,368	6	5	1
Parker	61,865	105	70	35
Platteville	3,930	10	9	1
Pueblo	112,618	256	200	56
Rifle	10,612	23	17	6
Rocky Ford	3,837	4	3	1
Salida	5,912	23	19	4
Severance	11,574	10	8	2
Sheridan	5,964	55	38	17
Silt	3,583	7	6	1
Silverthorne	4,870	19	17	2
Snowmass Village	3,093	13	10	3
South Fork	495	4	3	1
Steamboat Springs	13,593	38	24	14
Sterling	13,713	24	20	4
Telluride	2,590	13	9	4
Thornton	143,055	323	240	83
Timnath	9,063	17	15	2
Trinidad	8,350	35	24	11
Vail	4,657	62	31	31
Westminster	112,844	248	172	76
Wiggins	1,672	3	3	0
Windsor	38,498	62	49	13
Woodland Park	8,025	29	18	11
Wray	2,298	7	6	1
Yuma	3,444	9	7	2
CONNECTICUT				
Ansonia	18,750	44	34	10
Avon	18,806	42	33	9
Berlin	20,109	57	44	13
Bethel	20,728	54	41	13
Bloomfield	21,461	55	43	12
Branford	28,138	66	52	14
Bridgeport	148,395	330	287	43
Bristol	60,657	137	112	25
Brookfield	17,492	43	33	10
Canton	10,068	21	16	5
Cheshire	28,612	62	47	15
Clinton	13,566	37	27	10

Table 78. Full-Time Law Enforcement Employees, by Selected State and City, 2022—Continued

(Number.)

State/city	Population	Total law enforcement employees	Total officers	Total civilians
Coventry	12,252	19	15	4
Cromwell	14,360	37	27	10
Danbury	87,164	150	142	8
Darien	21,549	65	49	16
Derby	12,243	35	33	2
East Hampton	12,943	20	18	2
East Hartford	50,579	152	117	35
East Haven	27,725	76	61	15
East Lyme	18,984	37	28	9
Easton	7,613	20	15	5
East Windsor	11,148	34	24	10
Enfield	41,912	121	90	31
Fairfield	62,270	128	109	19
Farmington	26,618	58	43	15
Glastonbury	35,034	75	58	17
Granby	11,011	20	15	5
Greenwich	63,631	171	146	25
Groton	9,323	34	28	6
Groton Long Point	515	5	5	0
Groton Town	28,608	80	62	18
Guilford	22,022	43	36	7
Hamden	60,831	110	85	25
Hartford	120,196	415	391	24
Ledyard	15,340	32	23	9
Madison	17,581	46	32	14
Manchester	59,293	146	112	34
Meriden	60,332	140	121	19
Middlebury	7,793	14	12	2
Middletown	47,256	125	109	16
Milford	52,694	135	112	23
Monroe	18,772	51	41	10
Naugatuck	31,356	71	59	12
New Britain	73,621	161	155	6
New Canaan	20,924	51	46	5
New Haven	136,205	371	317	54
Newington	30,277	62	47	15
New London	27,667	81	64	17
New Milford	28,252	58	47	11
Newtown	27,918	59	45	14
North Branford	13,474	29	23	6
North Haven	24,119	66	56	10
Norwalk	91,414	207	176	31
Norwich	40,096	95	80	15
Orange	14,239	54	45	9
Plainfield	14,971	22	17	5
Plainville	17,413	48	40	8
Plymouth	11,655	24	22	2
Portland	9,499	13	12	1
Putnam	9,244	22	17	5
Redding	8,732	22	16	6
Ridgefield	25,048	49	42	7
Rocky Hill	20,692	52	41	11
Seymour	16,634	40	38	2
Shelton	42,189	63	54	9
Simsbury	25,135	51	40	11
Southington	43,564	88	70	18
South Windsor	26,695	60	45	15
Stamford	136,936	295	271	24
Stonington	18,549	52	38	14
Stratford	52,320	113	106	7
Suffield	15,890	28	19	9
Thomaston	7,449	16	13	3
Torrington	35,302	81	72	9
Trumbull	37,192	77	67	10
Vernon	30,584	58	45	13
Wallingford	44,099	89	69	20
Waterbury	113,464	297	248	49
Waterford	19,565	53	47	6
Watertown	22,122	50	40	10
West Hartford	63,934	147	125	22
West Haven	55,133	125	116	9
Weston	10,350	19	18	1
Westport	27,484	75	63	12
Wethersfield	27,038	58	46	12
Willimantic	17,777	51	42	9
Wilton	18,469	47	43	4
Winchester	10,199	24	21	3
Windsor	29,326	62	49	13
Windsor Locks	12,497	37	28	9
Wolcott	16,180	36	25	11
Woodbridge	9,020	32	23	9
DELAWARE				
Bethany Beach	1,032	12	11	1
Blades	1,270	2	2	0

Table 78. Full-Time Law Enforcement Employees, by Selected State and City, 2022—Continued

(Number.)

State/city	Population	Total law enforcement employees	Total officers	Total civilians
Bridgeville	2,761	9	8	1
Camden	4,852	9	8	1
Cheswold	1,989	4	4	0
Clayton	4,003	10	9	1
Dagsboro	939	6	6	0
Delaware City	1,881	4	3	1
Delmar	2,178	14	13	1
Dewey Beach	384	11	9	2
Dover	38,438	130	101	29
Ellendale	530	1	1	0
Elsmere	6,111	12	11	1
Felton	1,331	4	4	0
Fenwick Island	366	9	8	1
Frederica	1,086	1	1	0
Georgetown	7,667	19	15	4
Greenwood	1,062	2	2	0
Harrington	3,785	10	9	1
Laurel	4,178	16	15	1
Lewes	3,533	14	13	1
Middletown	25,044	45	39	6
Milford	13,326	46	33	13
Millsboro	7,386	20	18	2
Milton	3,548	10	9	1
Newark	31,015	86	66	20
New Castle	5,465	17	17	0
Newport	885	5	5	0
Ocean View	2,851	14	13	1
Rehoboth Beach	1,190	29	17	12
Seaford	8,526	34	27	7
Selbyville	3,104	10	9	1
Smyrna	13,361	42	31	11
South Bethany	490	5	5	0
Townsend	2,842	2	2	0
Wilmington	70,625	360	303	57
Wyoming	1,906	3	3	0
DISTRICT OF COLUMBIA				
Washington	671,803	4,059	3,425	634
FLORIDA				
Alachua	10,746	36	29	7
Altamonte Springs	44,833	110	94	16
Apopka	56,125	147	108	39
Arcadia	7,588	22	18	4
Astatula	1,973	8	8	0
Atlantic Beach	13,189	39	26	13
Atlantis	2,121	15	10	5
Auburndale	19,208	47	38	9
Aventura	38,484	123	91	32
Bal Harbour Village	2,945	34	25	9
Bay Harbor Islands	5,644	32	23	9
Belleair	4,343	15	13	2
Belle Isle	6,902	23	21	2
Belleview	5,726	15	13	2
Boca Raton	95,335	295	196	99
Bonifay	2,804	7	6	1
Bowling Green	2,478	6	6	0
Boynton Beach	79,551	170	138	32
Bradenton	56,316	143	109	34
Bradenton Beach	923	12	11	1
Cape Coral	213,074	332	243	89
Casselberry	29,255	63	53	10
Chattahoochee	3,324	10	8	2
Chiefland	2,379	14	12	2
Chipley	3,665	13	11	2
Clearwater	116,303	327	233	94
Clermont	45,785	87	78	9
Clewiston	7,534	22	16	6
Cocoa	19,618	91	61	30
Cocoa Beach	11,297	58	37	21
Coconut Creek	56,571	139	103	36
Cooper City	33,647	75	58	17
Coral Gables	47,525	269	192	77
Coral Springs	131,628	329	220	109
Cottondale	864	2	2	0
Crestview	28,098	43	36	7
Dania Beach	31,209	82	75	7
Davenport	12,393	16	15	1
Davie	104,215	275	197	78
Daytona Beach	77,130	270	201	69
Daytona Beach Shores	5,251	31	22	9
Deerfield Beach	85,964	141	132	9
DeFuniak Springs	6,620	30	22	8
DeLand	39,924	84	68	16
Delray Beach	66,308	229	149	80

Table 78. Full-Time Law Enforcement Employees, by Selected State and City, 2022—Continued

(Number.)

State/city	Population	Total law enforcement employees	Total officers	Total civilians
Doral	75,838	193	148	45
Dunnellon	1,991	11	10	1
Edgewater	23,367	35	30	5
Edgewood	2,641	13	10	3
Eustis	23,936	51	37	14
Fellsmere	4,978	10	9	1
Fernandina Beach	13,381	42	37	5
Flagler Beach	5,361	17	14	3
Florida City	12,485	45	35	10
Fort Lauderdale	180,554	106	85	21
Fort Myers	98,538	321	232	89
Fort Pierce	48,529	155	121	34
Fort Walton Beach	20,876	62	50	12
Fruitland Park	8,821	22	21	1
Gainesville	140,869	311	233	78
Golden Beach	935	25	20	5
Graceville	2,194	8	8	0
Green Cove Springs	9,933	30	24	6
Groveland	21,998	55	42	13
Gulf Breeze	6,665	30	22	8
Gulfport	11,659	30	25	5
Gulf Stream	950	11	11	0
Haines City	31,143	74	62	12
Hallandale Beach	40,919	125	86	39
Havana	1,713	14	10	4
Hialeah	218,839	354	290	64
Highland Beach	4,246	12	11	1
High Springs	6,540	20	19	1
Hillsboro Beach	1,937	19	16	3
Holly Hill	13,040	27	23	4
Hollywood	151,559	436	324	112
Holmes Beach	3,058	23	17	6
Homestead	80,633	149	116	33
Howey-in-the-Hills	1,656	9	9	0
Indialantic	3,075	17	11	6
Indian Creek Village	81	15	11	4
Indian Harbour Beach	8,950	29	20	9
Indian River Shores	4,421	23	18	5
Indian Shores	3,357	14	12	2
Interlachen	1,466	6	3	3
Jacksonville Beach	23,229	84	61	23
Juno Beach	3,746	18	16	2
Jupiter	60,557	148	116	32
Jupiter Inlet Colony	400	13	13	0
Jupiter Island	842	22	16	6
Kenneth City	4,967	15	14	1
Key Biscayne	14,256	46	36	10
Key Colony Beach	768	5	5	0
Key West	26,169	114	89	25
Kissimmee	79,715	237	154	83
Lady Lake	16,445	30	25	5
Lake Alfred	6,613	15	11	4
Lake City	12,503	54	38	16
Lake Clarke Shores	3,527	10	9	1
Lake Hamilton	1,571	7	6	1
Lake Helen	2,867	7	6	1
Lakeland	118,365	358	252	106
Lake Mary	16,469	51	43	8
Lake Placid	2,472	10	7	3
Lake Wales	16,793	52	45	7
Lantana	12,650	42	32	10
Largo	82,167	183	155	28
Lauderdale-by-the-Sea	6,038	27	25	2
Lauderdale Lakes	35,204	45	42	3
Lauderhill	72,654	175	125	50
Lawtey	650	3	3	0
Leesburg	28,610	90	64	26
Lighthouse Point	10,283	38	30	8
Live Oak	6,957	17	14	3
Longboat Key	7,648	19	16	3
Longwood	14,999	47	42	5
Lynn Haven	19,377	48	38	10
Madison	2,993	15	14	1
Maitland	18,471	59	52	7
Manalapan	415	11	11	0
Marco Island	16,137	46	38	8
Margate	57,455	146	110	36
Marianna	6,253	22	15	7
Mascotte	7,972	18	16	2
Medley	1,018	49	41	8
Melbourne	85,761	208	147	61
Melbourne Beach	3,231	11	10	1
Miami	437,900	1,688	1,269	419
Miami Beach	79,031	493	400	93
Miami Gardens	110,649	257	209	48

Table 78. Full-Time Law Enforcement Employees, by Selected State and City, 2022—Continued

(Number.)

State/city	Population	Total law enforcement employees	Total officers	Total civilians
Miami Shores	11,217	46	39	7
Miami Springs	13,215	55	45	10
Midway	3,422	5	4	1
Milton	10,755	22	16	6
Miramar	135,785	317	216	101
Monticello	2,564	12	8	4
Mount Dora	16,962	54	40	14
Naples	19,668	87	59	28
Neptune Beach	6,971	30	22	8
New Port Richey	17,249	54	40	14
New Smyrna Beach	31,839	67	42	25
Niceville	16,130	34	23	11
North Bay Village	7,798	37	26	11
North Lauderdale	43,807	67	60	7
North Miami	58,502	130	104	26
North Miami Beach	41,632	139	100	39
North Palm Beach	13,021	40	35	5
North Port	84,459	165	127	38
Oakland	3,470	15	13	2
Oakland Park	43,209	94	85	9
Ocala	64,596	299	202	97
Ocean Ridge	1,824	21	16	5
Ocoee	47,445	111	92	19
Okeechobee	5,442	30	23	7
Orange City	14,880	26	23	3
Orange Park	8,699	32	25	7
Orlando	310,713	1,030	790	240
Ormond Beach	43,860	88	69	19
Oviedo	39,027	76	68	8
Palatka	10,599	28	24	4
Palm Bay	125,766	225	155	70
Palm Beach	9,222	91	65	26
Palm Beach Gardens	59,646	173	116	57
Palmetto	13,621	43	29	14
Palm Springs	26,593	59	40	19
Panama City	35,384	127	88	39
Panama City Beach	18,629	97	76	21
Parker	5,096	9	8	1
Parkland	35,659	54	49	5
Pembroke Park	6,151	37	33	4
Pembroke Pines	167,816	345	251	94
Pensacola	53,006	221	182	39
Perry	6,932	22	20	2
Pinellas Park	53,045	135	108	27
Plantation	94,014	256	164	92
Plant City	39,615	84	68	16
Pompano Beach	110,733	270	240	30
Ponce Inlet	3,436	15	13	2
Port Orange	64,037	105	80	25
Port Richey	3,354	24	17	7
Port St. Joe	3,696	10	9	1
Port St. Lucie	228,855	322	251	71
Punta Gorda	20,401	57	39	18
Riviera Beach	38,554	147	107	40
Rockledge	28,961	81	61	20
Sanford	60,602	152	126	26
Sanibel	6,495	42	26	16
Sarasota	55,380	233	175	58
Satellite Beach	11,288	32	25	7
Sebastian	26,258	54	40	14
Sebring	11,245	43	37	6
Sewall's Point	2,046	10	9	1
Shalimar	747	3	3	0
Sneads	1,748	7	6	1
South Daytona	13,712	32	28	4
South Miami	11,597	51	46	5
Springfield	8,044	29	24	5
Starke	5,830	18	17	1
St. Augustine	14,875	64	59	5
St. Augustine Beach	7,100	19	16	3
St. Cloud	64,799	138	96	42
St. Petersburg	257,745	767	554	213
Stuart	17,663	62	46	16
Sunny Isles Beach	21,908	68	57	11
Sunrise	95,018	249	190	59
Surfside	5,418	34	30	4
Tallahassee	197,865	462	357	105
Tamarac	71,241	97	80	17
Tampa	390,145	1,195	929	266
Tarpon Springs	25,997	60	48	12
Tavares	20,241	29	26	3
Temple Terrace	27,392	66	48	18
Titusville	48,979	132	85	47
Treasure Island	6,537	24	19	5
Trenton	2,117	5	4	1

Table 78. Full-Time Law Enforcement Employees, by Selected State and City, 2022—Continued

(Number.)

State/city	Population	Total law enforcement employees	Total officers	Total civilians
Umatilla	3,733	9	8	1
Valparaiso	4,929	14	10	4
Vero Beach	17,038	76	55	21
Village of Pinecrest	17,690	67	49	18
Virginia Gardens	2,251	8	7	1
Welaka	730	2	2	0
West Melbourne	29,221	57	47	10
West Miami	6,911	28	23	5
West Palm Beach	117,393	387	292	95
Wildwood	17,167	40	34	6
Williston	3,140	17	11	6
Wilton Manors	11,202	47	33	14
Windermere	2,976	11	10	1
Winter Garden	45,963	110	83	27
Winter Haven	54,905	93	72	21
Winter Park	28,582	109	81	28
Winter Springs	38,160	60	53	7
Zephyrhills	19,106	49	34	15
GEORGIA				
Abbeville	2,663	5	4	1
Acworth	22,170	53	42	11
Adairsville	5,063	20	18	2
Alapaha	479	2	2	0
Albany	68,613	157	120	37
Alma	3,370	18	16	2
Alpharetta	66,629	136	122	14
Alto	993	5	2	3
Americus	15,808	41	33	8
Arcade	1,948	4	4	0
Athens-Clarke County	128,177	267	207	60
Atlanta	495,707	2,077	1,643	434
Auburn	8,658	20	16	4
Austell	7,867	32	24	8
Avondale Estates	3,440	13	13	0
Bainbridge	14,112	46	35	11
Ball Ground	2,876	6	6	0
Barnesville	6,449	19	19	0
Bartow	182	2	1	1
Baxley	5,016	14	11	3
Blackshear	3,572	19	16	3
Blairsville	538	10	9	1
Blakely	5,139	18	16	2
Bloomingdale	2,849	19	14	5
Blythe	747	3	3	0
Boston	1,212	6	5	1
Bowdon	2,190	8	7	1
Braselton	15,203	20	19	1
Braswell	366	7	4	3
Bremen	7,683	21	18	3
Brookhaven	55,614	84	75	9
Brooklet	2,015	6	5	1
Broxton	1,074	6	5	1
Brunswick	14,650	46	39	7
Buchanan	944	7	6	1
Buena Vista	1,478	3	3	0
Butler	1,797	7	6	1
Byron	5,953	25	23	2
Cairo	9,864	25	22	3
Calhoun	17,585	56	46	10
Camilla	5,001	20	17	3
Canon	666	1	1	0
Canton	35,813	53	44	9
Carrollton	27,844	91	77	14
Cartersville	23,293	58	48	10
Cave Spring	1,195	4	4	0
Cecil	287	3	2	1
Cedartown	10,397	35	31	4
Centerville	8,230	19	16	3
Chamblee	29,393	75	58	17
Chatsworth	4,775	22	20	2
Chickamauga	3,223	5	5	0
Clarkston	14,368	17	17	0
Claxton	2,549	17	11	6
Clayton	2,064	12	11	1
Cleveland	3,537	16	15	1
Cochran	5,077	14	13	1
Cohutta	798	4	4	0
College Park	13,917	95	67	28
Colquitt	1,910	13	13	0
Columbus	204,986	404	305	99
Conyers	17,709	102	75	27
Coolidge	534	1	1	0
Cordele	9,929	31	22	9
Cornelia	5,007	19	17	2

Table 78. Full-Time Law Enforcement Employees, by Selected State and City, 2022—Continued

(Number.)

State/city	Population	Total law enforcement employees	Total officers	Total civilians
Covington	14,549	69	56	13
Cumming	7,482	21	19	2
Dallas	14,801	43	30	13
Dalton	34,276	92	78	14
Danielsville	677	5	5	0
Davisboro	1,854	2	2	0
Dawson	4,229	12	7	5
Decatur	24,259	57	43	14
Demorest	1,927	10	7	3
Dillard	339	3	2	1
Doerun	713	6	5	1
Donalsonville	2,834	9	8	1
Doraville	11,185	64	46	18
Douglas	11,762	36	33	3
Douglasville	36,331	116	96	20
Dublin	16,111	56	49	7
Duluth	31,836	73	54	19
Dunwoody	50,271	65	53	12
East Dublin	2,482	7	6	1
East Ellijay	1,135	15	7	8
Eastman	5,538	14	12	2
East Point	38,080	132	94	38
Eatonton	6,568	20	12	8
Edison	1,237	5	4	1
Elberton	4,719	19	18	1
Ellaville	1,521	5	5	0
Ellijay	1,861	12	11	1
Emerson	1,451	12	11	1
Enigma	1,066	4	3	1
Eton	825	4	4	0
Euharlee	4,345	14	11	3
Fairburn	16,710	51	42	9
Fairmount	775	8	7	1
Fayetteville	19,619	57	50	7
Fitzgerald	8,960	33	23	10
Flowery Branch	10,843	23	21	2
Folkston	4,457	7	7	0
Forest Park	19,605	87	63	24
Forsyth	4,608	17	15	2
Fort Oglethorpe	10,626	33	30	3
Fort Valley	8,946	35	27	8
Franklin	926	8	8	0
Franklin Springs	1,125	3	3	0
Gainesville	44,314	102	87	15
Garden City	10,248	40	36	4
Glennville	3,731	7	5	2
Gordon	1,767	11	6	5
Grantville	3,446	13	12	1
Gray	3,406	15	15	0
Greensboro	3,662	21	17	4
Greenville	799	5	4	1
Griffin	23,862	83	64	19
Grovetown	17,161	29	23	6
Guyton	2,826	6	6	0
Hagan	939	4	3	1
Hahira	3,442	12	10	2
Hamilton	1,695	3	3	0
Hampton	8,308	21	19	2
Hapeville	6,543	43	29	14
Harlem	4,130	8	7	1
Hartwell	4,567	23	18	5
Hazlehurst	4,079	16	14	2
Helen	555	15	14	1
Hephzibah	3,778	6	5	1
Hiawassee	1,049	5	5	0
Hinesville	35,443	87	71	16
Hiram	5,203	23	18	5
Hoboken	484	3	1	2
Hogansville	3,180	23	15	8
Holly Springs	18,511	40	38	2
Homerville	2,309	9	7	2
Jacksonville	115	5	4	1
Jasper	4,371	17	15	2
Jefferson	14,664	27	25	2
Johns Creek	81,964	90	75	15
Kennesaw	32,974	75	65	10
Kingsland	19,650	38	35	3
Kingston	750	3	2	1
LaFayette	7,022	26	22	4
LaGrange	32,146	107	88	19
Lake City	3,042	15	13	2
Lakeland	2,726	11	9	2
Lake Park	1,406	4	3	1
Lavonia	2,170	15	14	1
Lawrenceville	30,618	90	68	22

Table 78. Full-Time Law Enforcement Employees, by Selected State and City, 2022—Continued

(Number.)

State/city	Population	Total law enforcement employees	Total officers	Total civilians
Leesburg	3,529	13	13	0
Lilburn	15,823	37	32	5
Locust Grove	10,394	31	27	4
Loganville	15,250	33	28	5
Louisville	2,336	6	6	0
Lovejoy	12,041	22	19	3
Lyons	4,175	19	16	3
Madison	5,410	18	16	2
Manchester	3,563	16	10	6
Marietta	62,059	166	128	38
Maysville	2,051	4	4	0
McDonough	31,292	55	47	8
McIntyre	568	3	3	0
McRae-Helena	5,873	12	11	1
Metter	4,001	13	13	0
Midway	2,227	7	5	2
Milledgeville	17,102	54	39	15
Millen	2,913	12	12	0
Milton	41,330	43	39	4
Monroe	15,569	51	48	3
Montezuma	3,056	13	11	2
Morrow	6,493	28	26	2
Moultrie	14,454	39	33	6
Mount Zion	2,021	8	7	1
Nashville	4,830	19	16	3
Newnan	43,932	94	82	12
Norcross	17,731	62	43	19
Norman Park	960	2	2	0
Ocilla	3,714	11	10	1
Oglethorpe	1,006	2	1	1
Omega	1,289	5	5	0
Oxford	2,275	2	2	0
Palmetto	5,084	18	16	2
Patterson	770	5	3	2
Peachtree City	39,301	60	55	5
Pearson	1,865	6	5	1
Pelham	3,380	9	7	2
Pendergrass	1,779	7	6	1
Perry	23,213	42	35	7
Pine Mountain	1,282	8	7	1
Plains	548	5	5	0
Pooler	28,328	69	58	11
Port Wentworth	12,684	43	36	7
Poulan	737	5	4	1
Quitman	4,097	12	10	2
Reidsville	2,467	8	6	2
Remerton	1,279	9	8	1
Reynolds	929	6	6	0
Richmond Hill	18,421	48	37	11
Rincon	11,050	20	18	2
Ringgold	3,444	10	10	0
Riverdale	14,771	41	32	9
Rochelle	1,167	7	6	1
Rockmart	4,877	23	21	2
Rome	37,778	91	81	10
Roswell	92,550	198	156	42
Royston	2,667	12	10	2
Sandersville	5,540	21	19	2
Sandy Springs	106,747	178	154	24
Savannah	239,089	511	411	100
Shiloh	421	2	1	1
Smyrna	55,735	110	73	37
Snellville	20,988	56	44	12
Social Circle	5,252	14	13	1
Soperton	2,823	8	7	1
South Fulton	110,102	133	116	17
Sparks	2,025	3	3	0
Sparta	1,315	11	6	5
Springfield	3,083	11	10	1
Stapleton	392	2	2	0
Statesboro	33,590	81	63	18
Statham	2,880	13	11	2
St. Marys	18,633	22	18	4
Stone Mountain	6,541	16	15	1
Summerville	4,387	15	13	2
Suwanee	22,911	50	39	11
Swainsboro	7,426	25	23	2
Sycamore	766	9	9	0
Sylvania	2,663	12	9	3
Sylvester	5,488	26	20	6
Tallapoosa	3,273	13	11	2
Tallulah Falls	201	1	1	0
Temple	6,168	16	13	3
Thomaston	9,681	27	22	5
Thomasville	18,836	59	52	7

394 CRIME IN THE UNITED STATES

Table 78. Full-Time Law Enforcement Employees, by Selected State and City, 2022—Continued

(Number.)

State/city	Population	Total law enforcement employees	Total officers	Total civilians
Thunderbolt	2,513	8	7	1
Toccoa	9,218	30	28	2
Trenton	2,224	8	8	0
Tunnel Hill	965	4	4	0
Twin City	1,683	2	2	0
Tybee Island	3,075	39	26	13
Tyrone	7,917	15	15	0
Union City	27,818	67	60	7
Valdosta	55,666	142	113	29
Varnell	2,182	13	13	0
Vidalia	10,656	30	20	10
Vienna	2,830	6	5	1
Villa Rica	18,592	52	43	9
Wadley	1,606	5	4	1
Walthourville	3,862	10	9	1
Warner Robins	82,409	154	96	58
Warwick	496	5	3	2
Waverly Hall	632	4	3	1
Waycross	13,630	65	52	13
Waynesboro	5,576	22	19	3
West Point	3,750	23	12	11
Whigham	420	3	2	1
White	661	3	3	0
Winder	19,401	35	28	7
Woodstock	37,325	58	51	7
Wrens	2,156	14	13	1
Zebulon	1,289	7	7	0
HAWAII				
Honolulu	994,799	2,261	1,857	404
IDAHO				
American Falls	4,661	9	7	2
Ashton	957	3	3	0
Bellevue	2,587	5	5	0
Blackfoot	12,437	32	29	3
Boise	239,074	367	288	79
Bonners Ferry	2,626	6	6	0
Buhl	4,744	11	9	2
Caldwell	66,940	82	68	14
Chubbuck	15,970	35	21	14
Coeur d'Alene	57,061	110	87	23
Cottonwood	875	1	1	0
Emmett	8,007	15	14	1
Filer	2,888	6	6	0
Fruitland	6,823	17	13	4
Garden City	12,279	36	28	8
Gooding	3,741	8	7	1
Grangeville	3,540	5	5	0
Hagerman	989	1	1	0
Hailey	9,789	14	13	1
Heyburn	3,684	6	6	0
Homedale	3,095	7	7	0
Idaho City	504	2	2	0
Idaho Falls	68,162	131	90	41
Jerome	12,806	21	18	3
Kellogg	2,443	10	8	2
Ketchum	3,606	12	11	1
Kimberly	5,025	9	9	0
Lewiston	34,711	66	45	21
McCall	4,007	13	10	3
Meridian	132,522	170	132	38
Middleton	10,845	11	10	1
Montpelier	2,720	6	5	1
Moscow	26,240	41	33	8
Mountain Home	16,357	28	24	4
Nampa	111,501	205	138	67
Orofino	3,310	5	4	1
Osburn	1,670	2	2	0
Parma	2,136	6	5	1
Payette	8,657	16	14	2
Pinehurst	1,784	1	1	0
Pocatello	57,914	139	95	44
Ponderay	1,653	8	7	1
Post Falls	46,306	68	47	21
Preston	5,932	9	8	1
Priest River	1,810	6	5	1
Rathdrum	11,250	18	15	3
Rexburg	35,711	42	33	9
Rigby	5,428	10	9	1
Rupert	6,107	14	13	1
Salmon	3,274	8	8	0
Sandpoint	9,429	25	21	4
Shelley	5,232	9	9	0
Soda Springs	3,146	6	6	0

Table 78. Full-Time Law Enforcement Employees, by Selected State and City, 2022—Continued

(Number.)

State/city	Population	Total law enforcement employees	Total officers	Total civilians
Spirit Lake	2,578	8	6	2
St. Anthony	3,809	6	6	0
Sun Valley	1,828	13	12	1
Twin Falls	54,648	99	74	25
Weiser	5,986	14	11	3
Wendell	2,940	4	4	0
Wilder	1,720	5	5	0
ILLINOIS				
Abingdon	2,861	4	3	1
Addison	35,039	137	66	71
Albany	853	1	1	0
Albers	1,090	2	1	1
Aledo	3,602	7	6	1
Algonquin	30,212	68	62	6
Alsip	18,246	39	36	3
Altamont	2,171	4	4	0
Alton	25,212	84	64	20
Anna	4,096	9	9	0
Annawan	874	1	1	0
Antioch	15,017	30	27	3
Arcola	2,874	6	5	1
Arlington Heights	74,648	136	108	28
Arthur	2,227	5	5	0
Assumption	1,172	1	1	0
Athens	1,923	6	6	0
Atwood	1,116	1	1	0
Auburn	4,463	5	5	0
Bannockburn	1,000	8	8	0
Barrington	10,614	27	23	4
Barrington Hills	4,024	20	16	4
Bartlett	40,020	74	58	16
Bartonville	5,789	17	12	5
Batavia	26,088	53	41	12
Bedford Park	584	37	35	2
Beecher	4,675	12	11	1
Belleville	41,291	95	72	23
Bellwood	17,972	52	48	4
Benton	6,669	14	13	1
Berwyn	54,654	210	117	93
Bethalto	9,311	16	15	1
Bloomingdale	22,447	50	37	13
Bloomington	78,340	148	121	27
Blue Island	21,577	48	41	7
Bolingbrook	73,364	144	120	24
Bourbonnais	18,780	29	27	2
Bradley	14,950	41	36	5
Braidwood	6,176	12	10	2
Breese	4,588	8	7	1
Brighton	2,172	4	4	0
Broadview	7,961	29	23	6
Brookfield	18,722	29	28	1
Buffalo Grove	42,468	72	59	13
Burbank	28,271	55	38	17
Burr Ridge	11,069	30	26	4
Cahokia Heights	17,403	23	18	5
Calumet Park	6,711	20	18	2
Cambridge	2,057	1	1	0
Campton Hills	10,802	9	9	0
Canton	13,291	30	20	10
Carbondale	21,612	77	50	27
Carlinville	5,500	16	11	5
Carlyle	3,200	8	7	1
Carmi	4,783	11	10	1
Carol Stream	38,920	80	64	16
Carpentersville	37,334	63	59	4
Carthage	2,457	4	4	0
Cary	17,892	27	25	2
Champaign	89,815	132	109	23
Channahon	14,006	31	27	4
Chatham	14,420	22	16	6
Chenoa	3,121	3	3	0
Cherry Valley	2,880	15	14	1
Chicago	2,652,124	12,263	11,678	585
Chicago Heights	26,393	88	70	18
Cicero	81,492	224	172	52
Clarendon Hills	8,560	15	13	2
Clinton	6,862	13	12	1
Colfax	974	1	1	0
Collinsville	24,131	61	42	19
Colona	5,009	15	13	2
Columbia	10,910	29	21	8
Cortland	4,404	6	6	0
Coulterville	832	2	2	0
Country Club Hills	16,100	41	34	7

Table 78. Full-Time Law Enforcement Employees, by Selected State and City, 2022—Continued

(Number.)

State/city	Population	Total law enforcement employees	Total officers	Total civilians
Countryside	6,159	27	24	3
Crest Hill	20,197	34	32	2
Crestwood	10,507	23	17	6
Crete	8,371	22	20	2
Crystal Lake	40,625	75	65	10
Dallas City	791	3	3	0
Danville	28,480	78	64	14
Darien	21,515	38	33	5
Decatur	68,789	145	135	10
Deerfield	18,981	54	39	15
DeKalb	40,555	77	60	17
Delavan	1,548	6	6	0
Des Plaines	58,425	107	92	15
Dixon	15,396	31	29	2
Downers Grove	49,186	85	67	18
Dupo	3,896	9	9	0
Durand	1,387	1	1	0
Dwight	3,989	9	8	1
East Dundee	3,091	15	14	1
East Hazel Crest	1,237	12	10	2
East Peoria	22,130	48	43	5
Edwardsville	25,117	62	45	17
Effingham	12,188	41	27	14
Eldorado	3,644	10	6	4
Elgin	113,205	265	185	80
Elk Grove Village	31,479	97	79	18
Elmhurst	45,005	78	61	17
Elmwood Park	23,485	41	35	6
Elwood	2,208	15	14	1
Evanston	76,259	178	131	47
Evergreen Park	19,103	78	59	19
Fairbury	3,585	8	8	0
Fairfield	4,724	11	8	3
Fairmont City	2,211	7	6	1
Fairview Heights	16,270	48	45	3
Farmer City	1,803	5	5	0
Farmington	2,293	5	5	0
Flossmoor	9,281	23	18	5
Fox Lake	10,876	35	29	6
Fox River Grove	4,684	9	9	0
Franklin Park	18,230	53	47	6
Freeburg	4,494	12	11	1
Freeport	23,411	57	39	18
Fulton	3,609	9	8	1
Galesburg	29,425	73	45	28
Geneseo	6,488	19	13	6
Geneva	21,152	44	35	9
Genoa	5,321	8	8	0
Germantown	1,312	2	2	0
Gilberts	8,339	10	9	1
Glen Carbon	13,822	39	27	12
Glencoe	8,567	34	28	6
Glendale Heights	32,440	67	52	15
Glenview	47,092	76	71	5
Glenwood	8,317	25	21	4
Golf	501	1	1	0
Granite City	27,273	69	56	13
Grantfork	344	6	6	0
Grant Park	1,252	4	4	0
Grayville	1,512	3	3	0
Greenfield	1,028	3	3	0
Greenup	1,338	4	4	0
Greenville	6,480	11	11	0
Gurnee	30,361	104	62	42
Hampshire	7,881	14	13	1
Hanover Park	36,222	82	60	22
Harvard	9,461	19	17	2
Havana	2,868	14	9	5
Hawthorn Woods	9,322	13	12	1
Hazel Crest	12,849	35	29	6
Henry	2,308	5	4	1
Herrin	12,174	32	21	11
Herscher	1,469	2	2	0
Heyworth	2,762	3	3	0
Hickory Hills	13,924	35	25	10
Highland	10,026	22	20	2
Highland Park	30,173	71	60	11
Hillsboro	5,860	8	8	0
Hillside	7,987	28	25	3
Hinckley	1,991	3	3	0
Hodgkins	1,452	23	20	3
Hoffman Estates	50,385	101	83	18
Homer Glen	24,524	22	22	0
Hometown	4,157	5	4	1
Homewood	18,634	42	37	5

Table 78. Full-Time Law Enforcement Employees, by Selected State and City, 2022—Continued

(Number.)

State/city	Population	Total law enforcement employees	Total officers	Total civilians
Hoopeston	4,782	14	10	4
Hopedale	809	1	1	0
Hudson	1,733	2	2	0
Huntley	28,223	43	35	8
Indian Head Park	3,935	11	10	1
Inverness	7,314	14	13	1
Itasca	9,335	25	21	4
Jacksonville	17,731	42	38	4
Jerseyville	8,271	22	16	6
Joliet	150,545	333	267	66
Kankakee	23,719	76	68	8
Kenilworth	2,404	9	8	1
Kildeer	4,240	10	9	1
Kingston	1,099	1	1	0
La Grange	15,699	30	24	6
La Grange Park	12,992	23	21	2
Lake Forest	19,201	41	36	5
Lake in the Hills	28,961	47	40	7
Lakemoor	6,285	15	14	1
Lake Villa	8,649	18	17	1
Lakewood	4,321	10	9	1
Lake Zurich	19,571	47	31	16
Lansing	27,828	72	54	18
La Salle	9,450	23	22	1
Leland	927	2	2	0
Lemont	17,394	30	25	5
Le Roy	3,448	7	7	0
Lincoln	13,119	28	26	2
Lincolnshire	7,931	26	23	3
Lincolnwood	12,946	40	33	7
Lindenhurst	14,242	15	14	1
Lisle	23,647	46	37	9
Litchfield	6,705	16	15	1
Livingston	761	2	1	1
Lockport	26,079	46	41	5
Lombard	43,447	74	63	11
Loves Park	23,222	41	38	3
Lovington	1,061	1	1	0
Machesney Park	22,558	20	20	0
Mackinaw	1,851	2	2	0
Mahomet	9,709	12	11	1
Manhattan	10,569	16	14	2
Manito	1,511	3	3	0
Manteno	8,985	22	21	1
Maple Park	1,506	1	1	0
Marengo	7,590	16	14	2
Markham	11,184	37	35	2
Marseilles	4,785	10	9	1
Maryville	8,194	17	16	1
Mason City	2,011	3	3	0
Matteson	18,324	41	36	5
Mattoon	16,809	43	39	4
Mazon	978	1	1	0
McHenry	27,610	77	48	29
Melrose Park	23,739	79	67	12
Mendota	6,942	15	14	1
Metropolis	5,849	22	16	6
Midlothian	13,721	32	29	3
Milan	4,994	16	15	1
Milledgeville	1,082	3	3	0
Millstadt	3,986	8	8	0
Mokena	19,829	35	33	2
Moline	42,009	82	75	7
Momence	3,026	8	7	1
Monee	5,090	19	18	1
Montgomery	22,257	31	26	5
Monticello	5,992	6	5	1
Morris	14,511	31	27	4
Morrisonville	1,030	2	1	1
Morton	17,169	22	20	2
Morton Grove	24,238	59	47	12
Mount Carmel	6,733	19	13	6
Mount Prospect	54,477	94	83	11
Mount Pulaski	1,516	2	2	0
Mount Zion	5,867	12	10	2
Mundelein	31,561	78	50	28
Neoga	1,367	3	3	0
New Athens	1,902	4	4	0
New Lenox	27,699	42	36	6
Newman	761	1	1	0
Newton	2,668	8	7	1
Nokomis	2,117	6	5	1
Normal	53,613	89	79	10
Norridge	14,786	43	36	7
Northbrook	34,039	93	66	27

Table 78. Full-Time Law Enforcement Employees, by Selected State and City, 2022—Continued

(Number.)

State/city	Population	Total law enforcement employees	Total officers	Total civilians
Northlake	12,440	49	34	15
North Pekin	1,449	6	6	0
North Riverside	7,106	27	25	2
Oak Brook	8,014	46	37	9
Oakbrook Terrace	2,699	21	18	3
Oak Forest	26,282	51	39	12
Oak Lawn	55,957	121	108	13
Oak Park	52,152	121	99	22
Oakwood	1,296	2	2	0
Oakwood Hills	2,085	4	4	0
O'Fallon	32,250	66	46	20
Okawville	1,357	2	2	0
Olney	8,681	12	11	1
Orion	1,732	2	2	0
Orland Hills	6,600	12	12	0
Orland Park	57,206	135	101	34
Oswego	35,932	62	52	10
Ottawa	18,696	50	35	15
Palatine	65,078	136	109	27
Palestine	1,224	2	2	0
Palos Heights	11,602	32	28	4
Palos Hills	17,790	34	31	3
Palos Park	4,819	12	11	1
Pana	5,218	12	8	4
Paris	8,026	18	12	6
Park City	7,843	12	10	2
Park Forest	20,896	57	41	16
Park Ridge	38,108	79	55	24
Pawnee	2,754	6	6	0
Paxton	4,444	8	8	0
Pecatonica	2,044	3	3	0
Pekin	31,252	64	55	9
Peoria	110,551	223	196	27
Petersburg	2,208	4	4	0
Pingree Grove	11,078	15	13	2
Plainfield	46,004	76	61	15
Plano	12,474	26	25	1
Pleasant Plains	804	1	1	0
Polo	2,246	3	2	1
Prairie Grove	1,963	2	2	0
Princeton	7,630	17	15	2
Prophetstown	1,922	4	4	0
Quincy	38,822	74	61	13
Rantoul	11,971	37	31	6
Richmond	2,125	7	7	0
Richton Park	12,259	24	21	3
River Forest	11,403	33	31	2
River Grove	10,504	30	29	1
Riverwoods	3,744	8	8	0
Robinson	7,189	16	15	1
Rochester	3,827	10	10	0
Rock Falls	8,687	23	20	3
Rockford	146,710	319	272	47
Rock Island	36,235	95	69	26
Rockton	7,738	16	14	2
Rolling Meadows	23,453	59	51	8
Romeoville	41,069	80	67	13
Roscoe	10,815	16	15	1
Roselle	22,402	40	30	10
Rosemont	3,779	95	79	16
Round Lake	18,531	29	27	2
Round Lake Beach	26,928	44	40	4
Round Lake Park	7,699	15	12	3
Roxana	1,438	7	6	1
Royalton	1,042	3	3	0
Rushville	3,010	5	5	0
Salem	7,136	26	18	8
Sandwich	7,167	14	12	2
San Jose	462	2	1	1
Sauget	134	12	11	1
Schaumburg	75,745	144	109	35
Sherman	4,603	7	7	0
Shiloh	14,616	21	20	1
Shorewood	18,326	37	33	4
Skokie	65,185	151	108	43
Sleepy Hollow	3,160	10	8	2
Smithton	3,969	8	8	0
Somonauk	1,774	4	4	0
South Barrington	4,973	20	17	3
South Beloit	7,893	16	15	1
South Elgin	23,995	36	30	6
Southern View	1,553	4	4	0
South Holland	20,626	46	41	5
South Pekin	971	2	2	0
South Roxana	1,884	5	5	0

Table 78. Full-Time Law Enforcement Employees, by Selected State and City, 2022—Continued

(Number.)

State/city	Population	Total law enforcement employees	Total officers	Total civilians
Springfield	112,549	260	232	28
Spring Grove	5,535	8	7	1
Spring Valley	5,415	12	11	1
St. Anne	1,111	4	4	0
St. Charles	32,973	75	59	16
Steger	9,325	15	14	1
Sterling	14,681	35	26	9
Stickney	6,841	31	28	3
Stone Park	4,386	18	12	6
Streamwood	37,923	69	57	12
Streator	12,303	22	20	2
Sugar Grove	9,211	10	10	0
Sullivan	4,385	10	8	2
Summit	10,658	32	30	2
Swansea	14,068	23	21	2
Sycamore	18,673	34	31	3
Taylorville	10,634	26	21	5
Thayer	620	1	1	0
Thornton	2,289	11	10	1
Tilton	2,584	7	7	0
Tinley Park	53,973	97	84	13
Tolono	3,489	4	4	0
Trenton	2,630	6	6	0
Troy	11,260	27	21	6
Tuscola	4,656	7	6	1
University Park	7,038	13	12	1
Vandalia	6,812	12	12	0
Vernon Hills	26,717	67	43	24
Vienna	1,491	3	3	0
Villa Park	21,752	47	37	10
Virden	3,159	9	5	4
Warrensburg	1,075	1	1	0
Washington	15,910	30	24	6
Watseka	4,587	12	11	1
Waukegan	88,073	198	153	45
Wayne	2,240	6	6	0
Westchester	16,171	36	31	5
West Chicago	25,172	51	46	5
West Dundee	7,727	25	22	3
Western Springs	13,175	23	19	4
Westmont	23,921	45	39	6
Westville	3,084	5	5	0
Wheaton	52,663	82	67	15
Wheeling	37,790	92	60	32
White Hall	2,313	9	5	4
Willowbrook	9,037	26	24	2
Wilmette	27,144	61	45	16
Winfield	10,460	18	15	3
Winnebago	2,885	5	5	0
Winnetka	12,277	31	26	5
Wood Dale	13,720	42	32	10
Woodridge	33,516	57	48	9
Wood River	10,350	29	18	11
Woodstock	25,778	43	39	4
Worden	1,092	2	2	0
Worth	10,507	29	27	2
Yorkville	23,635	36	33	3
Zion	24,348	53	50	3
INDIANA				
Albion	2,232	6	6	0
Anderson	54,965	122	103	19
Auburn	13,645	27	26	1
Austin	4,049	9	9	0
Avon	24,167	37	35	2
Bargersville	10,791	17	16	1
Batesville	7,308	18	13	5
Bedford	13,824	39	31	8
Bloomington	80,135	143	89	54
Bluffton	10,327	33	21	12
Brownsburg	31,072	5	5	0
Cannelton	1,530	4	4	0
Carmel	101,670	162	137	25
Cedar Lake	15,271	25	23	2
Cicero	5,537	9	9	0
Clarksville	21,890	58	52	6
Columbia City	10,027	22	21	1
Danville	10,925	24	22	2
Dyer	16,351	35	32	3
Edinburgh	4,431	13	12	1
Elwood	8,397	20	19	1
Evansville	115,719	291	264	27
Fishers	102,921	135	118	17
Fort Wayne	267,791	548	479	69
Franklin	25,714	60	52	8

Table 78. Full-Time Law Enforcement Employees, by Selected State and City, 2022—Continued

(Number.)

State/city	Population	Total law enforcement employees	Total officers	Total civilians
Fremont	2,092	4	3	1
Gas City	6,062	12	12	0
Goshen	34,697	74	62	12
Greenfield	24,596	45	42	3
Greenwood	65,813	74	66	8
Hammond	76,366	244	212	32
Highland	23,498	42	37	5
Hobart	29,374	79	68	11
Huntingburg	6,459	15	14	1
Huntington	17,030	34	32	2
Indianapolis	886,455	2,513	2,022	491
Jasper	16,699	33	25	8
Kendallville	10,153	29	19	10
Kokomo	59,776	107	87	20
Lebanon	17,042	45	42	3
Logansport	18,195	40	38	2
Loogootee	2,595	5	5	0
Lowell	11,204	19	18	1
Marion	28,108	67	55	12
Merrillville	36,457	67	61	6
Mount Vernon	6,380	19	18	1
Muncie	65,343	113	104	9
Munster	23,628	46	40	6
New Albany	37,198	78	67	11
New Haven	15,856	33	24	9
New Whiteland	5,597	9	8	1
Noblesville	72,070	107	96	11
North Webster	993	5	4	1
Pendleton	4,974	14	13	1
Pittsboro	4,145	10	9	1
Plainfield	36,189	70	63	7
Prince's Lakes	1,372	3	3	0
Remington	1,307	2	2	0
Richmond	35,783	73	65	8
Roseland	849	3	3	0
Schererville	29,628	65	50	15
Sellersburg	9,784	21	19	2
Seymour	21,415	64	45	19
Shirley	827	3	3	0
South Bend	103,179	291	221	70
St. John	22,496	26	24	2
Syracuse	3,063	10	9	1
Terre Haute	58,507	143	134	9
Vincennes	16,487	40	35	5
Walkerton	2,080	10	6	4
Warsaw	15,952	44	38	6
Washington	12,090	21	19	2
Westfield	54,552	75	69	6
West Lafayette	44,891	64	44	20
Westville	5,320	4	4	0
Whiteland	4,835	12	11	1
Whiting	4,532	16	14	2
Winona Lake	5,066	6	6	0
Zionsville	32,575	39	38	1
IOWA				
Adel	6,377	12	11	1
Albia	3,717	7	6	1
Algona	5,257	14	10	4
Altoona	21,830	43	40	3
Ames	66,852	78	53	25
Anamosa	5,411	9	8	1
Ankeny	72,315	94	69	25
Asbury	6,005	6	6	0
Atlantic	6,726	13	12	1
Audubon	2,018	3	3	0
Belle Plaine	2,340	5	5	0
Belmond	2,407	4	4	0
Bettendorf	39,548	57	50	7
Bloomfield	2,694	6	5	1
Blue Grass	1,666	5	5	0
Boone	12,491	17	16	1
Buffalo	1,168	8	8	0
Burlington	23,497	50	44	6
Camanche	4,587	8	8	0
Carlisle	4,225	9	8	1
Carroll	10,195	16	15	1
Carter Lake	3,768	15	10	5
Cedar Falls	40,291	72	71	1
Cedar Rapids	135,362	284	220	64
Centerville	5,303	14	8	6
Charles City	7,211	15	15	0
Cherokee	5,040	8	7	1
Clarinda	5,499	10	9	1
Clarion	2,754	5	5	0

Table 78. Full-Time Law Enforcement Employees, by Selected State and City, 2022—Continued

(Number.)

State/city	Population	Total law enforcement employees	Total officers	Total civilians
Clear Lake	7,501	17	12	5
Clinton	24,443	51	47	4
Clive	18,984	34	29	5
Colfax	2,246	4	4	0
Coralville	23,555	36	32	4
Council Bluffs	62,206	132	113	19
Creston	7,438	16	12	4
Davenport	100,437	182	155	27
Decorah	7,764	14	13	1
Denison	8,048	20	13	7
Denver	1,940	3	3	0
Des Moines	210,376	477	339	138
DeWitt	5,528	10	9	1
Dubuque	58,676	109	102	7
Dyersville	4,516	7	7	0
Dysart	1,242	3	3	0
Eldridge	6,770	11	10	1
Emmetsburg	3,612	7	6	1
Estherville	5,847	9	9	0
Evansdale	4,486	9	8	1
Fairfield	9,641	17	10	7
Fort Dodge	25,097	41	38	3
Fort Madison	10,084	26	23	3
Glenwood	5,195	10	9	1
Gowrie	952	1	1	0
Grinnell	9,474	16	14	2
Grundy Center	2,804	5	5	0
Hampton	4,295	6	5	1
Harlan	4,936	7	6	1
Hawarden	2,665	5	5	0
Hiawatha	7,109	15	15	0
Huxley	4,658	6	6	0
Independence	6,236	12	11	1
Indianola	15,817	28	22	6
Iowa City	74,749	102	80	22
Iowa Falls	5,023	14	10	4
Jefferson	4,119	8	8	0
Johnston	24,295	39	32	7
Keokuk	9,702	26	22	4
Knoxville	7,366	16	14	2
Lake City	1,721	4	4	0
Lansing	945	3	3	0
Le Claire	4,712	10	8	2
Le Mars	10,564	17	15	2
Manchester	5,134	16	9	7
Maquoketa	6,035	17	10	7
Marengo	2,411	4	4	0
Marion	41,793	57	45	12
Mar-Mac	1,152	2	2	0
Marshalltown	27,207	41	36	5
Mason City	27,032	45	38	7
Monroe	2,042	3	3	0
Monticello	4,071	8	7	1
Mount Pleasant	8,959	16	14	2
Mount Vernon-Lisbon	4,435	9	8	1
Muscatine	23,237	43	39	4
Nevada	7,112	13	11	2
New Hampton	3,392	6	6	0
North Liberty	21,131	25	23	2
Oelwein	5,788	13	11	2
Ogden	1,996	2	2	0
Orange City	6,220	8	8	0
Osage	3,528	7	6	1
Osceola	5,654	12	11	1
Oskaloosa	11,479	17	15	2
Ottumwa	25,249	49	39	10
Parkersburg	2,011	1	1	0
Pella	10,729	24	18	6
Perry	7,986	20	13	7
Polk City	5,920	8	8	0
Postville	2,434	4	4	0
Prairie City	1,713	2	2	0
Princeton	914	1	1	0
Red Oak	5,568	15	13	2
Rockwell City Police Department	2,257	5	5	0
Sabula	491	3	3	0
Sergeant Bluff	4,991	10	9	1
Sheldon	5,385	8	8	0
Shenandoah	4,861	11	9	2
Sioux Center	8,340	8	8	0
Sioux City	85,580	148	128	20
Spencer	11,440	30	20	10
State Center	1,388	1	1	0
Storm Lake	11,274	23	19	4
Tama	3,026	7	6	1

Table 78. Full-Time Law Enforcement Employees, by Selected State and City, 2022—Continued

(Number.)

State/city	Population	Total law enforcement employees	Total officers	Total civilians
Tipton	3,092	7	6	1
Toledo	2,308	6	6	0
Urbandale	46,284	63	54	9
Van Meter	1,589	4	4	0
Vinton	4,951	10	9	1
Walcott	1,547	8	8	0
Washington	7,209	13	12	1
Waterloo	66,504	129	120	9
Waukee	28,790	32	29	3
Waukon	3,706	7	6	1
Waverly	10,445	18	17	1
Webster City	7,689	19	12	7
West Branch	2,608	4	4	0
West Burlington	3,177	10	10	0
West Des Moines	70,701	94	85	9
West Union	2,421	1	1	0
Williamsburg	3,362	7	7	0
Wilton	2,867	7	7	0
Windsor Heights	5,108	14	13	1
KANSAS				
Abilene	6,489	17	14	3
Altamont	1,031	3	3	0
Andover	15,842	36	26	10
Anthony	1,993	5	4	1
Arkansas City	11,902	27	23	4
Arma	1,407	5	5	0
Atchison	10,650	25	24	1
Attica	493	1	1	0
Augusta	9,256	32	24	8
Baldwin City	4,955	13	11	2
Basehor	7,546	17	15	2
Baxter Springs	3,826	12	10	2
Bel Aire	8,599	14	13	1
Belleville	2,015	5	5	0
Beloit	3,396	9	7	2
Benton	942	1	1	0
Blue Rapids	917	2	2	0
Bonner Springs	7,731	23	20	3
Buhler	1,306	3	3	0
Burlingame	965	3	2	1
Burlington	2,637	9	7	2
Caldwell	1,015	3	3	0
Caney	1,745	11	7	4
Canton	691	1	1	0
Carbondale	1,339	3	3	0
Chanute	8,571	21	18	3
Chapman	1,381	3	3	0
Cheney	2,162	6	6	0
Cherryvale	2,146	8	7	1
Chetopa	911	4	4	0
Claflin	549	1	1	0
Clay Center	4,105	7	6	1
Clearwater	2,607	7	6	1
Coffeyville	8,788	30	23	7
Colby	5,488	13	12	1
Coldwater	668	1	1	0
Columbus	2,857	9	8	1
Colwich	1,457	4	4	0
Concordia	5,002	10	5	5
Conway Springs	1,115	3	3	0
Council Grove	2,116	8	7	1
Dodge City	27,641	54	41	13
Eastborough	746	6	6	0
Edwardsville	4,574	20	18	2
El Dorado	12,821	25	24	1
Ellinwood	1,970	5	5	0
Ellis	1,987	4	4	0
Elwood	1,118	3	3	0
Eudora	6,480	14	14	0
Fort Scott	7,501	20	20	0
Fredonia	2,090	6	5	1
Frontenac	3,415	12	10	2
Galena	2,737	11	10	1
Galva	869	1	1	0
Garden City	27,701	88	61	27
Garden Plain	939	2	2	0
Gardner	24,497	38	33	5
Garnett	3,150	8	8	0
Girard	2,517	8	6	2
Goddard	5,644	12	11	1
Goodland	4,459	10	9	1
Grandview Plaza	1,628	8	7	1
Great Bend	14,456	37	33	4
Greensburg	696	2	2	0

Table 78. Full-Time Law Enforcement Employees, by Selected State and City, 2022—Continued

(Number.)

State/city	Population	Total law enforcement employees	Total officers	Total civilians
Halstead	2,159	6	5	1
Hays	20,696	54	34	20
Herington	2,113	7	6	1
Hesston	3,493	9	8	1
Hiawatha	3,239	10	8	2
Hill City	1,394	4	4	0
Hillsboro	2,724	5	5	0
Hoisington	2,629	7	6	1
Holcomb	2,217	5	4	1
Holton	3,317	10	5	5
Horton	1,510	5	5	0
Hugoton	3,795	7	5	2
Humboldt	1,822	7	5	2
Hutchinson	39,424	105	71	34
Independence	8,402	26	18	8
Inman	1,309	3	3	0
Iola	5,302	18	17	1
Junction City	21,927	65	47	18
Kechi	2,265	1	1	0
Kingman	3,021	23	7	16
Kiowa	850	1	1	0
La Cygne	1,056	2	2	0
La Harpe	483	1	1	0
Lake Quivira	1,003	1	1	0
Lansing	11,200	19	18	1
Larned	3,607	8	8	0
Lawrence	95,580	175	145	30
Leavenworth	37,004	76	53	23
Leawood	33,596	78	57	21
Lenexa	59,289	144	92	52
Liberal	19,557	46	29	17
Lindsborg	3,474	7	6	1
Little River	475	1	1	0
Louisburg	5,023	9	8	1
Lyndon	1,061	1	1	0
Lyons	3,554	7	6	1
Macksville	469	1	1	0
Maize	6,275	20	19	1
Marion	1,897	5	5	0
Marquette	589	1	1	0
Marysville	3,405	9	8	1
McLouth	858	2	2	0
McPherson	13,853	39	34	5
Merriam	10,928	34	29	5
Minneapolis	1,974	5	5	0
Mission	9,787	32	29	3
Mission Hills	3,540	51	40	11
Moran	466	1	1	0
Mound City	658	13	13	0
Mount Hope	782	2	2	0
Mulberry	415	1	1	0
Mulvane	6,844	15	15	0
Neodesha	2,233	10	8	2
Newton	18,337	45	41	4
North Newton	1,824	4	4	0
Norton	2,702	8	7	1
Oakley	2,014	8	5	3
Oberlin	1,639	4	4	0
Olathe	144,646	215	191	24
Osage City	2,840	7	7	0
Osawatomie	4,285	15	14	1
Osborne	1,328	3	3	0
Oswego	1,650	5	5	0
Ottawa	12,586	33	29	4
Overbrook	996	1	1	0
Overland Park	196,626	313	246	67
Paola	5,808	18	13	5
Park City	8,565	20	18	2
Parsons	9,369	31	21	10
Pittsburg	20,774	70	42	28
Plainville	1,738	14	9	5
Pleasanton	1,244	3	3	0
Pratt	6,593	23	15	8
Roeland Park	6,762	16	15	1
Rose Hill	4,336	10	9	1
Rossville	1,093	3	2	1
Sabetha	2,517	8	4	4
Salina	46,161	84	63	21
Scott City	4,100	13	8	5
Scranton	651	1	1	0
Sedan	1,006	2	2	0
Sedgwick	1,598	3	2	1
Shawnee	67,617	115	93	22
Smith Center	1,580	2	2	0
South Hutchinson	2,479	7	7	0

Table 78. Full-Time Law Enforcement Employees, by Selected State and City, 2022—Continued

(Number.)

State/city	Population	Total law enforcement employees	Total officers	Total civilians
Spearville	801	1	1	0
Spring Hill	9,024	16	15	1
Stafford	923	4	4	0
Sterling	2,323	5	5	0
St. George	1,108	3	3	0
St. John	1,180	3	3	0
St. Marys	2,753	6	6	0
Tonganoxie	5,836	13	12	1
Topeka	125,658	308	261	47
Troy	952	2	2	0
Udall	655	3	3	0
Ulysses	5,764	11	10	1
Victoria	1,142	2	2	0
Wamego	4,885	9	8	1
Waterville	655	1	1	0
Wellington	7,641	19	16	3
Wellsville	1,922	6	5	1
Wichita	394,286	837	665	172
Winfield	11,713	29	24	5
Yates Center	1,326	4	4	0
KENTUCKY				
Adairville	876	2	2	0
Albany	1,749	8	7	1
Alexandria	10,416	17	14	3
Anchorage	2,470	14	10	4
Ashland	21,300	47	43	4
Audubon Park	1,411	4	4	0
Augusta	1,104	4	4	0
Bancroft	500	1	1	0
Barbourville	2,952	11	10	1
Bardstown	13,712	34	31	3
Beaver Dam	3,538	6	6	0
Bellefonte	902	5	5	0
Benton	4,771	8	8	0
Berea	16,229	35	32	3
Bloomfield	978	1	1	0
Bowling Green	74,427	158	125	33
Brandenburg	2,952	6	6	0
Brooksville	662	2	1	1
Brownsville	943	2	2	0
Burkesville	1,347	6	6	0
Burnside	699	6	6	0
Butler	626	1	1	0
Calvert City	2,521	8	7	1
Campbellsville	11,548	18	17	1
Carlisle	2,160	13	8	5
Carrollton	3,898	14	13	1
Catlettsburg	1,724	7	7	0
Cave City	2,347	8	8	0
Centertown	414	1	1	0
Central City	5,884	12	12	0
Clay	998	1	1	0
Clay City	1,204	3	3	0
Clinton	1,236	2	2	0
Cloverport	1,136	1	1	0
Coal Run Village	1,627	4	3	1
Cold Spring	6,272	13	13	0
Columbia	4,995	14	14	0
Corbin	7,762	26	22	4
Cynthiana	6,429	13	12	1
Danville	17,323	39	37	2
Dayton	5,685	13	12	1
Eddyville	2,323	4	4	0
Edgewood	8,372	17	17	0
Edmonton	1,696	7	7	0
Elizabethtown	32,437	87	66	21
Elkton	2,072	9	8	1
Elsmere	9,157	17	17	0
Eminence	2,702	8	8	0
Erlanger	24,147	46	43	3
Evarts	850	4	4	0
Falmouth	2,184	7	6	1
Ferguson	885	1	1	0
Flatwoods	7,231	10	10	0
Flemingsburg	2,943	10	10	0
Florence	32,341	73	70	3
Fort Mitchell	8,643	15	15	0
Fort Thomas	17,159	24	23	1
Fountain Run	217	1	1	0
Frankfort	28,559	68	53	15
Franklin	10,174	25	24	1
Fulton	2,387	7	7	0
Georgetown	38,213	67	61	6
Glasgow	15,194	38	33	5

Table 78. Full-Time Law Enforcement Employees, by Selected State and City, 2022—Continued

(Number.)

State/city	Population	Total law enforcement employees	Total officers	Total civilians
Grayson	3,683	12	11	1
Greensburg	2,220	6	6	0
Guthrie	1,334	3	3	0
Hardinsburg	2,416	6	6	0
Harlan	1,679	15	10	5
Harrodsburg	9,200	19	16	3
Hartford	2,667	6	6	0
Highland Heights	6,784	14	12	2
Hillview	8,721	22	21	1
Hopkinsville	30,528	90	57	33
Hustonville	388	1	1	0
Independence	29,211	40	38	2
Indian Hills	2,819	8	8	0
Irvine	2,317	5	5	0
Irvington	1,251	4	4	0
Jackson	2,179	13	9	4
Jamestown	1,842	10	9	1
Jeffersontown	28,519	70	54	16
Jenkins	1,855	2	2	0
Junction City	2,259	1	1	0
La Grange	10,348	19	16	3
Lakeside Park-Crestview Hills	6,227	13	12	1
Lancaster	3,996	13	13	0
Lawrenceburg	11,855	22	15	7
Leitchfield	6,433	19	18	1
Louisa	2,639	5	5	0
Louisville Metro	677,554	1,355	1,050	305
Ludlow	4,339	12	11	1
Madisonville	19,292	63	50	13
Maysville	8,672	33	24	9
Middlesboro	9,213	30	25	5
Middletown	9,600	19	18	1
Monticello	5,685	8	7	1
Morehead	7,030	32	23	9
Morganfield	3,202	7	7	0
Morgantown	2,459	8	8	0
Mount Sterling	7,544	24	22	2
Mount Vernon	2,409	10	10	0
Mount Washington	18,440	27	25	2
Muldraugh	1,028	3	3	0
Murray	17,506	41	35	6
Nicholasville	31,882	72	64	8
Oak Grove	7,810	29	22	7
Olive Hill	1,560	6	6	0
Owensboro	59,839	129	95	34
Owingsville	1,587	5	5	0
Paducah	26,050	87	79	8
Paintsville	4,313	12	11	1
Paris	10,174	35	32	3
Park Hills	3,158	8	8	0
Pineville	1,650	6	6	0
Pippa Passes	581	2	1	1
Powderly	782	2	2	0
Prestonsburg	4,034	30	21	9
Princeton	6,191	18	17	1
Raceland	2,321	7	7	0
Radcliff	22,931	39	31	8
Ravenna	559	1	1	0
Richmond	36,698	72	61	11
Russell	3,656	13	13	0
Russellville	7,257	22	21	1
Science Hill	657	3	3	0
Scottsville	4,368	28	18	10
Shepherdsville	14,440	42	40	2
Shively	15,438	37	31	6
Simpsonville	3,016	10	10	0
Smiths Grove	779	2	2	0
Somerset	12,170	47	42	5
Southgate	3,658	7	7	0
Springfield	2,854	13	6	7
Stanton	3,154	8	8	0
Strathmoor Village	673	1	1	0
Taylor Mill	6,821	9	8	1
Taylorsville	1,287	5	5	0
Trenton	327	1	1	0
Vanceburg	1,346	7	7	0
Versailles	27,242	38	37	1
Villa Hills	7,337	15	15	0
Vine Grove	6,843	6	6	0
Warsaw	1,740	6	6	0
Wayland	398	1	1	0
West Point	942	1	1	0
Wilder	3,125	9	9	0
Williamsburg	5,348	15	15	0
Williamstown	3,987	7	6	1

Table 78. Full-Time Law Enforcement Employees, by Selected State and City, 2022—Continued

(Number.)

State/city	Population	Total law enforcement employees	Total officers	Total civilians
Wilmore	6,081	10	9	1
Winchester	18,989	49	32	17
Woodlawn Park	931	1	1	0
LOUISIANA				
Abbeville	10,968	25	20	5
Addis	7,438	15	14	1
Alexandria	44,349	146	114	32
Amite	3,829	24	19	5
Arnaudville	999	10	6	4
Baker	12,303	38	27	11
Baldwin	1,693	3	3	0
Basile	1,192	6	6	0
Bastrop	9,291	15	15	0
Baton Rouge	219,913	812	577	235
Benton	2,061	10	9	1
Blanchard	3,383	9	8	1
Bossier City	63,078	193	157	36
Breaux Bridge	7,564	20	19	1
Broussard	14,103	37	34	3
Brusly	2,598	7	7	0
Bunkie	3,234	15	8	7
Carencro	12,505	37	35	2
Chataignier	262	6	5	1
Church Point	4,106	14	14	0
Clinton	1,342	21	21	0
Cottonport	1,954	6	6	0
Crowley	11,464	35	29	6
Delcambre	1,770	6	5	1
Denham Springs	9,361	34	26	8
De Quincy	2,758	17	13	4
De Ridder	9,674	33	28	5
Duson	1,296	7	7	0
Erath	2,002	12	8	4
Evergreen	207	1	1	0
Farmerville	3,308	12	12	0
Ferriday	3,041	16	11	5
Folsom	788	5	4	1
Franklin	6,408	28	26	2
French Settlement	1,129	4	4	0
Georgetown	277	5	4	1
Gonzales	12,869	47	42	5
Grambling	5,076	18	13	5
Greensburg	637	5	5	0
Greenwood	3,077	10	9	1
Gretna	17,358	135	98	37
Grosse Tete	526	2	1	1
Gueydan	1,124	5	5	0
Harahan	8,827	31	28	3
Haughton	4,457	14	13	1
Haynesville	1,884	9	8	1
Houma	32,762	102	84	18
Ida	212	1	1	0
Independence	1,666	8	8	0
Iowa	2,972	20	16	4
Jeanerette	4,655	9	4	5
Jena	3,760	7	6	1
Jennings	9,664	26	20	6
Kaplan	4,228	20	13	7
Kenner	64,419	201	139	62
Kentwood	2,200	12	11	1
Krotz Springs	894	8	5	3
Lafayette	121,546	320	275	45
Lake Arthur	2,648	10	9	1
Lake Charles	77,054	167	165	2
Lake Providence	3,661	15	8	7
Leesville	5,382	24	17	7
Lockport	2,469	8	5	3
Lutcher	2,966	4	3	1
Mamou	2,867	11	6	5
Mandeville	13,245	51	39	12
Mansfield	4,472	21	16	5
Maringouin	819	6	5	1
Marksville	4,843	19	13	6
Merryville	952	8	5	3
Moreauville	948	5	4	1
Morgan City	10,909	47	43	4
New Iberia	27,571	64	51	13
New Llano	2,056	8	4	4
New Orleans	370,128	1,144	945	199
Norwood	279	5	3	2
Oakdale	6,954	16	11	5
Oak Grove	1,580	6	6	0
Oberlin	1,343	7	5	2
Oil City	864	3	3	0

Table 78. Full-Time Law Enforcement Employees, by Selected State and City, 2022—Continued

(Number.)

State/city	Population	Total law enforcement employees	Total officers	Total civilians
Opelousas	15,447	50	36	14
Palmetto	95	2	1	1
Parks	634	5	5	0
Patterson	5,681	25	25	0
Pineville	14,407	72	64	8
Plain Dealing	888	6	2	4
Plaquemine	5,804	30	21	9
Pollock	399	5	4	1
Port Allen	4,984	16	15	1
Port Vincent	677	3	3	0
Rayne	7,100	24	21	3
Ringgold	1,330	6	6	0
Rosedale	618	9	5	4
Roseland	903	4	3	1
Ruston	22,435	47	35	12
Scott	8,111	27	25	2
Shreveport	180,763	520	456	64
Simmesport	1,425	4	4	0
St. Martinville	5,402	22	18	4
Sulphur	19,581	56	39	17
Sunset	3,087	13	7	6
Tallulah	5,975	10	3	7
Thibodaux	15,166	68	48	20
Tickfaw	651	6	6	0
Vidalia	3,771	36	27	9
Ville Platte	6,387	13	12	1
Vinton	2,973	16	10	6
Washington	732	4	3	1
Westlake	4,464	14	10	4
West Monroe	12,680	62	50	12
Westwego	8,266	37	36	1
White Castle	1,595	22	18	4
Wilson	354	10	5	5
Woodworth	1,698	9	7	2
Youngsville	16,985	40	35	5
Zachary	20,344	49	43	6
MAINE				
Ashland	1,184	4	4	0
Auburn	24,122	53	47	6
Augusta	19,013	54	42	12
Baileyville	1,334	1	1	0
Bangor	32,078	89	75	14
Bar Harbor	7,478	31	23	8
Bath	8,834	22	17	5
Belfast	7,037	18	15	3
Berwick	8,185	13	12	1
Biddeford	22,647	74	51	23
Boothbay Harbor	2,090	6	5	1
Brewer	9,634	25	23	2
Bridgton	5,640	9	8	1
Brunswick	21,888	42	32	10
Bucksport	5,080	14	10	4
Buxton	8,528	16	10	6
Calais	3,041	5	5	0
Camden	5,326	13	11	2
Cape Elizabeth	9,535	13	12	1
Caribou	7,352	14	13	1
Carrabassett Valley	698	1	1	0
Clinton	3,380	4	4	0
Cumberland	8,616	13	11	2
Damariscotta	2,332	6	5	1
Dexter	3,793	6	6	0
Dover-Foxcroft	4,537	5	5	0
East Millinocket	6,823	11	11	0
Eastport	1,282	4	4	0
Eliot	7,162	9	8	1
Ellsworth	8,676	22	18	4
Fairfield	6,507	12	12	0
Falmouth	12,695	28	19	9
Farmington	7,520	12	11	1
Fort Fairfield	3,267	4	4	0
Fort Kent	4,120	10	6	4
Freeport	8,802	17	15	2
Fryeburg	3,480	6	6	0
Gardiner	6,102	10	10	0
Gorham	18,482	27	24	3
Gouldsboro	1,768	3	3	0
Greenville	1,538	3	3	0
Hallowell	2,579	5	5	0
Hampden	7,864	11	10	1
Holden	3,312	7	7	0
Houlton	6,071	15	10	5
Islesboro	589	1	1	0
Jay	4,706	8	7	1

Table 78. Full-Time Law Enforcement Employees, by Selected State and City, 2022—Continued

(Number.)

State/city	Population	Total law enforcement employees	Total officers	Total civilians
Kennebunk	11,804	25	23	2
Kennebunkport	3,716	18	13	5
Kittery	10,279	27	22	5
Lewiston	36,488	90	77	13
Limestone	1,524	2	2	0
Lincoln	4,846	9	7	2
Lisbon	9,660	22	16	6
Livermore Falls	3,074	4	4	0
Machias	1,834	4	4	0
Madawaska	3,846	7	6	1
Mechanic Falls	3,112	5	5	0
Mexico	2,787	5	5	0
Milbridge	1,358	1	1	0
Milo	2,381	4	3	1
Monmouth	4,137	4	4	0
Newport	3,120	4	4	0
North Berwick	5,163	10	9	1
Norway	5,201	9	8	1
Oakland	6,300	11	10	1
Ogunquit	1,603	11	10	1
Old Orchard Beach	9,244	25	20	5
Old Town	7,372	18	17	1
Orono	11,651	13	12	1
Oxford	4,309	9	8	1
Paris	5,349	8	8	0
Phippsburg	2,200	1	1	0
Pittsfield	3,904	4	3	1
Portland	68,199	187	133	54
Presque Isle	8,746	21	16	5
Rangeley	1,253	2	2	0
Richmond	3,585	2	2	0
Rockland	7,081	15	13	2
Rockport	3,719	6	6	0
Rumford	5,929	13	12	1
Sabattus	5,113	6	5	1
Saco	20,936	45	30	15
Sanford	22,315	41	38	3
Scarborough	22,913	54	37	17
Searsport	2,663	5	5	0
Skowhegan	8,595	19	18	1
South Berwick	7,653	11	10	1
South Portland	27,445	55	48	7
Southwest Harbor	1,836	9	5	4
Thomaston	2,816	4	4	0
Topsham	9,680	15	14	1
Veazie	1,807	5	5	0
Waldoboro	5,314	7	7	0
Washburn	1,498	3	3	0
Waterville	15,972	38	27	11
Wells	11,760	31	21	10
Westbrook	20,741	46	40	6
Wilton	3,913	6	6	0
Windham	19,048	30	27	3
Winslow	7,970	13	12	1
Winter Harbor	479	1	1	0
Winthrop	6,168	16	10	6
Wiscasset	3,880	6	5	1
Yarmouth	9,009	14	13	1
York	13,977	38	26	12
MARYLAND				
Aberdeen	17,576	50	36	14
Annapolis	40,542	137	104	33
Baltimore	570,546	2,843	2,360	483
Baltimore City Sheriff	0	153	109	44
Bel Air	10,675	41	29	12
Berlin	5,103	16	11	5
Berwyn Heights	3,260	9	8	1
Bladensburg	9,419	37	24	13
Boonsboro	3,783	6	4	2
Bowie	57,068	71	57	14
Brentwood	3,724	5	4	1
Brunswick	8,279	16	16	0
Cambridge	13,072	36	32	4
Capitol Heights	3,946	10	8	2
Centreville	4,763	11	10	1
Chestertown	5,638	10	9	1
Cheverly	6,005	14	12	2
Chevy Chase Village	2,013	16	11	5
Colmar Manor	1,554	5	4	1
Cottage City	1,295	7	5	2
Crisfield	2,447	11	8	3
Cumberland	18,647	49	46	3
Delmar	3,971	13	12	1
Denton	4,827	11	10	1

Table 78. Full-Time Law Enforcement Employees, by Selected State and City, 2022—Continued

(Number.)

State/city	Population	Total law enforcement employees	Total officers	Total civilians
Edmonston	1,575	6	4	2
Elkton	15,806	49	43	6
Fairmount Heights	1,484	1	1	0
Federalsburg	2,836	10	9	1
Forest Heights	2,588	20	17	3
Frederick	80,985	183	141	42
Frostburg	7,024	18	13	5
Fruitland	5,888	22	17	5
Glenarden	6,247	21	19	2
Greenbelt	24,278	66	45	21
Greensboro	1,927	3	3	0
Hagerstown	43,548	97	78	19
Hampstead	6,342	10	9	1
Hancock	1,539	5	4	1
Havre de Grace	14,883	38	31	7
Hurlock	2,067	12	11	1
Hyattsville	20,623	57	38	19
Landover Hills	1,767	5	4	1
La Plata	10,672	27	21	6
Laurel	29,028	85	65	20
Manchester	5,477	8	7	1
Morningside	1,207	7	6	1
Mount Airy	9,831	11	9	2
Mount Rainier	8,112	23	21	2
New Carrollton	13,365	17	17	0
North East	4,100	16	13	3
Oakland	1,811	2	2	0
Ocean City	6,957	143	115	28
Ocean Pines	11,677	14	11	3
Oxford	613	2	2	0
Perryville	4,411	15	12	3
Pittsville	1,621	1	1	0
Pocomoke City	4,418	22	17	5
Princess Anne	3,438	15	12	3
Ridgely	1,620	4	4	0
Rising Sun	2,744	6	6	0
Riverdale Park	7,156	30	24	6
Rock Hall	1,195	3	3	0
Salisbury	33,063	113	82	31
Seat Pleasant	4,408	32	26	6
Smithsburg	3,153	5	4	1
Snow Hill	2,174	7	7	0
St. Michaels	1,080	11	10	1
Sykesville	4,361	10	9	1
Takoma Park	17,322	66	38	28
Taneytown	7,330	13	11	2
Thurmont	6,645	13	9	4
University Park	2,385	10	9	1
Upper Marlboro	638	6	5	1
Westminster	20,165	54	42	12
MASSACHUSETTS				
Abington	17,886	26	23	3
Acton	23,833	50	38	12
Acushnet	10,612	25	20	5
Adams	8,073	20	18	2
Agawam	28,536	61	50	11
Amesbury	17,276	38	32	6
Amherst	39,267	47	44	3
Andover	36,631	69	52	17
Aquinnah	465	4	4	0
Arlington	45,238	79	63	16
Ashburnham	6,402	19	15	4
Ashby	3,166	6	5	1
Ashfield	1,690	1	1	0
Ashland	18,373	29	22	7
Athol	11,938	26	19	7
Attleboro	46,942	89	74	15
Auburn	16,878	49	39	10
Avon	4,764	20	14	6
Ayer	8,368	31	19	12
Barnstable	50,501	146	119	27
Barre	5,555	11	10	1
Becket	1,934	6	6	0
Bedford	14,034	34	25	9
Belchertown	15,277	26	20	6
Bellingham	16,965	34	25	9
Belmont	26,557	56	43	13
Berkley	6,844	10	10	0
Berlin	4,137	11	10	1
Bernardston	2,846	4	4	0
Beverly	42,441	80	73	7
Billerica	41,110	94	63	31
Blackstone	9,222	22	18	4
Bolton	5,710	13	12	1

Table 78. Full-Time Law Enforcement Employees, by Selected State and City, 2022—Continued

(Number.)

State/city	Population	Total law enforcement employees	Total officers	Total civilians
Boston	638,925	2,782	2,112	670
Bourne	21,127	48	40	8
Boxborough	5,377	19	14	5
Boxford	8,134	12	12	0
Boylston	4,934	17	13	4
Braintree	38,835	111	91	20
Brewster	10,647	28	23	5
Bridgewater	8,820	46	42	4
Brockton	110,084	224	193	31
Brookfield	3,443	6	6	0
Brookline	62,825	161	123	38
Buckland	1,815	2	2	0
Burlington	25,783	74	66	8
Cambridge	117,044	299	260	39
Canton	24,717	45	45	0
Carlisle	5,149	14	10	4
Carver	12,215	22	17	5
Charlton	13,394	25	20	5
Chatham	6,844	25	19	6
Chelmsford	35,630	61	56	5
Chelsea	37,590	113	105	8
Cheshire	3,226	2	2	0
Chester	1,221	1	1	0
Chicopee	55,265	135	132	3
Cohasset	8,417	21	20	1
Concord	18,040	41	32	9
Dalton	6,273	12	11	1
Danvers	27,887	53	42	11
Dartmouth	34,192	86	68	18
Dedham	25,324	58	54	4
Deerfield	5,154	11	10	1
Dennis	15,200	56	46	10
Dighton	8,240	20	15	5
Douglas	9,146	19	15	4
Dover	5,902	18	18	0
Dracut	31,908	50	46	4
Dudley	11,914	17	16	1
Dunstable	3,333	9	8	1
Duxbury	16,861	33	31	2
East Bridgewater	15,142	31	24	7
East Brookfield	2,208	4	4	0
Eastham	5,939	22	17	5
Easthampton	15,914	37	29	8
East Longmeadow	16,458	30	27	3
Easton	25,463	41	38	3
Edgartown	5,485	19	17	2
Egremont	1,374	5	5	0
Erving	1,669	6	6	0
Essex	3,678	11	10	1
Everett	48,340	117	110	7
Fairhaven	15,987	41	35	6
Fall River	94,339	264	220	44
Falmouth	33,873	62	57	5
Fitchburg	41,791	94	78	16
Foxborough	18,549	42	39	3
Framingham	70,716	150	130	20
Franklin	33,107	55	53	2
Freetown	9,247	21	20	1
Gardner	21,231	44	27	17
Georgetown	8,409	18	13	5
Gill	1,535	2	2	0
Gloucester	30,301	67	60	7
Grafton	19,965	1	1	0
Granby	6,036	15	11	4
Great Barrington	7,143	15	14	1
Greenfield	17,203	42	29	13
Groton	11,074	28	20	8
Groveland	6,763	17	13	4
Hadley	5,244	23	17	6
Halifax	8,092	16	15	1
Hamilton	7,551	18	14	4
Hampden	4,948	11	11	0
Hanover	15,578	36	29	7
Hanson	11,196	26	25	1
Hardwick	2,672	7	7	0
Harvard	6,870	12	10	2
Harwich	13,891	38	30	8
Haverhill	67,359	123	108	15
Hingham	25,437	53	50	3
Hinsdale	1,905	5	5	0
Holbrook	11,350	27	26	1
Holden	19,998	38	22	16
Holland	2,585	2	2	0
Holliston	14,754	29	24	5
Holyoke	37,945	134	109	25

Table 78. Full-Time Law Enforcement Employees, by Selected State and City, 2022—Continued

(Number.)

State/city	Population	Total law enforcement employees	Total officers	Total civilians
Hopedale	6,021	17	13	4
Hopkinton	19,180	31	22	9
Hudson	19,623	46	35	11
Hull	10,676	30	26	4
Ipswich	13,735	28	24	4
Kingston	14,484	32	24	8
Lakeville	12,511	24	19	5
Lancaster	8,504	11	10	1
Lanesboro	3,021	6	6	0
Lawrence	88,422	180	162	18
Lee	5,740	9	8	1
Leicester	11,084	16	15	1
Lenox	5,105	10	10	0
Leominster	43,690	87	69	18
Leverett	1,861	3	3	0
Lexington	33,889	52	44	8
Lincoln	6,823	17	11	6
Littleton	10,154	30	21	9
Longmeadow	15,734	27	26	1
Lowell	113,277	312	242	70
Ludlow	20,971	47	35	12
Lunenburg	11,903	20	19	1
Lynn	101,056	195	176	19
Lynnfield	12,992	25	20	5
Malden	64,356	110	102	8
Manchester-by-the-Sea	5,365	17	13	4
Mansfield	23,932	48	38	10
Marblehead	20,289	42	33	9
Marion	5,567	18	17	1
Marlborough	40,722	78	67	11
Marshfield	27,064	48	45	3
Mashpee	15,730	46	38	8
Mattapoisett	6,932	20	18	2
Maynard	10,464	27	21	6
Medfield	13,107	17	13	4
Medford	64,122	115	97	18
Medway	13,261	25	25	0
Melrose	29,013	51	50	1
Mendon	6,307	16	14	2
Merrimac	6,726	13	9	4
Methuen	52,853	116	94	22
Middleboro	25,744	49	43	6
Middleton	9,790	18	17	1
Millbury	14,008	28	23	5
Milton	28,454	79	66	13
Montague	8,581	23	17	6
Monterey	1,091	3	3	0
Nahant	3,315	12	11	1
Nantucket	14,814	46	34	12
Natick	36,090	67	53	14
Needham	32,228	55	45	10
New Bedford	101,402	263	224	39
Newbury	6,717	14	11	3
Newburyport	18,366	34	31	3
Newton	86,710	176	139	37
Norfolk	11,621	23	21	2
North Adams	12,836	32	26	6
Northampton	29,150	68	61	7
North Andover	30,695	58	42	16
North Attleboro	31,071	58	41	17
Northborough	15,699	28	21	7
Northbridge	16,357	28	20	8
Northfield	2,877	4	4	0
North Reading	15,197	35	32	3
Norton	19,374	37	36	1
Norwell	11,866	25	22	3
Norwood	31,533	68	60	8
Oak Bluffs	5,653	18	16	2
Oakham	1,852	1	1	0
Orleans	6,546	25	19	6
Otis	1,628	2	2	0
Oxford	13,316	30	23	7
Palmer	12,393	26	18	8
Paxton	5,073	16	13	3
Peabody	54,091	104	87	17
Pelham	1,257	2	2	0
Pembroke	19,289	34	31	3
Pepperell	11,600	18	17	1
Pittsfield	43,496	113	91	22
Plainville	9,921	24	23	1
Plymouth	65,779	106	91	15
Plympton	3,075	10	10	0
Princeton	3,521	8	7	1
Provincetown	3,775	26	18	8
Quincy	101,434	273	238	35

Table 78. Full-Time Law Enforcement Employees, by Selected State and City, 2022—Continued

(Number.)

State/city	Population	Total law enforcement employees	Total officers	Total civilians
Randolph	32,477	67	57	10
Raynham	15,404	37	29	8
Reading	25,018	63	46	17
Rehoboth	12,936	35	27	8
Revere	56,961	115	106	9
Rockland	18,549	28	25	3
Rockport	6,961	22	18	4
Rowley	6,132	16	12	4
Rutland	9,316	14	13	1
Salem	45,345	100	87	13
Salisbury	9,238	27	17	10
Sandwich	21,013	44	34	10
Saugus	28,880	82	67	15
Scituate	20,147	39	37	2
Seekonk	15,692	40	38	2
Sharon	18,553	39	29	10
Sheffield	3,308	7	7	0
Shelburne	1,891	3	3	0
Sherborn	4,384	18	18	0
Shirley	7,228	13	11	2
Shrewsbury	39,745	72	55	17
Shutesbury	1,734	2	2	0
Somerset	18,317	41	33	8
Somerville	79,178	146	111	35
Southampton	6,177	14	10	4
Southborough	10,448	25	20	5
Southbridge	17,687	52	39	13
South Hadley	17,900	31	25	6
Southwick	9,229	24	18	6
Spencer	11,953	21	17	4
Springfield	155,046	556	475	81
Sterling	8,372	19	14	5
Stockbridge	1,997	8	7	1
Stoneham	22,660	45	37	8
Stoughton	29,204	69	59	10
Stow	6,989	14	11	3
Sturbridge	9,892	28	21	7
Sudbury	19,314	38	28	10
Sunderland	3,655	7	6	1
Sutton	9,418	21	16	5
Swampscott	15,268	30	29	1
Swansea	17,453	39	33	6
Taunton	60,062	129	119	10
Templeton	8,220	14	9	5
Tewksbury	30,656	101	61	40
Tisbury	5,079	16	14	2
Topsfield	6,581	13	12	1
Townsend	8,892	17	15	2
Truro	2,536	16	11	5
Tyngsboro	12,490	36	27	9
Upton	8,137	19	14	5
Uxbridge	14,418	28	22	6
Wakefield	27,263	47	46	1
Walpole	26,829	58	47	11
Waltham	63,525	175	148	27
Ware	10,295	20	20	0
Wareham	24,389	51	42	9
Warren	4,969	10	9	1
Watertown	35,088	85	71	14
Wayland	13,601	33	24	9
Webster	17,651	35	32	3
Wellesley	31,354	59	46	13
Wellfleet	3,725	20	15	5
Wenham	4,998	12	11	1
Westborough	21,562	39	37	2
West Bridgewater	8,087	27	23	4
West Brookfield	3,830	7	6	1
Westfield	40,691	83	80	3
Westford	24,270	51	47	4
Westminster	8,363	20	16	4
West Newbury	4,605	15	10	5
Weston	11,589	35	25	10
Westport	16,475	35	29	6
West Springfield	28,655	86	74	12
West Tisbury	3,757	11	10	1
Westwood	16,308	43	32	11
Weymouth	58,231	124	100	24
Whately	1,639	2	2	0
Wilbraham	14,600	28	27	1
Williamsburg	2,460	2	2	0
Wilmington	22,825	50	46	4
Winchendon	10,410	19	15	4
Winchester	22,496	50	39	11
Winthrop	17,954	32	31	1
Woburn	41,461	79	74	5

Table 78. Full-Time Law Enforcement Employees, by Selected State and City, 2022—Continued

(Number.)

State/city	Population	Total law enforcement employees	Total officers	Total civilians
Worcester	206,575	520	468	52
Worthington	1,176	1	1	0
Wrentham	12,343	22	21	1
Yarmouth	25,705	74	58	16
MICHIGAN				
Adrian	20,407	32	29	3
Adrian Township	6,325	3	3	0
Akron	367	1	1	0
Albion	7,940	19	14	5
Allegan	5,155	10	9	1
Allen Park	27,917	41	38	3
Alma	9,365	16	14	2
Almont	2,843	7	7	0
Alpena	10,146	18	16	2
Ann Arbor	120,549	139	111	28
Argentine Township	7,002	5	5	0
Armada	1,658	2	2	0
Auburn Hills	25,081	53	48	5
Augusta	846	8	6	2
Bad Axe	3,014	8	7	1
Bangor	1,988	6	6	0
Baraga	1,990	2	2	0
Baroda-Lake Township	4,187	8	7	1
Barry Township	3,469	3	3	0
Bath Township	13,456	14	13	1
Battle Creek	61,347	137	99	38
Bay City	32,249	52	47	5
Beaverton	1,150	4	4	0
Belding	6,153	9	8	1
Bellaire	1,029	2	2	0
Belleville	3,928	10	9	1
Bellevue	1,354	2	2	0
Benton Harbor	8,896	15	14	1
Benton Township	14,081	20	16	4
Berkley	15,006	40	29	11
Berrien Springs-Oronoko Township	9,422	10	9	1
Beverly Hills	10,467	26	24	2
Big Rapids	8,995	18	17	1
Birch Run	1,555	7	6	1
Birmingham	21,721	44	34	10
Blissfield	3,284	5	5	0
Bloomfield Hills	4,420	28	24	4
Bloomfield Township	43,805	81	63	18
Breckenridge	1,274	1	1	0
Bridgeport Township	9,975	10	9	1
Bridgman	2,062	5	5	0
Brighton	7,483	19	17	2
Bronson	2,311	5	4	1
Brown City	1,298	3	3	0
Brownstown Township	33,033	40	33	7
Buchanan	4,179	11	10	1
Buena Vista Township	7,588	12	11	1
Burton	29,373	38	35	3
Cadillac	10,413	15	14	1
Cambridge Township	5,681	4	4	0
Canton Township	98,582	136	88	48
Capac	1,972	3	3	0
Carleton	2,354	3	2	1
Caro	4,292	7	7	0
Carrollton Township	5,669	6	6	0
Carson City	1,131	1	1	0
Caseville	646	1	1	0
Caspian-Gaastra	1,119	1	1	0
Cass City	2,489	5	5	0
Cassopolis	1,689	5	5	0
Center Line	8,357	25	20	5
Central Lake	976	1	1	0
Charlevoix	2,351	8	7	1
Charlotte	9,175	16	15	1
Cheboygan	4,849	9	8	1
Chelsea	5,322	15	11	4
Chesaning	2,440	2	2	0
Chesterfield Township	45,519	61	48	13
Chikaming Township	2,741	7	6	1
Chocolay Township	5,976	4	3	1
Clare	3,290	7	7	0
Clayton Township	7,274	6	5	1
Clay Township	8,430	23	18	5
Clinton	2,497	4	4	0
Clinton Township	99,274	105	94	11
Clio	2,479	5	5	0
Coldwater	13,930	21	17	4
Coleman	1,262	2	2	0
Coloma Township	6,412	9	8	1

Table 78. Full-Time Law Enforcement Employees, by Selected State and City, 2022—Continued

(Number.)

State/city	Population	Total law enforcement employees	Total officers	Total civilians
Columbia Township	7,470	7	7	0
Constantine	1,968	4	3	1
Corunna	3,051	3	3	0
Covert Township	2,516	8	8	0
Croswell	2,312	5	5	0
Crystal Falls	1,596	2	2	0
Davison	5,058	7	6	1
Dearborn	107,197	222	181	41
Dearborn Heights	61,789	89	73	16
Detroit	626,757	3,080	2,381	699
DeWitt Township	15,557	17	16	1
Dowagiac	5,591	14	13	1
Dryden Township	4,797	4	4	0
Durand	4,033	6	6	0
East Jordan	2,254	5	5	0
East Lansing	46,660	59	41	18
Eastpointe	33,829	49	44	5
East Tawas	2,706	5	5	0
Eaton Rapids	5,184	10	9	1
Eau Claire	540	1	1	0
Ecorse	9,113	19	19	0
Elk Rapids	1,582	5	5	0
Elkton	791	1	1	0
Elsie	940	2	1	1
Emmett Township	11,607	17	15	2
Erie Township	4,293	2	2	0
Escanaba	12,404	36	32	4
Essexville	3,300	6	6	0
Evart	1,774	3	3	0
Fair Haven Township	1,087	1	1	0
Farmington	11,406	23	22	1
Farmington Hills	82,806	134	100	34
Fennville	1,733	2	1	1
Fenton	11,947	18	14	4
Ferndale	19,007	52	42	10
Flat Rock	10,369	21	19	2
Flint	80,059	130	96	34
Flint Township	31,097	43	36	7
Flushing	8,290	11	10	1
Flushing Township	10,586	11	11	0
Forsyth Township	6,260	11	9	2
Fowlerville	2,994	8	7	1
Frankenmuth	5,368	8	8	0
Frankfort	1,287	4	4	0
Franklin	3,113	11	11	0
Fraser	14,458	31	30	1
Fremont	4,559	10	9	1
Gagetown	317	1	1	0
Galien	524	2	1	1
Garden City	26,696	40	36	4
Garfield Township	997	1	1	0
Gaylord	4,340	13	12	1
Genesee Township	20,336	19	17	2
Gerrish Township	2,855	8	7	1
Gibraltar	4,899	10	9	1
Gladstone	5,246	13	12	1
Gladwin	3,101	6	6	0
Grand Blanc	7,970	19	17	2
Grand Blanc Township	40,115	48	41	7
Grand Haven	10,967	37	29	8
Grand Ledge	7,778	15	15	0
Grand Rapids	196,662	391	277	114
Grandville	15,847	27	25	2
Grant	956	3	3	0
Greenville	9,303	17	15	2
Grosse Ile Township	10,550	23	16	7
Grosse Pointe	5,519	23	23	0
Grosse Pointe Farms	9,890	37	32	5
Grosse Pointe Park	11,287	35	30	5
Grosse Pointe Shores	2,584	15	15	0
Grosse Pointe Woods	16,079	35	27	8
Hampton Township	9,564	10	10	0
Hamtramck	27,669	38	29	9
Hancock	4,515	9	9	0
Harbor Beach	1,589	4	4	0
Harbor Springs	1,289	9	7	2
Harper Woods	15,100	27	22	5
Hart	1,988	11	11	0
Hartford	2,483	5	5	0
Hastings	7,554	15	9	6
Hazel Park	14,849	38	34	4
Highland Park	8,802	12	8	4
Hillsdale	8,157	16	13	3
Holland	33,838	69	59	10
Holly	5,931	9	9	0

Table 78. Full-Time Law Enforcement Employees, by Selected State and City, 2022—Continued

(Number.)

State/city	Population	Total law enforcement employees	Total officers	Total civilians
Home Township	1,515	2	2	0
Houghton	7,644	11	10	1
Howell	10,104	16	14	2
Hudson	2,379	3	3	0
Huntington Woods	6,286	18	17	1
Huron Township	16,837	32	24	8
Imlay City	3,707	9	8	1
Inkster	25,447	33	22	11
Ionia	11,730	15	14	1
Iron Mountain	7,425	15	14	1
Iron River	3,001	3	3	0
Ironwood	5,021	12	12	0
Ishpeming	6,174	11	10	1
Ishpeming Township	3,421	1	1	0
Jackson	31,206	57	46	11
Jonesville	2,151	2	2	0
Kalamazoo	72,810	265	239	26
Kalamazoo Township	24,309	39	33	6
Kalkaska	2,122	6	6	0
Keego Harbor	2,741	5	5	0
Kentwood	53,977	74	57	17
Kingsford	5,100	18	18	0
Kingston	391	1	1	0
Kinross Township	5,986	2	2	0
Laingsburg	1,408	1	1	0
Lake Angelus	290	1	1	0
Lake Linden	1,047	1	1	0
Lake Odessa	2,138	3	2	1
Lake Orion	2,904	6	5	1
Lakeview	1,057	2	2	0
L'Anse	1,920	3	3	0
Lansing	112,567	243	192	51
Lansing Township	8,037	16	15	1
Lapeer	8,924	23	20	3
Lathrup Village	4,018	12	11	1
Laurium	1,942	3	3	0
Lawrence	1,013	4	4	0
Lawton	1,850	4	4	0
Leslie	1,929	4	4	0
Lexington	928	2	2	0
Lincoln Park	39,189	52	45	7
Lincoln Township	14,825	19	16	3
Linden	4,168	6	6	0
Litchfield	1,379	3	3	0
Livonia	93,517	167	135	32
Ludington	7,785	14	13	1
Mackinac Island	587	6	6	0
Mackinaw City	856	7	7	0
Madison Heights	28,079	48	48	0
Madison Township	8,404	5	5	0
Mancelona	1,378	1	1	0
Manistee	6,335	13	13	0
Manistique	2,809	8	8	0
Manton	1,378	1	1	0
Marine City	4,029	8	7	1
Marlette	1,850	5	5	0
Marquette	20,428	38	33	5
Mason	8,195	12	11	1
Mattawan	2,663	6	6	0
Mayville	909	2	1	1
Melvindale	12,524	18	17	1
Mendon	864	1	1	0
Menominee	8,314	17	16	1
Meridian Township	44,038	39	35	4
Metamora Township	4,438	5	5	0
Metro Police Authority of Genesee County	20,995	27	23	4
Midland	42,426	51	49	2
Milan	5,994	16	14	2
Milford	16,972	24	20	4
Millington	1,012	2	2	0
Monroe	20,266	41	36	5
Montague	2,437	4	4	0
Morrice	987	1	1	0
Mount Morris	3,113	5	5	0
Mount Morris Township	19,713	28	25	3
Mount Pleasant	21,363	34	27	7
Munising	1,968	5	5	0
Muskegon	37,615	81	70	11
Muskegon Heights	9,944	23	20	3
Muskegon Township	17,812	16	16	0
Napoleon Township	6,807	14	13	1
Nashville	1,598	2	2	0
Negaunee	4,652	9	9	0
Newaygo	2,487	10	7	3
New Baltimore	11,995	18	16	2

Table 78. Full-Time Law Enforcement Employees, by Selected State and City, 2022—Continued

(Number.)

State/city	Population	Total law enforcement employees	Total officers	Total civilians
New Buffalo	1,680	8	7	1
New Era	466	1	1	0
Niles	11,756	25	17	8
Northfield Township	8,438	13	11	2
North Muskegon	4,103	9	8	1
Northville Township	31,443	46	33	13
Norton Shores	25,226	41	36	5
Norway	2,802	6	6	0
Novi	66,936	97	73	24
Oakley	285	1	1	0
Oak Park	29,115	62	50	12
Ontwa Township-Edwardsburg	6,812	10	9	1
Orchard Lake	2,211	10	10	0
Otisville	812	1	1	0
Otsego	4,074	8	7	1
Ovid	1,467	3	3	0
Oxford	3,440	22	10	12
Pentwater	904	2	2	0
Perry	2,110	4	4	0
Petoskey	5,922	20	18	2
Pigeon	1,205	1	1	0
Pittsfield Township	39,298	42	40	2
Pleasant Ridge	2,584	7	7	0
Plymouth Township	27,426	44	29	15
Portage	48,811	66	56	10
Port Austin	659	2	2	0
Port Huron	28,675	62	54	8
Portland	3,954	5	5	0
Potterville	3,081	5	5	0
Prairieville Township	3,411	2	2	0
Quincy	1,560	2	2	0
Raisin Township	7,953	4	4	0
Reading	1,077	2	2	0
Redford Township	48,267	63	52	11
Reed City	2,518	5	4	1
Reese	1,251	2	2	0
Richfield Township, Roscommon County	3,588	5	5	0
Richland Township, Saginaw County	3,916	5	5	0
Richmond	5,784	13	10	3
River Rouge	7,028	24	17	7
Rochester	12,868	30	22	8
Rockwood	3,170	12	7	5
Rogers City	2,908	6	6	0
Romeo	3,711	12	8	4
Romulus	25,071	55	38	17
Roosevelt Park	4,186	7	5	2
Rose City	561	1	1	0
Roseville	46,719	74	71	3
Royal Oak	57,808	109	77	32
Saginaw	43,651	57	45	12
Saginaw Township	41,334	48	42	6
Saline	8,930	13	13	0
Sandusky	2,674	6	5	1
Saugatuck-Douglas	2,274	5	4	1
Sault Ste. Marie	13,412	25	22	3
Schoolcraft	1,443	3	3	0
Scottville	1,379	1	1	0
Sebewaing	1,717	4	4	0
Shelby Township	79,391	96	76	20
Shepherd	1,525	2	2	0
Somerset Township	4,531	3	3	0
Southfield	75,432	139	111	28
Southgate	29,769	48	38	10
South Haven	4,059	22	18	4
South Lyon	11,866	17	16	1
South Rockwood	1,589	2	2	0
Sparta	4,293	5	5	0
Spring Arbor Township	8,426	2	2	0
Springport Township	2,154	2	2	0
Stanton	1,370	2	2	0
St. Charles	1,971	3	3	0
St. Clair	5,450	8	8	0
St. Clair Shores	57,654	85	80	5
Sterling Heights	132,393	176	156	20
St. Ignace	2,300	5	5	0
St. Johns	7,640	12	10	2
St. Joseph	7,684	26	24	2
St. Joseph Township	9,772	13	12	1
St. Louis	6,842	9	7	2
Stockbridge	1,251	1	1	0
Sturgis	10,961	25	20	5
Sumpter Township	9,535	21	17	4
Sylvan Lake	1,693	5	5	0
Tawas City	1,865	4	4	0
Taylor	61,901	86	69	17

Table 78. Full-Time Law Enforcement Employees, by Selected State and City, 2022—Continued

(Number.)

State/city	Population	Total law enforcement employees	Total officers	Total civilians
Thomas Township	11,903	9	8	1
Three Oaks	1,384	2	2	0
Three Rivers	7,911	18	15	3
Tittabawassee Township	10,855	8	7	1
Traverse City	15,617	32	29	3
Trenton	18,108	32	31	1
Troy	86,548	156	111	45
Tuscarora Township	3,109	9	9	0
Ubly	839	1	1	0
Unadilla Township	3,385	3	3	0
Union City	1,723	5	5	0
Utica	5,129	16	14	2
Van Buren Township	30,103	57	43	14
Vassar	2,732	6	6	0
Vernon	719	1	1	0
Vicksburg	3,806	6	6	0
Walker	25,067	44	39	5
Warren	137,138	259	224	35
Waterford Township	69,851	82	55	27
Watervliet	1,635	5	5	0
Wayland	4,421	5	5	0
Wayne	17,284	26	23	3
West Bloomfield Township	65,271	108	77	31
West Branch	2,315	7	7	0
Westland	83,763	98	73	25
White Cloud	1,395	3	3	0
Whitehall	2,959	8	8	0
White Lake Township	31,001	38	28	10
White Pigeon	1,709	4	4	0
Williamston	3,780	8	6	2
Wixom	17,186	24	21	3
Wolverine Lake	4,460	7	7	0
Woodhaven	12,745	28	27	1
Wyandotte	24,414	50	37	13
Wyoming	76,726	112	93	19
Ypsilanti	19,872	29	23	6
Zeeland	5,670	13	11	2
Zilwaukee	1,515	1	1	0
MINNESOTA				
Ada	1,741	4	3	1
Adrian	1,189	2	2	0
Aitkin	2,092	8	7	1
Akeley	426	1	1	0
Albany	2,820	6	5	1
Albert Lea	18,338	32	28	4
Alexandria	14,564	28	25	3
Annandale	3,405	6	5	1
Anoka	17,864	41	31	10
Appleton	1,360	2	2	0
Apple Valley	55,145	58	50	8
Arlington	2,284	3	2	1
Atwater	1,108	1	1	0
Audubon	557	1	1	0
Austin	26,275	36	33	3
Avon	1,680	4	3	1
Babbitt	1,376	5	5	0
Bagley	1,276	2	2	0
Barnesville	2,799	6	5	1
Battle Lake	854	3	3	0
Baxter	9,024	16	15	1
Bayport	3,912	7	7	0
Becker	5,033	9	8	1
Belgrade/Brooten	1,368	3	3	0
Belle Plaine	7,440	13	11	2
Bemidji	15,317	38	34	4
Benson	3,359	8	7	1
Big Lake	12,625	16	14	2
Blackduck	829	1	1	0
Blaine	71,368	84	73	11
Blooming Prairie	1,941	3	3	0
Bloomington	88,745	156	122	34
Blue Earth	3,251	5	5	0
Bovey	808	2	2	0
Braham	1,793	6	5	1
Brainerd	14,398	31	25	6
Breckenridge	3,352	7	6	1
Breezy Point	2,741	7	6	1
Breitung Township	522	1	1	0
Brooklyn Center	32,094	46	37	9
Brooklyn Park	82,682	149	98	51
Brownton	717	1	1	0
Buffalo	16,531	20	17	3
Buffalo Lake	646	2	2	0
Burnsville	63,361	86	75	11

Table 78. Full-Time Law Enforcement Employees, by Selected State and City, 2022—Continued

(Number.)

State/city	Population	Total law enforcement employees	Total officers	Total civilians
Caledonia	2,807	6	5	1
Callaway	170	1	1	0
Cambridge	10,137	18	16	2
Canby	1,682	2	2	0
Cannon Falls	4,256	8	7	1
Centennial Lakes	11,649	16	14	2
Champlin	23,038	29	24	5
Chaska	28,204	34	29	5
Chatfield	2,994	5	5	0
Chisholm	4,686	12	11	1
Clearbrook	466	1	1	0
Cleveland	769	1	1	0
Cloquet	12,747	25	23	2
Cold Spring/Richmond	5,730	10	9	1
Coleraine	1,979	2	2	0
Columbia Heights	21,724	34	28	6
Coon Rapids	63,181	79	68	11
Corcoran	7,295	14	11	3
Cottage Grove	40,871	52	44	8
Crookston	7,214	17	15	2
Crosby	2,323	9	8	1
Crosslake	2,494	6	6	0
Crystal	22,175	40	34	6
Danube	453	1	1	0
Dawson/Boyd	1,590	3	3	0
Dayton	9,078	12	10	2
Deephaven	3,770	9	8	1
Deer River	902	4	4	0
Deerwood	598	3	3	0
Detroit Lakes	9,771	19	17	2
Dilworth	4,641	9	8	1
Duluth	86,144	173	135	38
Dundas	1,751	4	4	0
Eagan	68,518	85	70	15
Eagle Lake	3,275	3	3	0
East Grand Forks	9,002	22	21	1
East Range	3,650	9	8	1
Eden Prairie	62,008	92	70	22
Eden Valley	1,023	1	1	0
Edina	53,206	84	57	27
Elko New Market	4,995	6	6	0
Elk River	26,519	43	35	8
Ely	3,212	8	7	1
Emily	872	1	1	0
Eveleth	3,434	11	10	1
Fairfax	1,235	2	2	0
Fairmont	10,369	19	17	2
Faribault	24,417	40	33	7
Farmington	23,551	28	25	3
Fergus Falls	14,017	29	24	5
Floodwood	512	2	2	0
Foley	2,681	4	4	0
Forest Lake	20,512	29	26	3
Frazee	1,311	3	3	0
Fridley	31,095	54	46	8
Fulda	1,393	2	2	0
Gaylord	2,321	4	4	0
Gibbon	792	1	1	0
Gilbert	1,665	7	7	0
Glencoe	5,695	11	10	1
Glenwood	2,671	6	5	1
Glyndon	1,313	4	4	0
Golden Valley	21,424	32	17	15
Goodhue	1,261	3	3	0
Goodview	4,137	7	6	1
Grand Rapids	11,388	21	19	2
Granite Falls	2,681	8	7	1
Hallock	879	1	1	0
Hastings	21,772	34	29	5
Hawley	2,227	5	5	0
Hector	1,004	1	1	0
Henderson	975	1	1	0
Henning	861	1	1	0
Hermantown	10,218	19	16	3
Heron Lake	602	1	1	0
Hibbing	15,980	34	29	5
Hill City	620	1	1	0
Hokah	555	1	1	0
Hopkins	18,125	37	28	9
Houston	976	2	2	0
Howard Lake	2,170	3	3	0
Hutchinson	14,628	31	23	8
International Falls	5,657	12	12	0
Inver Grove Heights	35,294	48	42	6
Isanti	7,257	9	8	1

Table 78. Full-Time Law Enforcement Employees, by Selected State and City, 2022—Continued

(Number.)

State/city	Population	Total law enforcement employees	Total officers	Total civilians
Isle	836	4	4	0
Janesville	2,457	4	4	0
Jordan	6,890	12	10	2
Kasson	6,997	10	9	1
Keewatin	968	3	3	0
Kenyon	1,907	4	3	1
La Crescent	5,222	9	8	1
Lake City	5,318	11	10	1
Lake Crystal	2,536	3	3	0
Lakefield	1,730	3	3	0
Lake Park	721	2	2	0
Lakes Area	10,739	15	13	2
Lake Shore	1,108	2	2	0
Lakeville	75,548	73	63	10
Le Center	2,485	3	3	0
Lester Prairie	1,904	3	3	0
Le Sueur	4,174	9	8	1
Lewiston	1,517	3	3	0
Lino Lakes	21,997	31	27	4
Litchfield	6,490	11	10	1
Little Falls	9,025	17	15	2
Long Prairie	3,743	5	5	0
Lonsdale	4,908	8	7	1
Madelia	2,360	4	4	0
Madison Lake	1,264	3	3	0
Mankato	44,925	63	54	9
Maple Grove	70,935	86	69	17
Mapleton	2,193	5	5	0
Maplewood	47,144	60	52	8
Marshall	13,658	24	21	3
Medina	6,753	12	11	1
Melrose	3,604	6	5	1
Menahga	1,359	3	3	0
Mendota Heights	11,569	20	19	1
Milaca	3,092	8	7	1
Minneapolis	421,690	744	592	152
Minneota	1,367	1	1	0
Minnesota Lake	644	1	1	0
Minnetonka	52,309	69	58	11
Minnetrista	10,959	17	13	4
Montevideo	5,180	11	10	1
Montgomery	3,498	7	6	1
Moorhead	44,859	74	59	15
Moose Lake	2,565	5	5	0
Morgan	883	1	1	0
Motley	678	1	1	0
Mounds View	14,897	22	20	2
Mountain Lake	2,009	4	4	0
Nashwauk	962	4	4	0
New Brighton	26,408	36	29	7
New Hope	20,877	44	33	11
New Prague	8,354	13	11	2
New Richland	1,231	2	2	0
New Ulm	14,067	23	23	0
New York Mills	1,292	3	3	0
Nisswa	2,077	6	6	0
North Branch	11,439	15	13	2
Northfield	20,746	29	23	6
North Mankato	14,403	16	15	1
North St. Paul	15,208	19	17	2
Oakdale	27,681	42	35	7
Oak Park Heights	4,721	12	11	1
Olivia	2,327	4	4	0
Onamia	806	1	1	0
Orono	19,245	30	26	4
Osakis	1,729	3	3	0
Osseo	2,545	9	8	1
Owatonna	26,394	41	37	4
Parkers Prairie	1,006	2	2	0
Park Rapids	4,186	12	11	1
Paynesville	2,497	4	4	0
Pelican Rapids	2,571	5	5	0
Pequot Lakes	2,449	7	6	1
Perham	3,651	8	7	1
Pierz	1,407	2	2	0
Pillager	513	1	1	0
Pine River	902	3	3	0
Plainview	3,509	9	8	1
Plymouth	78,585	94	78	16
Preston	1,315	3	3	0
Princeton	4,949	14	12	2
Prior Lake	28,559	36	32	4
Proctor	3,077	8	7	1
Ramsey	28,562	29	26	3
Red Wing	16,962	31	26	5

Table 78. Full-Time Law Enforcement Employees, by Selected State and City, 2022—Continued

(Number.)

State/city	Population	Total law enforcement employees	Total officers	Total civilians
Redwood Falls	5,090	15	13	2
Renville	1,286	3	3	0
Rice	2,149	2	2	0
Richfield	36,079	55	45	10
Robbinsdale	13,907	27	21	6
Rochester	121,534	207	144	63
Rogers	13,438	24	20	4
Roseau	2,721	6	5	1
Rosemount	27,503	32	29	3
Roseville	42,031	63	54	9
Royalton	1,266	2	2	0
Rushford	1,825	3	3	0
Sartell	19,607	24	20	4
Sauk Centre	4,641	9	8	1
Sauk Rapids	13,860	19	18	1
Savage	33,372	44	34	10
Sebeka	742	2	2	0
Shakopee	45,122	60	48	12
Sherburn	1,063	4	4	0
Silver Bay	1,865	4	4	0
Slayton	1,987	6	5	1
Sleepy Eye	3,411	7	7	0
South Lake Minnetonka	12,391	19	16	3
South St. Paul	20,337	35	31	4
Springfield	2,002	5	5	0
Spring Grove	1,228	1	1	0
Spring Lake Park	7,163	14	11	3
St. Anthony	9,411	23	20	3
Staples	2,971	8	7	1
Starbuck	1,382	4	4	0
St. Charles	4,001	7	7	0
St. Cloud	68,925	140	111	29
St. Francis	8,502	13	11	2
Stillwater	19,388	29	24	5
St. James	4,677	9	8	1
St. Joseph	6,937	13	11	2
St. Louis Park	48,311	71	56	15
St. Paul	358,679	768	579	189
St. Paul Park	5,429	6	6	0
St. Peter	11,647	21	15	6
Thief River Falls	8,625	16	14	2
Tracy	2,069	3	3	0
Truman	1,084	2	2	0
Twin Valley	720	2	2	0
Two Harbors	3,624	10	9	1
Tyler	1,109	2	2	0
Verndale	508	1	1	0
Virginia	8,276	26	23	3
Wabasha	2,494	9	8	1
Wadena	4,339	10	9	1
Waite Park	8,349	25	20	5
Walker	958	3	3	0
Warroad	1,815	6	5	1
Waseca	9,253	18	16	2
Waterville	1,740	4	4	0
Wayzata	5,986	17	15	2
Wells	2,420	5	5	0
Westbrook	769	1	1	0
West Concord	848	1	1	0
West Hennepin	5,311	11	9	2
West St. Paul	21,113	41	36	5
Wheaton	1,400	2	2	0
White Bear Lake	27,700	34	30	4
Willmar	21,097	39	35	4
Windom	4,850	11	10	1
Winnebago	1,379	2	2	0
Winona	25,936	37	34	3
Winsted	2,197	4	4	0
Winthrop	1,329	4	4	0
Woodbury	78,531	78	67	11
Worthington	13,616	33	24	9
Wyoming	8,098	12	10	2
Zumbrota	3,865	7	7	0
MISSISSIPPI				
Aberdeen	4,812	21	15	6
Ackerman	1,515	5	5	0
Amory	6,439	32	25	7
Batesville	7,238	49	36	13
Bay Springs	1,569	7	7	0
Bay St. Louis	10,591	28	27	1
Biloxi	49,027	164	115	49
Booneville	8,676	22	17	5
Brandon	25,636	44	32	12
Brookhaven	11,901	41	29	12

Table 78. Full-Time Law Enforcement Employees, by Selected State and City, 2022—Continued

(Number.)

State/city	Population	Total law enforcement employees	Total officers	Total civilians
Bruce	1,616	5	5	0
Byhalia	1,350	13	9	4
Byram	12,299	40	27	13
Calhoun City	1,432	3	3	0
Canton	10,587	33	23	10
Charleston	1,713	19	8	11
Clarksdale	14,081	32	26	6
Cleveland	10,687	48	42	6
Clinton	27,001	72	52	20
Collins	2,232	18	14	4
Columbia	5,879	31	23	8
Corinth	14,216	36	31	5
Crenshaw	618	3	1	2
Crystal Springs	4,696	16	12	4
Derma	938	1	1	0
D'Iberville	13,810	36	33	3
Edwards	960	3	3	0
Ellisville	4,468	12	10	2
Eupora	1,956	7	6	1
Florence	4,680	23	16	7
Flowood	10,518	61	47	14
Forest	5,262	15	11	4
Fulton	4,005	12	12	0
Gautier	18,992	49	39	10
Greenville	28,128	71	46	25
Greenwood	13,692	45	30	15
Grenada	12,319	34	31	3
Gulfport	71,380	207	141	66
Guntown	2,416	5	5	0
Hattiesburg	46,862	136	96	40
Heidelberg	630	4	4	0
Hernando	17,622	62	48	14
Hollandale	2,227	10	5	5
Holly Springs	6,488	18	14	4
Horn Lake	26,729	59	41	18
Houston	3,751	10	10	0
Indianola	9,163	26	17	9
Inverness	821	4	4	0
Iuka	3,051	12	9	3
Jackson	146,738	378	248	130
Kosciusko	6,955	19	19	0
Laurel	17,066	66	46	20
Leland	3,798	20	11	9
Long Beach	16,944	47	33	14
Louisville	5,963	33	21	12
Lucedale	2,981	21	15	6
Lumberton	1,655	8	7	1
Macon	2,488	6	5	1
Madison	27,674	89	66	23
Mathiston	860	3	3	0
McComb	12,082	49	27	22
Mendenhall	2,159	8	5	3
Moss Point	11,962	30	21	9
New Albany	7,645	28	26	2
Oakland	463	2	1	1
Ocean Springs	18,361	44	36	8
Olive Branch	40,651	97	90	7
Oxford	26,975	108	86	22
Pascagoula	21,736	78	55	23
Pass Christian	6,032	26	19	7
Pearl	27,484	64	51	13
Pelahatchie	1,267	10	8	2
Petal	11,580	31	27	4
Philadelphia	6,956	29	25	4
Picayune	11,710	36	31	5
Pontotoc	5,771	24	22	2
Poplarville	2,808	9	9	0
Port Gibson	1,150	12	9	3
Purvis	1,951	13	11	2
Quitman	1,938	9	9	0
Raymond	1,838	4	4	0
Richland	7,245	34	28	6
Ridgeland	23,896	88	58	30
Ripley	5,333	15	14	1
Ruleville	2,526	4	4	0
Saltillo	4,900	13	13	0
Sandersville	628	8	8	0
Seminary	297	1	1	0
Senatobia	8,104	35	32	3
Smithville	523	1	1	0
Southaven	56,092	183	145	38
Starkville	24,720	69	58	11
Sumrall	1,929	6	6	0
Tunica	958	9	9	0
Tupelo	37,534	118	103	15

Table 78. Full-Time Law Enforcement Employees, by Selected State and City, 2022—Continued

(Number.)

State/city	Population	Total law enforcement employees	Total officers	Total civilians
Union	1,952	8	7	1
Utica	627	3	3	0
Vaiden	750	1	1	0
Vardaman	1,089	1	1	0
Verona	2,747	8	8	0
Vicksburg	20,381	59	43	16
Walls	1,374	5	5	0
Water Valley	3,296	11	10	1
Waveland	6,920	22	21	1
Waynesboro	4,530	12	12	0
West Point	9,893	31	25	6
Wiggins	4,324	20	15	5
Yazoo City	10,019	19	11	8
MISSOURI				
Adrian	1,734	5	5	0
Arcadia	606	3	3	0
Arnold	20,794	61	54	7
Ash Grove	1,506	5	5	0
Ashland	4,948	8	7	1
Aurora	7,329	22	16	6
Ballwin	30,630	58	47	11
Bates City	223	2	2	0
Bella Villa	737	4	4	0
Bel-Nor	1,371	5	5	0
Belton	24,395	64	40	24
Berkeley	8,078	32	26	6
Bernie	1,837	9	5	4
Bertrand	719	1	1	0
Bethany	2,894	6	6	0
Bloomfield	1,753	6	5	1
Bolivar	11,129	25	18	7
Boonville	7,882	28	21	7
Bourbon	1,543	4	4	0
Bowling Green	4,262	13	12	1
Branson	13,021	61	40	21
Branson West	480	7	7	0
Brookfield	4,068	12	10	2
Buckner	2,896	7	6	1
Buffalo	3,370	8	7	1
Butler	4,189	9	5	4
Byrnes Mill	3,160	14	12	2
Cabool	2,024	12	8	4
Calverton Park	1,129	7	7	0
Camdenton	4,074	16	14	2
Cameron	8,429	22	14	8
Campbell	1,535	4	4	0
Canton	2,640	4	3	1
Cape Girardeau	40,067	102	69	33
Cardwell	545	1	1	0
Carl Junction	8,355	15	11	4
Carrollton	3,389	7	6	1
Carterville	1,839	4	4	0
Caruthersville	5,288	17	15	2
Cassville	3,201	12	11	1
Centralia	4,729	14	9	5
Chaffee	3,017	12	7	5
Charleston	4,987	18	13	5
Chesterfield	49,451	111	96	15
Chillicothe	9,177	28	18	10
Clayton	16,851	56	47	9
Cleveland	643	1	1	0
Clever	3,101	6	5	1
Columbia	127,862	209	157	52
Concordia	2,331	9	9	0
Cottleville	5,828	15	15	0
Country Club Hills	1,004	5	5	0
Country Club Village	2,458	1	1	0
Crestwood	12,267	28	26	2
Creve Coeur	18,527	51	46	5
Crystal City	4,698	22	16	6
Delta	379	1	1	0
Des Peres	9,135	49	43	6
Dexter	7,854	24	18	6
Doniphan	1,703	13	8	5
East Prairie	2,955	12	7	5
Edgar Springs	202	1	1	0
Edmundson	851	12	11	1
El Dorado Springs	3,579	11	7	4
Ellisville	9,890	25	24	1
Ellsinore	432	1	1	0
Eureka	12,589	31	27	4
Excelsior Springs	10,608	29	16	13
Fair Grove	1,619	6	6	0
Fair Play	430	1	1	0

Table 78. Full-Time Law Enforcement Employees, by Selected State and City, 2022—Continued

(Number.)

State/city	Population	Total law enforcement employees	Total officers	Total civilians
Farmington	18,565	40	38	2
Fayette	2,725	5	5	0
Ferguson	18,178	42	32	10
Festus	13,036	40	29	11
Flordell Hills	711	6	6	0
Fordland	785	1	1	0
Fredericktown	4,353	13	12	1
Frontenac	4,067	22	21	1
Galena	469	4	2	2
Gideon	749	1	1	0
Gladstone	26,953	54	35	19
Glendale	6,104	11	11	0
Gower	1,511	2	2	0
Grain Valley	16,320	26	22	4
Granby	2,086	3	3	0
Grandview	25,542	62	50	12
Greenwood	6,077	6	6	0
Hamilton	1,693	5	5	0
Hannibal	17,028	40	31	9
Hardin	552	1	1	0
Hartville	598	3	3	0
Hayti	2,367	5	5	0
Herculaneum	5,118	12	11	1
Hermann	2,190	10	5	5
Higginsville	4,642	23	11	12
Hillsboro	3,497	12	11	1
Holcomb	599	1	1	0
Holden	2,206	8	6	2
Holts Summit	5,431	7	6	1
Hornersville	515	2	2	0
Houston	2,187	7	7	0
Huntsville	1,370	1	1	0
Iberia	717	5	4	1
Independence	121,255	322	230	92
Jackson	15,561	28	27	1
Joplin	51,989	122	97	25
Kansas City	508,856	1,624	1,119	505
Kearney	11,041	18	17	1
Kimberling City	2,385	5	5	0
Kirksville	17,515	31	28	3
Kirkwood	29,276	81	59	22
Ladue	8,948	28	27	1
La Grange	835	3	3	0
Lake Lafayette	286	1	1	0
Lake Lotawana	2,350	9	9	0
Lake Ozark	2,161	12	7	5
Lakeshire	1,529	4	4	0
Lake St. Louis	17,846	48	38	10
Lake Tapawingo	783	4	3	1
La Plata	1,251	3	3	0
Lebanon	15,143	41	29	12
Lee's Summit	103,976	198	145	53
Lexington	4,516	11	9	2
Licking	2,749	5	5	0
Lincoln	1,170	2	2	0
Lone Jack	1,578	9	8	1
Macon	5,480	9	7	2
Malden	3,568	15	11	4
Manchester	18,142	40	36	4
Maplewood	8,117	34	32	2
Marble Hill	1,336	6	5	1
Marceline	2,124	9	8	1
Marquand	193	1	1	0
Marshall	13,490	30	24	6
Marshfield	7,605	13	12	1
Maryland Heights	27,795	97	78	19
Maryville	10,791	29	20	9
Merriam Woods	2,025	2	2	0
Moline Acres	2,118	11	9	2
Monett	9,782	28	22	6
Monroe City	2,681	9	8	1
Moscow Mills	3,911	7	7	0
Mound City	1,015	2	2	0
Mountain Grove	4,530	15	15	0
Mountain View	2,578	9	7	2
Mount Vernon	4,555	11	11	0
Neosho	12,864	27	23	4
Nevada	8,182	25	22	3
New Haven	2,361	6	6	0
New London	957	2	2	0
New Madrid	2,654	17	9	8
Niangua	398	1	1	0
Nixa	24,860	45	39	6
North Kansas City	4,534	53	41	12
Northmoor	292	7	7	0

Table 78. Full-Time Law Enforcement Employees, by Selected State and City, 2022—Continued

(Number.)

State/city	Population	Total law enforcement employees	Total officers	Total civilians
Northwoods	3,877	28	13	15
Oak Grove	8,388	16	15	1
Odessa	5,546	14	12	2
Old Monroe	260	2	1	1
Olivette	8,387	24	23	1
Oronogo	2,654	6	6	0
Osage Beach	4,741	31	22	9
Overland	15,632	46	40	6
Owensville	2,750	8	7	1
Ozark	22,447	38	34	4
Pagedale	2,527	23	22	1
Palmyra	3,629	9	8	1
Parkville	8,412	15	14	1
Peculiar	6,037	13	12	1
Perry	673	1	1	0
Perryville	8,458	29	22	7
Pevely	5,998	22	14	8
Piedmont	1,859	7	7	0
Pilot Knob	648	1	1	0
Platte City	4,775	10	10	0
Pleasant Hill	8,811	17	11	6
Pleasant Valley	2,733	11	7	4
Poplar Bluff	16,181	52	42	10
Portageville	2,832	14	10	4
Raymore	25,351	39	25	14
Raytown	29,224	46	30	16
Republic	19,481	32	28	4
Rich Hill	1,246	2	2	0
Richland	1,726	5	4	1
Richmond Heights	9,120	40	39	1
Riverside	4,063	33	24	9
Riverview	2,352	11	10	1
Rockaway Beach	840	2	1	1
Rock Hill	4,689	11	10	1
Rock Port	1,251	3	3	0
Rogersville	4,972	10	10	0
Rolla	20,321	60	36	24
Salisbury	1,561	4	3	1
Savannah	5,032	6	6	0
Scott City	4,373	15	9	6
Sedalia	21,924	49	43	6
Seligman	843	1	1	0
Seneca	2,290	7	7	0
Seymour	1,854	9	9	0
Shelbina	1,551	5	4	1
Shrewsbury	6,280	21	19	2
Sikeston	16,024	72	48	24
Smithville	10,654	21	20	1
Southwest City	984	4	4	0
Sparta	1,965	5	5	0
Springfield	169,822	375	310	65
St. Ann	12,788	69	43	26
Steele	1,747	5	5	0
Steelville	1,373	6	6	0
Ste. Genevieve	4,686	10	10	0
St. John	6,538	23	21	2
St. Joseph	70,918	162	111	51
St. Louis	286,053	1,357	1,010	347
St. Peters	58,584	121	93	28
Strafford	2,633	6	6	0
St. Robert	5,399	25	17	8
Sugar Creek	3,177	21	17	4
Sullivan	6,811	26	19	7
Sunrise Beach	480	3	3	0
Sunset Hills	9,053	30	23	7
Tarkio	1,473	3	3	0
Thayer	1,861	12	8	4
Town and Country	11,479	29	28	1
Trenton	5,581	17	11	6
Union	12,575	26	25	1
University City	34,326	78	64	14
Velda City	1,165	6	6	0
Viburnum	636	2	2	0
Vienna	527	3	3	0
Vinita Park	8,852	43	41	2
Walnut Grove	640	2	2	0
Warrensburg	19,703	35	30	5
Warrenton	9,215	25	20	5
Warson Woods	1,997	9	9	0
Washington	15,175	32	30	2
Waynesville	5,419	12	11	1
Weatherby Lake	2,089	3	3	0
Webb City	13,433	24	20	4
Webster Groves	23,598	44	42	2
Wellsville	1,026	7	7	0

Table 78. Full-Time Law Enforcement Employees, by Selected State and City, 2022—Continued

(Number.)

State/city	Population	Total law enforcement employees	Total officers	Total civilians
Wentzville	46,018	102	82	20
West Plains	12,252	33	25	8
Willard	6,430	10	9	1
Willow Springs	2,173	10	9	1
Woodson Terrace	3,900	19	17	2
Wright City	5,360	12	11	1
MONTANA				
Baker	1,823	4	4	0
Belgrade	12,529	26	22	4
Billings	117,866	193	159	34
Bozeman	55,997	80	66	14
Bridger	712	3	3	0
Chinook	1,173	3	3	0
Colstrip	2,009	10	6	4
Columbia Falls	5,734	9	8	1
Columbus	1,863	6	5	1
Conrad	2,398	5	5	0
Cut Bank	3,053	9	8	1
Deer Lodge	2,949	6	6	0
Dillon	4,075	11	10	1
East Helena	1,973	6	5	1
Ennis	1,008	2	2	0
Eureka	1,489	3	3	0
Fairview	858	2	2	0
Fort Benton	1,510	3	3	0
Glasgow	3,183	10	6	4
Glendive	4,860	7	5	2
Great Falls	60,386	124	89	35
Hamilton	5,138	15	13	2
Hardin	3,656	7	6	1
Havre	9,270	22	17	5
Helena	33,896	71	48	23
Hot Springs	610	1	1	0
Kalispell	27,710	53	41	12
Laurel	7,139	20	13	7
Lewistown	6,135	24	13	11
Libby	3,055	6	6	0
Livingston	8,552	24	15	9
Manhattan	2,154	5	5	0
Miles City	8,437	18	17	1
Missoula	75,705	146	114	32
Plains	1,203	3	3	0
Polson	5,495	15	14	1
Red Lodge	2,450	7	7	0
Ronan City	2,255	5	5	0
Sidney	6,066	11	10	1
Stevensville	2,187	3	3	0
St. Ignatius	803	2	2	0
Thompson Falls	1,447	4	4	0
Troy	865	4	4	0
West Yellowstone	1,268	10	6	4
Whitefish	9,189	20	17	3
Wolf Point	2,620	6	5	1
NEBRASKA				
Albion	1,721	3	3	0
Alliance	7,807	24	14	10
Ashland	3,279	6	4	2
Aurora	4,631	10	9	1
Battle Creek	1,147	1	1	0
Bayard	1,139	3	3	0
Beatrice	12,164	38	23	15
Bellevue	63,178	121	109	12
Bennington	1,977	5	5	0
Blair	7,855	18	16	2
Bloomfield	985	2	2	0
Boys Town	413	10	10	0
Broken Bow	3,448	8	7	1
Burwell	1,108	1	1	0
Central City	3,038	5	4	1
Chadron	5,222	18	11	7
Columbus	24,158	41	35	6
Creighton	1,152	2	2	0
Crete	7,200	15	13	2
Emerson	814	1	1	0
Falls City	4,032	15	9	6
Fremont	27,586	47	39	8
Gering	8,372	18	17	1
Gordon	1,493	6	5	1
Gothenburg	3,372	9	7	2
Grand Island	51,733	93	73	20
Harvard	938	1	1	0
Hastings	24,930	41	31	10
Henderson	1,103	1	1	0

Table 78. Full-Time Law Enforcement Employees, by Selected State and City, 2022—Continued

(Number.)

State/city	Population	Total law enforcement employees	Total officers	Total civilians
Imperial	1,991	4	4	0
Kearney	34,186	78	62	16
Laurel	962	1	1	0
La Vista	16,515	46	40	6
Lexington	10,382	22	20	2
Lincoln	293,937	474	336	138
Madison	2,174	4	4	0
McCook	7,325	22	15	7
Milford	2,142	1	1	0
Minatare	715	2	2	0
Mitchell	1,516	4	4	0
Morrill	922	2	2	0
Nebraska City	7,212	14	13	1
Norfolk	25,048	56	35	21
North Platte	22,684	61	42	19
Omaha	483,462	968	827	141
O'Neill	3,536	9	8	1
Ord	2,114	4	4	0
Osmond	806	1	1	0
Papillion	23,874	51	47	4
Pierce	1,823	3	3	0
Plainview	1,264	2	2	0
Plattsmouth	6,710	17	14	3
Ralston	6,448	15	14	1
Randolph	868	1	1	0
Ravenna	1,430	1	1	0
Schuyler	6,476	12	10	2
Scottsbluff	15,224	35	30	5
Scribner	794	1	1	0
Seward	7,695	12	10	2
Sidney	6,469	13	11	2
South Sioux City	13,652	29	28	1
St. Paul	2,407	4	4	0
Superior	1,791	1	1	0
Sutton	1,430	3	3	0
Tekamah	1,708	5	5	0
Tilden	972	1	1	0
Valentine	2,605	5	4	1
Wahoo	4,983	7	7	0
Waterloo	911	5	5	0
Wayne	6,056	12	9	3
West Point	3,445	7	6	1
Wisner	1,252	2	2	0
Wymore	1,354	2	2	0
York	8,214	18	15	3
NEVADA				
Boulder City	14,848	53	37	16
Carlin	2,048	7	5	2
Elko	20,664	45	38	7
Fallon	9,359	33	24	9
Henderson	325,332	667	471	196
Las Vegas Metropolitan Police Department	1,667,961	5,686	4,102	1,584
Mesquite	21,732	63	43	20
North Las Vegas	284,422	394	282	112
Reno	273,671	420	346	74
Sparks	110,475	175	120	55
West Wendover	4,473	22	14	8
Winnemucca	8,775	29	24	5
Yerington	3,200	9	8	1
NEW HAMPSHIRE				
Alexandria	1,789	2	2	0
Allenstown	4,788	11	9	2
Alstead	1,909	2	2	0
Alton	6,054	14	12	2
Amherst	11,876	20	19	1
Andover	2,434	2	2	0
Antrim	2,683	8	6	2
Ashland	1,969	5	5	0
Atkinson	7,343	9	8	1
Auburn	6,090	12	10	2
Barnstead	5,024	7	6	1
Barrington	9,531	13	12	1
Bartlett	3,363	4	4	0
Bedford	23,845	48	36	12
Belmont	7,425	17	14	3
Bennington	1,506	2	2	0
Berlin	9,717	30	22	8
Bethlehem	2,543	6	6	0
Boscawen	4,008	9	8	1
Bow	8,429	13	12	1
Bradford	1,726	4	4	0
Brentwood	4,610	2	2	0
Bristol	3,303	10	9	1

Table 78. Full-Time Law Enforcement Employees, by Selected State and City, 2022—Continued

(Number.)

State/city	Population	Total law enforcement employees	Total officers	Total civilians
Brookline	5,774	9	8	1
Campton	3,418	8	6	2
Canaan	3,818	7	6	1
Candia	4,162	7	6	1
Canterbury	2,483	2	2	0
Carroll	812	4	4	0
Center Harbor	1,040	3	3	0
Charlestown	4,950	9	5	4
Chester	5,279	9	8	1
Chesterfield	3,638	6	5	1
Chichester	2,777	5	5	0
Claremont	13,153	25	18	7
Colebrook	2,051	4	4	0
Concord	44,305	102	81	21
Conway	10,334	32	23	9
Danville	4,596	5	5	0
Deerfield	4,934	9	8	1
Deering	1,912	1	1	0
Derry	34,290	67	55	12
Dover	33,453	71	43	28
Dublin	1,586	4	3	1
Dunbarton	3,112	6	6	0
Durham	15,550	24	21	3
East Kingston	2,427	6	5	1
Effingham	1,781	2	2	0
Enfield	4,540	7	6	1
Epping	7,274	19	18	1
Epsom	4,957	6	5	1
Exeter	16,155	32	24	8
Farmington	6,872	12	11	1
Fitzwilliam	2,437	4	3	1
Francestown	1,640	1	1	0
Franconia	1,101	4	4	0
Franklin	8,850	26	19	7
Freedom	1,767	2	2	0
Fremont	4,797	7	6	1
Gilford	7,880	25	19	6
Gilmanton	4,022	5	4	1
Goffstown	18,375	45	31	14
Gorham	2,641	11	7	4
Grafton	1,414	1	1	0
Grantham	3,497	6	5	1
Greenland	4,091	10	9	1
Greenville	1,970	3	3	0
Hampstead	9,058	10	10	0
Hampton	16,384	44	36	8
Hampton Falls	2,408	4	4	0
Hancock	1,756	4	4	0
Hanover	11,778	27	17	10
Haverhill	4,622	9	7	2
Hebron	649	1	1	0
Henniker	5,870	8	7	1
Hillsborough	5,968	23	15	8
Hinsdale	4,033	8	7	1
Holderness	2,037	6	6	0
Hollis	8,661	19	16	3
Hooksett	15,313	41	30	11
Hopkinton	6,079	8	7	1
Hudson	25,530	67	50	17
Jackson	1,099	4	4	0
Jaffrey	5,495	11	10	1
Keene	23,271	49	39	10
Kensington	2,090	7	6	1
Kingston	6,231	7	6	1
Laconia	17,109	54	44	10
Lancaster	3,209	9	7	2
Lebanon	15,702	46	33	13
Lee	4,634	8	7	1
Lincoln	1,652	15	9	6
Lisbon	1,651	4	4	0
Litchfield	8,556	12	10	2
Littleton	6,058	15	13	2
Londonderry	26,340	71	57	14
Loudon	5,781	8	7	1
Lyme	1,758	2	2	0
Lyndeborough	1,705	1	1	0
Madison	2,717	4	4	0
Manchester	114,650	307	251	56
Marlborough	2,163	3	3	0
Mason	1,450	1	1	0
Meredith	6,786	17	13	4
Merrimack	27,403	53	38	15
Middleton	1,860	3	3	0
Milford	16,331	28	23	5
Milton	4,530	3	2	1

Table 78. Full-Time Law Enforcement Employees, by Selected State and City, 2022—Continued

(Number.)

State/city	Population	Total law enforcement employees	Total officers	Total civilians
Mont Vernon	2,617	4	3	1
Moultonborough	5,235	7	6	1
Nashua	91,027	223	167	56
New Boston	6,216	11	10	1
Newbury	2,236	5	5	0
New Castle	999	4	4	0
New Durham	2,765	4	4	0
Newfields	1,761	4	4	0
New Hampton	2,433	6	5	1
Newington	817	11	9	2
New Ipswich	5,333	7	6	1
New London	4,354	14	9	5
Newmarket	9,417	20	13	7
Newport	6,411	16	11	5
Newton	4,834	9	8	1
Northfield	4,998	6	6	0
North Hampton	4,546	12	11	1
Northumberland	2,085	3	3	0
Northwood	4,670	7	6	1
Nottingham	5,358	8	7	1
Orford	1,253	1	1	0
Ossipee	4,565	9	8	1
Pelham	14,364	31	23	8
Pembroke	7,684	12	10	2
Peterborough	6,479	13	11	2
Piermont	778	1	1	0
Pittsfield	4,155	7	7	0
Plainfield	2,505	3	3	0
Plaistow	7,856	22	15	7
Plymouth	6,658	19	12	7
Portsmouth	22,513	84	64	20
Raymond	10,996	23	15	8
Rindge	6,633	10	9	1
Rochester	33,098	68	56	12
Rollinsford	2,646	5	5	0
Rumney	1,513	2	2	0
Rye	5,550	9	8	1
Salem	30,712	80	64	16
Sanbornton	3,072	6	5	1
Sandown	6,575	9	8	1
Sandwich	1,573	2	2	0
Seabrook	8,441	34	28	6
Somersworth	12,160	32	25	7
South Hampton	896	2	2	0
Springfield	1,316	2	2	0
Strafford	4,324	6	6	0
Stratham	7,844	13	12	1
Sugar Hill	662	2	2	0
Sunapee	3,457	5	4	1
Sutton	2,038	2	2	0
Swanzey	7,468	12	10	2
Tamworth	2,949	3	3	0
Thornton	2,785	6	5	1
Tilton	4,106	15	11	4
Troy	2,192	2	2	0
Tuftonboro	2,614	4	4	0
Wakefield	6,315	13	11	2
Walpole	3,729	5	4	1
Warner	2,969	3	2	1
Warren	840	1	1	0
Washington	1,221	1	1	0
Waterville Valley	510	7	7	0
Weare	9,213	12	11	1
Webster	1,976	2	2	0
Whitefield	2,563	7	6	1
Wilmot	1,444	1	1	0
Wilton	3,994	9	8	1
Winchester	4,246	2	1	1
Windham	15,994	25	18	7
Wolfeboro	6,710	19	13	6
Woodstock	1,454	3	3	0
NEW JERSEY				
Aberdeen Township	19,345	50	43	7
Absecon	9,153	29	26	3
Allendale	6,785	21	16	5
Allenhurst	470	11	9	2
Allentown	1,737	7	6	1
Alpha	2,348	39	38	1
Alpine	1,743	11	11	0
Andover Township	6,227	17	12	5
Asbury Park	15,209	93	89	4
Atlantic City	38,502	342	270	72
Atlantic Highlands	4,416	16	15	1
Audubon	8,665	18	17	1

Table 78. Full-Time Law Enforcement Employees, by Selected State and City, 2022—Continued
(Number.)

State/city	Population	Total law enforcement employees	Total officers	Total civilians
Audubon Park	983	25	24	1
Avalon	1,209	25	22	3
Avon-by-the-Sea	1,899	12	12	0
Barnegat Township	25,142	54	52	2
Barrington	7,013	19	17	2
Bay Head	967	10	9	1
Bayonne	66,990	225	187	38
Beach Haven	1,082	13	12	1
Beachwood	11,188	23	20	3
Bedminster Township	8,123	17	15	2
Belleville	37,348	108	102	6
Bellmawr	11,645	24	23	1
Belmar	5,868	32	25	7
Belvidere	2,531	7	7	0
Bergenfield	28,082	57	46	11
Berkeley Heights Township	13,096	32	29	3
Berkeley Township	45,006	97	75	22
Berlin	7,522	21	20	1
Berlin Township	5,975	20	19	1
Bernards Township	27,682	41	38	3
Bernardsville	7,786	28	22	6
Beverly	2,487	9	9	0
Blairstown Township	5,766	10	9	1
Bloomfield	52,663	146	123	23
Bloomingdale	7,616	19	18	1
Bogota	9,652	22	17	5
Boonton	8,805	24	23	1
Boonton Township	4,387	14	13	1
Bordentown City	3,990	14	13	1
Bordentown Township	12,095	33	31	2
Bound Brook	11,948	30	24	6
Bradley Beach	4,267	22	18	4
Branchburg Township	14,690	27	25	2
Brick Township	76,287	184	146	38
Bridgeton	26,524	75	64	11
Bridgewater Township	46,836	84	74	10
Brielle	4,985	20	19	1
Brigantine	7,642	44	34	10
Brooklawn	1,802	8	8	0
Buena	4,482	40	37	3
Burlington City	10,202	39	34	5
Burlington Township	23,927	53	43	10
Butler	8,203	16	15	1
Byram Township	8,128	15	15	0
Caldwell	8,734	21	20	1
Califon	1,016	35	32	3
Camden County Police Department	71,616	413	383	30
Cape May	2,845	26	24	2
Carlstadt	6,316	29	24	5
Carney's Point Township	8,763	23	21	2
Carteret	25,030	77	70	7
Cedar Grove Township	13,822	32	31	1
Chatham	9,307	24	20	4
Chatham Township	10,897	23	21	2
Cherry Hill Township	76,401	170	141	29
Chesilhurst	1,543	11	10	1
Chesterfield Township	9,599	13	12	1
Chester Township	7,711	25	24	1
Cinnaminson Township	17,302	32	32	0
Clark Township	15,308	56	45	11
Clayton	9,017	16	15	1
Clementon	5,318	17	16	1
Cliffside Park	25,531	50	49	1
Clifton	88,768	187	150	37
Clinton	2,795	12	12	0
Clinton Township	13,759	27	24	3
Closter	8,474	23	22	1
Collingswood	14,108	28	25	3
Colts Neck Township	9,967	27	25	2
Cranbury Township	3,989	21	20	1
Cranford Township	24,133	65	53	12
Cresskill	9,069	27	22	5
Deal	892	22	18	4
Delanco Township	4,805	15	14	1
Delaware Township	4,589	8	7	1
Delran Township	17,822	32	28	4
Demarest	4,812	17	17	0
Denville Township	17,119	42	34	8
Deptford Township	32,429	74	70	4
Dover	18,434	37	34	3
Dumont	18,533	39	31	8
Dunellen	7,525	20	19	1
Eastampton Township	6,319	21	20	1
East Brunswick Township	49,038	112	84	28
East Greenwich Township	12,353	23	22	1

Table 78. Full-Time Law Enforcement Employees, by Selected State and City, 2022—Continued

(Number.)

State/city	Population	Total law enforcement employees	Total officers	Total civilians
East Hanover Township	11,103	38	34	4
East Newark	2,383	13	7	6
East Orange	68,279	259	197	62
East Rutherford	9,904	38	37	1
East Windsor Township	29,788	48	43	5
Eatontown	13,607	50	38	12
Edgewater	14,793	38	33	5
Edgewater Park Township	8,904	18	16	2
Edison Township	108,050	233	185	48
Egg Harbor City	4,402	16	15	1
Egg Harbor Township	47,747	127	86	41
Elizabeth	134,065	448	343	105
Elk Township	4,441	14	13	1
Elmer	1,378	2	2	0
Elmwood Park	21,154	57	52	5
Emerson	7,215	25	22	3
Englewood	28,975	105	85	20
Englewood Cliffs	5,352	25	24	1
Englishtown	2,362	7	7	0
Essex Fells	2,144	13	13	0
Evesham Township	49,166	87	78	9
Ewing Township	37,408	91	76	15
Fairfield Township, Essex County	7,777	46	43	3
Fair Haven	6,156	13	13	0
Fair Lawn	35,424	71	62	9
Fairview	14,850	35	32	3
Fanwood	7,654	18	16	2
Far Hills	908	8	7	1
Flemington	4,923	17	17	0
Florence Township	12,747	33	31	2
Florham Park	13,685	36	31	5
Fort Lee	39,636	120	99	21
Franklin	4,983	17	16	1
Franklin Lakes	10,899	29	24	5
Franklin Township, Gloucester County	16,579	40	37	3
Franklin Township, Hunterdon County	3,303	6	6	0
Franklin Township, Somerset County	68,782	123	102	21
Freehold Borough	12,539	36	32	4
Freehold Township	35,791	70	66	4
Frenchtown	1,387	4	3	1
Galloway Township	37,961	89	62	27
Garfield	32,351	73	65	8
Garwood	4,358	20	16	4
Gibbsboro	2,208	10	9	1
Glassboro	21,115	52	48	4
Glen Ridge	7,620	28	23	5
Glen Rock	12,017	28	26	2
Gloucester City	11,430	37	35	2
Gloucester Township	65,848	163	136	27
Green Brook Township	7,314	24	23	1
Greenwich Township, Gloucester County	5,018	21	20	1
Greenwich Township, Warren County	5,490	12	12	0
Guttenberg	11,107	40	30	10
Hackensack	45,413	123	105	18
Hackettstown	10,389	18	17	1
Haddonfield	12,467	21	20	1
Haddon Heights	7,461	16	15	1
Haddon Township	15,358	25	24	1
Haledon	8,848	21	21	0
Hamburg	3,311	10	9	1
Hamilton Township, Atlantic County	28,658	80	53	27
Hamilton Township, Mercer County	91,408	203	171	32
Hammonton	14,861	33	28	5
Hanover Township	14,630	42	35	7
Harding Township	3,883	19	17	2
Hardyston Township	8,351	26	20	6
Harrington Park	5,206	11	11	0
Harrison	18,999	61	49	12
Harrison Township	13,886	24	23	1
Harvey Cedars	410	10	9	1
Hasbrouck Heights	12,005	30	28	2
Haworth	3,288	13	12	1
Hawthorne	19,163	42	36	6
Hazlet Township	20,547	46	43	3
High Bridge	3,641	9	9	0
Highland Park	14,914	34	27	7
Highlands	4,654	17	15	2
Hightstown	5,859	14	13	1
Hillsborough Township	42,893	65	57	8
Hillsdale	10,011	25	24	1
Hillside Township	22,026	75	66	9
Hi-Nella	923	9	9	0
Hoboken	56,882	148	134	14
Ho-Ho-Kus	4,195	21	16	5
Holland Township	5,233	10	9	1

Table 78. Full-Time Law Enforcement Employees, by Selected State and City, 2022—Continued

(Number.)

State/city	Population	Total law enforcement employees	Total officers	Total civilians
Holmdel Township	17,421	50	42	8
Hopatcong	14,561	35	28	7
Hopewell Township	17,339	38	30	8
Howell Township	54,073	110	93	17
Independence Township	5,510	11	10	1
Irvington	59,726	197	143	54
Island Heights	1,702	6	6	0
Jackson Township	60,762	126	106	20
Jamesburg	5,703	23	18	5
Jefferson Township	20,498	44	36	8
Jersey City	276,300	1,168	921	247
Keansburg	9,757	45	37	8
Kearny	38,906	116	109	7
Kenilworth	8,280	31	26	5
Keyport	7,205	24	23	1
Kinnelon	9,983	18	17	1
Lacey Township	29,903	57	44	13
Lakehurst	2,708	15	14	1
Lakewood Township	141,190	188	155	33
Lambertville	4,173	12	10	2
Laurel Springs	1,971	7	7	0
Lavallette	1,852	14	11	3
Lawnside	3,343	12	11	1
Lawrence Township, Mercer County	32,949	66	60	6
Lebanon Township	6,243	14	13	1
Leonia	9,198	24	21	3
Lincoln Park	10,904	32	26	6
Linden	43,652	182	140	42
Lindenwold	21,524	46	43	3
Linwood	6,950	18	16	2
Little Egg Harbor Township	21,498	62	45	17
Little Falls Township	13,220	37	29	8
Little Ferry	10,859	32	27	5
Little Silver	6,050	21	17	4
Livingston Township	30,844	82	72	10
Lodi	25,788	49	48	1
Logan Township	6,103	24	23	1
Long Beach Township	3,143	46	36	10
Long Branch	33,094	109	90	19
Long Hill Township	8,610	25	23	2
Longport	879	13	12	1
Lopatcong Township	10,057	15	14	1
Lower Alloways Creek Township	1,722	12	12	0
Lower Township	22,238	55	49	6
Lumberton Township	12,764	20	18	2
Lyndhurst Township	22,183	57	54	3
Madison	16,975	36	28	8
Magnolia	4,325	16	16	0
Mahwah Township	25,150	62	54	8
Manalapan Township	40,897	61	57	4
Manasquan	5,949	21	16	5
Manchester Township	46,265	123	72	51
Mansfield Township, Burlington County	8,868	16	14	2
Mansfield Township, Warren County	7,846	16	15	1
Mantoloking	324	10	9	1
Mantua Township	15,522	29	27	2
Manville	10,763	27	24	3
Maple Shade Township	19,911	41	37	4
Maplewood Township	25,088	75	63	12
Margate City	5,202	40	30	10
Marlboro Township	41,576	113	87	26
Matawan	9,734	24	23	1
Maywood	9,966	27	23	4
Medford Lakes	4,257	11	10	1
Medford Township	24,447	43	39	4
Mendham	4,975	13	12	1
Mendham Township	6,007	16	15	1
Merchantville	3,799	16	13	3
Metuchen	14,874	31	30	1
Middlesex Borough	14,423	32	29	3
Middle Township	20,845	60	54	6
Middletown Township	67,055	121	110	11
Midland Park	6,930	17	16	1
Millburn Township	22,417	64	58	6
Milltown	6,947	19	16	3
Millville	27,550	95	80	15
Monmouth Beach	3,242	13	12	1
Monroe Township, Gloucester County	38,222	76	71	5
Monroe Township, Middlesex County	48,097	89	68	21
Montclair	41,117	128	111	17
Montgomery Township	23,441	40	35	5
Montvale	8,436	30	28	2
Montville Township	22,415	47	42	5
Moonachie	3,093	22	20	2
Moorestown Township	21,420	38	34	4

Table 78. Full-Time Law Enforcement Employees, by Selected State and City, 2022—Continued

(Number.)

State/city	Population	Total law enforcement employees	Total officers	Total civilians
Morris Plains	6,138	18	16	2
Morristown	20,418	55	51	4
Morris Township	23,455	50	44	6
Mountain Lakes	4,666	14	13	1
Mountainside	7,019	27	22	5
Mount Arlington	5,908	16	15	1
Mount Ephraim	4,615	14	13	1
Mount Holly Township	9,968	26	23	3
Mount Laurel Township	46,518	83	76	7
Mount Olive Township	28,970	63	52	11
Mullica Township	5,798	16	15	1
National Park	3,080	46	43	3
Neptune City	4,620	19	18	1
Neptune Township	28,491	84	74	10
Netcong	3,973	14	13	1
Newark	304,311	1,323	1,118	205
New Brunswick	55,971	155	135	20
Newfield	1,806	40	37	3
New Hanover Township	6,507	3	3	0
New Milford	16,897	42	37	5
New Providence	13,548	26	24	2
Newton	8,593	27	22	5
North Arlington	16,259	39	32	7
North Bergen Township	58,378	139	125	14
North Brunswick Township	43,419	100	82	18
North Caldwell	6,556	20	16	4
Northfield	8,435	24	22	2
North Haledon	8,788	29	25	4
North Hanover Township	7,925	11	10	1
North Plainfield	22,394	55	46	9
Northvale	4,759	15	15	0
North Wildwood	3,602	37	28	9
Norwood	5,565	18	17	1
Nutley Township	29,445	81	72	9
Oakland	12,616	33	27	6
Oaklyn	3,908	14	13	1
Ocean City	11,258	78	69	9
Ocean Gate	2,000	13	12	1
Oceanport	6,119	16	15	1
Ocean Township, Monmouth County	28,119	76	61	15
Ocean Township, Ocean County	9,031	32	22	10
Ogdensburg	2,286	7	7	0
Old Bridge Township	67,876	122	99	23
Old Tappan	5,799	15	14	1
Oradell	8,139	23	22	1
Orange City	33,615	160	134	26
Palisades Park	19,991	41	38	3
Palmyra	7,418	16	15	1
Paramus	26,242	119	95	24
Park Ridge	10,040	45	23	22
Parsippany-Troy Hills Township	56,193	118	88	30
Passaic	69,003	184	160	24
Paterson	156,292	480	412	68
Paulsboro	6,292	22	20	2
Peapack-Gladstone	2,588	10	9	1
Pemberton Borough	1,363	6	6	0
Pemberton Township	26,759	51	46	5
Pennington	2,790	7	7	0
Pennsauken Township	37,198	89	85	4
Penns Grove	4,821	15	14	1
Pennsville Township	12,651	24	22	2
Pequannock Township	15,560	37	32	5
Perth Amboy	55,229	155	126	29
Phillipsburg	15,374	39	38	1
Pine Beach	2,201	7	6	1
Pine Hill	10,689	26	24	2
Piscataway Township	61,170	97	81	16
Pitman	8,837	17	16	1
Plainfield	55,494	167	139	28
Plainsboro Township	23,798	46	35	11
Pleasantville	20,603	63	55	8
Plumsted Township	8,582	15	14	1
Pohatcong Township	3,270	16	15	1
Point Pleasant	19,501	42	32	10
Point Pleasant Beach	4,903	31	25	6
Pompton Lakes	10,875	29	24	5
Princeton	30,797	59	51	8
Prospect Park	6,225	18	18	0
Rahway	30,149	93	78	15
Ramsey	14,621	38	31	7
Randolph Township	26,500	42	36	6
Raritan	10,609	22	21	1
Raritan Township	24,202	45	42	3
Readington Township	16,348	30	24	6
Red Bank	12,927	45	38	7

Table 78. Full-Time Law Enforcement Employees, by Selected State and City, 2022—Continued

(Number.)

State/city	Population	Total law enforcement employees	Total officers	Total civilians
Ridgefield	11,368	29	27	2
Ridgefield Park	13,067	45	38	7
Ridgewood	26,485	53	48	5
Ringwood	11,456	24	19	5
Riverdale	4,105	22	17	5
River Edge	11,950	27	24	3
Riverside Township	7,975	19	19	0
Riverton	2,755	6	6	0
River Vale Township	9,789	25	24	1
Robbinsville Township	15,303	36	28	8
Rochelle Park Township	5,841	27	23	4
Rockaway	6,589	18	17	1
Rockaway Township	26,377	62	51	11
Rockleigh	395	15	15	0
Roseland	6,149	23	22	1
Roselle	22,257	64	53	11
Roselle Park	13,825	36	34	2
Roxbury Township	23,293	43	42	1
Rumson	7,228	18	17	1
Runnemede	8,283	18	17	1
Rutherford	18,592	43	41	2
Saddle Brook Township	14,408	33	30	3
Saddle River	3,338	24	19	5
Salem	5,319	23	22	1
Sayreville	44,981	106	89	17
Scotch Plains Township	24,490	52	49	3
Sea Bright	1,453	11	11	0
Sea Girt	1,885	13	12	1
Sea Isle City	2,135	31	22	9
Seaside Heights	2,507	30	27	3
Seaside Park	1,486	14	13	1
Secaucus	20,519	94	78	16
Ship Bottom	1,135	15	13	2
Shrewsbury	4,188	21	16	5
Somerdale	5,531	19	18	1
Somers Point	10,467	36	29	7
Somerville	12,759	36	34	2
South Amboy	9,277	33	27	6
South Bound Brook	4,784	14	13	1
South Brunswick Township	46,442	111	87	24
South Hackensack Township	2,668	21	20	1
South Orange Village	18,029	51	45	6
South Plainfield	24,211	72	58	14
South River	15,877	42	32	10
South Toms River	3,752	12	11	1
Sparta Township	20,348	46	33	13
Spotswood	8,041	29	25	4
Springfield Township, Burlington County	3,222	11	10	1
Springfield Township, Union County	16,860	48	44	4
Spring Lake	2,807	14	14	0
Spring Lake Heights	4,888	15	15	0
Stafford Township	30,365	84	59	25
Stanhope	3,572	10	9	1
Stone Harbor	792	19	17	2
Stratford	6,954	15	15	0
Summit	22,414	52	48	4
Surf City	1,302	11	11	0
Teaneck Township	42,128	108	92	16
Tenafly	15,109	39	34	5
Tewksbury Township	5,918	14	13	1
Tinton Falls	19,556	44	42	2
Toms River Township	99,239	210	162	48
Totowa	10,813	33	28	5
Trenton	90,313	338	270	68
Tuckerton	3,682	14	13	1
Union Beach	5,732	22	19	3
Union City	63,312	190	165	25
Union Township	59,622	202	143	59
Upper Saddle River	8,248	21	17	4
Ventnor City	9,226	46	35	11
Vernon Township	22,623	41	32	9
Verona	14,272	35	29	6
Vineland	61,110	169	141	28
Voorhees Township	31,090	65	55	10
Waldwick	10,055	26	21	5
Wallington	11,749	21	21	0
Wall Township	26,458	84	65	19
Wanaque	11,089	29	24	5
Warren Township	15,747	38	31	7
Washington Township, Bergen County	9,225	29	24	5
Washington Township, Gloucester County	49,625	86	80	6
Washington Township, Morris County	18,172	35	32	3
Washington Township, Warren County	6,539	29	28	1
Watchung	6,468	34	28	6
Waterford Township	10,393	27	26	1

Table 78. Full-Time Law Enforcement Employees, by Selected State and City, 2022—Continued

(Number.)

State/city	Population	Total law enforcement employees	Total officers	Total civilians
Wayne Township	53,828	156	131	25
Weehawken Township	17,499	77	60	17
Westampton Township	9,099	26	24	2
West Amwell Township	3,033	7	7	0
West Caldwell Township	10,756	31	27	4
West Deptford Township	22,521	46	43	3
Westfield	30,628	76	61	15
West Long Branch	8,525	22	21	1
West Milford Township	24,373	52	45	7
West New York	52,021	136	125	11
West Orange	47,722	109	96	13
Westville	4,337	14	13	1
West Wildwood	541	7	7	0
West Windsor Township	29,452	61	49	12
Westwood	11,149	33	28	5
Wharton	7,225	26	24	2
Wildwood	5,105	49	39	10
Wildwood Crest	3,079	32	29	3
Willingboro Township	31,795	67	58	9
Winfield Township	1,395	10	10	0
Winslow Township	39,881	85	79	6
Woodbridge Township	102,980	276	213	63
Woodbury	10,108	30	27	3
Woodbury Heights	3,122	6	5	1
Woodcliff Lake	6,058	21	20	1
Woodland Park	13,171	36	31	5
Woodlynne	2,888	8	7	1
Wood-Ridge	10,057	24	21	3
Woodstown	3,692	10	9	1
Woolwich Township	13,625	33	31	2
Wyckoff Township	17,544	27	26	1
NEW MEXICO				
Alamogordo	31,946	75	46	29
Albuquerque	560,557	1,483	899	584
Angel Fire	1,215	5	4	1
Anthony	8,631	14	13	1
Artesia	12,084	41	26	15
Aztec	6,130	16	14	2
Bayard	2,070	5	4	1
Belen	7,460	22	21	1
Bernalillo	9,977	26	23	3
Bloomfield	7,335	27	22	5
Bosque Farms	4,099	14	13	1
Capitan	1,414	5	4	1
Carlsbad	31,532	101	69	32
Carrizozo	976	2	1	1
Cimarron	814	2	2	0
Clayton	2,779	13	5	8
Cloudcroft	786	4	4	0
Clovis	37,734	79	58	21
Corrales	8,652	16	13	3
Deming	14,883	35	32	3
Dexter	1,065	5	4	1
Edgewood	6,125	12	11	1
Espanola	10,460	39	28	11
Estancia	1,515	5	2	3
Eunice	2,931	12	10	2
Farmington	46,249	161	112	49
Gallup	21,228	62	49	13
Grants	9,199	18	16	2
Hagerman	974	5	4	1
Hatch	1,554	10	9	1
Hobbs	38,912	119	70	49
Hope	106	1	1	0
Hurley	1,232	4	3	1
Jal	2,099	16	8	8
Las Cruces	114,102	256	186	70
Las Vegas	13,151	41	25	16
Logan	966	4	4	0
Lordsburg	2,229	12	9	3
Los Alamos	19,227	69	31	38
Los Lunas	18,366	45	41	4
Loving	1,290	5	3	2
Lovington	11,179	26	21	5
Magdalena	795	3	3	0
Mesilla	1,788	9	7	2
Milan	2,567	8	6	2
Moriarty	1,973	11	9	2
Peralta	3,432	7	6	1
Questa	1,746	3	2	1
Raton	6,063	14	8	6
Red River	541	9	4	5
Rio Rancho	107,435	197	126	71
Roswell	47,625	112	90	22

Table 78. Full-Time Law Enforcement Employees, by Selected State and City, 2022—Continued

(Number.)

State/city	Population	Total law enforcement employees	Total officers	Total civilians
Ruidoso	7,846	33	20	13
Ruidoso Downs	2,664	12	8	4
Santa Clara	1,588	5	3	2
Santa Fe	88,705	179	142	37
Santa Rosa	2,846	15	9	6
San Ysidro	166	2	2	0
Silver City	9,468	35	30	5
Socorro	8,281	14	13	1
Springer	945	3	3	0
Sunland Park	17,441	27	25	2
Taos	6,613	24	20	4
Taos Ski Valley	79	4	4	0
Tatum	683	7	5	2
Texico	928	1	1	0
Truth or Consequences	6,060	15	10	5
Tucumcari	5,162	11	9	2
Tularosa	2,664	12	6	6
NEW YORK				
Addison Town and Village	2,349	3	3	0
Akron Village	2,889	1	1	0
Albany	98,104	373	294	79
Albion Village	5,620	14	13	1
Alfred Village	3,777	5	5	0
Allegany Village	1,571	3	3	0
Altamont Village	1,652	11	11	0
Amherst Town	123,527	187	154	33
Amityville Village	9,542	26	25	1
Amsterdam	18,199	43	39	4
Andover Village	904	1	1	0
Arcade Village	1,975	6	6	0
Ardsley Village	4,944	20	20	0
Asharoken Village	619	3	3	0
Attica Village	2,497	5	5	0
Auburn	26,531	74	63	11
Avon Village	3,328	5	5	0
Baldwinsville Village	7,712	14	13	1
Ballston Spa Village	5,088	4	4	0
Batavia	15,438	35	32	3
Bath Village	5,493	12	11	1
Beacon	13,729	36	32	4
Bedford Town	16,989	43	38	5
Bethlehem Town	34,872	52	37	15
Binghamton	47,259	135	124	11
Blooming Grove Town	13,073	19	18	1
Bolivar Village	1,023	1	1	0
Briarcliff Manor Village	7,391	19	19	0
Brighton Town	36,380	45	39	6
Brockport Village	6,924	14	13	1
Bronxville Village	6,444	21	21	0
Buchanan Village	2,227	7	7	0
Buffalo	275,710	921	759	162
Cairo Town	6,853	2	2	0
Caledonia Village	2,068	1	1	0
Cambridge Village	1,799	3	3	0
Camden Village	2,148	1	1	0
Camillus Town and Village	25,268	26	24	2
Canajoharie Village	2,085	5	5	0
Canandaigua	10,479	25	23	2
Canastota Village	4,541	4	4	0
Canisteo Village	2,179	2	2	0
Canton Village	7,046	10	9	1
Carmel Town	33,868	39	32	7
Carthage Village	3,328	4	4	0
Catskill Village	3,884	16	14	2
Cayuga Heights Village	3,977	8	7	1
Cazenovia Village	2,697	6	5	1
Central Square Village	1,843	6	6	0
Centre Island Village	394	7	7	0
Cheektowaga Town	79,606	156	121	35
Chester Town	8,571	15	15	0
Chester Village	4,079	15	14	1
Cicero Town	29,252	19	18	1
Clarkstown Town	80,487	188	164	24
Clayton Village	1,735	8	6	2
Cobleskill Village	4,206	11	11	0
Coeymans Town	7,161	3	2	1
Cohoes	17,890	34	32	2
Colchester Town	1,809	2	2	0
Colonie Town	81,035	159	114	45
Cooperstown Village	1,863	3	3	0
Corning	10,900	24	20	4
Cornwall-on-Hudson Village	3,056	3	3	0
Cornwall Town	9,840	11	9	2
Cortland	17,061	43	41	2

Table 78. Full-Time Law Enforcement Employees, by Selected State and City, 2022—Continued

(Number.)

State/city	Population	Total law enforcement employees	Total officers	Total civilians
Crawford Town	9,179	12	11	1
Croton-on-Hudson Village	8,114	22	20	2
Cuba Town	3,115	6	6	0
Dansville Village	4,332	6	6	0
Deerpark Town	7,531	6	6	0
Delhi Village	2,912	5	5	0
Depew Village	14,974	37	28	9
DeWitt Town	25,623	45	41	4
Dobbs Ferry Village	11,361	28	26	2
Dolgeville Village	2,028	4	4	0
Dryden Village	1,930	4	4	0
Dunkirk	12,530	38	37	1
East Aurora-Aurora Town	13,936	21	17	4
Eastchester Town	20,277	48	46	2
East Fishkill Town	29,769	33	26	7
East Greenbush Town	16,558	33	24	9
East Hampton Town	25,765	90	63	27
East Hampton Village	1,531	30	26	4
East Rochester Village	6,212	10	9	1
Eden Town	7,504	2	2	0
Ellicott Town	5,350	13	13	0
Ellicottville	1,306	5	5	0
Elmira	26,237	78	68	10
Elmira Heights Village	3,823	9	9	0
Elmira Town	5,645	5	5	0
Elmsford Village	5,114	23	20	3
Endicott Village	13,397	34	32	2
Evans Town	15,117	28	20	8
Fairport Village	5,378	11	10	1
Fallsburg Town	13,890	20	20	0
Floral Park Village	16,000	31	20	11
Florida Village	2,931	1	1	0
Fort Edward Village	3,145	5	5	0
Fort Plain Village	2,028	3	3	0
Frankfort Town	4,614	6	6	0
Frankfort Village	2,307	4	4	0
Franklinville Village	1,674	3	3	0
Fredonia Village	9,763	20	16	4
Freeport Village	44,003	116	103	13
Fulton City	11,292	35	34	1
Garden City Village	22,929	65	51	14
Gates Town	28,772	34	32	2
Geddes Town	10,323	20	17	3
Geneseo Village	8,123	9	9	0
Geneva	12,365	28	27	1
Glen Cove	28,004	57	53	4
Glens Falls	14,639	27	25	2
Glenville Town	22,061	27	26	1
Gloversville	15,030	33	31	2
Goshen Town	8,679	6	6	0
Goshen Village	5,777	23	20	3
Gouverneur Village	3,587	9	6	3
Granville Village	2,413	3	3	0
Great Neck Estates Village	2,919	17	14	3
Greece Town	95,525	108	96	12
Greenburgh Town	45,094	142	115	27
Greene Village	1,448	1	1	0
Greenwich Village	1,666	1	1	0
Greenwood Lake Village	3,042	7	5	2
Groton Village	2,183	1	1	0
Guilderland Town	35,488	54	40	14
Hamburg Town	47,939	65	62	3
Hamburg Village	9,787	15	14	1
Hamilton Village	3,726	4	4	0
Hammondsport Village	590	1	1	0
Hancock Village	914	1	1	0
Harriman Village	2,680	7	7	0
Harrison Town	28,928	83	71	12
Hastings-on-Hudson Village	8,381	19	19	0
Haverstraw Town	38,927	73	67	6
Hempstead Village	58,469	151	122	29
Herkimer Village	7,289	19	19	0
Highland Falls Village	3,728	9	6	3
Holley Village	1,718	2	2	0
Homer Village	3,127	6	5	1
Hoosick Falls Village	3,191	1	1	0
Hornell	8,088	23	22	1
Horseheads Village	6,401	10	9	1
Hudson	5,907	27	27	0
Hudson Falls Village	7,370	11	11	0
Hunter Town	3,083	3	3	0
Huntington Bay Village	1,433	5	5	0
Hyde Park Town	21,071	21	17	4
Ilion Village	7,629	17	14	3
Inlet Town	369	2	2	0

Table 78. Full-Time Law Enforcement Employees, by Selected State and City, 2022—Continued
(Number.)

State/city	Population	Total law enforcement employees	Total officers	Total civilians
Irondequoit Town	50,090	63	55	8
Irvington Village	6,449	25	23	2
Ithaca	31,576	60	52	8
Jamestown	28,208	71	61	10
Johnson City Village	15,107	45	41	4
Johnstown	8,139	25	24	1
Kenmore Village	14,995	29	25	4
Kensington Village	1,221	6	6	0
Kent Town	12,943	24	19	5
Kings Point Village	5,530	20	17	3
Kingston	24,203	79	72	7
Lackawanna	19,692	51	44	7
Lake Placid Village	2,235	14	12	2
Lake Success Village	2,808	22	19	3
Lakewood-Busti	7,434	12	11	1
Lancaster Town	39,305	66	51	15
Larchmont Village	6,448	24	23	1
Le Roy Village	4,263	10	9	1
Lewisboro Town	11,912	2	2	0
Lewiston Town and Village	15,781	15	14	1
Liberty Village	5,367	20	18	2
Little Falls	4,558	15	14	1
Liverpool Village	2,280	4	4	0
Lloyd Harbor Village	3,569	14	13	1
Lloyd Town	11,372	11	9	2
Lockport	20,642	49	47	2
Long Beach	34,651	83	66	17
Lowville Village	3,332	6	6	0
Lynbrook Village	20,200	56	49	7
Macedon Town and Village	9,247	6	5	1
Malone Village	5,274	13	13	0
Malverne Village	8,477	23	22	1
Mamaroneck Town	12,479	39	38	1
Mamaroneck Village	19,674	56	49	7
Manlius Town	25,533	39	35	4
Marlborough Town	8,900	11	8	3
Massena Village	10,165	27	22	5
Maybrook Village	3,184	4	4	0
Mechanicville	5,158	8	8	0
Medina Village	5,978	14	13	1
Menands Village	4,478	16	13	3
Middleport Village	1,710	4	4	0
Middletown	30,538	80	71	9
Mohawk Village	2,397	4	4	0
Monroe Village	9,552	22	19	3
Montgomery Town	9,563	16	13	3
Montgomery Village	3,816	3	3	0
Monticello Village	7,386	20	17	3
Moriah Town	4,672	1	1	0
Mount Hope Town	6,405	4	4	0
Mount Morris Village	2,817	4	4	0
Mount Pleasant Town	25,892	56	49	7
Mount Vernon	71,690	236	189	47
Newark Village	8,939	15	14	1
New Berlin Town	1,588	1	1	0
Newburgh	28,819	74	60	14
Newburgh Town	32,207	59	49	10
New Castle Town	17,777	39	37	2
New Hartford Town and Village	20,415	24	22	2
New Paltz Town and Village	14,732	30	26	4
New Rochelle	82,628	216	175	41
New Windsor Town	28,008	55	43	12
New York	8,236,567	48,584	34,012	14,572
New York Mills Village	3,197	5	5	0
Niagara Falls	48,129	160	146	14
Niagara Town	7,808	8	7	1
Niskayuna Town	23,403	30	27	3
North Castle Town	12,124	34	32	2
North Greenbush Town	13,323	17	15	2
Northport Village	7,352	21	18	3
North Syracuse Village	6,676	13	12	1
North Tonawanda	30,358	54	51	3
Norwich	6,716	21	21	0
Ocean Beach Village	171	4	4	0
Ogdensburg	9,933	23	20	3
Ogden Town	20,293	14	11	3
Old Brookville Village	2,070	15	14	1
Old Westbury Village	4,229	31	26	5
Olean	13,671	41	35	6
Oneida	10,268	32	28	4
Oneonta City	12,447	28	22	6
Orangetown Town	39,317	96	88	8
Orchard Park Town	29,775	46	36	10
Ossining Village	26,980	59	53	6
Owego Village	3,889	8	7	1

Table 78. Full-Time Law Enforcement Employees, by Selected State and City, 2022—Continued

(Number.)

State/city	Population	Total law enforcement employees	Total officers	Total civilians
Oxford Village	1,327	2	2	0
Oyster Bay Cove Village	4,192	14	14	0
Palmyra Village	3,286	6	5	1
Peekskill	26,178	62	53	9
Pelham Manor Village	5,587	25	25	0
Pelham Village	7,115	27	24	3
Penn Yan Village	5,036	14	13	1
Perry Village	3,664	6	6	0
Piermont Village	2,776	8	8	0
Plattsburgh City	19,904	45	38	7
Pleasantville Village	7,324	22	22	0
Port Chester Village	30,804	61	60	1
Port Dickinson Village	1,697	5	4	1
Port Jervis	8,738	33	32	1
Portville Village	900	1	1	0
Port Washington	20,071	70	62	8
Poughkeepsie	32,202	109	83	26
Pound Ridge Town	4,929	2	1	1
Pulaski Village	2,411	1	1	0
Quogue Village	1,687	15	14	1
Ramapo Town	107,404	124	105	19
Red Hook Village	1,956	4	4	0
Rensselaer City	9,292	33	23	10
Riverhead Town	36,064	106	89	17
Rochester	210,270	741	663	78
Rockville Centre Village	25,703	65	57	8
Rome	31,834	75	73	2
Rosendale Town	5,813	2	2	0
Rotterdam Town	30,569	41	39	2
Rye	16,243	42	37	5
Rye Brook Village	9,863	25	24	1
Sag Harbor Village	2,792	13	12	1
Salamanca	5,837	16	16	0
Sands Point Village	2,716	20	20	0
Saranac Lake Village	4,805	9	9	0
Saugerties Town	19,323	27	23	4
Scarsdale Village	17,747	48	43	5
Schenectady	67,101	179	154	25
Schodack Town	11,424	9	9	0
Scotia Village	7,253	14	13	1
Seneca Falls Town	8,894	20	18	2
Shandaken Town	2,896	3	3	0
Shawangunk Town	13,680	5	5	0
Shelter Island Town	3,293	14	12	2
Sherrill	3,001	3	3	0
Sidney Village	3,707	8	8	0
Skaneateles Village	2,546	5	4	1
Sleepy Hollow Village	12,088	30	30	0
Solvay Village	6,574	15	14	1
Southampton Town	59,691	140	101	39
Southampton Village	4,636	46	31	15
South Glens Falls Village	3,781	4	4	0
Southold Town	21,347	73	55	18
Spring Valley Village	33,044	62	57	5
Stony Point Town	14,749	27	26	1
Suffern Village	11,383	21	21	0
Syracuse	145,179	454	373	81
Tarrytown Village	11,587	37	33	4
Ticonderoga Town	4,739	7	7	0
Tonawanda	14,988	35	29	6
Tonawanda Town	56,698	143	99	44
Troy	50,106	145	136	9
Trumansburg Village	1,745	2	2	0
Tuckahoe Village	6,887	26	23	3
Tupper Lake Village	3,254	7	7	0
Tuxedo Park Village	639	4	3	1
Tuxedo Town	3,125	7	7	0
Ulster Town	12,803	25	22	3
Utica	63,906	181	165	16
Vestal Town	29,553	44	40	4
Walden Village	6,819	15	12	3
Wallkill Town	30,804	52	50	2
Wappingers Falls Village	6,077	6	4	2
Warsaw Village	3,632	5	5	0
Washingtonville Village	5,804	16	14	2
Waterford Town and Village	8,228	10	9	1
Waterloo Village	4,841	8	7	1
Watertown	24,558	64	61	3
Watervliet	10,194	28	26	2
Waverly Village	4,233	10	9	1
Webb Town	1,804	10	9	1
Webster Town and Village	45,230	38	31	7
Weedsport Village	1,790	1	1	0
Wellsville Village	4,595	12	11	1
Westfield Village	2,951	7	7	0

Table 78. Full-Time Law Enforcement Employees, by Selected State and City, 2022—Continued

(Number.)

State/city	Population	Total law enforcement employees	Total officers	Total civilians
Westhampton Beach Village	2,190	15	14	1
West Seneca Town	45,119	77	64	13
Whitehall Village	2,478	4	4	0
White Plains	59,488	206	195	11
Whitesboro Village	3,599	5	5	0
Whitestown Town	8,605	7	7	0
Windham Town	1,769	1	1	0
Woodbury Town	11,705	24	20	4
Woodstock Town	6,322	10	10	0
Yonkers	208,100	703	620	83
Yorktown Town	35,529	67	58	9
Yorkville Village	2,590	3	3	0
NORTH CAROLINA				
Aberdeen	9,528	27	25	2
Ahoskie	4,830	20	18	2
Albemarle	16,819	52	37	15
Andrews	1,707	9	8	1
Angier	6,127	18	18	0
Apex	66,024	116	92	24
Archdale	12,002	32	27	5
Asheboro	27,275	74	63	11
Asheville	93,729	207	165	42
Atlantic Beach	1,420	15	14	1
Ayden	5,068	21	17	4
Badin	2,049	2	2	0
Bailey	565	1	1	0
Bakersville	455	1	1	0
Bald Head Island	273	28	27	1
Banner Elk	1,037	6	5	1
Beaufort	4,678	19	18	1
Beech Mountain	678	15	10	5
Belhaven	1,405	8	7	1
Belmont	15,297	50	43	7
Benson	4,246	19	18	1
Bessemer City	5,569	15	15	0
Bethel	1,394	4	4	0
Beulaville	1,109	6	6	0
Biltmore Forest	1,433	17	10	7
Biscoe	1,868	10	9	1
Black Creek	681	2	2	0
Black Mountain	8,476	24	22	2
Bladenboro	1,643	6	6	0
Blowing Rock	1,399	17	13	4
Boiling Spring Lakes	6,349	14	12	2
Boiling Springs	4,553	11	11	0
Boone	18,007	38	36	2
Boonville	1,190	5	5	0
Brevard	7,778	26	22	4
Bridgeton	345	1	1	0
Broadway	1,300	4	4	0
Bryson City	1,445	7	7	0
Bunn	353	3	2	1
Burgaw	3,138	15	15	0
Burlington	60,069	162	111	51
Burnsville	1,658	8	8	0
Butner	8,618	40	31	9
Candor	813	3	3	0
Canton	4,433	20	14	6
Cape Carteret	2,273	6	6	0
Carolina Beach	6,652	32	30	2
Carrboro	21,190	35	32	3
Carthage	2,839	11	10	1
Cary	178,600	220	177	43
Caswell Beach	405	4	4	0
Catawba	706	1	1	0
Chadbourn	1,534	6	5	1
Chapel Hill	60,984	111	86	25
Charlotte-Mecklenburg[1]	955,466	2,207	1,668	539
Cherryville	6,194	17	12	5
China Grove	4,477	12	12	0
Chocowinity	720	3	3	0
Claremont	1,712	9	9	0
Clayton	30,036	57	53	4
Cleveland	862	6	6	0
Clinton	8,004	33	28	5
Coats	2,219	8	8	0
Columbus	1,020	10	9	1
Concord	109,660	214	185	29
Conover	8,525	29	26	3
Conway	726	2	2	0
Cornelius	31,781	76	60	16
Cramerton	5,441	18	18	0
Creedmoor	5,095	20	16	4
Dallas	6,086	18	16	2

Table 78. Full-Time Law Enforcement Employees, by Selected State and City, 2022—Continued

(Number.)

State/city	Population	Total law enforcement employees	Total officers	Total civilians
Davidson	15,189	28	26	2
Dobson	1,386	10	10	0
Drexel	1,757	5	5	0
Duck	770	15	14	1
Dunn	8,426	49	42	7
Durham	286,377	540	428	112
East Bend	634	2	2	0
East Spencer	1,581	4	3	1
Eden	15,253	47	43	4
Edenton	4,400	19	15	4
Elizabeth City	18,751	56	43	13
Elizabethtown	3,115	15	14	1
Elkin	4,045	20	16	4
Elon	11,369	21	20	1
Emerald Isle	3,940	22	20	2
Enfield	1,838	3	2	1
Erwin	4,662	11	10	1
Fair Bluff	720	2	2	0
Fairmont	2,169	8	8	0
Farmville	4,495	20	15	5
Fayetteville	208,980	551	360	191
Fletcher	8,059	15	14	1
Forest City	7,353	31	29	2
Four Oaks	2,440	8	7	1
Foxfire Village	1,352	4	4	0
Franklin	4,289	14	13	1
Franklinton	2,664	9	9	0
Fremont	1,184	3	3	0
Fuquay-Varina	39,037	69	59	10
Garner	32,577	79	71	8
Garysburg	869	2	2	0
Gaston	973	1	1	0
Gastonia	81,937	187	159	28
Gibsonville	9,049	20	19	1
Glen Alpine	1,524	4	4	0
Goldsboro	32,464	88	75	13
Graham	17,377	46	42	4
Granite Falls	4,920	14	12	2
Granite Quarry	3,023	10	10	0
Greensboro	298,719	719	573	146
Greenville	89,363	222	175	47
Grifton	2,495	7	7	0
Hamlet	6,009	18	18	0
Havelock	17,108	37	27	10
Haw River	2,271	10	10	0
Henderson	14,806	47	40	7
Hendersonville	15,122	61	46	15
Hickory	43,756	142	112	30
Highlands	1,102	13	12	1
High Point	114,280	253	214	39
Hillsborough	9,732	30	29	1
Holden Beach	950	9	8	1
Holly Ridge	4,639	13	12	1
Holly Springs	45,406	91	75	16
Hope Mills	17,843	46	40	6
Hot Springs	534	1	1	0
Hudson	3,769	13	12	1
Huntersville	62,105	105	94	11
Indian Beach	227	3	3	0
Jackson	413	1	1	0
Jacksonville	72,570	176	133	43
Jefferson	1,523	6	5	1
Jonesville	2,310	10	9	1
Kannapolis	55,480	105	83	22
Kenansville	687	1	1	0
Kernersville	27,076	86	65	21
Kill Devil Hills	7,911	34	28	6
King	7,213	28	25	3
Kings Mountain	11,624	41	32	9
Kinston	19,342	67	56	11
Kitty Hawk	3,813	19	18	1
Knightdale	19,659	36	33	3
Kure Beach	2,134	13	12	1
Lake Lure	1,375	10	9	1
Lake Royale	2,561	8	8	0
Lake Waccamaw	1,262	4	4	0
Landis	3,732	9	9	0
Laurel Park	2,237	7	7	0
Laurinburg	15,199	38	36	2
Leland	28,203	46	43	3
Lenoir	18,160	68	50	18
Lexington	19,544	66	53	13
Liberty	2,686	11	10	1
Lilesville	405	2	1	1
Lillington	4,603	15	14	1

Table 78. Full-Time Law Enforcement Employees, by Selected State and City, 2022—Continued

(Number.)

State/city	Population	Total law enforcement employees	Total officers	Total civilians
Lincolnton	11,651	37	34	3
Littleton	556	3	3	0
Locust	4,691	13	13	0
Long View	5,148	18	18	0
Louisburg	3,098	17	16	1
Lowell	3,740	10	9	1
Lumberton	18,583	86	76	10
Madison	2,112	16	16	0
Maggie Valley	1,702	12	10	2
Magnolia	833	2	2	0
Maiden	3,743	19	18	1
Manteo	1,647	10	9	1
Marion	7,633	29	27	2
Marshall	802	4	4	0
Mars Hill	2,039	5	5	0
Marshville	2,603	8	8	0
Matthews	29,739	64	53	11
Maxton	2,110	10	6	4
Mayodan	2,419	14	14	0
Maysville	838	2	2	0
Mebane	18,956	41	37	4
Micro	497	2	2	0
Middlesex	913	5	5	0
Mint Hill	26,728	43	40	3
Misenheimer	647	5	5	0
Monroe	35,204	100	90	10
Montreat	871	5	5	0
Mooresville	52,762	112	88	24
Morehead City	9,810	43	41	2
Morganton	17,568	59	48	11
Morrisville	32,600	46	44	2
Mount Airy	10,511	43	32	11
Mount Gilead	1,176	7	7	0
Mount Holly	18,177	40	32	8
Mount Olive	4,027	15	14	1
Murfreesboro	2,490	7	6	1
Murphy	1,640	14	13	1
Nags Head	3,218	24	22	2
Nashville	5,699	21	20	1
Navassa	1,660	4	4	0
New Bern	31,614	109	85	24
Newland	719	6	6	0
Newport	4,564	10	10	0
Newton	13,252	37	28	9
Newton Grove	564	2	2	0
Norlina	947	2	2	0
North Topsail Beach	1,001	14	12	2
Northwest	853	2	2	0
North Wilkesboro	4,215	21	20	1
Norwood	2,434	11	10	1
Oakboro	2,188	8	8	0
Oak Island	9,272	25	23	2
Ocean Isle Beach	944	12	11	1
Old Fort	817	3	3	0
Oriental	900	2	2	0
Oxford	8,895	21	18	3
Parkton	499	2	2	0
Pembroke	2,803	14	11	3
Pikeville	705	4	4	0
Pilot Mountain	1,432	11	10	1
Pinebluff	1,522	4	4	0
Pinehurst	18,426	30	25	5
Pine Knoll Shores	1,397	9	9	0
Pine Level	2,218	3	3	0
Pinetops	1,172	10	6	4
Pineville	10,718	51	34	17
Pink Hill	455	2	2	0
Pittsboro	4,662	14	14	0
Plymouth	3,204	9	8	1
Polkton	1,872	1	1	0
Princeton	1,422	4	4	0
Raeford	4,725	19	18	1
Raleigh	470,829	784	637	147
Ramseur	1,753	6	6	0
Randleman	4,647	14	14	0
Ranlo	4,621	12	11	1
Red Springs	3,102	16	15	1
Reidsville	14,481	56	49	7
Richlands	2,325	7	6	1
Rich Square	847	4	3	1
River Bend	2,868	6	6	0
Roanoke Rapids	15,025	36	32	4
Robbins	1,220	5	5	0
Robersonville	1,236	5	5	0
Rockingham	8,865	32	30	2

Table 78. Full-Time Law Enforcement Employees, by Selected State and City, 2022—Continued

(Number.)

State/city	Population	Total law enforcement employees	Total officers	Total civilians
Rockwell	2,331	7	7	0
Rocky Mount	53,668	165	131	34
Rolesville	10,549	21	20	1
Rose Hill	1,356	5	5	0
Rowland	884	7	6	1
Roxboro	8,079	35	29	6
Rutherfordton	3,622	15	15	0
Salisbury	35,938	80	67	13
Saluda	620	3	3	0
Sanford	31,083	85	64	21
Scotland Neck	1,617	6	6	0
Seagrove	238	2	2	0
Selma	6,843	23	22	1
Seven Devils	325	6	6	0
Shallotte	4,453	17	16	1
Sharpsburg	1,693	5	5	0
Shelby	21,989	83	72	11
Siler City	7,969	14	12	2
Smithfield	12,042	35	31	4
Snow Hill	1,532	4	4	0
Southern Pines	16,388	50	37	13
Southern Shores	3,237	12	11	1
Southport	4,253	13	12	1
Sparta	1,716	7	7	0
Spencer	3,327	11	10	1
Spindale	4,165	9	9	0
Spring Hope	1,309	5	5	0
Spring Lake	11,603	23	21	2
Spruce Pine	2,227	11	11	0
Stallings	16,758	25	23	2
Stanfield	1,636	4	4	0
Stanley	4,046	7	7	0
Stantonsburg	743	3	3	0
Star	812	2	2	0
Statesville	29,454	99	66	33
Stoneville	1,318	4	4	0
St. Pauls	2,050	18	14	4
Sugar Mountain	376	6	6	0
Sunset Beach	4,322	18	17	1
Surf City	4,338	25	24	1
Swansboro	3,920	11	10	1
Sylva	2,633	15	14	1
Tabor City	3,646	10	9	1
Tarboro	10,492	34	27	7
Taylorsville	2,328	13	13	0
Taylortown	665	3	3	0
Thomasville	27,270	69	64	5
Topsail Beach	492	10	9	1
Trent Woods	3,981	6	6	0
Troutman	3,889	17	16	1
Troy	2,915	8	7	1
Tryon	1,584	9	7	2
Valdese	4,663	14	13	1
Vanceboro	854	4	4	0
Vass	1,003	4	4	0
Wadesboro	5,036	22	17	5
Wagram	633	1	1	0
Wake Forest	51,385	101	77	24
Wallace	3,296	16	15	1
Walnut Creek	1,086	3	3	0
Warrenton	861	5	4	1
Warsaw	2,668	15	14	1
Washington	9,614	38	27	11
Waxhaw	22,613	32	30	2
Waynesville	10,225	47	36	11
Weaverville	4,689	17	16	1
Weldon	1,414	6	6	0
Wendell	13,408	24	19	5
West Jefferson	1,237	7	7	0
Whispering Pines	5,235	11	9	2
Whitakers	623	2	2	0
White Lake	847	6	6	0
Whiteville	4,630	21	15	6
Wilkesboro	3,567	24	22	2
Williamston	5,047	22	20	2
Wilmington	119,159	345	235	110
Wilson	47,518	125	109	16
Wilson's Mills	2,767	11	11	0
Windsor	3,304	9	9	0
Wingate	3,945	8	7	1
Winston-Salem	251,295	533	404	129
Winterville	10,725	25	22	3
Woodfin	8,097	15	14	1
Woodland	534	1	1	0
Wrightsville Beach	2,396	22	21	1

Table 78. Full-Time Law Enforcement Employees, by Selected State and City, 2022—Continued

(Number.)

State/city	Population	Total law enforcement employees	Total officers	Total civilians
Yadkinville	2,790	13	12	1
Youngsville	2,197	11	10	1
Zebulon	9,003	23	22	1
NORTH DAKOTA				
Berthold	463	1	1	0
Beulah	3,032	7	6	1
Bismarck	74,604	157	127	30
Bowman	1,394	4	4	0
Burlington	1,255	2	2	0
Carrington	2,029	4	4	0
Cavalier	1,228	3	3	0
Devils Lake	7,212	21	19	2
Dickinson	24,577	69	49	20
Drayton	737	1	1	0
Dunseith	624	4	4	0
Ellendale	1,067	2	2	0
Emerado	449	1	1	0
Fargo	127,649	195	175	20
Garrison	1,435	3	3	0
Grafton	4,117	9	8	1
Grand Forks	58,620	105	89	16
Harvey	1,586	1	1	0
Hazen	2,271	4	4	0
Jamestown	15,772	31	27	4
Kenmare	912	1	1	0
Killdeer	892	6	6	0
Lamoure	759	1	1	0
Lincoln	4,387	8	8	0
Mandan	24,666	48	40	8
Medora	119	3	3	0
Minot	47,278	100	73	27
Napoleon	752	1	1	0
New Town	2,713	6	5	1
Northwood	946	1	1	0
Oakes	1,778	4	4	0
Powers Lake	377	1	1	0
Ray	666	1	1	0
Rolette	478	2	2	0
Rolla	1,173	4	4	0
Rugby	2,505	3	3	0
Stanley	2,327	5	5	0
Steele	657	1	1	0
Surrey	1,343	2	2	0
Thompson	1,086	1	1	0
Tioga	1,922	5	4	1
Valley City	6,547	15	13	2
Wahpeton	7,956	19	17	2
Watford City	5,513	30	24	6
West Fargo	39,987	83	70	13
Williston	25,513	94	79	15
Wishek	852	2	2	0
OHIO				
Ada	5,238	8	8	0
Akron	188,534	484	446	38
American Township	12,355	3	3	0
Amherst	12,993	32	23	9
Andover	958	3	3	0
Ansonia	1,149	2	2	0
Apple Creek	1,194	4	4	0
Archbold	4,484	12	11	1
Ashland	19,193	37	29	8
Ashville	4,696	8	8	0
Athens	24,220	33	25	8
Aurora	17,486	36	28	8
Austintown	35,462	64	41	23
Avon	25,560	54	46	8
Avon Lake	25,846	34	29	5
Baltimore	2,993	6	6	0
Bath Township, Summit County	9,922	30	22	8
Beavercreek	46,749	61	44	17
Beaver Township	6,716	17	13	4
Bellefontaine	14,065	37	30	7
Belpre	6,649	12	8	4
Berea	18,736	35	32	3
Bethel	2,646	7	6	1
Bexley	13,497	38	31	7
Blanchester	4,234	9	8	1
Blue Ash	13,314	45	37	8
Bluffton	4,256	9	9	0
Boston Heights	1,393	8	8	0
Botkins	1,167	2	2	0
Bratenahl	1,399	15	15	0
Brewster	2,107	10	9	1

Table 78. Full-Time Law Enforcement Employees, by Selected State and City, 2022—Continued

(Number.)

State/city	Population	Total law enforcement employees	Total officers	Total civilians
Brimfield Township	11,450	20	18	2
Brooklyn Heights	1,481	17	17	0
Brookville	5,945	10	9	1
Brunswick	35,235	52	40	12
Bryan	8,560	24	18	6
Burton	1,404	4	4	0
Butler Township	8,219	22	21	1
Cambridge	9,978	33	27	6
Campbell	7,687	14	13	1
Canfield	7,551	28	19	9
Canton	70,070	200	156	44
Carrollton	3,101	8	8	0
Carroll Township	2,093	3	3	0
Cedarville	4,333	5	5	0
Celina	10,881	23	18	5
Centerville	25,249	58	42	16
Chagrin Falls	4,084	13	12	1
Chardon	5,215	19	14	5
Cincinnati	307,761	1,097	986	111
Circleville	14,274	27	19	8
Cleveland	363,764	1,509	1,308	201
Cleveland Heights	44,105	95	90	5
Clinton Township	4,353	13	12	1
Coldwater	4,676	11	10	1
Colerain Township	58,548	61	54	7
Columbiana	6,806	19	15	4
Columbus	907,196	2,096	1,716	380
Copley Township	18,244	27	26	1
Cortland	7,090	12	11	1
Covington	2,576	7	6	1
Cuyahoga Falls	50,607	90	74	16
Danville	1,013	3	3	0
Dayton	137,084	406	346	60
Deer Park	5,302	14	10	4
Defiance	16,923	34	31	3
Delaware	44,042	62	53	9
Delhi Township	28,476	34	31	3
Delta	3,374	7	6	1
Doylestown	3,011	8	7	1
Dresden	1,655	2	2	0
Dublin	48,799	117	70	47
East Cleveland	13,418	45	33	12
East Liverpool	9,796	19	15	4
Eaton	8,347	17	16	1
Elida	1,859	2	2	0
Elmore	1,353	5	5	0
Englewood	13,338	32	23	9
Euclid	48,344	111	99	12
Fairborn	34,725	69	50	19
Fairfax	1,738	11	10	1
Fairfield	44,215	85	65	20
Fairfield Township	22,636	25	23	2
Fairlawn	7,665	35	25	10
Findlay	39,881	80	63	17
Forest Park	19,824	41	34	7
Fort Loramie	1,596	2	2	0
Fort Recovery	1,475	1	1	0
Fostoria	13,066	25	21	4
Franklin	11,604	33	26	7
Frazeysburg	1,355	2	2	0
Fremont	15,757	28	26	2
Gahanna	35,167	63	57	6
Galion	10,338	21	18	3
Gallipolis	3,296	12	11	1
Garfield Heights	29,022	67	53	14
Garrettsville	2,475	6	6	0
Gates Mills	2,231	18	17	1
Geneva	5,896	16	13	3
Genoa Township	26,447	30	28	2
Georgetown	4,453	8	8	0
Germantown	5,798	11	10	1
German Township, Montgomery County	2,924	7	6	1
Glenwillow	1,001	6	6	0
Glouster	1,611	2	2	0
Goshen Township, Clermont County	16,296	22	22	0
Goshen Township, Mahoning County	3,046	10	9	1
Grandview Heights	8,254	25	19	6
Granville	5,741	14	11	3
Greenhills	3,658	11	10	1
Green Springs	1,227	3	3	0
Green Township	59,568	62	60	2
Grove City	42,248	81	61	20
Groveport	5,820	26	25	1
Hamilton	62,536	134	121	13
Harrison	13,097	26	24	2

Table 78. Full-Time Law Enforcement Employees, by Selected State and City, 2022—Continued

(Number.)

State/city	Population	Total law enforcement employees	Total officers	Total civilians
Hartville	3,331	7	7	0
Heath	10,641	27	19	8
Hebron	2,376	9	9	0
Hicksville	3,414	12	11	1
Highland Heights	8,536	31	24	7
Hills and Dales	248	3	3	0
Hillsboro	6,482	18	13	5
Hiram	956	3	3	0
Holland	1,797	8	8	0
Howland Township	17,177	17	16	1
Hubbard Township	5,319	7	7	0
Hudson	22,902	40	32	8
Hunting Valley	774	11	11	0
Ironton	10,312	15	14	1
Jackson	6,168	17	13	4
Jackson Township, Montgomery County	3,559	7	7	0
Johnstown	5,299	8	7	1
Kalida	1,436	1	1	0
Kent	27,723	57	43	14
Kenton	7,938	17	17	0
Kettering	57,107	109	81	28
Kirtland	6,899	13	12	1
Kirtland Hills	685	9	8	1
Lakemore	2,894	4	3	1
Lake Township	8,202	17	17	0
Lakewood	49,490	114	93	21
Lebanon	21,547	39	29	10
Leipsic	2,153	4	4	0
Lexington	4,863	15	11	4
Lima	35,633	93	75	18
Linndale	106	6	5	1
Lodi	2,765	7	6	1
Logan	7,377	21	17	4
London	10,646	23	19	4
Lorain	65,536	125	110	15
Lordstown	3,341	15	10	5
Louisville	9,497	13	13	0
Loveland	13,095	24	20	4
Lynchburg	1,526	2	2	0
Lyndhurst	13,682	38	29	9
Macedonia	12,248	33	23	10
Madison Township, Franklin County	18,785	19	18	1
Mansfield	47,845	117	80	37
Mantua	1,009	3	3	0
Marblehead	838	4	4	0
Mariemont	3,446	12	11	1
Marion	35,775	62	57	5
Mason	35,344	54	50	4
Massillon	32,320	36	34	2
McComb	1,551	1	1	0
Medina Township	9,286	12	11	1
Mentor	47,063	108	78	30
Mentor-on-the-Lake	7,072	14	10	4
Miamisburg	19,723	42	39	3
Miami Township, Clermont County	44,356	49	44	5
Miami Township, Montgomery County	30,750	42	38	4
Middletown	50,970	102	69	33
Midvale	660	2	2	0
Mifflin Township	2,563	3	3	0
Milan	1,363	3	3	0
Milford	6,456	21	19	2
Millersburg	3,187	8	8	0
Minerva Park	1,949	10	9	1
Minster	2,993	8	7	1
Mogadore	3,785	8	8	0
Monroe	17,817	48	38	10
Monroeville	1,287	5	5	0
Montgomery	10,766	23	20	3
Montpelier	3,865	10	9	1
Montville Township	13,304	16	16	0
Moraine	6,540	35	26	9
Mount Eaton	170	6	6	0
Mount Gilead	3,514	6	6	0
Mount Healthy	6,867	16	14	2
Mount Vernon	16,860	35	31	4
Munroe Falls	5,007	9	8	1
Napoleon	8,744	21	15	6
Navarre	1,832	5	5	0
New Albany	10,851	40	28	12
Newark	50,818	79	68	11
New Boston	2,267	11	8	3
New Bremen	2,948	8	8	0
Newburgh Heights	1,808	17	15	2
New Knoxville	917	1	1	0
New Lebanon	3,781	8	8	0

Table 78. Full-Time Law Enforcement Employees, by Selected State and City, 2022—Continued

(Number.)

State/city	Population	Total law enforcement employees	Total officers	Total civilians
New London	2,402	6	6	0
New Philadelphia	17,508	28	24	4
New Straitsville	653	2	1	1
Newton Falls	4,540	4	4	0
Newtown	2,650	9	8	1
Niles	18,344	44	37	7
North Olmsted	31,641	61	45	16
North Randall	939	11	11	0
North Ridgeville	36,968	45	38	7
North Royalton	30,687	52	36	16
Northwood	5,190	23	18	5
Norton	11,507	18	17	1
Norwalk	16,986	29	21	8
Oak Hill	1,399	4	4	0
Oakwood, Montgomery County	9,416	17	16	1
Oakwood, Paulding County	550	20	18	2
Oberlin	8,238	24	16	8
Obetz	6,074	20	19	1
Ontario	6,686	27	22	5
Orange Village	3,437	19	18	1
Oregon	19,800	45	43	2
Orrville	8,453	15	14	1
Orwell	1,530	5	5	0
Ottawa	4,397	9	9	0
Ottawa Hills	4,816	14	13	1
Ottoville	974	3	3	0
Owensville	795	4	3	1
Oxford	22,520	41	29	12
Oxford Township	2,279	4	4	0
Pandora	1,177	2	2	0
Parma	79,098	130	113	17
Parma Heights	20,306	38	34	4
Pataskala	18,283	24	23	1
Payne	1,180	2	2	0
Pepper Pike	6,834	16	16	0
Perkins Township	12,075	22	21	1
Perrysburg Township	13,666	33	26	7
Perry Township, Columbiana County	4,361	4	4	0
Perry Township, Montgomery County	3,256	6	6	0
Perry Township, Stark County	28,143	25	22	3
Pierce Township	15,277	20	18	2
Plain City	4,651	12	11	1
Plymouth	1,703	5	5	0
Poland Township	11,956	13	13	0
Pomeroy	1,546	5	4	1
Port Clinton	5,951	20	16	4
Portsmouth	17,896	53	42	11
Powell	14,407	22	20	2
Ravenna	11,299	36	23	13
Reading	11,177	23	20	3
Reynoldsburg	41,046	76	62	14
Richfield	3,695	26	18	8
Richmond Heights	10,546	22	19	3
Richwood	2,398	7	7	0
Riverside	24,322	30	28	2
Roaming Shores Village	1,589	4	4	0
Rockford	1,022	2	2	0
Rossford	6,324	18	17	1
Russell Township	5,447	11	10	1
Russellville	545	4	3	1
Salem	11,776	26	23	3
Saline Township	1,153	2	2	0
Sebring	4,154	12	8	4
Seven Hills	11,516	19	18	1
Shaker Heights	28,615	78	62	16
Sharon Township	2,331	8	8	0
Sharonville	13,879	49	39	10
Shawnee Hills	889	5	5	0
Shawnee Township	12,314	19	13	6
Sheffield Village	4,444	21	16	5
Shelby	9,303	16	13	3
Sidney	20,309	46	35	11
Silver Lake	2,486	8	7	1
Solon	23,680	59	50	9
South Euclid	21,360	39	35	4
South Russell	3,971	14	10	4
Spencerville	2,153	4	4	0
Springboro	19,431	34	30	4
Springdale	10,835	38	31	7
Springfield	58,725	128	114	14
Springfield Township, Hamilton County	35,363	54	49	5
Springfield Township, Summit County	14,025	17	15	2
Steubenville	17,869	43	38	5
St. Henry	2,608	4	4	0
Stow	34,244	53	45	8

Table 78. Full-Time Law Enforcement Employees, by Selected State and City, 2022—Continued

(Number.)

State/city	Population	Total law enforcement employees	Total officers	Total civilians
Streetsboro	17,908	34	27	7
Struthers	9,859	22	17	5
Sugarcreek	2,320	9	9	0
Sugarcreek Township	9,579	19	17	2
Sunbury	8,030	16	15	1
Swanton	3,853	9	8	1
Sylvania	19,055	37	32	5
Tallmadge	18,240	29	25	4
Toledo	266,984	648	591	57
Trenton	13,534	23	18	5
Troy	26,544	44	40	4
Twinsburg	19,402	47	33	14
Uhrichsville	5,177	10	10	0
Uniontown	3,304	15	10	5
Union Township, Clermont County	50,164	64	50	14
University Heights	13,701	32	30	2
Urbana	11,119	18	17	1
Valley View, Cuyahoga County	1,850	22	20	2
Vandalia	15,026	43	32	11
Van Wert	11,005	27	20	7
Vermilion	10,711	23	18	5
Vienna Township	3,974	8	8	0
Village of Leesburg	1,269	4	4	0
Wadsworth	24,546	36	27	9
Waite Hill	530	7	7	0
Walton Hills	1,997	16	12	4
Wapakoneta	9,742	23	18	5
Warren	38,943	64	59	5
Washington Court House	14,494	28	21	7
Waterville	6,022	5	5	0
Waterville Township	2,042	5	5	0
Wauseon	7,492	18	13	5
Waynesfield	735	1	1	0
Waynesville	2,778	8	7	1
Weathersfield	8,043	14	13	1
Wellington	4,842	12	9	3
Wellston	5,400	12	10	2
West Jefferson	4,293	20	15	5
West Lafayette	2,435	5	5	0
West Liberty	1,763	5	5	0
West Milton	4,742	9	9	0
West Salem	1,436	1	1	0
West Union	3,023	2	2	0
Whitehall	20,094	73	58	15
Whitehouse	5,042	12	12	0
Wickliffe	12,622	39	30	9
Williamsburg	2,590	6	6	0
Willoughby	23,853	57	43	14
Willowick	14,103	31	22	9
Wilmington	12,506	29	22	7
Wintersville	3,724	9	8	1
Wooster	26,750	48	44	4
Worthington	14,346	34	31	3
Wyoming	8,646	22	19	3
Xenia	25,513	71	45	26
Yellow Springs	3,710	13	8	5
Youngstown	59,944	174	130	44
Zanesville	24,703	84	53	31
OKLAHOMA				
Achille	411	1	1	0
Ada	16,946	35	32	3
Adair	732	4	3	1
Alex	494	1	1	0
Allen	788	1	1	0
Altus	18,757	54	41	13
Alva	4,991	7	6	1
Amber	429	2	2	0
Anadarko	5,865	21	20	1
Antlers	2,179	12	6	6
Apache	1,071	3	3	0
Arapaho	650	1	1	0
Arcadia	173	1	1	0
Ardmore	24,999	57	41	16
Arkoma	1,831	2	1	1
Atoka	3,210	19	17	2
Avant	298	1	1	0
Barnsdall	1,016	4	3	1
Bartlesville	37,479	90	70	20
Beaver	1,225	2	2	0
Beggs	1,178	9	2	7
Bernice	436	1	1	0
Bethany	20,322	37	27	10
Binger	436	2	2	0
Bixby	29,690	45	35	10

Table 78. Full-Time Law Enforcement Employees, by Selected State and City, 2022—Continued

(Number.)

State/city	Population	Total law enforcement employees	Total officers	Total civilians
Blackwell	6,089	21	14	7
Blair	730	1	1	0
Blanchard	9,488	5	5	0
Boise City	1,119	2	2	0
Bokchito	594	7	6	1
Bokoshe	404	2	2	0
Boley	950	2	1	1
Bristow	4,262	15	11	4
Broken Arrow	118,683	212	155	57
Broken Bow	4,270	21	17	4
Burns Flat	1,953	3	3	0
Cache	3,073	6	6	0
Caddo	1,048	4	4	0
Calera	2,998	11	10	1
Calumet	472	2	2	0
Calvin	321	3	2	1
Caney	204	4	3	1
Carnegie	1,428	14	6	8
Carney	558	2	2	0
Cashion	889	2	2	0
Catoosa	7,402	18	16	2
Chandler	2,913	12	7	5
Chattanooga	409	2	1	1
Checotah	3,077	12	9	3
Chelsea	1,991	6	4	2
Cherokee	1,507	3	3	0
Chickasha	16,031	29	19	10
Choctaw	12,228	17	16	1
Chouteau	2,095	14	7	7
Claremore	19,659	46	39	7
Clayton	557	6	2	4
Cleveland	3,243	6	6	0
Clinton	8,280	24	14	10
Coalgate	1,648	14	14	0
Colbert	1,066	5	4	1
Colcord	759	6	5	1
Collinsville	8,740	23	14	9
Comanche	1,396	7	6	1
Commerce	2,285	6	6	0
Cordell	2,770	3	3	0
Covington	460	1	1	0
Coweta	10,623	22	15	7
Crescent	1,355	6	4	2
Cushing	8,195	24	16	8
Cyril	855	2	2	0
Davenport	849	2	2	0
Davis	2,773	13	11	2
Del City	21,382	47	35	12
Depew	406	1	1	0
Dewar	761	2	2	0
Dewey	3,387	12	10	2
Dibble	943	4	3	1
Dickson	1,350	3	2	1
Disney	223	1	1	0
Drumright	2,539	7	7	0
Duke	395	1	1	0
Duncan	22,915	62	46	16
Durant	19,481	39	34	5
Earlsboro	608	3	3	0
Edmond	95,946	168	126	42
Eldorado	315	1	1	0
Elgin	3,782	7	7	0
Elk City	11,417	42	27	15
Elmore City	749	1	1	0
El Reno	18,385	44	31	13
Enid	49,990	101	75	26
Erick	978	2	1	1
Eufaula	2,777	11	11	0
Fairfax	1,109	3	1	2
Fairland	1,112	4	4	0
Fairview	2,658	5	5	0
Fletcher	1,232	2	2	0
Forest Park	1,042	2	2	0
Fort Gibson	3,818	14	13	1
Foyil	388	1	1	0
Frederick	3,560	5	3	2
Gans	250	2	2	0
Garber	710	1	1	0
Geary	969	13	6	7
Geronimo	1,171	1	1	0
Glenpool	13,983	32	22	10
Goodwell	1,059	2	2	0
Gore	941	9	9	0
Grandfield	934	2	2	0
Granite	1,753	4	4	0

Table 78. Full-Time Law Enforcement Employees, by Selected State and City, 2022—Continued

(Number.)

State/city	Population	Total law enforcement employees	Total officers	Total civilians
Grove	7,179	26	19	7
Guthrie	11,255	33	23	10
Guymon	12,292	20	18	2
Haileyville	706	2	2	0
Harrah	6,425	13	11	2
Hartshorne	1,904	7	5	2
Haskell	1,702	7	7	0
Haworth	283	1	1	0
Healdton	2,335	6	5	1
Heavener	3,009	10	9	1
Hennessey	2,154	9	5	4
Henryetta	5,619	17	12	5
Hinton	3,144	6	6	0
Hobart	3,344	14	7	7
Holdenville	5,788	4	4	0
Hollis	1,714	10	4	6
Hominy	3,244	7	4	3
Hooker	1,705	6	4	2
Howe	630	2	1	1
Hugo	5,215	22	15	7
Hulbert	516	3	3	0
Hydro	929	3	3	0
Idabel	7,043	25	19	6
Inola	1,884	6	5	1
Jay	2,410	16	10	6
Jenks	27,208	38	25	13
Jennings	290	1	1	0
Jones	2,991	10	10	0
Kansas	732	6	5	1
Kellyville	1,010	5	5	0
Keota	444	1	1	0
Kiefer	2,220	4	4	0
Kingfisher	4,832	13	12	1
Kingston	1,466	8	8	0
Kiowa	589	7	6	1
Konawa	1,299	3	3	0
Krebs	2,085	10	8	2
Lahoma	515	1	1	0
Langley	608	3	3	0
Langston	1,756	3	2	1
Laverne	1,170	8	3	5
Lawton	91,596	215	165	50
Lexington	1,989	10	6	4
Lindsay	2,895	11	5	6
Locust Grove	1,373	7	7	0
Lone Grove	5,109	8	6	2
Luther	1,491	7	7	0
Madill	4,031	11	11	0
Mangum	2,674	9	5	4
Mannford	3,279	12	8	4
Marble City	186	2	1	1
Marietta	2,847	10	8	2
Marlow	4,435	10	10	0
Maud	867	4	3	1
Maysville	1,091	4	3	1
McAlester	18,219	44	41	3
McLoud	4,265	10	10	0
Medford	882	2	2	0
Medicine Park	449	2	2	0
Meeker	1,017	5	5	0
Miami	12,904	41	30	11
Midwest City	57,826	123	101	22
Minco	1,523	4	4	0
Moore	63,421	108	100	8
Mooreland	1,143	5	3	2
Morris	1,304	4	4	0
Mounds	957	3	3	0
Mountain Park	312	2	2	0
Mountain View	729	2	2	0
Muldrow	3,350	13	8	5
Muskogee	36,713	92	84	8
Mustang	22,026	40	27	13
Newcastle	13,290	50	24	26
Newkirk	2,201	7	6	1
Nichols Hills	3,827	23	15	8
Nicoma Park	2,283	7	6	1
Ninnekah	800	3	2	1
Noble	7,746	19	13	6
Norman	128,878	221	159	62
North Enid	976	4	4	0
Nowata	3,480	9	6	3
Oilton	875	4	4	0
Okarche	1,163	7	6	1
Okeene	1,032	3	2	1
Okemah	3,045	13	8	5

Table 78. Full-Time Law Enforcement Employees, by Selected State and City, 2022—Continued

(Number.)

State/city	Population	Total law enforcement employees	Total officers	Total civilians
Oklahoma City	692,726	1,375	1,089	286
Okmulgee	11,408	23	20	3
Olustee	466	1	1	0
Oologah	1,316	5	5	0
Owasso	38,998	83	64	19
Panama	1,293	3	3	0
Paoli	586	1	1	0
Pauls Valley	6,066	15	13	2
Pawhuska	2,924	13	8	5
Pawnee	1,935	10	6	4
Perkins	3,318	8	8	0
Perry	4,537	20	14	6
Piedmont	8,318	12	10	2
Pocola	4,402	14	9	5
Ponca City	24,487	70	49	21
Pond Creek	893	1	1	0
Porum	608	5	4	1
Poteau	8,871	35	28	7
Prague	2,379	14	9	5
Pryor Creek	9,467	40	30	10
Purcell	6,647	24	19	5
Quinton	849	5	5	0
Ramona	540	5	4	1
Ratliff City	64	4	4	0
Rattan	280	2	2	0
Red Oak	518	1	1	0
Ringling	902	2	2	0
Roland	3,645	14	10	4
Rush Springs	1,008	4	4	0
Salina	1,078	5	4	1
Sallisaw	8,505	32	23	9
Sand Springs	20,006	43	33	10
Sapulpa	22,447	56	44	12
Savanna	619	9	7	2
Sawyer	344	1	1	0
Sayre	4,363	11	5	6
Seiling	827	1	1	0
Seminole	7,063	15	14	1
Shady Point	990	2	2	0
Shattuck	1,248	16	14	2
Shawnee	31,865	79	64	15
Skiatook	8,651	26	21	5
Snyder	1,241	2	2	0
South Coffeyville	680	4	4	0
Spavinaw	352	1	1	0
Spencer	3,890	6	5	1
Sperry	1,123	2	2	0
Spiro	2,135	5	5	0
Sterling	674	3	3	0
Stigler	2,699	11	7	4
Stillwater	48,384	112	78	34
Stilwell	3,651	20	14	6
Stratford	1,414	4	4	0
Stringtown	460	5	5	0
Stroud	2,772	14	9	5
Sulphur	4,841	15	13	2
Tahlequah	16,757	45	39	6
Talala	260	4	2	2
Talihina	919	8	6	2
Tecumseh	6,365	11	10	1
Texhoma	817	2	2	0
Thackerville	412	2	2	0
The Village	9,402	28	22	6
Thomas	1,126	1	1	0
Tipton	911	2	2	0
Tishomingo	2,974	9	8	1
Tonkawa	3,051	12	8	4
Tryon	389	2	1	1
Tulsa	410,135	1,015	824	191
Tupelo	322	2	2	0
Tushka	452	4	3	1
Tuttle	7,981	21	15	6
Tyrone	698	2	1	1
Union City	1,941	14	9	5
Valley Brook	650	8	8	0
Valliant	811	4	4	0
Velma	567	2	2	0
Verden	519	4	3	1
Verdigris	5,605	9	8	1
Vian	1,368	7	7	0
Vici	590	1	1	0
Vinita	5,170	14	10	4
Wagoner	8,071	17	13	4
Walters	2,361	6	5	1
Warner	1,554	5	5	0

Table 78. Full-Time Law Enforcement Employees, by Selected State and City, 2022—Continued

(Number.)

State/city	Population	Total law enforcement employees	Total officers	Total civilians
Warr Acres	10,439	31	25	6
Washington	695	6	2	4
Watonga	2,579	9	8	1
Watts	278	3	3	0
Waukomis	1,303	3	3	0
Waurika	1,921	7	5	2
Waynoka	716	4	3	1
Weatherford	11,891	38	27	11
Webbers Falls	340	5	5	0
Weleetka	794	6	4	2
Wellston	686	4	4	0
West Siloam Springs	989	10	9	1
Westville	1,361	12	7	5
Wetumka	1,152	5	4	1
Wewoka	3,077	8	8	0
Wilburton	2,321	7	6	1
Wilson	1,429	4	4	0
Wister	1,054	1	1	0
Woodward	11,876	27	23	4
Wright City	610	4	2	2
Wyandotte	497	10	9	1
Wynnewood	1,939	8	7	1
Wynona	369	1	1	0
Yale	1,089	7	4	3
Yukon	25,514	68	50	18
OREGON				
Albany	57,058	90	58	32
Ashland	21,797	30	25	5
Astoria	10,448	25	17	8
Baker City	10,259	18	15	3
Bandon	3,342	9	6	3
Banks	1,821	2	2	0
Beaverton	98,991	177	136	41
Bend	104,649	133	99	34
Black Butte	0	8	6	2
Boardman	4,005	12	11	1
Brookings	6,880	24	16	8
Burns	2,786	5	4	1
Canby	18,101	29	25	4
Cannon Beach	1,572	11	8	3
Carlton	2,243	4	4	0
Central Point	19,670	33	27	6
Coburg	1,314	5	5	0
Columbia City	1,958	2	2	0
Coos Bay	15,871	42	26	16
Coquille	4,042	8	7	1
Cornelius	14,107	16	15	1
Corvallis	60,031	109	72	37
Cottage Grove	10,622	26	13	13
Dallas	17,622	22	19	3
Eagle Point	10,035	14	12	2
Enterprise	2,144	5	4	1
Eugene	175,390	317	197	120
Florence	9,514	22	16	6
Forest Grove	26,016	37	31	6
Gaston	673	1	1	0
Gearhart	1,890	2	2	0
Gervais	2,597	8	7	1
Gladstone	11,946	18	15	3
Gold Beach	2,385	7	6	1
Grants Pass	39,519	86	53	33
Gresham	111,590	146	113	33
Hillsboro	106,345	177	132	45
Hood River	8,396	18	15	3
Hubbard	3,437	7	6	1
Independence	10,368	17	13	4
Jacksonville	3,011	8	7	1
John Day	1,691	5	4	1
Junction City	7,442	16	9	7
Keizer	38,958	48	42	6
King City	5,043	7	6	1
Klamath Falls	23,078	40	35	5
La Grande	13,174	34	19	15
Lake Oswego	40,044	73	47	26
Lebanon	19,456	38	27	11
Lincoln City	10,110	37	23	14
Madras	7,852	8	7	1
Malin	752	1	1	0
Manzanita	625	4	4	0
McMinnville	34,912	46	38	8
Medford	86,876	148	110	38
Milton-Freewater	7,119	16	11	5
Milwaukie	20,784	39	34	5
Molalla	10,179	20	17	3

Table 78. Full-Time Law Enforcement Employees, by Selected State and City, 2022—Continued

(Number.)

State/city	Population	Total law enforcement employees	Total officers	Total civilians
Monmouth	11,123	15	12	3
Mount Angel	3,403	7	6	1
Myrtle Creek	3,522	8	6	2
Myrtle Point	2,499	6	5	1
Newberg-Dundee	25,503	44	32	12
Newport	10,667	22	15	7
North Bend	10,256	20	17	3
North Plains	3,406	3	3	0
Nyssa	3,218	7	7	0
Oakridge	3,236	5	4	1
Ontario	11,638	30	25	5
Oregon City	37,192	53	44	9
Pendleton	16,780	28	24	4
Philomath	5,881	9	8	1
Phoenix	4,051	11	9	2
Pilot Rock	1,332	2	2	0
Portland	630,129	1,041	791	250
Prineville	11,586	34	23	11
Rainier	1,912	6	5	1
Redmond	37,472	61	51	10
Reedsport	4,346	13	7	6
Rogue River	2,427	6	5	1
Roseburg	23,973	42	37	5
Salem	179,661	221	176	45
Sandy	12,825	20	16	4
Scappoose	8,102	9	8	1
Seaside	7,357	27	18	9
Sherwood	20,102	33	29	4
Silverton	10,622	19	16	3
Springfield	62,217	101	55	46
Stanfield	2,153	1	1	0
Stayton	8,162	15	13	2
St. Helens	14,356	21	18	3
Sunriver	1,390	11	10	1
Sutherlin	8,662	19	15	4
Sweet Home	10,055	21	14	7
Talent	5,979	9	8	1
The Dalles	16,100	29	25	4
Tigard	56,550	85	70	15
Tillamook	5,314	13	11	2
Toledo	3,557	12	6	6
Tualatin	27,195	44	36	8
Turner	2,448	3	3	0
Umatilla	7,513	15	13	2
Vernonia	2,432	5	4	1
Warrenton	6,537	14	12	2
West Linn	26,842	29	23	6
Winston	5,701	13	12	1
Woodburn	26,117	46	36	10
Yamhill	1,165	6	3	3
PENNSYLVANIA				
Abington Township, Montgomery County	58,432	106	88	18
Adams Township, Butler County	14,954	17	17	0
Aldan	4,184	11	9	2
Aliquippa	9,041	10	9	1
Allegheny Township, Blair County	6,501	10	9	1
Allegheny Township, Westmoreland County	8,249	12	11	1
Allentown	125,917	235	216	19
Altoona	43,183	71	63	8
Amity Township	13,416	16	15	1
Archbald	7,377	9	9	0
Ashland	2,490	3	3	0
Ashley	2,596	5	5	0
Aspinwall	2,840	7	7	0
Aston Township	16,645	24	22	2
Athens	3,250	5	5	0
Avalon	4,639	6	6	0
Avoca	2,516	3	3	0
Avonmore Boro	889	1	1	0
Baldwin Borough	20,941	25	24	1
Baldwin Township	1,928	6	6	0
Bally	1,228	2	2	0
Bangor	5,149	8	8	0
Beaver	4,377	12	11	1
Beaver Falls	10,095	21	19	2
Bedford	2,835	4	4	0
Bedminster Township	7,514	9	8	1
Bell Acres	1,478	5	5	0
Bellefonte	6,032	11	10	1
Bellevue	8,091	14	13	1
Bellwood	1,798	3	3	0
Bensalem Township	62,782	129	103	26
Bentleyville	2,325	2	2	0
Berlin	1,976	2	2	0

Table 78. Full-Time Law Enforcement Employees, by Selected State and City, 2022—Continued

(Number.)

State/city	Population	Total law enforcement employees	Total officers	Total civilians
Bern Township	6,597	12	12	0
Berwick	10,360	19	18	1
Bessemer	1,058	1	1	0
Bethel Park	32,727	47	40	7
Bethel Township, Berks County	4,065	7	6	1
Bethlehem	75,619	149	145	4
Bethlehem Township	26,039	36	35	1
Biglerville	1,228	1	1	0
Birdsboro	5,103	8	7	1
Birmingham Township	4,070	6	6	0
Blairsville	3,230	5	5	0
Blair Township	4,719	5	5	0
Bloomsburg Town	12,601	23	18	5
Bonneauville	1,761	1	1	0
Brackenridge	3,159	4	4	0
Bradford	7,635	20	20	0
Bradford Township	4,800	5	5	0
Branch Township	2,406	2	2	0
Brecknock Township, Berks County	4,599	5	5	0
Briar Creek Township	3,014	5	5	0
Bridgeport	5,048	10	9	1
Bridgeville	4,675	10	8	2
Bridgewater	729	2	1	1
Brighton Township	8,762	13	13	0
Bristol	9,836	14	12	2
Bristol Township	54,196	70	61	9
Brockway	2,240	1	1	0
Brookhaven	8,200	13	12	1
Brookville	3,939	8	7	1
Brownsville	2,128	2	2	0
Bryn Athyn	1,264	4	4	0
Buckingham Township	20,941	21	19	2
Buffalo Township	7,974	9	9	0
Buffalo Valley Regional	12,610	17	16	1
Bushkill Township	8,690	16	15	1
Butler	13,112	24	23	1
Butler Township, Butler County	16,814	23	21	2
Butler Township, Luzerne County	9,819	11	10	1
Butler Township, Schuylkill County	5,619	5	5	0
Caernarvon Township, Berks County	4,306	10	9	1
Caln Township	14,351	16	15	1
Cambria Township	5,699	4	4	0
Cambridge Springs	2,491	3	3	0
Camp Hill	8,203	14	13	1
Canonsburg	9,636	18	17	1
Canton	1,720	1	1	0
Carbondale	8,803	9	9	0
Carlisle	20,237	31	29	2
Carnegie	7,915	14	13	1
Carrolltown	2,200	2	2	0
Carroll Township, Washington County	5,322	3	3	0
Carroll Township, York County	7,009	13	13	0
Carroll Valley	4,485	3	3	0
Castle Shannon	8,287	14	13	1
Catasauqua	6,489	11	10	1
Cecil Township	14,866	26	25	1
Center Township	11,589	20	19	1
Central Berks Regional	13,923	21	20	1
Central Bucks Regional	15,313	30	26	4
Chambersburg	22,383	39	35	4
Charleroi Regional	6,761	12	12	0
Chartiers Township	9,199	12	12	0
Cheltenham Township	37,355	68	63	5
Chester	32,382	80	77	3
Chippewa Township	8,214	9	8	1
Churchill	3,070	9	9	0
Clairton	6,020	12	12	0
Clarion	3,878	10	9	1
Clarks Summit	6,629	5	5	0
Clearfield	5,881	7	7	0
Cleona	2,009	5	5	0
Clifton Heights	6,760	13	12	1
Coaldale	2,435	3	3	0
Collegeville	4,981	8	8	0
Collier Township	8,939	17	16	1
Collingdale	8,775	14	13	1
Colonial Regional	18,933	27	25	2
Columbia	10,116	21	18	3
Conemaugh Township, Cambria County	1,913	1	1	0
Conemaugh Township, Somerset County	6,666	7	7	0
Conewago Township, Adams County	7,885	11	10	1
Conneaut Lake Regional	4,619	4	4	0
Connellsville	6,798	16	15	1
Conshohocken	9,262	21	19	2
Conway	3,596	5	5	0

Table 78. Full-Time Law Enforcement Employees, by Selected State and City, 2022—Continued

(Number.)

State/city	Population	Total law enforcement employees	Total officers	Total civilians
Coopersburg	2,496	7	7	0
Coplay	3,519	6	5	1
Coraopolis	5,405	15	11	4
Corry	6,123	11	10	1
Coudersport	2,336	3	3	0
Covington Township	2,236	4	4	0
Crafton	6,387	10	9	1
Cranberry Township	34,468	34	31	3
Cresson Township	2,777	1	1	0
Croyle Township	2,280	1	1	0
Cumberland Township, Adams County	7,064	10	10	0
Cumberland Township, Greene County	6,649	6	5	1
Cumru Township	15,622	27	26	1
Curwensville	2,533	3	3	0
Dallas	2,688	6	6	0
Dallas Township	9,198	14	13	1
Dalton	1,278	3	3	0
Danville	4,185	10	9	1
Darby	10,581	18	17	1
Darby Township	9,086	16	15	1
Darlington Township	1,777	2	2	0
Delmont	2,553	5	5	0
Derry	2,600	3	3	0
Derry Township, Dauphin County	24,896	38	36	2
Donegal Township	3,091	2	2	0
Donora	4,504	4	4	0
Dormont	8,018	14	13	1
Douglass Township, Berks County	3,706	6	6	0
Douglass Township, Montgomery County	10,648	12	11	1
Downingtown	8,302	27	24	3
Doylestown Township	17,799	22	20	2
Dublin Borough	2,181	2	2	0
DuBois	7,423	20	19	1
Duncansville	1,235	1	1	0
Dupont	2,552	4	4	0
Duryea	5,061	5	5	0
East Berlin	1,544	3	1	2
East Brandywine Township	10,191	19	17	2
East Cocalico Township	11,016	17	16	1
East Coventry Township	7,253	8	7	1
East Earl Township	8,142	5	5	0
Eastern Adams Regional	7,829	6	6	0
Eastern Berks Regional	10,264	15	13	2
Eastern Pike Regional	5,160	10	10	0
East Fallowfield Township	7,792	7	7	0
East Greenville	3,158	2	2	0
East Hempfield Township	26,625	38	34	4
East Lampeter Township	26,642	41	39	2
East Lansdowne	2,670	5	4	1
East Marlborough Township	7,741	2	2	0
East McKeesport	2,517	3	3	0
East Norriton Township	13,988	29	28	1
Easton	28,124	67	62	5
East Pennsboro Township	21,146	24	23	1
East Pikeland Township	8,478	11	11	0
East Taylor Township	2,385	1	1	0
Easttown Township	11,011	18	17	1
East Vincent Township	7,446	7	7	0
East Whiteland Township	15,617	24	23	1
Ebensburg	3,361	5	5	0
Economy	8,952	14	13	1
Eddystone	2,418	12	10	2
Edgewood	3,054	8	8	0
Edgeworth	1,637	5	3	2
Edinboro	4,864	9	9	0
Edwardsville	4,914	6	6	0
Elizabeth	1,780	1	1	0
Elizabethtown	11,531	20	18	2
Elizabeth Township	12,643	17	17	0
Elkland	1,809	2	2	0
Ellwood City	7,517	12	11	1
Emmaus	11,646	21	19	2
Emporium	1,898	2	2	0
Ephrata	34,448	36	32	4
Erie	93,363	207	183	24
Etna	3,345	7	7	0
Everett	1,761	4	2	2
Exeter Township, Berks County	25,492	35	33	2
Fairview Township, Luzerne County	4,697	6	6	0
Fairview Township, York County	17,772	20	18	2
Falls Township, Bucks County	34,541	57	51	6
Farrell	4,203	14	13	1
Fawn Township	2,142	2	2	0
Ferguson Township	19,360	25	23	2
Ferndale	1,520	1	1	0

Table 78. Full-Time Law Enforcement Employees, by Selected State and City, 2022—Continued

(Number.)

State/city	Population	Total law enforcement employees	Total officers	Total civilians
Findlay Township	6,511	27	20	7
Fleetwood	4,047	9	8	1
Forest City	4,866	2	2	0
Forks Township	16,440	25	24	1
Forty Fort	4,226	6	6	0
Foster Township, McKean County	3,906	5	5	0
Fountain Hill	4,838	11	10	1
Fox Chapel	5,208	11	11	0
Frackville	3,881	3	3	0
Franklin	5,989	20	16	4
Franklin Park	15,165	17	16	1
Franklin Township, Carbon County	4,469	5	5	0
Frazer Township	1,133	3	3	0
Freedom Township	2,985	3	3	0
Freeland	3,815	2	2	0
Freemansburg	2,850	4	4	0
Freeport	1,716	2	2	0
Galeton	976	1	1	0
Gallitzin	1,712	1	1	0
German Township	4,546	3	3	0
Gettysburg	7,407	13	12	1
Gilpin Township	2,380	4	4	0
Girard	2,969	4	4	0
Glenolden	7,119	11	10	1
Granville Township	4,626	10	8	2
Greencastle	4,200	6	6	0
Greenfield Township	2,273	2	2	0
Green Tree	4,809	9	9	0
Greenville	8,683	10	9	1
Grove City	7,824	13	12	1
Hampden Township	34,244	29	27	2
Hampton Township	18,105	22	20	2
Hanover	16,535	24	22	2
Harmar Township	3,059	8	8	0
Harmony Township	3,117	5	5	0
Harrisburg	50,201	165	129	36
Harrison Township	9,898	14	13	1
Hastings	4,083	2	2	0
Hatboro	8,228	19	16	3
Hatfield Township	22,227	31	29	2
Haverford Township	50,016	76	70	6
Hegins Township	3,363	1	1	0
Heidelberg	1,255	4	4	0
Hellam Township	10,910	13	12	1
Hellertown	6,095	8	8	0
Hemlock Township	4,792	9	9	0
Hempfield Township, Mercer County	3,686	8	7	1
Hermitage	16,089	33	30	3
Highspire	2,720	5	5	0
Hilltown Township	16,895	20	18	2
Hollidaysburg	5,522	10	8	2
Honey Brook	1,898	1	1	0
Hopewell Township	13,372	17	16	1
Horsham Township	26,539	47	40	7
Hughestown	1,334	2	2	0
Hughesville	2,130	3	3	0
Hummelstown	4,514	8	8	0
Huntingdon	6,859	13	12	1
Independence Township, Beaver County	2,203	2	2	0
Indiana	13,472	21	20	1
Indiana Township	7,293	10	10	0
Indian Lake	390	1	1	0
Ingram	3,296	4	4	0
Irwin	3,840	6	6	0
Jackson Township, Butler County	5,516	12	11	1
Jackson Township, Cambria County	4,176	5	5	0
Jackson Township, Luzerne County	4,815	9	9	0
Jeannette	8,636	14	13	1
Jefferson Hills Borough	12,314	23	21	2
Jenkins Township	4,389	5	5	0
Jenkintown	4,708	12	11	1
Jermyn	2,144	3	3	0
Jessup	4,512	6	6	0
Jim Thorpe	4,604	9	8	1
Johnsonburg	2,362	4	4	0
Johnstown	19,474	39	35	4
Kane	3,520	4	4	0
Kennedy Township	8,522	12	10	2
Kennett Square	5,911	15	12	3
Kennett Township	9,056	12	11	1
Kidder Township	1,840	8	8	0
Kingston	14,232	24	21	3
Kingston Township	7,110	13	13	0
Kiskiminetas Township	4,572	7	7	0
Kline Township	1,486	1	1	0

Table 78. Full-Time Law Enforcement Employees, by Selected State and City, 2022—Continued

(Number.)

State/city	Population	Total law enforcement employees	Total officers	Total civilians
Knox	1,098	1	1	0
Koppel	701	1	1	0
Kulpmont	2,734	1	1	0
Kutztown	4,159	14	12	2
Lake City	2,885	2	2	0
Lancaster	57,295	173	132	41
Lancaster Township, Butler County	3,344	5	5	0
Lansdale	19,033	32	26	6
Lansdowne	10,948	18	16	2
Lansford	4,212	4	4	0
Latrobe	7,934	15	14	1
Laureldale	4,265	4	4	0
Lawrence Park Township	3,762	9	9	0
Lawrence Township, Clearfield County	7,422	13	12	1
Lebanon	26,434	37	34	3
Leetsdale	1,141	5	5	0
Leet Township	1,579	5	5	0
Lehighton	5,315	12	11	1
Lehigh Township, Northampton County	10,770	13	12	1
Lehman Township	3,393	7	7	0
Lewistown	8,495	15	14	1
Liberty Township, Adams County	1,376	1	1	0
Ligonier Valley Regional	7,635	10	10	0
Limerick Township	20,764	32	29	3
Linesville	950	2	2	0
Lititz	9,559	16	14	2
Littlestown	4,790	9	9	0
Lock Haven	8,253	15	13	2
Locust Township	2,024	6	6	0
Logan Township	12,154	18	16	2
Lower Allen Township	20,288	29	26	3
Lower Burrell	11,576	18	17	1
Lower Chichester Township	3,371	5	5	0
Lower Gwynedd Township	12,085	23	22	1
Lower Heidelberg Township	6,404	9	8	1
Lower Makefield Township	33,355	45	41	4
Lower Merion Township	64,642	138	121	17
Lower Moreland Township	14,242	30	25	5
Lower Paxton Township	54,552	67	60	7
Lower Pottsgrove Township	12,446	22	20	2
Lower Providence Township	25,876	33	31	2
Lower Salford Township	16,095	21	19	2
Lower Saucon Township	11,068	16	15	1
Lower Southampton Township	20,555	35	32	3
Lower Swatara Township	9,567	14	13	1
Lower Windsor Township	7,567	11	10	1
Macungie	3,243	5	5	0
Mahanoy Township	3,047	2	2	0
Mahoning Township, Carbon County	4,327	6	6	0
Mahoning Township, Lawrence County	2,676	2	2	0
Mahoning Township, Montour County	4,588	8	7	1
Malvern	3,414	15	14	1
Manheim	5,025	18	17	1
Manheim Township	62,277	74	63	11
Manor	3,550	4	4	0
Manor Township, Armstrong County	4,125	5	5	0
Manor Township, Lancaster County	22,003	21	19	2
Marcus Hook	2,416	9	8	1
Marion Township, Beaver County	786	2	2	0
Marlborough Township	3,522	4	4	0
Marple Township	23,954	34	32	2
Martinsburg	1,841	3	3	0
Marysville	2,672	2	2	0
Masontown	3,192	2	2	0
Mayfield	1,753	2	2	0
McCandless	29,001	29	27	2
McDonald Borough	7,527	8	7	1
McKeesport	18,852	39	37	2
McKees Rocks	5,762	12	11	1
McSherrystown	3,085	4	4	0
Meadville	12,782	23	20	3
Mechanicsburg	9,696	15	14	1
Media	5,826	14	13	1
Mercer	1,953	5	5	0
Mercersburg	1,487	2	2	0
Meshoppen	1,230	2	2	0
Middleburg	1,310	2	2	0
Middlesex Township, Butler County	7,255	5	5	0
Middlesex Township, Cumberland County	7,129	12	11	1
Middletown	9,622	11	11	0
Middletown Township	45,742	65	58	7
Midland	2,374	4	4	0
Mifflinburg	3,394	8	7	1
Mifflin County Regional	21,093	15	15	0
Milford	1,149	2	2	0

Table 78. Full-Time Law Enforcement Employees, by Selected State and City, 2022—Continued

(Number.)

State/city	Population	Total law enforcement employees	Total officers	Total civilians
Millcreek Township, Erie County	53,467	82	66	16
Millcreek Township, Lebanon County	5,855	2	2	0
Millersville	7,570	13	11	2
Milton	6,549	9	8	1
Minersville	4,407	6	6	0
Mohnton	2,919	3	3	0
Monaca	5,488	10	10	0
Monessen	6,768	14	13	1
Monongahela	9,441	8	8	0
Monroeville	28,046	55	44	11
Montgomery Township	26,158	44	36	8
Montoursville	4,694	7	6	1
Moon Township	26,700	38	30	8
Moosic	5,991	11	11	0
Morrisville	9,753	9	9	0
Moscow	2,050	3	3	0
Mount Carmel	5,699	9	9	0
Mount Carmel Township	2,469	7	7	0
Mount Holly Springs	2,018	4	4	0
Mount Joy	8,314	13	12	1
Mount Lebanon	33,188	53	42	11
Mount Oliver	3,299	9	9	0
Mount Pleasant	4,185	4	4	0
Mount Pleasant Township	3,315	6	6	0
Mount Union	2,275	3	3	0
Muhlenberg Township	21,986	33	31	2
Muncy Township	1,180	2	2	0
Munhall	10,497	22	21	1
Murrysville	20,735	24	22	2
Nanticoke	10,611	17	16	1
Nanty Glo	2,472	2	2	0
Narberth	4,492	5	4	1
Nazareth	6,003	10	9	1
Nether Providence Township	14,361	18	17	1
New Brighton	8,617	10	10	0
New Britain Township	12,330	15	14	1
New Castle	21,614	39	37	2
New Cumberland	7,588	9	8	1
New Hanover Township	13,702	12	11	1
New Holland	12,822	19	18	1
New Hope	2,634	10	9	1
New Kensington	11,982	25	22	3
Newport Township	4,471	5	5	0
New Sewickley Township	7,046	14	13	1
Newtown	2,285	6	6	0
Newtown Township, Bucks County	23,080	36	32	4
Newville	1,389	3	3	0
New Wilmington	2,085	5	5	0
Norristown	35,888	75	63	12
Northampton	10,337	17	15	2
Northampton Township	39,796	51	44	7
North Belle Vernon	1,839	2	2	0
North Buffalo	2,658	1	1	0
North Catasauqua	2,950	7	7	0
North Cornwall Township	9,095	13	11	2
North Coventry Township	8,388	14	13	1
North East, Erie County	4,052	8	8	0
Northern Berks Regional	14,047	14	13	1
Northern Cambria Borough	3,505	5	5	0
Northern Lancaster County Regional	40,934	33	31	2
Northern Regional	38,417	40	39	1
Northern York County Regional	89,256	67	62	5
North Fayette Township	16,061	22	21	1
North Hopewell Township	2,714	2	2	0
North Huntingdon Township	31,709	36	30	6
North Lebanon Township	12,030	13	12	1
North Londonderry Township	8,937	10	9	1
North Middleton Township	12,391	12	11	1
North Strabane Township	16,162	26	25	1
Northumberland	3,880	6	6	0
North Versailles Township	11,549	27	22	5
North Wales	3,403	5	5	0
Northwest Lancaster County Regional	19,802	22	20	2
North Woodbury	2,415	1	1	0
Norwood	5,863	7	6	1
O'Hara Township	9,060	17	15	2
Oil City	9,422	16	14	2
Old Forge	8,598	7	7	0
Old Lycoming Township	4,963	10	9	1
Olyphant	5,402	10	10	0
Orwigsburg	3,007	6	6	0
Oxford	5,742	12	11	1
Palmerton	5,705	10	9	1
Palmer Township	22,392	37	35	2
Palmyra	7,714	12	11	1

Table 78. Full-Time Law Enforcement Employees, by Selected State and City, 2022—Continued

(Number.)

State/city	Population	Total law enforcement employees	Total officers	Total civilians
Parkesburg	5,149	10	9	1
Parkside	2,285	2	2	0
Parks Township	2,443	1	1	0
Patterson Township	4,355	4	4	0
Patton	1,695	2	2	0
Patton Township	15,769	22	20	2
Penbrook	3,254	7	7	0
Penndel	2,530	1	1	0
Penn Hills	40,172	55	53	2
Penn Township, Butler County	4,875	5	4	1
Penn Township, Westmoreland County	20,630	21	21	0
Penn Township, York County	17,972	26	24	2
Perkasie	9,110	20	18	2
Peters Township	23,148	26	25	1
Philadelphia	1,555,812	7,184	5,800	1,384
Phoenixville	19,477	32	31	1
Pine Creek Township	5,890	2	2	0
Pine Grove	2,064	2	2	0
Pittsburgh	303,137	880	837	43
Pittston Township	3,183	8	8	0
Plains Township	9,819	20	19	1
Pleasant Hills	8,283	20	18	2
Plum	26,644	31	29	2
Plymouth	5,747	9	9	0
Plymouth Township, Montgomery County	18,329	56	48	8
Pocono Mountain Regional	43,672	46	41	5
Pocono Township	10,997	23	22	1
Point Marion	1,122	1	1	0
Point Township	3,812	6	6	0
Port Allegany	2,069	3	3	0
Port Vue	3,642	4	4	0
Pottstown	23,376	57	44	13
Pottsville	13,367	24	23	1
Pulaski Township, Lawrence County	3,055	2	2	0
Punxsutawney	5,683	10	9	1
Pymatuning Township	3,064	8	5	3
Quarryville	2,876	6	6	0
Raccoon Township	2,739	3	3	0
Ralpho Township	4,184	6	6	0
Reading	97,698	184	158	26
Reading Township	5,816	2	2	0
Redstone Township	3,858	2	2	0
Reserve Township	3,166	6	6	0
Reynoldsville	2,501	1	1	0
Rice Township	3,701	6	6	0
Richland Township, Bucks County	14,102	19	17	2
Richland Township, Cambria County	11,991	22	21	1
Ridgway	3,980	7	6	1
Ridley Park	7,088	9	9	0
Ridley Township	30,612	33	30	3
Riverside	2,033	4	4	0
Roaring Brook Township	2,309	2	2	0
Roaring Spring	2,345	3	3	0
Robeson Township	7,650	6	6	0
Robinson Township, Allegheny County	15,400	29	28	1
Rochester	3,956	6	6	0
Rochester Township	2,650	3	3	0
Rockledge	2,619	5	5	0
Roseto	1,572	1	1	0
Ross Township	32,854	40	38	2
Rostraver Township	11,368	17	16	1
Royalton	1,131	1	1	0
Royersford	4,930	9	8	1
Rush Township	3,462	1	1	0
Sadsbury Township, Chester County	4,294	4	4	0
Salem Township, Luzerne County	4,034	8	8	0
Sandy Lake	640	1	1	0
Saxton	716	4	4	0
Sayre	6,503	16	14	2
Schuylkill Haven	5,275	8	8	0
Schuylkill Township, Chester County	8,787	13	11	2
Scottdale	4,349	6	6	0
Scott Township, Columbia County	5,537	9	9	0
Scott Township, Lackawanna County	4,635	6	6	0
Scranton	75,798	150	138	12
Selinsgrove	5,724	7	6	1
Sewickley Heights	833	4	4	0
Shaler Township	27,427	26	26	0
Shamokin	6,874	9	9	0
Sharon Hill	5,923	9	8	1
Sharpsville	4,197	8	8	0
Shenango Township, Lawrence County	7,079	9	9	0
Shenango Township, Mercer County	3,487	11	11	0
Shillington	5,467	9	8	1
Shinglehouse	1,089	1	1	0

Table 78. Full-Time Law Enforcement Employees, by Selected State and City, 2022—Continued

(Number.)

State/city	Population	Total law enforcement employees	Total officers	Total civilians
Shippingport	156	2	2	0
Shiremanstown	1,648	2	2	0
Silver Spring Township	20,806	23	22	1
Sinking Spring	4,279	7	6	1
Slatington	4,271	7	7	0
Slippery Rock	3,055	4	4	0
Smethport	1,399	2	2	0
Smith Township	4,192	5	5	0
Solebury Township	8,674	19	17	2
Souderton	7,249	9	8	1
South Beaver Township	2,637	5	5	0
South Buffalo Township	2,681	3	3	0
South Coatesville	1,687	3	3	0
Southern Clarion County Regional	3,213	2	2	0
Southern Regional York County	13,571	15	14	1
South Fayette Township	18,476	24	23	1
South Greensburg	2,101	2	2	0
South Lebanon Township	10,481	10	9	1
South Londonderry Township	8,833	9	9	0
South Park Township	13,715	15	14	1
South Strabane Township	9,654	21	20	1
Southwest Greensburg	2,183	2	2	0
Southwest Regional, Fayette County	1,501	1	1	0
South Whitehall Township	21,189	42	40	2
South Williamsport	7,389	10	10	0
Springdale	3,308	4	4	0
Springettsbury Township	27,064	35	32	3
Springfield Township, Bucks County	5,181	4	4	0
Springfield Township, Delaware County	24,732	37	34	3
Springfield Township, Montgomery County	20,839	30	29	1
Spring Garden Township	13,941	25	21	4
Spring Township, Berks County	28,431	31	30	1
Spring Township, Centre County	8,026	10	9	1
State College	55,998	68	57	11
St. Clair Township	1,320	2	2	0
St. Marys City	12,602	16	15	1
Stoneboro	939	1	1	0
Stonycreek Township	2,723	6	6	0
Stowe Township	6,258	11	11	0
Strasburg	3,103	6	6	0
Stroud Area Regional	36,044	57	49	8
Sugarcreek	4,739	3	3	0
Sugarloaf Township, Luzerne County	3,896	5	5	0
Summerhill Township	2,268	2	2	0
Summit Hill	3,172	5	5	0
Summit Township	2,116	1	1	0
Sunbury	9,624	11	10	1
Susquehanna Regional	15,362	17	15	2
Susquehanna Township, Dauphin County	26,699	45	42	3
Swatara Township	29,743	53	50	3
Sweden Township	857	1	1	0
Swoyersville	5,017	6	6	0
Tamaqua	6,945	9	8	1
Tarentum	4,235	10	10	0
Tatamy	1,329	2	2	0
Telford	4,905	7	6	1
Throop	4,089	8	8	0
Tiadaghton Valley Regional	7,712	13	13	0
Tilden Township	3,581	4	4	0
Tinicum Township, Bucks County	3,817	4	4	0
Tinicum Township, Delaware County	3,938	17	15	2
Titusville	5,192	13	12	1
Towamencin Township	17,985	27	25	2
Towanda	2,786	6	6	0
Trafford	3,259	6	6	0
Trainer	1,944	6	6	0
Tredyffrin Township	31,706	47	42	5
Troy	1,247	2	2	0
Tullytown	2,262	3	3	0
Tunkhannock	1,757	3	3	0
Tunkhannock Township, Wyoming County	5,665	7	7	0
Turtle Creek	4,986	6	6	0
Tyrone	5,377	8	7	1
Union City	2,889	3	2	1
Union Township, Lawrence County	4,925	11	11	0
Upper Allen Township	23,290	25	24	1
Upper Chichester Township	16,666	24	23	1
Upper Darby Township	84,407	145	132	13
Upper Dublin Township	27,081	44	38	6
Upper Gwynedd Township	17,179	24	22	2
Upper Macungie Township	27,057	33	30	3
Upper Makefield Township	8,848	19	18	1
Upper Merion Township	34,792	86	70	16
Upper Moreland Township	26,071	43	37	6
Upper Nazareth Township	8,282	12	11	1

Table 78. Full-Time Law Enforcement Employees, by Selected State and City, 2022—Continued

(Number.)

State/city	Population	Total law enforcement employees	Total officers	Total civilians
Upper Perkiomen	3,963	6	6	0
Upper Pottsgrove Township	5,955	8	8	0
Upper Providence Township, Delaware County	10,687	16	15	1
Upper Providence Township, Montgomery County	24,741	32	28	4
Upper Southampton Township	15,175	24	22	2
Upper Uwchlan Township	12,967	15	15	0
Upper Yoder Township	5,057	6	6	0
Uwchlan Township	19,028	24	23	1
Valley Township	7,935	10	10	0
Vandergrift	4,986	8	8	0
Verona	2,421	4	3	1
Versailles	1,439	2	2	0
Warminster Township	33,413	44	40	4
Warren	9,159	18	16	2
Warrington Township	25,899	40	38	2
Warwick Township, Bucks County	14,859	19	18	1
Washington Township, Fayette County	3,764	3	3	0
Washington Township, Franklin County	15,104	13	11	2
Washington Township, Northampton County	5,169	5	5	0
Washington Township, Westmoreland County	6,818	10	10	0
Washington, Washington County	13,135	33	31	2
Watsontown	2,237	5	5	0
Waverly Township	1,861	3	3	0
Waynesboro	10,925	19	17	2
Waynesburg	3,872	10	8	2
Wellsboro	3,449	7	7	0
Wesleyville	3,172	8	7	1
West Brandywine Township	7,612	10	9	1
West Brownsville	969	2	2	0
West Caln Township	8,914	6	6	0
West Chester	18,690	54	43	11
West Conshohocken	1,502	11	10	1
West Deer Township	12,214	15	14	1
West Earl Township	12,609	13	12	1
Westfield	1,108	1	1	0
West Goshen Township	23,293	35	31	4
West Hazleton	5,163	5	4	1
West Hempfield Township	20,301	24	23	1
West Hills Regional	9,943	12	11	1
West Lampeter Township	17,434	18	17	1
West Manchester Township	19,161	32	28	4
West Manheim Township	9,386	10	10	0
West Mead Township	4,953	2	2	0
West Mifflin	19,122	39	33	6
West Norriton Township	16,392	30	27	3
West Penn Township	4,458	3	2	1
West Pottsgrove Township	3,792	8	7	1
West Reading	4,512	16	14	2
West Shore Regional	7,783	13	12	1
Westtown-East Goshen Regional	32,631	39	34	5
West View	6,507	11	10	1
West Vincent Township	6,947	9	8	1
West Whiteland Township	19,944	31	29	2
Whitehall	14,775	26	20	6
Whitehall Township	29,250	51	46	5
White Haven Borough	1,168	2	2	0
Whitemarsh Township	20,098	40	35	5
White Oak	7,434	15	14	1
Whitpain Township	20,381	39	31	8
Wilkes-Barre	44,497	78	74	4
Wilkes-Barre Township	3,216	17	16	1
Wilkins Township	6,184	13	13	0
Williamsburg	1,222	2	2	0
Williamsport	27,498	51	48	3
Willistown Township	11,258	21	19	2
Windber	3,868	3	2	1
Woodward Township	2,465	3	3	0
Wright Township	5,744	8	7	1
Wyomissing	11,145	22	21	1
Yardley	2,588	5	5	0
Yeadon	11,894	18	17	1
York	44,901	115	100	15
York County Regional	12,612	66	60	6
Youngsville	1,697	2	2	0
Zelienople	3,795	10	9	1
Zerbe Township	1,786	1	1	0
RHODE ISLAND				
Barrington	17,364	30	25	5
Bristol	22,220	48	41	7
Burrillville	16,246	32	25	7
Central Falls	22,340	43	35	8
Charlestown	8,117	25	20	5
Coventry	35,730	64	51	13
Cranston	82,205	172	142	30

Table 78. Full-Time Law Enforcement Employees, by Selected State and City, 2022—Continued

(Number.)

State/city	Population	Total law enforcement employees	Total officers	Total civilians
Cumberland	36,345	52	41	11
East Greenwich	14,260	40	32	8
East Providence	46,655	95	80	15
Foster	4,454	9	6	3
Glocester	10,147	22	16	6
Hopkinton	8,486	16	11	5
Jamestown	5,545	19	14	5
Johnston	29,430	70	57	13
Lincoln	22,400	42	34	8
Little Compton	3,599	14	10	4
Middletown	16,898	41	37	4
Narragansett	14,653	53	40	13
Newport	25,039	89	75	14
New Shoreham	1,423	12	7	5
North Kingstown	28,008	58	53	5
North Providence	33,809	69	62	7
North Smithfield	12,538	29	25	4
Pawtucket	74,967	190	157	33
Portsmouth	17,716	38	36	2
Providence	189,064	500	424	76
Richmond	8,243	20	15	5
Scituate	10,385	24	18	6
Smithfield	21,762	57	44	13
South Kingstown	32,046	70	55	15
Tiverton	16,244	38	29	9
Warren	11,243	31	26	5
Warwick	82,966	216	174	42
Westerly	23,563	76	50	26
West Greenwich	6,727	18	14	4
West Warwick	31,227	55	44	11
Woonsocket	42,925	113	93	20
SOUTH CAROLINA				
Abbeville	4,868	18	17	1
Aiken	31,985	112	89	23
Allendale	2,626	2	2	0
Anderson	29,398	112	87	25
Andrews	2,526	6	4	2
Atlantic Beach	269	5	4	1
Aynor	1,048	4	3	1
Bamberg	3,019	9	7	2
Barnwell	4,468	16	14	2
Batesburg-Leesville	5,249	26	18	8
Beaufort	13,003	51	47	4
Belton	4,463	13	12	1
Bennettsville	6,891	31	29	2
Bishopville	2,899	11	9	2
Blacksburg	1,886	9	9	0
Blackville	1,952	8	7	1
Bluffton	36,064	60	52	8
Bonneau	419	1	1	0
Bowman	766	1	1	0
Branchville	966	3	2	1
Briarcliffe Acres	523	1	1	0
Burnettown	3,181	1	1	0
Calhoun Falls	1,726	8	7	1
Camden	8,044	38	32	6
Cameron	371	2	1	1
Campobello	715	9	8	1
Cayce	13,710	66	52	14
Central	5,335	12	11	1
Chapin	1,876	7	7	0
Charleston	152,324	503	415	88
Cheraw	4,920	29	21	8
Chesnee	866	6	5	1
Chester	5,222	19	16	3
Chesterfield	1,326	5	5	0
Clemson	18,174	43	32	11
Clinton	7,663	28	25	3
Clio	600	2	1	1
Clover	7,153	26	21	5
Columbia	137,768	369	289	80
Conway	23,664	71	61	10
Cottageville	700	6	6	0
Coward	746	1	1	0
Cowpens	2,104	10	9	1
Darlington	6,051	24	22	2
Denmark	3,124	9	8	1
Dillon	6,213	26	25	1
Due West	1,197	5	5	0
Duncan	4,241	21	20	1
Easley	23,786	64	53	11
Edgefield	2,416	12	12	0
Edisto Beach	1,024	6	6	0
Ehrhardt	450	2	1	1

Table 78. Full-Time Law Enforcement Employees, by Selected State and City, 2022—Continued

(Number.)

State/city	Population	Total law enforcement employees	Total officers	Total civilians
Elgin	1,603	8	7	1
Elloree	553	3	3	0
Estill	1,790	3	2	1
Eutawville	235	1	1	0
Fairfax	1,455	5	5	0
Florence	39,997	97	75	22
Folly Beach	2,041	26	20	6
Forest Acres	10,514	36	27	9
Fort Lawn	965	4	2	2
Fort Mill	31,023	61	52	9
Fountain Inn	11,523	37	29	8
Gaffney	12,291	38	33	5
Gaston	1,629	4	4	0
Georgetown	8,323	32	26	6
Gifford	263	4	1	3
Goose Creek	46,665	110	80	30
Great Falls	1,935	5	4	1
Greeleyville	378	1	1	0
Greenville	73,311	249	206	43
Greenwood	22,145	58	53	5
Greer	42,196	91	64	27
Hampton	2,727	15	14	1
Hanahan	22,320	28	26	2
Hardeeville	9,995	31	28	3
Harleyville	679	2	2	0
Hartsville	7,614	38	33	5
Hemingway	489	5	4	1
Holly Hill	1,254	8	8	0
Honea Path	3,793	14	13	1
Inman	3,111	12	12	0
Irmo	11,937	27	24	3
Isle of Palms	4,284	27	20	7
Iva	1,154	11	10	1
Jackson	1,561	3	3	0
Jamestown	71	3	2	1
Johnsonville	1,358	7	6	1
Johnston	2,081	8	7	1
Jonesville	832	3	3	0
Kingstree	3,122	11	10	1
Lake City	5,946	29	25	4
Lake View	744	4	4	0
Lamar	861	1	1	0
Lancaster	8,678	45	33	12
Landrum	2,587	13	10	3
Lane	473	1	1	0
Latta	1,270	5	5	0
Laurens	9,307	39	34	5
Lexington	24,880	61	58	3
Liberty	3,310	18	13	5
Loris	2,676	14	13	1
Lyman	6,437	12	12	0
Manning	3,830	20	20	0
Marion	6,232	20	16	4
Mauldin	26,576	49	42	7
McColl	2,051	3	3	0
McCormick	2,252	5	5	0
Moncks Corner	13,906	32	28	4
Mount Pleasant	93,951	178	154	24
Mullins	3,884	16	11	5
Myrtle Beach	38,117	284	212	72
Newberry	10,507	24	21	3
New Ellenton	2,274	6	5	1
Nichols	226	1	1	0
Ninety Six	2,074	9	9	0
North	680	3	3	0
North Augusta	24,957	81	63	18
North Charleston	119,198	401	325	76
North Myrtle Beach	19,888	116	82	34
Norway	277	1	1	0
Olanta	538	2	1	1
Orangeburg	12,307	84	45	39
Pageland	2,436	16	12	4
Pamplico	1,046	4	4	0
Pawleys Island	133	3	3	0
Pelion	622	3	3	0
Pendleton	3,608	4	4	0
Perry	198	2	1	1
Pickens	3,365	15	15	0
Pine Ridge	2,267	4	4	0
Port Royal	13,430	26	26	0
Prosperity	1,206	5	5	0
Quinby	904	1	1	0
Ridgeland	3,680	11	10	1
Ridge Spring	577	3	3	0
Ridgeville	1,539	2	2	0

Table 78. Full-Time Law Enforcement Employees, by Selected State and City, 2022—Continued

(Number.)

State/city	Population	Total law enforcement employees	Total officers	Total civilians
Rock Hill	74,047	199	152	47
Salem	121	1	1	0
Salley	334	2	1	1
Saluda	3,025	10	8	2
Santee	780	6	6	0
Scranton	638	1	1	0
Seneca	8,964	44	33	11
Simpsonville	25,847	57	47	10
Society Hill	433	1	1	0
South Congaree	2,391	6	6	0
Spartanburg	38,271	145	125	20
Springdale	2,749	11	10	1
Springfield	438	2	2	0
St. George	1,774	11	10	1
St. Stephen	1,533	4	3	1
Sullivans Island	1,870	13	11	2
Summerton	793	6	5	1
Summerville	51,423	149	120	29
Sumter	42,613	145	103	42
Surfside Beach	4,301	24	19	5
Swansea	737	4	3	1
Tega Cay	13,607	29	22	7
Timmonsville	2,085	6	6	0
Travelers Rest	7,836	26	20	6
Trenton	206	1	1	0
Union	7,977	25	23	2
Varnville	1,680	8	7	1
Wagener	653	3	3	0
Walhalla	4,121	15	14	1
Walterboro	5,432	28	27	1
Ware Shoals	1,696	6	6	0
Wellford	3,478	13	11	2
West Columbia	17,581	62	51	11
Westminster	2,374	7	7	0
West Pelzer	997	3	3	0
West Union	380	1	1	0
Whitmire	1,418	5	4	1
Williamston	4,172	15	15	0
Williston	2,882	10	9	1
Winnsboro	3,126	13	12	1
Woodruff	4,372	13	12	1
Yemassee	1,149	11	10	1
York	8,699	39	33	6
SOUTH DAKOTA				
Aberdeen	28,206	60	52	8
Alcester	774	2	2	0
Avon	573	1	1	0
Belle Fourche	5,799	15	13	2
Beresford	2,112	5	5	0
Box Elder	12,710	22	21	1
Brandon	10,914	14	13	1
Brookings	23,725	50	35	15
Burke	575	1	1	0
Canton	3,033	7	7	0
Centerville	929	2	2	0
Chamberlain	2,451	7	7	0
Clark	1,139	2	2	0
Deadwood	1,255	20	17	3
Eagle Butte	1,260	1	1	0
Elk Point	2,113	5	5	0
Faith	366	1	1	0
Flandreau	2,338	7	6	1
Freeman	1,317	2	2	0
Gettysburg	1,116	2	2	0
Gregory	1,175	2	2	0
Groton	1,379	4	4	0
Hot Springs	3,605	8	7	1
Huron	14,217	35	25	10
Jefferson	455	2	2	0
Lake Norden	618	3	3	0
Lead	2,965	8	7	1
Lennox	2,385	5	5	0
Madison	5,967	15	14	1
Martin	957	4	4	0
Menno	620	1	1	0
Milbank	3,458	6	6	0
Miller	1,302	4	4	0
Mitchell	15,579	36	26	10
Mobridge	3,154	13	7	6
Murdo	435	1	1	0
North Sioux City	2,987	10	9	1
Parkston	1,536	2	2	0
Philip	722	2	2	0
Pierre	13,977	35	21	14

Table 78. Full-Time Law Enforcement Employees, by Selected State and City, 2022—Continued
(Number.)

State/city	Population	Total law enforcement employees	Total officers	Total civilians
Platte	1,243	2	2	0
Rapid City	78,063	165	124	41
Scotland	770	1	1	0
Sioux Falls	199,879	317	282	35
Sisseton	2,389	5	5	0
Spearfish	12,517	31	19	12
Springfield	2,053	2	2	0
Sturgis	7,121	21	18	3
Summerset	3,059	8	7	1
Tea	6,894	10	9	1
Tripp	562	1	1	0
Tyndall	1,049	2	2	0
Vermillion	11,927	15	13	2
Viborg	805	1	1	0
Wagner	1,425	3	3	0
Watertown	22,832	61	41	20
Webster	1,689	3	2	1
Whitewood	908	6	5	1
Winner	2,834	9	9	0
Yankton	15,507	30	28	2
TENNESSEE				
Adamsville	2,244	7	6	1
Alamo	2,335	4	4	0
Alcoa	11,689	54	47	7
Alexandria	987	2	2	0
Algood	4,012	15	15	0
Ardmore	1,212	9	6	3
Ashland City	5,152	20	18	2
Athens	14,409	29	27	2
Atoka	10,345	24	23	1
Baileyton	452	3	3	0
Bartlett	56,928	176	134	42
Baxter	1,677	7	7	0
Bean Station	2,983	8	4	4
Belle Meade	2,593	20	15	5
Bells	2,501	5	5	0
Benton	1,506	7	6	1
Berry Hill	1,865	16	12	4
Big Sandy	484	1	1	0
Blaine	2,103	6	5	1
Bluff City	1,820	8	8	0
Bolivar	5,127	23	21	2
Bradford	989	5	5	0
Brentwood	45,581	79	61	18
Brighton	2,858	5	5	0
Bristol	27,862	93	75	18
Brownsville	9,578	42	37	5
Bruceton	1,496	5	5	0
Burns	1,783	1	1	0
Calhoun	549	3	3	0
Camden	3,711	19	13	6
Carthage	2,276	13	8	5
Caryville	2,179	4	4	0
Celina	1,382	5	3	2
Centerville	3,569	29	16	13
Chapel Hill	1,780	8	7	1
Charleston	678	4	4	0
Chattanooga	182,603	567	463	104
Church Hill	7,105	8	8	0
Clarksville	174,738	385	308	77
Cleveland	48,579	111	99	12
Clifton	2,614	5	5	0
Clinton	10,050	40	28	12
Collegedale	12,032	26	25	1
Collierville	51,439	147	112	35
Collinwood	918	4	4	0
Columbia	44,852	95	76	19
Cookeville	35,771	96	72	24
Coopertown	4,702	5	4	1
Cornersville	1,267	2	2	0
Covington	8,582	35	30	5
Cowan	1,779	4	4	0
Cross Plains	1,884	1	1	0
Crossville	12,487	45	42	3
Cumberland City	315	2	2	0
Dandridge	3,475	12	11	1
Dayton	7,170	20	18	2
Decatur	1,646	6	6	0
Decaturville	791	1	1	0
Decherd	2,369	14	13	1
Dickson	16,154	67	61	6
Dover	1,768	7	7	0
Dresden	3,026	8	7	1
Dunlap	5,644	15	13	2

Table 78. Full-Time Law Enforcement Employees, by Selected State and City, 2022—Continued

(Number.)

State/city	Population	Total law enforcement employees	Total officers	Total civilians
Dyer	2,312	7	6	1
Dyersburg	15,988	64	57	7
Eagleville	914	3	3	0
East Ridge	21,790	46	42	4
Elizabethton	13,868	45	41	4
Elkton	549	2	2	0
Englewood	1,519	6	5	1
Erin	1,209	8	6	2
Erwin	5,931	17	16	1
Estill Springs	2,266	7	7	0
Ethridge	548	2	1	1
Etowah	3,668	10	9	1
Fairview	9,844	22	22	0
Fayetteville	6,942	28	26	2
Franklin	87,081	153	140	13
Friendship	621	1	1	0
Gadsden	479	1	1	0
Gainesboro	913	4	4	0
Gallatin	49,220	96	84	12
Gallaway	502	4	4	0
Gates	661	5	5	0
Gatlinburg	3,873	55	45	10
Germantown	40,859	125	100	25
Gibson	361	2	1	1
Gleason	1,407	5	5	0
Goodlettsville	16,963	54	40	14
Gordonsville	1,385	6	5	1
Grand Junction	335	4	4	0
Graysville	1,479	4	3	1
Greenbrier	6,963	14	10	4
Greeneville	15,556	54	52	2
Greenfield	2,083	6	6	0
Halls	2,076	9	9	0
Harriman	5,984	20	19	1
Henderson	6,372	17	16	1
Hendersonville	62,475	152	136	16
Henry	442	2	2	0
Hohenwald	3,882	17	16	1
Hollow Rock	690	1	1	0
Humboldt	7,831	28	24	4
Huntingdon	4,432	20	16	4
Huntland	895	3	3	0
Jacksboro	2,313	5	5	0
Jackson	68,059	242	202	40
Jamestown	1,920	9	9	0
Jasper	3,626	9	9	0
Jefferson City	8,319	32	30	2
Jellico	2,131	8	7	1
Johnson City	71,987	153	139	14
Jonesborough	6,081	25	19	6
Kenton	1,184	3	3	0
Kimball	1,578	9	9	0
Kingsport	55,799	149	112	37
Kingston	6,067	13	12	1
Kingston Springs	2,803	6	6	0
Knoxville	194,724	478	380	98
Lafayette	5,650	28	19	9
La Follette	7,271	30	20	10
La Vergne	39,424	83	64	19
Lawrenceburg	11,874	34	29	5
Lebanon	43,321	131	98	33
Lenoir City	10,597	33	31	2
Lewisburg	12,659	31	30	1
Lexington	7,944	38	31	7
Livingston	4,047	20	14	6
Lookout Mountain	2,025	19	15	4
Loretto	1,783	5	5	0
Loudon	6,479	16	15	1
Madisonville	5,118	24	21	3
Manchester	13,045	38	34	4
Martin	10,562	37	29	8
Maryville	32,717	64	59	5
Mason	1,354	2	1	1
Maynardville	2,507	4	4	0
McEwen	1,735	3	3	0
McKenzie	5,451	16	11	5
McMinnville	13,952	42	39	3
Medina	5,338	10	10	0
Memphis	624,944	2,461	1,904	557
Metropolitan Nashville Police Department	679,562	1,827	1,389	438
Middleton	682	2	2	0
Milan	8,167	32	25	7
Millersville	6,239	17	14	3
Millington	10,461	30	20	10
Minor Hill	515	2	2	0

Table 78. Full-Time Law Enforcement Employees, by Selected State and City, 2022—Continued

(Number.)

State/city	Population	Total law enforcement employees	Total officers	Total civilians
Monteagle	1,375	7	7	0
Monterey	2,750	11	10	1
Morristown	30,988	82	77	5
Mosheim	2,488	3	3	0
Mountain City	2,467	10	10	0
Mount Carmel	5,522	7	7	0
Mount Juliet	41,849	95	72	23
Mount Pleasant	4,871	19	14	5
Munford	6,466	19	19	0
Murfreesboro	161,810	326	265	61
Newbern	3,296	12	12	0
New Johnsonville	1,851	6	5	1
New Market	1,369	3	2	1
Newport	6,972	32	28	4
New Tazewell	2,802	10	10	0
Niota	794	4	3	1
Nolensville	16,990	18	17	1
Norris	1,576	6	6	0
Oakland	10,004	22	20	2
Oak Ridge	32,243	73	58	15
Obion	964	2	2	0
Oliver Springs	3,305	17	12	5
Oneida	3,793	16	11	5
Paris	10,371	39	27	12
Parsons	2,074	6	6	0
Petersburg	537	1	1	0
Pigeon Forge	6,340	84	67	17
Pikeville	1,889	4	4	0
Piperton	2,696	8	8	0
Pittman Center	468	3	3	0
Plainview	2,118	2	2	0
Pleasant View	5,379	5	5	0
Portland	13,460	39	35	4
Pulaski	8,240	26	24	2
Puryear	708	2	1	1
Red Bank	11,862	26	24	2
Red Boiling Springs	1,199	5	5	0
Ridgely	1,787	5	5	0
Ripley	7,772	37	28	9
Rockwood	5,571	14	13	1
Rocky Top	3,594	7	7	0
Rogersville	4,665	15	14	1
Rossville	1,146	8	8	0
Rutherford	1,140	2	2	0
Rutledge	1,282	3	3	0
Savannah	7,207	21	19	2
Scotts Hill	875	2	2	0
Selmer	4,419	15	13	2
Sevierville	19,021	86	69	17
Sharon	952	3	1	2
Shelbyville	24,160	59	48	11
Signal Mountain	8,824	15	13	2
Smithville	5,242	15	14	1
Smyrna	57,595	103	84	19
Soddy-Daisy	13,112	36	28	8
Somerville	3,470	11	11	0
South Carthage	1,563	4	4	0
South Fulton	2,178	10	5	5
South Pittsburg	3,065	8	8	0
Sparta	4,993	14	13	1
Spencer	1,592	3	3	0
Spring City	1,965	9	8	1
Springfield	19,330	38	35	3
Spring Hill	56,232	67	63	4
St. Joseph	814	2	1	1
Sweetwater	6,345	21	20	1
Tazewell	2,360	13	12	1
Tellico Plains	761	5	5	0
Tiptonville	4,071	8	8	0
Townsend	598	6	6	0
Tracy City	1,424	3	3	0
Trenton	4,243	22	17	5
Trezevant	800	1	1	0
Trimble	535	1	1	0
Troy	1,392	5	5	0
Tullahoma	20,948	37	30	7
Tusculum	3,025	2	2	0
Unicoi	3,763	1	1	0
Union City	10,996	43	35	8
Vonore	1,600	10	9	1
Wartburg	897	4	4	0
Wartrace	674	1	1	0
Watertown	1,556	7	6	1
Waverly	4,342	13	12	1
Waynesboro	2,353	7	7	0

Table 78. Full-Time Law Enforcement Employees, by Selected State and City, 2022—Continued
(Number.)

State/city	Population	Total law enforcement employees	Total officers	Total civilians
Westmoreland	2,740	13	12	1
White Bluff	4,065	6	6	0
White House	14,290	27	19	8
White Pine	2,583	11	10	1
Whiteville	2,646	7	7	0
Whitwell	1,612	2	2	0
Winchester	9,703	27	25	2
Woodbury	2,713	9	9	0
TEXAS				
Abernathy	2,783	6	6	0
Abilene	125,186	278	215	63
Addison	17,531	71	61	10
Alamo	20,383	45	34	11
Alamo Heights	7,412	29	19	10
Alba	493	3	3	0
Alice	17,727	45	34	11
Allen	108,135	199	137	62
Alma	407	3	3	0
Alpine	5,757	14	8	6
Alton	19,391	36	29	7
Alvarado	5,504	24	19	5
Alvin	27,974	85	55	30
Amarillo	201,572	422	342	80
Andrews	13,233	23	22	1
Angleton	19,369	49	32	17
Anna	23,541	34	31	3
Anthony	3,662	21	18	3
Aransas Pass	8,056	41	27	14
Archer City	1,593	2	2	0
Arcola	2,260	10	9	1
Argyle	4,986	18	16	2
Arlington	391,591	870	679	191
Arp	953	6	6	0
Athens	12,986	34	24	10
Atlanta	5,443	13	7	6
Aubrey	7,873	24	23	1
Austin	965,234	2,178	1,527	651
Azle	13,615	44	31	13
Baird	1,529	4	4	0
Balch Springs	26,973	55	38	17
Balcones Heights	2,709	21	18	3
Ballinger	3,577	13	10	3
Bangs	1,541	4	3	1
Bartonville	1,812	6	6	0
Bastrop	11,101	30	25	5
Bay City	17,796	55	36	19
Baytown	81,477	219	161	58
Beaumont	110,898	312	244	68
Bedford	48,579	106	72	34
Bee Cave	8,870	21	19	2
Beeville	13,592	27	20	7
Bellaire	16,783	55	38	17
Bellmead	10,589	32	22	10
Bells	1,557	4	4	0
Bellville	4,066	12	11	1
Belton	24,188	56	42	14
Benbrook	24,739	44	34	10
Bertram	1,913	8	8	0
Beverly Hills	1,867	11	8	3
Big Sandy	1,295	5	5	0
Big Spring	25,254	47	34	13
Blanco	1,870	10	9	1
Blooming Grove	888	1	1	0
Blue Mound	2,325	7	6	1
Boerne	20,488	66	46	20
Bogata	1,098	3	3	0
Borger	12,366	31	29	2
Bovina	1,706	3	3	0
Bowie	5,659	21	14	7
Boyd	1,538	6	5	1
Brady	4,998	12	11	1
Brazoria	2,823	15	8	7
Breckenridge	5,294	16	9	7
Bremond	862	4	4	0
Brenham	18,785	38	34	4
Bridge City	9,495	20	15	5
Bridgeport	6,186	28	17	11
Brookshire	5,739	17	10	7
Brownfield	8,877	27	20	7
Brownsboro	1,242	3	3	0
Brownsville	188,906	294	220	74
Brownwood	18,751	57	34	23
Bruceville-Eddy	1,428	6	6	0
Bryan	87,935	184	149	35

Table 78. Full-Time Law Enforcement Employees, by Selected State and City, 2022—Continued

(Number.)

State/city	Population	Total law enforcement employees	Total officers	Total civilians
Buda	16,000	26	22	4
Buffalo	1,812	3	3	0
Bullard	4,062	15	11	4
Bulverde	6,268	17	16	1
Burkburnett	11,057	21	13	8
Burleson	55,356	92	81	11
Burnet	6,861	24	21	3
Cactus	3,058	15	12	3
Caddo Mills	3,568	10	10	0
Caldwell	4,249	10	9	1
Calvert	965	3	3	0
Cameron	5,415	14	10	4
Canton	4,408	21	15	6
Canyon	15,680	29	26	3
Carrollton	133,610	208	161	47
Carthage	6,558	22	16	6
Castle Hills	3,921	23	20	3
Castroville	3,052	11	10	1
Cedar Hill	48,483	85	65	20
Cedar Park	79,353	124	88	36
Celina	24,190	41	38	3
Center	5,111	22	15	7
Chandler	3,529	8	8	0
Charlotte	1,571	5	5	0
Childress	5,915	13	12	1
China Grove	1,128	5	5	0
Cibolo	34,159	43	37	6
Cisco	3,902	12	10	2
Clarksville	2,786	2	2	0
Cleburne	32,728	62	42	20
Clifton	3,526	8	7	1
Clint	925	2	2	0
Clute	10,557	38	25	13
Clyde	4,038	11	10	1
Cockrell Hill	3,687	23	17	6
Coffee City	246	6	6	0
Coleman	3,943	5	5	0
College Station	121,618	209	150	59
Colleyville	25,897	43	38	5
Collinsville	1,993	5	5	0
Columbus	3,598	12	11	1
Comanche	4,276	13	10	3
Combes	3,071	10	10	0
Commerce	8,876	25	18	7
Conroe	98,623	191	146	45
Converse	29,503	50	46	4
Coppell	42,021	54	47	7
Copperas Cove	37,841	68	47	21
Corinth	22,719	39	36	3
Corpus Christi	317,694	611	439	172
Corrigan	1,487	14	8	6
Corsicana	25,585	43	34	9
Crandall	4,671	18	18	0
Crane	3,485	15	10	5
Crockett	6,428	14	13	1
Crowley	20,362	41	26	15
Cuero	8,271	16	15	1
Cuney	115	3	2	1
Daingerfield	2,520	6	5	1
Dalhart	8,410	17	13	4
Dallas	1,286,121	3,733	3,060	673
Dalworthington Gardens	2,260	15	9	6
Dawson	844	1	1	0
Dayton	9,451	25	18	7
Decatur	7,147	33	25	8
Deer Park	33,022	88	60	28
De Leon	2,310	4	4	0
Denison	25,828	63	47	16
Denton	154,230	276	192	84
Denver City	4,346	12	7	5
DeSoto	55,956	118	75	43
Devine	4,483	14	10	4
Diboll	4,466	16	13	3
Dickinson	21,936	48	32	16
Dilley	3,318	14	13	1
Dimmitt	4,183	9	7	2
Donna	16,842	52	37	15
Double Oak	3,052	7	7	0
Driscoll	668	3	2	1
Dublin	3,469	11	10	1
Dumas	14,140	20	15	5
Duncanville	39,474	64	55	9
Eagle Pass	28,811	93	60	33
Early	3,161	11	9	2
Eastland	3,630	13	11	2

Table 78. Full-Time Law Enforcement Employees, by Selected State and City, 2022—Continued

(Number.)

State/city	Population	Total law enforcement employees	Total officers	Total civilians
East Mountain	937	3	2	1
Edcouch	2,708	7	7	0
Edgewood	1,649	4	4	0
Edinburg	104,987	240	163	77
Edna	5,976	12	10	2
El Campo	12,235	38	26	12
Electra	2,286	13	8	5
Elgin	11,245	24	20	4
Elmendorf	2,202	7	6	1
El Paso	678,232	1,403	1,133	270
Elsa	5,683	24	18	6
Emory	1,359	5	4	1
Ennis	22,254	49	37	12
Euless	59,901	135	90	45
Everman	5,993	24	18	6
Fairfield	2,939	12	8	4
Fair Oaks Ranch	11,119	26	23	3
Fairview	10,917	14	14	0
Falfurrias	4,754	12	10	2
Farmers Branch	36,595	103	80	23
Farmersville	4,024	11	9	2
Farwell	1,383	3	3	0
Fate	23,955	26	24	2
Ferris	2,893	17	10	7
Flatonia	1,348	6	6	0
Florence	1,218	5	5	0
Floresville	7,971	21	19	2
Flower Mound	78,167	142	98	44
Floydada	2,638	6	6	0
Forest Hill	13,685	32	24	8
Forney	31,105	52	36	16
Fort Stockton	8,411	29	20	9
Fort Worth	948,605	2,105	1,672	433
Franklin	1,781	6	6	0
Frankston	1,117	6	6	0
Fredericksburg	11,348	41	34	7
Freeport	10,500	41	28	13
Freer	2,454	9	6	3
Friendswood	40,851	83	63	20
Friona	4,121	8	3	5
Frisco	218,962	333	233	100
Fulshear	18,058	26	24	2
Gainesville	17,789	53	38	15
Galena Park	10,240	17	11	6
Galveston	52,920	184	142	42
Ganado	1,998	3	3	0
Garden Ridge	4,442	12	11	1
Garland	241,095	475	346	129
Garrison	791	1	1	0
Gatesville	17,154	31	19	12
Georgetown	83,371	125	93	32
George West	2,194	12	9	3
Giddings	5,144	22	16	6
Gilmer	4,997	19	15	4
Gladewater	6,174	21	16	5
Glenn Heights	18,398	33	23	10
Godley	2,245	6	6	0
Gonzales	7,089	26	19	7
Graham	8,823	20	19	1
Granbury	12,132	49	42	7
Grand Prairie	199,663	450	286	164
Grand Saline	3,236	10	9	1
Granger	1,204	4	4	0
Grapeland	1,504	5	5	0
Grapevine	50,988	144	95	49
Greenville	30,890	67	47	20
Groesbeck	3,638	9	9	0
Groves	16,682	27	23	4
Gun Barrel City	6,551	20	14	6
Gunter	2,449	6	6	0
Hallettsville	2,762	8	7	1
Hallsville	4,707	6	6	0
Haltom City	45,488	74	69	5
Hamilton	2,860	9	8	1
Hamlin	1,899	9	5	4
Harker Heights	34,001	61	49	12
Harlingen	72,047	184	138	46
Haskell	3,033	6	5	1
Hawkins	1,353	4	4	0
Hawley	575	2	2	0
Hearne	4,517	18	12	6
Heath	10,661	29	28	1
Hedwig Village	2,295	23	17	6
Helotes	9,263	35	28	7
Hempstead	6,388	23	16	7

Table 78. Full-Time Law Enforcement Employees, by Selected State and City, 2022—Continued

(Number.)

State/city	Population	Total law enforcement employees	Total officers	Total civilians
Henderson	13,567	40	32	8
Hereford	14,626	32	26	6
Hewitt	16,291	41	29	12
Hickory Creek	5,786	13	13	0
Hico	1,360	5	5	0
Hidalgo	14,468	45	35	10
Highland Park	8,732	74	60	14
Highland Village	15,988	41	30	11
Hill Country Village	939	15	11	4
Hillsboro	8,407	36	25	11
Hitchcock	7,502	19	18	1
Hollywood Park	3,091	16	15	1
Hondo	8,522	24	22	2
Honey Grove	1,789	6	6	0
Hooks	2,510	7	6	1
Horizon City	23,726	47	28	19
Horseshoe Bay	4,693	26	22	4
Houston	2,276,533	6,271	5,243	1,028
Howe	3,659	7	6	1
Hudson Oaks	2,547	13	12	1
Hughes Springs	1,542	4	4	0
Humble	16,085	79	63	16
Huntington	2,020	5	5	0
Huntsville	46,780	71	57	14
Hurst	39,796	112	71	41
Hutchins	5,594	27	20	7
Hutto	33,891	41	36	5
Idalou	2,118	4	4	0
Ingleside	10,207	39	24	15
Ingram	1,834	4	4	0
Iowa Colony	11,056	11	10	1
Iowa Park	6,595	18	11	7
Irving	254,141	533	380	153
Italy	2,038	6	5	1
Itasca	1,682	6	6	0
Jacinto City	9,190	24	17	7
Jacksboro	4,292	11	10	1
Jacksonville	14,196	42	29	13
Jamaica Beach	1,065	7	7	0
Jarrell	2,469	9	9	0
Jasper	7,706	26	19	7
Jefferson	1,830	7	6	1
Jersey Village	7,575	29	26	3
Jonestown	2,506	10	9	1
Josephine	4,711	10	10	0
Joshua	8,256	17	16	1
Jourdanton	4,179	10	9	1
Junction	2,536	8	7	1
Karnes City	3,271	9	8	1
Katy	25,511	91	71	20
Kaufman	7,829	19	16	3
Keene	6,355	15	13	2
Keller	45,080	88	51	37
Kemah	1,794	21	15	6
Kemp	1,237	6	5	1
Kempner	1,211	3	2	1
Kenedy	3,589	16	15	1
Kennedale	8,417	25	22	3
Kerens	1,518	5	5	0
Kermit	5,749	23	13	10
Kerrville	24,696	71	46	25
Kilgore	13,419	48	34	14
Killeen	159,546	294	237	57
Kingsville	24,802	67	38	29
Kirby	8,069	18	12	6
Knox City	1,047	3	3	0
Kountze	2,371	6	5	1
Kyle	57,724	91	58	33
Lacy-Lakeview	7,143	23	14	9
La Feria	6,791	16	12	4
Lago Vista	9,637	23	18	5
La Grange	4,455	15	14	1
La Grulla	1,208	5	4	1
Laguna Vista	3,673	9	9	0
La Joya	4,666	18	13	5
Lake Dallas	7,738	16	12	4
Lake Jackson	27,595	68	48	20
Lakeport	970	6	4	2
Lakeside	1,603	8	8	0
Lakeview, Harrison County	6,490	13	12	1
Lakeway	19,267	49	33	16
Lake Worth	4,652	41	30	11
La Marque	19,068	48	36	12
Lamesa	8,726	20	18	2
Lampasas	7,737	37	23	14

Table 78. Full-Time Law Enforcement Employees, by Selected State and City, 2022—Continued

(Number.)

State/city	Population	Total law enforcement employees	Total officers	Total civilians
Lancaster	40,615	54	49	5
La Porte	36,646	106	75	31
Laredo	256,973	618	515	103
La Vernia	1,224	11	11	0
La Villa	2,782	9	8	1
Lavon	6,277	16	15	1
League City	116,511	173	130	43
Leander	73,905	87	63	24
Leonard	2,085	6	6	0
Leon Valley	11,402	39	38	1
Levelland	12,579	35	27	8
Lewisville	113,568	232	166	66
Lexington	1,246	1	1	0
Liberty	8,790	23	13	10
Liberty Hill	6,909	15	14	1
Lindale	6,509	27	19	8
Linden	1,788	5	4	1
Little Elm	55,340	91	83	8
Littlefield	5,814	19	12	7
Live Oak	15,884	46	34	12
Livingston	5,937	28	20	8
Llano	3,406	7	6	1
Lockhart	15,068	34	22	12
Lockney	1,474	4	3	1
Log Cabin	820	4	4	0
Lone Star	1,412	4	3	1
Longview	81,811	199	155	44
Lorena	1,787	8	7	1
Los Fresnos	8,164	26	26	0
Lubbock	264,142	580	438	142
Lufkin	34,063	85	68	17
Luling	5,511	19	11	8
Lumberton	14,004	21	18	3
Lyford	2,237	1	1	0
Lytle	3,037	10	10	0
Madisonville	4,670	13	10	3
Magnolia	2,906	19	17	2
Manor	23,497	34	26	8
Mansfield	75,993	152	104	48
Manvel	14,821	39	31	8
Marble Falls	7,408	43	27	16
Marfa	1,749	5	5	0
Marion	1,045	4	4	0
Marlin	5,631	16	10	6
Marshall	22,628	63	51	12
Mathis	4,379	15	9	6
Maud	969	1	1	0
Maypearl	945	4	4	0
McAllen	145,510	420	282	138
McKinney	208,415	300	235	65
Meadows Place	4,591	19	17	2
Melissa	20,071	20	20	0
Memorial Villages	10,987	44	31	13
Memphis	2,086	2	2	0
Mercedes	16,365	47	39	8
Meridian	1,424	4	4	0
Merkel	2,431	4	4	0
Mesquite	147,226	312	230	82
Mexia	6,865	16	14	2
Midland	129,945	243	175	68
Midlothian	38,587	101	68	33
Miles	927	2	2	0
Milford	736	8	6	2
Mineola	5,031	20	13	7
Mineral Wells	15,010	39	27	12
Mission	86,577	217	170	47
Missouri City	75,323	126	93	33
Monahans	7,185	20	13	7
Mont Belvieu	8,902	31	22	9
Montgomery	2,679	13	11	2
Morgans Point Resort	4,789	7	7	0
Moulton	869	4	4	0
Mount Enterprise	508	1	1	0
Mount Pleasant	16,044	46	33	13
Mount Vernon	2,500	8	8	0
Muleshoe	5,066	12	6	6
Murphy	21,297	35	24	11
Mustang Ridge	991	8	7	1
Nacogdoches	32,055	80	55	25
Nash	3,847	9	9	0
Nassau Bay	5,105	14	13	1
Natalia	1,342	3	3	0
Navasota	8,459	32	22	10
Nederland	18,034	42	28	14
Needville	3,040	8	8	0

Table 78. Full-Time Law Enforcement Employees, by Selected State and City, 2022—Continued

(Number.)

State/city	Population	Total law enforcement employees	Total officers	Total civilians
New Boston	4,557	14	9	5
New Braunfels	107,017	166	134	32
Newton	1,997	4	4	0
Nolanville	6,560	14	13	1
Northeast	3,962	6	6	0
Northlake	8,513	23	21	2
North Richland Hills	70,108	209	121	88
Oak Ridge, Kaufman County	979	27	27	0
Oak Ridge North	3,011	17	17	0
Odem	2,277	6	4	2
Odessa	110,163	176	133	43
Olmos Park	2,151	19	19	0
Olney	3,033	9	7	2
Onalaska	3,225	16	10	6
Orange	19,056	58	42	16
Ore City	1,170	4	4	0
Overton	2,294	8	6	2
Ovilla	4,365	11	10	1
Oyster Creek	1,196	13	9	4
Palacios	4,425	11	9	2
Palestine	19,113	48	32	16
Palmer	2,510	12	11	1
Palmhurst	2,600	21	15	6
Palmview	15,919	33	24	9
Pampa	16,343	32	30	2
Panhandle	2,310	4	4	0
Pantego	2,497	18	13	5
Paris	24,392	68	43	25
Parker	6,144	10	9	1
Pasadena	145,954	346	270	76
Patton Village	1,799	9	9	0
Payne Springs	755	3	3	0
Pearland	125,894	241	170	71
Pearsall	7,661	18	15	3
Pecos	12,483	52	23	29
Pelican Bay	2,398	4	4	0
Penitas	6,348	16	15	1
Perryton	8,143	18	11	7
Petersburg	972	4	2	2
Pflugerville	67,817	124	91	33
Pharr	79,558	170	140	30
Pilot Point	4,892	14	13	1
Pinehurst	2,209	7	5	2
Pineland	910	3	3	0
Pittsburg	4,433	13	11	2
Plainview	19,554	41	33	8
Plano	289,847	631	407	224
Pleasanton	10,951	30	24	6
Point Comfort	565	3	3	0
Ponder	2,417	7	6	1
Port Aransas	3,286	29	20	9
Port Arthur	55,899	148	115	33
Port Isabel	5,165	21	16	5
Portland	20,742	49	32	17
Port Lavaca	11,048	24	18	6
Port Neches	13,293	25	21	4
Poteet	2,970	11	10	1
Prairie View	7,059	16	15	1
Primera	5,319	10	9	1
Princeton	22,867	32	30	2
Prosper	37,752	60	45	15
Queen City	1,410	6	6	0
Quitman	2,021	7	7	0
Rancho Viejo	2,867	8	8	0
Ranger	2,287	5	5	0
Raymondville	10,552	24	16	8
Red Oak	16,396	30	27	3
Refugio	2,866	10	9	1
Reno, Lamar County	3,457	6	5	1
Reno, Parker County	3,457	11	9	2
Rhome	1,839	8	8	0
Rice	1,259	5	4	1
Richardson	115,771	245	164	81
Richland	270	3	3	0
Richland Hills	8,385	24	20	4
Richmond	12,936	38	27	11
Richwood	4,730	10	10	0
Rio Grande City	15,705	43	30	13
Rio Hondo	2,012	7	7	0
River Oaks	7,420	22	15	7
Roanoke	10,024	40	29	11
Robinson	12,954	33	22	11
Robstown	10,155	32	24	8
Rockdale	5,473	16	11	5
Rockport	10,759	33	27	6

Table 78. Full-Time Law Enforcement Employees, by Selected State and City, 2022—Continued

(Number.)

State/city	Population	Total law enforcement employees	Total officers	Total civilians
Rockwall	51,724	104	81	23
Rogers	1,107	3	3	0
Rollingwood	1,398	9	8	1
Roma	11,547	35	26	9
Roman Forest	1,963	12	10	2
Roscoe	1,231	2	2	0
Rose City	333	3	2	1
Rosenberg	40,472	100	76	24
Round Rock	127,349	242	174	68
Rowlett	65,196	150	100	50
Royse City	18,613	35	31	4
Runaway Bay	1,764	5	5	0
Rusk	5,583	10	9	1
Sabinal	1,410	6	5	1
Sachse	31,317	49	34	15
Saginaw	23,993	46	36	10
Salado	2,395	8	8	0
San Angelo	99,243	212	169	43
San Antonio	1,465,608	3,126	2,373	753
San Augustine	1,844	9	8	1
San Benito	24,712	48	41	7
San Elizario	10,080	3	3	0
Sanger	9,877	19	18	1
San Juan	35,806	46	33	13
San Marcos	69,470	150	112	38
San Saba	3,197	5	5	0
Sansom Park Village	5,336	18	11	7
Santa Anna	1,029	4	4	0
Santa Fe	12,802	30	23	7
Savoy	747	2	2	0
Schertz	43,162	93	60	33
Schulenburg	2,742	10	8	2
Seabrook	13,544	38	27	11
Seadrift	997	3	3	0
Seagoville	19,389	39	28	11
Sealy	6,720	24	21	3
Seguin	32,452	82	59	23
Selma	11,824	34	30	4
Seminole	7,066	12	10	2
Seven Points	1,430	9	5	4
Seymour	2,590	6	4	2
Shallowater	2,917	6	6	0
Shavano Park	3,609	19	18	1
Shenandoah	3,682	27	26	1
Sherman	45,881	112	78	34
Shiner	2,183	8	8	0
Silsbee	6,831	23	17	6
Sinton	5,602	12	10	2
Slaton	5,752	13	10	3
Smithville	4,150	19	12	7
Snyder	11,179	20	17	3
Socorro	37,952	68	48	20
Somerset	1,777	5	5	0
Somerville	1,346	2	2	0
Sonora	2,432	8	6	2
Sour Lake	1,807	7	6	1
South Houston	15,613	41	28	13
Southlake	30,949	68	61	7
South Padre Island	2,048	37	28	9
Southside Place	1,820	11	7	4
Spearman	3,034	4	4	0
Splendora	1,860	18	17	1
Springtown	3,638	14	10	4
Spring Valley	4,209	27	22	5
Stafford	17,110	68	52	16
Stamford	3,005	7	6	1
Stanton	2,630	7	6	1
Stephenville	21,505	57	38	19
Stinnett	1,639	2	2	0
Stratford	1,973	3	3	0
Sudan	934	1	1	0
Sugar Land	107,989	193	172	21
Sullivan City	3,896	16	10	6
Sulphur Springs	16,128	39	29	10
Sunnyvale	8,381	22	21	1
Sunray	1,701	5	4	1
Sunrise Beach Village	787	6	6	0
Sunset Valley	637	13	12	1
Surfside Beach	669	8	8	0
Sweeny	3,566	9	8	1
Sweetwater	10,420	34	25	9
Taft	2,835	8	5	3
Tahoka	2,419	5	5	0
Tatum	1,357	2	2	0
Taylor	17,259	41	29	12

Table 78. Full-Time Law Enforcement Employees, by Selected State and City, 2022—Continued

(Number.)

State/city	Population	Total law enforcement employees	Total officers	Total civilians
Teague	3,497	7	7	0
Temple	88,484	175	139	36
Tenaha	995	1	1	0
Terrell	19,670	67	44	23
Terrell Hills	5,036	14	14	0
Texarkana	35,859	95	84	11
Texas City	56,311	118	92	26
The Colony	45,357	103	76	27
Thorndale	1,312	2	2	0
Tioga	1,220	4	4	0
Todd Mission	126	3	3	0
Tomball	13,322	60	44	16
Tom Bean	934	5	5	0
Tool	2,243	8	4	4
Trophy Club	13,794	25	21	4
Tulia	4,501	17	10	7
Tye	1,192	7	4	3
Tyler	108,422	242	193	49
Universal City	19,903	39	28	11
University Park	24,918	60	42	18
Uvalde	15,410	50	34	16
Valley Mills	1,256	4	4	0
Van	2,825	9	9	0
Van Alstyne	6,023	20	14	6
Vega	844	1	1	0
Venus	7,843	16	16	0
Vernon	9,945	26	16	10
Victoria	65,165	145	108	37
Vidor	9,671	31	24	7
Waco	140,911	343	254	89
Waelder	943	5	4	1
Wake Village	5,861	9	8	1
Waller	2,846	14	12	2
Wallis	1,302	9	9	0
Watauga	23,027	37	28	9
Waxahachie	45,422	97	76	21
Weatherford	36,796	80	59	21
Webster	11,952	71	50	21
Weimar	2,083	7	6	1
Weslaco	41,478	101	76	25
West	2,587	8	8	0
West Columbia	3,587	16	10	6
West Lake Hills	3,220	15	14	1
West Orange	3,418	12	10	2
Westover Hills	638	15	10	5
West University Place	14,524	33	25	8
Westworth	2,614	18	14	4
Wharton	8,627	28	19	9
Whitehouse	9,175	15	13	2
White Oak	6,147	20	16	4
White Settlement	17,954	42	32	10
Whitewright	1,774	2	2	0
Whitney	2,066	10	9	1
Wichita Falls	103,337	270	194	76
Willis	6,986	14	12	2
Willow Park	5,427	20	19	1
Wills Point	3,977	9	8	1
Wilmer	5,590	24	24	0
Windcrest	5,793	37	25	12
Wink	844	1	1	0
Winnsboro	3,581	15	11	4
Winters	2,363	7	6	1
Wolfforth	6,482	16	15	1
Woodbranch	1,497	5	3	2
Woodsboro	1,275	3	3	0
Woodville	2,471	11	10	1
Woodway	9,514	43	34	9
Wortham	1,015	4	4	0
Wylie	60,910	87	67	20
Yoakum	5,958	17	11	6
Zavalla	610	3	3	0
UTAH				
Alta	217	8	4	4
American Fork/Cedar Hills	45,310	58	51	7
Big Water	443	1	1	0
Blanding	3,295	6	5	1
Bluffdale	20,386	15	15	0
Bountiful	45,098	57	38	19
Brian Head	159	7	7	0
Brigham City	20,355	31	26	5
Cedar City	39,266	50	42	8
Centerville	16,719	23	20	3
Clearfield	32,586	43	30	13
Clinton	23,784	24	23	1

Table 78. Full-Time Law Enforcement Employees, by Selected State and City, 2022—Continued

(Number.)

State/city	Population	Total law enforcement employees	Total officers	Total civilians
Cottonwood Heights	32,191	46	39	7
Draper	53,049	57	47	10
East Carbon	1,531	4	4	0
Enoch	8,518	9	7	2
Ephraim	5,834	9	8	1
Fairview	1,278	2	2	0
Farmington	24,935	26	24	2
Grantsville	14,431	23	20	3
Harrisville	6,948	11	10	1
Heber	17,659	29	23	6
Helper	2,082	6	5	1
Herriman	60,138	52	42	10
Hildale	1,198	22	9	13
Hurricane	23,607	39	36	3
Kamas	2,250	2	2	0
Kanab	5,324	9	8	1
Kaysville	33,004	35	32	3
La Verkin	4,582	7	5	2
Layton	84,636	111	84	27
Lehi	83,071	68	62	6
Lindon	11,922	17	15	2
Logan	56,267	81	52	29
Lone Peak	30,258	19	16	3
Mantua	1,336	2	2	0
Mapleton	13,415	12	11	1
Moab	5,263	24	15	9
Mount Pleasant	3,836	5	5	0
Murray	48,884	92	78	14
Naples	2,383	6	5	1
Nephi	6,739	14	11	3
North Ogden	21,977	28	22	6
North Park	16,904	17	14	3
North Salt Lake	22,679	31	27	4
Ogden	86,870	183	144	39
Orem	97,430	123	96	27
Park City	8,516	38	33	5
Parowan	3,230	6	5	1
Payson	22,989	25	22	3
Perry	5,921	8	7	1
Pleasant Grove	38,095	32	28	4
Pleasant View	11,234	14	12	2
Price	8,230	20	16	4
Provo	114,120	143	114	29
Richfield	8,379	18	16	2
Riverdale	9,408	24	21	3
Riverton	44,920	40	36	4
Roosevelt	7,004	17	15	2
Roy	39,305	47	39	8
Salem	10,308	14	13	1
Salina	2,559	4	3	1
Salt Lake City	201,373	681	554	127
Sandy	93,102	150	118	32
Santa Clara/Ivins	18,275	18	15	3
Santaquin/Genola	18,616	17	15	2
Saratoga Springs	50,850	32	27	5
Smithfield	14,455	12	12	0
South Jordan	82,250	69	60	9
South Ogden	17,585	26	21	5
South Salt Lake	26,021	81	64	17
Spanish Fork	45,005	45	41	4
Spring City	998	1	1	0
Springdale	589	11	10	1
Springville	36,907	42	31	11
St. George	104,158	187	134	53
Sunset	5,557	8	7	1
Syracuse	34,354	25	23	2
Taylorsville City	58,059	71	63	8
Tooele	38,318	51	42	9
Tremonton Garland	13,682	16	14	2
Vernal	10,368	26	23	3
Washington	33,535	43	34	9
Wellington	1,587	3	3	0
Wendover	1,139	4	4	0
West Bountiful	5,981	12	11	1
West Jordan	115,900	158	124	34
West Valley	138,020	282	229	53
Willard	2,251	2	2	0
Woods Cross	11,846	19	18	1
VERMONT				
Barre	8,447	26	19	7
Barre Town	7,970	8	7	1
Bellows Falls	2,820	4	3	1
Bennington	15,301	30	20	10
Berlin	2,936	11	10	1

Table 78. Full-Time Law Enforcement Employees, by Selected State and City, 2022—Continued

(Number.)

State/city	Population	Total law enforcement employees	Total officers	Total civilians
Bradford	2,822	2	2	0
Brandon	4,112	6	5	1
Brattleboro	12,256	29	18	11
Bristol	3,730	3	3	0
Burlington	44,689	86	62	24
Chester	3,055	5	4	1
Colchester	17,710	37	28	9
Dover	1,859	8	7	1
Essex	22,481	33	26	7
Fair Haven	2,726	4	4	0
Hardwick	2,997	5	5	0
Hartford	10,863	27	17	10
Hinesburg	4,699	4	4	0
Killington	1,414	3	3	0
Ludlow	2,204	9	5	4
Lyndonville	1,200	2	2	0
Manchester	4,499	13	9	4
Middlebury	9,037	16	13	3
Milton	10,656	18	17	1
Montpelier	7,995	21	13	8
Morristown	5,610	12	12	0
Newport	4,433	18	13	5
Northfield	6,291	8	7	1
Norwich	3,681	3	2	1
Pittsford	2,879	1	1	0
Richmond	4,110	3	3	0
Royalton	2,794	2	2	0
Rutland	15,858	40	27	13
Rutland Town	3,929	5	4	1
Shelburne	7,903	16	9	7
South Burlington	20,307	45	33	12
Springfield	9,180	13	8	5
St. Albans	7,022	30	19	11
St. Johnsbury	7,404	15	9	6
Stowe	5,359	12	12	0
Swanton	6,813	8	8	0
Thetford	2,826	2	2	0
Vergennes	2,565	7	7	0
Weathersfield	2,887	2	2	0
Williston	10,067	21	17	4
Wilmington	2,310	8	6	2
Windsor	3,595	11	10	1
Winhall	1,180	9	8	1
Winooski	8,647	19	15	4
Woodstock	3,064	6	5	1
VIRGINIA				
Abingdon	8,265	28	25	3
Alexandria	150,957	382	301	81
Altavista	3,348	14	13	1
Amherst	2,152	7	6	1
Ashland	7,661	24	21	3
Bedford	6,681	26	23	3
Berryville	4,588	10	9	1
Big Stone Gap	5,155	11	10	1
Blacksburg	45,749	66	56	10
Blackstone	3,347	15	12	3
Bluefield	4,957	22	19	3
Bowling Green	1,187	2	2	0
Bridgewater	6,215	10	10	0
Bristol	16,909	75	54	21
Broadway	4,269	7	6	1
Brookneal	1,061	2	2	0
Buena Vista	6,605	16	15	1
Burkeville	419	1	1	0
Cape Charles	1,177	7	7	0
Cedar Bluff	1,038	4	3	1
Charlottesville	45,089	109	81	28
Chase City	2,037	9	8	1
Chatham	1,182	3	3	0
Chesapeake	253,745	524	394	130
Chilhowie	1,652	6	6	0
Chincoteague	3,284	16	12	4
Christiansburg	21,746	67	61	6
Clarksville	1,291	8	7	1
Clifton Forge	3,433	8	7	1
Clintwood	1,334	4	4	0
Coeburn	1,559	7	6	1
Colonial Beach	3,980	15	13	2
Colonial Heights	18,419	58	52	6
Covington	5,733	24	15	9
Crewe	2,257	6	5	1
Culpeper	20,836	54	46	8
Damascus	782	4	4	0
Danville	42,111	133	114	19

Table 78. Full-Time Law Enforcement Employees, by Selected State and City, 2022—Continued

(Number.)

State/city	Population	Total law enforcement employees	Total officers	Total civilians
Dayton	1,721	6	6	0
Dublin	2,636	8	7	1
Dumfries	5,659	15	14	1
Eastville	295	4	4	0
Elkton	3,008	8	7	1
Emporia	5,637	38	26	12
Exmore	1,432	7	7	0
Fairfax City	24,509	88	63	25
Falls Church	14,384	53	36	17
Farmville	7,216	28	26	2
Franklin	8,292	28	21	7
Fredericksburg	28,844	105	71	34
Front Royal	15,201	50	36	14
Galax	6,652	37	23	14
Gate City	2,015	4	4	0
Glade Spring	1,355	3	3	0
Glen Lyn	93	1	1	0
Gordonsville	1,466	7	7	0
Gretna	1,274	3	3	0
Grottoes	2,965	6	6	0
Grundy	805	5	5	0
Halifax	1,098	5	5	0
Hampton	138,843	398	271	127
Harrisonburg	51,363	110	86	24
Haymarket	1,559	6	6	0
Haysi	526	1	1	0
Herndon	24,070	66	48	18
Hillsville	2,856	13	12	1
Honaker	1,192	3	3	0
Hopewell	23,395	70	57	13
Hurt	1,250	2	2	0
Independence	1,005	3	3	0
Jonesville	862	2	2	0
Kenbridge	1,110	4	4	0
Kilmarnock	1,419	6	6	0
La Crosse	607	1	1	0
Lawrenceville	1,025	6	6	0
Lebanon	3,098	11	10	1
Leesburg	49,395	84	69	15
Lexington	7,628	18	14	4
Louisa	2,118	4	3	1
Luray	4,813	15	14	1
Lynchburg	79,421	185	140	45
Manassas	42,836	133	98	35
Manassas Park	16,923	38	29	9
Marion	5,711	22	21	1
Martinsville	13,660	45	41	4
Middleburg	666	7	6	1
Middletown	1,413	6	5	1
Mount Jackson	2,010	6	6	0
Narrows	2,038	5	5	0
New Market	2,180	6	6	0
Newport News	183,903	607	428	179
Norfolk	233,419	574	490	84
Norton	3,666	27	17	10
Occoquan	1,041	4	4	0
Onancock	1,156	4	4	0
Onley	532	3	3	0
Orange	5,254	16	14	2
Parksley	804	1	1	0
Pearisburg	2,812	9	8	1
Pembroke	1,124	3	3	0
Pennington Gap	1,595	5	5	0
Petersburg	33,546	96	71	25
Pocahontas	259	1	1	0
Poquoson	12,738	28	26	2
Portsmouth	98,003	215	160	55
Pulaski	8,944	29	25	4
Purcellville	9,103	17	15	2
Radford	16,978	47	38	9
Remington	638	1	1	0
Rich Creek	719	1	1	0
Richlands	5,158	14	11	3
Richmond	227,323	693	603	90
Roanoke	98,204	244	202	42
Rocky Mount	4,929	20	18	2
Rural Retreat	1,527	1	1	0
Salem	25,460	83	59	24
Saltville	1,774	6	6	0
Shenandoah	2,510	8	7	1
Smithfield	8,827	21	17	4
South Boston	7,884	27	25	2
South Hill	4,737	21	19	2
Stanley	1,721	5	5	0
Staunton	25,611	61	46	15

Table 78. Full-Time Law Enforcement Employees, by Selected State and City, 2022—Continued

(Number.)

State/city	Population	Total law enforcement employees	Total officers	Total civilians
Stephens City	2,109	3	3	0
St. Paul	838	7	7	0
Strasburg	7,270	18	16	2
Suffolk	98,065	235	169	66
Tappahannock	2,236	12	11	1
Tazewell	4,374	16	15	1
Timberville	3,013	6	6	0
Victoria	1,739	5	4	1
Vienna	16,194	47	38	9
Vinton	7,996	26	24	2
Virginia Beach	457,556	1,008	822	186
Warrenton	10,218	31	29	2
Warsaw	1,671	4	4	0
Waynesboro	22,903	48	38	10
Weber City	1,228	2	2	0
West Point	3,424	12	11	1
Williamsburg	15,790	41	39	2
Winchester	28,363	85	76	9
Windsor	2,876	7	7	0
Wintergreen	166	15	10	5
Wise	2,884	12	11	1
Woodstock	5,929	20	18	2
Wytheville	8,199	28	25	3
WASHINGTON				
Aberdeen	17,338	51	35	16
Airway Heights	10,803	23	22	1
Algona	3,194	9	8	1
Anacortes	17,990	31	24	7
Arlington	20,176	34	29	5
Asotin	1,192	1	1	0
Auburn	84,279	122	102	20
Bainbridge Island	24,336	29	22	7
Battle Ground	21,385	29	24	5
Bellevue	147,079	212	172	40
Bellingham	93,014	168	110	58
Black Diamond	7,021	14	12	2
Blaine	6,050	16	14	2
Bonney Lake	22,898	38	30	8
Bothell	47,407	108	70	38
Bremerton	44,256	75	58	17
Brewster	2,027	6	5	1
Brier	6,448	7	6	1
Buckley	5,982	13	11	2
Burien	50,159	69	46	23
Burlington	10,187	30	24	6
Camas	27,653	34	29	5
Carnation	2,170	2	2	0
Castle Rock	2,442	6	5	1
Centralia	18,993	35	26	9
Chehalis	7,870	19	15	4
Cheney	13,092	21	15	6
Chewelah	2,567	5	4	1
Clarkston	7,267	17	14	3
Cle Elum	3,198	10	8	2
Clyde Hill	3,083	10	9	1
Colfax	2,774	5	5	0
College Place	9,907	16	13	3
Colville	5,026	10	9	1
Connell	4,945	8	7	1
Cosmopolis	1,704	5	4	1
Coulee Dam	1,241	2	2	0
Covington	20,686	22	16	6
Des Moines	32,541	48	37	11
Dupont	10,024	14	12	2
Duvall	8,778	12	10	2
East Wenatchee	14,243	26	22	4
Eatonville	2,849	6	5	1
Edgewood	12,900	13	12	1
Edmonds	42,714	62	51	11
Ellensburg	19,822	37	29	8
Elma	3,509	9	7	2
Enumclaw	12,833	34	19	15
Ephrata	8,465	18	15	3
Everett	110,694	223	190	33
Everson	4,653	8	7	1
Federal Way	97,094	168	136	32
Ferndale	15,816	25	20	5
Fife	10,900	37	29	8
Fircrest	7,047	10	9	1
Forks	3,430	7	6	1
Garfield	566	1	1	0
Gig Harbor	12,301	23	21	2
Goldendale	3,551	9	7	2
Grand Coulee	1,919	8	8	0

Table 78. Full-Time Law Enforcement Employees, by Selected State and City, 2022—Continued

(Number.)

State/city	Population	Total law enforcement employees	Total officers	Total civilians
Grandview	10,901	22	17	5
Granger	3,704	10	9	1
Hoquiam	8,918	24	19	5
Issaquah	38,917	67	33	34
Kalama	3,061	8	7	1
Kelso	12,723	31	26	5
Kenmore	23,107	20	16	4
Kennewick	85,058	107	91	16
Kent	133,066	208	156	52
Kettle Falls	1,665	4	3	1
Kirkland	91,464	148	107	41
Kittitas	1,439	4	4	0
La Center	4,142	2	2	0
Lacey	55,101	68	57	11
Lake Forest Park	13,096	22	19	3
Lake Stevens	36,828	39	30	9
Lakewood	63,044	111	96	15
Langley	1,155	3	3	0
Liberty Lake	12,897	20	18	2
Long Beach	1,752	9	8	1
Longview	37,768	77	60	17
Lynden	16,275	23	19	4
Lynnwood	42,764	99	64	35
Mabton	1,938	2	2	0
Maple Valley	28,175	26	20	6
Marysville	71,395	101	60	41
Mattawa	3,927	7	7	0
McCleary	2,051	6	5	1
Medina	2,849	11	9	2
Mercer Island	25,121	38	34	4
Mill Creek	20,925	28	23	5
Milton	9,113	14	13	1
Monroe	20,309	40	31	9
Montesano	4,196	9	8	1
Morton	1,083	4	4	0
Moses Lake	25,709	51	43	8
Mountlake Terrace	21,589	35	27	8
Mount Vernon	35,511	53	39	14
Moxee	4,408	8	7	1
Mukilteo	21,009	36	30	6
Napavine	1,999	5	4	1
Newcastle	12,782	14	11	3
Newport	2,182	5	4	1
Normandy Park	6,519	10	9	1
Oak Harbor	24,858	37	28	9
Ocean Shores	7,446	14	10	4
Odessa	934	1	1	0
Olympia	56,214	107	68	39
Omak	5,063	14	10	4
Oroville	1,794	6	5	1
Orting	8,877	11	10	1
Othello	8,876	25	17	8
Pacific	6,966	10	9	1
Palouse	1,034	1	1	0
Pasco	79,899	96	86	10
Port Angeles	20,290	56	32	24
Port Orchard	16,351	27	23	4
Port Townsend	10,452	14	11	3
Poulsbo	11,814	24	20	4
Prosser	6,136	13	11	2
Pullman	32,848	41	30	11
Puyallup	42,580	94	67	27
Quincy	8,413	29	22	7
Raymond	3,201	7	6	1
Reardan	685	2	2	0
Redmond	79,403	116	78	38
Renton	103,619	145	116	29
Richland	63,081	79	61	18
Ridgefield	14,465	15	13	2
Ritzville	1,704	5	5	0
Roy	805	2	2	0
Royal City	1,828	4	4	0
Ruston	1,053	7	7	0
Sammamish	65,738	40	32	8
SeaTac	30,203	69	50	19
Seattle	729,691	1,418	1,077	341
Sedro Woolley	12,565	24	19	5
Selah	8,258	19	16	3
Sequim	8,439	24	18	6
Shelton	11,102	19	17	2
Shoreline	57,147	65	45	20
Snohomish	10,125	17	15	2
Snoqualmie	13,523	25	22	3
Soap Lake	1,708	7	6	1
South Bend	1,784	5	4	1

Table 78. Full-Time Law Enforcement Employees, by Selected State and City, 2022—Continued

(Number.)

State/city	Population	Total law enforcement employees	Total officers	Total civilians
Spokane	229,292	430	341	89
Spokane Valley	108,076	130	104	26
Stanwood	9,132	10	8	2
Steilacoom	6,690	11	10	1
Sumas	1,647	7	6	1
Sumner	10,681	26	21	5
Sunnyside	16,300	48	27	21
Tacoma	219,027	363	324	39
Tenino	2,042	6	5	1
Tieton	1,756	3	3	0
Toledo	663	2	1	1
Toppenish	8,717	14	11	3
Tukwila	21,473	87	65	22
Tumwater	26,227	39	32	7
Twisp	1,070	3	3	0
Union Gap	6,514	20	17	3
University Place	34,846	16	15	1
Vancouver	193,273	261	212	49
Walla Walla	33,899	73	44	29
Wapato	4,509	10	8	2
Warden	2,574	6	5	1
Washougal	16,902	25	21	4
Wenatchee	35,462	55	44	11
Westport	2,280	8	7	1
West Richland	17,557	24	20	4
White Salmon	2,663	8	6	2
Winlock	1,704	2	2	0
Winthrop	550	3	3	0
Woodinville	13,357	19	15	4
Woodland	6,544	16	14	2
Yakima	96,267	163	123	40
Yelm	10,749	20	14	6
Zillah	3,138	9	8	1
WEST VIRGINIA				
Alderson	962	4	3	1
Anmoore	503	3	3	0
Athens	926	1	1	0
Barboursville	4,264	25	23	2
Barrackville	1,203	1	1	0
Beckley	16,843	67	56	11
Belington	1,806	3	3	0
Belle	1,128	3	3	0
Benwood	1,229	11	6	5
Berkeley Springs	754	3	2	1
Bethlehem	2,538	5	5	0
Bluefield	9,411	34	28	6
Bradshaw	211	1	1	0
Bramwell	272	2	2	0
Bridgeport	9,206	40	36	4
Buckhannon	5,243	13	12	1
Burnsville	387	2	2	0
Cameron	823	2	2	0
Cedar Grove	688	1	1	0
Ceredo	1,372	6	6	0
Chapmanville	980	6	6	0
Charleston	47,350	180	157	23
Charles Town	6,524	16	14	2
Chesapeake	1,296	1	1	0
Chester	2,139	5	4	1
Clarksburg	15,581	44	39	5
Clendenin	849	4	4	0
Davy	216	1	1	0
Delbarton	406	2	2	0
Dunbar	7,218	16	15	1
East Bank	795	1	1	0
Eleanor	1,531	1	1	0
Elkins	6,865	15	13	2
Fairmont	18,121	40	35	5
Fairview	372	1	1	0
Fayetteville	2,815	15	13	2
Follansbee	2,760	7	7	0
Fort Gay	668	3	3	0
Gary	709	1	1	0
Gassaway	746	1	1	0
Gauley Bridge	535	1	1	0
Gilbert	319	3	3	0
Glasgow	693	1	1	0
Glen Dale	1,467	6	6	0
Glenville	1,106	3	2	1
Grafton	4,578	8	7	1
Grant Town	681	1	1	0
Granville	1,396	15	15	0
Hamlin	1,005	4	3	1
Harpers Ferry/Bolivar	1,298	3	3	0

Table 78. Full-Time Law Enforcement Employees, by Selected State and City, 2022—Continued
(Number.)

State/city	Population	Total law enforcement employees	Total officers	Total civilians
Harrisville	1,628	1	1	0
Hartford City	500	1	1	0
Hinton	2,231	4	3	1
Huntington	45,547	98	94	4
Hurricane	6,874	21	19	2
Iaeger	265	1	1	0
Kenova	2,940	14	10	4
Keyser	4,883	11	10	1
Kingwood	3,103	3	3	0
Lewisburg	3,821	16	14	2
Logan	1,369	11	8	3
Lumberport	701	2	2	0
Mabscott	1,298	2	2	0
Madison	2,779	3	3	0
Man	742	2	2	0
Mannington	1,934	2	2	0
Marlinton	979	1	1	0
Marmet	1,453	5	5	0
Martinsburg	18,911	51	40	11
Mason	846	6	5	1
Masontown	534	2	1	1
Matewan	393	1	1	0
McMechen	1,655	2	2	0
Milton	2,796	9	8	1
Monongah	1,011	1	1	0
Montgomery	1,240	6	5	1
Moorefield	2,459	9	8	1
Morgantown	29,279	83	71	12
Moundsville	7,885	17	13	4
Mount Hope	1,088	3	2	1
Mullens	1,421	3	3	0
New Haven	1,447	2	1	1
New Martinsville	5,168	14	9	5
Nitro	6,444	20	19	1
Nutter Fort	1,464	3	3	0
Oak Hill	7,941	22	18	4
Oceana	1,424	3	3	0
Paden City	2,424	5	4	1
Parkersburg	29,190	79	67	12
Parsons	1,295	1	1	0
Paw Paw	413	1	1	0
Pennsboro	1,034	1	1	0
Petersburg	2,247	1	1	0
Philippi	2,921	6	6	0
Piedmont	701	2	2	0
Pineville	630	3	3	0
Poca	872	2	2	0
Point Pleasant	3,983	9	8	1
Pratt	462	2	2	0
Princeton	5,746	19	17	2
Rainelle	1,193	2	1	1
Ranson	5,995	17	16	1
Ravenswood	3,838	11	10	1
Reedsville	565	2	1	1
Rhodell	135	2	1	1
Richwood	1,619	3	3	0
Ridgeley	581	4	3	1
Ripley	3,061	11	10	1
Rivesville	817	1	1	0
Romney	1,718	6	5	1
Rupert	856	1	1	0
Salem	1,454	5	5	0
Shepherdstown	1,504	6	5	1
Shinnston	2,285	6	4	2
Sistersville	1,356	3	3	0
Sophia	1,095	6	6	0
South Charleston	13,138	49	47	2
Spencer	2,022	5	5	0
St. Albans	10,463	28	25	3
Star City	1,825	8	7	1
St. Marys	1,815	5	4	1
Stonewood	1,772	2	2	0
Summersville	3,371	16	15	1
Sutton	847	1	1	0
Sylvester	159	1	1	0
Terra Alta	1,505	1	1	0
Triadelphia	651	1	1	0
Vienna	10,521	23	19	4
War	642	3	3	0
Wayne	1,411	2	2	0
Webster Springs	705	4	3	1
Weirton	18,544	43	39	4
Welch	1,858	3	3	0
Wellsburg	2,360	6	6	0
West Liberty	1,541	7	7	0

Table 78. Full-Time Law Enforcement Employees, by Selected State and City, 2022—Continued

(Number.)

State/city	Population	Total law enforcement employees	Total officers	Total civilians
West Logan	383	1	1	0
Weston	3,846	6	6	0
Westover	4,096	14	14	0
Wheeling	26,244	82	68	14
White Hall	705	5	5	0
White Sulphur Springs	2,173	10	8	2
Williamson	2,896	7	6	1
Williamstown	2,971	8	7	1
Winfield	2,386	7	7	0
WISCONSIN				
Adams	1,776	5	5	0
Albany	1,076	3	3	0
Algoma	3,205	5	5	0
Altoona	9,320	16	15	1
Amery	2,942	6	5	1
Antigo	7,947	18	15	3
Appleton	74,411	132	107	25
Arcadia	3,654	3	3	0
Argyle	798	1	1	0
Ashland	7,975	21	19	2
Ashwaubenon	16,833	56	50	6
Athens	1,059	1	1	0
Augusta	1,534	4	4	0
Avoca	556	1	1	0
Baraboo	12,312	59	27	32
Barneveld	1,318	1	1	0
Barron	3,644	6	6	0
Bayfield	590	6	3	3
Bayside	4,365	13	13	0
Beaver Dam	16,656	35	31	4
Belleville	2,614	7	6	1
Beloit	36,784	81	69	12
Beloit Town	7,895	16	14	2
Berlin	5,665	12	11	1
Big Bend	1,491	3	3	0
Birchwood	408	1	1	0
Black River Falls	3,495	7	6	1
Blair	1,291	2	2	0
Blanchardville	833	1	1	0
Bloomer	3,742	8	7	1
Bloomfield	6,677	14	6	8
Blue Mounds	935	2	1	1
Boscobel	3,291	7	7	0
Boyceville	1,094	7	7	0
Brillion	3,395	8	8	0
Brodhead	3,241	9	7	2
Brookfield	41,489	90	77	13
Brookfield Township	6,429	17	16	1
Brown Deer	12,817	33	30	3
Brownsville	610	1	1	0
Burlington	10,991	23	22	1
Butler	1,765	9	8	1
Caledonia	25,165	37	36	1
Campbellsport	1,902	2	2	0
Campbell Township	4,198	5	5	0
Cashton	1,150	2	2	0
Cedarburg	12,636	27	21	6
Chenequa	540	8	8	0
Chetek	2,160	5	4	1
Chilton	3,898	16	8	8
Chippewa Falls	14,832	27	24	3
Cleveland	1,599	1	1	0
Clinton	2,178	10	5	5
Clintonville	4,493	28	12	16
Colby-Abbotsford	4,312	9	8	1
Coleman	724	1	1	0
Colfax	1,175	2	2	0
Columbus	5,478	10	8	2
Cornell	1,448	3	3	0
Cottage Grove	7,328	16	14	2
Crandon	1,764	4	3	1
Crivitz	1,077	2	2	0
Cross Plains	4,011	7	6	1
Cuba City	2,173	8	4	4
Cudahy	17,702	41	33	8
Cumberland	2,269	8	8	0
Darlington	2,458	5	5	0
Deforest	10,869	25	22	3
Delafield	7,192	17	15	2
Delavan	10,193	29	26	3
Delavan Town	5,347	14	13	1
De Pere	25,382	43	39	4
Dodgeville	4,995	11	11	0
Durand	1,879	8	4	4

Table 78. Full-Time Law Enforcement Employees, by Selected State and City, 2022—Continued
(Number.)

State/city	Population	Total law enforcement employees	Total officers	Total civilians
Eagle River	1,695	7	6	1
Eagle Village	2,119	2	2	0
East Troy	4,748	8	8	0
Eau Claire	69,569	142	94	48
Edgar	1,456	1	1	0
Edgerton	5,954	11	10	1
Eleva	691	2	1	1
Elkhart Lake	957	4	3	1
Elkhorn	10,359	18	16	2
Elk Mound	979	1	1	0
Ellsworth	3,318	5	5	0
Elm Grove	6,512	22	16	6
Elroy	1,332	2	2	0
Evansville	5,840	12	10	2
Everest Metropolitan	17,819	33	30	3
Fall Creek	1,417	2	2	0
Fall River	1,802	4	3	1
Fennimore	2,783	6	6	0
Fitchburg	31,796	54	45	9
Fond du Lac	44,613	75	66	9
Fontana	2,777	8	7	1
Fort Atkinson	12,432	27	21	6
Fox Crossing	18,866	32	28	4
Fox Lake	1,578	3	3	0
Fox Point	6,749	17	16	1
Fox Valley Metro	23,894	29	27	2
Franklin	36,396	75	57	18
Frederic	1,123	2	2	0
Galesville	1,651	4	4	0
Geneva Town	5,484	8	7	1
Genoa City	2,997	6	5	1
Germantown	20,956	45	33	12
Gillett	1,282	4	4	0
Gilman	381	1	1	0
Glendale	13,004	88	41	47
Grafton	12,471	28	22	6
Grand Chute	23,871	41	36	5
Grand Rapids	7,628	8	6	2
Grantsburg	1,336	3	2	1
Green Bay	106,916	200	163	37
Greendale	14,459	43	30	13
Greenfield	36,924	80	61	19
Green Lake	995	8	4	4
Hales Corners	7,516	16	16	0
Hammond	1,851	4	3	1
Hartford	15,803	60	27	33
Hartford Township	3,399	1	1	0
Hartland	9,644	20	18	2
Hayward	2,566	8	7	1
Hazel Green	1,183	2	2	0
Highland	866	1	1	0
Hillsboro	1,463	3	3	0
Hobart-Lawrence	16,948	14	14	0
Holmen	11,058	15	13	2
Horicon	3,827	9	8	1
Hortonville	3,111	8	7	1
Hudson	15,571	33	30	3
Hurley	1,564	7	6	1
Independence	1,465	2	2	0
Iron Ridge	892	1	1	0
Iron River	1,258	6	3	3
Jackson	7,205	14	13	1
Janesville	66,242	117	104	13
Jefferson	7,709	15	12	3
Juneau	2,656	5	4	1
Kaukauna	17,288	27	26	1
Kenosha	98,841	217	204	13
Kewaskum	4,429	8	8	0
Kewaunee	2,774	6	6	0
Kiel	3,969	17	8	9
Kohler	2,184	9	8	1
Kronenwetter	8,530	8	7	1
La Crosse	51,727	112	89	23
Ladysmith	3,112	9	8	1
La Farge	720	1	1	0
Lake Delton	3,447	53	25	28
Lake Geneva	8,631	37	27	10
Lake Hallie	7,352	13	11	2
Lake Mills	6,662	22	20	2
Lancaster	3,911	7	6	1
Lena	530	2	1	1
Linn Township	2,734	8	8	0
Lodi	3,213	7	6	1
Lomira	2,680	2	2	0
Luxemburg	2,699	1	1	0

Table 78. Full-Time Law Enforcement Employees, by Selected State and City, 2022—Continued

(Number.)

State/city	Population	Total law enforcement employees	Total officers	Total civilians
Madison	269,546	611	500	111
Manawa	1,408	3	3	0
Manitowoc	34,688	76	65	11
Maple Bluff	1,326	8	6	2
Marathon City	1,560	3	3	0
Marinette	11,015	30	26	4
Marion	1,300	4	4	0
Markesan	1,386	4	4	0
Marshall Village	3,833	10	9	1
Marshfield	18,787	47	39	8
Mauston	4,294	12	10	2
Mayville	5,124	10	9	1
McFarland	9,555	33	16	17
Medford	4,298	9	8	1
Menasha	17,971	39	32	7
Menomonee Falls	39,312	74	61	13
Menomonie	16,781	32	26	6
Mequon	25,347	46	39	7
Merrill	9,341	26	23	3
Middleton	23,346	49	39	10
Milton	5,683	14	12	2
Milwaukee	561,743	1,593	1,593	0
Mineral Point	2,566	6	6	0
Minocqua	5,186	16	10	6
Mishicot	1,440	3	3	0
Mondovi	2,795	10	5	5
Monona	8,920	48	21	27
Monroe	10,461	32	26	6
Monticello	1,183	3	3	0
Mosinee	4,501	8	7	1
Mount Horeb	7,687	17	14	3
Mount Pleasant	27,625	60	54	6
Mukwonago	8,477	21	15	6
Mukwonago Town	7,792	7	6	1
Muscoda	1,301	3	3	0
Muskego	25,406	52	42	10
Neenah	27,706	52	40	12
Neillsville	2,348	14	7	7
Nekoosa	2,434	7	7	0
New Berlin	40,358	80	69	11
New Glarus	2,221	3	3	0
New Holstein	3,033	7	6	1
New Lisbon	1,745	4	4	0
New London	7,286	19	17	2
New Richmond	10,610	21	20	1
Niagara	1,582	4	4	0
North Fond du Lac	5,423	11	9	2
North Hudson	3,953	6	5	1
Norwalk	594	1	1	0
Oak Creek	35,995	85	60	25
Oconomowoc	18,531	33	26	7
Oconomowoc Lake	580	6	6	0
Oconomowoc Town	8,853	12	11	1
Oconto	4,589	20	10	10
Oconto Falls	2,961	7	7	0
Omro	3,662	9	8	1
Onalaska	18,807	33	31	2
Oregon	11,538	21	18	3
Orfordville	1,469	1	1	0
Osceola	2,849	6	5	1
Oshkosh	66,521	116	101	15
Osseo	1,778	4	4	0
Park Falls	2,379	7	7	0
Pepin	735	1	1	0
Peshtigo	3,362	6	6	0
Pewaukee Village	8,177	21	20	1
Phillips	1,512	5	5	0
Pittsville	835	2	2	0
Plainfield	937	2	1	1
Platteville	11,771	25	20	5
Pleasant Prairie	21,421	46	36	10
Plover	13,850	24	21	3
Plymouth	8,885	15	15	0
Portage	10,251	29	25	4
Port Edwards	1,748	3	3	0
Port Washington	12,867	26	21	5
Poynette	2,580	6	5	1
Prairie du Chien	5,461	13	13	0
Prescott	4,340	12	11	1
Princeton	1,280	4	4	0
Pulaski	4,020	8	7	1
Racine	76,679	210	180	30
Reedsburg	10,113	25	19	6
Rhinelander	8,341	19	17	2
Rib Lake	913	1	1	0

Table 78. Full-Time Law Enforcement Employees, by Selected State and City, 2022—Continued

(Number.)

State/city	Population	Total law enforcement employees	Total officers	Total civilians
Rice Lake	8,941	19	18	1
Richland Center	4,997	13	11	2
Rio	1,125	2	2	0
Ripon	7,793	16	14	2
Ripon Town	1,318	1	1	0
River Falls	17,169	29	26	3
River Hills	1,559	12	11	1
Rome Town	3,158	6	6	0
Rosendale	1,052	1	1	0
Rothschild	5,522	14	12	2
Sauk Prairie	4,572	15	13	2
Saukville	4,283	13	11	2
Seymour	3,512	6	6	0
Sharon	1,590	5	4	1
Shawano	9,240	44	21	23
Sheboygan	49,917	102	83	19
Sheboygan Falls	8,140	15	15	0
Shiocton	929	2	2	0
Shorewood	13,453	29	25	4
Shorewood Hills	2,113	7	6	1
Shullsburg	1,190	1	1	0
Siren	835	4	3	1
Slinger	6,201	14	13	1
Somerset	3,073	7	7	0
South Milwaukee	20,247	39	33	6
Sparta	9,901	27	24	3
Spencer	1,809	4	4	0
Spooner	2,492	8	7	1
Spring Green	1,522	1	1	0
Spring Valley	1,403	1	1	0
Stanley	3,800	6	6	0
St. Croix Falls	2,242	15	7	8
Stevens Point	25,777	50	45	5
St. Francis	9,758	22	21	1
Stoughton	12,948	30	24	6
Strum	1,056	2	2	0
Sturgeon Bay	9,758	24	22	2
Sturtevant	6,970	14	13	1
Summit	5,201	11	10	1
Sun Prairie	36,153	76	54	22
Superior	26,429	58	51	7
Theresa	1,255	2	2	0
Thiensville	3,302	9	8	1
Thorp	1,767	3	3	0
Three Lakes	2,481	5	5	0
Tomah	9,525	24	21	3
Tomahawk	3,432	10	9	1
Town of East Troy	4,068	5	4	1
Trempealeau	1,884	4	4	0
Twin Lakes	6,448	18	13	5
Two Rivers	11,273	31	26	5
Verona	14,413	25	23	2
Viroqua	4,421	12	10	2
Walworth	2,778	9	8	1
Washburn	2,060	5	5	0
Waterford Town	6,455	9	9	0
Waterloo	3,475	7	6	1
Watertown	22,885	54	39	15
Waukesha	71,147	155	124	31
Waunakee	14,914	23	21	2
Waupaca	6,436	17	16	1
Waupun	11,530	19	17	2
Wausau	39,349	85	75	10
Wautoma	2,252	7	6	1
Wauwatosa	47,149	116	92	24
Webster	707	3	3	0
West Allis	58,681	153	124	29
West Bend	31,773	68	53	15
Westby	2,360	5	5	0
Westfield	1,336	2	2	0
West Milwaukee	3,997	22	19	3
West Salem	5,271	11	10	1
Whitefish Bay	14,549	24	22	2
Whitehall	1,616	4	4	0
Whitewater	14,327	57	23	34
Wild Rose	799	1	1	0
Williams Bay	3,017	8	8	0
Wilton	520	2	1	1
Wind Point	1,629	1	1	0
Winneconne	2,515	4	4	0
Wisconsin Dells	3,448	22	17	5
Wisconsin Rapids	18,693	42	38	4
Woodruff	2,105	6	5	1

Table 78. Full-Time Law Enforcement Employees, by Selected State and City, 2022—Continued

(Number.)

State/city	Population	Total law enforcement employees	Total officers	Total civilians
WYOMING				
Afton	2,263	3	3	0
Buffalo	4,567	20	12	8
Casper	58,076	152	101	51
Cheyenne	64,941	126	104	22
Cody	10,281	25	22	3
Diamondville	530	2	2	0
Douglas	6,336	23	20	3
Evanston	11,886	30	25	5
Evansville	2,738	15	13	2
Gillette	32,320	81	57	24
Glenrock	2,396	13	7	6
Green River	11,435	30	25	5
Greybull	1,700	6	6	0
Hanna	687	1	1	0
Jackson	10,932	44	34	10
Kemmerer	2,440	7	7	0
Lander	7,580	20	18	2
Laramie	32,009	66	43	23
Lingle	401	1	1	0
Lusk	1,496	6	5	1
Medicine Bow	249	3	2	1
Mills	4,239	18	14	4
Moorcroft	981	4	3	1
Newcastle	3,176	9	3	6
Pine Bluffs	1,146	5	5	0
Powell	6,484	19	13	6
Rawlins	8,355	28	16	12
Riverton	10,623	37	27	10
Rock Springs	22,914	48	36	12
Saratoga	1,766	7	3	4
Sheridan	19,373	45	28	17
Thermopolis	2,691	10	5	5
Torrington	6,145	24	17	7
Upton	904	3	3	0
Wheatland	3,611	9	8	1
Worland	4,817	13	11	2

1 The employee data presented in this table for Charlotte-Mecklenburg represent only Charlotte-Mecklenburg Police Department and exclude Mecklenburg County Sheriff's Office.

Table 79. Full-Time Law Enforcement Employees, by Selected State and University or College, 2022

(Number.)

State and university/college	Student enrollment[1]	Law enforcement employees	Officers	Civilians
ALABAMA				
Alabama State University	4,478	28	20	8
Auburn University, Montgomery	6,141	15	10	5
Bevill State Community College	4,595	1	1	0
Bishop State Community College	3,549	7	6	1
Calhoun Community College	12,424	8	7	1
Central Alabama Community College	2,108	1	1	0
Coastal Alabama Community College	8,971	12	12	0
Enterprise State Community College	2,508	1	1	0
Faulkner University	3,670	9	8	1
Jacksonville State University	10,752	26	17	9
Jefferson State Community College	12,293	12	10	2
Lawson State Community College	4,239	7	6	1
Lurleen B. Wallace Community College	2,295	1	1	0
Samford University	6,160	17	15	2
Southern Union State Community College	5,789	7	5	2
Troy University	20,866	16	12	4
Tuskegee University	3,058	22	6	16
University of Alabama				
Birmingham	26,327	214	114	100
Huntsville	11,318	23	15	8
Tuscaloosa	41,992	121	67	54
University of Montevallo	2,960	20	10	10
University of North Alabama	10,003	13	9	4
University of South Alabama	16,311	21	15	6
University of West Alabama	8,711	14	8	6
Wallace Community College				
Dothan	5,088	3	3	0
Selma	2,104	3	1	2
Wallace State Community College	6,298	8	8	0
ALASKA				
University of Alaska				
Anchorage	19,093	17	10	7
Fairbanks	10,725	13	7	6
ARIZONA				
Arizona State University, Main Campus	161,117	123	75	48
Arizona Western College	9,712	11	7	4
Central Arizona College	6,317	15	13	2
Maricopa Community College[2]		81	69	12
Northern Arizona University	33,349	31	18	13
Pima Community College	32,802	49	26	23
University of Arizona	52,329	100	61	39
Yavapai College	8,393	8	7	1
ARKANSAS				
Arkansas State University				
Beebe	3,939	6	5	1
Jonesboro	18,451	23	18	5
Newport	4,280	3	3	0
Arkansas Tech University	12,257	20	17	3
Henderson State University	3,610	9	8	1
Northwest Arkansas Community College	10,242	16	12	4
Southern Arkansas University	5,209	10	9	1
Southern Arkansas University Tech	1,588	3	3	0
University of Arkansas				
Fayetteville	30,349	45	30	15
Little Rock	10,955	23	16	7
Medical Sciences	3,241	39	32	7
Monticello	3,293	9	8	1
Pine Bluff	2,898	19	14	5
Pulaski Technical College	6,967	12	11	1
University of Arkansas Community College at Morrilton	2,400	3	3	0
University of Central Arkansas	11,834	34	24	10
CALIFORNIA				
Allan Hancock College	14,876	12	4	8
California State Polytechnic University				
Humboldt	7,184	17	8	9
Pomona	31,745	46	19	27
San Luis Obispo	23,319	24	18	6
California State University				
Bakersfield	13,088	24	15	9
Channel Islands	8,370	21	16	5
Chico	18,141	22	14	8
Dominguez Hills	20,180	16	16	0
East Bay	18,567	21	14	7
Fresno	27,235	37	26	11
Fullerton	47,482	32	23	9
Long Beach	43,455	35	21	14
Los Angeles	29,167	40	18	22
Monterey Bay	8,273	26	16	10

Table 79. Full-Time Law Enforcement Employees, by Selected State and University or College, 2022 —Continued

(Number.)

State and university/college	Student enrollment[1]	Law enforcement employees	Officers	Civilians
Northridge	43,286	36	16	20
Sacramento	36,476	35	19	16
San Bernardino	21,793	25	14	11
San Jose	39,940	61	19	42
San Marcos	17,565	25	17	8
Stanislaus	12,470	21	14	7
Chaffey College	27,808	14	12	2
College of the Sequoias	15,729	7	6	1
Contra Costa Community College	49,068	33	22	11
Cuesta College	13,912	6	3	3
El Camino College	30,759	17	12	5
Foothill-De Anza College	56,506	17	10	7
Irvine Valley College	18,155	17	11	6
Marin Community College	6,494	7	5	2
Pasadena Community College	35,760	15	10	5
Riverside Community College	59,448	24	17	7
San Bernardino Community College	25,704	17	10	7
San Diego State University	38,811	52	34	18
San Francisco State University	31,072	39	15	24
San Jose/Evergreen Community College	26,623	18	6	12
Sonoma County Junior College	24,673	23	10	13
Sonoma State University	8,775	12	10	2
State Center Community College District	61,021	27	21	6
University of California				
Berkeley	45,584	93	46	47
Davis	41,743	68	42	26
Irvine	38,479	109	45	64
Los Angeles	47,499	112	56	56
Merced	9,488	33	17	16
Riverside	28,597	37	25	12
San Diego	41,682	74	36	38
San Francisco	3,313	75	58	17
Santa Barbara	28,222	44	30	14
Santa Cruz	20,781	32	18	14
Ventura County Community College District	50,633	14	13	1
West Valley-Mission College	23,203	14	9	5
COLORADO				
Adams State University	3,863	6	5	1
Aims Community College	10,162	2	2	0
Arapahoe Community College	16,340	8	7	1
Auraria Higher Education Center[3]		47	30	17
Colorado School of Mines	7,281	11	10	1
Colorado State University, Fort Collins	36,626	49	29	20
Fort Lewis College	3,899	11	9	2
Pikes Peak Community College	15,915	14	14	0
Red Rocks Community College	9,871	7	4	3
University of Colorado, Denver	30,432	53	22	31
University of Northern Colorado	13,818	23	16	7
CONNECTICUT				
Central Connecticut State University	12,467	24	17	7
Eastern Connecticut State University	5,054	21	13	8
Southern Connecticut State University	10,580	23	18	5
University of Connecticut, all campuses[2]		108	74	34
Western Connecticut State University	6,001	11	7	4
DELAWARE				
Delaware State University	5,230	30	10	20
University of Delaware	25,695	81	51	30
FLORIDA				
Florida A&M University	10,221	32	17	15
Florida Atlantic University	37,656	83	46	37
Florida Gulf Coast University	18,873	30	20	10
Florida International University	74,678	96	66	30
Florida Polytechnic University	1,498	13	11	2
Florida SouthWestern State College	20,209	32	19	13
Florida State University				
Panama City[2]		7	6	1
Tallahassee	49,091	83	58	25
New College of Florida	706	15	11	4
Northwest Florida State College	7,054	4	4	0
Tallahassee Community College	15,478	16	9	7
University of Central Florida	83,889	114	77	37
University of Florida	60,790	123	78	45
University of North Florida	20,138	42	32	10
University of South Florida				
St. Petersburg[2]		20	14	6
Tampa	59,918	71	44	27
University of West Florida	16,584	24	18	6

Table 79. Full-Time Law Enforcement Employees, by Selected State and University or College, 2022 —Continued

(Number.)

State and university/college	Student enrollment[1]	Law enforcement employees	Officers	Civilians
GEORGIA				
Abraham Baldwin Agricultural College	4,735	16	15	1
Agnes Scott College	1,130	17	11	6
Albany State University	7,702	31	20	11
Albany Technical College	4,191	4	4	0
Athens Technical College	5,778	3	2	1
Atlanta Technical College	4,973	4	2	2
Augusta Technical College	5,549	6	5	1
Augusta University	9,979	53	34	19
Berry College	2,308	13	8	5
Clark Atlanta University	4,123	43	14	29
Clayton State University	8,659	16	12	4
College of Coastal Georgia	4,303	12	12	0
Columbus State University	10,094	30	24	6
Dalton State College	5,513	12	9	3
Emory University	15,201	72	40	32
Fort Valley State University	3,202	18	8	10
Georgia College and State University	7,914	15	9	6
Georgia Gwinnett College	14,559	30	22	8
Georgia Highlands College	7,367	5	5	0
Georgia Institute of Technology	47,787	114	63	51
Georgia Military College	12,823	5	3	2
Georgia Northwestern Technical College	8,768	8	7	1
Georgia Piedmont Technical College	3,920	9	8	1
Georgia Southern University	31,082	65	46	19
Georgia Southwestern State University	3,926	9	8	1
Georgia State University	42,775	213	108	105
Gordon State College	3,908	9	8	1
Gwinnett Technical College	11,675	4	4	0
Kennesaw State University	48,071	86	53	33
Mercer University	10,403	28	20	8
Middle Georgia State University	10,346	28	22	6
Morehouse College	2,482	32	15	17
Piedmont College	3,055	8	5	3
Savannah Technical College	5,536	10	8	2
Southern Regional Technical College	5,685	6	4	2
Spelman College	2,286	33	24	9
University of Georgia	43,314	95	71	24
University of North Georgia	23,080	46	35	11
University of West Georgia	16,100	39	26	13
West Georgia Technical College	8,932	11	11	0
Young Harris College	1,620	4	4	0
ILLINOIS				
Chicago State University	3,246	22	19	3
College of DuPage	36,245	22	17	5
College of Lake County	20,233	31	20	11
Eastern Illinois University	10,562	12	11	1
Elgin Community College	11,788	18	16	2
Eureka College	551	2	2	0
Illinois Central College	11,132	18	7	11
Illinois State University	22,580	37	27	10
John Wood Community College	2,724	5	4	1
Joliet Junior College	20,745	24	14	10
Kankakee Community College	3,791	7	3	4
Lewis University	7,703	19	10	9
Lincoln Land Community College	8,670	15	12	3
McHenry County College	11,883	9	8	1
Millikin University	2,147	16	3	13
Moraine Valley Community College	17,693	24	17	7
Morton College	5,387	4	3	1
Northeastern Illinois University	8,778	20	15	5
Northern Illinois University	18,759	55	38	17
Oakton Community College	14,960	13	12	1
Richland Community College	3,499	6	2	4
Rock Valley College	8,551	12	9	3
Southern Illinois University, Carbondale	12,905	45	31	14
South Suburban College	7,210	12	8	4
Southwestern Illinois College	13,299	20	19	1
Triton College	14,714	15	10	5
University of Illinois				
Chicago	36,710	85	70	15
Urbana	59,691	109	66	43
Waubonsee Community College	13,452	9	8	1
IOWA				
Iowa State University	33,336	57	33	24
University of Iowa	33,345	78	40	38
University of Northern Iowa	10,888	18	15	3
KANSAS				
Emporia State University	7,245	7	7	0

Table 79. Full-Time Law Enforcement Employees, by Selected State and University or College, 2022 —Continued

(Number.)

State and university/college	Student enrollment[1]	Law enforcement employees	Officers	Civilians
Fort Hays State University	19,052	7	5	2
Garden City Community College	2,537	2	1	1
Kansas State University	22,693	26	16	10
Pittsburg State University	8,034	14	11	3
University of Kansas, Medical Center[2]		192	56	136
Washburn University	6,743	14	9	5
Wichita State University	17,430	38	25	13
KENTUCKY				
Morehead State University	10,581	17	11	6
Murray State University	10,570	21	14	7
University of Kentucky	32,446	174	54	120
University of Louisville	26,237	72	38	34
Western Kentucky University	20,304	28	19	9
LOUISIANA				
Delgado Community College	18,938	36	28	8
Dillard University	1,274	20	11	9
Grambling State University	6,351	23	14	9
Louisiana State University	13,967	7	7	0
Louisiana Tech University, Shreveport	12,841	20	18	2
McNeese State University	7,927	12	6	6
Southeastern Louisiana University	17,259	28	23	5
Southern University and A&M College, New Orleans	2,688	13	13	0
University of Louisiana				
Shreveport	4,114	3	3	0
Monroe	10,197	25	25	0
MAINE				
University of Maine				
Farmington	2,292	6	5	1
Orono	14,808	21	11	10
University of Southern Maine	10,662	17	9	8
MARYLAND				
Bowie State University	6,994	28	13	15
Coppin State University	2,573	22	11	11
Frostburg State University	5,432	22	17	5
Hagerstown Community College	4,996	5	3	2
Morgan State University	8,294	33	33	0
Prince George's County Community College	16,951	19	10	9
Salisbury University	8,759	27	17	10
Towson University	24,486	48	37	11
University of Maryland				
Baltimore City	24	176	72	104
Baltimore County	15,358	39	28	11
College Park	44,529	113	76	37
Eastern Shore	2,946	38	8	30
MASSACHUSETTS				
Amherst College	1,863	16	8	8
Assumption College	2,670	16	10	6
Babson College	3,877	28	19	9
Bentley University	5,541	30	20	10
Boston College	16,198	74	48	26
Boston University	40,492	60	47	13
Brandeis University	6,926	20	15	5
Bridgewater State University	12,652	28	21	7
Bristol Community College	8,925	5	5	0
Bunker Hill Community College	14,143	14	12	2
Clark University	3,766	14	11	3
College of the Holy Cross	3,051	25	17	8
Curry College	2,825	12	7	5
Dean College	1,401	15	3	12
Emerson College	5,883	19	15	4
Endicott College	5,081	17	13	4
Fisher College	2,299	11	6	5
Fitchburg State University	10,165	23	18	5
Framingham State University	7,568	12	10	2
Gordon College	2,263	8	6	2
Harvard University	39,981	87	64	23
Holyoke Community College	5,496	4	4	0
Massachusetts Bay Community College	6,236	8	8	0
Massachusetts College of Liberal Arts	1,765	11	4	7
Massachusetts Institute of Technology	12,217	61	59	2
Massasoit Community College	8,472	14	13	1
Merrimack College	6,233	15	10	5
Mount Wachusett Community College	4,343	9	8	1
Quinsigamond Community College	9,370	18	12	6
Salem State University	8,742	24	21	3
Simmons College	7,362	25	19	6
Smith College	2,979	18	10	8

Table 79. Full-Time Law Enforcement Employees, by Selected State and University or College, 2022 —Continued

(Number.)

State and university/college	Student enrollment[1]	Law enforcement employees	Officers	Civilians
Springfield College	3,250	29	19	10
Springfield Technical Community College	5,743	16	13	3
Stonehill College	2,574	18	13	5
University of Massachusetts				
Amherst	36,827	65	53	12
Dartmouth	9,244	21	14	7
Harbor Campus, Boston	19,398	26	21	5
Medical Center, Worcester	1,339	35	20	15
Wentworth Institute of Technology	5,319	23	18	5
Western New England University	3,951	26	12	14
Westfield State University	6,391	20	15	5
Worcester Polytechnic Institute	7,876	26	20	6
Worcester State University	7,737	19	14	5
MICHIGAN				
Central Michigan University	20,057	29	22	7
Delta College	9,738	12	6	6
Eastern Michigan University	19,451	41	31	10
Ferris State University	13,171	12	10	2
Grand Rapids Community College	18,142	18	14	4
Grand Valley State University	26,320	30	21	9
Kalamazoo Valley Community College	10,128	8	6	2
Kellogg Community College	5,335	3	3	0
Kirtland Community College	1,982	1	1	0
Lansing Community College	14,739	14	11	3
Macomb Community College	24,180	34	27	7
Michigan State University	54,245	108	68	40
Michigan Technological University	7,241	16	11	5
Mott Community College	7,479	31	21	10
Northern Michigan University	8,365	21	18	3
Oakland Community College	23,708	23	22	1
Oakland University	21,329	29	18	11
Schoolcraft College	13,994	18	13	5
University of Michigan				
Ann Arbor	50,002	73	59	14
Dearborn	10,105	26	13	13
Flint	8,032	30	16	14
Washtenaw Community College	18,734	13	6	7
Western Michigan University	22,035	48	33	15
MINNESOTA				
University of Minnesota				
Duluth	11,024	12	11	1
Morris	1,441	7	3	4
Twin Cities	62,309	101	47	54
MISSISSIPPI				
East Mississippi Community College				
Communiversity[2]		1	1	0
Golden Triangle[2]		6	4	2
West Point[2]		1	1	0
Holmes Community College				
Goodman	7,549	12	6	6
Grenada[2]		4	4	0
Ridgeland[2]		5	4	1
Jones County Junior College	6,213	5	5	0
Mississippi Delta Community College	5,205	14	13	1
Mississippi State University	25,760	46	24	22
Northeast Mississippi Community College	5,809	7	6	1
Northwest Mississippi Community College				
Desoto	9,427	3	3	0
Senatobia	9,427	15	14	1
Pearl River Community College				
Forrest	7,068	4	4	0
Poplarville[2]		10	8	2
University of Mississippi				
Medical Center[2]		80	57	23
Oxford	23,683	46	31	15
MISSOURI				
Missouri Southern State University	5,858	6	5	1
Missouri Western State University	5,390	8	7	1
Northwest Missouri State University	8,872	13	10	3
Southeast Missouri State University	11,387	20	11	9
St. Charles Community College	8,648	14	12	2
St. Louis Community College, Meramec	23,466	40	29	11
Truman State University	5,047	9	7	2
University of Central Missouri	14,187	22	15	7
University of Missouri				
Kansas City	18,650	30	21	9
St. Louis	17,406	21	15	6

Table 79. Full-Time Law Enforcement Employees, by Selected State and University or College, 2022 —Continued

(Number.)

State and university/college	Student enrollment[1]	Law enforcement employees	Officers	Civilians
MONTANA				
Montana State University	18,344	22	20	2
Montana State University, Billings	5,402	8	7	1
University of Montana	11,821	21	15	6
NEBRASKA				
Metropolitan Community College, Douglas County	21,101	27	23	4
University of Nebraska				
Kearney	7,556	13	10	3
Lincoln	27,390	57	25	32
Omaha	18,632	19	19	0
NEVADA				
University of Nevada, Reno	22,982	38	24	14
University Police Services	86,700	67	45	22
NEW HAMPSHIRE				
Plymouth State University	5,079	8	8	0
University of New Hampshire	15,585	35	18	17
NEW JERSEY				
Brookdale Community College	14,796	12	12	0
Essex County College	9,039	57	9	48
Kean University	16,448	42	23	19
Middlesex County College	15,190	16	9	7
Monmouth University	6,166	28	14	14
Montclair State University	24,137	44	33	11
New Jersey Institute of Technology	13,687	75	36	39
Princeton University	7,942	97	39	58
Rowan University	22,640	88	35	53
Rutgers University				
Camden	7,991	54	17	37
Newark	15,444	140	58	82
New Brunswick	56,771	140	55	85
Stevens Institute of Technology	8,436	23	21	2
Stockton University	11,788	39	21	18
The College of New Jersey	8,773	32	15	17
William Paterson University	11,681	34	25	9
NEW MEXICO				
Eastern New Mexico University	6,620	9	8	1
New Mexico Highlands University	3,409	17	7	10
New Mexico Institute of Mining and Technology	1,882	19	9	10
New Mexico Military Institute	570	6	6	0
New Mexico State University	16,089	44	17	27
University of New Mexico	24,776	65	43	22
Western New Mexico University	3,717	8	7	1
NEW YORK				
Cornell University	24,486	77	47	30
Ithaca College	6,034	35	15	20
State University of New York Police				
Albany	20,071	55	36	19
Alfred	3,977	16	11	5
Binghamton	19,919	52	35	17
Brockport	8,882	21	15	6
Buffalo	35,840	75	62	13
Buffalo State College	9,509	35	29	6
Canton	4,611	10	10	0
Cobleskill	2,372	12	11	1
Cortland	7,735	24	16	8
Delhi	3,438	16	12	4
Downstate Medical	2,415	97	21	76
Environmental Science	2,318	14	9	5
Farmingdale	12,415	32	22	10
Fredonia	4,387	19	15	4
Geneseo	5,276	22	16	6
Maritime	1,832	15	11	4
Morrisville	2,859	14	12	2
New Paltz	8,597	23	19	4
Old Westbury	5,954	24	20	4
Oneonta	7,123	26	16	10
Optometry	403	17	7	10
Oswego	8,882	20	15	5
Plattsburgh	5,906	22	15	7
Polytechnic Institute	3,439	17	12	5
Potsdam	3,442	14	10	4
Purchase	4,243	32	24	8
Stony Brook	34,254	150	67	83
Upstate Medical	1,623	121	21	100

Table 79. Full-Time Law Enforcement Employees, by Selected State and University or College, 2022 —Continued

(Number.)

State and university/college	Student enrollment[1]	Law enforcement employees	Officers	Civilians
NORTH CAROLINA				
Appalachian State University	21,706	48	31	17
Beaufort County Community College	1,902	4	4	0
Belmont Abbey College	1,634	8	8	0
Davidson College	2,029	11	8	3
Duke University	18,120	153	61	92
East Carolina University	32,009	63	50	13
Elizabeth City State University	2,351	22	13	9
Elon University	7,461	36	17	19
Fayetteville State University	8,658	35	15	20
Meredith College	1,970	12	3	9
Methodist University	2,075	19	7	12
North Carolina Agricultural and Technical State University	14,121	54	23	31
North Carolina Central University	9,000	46	25	21
North Carolina School of the Arts	1,085	23	16	7
North Carolina State University, Raleigh	40,482	70	50	20
Queens University	2,755	10	8	2
Saint Augustine's University	1,180	12	4	8
University of North Carolina				
Asheville	3,863	17	13	4
Chapel Hill	32,943	95	47	48
Charlotte	34,188	50	42	8
Greensboro	21,720	45	27	18
Pembroke	10,152	29	20	9
Wilmington	20,873	45	27	18
Wake Forest University	9,572	50	20	30
Western Carolina University	13,820	22	22	0
Winston-Salem State University	5,897	20	13	7
NORTH DAKOTA				
Bismarck State College	4,825	3	3	0
North Dakota State University	14,102	17	15	2
University of North Dakota	16,791	20	19	1
OHIO				
Capital University	4,447	14	8	6
Cleveland State University	18,165	48	25	23
Columbus State Community College	44,909	42	23	19
Hocking College	3,411	6	4	2
Kent State University	31,555	36	25	11
Lakeland Community College	7,732	11	8	3
Miami University	20,330	33	24	9
Ohio State University, Columbus	66,749	71	66	5
Ohio University	30,163	27	20	7
Otterbein University	3,085	9	9	0
University of Cincinnati	48,219	115	52	63
University of Rio Grande	2,950	5	4	1
University of Toledo	18,929	29	29	0
Walsh University	3,122	5	5	0
Wilberforce University	520	13	8	5
Wright State University	12,862	21	15	6
OKLAHOMA				
Bacone College	374	3	3	0
Cameron University	4,745	10	10	0
East Central University	4,326	5	5	0
Eastern Oklahoma State College	1,699	4	4	0
Langston University	2,207	14	11	3
Mid-America Christian University	2,617	6	6	0
Northeastern Oklahoma A&M College	2,148	5	4	1
Northeastern State University, Tahlequah	8,756	15	11	4
Northwestern Oklahoma State University	2,174	1	1	0
Oklahoma City Community College	17,029	33	25	8
Oklahoma City University	2,960	33	7	26
Oklahoma Panhandle State University	1,617	2	1	1
Oklahoma State University				
Main Campus	26,947	45	34	11
Okmulgee	3,017	6	6	0
Tulsa	1,442	8	7	1
Rogers State University	4,106	7	7	0
Seminole State College	1,886	3	3	0
Southeastern Oklahoma State University	7,208	7	6	1
Southern Nazarene University	2,883	6	4	2
Southwestern Oklahoma State University	5,664	8	6	2
Tulsa Community College	21,523	77	63	14
University of Central Oklahoma	16,527	22	15	7
University of Oklahoma				
Health Sciences Center	3,668	69	39	30
Norman	31,285	60	29	31

Table 79. Full-Time Law Enforcement Employees, by Selected State and University or College, 2022 —Continued

(Number.)

State and university/college	Student enrollment[1]	Law enforcement employees	Officers	Civilians
OREGON				
Oregon State University	38,654	47	13	34
Portland State University	29,053	26	10	16
University of Oregon	23,751	37	18	19
PENNSYLVANIA				
Allegheny College	1,743	14	9	5
Bloomsburg University	9,276	18	15	3
Bucknell University	3,815	19	10	9
California University	8,993	18	15	3
Chatham University	2,693	14	11	3
Cheyney University	687	12	6	6
Clarion University	5,270	9	6	3
Drexel University	27,010	77	49	28
East Stroudsburg University	6,500	16	13	3
Edinboro University	5,285	12	11	1
Franklin and Marshall College	2,365	22	16	6
Indiana University	11,427	19	13	6
Lehigh Career and Technical Institute[2]		1	1	0
Lincoln University	2,214	29	18	11
Mansfield University	2,110	9	8	1
Mercyhurst University	4,049	12	8	4
Millersville University	8,697	18	16	2
Moravian College	2,979	16	10	6
Pennsylvania State University				
Abington[2]		8	8	0
Altoona[2]		10	10	0
Beaver[2]		7	7	0
Behrend[2]		11	10	1
Berks[2]		10	9	1
Brandywine[2]		6	5	1
Dubois[2]		2	2	0
Fayette[2]		4	4	0
Greater Allegheny[2]		6	6	0
Great Valley[2]		2	2	0
Harrisburg[2]		6	6	0
Hazleton[2]		5	5	0
Lehigh Valley[2]		3	3	0
Mont Alto[2]		5	5	0
New Kensington[2]		4	4	0
Schuylkill[2]		6	6	0
University Park[2]		105	50	55
Wilkes-Barre[2]		3	3	0
Worthington Scranton[2]		4	4	0
York[2]		4	4	0
Point Park University	4,280	7	7	0
Saint Francis University	3,406	9	8	1
Shippensburg University	6,891	15	15	0
Slippery Rock University	9,984	11	10	1
University of Pittsburgh				
Bradford	2,331	6	5	1
Greensburg	1,557	11	10	1
Johnstown	2,459	12	9	3
Pittsburgh	35,479	122	69	53
University of Scranton	5,493	24	14	10
Villanova University	12,623	63	22	41
West Chester University	19,767	47	22	25
Wilkes University	6,605	29	17	12
York College of Pennsylvania	4,512	12	9	3
RHODE ISLAND				
Brown University	10,446	68	46	22
University of Rhode Island	20,720	46	28	18
SOUTH CAROLINA				
Benedict College	1,914	17	14	3
Bob Jones University	3,654	3	3	0
Clemson University	29,483	54	37	17
Coastal Carolina University	11,421	44	31	13
College of Charleston	12,326	41	21	20
Columbia College	1,674	11	9	2
Denmark Technical College	782	7	3	4
Erskine College	1,064	3	2	1
Francis Marion University	4,743	13	10	3
Furman University	2,714	22	15	7
Greenville Technical College	13,774	13	11	2
Lander University	3,857	21	12	9
Medical University of South Carolina	3,638	59	40	19
Midlands Technical College	11,804	8	7	1
Orangeburg-Calhoun Technical College	3,219	4	4	0
Presbyterian College	1,337	6	3	3
Spartanburg Methodist College	1,116	7	5	2

Table 79. Full-Time Law Enforcement Employees, by Selected State and University or College, 2022 —Continued

(Number.)

State and university/college	Student enrollment[1]	Law enforcement employees	Officers	Civilians
The Citadel	4,388	25	15	10
Tri-County Technical College	7,208	14	11	3
Trident Technical College	16,834	10	7	3
University of South Carolina				
Aiken	4,870	7	6	1
Beaufort	2,398	22	13	9
Columbia	38,770	92	65	27
Upstate	7,107	11	9	2
Winthrop University	6,589	17	14	3
Wofford College[2]		17	5	12
York Technical College	5,556	3	3	0
SOUTH DAKOTA				
South Dakota School of Mines and Technology	2,857	4	2	2
South Dakota State University	13,678	20	14	6
University of South Dakota	12,018	16	13	3
TENNESSEE				
Austin Peay State University	12,108	26	17	9
Chattanooga State Community College	9,510	10	6	4
Christian Brothers University	2,295	13	4	9
Cleveland State Community College	3,892	5	5	0
Columbia State Community College	8,037	6	3	3
East Tennessee State University	15,797	27	18	9
Jackson State Community College	5,595	2	2	0
Lincoln Memorial University	5,474	40	10	30
Middle Tennessee State University	25,626	47	37	10
Motlow State Community College	7,928	6	6	0
Nashville State Community College	9,537	20	2	18
Northeast State Community College	6,807	8	8	0
Pellissippi State Community College	13,051	18	15	3
Roane State Community College	6,544	22	11	11
Southwest Tennessee Community College	10,313	26	24	2
Tennessee State University	8,424	46	20	26
Tennessee Technological University	11,296	15	8	7
University of Memphis	25,700	56	35	21
University of Tennessee				
Chattanooga	12,675	34	20	14
Health Science Center	3,387	69	30	39
Knoxville	33,245	99	65	34
Martin	8,151	13	10	3
University of the South	1,940	13	10	3
Vanderbilt University	14,356	246	86	160
Volunteer State Community College	11,168	11	9	2
Walters State Community College	7,061	11	10	1
TEXAS				
Alvin Community College	7,481	14	13	1
Amarillo College	11,769	13	11	2
Angelo State University	12,391	20	16	4
Austin College	1,324	9	8	1
Austin Community College District	61,370	94	80	14
Baylor Health Care System[2]		142	56	86
Brazosport College	5,501	10	8	2
Central Texas College	18,388	8	7	1
Cisco College	4,445	2	1	1
Collin County Community College District	50,042	82	73	9
Concordia University	2,763	5	4	1
Dallas County Community College District	110,694	127	109	18
El Paso Community College	33,704	36	30	6
Grayson College	4,101	6	5	1
Hardin-Simmons University	2,279	6	3	3
Houston Community College	72,749	93	70	23
Kilgore College	6,886	5	4	1
Lamar University, Beaumont	22,837	62	19	43
Lone Star College System District	107,768	176	109	67
Lubbock Christian University	1,858	5	2	3
McLennan Community College	12,405	16	10	6
Midwestern State University	6,837	15	10	5
Odessa College	9,971	5	5	0
Panola College	3,277	4	4	0
Paris Junior College	6,148	5	5	0
Prairie View A&M University	10,303	41	31	10
Rice University	8,270	50	26	24
Sam Houston State University	24,652	41	26	15
San Jacinto College, Central Campus	41,796	45	35	10
Southern Methodist University	13,602	37	30	7
South Plains College	12,259	6	6	0
Southwestern Christian College	89	4	3	1
Southwestern University	1,549	7	6	1
St. Edwards University	4,006	9	6	3
Stephen F. Austin State University	14,155	37	21	16

Table 79. Full-Time Law Enforcement Employees, by Selected State and University or College, 2022 —Continued

(Number.)

State and university/college	Student enrollment[1]	Law enforcement employees	Officers	Civilians
St. Mary's University	3,683	19	16	3
St. Thomas University	4,297	11	10	1
Sul Ross State University	2,879	7	6	1
Tarleton State University	16,109	19	18	1
Texas A&M International University	9,961	23	19	4
Texas A&M University				
College Station	75,001	141	71	70
Commerce	14,782	32	20	12
San Antonio	8,124	19	13	6
Texas Christian University	11,957	44	27	17
Texas State Technical College				
Harlingen[2]		11	9	2
Waco	12,577	7	5	2
West Texas[2]		5	5	0
Texas State University, San Marcos	42,111	43	26	17
Texas Tech University, Lubbock	43,379	153	66	87
Texas Woman's University	20,404	36	18	18
Trinity Valley Community College	6,696	12	11	1
Tyler Junior College	15,918	17	9	8
University of Houston				
Central Campus	52,440	135	47	88
Clearlake	11,255	25	13	12
Downtown Campus	18,860	54	25	29
University of North Texas, Denton	47,297	67	45	22
University of Texas				
Arlington	60,276	87	43	44
Austin	53,502	122	81	41
Dallas	31,508	69	24	45
El Paso	29,288	47	25	22
Health Science Center, San Antonio	4,104	88	33	55
Health Science Center, Tyler[2]		26	8	18
Houston	7,375	318	73	245
Medical Branch	3,940	134	75	59
Permian Basin	7,561	25	16	9
Rio Grande Valley	44,634	79	46	33
San Antonio	38,737	93	43	50
Southwestern Medical School	2,538	126	41	85
Tyler	12,027	28	11	17
West Texas A&M University	11,481	23	15	8
UTAH				
Brigham Young University	40,688	23	19	4
Dixie State University	14,051	8	7	1
Snow College	7,064	3	3	0
Southern Utah University	17,896	7	6	1
University of Utah	38,804	50	46	4
Utah State University, Logan	32,967	29	17	12
Utah Valley University	43,749	35	20	15
Weber State University	36,680	13	11	2
VERMONT				
University of Vermont	15,499	27	14	13
VIRGINIA				
Christopher Newport University	5,034	35	20	15
College of William and Mary	9,959	25	21	4
Eastern Virginia Medical School	1,450	59	26	33
Emory and Henry College	1,414	7	4	3
George Mason University	46,687	62	42	20
Germanna Community College	10,510	25	2	23
Hampton University	3,807	35	11	24
James Madison University	23,827	44	30	14
J. Sargeant Reynolds Community College	11,534	11	9	2
Laurel Ridge Community College	8,449	4	4	0
Longwood University	5,771	17	13	4
Norfolk State University	6,041	43	21	22
Northern Virginia Community College	74,794	59	43	16
Old Dominion University	28,478	53	40	13
Radford University	13,511	25	21	4
Richard Bland College	2,655	6	4	2
Southwest Virginia Community College	2,996	2	2	0
Thomas Nelson Community College	9,652	6	4	2
University of Mary Washington	4,728	19	13	6
University of Richmond	4,357	34	22	12
University of Virginia	28,322	139	59	80
University of Virginia's College at Wise	3,423	10	9	1
Virginia Commonwealth University	32,089	111	87	24
Virginia Highlands Community College	2,729	2	2	0
Virginia Military Institute	1,744	12	11	1
Virginia Polytechnic Institute and State University	39,078	62	46	16
Virginia State University	8,654	37	24	13
Virginia Western Community College	7,827	16	8	8

Table 79. Full-Time Law Enforcement Employees, by Selected State and University or College, 2022 —Continued

(Number.)

State and university/college	Student enrollment[1]	Law enforcement employees	Officers	Civilians
WASHINGTON				
Central Washington University	13,401	16	14	2
Eastern Washington University	16,129	14	13	1
Evergreen State College	2,856	11	5	6
University of Washington	56,931	54	24	30
Washington State University				
Pullman	34,825	21	17	4
Vancouver[2]		6	3	3
Western Washington University	16,881	21	13	8
WEST VIRGINIA				
Bluefield State College	1,458	3	3	0
Concord University	2,257	8	5	3
Fairmont State University	4,252	12	8	4
Glenville State College	1,774	7	2	5
Marshall University	14,176	24	20	4
Potomac State College	1,541	5	4	1
Shepherd University	5,409	9	8	1
West Liberty University	3,070	7	7	0
West Virginia State University	5,025	6	5	1
West Virginia University				
Institute of Technology	1,879	7	6	1
Morgantown	29,152	62	46	16
WISCONSIN				
Marquette University	12,306	61	44	17
University of Wisconsin				
Eau Claire	11,937	11	10	1
Green Bay	11,192	11	10	1
La Crosse	11,344	16	11	5
Madison	48,646	126	60	66
Milwaukee	28,802	43	34	9
Oshkosh	17,570	17	12	5
Parkside	5,299	13	8	5
Platteville	8,418	9	8	1
River Falls	6,531	8	6	2
Stevens Point	9,293	14	8	6
Stout	9,006	10	9	1
Superior	3,170	7	6	1
Whitewater	14,126	17	15	2
WYOMING				
University of Wyoming	13,300	26	15	11

1 The student enrollment figures provided by the United States Department of Education are for the 2021 school year, the most recent available. The enrollment figures include full-time and part-time students.   2 Student enrollment figures were not available.

Table 80. Full-Time Law Enforcement Employees, by Selected State Metropolitan and Nonmetropolitan Counties, 2022

(Number.)

State/county	Law enforcement employees	Officers	Civilians
ALABAMA			
Metropolitan Counties			
Autauga	62	31	31
Baldwin	352	152	200
Bibb	12	11	1
Blount	68	47	21
Calhoun	85	50	35
Chilton	66	37	29
Colbert	58	33	25
Elmore	131	61	70
Etowah	118	57	61
Geneva	32	12	20
Greene	31	11	20
Hale	27	8	19
Henry	38	23	15
Houston	118	85	33
Jefferson	643	492	151
Lauderdale	53	45	8
Lawrence	54	27	27
Lee	180	88	92
Limestone	116	45	71
Lowndes	34	18	16
Madison	302	145	157
Mobile	551	197	354
Montgomery	160	118	42
Morgan	169	50	119
Pickens	27	12	15
Russell	111	38	73
Shelby	216	138	78
St. Clair	129	49	80
Tuscaloosa	227	106	121
Washington	23	10	13
Nonmetropolitan Counties			
Barbour	34	16	18
Bullock	13	6	7
Butler	15	13	2
Chambers	56	24	32
Cherokee	58	32	26
Choctaw	9	7	2
Clarke	42	16	26
Clay	27	13	14
Cleburne	28	13	15
Coffee	60	30	30
Conecuh	38	10	28
Coosa	22	10	12
Covington	32	27	5
Crenshaw	25	8	17
Cullman	150	83	67
Dale	52	31	21
Dallas	50	21	29
DeKalb	97	44	53
Escambia	61	24	37
Fayette	20	10	10
Franklin	55	23	32
Jackson	82	32	50
Lamar	18	8	10
Macon	50	20	30
Marengo	23	10	13
Marion	31	15	16
Marshall	92	53	39
Monroe	40	16	24
Perry	20	8	12
Pike	45	23	22
Randolph	44	18	26
Sumter	5	5	0
Talladega	92	40	52
Tallapoosa	54	24	30
Walker	82	40	42
Wilcox	14	9	5
Winston	25	10	15
ARIZONA			
Metropolitan Counties			
Cochise	115	87	28
Coconino	194	67	127
Maricopa	2,935	596	2,339
Mohave	254	88	166
Pima	913	534	379
Pinal	479	225	254
Yavapai	174	122	52
Yuma	305	82	223

Table 80. Full-Time Law Enforcement Employees, by Selected State Metropolitan and Nonmetropolitan Counties, 2022—Continued

(Number.)

State/county	Law enforcement employees	Officers	Civilians
Nonmetropolitan Counties			
Apache	27	15	12
Gila	115	45	70
Graham	75	22	53
Greenlee	46	15	31
La Paz	67	27	40
Navajo	139	54	85
Santa Cruz	83	33	50
ARKANSAS			
Metropolitan Counties			
Benton	265	185	80
Cleveland	13	8	5
Craighead	118	42	76
Crawford	73	33	40
Crittenden	131	39	92
Faulkner	158	55	103
Franklin	36	9	27
Garland	163	65	98
Grant	20	17	3
Jefferson	109	41	68
Lincoln	40	10	30
Little River	34	15	19
Lonoke	71	37	34
Madison	23	13	10
Miller	31	26	5
Perry	23	12	11
Poinsett	44	17	27
Pulaski	462	311	151
Saline	100	51	49
Sebastian	173	51	122
Washington	279	145	134
Nonmetropolitan Counties			
Arkansas	12	11	1
Ashley	32	17	15
Baxter	70	41	29
Boone	59	30	29
Bradley	10	7	3
Calhoun	13	7	6
Carroll	51	19	32
Chicot	7	6	1
Clark	25	16	9
Clay	6	6	0
Cleburne	50	26	24
Columbia	44	19	25
Conway	26	24	2
Cross	47	18	29
Dallas	26	6	20
Desha	7	6	1
Drew	14	13	1
Fulton	23	9	14
Greene	37	31	6
Hempstead	48	19	29
Hot Spring	31	29	2
Howard	26	13	13
Independence	51	34	17
Izard	41	24	17
Jackson	35	12	23
Johnson	47	24	23
Lafayette	23	15	8
Lawrence	37	18	19
Lee	10	10	0
Logan	49	14	35
Marion	16	14	2
Mississippi	85	39	46
Monroe	15	6	9
Montgomery	26	11	15
Nevada	28	6	22
Newton	21	10	11
Ouachita	56	26	30
Phillips	18	15	3
Pike	27	21	6
Polk	33	20	13
Pope	92	37	55
Prairie	28	8	20
Randolph	36	12	24
Scott	27	9	18
Searcy	22	8	14
Sevier	37	16	21
Sharp	28	14	14
St. Francis	47	22	25
Stone	25	11	14

Table 80. Full-Time Law Enforcement Employees, by Selected State Metropolitan and Nonmetropolitan Counties, 2022—Continued

(Number.)

State/county	Law enforcement employees	Officers	Civilians
Union	62	28	34
Van Buren	20	18	2
White	79	48	31
Woodruff	22	4	18
Yell	36	17	19
CALIFORNIA			
Metropolitan Counties			
Alameda	1,624	1,062	562
Butte	264	90	174
Contra Costa	906	617	289
El Dorado	337	161	176
Fresno	1,125	409	716
Imperial	271	187	84
Kern	1,046	694	352
Kings	294	92	202
Los Angeles	14,573	9,185	5,388
Madera	245	110	135
Marin	275	184	91
Merced	286	225	61
Monterey	432	283	149
Napa	150	111	39
Orange	3,580	1,896	1,684
Placer	520	250	270
Riverside	3,953	1,659	2,294
Sacramento	2,015	1,333	682
San Benito	58	25	33
San Bernardino	3,325	1,875	1,450
San Diego	3,977	2,343	1,634
San Francisco	871	677	194
San Joaquin	749	303	446
San Luis Obispo	418	307	111
San Mateo	676	300	376
Santa Barbara	659	453	206
Santa Clara	1,456	1,127	329
Santa Cruz	329	146	183
Shasta	179	124	55
Solano	506	163	343
Sonoma	556	218	338
Stanislaus	766	543	223
Sutter	121	96	25
Tulare	712	502	210
Ventura	1,203	744	459
Yolo	251	87	164
Yuba	168	130	38
Nonmetropolitan Counties			
Alpine	15	12	3
Amador	84	45	39
Calaveras	116	58	58
Colusa	65	44	21
Del Norte	49	20	29
Glenn	63	26	37
Humboldt	261	190	71
Inyo	74	37	37
Lake	116	83	33
Lassen	77	48	29
Mariposa	82	65	17
Mendocino	152	104	48
Modoc	30	11	19
Mono	43	38	5
Nevada	155	60	95
Plumas	53	30	23
Sierra	12	8	4
Siskiyou	72	57	15
Tehama	92	29	63
Trinity	44	34	10
Tuolumne	119	57	62
COLORADO			
Metropolitan Counties			
Adams	576	394	182
Boulder	382	103	279
Clear Creek	63	24	39
Douglas	597	402	195
El Paso	808	503	305
Gilpin	58	36	22
Jefferson	754	531	223
Larimer	472	227	245
Mesa	247	192	55
Pueblo	323	146	177
Teller	84	44	40
Weld	405	147	258

Table 80. Full-Time Law Enforcement Employees, by Selected State Metropolitan and Nonmetropolitan Counties, 2022—Continued

(Number.)

State/county	Law enforcement employees	Officers	Civilians
Nonmetropolitan Counties			
Alamosa	42	20	22
Archuleta	43	17	26
Bent	31	11	20
Chaffee	56	22	34
Costilla	15	8	7
Crowley	13	6	7
Delta	72	34	38
Eagle	65	49	16
Garfield	126	44	82
Huerfano	22	18	4
Jackson	7	3	4
Kiowa	8	6	2
Kit Carson	23	6	17
Lake	28	10	18
Las Animas	25	11	14
Logan	42	18	24
Moffat	36	32	4
Montezuma	61	26	35
Montrose	90	48	42
Otero	19	9	10
Ouray	9	8	1
Phillips	2	2	0
Pitkin	54	23	31
Prowers	30	12	18
Routt	49	45	4
Saguache	22	15	7
San Miguel	32	13	19
Sedgwick	3	2	1
Summit	107	48	59
Washington	31	9	22
Yuma	16	9	7
DELAWARE			
Metropolitan Counties			
New Castle County Police Department	459	368	91
FLORIDA			
Metropolitan Counties			
Alachua	370	246	124
Baker	61	42	19
Bay	301	230	71
Brevard	943	539	404
Broward	2,620	1,598	1,022
Charlotte	466	301	165
Citrus	319	202	117
Clay	662	294	368
Collier	971	578	393
Escambia	706	400	306
Flagler	268	182	86
Gadsden	57	40	17
Gilchrist	61	50	11
Hernando	559	370	189
Highlands	328	225	103
Hillsborough	3,308	1,315	1,993
Indian River	484	198	286
Jefferson	58	28	30
Lake	683	286	397
Lee	1,611	743	868
Leon	451	313	138
Levy	148	111	37
Manatee	1,218	563	655
Marion	843	532	311
Martin	402	274	128
Nassau	310	211	99
Okaloosa	467	322	145
Orange	2,206	1,602	604
Osceola	704	465	239
Palm Beach	3,646	1,677	1,969
Pasco	1,017	677	340
Pinellas	2,279	810	1,469
Polk	1,162	672	490
Santa Rosa	343	249	94
Sarasota	779	417	362
Seminole	1,190	440	750
St. Johns	571	367	204
St. Lucie	706	310	396
Sumter	264	164	100
Volusia	691	395	296
Walton	405	193	212
Nonmetropolitan Counties			
Bradford	82	41	41
Calhoun	25	21	4

Table 80. Full-Time Law Enforcement Employees, by Selected State Metropolitan and Nonmetropolitan Counties, 2022—Continued

(Number.)

State/county	Law enforcement employees	Officers	Civilians
Columbia	55	45	10
DeSoto	113	55	58
Dixie	80	38	42
Franklin	62	38	24
Glades	65	27	38
Gulf	43	31	12
Hamilton	62	24	38
Hardee	100	74	26
Hendry	148	80	68
Madison	59	41	18
Monroe	347	196	151
Okeechobee	198	88	110
Putnam	228	130	98
Suwannee	83	55	28
Taylor	79	54	25
Union	18	16	2
Washington	61	45	16
GEORGIA			
Metropolitan Counties			
Augusta-Richmond	583	345	238
Barrow	183	122	61
Bartow	206	169	37
Bibb	417	234	183
Brantley	43	19	24
Brooks	44	23	21
Bryan	95	53	42
Burke	133	80	53
Butts	102	60	42
Carroll	183	108	75
Catoosa	115	70	45
Chatham County Police Department	146	123	23
Cherokee	419	283	136
Clarke	141	100	41
Clayton County Police Department	413	316	97
Cobb	780	492	288
Cobb County Police Department	643	583	60
Columbia	330	203	127
Coweta	253	173	80
Crawford	30	13	17
Dawson	118	78	40
DeKalb	471	269	202
DeKalb County Police Department	803	586	217
Dougherty	244	92	152
Dougherty County Police Department	43	35	8
Douglas	330	207	123
Echols	9	9	0
Effingham	147	77	70
Fayette	214	135	79
Floyd County Police Department	88	82	6
Forsyth	448	363	85
Fulton	916	585	331
Fulton County Police Department	77	40	37
Glynn	159	61	98
Glynn County Police Department	111	97	14
Gwinnett	631	341	290
Gwinnett County Police Department	944	689	255
Hall	410	271	139
Haralson	81	45	36
Harris	76	54	22
Heard	36	19	17
Henry	289	223	66
Henry County Police Department	290	243	47
Houston	336	134	202
Jasper	47	28	19
Jones	71	35	36
Lamar	53	32	21
Lanier	14	8	6
Lee	89	42	47
Long	37	33	4
Lowndes	223	121	102
Madison	86	45	41
Marion	17	9	8
McDuffie	49	20	29
McIntosh	62	41	21
Meriwether	40	24	16
Monroe	112	68	44
Murray	89	50	39
Muscogee	305	185	120
Newton	239	149	90
Oconee	96	62	34
Oglethorpe	39	30	9
Paulding	279	169	110

Table 80. Full-Time Law Enforcement Employees, by Selected State Metropolitan and Nonmetropolitan Counties, 2022—Continued

(Number.)

State/county	Law enforcement employees	Officers	Civilians
Peach	57	30	27
Pickens	74	63	11
Pike	46	26	20
Rockdale	184	158	26
Spalding	177	101	76
Stewart	12	8	4
Twiggs	51	23	28
Walker	110	65	45
Walton	180	157	23
Whitfield	214	182	32
Worth	36	26	10
Nonmetropolitan Counties			
Atkinson	25	10	15
Baker	6	5	1
Baldwin	113	53	60
Banks	71	53	18
Ben Hill	47	24	23
Berrien	46	27	19
Bleckley	42	17	25
Bulloch	88	77	11
Calhoun	16	8	8
Camden	118	65	53
Candler	25	12	13
Charlton	35	20	15
Chattooga	44	26	18
Clay	10	9	1
Clinch	15	12	3
Coffee	124	51	73
Cook	52	31	21
Crisp	101	55	46
Decatur	60	28	32
Dodge	53	24	29
Dooly	63	32	31
Early	33	14	19
Elbert	53	26	27
Emanuel	44	40	4
Fannin	67	39	28
Franklin	63	39	24
Gilmer	101	63	38
Glascock	6	5	1
Gordon	116	77	39
Grady	24	21	3
Greene	54	32	22
Habersham	83	56	27
Hancock	36	10	26
Hart	52	30	22
Irwin	23	13	10
Jackson	153	92	61
Jeff Davis	37	15	22
Jefferson	52	27	25
Jenkins	20	10	10
Laurens	107	72	35
Lumpkin	84	46	38
Mitchell	48	22	26
Montgomery	27	15	12
Pierce	57	26	31
Polk	71	33	38
Polk County Police Department	40	37	3
Pulaski	23	10	13
Putnam	45	36	9
Quitman	6	4	2
Rabun	53	30	23
Schley	10	5	5
Screven	33	25	8
Seminole	34	25	9
Sumter	83	39	44
Tattnall	61	25	36
Taylor	21	9	12
Thomas	94	63	31
Towns	41	19	22
Treutlen	23	16	7
Troup	145	79	66
Turner	48	22	26
Union	47	42	5
Upson	65	35	30
Ware	97	44	53
Warren	10	8	2
Washington	44	41	3
Wayne	76	41	35
Webster	5	5	0
Wheeler	11	6	5
White	76	46	30

Table 80. Full-Time Law Enforcement Employees, by Selected State Metropolitan and Nonmetropolitan Counties, 2022—Continued

(Number.)

State/county	Law enforcement employees	Officers	Civilians
Wilcox	13	13	0
Wilkes	65	34	31
Wilkinson	26	13	13
HAWAII			
Metropolitan Counties			
Maui Police Department	371	277	94
Nonmetropolitan Counties			
Hawaii Police Department	548	424	124
Kauai Police Department	198	141	57
IDAHO			
Metropolitan Counties			
Ada	758	213	545
Bannock	120	43	77
Boise	23	15	8
Bonneville	192	73	119
Butte	5	5	0
Canyon	255	64	191
Franklin	16	10	6
Gem	37	14	23
Jefferson	60	23	37
Jerome	55	26	29
Kootenai	274	94	180
Nez Perce	72	24	48
Owyhee	32	15	17
Power	23	16	7
Twin Falls	121	42	79
Nonmetropolitan Counties			
Adams	21	9	12
Bear Lake	13	7	6
Benewah	26	16	10
Bingham	91	40	51
Blaine	44	33	11
Bonner	100	46	54
Boundary	33	12	21
Camas	6	4	2
Caribou	27	9	18
Cassia	75	53	22
Clark	7	2	5
Clearwater	27	15	12
Custer	15	8	7
Elmore	61	22	39
Fremont	40	20	20
Gooding	31	12	19
Idaho	40	20	20
Latah	51	29	22
Lemhi	24	8	16
Lewis	12	8	4
Lincoln	13	11	2
Madison	58	21	37
Minidoka	31	20	11
Oneida	14	9	5
Payette	44	13	31
Shoshone	46	20	26
Teton	18	11	7
Valley	44	20	24
Washington	30	11	19
ILLINOIS			
Metropolitan Counties			
Bond	23	12	11
Champaign	74	56	18
Clinton	35	15	20
Cook	5,002	1,564	3,438
DeKalb	97	37	60
Grundy	52	33	19
Henry	71	24	47
Jackson	91	31	60
Jersey	27	24	3
Kankakee	185	53	132
Kendall	95	50	45
Lake	426	167	259
Macon	168	47	121
Madison	164	82	82
Marshall	18	9	9
McHenry	349	104	245
McLean	135	51	84
Monroe	43	20	23
Peoria	150	63	87

Table 80. Full-Time Law Enforcement Employees, by Selected State Metropolitan and Nonmetropolitan Counties, 2022—Continued

(Number.)

State/county	Law enforcement employees	Officers	Civilians
Piatt	37	14	23
Sangamon	195	151	44
St. Clair	132	60	72
Tazewell	57	38	19
Vermilion	91	41	50
Will	641	218	423
Winnebago	332	106	226
Nonmetropolitan Counties			
Adams	32	28	4
Carroll	23	8	15
Cass	10	9	1
Christian	37	16	21
Clay	21	21	0
Crawford	33	11	22
DeWitt	36	27	9
Edwards	8	4	4
Effingham	47	20	27
Ford	27	21	6
Hancock	23	11	12
Henderson	16	7	9
Iroquois	30	17	13
Jo Daviess	39	19	20
La Salle	121	50	71
Lawrence	7	7	0
Livingston	65	30	35
Logan	48	20	28
Marion	37	15	22
McDonough	26	15	11
Montgomery	36	15	21
Morgan	26	13	13
Moultrie	11	11	0
Ogle	52	28	24
Pulaski	7	7	0
Putnam	15	9	6
Randolph	48	11	37
Saline	45	11	34
Scott	7	3	4
Shelby	32	13	19
Stephenson	34	24	10
Wabash	11	9	2
Warren	22	19	3
Wayne	21	11	10
Whiteside	66	35	31
INDIANA			
Metropolitan Counties			
Allen	316	138	178
Boone	104	42	62
Clark	135	40	95
Delaware	123	44	79
Elkhart	178	70	108
Hancock	98	47	51
Hendricks	134	61	73
Howard	129	40	89
Johnson	154	140	14
Lake	431	164	267
La Porte	156	62	94
Madison	103	42	61
Monroe	116	92	24
Morgan	69	54	15
Ohio	9	8	1
St. Joseph	288	112	176
Whitley	57	19	38
Nonmetropolitan Counties			
Daviess	59	24	35
Grant	75	43	32
Jackson	71	18	53
Jay	41	13	28
Knox	69	31	38
Kosciusko	112	37	75
LaGrange	62	21	41
Miami	54	17	37
Montgomery	75	26	49
Noble	66	54	12
Pulaski	14	14	0
Rush	40	32	8
Scott	36	18	18
Starke	36	13	23
Steuben	64	24	40
Wells	38	18	20

Table 80. Full-Time Law Enforcement Employees, by Selected State Metropolitan and Nonmetropolitan Counties, 2022—Continued

(Number.)

State/county	Law enforcement employees	Officers	Civilians
IOWA			
Metropolitan Counties			
Benton	37	14	23
Black Hawk	129	66	63
Boone	28	12	16
Bremer	35	14	21
Dallas	77	32	45
Dubuque	95	75	20
Guthrie	17	10	7
Harrison	22	11	11
Jasper	52	18	34
Johnson	95	76	19
Jones	28	11	17
Linn	202	132	70
Madison	18	9	9
Mills	28	13	15
Polk	514	155	359
Pottawattamie	210	55	155
Scott	161	53	108
Story	87	34	53
Warren	52	21	31
Washington	52	20	32
Woodbury	116	41	75
Nonmetropolitan Counties			
Adair	14	6	8
Adams	12	7	5
Allamakee	20	9	11
Appanoose	16	9	7
Audubon	12	6	6
Buchanan	33	13	20
Butler	18	12	6
Calhoun	13	8	5
Carroll	12	10	2
Cass	25	10	15
Cedar	38	14	24
Cerro Gordo	68	20	48
Cherokee	18	7	11
Chickasaw	17	10	7
Clarke	23	8	15
Clay	23	11	12
Clayton	32	13	19
Clinton	52	27	25
Crawford	14	11	3
Davis	7	6	1
Decatur	16	6	10
Delaware	26	14	12
Des Moines	28	23	5
Dickinson	20	9	11
Emmet	14	9	5
Fayette	39	12	27
Floyd	12	12	0
Franklin	11	8	3
Fremont	28	10	18
Greene	30	9	21
Hamilton	31	11	20
Hancock	10	8	2
Hardin	34	10	24
Henry	22	13	9
Howard	18	9	9
Humboldt	10	9	1
Ida	20	10	10
Iowa	27	12	15
Jefferson	22	11	11
Keokuk	12	7	5
Kossuth	25	10	15
Lee	44	18	26
Louisa	30	14	16
Lucas	10	4	6
Lyon	27	12	15
Mahaska	26	10	16
Marion	41	19	22
Marshall	55	21	34
Mitchell	17	7	10
Monona	23	12	11
Muscatine	84	24	60
O'Brien	29	9	20
Osceola	14	9	5
Palo Alto	17	8	9
Plymouth	36	13	23
Pocahontas	20	8	12
Poweshiek	23	12	11
Sac	22	10	12

Table 80. Full-Time Law Enforcement Employees, by Selected State Metropolitan and Nonmetropolitan Counties, 2022—Continued

(Number.)

State/county	Law enforcement employees	Officers	Civilians
Shelby	18	11	7
Sioux	40	14	26
Tama	24	14	10
Wapello	44	11	33
Wayne	19	8	11
Webster	50	20	30
Winneshiek	28	13	15
Worth	26	13	13
KANSAS			
Metropolitan Counties			
Butler	68	53	15
Douglas	148	76	72
Geary	74	38	36
Harvey	47	23	24
Jackson	42	19	23
Jefferson	45	26	19
Johnson	607	436	171
Leavenworth	103	57	46
Linn	46	21	25
Miami	63	38	25
Osage	44	30	14
Pottawatomie	42	27	15
Riley County Police Department	207	108	99
Sedgwick	250	191	59
Sumner	35	27	8
Wabaunsee	17	11	6
Nonmetropolitan Counties			
Anderson	19	9	10
Barber	8	6	2
Barton	40	19	21
Brown	21	8	13
Chase	7	3	4
Chautauqua	14	6	8
Cherokee	20	20	0
Cheyenne	7	6	1
Clay	17	7	10
Cloud	10	10	0
Coffey	43	16	27
Comanche	8	4	4
Cowley	45	24	21
Crawford	64	30	34
Decatur	3	3	0
Dickinson	26	21	5
Edwards	6	5	1
Elk	10	6	4
Ellis	25	20	5
Ellsworth	24	9	15
Finney	88	35	53
Ford	69	29	40
Franklin	29	25	4
Gove	6	4	2
Graham	8	3	5
Grant	15	6	9
Gray	10	4	6
Greeley	8	4	4
Greenwood	21	12	9
Hamilton	12	6	6
Haskell	15	10	5
Hodgeman	7	3	4
Kearny	17	9	8
Kiowa	15	6	9
Labette	22	20	2
Lane	9	4	5
Lincoln	13	8	5
Logan	5	5	0
Lyon	29	23	6
Marion	12	11	1
Marshall	27	11	16
McPherson	21	18	3
Meade	14	9	5
Morris	14	9	5
Neosho	28	15	13
Ness	11	7	4
Norton	10	6	4
Osborne	14	8	6
Ottawa	11	6	5
Pawnee	12	11	1
Phillips	13	8	5
Pratt	17	10	7
Reno	87	52	35
Republic	14	8	6

Table 80. Full-Time Law Enforcement Employees, by Selected State Metropolitan and Nonmetropolitan Counties, 2022—Continued

(Number.)

State/county	Law enforcement employees	Officers	Civilians
Rice	9	7	2
Rooks	14	9	5
Russell	18	11	7
Saline	47	38	9
Scott	8	4	4
Seward	25	17	8
Sherman	12	6	6
Smith	15	15	0
Stafford	11	6	5
Stanton	10	6	4
Trego	5	3	2
Wallace	8	4	4
Washington	19	8	11
Wichita	7	3	4
Wilson	15	11	4
Woodson	12	8	4
KENTUCKY			
Metropolitan Counties			
Boone	185	172	13
Bourbon	11	10	1
Boyd	40	29	11
Bullitt	74	40	34
Butler	9	6	3
Campbell	25	17	8
Carter	14	11	3
Christian	51	47	4
Daviess	43	37	6
Edmonson	6	4	2
Fayette	75	50	25
Grant	24	22	2
Hardin	58	43	15
Henderson	32	25	7
Jefferson	223	176	47
Jessamine	37	31	6
Kenton County Police Department	36	34	2
Larue	9	8	1
Meade	18	14	4
Oldham	21	18	3
Pendleton	6	5	1
Shelby	27	24	3
Trigg	9	6	3
Warren	111	54	57
Woodford	15	10	5
Nonmetropolitan Counties			
Adair	9	7	2
Anderson	20	16	4
Ballard	11	9	2
Bath	5	3	2
Breathitt	2	2	0
Breckinridge	9	7	2
Caldwell	6	3	3
Calloway	30	21	9
Carlisle	8	4	4
Casey	14	7	7
Crittenden	5	4	1
Cumberland	6	5	1
Elliott	7	3	4
Estill	8	6	2
Franklin	32	28	4
Fulton	5	4	1
Garrard	10	8	2
Graves	21	18	3
Harlan	17	14	3
Hart	24	22	2
Hickman	4	3	1
Hopkins	41	32	9
Jackson	8	6	2
Johnson	14	7	7
Knott	4	4	0
Knott County Police Department	1	1	0
Laurel	47	33	14
Lawrence	11	7	4
Lee	3	2	1
Leslie	11	10	1
Letcher	8	7	1
Lewis	11	9	2
Lincoln	7	6	1
Livingston	12	11	1
Lyon	7	6	1
Madison	41	37	4
Marion	12	8	4

Table 80. Full-Time Law Enforcement Employees, by Selected State Metropolitan and Nonmetropolitan Counties, 2022—Continued

(Number.)

State/county	Law enforcement employees	Officers	Civilians
Marshall	40	38	2
Mason	19	16	3
McCracken	50	45	5
Mercer	11	8	3
Metcalfe	6	4	2
Monroe	8	7	1
Montgomery	15	13	2
Morgan	11	10	1
Muhlenberg	19	17	2
Nelson	36	30	6
Nicholas	3	2	1
Ohio	17	14	3
Pike	19	10	9
Powell	5	3	2
Pulaski	43	35	8
Robertson	2	1	1
Rockcastle	7	4	3
Rowan	15	13	2
Russell	10	9	1
Simpson	25	19	6
Taylor	13	9	4
Todd	11	9	2
Trimble	3	3	0
Union	13	11	2
Washington	9	7	2
Wayne	16	14	2
Webster	6	4	2
Whitley	20	13	7
Wolfe	2	1	1
LOUISIANA			
Metropolitan Counties			
Acadia	102	66	36
Ascension	339	221	118
Assumption	96	53	43
Bossier	389	304	85
Caddo	565	341	224
Cameron	97	85	12
East Baton Rouge	779	641	138
Iberia	148	93	55
Iberville	137	82	55
Jefferson	1,276	850	426
Lafayette	728	404	324
Lafourche	280	233	47
Livingston	339	170	169
Morehouse	116	116	0
Ouachita	375	375	0
Rapides	519	402	117
St. Charles	352	248	104
St. Helena	46	44	2
St. Martin	196	95	101
St. Tammany	650	631	19
Terrebonne	313	253	60
Vermilion	134	110	24
West Feliciana	83	29	54
Nonmetropolitan Counties			
Allen	124	26	98
Avoyelles	108	27	81
Beauregard	144	106	38
Bienville	65	36	29
Caldwell	28	19	9
Catahoula	41	22	19
Concordia	23	23	0
Evangeline	70	47	23
Franklin	97	97	0
Jackson	80	80	0
Jefferson Davis	113	113	0
La Salle	65	25	40
Lincoln	2	2	0
Madison	39	39	0
Natchitoches	139	83	56
Richland	146	121	25
St. Landry	212	148	64
St. Mary	14	14	0
Vernon	111	52	59
Washington	79	66	13
Webster	19	19	0
West Carroll	18	9	9
MAINE			
Metropolitan Counties			
Androscoggin	39	36	3

Table 80. Full-Time Law Enforcement Employees, by Selected State Metropolitan and Nonmetropolitan Counties, 2022—Continued

(Number.)

State/county	Law enforcement employees	Officers	Civilians
Cumberland	74	62	12
Penobscot	52	48	4
Sagadahoc	20	18	2
York	33	30	3
Nonmetropolitan Counties			
Aroostook	25	18	7
Franklin	16	15	1
Hancock	48	27	21
Kennebec	28	25	3
Knox	21	19	2
Lincoln	24	22	2
Oxford	31	29	2
Piscataquis	10	9	1
Somerset	26	23	3
Waldo	42	23	19
Washington	20	18	2
MARYLAND			
Metropolitan Counties			
Allegany	40	37	3
Anne Arundel	98	75	23
Anne Arundel County Police Department	975	764	211
Baltimore County	80	67	13
Baltimore County Police Department	2,047	1,832	215
Calvert	199	164	35
Carroll	248	201	47
Cecil	180	82	98
Charles	487	302	185
Frederick	239	184	55
Harford	433	336	97
Howard	80	60	20
Howard County Police Department	687	476	211
Montgomery	172	143	29
Montgomery County Police Department	1,647	1,196	451
Prince George's County Police Department	1,668	1,444	224
Queen Anne's	71	63	8
Somerset	33	29	4
St. Mary's	381	208	173
Washington	255	103	152
Wicomico	111	89	22
Worcester	77	68	9
Nonmetropolitan Counties			
Caroline	41	37	4
Dorchester	43	39	4
Garrett	82	35	47
Kent	27	24	3
Talbot	44	41	3
MICHIGAN			
Metropolitan Counties			
Bay	88	39	49
Berrien	160	70	90
Calhoun	179	51	128
Cass	71	33	38
Clinton	61	26	35
Eaton	111	56	55
Genesee	259	116	143
Ingham	161	71	90
Ionia	42	19	23
Jackson	91	41	50
Kalamazoo	198	102	96
Kent	610	251	359
Lapeer	78	45	33
Livingston	124	59	65
Macomb	503	243	260
Midland	68	30	38
Monroe	162	90	72
Montcalm	51	24	27
Muskegon	109	49	60
Oakland	1,142	950	192
Ottawa	233	141	92
Saginaw	60	54	6
Shiawassee	55	22	33
St. Clair	186	81	105
Washtenaw	287	125	162
Wayne	682	583	99
Nonmetropolitan Counties			
Alcona	13	11	2
Alger	17	12	5
Allegan	109	61	48

Table 80. Full-Time Law Enforcement Employees, by Selected State Metropolitan and Nonmetropolitan Counties, 2022—Continued

(Number.)

State/county	Law enforcement employees	Officers	Civilians
Alpena	33	13	20
Antrim	50	20	30
Arenac	24	13	11
Baraga	6	4	2
Barry	55	30	25
Benzie	37	18	19
Branch	35	15	20
Charlevoix	40	23	17
Cheboygan	38	21	17
Chippewa	40	18	22
Clare	25	20	5
Crawford	27	13	14
Delta	45	18	27
Dickinson	34	13	21
Emmet	49	27	22
Gladwin	45	14	31
Gogebic	24	15	9
Grand Traverse	125	68	57
Gratiot	26	24	2
Hillsdale	38	22	16
Houghton	31	20	11
Huron	36	19	17
Iosco	23	6	17
Iron	20	9	11
Isabella	52	20	32
Kalkaska	43	17	26
Keweenaw	7	7	0
Lake	20	18	2
Leelanau	38	20	18
Lenawee	99	39	60
Luce	6	5	1
Manistee	38	17	21
Marquette	60	22	38
Mason	45	25	20
Mecosta	21	20	1
Menominee	36	35	1
Missaukee	15	14	1
Montmorency	13	13	0
Newaygo	72	28	44
Oceana	36	21	15
Ogemaw	40	18	22
Ontonagon	12	6	6
Osceola	30	17	13
Oscoda	18	12	6
Otsego	29	12	17
Presque Isle	17	15	2
Roscommon	39	25	14
Sanilac	58	26	32
Schoolcraft	11	4	7
St. Joseph	60	27	33
Tuscola	41	19	22
Van Buren	109	69	40
Wexford	38	16	22
MINNESOTA			
Metropolitan Counties			
Anoka	273	131	142
Benton	70	25	45
Blue Earth	71	33	38
Carlton	59	24	35
Carver	144	73	71
Chisago	86	44	42
Clay	88	35	53
Dakota	202	96	106
Dodge	40	24	16
Fillmore	31	20	11
Hennepin	843	313	530
Houston	34	15	19
Isanti	56	21	35
Lake	30	16	14
Le Sueur	50	23	27
Mille Lacs	71	35	36
Nicollet	40	16	24
Olmsted	194	80	114
Polk	48	32	16
Ramsey	442	230	212
Scott	147	52	95
Sherburne	282	77	205
Stearns	210	80	130
St. Louis	251	108	143
Wabasha	48	19	29
Washington	261	122	139
Wright	273	165	108

Table 80. Full-Time Law Enforcement Employees, by Selected State Metropolitan and Nonmetropolitan Counties, 2022—Continued

(Number.)

State/county	Law enforcement employees	Officers	Civilians
Nonmetropolitan Counties			
Aitkin	48	21	27
Becker	70	24	46
Beltrami	81	30	51
Big Stone	8	6	2
Brown	35	12	23
Cass	73	45	28
Chippewa	23	11	12
Clearwater	19	9	10
Cook	20	12	8
Cottonwood	23	10	13
Crow Wing	131	44	87
Douglas	84	36	48
Faribault	30	13	17
Freeborn	64	21	43
Goodhue	100	44	56
Grant	17	11	6
Hubbard	53	19	34
Itasca	68	28	40
Jackson	28	15	13
Kanabec	46	21	25
Kandiyohi	98	30	68
Kittson	11	5	6
Koochiching	20	10	10
Lac qui Parle	11	7	4
Lake of the Woods	14	7	7
Lincoln	13	7	6
Lyon	44	17	27
Mahnomen	21	15	6
Marshall	26	15	11
Martin	35	14	21
McLeod	63	26	37
Meeker	48	21	27
Morrison	56	22	34
Mower	81	32	49
Murray	19	13	6
Nobles	34	13	21
Norman	9	5	4
Otter Tail	85	39	46
Pennington	38	11	27
Pine	81	37	44
Pipestone	25	15	10
Pope	18	11	7
Red Lake	12	9	3
Redwood	33	15	18
Renville	41	17	24
Rice	67	31	36
Rock	19	14	5
Roseau	23	12	11
Sibley	30	13	17
Steele	31	25	6
Stevens	22	13	9
Swift	19	10	9
Todd	39	20	19
Traverse	14	6	8
Wadena	25	12	13
Waseca	32	14	18
Watonwan	19	8	11
Wilkin	18	7	11
Winona	53	22	31
Yellow Medicine	25	10	15
MISSISSIPPI			
Metropolitan Counties			
Copiah	31	24	7
Covington	18	16	2
DeSoto	295	161	134
Forrest	133	50	83
Hancock	126	66	60
Harrison	230	110	120
Hinds	298	75	223
Jackson	183	97	86
Lamar	100	48	52
Madison	90	76	14
Perry	25	13	12
Rankin	221	110	111
Simpson	56	21	35
Stone	27	22	5
Tate	45	25	20
Tunica	93	48	45
Yazoo	14	14	0

Table 80. Full-Time Law Enforcement Employees, by Selected State Metropolitan and Nonmetropolitan Counties, 2022—Continued

(Number.)

State/county	Law enforcement employees	Officers	Civilians
Nonmetropolitan Counties			
Adams	70	37	33
Alcorn	28	26	2
Attala	13	11	2
Calhoun	9	8	1
Carroll	10	9	1
Chickasaw	14	13	1
Choctaw	13	8	5
Claiborne	11	10	1
Clay	18	12	6
Coahoma	37	25	12
George	20	17	3
Greene	18	8	10
Grenada	10	9	1
Jasper	34	20	14
Jefferson	15	7	8
Jones	50	45	5
Kemper	18	14	4
Lafayette	51	49	2
Lauderdale	123	52	71
Leake	17	15	2
Lee	147	56	91
Leflore	64	20	44
Lincoln	58	28	30
Lowndes	110	58	52
Marion	22	16	6
Monroe	62	39	23
Montgomery	9	8	1
Neshoba	20	17	3
Newton	29	16	13
Noxubee	15	9	6
Oktibbeha	32	29	3
Panola	77	39	38
Pearl River	34	33	1
Pike	32	29	3
Pontotoc	37	22	15
Prentiss	36	19	17
Scott	55	30	25
Sharkey	9	5	4
Smith	23	12	11
Sunflower	57	14	43
Tallahatchie	21	9	12
Tishomingo	28	14	14
Union	42	23	19
Walthall	29	14	15
Warren	36	33	3
Washington	52	39	13
Wayne	27	12	15
Webster	9	7	2
Wilkinson	8	3	5
Winston	40	7	33
MISSOURI			
Metropolitan Counties			
Andrew	26	16	10
Bollinger	20	13	7
Boone	73	50	23
Caldwell	18	10	8
Callaway	55	39	16
Cape Girardeau	112	64	48
Cass	119	93	26
Christian	93	60	33
Clay	215	146	69
Clinton	31	19	12
Cooper	13	12	1
DeKalb	20	13	7
Franklin	167	123	44
Greene	552	193	359
Jackson	125	93	32
Jasper	122	70	52
Jefferson	233	163	70
Lafayette	53	30	23
Newton	72	42	30
Osage	19	9	10
Platte	121	87	34
Polk	41	25	16
Ray	30	16	14
St. Charles County Police Department	180	144	36
St. Louis County Police Department	1,208	868	340
Warren	67	34	33
Nonmetropolitan Counties			
Adair	26	10	16
Atchison	15	9	6

Table 80. Full-Time Law Enforcement Employees, by Selected State Metropolitan and Nonmetropolitan Counties, 2022—Continued

(Number.)

State/county	Law enforcement employees	Officers	Civilians
Barry	35	19	16
Barton	12	7	5
Benton	34	13	21
Butler	53	25	28
Carroll	9	8	1
Cedar	28	13	15
Clark	14	6	8
Crawford	43	26	17
Dade	12	7	5
Dent	42	14	28
Douglas	18	11	7
Dunklin	38	13	25
Grundy	16	6	10
Henry	42	20	22
Howell	49	30	19
Iron	13	8	5
Johnson	82	47	35
Laclede	66	26	40
Lawrence	41	30	11
Lewis	12	7	5
Linn	2	2	0
Madison	8	8	0
Mercer	9	4	5
Mississippi	17	7	10
Monroe	10	9	1
New Madrid	19	18	1
Nodaway	25	14	11
Oregon	10	5	5
Ozark	16	7	9
Pemiscot	49	21	28
Perry	34	23	11
Phelps	82	37	45
Pulaski	39	19	20
Ralls	16	14	2
Randolph	39	21	18
Reynolds	10	8	2
Ripley	11	9	2
Schuyler	8	6	2
Shannon	9	4	5
Shelby	13	6	7
St. Clair	68	50	18
Ste. Genevieve	85	54	31
St. Francois	115	102	13
Stoddard	42	19	23
Stone	56	45	11
Sullivan	4	4	0
Taney	61	44	17
Vernon	53	17	36
Washington	30	17	13
Wayne	28	9	19
Wright	23	7	16
MONTANA			
Metropolitan Counties			
Carbon	21	13	8
Cascade	229	199	30
Missoula	170	60	110
Stillwater	24	14	10
Yellowstone	174	60	114
Nonmetropolitan Counties			
Beaverhead	18	6	12
Big Horn	33	15	18
Blaine	14	8	6
Broadwater	24	12	12
Butte-Silver Bow	97	48	49
Carter	4	4	0
Chouteau	19	9	10
Custer	20	6	14
Daniels	8	4	4
Dawson	47	29	18
Deer Lodge	21	21	0
Fallon	9	4	5
Fergus	20	18	2
Flathead	108	57	51
Gallatin	138	66	72
Garfield	4	3	1
Glacier	24	12	12
Golden Valley	3	3	0
Granite	10	6	4
Hill	26	13	13
Jefferson	31	16	15
Judith Basin	6	5	1

Table 80. Full-Time Law Enforcement Employees, by Selected State Metropolitan and Nonmetropolitan Counties, 2022—Continued

(Number.)

State/county	Law enforcement employees	Officers	Civilians
Lake	46	22	24
Lewis and Clark	116	48	68
Liberty	9	5	4
Lincoln	41	20	21
Madison	22	15	7
McCone	5	4	1
Meagher	9	4	5
Mineral	20	8	12
Musselshell	14	7	7
Park	27	18	9
Petroleum	2	2	0
Phillips	11	6	5
Pondera	16	9	7
Powder River	8	4	4
Powell	10	5	5
Prairie	3	3	0
Ravalli	80	39	41
Richland	33	11	22
Roosevelt	43	14	29
Rosebud	26	14	12
Sanders	23	13	10
Sheridan	7	5	2
Sweet Grass	14	8	6
Teton	11	8	3
Toole	21	13	8
Valley	24	8	16
Wheatland	13	8	5
Wibaux	3	3	0
NEBRASKA			
Metropolitan Counties			
Cass	76	35	41
Dakota	19	17	2
Dixon	10	8	2
Douglas	237	148	89
Hall	42	30	12
Howard	14	7	7
Lancaster	107	77	30
Merrick	15	9	6
Sarpy	196	108	88
Saunders	23	14	9
Seward	22	18	4
Washington	61	30	31
Nonmetropolitan Counties			
Adams	44	16	28
Antelope	17	4	13
Arthur	1	1	0
Banner	2	2	0
Boone	13	5	8
Box Butte	15	6	9
Boyd	2	2	0
Brown	9	6	3
Buffalo	87	31	56
Burt	14	8	6
Butler	22	10	12
Cedar	5	5	0
Chase	10	5	5
Cherry	5	4	1
Cheyenne	21	10	11
Clay	11	6	5
Colfax	20	10	10
Cuming	6	5	1
Custer	9	8	1
Dawes	17	7	10
Dawson	65	27	38
Deuel	5	4	1
Dodge	24	20	4
Fillmore	13	6	7
Franklin	7	3	4
Frontier	8	4	4
Furnas	13	7	6
Gage	18	15	3
Garfield	2	2	0
Gosper	3	2	1
Grant	1	1	0
Greeley	3	2	1
Hamilton	22	9	13
Harlan	7	3	4
Hayes	1	1	0
Hitchcock	9	5	4
Holt	8	6	2
Hooker	2	2	0

Table 80. Full-Time Law Enforcement Employees, by Selected State Metropolitan and Nonmetropolitan Counties, 2022—Continued

(Number.)

State/county	Law enforcement employees	Officers	Civilians
Jefferson	28	14	14
Johnson	13	7	6
Kearney	10	5	5
Keith	17	7	10
Keya Paha	2	2	0
Kimball	8	2	6
Knox	14	5	9
Lincoln	67	23	44
Logan	2	2	0
Loup	1	1	0
Madison	21	16	5
McPherson	1	1	0
Morrill	14	9	5
Nance	8	7	1
Nemaha	12	12	0
Nuckolls	10	5	5
Otoe	30	15	15
Pawnee	4	3	1
Perkins	8	4	4
Phelps	24	7	17
Pierce	10	5	5
Platte	64	22	42
Polk	5	4	1
Red Willow	17	2	15
Richardson	26	9	17
Rock	8	4	4
Saline	52	20	32
Scotts Bluff	24	18	6
Sheridan	18	7	11
Sherman	6	4	2
Sioux	3	3	0
Stanton	10	9	1
Thayer	12	7	5
Thomas	2	1	1
Thurston	14	7	7
Valley	5	4	1
Wayne	6	5	1
Webster	11	6	5
Wheeler	2	2	0
York	15	13	2
NEVADA			
Metropolitan Counties			
Carson City	138	100	38
Storey	28	25	3
Washoe	734	433	301
Nonmetropolitan Counties			
Churchill	51	43	8
Douglas	123	108	15
Elko	78	63	15
Eureka	16	9	7
Humboldt	60	38	22
Lander	37	18	19
Lincoln	20	16	4
Lyon	94	72	22
Pershing	22	15	7
White Pine	32	26	6
NEW HAMPSHIRE			
Metropolitan Counties			
Hillsborough	31	21	10
Rockingham	44	23	21
Strafford	39	22	17
Nonmetropolitan Counties			
Belknap	18	9	9
Carroll	21	11	10
Cheshire	20	8	12
Grafton	25	10	15
Merrimack	44	13	31
Sullivan	9	8	1
NEW JERSEY			
Metropolitan Counties			
Atlantic	146	112	34
Bergen	614	508	106
Burlington	82	66	16
Camden	220	188	32
Cape May	170	135	35
Cumberland	57	49	8
Essex	451	383	68
Gloucester	113	103	10

Table 80. Full-Time Law Enforcement Employees, by Selected State Metropolitan and Nonmetropolitan Counties, 2022—Continued

(Number.)

State/county	Law enforcement employees	Officers	Civilians
Hudson	400	263	137
Hunterdon	45	40	5
Mercer	198	151	47
Middlesex	177	147	30
Monmouth	553	378	175
Morris	143	115	28
Ocean	266	148	118
Passaic	615	487	128
Salem	239	188	51
Somerset	200	179	21
Sussex	113	74	39
Union	301	256	45
Warren	22	18	4
NEW MEXICO			
Metropolitan Counties			
Bernalillo	417	304	113
Dona Ana	191	134	57
Sandoval	65	56	9
San Juan	111	82	29
Santa Fe	101	76	25
Torrance	22	16	6
Valencia	60	45	15
Nonmetropolitan Counties			
Catron	8	7	1
Chaves	47	38	9
Cibola	19	13	6
Colfax	15	12	3
Curry	24	12	12
De Baca	5	5	0
Eddy	64	54	10
Grant	39	34	5
Guadalupe	8	6	2
Harding	2	2	0
Hidalgo	10	8	2
Lea	80	69	11
Lincoln	31	19	12
Luna	35	31	4
McKinley	41	34	7
Mora	9	7	2
Otero	67	44	23
Quay	9	7	2
Rio Arriba	26	23	3
Roosevelt	14	10	4
San Miguel	10	8	2
Sierra	16	13	3
Socorro	14	12	2
Taos	32	29	3
Union	7	6	1
NEW YORK			
Metropolitan Counties			
Albany	212	135	77
Broome	81	59	22
Chemung	40	37	3
Dutchess	124	101	23
Erie	305	157	148
Herkimer	18	11	7
Jefferson	59	44	15
Livingston	57	52	5
Madison	52	41	11
Monroe	359	307	52
Nassau	3,390	2,494	896
Niagara	173	110	63
Oneida	117	86	31
Onondaga	257	216	41
Ontario	130	72	58
Orleans	41	26	15
Oswego	79	69	10
Putnam	96	82	14
Rensselaer	51	43	8
Rockland	166	80	86
Saratoga	209	156	53
Schenectady	24	18	6
Schoharie	35	21	14
Suffolk	366	245	121
Suffolk County Police Department	3,047	2,558	489
Tioga	53	33	20
Tompkins	48	43	5
Ulster	93	63	30
Warren	112	75	37
Washington	47	42	5

Table 80. Full-Time Law Enforcement Employees, by Selected State Metropolitan and Nonmetropolitan Counties, 2022—Continued

(Number.)

State/county	Law enforcement employees	Officers	Civilians
Wayne	75	68	7
Westchester Public Safety	348	278	70
Yates	43	26	17
Nonmetropolitan Counties			
Allegany	44	23	21
Cattaraugus	81	54	27
Cayuga	41	34	7
Chautauqua	108	66	42
Chenango	24	24	0
Clinton	31	26	5
Columbia	66	50	16
Cortland	39	36	3
Delaware	25	18	7
Essex	27	24	3
Franklin	4	2	2
Fulton	42	27	15
Genesee	80	51	29
Greene	45	35	10
Hamilton	7	6	1
Lewis	22	22	0
Montgomery	56	36	20
Otsego	20	20	0
Schuyler	18	15	3
Seneca	35	35	0
Steuben	50	40	10
St. Lawrence	42	37	5
Sullivan	59	59	0
Wyoming	44	31	13
NORTH CAROLINA			
Metropolitan Counties			
Alamance	265	154	111
Alexander	81	35	46
Anson	57	30	27
Brunswick	325	188	137
Buncombe	255	210	45
Burke	127	87	40
Cabarrus	369	225	144
Caldwell	134	87	47
Camden	23	19	4
Catawba	231	160	71
Chatham	150	80	70
Craven	154	102	52
Cumberland	459	223	236
Currituck	87	67	20
Davidson	180	121	59
Davie	118	79	39
Durham	361	173	188
Edgecombe	123	53	70
Forsyth	489	255	234
Franklin	112	82	30
Gaston	237	106	131
Gaston County Police Department	244	134	110
Gates	15	14	1
Granville	99	57	42
Guilford	580	261	319
Harnett	127	91	36
Haywood	138	71	67
Henderson	220	146	74
Hoke	117	68	49
Iredell	275	178	97
Johnston	149	124	25
Jones	27	17	10
Lincoln	190	132	58
Madison	47	23	24
Mecklenburg[1]	889	267	622
Nash	131	84	47
New Hanover	565	391	174
Onslow	273	147	126
Orange	159	88	71
Pamlico	50	22	28
Pender	115	74	41
Person	78	51	27
Pitt	314	114	200
Randolph	253	183	70
Rockingham	130	89	41
Rowan	178	115	63
Stokes	84	55	29
Union	330	238	92
Wake	792	332	460
Wayne	213	126	87
Yadkin	69	37	32

Table 80. Full-Time Law Enforcement Employees, by Selected State Metropolitan and Nonmetropolitan Counties, 2022—Continued

(Number.)

State/county	Law enforcement employees	Officers	Civilians
Nonmetropolitan Counties			
Alleghany	44	26	18
Ashe	71	36	35
Avery	49	26	23
Beaufort	78	48	30
Bertie	29	22	7
Bladen	98	53	45
Carteret	113	68	45
Caswell	51	35	16
Cherokee	58	35	23
Chowan	38	17	21
Clay	26	21	5
Cleveland	198	116	82
Columbus	101	94	7
Dare	146	69	77
Duplin	83	61	22
Graham	37	21	16
Greene	23	20	3
Halifax	66	63	3
Hertford	56	24	32
Hyde	17	16	1
Jackson	66	62	4
Lee	115	79	36
Lenoir	61	54	7
Macon	73	53	20
Martin	45	39	6
McDowell	82	54	28
Mitchell	21	20	1
Montgomery	46	27	19
Moore	173	84	89
Northampton	58	35	23
Pasquotank	58	50	8
Perquimans	28	24	4
Polk	57	34	23
Richmond	82	59	23
Robeson	218	138	80
Rutherford	115	80	35
Sampson	132	93	39
Scotland	64	36	28
Stanly	99	62	37
Surry	139	86	53
Swain	42	30	12
Transylvania	84	61	23
Tyrrell	15	13	2
Vance	77	42	35
Warren	57	26	31
Washington	32	12	20
Watauga	77	49	28
Wilkes	142	80	62
Wilson	113	71	42
Yancey	55	28	27
NORTH DAKOTA			
Metropolitan Counties			
Burleigh	64	54	10
Cass	152	101	51
Grand Forks	41	34	7
Morton	42	35	7
Oliver	5	4	1
Nonmetropolitan Counties			
Adams	6	5	1
Barnes	10	9	1
Benson	5	5	0
Billings	7	7	0
Bottineau	17	9	8
Bowman	5	4	1
Burke	5	5	0
Cavalier	12	7	5
Dickey	3	2	1
Divide	6	5	1
Dunn	23	21	2
Eddy	5	5	0
Emmons	6	5	1
Foster	3	3	0
Golden Valley	5	4	1
Grant	6	6	0
Griggs	4	3	1
Hettinger	8	7	1
Kidder	4	3	1
Lamoure	5	4	1
Logan	3	3	0
McHenry	8	8	0

Table 80. Full-Time Law Enforcement Employees, by Selected State Metropolitan and Nonmetropolitan Counties, 2022—Continued

(Number.)

State/county	Law enforcement employees	Officers	Civilians
McIntosh	3	3	0
McKenzie	56	37	19
McLean	43	27	16
Mercer	29	16	13
Mountrail	24	11	13
Nelson	6	5	1
Pembina	14	9	5
Pierce	38	4	34
Ramsey	11	10	1
Renville	8	7	1
Richland	35	15	20
Rolette	22	9	13
Sargent	6	5	1
Sheridan	4	3	1
Sioux	1	1	0
Slope	1	1	0
Stark	33	28	5
Steele	3	3	0
Towner	5	4	1
Traill	14	10	4
Walsh	20	12	8
Ward	96	42	54
Wells	5	4	1
OHIO			
Metropolitan Counties			
Allen	94	53	41
Butler	377	145	232
Clark	204	105	99
Clermont	213	95	118
Cuyahoga	1,066	187	879
Delaware	224	117	107
Fairfield	158	105	53
Fulton	24	22	2
Geauga	119	48	71
Greene	145	62	83
Hamilton	832	418	414
Hocking	43	39	4
Jefferson	72	36	36
Licking	234	100	134
Madison	51	36	15
Mahoning	221	188	33
Medina	151	58	93
Miami	116	56	60
Montgomery	451	223	228
Morrow	49	21	28
Perry	26	17	9
Pickaway	99	42	57
Portage	176	84	92
Stark	237	116	121
Summit	342	283	59
Trumbull	75	65	10
Union	69	46	23
Warren	198	101	97
Nonmetropolitan Counties			
Ashland	93	46	47
Ashtabula	89	39	50
Athens	43	37	6
Auglaize	74	28	46
Champaign	31	27	4
Columbiana	44	31	13
Coshocton	62	40	22
Crawford	63	28	35
Darke	61	30	31
Defiance	25	23	2
Erie	96	49	47
Fayette	53	24	29
Gallia	43	25	18
Guernsey	58	28	30
Hancock	102	41	61
Henry	25	18	7
Huron	73	29	44
Jackson	17	12	5
Knox	73	45	28
Marion	62	36	26
Mercer	60	25	35
Monroe	63	28	35
Morgan	15	5	10
Muskingum	131	80	51
Noble	43	21	22
Paulding	44	28	16
Preble	60	26	34

Table 80. Full-Time Law Enforcement Employees, by Selected State Metropolitan and Nonmetropolitan Counties, 2022—Continued

(Number.)

State/county	Law enforcement employees	Officers	Civilians
Ross	102	52	50
Scioto	96	46	50
Seneca	85	22	63
Van Wert	45	24	21
Vinton	23	12	11
Washington	110	51	59
Wayne	75	50	25
Williams	23	20	3
Wyandot	28	19	9
OKLAHOMA			
Metropolitan Counties			
Canadian	100	65	35
Cleveland	213	113	100
Comanche	41	31	10
Cotton	10	5	5
Creek	87	39	48
Garfield	37	28	9
Grady	46	34	12
Lincoln	34	19	15
Logan	55	35	20
McClain	43	30	13
Oklahoma	218	161	57
Okmulgee	17	15	2
Osage	72	36	36
Pawnee	28	9	19
Rogers	43	38	5
Sequoyah	42	26	16
Tulsa	568	219	349
Wagoner	73	38	35
Nonmetropolitan Counties			
Adair	32	12	20
Alfalfa	11	5	6
Atoka	23	12	11
Beaver	8	8	0
Beckham	36	13	23
Blaine	23	12	11
Bryan	46	23	23
Caddo	15	14	1
Carter	57	21	36
Cherokee	34	27	7
Choctaw	7	6	1
Cimarron	8	2	6
Coal	8	5	3
Craig	27	13	14
Custer	38	12	26
Delaware	46	25	21
Dewey	30	7	23
Ellis	8	6	2
Garvin	29	13	16
Grant	14	8	6
Greer	10	3	7
Harmon	3	2	1
Harper	8	4	4
Haskell	10	10	0
Hughes	17	9	8
Jackson	38	12	26
Jefferson	15	3	12
Johnston	22	11	11
Kay	26	18	8
Kingfisher	31	13	18
Kiowa	12	11	1
Latimer	11	9	2
Le Flore	24	21	3
Love	14	13	1
Major	19	5	14
Marshall	35	13	22
Mayes	60	31	29
McCurtain	24	19	5
McIntosh	15	14	1
Murray	17	8	9
Muskogee	35	29	6
Noble	21	11	10
Nowata	9	4	5
Okfuskee	24	8	16
Ottawa	14	11	3
Payne	88	47	41
Pittsburg	60	24	36
Pontotoc	19	17	2
Pottawatomie	33	29	4
Pushmataha	17	7	10
Roger Mills	12	7	5

Table 80. Full-Time Law Enforcement Employees, by Selected State Metropolitan and Nonmetropolitan Counties, 2022—Continued

(Number.)

State/county	Law enforcement employees	Officers	Civilians
Seminole	17	13	4
Stephens	23	19	4
Texas	31	12	19
Tillman	4	4	0
Washington	61	29	32
Washita	34	6	28
Woods	15	7	8
Woodward	29	12	17
OREGON			
Metropolitan Counties			
Benton	83	34	49
Clackamas	423	194	229
Columbia	61	21	40
Deschutes	234	178	56
Jackson	184	126	58
Josephine	87	27	60
Lane	292	75	217
Linn	175	125	50
Marion	327	88	239
Multnomah	740	126	614
Polk	69	27	42
Washington	555	250	305
Yamhill	90	40	50
Nonmetropolitan Counties			
Baker	45	33	12
Clatsop	84	66	18
Coos	79	21	58
Crook	63	43	20
Douglas	139	67	72
Gilliam	10	9	1
Grant	23	23	0
Harney	19	14	5
Hood River	49	24	25
Jefferson	32	29	3
Klamath	47	35	12
Lake	30	29	1
Lincoln	91	30	61
Malheur	52	25	27
Morrow	39	34	5
Sherman	7	6	1
Tillamook	59	45	14
Umatilla	101	34	67
Union	41	17	24
Wallowa	10	5	5
Wasco	27	15	12
Wheeler	3	3	0
PENNSYLVANIA			
Metropolitan Counties			
Adams	19	15	4
Allegheny	196	165	31
Allegheny County Police Department	232	216	16
Beaver	32	27	5
Berks	101	89	12
Blair	28	25	3
Bucks	79	64	15
Butler	30	27	3
Cambria	28	23	5
Carbon	21	17	4
Centre	27	23	4
Chester	66	50	16
Cumberland	40	33	7
Erie	44	37	7
Franklin	36	32	4
Lancaster	51	45	6
Lehigh	80	72	8
Lycoming	23	17	6
Mercer	17	14	3
Monroe	45	21	24
Pike	19	15	4
Washington	40	37	3
Westmoreland	67	61	6
Wyoming	6	4	2
York	108	101	7
Nonmetropolitan Counties			
Bradford	11	9	
Clarion	8	6	
Indiana	23	21	
Jefferson	10	8	
Lawrence	20	15	

Table 80. Full-Time Law Enforcement Employees, by Selected State Metropolitan and Nonmetropolitan Counties, 2022—Continued

(Number.)

State/county	Law enforcement employees	Officers	Civilians
Schuylkill	22	18	
Tioga	7	5	
Wayne	11	11	
SOUTH CAROLINA			
Metropolitan Counties			
Aiken	234	137	97
Anderson	431	259	172
Beaufort	277	188	89
Berkeley	229	184	45
Calhoun	28	26	2
Charleston	586	247	339
Chester	113	57	56
Clarendon	74	66	8
Darlington	121	70	51
Dorchester	271	160	111
Edgefield	72	39	33
Fairfield	58	49	9
Florence	271	147	124
Greenville	629	530	99
Horry	91	70	21
Horry County Police Department	303	270	33
Jasper	54	44	10
Kershaw	82	71	11
Lancaster	195	135	60
Laurens	112	61	51
Lexington	403	285	118
Pickens	176	153	23
Richland	618	546	72
Saluda	39	27	12
Spartanburg	362	330	32
Sumter	130	103	27
York	424	187	237
Nonmetropolitan Counties			
Abbeville	57	36	21
Allendale	12	10	2
Bamberg	11	11	0
Barnwell	97	37	60
Cherokee	103	62	41
Chesterfield	69	56	13
Colleton	108	51	57
Dillon	53	41	12
Georgetown	137	90	47
Greenwood	128	74	54
Hampton	43	40	3
Lee	25	21	4
Marion	66	36	30
Marlboro	49	31	18
McCormick	23	21	2
Newberry	104	52	52
Oconee	189	103	86
Orangeburg	108	85	23
Union	37	32	5
Williamsburg	38	35	3
SOUTH DAKOTA			
Metropolitan Counties			
Lincoln	47	33	14
McCook	8	7	1
Meade	47	17	30
Minnehaha	251	84	167
Pennington	370	101	269
Turner	11	9	2
Union	29	8	21
Nonmetropolitan Counties			
Aurora	5	4	1
Beadle	22	5	17
Bennett	5	3	2
Bon Homme	8	3	5
Brookings	36	17	19
Brown	86	19	67
Brule	13	4	9
Buffalo	1	1	0
Butte	13	6	7
Campbell	3	3	0
Charles Mix	26	11	15
Clark	3	3	0
Clay	17	9	8
Codington	31	12	19
Corson	5	5	0
Custer	13	12	1

Table 80. Full-Time Law Enforcement Employees, by Selected State Metropolitan and Nonmetropolitan Counties, 2022—Continued

(Number.)

State/county	Law enforcement employees	Officers	Civilians
Davison	11	8	3
Day	9	4	5
Deuel	5	4	1
Dewey	4	4	0
Douglas	4	4	0
Edmunds	9	4	5
Fall River	22	7	15
Faulk	14	5	9
Grant	9	5	4
Gregory	5	4	1
Haakon	2	2	0
Hamlin	6	6	0
Hand	4	3	1
Hanson	3	3	0
Harding	3	2	1
Hughes	45	8	37
Hutchinson	4	3	1
Hyde	1	1	0
Jackson	2	1	1
Jerauld	4	4	0
Jones	2	2	0
Kingsbury	6	4	2
Lake	16	7	9
Lawrence	43	18	25
Lyman	5	4	1
Marshall	9	4	5
McPherson	3	3	0
Mellette	4	3	1
Miner	4	3	1
Moody	10	6	4
Oglala Lakota	2	2	0
Perkins	8	7	1
Potter	3	2	1
Roberts	30	8	22
Sanborn	4	3	1
Spink	11	7	4
Stanley	7	6	1
Sully	3	3	0
Tripp	4	3	1
Walworth	8	2	6
Yankton	32	10	22
Ziebach	2	2	0
TENNESSEE			
Metropolitan Counties			
Anderson	211	68	143
Blount	302	180	122
Bradley	213	106	107
Campbell	66	34	32
Cannon	41	15	26
Carter	91	50	41
Cheatham	86	52	34
Chester	41	17	24
Crockett	35	14	21
Dickson	152	76	76
Fayette	89	49	40
Gibson	85	44	41
Grainger	35	21	14
Hamblen	93	39	54
Hamilton	410	170	240
Hartsville/Trousdale	27	20	7
Hawkins	111	66	45
Jefferson	92	47	45
Knox	837	373	464
Loudon	112	108	4
Macon	68	33	35
Madison	265	120	145
Marion	49	31	18
Maury	168	92	76
Montgomery	390	161	229
Morgan	49	25	24
Polk	65	27	38
Roane	90	51	39
Robertson	136	66	70
Rutherford	445	242	203
Sequatchie	22	20	2
Shelby	1,540	620	920
Smith	60	30	30
Stewart	55	24	31
Sullivan	303	132	171
Sumner	280	133	147
Tipton	66	62	4
Unicoi	53	23	30

Table 80. Full-Time Law Enforcement Employees, by Selected State Metropolitan and Nonmetropolitan Counties, 2022—Continued

(Number.)

State/county	Law enforcement employees	Officers	Civilians
Union	55	32	23
Washington	242	97	145
Williamson	292	182	110
Wilson	273	143	130
Nonmetropolitan Counties			
Bedford	61	54	7
Benton	53	20	33
Bledsoe	34	12	22
Carroll	72	29	43
Claiborne	80	44	36
Clay	23	14	9
Cocke	87	44	43
Coffee	120	55	65
Cumberland	115	61	54
Decatur	32	16	16
DeKalb	49	48	1
Dyer	106	38	68
Fentress	36	23	13
Franklin	77	41	36
Giles	69	40	29
Greene	172	76	96
Grundy	28	14	14
Hancock	63	23	40
Hardeman	51	29	22
Hardin	62	33	29
Haywood	42	20	22
Henderson	60	31	29
Henry	69	32	37
Hickman	49	28	21
Houston	24	8	16
Humphreys	50	26	24
Jackson	29	15	14
Johnson	43	21	22
Lake	19	8	11
Lauderdale	58	23	35
Lawrence	60	49	11
Lewis	40	16	24
Lincoln	85	41	44
Marshall	51	29	22
McMinn	91	41	50
McNairy	46	25	21
Meigs	27	21	6
Monroe	56	48	8
Moore	32	17	15
Obion	66	35	31
Overton	60	31	29
Perry	26	16	10
Pickett	18	13	5
Putnam	165	76	89
Rhea	91	38	53
Scott	68	28	40
Sevier	202	104	98
Van Buren	19	3	16
Warren	113	54	59
Wayne	51	19	32
Weakley	48	26	22
White	81	41	40
TEXAS			
Metropolitan Counties			
Armstrong	7	4	3
Atascosa	101	44	57
Austin	74	38	36
Bandera	72	33	39
Bastrop	181	80	101
Bell	380	112	268
Bexar	1,609	592	1,017
Bowie	42	35	7
Brazoria	357	146	211
Brazos	223	96	127
Burleson	50	27	23
Caldwell	87	35	52
Callahan	18	7	11
Cameron	356	106	250
Carson	24	10	14
Chambers	68	59	9
Clay	31	16	15
Collin	529	139	390
Comal	348	159	189
Coryell	65	31	34
Crosby	20	10	10
Dallas	2,205	378	1,827

Table 80. Full-Time Law Enforcement Employees, by Selected State Metropolitan and Nonmetropolitan Counties, 2022—Continued

(Number.)

State/county	Law enforcement employees	Officers	Civilians
Denton	414	183	231
Ector	202	83	119
Ellis	217	89	128
El Paso	952	292	660
Falls	24	10	14
Fort Bend	743	532	211
Galveston	466	287	179
Goliad	32	19	13
Grayson	169	55	114
Gregg	227	101	126
Hardin	77	37	40
Harris	4,637	2,260	2,377
Harrison	100	47	53
Hays	403	172	231
Hidalgo	850	295	555
Hudspeth	41	15	26
Hunt	134	46	88
Irion	12	6	6
Jefferson	370	325	45
Johnson	135	92	43
Jones	35	8	27
Kaufman	226	77	149
Kendall	103	54	49
Lampasas	36	16	20
Liberty	174	79	95
Lubbock	507	180	327
Lynn	23	11	12
Martin	17	9	8
McLennan	476	111	365
Medina	93	53	40
Midland	197	78	119
Montgomery	918	505	413
Nueces	231	48	183
Oldham	11	6	5
Orange	131	63	68
Parker	132	95	37
Potter	228	91	137
Randall	203	87	116
Robertson	44	16	28
Rockwall	137	54	83
Rusk	70	36	34
Smith	350	146	204
Sterling	5	5	0
Tarrant	1,391	370	1,021
Taylor	234	80	154
Tom Green	186	170	16
Travis	1,423	412	1,011
Upshur	83	47	36
Victoria	197	113	84
Waller	126	76	50
Webb	334	144	190
Wichita	193	66	127
Williamson	226	169	57
Wilson	73	36	37
Wise	128	60	68
Nonmetropolitan Counties			
Andrews	54	18	36
Angelina	82	32	50
Aransas	71	22	49
Bailey	26	11	15
Baylor	5	2	3
Bee	57	21	36
Blanco	30	15	15
Borden	4	3	1
Bosque	46	23	23
Brewster	20	19	1
Briscoe	4	4	0
Brooks	36	17	19
Brown	66	31	35
Burnet	146	57	89
Calhoun	63	26	37
Camp	18	8	10
Cass	49	19	30
Castro	21	7	14
Cherokee	65	33	32
Childress	21	4	17
Cochran	13	6	7
Coke	6	5	1
Coleman	18	5	13
Collingsworth	3	3	0
Colorado	44	21	23
Comanche	32	9	23

Table 80. Full-Time Law Enforcement Employees, by Selected State Metropolitan and Nonmetropolitan Counties, 2022—Continued

(Number.)

State/county	Law enforcement employees	Officers	Civilians
Concho	15	8	7
Cooke	84	34	50
Crane	22	9	13
Crockett	12	7	5
Dallam	7	6	1
Dawson	22	9	13
Deaf Smith	60	11	49
Delta	21	10	11
DeWitt	46	14	32
Donley	11	6	5
Duval	41	23	18
Eastland	33	13	20
Edwards	15	7	8
Erath	71	34	37
Fannin	23	20	3
Fayette	53	30	23
Fisher	16	6	10
Floyd	10	5	5
Foard	3	2	1
Franklin	29	29	0
Freestone	37	18	19
Gaines	42	17	25
Garza	36	8	28
Gillespie	54	32	22
Glasscock	6	5	1
Gonzales	50	19	31
Gray	41	14	27
Grimes	52	27	25
Hall	9	3	6
Hamilton	18	10	8
Hansford	13	7	6
Hardeman	11	6	5
Hartley	7	6	1
Haskell	7	2	5
Hemphill	16	8	8
Henderson	161	76	85
Hill	74	32	42
Hockley	16	14	2
Hood	133	44	89
Hopkins	70	28	42
Houston	49	22	27
Howard	67	25	42
Hutchinson	36	14	22
Jack	30	14	16
Jackson	38	14	24
Jasper	46	21	25
Jeff Davis	5	4	1
Jim Hogg	38	33	5
Jim Wells	65	56	9
Karnes	64	31	33
Kenedy	16	10	6
Kerr	112	51	61
Kimble	20	11	9
King	2	2	0
Kleberg	66	22	44
Lamar	75	34	41
Lamb	27	10	17
La Salle	119	24	95
Lavaca	32	13	19
Lee	44	17	27
Leon	40	24	16
Limestone	68	21	47
Lipscomb	13	5	8
Llano	46	26	20
Loving	10	7	3
Madison	39	18	21
Marion	9	8	1
Mason	13	8	5
Matagorda	72	33	39
Maverick	75	61	14
McCulloch	27	8	19
Milam	74	28	46
Mills	22	9	13
Montague	30	13	17
Moore	49	18	31
Morris	23	9	14
Motley	2	2	0
Nacogdoches	81	39	42
Navarro	118	46	72
Newton	9	9	0
Nolan	39	16	23
Ochiltree	25	8	17
Palo Pinto	52	24	28

Table 80. Full-Time Law Enforcement Employees, by Selected State Metropolitan and Nonmetropolitan Counties, 2022—Continued

(Number.)

State/county	Law enforcement employees	Officers	Civilians
Panola	62	34	28
Parmer	19	6	13
Polk	104	43	61
Presidio	26	6	20
Rains	28	21	7
Reagan	29	14	15
Real	11	5	6
Red River	27	10	17
Refugio	46	17	29
Roberts	6	5	1
Runnels	34	6	28
Sabine	20	10	10
San Augustine	21	12	9
Schleicher	10	4	6
Scurry	44	10	34
Shackelford	17	6	11
Shelby	36	15	21
Somervell	42	21	21
Starr	113	45	68
Stephens	20	6	14
Sutton	13	5	8
Swisher	10	9	1
Terrell	4	3	1
Terry	35	9	26
Throckmorton	5	1	4
Titus	64	24	40
Trinity	20	13	7
Tyler	30	17	13
Upton	23	11	12
Uvalde	66	25	41
Val Verde	77	51	26
Van Zandt	51	20	31
Walker	81	44	37
Ward	44	20	24
Washington	56	32	24
Wharton	75	44	31
Wheeler	31	12	19
Wilbarger	20	8	12
Willacy	33	19	14
Winkler	28	12	16
Wood	45	33	12
Yoakum	22	21	1
Young	32	12	20
Zapata	75	63	12
Zavala	43	21	22
UTAH			
Metropolitan Counties			
Box Elder	77	26	51
Cache	155	134	21
Davis	289	82	207
Juab	28	14	14
Morgan	16	14	2
Salt Lake County Unified Police Department	402	320	82
Tooele	89	26	63
Utah	421	178	243
Washington	162	43	119
Weber	312	224	88
Nonmetropolitan Counties			
Beaver	78	23	55
Carbon	50	25	25
Daggett	6	5	1
Duchesne	64	24	40
Emery	36	24	12
Garfield	32	14	18
Grand	40	18	22
Iron	88	35	53
Kane	53	27	26
Millard	53	28	25
Piute	6	5	1
Rich	10	5	5
San Juan	39	20	19
Sanpete	63	29	34
Sevier	60	48	12
Summit	111	66	45
Uintah	93	29	64
Wasatch	74	38	36
Wayne	5	4	1
VERMONT			
Metropolitan Counties			
Chittenden	14	12	2

Table 80. Full-Time Law Enforcement Employees, by Selected State Metropolitan and Nonmetropolitan Counties, 2022—Continued

(Number.)

State/county	Law enforcement employees	Officers	Civilians
Franklin	20	19	1
Grand Isle	7	5	2
Nonmetropolitan Counties			
Addison	9	8	1
Bennington	7	4	3
Caledonia	6	5	1
Essex	5	5	0
Lamoille	25	11	14
Orange	16	12	4
Orleans	20	14	6
Rutland	22	17	5
Washington	9	7	2
Windham	21	14	7
Windsor	19	16	3
VIRGINIA			
Metropolitan Counties			
Albemarle County Police Department	168	142	26
Amelia	30	20	10
Amherst	51	43	8
Appomattox	24	22	2
Arlington County Police Department	419	316	103
Augusta	93	83	10
Bedford	94	86	8
Botetourt	108	92	16
Campbell	92	83	9
Charles City	19	12	7
Chesterfield County Police Department	672	542	130
Clarke	31	18	13
Craig	12	7	5
Culpeper	111	98	13
Dinwiddie	50	45	5
Fairfax County Police Department	1,602	1,304	298
Fauquier	174	131	43
Fluvanna	62	44	18
Franklin	96	54	42
Frederick	164	150	14
Giles	34	25	9
Gloucester	101	83	18
Goochland	66	49	17
Greene	53	34	19
Hanover	263	244	19
Henrico County Police Department	811	662	149
Isle of Wight	57	53	4
James City County Police Department	94	89	5
King and Queen	24	16	8
King William	34	24	10
Loudoun	695	550	145
Madison	33	20	13
Mathews	21	12	9
Montgomery	121	115	6
Nelson	23	20	3
New Kent	62	44	18
Powhatan	55	48	7
Prince George County Police Department	84	58	26
Prince William County Police Department	778	619	159
Pulaski	58	55	3
Rappahannock	22	16	6
Roanoke County Police Department	145	132	13
Rockingham	211	188	23
Scott	46	39	7
Southampton	89	76	13
Spotsylvania	260	222	38
Stafford	276	208	68
Sussex	51	44	7
Warren	76	59	17
Washington	91	74	17
York	123	109	14
Nonmetropolitan Counties			
Accomack	35	29	6
Alleghany	73	53	20
Bath	24	15	9
Bland	23	14	9
Brunswick	45	34	11
Buchanan	50	36	14
Buckingham	29	20	9
Caroline	69	51	18
Carroll	44	38	6
Charlotte	39	19	20
Cumberland	23	18	5
Dickenson	37	23	14

Table 80. Full-Time Law Enforcement Employees, by Selected State Metropolitan and Nonmetropolitan Counties, 2022—Continued

(Number.)

State/county	Law enforcement employees	Officers	Civilians
Essex	24	17	7
Floyd	37	27	10
Grayson	31	26	5
Greensville	38	28	10
Halifax	40	37	3
Henry	217	197	20
Highland	9	6	3
King George	63	41	22
Lancaster	43	30	13
Lee	41	30	11
Louisa	73	52	21
Lunenburg	19	13	6
Mecklenburg	51	49	2
Middlesex	22	14	8
Northampton	69	59	10
Northumberland	33	21	12
Nottoway	27	18	9
Orange	52	47	5
Page	72	64	8
Patrick	72	57	15
Pittsylvania	120	66	54
Prince Edward	32	26	6
Richmond	23	15	8
Rockbridge	45	42	3
Russell	54	40	14
Shenandoah	84	77	7
Smyth	55	43	12
Surry	27	14	13
Tazewell	82	57	25
Westmoreland	46	30	16
Wise	76	59	17
Wythe	65	56	9
WASHINGTON			
Metropolitan Counties			
Asotin	23	12	11
Benton	82	68	14
Chelan	74	58	16
Clark	225	128	97
Cowlitz	64	45	19
Douglas	38	32	6
Franklin	87	30	57
King	224	171	53
Kitsap	251	122	129
Pierce	312	252	60
Skagit	128	54	74
Skamania	37	34	3
Snohomish	361	294	67
Spokane	154	127	27
Stevens	64	31	33
Thurston	237	92	145
Walla Walla	38	29	9
Whatcom	182	85	97
Yakima	92	59	33
Nonmetropolitan Counties			
Adams	34	16	18
Clallam	47	36	11
Columbia	13	12	1
Ferry	23	8	15
Garfield	14	8	6
Grant	117	54	63
Grays Harbor	93	63	30
Island	70	38	32
Jefferson	49	24	25
Kittitas	99	50	49
Klickitat	36	17	19
Lewis	103	40	63
Lincoln	24	14	10
Mason	88	48	40
Okanogan	72	24	48
Pacific	44	15	29
Pend Oreille	33	14	19
San Juan	32	19	13
Wahkiakum	20	9	11
Whitman	34	17	17
WEST VIRGINIA			
Metropolitan Counties			
Berkeley	74	64	10
Boone	20	18	2
Brooke	20	18	2
Cabell	48	44	4

Table 80. Full-Time Law Enforcement Employees, by Selected State Metropolitan and Nonmetropolitan Counties, 2022—Continued

(Number.)

State/county	Law enforcement employees	Officers	Civilians
Clay	3	3	0
Fayette	41	34	7
Hampshire	24	20	4
Hancock	35	32	3
Jackson	24	16	8
Jefferson	37	31	6
Kanawha	130	104	26
Lincoln	4	4	0
Marshall	31	29	2
Mineral	21	16	5
Monongalia	86	35	51
Morgan	14	13	1
Ohio	36	30	6
Preston	22	20	2
Putnam	46	33	13
Raleigh	69	53	16
Wayne	24	21	3
Wirt	6	3	3
Wood	58	34	24
Nonmetropolitan Counties			
Barbour	14	13	1
Braxton	10	8	2
Calhoun	6	4	2
Doddridge	11	10	1
Gilmer	4	2	2
Grant	14	13	1
Greenbrier	29	28	1
Hardy	16	11	5
Harrison	59	54	5
Lewis	14	12	2
Logan	24	22	2
Marion	41	29	12
Mason	17	15	2
McDowell	11	11	0
Mercer	34	28	6
Mingo	19	18	1
Monroe	13	10	3
Nicholas	22	19	3
Pendleton	5	4	1
Pleasants	8	7	1
Pocahontas	10	5	5
Randolph	29	18	11
Ritchie	15	10	5
Roane	9	6	3
Summers	11	10	1
Taylor	15	9	6
Tucker	8	5	3
Tyler	24	13	11
Upshur	14	12	2
Webster	6	4	2
Wetzel	7	6	1
Wyoming	19	18	1
WISCONSIN			
Metropolitan Counties			
Brown	311	169	142
Calumet	57	30	27
Chippewa	93	47	46
Dane	525	414	111
Douglas	74	30	44
Eau Claire	110	43	67
Fond du Lac	128	64	64
Green	58	30	28
Iowa	48	23	25
Kenosha	355	145	210
Kewaunee	36	36	0
La Crosse	105	40	65
Lincoln	68	30	38
Marathon	168	72	96
Milwaukee	554	290	264
Oconto	69	31	38
Outagamie	156	59	97
Ozaukee	108	77	31
Pierce	40	39	1
Racine	275	162	113
Rock	202	102	100
Sheboygan	182	65	117
St. Croix	110	79	31
Washington	172	78	94
Waukesha	361	175	186
Winnebago	177	125	52

Table 80. Full-Time Law Enforcement Employees, by Selected State Metropolitan and Nonmetropolitan Counties, 2022—Continued

(Number.)

State/county	Law enforcement employees	Officers	Civilians
Nonmetropolitan Counties			
Adams	54	30	24
Ashland	48	23	25
Barron	73	34	39
Bayfield	46	22	24
Buffalo	24	12	12
Burnett	34	34	0
Clark	59	30	29
Crawford	34	26	8
Dodge	157	54	103
Door	60	56	4
Dunn	57	28	29
Florence	22	11	11
Forest	35	23	12
Grant	56	30	26
Green Lake	43	20	23
Iron	22	11	11
Jackson	49	23	26
Jefferson	111	87	24
Juneau	57	45	12
Lafayette	29	29	0
Langlade	42	17	25
Manitowoc	106	66	40
Marinette	61	34	27
Menominee	16	10	6
Monroe	65	27	38
Oneida	113	34	79
Pepin	21	20	1
Polk	79	32	47
Portage	104	48	56
Price	34	20	14
Richland	30	30	0
Rusk	34	31	3
Sauk	136	107	29
Sawyer	40	23	17
Shawano	92	38	54
Trempealeau	59	28	31
Vilas	68	37	31
Walworth	192	76	116
Washburn	35	18	17
Waupaca	102	48	54
Waushara	58	30	28
Wood	75	46	29
WYOMING			
Metropolitan Counties			
Laramie	162	46	116
Natrona	157	114	43
Nonmetropolitan Counties			
Albany	50	22	28
Big Horn	42	19	23
Campbell	148	57	91
Carbon	49	18	31
Converse	40	38	2
Crook	23	15	8
Fremont	94	41	53
Goshen	26	8	18
Hot Springs	13	11	2
Johnson	32	28	4
Lincoln	49	22	27
Niobrara	16	10	6
Park	60	21	39
Platte	39	32	7
Sheridan	54	19	35
Sublette	70	54	16
Sweetwater	82	62	20
Teton	69	31	38
Uinta	44	16	28
Washakie	15	8	7
Weston	16	14	2

1 The employee data presented in this table for Mecklenburg represent only Mecklenburg County Sheriff's Office employees and exclude Charlotte-Mecklenburg Police Department employees.

Table 81. Full-Time Law Enforcement Employees, by Selected State and Agency, 2022

(Number.)

State/agency	Law enforcement employees	Officers	Civilians
ALABAMA			
State Agencies			
Alabama Department of Mental Health	4	3	1
Alabama Law Enforcement Agency	1,333	745	588
Department of Corrections Investigations and Intelligence Division	121	93	28
State Fire Marshal	43	36	7
Tannehill Ironworks Historic State Park	1	1	0
Taylor Hardin Secure Medical Facility	14	12	2
Tribal Agencies			
Poarch Creek Tribal	55	44	11
Other Agencies			
Dothan-Houston County Airport Authority	5	4	1
Huntsville International Airport	23	17	6
Mobile Regional Airport	17	11	6
Montgomery Airport	16	14	2
Trussville Fire Department Fire and Explosion Investigation Unit	3	3	0
ALASKA			
Other Agencies			
Fairbanks International Airport	33	26	7
Ted Stevens Anchorage International Airport	64	57	7
ARIZONA			
Tribal Agencies			
Ak-Chin Tribal	49	14	35
Cocopah Tribal	19	12	7
Colorado River Tribal	23	15	8
Fort Apache Agency	3	3	0
Fort McDowell Tribal	21	15	6
Fort Mojave Tribal	30	13	17
Gila River Indian Community	150	113	37
Hopi Resource Enforcement Agency	30	16	14
Hopi Tribal	2	2	0
Hualapai Tribal	19	17	2
Kaibab Paiute Tribal	1	1	0
Navajo Nation	268	194	74
Pascua Yaqui Tribal	65	24	41
San Carlos Agency	2	2	0
San Carlos Apache	56	29	27
Tonto Apache Tribal	9	9	0
Truxton Canon Agency	8	4	4
White Mountain Apache Tribal	51	28	23
Yavapai-Apache Nation	16	13	3
Yavapai-Prescott Tribal	12	9	3
Other Agencies			
Tucson Airport Authority	54	25	29
ARKANSAS			
State Agencies			
Camp Robinson	31	10	21
State Capitol Police	32	29	3
Other Agencies			
Fort Smith Public Schools	11	10	1
Northwest Arkansas Regional Airport	21	14	7
Pottsville School District	4	4	0
CALIFORNIA			
State Agencies			
Atascadero State Hospital	164	150	14
California State Fair	2	1	1
California State Parks, Capital	567	524	43
Coalinga State Hospital	258	241	17
Fairview Developmental Center	5	5	0
Metropolitan State Hospital	136	121	15
Napa State Hospital	103	103	0
Patton State Hospital	113	100	13
Porterville Developmental Center	62	53	9
Tribal Agencies			
Bear River Band	9	7	2
Blue Lake Tribal	7	1	6
Hoopa Valley Tribal	14	7	7
La Jolla Tribal	2	2	0
Los Coyotes Tribal	1	1	0
San Pasqual Band of Mission Indians Tribal	10	10	0
Sycuan Tribal	21	14	7
Table Mountain Rancheria	27	19	8
Tule River Tribal	11	5	6
Yurok Tribal	15	12	3

Table 81. Full-Time Law Enforcement Employees, by Selected State and Agency, 2022—Continued

(Number.)

State/agency	Law enforcement employees	Officers	Civilians
Other Agencies			
Clovis Unified School District	16	14	2
East Bay Regional Park District	88	59	29
Fontana Unified School District	73	13	60
Kern High School District	36	32	4
Port of San Diego Harbor	148	119	29
San Bernardino Unified School District	94	24	70
San Francisco Bay Area Rapid Transit, Contra Costa County	348	212	136
Shasta County Marshal	29	23	6
Stockton Unified School District	35	24	11
Twin Rivers Unified School District	21	14	7
Union Pacific Railroad, Alameda County	42	42	0
COLORADO			
State Agencies			
Colorado Bureau of Investigation	287	48	239
Colorado Mental Health Institute	3	3	0
Division of Gaming Criminal Enforcement and Investigations Section			
Cripple Creek	18	10	8
Golden	48	18	30
Tribal Agencies			
Southern Ute Tribal	26	15	11
Ute Mountain Tribal	17	10	7
Other Agencies			
Southwest Drug Task Force	8	7	1
CONNECTICUT			
State Agencies			
Department of Energy and Environmental Protection	53	44	9
Department of Motor Vehicles	47	47	0
State Capitol Police	35	26	9
Tribal Agencies			
Mashantucket Pequot Tribal	35	24	11
Mohegan Tribal	37	29	8
Other Agencies			
Metropolitan Transportation Authority	39	38	1
DELAWARE			
State Agencies			
Alcohol and Tobacco Enforcement	17	16	1
Animal Welfare, New Castle County	31	24	7
Attorney General			
Kent County	86	8	78
New Castle County	364	28	336
Sussex County	64	1	63
Environmental Control	16	15	1
Fish and Wildlife	29	23	6
Park Rangers	25	25	0
River and Bay Authority	58	48	10
State Capitol Police	80	65	15
State Fire Marshal	50	19	31
Other Agencies			
Wilmington Fire Department	13	9	4
DISTRICT OF COLUMBIA			
Other Agencies			
Metro Transit Police	568	389	179
FLORIDA			
State Agencies			
Capitol Police	78	65	13
Department of Corrections, Office of the Inspector General, Leon County	188	114	74
Department of Law Enforcement			
Duval County, Jacksonville	126	45	81
Escambia County, Pensacola	87	30	57
Hillsborough County, Tampa	162	57	105
Lee County, Fort Myers	82	35	47
Leon County, Tallahassee	911	115	796
Miami-Dade County, Miami	83	59	24
Orange County, Orlando	184	61	123
Division of Alcoholic Beverages and Tobacco, Leon County	140	83	57
Fish and Wildlife Conservation Commission			
Jefferson County	40	26	14
Leon County	996	818	178
Tribal Agencies			
Miccosukee Tribal	63	50	13
Seminole Tribal	219	156	63

Table 81. Full-Time Law Enforcement Employees, by Selected State and Agency, 2022—Continued

(Number.)

State/agency	Law enforcement employees	Officers	Civilians
Other Agencies			
Clay County School Board	46	45	1
Duval County Schools	157	108	49
Florida School for the Deaf and Blind	19	11	8
Fort Lauderdale Airport	106	85	21
Jacksonville Aviation Authority	32	32	0
Lee County Port Authority	68	47	21
Melbourne International Airport	15	13	2
Miami-Dade County Public Schools	521	473	48
Northwest Florida Beaches International Airport	22	15	7
Palm Beach County School District	304	245	59
Putnam County School District	2	1	1
Sarasota County Schools	61	59	2
Sarasota-Manatee Airport Authority	16	14	2
Tampa International Airport	138	77	61
Volusia County Beach Safety	78	61	17
GEORGIA			
State Agencies			
Georgia Bureau of Investigation, Headquarters	997	299	698
Georgia Department of Transportation, Office of Investigations	4	4	0
Georgia Forestry Commission	7	6	1
Georgia Public Safety Training Center	177	70	107
Georgia World Congress	28	19	9
Ports Authority, Savannah	180	138	42
Roosevelt Institute Facility Police	6	6	0
State Board of Workers Compensation Fraud Investigation Division	10	6	4
Other Agencies			
Atlanta Public Schools	95	94	1
Augusta Board of Education	31	26	5
Bibb County Board of Education	25	19	6
Cherokee County Board of Education	30	25	5
Cherokee County Marshal	21	12	9
Cobb County Board of Education	72	69	3
Decatur County Schools	8	8	0
DeKalb County School System	208	64	144
Dougherty County Board of Education	20	17	3
Fayette County Marshal	6	4	2
Forsyth County Fire Investigation Unit	3	3	0
Fulton County Marshal	72	56	16
Fulton County School System	72	71	1
Glynn County School System	27	26	1
Grady County Schools	7	7	0
Gwinnett County Public Schools	110	99	11
Hall County Marshal	15	14	1
Hartsfield-Jackson Atlanta International Airport	137	132	5
Metropolitan Atlanta Rapid Transit Authority	328	241	87
Muscogee County Schools	29	23	6
Paulding County Marshal	10	9	1
Richmond County Marshal	63	51	12
Stone Mountain Park	18	16	2
Turner County Schools	3	1	2
Twiggs County Board of Education	2	2	0
Washington County Board of Education	7	7	0
IDAHO			
State Agencies			
Attorney General	28	20	8
Idaho State Lottery Security Division	7	3	4
Tribal Agencies			
Fort Hall Tribal	30	15	15
Kootenai Tribal	2	2	0
Nez Perce Tribal	22	16	6
ILLINOIS			
State Agencies			
Illinois Department of Revenue	34	34	0
Illinois Liquor Control Commission	28	6	22
Secretary of State Police	292	152	140
Other Agencies			
Alton & Southern Railway	7	7	0
Belt Railway	7	7	0
Fox Valley Park District	3	2	1
McHenry County Conservation District	12	11	1
Naperville Park District	5	3	2
Peoria Park District	5	4	1
Rockford Park District	12	11	1
Terminal Railroad Association	5	5	0
Tri-County Drug Enforcement Narcotics Team	11	11	0
Will County Forest Preserve	14	13	1

Table 81. Full-Time Law Enforcement Employees, by Selected State and Agency, 2022—Continued

(Number.)

State/agency	Law enforcement employees	Officers	Civilians
INDIANA			
State Agencies			
Indiana State Excise Police	75	68	7
Other Agencies			
Linton-Stockton School Corporation	10	10	0
IOWA			
Other Agencies			
Eastern Iowa Airport Public Safety	13	13	0
Southeast Iowa Interagency Drug Task Force	49	39	10
KANSAS			
State Agencies			
Kansas Alcoholic Beverage Control	37	18	19
Kansas Department of Wildlife and Parks	168	166	2
Kansas Lottery Security Division	6	4	2
Kansas Racing Commission, Security Division	61	48	13
State Fire Marshal	13	11	2
Tribal Agencies			
Iowa Tribal	4	3	1
Kickapoo Tribal	5	5	0
Potawatomi Tribal	28	18	10
Sac and Fox Tribal	5	4	1
Other Agencies			
Blue Valley School District	11	11	0
El Dorado School District	2	2	0
Johnson County Park	25	24	1
Metropolitan Topeka Airport Authority	20	15	5
Unified School District			
Goddard	7	7	0
Kansas City	49	32	17
Nickerson/South Hutchinson	1	1	0
Seaman	4	4	0
Shawnee Heights	2	2	0
KENTUCKY			
State Agencies			
Alcohol Beverage Control			
Enforcement Division	38	36	2
Investigative Division	16	8	8
Department of Agriculture Animal Health Enforcement Division	4	4	0
Fish and Wildlife Enforcement	112	108	4
Kentucky Horse Park	8	8	0
Kentucky State Park Rangers Division	40	40	0
Other Agencies			
Barren County Drug Task Force	4	3	1
Bourbon County Schools	3	3	0
Cincinnati-Northern Kentucky International Airport	78	45	33
Clark County School System	10	10	0
Fayette County Schools	79	74	5
Jefferson County School District	32	15	17
Lake Cumberland Area Drug Enforcement Task Force	4	3	1
Louisville Regional Airport Authority	34	31	3
McCracken County Public Schools	8	8	0
Montgomery County School District	5	4	1
Northern Kentucky Drug Strike Force	4	3	1
Warren County Drug Task Force	3	2	1
LOUISIANA			
State Agencies			
Tensas Basin Levee District	3	2	1
Tribal Agencies			
Chitimacha Tribal	13	11	2
Coushatta Tribal	23	16	7
Tunica-Biloxi Tribal	14	13	1
MAINE			
State Agencies			
Bureau of Capitol Police	18	11	7
Drug Enforcement Agency	2	1	1
State Fire Marshal	38	17	21
Tribal Agencies			
Passamaquoddy Indian Township	13	6	7
Passamaquoddy Pleasant Point Tribal	6	6	0
Penobscot Nation	8	6	2

Table 81. Full-Time Law Enforcement Employees, by Selected State and Agency, 2022—Continued

(Number.)

State/agency	Law enforcement employees	Officers	Civilians
MARYLAND			
State Agencies			
Comptroller of the Treasury, Field Enforcement Division	35	13	22
Department of Public Safety and Correctional Services, Internal Investigation Division	130	83	47
General Services			
Annapolis, Anne Arundel County	191	79	112
Baltimore City	102	30	72
Natural Resources Police	329	261	68
State Fire Marshal	65	42	23
Transit Administration	198	147	51
Transportation Authority	516	424	92
Other Agencies			
Maryland-National Capital Park Police			
Montgomery County	112	90	22
Prince George's County	125	106	19
MASSACHUSETTS			
State Agencies			
Division of Law Enforcement, Environmental Police	129	94	35
Tribal Agencies			
Wampanoag Tribe of Gay Head	2	2	0
Other Agencies			
Massachusetts General Hospital	154	28	126
MICHIGAN			
State Agencies			
Department of Natural Resources, Law Enforcement Division	245	215	30
Tribal Agencies			
Bay Mills Tribal	9	8	1
Grand Traverse Tribal	16	11	5
Gun Lake Tribal	21	19	2
Hannahville Tribal	13	12	1
Keweenaw Bay Tribal	11	9	2
Little Traverse Bay Bands of Odawa Indians	11	8	3
Nottawaseppi Huron Band of Potawatomi	20	19	1
Pokagon Tribal	46	43	3
Other Agencies			
Bishop International Airport	14	13	1
Capitol Region Airport Authority	10	10	0
Genesee County Parks and Recreation	4	4	0
Gerald R. Ford International Airport	22	20	2
Wayne County Airport	115	90	25
MINNESOTA			
State Agencies			
Bureau of Criminal Apprehension	388	94	294
Capitol Security, St. Paul	81	19	62
Department of Natural Resources, Enforcement Division	230	199	31
Tribal Agencies			
Fond du Lac Tribal	22	20	2
Leech Lake Band of Ojibwe	47	25	22
Lower Sioux Tribal	4	3	1
Mille Lacs Tribal	26	21	5
Nett Lake Tribal	5	4	1
Red Lake Agency	49	34	15
Upper Sioux Community	4	4	0
White Earth Tribal	29	20	9
Other Agencies			
Metropolitan Transit Commission	135	109	26
Minneapolis-St. Paul International Airport	148	84	64
Three Rivers Park District	12	11	1
MISSISSIPPI			
State Agencies			
Reservoir Police Department	17	16	1
State Capitol Police	115	103	12
Tribal Agencies			
Choctaw Tribal	33	24	9
Other Agencies			
Forrest General Hospital	28	19	9
MISSOURI			
State Agencies			
Capitol Police	30	25	5
Department of Revenue, Compliance and Investigation Bureau	17	14	3

Table 81. Full-Time Law Enforcement Employees, by Selected State and Agency, 2022—Continued

(Number.)

State/agency	Law enforcement employees	Officers	Civilians
Department of Social Services, State Technical Assistance Team	24	16	8
Division of Alcohol and Tobacco Control	39	25	14
State Fire Marshal	20	19	1
State Park Rangers	48	47	1
Other Agencies			
Blue Spring Public Schools	21	19	2
Jackson County Drug Task Force	21	18	3
Jackson County Park Rangers	20	18	2
Kansas City International Airport	79	41	38
St. Charles Regional Drug Task Force	12	12	0
Terminal Railroad	5	5	0
Willard Public Schools	3	3	0
MONTANA			
State Agencies			
Gambling Investigations Bureau	34	14	20
Tribal Agencies			
Blackfeet Agency	27	14	13
Crow Agency	18	14	4
Fort Belknap Tribal	15	9	6
Fort Peck Assiniboine and Sioux Tribes	23	21	2
Northern Cheyenne Agency	10	8	2
Rocky Boy's Tribal	23	12	11
NEBRASKA			
State Agencies			
Nebraska State Fire Marshal	9	8	1
Tribal Agencies			
Omaha Tribal	24	6	18
Santee Tribal	5	5	0
Winnebago Tribal	6	3	3
NEVADA			
State Agencies			
Attorney General Investigations Division	341	46	295
Department of Wildlife, Law Enforcement Division	41	28	13
Nevada Gaming Control Board			
Clark County	80	59	21
Elko County	4	3	1
Carson City County	4	3	1
Washoe County	19	18	1
Secretary of State Securities Division Enforcement Section	7	6	1
State Fire Marshal	8	7	1
Tribal Agencies			
Eastern Nevada Agency	16	4	12
Fallon Tribal	7	6	1
Las Vegas Paiute Tribal	18	10	8
Lovelock Paiute Tribal	6	6	0
Moapa Tribal	16	11	5
Pyramid Lake Tribal	17	14	3
Reno-Sparks Indian Colony	14	12	2
Walker River Tribal	5	4	1
Washoe Tribal	15	9	6
Western Nevada Agency	5	4	1
Western Shoshone Tribal	3	3	0
Yerington Paiute Tribal	2	2	0
Other Agencies			
City of Las Vegas Department of Public Safety	390	102	288
Clark County Fire Department	8	8	0
Clark County School District	215	174	41
Las Vegas Fire and Rescue, Arson Bomb Unit	13	13	0
Reno Municipal Court Marshal	12	10	2
Reno Tahoe Airport Authority	23	22	1
NEW HAMPSHIRE			
State Agencies			
Liquor Commission	33	20	13
NEW JERSEY			
State Agencies			
Department of Corrections	6,819	5,177	1,642
Department of Human Services	77	63	14
Division of Fish and Wildlife	55	52	3
New Jersey Transit Police	337	298	39
Palisades Interstate Parkway	34	33	1
Port Authority of New York and New Jersey	1,917	1,736	181
State Park Police	81	80	1

Table 81. Full-Time Law Enforcement Employees, by Selected State and Agency, 2022—Continued

(Number.)

State/agency	Law enforcement employees	Officers	Civilians
Other Agencies			
Delaware River Port Authority Police Department	143	122	21
Park Police			
Morris County	22	21	1
Union County	100	67	33
Prosecutor			
Atlantic County	168	73	95
Bergen County	252	104	148
Burlington County	132	44	88
Camden County	271	185	86
Cape May County	90	41	49
Cumberland County	107	40	67
Essex County	249	123	126
Gloucester County	109	34	75
Hudson County	248	101	147
Hunterdon County	52	25	27
Mercer County	169	59	110
Middlesex County	213	72	141
Monmouth County	265	78	187
Morris County	157	65	92
Ocean County	176	66	110
Passaic County	171	75	96
Salem County	60	20	40
Somerset County	129	56	73
Sussex County	55	37	18
Union County	168	76	92
Warren County	60	19	41
NEW MEXICO			
Tribal Agencies			
Acoma Tribal	22	15	7
Isleta Tribal	53	31	22
Jemez Pueblo	12	10	2
Jicarilla Apache Tribal	31	18	13
Laguna Tribal	41	31	10
Mescalero Tribal	21	12	9
Northern Pueblos Agency	12	11	1
Ohkay Owingeh Tribal	9	8	1
Pojoaque Tribal	31	21	10
Ramah Navajo Tribal	9	7	2
Santa Ana Tribal	27	25	2
Santa Clara Pueblo	20	9	11
Southern Pueblos Agency	19	12	7
Taos Pueblo	8	7	1
Tesuque Pueblo	11	6	5
Zia Pueblo	6	5	1
Zuni Tribal	32	20	12
NEW YORK			
State Agencies			
State Park			
Allegany Region	12	10	2
Central Region	14	12	2
Finger Lakes Region	13	10	3
Genesee Region	15	14	1
Long Island Region	47	43	4
New York City Region	8	6	2
Niagara Region	29	27	2
Palisades Region	16	15	1
Saratoga/Capital Region	80	75	5
Statewide	101	94	7
Taconic Region	5	4	1
Thousand Island Region	11	10	1
Tribal Agencies			
Oneida Indian Nation	43	37	6
St. Regis Tribal	31	26	5
Other Agencies			
New York City Department of Environmental Protection Police, Ashokan Precinct	236	205	31
New York City Metropolitan Transportation Authority	1,151	1,095	56
Niagara Frontier Transportation Authority	85	81	4
Onondaga County Parks	1	1	0
NORTH CAROLINA			
State Agencies			
Cherry Hospital	15	14	1
Department of Health and Human Resources	7	7	0
Department of Wildlife	219	206	13
Division of Alcohol Law Enforcement	111	96	15
Division of Marine Fisheries	58	49	9
North Carolina Arboretum	4	4	0
North Carolina State Bureau of Investigation	404	247	157
State Capitol Police	99	66	33

Table 81. Full-Time Law Enforcement Employees, by Selected State and Agency, 2022—Continued

(Number.)

State/agency	Law enforcement employees	Officers	Civilians
State Fairgrounds	5	2	3
State Park Rangers			
Carolina Beach	4	4	0
Carvers Creek	6	3	3
Chimney Rock	8	4	4
Cliffs of the Neuse	4	4	0
Crowders Mountain	10	5	5
Dismal Swamp	5	3	2
Elk Knob	5	3	2
Eno River	9	5	4
Falls Lake Recreation Area	14	10	4
Fort Fisher	5	4	1
Fort Macon	6	5	1
Goose Creek	5	4	1
Gorges	4	4	0
Grandfather Mountain	2	1	1
Hammocks Beach	5	5	0
Hanging Rock	5	5	0
Haw River	9	9	0
Jockey's Ridge	5	5	0
Jones Lake	4	4	0
Jordan Lake State Recreation Area	15	10	5
Kerr Lake	22	8	14
Lake James	5	5	0
Lake Norman	8	5	3
Lake Waccamaw	6	3	3
Lumber River	7	3	4
Medoc Mountain	2	2	0
Merchants Millpond	3	2	1
Morrow Mountain	5	4	1
Mount Mitchell	8	2	6
New River-Mount Jefferson	6	6	0
Pettigrew	6	3	3
Pilot Mountain	6	6	0
Raven Rock	5	3	2
Singletary Lake	5	2	3
South Mountains	8	7	1
Stone Mountain	11	6	5
Weymouth Woods/Sandhills Nature Preserve	5	2	3
William B. Umstead	12	7	5
Tribal Agencies			
Cherokee Tribal	95	67	28
Other Agencies			
Asheville Regional Airport	22	18	4
Moore County Schools	12	12	0
Nash County Alcoholic Beverage Control Enforcement	1	1	0
North Carolina General Assembly	41	24	17
North Carolina Museum of Art Park Police	2	2	0
North Carolina State Port Authority, Division 1	7	6	1
Piedmont Triad International Airport	33	24	9
Raleigh-Durham International Airport	41	40	1
Triad Municipal Alcoholic Beverage Control Law Enforcement	6	5	1
University of North Carolina Hospitals	122	37	85
WakeMed Campus Police	87	41	46
NORTH DAKOTA			
State Agencies			
North Dakota Bureau of Criminal Investigation	57	57	0
Tribal Agencies			
Fort Totten Agency	14	7	7
Standing Rock Agency	32	13	19
Three Affiliated Tribes	39	26	13
Turtle Mountain Agency	43	22	21
OHIO			
Other Agencies			
Clark County Park District	1	1	0
Hamilton County Park District	35	33	2
Holden Arboretum	4	4	0
Lake Metroparks	14	13	1
Muskingum Watershed Conservancy District	16	16	0
Port Columbus International Airport	54	44	10
Preservation Parks of Delaware County	7	7	0
Toledo Metropolitan Park District	29	29	0
OKLAHOMA			
State Agencies			
Capitol Park Police	55	10	45
Grand River Dam Authority Lake Patrol	54	36	18
Oklahoma Department of Corrections	72	66	6

Table 81. Full-Time Law Enforcement Employees, by Selected State and Agency, 2022—Continued

(Number.)

State/agency	Law enforcement employees	Officers	Civilians
State Bureau of Investigation	345	97	248
State Park Rangers	40	40	0
Tribal Agencies			
Absentee Shawnee Tribal	14	12	2
Anadarko Agency	13	8	5
Cherokee Nation	80	64	16
Chickasaw Nation	119	95	24
Choctaw Nation	98	89	9
Citizen Potawatomi Nation	36	26	10
Comanche Nation	27	19	8
Concho Agency	8	8	0
Eastern Shawnee Tribal	18	17	1
Iowa Tribal	12	7	5
Kaw Tribal	8	7	1
Keetoowah Tribal	8	5	3
Kickapoo Tribal	15	14	1
Miami Agency	4	4	0
Miami Tribal	5	5	0
Muscogee Nation Tribal	92	78	14
Osage Nation	17	15	2
Otoe-Missouria Tribal	13	7	6
Pawnee Tribal	6	5	1
Ponca Tribal	3	3	0
Quapaw Tribal	28	27	1
Sac and Fox Tribal	11	11	0
Seminole Nation Lighthorse	12	10	2
Tonkawa Tribal	8	6	2
Wyandotte Nation	12	11	1
Other Agencies			
Beggs Public Schools	2	2	0
District 1 Narcotics Task Force	5	5	0
District 8 Narcotics Task Force	3	3	0
Jenks Public Schools	8	7	1
Lawton Public Schools	14	13	1
Muskogee City Schools	8	7	1
Okmulgee County Criminal Justice Authority	104	21	83
Putnam City Campus	16	12	4
Victory Life	1	1	0
OREGON			
State Agencies			
Liquor Commission			
Benton County	3	3	0
Coos County	2	1	1
Deschutes County	12	9	3
Douglas County	1	1	0
Jackson County	19	18	1
Klamath County	1	1	0
Lane County	13	12	1
Marion County	5	5	0
Multnomah County	25	25	0
Umatilla County	2	2	0
Tribal Agencies			
Burns Paiute Tribal	2	2	0
Columbia River Inter-Tribal Fisheries Enforcement	25	18	7
Coos, Lower Umpqua, and Siuslaw Tribal	5	4	1
Coquille Tribal	3	3	0
Cow Creek Tribal	6	5	1
Grand Ronde Tribal	14	13	1
Umatilla Tribal	20	13	7
Other Agencies			
Hillsboro School District	1	1	0
Port of Portland	66	47	19
PENNSYLVANIA			
State Agencies			
Pennsylvania Fish and Boat Commission	94	86	8
State Capitol Police	103	85	18
State Park Rangers			
Bald Eagle	6	6	0
Beltzville	4	4	0
Bendigo	1	1	0
Black Moshannon	2	2	0
Caledonia	1	1	0
Canoe Creek	1	1	0
Chapman	1	1	0
Clear Creek	5	5	0
Codorus	12	3	9
Cook Forest	5	5	0
Cowans Gap	2	2	0

Table 81. Full-Time Law Enforcement Employees, by Selected State and Agency, 2022—Continued

(Number.)

State/agency	Law enforcement employees	Officers	Civilians
Evansburg	2	2	0
Fort Washington	3	3	0
Frances Slocum	3	3	0
French Creek	6	6	0
Gifford Pinchot	4	3	1
Greenwood Furnace	4	2	2
Hickory Run	10	5	5
Hills Creek	3	3	0
Jacobsburg Environmental Education Center	1	1	0
Jennings Environmental Education Center	1	1	0
Kettle Creek	1	1	0
Kings Gap Environmental Education Center	1	1	0
Laurel Hill	6	6	0
Linn Run	1	1	0
Little Buffalo	4	4	0
Little Pine	1	1	0
Lyman Run	2	2	0
Maurice K. Goddard	2	1	1
Memorial Lake	3	3	0
Mount Pisgah	3	1	2
Neshaminy	6	2	4
Ohiopyle	5	5	0
Oil Creek	3	1	2
Parker Dam	2	2	0
Pine Grove Furnace	1	1	0
Point	3	3	0
Presque Isle	5	5	0
Prince Gallitzin	2	2	0
Promised Land	4	4	0
Pymatuning	11	6	5
Raccoon Creek	14	5	9
Raymond B. Winter	1	1	0
Reeds Gap	5	1	4
Ricketts Glen	4	4	0
Ridley Creek	4	4	0
Ryerson Station	8	1	7
Shikellamy	1	1	0
Sinnemahoning	7	2	5
Sizerville	1	1	0
Susquehannock	1	1	0
Tuscarora	2	2	0
White Clay	4	4	0
Worlds End	4	2	2
Yellow Creek	1	1	0
Other Agencies			
Adams County Drug Task Force	2	2	0
Allegheny County District Attorney, Investigation Division	31	25	6
Allegheny County Housing Authority	11	10	1
Allegheny County Port Authority	54	41	13
Cambria County District Attorney's Office	6	6	0
County Detective			
Adams County	3	3	0
Beaver County	10	8	2
Berks County	39	33	6
Bucks County	27	21	6
Butler County	4	4	0
Chester County	27	24	3
Dauphin County	10	9	1
Erie County	11	9	2
Indiana County	2	2	0
Lackawanna County	13	13	0
Lawrence County	11	10	1
Lebanon County	5	5	0
Luzerne County	17	16	1
McKean County	7	2	5
Montgomery County	53	39	14
Pike County	4	4	0
Schuylkill County	23	6	17
Wayne County	4	4	0
Westmoreland County	55	15	40
Wyoming County	4	4	0
York County	21	18	3
Cumberland County District Attorney	11	7	4
Delaware County District Attorney, Criminal Investigation Division	55	42	13
Delaware County Park	71	69	2
Fort Indiantown Gap	21	14	7
Harrisburg International Airport	15	11	4
Lancaster County Detectives Drug Task Force	28	26	2
Lehigh County District Attorney	38	37	1
Lehigh Valley International Airport	11	11	0
Westmoreland County Park	37	36	1
Wilkes-Barre Area School District	7	7	0

Table 81. Full-Time Law Enforcement Employees, by Selected State and Agency, 2022—Continued

(Number.)

State/agency	Law enforcement employees	Officers	Civilians
RHODE ISLAND			
State Agencies			
Department of Environmental Management	40	30	10
Tribal Agencies			
Narragansett Tribal	3	2	1
Other Agencies			
T.F. Green International Airport	34	26	8
SOUTH CAROLINA			
State Agencies			
Bureau of Protective Services	79	73	6
Department of Health and Environmental Control Drug Control, Richland County	40	32	8
Department of Mental Health	88	73	15
Department of Natural Resources			
Abbeville County	3	3	0
Aiken County	3	3	0
Allendale County	2	2	0
Anderson County	6	6	0
Bamberg County	3	3	0
Barnwell County	3	3	0
Beaufort County	9	9	0
Berkeley County	8	8	0
Calhoun County	3	3	0
Charleston County	37	32	5
Cherokee County	4	4	0
Chester County	4	4	0
Chesterfield County	4	4	0
Clarendon County	5	5	0
Colleton County	3	3	0
Darlington County	4	4	0
Dillon County	3	3	0
Dorchester County	4	4	0
Edgefield County	4	4	0
Fairfield County	4	4	0
Florence County	8	7	1
Georgetown County	7	7	0
Greenville County	6	5	1
Greenwood County	4	4	0
Hampton County	4	4	0
Horry County	11	11	0
Jasper County	3	3	0
Kershaw County	3	3	0
Lancaster County	3	3	0
Laurens County	4	4	0
Lee County	3	2	1
Lexington County	31	12	19
Marion County	4	4	0
Marlboro County	3	3	0
McCormick County	3	3	0
Newberry County	3	3	0
Oconee County	6	6	0
Orangeburg County	6	6	0
Pickens County	12	8	4
Richland County	67	53	14
Saluda County	4	4	0
Spartanburg County	4	3	1
Sumter County	4	4	0
Union County	3	3	0
Williamsburg County	6	6	0
York County	3	2	1
Forestry Commission			
Aiken County	2	2	0
Anderson County	1	1	0
Bamberg County	1	1	0
Cherokee County	1	1	0
Chesterfield County	3	3	0
Colleton County	2	2	0
Darlington County	1	1	0
Dorchester County	1	1	0
Fairfield County	1	1	0
Florence County	1	1	0
Greenville County	1	1	0
Hampton County	1	1	0
Horry County	1	1	0
Kershaw County	2	2	0
Laurens County	2	2	0
Lexington County	3	3	0
Marlboro County	1	1	0
Newberry County	1	1	0
Oconee County	1	1	0
Orangeburg County	4	4	0
Pickens County	1	1	0

Table 81. Full-Time Law Enforcement Employees, by Selected State and Agency, 2022—Continued

(Number.)

State/agency	Law enforcement employees	Officers	Civilians
Richland County	3	3	0
Spartanburg County	1	1	0
Sumter County	1	1	0
Williamsburg County	3	3	0
Santee Cooper	8	7	1
South Carolina School for the Deaf and Blind	1	1	0
State Museum	4	1	3
State Ports Authority	90	28	62
State Transport Police			
Abbeville County	1	1	0
Aiken County	2	2	0
Allendale County	1	1	0
Anderson County	4	4	0
Bamberg County	1	1	0
Barnwell County	1	1	0
Berkeley County	1	1	0
Chester County	1	1	0
Chesterfield County	1	1	0
Clarendon County	1	1	0
Colleton County	1	1	0
Darlington County	1	1	0
Dillon County	1	1	0
Dorchester County	7	7	0
Edgefield County	2	2	0
Florence County	7	6	1
Greenville County	4	4	0
Greenwood County	9	9	0
Hampton County	2	2	0
Horry County	2	2	0
Lexington County	16	13	3
Marion County	3	3	0
Marlboro County	1	1	0
Newberry County	2	2	0
Oconee County	2	2	0
Orangeburg County	2	1	1
Pickens County	3	3	0
Richland County	24	7	17
Saluda County	1	1	0
Spartanburg County	8	7	1
Union County	1	1	0
Williamsburg County	1	1	0
York County	11	11	0
United States Department of Energy, Savannah River Plant	56	45	11
Tribal Agencies			
Catawba Nation	2	2	0
Other Agencies			
Atlantic Railways	2	2	0
Charleston County Aviation Authority	66	37	29
Columbia Metropolitan Airport	18	18	0
Florence Regional Airport	8	8	0
Greenville Hospital, Greenville	31	31	0
Greenville-Spartanburg International Airport	20	19	1
Lexington County Medical Center	62	26	36
SOUTH DAKOTA			
State Agencies			
Division of Criminal Investigation	183	49	134
Tribal Agencies			
Cheyenne River Tribal	65	21	44
Crow Creek Tribal	10	6	4
Flandreau Santee Sioux Tribal	3	3	0
Lower Brule Tribal	21	9	12
Pine Ridge Sioux Tribal	76	50	26
Rosebud Tribal	42	36	6
Sisseton-Wahpeton Tribal	24	16	8
Yankton Tribal	25	5	20
TENNESSEE			
State Agencies			
Alcoholic Beverage Commission	58	48	10
Department of Agriculture, Agricultural Crime Unit	6	6	0
Department of Correction, Internal Affairs	39	25	14
TennCare Office of Inspector General	47	19	28
Tennessee Bureau of Investigation	625	411	214
Tennessee Department of Revenue, Special Investigations Unit	43	31	12
Wildlife Resources Agency			
Region 1	48	44	4
Region 2	91	61	30
Region 3	47	44	3
Region 4	53	50	3

Table 81. Full-Time Law Enforcement Employees, by Selected State and Agency, 2022—Continued

(Number.)

State/agency	Law enforcement employees	Officers	Civilians
Other Agencies			
7th Judicial District Crime Task Force	7	7	0
Chattanooga Housing Authority	5	4	1
Chattanooga Metropolitan Airport	13	8	5
Dickson City Park Ranger Division	2	2	0
Drug Task Force	3	3	0
2nd Judicial District	6	5	1
3rd Judicial District	4	4	0
4th Judicial District	1	1	0
9th Judicial District	6	6	0
10th Judicial District	1	1	0
12th Judicial District	4	3	1
14th Judicial District	2	2	0
15th Judicial District	13	2	11
18th Judicial District	3	2	1
19th Judicial District	8	7	1
21st Judicial District	1	1	0
22nd Judicial District	1	1	0
23rd Judicial District	7	7	0
24th Judicial District	2	1	1
25th Judicial District	1	1	0
31st Judicial District	2	2	0
Knoxville Metropolitan Airport	48	27	21
Memphis-Shelby County Airport Authority	59	46	13
Metropolitan Nashville Park Police	16	16	0
Nashville International Airport	111	86	25
Tri-Cities Regional Airport	15	14	1
West Tennessee Violent Crime Task Force	7	6	1
TEXAS			
Other Agencies			
Amarillo International Airport	12	12	0
Dallas-Fort Worth International Airport	218	199	19
Ector County Hospital District	18	12	6
Elm Ridge	20	18	2
Hidalgo County Constable, Precinct 1	19	17	2
Hospital District, Tarrant County	72	43	29
Houston Metropolitan Transit Authority	284	204	80
Independent School District			
Aldine	74	62	12
Alief	49	43	6
Alvin	50	40	10
Angleton	18	16	2
Anna	5	5	0
Aubrey	5	5	0
Austin	74	62	12
Barbers Hill	11	10	1
Bastrop	20	17	3
Bay City	9	8	1
Blooming Grove	2	2	0
Brazosport	22	21	1
Bridge City	3	3	0
Brownsboro	2	2	0
Brownsville	151	62	89
Burkburnett	5	5	0
Calhoun County	3	3	0
Castleberry	6	6	0
Centerpoint	2	2	0
Central	7	5	2
Coldspring-Oakhurst	8	8	0
Columbia-Brazoria	6	6	0
Conroe	118	82	36
Corsicana	17	12	5
Crowley	15	13	2
Dumas	2	2	0
Duncanville	28	4	24
Ector County	29	27	2
Edinburg	111	80	31
El Paso	44	36	8
Farmersville	6	6	0
Floresville	7	6	1
Fort Bend	92	69	23
Gonzales	2	2	0
Hallsville	11	8	3
Houston	235	194	41
Hudson	5	4	1
Humble	67	45	22
Huntington	5	5	0
Hutto	8	8	0
Idalou	1	1	0
Jonesboro	1	1	0
Judson	26	25	1
Katy	89	66	23
Killeen	28	27	1

Table 81. Full-Time Law Enforcement Employees, by Selected State and Agency, 2022—Continued

(Number.)

State/agency	Law enforcement employees	Officers	Civilians
Klein	72	50	22
Kopperl	1	1	0
Lamar Consolidated	31	30	1
Lancaster	12	9	3
Laredo	115	41	74
Liberty Hill	9	8	1
Lufkin	17	12	5
Lyford	6	6	0
Malakoff	3	3	0
Mansfield	63	54	9
Marlin	2	2	0
McAllen	74	62	12
Midland	24	19	5
Montgomery County	16	15	1
Northside	115	94	21
Pasadena	40	33	7
Pecos Barstow Toyah	11	9	2
Pflugerville	28	25	3
Pilot Point	3	3	0
Pleasanton	5	5	0
Point Isabel	7	4	3
Rio Grande City	80	20	60
Roma	12	11	1
Round Rock	29	24	5
Royal	5	4	1
San Antonio	67	59	8
Santa Fe	17	9	8
Santa Rosa	6	3	3
Sealy	5	5	0
Socorro	63	55	8
Spring	67	51	16
Spring Branch	61	48	13
Taft	2	2	0
Tatem	1	1	0
Terrell	6	6	0
Trinity	3	3	0
United	217	84	133
Van Vleck	1	1	0
Vensus	1	1	0
Warren	1	1	0
West Hardin	1	1	0
Wharton	6	3	3
Whitesboro	1	1	0
Wichita Falls	10	9	1
Independent School System, Nacogdoches	9	8	1
Kaufman County Constable, Precinct 2	25	24	1
Montgomery County Constable			
Precinct 1	59	54	5
Precinct 3	63	58	5
Montgomery County Constable's Office	50	47	3
Pewitt Consolidated Independent School District	2	2	0
Port of Brownsville	24	13	11
Port of Houston Authority	46	33	13
Sabine County Constable, Precinct 2	1	1	0
University Medical Center	14	10	4
UTAH			
State Agencies			
Department of Natural Resources, Outdoor Rec	11	8	3
Parks and Recreation	64	63	1
Utah Division of Forestry, Fire, and State Lands	2	2	0
Utah Tax Commission Motor Vehicle Division, Vehicle Investigation Section	33	17	16
Wildlife Resources	86	76	10
Tribal Agencies			
Uintah and Ouray Tribal	24	12	12
Other Agencies			
Cache-Rich Drug Task Force	5	5	0
Granite School District	30	22	8
Utah County Attorney, Investigations Division	9	7	2
Utah Transit Authority	82	76	6
VERMONT			
State Agencies			
Attorney General	6	6	0
Capitol Police	5	5	0
Department of Motor Vehicles	50	27	23
Fish and Wildlife Department, Law Enforcement Division	41	39	2
Secretary of State, Investigations Unit	5	5	0
VIRGINIA			
State Agencies			
Alcoholic Beverage Control Commission	263	83	180

Table 81. Full-Time Law Enforcement Employees, by Selected State and Agency, 2022—Continued

(Number.)

State/agency	Law enforcement employees	Officers	Civilians
Department of Conservation and Recreation	93	93	0
Department of Game and Inland Fisheries, Enforcement Division	165	147	18
Department of Motor Vehicles	82	71	11
Virginia Marine Resources Commission Law Enforcement Division	75	67	8
Virginia State Capitol	71	56	15
Other Agencies			
Norfolk Airport Authority	43	35	8
Port Authority, Norfolk	53	41	12
Reagan National Airport	274	218	56
Richmond International Airport	23	23	0
WASHINGTON			
State Agencies			
State Gambling Commission, Enforcement Unit	96	49	47
State Insurance Commissioner, Special Investigations Unit	11	9	2
Washington State Parks and Recreation Law Enforcement	193	84	109
Tribal Agencies			
Chehalis Tribal	33	15	18
Colville Tribal	34	24	10
Elwha Klallam Tribal	12	11	1
Jamestown S'Klallam Tribal	4	3	1
Kalispel Tribal	28	23	5
La Push Tribal	7	7	0
Lummi Tribal	24	21	3
Makah Tribal	19	10	9
Muckleshoot Tribal	16	14	2
Nisqually Tribal	24	20	4
Nooksack Tribal	7	7	0
Port Gamble S'Klallam Tribal	17	17	0
Puyallup Tribal	38	18	20
Quinault Indian Nation	16	7	9
Sauk-Suiattle Tribal	6	6	0
Shoalwater Bay Tribal	5	4	1
Skokomish Tribal	5	4	1
Snoqualmie Tribal	3	2	1
Spokane Agency	20	12	8
Squaxin Island Tribal	12	11	1
Stillaguamish Tribal	13	13	0
Suquamish Tribal	16	14	2
Swinomish Tribal	13	7	6
Tulalip Tribal	60	41	19
Upper Skagit Tribal	7	7	0
Yakama Nation	50	36	14
Other Agencies			
Port of Seattle	130	99	31
WEST VIRGINIA			
State Agencies			
Capitol Protective Services	47	26	21
Department of Natural Resources			
Barbour County	1	1	0
Berkeley County	2	2	0
Braxton County	2	2	0
Brooke County	1	1	0
Calhoun County	2	2	0
Clay County	1	1	0
Doddridge County	2	2	0
Fayette County	2	2	0
Gilmer County	1	1	0
Grant County	2	2	0
Greenbrier County	3	3	0
Hampshire County	5	4	1
Hancock County	1	1	0
Hardy County	2	2	0
Harrison County	1	1	0
Jackson County	2	2	0
Jefferson County	1	1	0
Kanawha County	19	13	6
Lewis County	1	1	0
Lincoln County	2	2	0
Logan County	1	1	0
Marion County	7	6	1
Marshall County	1	1	0
Mason County	1	1	0
McDowell County	1	1	0
Mercer County	2	2	0
Mineral County	1	1	0
Mingo County	1	1	0
Monongalia County	2	2	0
Monroe County	2	2	0
Morgan County	1	1	0

Table 81. Full-Time Law Enforcement Employees, by Selected State and Agency, 2022—Continued

(Number.)

State/agency	Law enforcement employees	Officers	Civilians
Nicholas County	1	1	0
Ohio County	1	1	0
Pendleton County	1	1	0
Pleasants County	1	1	0
Pocahontas County	1	1	0
Preston County	3	3	0
Putnam County	3	3	0
Raleigh County	6	5	1
Randolph County	2	2	0
Ritchie County	1	1	0
Roane County	2	2	0
Summers County	3	3	0
Taylor County	1	1	0
Tucker County	2	2	0
Tyler County	1	1	0
Upshur County	4	3	1
Wayne County	2	2	0
Webster County	2	2	0
Wetzel County	1	1	0
Wirt County	1	1	0
Wood County	6	5	1
Wyoming County	1	1	0
State Fire Marshal, Kanawha County	47	31	16
Other Agencies			
Central West Virginia Drug Task Force	2	1	1
Greenbrier County Drug and Violent Crime Task Force	4	3	1
Harrison County Drug and Violent Crime Task Force	7	7	0
Huntington Drug and Violent Crime Task Force	4	3	1
Kanawha County Parks and Recreation	3	3	0
Logan County Drug and Violent Crime Task Force	7	6	1
Metropolitan Drug Enforcement Network Team	3	3	0
Mon Metro Drug Task Force	4	3	1
Potomac Highlands Drug and Violent Crime Task Force	4	4	0
Three Rivers Drug and Violent Crime Task Force	2	2	0
WISCONSIN			
State Agencies			
Capitol Police	50	38	12
Department of Natural Resources	238	206	32
Division of Criminal Investigation, Madison	143	88	55
State Fair Park Police	5	4	1
Tribal Agencies			
Lac Courte Oreilles Tribal	14	12	2
Lac du Flambeau Tribal	13	11	2
Menominee Tribal	25	18	7
Oneida Tribal	26	19	7
Red Cliff Tribal	9	6	3
St. Croix Tribal	13	9	4
Stockbridge Munsee Tribal	5	5	0
WYOMING			
State Agencies			
Wyoming Division of Criminal Investigation	86	37	49
Tribal Agencies			
Wind River Agency	22	17	5
PUERTO RICO			
Puerto Rico	12,495	11,797	698

SECTION VI

HATE CRIMES

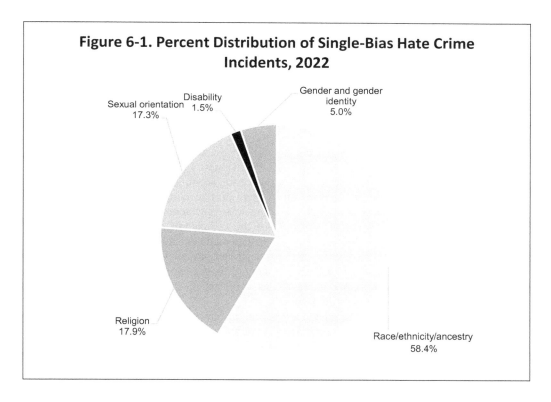

Figure 6-1. Percent Distribution of Single-Bias Hate Crime Incidents, 2022

Sexual orientation 17.3%

Disability 1.5%

Gender and gender identity 5.0%

Religion 17.9%

Race/ethnicity/ancestry 58.4%

The Federal Bureau of Investigation (FBI) began the procedures for implementing, collecting, and managing hate crime data after Congress passed the Hate Crime Statistics Act in 1990. This act required the collection of data "about crimes that manifest evidence of prejudice based on race, religion, sexual orientation, or ethnicity." Beginning in 2013, law enforcement agencies could submit hate crime data in accordance with a number of program modifications. In 1994, the Hate Crime Statistics Act was amended to include bias against persons with disabilities. The Church Arson Prevention Act, which was signed into law in July 1996, removed the sunset clause from the original statute and mandated that the collection of hate crime data become a permanent part of the UCR program. In 2009, Congress further amended the Hate Crime Statistics Act by passing the Matthew Shepard and James Byrd, Jr., Hate Crime Prevention Act. The amendment includes the collection of data for crimes motivated by bias against a particular gender and gender identity, as well as for crimes committed by, and crimes directed against, juveniles. In response to the Shepard/Byrd Act, the FBI modified its data collection so that reporting agencies could indicate whether hate crimes were committed by, or directed against, juveniles.

Definitions

Hate crimes include any crime motivated by bias against race, religion, sexual orientation, ethnicity/national origin, and/or disability. Because motivation is subjective, it is sometimes difficult to know with certainty whether a crime resulted from

the offender's bias. Moreover, the presence of bias alone does not necessarily mean that a crime can be considered a hate crime. Only when law enforcement investigation reveals sufficient evidence to lead a reasonable and prudent person to conclude that the offender's actions were motivated, in whole or in part, by his or her bias should an incident be reported as a hate crime.

Data Collection

The UCR (Uniform Crime Reporting) program collects data about both single-bias and multiple-bias hate crimes. A single-bias incident is defined as an incident in which one or more offense types are motivated by the same bias. A multiple-bias incident is defined as an incident in which more than one offense type occurs and at least two offense types are motivated by different biases.

A table enumerating selected places in the United States that did not report hate crimes in 2022 is available on the FBI's Crime Data Explorer at https://cde.ucr.cjis.gov/LATEST/webapp/#/pages/downloads#datasets.

CRIMES AGAINST PERSONS, PROPERTY, OR SOCIETY

The UCR program's data collection guidelines stipulate that a hate crime may involve multiple offenses, victims, and offenders within one incident; therefore, the Hate Crime

Statistics program is incident-based. According to UCR counting guidelines:

- One offense is counted for each victim in *crimes against persons*

- One offense is counted for each offense type in *crimes against property*

- One offense is counted for each offense type in *crimes against society*

VICTIMS

In the UCR program, the victim of a hate crime may be an individual, a business, an institution, or society as a whole.

OFFENDERS

According to the UCR program, the term *known offender* does not imply that the suspect's identity is known; rather, the term indicates that some aspect of the suspect was identified, thus distinguishing the suspect from an unknown offender. Law enforcement agencies specify the number of offenders, and when possible, the race of the offender or offenders as a group.

RACE/ETHNICITY

The UCR program uses the following racial designations in its Hate Crime Statistics program: White; Black; American Indian or Alaskan Native; Asian; Native Hawaiian or Other Pacific Islander; and Multiple Races, Group. In addition, the UCR program uses the ethnic designations of Hispanic or Latino and Not Hispanic or Latino.

The law enforcement agencies that voluntarily participate in the Hate Crime Statistics program collect details about an offender's bias motivation associated with 11 offense types already being reported to the UCR program: murder and nonnegligent manslaughter, rape, aggravated assault, simple assault, and intimidation (crimes against persons); and robbery, burglary, larceny-theft, motor vehicle theft, arson, and destruction/damage/vandalism (crimes against property). The law enforcement agencies that participate in the UCR program via the National Incident-Based Reporting System (NIBRS) collect data about additional offenses for *crimes against persons* and *crimes against property*. These data appear in the category of other. These agencies also collect hate crime data for the category called *crimes against society*, which includes drug or narcotic offenses, gambling offenses, prostitution offenses, and weapon law violations.

National Volume and Percent Distribution

In 2022, hate crime statistics were collected from 14,660 (of 18,888) law enforcement agencies. These law enforcement agencies reported 11,634 hate crime incidents involving 13,337 offenses. Of these, 11,288 were single-bias incidents. An analysis of the single-bias incidents revealed that approximately 58.4 percent were racially/ethnically/ancestrally motivated, 17.9 percent resulted from sexual orientation bias, 17.3 percent were motivated by religious bias, 5.0 percent were motivated by gender and gender-identity bias, and 1.5 percent were prompted by a disability bias. (Table 82)

The largest proportion of the 6,567 single-bias hate crime incidents that were racially motivated resulted from an anti-Black or African American bias (52.1 percent), followed by an anti-White basis (14.7 percent). Bias against people of more than one race accounted for 3.5 percent of incidents, while anti-Asian bias accounted for an increased 7.6 percent of racially motivated incidents. Anti-Arab bias accounted for 1.4 percent of these incidents, anti–Native Hawaiian and Other Pacific Islander accounted for 0.4 percent of these incidents, and anti–American Indian or Alaska Native bias accounted for 3.0 percent of these incidents. Approximately 11.2 percent of crimes were classified as an anti–Hispanic or Latino bias. (Table 82)

Hate crimes motivated by religious bias accounted for 2,042 incidents reported by law enforcement. A breakdown of these incidents revealed that more than half (54.9 percent) were motivated by anti-Jewish bias. Approximately 8.9 percent were anti-Sikh, 7.7 percent by anti-Islamic (Muslim) bias, 3.8 percent were anti—Eastern Orthodox (Russian, Greek, or other), 5.2 percent were anti-Catholic, 3.1 percent were anti-Protestant, 4.5 percent were anti—other Christian, 2.1 percent were anti–multiple religions or groups, 1.0 percent were anti-Buddhist, 0.7 percent were anti-atheism/agnosticism/etc., 1.5 percent were anti–Church of Jesus Christ (renamed in 2022 from anti-Mormon), 1.2 percent were anti-Hindu, 0.7 percent were anti—Jehovah's Witness, and the remainder, 4.8 percent, of offenses were based on a bias against other religions—those not specified. (Table 82)

In 2022, 1,944 incidents were committed on the basis of sexual orientation bias. Of the offenses based on sexual orientation, 32.0 percent were classified as having an anti–lesbian, gay, bisexual, or transgender (mixed group) bias; 55.3 percent were classified as having an anti–gay (male) bias; 9.8 percent had an anti–lesbian basis; 1.8 percent had an anti-bisexual bias; and 1.1 percent had an anti-heterosexual bias. (Table 82)

Hate crime incidents committed based on disability totaled 172 incidents in 2022. The majority (56.7 percent) were classified as anti-mental disability, with the rest (43.3 percent) classified as anti–physical disability. (Table 82)

Of the 469 gender identity bias incidents reported, 338 (72.1 percent) were anti-transgender and 131 (27.9 percent) were anti–gender nonconforming. Of the 95 gender bias offenses reported, 77 (81.1 percent) were anti-female and 18 (18.9 percent) were anti-male. (Table 82)

Crimes Against Persons

Law enforcement agencies reported 7,572 hate crime incidents against persons in 2022. Approximately 45.6 percent involved intimidation, 35.8 percent involved simple assault, and 17.4 percent involved aggravated assault. There were 15 murders, 21 rapes, and 2 incidents of human trafficking. (Table 83)

Crimes Against Property

In 2022, hate crime incidents against property totaled 4,243. Approximately 72.8 percent of offenses involved destruction, damage, or vandalism. The remaining 27.2 percent of crimes against property consisted of robbery, burglary, larceny-theft, motor vehicle theft, arson, and other crimes. (Table 83)

Offenders and Bias Motivation

Of the 13,337 total offenses committed in 2022, White (40.6 percent) and Black or African American (15.8 percent) represented the highest proportions of offenders, accounting for over 55 percent of this group. Persons of Hispanic or Latino ethnicity committed approximately 6.6 percent of offenses. Of the 33 single-bias incident murders committed, 13 were motivated by anti–Black or African American bias; 9 by

anti–lesbian, gay, bisexual, or transgender (mixed group) bias; 4 by anti-Islamic (Muslim) bias; 2 by anti-transgender bias; and 1 each by anti-White, anti–Hispanic or Latino, anti–other race/ethnicity/ancestry bias, anti-female bias, and anti–gender non-conforming bias. One murders encompassed multiple biases. The greatest proportions of destruction/damage/vandalism had an anti–Black or African American bias (29.9 percent) or an anti-Jewish bias (23.7 percent). More than four out of five known offenders were adults (18 years old or over). (Tables 84, 85, and 90)

Victims

Of the 13,337 reported offenses in 2021, the vast majority of victims were individuals (81.3 percent). Businesses and financial institutions represented 5.9 percent of the total, society/public represented 2.1 percent of the total, government represented 4.0 percent of the total, religious organizations represented 2.2 percent of the total, and other/unknown/multiple comprised the remaining 4.5 percent. The greatest number of adult and juvenile victims were the same for the race/ethnicity/ancestry (anti-Black or anti–African American), sexual orientation (anti-gay [male]), and religion (anti-Jewish) categories. (Tables 87 and 88) Over 40 percent of all incidents occurred either in a residence/home (26.8 percent) or on a highway, road, alley, street, or sidewalk (15.7 percent). (Table 91)

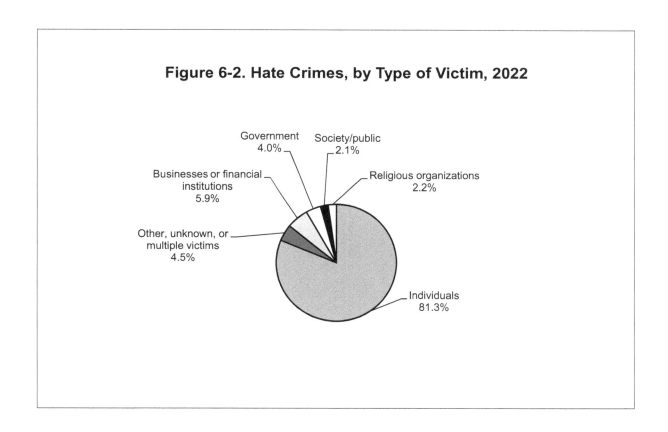

Figure 6-2. Hate Crimes, by Type of Victim, 2022

Table 82. Incidents, Offenses, Victims, and Known Offenders, by Bias Motivation, 2022

(Number.)

Bias motivation	Incidents	Offenses	Victims[1]	Known offenders[2]
Total	11,634	13,337	13,711	10,299
Single-Bias Incidents	11,288	12,913	13,278	10,046
Race/Ethnicity/Ancestry:	6,567	7,677	7,852	5,980
Anti-White	966	1,102	1,126	892
Anti–Black or African American	3,421	4,000	4,075	3,017
Anti–American Indian or Alaska Native	194	209	217	196
Anti-Asian	499	579	602	466
Anti–Native Hawaiian or Other Pacific Islander	26	29	30	23
Anti–multiple races, group	232	271	287	175
Anti-Arab	92	105	105	82
Anti–Hispanic or Latino	738	937	958	778
Anti–other race/ethnicity/ancestry	399	445	452	351
Religion:	2,042	2,199	2,293	1,527
Anti-Jewish	1,122	1,194	1,217	769
Anti-Catholic	107	110	113	77
Anti-Protestant	63	68	71	59
Anti-Islamic (Muslim)	158	179	200	136
Anti–other religion	91	100	103	85
Anti–multiple religions,group	42	48	62	28
Anti–Church of Jesus Christ[3]	30	34	37	15
Anti–Jehovah's Witness	14	14	14	9
Anti–Eastern Orthodox (Russian, Greek, other)	78	83	91	73
Anti–other Christian	97	111	117	69
Anti-Buddhist	20	21	23	16
Anti-Hindu	25	29	29	27
Anti-Sikh	181	192	198	150
Anti–atheism/agnosticism/etc.	14	16	18	14
Sexual Orientation:	1,944	2,210	2,289	1,842
Anti-gay (male)	1,075	1,194	1,217	1,115
Anti-lesbian	190	211	216	162
Anti–lesbian, gay, bisexual, or transgender (mixed group)	622	745	796	509
Anti-heterosexual	22	23	23	23
Anti-bisexual	35	37	37	33
Disability:	171	191	194	179
Anti-physical	74	83	83	72
Anti-mental	97	108	111	107
Gender:	95	121	123	81
Anti-male	18	22	22	13
Anti-female	77	99	101	68
Gender Identity:	469	515	527	437
Anti-transgender	338	374	382	335
Anti–gender non-conforming	131	141	145	102
Multiple-Bias Incidents[4]	346	424	433	253

1 The term *victim* may refer to an individual, business/financial institution, government entity, religious organization, or society/public as a whole.   2 The term *known offender* does not imply the suspect's identity is known; rather, the term indicates some aspect of the suspect was identified, thus distinguishing the suspect from an unknown offender.   3 The anti-Mormon religious bias has been renamed anti–Church of Jesus Christ.   4 A multiple-bias incident is an incident in which one or more offense types are motivated by two or more biases.

Table 83. Incidents, Offenses, Victims, and Known Offenders, by Offense Type, 2022

(Number.)

Offense type	Incidents[1]	Offenses	Victims[2]	Known offenders[3]
Total	11,634	13,337	13,711	10,299
Crimes Against Persons	7,572	8,810	8,810	7,753
Murder and nonnegligent manslaughter	15	33	33	19
Rape	21	21	21	28
Aggravated assault	1,321	1,561	1,561	1,525
Simple assault	2,707	3,111	3,111	3,104
Intimidation	3,450	4,023	4,023	2,997
Human trafficking	2	2	2	1
Other[4]	56	59	59	79
Crimes Against Property	4,243	4,245	4,619	2,723
Robbery	169	169	190	284
Burglary	169	169	195	130
Larceny-theft	561	562	605	337
Motor vehicle theft	62	62	65	42
Arson	51	51	72	47
Destruction/damage/vandalism	3,088	3,088	3,326	1,772
Other[4]	143	144	166	111
Crimes Against Society[4]	270	282	282	312

1 The actual number of incidents is 11,634. However, the column figures will not add to the total because incidents may include more than one offense type, and these are counted in each appropriate offense type category.   2 The term victim may refer to an individual, business/financial institution, government entity, religious organization, or society/public as a whole.   3 The term known offender does not imply the suspect's identity is known; rather, the term indicates some aspect of the suspect was identified, thus distinguishing the suspect from an unknown offender. The actual number of known offenders is 10,299. However, the column figures will not add to the total because some offenders are responsible for more than one offense type, and are, therefore, counted more than once in this table.   4 The figures shown include additional offenses collected in the National Incident-Based Reporting System.

Table 84. Offenses, Known Offender's Race and Ethnicity, by Offense Type, 2022

(Number.)

Bias motivation	Total offenses	Known offender's race							Known offender's ethnicity[1]				Unknown offender
		White	Black or African American	American Indian or Alaska Native	Asian	Native Hawaiian or Other Pacific Islander	Group of multiple races	Unknown race	Hispanic or Latino	Not Hispanic or Latino	Group of multiple ethnicities	Unknown ethnicity	
Total	13,337	5,420	2,102	93	164	24	450	1,662	882	3,902	335	2,255	3,422
Crimes Against Persons	8,810	4,362	1,686	76	135	22	369	858	708	3,180	256	1,683	1,302
Murder and nonnegligent manslaughter	33	22	4	0	0	0	0	7	2	13	0	16	0
Rape	21	9	6	0	0	0	2	4	3	8	1	2	0
Aggravated assault	1,561	772	387	20	19	2	72	153	201	565	46	315	136
Simple assault	3,111	1,527	768	32	44	7	202	273	288	1,205	139	455	258
Intimidation	4,023	2,003	501	24	70	13	91	416	211	1,363	69	879	905
Human trafficking	2	0	0	0	1	0	0	0	0	1	0	0	1
Other[2]	59	29	20	0	1	0	2	5	3	25	1	16	2
Crimes Against Property	4,245	897	333	14	28	2	73	790	153	608	70	520	2,108
Robbery	169	43	71	3	3	0	13	15	21	63	8	35	21
Burglary	169	43	19	0	0	0	0	32	6	23	5	31	75
Larceny-theft	562	128	54	4	1	0	6	78	20	92	15	61	291
Motor vehicle theft	62	13	10	0	1	0	0	14	2	12	1	12	24
Arson	51	19	6	0	2	0	3	6	3	18	1	8	15
Destruction/damage/ vandalism	3,088	609	147	6	21	1	50	619	94	361	35	349	1,635
Other[2]	144	42	26	1	0	1	1	26	7	39	5	24	47
Crimes Against Society[2]	282	161	83	3	1	0	8	14	21	114	9	52	12

1 The sum of offenses by the known offender's ethnicity does not equal the sum of offenses by the known offender's race because not all law enforcement agencies that report offender race data also report offender ethnicity data.   2 The figures shown include additional offenses collected in the National Incident-Based Reporting System.

Table 85. Offenses, Offense Type, by Bias Motivation, 2022

(Number.)

Bias motivation	Total offenses	Crimes against persons						
		Murder and nonnegligent manslaughter	Rape	Aggravated assault	Simple assault	Intimidation	Human trafficking	Other[1]
Total	13,337	33	21	1,561	3,111	4,023	2	59
Single-Bias Incidents	12,913	33	20	1,525	3,042	3,846	2	58
Race/Ethnicity/Ancestry:	7,677	16	10	1,019	1,924	2,514	1	23
Anti-White	1,102	1	3	155	323	259	0	6
Anti–Black or African American	4,000	13	4	501	875	1,482	0	7
Anti–American Indian or Alaska Native	209	0	0	21	31	20	0	2
Anti-Asian	579	0	0	79	190	191	1	1
Anti–Native Hawaiian or Other Pacific Islander	29	0	0	5	5	5	0	0
Anti–multiple races, group	271	0	1	13	44	75	0	1
Anti-Arab	105	0	0	15	29	47	0	0
Anti–Hispanic or Latino	937	1	2	190	306	297	0	4
Anti–other race/ethnicity/ancestry	445	1	0	40	121	138	0	2
Religion:	2,199	4	2	103	223	497	0	8
Anti-Jewish	1,194	0	0	36	103	322	0	5
Anti-Catholic	110	0	0	2	6	7	0	0
Anti-Protestant	68	0	0	3	6	8	0	0
Anti-Islamic (Muslim)	179	4	0	19	41	76	0	0
Anti–other religion	100	0	0	12	10	22	0	1
Anti–multiple religions, group	48	0	1	2	1	4	0	0
Anti–Church of Jesus Christ[2]	34	0	0	0	2	2	0	0
Anti–Jehovah's Witness	14	0	0	1	3	3	0	1
Anti–Eastern Orthodox (Russian, Greek, other)	83	0	0	2	10	17	0	0
Anti–other Christian	111	0	0	2	8	18	0	0
Anti-Buddhist	21	0	0	0	1	0	0	0
Anti-Hindu	29	0	0	3	6	10	0	0
Anti-Sikh	192	0	1	19	24	6	0	1
Anti–atheism/agnosticism/etc.	16	0	0	2	2	2	0	0
Sexual Orientation:	2,210	9	4	288	646	644	0	19
Anti-gay (male)	1,194	0	1	168	421	344	0	10
Anti-lesbian	211	0	2	23	57	84	0	1
Anti–lesbian, gay, bisexual, or transgender (mixed group)	745	9	0	86	152	203	0	5
Anti-heterosexual	23	0	1	4	5	4	0	1
Anti-bisexual	37	0	0	7	11	9	0	2
Disability:	191	0	0	24	62	30	0	1
Anti-physical	83	0	0	5	30	12	0	0
Anti-mental	108	0	0	19	32	18	0	1
Gender:	121	1	1	19	27	41	0	1
Anti-male	22	0	0	2	7	2	0	0
Anti-female	99	1	1	17	20	39	0	1
Gender Identity:	515	3	3	72	160	120	1	6
Anti-transgender	374	2	2	60	123	95	1	6
Anti–gender non-conforming	141	1	1	12	37	25	0	0
Multiple-Bias Incidents[3]	424	0	1	36	69	177	0	1

1 The figures shown include additional offenses collected in the National Incident-Based Reporting System.
2 The anti-Mormon religious bias has been renamed anti–Church of Jesus Christ.
3 A *multiple-bias incident* is an incident in which one or more offense types are motivated by two or more biases.

Table 85. Offenses, Offense Type, by Bias Motivation, 2022—Continued

(Number.)

Bias motivation	Crimes against property							Crimes against society[1]
	Robbery	Burglary	Larceny- theft	Motor vehicle theft	Arson	Destruction/ damage/ vandalism	Other[1]	
Total	169	169	562	62	51	3,088	144	282
Single-Bias Incidents	168	164	555	62	48	2,965	144	281
Race/Ethnicity/Ancestry:	112	84	249	44	16	1,421	76	168
Anti-White	31	20	97	16	2	119	28	42
Anti–Black or African American	29	30	67	14	7	888	15	68
Anti–American Indian or Alaska Native	1	6	43	9	1	29	15	31
Anti-Asian	19	8	12	0	1	72	0	5
Anti–Native Hawaiian or Other Pacific Islander	0	4	2	0	0	1	3	4
Anti–multiple races, group	2	3	4	1	0	121	3	3
Anti-Arab	1	1	2	0	0	7	1	2
Anti–Hispanic or Latino	23	9	9	2	5	77	5	7
Anti–other race/ethnicity/ancestry	6	3	13	2	0	107	6	6
Religion:	10	47	125	15	22	1,037	41	65
Anti-Jewish	2	5	13	0	2	704	0	2
Anti-Catholic	0	2	7	1	6	75	3	1
Anti-Protestant	0	2	14	1	2	23	1	8
Anti-Islamic (Muslim)	1	7	1	0	2	26	1	1
Anti–other religion	1	3	8	0	0	36	3	4
Anti–multiple religions,group	0	2	5	1	2	26	0	4
Anti–Church of Jesus Christ[2]	0	6	2	0	2	19	1	0
Anti–Jehovah's Witness	0	0	1	0	0	4	1	0
Anti–Eastern Orthodox (Russian, Greek, other)	0	4	10	4	0	15	6	15
Anti–other Christian	1	5	7	0	5	61	2	2
Anti-Buddhist	1	3	3	0	0	8	2	3
Anti-Hindu	0	0	0	0	0	8	0	2
Anti-Sikh	4	8	48	8	0	32	19	22
Anti–atheism/agnosticism/etc.	0	0	6	0	1	0	2	1
Sexual Orientation:	33	15	106	1	8	411	8	18
Anti-gay (male)	30	7	25	1	2	174	5	6
Anti-lesbian	1	2	6	0	0	31	0	4
Anti–lesbian, gay, bisexual, or transgender (mixed group)	2	5	70	0	6	199	3	5
Anti-heterosexual	0	1	1	0	0	3	0	3
Anti-bisexual	0	0	4	0	0	4	0	0
Disability:	1	8	23	0	1	21	11	9
Anti-physical	1	3	10	0	0	11	6	5
Anti-mental	0	5	13	0	1	10	5	4
Gender:	0	2	8	0	1	13	2	5
Anti-male	0	1	3	0	0	4	1	2
Anti-female	0	1	5	0	1	9	1	3
Gender Identity:	12	8	44	2	0	62	6	16
Anti-transgender	11	5	24	2	0	37	1	5
Anti–gender non-conforming	1	3	20	0	0	25	5	11
Multiple-Bias Incidents[3]	1	5	7	0	3	123	0	1

1 The figures shown include additional offenses collected in the National Incident-Based Reporting System.   2 The anti-Mormon religious bias has been renamed anti–Church of Jesus Christ.   3 A *multiple-bias incident* is an incident in which one or more offense types are motivated by two or more biases.

Table 86. Offenses, Known Offender's Race and Ethnicity, by Bias Motivation, 2022

(Number.)

Bias motivation	Total offenses	White	Black or African American	American Indian or Alaska Native	Asian	Native Hawaiian or Other Pacific Islander	Group of multiple races	Unknown race	Hispanic or Latino	Not Hispanic or Latino	Group of multiple ethnicities	Unknown ethnicity	Unknown offender
					Known offender's race					Known offender's ethnicity[1]			
Total	13,337	5,420	2,102	93	164	24	450	1,662	882	3,902	335	2,255	3,422
Single-Bias Incidents	12,913	5,282	2,061	90	160	24	423	1,617	862	3,802	325	2,150	3,256
Race/Ethnicity/Ancestry:	7,677	3,525	1,192	66	92	19	274	742	523	2,463	198	1,319	1,767
Anti-White	1,102	232	487	19	11	5	23	71	56	425	28	152	254
Anti–Black or African American	4,000	2,118	248	20	40	3	185	415	285	1,187	104	693	971
Anti–American Indian or Alaska Native	209	83	26	13	2	0	3	22	15	64	10	32	60
Anti-Asian	579	222	134	4	13	3	16	72	39	167	7	109	115
Anti–Native Hawaiian or Other Pacific Islander	29	10	5	0	0	1	0	3	3	6	3	2	10
Anti–multiple races, group	271	110	30	0	1	1	9	20	14	64	8	49	100
Anti-Arab	105	55	20	0	1	0	1	10	7	22	3	32	18
Anti–Hispanic or Latino	937	525	183	4	11	6	23	63	67	413	24	183	122
Anti–other race/ethnicity/ancestry	445	170	59	6	13	0	14	66	37	115	11	67	117
Religion:	2,199	601	235	6	41	2	39	525	80	425	42	311	750
Anti-Jewish	1,194	255	78	1	24	0	13	370	24	161	9	146	453
Anti-Catholic	110	37	6	0	1	0	3	16	5	11	3	19	47
Anti-Protestant	68	15	10	0	0	0	7	15	11	18	1	6	21
Anti-Islamic (Muslim)	179	68	32	1	5	1	6	29	7	50	7	35	37
Anti–other religion	100	40	12	0	3	0	1	19	11	15	1	25	25
Anti–multiple religions, group	48	15	7	0	0	0	1	7	0	9	4	9	18
Anti–Church of Jesus Christ[2]	34	7	5	0	0	1	0	4	2	10	0	5	17
Anti–Jehovah's Witness	14	7	0	0	1	0	0	1	0	4	0	2	5
Anti–Eastern Orthodox (Russian, Greek, other)	83	38	21	0	1	0	0	8	2	33	3	7	15
Anti–other Christian	111	30	14	1	2	0	2	20	4	30	3	15	42
Anti-Buddhist	21	5	1	1	0	0	0	6	1	4	0	6	8
Anti-Hindu	29	13	3	0	2	0	2	3	1	7	0	6	6
Anti-Sikh	192	62	46	2	2	0	3	25	10	67	10	28	52
Anti-atheism/agnosticism/etc.	16	9	0	0	0	0	1	2	2	6	1	2	4
Sexual Orientation:	2,210	820	455	13	18	2	80	263	195	653	59	382	559
Anti-gay (male)	1,194	463	300	4	12	2	52	137	113	394	30	211	224
Anti-lesbian	211	87	33	1	3	0	5	22	24	49	3	41	60
Anti–lesbian, gay, bisexual, or transgender (mixed group)	745	243	112	8	2	0	21	99	53	194	24	121	260
Anti-heterosexual	23	9	3	0	1	0	2	2	3	7	2	0	6
Anti-bisexual	37	18	7	0	0	0	0	3	2	9	0	9	9
Disability:	191	84	29	0	2	0	12	26	7	56	10	36	38
Anti-physical	83	32	17	0	0	0	6	11	3	27	3	18	17
Anti-mental	108	52	12	0	2	0	6	15	4	29	7	18	21
Gender:	121	67	22	2	0	0	3	6	3	51	4	24	21
Anti-male	22	8	4	0	0	0	0	3	1	3	0	7	7
Anti-female	99	59	18	2	0	0	3	3	2	48	4	17	14
Gender Identity:	515	185	128	3	7	1	15	55	54	154	12	78	121
Anti-transgender	374	127	108	0	6	1	14	43	35	119	11	59	75
Anti–gender non-conforming	141	58	20	3	1	0	1	12	19	35	1	19	46
Multiple-Bias Incidents[3]	424	138	41	3	4	0	27	45	20	100	10	105	166

1 The aggregate of offenses by the known offender's ethnicity does not equal the aggregate of offenses by the known offender's race because not all law enforcement agencies that report offender race data also report offender ethnicity data. 2 The anti–Mormon religious bias has been renamed anti–Church of Jesus Christ. 3 A *multiple-bias incident* is an incident in which one or more offense types are motivated by two or more biases.

Table 87. Offenses, Victim Type, by Offense Type, 2022

(Number.)

Offense type	Total offenses	Victim type					
		Individual	Business/ financial institution	Government	Religious organization	Society/ public[1]	Other/ unknown/ multiple
Total	13,337	10,842	790	537	289	282	597
Crimes against persons[2]	8,810	8,810	0	0	0	0	0
Crimes against property	4,245	2,032	790	537	289	0	597
Robbery	169	151	3	0	0	0	15
Burglary	169	111	25	5	14	0	14
Larceny-theft	562	404	118	7	16	0	17
Motor vehicle theft	62	56	5	0	0	0	1
Arson	51	17	8	3	18	0	5
Destruction/damage/vandalism	3,088	1,187	604	512	240	0	545
Other[2]	144	106	27	10	1	0	0
Crimes against society[2]	282	NA	NA	NA	NA	282	NA

NA = Not available.
1 The victim type *society/public* is collected only in National Incident-Based Reporting System (NIBRS).   2 The figures shown include additional offenses collected in the NIBRS.

Table 88. Victims, Offense Type, by Bias Motivation, 2022

(Number.)

Bias motivation	Total victims[1]	Total number of adult victims[2]	Total number of juvenile victims[2]	Crimes against persons						
				Murder and nonnegligent manslaughter	Rape	Aggravated assault	Simple assault	Human trafficking	Intimidation	Other[3]
Total	13,711	10,001	1,582	33	21	1,561	3,111	4,023	2	59
Single-Bias Incidents	13,278	9,682	1,514	33	20	1,525	3,042	3,846	2	58
Race/Ethnicity/Ancestry:	7,852	6,122	964	16	10	1,019	1,924	2,514	1	23
Anti-White	1,126	919	104	1	3	155	323	259	0	6
Anti–Black or African American	4,075	3,040	593	13	4	501	875	1,482	0	7
Anti–American Indian or Alaska Native	217	150	11	0	0	21	31	20	0	2
Anti-Asian	602	474	44	0	0	79	190	191	1	1
Anti–Native Hawaiian or Other Pacific Islander	30	22	3	0	0	5	5	5	0	0
Anti–multiple races, group	287	197	24	0	1	13	44	75	0	1
Anti-Arab	105	93	13	0	0	15	29	47	0	0
Anti–Hispanic or Latino	958	885	133	1	2	190	306	297	0	4
Anti–other race/ethnicity/ancestry	452	342	39	1	0	40	121	138	0	2
Religion:	2,293	1,110	136	4	2	103	223	497	0	8
Anti-Jewish	1,217	513	82	0	0	36	103	322	0	5
Anti-Catholic	113	31	0	0	0	2	6	7	0	0
Anti-Protestant	71	34	1	0	0	3	6	8	0	0
Anti-Islamic (Muslim)	200	142	26	4	0	19	41	76	0	0
Anti–other religion	103	57	6	0	0	12	10	22	0	1
Anti–multiple religions,group	62	28	0	0	1	2	1	4	0	0
Anti–Church of Jesus Christ[4]	37	14	0	0	0	0	2	2	0	0
Anti–Jehovah's Witness	14	8	2	0	0	1	3	3	0	1
Anti–Eastern Orthodox (Russian, Greek, other)	91	57	4	0	0	2	10	17	0	0
Anti–other Christian	117	52	2	0	0	2	8	18	0	0
Anti-Buddhist	23	11	0	0	0	0	1	0	0	0
Anti-Hindu	29	19	3	0	0	3	6	10	0	0
Anti-Sikh	198	132	9	0	1	19	24	6	0	1
Anti–atheism/agnosticism/etc.	18	12	1	0	0	2	2	2	0	0
Sexual Orientation:	2,289	1,837	284	9	4	288	646	644	0	19
Anti-gay (male)	1,217	1,005	123	0	1	168	421	344	0	10
Anti-lesbian	216	168	38	0	2	23	57	84	0	1
Anti–lesbian, gay, bisexual, or transgender (mixed group)	796	623	113	9	0	86	152	203	0	5
Anti-heterosexual	23	12	5	0	1	4	5	4	0	1
Anti-bisexual	37	29	5	0	0	7	11	9	0	2
Disability:	194	126	42	0	0	24	62	30	0	1
Anti-physical	83	51	16	0	0	5	30	12	0	0
Anti-mental	111	75	26	0	0	19	32	18	0	1
Gender:	123	103	8	1	1	19	27	41	0	1
Anti-male	22	15	1	0	0	2	7	2	0	0
Anti-female	101	88	7	1	1	17	20	39	0	1
Gender Identity:	527	384	80	3	3	72	160	120	1	6
Anti-transgender	382	291	53	2	2	60	123	95	1	6
Anti–gender non-conforming	145	93	27	1	1	12	37	25	0	0
Multiple-Bias Incidents[5]	433	319	68	0	1	36	69	177	0	1

NOTE: The aggregate of adult and juvenile individual victims does not equal the total number of victims because total victims include individuals, businesses/financial institutions, government entities, religious organizations, and society/public as a whole. In addition, the aggregate of adult and juvenile individual victims does not equal the aggregate of victims of crimes against persons because not all law enforcement agencies report the ages of individual victims.
1 The term *victim* may refer to an individual, business/financial institution, government entity, religious organization, or society/public as a whole.   2 The figures shown are individual victims only.   3 The figures shown include additional offenses collected in the National Incident-Based Reporting System.   4 The anti-Mormon religious bias has been renamed anti–Church of Jesus Christ.   5 A *multiple-bias incident* is an incident in which one or more offense types are motivated by two or more biases.

Table 88. Victims, Offense Type, by Bias Motivation, 2022—Continued

(Number.)

Bias motivation	Crimes against property							Crimes against society[3]
	Robbery	Burglary	Larceny- theft	Motor vehicle theft	Arson	Destruction/ damage/ vandalism	Other[3]	
Total	190	195	605	65	72	3,326	166	282
Single-Bias Incidents	189	190	598	65	68	3,195	166	281
Race/Ethnicity/Ancestry:	127	102	263	47	27	1,523	88	168
Anti-White	34	22	99	18	7	123	34	42
Anti–Black or African American	33	32	70	14	12	948	16	68
Anti–American Indian or Alaska Native	1	9	45	9	1	29	18	31
Anti-Asian	20	13	17	0	1	84	0	5
Anti–Native Hawaiian or Other Pacific Islander	0	4	2	0	0	2	3	4
Anti–multiple races, group	2	5	4	1	0	134	4	3
Anti-Arab	1	1	2	0	0	7	1	2
Anti–Hispanic or Latino	30	13	10	2	6	85	5	7
Anti–other race/ethnicity/ancestry	6	3	14	3	0	111	7	6
Religion:	12	50	137	15	29	1,106	42	65
Anti-Jewish	3	5	13	0	2	726	0	2
Anti-Catholic	0	2	7	1	6	78	3	1
Anti-Protestant	0	2	16	1	2	24	1	8
Anti-Islamic (Muslim)	2	8	3	0	7	37	2	1
Anti–other religion	1	3	9	0	0	38	3	4
Anti–multiple religions,group	0	2	5	1	2	40	0	4
Anti–Church of Jesus Christ[4]	0	7	3	0	2	20	1	0
Anti–Jehovah's Witness	0	0	1	0	0	4	1	0
Anti–Eastern Orthodox (Russian, Greek, other)	0	4	10	4	0	23	6	15
Anti–other Christian	1	5	7	0	5	67	2	2
Anti-Buddhist	1	4	3	0	0	9	2	3
Anti-Hindu	0	0	0	0	0	8	0	2
Anti-Sikh	4	8	54	8	0	32	19	22
Anti–atheism/agnosticism/etc.	0	0	6	0	3	0	2	1
Sexual Orientation:	35	18	121	1	9	461	16	18
Anti-gay (male)	32	9	27	1	2	191	5	6
Anti-lesbian	1	2	6	0	0	36	0	4
Anti–lesbian, gay, bisexual, or transgender (mixed group)	2	6	83	0	7	227	11	5
Anti-heterosexual	0	1	1	0	0	3	0	3
Anti-bisexual	0	0	4	0	0	4	0	0
Disability:	1	9	23	0	1	22	12	9
Anti-physical	1	3	10	0	0	11	6	5
Anti-mental	0	6	13	0	1	11	6	4
Gender:	0	2	9	0	2	13	2	5
Anti-male	0	1	3	0	0	4	1	2
Anti-female	0	1	6	0	2	9	1	3
Gender Identity:	14	9	45	2	0	70	6	16
Anti-transgender	13	6	25	2	0	41	1	5
Anti–gender non-conforming	1	3	20	0	0	29	5	11
Multiple-Bias Incidents[5]	1	5	7	0	4	131	0	1

NOTE: The aggregate of adult and juvenile individual victims does not equal the total number of victims because total victims include individuals, businesses/financial institutions, government entities, religious organizations, and society/public as a whole. In addition, the aggregate of adult and juvenile individual victims does not equal the aggregate of victims of crimes against persons because not all law enforcement agencies report the ages of individual victims.
1 The term victim may refer to an individual, business/financial institution, government entity, religious organization, or society/public as a whole.   2 The figures shown are individual victims only.   3 The figures shown include additional offenses collected in the National Incident-Based Reporting System.   4 The anti-Mormon religious bias has been renamed anti–Church of Jesus Christ.   5 A multiple-bias incident is an incident in which one or more offense types are motivated by two or more biases.

Table 89. Incidents, Victim Type, by Bias Motivation, 2022

(Number.)

Bias motivation	Total incidents	Victim type					
		Individual	Business/ financial institution	Government	Religious organization	Society/ public[1]	Other/ unknown/ multiple
Total	11,634	9,195	763	521	259	221	675
Single-Bias Incidents	11,288	8,948	745	488	248	221	638
Race/ethnicity/qncestry	6,567	5,524	350	278	20	119	276
Religion	2,042	1,055	276	148	212	59	292
Sexual orientation	1,944	1,738	66	52	13	14	61
Disability	171	141	18	2	1	8	1
Gender	95	80	7	2	0	5	1
Gender identity	469	410	28	6	2	16	7
Multiple-Bias Incidents[2]	346	247	18	33	11	0	37

1 The victim type *society/public* is collected only in the National Incident-Based Reporting System.   2 A *multiple-bias incident* is an incident in which one or more offense types are motivated by two or more biases.

Table 90. Known Offenders,[1] by Known Offender's Race, Ethnicity, and Age, 2022

(Number.)

Race/ethnicity/age	Total
Race	10,299
White	5,250
Black or African American	2,167
American Indian or Alaska Native	86
Asian	164
Native Hawaiian or Other Pacific Islander	21
Group of multiple races[2]	821
Unknown race	1,790
Ethnicity[3]	7,671
Hispanic or Latino	985
Not Hispanic or Latino	3,749
Group of multiple ethnicities[4]	658
Unknown ethnicity	2,279
Age[3]	8,487
Total known offenders 18 and over	6,842
Total known offenders under 18	1,645

1 The term *known offender* does not imply the suspect's identity is known; rather, the term indicates some aspect of the suspect was identified, thus distinguishing the suspect from an unknown offender.   2 The term *group of multiple races* is used to describe a group of offenders of varying races.   3 The total number of known offenders by age and the total number of known offenders by ethnicity do not equal the total number of known offenders by race because not all law enforcement agencies report the age and/or ethnicity of the known offenders.   4 The term *group of multiple ethnicities* is used to describe a group of offenders of varying ethnicities.

Table 91. Incidents, Bias Motivation, by Location, 2022

(Number.)

Location	Total incidents	Race/ethnicity/ ancestry	Religion	Sexual orientation	Disability	Gender	Gender identity	Multiple- bias incidents[1]
Total	11,634	6,567	2,042	1,944	171	95	469	346
Abandoned/condemned structure	10	6	1	2	0	0	0	1
Air/bus/train terminal	181	112	18	29	2	2	8	10
Amusement park	9	6	2	1	0	0	0	0
Arena/stadium/fairgrounds/coliseum	16	8	2	3	1	0	0	2
ATM separate from bank	2	2	0	0	0	0	0	0
Auto dealership new/used	11	6	4	0	0	0	1	0
Bank/savings and loan	35	20	6	4	3	0	1	1
Bar/nightclub	172	75	15	65	2	0	9	6
Camp/campground	19	11	4	4	0	0	0	0
Church/synagogue/temple/mosque	419	45	332	20	0	0	3	19
Commercial office building	241	145	41	31	6	2	6	10
Community center	46	14	20	7	2	1	1	1
Construction site	40	26	9	2	0	0	1	2
Convenience store	205	143	22	26	2	1	8	3
Cyberspace	122	48	23	28	2	1	13	7
Daycare facility	10	6	2	1	0	0	1	0
Department/discount store	146	91	21	19	8	0	6	1
Dock/wharf/freight/modal terminal	11	8	1	2	0	0	0	0
Drug store/doctor's office/hospital	165	111	15	15	4	3	9	8
Farm facility	3	1	1	0	0	1	0	0
Field/woods	58	29	15	6	0	3	2	3
Gambling facility/casino/race track	13	10	0	1	0	1	1	0
Government/public building	180	119	25	20	2	4	6	4
Grocery/supermarket	153	107	21	16	1	0	5	3
Highway/road/alley/street/sidewalk	1,823	1,146	208	313	19	14	91	32
Hotel/motel/etc.	115	80	10	12	0	4	5	4
Industrial site	17	10	3	2	0	0	1	1
Jail/prison/penitentiary/corrections facility	147	88	9	34	5	1	6	4
Lake/waterway/beach	27	19	2	4	0	0	1	1
Liquor store	21	16	2	2	0	0	1	0
Park/playground	386	197	85	55	2	6	10	31
Parking/drop lot/garage	676	445	70	103	5	5	28	20
Rental storage facility	18	11	5	0	1	0	1	0
Residence/home	3,115	1,729	415	666	53	33	147	72
Rest area	3	3	0	0	0	0	0	0
Restaurant	314	208	22	58	4	1	10	11
School/college[2]	129	72	25	24	1	0	6	1
School—college/university	274	124	52	63	2	3	12	18
School—elementary/secondary	788	469	120	109	27	0	21	42
Service/gas station	146	107	14	16	1	0	5	3
Shelter—mission/homeless	22	10	2	6	0	0	4	0
Shopping mall	43	30	4	3	1	0	3	2
Specialty store (TV, fur, etc.)	122	81	16	16	1	0	3	5
Tribal lands	7	5	0	0	0	2	0	0
Other/unknown	1,146	551	374	153	13	6	33	16
Multiple locations	28	17	4	3	1	1	0	2

1 A *multiple-bias incident* is an incident in which one or more offense types are motivated by two or more biases.   2 The location designation *School/college* has been retained for agencies that have not updated their records management systems to include the new location designations of *School—college/university* and *School—elementary/secondary*, which allow for more specificity in reporting.

Table 92. Offenses, Offense Type, by Participating State, Territory, and Federal, 2022

(Number.)

Participating state/ territory/federal	Total offenses	Crimes against persons							Crimes against property							Crimes against society[1]
		Murder and nonnegligent manslaughter	Rape	Aggravated assault	Simple assault	Intimidation	Human trafficking	Other[1]	Robbery	Burglary	Larceny-theft	Motor vehicle theft	Arson	Destruction/ damage/ vandalism	Other[1]	
Total	13,337	33	21	1,561	3,111	4,023	2	59	169	169	562	62	51	3,088	144	282
Alabama	254	1	2	31	66	37	0	0	1	10	29	5	1	45	11	15
Alaska	5	0	0	0	0	1	0	0	0	0	0	0	0	4	0	0
Arizona	225	0	0	36	75	58	0	1	2	3	4	0	3	42	0	1
Arkansas	38	0	0	7	8	8	0	0	0	0	5	0	0	4	2	4
California	2,261	3	3	435	538	510	0	6	72	12	18	2	13	638	3	8
Colorado	389	5	0	50	98	99	0	0	3	10	24	4	3	77	11	5
Connecticut	101	0	0	6	27	36	0	0	0	2	3	0	3	21	2	1
Delaware	16	0	0	0	2	4	0	0	0	0	0	0	0	10	0	0
District of Columbia	167	0	0	20	69	51	0	2	2	1	0	0	0	22	0	0
Florida	166	0	0	35	66	14	0	0	2	2	4	0	0	40	1	2
Georgia	225	0	1	20	75	62	0	4	1	4	7	4	1	37	6	3
Hawaii	36	0	0	11	6	18	0	0	1	0	0	0	0	0	0	0
Idaho	47	0	0	10	10	17	0	1	0	1	2	0	1	4	1	0
Illinois	382	0	1	28	91	112	0	2	6	5	29	1	0	95	8	4
Indiana	194	2	0	15	57	67	0	0	1	1	12	0	0	25	4	10
Iowa	77	0	0	7	11	26	0	1	0	2	4	1	0	25	0	0
Kansas	134	0	1	9	17	31	0	1	0	2	11	1	1	38	6	16
Kentucky	181	1	0	11	51	75	0	2	1	4	6	0	0	28	0	2
Louisiana	80	0	0	1	29	8	0	5	1	1	9	0	0	10	2	14
Maine	92	0	0	1	15	43	0	0	0	1	7	0	0	25	0	0
Maryland	242	0	0	38	67	23	0	0	5	2	12	2	1	82	3	7
Massachusetts	525	0	0	71	126	165	0	1	5	1	13	0	1	139	3	0
Michigan	502	0	1	59	122	198	0	2	3	9	21	3	2	66	3	13
Minnesota	198	0	0	29	63	46	0	2	2	2	2	0	2	49	1	0
Mississippi	32	0	0	3	12	5	0	0	0	0	3	1	0	1	2	5
Missouri	252	2	1	55	60	63	0	3	1	6	13	5	0	35	4	4
Montana	16	0	0	4	3	4	0	0	1	0	0	0	0	4	0	0
Nebraska	82	0	0	9	18	27	0	0	1	1	9	0	0	15	0	2
Nevada	115	0	0	23	26	21	0	1	1	3	3	2	0	30	1	4
New Hampshire	30	0	0	0	4	7	0	0	0	1	1	0	0	16	0	1
New Jersey	1,193	1	0	12	73	827	0	0	4	2	9	0	1	259	0	5
New Mexico	50	0	1	11	9	16	0	0	1	0	4	1	0	6	0	1
New York	964	0	1	90	282	115	0	0	12	10	21	0	2	428	0	3
North Carolina	358	0	0	29	77	104	0	5	2	13	15	3	3	69	15	23
North Dakota	29	0	0	1	5	22	0	0	0	0	0	0	0	1	0	0
Ohio	591	0	6	44	123	143	1	2	2	22	81	11	2	100	17	37
Oklahoma	79	0	0	12	20	36	0	0	1	0	3	0	1	6	0	0
Oregon	364	0	0	59	80	107	0	1	3	6	6	0	2	84	1	15
Pennsylvania	313	0	0	27	70	135	0	1	6	3	15	1	1	47	5	2
Rhode Island	17	0	0	0	2	7	0	0	0	0	0	0	0	8	0	0
South Carolina	68	0	0	3	15	14	0	0	0	1	6	1	0	12	3	13
South Dakota	19	0	0	2	7	4	0	0	0	0	0	0	0	4	0	2
Tennessee	126	0	1	16	39	43	0	1	2	0	1	0	0	19	1	3
Texas	669	2	1	86	166	172	0	5	12	13	54	3	2	119	13	21
Utah	131	0	0	5	37	18	0	0	0	2	14	0	1	48	1	5
Vermont	54	1	0	4	13	10	0	1	0	0	7	0	1	16	0	1
Virginia	211	0	0	8	81	44	0	1	1	3	3	0	1	64	2	3
Washington	652	0	1	71	129	272	0	2	8	6	34	8	1	113	2	5
West Virginia	59	0	0	3	14	7	0	0	0	2	15	1	0	8	3	6
Wisconsin	163	0	0	21	29	39	0	1	1	0	22	1	1	32	3	13
Wyoming	29	0	0	1	15	6	0	0	0	0	1	0	0	6	0	0
Territory																
Guam	6	0	0	0	1	2	0	0	0	0	0	1	0	1	1	0
Federal																
Federal Bureau of Investigation	104	15	0	32	1	36	1	5	2	0	0	0	0	7	3	2
National Institute of Health	2	0	0	0	0	1	0	0	0	0	0	0	0	1	0	0
United States Air Force Security Police	7	0	0	0	3	2	0	0	0	0	0	0	0	2	0	0
United States Department of Veterans Affairs Police Service	11	0	0	0	8	3	0	0	0	0	0	0	0	0	0	0
United States Forest Service	2	0	0	0	0	0	0	0	0	0	0	0	0	1	0	1
United States Treasury Inspector General for Tax Administration	2	0	0	0	0	2	0	0	0	0	0	0	0	0	0	0

1 The figures shown include additional offenses collected in the National Incident-Based Reporting System.

Table 93. Agency Hate Crime Reporting, by Participating State, Territory, and Federal, 2022

(Number.)

State/federal	Number of participating agencies	Population covered	Agencies submitting incident reports	Total number of incidents reported
Total	14,631	305,468,626	3,109	11,634
Alabama	404	4,519,862	68	227
Alaska	33	730,233	3	5
Arizona	100	6,282,390	36	206
Arkansas	294	2,986,257	20	35
California	819	38,957,207	340	2,088
Colorado	234	5,825,547	72	317
Connecticut	107	3,626,205	39	88
Delaware	63	1,018,396	8	16
District of Columbia	2	671,803	2	151
Florida	226	14,416,328	40	150
Georgia	456	10,212,747	62	188
Hawaii	3	1,233,842	3	32
Idaho	111	1,938,529	13	37
Illinois	520	10,010,597	85	318
Indiana	209	5,603,871	62	167
Iowa	228	2,968,878	34	70
Kansas	327	2,675,833	65	122
Kentucky	431	4,509,571	55	124
Louisiana	148	3,428,406	32	65
Maine	131	1,384,006	45	81
Maryland	95	4,898,180	42	200
Massachusetts	384	6,947,897	99	433
Michigan	603	9,616,858	167	405
Minnesota	408	5,711,489	68	168
Mississippi	152	1,791,767	20	28
Missouri	498	6,077,481	91	195
Montana	110	1,121,153	7	14
Nebraska	262	1,943,315	25	63
Nevada	55	3,162,409	23	98
New Hampshire	213	1,378,928	20	29
New Jersey	431	8,367,147	233	1,098
New Mexico	95	1,813,146	16	39
New York	559	19,539,474	101	935
North Carolina	407	10,235,931	129	310
North Dakota	111	779,261	10	17
Ohio	638	10,916,774	151	528
Oklahoma	461	4,019,800	48	63
Oregon	212	4,079,739	55	290
Pennsylvania	465	8,034,859	67	278
Rhode Island	49	1,093,734	12	16
South Carolina	462	5,271,145	38	60
South Dakota	107	830,169	9	16
Tennessee	399	7,047,629	50	94
Texas	1,063	29,643,845	195	587
Utah	135	3,325,856	46	104
Vermont	86	647,064	24	49
Virginia	410	8,682,813	55	182
Washington	246	7,730,372	99	530
West Virginia	214	1,541,815	30	51
Wisconsin	362	5,610,301	78	143
Wyoming	50	453,931	10	23
Territory				
Guam[1]	1	153,836	1	6
Federal[2]				
Board of Governors of the Federal Reserve System and the Consumer Financial Protection Bureau, Office of Inspector General	1		0	0
Central Intelligence Agency, Security Protective Service	1		0	0
Commodity Futures Trading Commission, Office of Inspector General	1		0	0
Corporation for National and Community Service, Office of Inspector General	1		0	0
Defense Intelligence Agency	1		0	0
Department of Veterans Affairs, Office of Inspector General	1		0	0
Drug Enforcement Administration, Wilmington Resident Office	1		0	0
Export-Import Bank of the United States, Office of Inspector General	1		0	0
Federal Bureau of Investigation	1		1	72
Federal Communications Commission, Office of Inspector General	1		0	0
Federal Emergency Management Agency	1		0	0
Federal Housing Finance Agency, Office of Inspector General	1		0	0

Table 93. Agency Hate Crime Reporting, by Participating State, Territory, and Federal, 2022—Continued

(Number.)

State/federal	Number of participating agencies	Population covered	Agencies submitting incident reports	Total number of incidents reported
Library of Congress, Office of Inspector General	1		0	0
National Institute of Health	1		1	2
National Security Agency Police	1		0	0
Peace Corps, Office of Inspector General	1		0	0
Pentagon Force Protection Agency	1		0	0
Smithsonian Institution, Office of Inspector General	1		0	0
Special Inspector General for Afghanistan Reconstruction	1		0	0
Tennessee Valley Authority, Office of Inspector General	1		0	0
United States Agency for International Development, Office of Inspector General	1		0	0
United States Air Force, Office of Special Investigations	1		0	0
United States Air Force Security Police	1		1	6
United States Department of Agriculture, Office of Inspector General	1		0	0
United States Department of Defense, Office of Inspector General	1		0	0
United States Department of Education, Office of Inspector General	1		0	0
United States Department of Housing and Urban Development, Office of Inspector General	1		0	0
United States Department of Justice, Office of Inspector General	1		0	0
United States Department of State, Office of Inspector General	1		0	0
United States Department of the Interior	1		0	0
United States Department of Transportation, Office of Inspector General	1		0	0
United States Department of Veterans Affairs Police Service	1		1	11
United States Environmental Protection Agency, Office of Inspector General	1		0	0
United States Federal Deposit Insurance Corporation, Office of Inspector General	1		0	0
United States Forest Service	1		1	2
United States General Services Administration, Office of Inspector General	1		0	0
United States National Archives and Records Administration, Office of Inspector General	1		0	0
United States Nuclear Regulatory Commission, Office of Inspector General	1		0	0
United States Office of Personnel Management, Office of the Inspector General	1		0	0
United States Railroad Retirement Board, Office of Inspector General	1		0	0
United States Securities and Exchange Commission, Office of Inspector General	1		0	0
United States Treasury Inspector General for Tax Administration	1		1	2

1 The population attributed to this agency is from the United States Census Bureau 2020 Census of Guam.   2 Population estimates are not attributed to the federal agencies.

Table 94. Hate Crime Incidents Per Bias Motivation and Quarter, by Selected State, Territory, Federal, and Agency, 2022

(Number.)

State/agency	Number of incidents per bias motivation						Number of incidents per quarter				Population[1]
	Race/ Ethnicity/ Ancestry	Religion	Sexual orientation	Disability	Gender	Gender Identity	1st quarter	2nd quarter	3rd quarter	4th quarter	
ALABAMA	142	67	20	3	3	9					
Cities	101	53	15	2	3	8					
Abbeville	1	0	0	0	0	0	1	0	0	0	2,390
Adamsville	1	0	0	0	0	0	1	0	0	0	4,233
Alexander City	0	1	0	0	0	0	0	0	1	0	14,476
Andalusia	1	0	0	0	0	0	0	0	0	1	8,699
Anniston	1	0	0	0	0	0	1	0	0	0	21,007
Atmore	1	0	0	0	0	0	0	0	1	0	8,536
Auburn	0	0	1	0	0	0	0	0	1	0	80,759
Bessemer[2]	2	3	0	0	0	0	2	0	1	1	25,265
Birmingham[2]	2	32	4	1	0	6	13	6	15	7	195,050
Brent	1	0	0	0	0	0	1	0	0	0	2,995
Camp Hill	1	0	0	0	0	0	0	1	0	0	977
Carbon Hill	1	0	0	0	0	0	0	0	1	0	1,714
Chickasaw	2	1	0	0	0	0	0	1	1	1	6,333
Citronelle	1	0	0	0	0	0	1	0	0	0	3,916
Clayhatchee	1	0	0	0	0	0	0	0	1	0	473
Cordova	0	0	1	0	0	0	0	1	0	0	1,663
Courtland	1	0	0	0	0	0	0	0	0	1	584
Cullman	2	0	0	0	0	0	0	1	1	0	19,065
Dauphin Island	0	1	0	0	0	0	0	0	0	1	1,843
Decatur	2	2	0	0	0	0	0	3	0	1	57,831
Dora	1	0	0	0	0	0	0	0	0	1	2,281
Dothan	1	0	1	0	0	0	1	0	1	0	71,196
Enterprise	1	0	1	0	0	0	2	0	0	0	29,936
Flomaton[2]	1	1	0	0	0	0	0	0	0	1	1,455
Florence	5	0	1	0	0	0	2	3	1	0	40,063
Fort Payne	1	0	1	0	0	0	0	0	1	1	14,845
Fultondale[2]	2	0	0	0	0	0	0	0	1	0	9,699
Gardendale	3	1	0	0	0	0	1	1	1	1	16,861
Haleyville	0	1	0	0	0	0	0	0	0	1	4,366
Headland	2	0	0	0	0	0	1	0	0	1	5,320
Hoover	0	1	0	1	0	0	1	1	0	0	92,491
Huntsville	16	2	2	0	0	2	0	7	7	8	218,897
Jackson	1	0	0	0	0	0	0	0	0	1	4,576
Jasper	0	0	1	0	0	0	1	0	0	0	14,312
Jemison	1	0	0	0	0	0	0	1	0	0	2,662
Lanett	1	0	0	0	0	0	0	0	1	0	6,716
Leeds	3	0	0	0	0	0	0	1	0	2	12,206
Mobile	4	0	2	0	0	0	3	2	0	1	239,323
Monroeville	1	0	0	0	0	0	0	0	0	1	5,797
Muscle Shoals[2]	3	0	0	0	0	0	0	0	0	2	16,917
Northport[2]	3	0	0	0	1	0	0	1	1	1	30,901
Prattville	1	1	0	0	0	0	1	0	0	1	38,679
Prichard	2	0	0	0	0	0	1	0	1	0	18,936
Rainbow City[2]	3	0	0	0	0	0	2	0	0	0	10,150
Repton	1	0	0	0	0	0	0	0	0	1	230
Robertsdale	1	0	0	0	0	0	0	0	0	1	7,116
Saraland	2	0	0	0	0	0	1	1	0	0	16,459
Selma[2]	2	0	0	0	2	0	0	0	2	1	17,296
Talladega	11	1	0	0	0	0	0	1	0	11	15,448
Tarrant	3	2	0	0	0	0	2	2	0	1	5,913
Thorsby	1	0	0	0	0	0	1	0	0	0	2,117
Weaver	2	0	0	0	0	0	0	1	1	0	3,394
Winfield[2]	0	3	0	0	0	0	0	0	1	0	4,805
Woodstock	1	0	0	0	0	0	0	1	0	0	1,691
Universities and Colleges	1	0	2	0	0	0					
Jacksonville State University	0	0	1	0	0	0	0	0	1	0	10,752
Jefferson State Community College	0	0	1	0	0	0	0	0	1	0	12,293
Troy University	1	0	0	0	0	0	0	0	1	0	20,866
Metropolitan Counties	38	14	2	1	0	1					
Chilton	0	2	0	0	0	0	0	1	0	1	
Colbert	1	0	0	0	0	0	0	0	0	1	
Elmore	0	1	0	0	0	0	1	0	0	0	
Houston	0	1	0	0	0	0	0	0	0	1	
Jefferson[2]	22	7	1	1	0	1	11	7	6	6	
Lawrence	1	0	0	0	0	0	0	1	0	0	
Madison	5	2	0	0	0	0	0	2	5	0	
Mobile[2]	7	1	0	0	0	0	3	2	0	1	
Russell	2	0	1	0	0	0	0	0	1	2	
Nonmetropolitan Counties	2	0	1	0	0	0					
Marshall	1	0	1	0	0	0	0	0	1	1	
Tallapoosa	1	0	0	0	0	0	1	0	0	0	
ALASKA	0	4	1	0	0	0					
Cities	0	4	1	0	0	0					
Anchorage	0	3	0	0	0	0	1	1	1		285,821

Table 94. Hate Crime Incidents Per Bias Motivation and Quarter, by Selected State, Territory, Federal, and Agency, 2022—Continued

(Number.)

State/agency	Number of incidents per bias motivation						Number of incidents per quarter				Population[1]
	Race/ Ethnicity/ Ancestry	Religion	Sexual orientation	Disability	Gender	Gender Identity	1st quarter	2nd quarter	3rd quarter	4th quarter	
Kodiak	0	0	1	0	0	0	0	0	1	0	5,357
Wasilla	0	1	0	0	0	0	0	0	0	1	9,809
ARIZONA	138	27	42	2	5	14					
Cities	123	21	40	2	5	12					
Apache Junction	0	0	1	0	0	0	0	1	0	0	41,099
Buckeye	1	1	1	0	0	0	2	0	1	0	110,002
Bullhead City	1	0	0	0	0	0			1	0	42,953
Camp Verde	2	0	0	0	0	0	1	0	0	1	12,362
Casa Grande	2	0	0	0	0	0	1	0	1	0	61,271
Colorado City[2]	0	0	2	0	0	0		0	1	0	2,560
El Mirage	1	0	0	0	0	0	0	0	0	1	36,039
Glendale	5	4	1	0	0	0	2	1	1	6	250,466
Goodyear	2	0	0	0	0	0	1	1	0	0	107,212
Lake Havasu City	1	0	1	0	0	0	0	0	2	0	59,166
Marana	1	0	0	0	0	0	1	0	0	0	57,119
Maricopa[2]	2	0	2	0	0	0	1	0	2	0	66,525
Mesa[2]	11	1	2	0	1	1	5	3	4	3	513,116
Parker	0	0	1	0	0	0	0	0	1	0	3,263
Payson	0	1	0	0	0	0	0	0	1	0	16,638
Phoenix[2]	77	9	24	0	3	10	26	21	31	28	1,637,902
Prescott[2]	3	0	1	0	0	0	1	1	0	1	47,878
Prescott Valley	1	0	1	0	0	0	0	1	1	0	49,422
Queen Creek	1	0	0	0	0	0	0	1	0	0	72,229
Sahuarita	4	0	0	0	0	1	1	1	3	0	36,229
Show Low	1	0	1	0	1	0	0	2	1	0	12,157
Sierra Vista	1	0	0	0	0	0	0	0	1	0	45,611
Snowflake-Taylor	0	1	0	0	0	0	0	0	0	1	10,834
Surprise	1	0	0	0	0	0	0	1	0	0	154,128
Tempe	3	4	1	0	0	0	3	4	0	1	187,473
Williams[2]	1	0	1	0	0	0	0	0	0	1	3,316
Yuma	1	0	0	2	0	0	0	0	3	0	98,164
Universities and Colleges	1	0	0	0	0	0					
University of Arizona	1	0	0	0	0	0			1		52,329
Metropolitan Counties	10	5	1	0	0	1					
Mohave	1	0	1	0	0	0	0	1	0	1	
Pima	5	5	0	0	0	1	2	3	3	3	
Pinal	2	0	0	0	0	0	0	0	2	0	
Yavapai	2	0	0	0	0	0	1	0	1	0	
Nonmetropolitan Counties	0	1	0	0	0	0					
La Paz	0	1	0	0	0	0	0	0	1	0	
Tribal Agencies	4	0	1	0	0	1					
Gila River Indian Community	2	0	1	0	0	1	2	1	0	1	
Pascua Yaqui Tribal	1	0	0	0	0	0	0	1	0	0	
Truxton Canon Agency	1	0	0	0	0	0	0	1	0	0	
ARKANSAS	22	4	3	3	0	3					
Cities	9	2	1	0	0	1					
Benton	1	1	0	0	0	0	0	0	1	1	36,282
Centerton	1	0	0	0	0	1	1	1	0	0	21,927
Conway	1	0	0	0	0	0	0	0	0	1	66,487
Fayetteville	1	0	0	0	0	0	0	0	1	0	96,456
Hot Springs	1	0	0	0	0	0	0	0	0	1	38,174
Malvern	1	1	0	0	0	0	0	0	1	1	10,824
Searcy	1	0	1	0	0	0	1	0	1	0	23,175
Siloam Springs	1	0	0	0	0	0	1	0	0	0	17,957
Springdale	1	0	0	0	0	0	0	0	0	1	90,892
Universities and Colleges	1	0	1	0	0	0					
University of Arkansas											
Fayetteville	0	0	1	0	0	0	0	0	1	0	30,349
Medical Sciences	1	0	0	0	0	0	0	0	1	0	3,241
Metropolitan Counties	5	2	1	2	0	2					
Benton	1	1	0	0	0	0	0	1	0	1	
Perry	1	0	0	0	0	0	0	0	0	1	
Poinsett	0	0	0	1	0	0	0	0	0	1	
Pulaski	3	0	0	0	0	2	1	2	1	1	
Saline	0	1	1	0	0	0	0	0	0	2	
Washington	0	0	0	1	0	0	0	0	1	0	
Nonmetropolitan Counties	7	0	0	1	0	0					
Cross	1	0	0	0	0	0					
Mississippi	5	0	0	1	0	0	0	0	1	0	
Van Buren	1	0	0	0	0	0	1	3	0	2	

Table 94. Hate Crime Incidents Per Bias Motivation and Quarter, by Selected State, Territory, Federal, and Agency, 2022—Continued

(Number.)

State/agency	Number of incidents per bias motivation						Number of incidents per quarter				Population[1]
	Race/Ethnicity/Ancestry	Religion	Sexual orientation	Disability	Gender	Gender Identity	1st quarter	2nd quarter	3rd quarter	4th quarter	
CALIFORNIA	1,367	318	416	11	15	74					
Cities	1,203	285	362	11	12	72					
Agoura Hills	0	1	0	0	0	0	0	0		1	19,397
Alameda	3	0	3	0	0	0	0	1	5	0	74,441
Albany	4	0	1	0	0	1	1	0	0	5	19,011
Alhambra	4	0	0	0	0	0	0	3	0	1	79,703
Aliso Viejo	1	0	0	0	0	0	0	0	0	1	51,477
Anaheim[2]	1	1	0	0	0	0	1	0	0	0	344,795
Antioch	2	1	1	0	0	0	1	1	1	1	114,338
Apple Valley[2]	2	0	0	0	0	0	0			1	76,520
Arcadia	2	0	0	0	0	0	1	1	0	0	54,202
Arroyo Grande	0	0	1	0	0	0	1	0	0	0	18,492
Atascadero	1	0	1	0	0	0	1	1	0	0	29,679
Atherton	2	2	0	0	0	0	0	0	2	2	6,704
Atwater	2	1	0	0	0	0	0	1	2	0	32,157
Auburn	2	0	0	0	0	0	0	0	1	1	13,933
Azusa	2	0	0	0	0	0	1			1	47,754
Bakersfield[2]	2	2	2	0	0	1	2	2	1	1	411,873
Baldwin Park	2	0	0	0	0	0	0	1	0	1	69,205
Banning	2	0	0	0	0	0	0	2	0	0	31,050
Barstow	1	0	0	0	0	0	0	1			25,465
Beaumont	2	0	1	0	0	0	0	1	1	1	57,067
Bell	0	1	0	0	0	0	0	0	1	0	32,140
Bellflower	2	0	0	0	0	0	0	1	1		75,830
Bell Gardens	0	0	1	0	0	0	0	0	1	0	37,720
Berkeley[2]	28	3	9	0	0	2	11	9	9	11	114,872
Beverly Hills	3	3	0	0	0	0	2	1	2	1	31,163
Blythe	2	0	0	0	0	0	0	0	1	1	17,853
Brawley	2	0	0	0	0	0	0	0	0	2	26,650
Burbank[2]	8	0	3	0	0	0	0	3	2	4	103,516
Burlingame	4	0	0	0	0	0	0	0	2	2	29,003
Calabasas	0	1	0	0	0	0	0	0	1		22,628
Camarillo	2	0	0	0	0	0	0	1	1		70,872
Campbell	0	1	2	0	0	0	1	1	1		41,605
Carlsbad	2	0	0	0	0	0	1	0	1	0	115,531
Carson	1	0	0	0	0	0	0	0	1		92,021
Cathedral City	2	0	1	0	0	0	1		2		52,871
Central Marin	2	0	1	0	0	0	1	1	0	1	35,543
Ceres	3	0	0	0	0	0	0		1	2	49,282
Cerritos	0	1	1	0	0	0	0	0	2		47,325
Chico[2]	1	1	3	0	0	2	3	0	1	2	102,499
Chino	1	0	0	0	0	0	1	0	0	0	94,611
Chino Hills	0	1	0	0	0	0	0			1	78,786
Chowchilla[2]	2	0	0	0	0	1	0	2	0	0	19,195
Chula Vista	4	3	1	0	0	1	1	2	5	1	277,976
Citrus Heights	2	3	0	0	0	0	4	0	1	0	86,896
Claremont	1	0	0	0	0	0	0	0	1	0	35,068
Clearlake[2]	8	1	1	0	0	0	2	1	3	2	16,901
Clovis	0	0	2	0	0	0	0	0	1	1	125,348
Compton	1	0	0	0	0	0	0	1			91,625
Corning	0	0	0	1	0	0	0		1	0	8,191
Corona	2	0	0	0	0	0	1	1	0	0	161,946
Coronado	1	0	0	0	1	0	0	1	1	0	19,706
Costa Mesa	3	0	2	0	0	0	1	1	2	1	109,785
Covina	2	0	0	0	0	0	1	1	0	0	49,590
Crescent City	1	1	1	0	0	0	0	0	2	1	6,732
Culver City[2]	2	1	0	0	0	0	1	0	0	1	39,271
Cupertino	1	0	0	0	0	0	0	1			56,950
Cypress	4	0	0	0	0	0	3	0	0	1	49,588
Daly City	3	0	0	0	0	0	1	2	0	0	98,021
Dana Point	1	0	0	0	0	0	0	1	0	0	32,534
Davis	10	2	2	0	0	0	4	3	3	4	66,939
Delano	7	0	0	0	0	0	1	1	3	2	52,484
Desert Hot Springs	0	0	1	0	0	0	0		0	1	32,923
Diamond Bar	2	0	0	0	0	0	1	0		1	52,713
Downey	0	0	1	0	0	0	0	0	1		109,226
El Cajon[2]	3	0	1	0	0	0	2	1	0	0	104,693
El Centro	2	0	0	0	0	0	0	2	0	0	44,076
El Cerrito[2]	2	2	2	0	0	1	0	1	1	4	25,718
Elk Grove	2	0	0	0	0	0	1	0	1	0	180,372
El Monte	4	0	0	0	0	0	1	2	0	1	104,695
El Segundo	1	1	0	0	0	0	0	0	1	1	16,550
Emeryville	1	0	2	0	0	0	0	1	0	2	12,781
Encinitas	2	1	0	0	0	0	1	0	1	1	61,488
Escondido	0	1	1	0	0	0	0	0	1	1	150,072
Eureka	1	0	0	0	0	0	0	0		1	26,465
Fairfax	0	1	0	0	0	0	0	1	0	0	7,477
Fairfield[2]	5	0	3	1	0	0	2	3	1	1	119,583
Ferndale	2	0	0	0	0	1	0	2	1	0	1,399

Table 94. Hate Crime Incidents Per Bias Motivation and Quarter, by Selected State, Territory, Federal, and Agency, 2022—Continued

(Number.)

State/agency	Number of incidents per bias motivation						Number of incidents per quarter				Population[1]
	Race/ Ethnicity/ Ancestry	Religion	Sexual orientation	Disability	Gender	Gender Identity	1st quarter	2nd quarter	3rd quarter	4th quarter	
Folsom	5	1	0	1	0	0	4	0	0	3	83,011
Fontana	1	0	0	0	0	0	0	0	0	1	212,730
Fortuna	0	1	0	0	0	1	0	0	1	1	12,481
Foster City[2]	3	2	0	0	0	1	3	0	1	1	31,389
Fremont[2]	8	1	0	0	0	0	2	1	4	1	223,430
Fresno[2]	14	2	5	0	0	1	4	3	3	6	546,871
Fullerton[2]	6	1	0	0	0	0	0	2	3	1	140,587
Galt	1	0	0	0	0	0	0	0	0	1	25,463
Gardena[2]	6	0	1	0	0	0	1	1	1	1	58,535
Garden Grove	0	2	0	0	0	0	1	1	0	0	169,157
Glendale	2	0	1	0	0	0	1	1		1	188,599
Gridley	1	0	0	0	0	0	0		1	0	7,349
Hanford	2	0	0	0	0	0	1	0	1	0	58,990
Hawaiian Gardens	2	0	0	0	0	0	2	0			13,510
Hawthorne	2	0	0	0	0	0	0	0	1	1	84,283
Hayward	3	0	0	0	0	1	1	0	2	1	156,458
Healdsburg	1	0	0	0	0	0	0	0	0	1	11,229
Hemet[2]	1	0	2	0	0	0	1	0	0	1	91,046
Hercules	1	0	0	0	0	0	0	0	1	0	26,157
Highland[2]	3	0	0	0	0	0	0	0	2		57,248
Hillsborough	0	0	1	0	0	0	0	1	0	0	10,678
Hollister	1	0	0	0	0	0	0	0	1	0	44,823
Huntington Beach[2]	5	1	3	0	0	0	3	3	1		194,618
Huntington Park	1	0	0	0	0	0	1	0			52,507
Industry	1	0	0	0	0	0	1	0			241
Irvine[2]	14	3	3	0	0	0	3	5	6	5	311,696
Irwindale	1	0	0	0	0	0	0	0	1	0	1,410
Kingsburg	0	1	0	0	0	0	0	1			12,879
La Canada Flintridge	1	0	0	0	0	0	0	1			19,682
Lafayette	1	0	0	0	0	0	0	0	1	0	25,031
Laguna Beach	0	0	1	0	0	0	0	0	1		22,559
Laguna Niguel[2]	2	0	0	0	0	0	0	0	1	0	64,119
Laguna Woods	0	1	0	0	0	0	1	0	0	0	17,249
La Habra	1	0	0	0	0	0	0	0	0	1	62,082
Lake Forest	1	0	0	0	0	0	0	0	0	1	85,480
Lakeport[2]	0	0	5	0	0	0	1	2	0	1	5,171
Lakewood	5	0	0	0	0	0	1	4			78,858
Lancaster	4	0	0	0	0	0	0	1	3		167,481
La Palma	1	0	0	0	0	0	1	0	0	0	15,236
La Verne	1	0	0	1	0	0	0	1	1	0	30,060
Lawndale	0	0	1	0	0	0	1	0			30,480
Lemon Grove	0	1	0	0	0	0	0	0	0	1	27,208
Livermore	2	1	2	0	0	0	1	1	1	2	85,151
Livingston	1	0	0	0	0	0	0	1	0	0	14,897
Loma Linda[2]	2	0	0	0	0	0	0	0	1		25,350
Lomita	2	0	0	0	0	0	1	1			19,981
Lompoc[2]	1	0	0	0	1	0	0	0	0	1	43,363
Long Beach[2]	10	1	4	0	0	1	2	5	4	3	447,528
Los Altos	3	1	1	0	1	0	1	1	2	2	29,847
Los Angeles[2]	356	95	120	3	1	35	118	203	156	132	3,809,182
Los Banos	1	0	0	0	0	0	0	0	1	0	47,398
Los Gatos[2]	3	0	3	0	0	0	1	1	1	2	31,640
Lynwood	2	0	1	0	0	0	1			2	64,142
Madera	0	0	2	0	0	1	1	0	1	1	69,395
Malibu	1	1	0	0	0	0	0	1	1		10,226
Manhattan Beach	9	6	0	0	0	0	7	2	3	3	33,888
Manteca	1	0	0	0	0	0	0	1			87,677
Marina	1	0	0	0	0	0	0	1	0	0	22,651
Martinez	3	0	1	0	0	0	0	1	1	2	36,498
Marysville	0	0	1	0	0	0	1	0	0	0	12,711
Menlo Park	4	2	1	0	0	0	0	2	3	2	31,332
Merced	0	0	1	0	0	0	0	0	1	0	92,191
Mission Viejo	0	0	1	0	0	0	0	1	0	0	91,382
Modesto[2]	3	2	3	0	0	0	2	2	1	1	219,083
Monrovia	1	0	0	0	0	0	0	1	0	0	37,104
Montclair[2]	1	0	0	0	0	1	0	1	0	0	38,203
Montebello	1	0	0	0	0	0	0	0		1	59,909
Monterey	4	0	1	0	0	0	2	2	0	1	29,709
Monterey Park	2	0	0	0	0	0	0	1	0	1	58,352
Moraga	0	0	0	0	0	1	0	1	0	0	16,550
Moreno Valley	1	0	0	0	0	0	0	1			214,014
Morgan Hill	1	2	0	0	0	0	3	0	0	0	45,134
Mountain View	10	2	4	0	1	0	1	6	5	5	80,588
National City	0	0	1	1	0	0	0	0	0	2	55,676
Newark	0	0	2	0	0	0	0	1	1	0	46,861
Newport Beach	0	0	1	0	0	1	0			2	84,254
Norwalk	1	0	0	0	0	0	1	0			98,259
Oakdale[2]	0	4	0	0	1	0	0	1	1	2	23,284
Oakland[2]	9	2	4	0	0	0	1	5	6	2	428,374

Table 94. Hate Crime Incidents Per Bias Motivation and Quarter, by Selected State, Territory, Federal, and Agency, 2022—Continued

(Number.)

State/agency	Number of incidents per bias motivation						Number of incidents per quarter				Population[1]
	Race/ Ethnicity/ Ancestry	Religion	Sexual orientation	Disability	Gender	Gender Identity	1st quarter	2nd quarter	3rd quarter	4th quarter	
Oakley	1	0	0	0	0	0	0	0	1	0	44,061
Oceanside	6	0	0	0	0	0	1	2	2	1	171,844
Orange	2	1	0	0	0	0	1	0	1	1	135,862
Orinda	0	1	0	0	0	0	0	0	0	1	19,441
Oxnard	2	0	1	0	0	0	0	0	1	2	201,517
Pacifica	1	0	1	0	0	0	0	1	1	0	35,742
Palmdale	6	2	2	0	0	0	3	4		3	162,316
Palm Desert[2]	3	0	0	0	0	0	0	1			51,918
Palm Springs	6	0	0	0	0	0	2	4			45,463
Palo Alto	10	0	0	0	0	0	2	4	3	1	64,922
Parlier	2	0	0	1	0	0	0	0	3		14,760
Pasadena	1	1	1	0	0	0	2	0	1	0	133,312
Petaluma[2]	10	1	0	0	1	0	1	6	1	3	59,129
Pico Rivera[2]	1	0	1	0	0	2	1	0	2		59,557
Pinole	1	0	0	0	0	0	0	0	1	0	18,651
Pismo Beach[2]	3	0	1	0	0	0	0		1	2	8,015
Placerville[2]	3	0	0	0	0	0	0	1	1	0	10,951
Pleasant Hill	1	0	0	0	0	0	0	1	0	0	34,060
Pomona	1	2	1	0	0	0	2	0	1	1	145,600
Port Hueneme	0	1	0	0	0	0	1	0			21,545
Rancho Cordova	2	0	0	0	0	0	1	1			81,041
Rancho Mirage[2]	2	0	0	0	0	0	0	0	1		17,598
Rancho Palos Verdes	1	0	0	0	0	0	0	1			40,403
Redding[2]	6	0	0	0	0	0	3	0	2		93,531
Redlands	1	0	0	0	0	0	0	0	1	0	73,554
Redondo Beach[2]	13	2	0	0	0	0	3	4	2	5	68,332
Redwood City	4	1	2	0	0	0	1	0	3	3	79,182
Rialto	4	0	0	0	0	0	1	1	1	1	104,589
Richmond[2]	5	0	0	0	0	0	0	1	2	1	115,043
Ridgecrest	1	0	0	0	0	0	1	0	0	0	28,290
Riverside	8	3	1	0	0	0	5	1	5	1	319,889
Rocklin	2	0	0	0	0	0	1	0	1	0	74,168
Rohnert Park	1	0	0	0	0	0	1	0	0		44,479
Rosemead	1	0	0	0	0	0	0	0		1	49,368
Roseville	3	1	5	0	0	0	4	2	3		155,448
Sacramento	48	5	28	0	0	3	17	33	24	10	526,671
Salinas	1	1	1	0	0	0	0	1	1	1	162,187
San Bernardino	2	0	0	0	0	0	0	2			222,623
San Bruno	1	0	0	0	0	0	1	0	0	0	40,817
San Clemente	1	0	0	0	0	0	0	0	1	0	63,449
San Diego[2]	22	10	9	1	0	1	13	10	11	6	1,377,838
San Fernando	2	0	0	0	0	0	0	0	2		23,501
San Francisco[2]	15	9	9	0	1	3	11	11	5	9	764,693
San Jose[2]	83	9	23	0	0	2	15	32	33	28	956,814
San Juan Capistrano[2]	2	0	0	0	0	0	1	0	0	0	34,698
San Leandro	0	0	1	0	0	0	1	0			86,465
San Luis Obispo[2]	10	2	1	0	0	1	2	4	1	6	47,990
San Marcos	1	0	0	0	0	0	1	0	0	0	94,879
San Mateo	11	0	1	0	0	0	0	5	2	5	99,184
San Pablo[2]	0	0	2	0	0	0	0	0	1	0	31,498
San Rafael	3	0	1	0	0	0	0	2	2	0	60,386
Santa Ana[2]	10	19	2	0	0	2	12	11	7	2	308,995
Santa Barbara	1	0	0	0	0	0	0	1	0	0	87,817
Santa Clara[2]	4	2	0	0	0	0	1	0	4	0	126,877
Santa Clarita	8	3	1	0	0	0	3	6	1	2	220,765
Santa Cruz	5	1	3	0	0	0	1	1	4	3	61,650
Santa Maria	2	0	1	0	0	0	0	0	2	1	109,518
Santa Monica[2]	5	2	1	0	0	0	1	1	3	2	89,527
Santa Paula	1	0	0	0	0	0	1	0	0	0	30,851
Santa Rosa[2]	3	5	0	0	0	1	1	1	3	2	175,999
Santee	1	1	0	0	0	0	0	0	1	1	59,351
Saratoga	3	0	0	0	0	0	0			3	29,306
Scotts Valley	3	1	0	0	0	0	0	1	1	2	12,196
Seal Beach[2]	2	2	0	0	0	0	1	0	1	1	24,665
Sebastopol	0	1	0	0	0	0	0	0	1	0	7,393
Simi Valley[2]	9	1	0	0	0	0	6	1	1	1	125,585
Solana Beach	1	0	0	0	0	0	0	1	0	0	12,778
Sonora	0	1	0	0	0	0	0	0	1		5,025
South El Monte	1	0	0	0	0	0	0			1	19,523
South Gate	1	0	0	0	0	0	1	0			89,698
South Lake Tahoe	0	0	1	0	0	0	0		0	1	21,525
South Pasadena[2]	2	1	1	0	0	0	0	1	1	1	25,744
South San Francisco	2	2	1	0	1	0	4	1	1	0	62,427
Stanton	1	0	0	0	0	0	0	0	0	1	38,038
Stockton[2]	12	4	2	0	0	1	6	2	4	5	323,501
Suisun City	2	0	1	0	0	0	0	1	0	2	28,917
Sunnyvale[2]	15	0	1	0	2	0	0	2	2	11	148,739
Susanville[2]	0	1	3	0	0	0	0	2	1	0	16,493
Taft	0	0	1	0	0	0	0	1	0	0	8,674

Table 94. Hate Crime Incidents Per Bias Motivation and Quarter, by Selected State, Territory, Federal, and Agency, 2022—Continued

(Number.)

State/agency	Number of incidents per bias motivation						Number of incidents per quarter				Population[1]
	Race/ Ethnicity/ Ancestry	Religion	Sexual orientation	Disability	Gender	Gender Identity	1st quarter	2nd quarter	3rd quarter	4th quarter	
Tehachapi	3	1	0	0	0	0	0	1	2	1	13,212
Temple City	1	0	0	0	0	0	1	0			35,103
Thousand Oaks	2	0	1	0	0	0	0	0	1	2	124,862
Torrance[2]	11	0	0	0	0	0	1	3	3	3	140,499
Tracy	2	0	2	0	0	0	0	1	1	2	97,219
Turlock	1	0	1	0	0	0	0	0	1	1	72,753
Tustin[2]	4	0	1	1	0	0	0	3	1	1	78,841
Union City[2]	7	1	1	0	0	0	2	3	2	1	66,947
Upland[2]	5	0	1	0	0	0	0	2	1	2	79,430
Vacaville	1	0	1	0	0	0	0	0	1	1	103,486
Vallejo	2	0	0	0	1	0	0	0	1	2	123,940
Ventura	1	0	0	0	0	0	1	0	0	0	109,439
Victorville	2	0	0	0	0	0	0	2			137,169
Visalia[2]	7	1	2	0	0	0	4	2	2	1	144,137
Vista	1	0	0	0	0	0	1	0	0	0	98,802
Walnut	2	1	0	0	0	0	2	1			27,253
Walnut Creek	2	0	0	0	0	0	1	1			69,417
Watsonville[2]	0	1	2	0	0	0	1	0		1	51,517
Weed	1	0	0	0	0	0	0		0	1	2,888
West Covina[2]	2	2	0	0	0	0	0	0	1	0	104,739
West Hollywood[2]	5	5	9	0	0	1	3	7	6	3	34,185
Westminster[2]	6	0	0	0	0	0	1	0	1	1	89,490
Wheatland	1	0	0	0	0	0	0	0	1		3,804
Woodland	2	1	1	0	0	1	0	3	2	0	61,883
Yorba Linda	1	0	0	0	0	0	1	0	0	0	67,550
Yuba City	0	0	1	0	0	0	0	1	0	0	69,122
Yucca Valley	1	0	0	0	0	0	0	1			21,890
Universities and Colleges	48	10	13	0	0	0					
California State Polytechnic University, Humboldt	0	0	2	0	0	0	0	0	1	1	7,184
California State University											
Chico	2	0	1	0	0	0	1	2	0	0	18,141
Fullerton	1	0	0	0	0	0	0		0	1	47,482
Monterey Bay	0	0	1	0	0	0	1	0	0	0	8,273
Northridge	1	0	0	0	0	0	0	0	0	1	43,286
San Jose[2]	10	0	0	0	0	0	0	1	2	6	39,940
San Marcos	10	0	0	0	0	0	0	1	9	0	17,565
Stanislaus[2]	1	1	0	0	0	0	0	0	0	1	12,470
Chaffey College	1	0	0	0	0	0	0	0	0	1	27,808
Foothill-De Anza College	0	0	1	0	0	0	0	0	0	1	56,506
Los Rios Community College[3]	0	1	1	0	0	0			1	1	
Pasadena Community College	3	3	0	0	0	0	2			4	35,760
Riverside Community College	1	0	0	0	0	0	0	0	1		59,448
San Diego State University	0	2	1	0	0	0	1	1		1	38,811
San Francisco State University	1	0	2	0	0	0	2	0	1	0	31,072
Sonoma State University	1	0	0	0	0	0	0	1	0	0	8,775
University of California											
Berkeley[2]	5	0	1	0	0	0	0	0	3	2	45,584
Davis	1	0	0	0	0	0	0	1	0	0	41,743
Irvine	1	0	0	0	0	0	0	0	0	1	38,479
Los Angeles	2	0	1	0	0	0	1	0	1	1	47,499
Riverside	2	0	1	0	0	0	0	0	3	0	28,597
San Francisco	1	0	0	0	0	0	1	0	0	0	3,313
Santa Barbara	1	0	0	0	0	0	0	1	0	0	28,222
Santa Cruz[2]	3	2	1	0	0	0	3	0	1	1	20,781
Ventura County Community College District	0	1	0	0	0	0	0	0	1	0	50,633
Metropolitan Counties	90	16	33	0	3	2					
Alameda	2	0	2	0	0	0	0	0	1	3	
Butte	0	1	1	0	0	0	0	2	0	0	
Contra Costa	2	1	0	0	0	0	0	0	1	2	
El Dorado	2	0	3	0	3	2	2	2	3	3	
Fresno[2]	3	0	0	0	0	0	0	2			
Kern[2]	3	0	0	0	0	0	0	1	1		
Kings	2	0	0	0	0	0	1	1	0	0	
Los Angeles	18	4	5	0	0	0	5	9	9	4	
Madera	1	2	0	0	0	0	0	1	2	0	
Merced	1	0	0	0	0	0	0	0	1	0	
Monterey	1	0	0	0	0	0	1	0	0	0	
Napa	0	0	1	0	0	0	0	0	1	0	
Orange	1	0	0	0	0	0	0	0	1	0	
Placer	2	0	1	0	0	0	0	2		1	
Riverside	1	0	0	0	0	0	0	1			
Sacramento	5	2	2	0	0	0	3	2	4		
San Bernardino[2]	5	0	3	0	0	0	1	3	2		
San Diego[2]	13	0	4	0	0	0	8	3	2	2	
San Luis Obispo	0	1	0	0	0	0	0	0	1	0	
San Mateo	3	2	2	0	0	0	0	1	3	3	
Santa Barbara[2]	7	1	5	0	0	0	4	2	4	2	

Table 94. Hate Crime Incidents Per Bias Motivation and Quarter, by Selected State, Territory, Federal, and Agency, 2022—Continued

(Number.)

State/agency	Number of incidents per bias motivation						Number of incidents per quarter				
	Race/ Ethnicity/ Ancestry	Religion	Sexual orientation	Disability	Gender	Gender Identity	1st quarter	2nd quarter	3rd quarter	4th quarter	Population[1]
Santa Clara	3	1	1	0	0	0	1	1		3	
Santa Cruz[2]	5	1	2	0	0	0	2	3	0	1	
Solano	1	0	0	0	0	0	1	0			
Sonoma	2	0	0	0	0	0	0	2	0	0	
Sutter	1	0	0	0	0	0	0			1	
Tulare	1	0	0	0	0	0	0	1			
Ventura	1	0	1	0	0	0	2	0			
Yolo	1	0	0	0	0	0	0	0	1		
Yuba[2]	3	0	0	0	0	0	1			1	
Nonmetropolitan Counties	4	4	4	0	0	0					
Amador	0	0	1	0	0	0	0	0	1	0	
Humboldt	0	0	2	0	0	0	0	0	1	1	
Lake	1	0	0	0	0	0	0	0	0	1	
Lassen	0	1	1	0	0	0	0	1	1	0	
Mariposa	1	0	0	0	0	0	0	0	0	1	
Nevada	1	0	0	0	0	0	0	0	1	0	
Tehama	0	2	0	0	0	0	0	0	0	2	
Trinity	1	1	0	0	0	0	1	1	0	0	
State Police Agencies	3	0	0	0	0	0					
Highway Patrol											
Bishop Area Office	1	0	0	0	0	0	0	0	0	1	
Capitol Protection Section	2	0	0	0	0	0	1	1	0	0	
Other Agencies	19	3	4	0	0	0					
Atascadero State Hospital	1	0	0	0	0	0	0	0	1	0	
Coalinga State Hospital	1	0	0	0	0	0	1	0	0	0	
East Bay Regional Park District	1	3	0	0	0	0	1	2	1	0	
Kern High School District	3	0	1	0	0	0	1	1	1	1	
Metropolitan State Hospital	2	0	0	0	0	0	0	0	2	0	
Napa State Hospital	1	0	0	0	0	0	0	0	0	1	
Patton State Hospital	2	0	1	0	0	0	0	1	2	0	
Porterville Developmental Center	1	0	0	0	0	0	0	0	1	0	
Port of San Diego Harbor	4	0	0	0	0	0	0	1	2	1	
San Bernardino Unified School District	1	0	0	0	0	0	0	0	1	0	
Santa Clara Transit District	2	0	0	0	0	0	0	1		1	
Stockton Unified School District	0	0	1	0	0	0	0	1	0	0	
Twin Rivers Unified School District	0	0	1	0	0	0	1	0	0	0	
COLORADO	201	46	71	4	1	20					
Cities	163	41	65	3	1	14					
Alamosa	1	0	0	0	0	0	0	1	0	0	9,874
Arvada	0	0	1	0	0	1	0	1	0	1	122,403
Aspen	1	0	0	0	0	0	0	0	0	1	6,910
Aurora[2]	15	1	3	0	0	1	2	10	3	2	392,134
Avon	2	0	0	0	0	0	0	1	1	0	5,968
Bayfield	1	0	0	1	0	0	1	0	0	1	2,929
Black Hawk	1	0	0	0	0	0	0	0	1	0	129
Boulder[2]	4	3	1	0	1	0	1	3	1	2	103,099
Brighton	1	0	0	0	0	0	0	0	0	1	41,205
Canon City	0	1	1	0	0	0	0	1	0	1	17,582
Carbondale	0	0	1	0	0	0	0	1	0	0	6,528
Castle Rock	2	0	2	0	0	0	2	0	2	0	79,102
Centennial[2]	27	5	1	0	0	0	5	9	9	7	105,849
Colorado Springs	8	2	4	0	0	0	3	0	5	6	487,728
Commerce City	1	0	0	0	0	0	1	0	0	0	65,817
Delta	0	0	0	1	0	0	0	1	0	0	9,373
Denver[2]	35	12	34	1	0	5	15	15	23	29	705,264
Durango	2	2	1	0	0	0	3	2	0		19,402
Englewood	2	0	0	0	0	0	2	0	0	0	33,452
Erie	3	0	1	0	0	0	0	2	1	1	32,832
Evans	0	0	0	0	0	1	0	1	0	0	22,333
Federal Heights	1	1	0	0	0	0	1	1	0	0	13,987
Firestone[2]	1	1	1	0	0	0	0	0	1	0	17,971
Fort Collins[2]	7	1	1	0	0	1	3	0	3	2	168,045
Frisco	0	0	1	0	0	0	0	1	0	0	2,858
Garden City	1	0	0	0	0	0	0	0	1	0	256
Glendale	3	0	0	0	0	0	1	2	0	0	4,502
Glenwood Springs	1	0	0	0	0	1	0	0	2	0	10,664
Grand Junction	4	0	1	0	0	0	1	4	0	0	68,126
Greeley	2	0	0	0	0	0	0	0	1	1	109,258
Gunnison	1	0	0	0	0	0	0	0	0	1	6,914
Johnstown	1	0	0	0	0	0	0	0	0	1	19,093
Lafayette	2	1	0	0	0	0	3	0	0	0	31,204
La Junta	1	0	0	0	0	0	0	0	1	0	7,264
Lakewood	0	0	1	0	0	0	0	0	0	1	157,068
Littleton	0	0	1	0	0	0	1	0	0	0	44,821
Lone Tree	6	0	0	0	0	0	1	3	2	0	14,204

Table 94. Hate Crime Incidents Per Bias Motivation and Quarter, by Selected State, Territory, Federal, and Agency, 2022—Continued

(Number.)

State/agency	Number of incidents per bias motivation						Number of incidents per quarter				Population[1]
	Race/ Ethnicity/ Ancestry	Religion	Sexual orientation	Disability	Gender	Gender Identity	1st quarter	2nd quarter	3rd quarter	4th quarter	
Longmont[2]	8	4	0	0	0	0	2	0	5	2	101,159
Louisville	2	1	0	0	0	0	0	1	2	0	20,587
Loveland	0	0	1	0	0	1	0	2	0	0	77,770
Mancos	0	0	1	0	0	0	1	0	0		1,240
Montrose	1	0	3	0	0	0	1	2	1	0	20,944
Monument	0	1	0	0	0	0	0	0	1	0	11,300
Parker	3	0	0	0	0	1	0	1	0	3	61,865
Pueblo	1	0	0	0	0	0	0	1	0	0	112,618
Rifle	2	0	0	0	0	0	0	1	1	0	10,612
Sheridan	1	0	0	0	0	0	0	0	1	0	5,964
Steamboat Springs	0	2	1	0	0	0	0	1	1	1	13,593
Sterling	0	0	1	0	0	0	1	0	0	0	13,713
Telluride[2]	0	2	0	0	0	0	0	1	0	0	2,590
Thornton[2]	4	0	1	0	0	0	0	1	1	1	143,055
Timnath	1	0	0	0	0	0	0	0	0	1	9,063
Trinidad	2	0	0	0	0	0	1	1	0	0	8,350
Westminster	1	0	0	0	0	0	0	1	0	0	112,844
Wheat Ridge	0	0	1	0	0	1	2	0	0	0	33,104
Windsor	0	1	0	0	0	1	2	0	0	0	38,498
Universities and Colleges	3	0	2	0	0	0					
Adams State University[2]	2	0	1	0	0	0	0	0	0	2	3,863
University of Colorado, Boulder	0	0	1	0	0	0	0	0	0	1	41,927
University of Northern Colorado	1	0	0	0	0	0	1	0	0	0	13,818
Metropolitan Counties	31	5	4	1	0	3					
Adams	2	0	0	0	0	1	2	0	1	0	
Arapahoe[2]	18	2	0	0	0	0	4	2	7	5	
Boulder	1	1	0	0	0	0	1	1	0	0	
Douglas	1	0	2	1	0	0	0	0	2	2	
Gilpin	2	0	0	0	0	0	1	1	0	0	
Jefferson	2	2	1	0	0	1	0	1	4	1	
Larimer	3	0	0	0	0	1	2	0	0	2	
Mesa	2	0	0	0	0	0	0	1	1	0	
Park	0	0	1	0	0	0	1	0	0	0	
Nonmetropolitan Counties	3	0	0	0	0	3					
Las Animas	0	0	0	0	0	3	1	0	1	1	
Saguache	1	0	0	0	0	0	0	1	0	0	
Summit	2	0	0	0	0	0	1	0	0	1	
Tribal Agencies	1	0	0	0	0	0					
Ute Mountain Tribal	1	0	0	0	0	0	0	0	1	0	
CONNECTICUT	61	18	16	1	0	2					
Cities	55	17	12	1	0	2					
Bethel	1	0	0	0	0	0	1	0	0	0	20,728
Bridgeport	1	1	1	0	0	0	1	1	0	1	148,395
Cromwell	1	0	0	0	0	0	0	0	0	1	14,360
Danbury	1	0	0	0	0	0	0	0	0	1	87,164
Derby	2	0	0	0	0	0	0	1	1	0	12,243
East Haven[2]	0	2	0	0	0	0	0	0	1	0	27,725
Enfield	1	0	0	0	0	0	0	0	1	0	41,912
Fairfield	3	0	0	0	0	0	2	1	0	0	62,270
Farmington	0	1	0	0	0	0	0	0	0	1	26,618
Glastonbury	1	0	0	0	0	0	0	0	1	0	35,034
Greenwich	1	1	0	0	0	0	0	1	1	0	63,631
Hamden	1	1	0	0	0	0	0	0	0	2	60,831
Madison[2]	1	0	0	1	0	0	1	0	0	0	17,581
Manchester	3	0	1	0	0	0	0	3	1	0	59,293
Meriden	1	0	0	0	0	0	0	0	0	1	60,332
Middlebury	1	0	0	0	0	0	0	0	0	1	7,793
Middletown	1	0	0	0	0	0	1	0	0	0	47,256
Milford	1	0	1	0	0	0	0	0	1	1	52,694
New Britain[2]	6	8	2	0	0	2	8	2	4	1	73,621
New Haven	1	0	2	0	0	0	0	0	1	2	136,205
New London	0	1	0	0	0	0	1	0	0	0	27,667
Norwalk	0	0	1	0	0	0	0	0	0	1	91,414
Norwich	1	0	0	0	0	0	0	1	0	0	40,096
Orange[2]	3	0	1	0	0	0	0	1	2	0	14,239
Plainville	1	0	0	0	0	0	0	1	0	0	17,413
Simsbury	1	0	0	0	0	0	0	0	0	1	25,135
Stamford	5	0	0	0	0	0	1	2	0	2	136,936
Stratford	1	0	0	0	0	0	0	1	0	0	52,320
Suffield[2]	3	0	0	0	0	0	1	1	0	0	15,890
Torrington	5	1	1	0	0	0	1	3	0	3	35,302
Watertown	1	0	0	0	0	0	1	0	0	0	22,122
West Hartford	1	0	0	0	0	0	1	0	0	0	63,934
Wethersfield[2]	1	1	2	0	0	0	0	2	0	0	27,038

Table 94. Hate Crime Incidents Per Bias Motivation and Quarter, by Selected State, Territory, Federal, and Agency, 2022—Continued

(Number.)

State/agency	Race/ Ethnicity/ Ancestry	Religion	Sexual orientation	Disability	Gender	Gender Identity	1st quarter	2nd quarter	3rd quarter	4th quarter	Population[1]
Willimantic	2	0	0	0	0	0	2	0	0	0	17,777
Windsor Locks	1	0	0	0	0	0	1	0	0	0	12,497
Woodbridge	1	0	0	0	0	0	0	0	1	0	9,020
Universities and Colleges	1	0	3	0	0	0					
Central Connecticut State University	0	0	1	0	0	0	0	0	0	1	12,467
Yale University	1	0	2	0	0	0	1	0	0	2	13,555
State Police Agencies	5	1	1	0	0	0					
Connecticut State Police[2]	5	1	1	0	0	0	1	3	1	1	
DELAWARE	10	4	2	0	0	0					
Cities	3	0	1	0	0	0					
Delaware City	1	0	0	0	0	0	1	0	0	0	1,881
Milford	0	0	1	0	0	0	0	0	0	1	13,326
Ocean View	1	0	0	0	0	0	0	1	0	0	2,851
Smyrna	1	0	0	0	0	0	0	1	0	0	13,361
Universities and Colleges	3	4	1	0	0	0					
University of Delaware	3	4	1	0	0	0	1	4	1	2	25,695
Metropolitan Counties	2	0	0	0	0	0					
New Castle County Police Department	2	0	0	0	0	0	1	0	1	0	
State Police Agencies	2	0	0	0	0	0					
State Police											
New Castle County	1	0	0	0	0	0	0	0	0	1	
Sussex County	1	0	0	0	0	0	0	0	0	1	
DISTRICT OF COLUMBIA	72	4	52	1	0	23					
Cities	52	4	47	0	0	22					
Washington	52	4	47	0	0	22	16	48	32	29	671,803
Other Agencies	20	0	5	1	0	1					
Metro Transit Police[2]	20	0	5	1	0	1	7	6	6	7	
FLORIDA	82	38	37	0	0	4					
Cities	36	19	11	0	0	2					
Aventura	0	2	0	0	0	0	1	0	0	1	38,484
Clearwater	2	1	0	0	0	0	0			3	116,303
Davie	1	1	0	0	0	0	0	1	1	0	104,215
Dunedin	0	0	1	0	0	0	0	1	0	0	35,871
Hallandale Beach	1	0	0	0	0	0	0	1			40,919
Homestead	0	0	1	0	0	0			1		80,633
Kissimmee	1	0	0	0	0	0	0	1	0	0	79,715
Largo	4	1	1	0	0	0	1	2	2	1	82,167
Miami	3	2	1	0	0	0		2	2	2	437,900
Miami Beach	0	7	5	0	0	1	5	4	4		79,031
Miami Shores	0	1	0	0	0	0	0	0	1		11,217
Miramar	1	0	0	0	0	0	0	1			135,785
Ocala	2	1	0	0	0	0	1	0	2	0	64,596
Orlando	3	0	1	0	0	0	1		1	2	310,713
Port St. Lucie	1	0	0	0	0	0	1				228,855
South Daytona	2	0	0	0	0	0	1	1			13,712
St. Augustine	1	0	1	0	0	0	1	0	0	1	14,875
St. Petersburg	4	2	0	0	0	0	5	1			257,745
Sunny Isles Beach	6	0	0	0	0	0	0	1	2	3	21,908
Tallahassee	2	0	0	0	0	0	0	2			197,865
Tampa	2	1	0	0	0	0	1	1	0	1	390,145
Titusville	0	0	0	0	0	1	0	0	1		48,979
Universities and Colleges	1	0	3	0	0	0					
Florida State University, Tallahassee	1	0	1	0	0	0	0	0	1	1	49,091
University of Florida	0	0	2	0	0	0	0	0	2	0	60,790
Metropolitan Counties	45	19	22	0	0	2					
Alachua[2]	3	0	0	0	0	0	1	0	0	1	
Collier[2]	1	1	3	0	0	1	1	1	0	0	
Flagler	1	0	2	0	0	0	3	0			
Jacksonville Sheriff's Office[2]	5	2	2	0	0	0	4	0	3	1	
Lee	8	2	2	0	0	0	4	3	3	2	
Marion	3	0	1	0	0	0	0	2	0	2	
Miami-Dade[2]	13	10	6	0	0	1	8	5	7	6	
Orange	2	2	3	0	0	0	5	1		1	
Palm Beach	0	0	1	0	0	0	0	0	1		
Pinellas	1	0	0	0	0	0	1	0	0	0	
Polk	1	0	0	0	0	0	1				
Sarasota[2]	3	2	0	0	0	0	2	2	0	0	
Seminole	1	0	0	0	0	0	0			1	
St. Johns	3	0	0	0	0	0	1	1	0	1	
Volusia	0	0	2	0	0	0	1	1			

Table 94. Hate Crime Incidents Per Bias Motivation and Quarter, by Selected State, Territory, Federal, and Agency, 2022—Continued

(Number.)

State/agency	Number of incidents per bias motivation						Number of incidents per quarter				Population[1]
	Race/ Ethnicity/ Ancestry	Religion	Sexual orientation	Disability	Gender	Gender Identity	1st quarter	2nd quarter	3rd quarter	4th quarter	
Tribal Agencies	0	0	1	0	0	0					
Seminole Tribal	0	0	1	0	0	0	1	0	0	0	
GEORGIA	126	24	31	5	5	6					
Cities	61	16	11	3	1	6					
Albany	0	0	1	0	0	0	1	0	0	0	68,613
Athens-Clarke County[2]	1	5	0	1	0	1	0	0	1	6	128,177
Atlanta	2	0	0	0	0	0	0	2	0	0	495,707
Bloomingdale	1	0	0	0	0	0	0	0	1	0	2,849
Brookhaven	8	5	1	0	0	0	2	1	4	7	55,614
Carrollton	1	0	0	0	0	0	0	1	0	0	27,844
Cartersville	1	0	0	0	0	0	1	0	0	0	23,293
Cedartown	1	0	0	0	0	0	0	0	1	0	10,397
Chamblee	2	0	0	0	0	0	0	0	2	0	29,393
College Park	0	0	1	0	0	0	1	0	0	0	13,917
Decatur	1	1	0	0	0	0	0	1	0	1	24,259
Dunwoody	2	0	0	0	0	0	0	2	0	0	50,271
Folkston	1	0	0	0	0	0	0	0	1	0	4,457
Gainesville	5	1	0	0	0	0	0	1	1	4	44,314
Greenville[2]	4	0	0	0	0	0	1	1	1	0	799
Griffin	1	0	0	0	0	0	0	1	0	0	23,862
Hephzibah	0	0	0	1	0	0	0	0	1	0	3,778
Hinesville	0	1	0	0	0	0	0	0	0	1	35,443
Hiram	2	0	0	0	0	0	0	0	0	2	5,203
Jefferson	0	0	1	0	0	0	0	0	1	0	14,664
Johns Creek	1	1	0	0	0	0	0	0	2	0	81,964
Lithonia	15	0	0	0	1	4	16	1	2	1	2,585
Loganville[2]	0	0	2	0	0	0	1	0	0	0	15,250
Marietta[2]	5	0	1	0	0	0	1	2	1	1	62,059
Rome	2	0	0	0	0	0	2	0	0	0	37,778
Sandy Springs	0	2	2	1	0	0	1	2	2	0	106,747
Smyrna	3	0	0	0	0	0	2	1	0	0	55,735
Statesboro	0	0	0	0	0	1	0	1	0	0	33,590
Suwanee	2	0	0	0	0	0	0	1	1	0	22,911
Thomasville	0	0	1	0	0	0	0	1	0	0	18,836
Toccoa	0	0	1	0	0	0	0	0	1	0	9,218
Universities and Colleges	6	1	1	0	0	0					
Emory University	1	0	0	0	0	0	1	0	0	0	15,201
Georgia College and State University	1	0	0	0	0	0	0	0	0	1	7,914
Spelman College	3	0	0	0	0	0	2	0	0	1	2,286
University of Georgia	0	1	0	0	0	0	0	0	1	0	43,314
University of West Georgia	1	0	0	0	0	0	0	1	0	0	16,100
Young Harris College	0	0	1	0	0	0	0	0	0	1	1,620
Metropolitan Counties	51	4	15	0	2	0					
Carroll	4	0	1	0	0	0	0	1	1	3	
Cobb	0	0	2	0	0	0	0	2	0	0	
Cobb County Police Department	22	2	1	0	0	0	5	8	8	4	
DeKalb County Police Department	1	0	0	0	0	0	0	0	0	1	
Fayette	1	0	0	0	0	0	1	0	0	0	
Floyd County Police Department	1	0	1	0	0	0	2	0	0	0	
Forsyth	1	0	2	0	0	0	0	3	0	0	
Fulton County Police Department	1	0	0	0	0	0	1	0	0	0	
Glynn County Police Department	1	0	0	0	0	0	1	0	0	0	
Gwinnett	0	0	1	0	0	0	0	0	0	1	
Gwinnett County Police Department[2]	13	2	7	0	2	0	1	10	7	3	
Hall	2	0	0	0	0	0	1	1	0	0	
McIntosh	1	0	0	0	0	0	0	0	0	1	
Oconee	1	0	0	0	0	0	0	1	0	0	
Paulding	2	0	0	0	0	0	0	2	0	0	
Nonmetropolitan Counties	3	1	2	0	0	0					
Ben Hill	1	0	0	0	0	0	0	0	0	1	
Camden	1	0	0	0	0	0	0	1	0	0	
Crisp	0	1	0	0	0	0	1	0	0	0	
Dodge	0	0	1	0	0	0	0	1	0	0	
Habersham	1	0	0	0	0	0	0	0	1	0	
Rabun	0	0	1	0	0	0	0	1	0	0	
Other Agencies	5	2	2	2	2	0					
Chatham County Board of Education	3	0	0	0	0	0	0	0	1	2	
Cobb County Board of Education[2]	0	0	2	2	2	0	0	0	0	4	
Fulton County School System	1	2	0	0	0	0	1	0	0	2	
Georgia World Congress	1	0	0	0	0	0	0	0	0	1	
HAWAII	26	1	2	3	0	1					
Cities	19	0	2	2	0	1					
Honolulu[2]	19	0	2	2	0	1	7	8	4	4	994,799

Table 94. Hate Crime Incidents Per Bias Motivation and Quarter, by Selected State, Territory, Federal, and Agency, 2022—Continued

(Number.)

State/agency	Number of incidents per bias motivation						Number of incidents per quarter				Population[1]
	Race/Ethnicity/Ancestry	Religion	Sexual orientation	Disability	Gender	Gender Identity	1st quarter	2nd quarter	3rd quarter	4th quarter	
Metropolitan Counties	0	1	0	0	0	0					
Maui Police Department	0	1	0	0	0	0	1	0	0		
Nonmetropolitan Counties	7	0	0	1	0	0					
Kauai Police Department	7	0	0	1	0	0	1	4	3	0	
IDAHO	28	3	9	0	0	0					
Cities	24	1	9	0	0	0					
Blackfoot	1	0	0	0	0	0	0	0	1	0	12,437
Boise[2]	10	0	4	0	0	0	3	2	3	5	239,074
Chubbuck	1	1	0	0	0	0	0	0	1	1	15,970
Coeur d'Alene	1	0	0	0	0	0	0	0	1	0	57,061
Meridian[2]	2	0	0	0	0	0	1	0	0	0	132,522
Mountain Home	1	0	0	0	0	0	1	0	0	0	16,357
Nampa[2]	5	0	4	0	0	0	1	1	4	2	111,501
Pocatello	0	0	1	0	0	0	1	0	0	0	57,914
Rexburg	1	0	0	0	0	0	0	0	0	1	35,711
Twin Falls	2	0	0	0	0	0	1	1	0	0	54,648
Metropolitan Counties	3	1	0	0	0	0					
Ada	3	1	0	0	0	0	1	0	3	0	
Nonmetropolitan Counties	0	1	0	0	0	0					
Valley	0	1	0	0	0	0	0	0	1	0	
Tribal Agencies	1	0	0	0	0	0					
Fort Hall Tribal	1	0	0	0	0	0	1	0	0	0	
ILLINOIS	190	68	75	1	3	9					
Cities	170	62	72	1	3	7					
Aledo	0	0	1	0	0	0	1	0	0	0	3,602
Alton	2	0	0	0	0	0	0	1	0	1	25,212
Antioch	1	0	0	0	0	0				1	15,017
Arcola	0	1	0	0	0	0	1	0	0	0	2,874
Bartonville	1	0	0	0	0	0	0	1	0	0	5,789
Batavia[2]	0	0	7	0	0	0	0	4	0	0	26,088
Berwyn	0	0	1	0	0	0	1	0	0	0	54,654
Bolingbrook	0	2	0	0	0	0	0	2	0	0	73,364
Calumet Park	25	0	0	0	0	1	6	8	5	7	6,711
Chicago[2]	67	37	31	0	0	5	37	35	31	26	2,652,124
Chicago Heights[2]	5	0	2	0	1	0	1	2	3	0	26,393
Cicero	2	0	0	0	0	0	0	0	2	0	81,492
Collinsville	0	0	1	0	0	0	0	0	1	0	24,131
Country Club Hills	1	0	0	0	0	0				1	16,100
Decatur[2]	0	0	3	0	0	0	1	0	0	0	68,789
DeKalb	0	0	1	0	0	0	1	0	0	0	40,555
East Moline	1	0	0	0	0	0	0	0	0	1	20,922
Evanston	1	0	1	0	0	0	0	0	2	0	76,259
Forest Park	1	0	0	0	0	0	0	0	0	1	13,740
Franklin Park	1	0	0	0	0	0	0	0	0	1	18,230
Geneva	0	0	6	0	0	0	0	0	4	2	21,152
Glencoe[2]	0	1	2	0	0	0	0	2	0	0	8,567
Glenview	0	3	0	0	0	0	3	0	0	0	47,092
Grayslake	1	0	0	0	0	0	1	0	0	0	24,519
Gurnee	1	0	0	0	0	0	0	0	0	1	30,361
Hazel Crest	2	0	1	0	0	0	0	2	0	1	12,849
Highland Park	0	1	2	0	0	0	2	1	0	0	30,173
Hillsboro	0	0	1	0	0	0	0	0	1	0	5,860
Hoffman Estates	1	0	0	0	0	0	0	0	0	1	50,385
Homer Glen[2]	1	2	0	0	0	0	0	1	1	0	24,524
Homewood	0	1	0	0	0	0	0	0	1	0	18,634
Huntley	2	0	1	1	0	0	0	2	1	1	28,223
Johnsburg	1	0	0	0	0	0	0	0	1	0	6,395
Joliet	7	3	2	0	0	0	1	3	7	1	150,545
Lake in the Hills	1	0	2	0	0	0	0	0	3	0	28,961
Lansing	1	0	0	0	0	0	0	0	0	1	27,828
Litchfield	1	0	0	0	0	0	0	0	0	1	6,705
Marshall	1	0	0	0	0	0	0	0	0	1	3,867
Melrose Park	1	0	0	0	0	0	0	1	0	0	23,739
Milan	1	0	0	0	0	0	0	1	0	0	4,994
Mokena[2]	2	1	0	0	0	0	0	2	0	0	19,829
Moline	1	2	1	0	0	0	0	1	3	1	42,009
Monmouth	1	0	0	0	1	0	0	0	0	1	8,652
Morris	1	0	0	0	0	0	0	0	0	1	14,511
Mount Prospect[2]	1	1	0	0	0	0	0	0	1	0	54,477
New Lenox	2	0	0	0	0	0	1	1	0	0	27,699
Niles	0	1	0	0	0	0	0	0	1	0	29,784
Normal	0	0	3	0	0	1	0	1	1	2	53,613
Northbrook	1	0	0	0	0	0			1	0	34,039

Table 94. Hate Crime Incidents Per Bias Motivation and Quarter, by Selected State, Territory, Federal, and Agency, 2022—Continued

(Number.)

State/agency	Number of incidents per bias motivation						Number of incidents per quarter				Population[1]
	Race/ Ethnicity/ Ancestry	Religion	Sexual orientation	Disability	Gender	Gender Identity	1st quarter	2nd quarter	3rd quarter	4th quarter	
Oak Lawn	0	0	1	0	0	0	1	0	0	0	55,957
Oak Park	1	0	0	0	0	0	0	0	0	1	52,152
Ottawa	1	0	0	0	0	0	0	0	0	1	18,696
Palatine	2	0	0	0	0	0	0	0	1	1	65,078
Park Forest	0	1	0	0	0	0	0	0	0	1	20,896
Plainfield	1	0	0	0	0	0	0	0	1	0	46,004
Richton Park	1	1	0	0	0	0		1	1	0	12,259
River Grove	1	0	0	0	0	0	0	1	0	0	10,504
Rock Falls[2]	3	0	0	0	0	0	0	0	1	1	8,687
Rock Island[2]	6	1	1	0	0	0	1	0	5	1	36,235
Rolling Meadows[2]	3	0	0	0	0	0	0	2	0	0	23,453
Roxana	1	0	0	0	0	0	0	1	0	0	1,438
Schaumburg[2]	2	0	0	0	0	0	0	0	0	1	75,745
Skokie	0	1	0	0	0	0	1	0	0	0	65,185
South Elgin	1	0	0	0	0	0	0	0	0	1	23,995
Steger	1	1	1	0	0	0	1	0	1	1	9,325
Streamwood[2]	3	0	0	0	0	0	0	0	1	1	37,923
Summit	1	0	0	0	0	0		0	0	1	10,658
Urbana	0	0	0	0	1	0	1	0			38,990
Washington	1	0	0	0	0	0	0	0	0	1	15,910
Wood River	1	1	0	0	0	0	0	2	0	0	10,350
Yorkville	1	0	0	0	0	0	1	0	0	0	23,635
Universities and Colleges	2	2	0	0	0	0					
University of Illinois											
Chicago[2]	1	1	0	0	0	0	0	0	0	1	36,710
Urbana	1	1	0	0	0	0	1	1	0	0	59,691
Metropolitan Counties	16	2	2	0	0	0					
Calhoun	1	0	0	0	0	0	0	0	1	0	
Jackson	0	1	0	0	0	0	1	0	0	0	
Madison	2	0	0	0	0	0	0	1	1	0	
Rock Island	11	0	0	0	0	0	0	3	4	4	
Tazewell	1	0	0	0	0	0	0	0	0	1	
Vermilion	1	0	0	0	0	0	1	0	0	0	
Will	0	1	2	0	0	0	1	0	0	2	
Nonmetropolitan Counties	2	1	1	0	0	0					
Effingham	1	0	0	0	0	0	1	0	0	0	
Jasper	1	0	0	0	0	0		0	0	1	
Livingston	0	0	1	0	0	0	0	0	0	1	
Stephenson	0	1	0	0	0	0	0	0	1	0	
State Police Agencies	0	1	0	0	0	2					
Illinois State Police	0	1	0	0	0	2	0	2	0	1	
INDIANA	117	17	30	1	1	8					
Cities	98	16	25	1	1	6					
Albion	0	0	1	0	0	0	0	1	0	0	2,232
Anderson	1	0	0	0	0	0	0	1	0	0	54,965
Angola	1	0	0	0	0	0	0	1	0	0	9,022
Auburn	1	0	0	0	0	0	0	0	1	0	13,645
Avon[2]	2	1	0	0	0	0	0	1	1	0	24,167
Bloomfield	1	0	0	0	0	0	0	0	1	0	2,246
Bloomington	1	2	1	0	0	0	2	0	2	0	80,135
Bristol	0	1	0	0	0	0	0	0	0	1	1,783
Carmel	1	0	0	0	0	0	0	1	0	0	101,670
Crawfordsville	2	0	0	0	0	0	0	0	1	1	16,449
Crown Point	0	0	2	0	0	1	2	0	0	1	34,731
Danville	2	0	0	0	0	0	0	1	0	1	10,925
East Chicago	6	0	0	0	0	0	4	0	2	0	25,941
Elkhart	2	0	0	0	0	0	1	1	0	0	53,947
Evansville	1	0	1	0	0	0	1	0	0	1	115,719
Fort Wayne	13	0	0	0	0	0	0	4	3	6	267,791
Frankfort	1	0	0	0	0	0	0	0	0	1	16,572
Franklin	1	1	0	0	0	0	0	1	1	0	25,714
Fremont	1	0	0	0	0	0	0	0	1	0	2,092
Goshen	0	2	1	0	0	0	1	1	1	0	34,697
Griffith	2	1	0	0	0	1	0	1	1	2	16,218
Hammond	6	1	1	0	0	0	2	4	1	1	76,366
Hartford City	0	0	1	0	0	0	0	0	1	0	6,060
Hobart	1	2	0	0	0	0	0	1	2	0	29,374
Huntingburg	0	1	0	0	0	0	0	0	0	1	6,459
Huntington	2	0	0	0	0	0	1	1	0	0	17,030
Indianapolis[2]	13	1	9	0	0	0	8	5	4	5	886,455
Jasper[2]	2	0	0	0	0	0	0	0	0	1	16,699
Jeffersonville	1	0	1	0	0	1	0	1	2	0	51,150
Kendallville	1	0	0	0	0	0	0	1	0	0	10,153
Kokomo	1	0	0	0	0	0	1	0	0	0	59,776
Lafayette[2]	7	1	3	0	0	1	4	1	5	1	70,861

Table 94. Hate Crime Incidents Per Bias Motivation and Quarter, by Selected State, Territory, Federal, and Agency, 2022—Continued

(Number.)

State/agency	Number of incidents per bias motivation						Number of incidents per quarter				Population[1]
	Race/ Ethnicity/ Ancestry	Religion	Sexual orientation	Disability	Gender	Gender Identity	1st quarter	2nd quarter	3rd quarter	4th quarter	
Lawrence	1	0	0	0	0	0	1	0	0	0	49,421
Lawrenceburg	0	0	0	0	1	0	0	1	0	0	5,142
Linton	0	0	1	0	0	0	1	0	0	0	5,147
Michigan City	1	0	1	0	0	1	0	2	1	0	32,051
New Haven	2	0	0	1	0	0	1	0	1	1	15,856
North Vernon	0	0	1	0	0	0	1	0	0	0	6,455
Plainfield	2	0	0	0	0	0	0	1	1	0	36,189
Portage	3	0	0	0	0	0	0	3	0	0	38,438
Sellersburg[2]	4	0	0	0	0	0	2	0	1	0	9,784
South Bend	1	0	0	0	0	0	1	0	0	0	103,179
Speedway	1	0	1	0	0	0	0	0	2	0	13,612
Terre Haute	4	2	0	0	0	0	2	2	1	1	58,507
Valparaiso	2	0	0	0	0	0	0	0	1	1	34,708
Westfield	2	0	0	0	0	0	1	1	0	0	54,552
West Lafayette	1	0	0	0	0	1	1	1	0	0	44,891
Zionsville	1	0	0	0	0	0	0	0	0	1	32,575
Universities and Colleges	0	0	1	0	0	0					
Purdue University	0	0	1	0	0	0	0	0	0	1	51,304
Metropolitan Counties	5	1	0	0	0	1					
Hamilton	2	0	0	0	0	0	0	1	0	1	
Hancock	1	0	0	0	0	1	0	1	1	0	
Hendricks	0	1	0	0	0	0	0	1	0	0	
Warrick	2	0	0	0	0	0	1	0	1	0	
Nonmetropolitan Counties	4	0	3	0	0	0					
Blackford[2]	1	0	1	0	0	0	1			0	
Cass	1	0	0	0	0	0	0	1	0		
Gibson	1	0	0	0	0	0	0	0	0	1	
Greene	0	0	1	0	0	0	0	0	1	0	
Jennings	0	0	1	0	0	0	0	1	0	0	
Wells	1	0	0	0	0	0	0	0	1	0	
State Police Agencies	9	0	0	0	0	1					
Indiana State Police[2]	9	0	0	0	0	1	1	2	3	3	
Other Agencies	1	0	1	0	0	0					
Indiana Gaming Commission	1	0	0	0	0	0	0	0	1	0	
Indianapolis International Airport	0	0	1	0	0	0	0	0	0	1	
IOWA	41	8	18	2	1	3					
Cities	34	7	13	1	1	2					
Altoona	1	0	0	0	0	0	0	1	0	0	21,830
Ames	0	0	1	0	0	0	0	1	0	0	66,852
Ankeny	2	0	1	0	0	0	1	2	0	0	72,315
Atlantic	0	0	2	0	0	0	1	1	0	0	6,726
Bettendorf[2]	0	0	2	0	0	0	0	0	0	1	39,548
Camanche	1	0	0	0	0	0	0	0	0	1	4,587
Carlisle	0	0	1	0	0	0	0	0	0	1	4,225
Clinton	2	1	1	0	0	0	0	1	2	1	24,443
Council Bluffs	2	0	0	0	0	0	1	1	0	0	62,206
Creston	1	0	1	0	0	0	1	1	0	0	7,438
Des Moines	3	2	0	0	1	0	0	6			210,376
DeWitt	1	0	0	0	0	0	0	0	1	0	5,528
Dyersville	2	0	0	0	0	0	0	0	0	2	4,516
Fairfield	1	0	0	0	0	0	0	0	0	1	9,641
Fort Dodge	1	0	0	0	0	0	0	0	1	0	25,097
Grundy Center	0	0	0	1	0	0	0	0	0	1	2,804
Hiawatha	1	0	0	0	0	0	0	0	1	0	7,109
Iowa City	0	0	0	0	0	1	0	0	0	1	74,749
Keokuk	1	0	0	0	0	0	0	0	0	1	9,702
Knoxville	1	0	0	0	0	0	0	0	0	1	7,366
Marion[2]	6	4	0	0	0	1	0	1	9	0	41,793
North Liberty	1	0	1	0	0	0	0	2	0	0	21,131
Ottumwa	1	0	0	0	0	0	0	0	1	0	25,249
Sioux City	2	0	0	0	0	0	0	0	2	0	85,580
Waukee	3	0	0	0	0	0	0	1	2	0	28,790
Waukon	0	0	1	0	0	0	0	1	0	0	3,706
West Des Moines	1	0	2	0	0	0	1	2	0	0	70,701
Universities and Colleges	2	0	1	0	0	1					
University of Iowa	2	0	1	0	0	1	1	3	0	0	33,345
Metropolitan Counties	1	1	2	1	0	0					
Polk	1	1	2	1	0	0	0	1	1	3	
Nonmetropolitan Counties	4	0	2	0	0	0					
Iowa	1	0	0	0	0	0	1	0	0	0	

Table 94. Hate Crime Incidents Per Bias Motivation and Quarter, by Selected State, Territory, Federal, and Agency, 2022—Continued

(Number.)

State/agency	Number of incidents per bias motivation						Number of incidents per quarter				Population[1]
	Race/ Ethnicity/ Ancestry	Religion	Sexual orientation	Disability	Gender	Gender Identity	1st quarter	2nd quarter	3rd quarter	4th quarter	
Keokuk[2]	0	0	2	0	0	0	0	0	1	0	
Lucas	1	0	0	0	0	0	0	1	0	0	
Poweshiek	1	0	0	0	0	0	0	1	0	0	
Sac	1	0	0	0	0	0	1	0	0	0	
KANSAS	58	45	15	4	1	5					
Cities	39	30	9	2	1	4					
Atchison	0	1	0	0	0	0	0	1	0	0	10,650
Augusta	0	1	0	0	0	0	0	0	0	1	9,256
Belleville	1	0	0	0	0	0	0	0	0	1	2,015
Beloit	1	0	0	0	0	0	1	0	0	0	3,396
Coffeyville	0	1	0	0	1	0	1	0	1	0	8,788
Colby	0	1	0	0	0	0	0	1	0	0	5,488
Dodge City	2	0	0	0	0	0	1	1	0	0	27,641
Edwardsville	0	1	0	0	0	0	0	1	0	0	4,574
Galena	1	0	0	0	0	0	0	0	1	0	2,737
Garden City[2]	0	0	0	2	0	0	0	0	0	1	27,701
Gardner	2	0	0	0	0	0	0	0	2	0	24,497
Goddard	0	0	1	0	0	0	0	0	0	1	5,644
Grandview Plaza	1	0	0	0	0	0	0	1	0		1,628
Great Bend	0	1	0	0	0	0	0	1	0	0	14,456
Independence	0	0	1	0	0	0	1	0	0	0	8,402
Kechi	0	1	0	0	0	0	1	0	0	0	2,265
Leavenworth	0	2	0	0	0	0	0	0	2	0	37,004
Leawood	4	1	0	0	0	0	3	1	1	0	33,596
Liberal	1	1	0	0	0	0	1	1	0	0	19,557
Maize	1	1	0	0	0	0	0	1	0	1	6,275
Mulvane	0	0	1	0	0	0	0	0	0	1	6,844
Newton	0	1	1	0	0	0	1	0	1	0	18,337
Olathe	4	0	1	0	0	0	0	2	1	2	144,646
Osage City	0	2	0	0	0	0	1	1	0	0	2,840
Overland Park	2	5	2	0	0	0	0	5	2	2	196,626
Park City	1	0	0	0	0	0	0	0	1	0	8,565
Rose Hill	0	1	0	0	0	0	0	0	1	0	4,336
Salina[2]	6	0	0	0	0	0	2	1	1	1	46,161
Shawnee	1	0	0	0	0	1	0	0	1	1	67,617
Spring Hill	1	0	0	0	0	0	0	0	0	1	9,024
Topeka[2]	3	3	0	0	0	3	2	3	2	1	125,658
Valley Center	2	2	0	0	0	0	1	2	1	0	7,463
Wellington	0	1	0	0	0	0	1	0	0	0	7,641
Wichita	5	3	2	0	0	0	4	5	1	0	394,286
Universities and Colleges	0	1	0	0	0	0					
University of Kansas, Medical Center[3]	0	1	0	0	0	0	0	1	0	0	
Metropolitan Counties	8	7	0	1	0	1					
Butler	1	0	0	0	0	0	0	0	1	0	
Leavenworth[2]	0	2	0	0	0	0	0	1	0	0	
Linn	1	0	0	0	0	0	1	0	0	0	
Pottawatomie	0	1	0	0	0	0	0	1	0	0	
Riley County Police Department	0	0	0	1	0	0	0	0	0	1	
Sedgwick	0	3	0	0	0	1	1	0	1	2	
Shawnee[2]	3	0	0	0	0	0	0	2	0	0	
Sumner	2	0	0	0	0	0	0	0	1	1	
Wyandotte	1	1	0	0	0	0	1	0	1	0	
Nonmetropolitan Counties	10	6	3	1	0	0					
Barton[2]	0	0	2	0	0	0	0	1	0	0	
Dickinson	0	1	0	0	0	0	0	1	0	0	
Edwards	1	0	0	0	0	0	0	0	1	0	
Finney	1	0	0	0	0	0	0	0	1	0	
Ford	1	0	0	0	0	0	0	0	0	1	
Franklin	1	0	0	0	0	0	0	0	0	1	
Greenwood	1	0	0	0	0	0	0	0	1	0	
Haskell	0	1	0	0	0	0	0	0	0	1	
Kiowa	1	0	0	0	0	0	0	0	1	0	
Labette	0	1	0	0	0	0	0	0	1	0	
Lane	0	0	0	1	0	0	0	0	1	0	
Montgomery	0	1	0	0	0	0	0	1	0	0	
Neosho	0	1	0	0	0	0	0	0	1	0	
Norton	1	0	0	0	0	0	0	1	0	0	
Phillips	0	0	1	0	0	0	1	0	0	0	
Reno	1	1	0	0	0	0	0	1	1	0	
Saline	1	0	0	0	0	0	1	0	0	0	
Washington	1	0	0	0	0	0	0	0	0	1	
State Police Agencies	0	1	1	0	0	0					
Highway Patrol											
Troop C	0	0	1	0	0	0	0	0	0	1	
Troop G	0	1	0	0	0	0	0	0	1	0	

Table 94. Hate Crime Incidents Per Bias Motivation and Quarter, by Selected State, Territory, Federal, and Agency, 2022—Continued

(Number.)

State/agency	Number of incidents per bias motivation						Number of incidents per quarter				Population[1]
	Race/ Ethnicity/ Ancestry	Religion	Sexual orientation	Disability	Gender	Gender Identity	1st quarter	2nd quarter	3rd quarter	4th quarter	
Tribal Agencies	1	0	2	0	0	0					
Potawatomi Tribal	1	0	2	0	0	0	1	1	0	1	
KENTUCKY	91	15	33	2	1	7					
Cities	62	12	31	1	1	7					
Alexandria	1	0	0	0	0	0	0	0	1	0	10,416
Ashland[2]	2	0	1	0	0	0	0	0	2	0	21,300
Bowling Green	2	0	2	0	0	0	0	1	0	3	74,427
Cadiz	1	0	0	0	0	0	1	0	0	0	2,840
Corbin[2]	1	0	2	0	0	0	0	0	0	2	7,762
Covington	0	0	1	0	0	0	0	0	0	1	40,657
Elizabethtown	1	0	0	0	0	0	0	0	1	0	32,437
Florence	0	0	0	0	0	1	0	0	0	1	32,341
Fort Mitchell	0	0	1	0	0	0	1	0	0	0	8,643
Frankfort	2	0	0	0	0	0	0	1	1	0	28,559
Franklin	0	0	1	0	0	0	0	1	0	0	10,174
Harrodsburg	1	0	0	0	0	0	0	1	0	0	9,200
Hazard[2]	2	0	0	0	0	0	0	0	0	1	5,011
La Grange	1	1	0	0	0	0	2	0	0	0	10,348
Lancaster	1	0	0	0	0	0	0	1	0	0	3,996
Lebanon	0	0	1	0	0	0	0	0	0	1	6,473
Leitchfield[2]	2	0	1	0	0	0	1	1	0	0	6,433
Lexington[2]	8	2	8	0	1	3	4	6	2	2	320,983
Louisville Metro[2]	18	3	2	1	0	0	0	6	4	12	677,554
Lyndon[2]	0	2	2	0	0	0	0	1	0	0	2,831
Madisonville	1	0	0	0	0	0	0	0	0	1	19,292
Murray	1	0	1	0	0	0	0	1	1	0	17,506
Nicholasville[2]	4	0	4	0	0	1	1	3	0	2	31,882
Oak Grove	1	0	0	0	0	0	0	0	1	0	7,810
Owensboro	3	0	1	0	0	2	1	4	0	1	59,839
Owingsville	1	0	0	0	0	0	0	0	1	0	1,587
Paducah	2	0	0	0	0	0	0	0	2	0	26,050
Pikeville	1	0	0	0	0	0	0	0	0	1	7,190
Richmond[2]	1	2	1	0	0	0	1	1	0	1	36,698
Scottsville	0	1	0	0	0	0	0	1	0	0	4,368
Shively	2	0	0	0	0	0	1	1	0	0	15,438
Simpsonville	1	0	0	0	0	0	0	0	0	1	3,016
Taylor Mill	1	0	0	0	0	0	1	0	0	0	6,821
West Buechel	0	0	1	0	0	0	1	0	0	0	1,352
Wilmore	0	1	1	0	0	0	0	1	1	0	6,081
Universities and Colleges	5	0	1	0	0	0					
Eastern Kentucky University	1	0	0	0	0	0	1	0	0	0	16,847
University of Kentucky	3	0	0	0	0	0	0	0	0	3	32,446
Western Kentucky University	1	0	1	0	0	0	0	1	0	1	20,304
Metropolitan Counties	12	2	1	1	0	0					
Boone	1	0	0	0	0	0	0	1	0	0	
Daviess	0	2	0	1	0	0	0	3	0	0	
Grant	2	0	0	0	0	0	1	1	0	0	
Hardin	1	0	0	0	0	0	0	0	0	1	
Kenton County Police Department	2	0	0	0	0	0	0	0	2	0	
Oldham County Police Department	2	0	0	0	0	0	0	0	2	0	
Spencer[2]	1	0	1	0	0	0	0	1	0	0	
Warren[2]	3	0	0	0	0	0	1	1	0	1	
Nonmetropolitan Counties	6	0	0	0	0	0					
Crittenden	1	0	0	0	0	0	0	1	0	0	
Franklin	1	0	0	0	0	0	0	0	1	0	
Garrard	1	0	0	0	0	0	1	0	0	0	
Livingston	1	0	0	0	0	0	0	0	0	1	
Madison	2	0	0	0	0	0	0	0	0	2	
State Police Agencies	5	1	0	0	0	0					
State Police											
Columbia	1	0	0	0	0	0	0	0	0	1	
Henderson	0	1	0	0	0	0	0	1	0	0	
Richmond[2]	4	0	0	0	0	0	1	0	0	0	
Other Agencies	1	0	0	0	0	0					
Bourbon County Schools	1	0	0	0	0	0	0	0	1	0	
LOUSIANA	49	14	11	0	1	0					
Cities	12	4	1	0	0	0					
Baton Rouge	1	1	0	0	0	0	0	1	0	1	219,913
Blanchard	1	0	0	0	0	0	0	0	0	1	3,383
Bogalusa	1	0	0	0	0	0	0	0	0	1	10,461
Broussard	1	0	0	0	0	0	0	0	1	0	14,103
Covington[2]	0	3	0	0	0	0	1	0	0	0	11,543

Table 94. Hate Crime Incidents Per Bias Motivation and Quarter, by Selected State, Territory, Federal, and Agency, 2022—Continued

(Number.)

State/agency	Race/ Ethnicity/ Ancestry	Religion	Sexual orientation	Disability	Gender	Gender Identity	1st quarter	2nd quarter	3rd quarter	4th quarter	Population[1]
De Ridder	1	0	0	0	0	0	0	0	1	0	9,674
Kenner	1	0	0	0	0	0	0	1	0	0	64,419
Marksville	2	0	0	0	0	0	2	0	0	0	4,843
Monroe	0	0	1	0	0	0	0	0	1	0	46,908
Opelousas	1	0	0	0	0	0	0	0	1	0	15,447
Vidalia	2	0	0	0	0	0	0	2	0	0	3,771
Vinton	1	0	0	0	0	0	1	0	0	0	2,973
Universities and Colleges	1	0	0	0	0	0					
Louisiana State University, Health Sciences Center, Shreveport	1	0	0	0	0	0	1	0	0	0	1,150
Metropolitan Counties	30	10	7	0	0	0					
Ascension	0	1	0	0	0	0	0	0	0	1	
Bossier[2]	4	0	0	0	0	0	0	0	1	1	
Calcasieu	1	0	2	0	0	0	0	1	1	1	
De Soto[2]	0	2	0	0	0	0	0	1	0	0	
East Baton Rouge	0	1	0	0	0	0	0	0	1	0	
East Feliciana	1	0	0	0	0	0	1	0	0	0	
Lafourche	1	0	0	0	0	0	0	0	1	0	
Rapides	2	0	1	0	0	0	1	0	2	0	
St. Bernard	0	1	0	0	0	0	0	0	0	1	
St. Charles	0	0	2	0	0	0	1	1	0	0	
St. John the Baptist	2	0	0	0	0	0	0	0	0	2	
St. Tammany[2]	3	1	0	0	0	0	2	1	0	0	
Tangipahoa[2]	16	4	2	0	0	0	4	4	6	4	
Nonmetropolitan Counties	5	0	3	0	0	0					
Catahoula	1	0	0	0	0	0	1	0	0	0	
Evangeline	3	0	0	0	0	0	2	1	0	0	
Jefferson Davis	1	0	1	0	0	0	0	2	0	0	
St. Landry	0	0	1	0	0	0	0	1	0	0	
Webster	0	0	1	0	0	0	1	0	0	0	
Tribal Agencies	1	0	0	0	1	0					
Coushatta Tribal	1	0	0	0	1	0	1	1	0	0	
MAINE	37	11	22	2	3	7					
Cities	27	10	19	2	2	6					
Auburn	1	0	0	0	0	0	1	0	0	0	24,122
Augusta	2	3	1	0	0	0	1	4	0	1	19,013
Bangor	2	0	0	0	0	1	0	0	1	2	32,078
Bar Harbor	0	1	0	0	0	0	0	0	1	0	7,478
Biddeford	4	0	0	0	0	0	3	0	0	1	22,647
Brewer	1	0	0	0	0	0	0	0	0	1	9,634
Brunswick	2	0	1	0	0	0	1	1	0	1	21,888
Bucksport	0	0	1	0	0	0	0	1	0	0	5,080
Buxton	1	0	0	0	0	0	0	0	0	1	8,528
Cumberland	1	0	0	0	1	0	0	1	1	0	8,616
Damariscotta	0	0	2	0	0	0	0	0	0	2	2,332
Fort Kent	0	0	0	0	0	3	0	1	2	0	4,120
Gardiner	0	0	1	0	0	0	0	1	0	0	6,102
Gorham	0	0	1	0	0	0	0	1	0	0	18,482
Hallowell	0	0	1	0	0	0	0	0	1	0	2,579
Houlton	0	0	0	0	1	0	0	1	0	0	6,071
Jay	1	0	0	0	0	0	0	0	0	1	4,706
Kittery	1	0	0	0	0	0	0	0	1	0	10,279
Milo	0	0	0	1	0	0	0	0	0	1	2,381
Old Town	0	2	0	0	0	0	0	1	0	1	7,372
Oxford	0	1	0	0	0	0	0	1	0	0	4,309
Paris	0	0	1	0	0	0	0	1	0	0	5,349
Portland	1	1	3	0	0	0	2	3	0	0	68,199
Presque Isle	0	0	0	0	0	1	0	0	1	0	8,746
Rockland	1	0	1	0	0	0	1	0	1	0	7,081
Rumford	0	0	1	0	0	1	2	0	0	0	5,929
Saco	0	0	1	0	0	0	0	1	0	0	20,936
Sanford	2	0	3	0	0	0	1	1	1	2	22,315
Scarborough	1	0	0	0	0	0	1	0	0	0	22,913
Southwest Harbor	0	1	0	0	0	0	0	1	0	0	1,836
Thomaston	0	0	0	1	0	0	0	0	1	0	2,816
Topsham	1	1	0	0	0	0	0	1	0	1	9,680
Windham	1	0	0	0	0	0	0	0	0	1	19,048
Winslow	1	0	0	0	0	0	1	0	0	0	7,970
Winter Harbor	0	0	1	0	0	0	1	0	0	0	479
Wiscasset	1	0	0	0	0	0	0	0	0	1	3,880
York	2	0	0	0	0	0	0	2	0	0	13,977
Universities and Colleges	1	0	0	0	0	0					
University of Maine, Orono	1	0	0	0	0	0	0	0	0	1	14,808

Table 94. Hate Crime Incidents Per Bias Motivation and Quarter, by Selected State, Territory, Federal, and Agency, 2022—Continued

(Number.)

State/agency	Number of incidents per bias motivation						Number of incidents per quarter				Population[1]
	Race/ Ethnicity/ Ancestry	Religion	Sexual orientation	Disability	Gender	Gender Identity	1st quarter	2nd quarter	3rd quarter	4th quarter	
Metropolitan Counties	6	1	1	0	0	0					
Cumberland	1	0	0	0	0	0	0	1	0	0	
Penobscot	1	0	1	0	0	0	0	1	0	1	
York[2]	4	1	0	0	0	0	0	0	2	2	
Nonmetropolitan Counties	2	0	2	0	1	1					
Knox	1	0	0	0	1	1	0	1	0	2	
Oxford	1	0	1	0	0	0	0	0	1	1	
Washington	0	0	1	0	0	0	0	0	1	0	
State Police Agencies	1	0	0	0	0	0					
State Police	1	0	0	0	0	0	0	1	0	0	
MARYLAND	130	45	30	6	2	8					
Cities	34	15	14	2	1	6					
Baltimore[2]	24	10	11	1	1	4	9	13	14	9	570,546
Bowie	1	0	0	0	0	0	0	0	1	0	57,068
Cumberland	0	1	0	0	0	0	0	1	0	0	18,647
Easton[2]	2	0	0	1	0	1	2	0	0	0	17,237
Frederick	1	0	0	0	0	1	0	0	1	1	80,985
Hagerstown	3	4	1	0	0	0	2	2	1	3	43,548
Hancock	0	0	1	0	0	0	0	1	0	0	1,539
Salisbury	1	0	1	0	0	0	0	1	1	0	33,063
Smithsburg	1	0	0	0	0	0	0	0	1	0	3,153
Takoma Park	1	0	0	0	0	0	0	0	1	0	17,322
Universities and Colleges	2	1	1	0	0	0					
Frostburg State University	0	0	1	0	0	0	0	0	0	1	5,432
Towson University	2	0	0	0	0	0	0	0	1	1	24,486
University of Maryland, Baltimore County	0	1	0	0	0	0	0	0	1	0	15,358
Metropolitan Counties	64	26	14	3	1	2					
Baltimore County Police Department[2]	35	23	8	2	0	1	6	26	22	9	
Cecil	1	0	0	0	0	0	0	0	1	0	
Charles	8	1	2	0	0	0	5	2	3	1	
Frederick	5	0	1	0	0	0	4	0	2	0	
Howard County Police Department[2]	11	1	2	0	0	1	1	5	5	3	
Montgomery County Police Department	0	1	0	0	0	0	0	0	0	1	
Prince George's County Police Department	1	0	0	0	0	0	0	0	1	0	
St. Mary's	2	0	1	1	0	0	1	1	1	1	
Washington	1	0	0	0	1	0	0	1	0	1	
Nonmetropolitan Counties	1	0	0	0	0	0					
Garrett	1	0	0	0	0	0	0	1	0	0	
State Police Agencies	23	2	1	1	0	0					
Maryland State Police Statewide[2]	4	0	1	0	0	0	0	3	0	0	
State Police											
Allegany County	1	0	0	0	0	0	0	1	0	0	
Anne Arundel County	1	0	0	0	0	0	0	1	0	0	
Baltimore County	1	0	0	0	0	0	0	1	0	0	
Caroline County	0	1	0	0	0	0	0	1	0	0	
Carroll County	1	1	0	0	0	0	0	0	1	1	
Cecil County[2]	5	0	0	0	0	0	0	1	3	0	
Dorchester County[2]	2	0	0	0	0	0	0	0	1	0	
Garrett County	1	0	0	0	0	0	0	0	1	0	
Prince Georges County[2]	2	0	0	0	0	0	0	1	0	0	
Queen Annes's County	0	0	0	1	0	0	0	1	0	0	
Somerset County[2]	2	0	0	0	0	0	1	0	0	0	
St. Mary's County	1	0	0	0	0	0	1	0	0	0	
Washington County	1	0	0	0	0	0	1	0	0	0	
Wicomico County	1	0	0	0	0	0	1	0	0	0	
Other Agencies	6	1	0	0	0	0					
Department of Public Safety and Correctional Services, Internal Investigation Division	1	0	0	0	0	0	0	1	0	0	
Natural Resources Police	1	1	0	0	0	0	0	0	2	0	
Transit Administration	2	0	0	0	0	0	0	1	1	0	
Transportation Authority	2	0	0	0	0	0	0	0	0	2	
MASSACHUSETTS	257	98	94	0	5	23					
Cities	251	92	87	0	5	22					
Amesbury	0	1	0	0	0	0	0	0	1	0	17,276
Andover[2]	3	2	0	0	0	0	0	0	1	3	36,631
Arlington	1	2	2	0	0	0	1	3	1	0	45,238
Attleboro	2	0	0	0	0	0	1	0	1	0	46,942
Ayer	1	0	0	0	0	0	1	0	0	0	8,368
Barnstable	2	0	0	0	0	0	2	0	0	0	50,501
Barre	1	0	0	0	0	0	0	1	0	0	5,555

Table 94. Hate Crime Incidents Per Bias Motivation and Quarter, by Selected State, Territory, Federal, and Agency, 2022—Continued

(Number.)

State/agency	Number of incidents per bias motivation						Number of incidents per quarter				
	Race/ Ethnicity/ Ancestry	Religion	Sexual orientation	Disability	Gender	Gender Identity	1st quarter	2nd quarter	3rd quarter	4th quarter	Population[1]
Bedford	0	1	0	0	0	0	0	0	0	1	14,034
Belchertown	0	1	0	0	0	0	0	0	0	1	15,277
Belmont	0	0	0	0	1	0	0	1	0	0	26,557
Boston[2]	93	25	42	0	2	10	38	44	38	36	638,925
Braintree	0	0	0	0	0	2	2	0	0	0	38,835
Brookline	1	1	1	0	0	1	1	3	0	0	62,825
Cambridge[2]	34	9	7	0	0	3	15	8	10	15	117,044
Carlisle	1	1	0	0	0	0	1	1	0	0	5,149
Chelmsford[2]	0	0	2	0	0	0	0	1	0	0	35,630
Chelsea	0	1	1	0	0	0	2	0	0	0	37,590
Cohasset	1	0	0	0	0	0	0	0	1	0	8,417
Concord	1	0	0	0	0	0	0	0	1	0	18,040
Danvers	0	0	0	0	0	1	0	0	1	0	27,887
Dedham	1	0	0	0	0	0	0	0	1	0	25,324
Dennis	1	0	1	0	0	0	0	0	1	1	15,200
Dighton[2]	2	1	0	0	0	0	1	1	0	0	8,240
Douglas	0	1	0	0	0	0	0	1	0	0	9,146
Everett	1	1	0	0	0	0	1	0	0	1	48,340
Fairhaven	1	0	1	0	0	0	1	1	0	0	15,987
Falmouth	0	1	1	0	0	0	1	1	0	0	33,873
Framingham[2]	4	1	1	0	0	0	0	2	1	2	70,716
Franklin	2	0	0	0	0	0	1	0	1	0	33,107
Great Barrington	1	0	0	0	0	0	1	0	0	0	7,143
Groveland	1	0	0	0	0	0	0	1	0	0	6,763
Harwich	0	0	1	0	0	0	1	0	0	0	13,891
Haverhill[2]	3	0	2	0	0	0	1	2	0	0	67,359
Hingham[2]	1	2	0	0	0	0	0	0	0	2	25,437
Holbrook[2]	4	0	0	0	0	0	1	1	0	1	11,350
Hull	0	1	0	0	0	0	0	0	0	1	10,676
Ipswich	1	0	0	0	0	0	0	0	1	0	13,735
Lakeville	1	0	0	0	0	0	0	0	0	1	12,511
Lawrence	0	1	0	0	0	0	0	0	0	1	88,422
Lincoln	1	0	1	0	0	0	0	2	0	0	6,823
Lowell	1	0	0	0	0	0	0	0	1	0	113,277
Ludlow	0	0	0	0	0	1	0	1	0	0	20,971
Lynn	6	4	0	0	0	0	0	4	3	3	101,056
Malden	3	0	0	0	0	0	1	0	1	1	64,356
Manchester-by-the-Sea	1	0	2	0	0	0	1	2	0	0	5,365
Marblehead	0	6	0	0	0	1	5	1	1	0	20,289
Medford	2	1	0	0	0	0	0	2	1	0	64,122
Milford	1	0	0	0	0	0	0	1	0	0	30,360
Natick	0	1	0	0	0	0	1	0	0	0	36,090
New Bedford	1	0	0	0	0	0	0	0	0	1	101,402
Newburyport	1	0	0	0	0	0	0	1	0	0	18,366
Newton[2]	10	8	3	0	1	1	6	4	4	5	86,710
Norfolk	0	1	1	0	0	0	0	0	1	1	11,621
Northampton[2]	2	2	0	0	0	0	0	0	0	1	29,150
North Attleboro	0	0	1	0	0	0	1	0	0	0	31,071
North Reading	1	0	0	0	0	0	0	0	0	1	15,197
Norwood	0	1	0	0	0	0	0	1	0	0	31,533
Oakham	1	0	0	0	0	0	0	1	0	0	1,852
Oxford	0	0	1	0	0	0	0	1	0	0	13,316
Pembroke[2]	1	1	0	0	0	0	0	1	0	0	19,289
Pittsfield	1	0	0	0	0	0	0	1	0	0	43,496
Plymouth[2]	5	0	0	0	0	1	3	0	1	0	65,779
Provincetown[2]	4	0	1	0	0	0	0	2	2	0	3,775
Quincy[2]	10	3	2	0	0	0	4	3	4	2	101,434
Reading	1	0	0	0	0	0	0	0	0	1	25,018
Revere	1	1	0	0	0	0	0	1	1	0	56,961
Rowley	1	0	0	0	0	0	0	0	0	1	6,132
Rutland	1	0	0	0	0	0	0	0	0	1	9,316
Salem	1	2	1	0	0	0	1	3	0	0	45,345
Shrewsbury	1	0	1	0	0	0	1	0	1	0	39,745
Somerville[2]	7	2	0	0	0	1	1	2	2	3	79,178
Southbridge	1	0	0	0	0	0	0	0	0	1	17,687
Southwick	0	0	1	0	0	0	0	1	0	0	9,229
Springfield	2	0	1	0	0	0	1	0	2	0	155,046
Stoughton	0	1	0	0	0	0	0	0	0	1	29,204
Stow	2	1	0	0	0	0	1	0	1	1	6,989
Swampscott	1	1	0	0	0	0	0	1	0	1	15,268
Taunton	1	0	0	0	0	0	0	0	1	0	60,062
Tyngsboro	1	0	0	0	0	0	0	0	0	1	12,490
Uxbridge	1	1	0	0	0	0	0	1	0	1	14,418
Wakefield	1	0	0	0	0	0	0	1	0	0	27,263
Waltham	1	0	0	0	0	0	0	0	0	1	63,525
Wayland	1	0	0	0	0	0	0	0	0	1	13,601
Webster	0	0	1	0	0	0	0	0	1	0	17,651
Wenham	1	0	0	0	0	0	1	0	0	0	4,998
Westfield	1	0	5	0	0	0	1	2	2	1	40,691

Table 94. Hate Crime Incidents Per Bias Motivation and Quarter, by Selected State, Territory, Federal, and Agency, 2022—Continued

(Number.)

State/agency	Number of incidents per bias motivation						Number of incidents per quarter				Population[1]
	Race/ Ethnicity/ Ancestry	Religion	Sexual orientation	Disability	Gender	Gender Identity	1st quarter	2nd quarter	3rd quarter	4th quarter	
Williamstown	1	0	0	0	0	0	0	0	0	1	8,020
Wilmington	1	0	0	0	0	0	0	0	1	0	22,825
Worcester	3	0	2	0	0	0	2	1	1	1	206,575
Wrentham	0	2	0	0	0	0	0	0	2	0	12,343
Yarmouth	2	0	1	0	1	0	1	1	1	1	25,705
Universities and Colleges	6	6	7	0	0	1					
Bentley University	0	1	1	0	0	0	1	0	0	1	5,541
Boston University	0	1	2	0	0	0	1	0	0	2	40,492
College of the Holy Cross	2	0	1	0	0	0	2	1	0	0	3,051
Dean College	3	0	0	0	0	0	2	0	0	1	1,401
Northeastern University	0	0	1	0	0	0	1	0	0	0	31,124
University of Massachusetts, Amherst	0	0	1	0	0	0	0	0	1	0	36,827
Wellesley College	1	4	0	0	0	0	1	2	1	1	2,405
Worcester Polytechnic Institute	0	0	1	0	0	1	0	0	0	2	7,876
MICHIGAN	276	52	68	5	7	14					
Cities	213	43	48	5	4	9					
Ann Arbor	1	0	0	0	0	2	0	3	0	0	120,549
Armada	0	0	1	0	0	0	0	0	1	0	1,658
Auburn Hills	0	0	1	0	0	0	0	1	0	0	25,081
Bad Axe	1	0	1	0	0	0	0	0	0	2	3,014
Bath Township	1	0	0	0	0	0	0	0	0	1	13,456
Benton Township	0	0	0	0	0	1	0	0	0	1	14,081
Bloomfield Township	1	2	0	0	0	0	0	1	1	1	43,805
Bridgeport Township	1	0	0	0	0	0	0	0	0	1	9,975
Burton[2]	3	0	0	0	0	0	1	1	0	0	29,373
Caro	1	0	0	0	0	0	1	0	0	0	4,292
Cass City	1	0	0	0	0	0	0	0	0	1	2,489
Cassopolis	1	0	0	0	0	0	0	1	0	0	1,689
Center Line	1	0	0	0	0	0	1	0	0	0	8,357
Charlevoix	1	0	1	0	0	0	0	1	1	0	2,351
Charlotte	1	0	0	0	0	0	0	0	1	0	9,175
Chelsea	0	0	2	0	0	0	0	0	0	2	5,322
Clayton Township	0	0	1	0	0	0	0	1	0	0	7,274
Clinton Township	2	0	0	0	0	0	0	0	2	0	99,274
Coldwater	2	0	1	0	0	0	0	2	0	1	13,930
Colon	0	0	1	0	0	0	0	1	0	0	1,191
Columbia Township	0	1	0	0	0	0	0	0	1	0	7,470
Commerce Township	2	0	0	0	0	0	0	0	1	1	38,873
Dearborn	3	0	0	0	0	0	0	3	0	0	107,197
Dearborn Heights	4	3	0	0	0	0	0	0	3	4	61,789
Detroit[2]	21	2	15	0	1	0	5	12	13	7	626,757
DeWitt Township	2	0	0	0	0	0	0	2	0	0	15,557
East Lansing	2	2	1	0	0	0	1	0	2	2	46,660
Eastpointe	4	0	0	0	0	0	1	3	0	0	33,829
Ecorse	0	0	1	0	0	1	0	0	2	0	9,113
Escanaba	1	0	2	0	0	0	0	2	1	0	12,404
Farmington Hills	4	2	0	0	0	0	2	1	1	2	82,806
Ferndale	1	0	0	0	0	0	0	0	0	1	19,007
Flint	17	1	1	3	1	0	9	4	8	2	80,059
Flint Township	1	0	0	0	0	0	0	0	1	0	31,097
Frankenmuth[2]	2	0	0	0	0	0	0	0	0	1	5,368
Fraser	2	0	0	0	0	0	0	2	0	0	14,458
Garden City	1	0	0	0	0	0	0	0	1	0	26,696
Gaylord	1	0	0	0	0	0	1	0	0	0	4,340
Gladwin	1	0	0	0	0	0	0	0	0	1	3,101
Grand Blanc Township	2	0	0	0	0	0	0	2	0	0	40,115
Grandville	1	0	0	0	0	0	0	0	1	0	15,847
Grayling	0	0	1	0	0	0	0	1	0	0	1,865
Hancock	1	2	0	0	0	0	1	0	2	0	4,515
Hastings	0	0	1	0	0	0	0	1	0	0	7,554
Highland Park	16	0	0	0	1	1	4	7	6	1	8,802
Hillsdale	1	0	0	0	0	0	0	0	1	0	8,157
Hudson	1	0	0	0	0	0	0	1	0	0	2,379
Huron Township	1	0	0	0	0	0	0	1	0	0	16,837
Imlay City	1	0	0	0	0	0	0	1	0	0	3,707
Inkster	2	1	0	0	0	0	0	1	2	0	25,447
Ishpeming	1	0	0	0	0	0	0	0	0	1	6,174
Kentwood	1	0	0	1	1	0	0	0	0	3	53,977
Lansing	1	0	1	0	0	0	0	2	0	0	112,567
Lapeer	1	0	0	0	0	0	0	1	0	0	8,924
Lawrence	1	0	0	0	0	0	0	0	1	0	1,013
Lincoln Park	1	0	1	0	0	0	2	0	0	0	39,189
Livonia	1	0	1	0	0	0	0	0	1	1	93,517
Ludington	0	0	1	0	0	0	0	1	0	0	7,785
Madison Heights	1	0	0	0	0	1	1	0	1	0	28,079
Manistique	2	0	0	0	0	0	0	0	2	0	2,809
Marine City	1	0	0	0	0	0	0	1	0	0	4,029

Table 94. Hate Crime Incidents Per Bias Motivation and Quarter, by Selected State, Territory, Federal, and Agency, 2022—Continued

(Number.)

State/agency	Number of incidents per bias motivation						Number of incidents per quarter				Population[1]
	Race/ Ethnicity/ Ancestry	Religion	Sexual orientation	Disability	Gender	Gender Identity	1st quarter	2nd quarter	3rd quarter	4th quarter	
Marysville	1	0	0	0	0	0	1	0	0	0	9,897
Mason	1	0	0	0	0	0	0	0	0	1	8,195
Melvindale	1	0	0	0	0	0	0	0	0	1	12,524
Meridian Township	0	17	0	0	0	0	0	17	0	0	44,038
Metamora Township	0	0	1	0	0	0	0	0	1	0	4,438
Montague	1	0	0	0	0	0	0	0	0	1	2,437
Newaygo	0	1	0	0	0	0	0	0	1	0	2,487
New Buffalo	1	0	0	0	0	0	0	0	1	0	1,680
Niles	1	0	0	0	0	0	1	0	0	0	11,756
Northville Township	1	0	0	0	0	0	0	1	0	0	31,443
Oakland Township	0	1	0	0	0	0	0	0	0	1	20,234
Ontwa Township-Edwardsburg	0	0	0	0	0	1	0	0	1	0	6,812
Owosso	1	0	0	0	0	0	0	0	1	0	14,581
Oxford	0	1	0	0	0	0	0	0	1	0	3,440
Pittsfield Township	1	0	0	0	0	0	0	0	1	0	39,298
Plymouth Township	1	0	0	0	0	0	0	0	1	0	27,426
Pontiac	1	0	2	0	0	0	0	0	1	2	60,581
Port Huron	1	0	0	0	0	0	0	0	1	0	28,675
Portland	1	0	0	0	0	0	0	0	0	1	3,954
Redford Township	1	0	0	0	0	0	1	0	0	0	48,267
Reed City	1	0	0	0	0	0	1	0	0	0	2,518
Richland Township, Saginaw County[2]	2	0	0	0	0	0	0	1	0	0	3,916
Riverview	1	0	0	0	0	0	0	0	1	0	12,274
Rochester	1	0	0	0	0	0	0	0	0	1	12,868
Rochester Hills	3	0	0	0	0	0	0	2	0	1	75,921
Romeo	1	0	0	0	0	0	0	1	0	0	3,711
Romulus	1	0	0	0	0	0	1	0	0	0	25,071
Roosevelt Park	1	0	0	0	0	0	0	1	0	0	4,186
Rose City	1	0	0	0	0	0	0	1	0	0	561
Roseville[2]	6	0	0	0	0	0	3	1	0	1	46,719
Royal Oak	1	0	0	0	0	0	1	0	0	0	57,808
Saginaw	1	0	0	0	0	0	0	1	0	0	43,651
Saline	1	0	0	0	0	0	1	0	0	0	8,930
Shelby Township	1	0	1	0	0	1	1	1	1	0	79,391
Southfield	1	1	0	0	0	0	1	0	0	1	75,432
Southgate	1	0	0	0	0	0	1	0	0	0	29,769
South Haven	0	0	1	0	0	0	0	0	1	0	4,059
Springport Township	0	0	2	0	0	0	1	1	0	0	2,154
St. Clair Shores	2	0	0	0	0	0	0	1	0	1	57,654
Sterling Heights[2]	13	1	5	0	0	0	1	4	7	5	132,393
St. Johns	1	0	0	0	0	0	0	0	0	1	7,640
St. Joseph	0	0	0	0	0	1	0	0	0	1	7,684
St. Louis	0	0	0	1	0	0	0	1	0	0	6,842
Sylvan Lake	1	0	0	0	0	0	0	1	0	0	1,693
Taylor	1	0	0	0	0	0	0	1	0	0	61,901
Thomas Township	1	0	0	0	0	0	0	1	0	0	11,903
Troy	0	1	0	0	0	0	1	0	0	0	86,548
Walker	1	0	0	0	0	0	0	0	0	1	25,067
Warren[2]	12	1	0	0	0	0	1	1	5	4	137,138
Waterford Township	1	0	0	0	0	0	0	0	0	1	69,851
West Bloomfield Township	5	3	1	0	0	0	0	2	3	4	65,271
Wixom	1	0	0	0	0	0	0	0	1	0	17,186
Woodhaven	1	0	0	0	0	0	0	0	1	0	12,745
Wyoming[2]	10	0	0	0	0	0	1	6	0	2	76,726
Ypsilanti	1	0	0	0	0	0	0	0	1	0	19,872
Universities and Colleges	5	6	1	0	2	0					
Michigan State University	2	3	1	0	1	0	1	2	2	2	54,245
Oakland Community College	0	0	0	0	1	0	0	0	0	1	23,708
University of Michigan, Ann Arbor	2	2	0	0	0	0	1	0	2	1	50,002
Washtenaw Community College	1	0	0	0	0	0	0	0	0	1	18,734
Western Michigan University	0	1	0	0	0	0	0	1	0	0	22,035
Metropolitan Counties	24	1	11	0	1	4					
Bay	0	0	1	0	0	0	0	1	0	0	
Berrien	1	0	0	0	0	1	0	0	1	1	
Calhoun	3	0	0	0	1	0	2	0	0	2	
Cass	1	1	0	0	0	0	2	0	0	0	
Eaton	1	0	0	0	0	0	0	0	1	0	
Genesee	2	0	0	0	0	0	0	0	2	0	
Ingham	1	0	1	0	0	0	2	0	0	0	
Jackson	0	0	1	0	0	0	0	0	1	0	
Kent	3	0	2	0	0	2	1	0	2	4	
Lapeer	2	0	0	0	0	0	0	0	0	2	
Muskegon	1	0	0	0	0	0	1	0	0	0	
Oakland	1	0	0	0	0	0	0	0	0	1	
Ottawa[2]	2	0	2	0	0	0	0	1	0	2	
Saginaw	2	0	0	0	0	0	0	1	1	0	
Washtenaw	4	0	4	0	0	1	0	4	2	3	

Table 94. Hate Crime Incidents Per Bias Motivation and Quarter, by Selected State, Territory, Federal, and Agency, 2022—Continued

(Number.)

State/agency	Race/ Ethnicity/ Ancestry	Religion	Sexual orientation	Disability	Gender	Gender Identity	1st quarter	2nd quarter	3rd quarter	4th quarter	Population[1]
Nonmetropolitan Counties	8	0	3	0	0	1					
Allegan	1	0	0	0	0	0	0	1	0	0	
Emmet	0	0	1	0	0	0	0	0	0	1	
Gladwin	1	0	0	0	0	0	0	1	0	0	
Grand Traverse	1	0	0	0	0	0	1	0	0	0	
Hillsdale	0	0	1	0	0	0	0	0	1	0	
Huron	1	0	0	0	0	0	0	0	0	1	
Isabella	1	0	0	0	0	0	0	0	0	1	
Kalkaska	0	0	0	0	0	1	1	0	0	0	
Oceana	1	0	0	0	0	0	0	0	0	1	
Sanilac	0	0	1	0	0	0	0	0	1	0	
Tuscola	1	0	0	0	0	0	0	1	0	0	
Van Buren	1	0	0	0	0	0	1	0	0	0	
State Police Agencies	17	1	2	0	0	0					
State Police											
Allegan County	1	0	0	0	0	0	0	0	1	0	
Calhoun County	1	0	0	0	0	0	0	0	1	0	
Delta County	1	0	0	0	0	0	0	1	0	0	
Eaton County	1	0	0	0	0	0	0	0	0	1	
Emmet County	1	0	0	0	0	0	0	1	0	0	
Ingham County	1	0	0	0	0	0	0	1	0	0	
Iosco County	1	0	0	0	0	0	0	0	0	1	
Kalkaska County	0	0	1	0	0	0	0	0	0	1	
Leelanau County	0	0	1	0	0	0	0	0	1	0	
Montcalm County	1	0	0	0	0	0	0	0	1	0	
Muskegon County	2	0	0	0	0	0	1	0	1	0	
Newaygo County	1	0	0	0	0	0	0	0	1	0	
Oakland County	1	0	0	0	0	0	0	0	0	1	
Washtenaw County[2]	4	0	0	0	0	0	0	2	0	0	
Wayne County	1	1	0	0	0	0	0	1	1	0	
Tribal Agencies	8	0	3	0	0	0					
Hannahville Tribal	2	0	3	0	0	0	0	0	5	0	
Saginaw Chippewa Tribal[2]	6	0	0	0	0	0	2	1	0	0	
Other Agencies	1	1	0	0	0	0					
Department of Natural Resources Law Enforcement Division	0	1	0	0	0	0	0	0	0	1	
Huron-Clinton Metropolitan Authority, Stony Creek Metropark	1	0	0	0	0	0	0	1	0	0	
MINNESTOA	109	27	36	1	3	9					
Cities	90	24	33	1	1	8					
Alexandria	1	1	0	0	0	0	0	0	1	1	14,564
Austin	1	0	0	0	0	0	1	0	0	0	26,275
Avon	1	0	0	0	0	0	0	1	0	0	1,680
Bemidji[2]	4	0	1	0	0	0	0	0	3	1	15,317
Benson	1	0	0	0	0	0	1	0	0	0	3,359
Blaine	1	0	0	0	0	0	1	0	0	0	71,368
Bloomington	2	0	1	0	0	0	3	0	0	0	88,745
Brooklyn Center	1	0	0	0	0	0	0	1	0	0	32,094
Brooklyn Park[2]	4	0	0	0	0	1	2	0	0	1	82,682
Buffalo	0	0	1	0	0	0	0	1	0	0	16,531
Burnsville[2]	2	0	0	1	1	0	0	1	1	1	63,361
Chaska[2]	0	0	1	0	0	1	0	1	0	0	28,204
Cloquet	0	1	0	0	0	0	0	1	0	0	12,747
Duluth[2]	1	0	4	0	0	0	0	1	2	1	86,144
East Grand Forks	0	1	0	0	0	0	0	1	0	0	9,002
Eden Prairie	1	0	0	0	0	0	1	0	0	0	62,008
Edina	0	1	1	0	0	0	0	2	0	0	53,206
Elk River	2	0	1	0	0	1	0	3	0	1	26,519
Fairmont	1	0	0	0	0	0	1	0	0	0	10,369
Farmington[2]	2	0	0	0	0	0	0	0	1	0	23,551
Foley	1	0	0	0	0	0	1	0	0	0	2,681
Frazee	0	0	1	0	0	0	0	1	0	0	1,311
Fridley	1	0	0	0	0	0	1	0	0	0	31,095
Hopkins	2	2	0	0	0	0	0	2	1	1	18,125
International Falls	0	0	1	0	0	0	0	0	1	0	5,657
Inver Grove Heights	3	0	0	0	0	0	1	0	1	1	35,294
Lakeville	1	4	0	0	0	0	1	1	0	3	75,548
Mankato	0	1	0	0	0	0	0	1	0	0	44,925
Maple Grove	1	0	0	0	0	0	0	1	0	0	70,935
Maplewood[2]	5	0	0	0	0	1	1	1	3	0	47,144
Mendota Heights	1	0	0	0	0	0	0	0	1	0	11,569
Minneapolis[2]	8	1	7	0	0	1	4	4	3	5	421,690
Minnetonka	1	0	0	0	0	0	0	1	0	0	52,309
Mounds View	1	0	0	0	0	0	1	0	0	0	14,897
North Branch[2]	1	0	1	0	0	0	0	0	0	1	11,439

Table 94. Hate Crime Incidents Per Bias Motivation and Quarter, by Selected State, Territory, Federal, and Agency, 2022—Continued

(Number.)

State/agency	Number of incidents per bias motivation						Number of incidents per quarter				Population[1]
	Race/ Ethnicity/ Ancestry	Religion	Sexual orientation	Disability	Gender	Gender Identity	1st quarter	2nd quarter	3rd quarter	4th quarter	
Prior Lake	0	1	1	0	0	0	0	2	0	0	28,559
Robbinsdale	0	0	0	0	0	1	0	0	1	0	13,907
Rochester	4	1	0	0	0	0	1	1	2	1	121,534
Roseville	8	0	1	0	0	0	4	2	1	2	42,031
Sartell	0	1	0	0	0	0	0	0	1	0	19,607
Savage	1	0	0	0	0	1	1	1	0	0	33,372
Shakopee	1	0	0	0	0	0	0	0	1	0	45,122
Slayton	1	0	0	0	0	0	0	1	0	0	1,987
South St. Paul	1	0	0	0	0	0	0	0	1	0	20,337
St. Cloud	6	2	1	0	0	0	1	4	3	1	68,925
St. Louis Park[2]	4	2	3	0	0	0	0	4	4	0	48,311
St. Paul[2]	7	4	6	0	0	1	6	8	1	2	277,533
St. Peter	1	0	1	0	0	0	1	1	0	0	11,647
Virginia	0	1	0	0	0	0	1	0	0	0	8,276
West St. Paul	1	0	0	0	0	0	1	0	0	0	21,113
White Bear Lake	1	0	0	0	0	0	0	1	0	0	27,700
Woodbury	3	0	0	0	0	0	0	0	2	1	78,531
Universities and Colleges	3	1	0	0	0	0					
University of Minnesota, Twin Cities[2]	3	1	0	0	0	0	0	0	1	0	62,309
Metropolitan Counties	9	1	1	0	2	1					
Carver	1	0	0	0	0	0	0	0	0	1	
Dodge	1	0	0	0	0	0	0	0	0	1	
Lake	1	0	0	0	0	0	1	0	0	0	
Olmsted	2	0	1	0	0	0	0	1	1	1	
Ramsey[2]	3	0	0	0	2	1	1	1	0	3	
Sherburne	0	1	0	0	0	0	0	0	0	1	
Wright	1	0	0	0	0	0	0	0	1	0	
Nonmetropolitan Counties	5	0	1	0	0	0					
Cass	1	0	0	0	0	0	0	1	0	0	
Clearwater	0	0	1	0	0	0	0	0	0	1	
Kandiyohi	1	0	0	0	0	0	0	0	1	0	
Mahnomen	1	0	0	0	0	0	0	1	0	0	
Todd	1	0	0	0	0	0	0	0	0	1	
Waseca	1	0	0	0	0	0	1	0	0	0	
Other Agencies	2	1	1	0	0	0					
Metropolitan Transit Commission	1	0	1	0	0	0	0	0	1	1	
Minneapolis-St. Paul International Airport[2]	1	1	0	0	0	0	1	0	0	0	
MISSISSIPPI	16	1	4	5	1	2					
Cities	7	1	2	4	0	1					
Brandon	1	0	0	0	0	0	0	0	1	0	25,636
Cleveland	1	0	0	0	0	0	0	0	0	1	10,687
Corinth	0	0	0	0	0	1	0	0	0	1	14,216
Gautier	1	1	0	0	0	0	0	1	0	1	18,992
Guntown	0	0	1	0	0	0	1	0	0	0	2,416
Hattiesburg	2	0	1	0	0	0	0	1	2	0	46,862
Olive Branch	1	0	0	0	0	0	1	0	0	0	40,651
Tupelo	1	0	0	0	0	0	1	0	0	0	37,534
Vicksburg[2]	0	0	0	4	0	0	0	1	1	1	20,381
Metropolitan Counties	4	0	1	0	0	0					
DeSoto	1	0	0	0	0	0	1	0	0	0	
Hancock	1	0	0	0	0	0	0	0	0	1	
Harrison	0	0	1	0	0	0	0	0	1	0	
Lamar	2	0	0	0	0	0	0	0	1	1	
Nonmetropolitan Counties	5	0	1	1	1	1					
Bolivar	0	0	0	0	0	1	0	1	0	0	
Leake	1	0	0	0	0	0	0	0	0	1	
Marion	3	0	0	0	0	0	1	1	1	0	
Pontotoc	0	0	1	0	0	0	0	0	1	0	
Sunflower	1	0	0	0	0	0	0	0	0	1	
Tishomingo	0	0	0	0	1	0	0	0	0	1	
Winston	0	0	0	1	0	0	0	0	0	1	
MISSOURI	119	35	29	4	4	8					
Cities	90	23	23	2	1	5					
Arnold	2	1	0	0	0	0	0	2	0	1	20,794
Battlefield	1	0	0	0	0	0	1	0	0	0	6,078
Bellefontaine Neighbors	1	0	0	0	0	0	0	0	0	1	10,524
Belton	1	3	0	0	0	0	0	2	0	2	24,395
Branson[2]	1	0	1	0	0	0	0	1	0	0	13,021
Bridgeton	0	1	0	0	0	0	0	1	0	0	11,342
Camdenton	1	0	0	0	0	0	0	1	0	0	4,074
Carthage	1	0	0	0	0	0	0	0	0	1	15,510

Table 94. Hate Crime Incidents Per Bias Motivation and Quarter, by Selected State, Territory, Federal, and Agency, 2022—Continued

(Number.)

State/agency	Race/ Ethnicity/ Ancestry	Religion	Sexual orientation	Disability	Gender	Gender Identity	1st quarter	2nd quarter	3rd quarter	4th quarter	Population[1]
Charleston	1	0	0	0	0	0	1	0	0	0	4,987
Chesterfield	0	1	0	0	0	0	1	0	0	0	49,451
Clarkson Valley	1	0	0	0	0	0	0	1	0	0	2,571
Cottleville	1	0	0	0	0	0	0	1	0	0	5,828
Creve Coeur	0	0	0	1	0	0	0	0	1	0	18,527
Cuba	1	0	0	0	0	0	0	0	1	0	3,153
Farmington	3	2	1	0	0	0	0	3	2	1	18,565
Ferguson	0	1	0	0	0	0	0	0	0	1	18,178
Festus	0	1	0	0	0	0	1	0	0	0	13,036
Florissant	0	1	0	0	0	0	0	0	1	0	51,565
Frontenac	1	0	0	0	0	0	1	0	0	0	4,067
Grandview	0	1	0	0	0	0	1	0	0	0	25,542
Greenwood	0	0	0	0	0	1	0	1	0	0	6,077
Hannibal	1	0	1	0	0	0	2	0	0	0	17,028
Hazelwood	1	0	0	0	0	0	0	0	1	0	25,029
Huntsville	1	0	0	0	0	0	0	0	1	0	1,370
Independence	2	0	0	0	0	0	0	0	2	0	121,255
Jonesburg	1	0	0	0	0	0	0	1	0	0	776
Kansas City	28	3	8	0	0	3	4	10	17	11	508,856
Lake St. Louis	1	0	0	0	0	0	0	0	0	1	17,846
Lebanon	2	0	0	0	0	0	0	0	1	1	15,143
Lee's Summit	4	0	0	0	0	0	2	0	0	2	103,976
Liberty	1	0	0	0	0	0				1	30,470
Macon	0	1	0	0	0	0	0	0	0	1	5,480
Malden	2	0	0	0	0	0	0	0	0	2	3,568
Maplewood[2]	0	0	2	0	0	0	0	1	0	0	8,117
Matthews	0	0	1	0	0	0	0	1	0	0	509
Moberly	2	0	0	0	0	0	0	0	1	1	13,998
Monroe City	1	0	0	0	0	0	0	1	0	0	2,681
Mountain Grove	1	0	0	0	0	0	1	0	0	0	4,530
North Kansas City	1	0	0	0	0	0	0	1	0	0	4,534
O'Fallon	1	0	1	0	0	0	1	1	0	0	95,689
Overland	1	0	0	0	0	0	0	1	0	0	15,632
Raytown	1	0	0	0	0	0	1	0	0	0	29,224
Rolla	2	0	1	0	0	0	1	0	2	0	20,321
Shrewsbury	1	0	0	0	0	0	0	0	0	1	6,280
Sikeston	1	0	1	0	0	0	1	0	0	1	16,024
St. Ann	2	0	0	0	0	0	1	1	0	0	12,788
St. Charles	0	0	0	0	1	0	1	0	0	0	71,079
St. Clair	1	0	1	0	0	0	0	0	1	1	4,746
St. James	1	0	0	0	0	0	1	0	0	0	4,010
St. John	1	0	0	0	0	0	0	1	0	0	6,538
St. Joseph	1	1	0	0	0	1	0	1	2	0	70,918
St. Louis[2]	6	0	5	0	0	0	1	3	3	3	286,053
St. Peters	2	0	0	1	0	0	1	0	0	2	58,584
St. Robert	1	0	0	0	0	0	1	0	0	0	5,399
Sunset Hills	1	0	0	0	0	0	0	0	0	1	9,053
Union	0	2	0	0	0	0	0	0	1	1	12,575
Velda City	1	0	0	0	0	0	1	0	0	0	1,165
Vinita Park	1	4	0	0	0	0	0	2	1	2	8,852
Universities and Colleges	4	0	2	0	0	0					
Missouri University of Science and Technology	1	0	0	0	0	0	1	0	0	0	8,165
Northwest Missouri State University[2]	2	0	1	0	0	0	0	0	1	1	8,872
Truman State University	1	0	0	0	0	0	0	0	0	1	5,047
University of Missouri, Kansas City	0	0	1	0	0	0	0	0	0	1	18,650
Metropolitan Counties	14	8	1	1	0	3					
Boone	1	0	0	0	0	0	0	0	1	0	
Cape Girardeau	1	0	0	0	0	0	1	0	0	0	
Clay	1	0	0	0	0	0	0	0	0	1	
DeKalb	1	0	0	0	0	0	0	1	0	1	
Franklin	0	1	0	0	0	0	0	1	0	0	
Jackson	2	0	0	0	0	0	0	2	0	0	
Jasper	0	2	0	0	0	0	0	0	2	0	
Lincoln	2	0	0	0	0	0	2	0	0	0	
Platte	2	1	0	1	0	0	1	2	0	1	
St. Charles	1	0	0	0	0	0	0	1	0	0	
St. Charles County Police Department	0	1	0	0	0	2	0	3	0	1	
St. Louis County Police Department	3	2	1	0	0	1	1	4	1	1	
Webster	0	1	0	0	0	0	0	0	1	0	
Nonmetropolitan Counties	11	4	3	1	3	0					
Barry	0	0	1	0	0	0	1	0	0	0	
Butler	1	0	0	0	0	0	0	1	0	0	
Camden	1	1	1	0	0	0	0	2	0	1	
Cedar	1	0	0	0	0	0	0	0	0	1	
Chariton	0	1	0	0	0	0	0	1	0	0	
Grundy	0	1	0	0	0	0	0	0	1	0	

Table 94. Hate Crime Incidents Per Bias Motivation and Quarter, by Selected State, Territory, Federal, and Agency, 2022—Continued

(Number.)

State/agency	Number of incidents per bias motivation						Number of incidents per quarter				Population[1]
	Race/ Ethnicity/ Ancestry	Religion	Sexual orientation	Disability	Gender	Gender Identity	1st quarter	2nd quarter	3rd quarter	4th quarter	
Madison	1	0	0	0	0	0	0	0	1	0	
Montgomery	0	0	0	0	1	0	0	1	0	0	
Morgan	1	0	0	0	0	0	0	0	1		
Pike	0	1	0	0	0	0	0	0	0	1	
Schuyler	0	0	0	0	1	0	0	1	0	0	
Ste. Genevieve	1	0	0	1	0	0	1	0	0	1	
St. Francois	2	0	0	0	1	0	0	1	0	2	
Stone	2	0	0	0	0	0	0	1	1	0	
Taney	0	0	1	0	0	0	0	1	0	0	
Washington	1	0	0	0	0	0	0	0	0	1	
MONTANA	13	0	2	0	0	0					
Cities	10	0	2	0	0	0					
Billings	3	0	0	0	0	0	0	1	1	1	117,866
Bozeman	1	0	0	0	0	0	0	0	0	1	55,997
Great Falls[2]	5	0	1	0	0	0	1	1	1	2	60,386
Helena	1	0	0	0	0	0	0	1	0	0	33,896
Kalispell	0	0	1	0	0	0	0	0	0	1	27,710
Montana State University	2	0	0	0	0	0	0	1	0	1	18,344
Roosevelt	1	0	0	0	0	0	0	0	0	1	
NEBRASKA	49	4	12	0	2	3					
Cities	37	2	9	0	2	3					
Albion	1	0	0	0	0	0	1	0	0	0	1,721
Alliance	0	0	1	0	0	0	0	1	0	0	7,807
Beatrice	1	0	0	0	0	0	0	1	0	0	12,164
Chadron	1	0	1	0	0	0	0	0	0	2	5,222
Columbus	1	0	0	0	0	0	0	1	0	0	24,158
Falls City[2]	5	0	0	0	0	0	0	1	0	0	4,032
Gering	0	0	1	0	0	0	1	0	0	0	8,372
Grand Island	2	0	0	0	0	0	0	0	0	2	51,733
Hastings	1	0	0	0	0	0	0	0	1	0	24,930
Lincoln	8	1	0	0	0	3	0	1	7	4	293,937
McCook	1	0	1	0	0	0	0	1	0	1	7,325
Nebraska City	1	0	1	0	0	0	1	1	0	0	7,212
Norfolk	1	0	0	0	0	0	1	0	0	0	25,048
North Platte	0	0	1	0	0	0	0	0	0	1	22,684
Omaha	14	1	2	0	0	0	9	2	4	2	483,462
Scottsbluff	0	0	1	0	0	0	1	0	0	0	15,224
York	0	0	0	0	2	0	0	0	1	1	8,214
Universities and Colleges	4	1	2	0	0	0					
Metropolitan Community College, Douglas County	1	0	0	0	0	0	1	0	0	0	21,101
University of Nebraska, Lincoln[2]	3	1	2	0	0	0	1	0	2	0	27,390
Metropolitan Counties	3	0	0	0	0	0					
Douglas	3	0	0	0	0	0	1	0	1	1	
Nonmetropolitan Counties	5	0	0	0	0	0					
Dodge	1	0	0	0	0	0	1	0	0	0	
Jefferson	3	0	0	0	0	0	0	1	1	1	
Scotts Bluff	1	0	0	0	0	0	0	0	1	0	
State Police Agencies	0	1	1	0	0	0					
State Patrol											
Butler County	0	0	1	0	0	0	0	0	0	1	
Hall County	0	1	0	0	0	0	0	0	0	1	
NEVADA	66	15	18	0	2	6					
Cities	45	10	12	0	0	4					
Las Vegas Metropolitan Police Department[2]	28	5	10	0	0	2	10	10	11	9	1,667,961
Mesquite	0	0	0	0	0	1	0	0	0	1	21,732
North Las Vegas[2]	7	1	0	0	0	0	0	2	2	3	284,422
Reno[2]	8	4	2	0	0	1	6	4	4	0	273,671
Winnemucca	2	0	0	0	0	0	0	0	1	1	8,775
Universities and Colleges	2	2	0	0	0	0					
University of Nevada, Reno	2	2	0	0	0	0	2	1	1	0	22,982
Metropolitan Counties	4	0	2	0	0	0					
Carson City	1	0	1	0	0	0	0	0	2	0	
Storey	1	0	0	0	0	0	0	0	0	1	
Washoe	2	0	1	0	0	0	0	0	3	0	
Nonmetropolitan Counties	8	3	3	0	0	2					
Churchill	2	1	0	0	0	0	2	0	1	0	
Douglas	1	0	0	0	0	0	0	0	1	0	

Table 94. Hate Crime Incidents Per Bias Motivation and Quarter, by Selected State, Territory, Federal, and Agency, 2022—Continued

(Number.)

State/agency	Number of incidents per bias motivation						Number of incidents per quarter				Population[1]
	Race/ Ethnicity/ Ancestry	Religion	Sexual orientation	Disability	Gender	Gender Identity	1st quarter	2nd quarter	3rd quarter	4th quarter	
Elko	0	0	2	0	0	0	0	1	1	0	
Lander	0	0	0	0	0	1	0	1	0	0	
Lyon	1	0	1	0	0	1	1	1	1	0	
Mineral	2	0	0	0	0	0	0	0	2	0	
Nye	0	2	0	0	0	0	0	0	0	2	
White Pine[2]	2	0	0	0	0	0	0	0	1	0	
State Police Agencies	3	0	1	0	0	0					
Highway Patrol											
Northeastern Division[2]	2	0	0	0	0	0	0	0	0	1	
Northwestern Division	1	0	0	0	0	0	0	0	1	0	
Southern Division	0	0	1	0	0	0	0	1	0	0	
Tribal Agencies	1	0	0	0	2	0					
Pyramid Lake Tribal	1	0	0	0	2	0	0	1	2	0	
Other Agencies	3	0	0	0	0	0					
Capitol Police	1	0	0	0	0	0	0	0	1	0	
Washoe County School District	2	0	0	0	0	0	0	0	1	1	
NEW HAMPSHIRE	14	5	10	0	1	0					
Cities	11	4	9	0	1	0					
Alton	0	0	1	0	0	0	1	0	0	0	6,054
Concord	2	1	0	0	0	0	0	0	2	1	44,305
Durham	1	0	0	0	0	0	0	0	0	1	15,550
Exeter	0	0	1	0	0	0	0	1	0	0	16,155
Gilmanton	0	0	0	0	1	0	0	0	1	0	4,022
Hampton	1	0	0	0	0	0	0	1	0	0	16,384
Hooksett	0	0	1	0	0	0	1	0	0	0	15,313
Keene	0	2	0	0	0	0	1	0	0	1	23,271
Laconia	1	0	0	0	0	0	1	0	0	0	17,109
Lebanon	1	0	0	0	0	0	1	0	0	0	15,702
Madbury	1	0	0	0	0	0	0	0	1	0	1,938
Manchester	3	0	1	0	0	0	0	1	0	3	114,650
Newmarket	0	1	1	0	0	0	2	0	0	0	9,417
Portsmouth	0	0	2	0	0	0	1	1	0	0	22,513
Somersworth	0	0	1	0	0	0	0	1	0	0	12,160
Stratham	0	0	1	0	0	0	1	0	0	0	7,844
Weare	1	0	0	0	0	0	0	1	0	0	9,213
Universities and Colleges	2	1	0	0	0	0					
Plymouth State University	1	1	0	0	0	0	1	1	0	0	5,079
University of New Hampshire	1	0	0	0	0	0	1	0	0	0	15,585
State Police Agencies	1	0	1	0	0	0					
State Police, Cheshire County[2]	1	0	1	0	0	0	0	0	0	1	
NEW JERSEY	726	305	174	12	9	56					
Cities	671	273	156	12	8	51					
Asbury Park[2]	1	0	2	0	0	1		2		1	15,209
Atlantic Highlands	2	0	1	0	0	0		1	2		4,416
Barnegat Township	1	0	0	0	0	0	0	0	1	0	25,142
Barrington	1	0	0	0	0	0	1	0	0	0	7,013
Bayonne	0	0	1	0	0	0		1			66,990
Beachwood	4	2	0	0	0	0	2	0	0	4	11,188
Bedminster Township	3	0	0	0	0	0	2	1			8,123
Belvidere[2]	1	1	0	0	0	0				1	2,531
Bergenfield[2]	3	1	3	0	0	0	1	1	1	2	28,082
Berkeley Township[2]	2	1	1	0	0	1	2	1	1		45,006
Bernardsville	1	0	0	0	0	0	0	0	0	1	7,786
Blairstown Township	2	0	2	0	0	0	1	2		1	5,766
Bloomingdale	2	0	0	0	0	0	0	0	0	2	7,616
Bordentown Township	1	0	0	0	0	0		0	0	1	12,095
Branchburg Township[2]	2	1	2	0	0	0	1	2	1		14,690
Brick Township[2]	6	4	5	0	0	2	2	5	1	4	76,287
Burlington Township[2]	3	0	0	0	0	0	0	0	0	2	23,927
Butler	2	0	0	0	0	0		1		1	8,203
Camden County Police Department	0	0	1	0	0	0			1		71,616
Cedar Grove Township	2	0	0	0	0	0	0	2	0	0	13,822
Chatham Township[2]	4	0	0	0	0	0	1		2		10,897
Cherry Hill Township[2]	31	8	6	0	0	1	3	19	8	11	76,401
Clark Township	3	0	0	0	0	0	0	1	1	1	15,308
Clifton[2]	21	6	0	0	1	0	14	5	2	1	88,768
Clinton Township[2]	6	4	1	0	0	0	3	4	1	1	13,759
Closter	1	0	0	0	0	0	0	0	1	0	8,474
Colts Neck Township	2	1	0	0	0	0		1		2	9,967
Cranford Township	1	0	0	0	0	3	0	3	1	0	24,133
Deal	0	1	0	0	0	0	0	0	1	0	892
Delanco Township	1	0	0	0	0	0		1			4,805

Table 94. Hate Crime Incidents Per Bias Motivation and Quarter, by Selected State, Territory, Federal, and Agency, 2022—Continued

(Number.)

State/agency	Number of incidents per bias motivation						Number of incidents per quarter				Population[1]
	Race/ Ethnicity/ Ancestry	Religion	Sexual orientation	Disability	Gender	Gender Identity	1st quarter	2nd quarter	3rd quarter	4th quarter	
Delran Township	1	1	0	0	0	0	0	0	1	1	17,822
Demarest	0	0	1	0	0	0	1				4,812
Denville Township	0	3	1	0	0	1	3	1	0	1	17,119
Deptford Township	0	1	0	0	0	0				1	32,429
Dover[2]	1	4	0	0	0	0	1	0	2	0	18,434
Dumont	4	0	1	0	0	0	1	2	2	0	18,533
East Brunswick Township	1	1	0	0	0	0	1	0	0	1	49,038
East Newark[2]	2	1	0	0	0	0		1			2,383
East Rutherford	1	1	0	0	0	0	1	1			9,904
East Windsor Township	3	0	0	0	0	0		2		1	29,788
Eatontown	2	0	0	0	0	0	0	1	0	1	13,607
Edison Township[2]	10	5	4	0	0	0	3	2	4	7	108,050
Elizabeth	2	1	0	0	0	1	1	1	0	2	134,065
Englewood	1	0	0	0	0	0	0	0	0	1	28,975
Englishtown	1	0	0	0	0	0			1		2,362
Evesham Township	3	2	1	0	0	1	2	2	3	0	49,166
Fair Lawn	0	2	0	0	0	0	1			1	35,424
Fairview	1	0	1	0	0	1		2		1	14,850
Fanwood	1	0	0	0	0	0		0	0	1	7,654
Florence Township	0	0	1	0	0	0			1		12,747
Fort Lee[2]	5	1	4	2	1	0	3	4	1	1	39,636
Franklin	1	0	0	0	0	0	0	0	0	1	4,983
Franklin Lakes	1	0	0	0	0	0	1	0	0	0	10,899
Franklin Township, Somerset County	5	1	0	0	0	0		2	1	3	68,782
Freehold Borough[2]	1	1	0	0	0	0	0	1	0	0	12,539
Freehold Township[2]	1	2	0	0	0	0		1		1	35,791
Frenchtown	0	0	14	0	0	0			14		1,387
Garfield	1	0	0	0	0	0	1	0	0	0	32,351
Gloucester Township[2]	4	2	0	0	0	2	3	2	1	0	65,848
Green Brook Township	1	0	0	0	0	0	1				7,314
Greenwich Township, Gloucester County	2	0	0	0	0	0				2	5,018
Greenwich Township, Warren County	0	0	1	0	0	0				1	5,490
Hackensack	5	1	1	0	0	0	2	2	0	3	45,413
Hackettstown	0	0	1	0	0	0				1	10,389
Haddonfield	2	4	0	0	0	0	2	3	1	0	12,467
Haddon Township	1	0	0	0	0	0	0	0	0	1	15,358
Hamilton Township, Mercer County	1	0	0	0	0	0	1	0	0	0	91,408
Hanover Township	1	0	0	0	0	0	0	0	0	1	14,630
Harding Township	0	1	0	0	0	0				1	3,883
Hardyston Township	0	1	0	0	0	0	0	0	1	0	8,351
Hasbrouck Heights	2	0	1	0	0	0		2	1		12,005
High Bridge	2	0	0	0	0	0			1	1	3,641
Highland Park[2]	1	2	0	0	0	0	0	2	0	0	14,914
Highlands	1	0	0	0	0	0		1			4,654
Hightstown	3	0	1	0	0	0	1	0	0	3	5,859
Hillsborough Township	2	0	1	1	0	3	5	2	0	0	42,893
Hillsdale	1	0	0	0	0	0		1			10,011
Hillside Township	2	1	0	0	0	0	0	0	2	1	22,026
Ho-Ho-Kus	0	1	0	0	0	0	0	0	0	1	4,195
Holmdel Township	1	0	0	0	0	0	1				17,421
Hopewell Township	1	0	2	0	0	0	0	0	0	3	17,339
Howell Township[2]	31	17	4	1	0	2	7	12	8	18	54,073
Jackson Township	0	1	0	0	0	0	0	0	0	1	60,762
Jersey City	3	2	0	0	0	3	1	3	2	2	276,300
Keansburg[2]	11	1	0	0	0	0	3	3	2	3	9,757
Kearny	0	1	1	0	0	0		1	1		38,906
Keyport	1	0	0	0	0	0		1	0	0	7,205
Lacey Township[2]	9	2	0	0	0	0	3	4	1	1	29,903
Lakewood Township[2]	13	33	2	0	0	0	7	4	11	18	141,190
Lawrence Township, Mercer County	6	1	0	0	0	0	1	4	0	2	32,949
Linden	7	6	0	0	0	0	3	3	6	1	43,652
Lindenwold	0	1	0	0	0	0	0	0	1	0	21,524
Little Egg Harbor Township	0	0	1	0	0	0	0	1	0	0	21,498
Little Falls Township	0	1	1	0	0	0				2	13,220
Livingston Township[2]	4	5	0	0	0	0	0	1	4	2	30,844
Long Beach Township	0	1	0	0	0	0		0	1	0	3,143
Long Branch[2]	4	0	1	0	0	0	1		2	1	33,094
Long Hill Township	1	0	0	0	0	0	1				8,610
Lopatcong Township[2]	3	1	0	0	0	0		1	1	1	10,057
Lower Township[2]	2	1	0	0	0	2	0	1	1	2	22,238
Lyndhurst Township	2	0	0	0	0	0	0	2	0	0	22,183
Magnolia	1	0	0	0	0	0	0	1	0	0	4,325
Mahwah Township[2]	4	0	1	0	0	0		1	2	1	25,150
Manalapan Township[2]	7	6	2	0	0	0	1	2	2	6	40,897
Manchester Township	1	1	1	0	0	0	1	2	0	0	46,265
Mansfield Township, Burlington County	0	1	0	0	0	0			0	1	8,868
Mansfield Township, Warren County[2]	1	0	0	0	1	0				1	7,846
Manville	3	0	0	0	0	0	1		2		10,763
Maple Shade Township[2]	6	2	0	0	0	0	2	3	1	1	19,911

Table 94. Hate Crime Incidents Per Bias Motivation and Quarter, by Selected State, Territory, Federal, and Agency, 2022—Continued

(Number.)

State/agency	Race/ Ethnicity/ Ancestry	Religion	Sexual orientation	Disability	Gender	Gender Identity	1st quarter	2nd quarter	3rd quarter	4th quarter	Population[1]
Margate City	0	0	1	0	0	0	1				5,202
Marlboro Township[2]	8	0	2	1	0	1	2	2	3	4	41,576
Medford Lakes[2]	0	3	0	0	0	0	0	0	2	0	4,257
Medford Township	4	2	2	0	0	0	5	1	1	1	24,447
Mendham	1	0	0	0	0	0				1	4,975
Middle Township	1	0	0	0	0	1	0	1	0	1	20,845
Middletown Township[2]	16	7	2	0	0	0	1	8	6	5	67,055
Midland Park	0	1	0	0	0	1	0	1	0	1	6,930
Monmouth Beach	1	0	1	0	0	0		1	1		3,242
Monroe Township, Middlesex County[2]	12	4	0	1	0	1	1	4	6	5	48,097
Montclair	11	3	0	0	0	1	5	5	2	3	41,117
Moorestown Township	2	0	0	0	0	0	0	2	0	0	21,420
Morris Plains[2]	2	1	2	0	1	0		1	1	1	6,138
Morristown[2]	3	2	2	0	0	1	0	2	0	2	20,418
Morris Township	2	1	0	0	0	0	1	2			23,455
Mount Laurel Township[2]	5	0	3	0	0	0	0	3	2	2	46,518
Mount Olive Township	2	0	0	0	0	0	0	2	0	0	28,970
Neptune City	1	0	0	0	0	0		1			4,620
Neptune Township[2]	21	1	9	1	0	1	5	5	13	5	28,491
Netcong[2]	1	0	1	0	1	0				1	3,973
New Brunswick[2]	8	2	0	0	0	3	2	5	3	2	55,971
New Providence	2	0	0	0	0	0		1		1	13,548
North Arlington	1	0	0	0	0	0			0	1	16,259
Northfield	1	0	0	0	0	0	1				8,435
North Haledon	1	0	0	0	0	0	1	0	0	0	8,788
North Hanover Township	1	0	0	1	0	0		0	2	0	7,925
Northvale	1	0	0	0	0	0				1	4,759
Norwood[2]	2	1	0	0	0	0			2		5,565
Ocean Gate	1	0	0	0	0	0	0	0	0	1	2,000
Ocean Township, Monmouth County[2]	10	17	3	0	0	1	13	7	5	4	28,119
Ocean Township, Ocean County	0	1	0	0	0	0	0	0	1	0	9,031
Old Bridge Township	5	3	1	0	0	0	5	3	1		67,876
Palisades Park[2]	0	0	1	0	0	1	1				19,991
Paramus	2	2	1	0	0	0	1	0	3	1	26,242
Park Ridge	0	0	0	0	0	1	0	0	1	0	10,040
Passaic	4	7	2	0	0	0	5	3	4	1	69,003
Paterson	3	1	3	0	0	1	2	3	1	2	156,292
Pemberton Township	6	0	3	0	0	1		6	3	1	26,759
Pennington	1	0	0	0	0	0	0	1	0	0	2,790
Pennsauken Township	1	0	0	0	0	0	1	0	0	0	37,198
Pequannock Township[2]	3	1	1	0	0	0	2			1	15,560
Perth Amboy[2]	2	2	0	0	0	0		3			55,229
Phillipsburg	3	0	0	0	0	0	2		1		15,374
Pine Beach	0	1	0	0	0	0		1	0	0	2,201
Piscataway Township[2]	8	1	1	0	0	0	1	3		4	61,170
Plainfield	0	0	1	0	0	0		1			55,494
Plainsboro Township[2]	2	2	1	0	0	0	1	2		1	23,798
Pleasantville	1	0	0	0	0	0			1		20,603
Plumsted Township	9	0	0	0	0	0	2	2		5	8,582
Point Pleasant	1	1	0	0	0	0			1	1	19,501
Princeton	6	1	0	1	0	0	3	5	0	0	30,797
Prospect Park	1	1	0	0	0	0		1	1		6,225
Ramsey[2]	2	0	1	0	0	0			1	1	14,621
Randolph Township[2]	8	0	1	0	0	0	2	1	1	2	26,500
Raritan Township[2]	3	2	1	0	0	0	1		1	2	24,202
Readington Township[2]	1	0	1	0	0	0	1				16,348
Red Bank[2]	1	1	0	0	0	0	1				12,927
Ridgefield[2]	2	1	1	0	0	0	1		1	1	11,368
Ridgefield Park	1	0	0	0	0	0	1	0	0	0	13,067
Ridgewood	1	2	0	0	0	0	0	3	0	0	26,485
Ringwood[2]	2	1	1	0	0	0	0	0	1	1	11,456
River Vale Township	1	0	0	0	0	0	0	1	0	0	9,789
Robbinsville Township	0	1	0	0	0	0	0	0	0	1	15,303
Rochelle Park Township	1	0	0	0	0	0	1	0	0	0	5,841
Roselle	8	0	0	0	0	0	1	2	2	3	22,257
Rutherford	1	1	1	0	0	0	0	2	0	1	18,592
Saddle Brook Township	1	1	0	0	0	0		2			14,408
Sayreville[2]	10	2	1	2	0	0	2	3		5	44,981
Scotch Plains Township	0	0	1	0	0	0	0	1	0	0	24,490
Secaucus	3	0	0	0	0	0	0	1	2	0	20,519
Somerville	3	0	1	0	0	0	1	1	1	1	12,759
South Amboy[2]	1	0	1	0	1	1	0	1	0	0	9,277
South Bound Brook	2	0	0	0	0	0			1	1	4,784
South Brunswick Township	0	1	1	0	0	0	0	0	0	2	46,442
South Plainfield	3	0	0	0	0	0	2	0	1	0	24,211
Sparta Township	6	2	0	0	0	2	4	3	0	3	20,348
Spotswood	3	0	0	0	0	0	1	2			8,041
Summit[2]	9	3	2	0	0	0	2	6	3	2	22,414
Swedesboro	0	0	1	0	0	0				1	2,749

Table 94. Hate Crime Incidents Per Bias Motivation and Quarter, by Selected State, Territory, Federal, and Agency, 2022—Continued

(Number.)

State/agency	Number of incidents per bias motivation						Number of incidents per quarter				Population[1]
	Race/ Ethnicity/ Ancestry	Religion	Sexual orientation	Disability	Gender	Gender Identity	1st quarter	2nd quarter	3rd quarter	4th quarter	
Tenafly	1	0	0	0	0	1	1			1	15,109
Tinton Falls[2]	1	0	1	0	0	2		1		2	19,556
Toms River Township[2]	5	8	5	0	0	2	0	4	6	9	99,239
Trenton[2]	3	2	1	0	1	2		2	1		90,313
Union City[2]	6	6	2	0	0	2	2	3	7		63,312
Union Township	1	0	0	0	0	0		1	0	0	59,622
Upper Saddle River	1	0	0	0	0	0	1				8,248
Voorhees Township	1	1	0	0	0	0	0	1	0	1	31,090
Washington Township, Gloucester County[2]	27	2	4	0	1	0	6	6	9	9	49,625
Washington Township, Morris County	1	0	0	0	0	0	1				18,172
Washington Township, Warren County	1	0	0	0	0	0	1				6,539
Westampton Township	7	1	0	0	0	0	4	0	3	1	9,099
West Amwell Township	1	1	0	0	0	0	1			1	3,033
West Caldwell Township	0	0	1	0	0	0		1			10,756
West New York[2]	5	4	0	0	0	0	0	3	2	0	52,021
Westville	0	0	1	0	0	0	1				4,337
West Windsor Township[2]	6	3	0	0	0	0	2	3	1	2	29,452
Willingboro Township	4	0	0	0	0	0	0	2	0	2	31,795
Woodbridge Township[2]	13	4	4	1	0	0	1	7	5	3	102,980
Woodbury[2]	18	0	4	0	0	0	4	4	10	2	10,108
Woodland Park	3	0	0	0	0	0	1	0	2	0	13,171
Wood-Ridge[2]	2	0	0	0	0	0			0	1	10,057
Wyckoff Township	1	0	0	0	0	0	0	0	0	1	17,544
Universities and Colleges	13	13	5	0	0	1					
Brookdale Community College	0	1	0	0	0	0			1		14,796
Kean University	2	0	0	0	0	1		2	1	0	16,448
Monmouth University	1	0	0	0	0	0	1				6,166
Princeton University	1	1	3	0	0	0	3	0	0	2	7,942
Rutgers University											
Newark	1	0	0	0	0	0	1	0	0	0	15,444
New Brunswick	1	1	0	0	0	0	0	0	2	0	56,771
Stockton University	1	0	0	0	0	0	0	0	1	0	11,788
William Paterson University[2]	6	10	2	0	0	0	6	4	2	1	11,681
Metropolitan Counties	20	4	6	0	0	1					
Bergen[2]	4	2	1	0	0	0	2	1	2		
Essex[2]	1	1	1	0	0	1	2	1	1		
Hudson[2]	4	0	0	0	0	0					
Morris	0	1	0	0	0	0			1		
Somerset[2]	11	0	4	0	0	0	3	3	4	2	
State Police Agencies	4	0	0	0	0	1					
State Police	4	0	0	0	0	1	3	2	0		
Other Agencies	18	15	7	0	1	2					
Department of Corrections[2]	1	1	1	0	0	0		1	1		
New Jersey Transit Police[2]	4	8	1	0	0	1	1	3	4	5	
Park Police, Union County	1	1	1	0	0	0	1	2			
Port Authority of New York and New Jersey[2]	4	2	1	0	0	1	3	1	2	1	
Prosecutor											
Hunterdon County[2]	1	1	0	0	0	0	1				
Union County[2]	2	0	0	0	1	0					
Warren County[2]	1	0	1	0	0	0		1			
State Park Police[2]	4	2	2	0	0	0		4		1	
NEW MEXICO	24	5	8	1	1	2					
Cities	16	4	5	1	0	1					
Albuquerque	0	0	1	0	0	0	0	0	0	1	560,557
Artesia[2]	2	0	0	0	0	0	0	0	1	0	12,084
Bosque Farms	0	1	0	0	0	0	1	0	0	0	4,099
Carlsbad	1	0	0	0	0	0	1	0	0	0	31,532
Clovis	8	1	1	0	0	0	0	0	7	3	37,734
Las Cruces	2	1	2	1	0	0	3	2	0	1	114,102
Milan	0	0	0	0	0	1	0	1	0	0	2,567
Rio Rancho	1	0	0	0	0	0	0	1	0	0	107,435
Santa Fe	0	1	1	0	0	0	0	0	1	1	88,705
Truth or Consequences	2	0	0	0	0	0	1	0	1	0	6,060
Universities and Colleges	0	1	0	0	0	1					
New Mexico State University	0	1	0	0	0	1	0	0	1	1	16,089
Metropolitan Counties	6	0	1	0	0	0					
Bernalillo[2]	3	0	1	0	0	0					
Valencia	3	0	0	0	0	0	1	0	0	2	
Nonmetropolitan Counties	1	0	2	0	1	0					
De Baca	0	0	2	0	1	0	1	2	0	0	
Sierra	1	0	0	0	0	0	0	0	0	1	

Table 94. Hate Crime Incidents Per Bias Motivation and Quarter, by Selected State, Territory, Federal, and Agency, 2022—Continued

(Number.)

State/agency	Number of incidents per bias motivation						Number of incidents per quarter				Population[1]
	Race/ Ethnicity/ Ancestry	Religion	Sexual orientation	Disability	Gender	Gender Identity	1st quarter	2nd quarter	3rd quarter	4th quarter	
Tribal Agencies	1	0	0	0	0	0					
Pojoaque Tribal	1	0	0	0	0	0	1	0	0	0	
NEW YORK	386	421	123	4	0	19					
Cities	280	344	101	3	0	16					
Albany[2]	28	2	3	0	0	0	6	7	8	4	98,104
Amherst Town	1	0	0	0	0	0	0	0	1		123,527
Beacon	0	0	1	0	0	0	0	1	0	0	13,729
Bethlehem Town	2	0	0	0	0	0	0	0	1	1	34,872
Brighton Town[2]	0	3	0	0	0	0	0	1	0	1	36,380
Buffalo[2]	9	1	2	0	0	0	4	2	4	1	275,710
Canandaigua	1	0	0	0	0	0	0	0	1		10,479
Canton Village	1	0	0	0	0	0	0	1	0	0	7,046
Clarkstown Town[2]	2	4	0	0	0	0	1	2	1	1	80,487
Colonie Town	1	1	1	0	0	0	1	1	1	0	81,035
Dobbs Ferry Village	1	0	1	0	0	0	0		1	1	11,361
East Aurora-Aurora Town	0	1	0	0	0	0	0			1	13,936
Goshen Village	0	1	0	0	0	0	0	0	1		5,777
Greenburgh Town	1	0	1	0	0	0	0	1	1	0	45,094
Guilderland Town	1	0	0	0	0	0	0	1			35,488
Hempstead Village[2]	2	0	0	0	0	0	0	0	1	0	58,469
Hyde Park Town	0	0	1	0	0	0	1	0	0	0	21,071
Kingston	0	4	1	0	0	0	1	1	3		24,203
Lynbrook Village	1	1	0	0	0	0	0	1		1	20,200
Massena Village	1	0	0	0	0	0	0	0	1	0	10,165
Newburgh	2	0	0	0	0	0	0	2			28,819
Newburgh Town	0	1	0	0	0	0	0	0	1		32,207
New Rochelle	0	2	0	0	0	0	1	0	0	1	82,628
New York	196	303	78	0	0	15	190	155	146	101	8,236,567
Niagara Falls	1	0	0	0	0	0	0	0	0	1	48,129
Niagara Town[2]	1	0	0	3	0	0	0	1	0	1	7,808
North Greenbush Town	1	0	0	0	0	0	0	1			13,323
Ogden Town[2]	0	0	2	0	0	0	0	1	0	0	20,293
Olean	2	0	0	0	0	0	2	0	0	0	13,671
Ossining Village	0	1	0	0	0	0	0	1			26,980
Oswego City	1	0	0	0	0	0	1	0	0	0	17,299
Pelham Manor Village	1	0	0	0	0	0	0	0	1		5,587
Poughkeepsie	1	2	0	0	0	0	3	0			32,202
Poughkeepsie Town	1	0	0	0	0	0	1	0	0	0	40,966
Ramapo Town	0	8	0	0	0	0	1	1	5	1	107,404
Rochester	4	0	4	0	0	1	0	5	0	4	210,270
Salamanca	1	0	0	0	0	0	1	0			5,837
Saranac Lake Village	1	0	0	0	0	0	0	1			4,805
Schenectady[2]	3	5	1	0	0	0	1	5	1	1	67,101
Scotia Village	1	0	0	0	0	0	0	1			7,253
South Glens Falls Village	1	0	0	0	0	0	0	0	1		3,781
Stony Point Town	1	0	0	0	0	0	0	0	0	1	14,749
Utica	2	0	0	0	0	0	0	2	0	0	63,906
Vestal Town	2	1	1	0	0	0	2	1	0	1	29,553
Waterloo Village	1	0	0	0	0	0	0	1	0	0	4,841
Watervliet	1	0	0	0	0	0	1				10,194
White Plains	1	0	1	0	0	0	0		1	1	59,488
Yonkers	1	3	0	0	0	0	3	0	1	0	208,100
Yorktown Town	1	0	3	0	0	0	0	2	2	0	35,529
Universities and Colleges	5	3	0	0	0	0					
Cornell University	2	0	0	0	0	0	1	1	0	0	24,486
State University of New York Police											
Albany	0	1	0	0	0	0	0			1	20,071
Buffalo	0	2	0	0	0	0	2	0	0	0	35,847
Plattsburgh	1	0	0	0	0	0	1	0			5,906
Potsdam	1	0	0	0	0	0	0	1			3,442
Stony Brook	1	0	0	0	0	0	1	0	0	0	34,254
Metropolitan Counties	35	41	9	0	0	1					
Broome	1	0	0	0	0	0	0	0	0	1	
Erie	1	0	0	0	0	0	1	0			
Monroe[2]	0	3	0	0	0	0	0	0	1	0	
Nassau	22	31	3	0	0	0	15	20	9	12	
Niagara	1	0	0	0	0	0	0	1	0		
Saratoga	0	0	2	0	0	0	0	0	1	1	
Schoharie	1	0	0	0	0	0	0	0	1	0	
Suffolk County Police Department	8	7	4	0	0	1	3	9	5	3	
Westchester Public Safety	1	0	0	0	0	0	1	0			
Nonmetropolitan Counties	0	0	1	0	0	0					
Montgomery	0	0	1	0	0	0	0	0	0	1	
State Police Agencies	44	14	9	1	0	2					
State Police											

Table 94. Hate Crime Incidents Per Bias Motivation and Quarter, by Selected State, Territory, Federal, and Agency, 2022—Continued

(Number.)

State/agency	Number of incidents per bias motivation						Number of incidents per quarter				Population[1]
	Race/ Ethnicity/ Ancestry	Religion	Sexual orientation	Disability	Gender	Gender Identity	1st quarter	2nd quarter	3rd quarter	4th quarter	
Albany County	1	0	0	0	0	0	0			1	
Broome County	2	0	1	0	0	0	1	1	1		
Cattaraugus County	4	0	0	0	0	0	0	1	3		
Cayuga County	6	0	0	0	0	0	0	4	2		
Chautauqua County	1	0	0	0	0	0	1	0			
Delaware County	1	0	0	0	0	0	1	0			
Dutchess County	1	0	0	0	0	1	0		1	1	
Erie County	1	0	0	0	0	0	0			1	
Essex County	1	0	0	0	0	0	0			1	
Franklin County	3	0	0	0	0	0	2	0	1		
Fulton County	1	0	0	1	0	0	0	0	2		
Genesee County	0	0	1	0	0	0	0	0	1		
Greene County	1	0	0	0	0	0	0	1			
Hamilton County	2	0	0	0	0	0	1	1			
Jefferson County	0	0	0	0	0	1	0	0	1		
Montgomery County	0	1	0	0	0	0	0	0	1		
Nassau County	2	0	0	0	0	0	0	2			
Oneida County	2	0	1	0	0	0	1	1	1		
Onondaga County	2	1	0	0	0	0	1	1	1		
Ontario County	1	0	0	0	0	0	0	0	1		
Orange County	0	2	1	0	0	0	0	3			
Oswego County	0	1	0	0	0	0	0			1	
Otsego County	1	0	0	0	0	0	0	0	1		
Rensselaer County	0	1	0	0	0	0	0	1			
Saratoga County	1	0	0	0	0	0	0	1			
Schoharie County	1	0	0	0	0	0	0	0	1		
St. Lawrence County	1	0	1	0	0	0	0			2	
Suffolk County	5	1	0	0	0	0	1	5			
Sullivan County	1	1	0	0	0	0	0		1	1	
Westchester County	3	5	3	0	0	0	4	3	3	1	
Wyoming County	0	0	1	0	0	0	0	1			
Other Agencies	22	19	3	0	0	0					
New York City Metropolitan Transportation Authority	14	16	3	0	0	0	8	14	4	7	
State Park											
Finger Lakes Region	4	1	0	0	0	0	0	3	2		
Genesee Region	0	1	0	0	0	0	0	1			
Long Island Region	4	0	0	0	0	0	0	4			
Statewide	0	1	0	0	0	0	0			1	
NORTH CAROLINA	187	77	54	8	2	2					
Cities	117	39	42	5	2	1					
Ahoskie	0	1	0	0	0	0	0	0	0	1	4,830
Albemarle[2]	2	0	0	0	0	0	1	0	0	0	16,819
Apex	0	0	2	0	0	0	1	0	0	1	66,024
Asheboro	1	1	0	0	0	0	1	1	0	0	27,275
Asheville	6	0	6	0	0	0	2	4	2	4	93,729
Bald Head Island	1	0	0	0	0	0	0	0	1	0	273
Beulaville	0	1	0	0	0	0	0	0	0	1	1,109
Biltmore Forest	0	1	0	0	0	0	0	1	0	0	1,433
Boiling Spring Lakes[2]	2	0	0	0	0	1	0	1	0	1	6,349
Burlington[2]	5	0	1	0	0	0	0	3	1	1	60,069
Canton	0	1	0	0	0	0	1	0	0	0	4,433
Charlotte-Mecklenburg[2]	16	5	8	1	0	0	6	6	6	5	955,466
Clayton	2	0	0	0	0	0	1	0	0	1	30,036
Concord	2	0	0	0	0	0	1	1	0	0	109,660
Cornelius	0	0	1	0	0	0	0	0	1	0	31,781
Durham	3	1	2	0	0	0	3	0	3	0	286,377
Emerald Isle	1	0	0	0	0	0	0	0	1	0	3,940
Fayetteville[2]	8	0	1	0	1	0	1	1	4	2	208,980
Fletcher	1	0	0	0	0	0	0	0	1	0	8,059
Gastonia	0	1	0	1	0	0	0	0	1	1	81,937
Gibsonville	1	0	0	0	0	0	1	0	0	0	9,049
Granite Falls	0	2	0	0	0	0	0	1	1	0	4,920
Greensboro[2]	8	1	8	1	0	0	2	5	8	1	298,719
Greenville[2]	2	1	0	1	0	0	0	1	2	0	89,363
Hendersonville	1	1	1	0	0	0	0	0	0	3	15,122
High Point	0	0	1	0	0	0	0	0	0	1	114,280
Hope Mills	2	0	0	0	0	0	0	0	2	0	17,843
Jacksonville	1	0	0	0	0	0	1	0	0	0	72,570
Jonesville	0	1	0	0	0	0	0	0	0	1	2,310
Kannapolis	0	0	0	1	0	0	1	0	0	0	55,480
Kernersville	2	0	0	0	0	0	1	0	1	0	27,076
Knightdale	1	0	0	0	0	0	0	1	0	0	19,659
Leland	1	0	0	0	0	0	0	1	0	0	28,203
Lexington	1	0	0	0	0	0	0	0	1	0	19,544
Lincolnton	3	0	0	0	0	0	1	0	2	0	11,651
Long View	0	1	0	0	0	0	0	0	1	0	5,148
Lumberton	0	3	1	0	0	0	0	3	0	1	18,583

Table 94. Hate Crime Incidents Per Bias Motivation and Quarter, by Selected State, Territory, Federal, and Agency, 2022—Continued

(Number.)

State/agency	Number of incidents per bias motivation						Number of incidents per quarter				Population[1]
	Race/Ethnicity/Ancestry	Religion	Sexual orientation	Disability	Gender	Gender Identity	1st quarter	2nd quarter	3rd quarter	4th quarter	
Matthews	1	0	0	0	0	0	0	1	0	0	29,739
Mint Hill	0	1	0	0	0	0	0	0	0	1	26,728
Mooresville	1	0	0	0	0	0	0	1	0	0	52,762
Morehead City	2	0	0	0	0	0	0	0	0	2	9,810
Mount Airy	0	1	0	0	0	0	1	0	0	0	10,511
Mount Gilead	0	1	0	0	0	0	0	0	0	1	1,176
Murphy	0	0	1	0	0	0	0	1			1,640
Pineville	1	2	0	0	0	0	3	0	0	0	10,718
Pittsboro	1	0	0	0	0	0	0	0	1	0	4,662
Raleigh[2]	18	2	6	0	1	0	4	11	5	6	470,829
Reidsville	2	0	0	0	0	0	0	0	2	0	14,481
Roxboro	0	0	1	0	0	0	0	0	0	1	8,079
Salisbury	3	0	0	0	0	0	1	1	1	0	35,938
Shallotte	0	1	0	0	0	0	0	0	1	0	4,453
Siler City	1	7	0	0	0	0	1	1	5	1	7,969
Stallings	1	0	0	0	0	0	0	0	0	1	16,758
Statesville	0	1	0	0	0	0	0	1	0		29,454
Surf City	1	0	0	0	0	0	0	0	1	0	4,338
Troutman	1	0	0	0	0	0	0	0	0	1	3,889
Warrenton	1	0	0	0	0	0	0	1	0	0	861
Warsaw	1	0	0	0	0	0	0	0	0	1	2,668
Washington	2	1	0	0	0	0	2	0	0	1	9,614
Wilkesboro	0	0	1	0	0	0	0	1	0	0	3,567
Wilmington	1	0	0	0	0	0	0	0	1	0	119,159
Wilson	1	0	0	0	0	0	0	0	1	0	47,518
Winston-Salem[2]	4	0	0	0	0	0	0	0	1	2	251,295
Woodfin	0	0	1	0	0	0	1	0	0	0	8,097
Zebulon	1	0	0	0	0	0	0	0	0	1	9,003
Universities and Colleges	4	0	0	0	0	1					
Elizabeth City State University	1	0	0	0	0	0	1	0	0	0	2,351
North Carolina Central University	1	0	0	0	0	0	1	0	0	0	9,000
North Carolina State University, Raleigh	1	0	0	0	0	0	0	0	0	1	40,482
University of North Carolina, Chapel Hill	1	0	0	0	0	0	0	0	1	0	32,943
Western Carolina University	0	0	0	0	0	1	0	0	1	0	13,820
Metropolitan Counties	48	15	7	3	0	0					
Alamance	1	0	0	0	0	0	0	1	0	0	
Anson	1	0	0	0	0	0	0	1	0		
Brunswick	0	1	0	0	0	0	0	0	1	0	
Buncombe	3	0	3	1	0	0	3	2	1	1	
Burke	2	1	0	0	0	0	0	1	1	1	
Cabarrus	2	0	0	0	0	0	0	1	0	1	
Camden	1	0	0	0	0	0	1	0	0		
Catawba	0	1	0	0	0	0	0	1	0	0	
Chatham	1	0	0	0	0	0	0	0	1	0	
Craven	1	0	0	0	0	0	0	1	0	0	
Currituck	2	0	2	0	0	0	2	1	1	0	
Davidson	2	0	0	0	0	0	0	1	1	0	
Durham[2]	2	0	0	0	0	0	0	0	0	1	
Edgecombe	1	0	0	0	0	0	0	0	1	0	
Forsyth	5	1	1	0	0	0	0	2	3	2	
Franklin	0	1	0	0	0	0	0	0	1		
Guilford	1	1	0	0	0	0	0	0	0	2	
Harnett	4	0	0	0	0	0	1	0	1	2	
Haywood	0	1	0	0	0	0	0	0	0	1	
Henderson	1	0	0	0	0	0	0	1	0	0	
Hoke	0	4	0	0	0	0	0	4	0	0	
Lincoln	1	0	0	0	0	0	0	0	1	0	
Nash	0	1	1	0	0	0	0	1	1	0	
New Hanover	1	0	0	0	0	0	0	0	0	1	
Pamlico	1	0	0	0	0	0	0	0	0	1	
Pender[2]	0	1	0	2	0	0	0	2	0	0	
Person	0	2	0	0	0	0	0	1	1	0	
Pitt	1	0	0	0	0	0	0	0	1	0	
Randolph	1	0	0	0	0	0	0	1	0	0	
Union	12	0	0	0	0	0	6	2	2	2	
Wake	1	0	0	0	0	0	0	0	1	0	
Nonmetropolitan Counties	15	22	5	0	0	0					
Ashe	0	1	0	0	0	0	0	0	0	1	
Avery	0	1	0	0	0	0	0	0	0	1	
Carteret	0	0	1	0	0	0	0	1	0		
Cherokee	1	0	0	0	0	0	0	0	1	0	
Chowan	0	1	0	0	0	0	0	0	1	0	
Clay	0	3	0	0	0	0	0	0	1	2	
Cleveland	1	0	0	0	0	0	0	1	0	0	
Halifax	1	0	0	0	0	0	0	0	1	0	
Hertford	1	0	0	0	0	0	0	0	0	1	

Table 94. Hate Crime Incidents Per Bias Motivation and Quarter, by Selected State, Territory, Federal, and Agency, 2022—Continued

(Number.)

State/agency	Race/Ethnicity/Ancestry	Religion	Sexual orientation	Disability	Gender	Gender Identity	1st quarter	2nd quarter	3rd quarter	4th quarter	Population[1]
Jackson	1	0	1	0	0	0	1	1	0	0	
Lee	0	1	0	0	0	0	0	1	0	0	
Macon	1	0	0	0	0	0	0	0	1	0	
Montgomery	1	6	0	0	0	0	1	1	3	2	
Pasquotank	2	0	0	0	0	0	0	0	0	2	
Richmond	0	2	0	0	0	0	0	0	0	2	
Robeson	1	0	0	0	0	0	1	0	0	0	
Scotland	0	1	0	0	0	0	0	0	0	1	
Surry	1	3	0	0	0	0	0	0	2	2	
Swain	2	0	1	0	0	0	1	0	2	0	
Transylvania	1	0	0	0	0	0	0	0	1	0	
Warren	0	1	0	0	0	0	0	0	0	1	
Washington	0	0	1	0	0	0	1	0	0	0	
Watauga	0	1	1	0	0	0	0	0	1	1	
Wilson	1	0	0	0	0	0	0	0	1	0	
Yancey	0	1	0	0	0	0	0	0	1	0	
Other Agencies	3	1	0	0	0	0					
Raleigh-Durham International Airport[2]	1	1	0	0	0	0	0	0	0	1	
University of North Carolina Hospitals	1	0	0	0	0	0	1	0	0	0	
WakeMed Campus Police	1	0	0	0	0	0	0	0	0	1	
NORTH DAKOTA	16	0	1	0	0	0					
Cities	12	0	1	0	0	0					
Bismarck	6	0	0	0	0	0	1	0	3	2	74,604
Dickinson	1	0	0	0	0	0	1	0	0	0	24,577
Fargo	1	0	0	0	0	0	0	0	0	1	127,649
Grand Forks	1	0	1	0	0	0	0	0	2	0	58,620
Lincoln	2	0	0	0	0	0	0	1	1	0	4,387
Lisbon	1	0	0	0	0	0	0	1	0	0	2,177
Metropolitan Counties	1	0	0	0	0	0					
Grand Forks	1	0	0	0	0	0	1	0	0	0	
Nonmetropolitan Counties	3	0	0	0	0	0					
Benson	1	0	0	0	0	0	0	0	0	1	
Emmons	1	0	0	0	0	0	1	0	0	0	
Griggs	1	0	0	0	0	0	1	0	0	0	
OHIO	312	67	81	41	2	45					
Cities	261	42	72	32	1	39					
Akron[2]	11	5	0	1	0	2	4	4	4	6	188,534
American Township	2	0	0	0	0	1	0	1	2	0	12,355
Archbold	0	0	0	1	0	0	0	0	1	0	4,484
Ashland	0	0	1	1	0	0	1	0	1	0	19,193
Barberton	3	0	0	0	0	0	0	1	1	1	24,840
Bath Township, Summit County	0	0	0	2	0	0	0	0	0	2	9,922
Bay Village	0	0	0	1	0	0	0	1	0	0	15,826
Bazetta Township	0	0	0	2	0	0	1	0	0	1	5,916
Bexley	1	0	0	0	0	0	0	1	0	0	13,497
Blue Ash	1	0	0	0	0	0	1	0	0	0	13,314
Boardman	5	1	0	0	0	0	2	1	0	3	39,490
Brecksville	0	0	0	1	0	0	1	0	0	0	13,466
Brewster	1	0	0	0	0	0	0	1	0	0	2,107
Brimfield Township	1	0	0	0	0	0	0	0	0	1	11,450
Brookville	0	1	0	0	0	0	0	1	0	0	5,945
Butler Township	1	1	3	0	0	0	0	0	2	3	8,219
Byesville	1	0	0	0	0	0	0	0	1	0	2,352
Cambridge	1	0	0	0	0	0	0	1	0	0	9,978
Carrollton	0	0	1	0	0	0	0	1	0	0	3,101
Cincinnati	3	1	1	0	0	0	2	2	1	0	307,761
Clayton	1	0	0	0	0	0	0	0	0	1	13,228
Cleveland[2]	31	3	5	1	0	18	13	18	16	10	363,764
Columbus[2]	30	5	17	2	0	4	16	18	11	6	907,196
Copley Township	1	0	0	0	0	0	0	0	1	0	18,244
Cuyahoga Falls	3	1	0	0	0	0	1	3	0	0	50,607
Dayton	1	1	0	0	0	0	1	0	0	1	137,084
Delaware[2]	3	2	2	0	0	0	1	2	3	0	44,042
Delhi Township	0	0	1	0	0	0	0	0	1	0	28,476
Dennison	0	0	1	0	0	0	0	1	0	0	2,658
East Cleveland	45	0	0	0	0	0	15	19	11	0	13,418
East Liverpool	0	0	1	0	0	0	0	1	0	0	9,796
Elyria	3	1	0	0	0	1	1	1	0	3	52,902
Englewood	1	0	0	0	0	0	0	0	1	0	13,338
Fairfax	1	0	0	1	0	0	0	1	0	1	1,738
Felicity	1	0	0	0	0	0	0	1	0	0	652
Franklin	3	0	0	0	0	0	1	1	0	1	11,604
Gahanna	1	1	0	0	0	0	0	0	1	1	35,167
Garfield Heights	3	0	1	3	0	0	1	2	2	2	29,022
Germantown	1	0	0	0	0	0	0	0	1	0	5,798

Table 94. Hate Crime Incidents Per Bias Motivation and Quarter, by Selected State, Territory, Federal, and Agency, 2022—Continued

(Number.)

State/agency	Number of incidents per bias motivation						Number of incidents per quarter				Population[1]
	Race/ Ethnicity/ Ancestry	Religion	Sexual orientation	Disability	Gender	Gender Identity	1st quarter	2nd quarter	3rd quarter	4th quarter	
Goshen Township, Mahoning County	2	0	0	0	0	0	0	0	1	1	3,046
Greenfield	1	0	0	0	0	0	0	0	0	1	4,334
Green Township[2]	2	0	0	0	0	0	1	0	0	0	59,568
Grove City	1	4	1	0	0	0	2	3	1	0	42,248
Hamilton	5	0	1	0	0	0	1	2	2	1	62,536
Hillsboro	1	0	0	0	0	0	0	1	0	0	6,482
Huber Heights	3	0	1	1	0	0	0	1	3	1	43,233
Ironton	0	0	1	0	0	0	0	1	0	0	10,312
Jackson	1	0	0	0	0	0	0	0	0	1	6,168
Jackson Township, Stark County[2]	0	0	3	0	0	0	1	1	1	0	42,745
Kent	0	0	1	0	0	0	0	0	0	1	27,723
Kenton	0	0	0	0	0	1	0	1	0	0	7,938
Kettering[2]	2	2	0	0	0	0	0	1	2	0	57,107
Kirtland	0	0	1	0	0	0	1	0	0	0	6,899
Lakewood	1	0	0	0	0	0	0	0	0	1	49,490
Lancaster[2]	2	0	1	0	0	0	1	1	0	0	40,937
Lebanon	1	0	0	0	0	0	0	0	1	0	21,547
Lima	1	1	1	2	0	0	2	2	1	0	35,633
Logan	1	0	0	0	0	0	0	1	0		7,377
Lyndhurst	1	0	0	0	0	0	1	0	0	0	13,682
Mason	3	0	0	0	0	0	0	2	1	0	35,344
Maumee	1	0	0	0	0	0	0	0	1	0	13,725
Mayfield Heights	0	0	1	0	0	0	0	1	0	0	19,813
Medina	0	1	0	0	0	0	0	0	1	0	25,921
Miamisburg	1	0	0	0	0	0	1	0	0	0	19,723
Middletown	4	0	1	3	0	0	1	1	4	2	50,970
Minster	0	0	2	0	0	0	0	0	2	0	2,993
Mogadore	1	0	0	0	0	1	1	0	1	0	3,785
Monroe	0	0	0	2	0	0	0	1	0	1	17,817
Montgomery	0	0	0	1	0	0	1	0	0	0	10,766
Montville Township	0	1	0	0	0	0	0	0	0	1	13,304
Mount Vernon	0	1	0	0	0	0	0	1	0	0	16,860
Napoleon	1	0	1	0	0	0	1	0	0	1	8,744
New Albany	1	0	0	0	0	0	0	0	1	0	10,851
Newark	2	0	0	0	0	0	1	0	0	1	50,818
New Lebanon	1	0	1	0	0	0	0	1	0	1	3,781
New Philadelphia	1	0	0	0	0	0	0	1	0	0	17,508
New Washington	1	0	0	0	0	0	0	1	0	0	857
North Canton[2]	3	0	1	0	0	0	1	1	1	0	17,855
Obetz[2]	2	0	0	1	0	0	1	0	1	0	6,074
Perrysburg	1	0	0	0	0	0	1	0	0	0	25,165
Perry Township, Stark County	3	0	0	0	0	0	2	0	0	1	28,143
Pickerington	0	0	2	0	0	0	0	2	0	0	24,647
Port Clinton	1	0	0	1	0	0	0	1	0	1	5,951
Portsmouth	2	0	1	0	0	0	1	1	0	1	17,896
Richwood	1	0	0	0	0	0	0	1	0	0	2,398
Riverside	1	1	0	0	0	0	0	0	2	0	24,322
Rocky River	0	0	1	0	0	0	0	1	0	0	21,309
Russells Point	0	0	0	1	0	0	1	0	0	0	1,320
Sebring[2]	3	0	0	0	0	0	2	0	0	0	4,154
Sharonville	1	0	0	0	0	0	0	0	1	0	13,879
Springboro	1	0	0	0	0	0	0	0	1	0	19,431
Springfield[2]	9	0	3	0	0	4	3	2	6	4	58,725
Springfield Township, Hamilton County	0	0	0	2	0	0	0	0	1	1	35,363
Steubenville	2	0	0	0	0	0	1	1	0	0	17,869
Stow	1	1	0	0	0	0	1	1	0	0	34,244
Streetsboro	1	0	0	0	0	0	0	1	0	0	17,908
Sylvania Township	0	1	0	0	0	0	1	0	0	0	31,833
Tipp City	1	0	0	0	0	0	0	0	1	0	10,375
Toledo	1	1	1	0	0	0	0	2	2	0	266,984
Trotwood	4	1	0	0	0	0	0	1	2	2	22,930
Troy	0	0	1	0	0	0	0	0	0	1	26,544
Uhrichsville	1	0	0	0	0	0	0	1	0	0	5,177
Union	1	0	0	0	0	0	0	0	0	1	6,865
Union Township, Clermont County	2	0	0	0	0	0	1	1	0	0	50,164
Vandalia	1	0	0	0	0	0	0	1	0	0	15,026
Wadsworth	0	0	1	0	0	0	1	0	0	0	24,546
Wapakoneta	0	0	2	0	0	0	0	1	1	0	9,742
Waterville	0	0	0	1	0	0	0	0	1	0	6,022
Waverly	1	0	0	0	0	0	0	0	1	0	4,139
West Carrollton	1	0	1	0	0	0	1	1	0	0	12,951
West Chester Township	6	0	1	0	1	6	4	1	5	4	62,374
West Jefferson	1	0	0	0	0	0	0	0	0	1	4,293
Worthington	2	1	1	0	0	0	2	1	0	1	14,346
Youngstown	4	3	0	0	0	1	1	0	3	4	59,944
Zanesville	1	0	5	1	0	0	1	3	3	0	24,703
Universities and Colleges	9	4	1	0	0	0					
Kent State University	1	2	0	0	0	0	0	2	1	0	31,555

Table 94. Hate Crime Incidents Per Bias Motivation and Quarter, by Selected State, Territory, Federal, and Agency, 2022—Continued

(Number.)

State/agency	Race/ Ethnicity/ Ancestry	Religion	Sexual orientation	Disability	Gender	Gender Identity	1st quarter	2nd quarter	3rd quarter	4th quarter	Population[1]
Ohio State University, Columbus[2]	8	1	1	0	0	0	1	3	0	5	66,749
Ohio University	0	1	0	0	0	0	1	0	0	0	30,163
Metropolitan Counties	29	16	4	2	0	5					
Belmont	1	0	0	0	0	0	0	0	1	0	
Butler[2]	2	1	0	0	0	0	2	0	0	0	
Delaware	1	3	1	0	0	0	1	1	3	0	
Greene	3	0	0	0	0	0	0	0	0	3	
Hamilton	2	1	1	0	0	2	3	2	0	1	
Jefferson	1	0	0	0	0	0	0	0	1	0	
Licking	1	0	0	0	0	0	0	0	1	0	
Lorain	1	2	0	0	0	0	2	0	0	1	
Madison	0	0	1	0	0	0	1	0	0	0	
Mahoning	3	0	0	0	0	0	1	2			
Medina	0	1	0	0	0	1	0	1	1		
Miami	2	0	0	0	0	0	1	0	1	0	
Montgomery	2	3	1	1	0	0	1	3	3	0	
Pickaway	1	2	0	0	0	0	1	2	0	0	
Portage	2	0	0	0	0	0	0	2	0	0	
Summit	4	3	0	1	0	2	1	4	4	1	
Warren	3	0	0	0	0	0	0	0	1	2	
Nonmetropolitan Counties	11	5	3	7	1	1					
Ashland	2	0	0	0	0	0	0	0	1	1	
Athens	0	1	0	0	0	0	1	0	0	0	
Columbiana	1	0	0	2	0	0	2	0	1	0	
Coshocton	0	0	1	0	0	0	0	0	0	1	
Darke	1	0	0	0	0	0	1	0	0	0	
Defiance	0	2	0	0	0	0	0	0	1	1	
Hancock	1	0	0	0	0	0	0	1	0	0	
Knox	1	0	0	0	0	0	0	0	1	0	
Logan	1	0	0	1	0	0	1	0	1	0	
Mercer	0	0	0	1	0	0	0	1	0	0	
Muskingum	1	0	1	0	0	0	0	1	1		
Ross	1	0	0	0	0	0	1	0	0	0	
Scioto	0	0	0	2	0	0	0	1	1	0	
Tuscarawas	0	2	1	0	1	1	3	1	0	1	
Wayne	2	0	0	1	0	0	1	0	2	0	
Other Agencies	2	0	1	0	0	0					
Ohio Department of Natural Resources	2	0	1	0	0	0	1	1	1	0	
OKLAHOMA	43	4	12	2	0	2					
Cities	35	3	12	2	0	2					
Altus	1	0	0	0	0	0	0	0	1	0	18,757
Antlers	0	0	1	0	0	0	0	0	1	0	2,179
Binger	0	0	1	0	0	0	0	0	1	0	436
Bixby	1	0	0	0	0	0	0	0	1	0	29,690
Blackwell	1	0	0	0	0	0	0	1	0	0	6,089
Blanchard	0	0	1	0	0	0	0	1	0	0	9,488
Broken Bow	1	0	0	0	0	0	0	0	1	0	4,270
Claremore	0	0	1	0	0	0	0	1	0	0	19,659
Coweta	1	0	0	0	0	0	0	1	0	0	10,623
Cushing	1	0	0	0	0	0	0	0	1	0	8,195
Edmond	0	1	0	0	0	0	0	0	1	0	95,946
Elk City	1	0	0	0	0	0	0	0	0	1	11,417
Elmore City	1	0	0	0	0	0	0	0	0	1	749
Enid	1	0	0	0	0	0	0	1	0	0	49,990
Fairview	0	0	1	0	0	0	1	0	0	0	2,658
Guymon	1	0	1	0	0	0	2	0	0	0	12,292
Harrah	1	0	0	0	0	0	0	0	1	0	6,425
Hominy	1	0	0	0	0	0	1	0	0	0	3,244
Jenks	0	0	1	0	0	0	0	1	0	0	27,208
Lawton	1	0	0	0	0	0	0	1	0	0	91,596
Lexington	1	0	0	0	0	0	0	0	0	1	1,989
Madill	0	0	0	0	0	1	0	1	0	0	4,031
McAlester	1	0	0	0	0	0	0	0	0	1	18,219
Moore	0	0	0	1	0	0	0	1	0	0	63,421
Muskogee	1	0	0	0	0	0	0	0	1	0	36,713
Norman	2	0	0	0	0	0	1	1	0	0	128,878
Oklahoma City	6	0	2	0	0	0	0	6	2	0	692,726
Pawhuska	1	0	0	0	0	0	0	0	1	0	2,924
Pryor Creek	1	0	0	0	0	0	0	1	0	0	9,467
Purcell	1	0	0	0	0	0	1	0	0	0	6,647
Sapulpa	1	0	0	0	0	0	1	0	0	0	22,447
Seminole	0	0	1	0	0	0	0	0	0	1	7,063
Shawnee	1	1	0	0	0	0	0	1	1	0	31,865
Skiatook	1	0	0	0	0	0	0	1	0	0	8,651

Table 94. Hate Crime Incidents Per Bias Motivation and Quarter, by Selected State, Territory, Federal, and Agency, 2022—Continued

(Number.)

State/agency	Number of incidents per bias motivation						Number of incidents per quarter				Population[1]
	Race/Ethnicity/Ancestry	Religion	Sexual orientation	Disability	Gender	Gender Identity	1st quarter	2nd quarter	3rd quarter	4th quarter	
Stillwater	1	0	0	0	0	0	0	0	0	1	48,384
Tecumseh	1	0	0	0	0	0	1	0	0	0	6,365
The Village	0	1	0	0	0	0	1	0	0	0	9,402
Tulsa	0	0	1	0	0	0	0	0	0	1	410,135
Vinita	1	0	0	0	0	0	0	1	0	0	5,170
Wetumka	1	0	0	0	0	0	0	0	0	1	1,152
Woodward	1	0	1	1	0	1	0	2	0	2	11,876
Universities and Colleges	0	1	0	0	0	0					
University of Oklahoma, Norman	0	1	0	0	0	0	1	0	0	0	31,285
Metropolitan Counties	2	0	0	0	0	0					
Logan	1	0	0	0	0	0	1	0	0	0	
Rogers	1	0	0	0	0	0	0	1	0	0	
Nonmetropolitan Counties	4	0	0	0	0	0					
Craig	1	0	0	0	0	0	0	0	0	1	
Pottawatomie	3	0	0	0	0	0	1	2	0	0	
Tribal Agencies	2	0	0	0	0	0					
Citizen Potawatomi Nation	1	0	0	0	0	0	0	0	1	0	
Seminole Nation Lighthorse	1	0	0	0	0	0	0	1	0	0	
OREGON	203	34	77	4	7	14					
Cities	156	27	47	4	4	8					
Albany[2]	13	0	3	0	0	0	2	5	3	5	57,058
Beaverton[2]	3	0	0	0	0	0	0	1	1	0	98,991
Bend	9	2	0	0	0	0	2	1	6	2	104,649
Canby	1	0	1	0	0	0	0	0	0	2	18,101
Central Point	0	0	0	0	1	0	1	0	0	0	19,670
Corvallis	3	0	1	0	0	1	1	3	1	0	60,031
Dallas	1	0	0	0	0	0	0	0	0	1	17,622
Eugene[2]	15	1	6	0	0	0	1	5	6	9	175,390
Forest Grove	1	0	1	0	0	0	0	0	2	0	26,016
Grants Pass	1	0	0	0	0	0	0	0	1	0	39,519
Gresham[2]	6	1	0	1	1	0	2	1	0	3	111,590
Hermiston	1	0	0	0	0	0	0	0	0	1	19,438
Hillsboro[2]	8	6	1	0	0	0	2	6	3	0	106,345
Hood River	1	0	0	0	0	0	1	0	0	0	8,396
Independence	0	0	1	0	0	0	1	0	0	0	10,368
McMinnville	1	1	0	0	0	0	0	1	1	0	34,912
Medford	2	0	1	0	0	0	1	0	1	1	86,876
Molalla	1	0	0	0	0	0	1	0	0	0	10,179
Newport	0	0	1	0	0	0	0	1	0	0	10,667
Ontario	1	0	0	0	0	0	0	1	0	0	11,638
Oregon City	7	0	0	0	0	0	3	1	2	1	37,192
Pendleton	1	0	1	0	0	0	0	1	1	0	16,780
Portland[2]	34	7	11	1	1	2	8	7	19	13	630,129
Reedsport	1	0	0	0	0	0	1	0	0	0	4,346
Roseburg	1	0	0	0	0	0	0	0	1	0	23,973
Salem[2]	22	5	11	0	0	1	4	10	9	6	179,661
Sherwood	1	0	1	0	1	0	1	0	0	2	20,102
Springfield	4	0	0	1	0	2	0	3	2	2	62,217
Sweet Home	1	0	1	0	0	0	1	1	0	0	10,055
The Dalles	1	0	0	0	0	0	1	0	0	0	16,100
Tigard	13	3	2	1	0	1	8	5	3	4	56,550
Tualatin	2	0	1	0	0	0	1	0	2	0	27,195
Warrenton	0	0	1	0	0	0	0	1	0	0	6,537
West Linn[2]	0	0	2	0	0	0	0	1	0	0	26,842
Winston	0	1	0	0	0	0	0	1	0	0	5,701
Woodburn	0	0	0	0	0	1	0	0	1	0	26,117
Universities and Colleges	4	0	0	0	0	2					
Oregon State University	4	0	0	0	0	2	2	2	0	2	38,654
Metropolitan Counties	36	3	22	0	2	4					
Clackamas[2]	14	1	16	0	0	2	4	5	8	4	
Josephine	1	0	0	0	0	0	0	1	0	0	
Linn	1	0	0	0	0	0	1	0	0	0	
Multnomah[2]	6	0	1	0	0	0	0	2	2	1	
Polk	2	0	0	0	0	0	0	0	0	2	
Washington[2]	12	2	5	0	2	2	6	6	2	6	
Nonmetropolitan Counties	1	4	4	0	1	0					
Klamath	0	1	0	0	0	0	0	0	1	0	
Sherman	1	0	0	0	1	0	0	0	2	0	
Umatilla	0	1	0	0	0	0	0	1	0	0	
Wasco[2]	0	2	4	0	0	0	0	2	1	1	

Table 94. Hate Crime Incidents Per Bias Motivation and Quarter, by Selected State, Territory, Federal, and Agency, 2022—Continued

(Number.)

State/agency	Race/ Ethnicity/ Ancestry	Religion	Sexual orientation	Disability	Gender	Gender Identity	1st quarter	2nd quarter	3rd quarter	4th quarter	Population[1]
State Police Agencies	5	0	4	0	0	0					
State Police											
Clatsop County	1	0	0	0	0	0	0	1	0	0	
Columbia County	1	0	0	0	0	0	0	1	0	0	
Douglas County	0	0	1	0	0	0	0	0	0	1	
Gilliam County	1	0	0	0	0	0	1	0	0	0	
Malheur County	0	0	3	0	0	0	1	2	0	0	
Marion County	1	0	0	0	0	0	0	0	0	1	
Washington County	1	0	0	0	0	0	0	0	1	0	
Other Agencies	1	0	0	0	0	0					
Port of Portland	1	0	0	0	0	0	0	0	1	0	
PENNSYLVANIA	199	41	46	7	1	3					
Cities	153	32	36	5	0	2					
Abington Township, Montgomery County	1	0	0	0	0	0	1	0			58,432
Carlisle	1	0	0	0	0	0	0	1	0	0	20,237
Cecil Township	1	0	0	0	0	0		1	0	0	14,866
Derry Township, Dauphin County	1	1	0	0	0	0	0	1	1	0	24,896
East Earl Township	0	1	0	0	0	0	0	0	0	1	8,142
Erie	1	0	0	1	0	1	1	1	1	0	93,363
Ferguson Township	1	0	0	0	0	0		1			19,360
Jefferson Hills Borough[2]	0	2	0	0	0	0	0	0	1	0	12,314
Kennett Square	0	2	0	0	0	0			2		5,911
Mount Lebanon	1	0	0	0	0	0	0	1	0	0	33,188
New Cumberland	1	0	0	0	0	0	0	0	0	1	7,588
Philadelphia[2]	111	16	28	1	0	0	52	35	30	33	1,555,812
Pittsburgh	12	5	4	0	0	0	3	4	11	3	303,137
Reading	2	0	0	0	0	0	1	1	0	0	97,698
Richland Township, Cambria County	1	0	0	0	0	0				1	11,991
Scranton	3	2	0	3	0	1	1	3	2	3	75,798
South Londonderry Township	1	0	0	0	0	0	1	0	0	0	8,833
State College[2]	4	0	0	0	0	0	0	2			55,998
St. Marys City	0	1	0	0	0	0	0	0	0	1	12,602
Sugarcreek[2]	3	0	0	0	0	0		1	1		4,739
Susquehanna Township, Dauphin County	1	0	0	0	0	0			1	0	26,699
Upper Moreland Township[2]	4	1	0	0	0	0	0		1	1	26,071
Washington Township, Franklin County	0	1	0	0	0	0	0	0	1	0	15,104
Waynesboro	2	0	1	0	0	0	0	2	0	1	10,925
West Hills Regional	0	0	2	0	0	0	2				9,943
West Shore Regional	0	0	1	0	0	0	0	1	0	0	7,783
Whitemarsh Township	1	0	0	0	0	0	1				20,098
Universities and Colleges	7	0	5	0	0	0					
Edinboro University[2]	2	0	0	0	0	0				1	5,285
Juniata College	0	0	2	0	0	0			2		1,440
Pennsylvania State University											
Abington[2,3]	2	0	1	0	0	0	0			1	
Brandywine[3]	0	0	1	0	0	0		0	1		
Hazleton[3]	0	0	1	0	0	0				1	
University Park[3]	1	0	0	0	0	0	1				
York[3]	1	0	0	0	0	0	1				
Villanova University	1	0	0	0	0	0				1	12,623
State Police Agencies	39	9	5	2	1	1					
State Police											
Adams County[2]	2	0	0	0	0	0	0	1	0	0	
Bedford County	1	0	0	0	0	0	0	0	1	0	
Blair County	2	0	0	0	0	0	1	0	1	0	
Cambria County	1	0	0	0	0	0	0	0	1	0	
Chester County	1	0	0	0	0	0	0	1	0	0	
Clarion County[2]	2	0	0	0	0	0	0	0	1	0	
Clearfield County	0	1	0	0	0	0	0	1	0	0	
Crawford County	0	0	0	1	0	0	0	1	0	0	
Cumberland County	2	0	0	0	0	0	0	0	0	2	
Delaware County	2	0	0	0	0	0	0	0	2	0	
Elizabethville	1	0	0	0	0	0	0	1	0	0	
Fayette County	1	0	1	1	0	0	0	1	1	1	
Franklin County	3	0	2	0	0	0	2	1	1	1	
Indiana County	1	0	0	0	0	0	0	1	0	0	
Jefferson County	0	2	0	0	0	0	0	2	0	0	
Juniata County	1	0	0	0	0	0	0	1	0	0	
Lancaster County	2	0	1	0	0	0	2	1	0	0	
Lebanon County	0	2	0	0	0	0	0	1	0	1	
Lehigh County	0	1	0	0	0	0	0	0	0	1	
Luzerne County[2]	2	0	0	0	0	0	0	0	1	0	
Lycoming County	1	1	0	0	0	0	0	1	1	0	
Mercer County	1	0	0	0	0	0	1	0	0	0	
Monroe County	4	0	0	0	0	0	0	1	1	2	

Table 94. Hate Crime Incidents Per Bias Motivation and Quarter, by Selected State, Territory, Federal, and Agency, 2022—Continued

(Number.)

State/agency	Race/Ethnicity/Ancestry	Religion	Sexual orientation	Disability	Gender	Gender Identity	1st quarter	2nd quarter	3rd quarter	4th quarter	Population[1]
Montour County	0	0	0	0	1	0	0	1	0	0	
Northumberland County	1	0	0	0	0	0	0	0	1	0	
Perry County	1	0	1	0	0	0	0	2	0	0	
Philadelphia County	2	0	0	0	0	1	0	2	0	1	
Skippack	2	0	0	0	0	0	0	0	1	1	
Susquehanna County	1	0	0	0	0	0	0	1	0	0	
Venango County	1	0	0	0	0	0	0	0	0	1	
Washington County	0	1	0	0	0	0	0	0	0	1	
Wayne County	1	1	0	0	0	0	0	0	1	1	
RHODE ISLAND	4	9	2	0	1	0					
Cities	4	9	2	0	1	0					
Barrington	1	1	0	0	0	0	0	0	0	2	17,364
Charlestown	1	0	0	0	0	0	0	1	0	0	8,117
Coventry	0	1	0	0	0	0	1	0	0	0	35,730
East Providence	0	1	0	0	0	0	1	0	0	0	46,655
Johnston	0	0	1	0	0	0	0	1	0	0	29,430
Narragansett	0	1	0	0	0	0	1	0	0	0	14,653
North Providence	0	1	0	0	1	0	0	0	2	0	33,809
Pawtucket	1	1	0	0	0	0	0	2	0	0	74,967
Portsmouth	0	1	0	0	0	0	1	0	0	0	17,716
Providence	0	1	0	0	0	0	0	0	1	0	189,064
Smithfield	1	0	0	0	0	0	0	0	0	1	21,762
Warren	0	1	1	0	0	0	1	0	0	1	11,243
SOUTH CAROLINA	40	13	10	0	0	2					
Cities	25	12	7	0	0	0					
Andrews	0	1	0	0	0	0	0	1	0	0	2,526
Atlantic Beach	1	0	0	0	0	0	0	1	0	0	269
Bennettsville	2	0	0	0	0	0	1	1	0	0	6,891
Blackville	0	1	0	0	0	0	0	0	1	0	1,952
Calhoun Falls[2]	8	0	0	0	0	0	1	0	4	2	1,726
Cayce	1	0	0	0	0	0	1	0	0	0	13,710
Charleston[2]	0	4	1	0	0	0	1	0	2	0	152,324
Cheraw	0	0	1	0	0	0	0	0	0	1	4,920
Chester	1	0	0	0	0	0	1	0	0	0	5,222
Clemson	0	1	0	0	0	0	0	0	1	0	18,174
Denmark	1	0	0	0	0	0	0	1	0	0	3,124
Elloree	1	0	0	0	0	0	0	0	0	1	553
Florence	2	0	2	0	0	0	1	0	2	1	39,997
Goose Creek	0	3	0	0	0	0	0	0	1	2	46,665
Greenwood	1	0	0	0	0	0	0	0	0	1	22,145
Hardeeville	0	1	0	0	0	0	0	0	0	1	9,995
Jonesville	1	0	0	0	0	0	0	0	1	0	832
Lake City	1	0	0	0	0	0	1	0	0	0	5,946
Mauldin	1	0	0	0	0	0	0	1	0	0	26,576
Moncks Corner	0	0	1	0	0	0	0	0	1	0	13,906
North Myrtle Beach	1	0	0	0	0	0	0	1	0	0	19,888
Ridge Spring	1	0	0	0	0	0	0	1	0	0	577
Rock Hill	0	1	1	0	0	0	0	2	0	0	74,047
Simpsonville	1	0	1	0	0	0	0	1	0	1	25,847
Wellford	1	0	0	0	0	0	1	0	0	0	3,478
Universities and Colleges	4	0	2	0	0	0					
Benedict College[2]	4	0	0	0	0	0	3	0	0	0	1,914
Clemson University[2]	0	0	2	0	0	0	0	0	0	1	29,483
Metropolitan Counties	8	1	1	0	0	2					
Aiken	1	0	0	0	0	1	2	0			
Charleston	2	1	0	0	0	0	0	1	1	1	
Clarendon	1	0	0	0	0	0	0	0	0	1	
Horry County Police Department	1	0	0	0	0	0	0	0	0	1	
Lexington	1	0	0	0	0	0	0	0	0	1	
Pickens	0	0	1	0	0	0	1	0	0	0	
Richland	1	0	0	0	0	1	1	0	1	0	
York	1	0	0	0	0	0	0	0	1	0	
Nonmetropolitan Counties	2	0	0	0	0	0					
Greenwood	1	0	0	0	0	0	0	0	1	0	
Hampton	1	0	0	0	0	0	0	1	0	0	
Other Agencies	1	0	0	0	0	0					
Lexington County Medical Center	1	0	0	0	0	0	0	0	1	0	
SOUTH DAKOTA	11	2	6	0	0	0					
Cities	7	2	6	0	0	0					
Aberdeen	2	0	1	0	0	0	2	0	0	1	28,206
Rapid City	0	0	1	0	0	0	0	0	1	0	78,063
Sioux Falls	4	0	2	0	0	0	2	1	0	3	199,879

Table 94. Hate Crime Incidents Per Bias Motivation and Quarter, by Selected State, Territory, Federal, and Agency, 2022—Continued

(Number.)

State/agency	Race/ Ethnicity/ Ancestry	Religion	Sexual orientation	Disability	Gender	Gender Identity	1st quarter	2nd quarter	3rd quarter	4th quarter	Population[1]
Sturgis	1	0	0	0	0	0	0	0	1	0	7,121
Tea[2]	0	2	2	0	0	0	0	1	0	0	6,894
Metropolitan Counties	1	0	0	0	0	0					
Pennington	1	0	0	0	0	0	1	0	0	0	
Nonmetropolitan Counties	1	0	0	0	0	0					
Brookings	1	0	0	0	0	0	0	1	0	0	
Tribal Agencies	2	0	0	0	0	0					
Cheyenne River Tribal	1	0	0	0	0	0	1	0	0	0	
Crow Creek Tribal	1	0	0	0	0	0	0	0	1	0	
TENNESSEE	75	9	8	6	1	1					
Cities	52	8	7	4	1	1					
Alcoa	1	0	0	0	0	0	0	0	1	0	11,689
Atoka	1	0	0	0	0	0	0	0	1	0	10,345
Bolivar	0	0	1	0	0	0	0	0	1	0	5,127
Carthage	1	0	0	0	0	0	1	0	0	0	2,276
Chattanooga	1	0	0	0	0	0	0	1	0	0	182,603
Cleveland[2]	7	1	0	0	0	0	2	4	1	0	48,579
Collegedale	1	0	0	0	0	0	0	0	1	0	12,032
Collierville	1	0	0	0	0	1	0	1	1	0	51,439
Covington	0	0	0	2	0	0	0	0	2	0	8,582
Crossville	1	0	0	0	0	0	0	0	0	1	12,487
Dickson	1	0	0	0	0	0	0	1	0	0	16,154
Franklin	1	3	0	0	0	0	1	0	2	1	87,081
Jonesborough	1	0	0	0	0	0	0	1	0	0	6,081
Knoxville	1	0	1	0	0	0	1	0	0	1	194,724
La Vergne	2	0	0	0	0	0	0	1	0	1	39,424
Lawrenceburg	1	0	0	0	0	0	0	1	0	0	11,874
Lebanon	5	0	0	0	0	0	0	1	2	2	43,321
Maryville	1	0	0	0	0	0	0	0	1	0	32,717
Memphis[2]	11	0	2	0	1	0	2	2	2	7	624,944
Metropolitan Nashville Police Department	1	1	1	0	0	0	3	0	0	0	679,562
Millington	1	0	0	1	0	0	0	0	1	1	10,461
Monteagle	1	0	0	0	0	0	0	0	0	1	1,375
Morristown	1	0	0	0	0	0	0	0	0	1	30,988
Mount Juliet[2]	0	2	0	0	0	0	0	1	0	0	41,849
Munford	1	0	0	0	0	0	0	0	0	1	6,466
Murfreesboro	2	0	0	0	0	0	1	0	0	1	161,810
Oakland[2]	1	1	0	0	0	0	0	0	0	1	10,004
Rogersville	0	0	1	0	0	0	1	0	0	0	4,665
Rossville	2	0	0	0	0	0	0	1	0	1	1,146
Selmer	1	0	0	0	0	0	1	0	0	0	4,419
Sevierville	2	0	0	0	0	0	0	0	1	1	19,021
Spring City	0	0	0	1	0	0	1	0	0	0	1,965
Vonore	1	0	0	0	0	0	0	0	1	0	1,600
White Bluff	0	0	1	0	0	0	0	1	0	0	4,065
Universities and Colleges	2	0	0	0	0	0					
Columbia State Community College	1	0	0	0	0	0	0	0	1	0	8,037
University of Tennessee, Knoxville	1	0	0	0	0	0	1	0	0	0	33,245
Metropolitan Counties	14	0	1	2	0	0					
Dickson	1	0	0	0	0	0	0	1	0	0	
Fayette	1	0	0	0	0	0	0	0	1	0	
Hamilton	4	0	0	0	0	0	0	0	3	1	
Knox	1	0	0	0	0	0	0	1	0	0	
Montgomery	1	0	0	0	0	0	0	1	0	0	
Rutherford	1	0	0	0	0	0	0	0	1	0	
Shelby	3	0	0	1	0	0	2	0	1	1	
Sullivan	1	0	0	1	0	0	1	1	0	0	
Tipton	0	0	1	0	0	0	0	0	0	1	
Williamson	1	0	0	0	0	0	0	1	0	0	
Nonmetropolitan Counties	3	1	0	0	0	0					
Greene	1	0	0	0	0	0	0	0	0	1	
Monroe	1	1	0	0	0	0	1	1	0	0	
Obion	1	0	0	0	0	0	0	0	1	0	
State Police Agencies	4	0	0	0	0	0					
Department of Safety[2]	4	0	0	0	0	0	0	0	0	2	
TEXAS	350	76	127	15	7	41					
Cities	279	61	100	7	3	32					
Addison	1	0	0	0	0	0	0	0	0	1	17,531
Alice	0	1	0	0	0	0	1	0	0	0	17,727
Allen	1	0	0	0	0	0	0	0	0	1	108,135

Table 94. Hate Crime Incidents Per Bias Motivation and Quarter, by Selected State, Territory, Federal, and Agency, 2022—Continued

(Number.)

State/agency	Number of incidents per bias motivation						Number of incidents per quarter				Population[1]
	Race/ Ethnicity/ Ancestry	Religion	Sexual orientation	Disability	Gender	Gender Identity	1st quarter	2nd quarter	3rd quarter	4th quarter	
Alvarado	2	0	0	0	0	0	0	1	0	1	5,504
Amarillo	0	0	1	0	0	0	0	1	0	0	201,572
Anna	2	0	0	0	0	0	0	1	0	1	23,541
Aransas Pass	1	0	0	0	0	0	0	0	0	1	8,056
Arlington[2]	8	1	6	0	0	1	2	7	3	3	391,591
Austin[2]	22	7	16	0	0	3	9	9	13	16	965,234
Balcones Heights	1	0	0	0	0	0	0	0	0	1	2,709
Bastrop[2]	1	0	0	0	1	0	0	0	0	1	11,101
Beaumont	2	0	1	0	0	0	0	2	1	0	110,898
Bedford	0	0	1	0	0	0	0	0	0	1	48,579
Bellaire	0	2	0	0	0	0	0	1	1	0	16,783
Bellmead	2	0	0	0	0	0	0	2	0	0	10,589
Boerne[2]	0	0	2	0	0	1	0	1	0	0	20,488
Brenham	0	4	0	0	0	0	0	1	1	2	18,785
Bridgeport	0	1	0	0	0	0	0	0	1	0	6,186
Brownsville	1	1	0	0	0	1	0	0	2	1	188,906
Brownwood	0	0	1	0	0	0	0	0	1	0	18,751
Bryan	1	0	0	0	0	0	1	0			87,935
Burleson	1	0	0	0	0	0	0	1	0	0	55,356
Carrollton	1	0	1	0	0	0	1	0	0	1	133,610
Castle Hills	1	0	0	0	0	0	1	0	0	0	3,921
Cedar Park	1	0	2	0	0	0	1	0	2	0	79,353
Cisco	0	0	1	0	0	0	0	1	0	0	3,902
College Station	1	0	0	0	0	1	1	0	0	1	121,618
Commerce	2	0	0	0	0	0	0	0	0	2	8,876
Copperas Cove	1	0	0	0	0	0	0	0	0	1	37,841
Corpus Christi	1	0	0	0	0	0	0	1	0	0	317,694
Corsicana	1	0	2	0	0	0	0	2	1	0	25,585
Crowley	1	0	0	0	0	0	0	0	1	0	20,362
Dallas[2]	17	4	8	0	0	2	6	15	5	3	1,286,121
Dayton	1	0	0	0	0	0	0	0	0	1	9,451
Del Rio	1	0	1	0	0	0	0	1	1	0	34,495
Denton[2]	4	0	2	0	0	0	2	0	1	2	154,230
DeSoto	2	0	0	0	0	0	0	1	0	1	55,956
Dickinson	1	0	0	0	0	0	0	0	0	1	21,936
Eagle Pass	1	0	0	0	0	0	1	0	0	0	28,811
Electra	1	1	0	0	0	0	1	0	0	1	2,286
El Paso	2	0	2	0	0	1	0	0	2	3	678,232
Euless	1	0	1	0	0	0	0	1	0	1	59,901
Florence	1	0	0	0	0	0	0	0	0	1	1,218
Floresville	1	0	0	0	0	0	1	0	0	0	7,971
Forney	2	0	0	0	0	0	0	0	1	1	31,105
Fort Worth	3	0	0	0	0	0	3	0	0	0	948,605
Friendswood	0	1	0	0	0	0	1	0	0	0	40,851
Frisco	1	0	0	0	0	0	0	1	0	0	218,962
Fulshear	1	0	0	0	0	0	0	0	0	1	18,058
Galveston	1	0	3	1	0	0	2	2	1	0	52,920
Garland	1	0	0	0	0	0	0	1	0	0	241,095
Georgetown	1	0	0	0	0	0	0	0	1	0	83,371
Gladewater	1	0	0	0	0	0	0	0	0	1	6,174
Graham	1	0	0	0	0	0	0	0	1	0	8,823
Granbury	1	0	0	0	0	0	0	0	0	1	12,132
Greenville	2	0	0	0	0	0	0	0	1	1	30,890
Gun Barrel City	1	0	0	0	0	0	0	0	1	0	6,551
Haltom City	0	1	1	0	0	0	1	0	0	1	45,488
Hamilton	1	0	0	0	0	0	0	1	0	0	2,860
Hedwig Village	1	0	0	0	0	0	0	0	1	0	2,295
Hewitt	1	0	0	0	0	0	0	0	1	0	16,291
Hooks[2]	0	1	1	0	0	0	0	1	0	0	2,510
Houston[2]	50	3	13	0	0	8	10	5	9	47	2,276,533
Hudson Oaks	1	0	0	0	0	0	1	0	0	0	2,547
Humble	1	0	0	0	0	0	0	0	0	1	16,085
Irving[2]	0	0	1	0	0	1	0	0	1	0	254,141
Jersey Village	1	0	0	0	0	0	0	0	1	0	7,575
Jourdanton	0	0	0	0	0	1	0	0	1	0	4,179
Kennedale	1	0	0	0	0	0	0	0	1	0	8,417
Killeen	0	0	1	0	0	0	0	0	0	1	159,546
Kingsville	2	0	0	0	0	0	0	0	1	1	24,802
Kyle	2	0	0	0	0	0	0	0	0	2	57,724
Lake Jackson	0	0	1	0	0	0	1	0	0	0	27,595
Lakeview, Harrison County	0	1	0	1	0	0	0	0	2	0	6,490
Lampasas	1	0	0	0	0	0	0	0	0	1	7,737
Lancaster	0	0	1	0	0	0	0	0	1	0	40,615
Laredo[2]	5	0	1	0	0	1	1	0	0	5	256,973
Lavon	1	0	0	0	0	0	0	1	0	0	6,277
League City	0	0	1	0	0	0	1	0	0	0	116,511
Leander	6	0	0	0	0	0	3	3	0	0	73,905
Leon Valley	1	0	0	0	0	0	0	0	0	1	11,402
Levelland	1	0	0	0	0	0	0	0	1	0	12,579

Table 94. Hate Crime Incidents Per Bias Motivation and Quarter, by Selected State, Territory, Federal, and Agency, 2022—Continued

(Number.)

State/agency	Race/ Ethnicity/ Ancestry	Religion	Sexual orientation	Disability	Gender	Gender Identity	1st quarter	2nd quarter	3rd quarter	4th quarter	Population[1]
	Number of incidents per bias motivation						Number of incidents per quarter				
Lewisville	2	0	0	0	0	0	0	2	0	0	113,568
Live Oak	1	0	0	0	0	0	1	0	0	0	15,884
Livingston	1	1	0	0	0	0	0	2	0	0	5,937
Lockhart	2	0	0	0	0	0	0	0	2	0	15,068
Longview	1	0	0	0	0	0	0	0	1	0	81,811
Lubbock	1	0	0	0	0	1	2	0	0	0	264,142
Lufkin	1	0	0	0	0	0	0	1	0	0	34,063
Madisonville[2]	2	0	0	0	0	0	1	0	0	0	4,670
Mansfield	1	0	0	0	0	0	0	0	0	1	75,993
Marlin[2]	2	0	0	0	1	0	0	1	0	1	5,631
Marshall	1	0	0	0	0	0	0	1	0	0	22,628
McAllen	0	0	1	0	0	0	0	0	0	1	145,510
McKinney	7	0	0	0	0	0	1	0	6	0	208,415
Midland	2	0	0	0	0	0	0	0	2	0	129,945
Mission	1	2	0	0	0	0	1	0	0	2	86,577
Missouri City	0	1	0	0	0	0	0	1	0	0	75,323
Mount Pleasant	1	0	0	0	0	0	0	0	1	0	16,044
New Braunfels	3	0	4	0	0	1	2	3	2	1	107,017
Odessa	3	0	1	0	0	0	3	0	0	1	110,163
Orange	2	3	0	2	0	0	5	2	0	0	19,056
Palestine	0	1	0	0	0	0	0	0	0	1	19,113
Palmview	0	0	1	0	0	0	0	0	1	0	15,919
Pampa	1	0	0	0	0	0	0	1	0	0	16,343
Pasadena	0	0	1	0	0	0	1	0	0	0	145,954
Pearland[2]	0	0	0	0	0	2	0	1	0	0	125,894
Pearsall	0	0	1	0	0	0	0	1	0	0	7,661
Perryton[2]	2	0	0	0	0	0	1	0	0	0	8,143
Pflugerville	1	1	0	0	0	0	0	2	0	0	67,817
Pharr	0	1	0	0	0	0	0	1	0	0	79,558
Plainview	1	0	0	0	0	0	0	1	0	0	19,554
Plano[2]	2	0	0	0	0	0	0	0	1	0	289,847
Port Arthur	0	1	0	0	0	0	0	0	1	0	55,899
Port Isabel	2	0	0	0	0	0	0	0	1	1	5,165
Port Neches	2	0	0	0	0	0	1	0	0	1	13,293
Prairie View	1	0	0	0	0	0	0	1	0	0	7,059
Red Oak	0	0	1	0	0	0	0	0	0	1	16,396
Reno, Parker County[2]	0	4	0	0	0	0	0	1	0	0	3,457
Rio Grande City	0	0	0	0	0	1	0	0	0	1	15,705
River Oaks	0	0	1	0	0	0	0	0	1	0	7,420
Robinson	1	0	0	0	0	0	0	0	1	0	12,954
Round Rock	2	0	0	0	0	0	0	0	1	1	127,349
San Angelo	0	0	1	0	0	0	0	1	0	0	99,243
San Antonio[2]	24	3	12	2	1	3	10	17	9	6	1,465,608
Sanger	1	0	0	0	0	0	0	0	0	1	9,877
San Juan	1	0	0	0	0	0	0	0	0	1	35,806
San Marcos	7	0	0	1	0	0	0	0	6	2	69,470
Selma[2]	2	0	0	0	0	0	0	0	0	1	11,824
Sherman	1	0	0	0	0	0	0	1	0	0	45,881
Splendora	0	0	0	0	0	1	0	0	1	0	1,860
Stafford	0	1	0	0	0	0	0	1	0	0	17,110
Stephenville	0	0	1	0	0	0	0	0	1	0	21,505
Sugar Land	1	2	0	0	0	0	1	0	1	1	107,989
Sweetwater	1	0	0	0	0	0	0	0	1	0	10,420
Tahoka	0	2	0	0	0	0	0	2	0	0	2,419
Temple	1	0	0	0	0	0	0	0	0	1	88,484
Texarkana	0	0	1	0	0	0	0	1	0	0	35,859
Tomball	1	0	0	0	0	0	1	0	0	0	13,322
Tyler	3	1	0	0	0	0	2	1	1	0	108,422
Uvalde	1	0	0	0	0	0	0	1	0	0	15,410
Watauga	1	3	1	0	0	0	0	2	3	0	23,027
Waxahachie	2	0	0	0	0	0	2	0	0	0	45,422
Weslaco	1	3	1	0	0	2	1	2	3	1	41,478
West University Place	0	2	0	0	0	0	0	0	0	2	14,524
Winters	1	0	0	0	0	0	0	0	0	1	2,363
Universities and Colleges	12	2	5	0	2	1					
Austin Community College District	0	0	1	0	0	0	0	1	0	0	61,370
Lone Star College System District	0	0	1	0	0	0	0	0	0	1	107,768
Rice University	1	0	0	0	1	1	0	1	1	1	8,270
Stephen F. Austin State University	1	0	0	0	0	0	0	1	0	0	14,155
Texas State University, San Marcos[2]	7	2	1	0	0	0	1	0	5	2	42,111
University of Houston, Central Campus	1	0	0	0	0	0	1	0	0	0	52,440
University of Texas											
Arlington	0	0	1	0	0	0	0	0	1	0	60,276
Austin	1	0	0	0	1	0	1	1	0	0	53,502
Houston	1	0	1	0	0	0	1	1	0	0	7,375
Metropolitan Counties	32	11	19	8	2	5					
Bandera	1	0	0	0	0	0	0	0	1	0	
Brazoria	0	0	3	0	0	0	1	0	1	1	

Table 94. Hate Crime Incidents Per Bias Motivation and Quarter, by Selected State, Territory, Federal, and Agency, 2022—Continued

(Number.)

State/agency	Number of incidents per bias motivation						Number of incidents per quarter				Population[1]
	Race/ Ethnicity/ Ancestry	Religion	Sexual orientation	Disability	Gender	Gender Identity	1st quarter	2nd quarter	3rd quarter	4th quarter	
Cameron	2	0	0	0	0	0	1	0	0	1	
Chambers	0	0	0	0	1	0	0	1	0	0	
Comal	1	0	0	0	0	0	0	1	0	0	
Fort Bend	1	0	0	0	0	0	0	1	0	0	
Galveston	1	0	2	2	0	0	0	0	3	2	
Harris[2]	15	3	5	3	1	4	2	7	8	13	
Hays	1	0	0	0	0	0	0	0	1	0	
Jones	0	1	0	0	0	0	0	0	1	0	
Lubbock	3	3	1	2	0	1	2	4	3	1	
Randall	1	0	1	0	0	0	0	0	1	1	
Tarrant	0	1	5	0	0	0	1	2	3	0	
Travis	3	1	2	1	0	0	3	1	2	1	
Upshur	0	2	0	0	0	0	1	0	1	0	
Williamson	3	0	0	0	0	0	1	1	1	0	
Nonmetropolitan Counties	13	1	1	0	0	2					
Angelina	0	1	0	0	0	0	0	0	1	0	
Bee	1	0	0	0	0	0	0	0	1	0	
Brown	1	0	0	0	0	0	0	0	0	1	
Burnet	1	0	0	0	0	0	0	0	1	0	
Cherokee	2	0	0	0	0	0	1	1	0	0	
Dawson	0	0	1	0	0	0	0	0	1	0	
Eastland	1	0	0	0	0	0	0	1	0	0	
Fisher	0	0	0	0	0	1	1	0	0	0	
Henderson	0	0	0	0	0	1	0	1	0	0	
Maverick	5	0	0	0	0	0	1	1	2	1	
Nolan	1	0	0	0	0	0	0	0	1	0	
Red River	1	0	0	0	0	0	0	0	0	1	
Other Agencies	14	1	2	0	0	1					
Dallas-Fort Worth International Airport	2	0	0	0	0	0	1	0	0	1	
Hospital District, Tarrant County	1	0	0	0	0	0	1	0	0	0	
Independent School District											
Austin	1	0	0	0	0	0	1	0	0	0	
Calhoun County	1	0	0	0	0	0	0	0	0	1	
Fort Bend	3	0	0	0	0	0	0	1	1	1	
Houston	2	0	0	0	0	0	0	0	1	1	
Hutto	0	0	0	0	0	1	0	0	0	1	
Katy	0	1	0	0	0	0	0	1	0	0	
Killeen	1	0	0	0	0	0	0	1	0	0	
Mansfield	1	0	0	0	0	0	0	0	0	1	
Round Rock	1	0	1	0	0	0	1	0	0	1	
Montgomery County Constable, Precinct[3]	1	0	1	0	0	0	0	0	1	1	
UTAH	41	28	36	3	0	5					
Cities	25	24	27	1	0	1					
American Fork/Cedar Hills	0	1	0	0	0	0	0	0	0	1	45,310
Blanding	1	0	0	0	0	0	0	0	1	0	3,295
Cedar City	1	1	0	0	0	0	0	1	0	1	39,266
Grantsville	2	0	1	0	0	0	1	1	0	1	14,431
Helper	1	0	0	0	0	0	0	0	0	1	2,082
Hurricane	0	0	1	0	0	0	0	0	1	0	23,607
Layton	0	0	0	0	0	1	0	0	1	0	84,636
Lehi	1	1	0	0	0	0	2				83,071
Lindon	0	1	0	0	0	0	0	1	0	0	11,922
Logan	2	1	0	0	0	0	0	0	1	2	56,267
Lone Peak	2	3	2	0	0	0	0	2	4	1	30,258
Moab	0	0	1	0	0	0	0	0	1	0	5,263
Nephi	1	0	0	0	0	0	0	1	0	0	6,739
North Ogden	0	0	2	0	0	0	1	1	0	0	21,977
Orem[2]	0	4	6	0	0	0	2	4	1	0	97,430
Park City	0	2	0	0	0	0	1	0	0	1	8,516
Payson	1	0	0	0	0	0	0	0	0	1	22,989
Perry	0	1	0	0	0	0	0	0	0	1	5,921
Roosevelt	1	0	0	0	0	0	1	0	0	0	7,004
Salt Lake City[2]	1	1	3	0	0	0	0	2	0	1	201,373
Santaquin/Genola[2]	2	0	0	0	0	0	0	0	1	0	18,616
Smithfield	0	1	0	0	0	0	0	1	0	0	14,455
South Salt Lake	0	0	1	0	0	0	0	1	0	0	26,021
Springdale	0	0	1	0	0	0	0	0	0	1	589
Springville	2	1	2	1	0	0	1	4	0	1	36,907
Sunset	0	4	0	0	0	0	1	1	0	2	5,557
Tooele[2]	1	2	0	0	0	0	0	0	1	1	38,318
Tremonton Garland	2	0	0	0	0	0	1	0	0	1	13,682
Vernal	1	0	5	0	0	0	1	3	2	0	10,368
Washington	0	0	1	0	0	0	0	0	0	1	33,535
Wellington	1	0	0	0	0	0	0	0	1	1	1,587
West Jordan	1	0	0	0	0	0	1	0	0	0	115,900
West Valley	1	0	1	0	0	0	1	1	0	0	138,020

Table 94. Hate Crime Incidents Per Bias Motivation and Quarter, by Selected State, Territory, Federal, and Agency, 2022—Continued

(Number.)

State/agency	Number of incidents per bias motivation						Number of incidents per quarter				
	Race/ Ethnicity/ Ancestry	Religion	Sexual orientation	Disability	Gender	Gender Identity	1st quarter	2nd quarter	3rd quarter	4th quarter	Population[1]
Universities and Colleges	6	0	3	0	0	1					
Snow College	1	0	0	0	0	0	0	0	0	1	7,064
University of Utah	5	0	2	0	0	1	1	4	3	0	38,804
Weber State University	0	0	1	0	0	0	1	0	0	0	36,680
Metropolitan Counties	2	3	2	0	0	1					
Morgan[2]	0	2	0	0	0	0	1	0	0	0	
Tooele	1	0	0	0	0	0	0	1	0	0	
Weber[2]	1	1	2	0	0	1	1	1	1	1	
Nonmetropolitan Counties	2	1	0	1	0	0					
Beaver	0	1	0	0	0	0	0	0	1	0	
Carbon	0	0	0	1	0	0	1	0	0	0	
Iron	1	0	0	0	0	0	0	1	0	0	
Sevier	1	0	0	0	0	0	0	1	0	0	
Other Agencies	6	0	4	1	0	2					
Granite School District	2	0	0	0	0	2	1	1	1	1	
Utah Transit Authority	3	0	4	1	0	0	0	1	4	3	
Wildlife Resources	1	0	0	0	0	0	0	1	0	0	
VERMONT	34	5	12	1	0	0					
Cities	27	2	5	1	0	0					
Barre	1	0	0	0	0	0	0	0	0	1	8,447
Bennington[2]	4	0	0	1	0	0	1	2	0	1	15,301
Berlin	2	0	0	0	0	0	1	0	0	1	2,936
Brattleboro	2	0	0	0	0	0	1	0	0	1	12,256
Burlington	3	0	2	0	0	0	0	3	0	2	44,689
Colchester	1	0	0	0	0	0	1	0	0	0	17,710
Essex[2]	2	0	0	0	0	0	0	0	0	1	22,481
Hartford	1	1	1	0	0	0	0	2	1	0	10,863
Northfield	1	0	0	0	0	0	0	0	0	1	6,291
Norwich	1	0	0	0	0	0	0	0	1	0	3,681
Rutland	2	0	0	0	0	0	0	1	0	1	15,858
South Burlington	1	0	1	0	0	0	0	1	1	0	20,307
St. Albans	2	0	0	0	0	0	2	0	0	0	7,022
St. Johnsbury	2	1	0	0	0	0	0	1	1	1	7,404
Stowe	2	0	0	0	0	0	0	0	1	1	5,359
Winooski	0	0	1	0	0	0	0	1	0	0	8,647
Universities and Colleges	0	2	0	0	0	0					
University of Vermont	0	2	0	0	0	0	1	0	0	1	15,499
Nonmetropolitan Counties	1	0	0	0	0	0					
Lamoille	1	0	0	0	0	0	0	0	1	0	
State Police Agencies	6	1	7	0	0	0					
State Police											
Berlin	1	1	0	0	0	0	0	0	2	0	
New Haven	0	0	1	0	0	0	1	0	0	0	
Royalton	1	0	0	0	0	0	1	0	0	0	
St. Albans[2]	2	0	5	0	0	0	0	1	5	0	
Westminster	1	0	1	0	0	0	0	1	1	0	
Williston	1	0	0	0	0	0	0	0	1	0	
VIRGINIA	125	18	41	2	1	6					
Cities	23	4	15	2	0	6					
Alexandria	1	0	0	0	0	0	1	0	0	0	150,957
Chesapeake	1	1	0	0	0	1	1	0	2	0	253,745
Colonial Beach	0	0	0	1	0	0	0	0	0	1	3,980
Colonial Heights	1	0	0	0	0	0	1	0	0	0	18,419
Fredericksburg[2]	0	0	2	0	0	0	0	0	0	1	28,844
Harrisonburg	1	0	0	0	0	0	1	0	0	1	51,363
Hopewell[2]	2	0	0	0	0	0	0	0	0	1	23,395
Leesburg	7	2	5	1	0	0	3	3	4	5	49,395
Manassas	0	0	1	0	0	0	0	0	0	1	42,836
Manassas Park	0	0	1	0	0	0	0	1	0	0	16,923
Martinsville	0	0	0	0	0	1	0	0	0	1	13,660
Newport News	1	0	0	0	0	2	3	0	0	0	183,903
Norfolk	1	0	1	0	0	1	1	2	0	0	233,419
Poquoson	1	1	0	0	0	0	0	2	0	0	12,738
Portsmouth	2	0	1	0	0	0	0	0	0	3	98,003
Purcellville	1	0	0	0	0	0	1	0	0	0	9,103
Richmond	1	0	0	0	0	0	0	0	0	1	227,323
Strasburg	1	0	0	0	0	0	0	0	1	0	7,270
Suffolk	1	0	2	0	0	0	1	0	1	1	98,065
Virginia Beach	1	0	1	0	0	1	0	3	0	0	457,556
West Point	0	0	1	0	0	0	0	1	0	0	3,424
Universities and Colleges	6	0	4	0	0	0					
Christopher Newport University	1	0	0	0	0	0	0	1	0	0	5,034

Table 94. Hate Crime Incidents Per Bias Motivation and Quarter, by Selected State, Territory, Federal, and Agency, 2022—Continued

(Number.)

State/agency	Number of incidents per bias motivation						Number of incidents per quarter				
	Race/ Ethnicity/ Ancestry	Religion	Sexual orientation	Disability	Gender	Gender Identity	1st quarter	2nd quarter	3rd quarter	4th quarter	Population[1]
Hampton University	1	0	0	0	0	0	1	0	0	0	3,807
James Madison University[2]	0	0	3	0	0	0	0	0	0	2	23,827
Longwood University	2	0	0	0	0	0	0	0	1	1	5,771
University of Richmond	1	0	0	0	0	0	0	0	1	0	4,357
University of Virginia	1	0	1	0	0	0	0	1	1	0	28,322
Metropolitan Counties	90	8	21	0	0	0					
Albemarle County Police Department	1	0	0	0	0	0	0	0	1	0	
Arlington County Police Department	2	0	0	0	0	0	1	0	1	0	
Augusta	0	0	1	0	0	0	0	0	1	0	
Bedford	1	0	0	0	0	0	0	0	0	1	
Chesterfield County Police Department[2]	13	2	3	0	0	0	2	3	7	5	
Fairfax County Police Department[2]	43	4	8	0	0	0	6	14	20	14	
Frederick	2	0	0	0	0	0	0	0	0	2	
Gloucester	0	0	2	0	0	0	1	1	0	0	
Greene[2]	2	0	0	0	0	0	0	0	1	0	
Hanover	2	1	0	0	0	0	0	0	3	0	
Henrico County Police Department	5	0	0	0	0	0	2	2	0	1	
James City County Police Department	0	1	0	0	0	0	1	0	1	0	
Loudoun[2]	8	0	3	0	0	0	3	1	4	2	
Montgomery	1	0	0	0	0	0	1	0	0	0	
New Kent	1	0	0	0	0	0	1	0	0	0	
Prince George County Police Department	2	0	2	0	0	0	2	1	0	1	
Roanoke County Police Department	1	0	0	0	0	0	0	0	0	1	
Rockingham	1	0	0	0	0	0	0	1	0	0	
Stafford	2	0	1	0	0	0	0	2	1	0	
York[2]	3	0	1	0	0	0	1	1	0	1	
Nonmetropolitan Counties	3	5	0	0	0	0					
Henry	1	0	0	0	0	0	0	1	0	0	
Patrick[2]	0	2	0	0	0	0	0	0	1	0	
Smyth[2]	0	3	0	0	0	0	0	0	0	1	
Surry	1	0	0	0	0	0	0	0	0	1	
Wythe	1	0	0	0	0	0	1	0	0	0	
State Police Agencies	2	0	0	0	1	0					
State Police											
Fairfax County	2	0	0	0	0	0	1	0	1	0	
Hampton	0	0	0	0	1	0	0	0	0	1	
Other Agencies	1	1	1	0	0	0					
Reagan National Airport	1	1	1	0	0	0	1	0	0	2	
WASHINGTON	373	57	103	6	11	40					
Cities	315	48	88	3	11	37					
Airway Heights	2	0	0	0	0	0	1	0	1	0	10,803
Auburn	0	0	0	0	0	1	0	0	0	1	84,279
Bainbridge Island	1	0	0	0	0	0	1	0	0	0	24,336
Bellevue	16	3	3	0	1	0	1	7	7	8	147,079
Bellingham[2]	9	1	3	0	0	0	2	2	6	2	93,014
Blaine	1	0	0	0	0	0	0	1	0	0	6,050
Bonney Lake	1	0	0	0	0	0	0	0	0	1	22,898
Bothell	2	0	0	0	0	0	0	1	1	0	47,407
Bremerton	0	0	0	0	0	1	0	0	1	0	44,256
Burien[2]	4	2	4	0	0	0	2	2	3	2	50,159
Burlington	1	0	0	0	0	0	1	0	0	0	10,187
Cheney	1	0	2	0	0	0	0	1	1	1	13,092
Colville	1	0	0	0	0	0	0	0	1	0	5,026
Covington	1	0	0	0	0	0	1	0	0	0	20,686
Edmonds	1	0	0	0	0	0	1	0	0	0	42,714
Everett[2]	8	1	1	0	0	0	1	3	3	2	110,694
Federal Way[2]	5	0	1	0	0	0	1	2	0	2	97,094
Ferndale	0	1	1	0	0	0	0	0	1	1	15,816
Fircrest	0	1	0	0	0	0	1	0	0	0	7,047
Issaquah	1	0	0	0	0	0	0	1	0	0	38,917
Kalama	1	0	1	0	0	0	0	2	0	0	3,061
Kelso	1	0	1	0	0	0	0	2	0	0	12,723
Kenmore	1	0	0	0	0	0	0	0	1	0	23,107
Kennewick	3	1	1	0	0	0	0	2	1	2	85,058
Kent[2]	13	0	0	0	0	0	3	3	4	1	133,066
Kirkland[2]	3	0	0	0	0	0	1	0	1	0	91,464
Lacey[2]	2	0	0	0	0	0	0	0	0	1	55,101
Lake Forest Park	2	0	0	0	0	0	1	0	1	0	13,096
Lake Stevens[2]	2	0	0	0	0	0	0	0	0	1	36,828
Lakewood	1	1	2	0	0	0	0	1	2	1	63,044
Liberty Lake	0	1	0	0	0	0	0	1	0	0	12,897
Longview[2]	8	0	0	0	0	1	1	3	1	2	37,768
Lynnwood	2	1	1	0	0	0	0	4	0	0	42,764
Maple Valley	1	0	0	0	0	0	0	0	0	1	28,175

Table 94. Hate Crime Incidents Per Bias Motivation and Quarter, by Selected State, Territory, Federal, and Agency, 2022—Continued

(Number.)

State/agency	Number of incidents per bias motivation						Number of incidents per quarter				Population[1]
	Race/ Ethnicity/ Ancestry	Religion	Sexual orientation	Disability	Gender	Gender Identity	1st quarter	2nd quarter	3rd quarter	4th quarter	
Marysville	3	0	1	0	0	0	2	2	0	0	71,395
Mercer Island	1	0	0	0	0	0	0	0	0	1	25,121
Mill Creek[2]	2	0	0	0	0	0	0	1	0	0	20,925
Milton	1	0	0	0	0	1	1	1	0	0	9,113
Monroe	5	0	2	0	0	0	3	3	1	0	20,309
Montesano	1	0	0	0	0	0	0	0	0	1	4,196
Moses Lake	0	0	0	0	1	0	0	1	0	0	25,709
Mountlake Terrace[2]	2	1	0	0	0	0	0	2	0	0	21,589
Mount Vernon	1	0	0	0	0	0	0	1	0	0	35,511
Mukilteo	2	0	1	0	0	0	1	1	0	1	21,009
Newcastle	1	0	0	0	0	0	0	1	0	0	12,782
Oak Harbor	1	0	0	0	0	0	0	0	0	1	24,858
Olympia	3	0	0	0	0	0	2	0	1	0	56,214
Pacific	1	0	0	0	0	0	0	0	0	1	6,966
Pasco	1	0	1	1	0	0	0	2	0	1	79,899
Port Townsend	3	1	0	0	0	1	0	0	3	2	10,452
Quincy	2	0	0	0	0	0	0	1	1	0	8,413
Redmond	3	0	0	0	0	0	0	2	1	0	79,403
Renton[2]	2	3	1	0	0	0	1	2	1	1	103,619
Richland	2	1	1	0	0	0	0	1	0	3	63,081
Ridgefield	1	0	0	0	0	0	1	0	0	0	14,465
Sammamish	1	0	0	0	0	0	0	1	0	0	65,738
Seattle[2]	72	14	27	0	7	6	26	30	36	16	729,691
Sequim	0	1	0	0	0	0	0	0	1	0	8,439
Shelton	3	1	0	0	0	0	1	0	1	2	11,102
Shoreline[2]	4	1	1	0	0	2	1	3	3	0	57,147
Spokane[2]	11	0	2	0	0	0	3	2	7	0	229,292
Spokane Valley	2	1	0	0	0	4	0	3	1	3	108,076
Sunnyside	1	0	0	0	0	0	0	1	0	0	16,300
Tacoma	10	0	1	0	0	3	3	4	5	2	219,027
Toppenish	2	0	0	0	0	0	0	0	2	0	8,717
Tukwila	11	2	0	0	0	1	0	3	8	3	21,473
Tumwater	1	0	0	0	0	0	1	0	0	0	26,227
Union Gap	0	1	0	0	0	0	0	0	1	0	6,514
University Place	0	0	2	0	0	0	0	1	1	0	34,846
Vancouver[2]	62	6	25	2	2	16	20	30	27	16	193,273
Walla Walla	0	1	1	0	0	0	1	1	0	0	33,899
Woodinville	1	0	0	0	0	0	0	0	1	0	13,357
Yakima	1	1	1	0	0	0	1	0	1	1	96,267
Universities and Colleges	8	2	1	0	0	0					
University of Washington[2]	6	1	1	0	0	0	2	1	2	2	56,931
Washington State University, Pullman	1	0	0	0	0	0	1	0	0	0	34,825
Western Washington University	1	1	0	0	0	0	0	0	2	0	16,881
Metropolitan Counties	38	5	11	2	0	2					
Benton	0	0	1	0	0	0	0	1	0	0	
Cowlitz	0	0	0	0	0	1	1	0	0	0	
Franklin	1	0	0	0	0	0	0	1	0	0	
King[2]	20	2	5	1	0	1	7	4	7	8	
Pierce	6	0	1	0	0	0	2	1	1	3	
Skagit	2	0	0	0	0	0	2	0	0	0	
Snohomish[2]	1	2	2	0	0	0	0	1	1	2	
Spokane	1	0	0	1	0	0	0	1	0	1	
Thurston	1	0	0	0	0	0	1	0	0	0	
Whatcom	3	0	2	0	0	0	3	1	0	1	
Yakima	3	1	0	0	0	0	0	1	1	2	
Nonmetropolitan Counties	2	2	3	1	0	1					
Adams	1	0	0	0	0	0	0	1	0	0	
Grant	0	0	0	1	0	0	0	1	0	0	
Island	0	0	1	0	0	0	0	0	1	0	
Jefferson	0	0	0	0	0	1	1	0	0	0	
Kittitas	0	1	0	0	0	0	0	0	0	1	
Okanogan	0	1	0	0	0	0	0	1	0	0	
Pacific	0	0	1	0	0	0	0	1	0	0	
Pend Oreille	1	0	0	0	0	0	0	1	0	0	
San Juan	0	0	1	0	0	0	1	0	0	0	
Tribal Agencies	7	0	0	0	0	0					
Squaxin Island Tribal	1	0	0	0	0	0	0	0	0	1	
Tulalip Tribal	6	0	0	0	0	0	1	2	3	0	
Other Agencies	3	0	0	0	0	0					
Washington State Parks and Recreation Law Enforcement[2]	3	0	0	0	0	0	0	0	1	1	
WEST VIRGINIA	23	18	9	2	0	2					
Cities	12	11	5	1	0	2					
Bridgeport	0	1	0	0	0	0	0	0	0	1	9,206

Table 94. Hate Crime Incidents Per Bias Motivation and Quarter, by Selected State, Territory, Federal, and Agency, 2022—Continued

(Number.)

State/agency	Number of incidents per bias motivation						Number of incidents per quarter				Population[1]
	Race/ Ethnicity/ Ancestry	Religion	Sexual orientation	Disability	Gender	Gender Identity	1st quarter	2nd quarter	3rd quarter	4th quarter	
Ceredo	0	1	0	0	0	0	1	0	0	0	1,372
Charleston	3	3	1	0	0	0	1	2	2	2	47,350
Clarksburg	0	1	0	0	0	0	1	0	0	0	15,581
Moorefield	2	0	0	0	0	0	0	0	2	0	2,459
Morgantown[2]	0	0	3	0	0	0	0	0	0	2	29,279
Moundsville	1	0	0	0	0	0	1	0	0	0	7,885
Parkersburg	0	4	0	0	0	2	4	0	0	2	29,190
Philippi	0	1	0	0	0	0	1	0	0	0	2,921
Vienna	0	0	0	1	0	0	1	0	0	0	10,521
Weirton	2	0	0	0	0	0	0	0	0	2	18,544
Wheeling	3	0	1	0	0	0	1	1	1	1	26,244
White Hall	1	0	0	0	0	0	0	1	0	0	705
Metropolitan Counties	2	3	2	1	0	0					
Brooke	0	0	1	0	0	0	0	0	1	0	
Cabell	1	0	1	0	0	0	1	1	0	0	
Fayette	0	0	0	1	0	0	0	1	0	0	
Kanawha	0	1	0	0	0	0	0	1	0	0	
Monongalia	1	2	0	0	0	0	0	1	1	1	
Nonmetropolitan Counties	3	1	0	0	0	0					
Harrison	0	1	0	0	0	0	0	0	1	0	
Mason[2]	2	0	0	0	0	0	1	0	0	0	
Wetzel	1	0	0	0	0	0	0	0	1	0	
State Police Agencies	6	3	2	0	0	0					
State Police											
Huntington	0	0	1	0	0	0	1	0	0	0	
Kearneysville	1	0	0	0	0	0	0	0	0	1	
Martinsburg	1	0	0	0	0	0	0	0	0	1	
Moorefield[2]	1	2	0	0	0	0	0	0	0	2	
Morgantown	0	1	0	0	0	0	0	1	0	0	
Moundsville	0	0	1	0	0	0	1	0	0	0	
Princeton	1	0	0	0	0	0	0	1	0	0	
South Charleston	1	0	0	0	0	0	0	1	0	0	
Wayne	1	0	0	0	0	0	0	1	0	0	
WISCONSIN	72	29	28	6	9	8					
Cities	54	23	24	4	4	6					
Algoma	0	1	0	0	0	0	0	1	0	0	3,205
Altoona	0	0	0	0	0	1	0	0	1	0	9,320
Ashland	1	0	1	0	0	0	2	0	0	0	7,975
Beloit	1	0	1	0	0	0	0	0	1	1	36,784
Brookfield	1	0	0	0	0	0	0	0	0	1	41,489
Clinton	1	0	0	0	0	0	0	1	0	0	2,178
Columbus	0	0	0	0	1	0	0	0	1	0	5,478
Cottage Grove	1	0	0	0	0	0	0	1	0	0	7,328
Darlington	1	0	0	0	0	0	0	0	1	0	2,458
Delafield	0	0	0	0	0	1	1	0	0	0	7,192
Eau Claire	1	1	2	0	1	2	2	4	0	1	69,569
Elk Mound	0	0	0	2	0	0	2	0	0	0	979
Fitchburg	2	2	2	0	0	1	3	2	2	0	31,796
Fond du Lac	1	0	0	0	0	0	0	0	1	0	44,613
Janesville	1	0	0	0	0	0	0	1	0	0	66,242
Kaukauna	1	0	0	0	0	0	0	0	0	1	17,288
Kenosha	5	0	1	0	0	0	1	1	1	3	98,841
La Crosse[2]	3	1	0	0	0	0	0	1	1	0	51,727
Lake Hallie[2]	1	1	1	0	0	0	1	0	0	0	7,352
Luxemburg	1	0	0	0	0	0	0	1	0	0	2,699
Madison	4	4	2	0	0	0	2	2	5	1	269,546
Manitowoc	0	1	0	0	0	0	0	0	0	1	34,688
Menomonie	1	0	0	0	0	0	0	1	0	0	16,781
Milwaukee	1	1	3	0	0	0	0	2	1	2	561,743
Minocqua	0	1	0	0	0	0	0	0	0	1	5,186
Monona	1	0	0	0	0	0	0	0	0	1	8,920
Mount Horeb	0	1	0	0	0	0	1	0	0	0	7,687
Neenah	1	0	0	0	0	0	0	0	1	0	27,706
New Berlin	1	1	0	0	0	0	0	1	0	1	40,358
New Holstein	1	0	0	0	0	0	0	1	0	0	3,033
New London	1	0	0	0	0	0	1	0	0	0	7,286
New Richmond	0	1	0	0	0	0	0	1	0	0	10,610
Onalaska	1	0	0	0	0	0	1	0	0	0	18,807
Oregon	1	0	0	0	0	0	0	0	0	1	11,538
Oshkosh	3	1	1	1	0	0	2	1	2	1	66,521
Phillips	1	0	0	0	0	0	0	0	0	1	1,512
Platteville	1	0	1	0	0	1	0	2	0	1	11,771
Plover	1	0	0	0	0	0	0	1	0	0	13,850
Port Washington	0	0	1	0	0	0	0	0	0	1	12,867
Reedsburg	0	0	0	0	1	0	0	0	1	0	10,113

Table 94. Hate Crime Incidents Per Bias Motivation and Quarter, by Selected State, Territory, Federal, and Agency, 2022—Continued

(Number.)

State/agency	Number of incidents per bias motivation						Number of incidents per quarter				Population[1]
	Race/ Ethnicity/ Ancestry	Religion	Sexual orientation	Disability	Gender	Gender Identity	1st quarter	2nd quarter	3rd quarter	4th quarter	
River Falls	0	0	2	0	0	0	0	2	0	0	17,169
Sheboygan	0	1	0	0	0	0	1	0	0	0	49,917
Shorewood Hills	0	1	0	0	0	0	0	1	0	0	2,113
Sparta	1	1	1	0	0	1	1	2	1	0	9,901
Stevens Point[2]	0	0	2	0	0	0	0	0	1	0	25,777
Sun Prairie	2	0	1	0	0	0	0	1	1	1	36,153
Superior	1	0	0	0	0	0	0	0	0	1	26,429
Three Lakes	0	2	0	0	0	0	0	1	1	0	2,481
Tomahawk	1	0	0	0	0	0	0	0	1	0	3,432
Verona[2]	1	1	0	0	0	0	1	0	0	0	14,413
Watertown	1	0	1	0	0	0	0	0	1	1	22,885
Waupun	1	0	0	0	0	0	0	0	0	1	11,530
Wausau	1	0	0	0	0	0	1	0	0	0	39,349
West Allis	3	0	0	0	0	0	3	0	0	0	58,681
Whitewater	0	0	1	0	0	0	0	1	0	0	14,327
Wisconsin Rapids	1	0	0	1	0	0	1	0	1	0	18,693
Universities and Colleges	4	2	1	1	0	1					
University of Wisconsin											
Eau Claire	0	0	0	0	0	1	1	0	0	0	11,937
La Crosse[2]	1	1	1	0	0	0	1	0	0	1	11,344
Madison[2]	3	1	0	0	0	0	0	1	2	0	48,646
Stout	0	0	0	1	0	0	0	1	0	0	9,006
Metropolitan Counties	8	2	1	0	0	1					
Calumet	1	0	0	0	0	0	0	1	0	0	
Chippewa	0	1	1	0	0	0	1	0	1	0	
Columbia[2]	2	1	0	0	0	0	1	0	1	0	
Dane	1	0	0	0	0	1	0	1	1	0	
Rock	2	0	0	0	0	0	1	1	0	0	
St. Croix	1	0	0	0	0	0	0	0	1	0	
Winnebago	1	0	0	0	0	0	0	0	0	1	
Nonmetropolitan Counties	6	2	2	1	5	0					
Barron	1	0	0	0	0	0	0	1	0	0	
Crawford	1	0	0	0	0	0	0	0	1	0	
Door	0	1	0	0	0	0	0	0	1	0	
Juneau	1	0	0	0	0	0	1	0	0	0	
Marinette	0	1	0	0	0	0	0	0	0	1	
Menominee	0	0	0	0	1	0	0	1	0	0	
Polk	0	0	0	1	4	0	1	1	2	1	
Portage	1	0	1	0	0	0	0	0	1	1	
Richland	0	0	1	0	0	0	1	0	0	0	
Waupaca	1	0	0	0	0	0	0	0	1	0	
Wood	1	0	0	0	0	0	1	0	0	0	
WYOMING	11	3	8	0	2	1					
Cities	8	3	6	0	2	1					
Cheyenne	3	2	0	0	1	1	2	3	1	1	64,941
Gillette	0	1	0	0	0	0	0	0	1	0	32,320
Green River	0	0	2	0	0	0	0	1	0	1	11,435
Laramie	0	0	3	0	0	0	2	0	1	0	32,009
Newcastle[2]	2	0	0	0	1	0	0	0	1	0	3,176
Rock Springs	2	0	0	0	0	0	1	1	0	0	22,914
Sheridan	1	0	1	0	0	0	0	2	0	0	19,373
Universities and Colleges	1	0	2	0	0	0					
University of Wyoming	1	0	2	0	0	0	1	0	2	0	13,300
Nonmetropolitan Counties	2	0	0	0	0	0					
Park	1	0	0	0	0	0	0	0	1	0	
Sweetwater	1	0	0	0	0	0	0	0	0	1	
TERRITORIES											
Other Agencies	4	2	0	0	0	0					
Guam Police Department	4	2	0	0	0	0	1	3	0	2	
FEDERAL											
Federal Agencies	49	22	15	1	8	10					
Federal Bureau of Investigation[2]	36	20	12	0	3	9	18	15	20	19	
National Institute of Health	1	0	1	0	0	0	1	1	0	0	
United States Air Force Security Police[2]	3	1	0	0	3	0	2	0	1	3	
United States Department of Veterans Affairs Police Service	5	0	2	1	2	1		0	0	11	
United States Forest Service	1	1	0	0	0	0	0	0	1	1	
United States Treasury Inspector General for Tax Administration[2]	3	0	0	0	0	0	0	1	1	0	

1 Population figures are published only for the cities. The figures listed for the universities and colleges are student enrollment and were provided by the United States Department of Education for the 2021 school year, the most recent available. The enrollment figures include full-time and part-time students.   2 The figures shown include at least one incident reported with more than one bias motivation.   3 Student enrollment figures were not available.

APPENDIXES

APPENDIX I. METHODOLOGY

Submitting UCR data to the FBI is a collective effort on the part of city, university/college, county, state, tribal, and federal law enforcement agencies to present a nationwide view of crime. Participating agencies throughout the country voluntarily provide reports on crimes known to the police and on persons arrested. For the most part, agencies submit monthly crime reports, using uniform offense definitions, to a centralized repository within their state. The state UCR Program then forwards the data to the FBI's UCR Program. Agencies in states that do not have a state UCR Program submit their data directly to the FBI. Staff members review the information for accuracy and reasonableness. [The FBI distributes the data presentations, special studies, and other publications compiled from the data to all who are interested in knowing about crime in the nation.] The national UCR Program is housed in the Operational Programs (OP) Branch of the FBI's Criminal Justice Information Services (CJIS) Division. Within the OP Branch, four units (the Crime Statistics Management Unit [CSMU], the CJIS Audit Unit, the Multimedia Productions Group [MPG]), and the CJIS Training and Advisory Process [CTAP] Unit), are involved in the day-to-day administration of the program.

Criteria for State UCR programs

The criteria established for state programs ensure consistency and comparability in the data submitted to the national program, as well as regular and timely reporting. These criteria are:

- A UCR Program must conform to the FBI UCR Program's submission standards, definitions, specifications, and required deadlines.

- A UCR Program must establish data integrity procedures and have personnel assigned to assist contributing agencies in quality assurance practices and crime reporting procedures. Data integrity procedures should include crime trend assessments, offense classification verification, and technical specification validation.

- A UCR Program's submissions must cover more than 50 percent of the law enforcement agencies within its established reporting domain and be willing to cover any and all UCR-contributing agencies that wish to use the UCR Program from within its domain. (An agency wishing to become a UCR Program must be willing to report for all of the agencies within the state.)

- A UCR Program must furnish the FBI UCR Program with all of the UCR data collected by the law enforcement agencies within its domain.

These requirements do not prohibit the state from gathering other statistical data beyond the national collection.

Data Completeness and Quality

National program staff members contact the state UCR program in connection with crime-reporting matters and, when necessary and approved by the state, they contact individual contributors within the state. To fulfill its responsibilities in connection with the UCR program, the FBI reviews and edits individual agency reports for completeness and quality. Upon request, they conduct training programs within the state on law enforcement record-keeping and crime-reporting procedures. The FBI conducts an audit of each state's UCR data collection procedures once every three years, in accordance with audit standards established by the federal government. Should circumstances develop in which the state program does not comply with the aforementioned requirements, the national program may institute a direct collection of data from law enforcement agencies within the state.

During a review of publication processes, the UCR Program staff analyzed Web statistics from previous editions of *Crime in the United States* (*CIUS*) to determine the tables that users access the most. Based on these criteria, the UCR Program streamlined the 2016 edition by reducing the number of tables from 81 to 29. The publication, however, still presents the major topics (offenses known, clearances, and persons arrested) that readers have come to expect. On June 30, 2017, the UCR Program launched the Crime Data Explorer (CDE), which provides law enforcement and the general public with crime data at the agency, state, and national levels. Offering multiple pathways to reported crime data, the CDE provides data visualizations of high-level trends and incident data with more detailed perspectives through downloads and a system enabling developers to create software applications. Planned enhancements to the CDE include additional tools to create dynamic data presentations, progressing beyond the static data tables of *CIUS* and the National Incident-Based Reporting System (NIBRS).

Beginning January 1, 2017, the UCR Program discontinued collecting rape data via the SRS according to the legacy definition. Therefore, the 2016 editions of *CIUS* and *Hate Crime Statistics* are the final publications which include the legacy definition of rape. Only rape data submitted under the revised definition will be published for 2017 and subsequent years. This change did not affect agencies that submit rape data via NIBRS.

Reporting Procedures

Offenses known and value of property. Law enforcement agencies tabulate the number of Part I offenses reported based on records of all reports of crime received from victims, officers who discover infractions, or other sources, and submit these reports each month to the FBI directly or through their state UCR programs. Part I offenses include murder and nonnegligent manslaughter, forcible rape, robbery, aggravated assault, burglary, larceny-theft, motor vehicle theft, and arson. Each month, law enforcement agencies also submit to the FBI the value of property stolen and recovered in connection with the offenses and detailed information pertaining to criminal homicide.

Unfounded offenses and clearances. When, through investigation, an agency determines that complaints of crimes are unfounded or false, the agency eliminates that offense from its crime tally through an entry on the monthly report. The report also provides the total number of actual Part I offenses, the number of offenses cleared, and the number of clearances that involve only offenders under the age of 18. (Law enforcement can clear crimes in one of two ways: by the arrest of at least one person who is charged and turned over to the court for prosecution or by exceptional means—when some element beyond law enforcement's control precludes the arrest of a known offender.)

Persons arrested. In addition to reporting Part I offenses each month, law enforcement agencies also provide data on the age, sex, and race of persons arrested for Part I and Part II offenses. Part II offenses encompass all crimes, except traffic violations, that are not classified as Part I offenses.

Officers killed or assaulted. Each month, law enforcement agencies also report information to the UCR program regarding law enforcement officers killed or assaulted, and each year they report the number of full-time sworn and civilian law enforcement personnel employed as of October 31.

Hate crimes. At the end of each quarter, law enforcement agencies report summarized data on hate crimes; that is specific offenses that were motivated by an offender's bias against the perceived race, religion, ethnic or national origin, sexual orientation, or physical or mental disability of the victim. Those agencies participating in the UCR program's National Incident-Based Reporting System (NIBRS) submit hate crime data monthly.

Editing Procedures

The UCR program thoroughly examines each report it receives for arithmetical accuracy and for deviations in crime data from month to month and from present to past years that may indicate errors. UCR staff members compare an agency's monthly reports with its previous submissions and with reports from similar agencies to identify any unusual fluctuations in the agency's crime count. Considerable variations in crime levels may indicate modified records procedures, incomplete reporting, or changes in the jurisdiction's geopolitical structure.

Evaluation of trends. Data reliability is a high priority of the FBI, which brings any deviations or arithmetical adjustments to the attention of state UCR programs or the submitting agencies. Typically, FBI staff members study the monthly reports to evaluate periodic trends prepared for individual reporting units. Any significant increase or decrease becomes the subject of a special inquiry. Changes in crime reporting procedures or annexations that affect an agency's jurisdiction can influence the level of reported crime. When this occurs, the FBI excludes the figures for specific crime categories or totals, if necessary, from the trend tabulations.

Training for contributors. In addition to the evaluation of trends, the FBI provides training seminars and instructional materials on crime reporting procedures to assist contributors in complying with UCR standards. Throughout the country, representatives from the national program coordinate with representatives of state programs and law enforcement personnel and hold training sessions to explain the purpose of the program, the rules of uniform classification and scoring, and the methods of assembling the information for reporting. When an individual agency has specific problems with compiling its crime statistics and its remedial efforts are unsuccessful, personnel from the FBI's Criminal Justice Information Services Division may visit the contributor to aid in resolving the problems.

UCR Handbook. The national UCR program publishes the *Uniform Crime Reporting (UCR) Handbook*, which details procedures for classifying and scoring offenses and serves as the contributing agencies' basic resource for preparing reports. The national staff also produces letters to UCR contributors, state program bulletins, and UCR newsletters as needed. These publications provide policy updates and new information, as well as clarification of reporting issues.

The final responsibility for data submissions rests with the individual contributing law enforcement agency. Although the FBI makes every effort through its editing procedures, training practices, and correspondence to ensure the validity of the data it receives, the accuracy of the statistics depends primarily on the adherence of each contributor to the established standards of reporting. Deviations from these established standards that cannot be resolved by the national UCR program may be brought to the attention of the Criminal Justice Information Systems Committees of the International Association of Chiefs of Police and the National Sheriffs' Association.

NIBRS Conversion

All state programs are certified to provide their UCR data in the expanded National Incident-Based Reporting System (NIBRS) format. The UCR program is currently in full transition/migration to NIBRS, as seen on the FBI's Crime Data Explorer.

Crime Trends

By showing fluctuations from year to year, trend statistics offer the data user an added perspective from which to study crime. Percent change tabulations in this publication are computed only for reporting agencies that provided comparable data for the periods under consideration. The FBI excludes from the trend calculations all figures except those received for common months from common agencies. Also excluded are unusual fluctuations of data that the FBI determines are the result of such variables as improved records procedures, annexations, and so on.

Caution to Users

Data users should exercise care in making any direct comparison between data in this publication and those in prior issues of *Crime in the United States*. Because of differing levels of participation from year to year and reporting problems that require the FBI to estimate crime counts for certain contributors, some data may not be comparable. In addition, this publication may contain updates to data provided in prior years' publications.

Offense Estimation

Some tables in this publication contain statistics for the entire United States. Because not all law enforcement agencies provide data for complete reporting periods, the FBI includes estimated crime numbers in these presentations. The FBI estimates data for three areas: Metropolitan Statistical Areas (MSAs), cities outside MSAs, and nonmetropolitan counties; and computes estimates for participating agencies that do not provide 12 months of complete data. For agencies supplying 3 to 11 months of data, the national UCR program estimates for the missing data by following a standard estimation procedure using the data provided by the agency. If an agency has supplied less than 3 months of data, the FBI computes estimates by using the known crime figures of similar areas within a state and assigning the same proportion of crime volumes to nonreporting agencies. The estimation process considers the following: population size covered by the agency; type of jurisdiction; for example, police department versus sheriff's office; and geographic location.

Estimation of State-Level Data

In response to various circumstances, the FBI calculates estimated offense totals for certain states. For example, some states do not provide forcible rape figures in accordance with UCR guidelines. In addition, problems at the state level have, at times, resulted in no useable data. Also, the conversion of the National Incident-Based Reporting System (NIBRS) data to Summary data has contributed to the need for unique estimation procedures.

APPENDIX II. OFFENSE DEFINITIONS

The Uniform Crime Reporting (UCR) program divides offenses into two groups. Contributing agencies submit information on the number of Part I offenses known to law enforcement; those offenses cleared by arrest or exceptional means; and the age, sex, and race of persons arrested for each of these offenses. Contributors provide only arrest data for Part II offenses. These are definitions of offenses set forth by the UCR.

The UCR program collects data on Part I offenses to measure the level and scope of crime occurring throughout the nation. The program's founders chose these offenses because (1) they are serious crimes, (2) they occur with regularity in all areas of the country, and (3) they are likely to be reported to police.

Part I offenses include murder and nonnegligent manslaughter, rape, robbery, aggravated assault, burglary, larceny-theft, motor vehicle theft, and arson.

Murder and Nonnegligent Manslaughter. The willful (non-negligent) killing of one human being by another. Deaths caused by negligence, attempts to kill, assaults to kill, suicides, and accidental deaths are excluded. The program classifies justifiable homicides separately and limits the definition to (1) the killing of a felon by a law enforcement officer in the line of duty; or (2) the killing of a felon, during the commission of a felony, by a private citizen. b. Manslaughter by negligence: the killing of another person through gross negligence. Deaths of persons due to their own negligence, accidental deaths not resulting from gross negligence, and traffic fatalities are excluded.

Rape. In 2013, the FBI UCR Program began collecting rape data under a revised definition within the Summary Reporting System. Previously, offense data for forcible rape were collected under the legacy UCR definition: the carnal knowledge of a female forcibly and against her will. Beginning with the 2013 data year, the term "forcible" was removed from the offense title, and the definition was changed. The revised UCR definition of rape is: penetration, no matter how slight, of the vagina or anus with any body part or object, or oral penetration by a sex organ of another person, without the consent of the victim. Attempts or assaults to commit rape are also included in the statistics presented here; however, statutory rape and incest are excluded. In 2016, the FBI director approved the recommendation to discontinue the reporting of rape data using the UCR legacy definition beginning in 2017.

However, to maintain the 20-year trend in Table 1, national estimates for rape under the legacy definition are provided along with estimates under the revised definition for 2017. The UCR Program counts one offense for each victim of a rape, attempted rape, or assault with intent to rape, regardless of the victim's age. Non-consensual sexual relations involving a familial member is considered rape, not incest. All other crimes of a sexual nature are considered to be Part II offenses; as such, the UCR Program collects only arrest data for those crimes. The offense of statutory rape, in which no force is used but the female victim is under the age of consent, is included in the arrest total for the sex offenses category.

Robbery. The taking or attempted taking of anything of value from the care, custody, or control of a person or persons by force or threat of force or violence and/or by putting the victim in fear.

Aggravated assault. An unlawful attack by one person upon another for the purpose of inflicting severe or aggravated bodily injury. This type of assault usually is accompanied by the use of a weapon or by means likely to produce death or great bodily harm. Simple assaults are excluded.

Burglary (breaking or entering). The unlawful entry of a structure to commit a felony or a theft. Attempted forcible entry is included.

Larceny-theft (except motor vehicle theft). The unlawful taking, carrying, leading, or riding away of property from the possession or constructive possession of another. Examples are thefts of bicycles or automobile parts and accessories, shoplifting, pocket-picking, or the stealing of any property or article that is not taken by force and violence or by fraud. Attempted larcenies are included. Embezzlement, confidence games, forgery, worthless checks, and the like, are excluded.

Motor vehicle theft. The theft or attempted theft of a motor vehicle. A motor vehicle is self-propelled and runs on land surface and not on rails. Motorboats, construction equipment, airplanes, and farming equipment are specifically excluded from this category.

Arson. Any willful or malicious burning or attempt to burn, with or without intent to defraud, a dwelling house, public building, motor vehicle, aircraft, personal property of another, and the like.

APPENDIX III. GEOGRAPHIC AREA DEFINITIONS

The program collects crime data and supplemental information that make it possible to generate a variety of statistical compilations, including data presented by reporting areas. These statistics enable data users to analyze local crime data in conjunction with those for areas of similar geographic location or population size. The reporting areas that the program uses in its data breakdowns include community types, population groups, and regions and divisions. For community types, the program considers proximity to metropolitan areas using the designations established by the U.S. Office of Management and Budget (OMB). (Generally, sheriffs, county police, and state police report crimes within counties but outside of cities; local police report crimes within city limits.) The number of inhabitants living in a locale (based on the U.S. Census Bureau's figures) determines the population group into which the program places it. For its geographic breakdowns, the program divides the United States into regions and divisions.

Regions and Divisions

The map below illustrates the nine divisions that make up the four regions of the United States. The program uses this widely recognized geographic organization when compiling the nation's crime data. The regions and divisions are as follows:

NORTHEAST

New England: Connecticut, Maine, Massachusetts, New Hampshire, Rhode Island, and Vermont

Middle Atlantic: New York, New Jersey, and Pennsylvania

MIDWEST

East North Central: Illinois, Indiana, Michigan, Ohio, and Wisconsin

West North Central: Iowa, Kansas, Minnesota, Missouri, Nebraska, North Dakota, and South Dakota

SOUTH

South Atlantic: Delaware, District of Columbia, Florida, Georgia, Maryland, North Carolina, South Carolina, Virginia, and West Virginia

East South Central: Alabama, Kentucky, Mississippi, and Tennessee

West South Central: Arkansas, Louisiana, Oklahoma, and Texas

WEST

Mountain: Arizona, Colorado, Idaho, Montana, Nevada, New Mexico, Utah, and Wyoming

Pacific: Alaska, California, Hawaii, Oregon, and Washington

APPENDIX IV. THE NATION'S TWO CRIME MEASURES

The Department of Justice administers two statistical programs to measure the magnitude, nature, and impact of crime in the nation: the Uniform Crime Reporting (UCR) program and the National Crime Victimization Survey (NCVS). Each of these programs produces valuable information about aspects of the nation's crime problem. Because the UCR and NCVS programs are conducted for different purposes, use different methods, and focus on somewhat different aspects of crime, the information they produce together provides a more comprehensive panorama of the nation's crime problem than either could produce alone.

Uniform Crime Reporting (UCR) program

The UCR program, administered by the Federal Bureau of Investigation (FBI), was created in 1929 and collects information on the following crimes reported to law enforcement authorities: murder and nonnegligent manslaughter, forcible rape, robbery, aggravated assault, burglary, larceny-theft, motor vehicle theft, and arson. Law enforcement agencies also report arrest data for 20 additional crime categories.

The UCR program compiles data from monthly law enforcement reports and from individual crime incident records transmitted directly to the FBI or to centralized state agencies that report to the FBI. The program thoroughly examines each report it receives for reasonableness, accuracy, and deviations that may indicate errors. Large variations in crime levels may indicate modified records procedures, incomplete reporting, or changes in a jurisdiction's boundaries. To identify any unusual fluctuations in an agency's crime counts, the program compares monthly reports to previous submissions of the agency and to those for similar agencies.

The FBI annually publishes its findings in a preliminary release in the spring of the following calendar year, followed by a detailed annual report, *Crime in the United States*, issued in the fall. (The printed copy of *Crime in the United States* is now published by Bernan.) In addition to crime counts and trends, this report includes data on crimes cleared, persons arrested (age, sex, and race), law enforcement personnel (including the number of sworn officers killed or assaulted), and the characteristics of homicides (including age, sex, and race of victims and offenders; victim-offender relationships; weapons used; and circumstances surrounding the homicides). Other periodic reports are also available from the UCR program.

The state and local law enforcement agencies participating in the UCR program are continually converting to the more comprehensive and detailed National Incident-Based Reporting System (NIBRS).

The UCR program presents crime counts for the nation as a whole, as well as for regions, states, counties, cities, towns, tribal law enforcement areas, and colleges and universities. This allows for studies among neighboring jurisdictions and among those with similar populations and other common characteristics.

National Crime Victimization Survey

The NCVS, conducted by the Bureau of Justice Statistics (BJS), began in 1973. It provides a detailed picture of crime incidents, victims, and trends. After a substantial period of research, the BJS completed an intensive methodological redesign of the survey in 1993. It conducted this redesign to improve the questions used to uncover crime, update the survey methods, and broaden the scope of crimes measured. The redesigned survey collects detailed information on the frequency and nature of the crimes of rape, sexual assault, personal robbery, aggravated and simple assault, household burglary, theft, and motor vehicle theft. It does not measure homicide or commercial crimes (such as burglaries of stores).

Twice a year, Census Bureau personnel interview household members in a nationally representative sample of approximately 90,000 households (about 160,000 people). Households stay in the sample for 3 years, and new households rotate into the sample on an ongoing basis.

The NCVS collects information on crimes suffered by individuals and households, whether or not those crimes were reported to law enforcement. It estimates the proportion of each crime type reported to law enforcement, and it summarizes the reasons that victims give for reporting or not reporting.

The survey provides information about victims (age, sex, race, ethnicity, marital status, income, and educational level); offenders (sex, race, approximate age, and victim-offender relationship); and crimes (time and place of occurrence, use of weapons, nature of injury, and economic consequences). Questions also cover victims' experiences with the criminal justice system, self-protective measures used by victims, and possible substance abuse by offenders. Supplements are added to the survey periodically to obtain detailed information on specific topics, such as school crime.

The BJS published the first data from the redesigned NCVS in a June 1995 bulletin. The publication of NCVS data includes *Criminal Victimization in the United States*, an annual report that covers the broad range of detailed information collected by the NCVS. The bureau also publishes detailed reports on topics such as crime against women, urban crime, and gun use in crime. The National Archive of Criminal Justice Data at the University of Michigan archives the NCVS data files to help researchers perform independent analyses.

Comparing the UCR program and the NCVS

Because the BJS designed the NCVS to complement the UCR program, the two programs share many similarities. As much as their different collection methods permit, the two measure the same subset of serious crimes with the same definitions. Both programs cover rape, robbery, aggravated assault, burglary, theft, and motor vehicle theft; both define rape, robbery, theft, and motor vehicle theft virtually identically. (Although rape is defined analogously, the UCR program measures the crime against women only, and the NCVS measures it against both sexes.)

There are also significant differences between the two programs. First, the two programs were created to serve different purposes. The UCR program's primary objective is to provide a reliable set of criminal justice statistics for law enforcement administration, operation, and management. The BJS established the NCVS to provide previously unavailable information about crime (including crime not reported to police), victims, and offenders.

Second, the two programs measure an overlapping but non-identical set of crimes. The NCVS includes crimes both reported and not reported to law enforcement. The NCVS excludes—but the UCR program includes—homicide, arson, commercial crimes, and crimes committed against children under 12 years of age. The UCR program captures crimes reported to law enforcement but collects only arrest data for simple assaults and sexual assaults other than forcible rape.

Third, because of methodology, the NCVS and UCR have different definitions of some crimes. For example, the UCR defines burglary as the unlawful entry or attempted entry of a structure to commit a felony or theft. The NCVS, not wanting to ask victims to ascertain offender motives, defines burglary as the entry or attempted entry of a residence by a person who had no right to be there.

Fourth, for property crimes (burglary, theft, and motor vehicle theft), the two programs calculate crime rates using different bases. The UCR program rates for these crimes are per capita (number of crimes per 100,000 persons), whereas the NCVS rates for these crimes are per household (number of crimes per 1,000 households).

Because the number of households may not grow at the same annual rate as the total population, trend data for rates of property crimes measured by the two programs may not be comparable. In addition, some differences in the data from the two programs may result from sampling variation in the NCVS and from estimating for nonresponsiveness in the UCR program.

The BJS derives the NCVS estimates from interviewing a sample and are, therefore, subject to a margin of error. The bureau uses rigorous statistical methods to calculate confidence intervals around all survey estimates, and describes trend data in the NCVS reports as genuine only if there is at least a 90-percent certainty that the measured changes are not the result of sampling variation. The UCR program bases its data on the actual counts of offenses reported by law enforcement agencies. In some circumstances, the UCR program estimates its data for nonparticipating agencies or those reporting partial data. Apparent discrepancies between statistics from the two programs can usually be accounted for by their definitional and procedural differences, or resolved by comparing NCVS sampling variations (confidence intervals) of crimes said to have been reported to police with UCR program statistics.

For most types of crimes measured by both the UCR program and the NCVS, analysts familiar with the programs can exclude those aspects of crime not common to both from analysis. Resulting long-term trend lines can be brought into close concordance. The impact of such adjustments is most striking for robbery, burglary, and motor vehicle theft, whose definitions most closely coincide.

With robbery, the BJS bases the NCVS victimization rates on only those robberies reported to the police. It is also possible to remove UCR program robberies of commercial establishments, such as gas stations, convenience stores, and banks, from analysis. When users compare the resulting NCVS police-reported robbery rates and the UCR program noncommercial robbery rates, the results reveal closely corresponding long-term trends.

Conclusion

Each program has unique strengths. The UCR program provides a measure of the number of crimes reported to law enforcement agencies throughout the country. The program's Supplementary Homicide Reports provide the most reliable, timely data on the extent and nature of homicides in the nation. The NCVS is the primary source of information on the characteristics of criminal victimization and on the number and types of crimes not reported to law enforcement authorities.

By understanding the strengths and limitations of each program, it is possible to use the UCR program and NCVS to achieve a greater understanding of crime trends and the nature of crime in the United States. For example, changes in police procedures, shifting attitudes towards crime and police, and other societal changes can affect the extent to which people report and law enforcement agencies record crime. NCVS and UCR program data can be used in concert to explore why trends in reported and police-recorded crime may differ.

Appendix V. Calculations by Population, Tables 16, 17, 18, 19

Due to a system upgrade in 2019, the FBI calculates rates for each offense based on the individual offenses and population that were published for each agency in tables 8-11. (Previous to 2019, when agencies were published in tables 8-11, but they had one or two offenses removed from publication due to not meeting UCR publication guidelines, the agency's data was not used to calculate rates for this table.) This table provides the rate per 100,000 inhabitants and the number of offenses known to law enforcement for violent crimes (murder and nonnegligent manslaughter, rape, robbery, and aggravated assault) and property crimes (burglary, larceny-theft, and motor vehicle theft) nationally and by city and county groupings for law enforcement agencies submitting 12 months of publishable data for 2019. For the 2019 population estimates used in this table, the FBI computed individual rates of growth from one year to the next for every city/town and county using 2010 decennial population counts and 2011 through 2018 population estimates from the U.S. Census Bureau. Each agency's rates of growth were averaged; that average was then applied and added to its 2018 Census population estimate to derive the agency's 2019 population estimate.

The UCR Program does not have sufficient data to publish arson offenses in this table.

Group VI city classifications include universities and colleges to which no population is attributed. The nonmetropolitan counties classification includes state police agencies that report aggregately for the entire state. Metropolitan and nonmetropolitan counties include state police to which no population is attributed. Suburban areas include law enforcement agencies in cities with fewer than 50,000 inhabitants and county law enforcement agencies that are within a Metropolitan Statistical Area. Suburban areas exclude all metropolitan agencies associated with a principal city. The agencies associated with suburban areas also appear in other groups within this The FBI derived the offense rates by first dividing the individual offense counts by the individual populations covered by contributing agencies for which 12 months of publishable data were supplied and then multiplying the resulting figure by 100,000.

Populations Used to Calculate Violent Crime Rates, by Population Group, Beginning in 2019

	Violent crime total		Murder/nonnegligent manslaughter		Rape		Robbery		Aggravated assault	
	Agency count	Population	Agency count	Population	Agency count	Population	Agency count	Population	Agency count	Population
Total	12,730	279,536,935	12,721	279,321,521	12,709	279,018,775	12,729	279,424,554	12,728	279,497,051
Total, Cities	9,195	194,512,905	9,192	194,342,817	9,180	194,253,008	9,194	194,400,524	9,193	194,473,021
GROUP I (250,000 and over)	83	60,188,585	83	60,188,585	83	60,188,585	83	60,188,585	83	60,188,585
Cities with 1,000,000 or over	10	26,216,990	10	26,216,990	10	26,216,990	10	26,216,990	10	26,216,990
Cities with 500,000 through 999,999	24	17,433,188	24	17,433,188	24	17,433,188	24	17,433,188	24	17,433,188
Cities with 250,000 through 499,999	49	16,538,407	49	16,538,407	49	16,538,407	49	16,538,407	49	16,538,407
GROUP II (100,000 to 249,999)	212	30,850,549	211	30,740,351	211	30,740,351	211	30,740,351	212	30,850,549
GROUP III (50,000 to 99,999)	458	31,931,708	458	31,931,708	458	31,931,708	458	31,931,708	458	31,931,708
GROUP IV (25,000 to 49,999)	803	27,996,450	803	27,996,450	803	27,996,450	803	27,996,450	803	27,996,450
GROUP V (10,000 to 24,999)	1,563	25,119,823	1,563	25,119,823	1,559	25,119,823	1,563	25,119,823	1,561	25,079,939
GROUP VI (under 10,000)	6,076	18,425,790	6,075	18,416,052	6,066	18,389,166	6,076	18,425,790	6,076	18,425,790
Metropolitan counties	1,608	65,156,789	1,604	65,134,008	1,604	65,134,008	1,608	65,156,789	1,608	65,156,789
Nonmetropolitan counties	1,927	19,867,241	1,925	19,844,696	1,925	19,844,696	1,927	19,867,241	1,927	19,867,241
Suburban areas	6,971	118,340,932	6,967	118,318,151	6,961	118,092,494	6,971	118,340,932	6,970	118,320,268

Populations Used to Calculate Property Crime Rates, by Population Group, Beginning in 2019

	Property crime total		Burglary		Larceny-theft		Motor vehicle theft	
	Agency count	Population	Agency count	Population	Agency count	Population	Agency count	Population
Total	12,730	279,536,935	12,704	278,387,019	12,720	279,320,446	12,726	278,744,544
Total, Cities	9,195	194,512,905	9,182	193,726,208	9,187	194,354,748	9,191	193,720,514
GROUP I (250,000 and over)	83	60,188,585	82	59,626,665	83	60,188,585	82	59,626,665
Cities with 1,000,000 or over	10	26,216,990	10	26,216,990	10	26,216,990	10	26,216,990
Cities with 500,000 through 999,999	24	17,433,188	23	16,871,268	24	17,433,188	23	16,871,268
Cities with 250,000 through 499,999	49	16,538,407	49	16,538,407	49	16,538,407	49	16,538,407
GROUP II (100,000 to 249,999)	212	30,850,549	211	30,740,351	211	30,740,351	211	30,740,351
GROUP III (50,000 to 99,999)	458	31,931,708	458	31,931,708	457	31,865,408	457	31,865,408
GROUP IV (25,000 to 49,999)	803	27,996,450	798	27,827,090	802	27,971,438	803	27,996,450
GROUP V (10,000 to 24,999)	1,563	25,119,823	1,561	251,088,221	1,560	25,064,398	1,562	251,100,993
GROUP VI (under 10,000)	6,076	18,425,790	6,071	18,401,975	6,073	18,414,370	6,075	18,423,524
Metropolitan counties	1,608	65,156,789	1,596	64,083,397	1,607	65,112,211	1,608	65,156,789
Nonmetropolitan counties	1,927	19,867,241	1,926	19,857,414	1,926	19,853,487	1,927	19,867,241
Suburban areas	6,971	118,340,932	6,952	117,846,365	6,965	118,236,886	6,970	118,322,103

AGE

Arrests, cities, distribution by age, 311

Arrests, distribution by age, 293–302

Arrests, metropolitan counties, 322, 324

Arrests, nonmetropolitan counties, 333, 335

Arrests, persons under 15, 18, 21, and 25, 302

Arrests, states and age, 354

Arrest trends, cities, 309, 310

Arrest trends, five-year, 289, 290

Arrest trends, metropolitan counties, 320, 321

Arrest trends, nonmetropolitan counties, 331, 332

Arrest trends, suburban areas, 342–346

Arrest trends, ten-year, 287, 288

Arrest trends, year over previous year, 291, 292

City arrests, distribution by age, 311

City arrests, persons under 15, 18, 21, and 25, 313

City arrest trends, by age, 309–311

County arrests, metropolitan counties, 322, 324

County arrests, nonmetropolitan counties, 333, 335

County arrest trends, metropolitan counties, 320, 321

County arrest trends, nonmetropolitan counties, 331, 332

Female arrests, distribution by age, 299

Hate crimes

    known offenders, by age, 564

Male arrests, distribution by age, 296

Offenses cleared by arrest or exceptional means, persons under 18, 274

Suburban area arrest trends, by age, 342–346

AGENCIES

Crime trends, additional information, 250

Crime trends, by population group, 247

Hate crimes

    incidents per bias motivation and quarter, 569

    offense types, 566

    participating states and Federal agencies, 567

    reporting of hate crimes, 567

Law enforcement employees, 370–533

Offenses known to law enforcement, by tribal, and other agencies, 222

AGGRAVATED ASSAULT

Arrests, by geographic region, 284

Arrests, by population group, 285

Arrests, by state, 354

Arrests, cities, distribution by age, 311

Arrests, cities, distribution by ethnicity, 318

Arrests, cities, distribution by race, 315

Arrests, cities, distribution by sex, 314

Arrests, cities, persons under 15, 18, 21, and 25, 313

Arrests, distribution by age, 293–302

Arrests, distribution by ethnicity, 307

Arrests, distribution by race, 304

Arrests, distribution by sex, 288, 290, 303

Arrests, estimated number of, 283

Arrests, females, distribution by age, 299

Arrests, males, distribution by age, 296

Arrests, metropolitan counties, distribution by age, 322

Arrests, metropolitan counties, distribution by ethnicity, 329

Arrests, metropolitan counties, distribution by race, 326

Arrests, metropolitan counties, distribution by sex, 325

Arrests, metropolitan counties, persons under 15, 18, 21, and 25, 324

Arrests, nonmetropolitan counties, distribution by age, 333

Arrests, nonmetropolitan counties, distribution by ethnicity, 337

Arrests, nonmetropolitan counties, distribution by race, 339

Arrests, nonmetropolitan counties, distribution by sex, 336

Arrests, nonmetropolitan counties, persons under 15, 18, 21, and 25, 335

Arrests, suburban areas, distribution by age, 342–346

Arrests, suburban areas, distribution by ethnicity, 351

Arrests, suburban areas, distribution by race, 348

Arrests, suburban areas, distribution by sex, 347

Arrests, suburban areas, persons under 15, 18, 21, and 25, 346

Arrests of persons under 15, 18, 21, and 25, 302

Arrest trends, cities, 309

Arrest trends, current year over previous, 291, 292

Arrest trends, metropolitan counties, 320, 321

Arrest trends, nonmetropolitan counties, 331, 332

Arrest trends, suburban areas, 342, 343

Arrest trends, ten-year, 287, 288

Community type, 37

Crime, by metropolitan statistical area, 54

Crime, by state and area, 46

Crime in the U.S., by volume and rate, 35

Crimes per 100,000 inhabitants, by cities, 254

Crimes per 100,000 inhabitants, by counties, 255

Crimes per 100,000 population, by population group, 252, 257

Crime trends, additional information, 250

Crime trends, by population group, 247

Crime trends, cities by population group, 248

Crime trends, counties by population group, 249

Hate crimes, 555, 556, 557, 561

Incidents cleared by offense category, 269

Offenses by state and type of weapon, 261

Offenses cleared by arrest or exceptional means, by population group, 270–274

Offenses cleared by arrest or exceptional means, by region, 271

Offenses cleared by arrest or exceptional means, persons under 18, 274

Offenses known to law enforcement, by counties, 190

Offenses known to law enforcement, by selected state, 84

Offenses known to law enforcement, by tribal, and other agencies, 222

Offenses known to law enforcement, by university and college, 181

Population and offense distribution, by region, 37, 38

Universities and colleges, 181

ALABAMA

Aggravated assault, by state and type of weapon, 261

Arrests, numbers and types of offenses, 354

Crime, by metropolitan statistical area, 54

Crime, by state and area, 46

Hate crimes, 566, 567, 569
Law enforcement employees, 370–533
Murder, by state and type of weapon, 259
Offenses known to law enforcement, by agencies, 222
Offenses known to law enforcement, by counties, 190
Offenses known to law enforcement, by selected state, 84
Offenses known to law enforcement, by university and
    college, 181
Robbery, by state and type of weapon, 260

ALASKA
Aggravated assault, by state and type of weapon, 261
Arrests, numbers and types of offenses, 354
Crime, by metropolitan statistical area, 54
Crime, by state and area, 46
Hate crimes, 566, 567, 569
Law enforcement employees, 370–533
Murder, by state and type of weapon, 259
Offenses known to law enforcement, by agencies, 222
Offenses known to law enforcement, by selected state, 84
Offenses known to law enforcement, by university and
    college, 181
Robbery, by state and type of weapon, 260

ALASKAN NATIVES
Generally
    see RACE

ALCOHOLIC BEVERAGES
Driving under the influence
    see DRIVING UNDER THE INFLUENCE
Drunkenness
    see DRUNKENNESS
Liquor law violations
    see LIQUOR LAW VIOLATIONS

ANCESTRY
Hate crimes generally
    see HATE CRIMES

ANIMAL CRUELTY
Incidents cleared by offense category, 269

ARIZONA
Aggravated assault, by state and type of weapon, 261
Arrests, numbers and types of offenses, 354
Crime, by metropolitan statistical area, 54
Crime, by state and area, 46
Hate crimes, 566, 567, 569
Law enforcement employees, 370–533
Murder, by state and type of weapon, 259
Offenses known to law enforcement, by agencies, 222
Offenses known to law enforcement, by counties, 190
Offenses known to law enforcement, by selected state, 84
Offenses known to law enforcement, by university and
    college, 181
Robbery, by state and type of weapon, 260

ARKANSAS
Aggravated assault, by state and type of weapon, 261
Arrests, numbers and types of offenses, 354
Crime, by metropolitan statistical area, 54
Crime, by state and area, 46
Hate crimes, 566, 567, 569
Law enforcement employees, 370–533

Murder, by state and type of weapon, 259
Offenses known to law enforcement, by agencies, 222
Offenses known to law enforcement, by counties, 190
Offenses known to law enforcement, by selected state, 84
Offenses known to law enforcement, by university and
    college, 181
Robbery, by state and type of weapon, 260

ARRESTS
Distribution by age, 311
Distribution by ethnicity, 307
Distribution by race, 304
Distribution by sex, 303
Estimated number of arrests, 283
Persons under 15, 18, 21, and 25 years, 313

ARRESTS, DISTRIBUTION BY AGE
City arrests, 311
Female arrests, 299
Male arrests, 296
Metropolitan counties, 322, 324
Nonmetropolitan counties, 333
Numbers and percentages generally, 293–302
Offenses cleared by arrest or exceptional means, persons
    under 18, 274
Persons under 15, 18, 21, and 25 years, 302
Police disposition of juvenile offenders taken into custody,
    353
Suburban areas, 342–346

ARRESTS, DISTRIBUTION BY ETHNICITY
Cities, 318
Metropolitan counties, 329
Nonmetropolitan counties, 337
Numbers and percentages, 307
Suburban areas, 351

ARRESTS, DISTRIBUTION BY RACE
Metropolitan counties, 326
Nonmetropolitan counties, 339
Numbers and percentages, 304
Offense categories, 304
Suburban areas, 348

ARRESTS, DISTRIBUTION BY SEX
City arrests, 314
Metropolitan counties, 325
Nonmetropolitan counties, 336
Numbers and percentages, 288, 290, 303
Suburban areas, 347

ARRESTS, GEOGRAPHIC REGIONS
Number and rate, 284

ARRESTS, METROPOLITAN COUNTIES
Distribution by age, 320, 321
Distribution by ethnicity, 329
Distribution by race, 326
Distribution by sex, 325
Persons under 15, 18, 21, and 25 years, 324

ARRESTS, NONMETROPOLITAN COUNTIES
Distribution by age, 331, 332
Distribution by ethnicity, 337
Distribution by race, 339
Distribution by sex, 336

Persons under 15, 18, 21, and 25 years, 335

ARRESTS, POPULATION GROUPS
Estimated number of arrests, 283
Number and rates, 285

ARRESTS, STATE TOTALS
Numbers and types of offenses, 354

ARRESTS, SUBURBAN AREAS
Distribution by age, 342–346
Distribution by ethnicity, 351
Distribution by race, 348
Distribution by sex, 347
Persons under 15, 18, 21, and 25 years, 346

ARREST TRENDS, CITIES
Age, 309–311
Numbers and percentages generally, 309
Sex, 310

ARREST TRENDS, METROPOLITAN COUNTIES
Numbers and percentages generally, 320, 321

ARREST TRENDS, NATIONALLY
Current year over previous year, 291, 292
Estimated number of arrests, 283
Five-year arrest trends, by age, 289, 290
Ten-year arrest trends, generally, 287, 288

ARREST TRENDS, NONMETROPOLITAN COUNTIES
Numbers and percentages, 331, 332

ARREST TRENDS, SUBURBAN AREAS
Numbers and percentages generally, 342, 343

ARREST TRENDS, YEAR OVER PREVIOUS YEAR
Numbers and percentages generally, 291, 292

ARSON
Arrests, by geographic region, 284
Arrests, by population group, 285
Arrests, by state, 354
Arrests, cities, distribution by age, 311
Arrests, cities, distribution by ethnicity, 318
Arrests, cities, distribution by race, 315
Arrests, cities, distribution by sex, 314
Arrests, cities, persons under 15, 18, 21, and 25, 313
Arrests, distribution by age, 293–302
Arrests, distribution by ethnicity, 307
Arrests, distribution by race, 304
Arrests, distribution by sex, 288, 290, 303
Arrests, estimated number of, 283
Arrests, females, distribution by age, 299
Arrests, males, distribution by age, 296
Arrests, metropolitan counties, distribution by age, 322
Arrests, metropolitan counties, distribution by ethnicity, 329
Arrests, metropolitan counties, distribution by race, 326
Arrests, metropolitan counties, distribution by sex, 325
Arrests, metropolitan counties, persons under 15, 18, 21, and 25, 324
Arrests, nonmetropolitan counties, distribution by age, 333
Arrests, nonmetropolitan counties, distribution by ethnicity, 337
Arrests, nonmetropolitan counties, distribution by race, 339
Arrests, nonmetropolitan counties, distribution by sex, 336
Arrests, nonmetropolitan counties, persons under 15, 18, 21, and 25, 335

Arrests, suburban areas, distribution by age, 342–346
Arrests, suburban areas, distribution by ethnicity, 351
Arrests, suburban areas, distribution by race, 348
Arrests, suburban areas, distribution by sex, 347
Arrests, suburban areas, persons under 15, 18, 21, and 25, 346
Arrests of persons under 15, 18, 21, and 25, 302
Arrest trends, cities, 309
Arrest trends, current year over previous, 291, 292
Arrest trends, five-year, 289, 290
Arrest trends, metropolitan counties, 320, 321
Arrest trends, nonmetropolitan counties, 331, 332
Arrest trends, suburban areas, 342, 343
Arrest trends, ten-year, 287, 288
Crime trends, additional information, 250
Crime trends, by population group, 247
Crime trends, cities by population group, 248
Crime trends, counties by population group, 249
Hate crimes, 555, 556, 560
Incidents cleared by offense category, 269
Offenses cleared by arrest or exceptional means, by population group, 270–274
Offenses cleared by arrest or exceptional means, by region, 271
Offenses cleared by arrest or exceptional means, persons under 18, 274
Offenses known to law enforcement, by counties, 190
Offenses known to law enforcement, by selected state, 84
Offenses known to law enforcement, by tribal, and other agencies, 222
Offenses known to law enforcement, by university and college, 181

ASIAN ORIGIN
Generally
see RACE

ASSAULT
Aggravated assault
see AGGRAVATED ASSAULT

BIAS MOTIVATION
Hate crimes
see HATE CRIMES

BURGLARY
Arrests, by geographic region, 284
Arrests, by population group, 285
Arrests, by state, 354
Arrests, cities, distribution by age, 311
Arrests, cities, distribution by ethnicity, 318
Arrests, cities, distribution by race, 315
Arrests, cities, distribution by sex, 314
Arrests, cities, persons under 15, 18, 21, and 25, 313
Arrests, distribution by age, 293–302
Arrests, distribution by ethnicity, 307
Arrests, distribution by race, 304
Arrests, distribution by sex, 288, 290, 303
Arrests, estimated number of, 283
Arrests, females, distribution by age, 299
Arrests, males, distribution by age, 296
Arrests, metropolitan counties, distribution by age, 322

Arrests, metropolitan counties, distribution by ethnicity, 329
Arrests, metropolitan counties, distribution by race, 326
Arrests, metropolitan counties, distribution by sex, 325
Arrests, metropolitan counties, persons under 15, 18, 21, and 25, 324
Arrests, nonmetropolitan counties, distribution by age, 333
Arrests, nonmetropolitan counties, distribution by ethnicity, 337
Arrests, nonmetropolitan counties, distribution by race, 339
Arrests, nonmetropolitan counties, distribution by sex, 336
Arrests, nonmetropolitan counties, persons under 15, 18, 21, and 25, 335
Arrests, suburban areas, distribution by age, 342–346
Arrests, suburban areas, distribution by ethnicity, 351
Arrests, suburban areas, distribution by race, 348
Arrests, suburban areas, distribution by sex, 347
Arrests, suburban areas, persons under 15, 18, 21, and 25, 346
Arrests of persons under 15, 18, 21, and 25, 302
Arrest trends, cities, 309
Arrest trends, current year over previous, 291, 292
Arrest trends, five-year, 289, 290
Arrest trends, metropolitan counties, 320, 321
Arrest trends, nonmetropolitan counties, 331, 332
Arrest trends, suburban areas, 342, 343
Arrest trends, ten-year, 287, 288
Community type, 37
Crime, by metropolitan statistical area, 54
Crime, by state and area, 46
Crime in the U.S., by volume and rate, 35
Crimes per 100,000 inhabitants, by cities, 254
Crimes per 100,000 inhabitants, by counties, 255
Crimes per 100,000 population, by population group, 252, 257
Crime trends, additional information, 250
Crime trends, by population group, 247
Crime trends, cities by population group, 248
Crime trends, counties by population group, 249
Hate crimes, 555, 556, 560
Incidents cleared by offense category, 269
Offense analysis, 83, 262
Offenses cleared by arrest or exceptional means, by population group, 270–274
Offenses cleared by arrest or exceptional means, by region, 271
Offenses cleared by arrest or exceptional means, persons under 18, 274
Offenses known to law enforcement, by counties, 190
Offenses known to law enforcement, by selected state, 84
Offenses known to law enforcement, by tribal, and other agencies, 222
Offenses known to law enforcement, by university and college, 181
Population and offense distribution, by region, 37, 38
Universities and colleges, 181

CALIFORNIA
Aggravated assault, by state and type of weapon, 261
Arrests, numbers and types of offenses, 354
Crime, by metropolitan statistical area, 54

Crime, by state and area, 46
Hate crimes, 566, 567, 569
Law enforcement employees, 370–533
Murder, by state and type of weapon, 259
Offenses known to law enforcement, by agencies, 222
Offenses known to law enforcement, by counties, 190
Offenses known to law enforcement, by selected state, 84
Offenses known to law enforcement, by university and college, 181
Robbery, by state and type of weapon, 260

CHILDREN
Police disposition of juveniles taken into custody, 353

CITIES
Arrests, by population group, 285
Arrests, distribution by age, 311
Arrests, distribution by ethnicity, 318
Arrests, distribution by race, 315
Arrests, distribution by sex, 314
Arrests, persons under 15, 18, 21, and 25, 313
Arrest trends, by age and sex, 309, 310
Arrest trends for cities, 309
Crime, by community type, 37
Crime, by metropolitan statistical area, 54
Crime, by state and area, 46
Crimes per 100,000 population, 252, 257
Crime trends, additional information, 250
Crime trends, by population group, 247
Crime trends, by suburban and nonsuburban cities, 248
Hate crimes, 569
Law enforcement employees, 366–374
Number of crimes per 100,000 inhabitants, 254
Offenses cleared by arrest or exceptional means, by population group, 270, 272
Offenses cleared by arrest or exceptional means, persons under 18, 274
Offenses known to law enforcement, by selected state and city, 84
Police disposition of juvenile offenders taken into custody, 353

CLOTHING AND FURS
Property stolen and recovered, 263

COLLEGES
Hate crimes, 569
Offenses known to law enforcement, by university and college, 181

COLORADO
Aggravated assault, by state and type of weapon, 261
Arrests, numbers and types of offenses, 354
Crime, by metropolitan statistical area, 54
Crime, by state and area, 46
Hate crimes, 566, 567, 569
Law enforcement employees, 370–533
Murder, by state and type of weapon, 259
Offenses known to law enforcement, by agencies, 222
Offenses known to law enforcement, by counties, 190
Offenses known to law enforcement, by selected state, 84
Offenses known to law enforcement, by university and college, 181
Robbery, by state and type of weapon, 260

COMMUNITIES
Crime in the U.S., by community type, 37
CONCEALED CARRY VIOLATIONS
see FIREARMS OFFENSES
CONNECTICUT
Aggravated assault, by state and type of weapon, 261
Arrests, numbers and types of offenses, 354
Crime, by metropolitan statistical area, 54
Crime, by state and area, 46
Hate crimes, 566, 567, 569
Law enforcement employees, 370–533
Murder, by state and type of weapon, 259
Offenses known to law enforcement, by agencies, 222
Offenses known to law enforcement, by selected state, 84
Offenses known to law enforcement, by university and
    college, 181
Robbery, by state and type of weapon, 260
CONSUMABLE GOODS
Property stolen and recovered, 263
CONTROLLED SUBSTANCES
Drug abuse violations
    see DRUG ABUSE VIOLATIONS
COUNTERFEITING
see FORGERY AND COUNTERFEITING
COUNTIES
Arrests, by population group, 285
Arrests, distribution by age, 333, 335
Arrests, distribution by ethnicity, 329, 337
Arrests, distribution by race, 326, 339
Arrests, distribution by sex, 336
Arrests, metropolitan counties, 322, 324
Arrests, nonmetropolitan counties, 333, 335
Arrests of persons under 15, 18, 21, and 25, 324, 335
Arrest trends for metropolitan counties, 320, 321
Arrest trends for nonmetropolitan counties, 331, 332
Crime, by community type, 37
Crime, by metropolitan statistical area, 54
Crime, by state and area, 46
Crimes per 100,000 population, 252, 257
Crime trends, additional information, 250
Crime trends, by metropolitan and nonmetropolitan
    counties, 249
Crime trends, by population group, 247
Hate crimes, 569
Law enforcement employees, 368, 369
Number of crimes per 100,000 inhabitants, 255, 257
Offenses cleared by arrest or exceptional means, by
    population group, 270, 272
Offenses cleared by arrest or exceptional means, persons
    under 18, 274
Offenses known to law enforcement, by counties, 190
Police disposition of juvenile offenders taken into custody,
    353
CRIME, METROPOLITAN STATISTICAL AREAS
Numbers and percentages, 54
CRIME, NATIONALLY
Community type, 37
Population and offense distribution, by region, 37, 38
Volume and rate, 35

CRIME, OFFENSE ANALYSIS
Numbers, 83, 262
CRIME, STATES
see STATE CRIME TOTALS
CRIMES PER 100,000 POPULATION
Population group numbers and rates, 252, 254, 255, 257
CRIME TRENDS
Cities, additional information, 250
Cities, by population group, 248
Counties, additional information, 250
Counties, by population group, 249
Population groups, 247–249
CURFEW AND LOITERING LAW VIOLATIONS
Arrests, by geographic region, 284
Arrests, by population group, 285
Arrests, cities, distribution by age, 311
Arrests, cities, distribution by ethnicity, 318
Arrests, cities, distribution by race, 315
Arrests, cities, distribution by sex, 314
Arrests, cities, persons under 15, 18, 21, and 25, 313
Arrests, distribution by age, 293–302
Arrests, distribution by ethnicity, 307
Arrests, distribution by race, 304
Arrests, distribution by race, 304
Arrests, distribution by sex, 288, 290, 303
Arrests, estimated number of, 283
Arrests, females, distribution by age, 299
Arrests, males, distribution by age, 296
Arrests, metropolitan counties, distribution by age, 322
Arrests, metropolitan counties, distribution by ethnicity, 329
Arrests, metropolitan counties, distribution by race, 326
Arrests, metropolitan counties, distribution by sex, 325
Arrests, metropolitan counties, persons under 15, 18, 21, and
    25, 324
Arrests, nonmetropolitan counties, distribution by age, 333
Arrests, nonmetropolitan counties, distribution by ethnicity, 337
Arrests, nonmetropolitan counties, distribution by race, 339
Arrests, nonmetropolitan counties, distribution by sex, 336
Arrests, nonmetropolitan counties, persons under 15, 18, 21,
    and 25, 335
Arrests, suburban areas, distribution by age, 342–346
Arrests, suburban areas, distribution by ethnicity, 351
Arrests, suburban areas, distribution by race, 348
Arrests, suburban areas, distribution by sex, 347
Arrests, suburban areas, persons under 15, 18, 21, and 25, 346
Arrests of persons under 15, 18, 21, and 25, 302
Arrest trends, cities, 309
Arrest trends, current year over previous, 291, 292
Arrest trends, five-year, 289, 290
Arrest trends, metropolitan counties, 320, 321
Arrest trends, nonmetropolitan counties, 331, 332
Arrest trends, suburban areas, 342, 343
Arrest trends, ten-year, 287, 288
CURRENCY
Property stolen and recovered, 263

DELAWARE
Aggravated assault, by state and type of weapon, 261
Arrests, numbers and types of offenses, 354

Crime, by metropolitan statistical area, 54
Crime, by state and area, 46
Hate crimes, 566, 567, 569
Law enforcement employees, 370–533
Murder, by state and type of weapon, 259
Offenses known to law enforcement, by agencies, 222
Offenses known to law enforcement, by counties, 190
Offenses known to law enforcement, by selected state, 84
Offenses known to law enforcement, by university and
    college, 181
Robbery, by state and type of weapon, 260

DISABLED PERSONS
Hate crimes
    see HATE CRIMES

DISORDERLY CONDUCT
Arrests, by geographic region, 284
Arrests, by population group, 285
Arrests, cities, distribution by age, 311
Arrests, cities, distribution by ethnicity, 318
Arrests, cities, distribution by race, 315
Arrests, cities, distribution by sex, 314
Arrests, cities, persons under 15, 18, 21, and 25, 313
Arrests, distribution by age, 293–302
Arrests, distribution by ethnicity, 307
Arrests, distribution by race, 304
Arrests, distribution by sex, 288, 290, 303
Arrests, estimated number of, 283
Arrests, females, distribution by age, 299
Arrests, males, distribution by age, 296
Arrests, metropolitan counties, distribution by age, 322
Arrests, metropolitan counties, distribution by ethnicity, 329
Arrests, metropolitan counties, distribution by race, 326
Arrests, metropolitan counties, distribution by sex, 325
Arrests, metropolitan counties, persons under 15, 18, 21, and
    25, 324
Arrests, nonmetropolitan counties, distribution by age, 333
Arrests, nonmetropolitan counties, distribution by ethnicity,
    337
Arrests, nonmetropolitan counties, distribution by race, 339
Arrests, nonmetropolitan counties, distribution by sex, 336
Arrests, nonmetropolitan counties, persons under 15, 18, 21,
    and 25, 335
Arrests, suburban areas, distribution by age, 342–346
Arrests, suburban areas, distribution by ethnicity, 351
Arrests, suburban areas, distribution by race, 348
Arrests, suburban areas, distribution by sex, 347
Arrests, suburban areas, persons under 15, 18, 21, and 25, 346
Arrests of persons under 15, 18, 21, and 25, 302
Arrest trends, cities, 309
Arrest trends, current year over previous, 291, 292
Arrest trends, five-year, 289, 290
Arrest trends, metropolitan counties, 320, 321
Arrest trends, nonmetropolitan counties, 331, 332
Arrest trends, suburban areas, 342, 343
Arrest trends, ten-year, 287, 288

DISTRICT OF COLUMBIA
Aggravated assault, by state and type of weapon, 261
Arrests, numbers and types of offenses, 354
Crime, by metropolitan statistical area, 54

Crime, by state and area, 46
Hate crimes, 566, 567, 569
Law enforcement employees, 370–533
Murder, by state and type of weapon, 259
Offenses known to law enforcement, by selected state, 84
Robbery, by state and type of weapon, 260

DRIVING UNDER THE INFLUENCE
Arrests, by geographic region, 284
Arrests, by population group, 285
Arrests, cities, distribution by age, 311
Arrests, cities, distribution by ethnicity, 318
Arrests, cities, distribution by race, 315
Arrests, cities, distribution by sex, 314
Arrests, cities, persons under 15, 18, 21, and 25, 313
Arrests, distribution by age, 293–302
Arrests, distribution by ethnicity, 307
Arrests, distribution by race, 304
Arrests, distribution by sex, 288, 290, 303
Arrests, estimated number of, 283
Arrests, females, distribution by age, 299
Arrests, males, distribution by age, 296
Arrests, metropolitan counties, distribution by age, 322
Arrests, metropolitan counties, distribution by ethnicity, 329
Arrests, metropolitan counties, distribution by race, 326
Arrests, metropolitan counties, distribution by sex, 325
Arrests, metropolitan counties, persons under 15, 18, 21, and
    25, 324
Arrests, nonmetropolitan counties, distribution by age, 333
Arrests, nonmetropolitan counties, distribution by ethnicity,
    337
Arrests, nonmetropolitan counties, distribution by race, 339
Arrests, nonmetropolitan counties, distribution by sex, 336
Arrests, nonmetropolitan counties, persons under 15, 18, 21,
    and 25, 335
Arrests, suburban areas, distribution by age, 342–346
Arrests, suburban areas, distribution by ethnicity, 351
Arrests, suburban areas, distribution by race, 348
Arrests, suburban areas, distribution by sex, 347
Arrests, suburban areas, persons under 15, 18, 21, and 25, 346
Arrests of persons under 15, 18, 21, and 25, 302
Arrest trends, cities, 309
Arrest trends, current year over previous, 291, 292
Arrest trends, five-year, 289, 290
Arrest trends, metropolitan counties, 320, 321
Arrest trends, nonmetropolitan counties, 331, 332
Arrest trends, suburban areas, 342, 343
Arrest trends, ten-year, 287, 288

DRUG ABUSE VIOLATIONS
Arrests, by geographic region, 284
Arrests, by population group, 285
Arrests, cities, distribution by age, 311
Arrests, cities, distribution by ethnicity, 318
Arrests, cities, distribution by race, 315
Arrests, cities, distribution by sex, 314
Arrests, cities, persons under 15, 18, 21, and 25, 313
Arrests, distribution by age, 293–302
Arrests, distribution by ethnicity, 307
Arrests, distribution by race, 304
Arrests, distribution by sex, 288, 290, 303

Arrests, estimated number of, 283
Arrests, females, distribution by age, 299
Arrests, males, distribution by age, 296
Arrests, metropolitan counties, distribution by age, 322
Arrests, metropolitan counties, distribution by ethnicity, 329
Arrests, metropolitan counties, distribution by race, 326
Arrests, metropolitan counties, distribution by sex, 325
Arrests, metropolitan counties, persons under 15, 18, 21, and 25, 324
Arrests, nonmetropolitan counties, distribution by age, 333
Arrests, nonmetropolitan counties, distribution by ethnicity, 337
Arrests, nonmetropolitan counties, distribution by race, 339
Arrests, nonmetropolitan counties, distribution by sex, 336
Arrests, nonmetropolitan counties, persons under 15, 18, 21, and 25, 335
Arrests, suburban areas, distribution by age, 342–346
Arrests, suburban areas, distribution by ethnicity, 351
Arrests, suburban areas, distribution by race, 348
Arrests, suburban areas, distribution by sex, 347
Arrests, suburban areas, persons under 15, 18, 21, and 25, 346
Arrests of persons under 15, 18, 21, and 25, 302
Arrest trends, cities, 309
Arrest trends, current year over previous, 291, 292
Arrest trends, five-year, 289, 290
Arrest trends, metropolitan counties, 320, 321
Arrest trends, nonmetropolitan counties, 331, 332
Arrest trends, suburban areas, 342, 343
Arrest trends, ten-year, 287, 288
Incidents cleared by offense category, 269

DRUNKENNESS
Arrests, by geographic region, 284
Arrests, by population group, 285
Arrests, cities, distribution by age, 311
Arrests, cities, distribution by ethnicity, 318
Arrests, cities, distribution by race, 315
Arrests, cities, distribution by sex, 314
Arrests, cities, persons under 15, 18, 21, and 25, 313
Arrests, distribution by age, 293–302
Arrests, distribution by ethnicity, 307
Arrests, distribution by race, 304
Arrests, distribution by sex, 288, 290, 303
Arrests, estimated number of, 283
Arrests, females, distribution by age, 299
Arrests, males, distribution by age, 296
Arrests, metropolitan counties, distribution by age, 322
Arrests, metropolitan counties, distribution by ethnicity, 329
Arrests, metropolitan counties, distribution by race, 326
Arrests, metropolitan counties, distribution by sex, 325
Arrests, metropolitan counties, persons under 15, 18, 21, and 25, 324
Arrests, nonmetropolitan counties, distribution by age, 333
Arrests, nonmetropolitan counties, distribution by ethnicity, 337
Arrests, nonmetropolitan counties, distribution by race, 339
Arrests, nonmetropolitan counties, distribution by sex, 336
Arrests, nonmetropolitan counties, persons under 15, 18, 21, and 25, 335
Arrests, suburban areas, distribution by age, 342–346

Arrests, suburban areas, distribution by ethnicity, 351
Arrests, suburban areas, distribution by race, 348
Arrests, suburban areas, distribution by sex, 347
Arrests, suburban areas, persons under 15, 18, 21, and 25, 346
Arrests of persons under 15, 18, 21, and 25, 302
Arrest trends, cities, 309
Arrest trends, current year over previous, 291, 292
Arrest trends, five-year, 289, 290
Arrest trends, metropolitan counties, 320, 321
Arrest trends, nonmetropolitan counties, 331, 332
Arrest trends, suburban areas, 342, 343
Arrest trends, ten-year, 287, 288

EMBEZZLEMENT
Arrests, by geographic region, 284
Arrests, by population group, 285
Arrests, cities, distribution by age, 311
Arrests, cities, distribution by ethnicity, 318
Arrests, cities, distribution by race, 315
Arrests, cities, distribution by sex, 314
Arrests, cities, persons under 15, 18, 21, and 25, 313
Arrests, distribution by age, 293–302
Arrests, distribution by ethnicity, 307
Arrests, distribution by race, 304
Arrests, distribution by sex, 288, 290, 303
Arrests, estimated number of, 283
Arrests, females, distribution by age, 299
Arrests, males, distribution by age, 296
Arrests, metropolitan counties, distribution by age, 322
Arrests, metropolitan counties, distribution by ethnicity, 329
Arrests, metropolitan counties, distribution by race, 326
Arrests, metropolitan counties, distribution by sex, 325
Arrests, metropolitan counties, persons under 15, 18, 21, and 25, 324
Arrests, nonmetropolitan counties, distribution by age, 333
Arrests, nonmetropolitan counties, distribution by ethnicity, 337
Arrests, nonmetropolitan counties, distribution by race, 339
Arrests, nonmetropolitan counties, distribution by sex, 336
Arrests, nonmetropolitan counties, persons under 15, 18, 21, and 25, 335
Arrests, suburban areas, distribution by age, 342–346
Arrests, suburban areas, distribution by ethnicity, 351
Arrests, suburban areas, distribution by race, 348
Arrests, suburban areas, distribution by sex, 347
Arrests, suburban areas, persons under 15, 18, 21, and 25, 346
Arrests of persons under 15, 18, 21, and 25, 302
Arrest trends, cities, 309
Arrest trends, current year over previous, 291, 292
Arrest trends, five-year, 289, 290
Arrest trends, metropolitan counties, 320, 321
Arrest trends, nonmetropolitan counties, 331, 332
Arrest trends, suburban areas, 342, 343
Arrest trends, ten-year, 287, 288
Incidents cleared by offense category, 269

ETHNICITY
Arrests, distribution by ethnicity, 307
Arrests, nonmetropolitan counties, 337
City arrests, distribution by ethnicity, 318

County arrests, distribution by ethnicity, 329, 337
Hate crimes generally
  see HATE CRIMES
Race
  see RACE
Suburban area arrests, distribution by ethnicity, 351

FEMALES
Generally
  see SEX
FIREARMS OFFENSES
Aggravated assault, by state and type of weapon, 261
Arrests, by geographic region, 284
Arrests, by population group, 285
Arrests, cities, distribution by age, 311
Arrests, cities, distribution by ethnicity, 318
Arrests, cities, distribution by sex, 314
Arrests, cities, persons under 15, 18, 21, and 25, 313
Arrests, distribution by age, 293–302
Arrests, distribution by ethnicity, 307
Arrests, distribution by race, 304
Arrests, distribution by sex, 288, 290, 303
Arrests, estimated number of, 283
Arrests, females, distribution by age, 299
Arrests, males, distribution by age, 296
Arrests, metropolitan counties, distribution by ethnicity, 329
Arrests, metropolitan counties, distribution by race, 326
Arrests, metropolitan counties, distribution by sex, 325
Arrests, metropolitan counties, persons under 15, 18, 21, and 25, 324
Arrests, nonmetropolitan counties, distribution by age, 333
Arrests, nonmetropolitan counties, distribution by ethnicity, 337
Arrests, nonmetropolitan counties, distribution by race, 339
Arrests, nonmetropolitan counties, distribution by sex, 336
Arrests, nonmetropolitan counties, persons under 15, 18, 21, and 25, 335
Arrests, suburban areas, distribution by age, 342–346
Arrests, suburban areas, distribution by ethnicity, 351
Arrests, suburban areas, distribution by race, 348
Arrests, suburban areas, distribution by sex, 347
Arrests, suburban areas, persons under 15, 18, 21, and 25, 346
Arrests of persons under 15, 18, 21, and 25, 302
Arrest trends, cities, 309
Arrest trends, current year over previous, 291, 292
Arrest trends, metropolitan counties, 320, 321
Arrest trends, nonmetropolitan counties, 331, 332
Arrest trends, suburban areas, 342, 343
Murder, by state and type of weapon, 259
Property stolen and recovered, 263
Robbery, by state and type of weapon, 260
FLORIDA
Aggravated assault, by state and type of weapon, 261
Arrests, numbers and types of offenses, 354
Crime, by metropolitan statistical area, 54
Crime, by state and area, 46
Hate crimes, 566, 567, 569
Law enforcement employees, 370–533
Murder, by state and type of weapon, 259

Offenses known to law enforcement, by agencies, 222
Offenses known to law enforcement, by counties, 190
Offenses known to law enforcement, by selected state, 84
Offenses known to law enforcement, by university and college, 181
Robbery, by state and type of weapon, 260
FORCIBLE RAPE
Arrests, by geographic region, 284
Arrests, by population group, 285
Arrests, by state, 354
Arrests, cities, distribution by age, 311
Arrests, cities, distribution by ethnicity, 318
Arrests, cities, distribution by race, 315
Arrests, cities, distribution by sex, 314
Arrests, cities, persons under 15, 18, 21, and 25, 313
Arrests, distribution by age, 293–302
Arrests, distribution by ethnicity, 307
Arrests, distribution by race, 304
Arrests, distribution by sex, 288, 290, 303
Arrests, estimated number of, 283
Arrests, females, distribution by age, 299
Arrests, males, distribution by age, 296
Arrests, metropolitan counties, distribution by age, 322
Arrests, metropolitan counties, distribution by ethnicity, 329
Arrests, metropolitan counties, distribution by race, 326
Arrests, metropolitan counties, distribution by sex, 325
Arrests, metropolitan counties, persons under 15, 18, 21, and 25, 324
Arrests, nonmetropolitan counties, distribution by age, 333
Arrests, nonmetropolitan counties, distribution by ethnicity, 337
Arrests, nonmetropolitan counties, distribution by race, 339
Arrests, nonmetropolitan counties, distribution by sex, 336
Arrests, nonmetropolitan counties, persons under 15, 18, 21, and 25, 335
Arrests, suburban areas, distribution by age, 342–346
Arrests, suburban areas, distribution by ethnicity, 351
Arrests, suburban areas, distribution by race, 348
Arrests, suburban areas, distribution by sex, 347
Arrests, suburban areas, persons under 15, 18, 21, and 25, 346
Arrests of persons under 15, 18, 21, and 25, 302
Arrest trends, cities, 309
Arrest trends, current year over previous, 291, 292
Arrest trends, five-year, 289, 290
Arrest trends, metropolitan counties, 320, 321
Arrest trends, nonmetropolitan counties, 331, 332
Arrest trends, suburban areas, 342, 343
Arrest trends, ten-year, 287, 288
Community type, 37
Crime, by metropolitan statistical area, 54
Crime, by state and area, 46
Crime in the U.S., by volume and rate, 35
Crimes per 100,000 inhabitants, by cities, 254
Crimes per 100,000 inhabitants, by counties, 255
Crimes per 100,000 population, by population group, 252, 257
Crime trends, additional information, 250
Crime trends, by population group, 247
Crime trends, cities by population group, 248

Crime trends, counties by population group, 249
Hate crimes, 555, 556, 557, 561
Offense analysis, 83, 262
Offenses cleared by arrest or exceptional means, by population group, 270–274
Offenses cleared by arrest or exceptional means, by region, 271
Offenses cleared by arrest or exceptional means, persons under 18, 274
Offenses known to law enforcement, by counties, 190
Offenses known to law enforcement, by selected state, 84
Offenses known to law enforcement, by tribal, and other agencies, 222
Offenses known to law enforcement, by university and college, 181
Population and offense distribution, by region, 37, 38
Universities and colleges, 181

FORGERY AND COUNTERFEITING
Arrests, by geographic region, 284
Arrests, by population group, 285
Arrests, cities, distribution by age, 311
Arrests, cities, distribution by ethnicity, 318
Arrests, cities, distribution by race, 315
Arrests, cities, distribution by sex, 314
Arrests, cities, persons under 15, 18, 21, and 25, 313
Arrests, distribution by age, 293–302
Arrests, distribution by ethnicity, 307
Arrests, distribution by race, 304
Arrests, distribution by sex, 288, 290, 303
Arrests, estimated number of, 283
Arrests, females, distribution by age, 299
Arrests, males, distribution by age, 296
Arrests, metropolitan counties, distribution by age, 322
Arrests, metropolitan counties, distribution by ethnicity, 329
Arrests, metropolitan counties, distribution by race, 326
Arrests, metropolitan counties, distribution by sex, 325
Arrests, metropolitan counties, persons under 15, 18, 21, and 25, 324
Arrests, nonmetropolitan counties, distribution by age, 333
Arrests, nonmetropolitan counties, distribution by ethnicity, 337
Arrests, nonmetropolitan counties, distribution by race, 339
Arrests, nonmetropolitan counties, distribution by sex, 336
Arrests, nonmetropolitan counties, persons under 15, 18, 21, and 25, 335
Arrests, suburban areas, distribution by age, 342–346
Arrests, suburban areas, distribution by ethnicity, 351
Arrests, suburban areas, distribution by race, 348
Arrests, suburban areas, distribution by sex, 347
Arrests, suburban areas, persons under 15, 18, 21, and 25, 346
Arrests of persons under 15, 18, 21, and 25, 302
Arrest trends, cities, 309
Arrest trends, current year over previous, 291, 292
Arrest trends, five-year, 289, 290
Arrest trends, metropolitan counties, 320, 321
Arrest trends, nonmetropolitan counties, 331, 332
Arrest trends, suburban areas, 342, 343
Arrest trends, ten-year, 287, 288
Incidents cleared by offense category, 269

FRAUD
Arrests, by geographic region, 284
Arrests, by population group, 285
Arrests, cities, distribution by age, 311
Arrests, cities, distribution by ethnicity, 318
Arrests, cities, distribution by race, 315
Arrests, cities, distribution by sex, 314
Arrests, cities, persons under 15, 18, 21, and 25, 313
Arrests, distribution by age, 293–302
Arrests, distribution by ethnicity, 307
Arrests, distribution by race, 304
Arrests, distribution by sex, 288, 290, 303
Arrests, estimated number of, 283
Arrests, females, distribution by age, 299
Arrests, males, distribution by age, 296
Arrests, metropolitan counties, distribution by age, 322
Arrests, metropolitan counties, distribution by ethnicity, 329
Arrests, metropolitan counties, distribution by race, 326
Arrests, metropolitan counties, distribution by sex, 325
Arrests, metropolitan counties, persons under 15, 18, 21, and 25, 324
Arrests, nonmetropolitan counties, distribution by age, 333
Arrests, nonmetropolitan counties, distribution by ethnicity, 337
Arrests, nonmetropolitan counties, distribution by race, 339
Arrests, nonmetropolitan counties, distribution by sex, 336
Arrests, nonmetropolitan counties, persons under 15, 18, 21, and 25, 335
Arrests, suburban areas, distribution by age, 342–346
Arrests, suburban areas, distribution by ethnicity, 351
Arrests, suburban areas, distribution by race, 348
Arrests, suburban areas, distribution by sex, 347
Arrests, suburban areas, persons under 15, 18, 21, and 25, 346
Arrests of persons under 15, 18, 21, and 25, 302
Arrest trends, cities, 309
Arrest trends, current year over previous, 291, 292
Arrest trends, five-year, 289, 290
Arrest trends, metropolitan counties, 320, 321
Arrest trends, nonmetropolitan counties, 331, 332
Arrest trends, suburban areas, 342, 343
Arrest trends, ten-year, 287, 288
Incidents cleared by offense category, 269

GAMBLING
Arrests, by geographic region, 284
Arrests, by population group, 285
Arrests, cities, distribution by age, 311
Arrests, cities, distribution by ethnicity, 318
Arrests, cities, distribution by race, 315
Arrests, cities, distribution by sex, 314
Arrests, cities, persons under 15, 18, 21, and 25, 313
Arrests, distribution by age, 293–302
Arrests, distribution by ethnicity, 307
Arrests, distribution by race, 304
Arrests, distribution by sex, 288, 290, 303
Arrests, estimated number of, 283
Arrests, females, distribution by age, 299
Arrests, males, distribution by age, 296
Arrests, metropolitan counties, distribution by age, 322

Arrests, metropolitan counties, distribution by ethnicity, 329
Arrests, metropolitan counties, distribution by race, 326
Arrests, metropolitan counties, distribution by sex, 325
Arrests, metropolitan counties, persons under 15, 18, 21, and 25, 324
Arrests, nonmetropolitan counties, distribution by age, 333
Arrests, nonmetropolitan counties, distribution by ethnicity, 337
Arrests, nonmetropolitan counties, distribution by race, 339
Arrests, nonmetropolitan counties, distribution by sex, 336
Arrests, nonmetropolitan counties, persons under 15, 18, 21, and 25, 335
Arrests, suburban areas, distribution by age, 342–346
Arrests, suburban areas, distribution by ethnicity, 351
Arrests, suburban areas, distribution by race, 348
Arrests, suburban areas, distribution by sex, 347
Arrests, suburban areas, persons under 15, 18, 21, and 25, 346
Arrests of persons under 15, 18, 21, and 25, 302
Arrest trends, cities, 309
Arrest trends, current year over previous, 291, 292
Arrest trends, five-year, 289, 290
Arrest trends, metropolitan counties, 320, 321
Arrest trends, nonmetropolitan counties, 331, 332
Arrest trends, suburban areas, 342, 343
Arrest trends, ten-year, 287, 288
Incidents cleared by offense category, 269

GENDER
Hate crimes generally
see HATE CRIMES

GEOGRAPHIC DIVISIONS
Crime in the U.S. by geographic division, 38

GEORGIA
Aggravated assault, by state and type of weapon, 261
Arrests, numbers and types of offenses, 354
Crime, by metropolitan statistical area, 54
Crime, by state and area, 46
Hate crimes, 566, 567, 569
Law enforcement employees, 370–533
Murder, by state and type of weapon, 259
Offenses known to law enforcement, by agencies, 222
Offenses known to law enforcement, by counties, 190
Offenses known to law enforcement, by selected state, 84
Offenses known to law enforcement, by university and college, 181
Robbery, by state and type of weapon, 260

GUAM
Hate crimes, 566, 567, 569
Murder, by type of weapon, 259

HANDGUNS
see FIREARMS OFFENSES

HATE CRIMES
Age
known offenders, by age, 564
Agencies
incidents per bias motivation and quarter, 569
participating states and Federal agencies, 567
Bias motivation
incidents, victim type, by bias motivation, 563

known offender's race, ethnicity, and age, 556, 559, 564
location of incidents, 565
multiple-bias incidents, 554, 557, 559, 561, 563
number of victims and offense type by, 554–563
offense type, 557, 559
single-bias incidents, 554, 557, 559, 561, 563
states and agencies, 569
Cities, 569
Counties, 569
Ethnicity
known offender's race and ethnicity, 556, 559, 564
Location of incidents and bias motivation, 565
Offense type
by bias motivation, 557, 559, 563
by state, 566, 567, 569
incidents, offenses, victims, and known offenders by, 555, 560
incidents, offenses, victims, and known offenders, 554
known offender's race, ethnicity, and age, 556, 559, 564
location of incidents, 565
victim type by, 554–563
Race
known offender's race and ethnicity, 556, 559, 564
State crime totals
offense type by state, 566, 567, 569
Victim types, 554–563

HAWAII
Aggravated assault, by state and type of weapon, 261
Arrests, numbers and types of offenses, 354
Crime, by metropolitan statistical area, 54
Crime, by state and area, 46
Hate crimes, 566, 567, 569
Law enforcement employees, 370–533
Murder, by state and type of weapon, 259
Offenses known to law enforcement, by counties, 190
Robbery, by state and type of weapon, 260

HISPANIC ORIGIN
Generally
see RACE

HOMICIDE
Murder and nonnegligent manslaughter
see MURDER AND NONNEGLIGENT MANSLAUGHTER

HOUSEHOLD GOODS
Property stolen and recovered, 263

HUMAN TRAFFICKING
Hate crimes, 555, 556, 557, 561
Incidents cleared by offense category, 269

IDAHO
Aggravated assault, by state and type of weapon, 261
Arrests, numbers and types of offenses, 354
Crime, by metropolitan statistical area, 54
Crime, by state and area, 46
Hate crimes, 566, 567, 569
Law enforcement employees, 370–533
Murder, by state and type of weapon, 259
Offenses known to law enforcement, by counties, 190
Offenses known to law enforcement, by selected state, 84

Offenses known to law enforcement, by university and college, 181
Offenses know to law enforcement, by agencies, 222
Robbery, by state and type of weapon, 260

ILLINOIS
Aggravated assault, by state and type of weapon, 261
Arrests, numbers and types of offenses, 354
Crime, by metropolitan statistical area, 54
Crime, by state and area, 46
Hate crimes, 566, 567, 569
Law enforcement employees, 370–533
Murder, by state and type of weapon, 259
Offenses known to law enforcement, by agencies, 222
Offenses known to law enforcement, by counties, 190
Offenses known to law enforcement, by selected state, 84
Offenses known to law enforcement, by university and college, 181
Robbery, by state and type of weapon, 260

INDIANA
Aggravated assault, by state and type of weapon, 261
Arrests, numbers and types of offenses, 354
Crime, by metropolitan statistical area, 54
Crime, by state and area, 46
Hate crimes, 566, 567, 569
Law enforcement employees, 370–533
Murder, by state and type of weapon, 259
Offenses known to law enforcement, by agencies, 222
Offenses known to law enforcement, by counties, 190
Offenses known to law enforcement, by selected state, 84
Offenses known to law enforcement, by university and college, 181
Robbery, by state and type of weapon, 260

INTIMIDATION
Hate crimes, 555, 556, 557, 561

IOWA
Aggravated assault, by state and type of weapon, 261
Arrests, numbers and types of offenses, 354
Crime, by metropolitan statistical area, 54
Crime, by state and area, 46
Hate crimes, 566, 567, 569
Law enforcement employees, 370–533
Murder, by state and type of weapon, 259
Offenses known to law enforcement, by agencies, 222
Offenses known to law enforcement, by counties, 190
Offenses known to law enforcement, by selected state, 84
Offenses known to law enforcement, by university and college, 181
Robbery, by state and type of weapon, 260

JEWELRY
Property stolen and recovered, 263

JUVENILES
Police disposition of juvenile offenders taken into custody, 353

KANSAS
Aggravated assault, by state and type of weapon, 261
Arrests, numbers and types of offenses, 354
Crime, by metropolitan statistical area, 54

Crime, by state and area, 46
Hate crimes, 566, 567, 569
Law enforcement employees, 370–533
Murder, by state and type of weapon, 259
Offenses known to law enforcement, by agencies, 222
Offenses known to law enforcement, by counties, 190
Offenses known to law enforcement, by selected state, 84
Offenses known to law enforcement, by university and college, 181
Robbery, by state and type of weapon, 260

KENTUCKY
Aggravated assault, by state and type of weapon, 261
Arrests, numbers and types of offenses, 354
Crime, by metropolitan statistical area, 54
Crime, by state and area, 46
Hate crimes, 566, 567, 569
Law enforcement employees, 370–533
Murder, by state and type of weapon, 259
Offenses known to law enforcement, by agencies, 222
Offenses known to law enforcement, by counties, 190
Offenses known to law enforcement, by selected state, 84
Offenses known to law enforcement, by university and college, 181
Robbery, by state and type of weapon, 260

KIDNAPPING
Incidents cleared by offense category, 269

KNIFE OFFENSES
Aggravated assault, by state and type of weapon, 261
Arrests, by geographic region, 284
Arrests, by population group, 285
Arrests, cities, distribution by age, 311
Arrests, cities, distribution by ethnicity, 318
Arrests, cities, distribution by sex, 314
Arrests, cities, persons under 15, 18, 21, and 25, 313
Arrests, distribution by age, 293–302
Arrests, distribution by ethnicity, 307
Arrests, distribution by race, 304
Arrests, distribution by sex, 288, 290, 303
Arrests, females, distribution by age, 299
Arrests, males, distribution by age, 296
Arrests, metropolitan counties, distribution by ethnicity, 329
Arrests, metropolitan counties, distribution by race, 326
Arrests, metropolitan counties, distribution by sex, 325
Arrests, metropolitan counties, persons under 15, 18, 21, and 25, 324
Arrests, nonmetropolitan counties, distribution by age, 333
Arrests, nonmetropolitan counties, distribution by ethnicity, 337
Arrests, nonmetropolitan counties, distribution by race, 339
Arrests, nonmetropolitan counties, distribution by sex, 336
Arrests, nonmetropolitan counties, persons under 15, 18, 21, and 25, 335
Arrests, suburban areas, distribution by age, 342–346
Arrests, suburban areas, distribution by ethnicity, 351
Arrests, suburban areas, distribution by race, 348
Arrests, suburban areas, distribution by sex, 347
Arrests, suburban areas, persons under 15, 18, 21, and 25, 346
Arrests of persons under 15, 18, 21, and 25, 302
Arrest trends, cities, 309

Arrest trends, metropolitan counties, 320, 321
Arrest trends, nonmetropolitan counties, 331, 332
Arrest trends, suburban areas, 342, 343
Murder, by state and type of weapon, 259
Robbery, by state and type of weapon, 260

LARCENY-THEFT
Arrests, by geographic region, 284
Arrests, by population group, 285
Arrests, by state, 354
Arrests, cities, distribution by age, 311
Arrests, cities, distribution by ethnicity, 318
Arrests, cities, distribution by race, 315
Arrests, cities, distribution by sex, 314
Arrests, cities, persons under 15, 18, 21, and 25, 313
Arrests, distribution by age, 293–302
Arrests, distribution by ethnicity, 307
Arrests, distribution by race, 304
Arrests, distribution by sex, 288, 290, 303
Arrests, estimated number of, 283
Arrests, females, distribution by age, 299
Arrests, males, distribution by age, 296
Arrests, metropolitan counties, distribution by age, 322
Arrests, metropolitan counties, distribution by ethnicity, 329
Arrests, metropolitan counties, distribution by race, 326
Arrests, metropolitan counties, distribution by sex, 325
Arrests, metropolitan counties, persons under 15, 18, 21, and 25, 324
Arrests, nonmetropolitan counties, distribution by age, 333
Arrests, nonmetropolitan counties, distribution by ethnicity, 337
Arrests, nonmetropolitan counties, distribution by race, 339
Arrests, nonmetropolitan counties, distribution by sex, 336
Arrests, nonmetropolitan counties, persons under 15, 18, 21, and 25, 335
Arrests, suburban areas, distribution by age, 342–346
Arrests, suburban areas, distribution by ethnicity, 351
Arrests, suburban areas, distribution by race, 348
Arrests, suburban areas, distribution by sex, 347
Arrests, suburban areas, persons under 15, 18, 21, and 25, 346
Arrests of persons under 15, 18, 21, and 25, 302
Arrest trends, cities, 309
Arrest trends, current year over previous, 291, 292
Arrest trends, five-year, 289, 290
Arrest trends, metropolitan counties, 320, 321
Arrest trends, nonmetropolitan counties, 331, 332
Arrest trends, suburban areas, 342, 343
Arrest trends, ten-year, 287, 288
Community type, 37
Crime, by metropolitan statistical area, 54
Crime, by state and area, 46
Crime in the U.S., by volume and rate, 35
Crimes per 100,000 inhabitants, by cities, 254
Crimes per 100,000 inhabitants, by counties, 255
Crimes per 100,000 population, by population group, 252, 257
Crime trends, by population group, 247
Crime trends, cities by population group, 248
Crime trends, counties by population group, 249
Hate crimes, 555, 556, 560

Incidents cleared by offense category, 269
Offense analysis, 83, 262
Offenses cleared by arrest or exceptional means, by population group, 270
Offenses cleared by arrest or exceptional means, by region, 271
Offenses cleared by arrest or exceptional means, persons under 18, 274
Offenses known to law enforcement, by counties, 190
Offenses known to law enforcement, by selected state, 84
Offenses known to law enforcement, by tribal, and other agencies, 222
Offenses known to law enforcement, by university and college, 181
Population and offense distribution, by region, 37, 38
Universities and colleges, 181

LATINO ORIGIN
Generally
see RACE

LAW ENFORCEMENT
Offenses known to, by counties, 190
Offenses known to, by selected state, 84
Offenses known to, by tribal and other agencies, 222
Offenses known to, by university and college, 181

LAW ENFORCEMENT EMPLOYEES
Full-time civilian employees, by population group, 369
Full-time employees, 366–374
Full-time employees, by region, geographic division, and group, 364
Full-time employees, by state, 370–533
Full-time employees, percent male and female, 368
Full-time employees, range in rate, 366

LAW ENFORCEMENT OFFICERS
Full-time officers, by region, geographic division, and group, 365
Full-time officers, by state, 370–533
Full-time officers, range in rate, 367

LIQUOR LAW VIOLATIONS
Arrests, by geographic region, 284
Arrests, by population group, 285
Arrests, cities, distribution by age, 311
Arrests, cities, distribution by ethnicity, 318
Arrests, cities, distribution by race, 315
Arrests, cities, distribution by sex, 314
Arrests, cities, persons under 15, 18, 21, and 25, 313
Arrests, distribution by age, 293–302
Arrests, distribution by ethnicity, 307
Arrests, distribution by race, 304
Arrests, distribution by sex, 288, 290, 303
Arrests, estimated number of, 283
Arrests, females, distribution by age, 299
Arrests, males, distribution by age, 296
Arrests, metropolitan counties, distribution by age, 322
Arrests, metropolitan counties, distribution by ethnicity, 329
Arrests, metropolitan counties, distribution by race, 326
Arrests, metropolitan counties, distribution by sex, 325
Arrests, metropolitan counties, persons under 15, 18, 21, and 25, 324
Arrests, nonmetropolitan counties, distribution by age, 333

Arrests, nonmetropolitan counties, distribution by ethnicity, 337

Arrests, nonmetropolitan counties, distribution by race, 339

Arrests, nonmetropolitan counties, distribution by sex, 336

Arrests, nonmetropolitan counties, persons under 15, 18, 21, and 25, 335

Arrests, suburban areas, distribution by age, 342–346

Arrests, suburban areas, distribution by ethnicity, 351

Arrests, suburban areas, distribution by race, 348

Arrests, suburban areas, distribution by sex, 347

Arrests, suburban areas, persons under 15, 18, 21, and 25, 346

Arrests of persons under 15, 18, 21, and 25, 302

Arrest trends, cities, 309

Arrest trends, current year over previous, 291, 292

Arrest trends, five-year, 289, 290

Arrest trends, metropolitan counties, 320, 321

Arrest trends, nonmetropolitan counties, 331, 332

Arrest trends, suburban areas, 342, 343

Arrest trends, ten-year, 287, 288

LIVESTOCK

Property stolen and recovered, 263

LOITERING

see CURFEW AND LOITERING LAW VIOLATIONS

LOUISIANA

Aggravated assault, by state and type of weapon, 261

Arrests, numbers and types of offenses, 354

Crime, by metropolitan statistical area, 54

Crime, by state and area, 46

Hate crimes, 566, 567, 569

Law enforcement employees, 370–533

Murder, by state and type of weapon, 259

Offenses known to law enforcement, by agencies, 222

Offenses known to law enforcement, by counties, 190

Offenses known to law enforcement, by selected state, 84

Offenses known to law enforcement, by university and college, 181

Robbery, by state and type of weapon, 260

MAINE

Aggravated assault, by state and type of weapon, 261

Arrests, numbers and types of offenses, 354

Crime, by metropolitan statistical area, 54

Crime, by state and area, 46

Hate crimes, 566, 567, 569

Law enforcement employees, 370–533

Murder, by state and type of weapon, 259

Offenses known to law enforcement, by agencies, 222

Offenses known to law enforcement, by counties, 190

Offenses known to law enforcement, by selected state, 84

Offenses known to law enforcement, by university and college, 181

Robbery, by state and type of weapon, 260

MALES

Generally

see SEX

MANSLAUGHTER

Murder and nonnegligent manslaughter

see MURDER AND NONNEGLIGENT MANSLAUGHTER

MARYLAND

Aggravated assault, by state and type of weapon, 261

Arrests, numbers and types of offenses, 354

Crime, by metropolitan statistical area, 54

Crime, by state and area, 46

Hate crimes, 566, 567, 569

Law enforcement employees, 370–533

Murder, by state and type of weapon, 259

Offenses known to law enforcement, by agencies, 222

Offenses known to law enforcement, by counties, 190

Offenses known to law enforcement, by selected state, 84

Offenses known to law enforcement, by university and college, 181

Robbery, by state and type of weapon, 260

MASSACHUSETTS

Aggravated assault, by state and type of weapon, 261

Arrests, numbers and types of offenses, 354

Crime, by metropolitan statistical area, 54

Crime, by state and area, 46

Hate crimes, 566, 567, 569

Law enforcement employees, 370–533

Murder, by state and type of weapon, 259

Offenses known to law enforcement, by agencies, 222

Offenses known to law enforcement, by selected state, 84

Offenses known to law enforcement, by university and college, 181

Robbery, by state and type of weapon, 260

METROPOLITAN STATISTICAL AREAS

Cities

see CITIES

Counties

see COUNTIES

Crime, by community type, 37

Crime, by state and area, 46

Crime, numbers and percentages, 54

Crimes per 100,000 inhabitants, 252, 254

Police disposition of juvenile offenders taken into custody, 353

MICHIGAN

Aggravated assault, by state and type of weapon, 261

Arrests, numbers and types of offenses, 354

Crime, by metropolitan statistical area, 54

Crime, by state and area, 46

Hate crimes, 566, 567, 569

Law enforcement employees, 370–533

Murder, by state and type of weapon, 259

Offenses known to law enforcement, by agencies, 222

Offenses known to law enforcement, by counties, 190

Offenses known to law enforcement, by selected state, 84

Offenses known to law enforcement, by university and college, 181

Robbery, by state and type of weapon, 260

MINNESOTA

Aggravated assault, by state and type of weapon, 261

Arrests, numbers and types of offenses, 354

Crime, by metropolitan statistical area, 54

Crime, by state and area, 46

Hate crimes, 566, 567, 569

Law enforcement employees, 370–533

Murder, by state and type of weapon, 259
Offenses known to law enforcement, by agencies, 222
Offenses known to law enforcement, by counties, 190
Offenses known to law enforcement, by selected state, 84
Offenses known to law enforcement, by university and
    college, 181
Robbery, by state and type of weapon, 260

MINORS
Arrests of persons under 15, 18, 21, and 25, 302
Offenses cleared by arrest or exceptional means, persons
    under 18, 274
Police disposition of juvenile offenders taken into custody,
    353

MISSISSIPPI
Aggravated assault, by state and type of weapon, 261
Arrests, numbers and types of offenses, 354
Crime, by metropolitan statistical area, 54
Crime, by state and area, 46
Hate crimes, 566, 567, 569
Law enforcement employees, 370–533
Murder, by state and type of weapon, 259
Offenses known to law enforcement, by agencies, 222
Offenses known to law enforcement, by counties, 190
Offenses known to law enforcement, by selected state, 84
Offenses known to law enforcement, by university and
    college, 181
Robbery, by state and type of weapon, 260

MISSOURI
Aggravated assault, by state and type of weapon, 261
Arrests, numbers and types of offenses, 354
Crime, by metropolitan statistical area, 54
Crime, by state and area, 46
Hate crimes, 566, 567, 569
Law enforcement employees, 370–533
Murder, by state and type of weapon, 259
Offenses known to law enforcement, by agencies, 222
Offenses known to law enforcement, by counties, 190
Offenses known to law enforcement, by selected state, 84
Offenses known to law enforcement, by university and
    college, 181
Robbery, by state and type of weapon, 260

MONTANA
Aggravated assault, by state and type of weapon, 261
Arrests, numbers and types of offenses, 354
Crime, by metropolitan statistical area, 54
Crime, by state and area, 46
Hate crimes, 566, 567, 569
Law enforcement employees, 370–533
Murder, by state and type of weapon, 259
Offenses known to law enforcement, by agencies, 222
Offenses known to law enforcement, by counties, 190
Offenses known to law enforcement, by selected state, 84
Offenses known to law enforcement, by university and
    college, 181
Robbery, by state and type of weapon, 260

MOTOR VEHICLE THEFT
Arrests, by geographic region, 284
Arrests, by population group, 285
Arrests, by state, 354

Arrests, cities, distribution by age, 311
Arrests, cities, distribution by ethnicity, 318
Arrests, cities, distribution by race, 315
Arrests, cities, distribution by sex, 314
Arrests, cities, persons under 15, 18, 21, and 25, 313
Arrests, distribution by age, 293–302
Arrests, distribution by ethnicity, 307
Arrests, distribution by race, 304
Arrests, distribution by sex, 288, 290, 303
Arrests, estimated number of, 283
Arrests, females, distribution by age, 299
Arrests, males, distribution by age, 296
Arrests, metropolitan counties, distribution by age, 322
Arrests, metropolitan counties, distribution by ethnicity, 329
Arrests, metropolitan counties, distribution by race, 326
Arrests, metropolitan counties, distribution by sex, 325
Arrests, metropolitan counties, persons under 15, 18, 21, and
    25, 324
Arrests, nonmetropolitan counties, distribution by age, 333
Arrests, nonmetropolitan counties, distribution by ethnicity,
    337
Arrests, nonmetropolitan counties, distribution by race, 339
Arrests, nonmetropolitan counties, distribution by sex, 336
Arrests, nonmetropolitan counties, persons under 15, 18, 21,
    and 25, 335
Arrests, suburban areas, distribution by age, 342–346
Arrests, suburban areas, distribution by ethnicity, 351
Arrests, suburban areas, distribution by race, 348
Arrests, suburban areas, distribution by sex, 347
Arrests, suburban areas, persons under 15, 18, 21, and 25, 346
Arrests of persons under 15, 18, 21, and 25, 302
Arrest trends, cities, 309
Arrest trends, current year over previous, 291, 292
Arrest trends, five-year, 289, 290
Arrest trends, metropolitan counties, 320, 321
Arrest trends, nonmetropolitan counties, 331, 332
Arrest trends, suburban areas, 342, 343
Arrest trends, ten-year, 287, 288
Community type, 37
Crime, by metropolitan statistical area, 54
Crime, by state and area, 46
Crime in the U.S., by volume and rate, 35
Crimes per 100,000 inhabitants, by cities, 254
Crimes per 100,000 inhabitants, by counties, 255
Crimes per 100,000 population, by population group, 252,
    257
Crime trends, additional information, 250
Crime trends, by population group, 247
Crime trends, cities by population group, 248
Crime trends, counties by population group, 249
Hate crimes, 555, 556, 560
Incidents cleared by offense category, 269
Offense analysis, 83, 262
Offenses cleared by arrest or exceptional means, by
    population group, 270–274
Offenses cleared by arrest or exceptional means, by region,
    271
Offenses cleared by arrest or exceptional means, persons
    under 18, 274

Offenses known to law enforcement, by counties, 190
Offenses known to law enforcement, by selected state, 84
Offenses known to law enforcement, by tribal, and other agencies, 222
Offenses known to law enforcement, by university and college, 181
Population and offense distribution, by region, 37, 38
Property stolen and recovered, 263
Universities and colleges, 181

MULTIPLE-BIAS INCIDENTS
Hate crimes, 554, 557, 559, 561, 563

MURDER AND NONNEGLIGENT MANSLAUGHTER
Arrests, by geographic region, 284
Arrests, by population group, 285
Arrests, by state, 354
Arrests, cities, distribution by age, 311
Arrests, cities, distribution by ethnicity, 318
Arrests, cities, distribution by race, 315
Arrests, cities, distribution by sex, 314
Arrests, cities, persons under 15, 18, 21, and 25, 313
Arrests, distribution by age, 293–302
Arrests, distribution by ethnicity, 307
Arrests, distribution by race, 304
Arrests, distribution by race, 304
Arrests, distribution by sex, 288, 290, 303
Arrests, estimated number of, 283
Arrests, females, distribution by age, 299
Arrests, males, distribution by age, 296
Arrests, metropolitan counties, distribution by age, 322
Arrests, metropolitan counties, distribution by ethnicity, 329
Arrests, metropolitan counties, distribution by race, 336
Arrests, metropolitan counties, distribution by sex, 325
Arrests, metropolitan counties, persons under 15, 18, 21, and 25, 324
Arrests, nonmetropolitan counties, distribution by age, 333
Arrests, nonmetropolitan counties, distribution by ethnicity, 337
Arrests, nonmetropolitan counties, distribution by race, 339
Arrests, nonmetropolitan counties, distribution by sex, 336
Arrests, nonmetropolitan counties, persons under 15, 18, 21, and 25, 335
Arrests, suburban areas, distribution by age, 342–346
Arrests, suburban areas, distribution by ethnicity, 351
Arrests, suburban areas, distribution by race, 348
Arrests, suburban areas, distribution by sex, 347
Arrests, suburban areas, persons under 15, 18, 21, and 25, 346
Arrests of persons under 15, 18, 21, and 25, 302
Arrest trends, cities, 309
Arrest trends, current year over previous, 291, 292
Arrest trends, five-year, 289, 290
Arrest trends, metropolitan counties, 320, 321
Arrest trends, nonmetropolitan counties, 331, 332
Arrest trends, suburban areas, 342, 343
Arrest trends, ten-year, 287, 288
Community type, 37
Crime, by metropolitan statistical area, 54
Crime, by state and area, 46
Crime in the U.S., by volume and rate, 35

Crimes per 100,000 inhabitants, by cities, 254
Crimes per 100,000 inhabitants, by counties, 255
Crimes per 100,000 population, by population group, 252
Crime trends, by population group, 247
Crime trends, cities by population group, 248
Crime trends, counties by population group, 249
Hate crimes, 555, 556, 557, 561
Incidents cleared by offense category, 269
Offense analysis, 83, 262
Offenses by state and type of weapon, 259
Offenses cleared by arrest or exceptional means, by population group, 270
Offenses cleared by arrest or exceptional means, by region, 271
Offenses cleared by arrest or exceptional means, persons under 18, 274
Offenses known to law enforcement, by counties, 190
Offenses known to law enforcement, by selected state, 84
Offenses known to law enforcement, by tribal, and other agencies, 222
Offenses known to law enforcement, by university and college, 181
Population and offense distribution, by region, 37, 38
Universities and colleges, 181

NATIONAL ORIGIN
Hate crimes generally
  see HATE CRIMES
NATIVE AMERICANS
Generally
  see RACE
NEBRASKA
Aggravated assault, by state and type of weapon, 261
Arrests, numbers and types of offenses, 354
Crime, by metropolitan statistical area, 54
Crime, by state and area, 46
Hate crimes, 566, 567, 569
Law enforcement employees, 370–533
Murder, by state and type of weapon, 259
Offenses known to law enforcement, by agencies, 222
Offenses known to law enforcement, by counties, 190
Offenses known to law enforcement, by selected state, 84
Offenses known to law enforcement, by university and college, 181
Robbery, by state and type of weapon, 260
NEVADA
Aggravated assault, by state and type of weapon, 261
Arrests, numbers and types of offenses, 354
Crime, by metropolitan statistical area, 54
Crime, by state and area, 46
Hate crimes, 566, 567, 569
Law enforcement employees, 370–533
Murder, by state and type of weapon, 259
Offenses known to law enforcement, by agencies, 222
Offenses known to law enforcement, by counties, 190
Offenses known to law enforcement, by selected state, 84
Offenses known to law enforcement, by university and college, 181
Robbery, by state and type of weapon, 260

NEW HAMPSHIRE
Aggravated assault, by state and type of weapon, 261
Arrests, numbers and types of offenses, 354
Crime, by metropolitan statistical area, 54
Crime, by state and area, 46
Hate crimes, 566, 567, 569
Law enforcement employees, 370–533
Murder, by state and type of weapon, 259
Offenses known to law enforcement, by agencies, 222
Offenses known to law enforcement, by counties, 190
Offenses known to law enforcement, by selected state, 84
Offenses known to law enforcement, by university and
college, 181
Robbery, by state and type of weapon, 260
NEW JERSEY
Aggravated assault, by state and type of weapon, 261
Arrests, numbers and types of offenses, 354
Crime, by metropolitan statistical area, 54
Crime, by state and area, 46
Hate crimes, 566, 567, 569
Law enforcement employees, 370–533
Murder, by state and type of weapon, 259
Offenses known to law enforcement, by agencies, 222
Offenses known to law enforcement, by counties, 190
Offenses known to law enforcement, by selected state, 84
Offenses known to law enforcement, by university and
college, 181
Robbery, by state and type of weapon, 260
NEW MEXICO
Aggravated assault, by state and type of weapon, 261
Arrests, numbers and types of offenses, 354
Crime, by metropolitan statistical area, 54
Crime, by state and area, 46
Hate crimes, 566, 567, 569
Law enforcement employees, 370–533
Murder, by state and type of weapon, 259
Offenses known to law enforcement, by agencies, 222
Offenses known to law enforcement, by counties, 190
Offenses known to law enforcement, by selected state, 84
Offenses known to law enforcement, by university and
college, 181
Robbery, by state and type of weapon, 260
NEW YORK
Aggravated assault, by state and type of weapon, 261
Arrests, numbers and types of offenses, 354
Crime, by metropolitan statistical area, 54
Crime, by state and area, 46
Hate crimes, 566, 567, 569
Law enforcement employees, 370–533
Murder, by state and type of weapon, 259
Offenses known to law enforcement, by agencies, 222
Offenses known to law enforcement, by counties, 190
Offenses known to law enforcement, by selected state, 84
Offenses known to law enforcement, by university and
college, 181
Robbery, by state and type of weapon, 260
NONNEGLIGENT MANSLAUGHTER
see MURDER AND NONNEGLIGENT
MANSLAUGHTER

NORTH CAROLINA
Aggravated assault, by state and type of weapon, 261
Arrests, numbers and types of offenses, 354
Crime, by metropolitan statistical area, 54
Crime, by state and area, 46
Hate crimes, 566, 567, 569
Law enforcement employees, 370–533
Murder, by state and type of weapon, 259
Offenses known to law enforcement, by agencies, 222
Offenses known to law enforcement, by counties, 190
Offenses known to law enforcement, by selected state, 84
Offenses known to law enforcement, by university and
college, 181
Robbery, by state and type of weapon, 260
NORTH DAKOTA
Aggravated assault, by state and type of weapon, 261
Arrests, numbers and types of offenses, 354
Crime, by metropolitan statistical area, 54
Crime, by state and area, 46
Hate crimes, 566, 567, 569
Law enforcement employees, 370–533
Murder, by state and type of weapon, 259
Offenses known to law enforcement, by agencies, 222
Offenses known to law enforcement, by counties, 190
Offenses known to law enforcement, by selected state, 84
Offenses known to law enforcement, by university and
college, 181
Robbery, by state and type of weapon, 260

OFFENSE ANALYSIS
Figures, 83
Number and percent change, 262
OFFENSES CLEARED
Persons under 18, by population group, 274
Population group numbers and percentages, 270–274
Region and geographic numbers and percentages, 271
OFFENSES REPORTED
Aggravated assault, by state and type of weapon, 261
Arrests, by geographic region, 284
Arrests, by population group, 285
Arrests, cities, distribution by age, 311
Arrests, cities, distribution by ethnicity, 318
Arrests, cities, distribution by sex, 314
Arrests, cities, persons under 15, 18, 21, and 25, 313
Arrests, distribution by age, 293–302
Arrests, distribution by ethnicity, 307
Arrests, distribution by race, 304
Arrests, distribution by race, 304
Arrests, distribution by sex, 288, 290, 303
Arrests, females, distribution by age, 299
Arrests, males, distribution by age, 296
Arrests, metropolitan counties, distribution by ethnicity, 329
Arrests, metropolitan counties, distribution by race, 326
Arrests, metropolitan counties, distribution by sex, 325
Arrests, metropolitan counties, persons under 15, 18, 21, and
25, 324
Arrests, nonmetropolitan counties, distribution by age, 333
Arrests, nonmetropolitan counties, distribution by ethnicity,
337

Arrests, nonmetropolitan counties, distribution by race, 339

Arrests, nonmetropolitan counties, distribution by sex, 336

Arrests, nonmetropolitan counties, persons under 15, 18, 21, and 25, 335

Arrests, suburban areas, distribution by age, 342–346

Arrests, suburban areas, distribution by ethnicity, 351

Arrests, suburban areas, distribution by race, 348

Arrests, suburban areas, distribution by sex, 347

Arrests, suburban areas, persons under 15, 18, 21, and 25, 346

Arrests of persons under 15, 18, 21, and 25, 302

Arrest trends, cities, 309

Arrest trends, metropolitan counties, 320, 321

Arrest trends, nonmetropolitan counties, 331, 332

Arrest trends, suburban areas, 342, 343

Crime, by metropolitan statistical area, 54

Crime, by state and area, 46

Crime in the U.S., by volume and rate, 35

Crimes per 100,000 population, by population group, 252, 257

Crime trends, additional information, 250

Crime trends, by population group, 247

Crime trends, cities by population group, 248

Crime trends, counties by population group, 249

Murder, by state and type of weapon, 259

Offense analysis, 83, 262

Offenses known to law enforcement, by counties, 190

Offenses known to law enforcement, by selected state, 84

Offenses known to law enforcement, by tribal, and other agencies, 222

Offenses known to law enforcement, by university and college, 181

Robbery, by state and type of weapon, 260

OFFICE EQUIPMENT

Property stolen and recovered, 263

OHIO

Aggravated assault, by state and type of weapon, 261

Arrests, numbers and types of offenses, 354

Crime, by metropolitan statistical area, 54

Crime, by state and area, 46

Hate crimes, 566, 567, 569

Law enforcement employees, 370–533

Murder, by state and type of weapon, 259

Offenses known to law enforcement, by agencies, 222

Offenses known to law enforcement, by counties, 190

Offenses known to law enforcement, by selected state, 84

Offenses known to law enforcement, by university and college, 181

Robbery, by state and type of weapon, 260

OKLAHOMA

Aggravated assault, by state and type of weapon, 261

Arrests, numbers and types of offenses, 354

Crime, by metropolitan statistical area, 54

Crime, by state and area, 46

Hate crimes, 566, 567, 569

Law enforcement employees, 370–533

Murder, by state and type of weapon, 259

Offenses known to law enforcement, by agencies, 222

Offenses known to law enforcement, by counties, 190

Offenses known to law enforcement, by selected state, 84

Offenses known to law enforcement, by university and college, 181

Robbery, by state and type of weapon, 260

OREGON

Aggravated assault, by state and type of weapon, 261

Arrests, numbers and types of offenses, 354

Crime, by metropolitan statistical area, 54

Crime, by state and area, 46

Hate crimes, 566, 567, 569

Law enforcement employees, 370–533

Murder, by state and type of weapon, 259

Offenses known to law enforcement, by agencies, 222

Offenses known to law enforcement, by counties, 190

Offenses known to law enforcement, by selected state, 84

Offenses known to law enforcement, by university and college, 181

Robbery, by state and type of weapon, 260

PACIFIC ISLANDERS

Generally

see RACE

PENNSYLVANIA

Aggravated assault, by state and type of weapon, 261

Arrests, numbers and types of offenses, 354

Crime, by metropolitan statistical area, 54

Crime, by state and area, 46

Hate crimes, 566, 567, 569

Law enforcement employees, 370–533

Murder, by state and type of weapon, 259

Offenses known to law enforcement, by agencies, 222

Offenses known to law enforcement, by counties, 190

Offenses known to law enforcement, by selected state, 84

Offenses known to law enforcement, by university and college, 181

Robbery, by state and type of weapon, 260

POLICE

see LAW ENFORCEMENT

PORNOGRAPHY

Incidents cleared by offense category, 269

PRECIOUS METALS

Property stolen and recovered, 263

PROPERTY CRIME

Arrests, by geographic region, 284

Arrests, by population group, 285

Arrests, by state, 354

Arrests, cities, distribution by age, 311

Arrests, cities, distribution by ethnicity, 318

Arrests, cities, distribution by race, 315

Arrests, cities, distribution by sex, 314

Arrests, cities, persons under 15, 18, 21, and 25, 313

Arrests, distribution by age, 293–302

Arrests, distribution by ethnicity, 307

Arrests, distribution by race, 304

Arrests, distribution by sex, 288, 290, 303

Arrests, estimated number of, 283

Arrests, females, distribution by age, 299

Arrests, males, distribution by age, 296

Arrests, metropolitan counties, distribution by age, 322

Arrests, metropolitan counties, distribution by ethnicity, 329

Arrests, metropolitan counties, distribution by race, 326
Arrests, metropolitan counties, distribution by sex, 325
Arrests, metropolitan counties, persons under 15, 18, 21, and 25, 324
Arrests, nonmetropolitan counties, distribution by age, 333
Arrests, nonmetropolitan counties, distribution by ethnicity, 337
Arrests, nonmetropolitan counties, distribution by race, 339
Arrests, nonmetropolitan counties, distribution by sex, 336
Arrests, nonmetropolitan counties, persons under 15, 18, 21, and 25, 335
Arrests, suburban areas, distribution by age, 342–346
Arrests, suburban areas, distribution by ethnicity, 351
Arrests, suburban areas, distribution by race, 348
Arrests, suburban areas, distribution by sex, 347
Arrests, suburban areas, persons under 15, 18, 21, and 25, 346
Arrests of persons under 15, 18, 21, and 25, 302
Arrest trends, cities, 309
Arrest trends, current year over previous, 291, 292
Arrest trends, metropolitan counties, 320, 321
Arrest trends, nonmetropolitan counties, 331, 332
Arrest trends, suburban areas, 342, 343
Community type, 37
Crime, by metropolitan statistical area, 54
Crime, by state and area, 46
Crime in the U.S., by volume and rate, 35
Crimes per 100,000 inhabitants, by cities, 254
Crimes per 100,000 inhabitants, by counties, 255
Crimes per 100,000 population, by population group, 252, 257
Crime trends, by population group, 247
Crime trends, cities by population group, 248
Crime trends, counties by population group, 249
Hate crimes, 555, 556
Offense analysis, number and percent change, 262
Offenses cleared by arrest or exceptional means, by population group, 270
Offenses cleared by arrest or exceptional means, by region, 271
Offenses cleared by arrest or exceptional means, persons under 18, 274
Offenses known to law enforcement, by counties, 190
Offenses known to law enforcement, by selected state, 84
Offenses known to law enforcement, by tribal, and other agencies, 222
Offenses known to law enforcement, by university and college, 181
Population and offense distribution, by region, 37, 38
Property stolen and recovered, by type and value, 263
Universities and colleges, 181
PROSTITUTION AND COMMERCIALIZED VICE
Arrests, by geographic region, 284
Arrests, by population group, 285
Arrests, cities, distribution by age, 311
Arrests, cities, distribution by ethnicity, 318
Arrests, cities, distribution by race, 315
Arrests, cities, distribution by sex, 314
Arrests, cities, persons under 15, 18, 21, and 25, 313
Arrests, distribution by age, 293–302

Arrests, distribution by ethnicity, 307
Arrests, distribution by race, 304
Arrests, distribution by sex, 288, 290, 303
Arrests, estimated number of, 283
Arrests, females, distribution by age, 299
Arrests, males, distribution by age, 296
Arrests, metropolitan counties, distribution by age, 322
Arrests, metropolitan counties, distribution by ethnicity, 329
Arrests, metropolitan counties, distribution by race, 326
Arrests, metropolitan counties, distribution by sex, 325
Arrests, metropolitan counties, persons under 15, 18, 21, and 25, 324
Arrests, nonmetropolitan counties, distribution by age, 333
Arrests, nonmetropolitan counties, distribution by ethnicity, 337
Arrests, nonmetropolitan counties, distribution by race, 339
Arrests, nonmetropolitan counties, distribution by sex, 336
Arrests, nonmetropolitan counties, persons under 15, 18, 21, and 25, 335
Arrests, suburban areas, distribution by age, 342–346
Arrests, suburban areas, distribution by ethnicity, 351
Arrests, suburban areas, distribution by race, 348
Arrests, suburban areas, distribution by sex, 347
Arrests, suburban areas, persons under 15, 18, 21, and 25, 346
Arrests of persons under 15, 18, 21, and 25, 302
Arrest trends, cities, 309
Arrest trends, current year over previous, 291, 292
Arrest trends, five-year, 289, 290
Arrest trends, metropolitan counties, 320, 321
Arrest trends, nonmetropolitan counties, 331, 332
Arrest trends, suburban areas, 342, 343
Arrest trends, ten-year, 287, 288
Incidents cleared by offense category, 269
PUERTO RICO
Full-time law enforcement employees, by selected state and agency, 533

RACE
Arrests, cities, distribution by race, 315
Arrests, distribution by race, 304
Arrests, nonmetropolitan counties, 339
County arrests, distribution by race, 326, 339
Hate crimes generally
    see HATE CRIMES
Suburban area arrests, distribution by race, 348
RAPE
Forcible rape
    see FORCIBLE RAPE
Sex offenses
    see SEX OFFENSES
RATES OF CRIME
Crime, by metropolitan statistical area, 54
Crime, by state and area, 46
Crime in the U.S., by volume and rate, 35
Crimes per 100,000 population, by population group, 252, 257
Murder, by state and type of weapon, 259
Offense analysis, 83, 262
Property crime, 35

Robbery, by state and type of weapon, 260
Violent crime, 35
REGIONS
Arrests, by geographic region, 284
Crime in the U.S. by region, 37, 38
Full-time law enforcement employees by region, 364
Full-time law-enforcement officers by region, 365
Offenses cleared by arrest or exception means, by region, 271
RELIGION
Hate crimes generally
see HATE CRIMES
RHODE ISLAND
Aggravated assault, by state and type of weapon, 261
Arrests, numbers and types of offenses, 354
Crime, by metropolitan statistical area, 54
Crime, by state and area, 46
Hate crimes, 566, 567, 569
Law enforcement employees, 370–533
Murder, by state and type of weapon, 259
Offenses known to law enforcement, by agencies, 222
Offenses known to law enforcement, by selected state, 84
Offenses known to law enforcement, by university and college, 181
Robbery, by state and type of weapon, 260
RIFLES
see FIREARMS OFFENSES
ROBBERY
Arrests, by geographic region, 284
Arrests, by population group, 285
Arrests, by state, 354
Arrests, cities, distribution by age, 311
Arrests, cities, distribution by ethnicity, 318
Arrests, cities, distribution by race, 315
Arrests, cities, distribution by sex, 314
Arrests, cities, persons under 15, 18, 21, and 25, 313
Arrests, distribution by age, 293–302
Arrests, distribution by ethnicity, 307
Arrests, distribution by race, 304
Arrests, distribution by sex, 288, 290, 303
Arrests, estimated number of, 283
Arrests, females, distribution by age, 299
Arrests, males, distribution by age, 296
Arrests, metropolitan counties, distribution by age, 322
Arrests, metropolitan counties, distribution by ethnicity, 329
Arrests, metropolitan counties, distribution by race, 326
Arrests, metropolitan counties, distribution by sex, 325
Arrests, metropolitan counties, persons under 15, 18, 21, and 25, 324
Arrests, nonmetropolitan counties, distribution by age, 333
Arrests, nonmetropolitan counties, distribution by ethnicity, 337
Arrests, nonmetropolitan counties, distribution by race, 339
Arrests, nonmetropolitan counties, distribution by sex, 336
Arrests, nonmetropolitan counties, persons under 15, 18, 21, and 25, 335
Arrests, suburban areas, distribution by age, 342–346
Arrests, suburban areas, distribution by ethnicity, 351
Arrests, suburban areas, distribution by race, 348
Arrests, suburban areas, distribution by sex, 347
Arrests, suburban areas, persons under 15, 18, 21, and 25, 346
Arrests of persons under 15, 18, 21, and 25, 302
Arrest trends, cities, 309
Arrest trends, current year over previous, 291, 292
Arrest trends, five-year, 289, 290
Arrest trends, metropolitan counties, 320, 321
Arrest trends, nonmetropolitan counties, 331, 332
Arrest trends, suburban areas, 342, 343
Arrest trends, ten-year, 287, 288
Community type, 37
Crime, by metropolitan statistical area, 54
Crime, by state and area, 46
Crime in the U.S., by volume and rate, 35
Crimes per 100,000 inhabitants, by cities, 254
Crimes per 100,000 inhabitants, by counties, 255
Crimes per 100,000 population, by population group, 252, 257
Crime trends, additional information, 250
Crime trends, by population group, 247
Crime trends, cities by population group, 248
Crime trends, counties by population group, 249
Hate crimes, 555, 556, 560
Incidents cleared by offense category, 269
Offense analysis, 83, 262
Offenses, by state and type of weapon, 260
Offenses cleared by arrest or exceptional means, by population group, 270–274
Offenses cleared by arrest or exceptional means, by region, 271
Offenses cleared by arrest or exceptional means, persons under 18, 274
Offenses known to law enforcement, by counties, 190
Offenses known to law enforcement, by selected state, 84
Offenses known to law enforcement, by university and college, 181
Population and offense distribution, by region, 37, 38
Universities and colleges, 181
SEX
Arrests, cities, distribution by sex, 314
Arrests, distribution by sex, 288, 290, 303
Arrests, metropolitan counties, distribution by sex, 325
Arrest trends, cities, 310
Arrest trends, current year over previous, 292
Arrest trends, metropolitan counties, 321
Arrest trends, nonmetropolitan counties, 331, 332
Arrest trends, suburban areas, 343, 347
City arrests, distribution by sex, 314
County arrests, distribution by sex, 325, 336
County arrest trends, metropolitan counties, 325
County arrest trends, nonmetropolitan counties, 336
Female arrests, distribution by age, 299
Hate crimes
see HATE CRIMES
Law enforcement employees
full-time employees, percent male and female, 368
Male arrests, distribution by age, 296
Suburban area arrests, distribution by sex, 347
Suburban area arrest trends, by sex, 343

SEX OFFENSES
Arrests, by geographic region, 284
Arrests, by population group, 285
Arrests, cities, distribution by age, 311
Arrests, cities, distribution by ethnicity, 318
Arrests, cities, distribution by race, 315
Arrests, cities, distribution by sex, 314
Arrests, cities, persons under 15, 18, 21, and 25, 313
Arrests, distribution by age, 293–302
Arrests, distribution by ethnicity, 307
Arrests, distribution by race, 304
Arrests, distribution by sex, 288, 290, 303
Arrests, estimated number of, 283
Arrests, females, distribution by age, 299
Arrests, males, distribution by age, 296
Arrests, metropolitan counties, distribution by age, 322
Arrests, metropolitan counties, distribution by ethnicity, 329
Arrests, metropolitan counties, distribution by race, 326
Arrests, metropolitan counties, distribution by sex, 325
Arrests, metropolitan counties, persons under 15, 18, 21, and 25, 324
Arrests, nonmetropolitan counties, distribution by age, 333
Arrests, nonmetropolitan counties, distribution by ethnicity, 337
Arrests, nonmetropolitan counties, distribution by race, 339
Arrests, nonmetropolitan counties, distribution by sex, 336
Arrests, nonmetropolitan counties, persons under 15, 18, 21, and 25, 335
Arrests, suburban areas, distribution by age, 342–346
Arrests, suburban areas, distribution by ethnicity, 351
Arrests, suburban areas, distribution by race, 348
Arrests, suburban areas, distribution by sex, 347
Arrests, suburban areas, persons under 15, 18, 21, and 25, 346
Arrests of persons under 15, 18, 21, and 25, 302
Arrest trends, cities, 309
Arrest trends, current year over previous, 291, 292
Arrest trends, five-year, 289, 290
Arrest trends, metropolitan counties, 320, 321
Arrest trends, nonmetropolitan counties, 331, 332
Arrest trends, suburban areas, 342, 343
Arrest trends, ten-year, 287, 288
Crime in the U.S., by volume and rate, 35
Forcible rape
    see FORCIBLE RAPE
Incidents cleared by offense category, 269
SEXUAL ORIENTATION
Hate crimes generally
    see HATE CRIMES
SHOTGUNS
    see FIREARMS OFFENSES
SINGLE-BIAS INCIDENTS
Hate crimes, 554, 557, 559, 561, 563
SOUTH CAROLINA
Aggravated assault, by state and type of weapon, 261
Arrests, numbers and types of offenses, 354
Crime, by metropolitan statistical area, 54
Crime, by state and area, 46
Hate crimes, 566, 567, 569
Law enforcement employees, 370–533

Murder, by state and type of weapon, 259
Offenses known to law enforcement, by agencies, 222
Offenses known to law enforcement, by counties, 190
Offenses known to law enforcement, by selected state, 84
Offenses known to law enforcement, by university and college, 181
Robbery, by state and type of weapon, 260
SOUTH DAKOTA
Aggravated assault, by state and type of weapon, 261
Arrests, numbers and types of offenses, 354
Crime, by metropolitan statistical area, 54
Crime, by state and area, 46
Hate crimes, 566, 567, 569
Law enforcement employees, 370–533
Murder, by state and type of weapon, 259
Offenses known to law enforcement, by agencies, 222
Offenses known to law enforcement, by counties, 190
Offenses known to law enforcement, by selected state, 84
Offenses known to law enforcement, by university and college, 181
Robbery, by state and type of weapon, 260
STATE ARREST TOTALS
Numbers and types of offenses, 354
STATE CRIME TOTALS
Aggravated assault, by state and type of weapon, 261
Crime, by state and area, 46
Crime in the U.S. by state, 38, 46
Hate crimes
    offenses by state, 566, 567, 569
Murder, by state and type of weapon, 259
Offenses known to law enforcement, by counties, 190
Offenses known to law enforcement, by selected state, 84
Offenses known to law enforcement, by tribal, and other agencies, 222
Offenses known to law enforcement, by university and college, 181
Robbery, by state and type of weapon, 260
STOLEN PROPERTY
Arrests, by geographic region, 284
Arrests, by population group, 285
Arrests, cities, distribution by age, 311
Arrests, cities, distribution by ethnicity, 318
Arrests, cities, distribution by race, 315
Arrests, cities, distribution by sex, 314
Arrests, cities, persons under 15, 18, 21, and 25, 313
Arrests, distribution by age, 293–302
Arrests, distribution by ethnicity, 307
Arrests, distribution by race, 304
Arrests, distribution by sex, 288, 290, 303
Arrests, estimated number of, 283
Arrests, females, distribution by age, 299
Arrests, males, distribution by age, 296
Arrests, metropolitan counties, distribution by age, 322
Arrests, metropolitan counties, distribution by ethnicity, 329
Arrests, metropolitan counties, distribution by race, 326
Arrests, metropolitan counties, distribution by sex, 325
Arrests, metropolitan counties, persons under 15, 18, 21, and 25, 324
Arrests, nonmetropolitan counties, distribution by age, 333

Arrests, nonmetropolitan counties, distribution by ethnicity, 337
Arrests, nonmetropolitan counties, distribution by race, 339
Arrests, nonmetropolitan counties, distribution by sex, 336
Arrests, nonmetropolitan counties, persons under 15, 18, 21, and 25, 335
Arrests, suburban areas, distribution by age, 342–346
Arrests, suburban areas, distribution by ethnicity, 351
Arrests, suburban areas, distribution by race, 348
Arrests, suburban areas, distribution by sex, 347
Arrests, suburban areas, persons under 15, 18, 21, and 25, 346
Arrests of persons under 15, 18, 21, and 25, 302
Arrest trends, cities, 309
Arrest trends, current year over previous, 291, 292
Arrest trends, five-year, 289, 290
Arrest trends, metropolitan counties, 320, 321
Arrest trends, nonmetropolitan counties, 331, 332
Arrest trends, suburban areas, 342, 343
Arrest trends, ten-year, 287, 288
Incidents cleared by offense category, 269
Property stolen and recovered, by type and value, 263
Type and value, 263

STUDENT ENROLLMENT
Offenses known to law enforcement, by university and college, 181

SUBURBAN AREAS
Arrests, distribution by age, 342–346
Arrests, distribution by ethnicity, 351
Arrests, distribution by race, 348
Arrests, distribution by sex, 347
Arrests of persons under 15, 18, 21, and 25 years, 346
Arrest trends, 342, 343
Crimes per 100,000 population, 252, 257
Crime trends, by suburban and nonsuburban cities, 248
Law enforcement employees, 366–374
Number of crimes per 100,000 inhabitants, 254
Offenses cleared by arrest or exceptional means, by population group, 270, 272
Offenses cleared by arrest or exceptional means, persons under 18, 274
Police disposition of juvenile offenders taken into custody, 353

SUSPICION
Arrests, by geographic region, 284
Arrests, by population group, 285
Arrests, cities, distribution by age, 311
Arrests, cities, distribution by ethnicity, 318
Arrests, cities, distribution by race, 315
Arrests, cities, distribution by sex, 314
Arrests, cities, persons under 15, 18, 21, and 25, 313
Arrests, distribution by age, 293–302
Arrests, distribution by ethnicity, 307
Arrests, distribution by race, 304
Arrests, distribution by sex, 288, 290, 303
Arrests, estimated number of, 283
Arrests, females, distribution by age, 299
Arrests, males, distribution by age, 296
Arrests, metropolitan counties, distribution by age, 322
Arrests, metropolitan counties, distribution by ethnicity, 329
Arrests, metropolitan counties, distribution by race, 326

Arrests, metropolitan counties, distribution by sex, 325
Arrests, metropolitan counties, persons under 15, 18, 21, and 25, 324
Arrests, nonmetropolitan counties, distribution by age, 333
Arrests, nonmetropolitan counties, distribution by ethnicity, 337
Arrests, nonmetropolitan counties, distribution by race, 339
Arrests, nonmetropolitan counties, distribution by sex, 336
Arrests, nonmetropolitan counties, persons under 15, 18, 21, and 25, 335
Arrests, suburban areas, distribution by age, 342–346
Arrests, suburban areas, distribution by ethnicity, 351
Arrests, suburban areas, distribution by race, 348
Arrests, suburban areas, distribution by sex, 347
Arrests, suburban areas, persons under 15, 18, 21, and 25, 346
Arrests of persons under 15, 18, 21, and 25, 302
Arrest trends, cities, 309
Arrest trends, current year over previous, 291, 292
Arrest trends, five-year, 289, 290
Arrest trends, metropolitan counties, 320, 321
Arrest trends, nonmetropolitan counties, 331, 332
Arrest trends, suburban areas, 342, 343
Arrest trends, ten-year, 287, 288

TELEVISIONS, RADIOS, AND STEREOS
Property stolen and recovered, 263

TENNES *see*
Aggravated assault, by state and type of weapon, 261
Arrests, numbers and types of offenses, 354
Crime, by metropolitan statistical area, 54
Crime, by state and area, 46
Hate crimes, 566, 567, 569
Law enforcement employees, 370–533
Murder, by state and type of weapon, 259
Offenses known to law enforcement, by agencies, 222
Offenses known to law enforcement, by counties, 190
Offenses known to law enforcement, by selected state, 84
Offenses known to law enforcement, by university and college, 181
Robbery, by state and type of weapon, 260

TEXAS
Aggravated assault, by state and type of weapon, 261
Arrests, numbers and types of offenses, 354
Crime, by metropolitan statistical area, 54
Crime, by state and area, 46
Hate crimes, 566, 567, 569
Law enforcement employees, 370–533
Murder, by state and type of weapon, 259
Offenses known to law enforcement, by agencies, 222
Offenses known to law enforcement, by counties, 190
Offenses known to law enforcement, by selected state, 84
Offenses known to law enforcement, by university and college, 181
Robbery, by state and type of weapon, 260

THEFT
Burglary
see BURGLARY
Embezzlement
see EMBEZZLEMENT

Larceny-theft
  see LARCENY-THEFT
Motor vehicle theft
  see MOTOR VEHICLE THEFT
Robbery
  see ROBBERY
Stolen property
  see STOLEN PROPERTY

TRENDS IN CRIME
  Crime in the U.S., by volume and rate, 35
  Crime trends, by population group, 247
  Crime trends, cities by population group, 248
  Crime trends, counties by population group, 249
  Offense analysis, 83, 262

TRIBAL AGENCIES
  Full-time law enforcement employees, by selected state and
    agency, 533
  Hate crimes, 569
  Offenses known to law enforcement, by tribal, and other
    agencies, 222

UNIVERSITIES
  Hate crimes, 569
  Offenses known to law enforcement, by university and
    college, 181

UTAH
  Aggravated assault, by state and type of weapon, 261
  Arrests, numbers and types of offenses, 354
  Crime, by metropolitan statistical area, 54
  Crime, by state and area, 46
  Hate crimes, 566, 567, 569
  Law enforcement employees, 370–533
  Murder, by state and type of weapon, 259
  Offenses known to law enforcement, by agencies, 222
  Offenses known to law enforcement, by counties, 190
  Offenses known to law enforcement, by selected state, 84
  Offenses known to law enforcement, by university and
    college, 181
  Robbery, by state and type of weapon, 260

VAGRANCY
  Arrests, by geographic region, 284
  Arrests, by population group, 285
  Arrests, cities, distribution by age, 311
  Arrests, cities, distribution by ethnicity, 318
  Arrests, cities, distribution by race, 315
  Arrests, cities, distribution by sex, 314
  Arrests, cities, persons under 15, 18, 21, and 25, 313
  Arrests, distribution by age, 293–302
  Arrests, distribution by ethnicity, 307
  Arrests, distribution by race, 304
  Arrests, distribution by sex, 288, 290, 303
  Arrests, estimated number of, 283
  Arrests, females, distribution by age, 299
  Arrests, males, distribution by age, 296
  Arrests, metropolitan counties, distribution by age, 322
  Arrests, metropolitan counties, distribution by ethnicity, 329
  Arrests, metropolitan counties, distribution by race, 326
  Arrests, metropolitan counties, distribution by sex, 325

  Arrests, metropolitan counties, persons under 15, 18, 21, and
    25, 324
  Arrests, nonmetropolitan counties, distribution by age, 333
  Arrests, nonmetropolitan counties, distribution by ethnicity,
    337
  Arrests, nonmetropolitan counties, distribution by race, 339
  Arrests, nonmetropolitan counties, distribution by sex, 336
  Arrests, nonmetropolitan counties, persons under 15, 18, 21,
    and 25, 335
  Arrests, suburban areas, distribution by age, 342–346
  Arrests, suburban areas, distribution by ethnicity, 351
  Arrests, suburban areas, distribution by race, 348
  Arrests, suburban areas, distribution by sex, 347
  Arrests, suburban areas, persons under 15, 18, 21, and 25, 346
  Arrests of persons under 15, 18, 21, and 25, 302
  Arrest trends, cities, 309
  Arrest trends, current year over previous, 291, 292
  Arrest trends, five-year, 289, 290
  Arrest trends, metropolitan counties, 320, 321
  Arrest trends, nonmetropolitan counties, 331, 332
  Arrest trends, suburban areas, 342, 343
  Arrest trends, ten-year, 287, 288

VANDALISM
  Arrests, by geographic region, 284
  Arrests, by population group, 285
  Arrests, cities, distribution by age, 311
  Arrests, cities, distribution by ethnicity, 318
  Arrests, cities, distribution by race, 315
  Arrests, cities, distribution by sex, 314
  Arrests, cities, persons under 15, 18, 21, and 25, 313
  Arrests, distribution by age, 293–302
  Arrests, distribution by ethnicity, 307
  Arrests, distribution by race, 304
  Arrests, distribution by sex, 288, 290, 303
  Arrests, estimated number of, 283
  Arrests, females, distribution by age, 299
  Arrests, males, distribution by age, 296
  Arrests, metropolitan counties, distribution by age, 322
  Arrests, metropolitan counties, distribution by ethnicity, 329
  Arrests, metropolitan counties, distribution by race, 326
  Arrests, metropolitan counties, distribution by sex, 325
  Arrests, metropolitan counties, persons under 15, 18, 21, and
    25, 324
  Arrests, nonmetropolitan counties, distribution by age, 333
  Arrests, nonmetropolitan counties, distribution by ethnicity,
    337
  Arrests, nonmetropolitan counties, distribution by race, 339
  Arrests, nonmetropolitan counties, distribution by sex, 336
  Arrests, nonmetropolitan counties, persons under 15, 18, 21,
    and 25, 335
  Arrests, suburban areas, distribution by age, 342–346
  Arrests, suburban areas, distribution by ethnicity, 351
  Arrests, suburban areas, distribution by race, 348
  Arrests, suburban areas, distribution by sex, 347
  Arrests, suburban areas, persons under 15, 18, 21, and 25, 346
  Arrests of persons under 15, 18, 21, and 25, 302
  Arrest trends, cities, 309
  Arrest trends, current year over previous, 291, 292
  Arrest trends, five-year, 289, 290

Arrest trends, metropolitan counties, 320, 321
Arrest trends, nonmetropolitan counties, 331, 332
Arrest trends, suburban areas, 342, 343
Arrest trends, ten-year, 287, 288
Hate crimes, 555, 556, 560
Incidents cleared by offense category, 269

VERMONT
Aggravated assault, by state and type of weapon, 261
Arrests, numbers and types of offenses, 354
Crime, by metropolitan statistical area, 54
Crime, by state and area, 46
Hate crimes, 566, 567, 569
Law enforcement employees, 370–533
Murder, by state and type of weapon, 259
Offenses known to law enforcement, by agencies, 222
Offenses known to law enforcement, by counties, 190
Offenses known to law enforcement, by selected state, 84
Offenses known to law enforcement, by university and
    college, 181
Robbery, by state and type of weapon, 260

VICE OFFENSES
see PROSTITUTION AND COMMERCIALIZED VICE

VIOLENT CRIME
Arrests, by geographic region, 284
Arrests, by population group, 285
Arrests, by state, 354
Arrests, cities, distribution by age, 311
Arrests, cities, distribution by ethnicity, 318
Arrests, cities, distribution by race, 315
Arrests, cities, distribution by sex, 314
Arrests, cities, persons under 15, 18, 21, and 25, 313
Arrests, distribution by age, 293–302
Arrests, distribution by ethnicity, 307
Arrests, distribution by race, 304
Arrests, distribution by sex, 288, 290, 303
Arrests, estimated number of, 283
Arrests, females, distribution by age, 299
Arrests, males, distribution by age, 296
Arrests, metropolitan counties, distribution by age, 322
Arrests, metropolitan counties, distribution by race, 326
Arrests, metropolitan counties, distribution by sex, 325
Arrests, metropolitan counties, persons under 15, 18, 21, and
    25, 324
Arrests, nonmetropolitan counties, distribution by age, 333
Arrests, nonmetropolitan counties, distribution by ethnicity,
    337
Arrests, nonmetropolitan counties, distribution by race, 339
Arrests, nonmetropolitan counties, distribution by sex, 336
Arrests, nonmetropolitan counties, persons under 15, 18, 21,
    and 25, 335
Arrests, suburban areas, distribution by age, 342–346
Arrests, suburban areas, distribution by ethnicity, 351
Arrests, suburban areas, distribution by race, 348
Arrests, suburban areas, distribution by sex, 347
Arrests, suburban areas, persons under 15, 18, 21, and 25,
    346
Arrests of persons under 15, 18, 21, and 25, 302
Arrest trends, cities, 309
Arrest trends, five-year, 289, 290

Arrest trends, metropolitan counties, 320, 321
Arrest trends, nonmetropolitan counties, 331, 332
Arrest trends, suburban areas, 342, 343
Arrest trends, ten-year, 287, 288
Community type, 37
Crime, by metropolitan statistical area, 54
Crime, by state and area, 46
Crime in the U.S., by volume and rate, 35
Crimes per 100,000 inhabitants, by cities, 254
Crimes per 100,000 inhabitants, by counties, 255
Crimes per 100,000 population, by population group, 252,
    257
Crime trends, by population group, 247
Crime trends, cities by population group, 248
Crime trends, counties by population group, 249
Offense analysis, number and percent change, 262
Offenses cleared by arrest or exceptional means, by
    population group, 270–274
Offenses cleared by arrest or exceptional means, by region,
    271
Offenses cleared by arrest or exceptional means, persons
    under 18, 274
Offenses known to law enforcement, by counties, 190
Offenses known to law enforcement, by selected state, 84
Offenses known to law enforcement, by tribal, and other
    agencies, 222
Offenses known to law enforcement, by university and
    college, 181
Population and offense distribution, by region, 37, 38
Universities and colleges, 181

VIRGINIA
Aggravated assault, by state and type of weapon, 261
Arrests, numbers and types of offenses, 354
Crime, by metropolitan statistical area, 54
Crime, by state and area, 46
Hate crimes, 566, 567, 569
Law enforcement employees, 370–533
Murder, by state and type of weapon, 259
Offenses known to law enforcement, by agencies, 222
Offenses known to law enforcement, by counties, 190
Offenses known to law enforcement, by selected state, 84
Offenses known to law enforcement, by university and
    college, 181
Robbery, by state and type of weapon, 260

VOLUME OF CRIME
Aggravated assault, by state and type of weapon, 261
Crime, by metropolitan statistical area, 54
Crime, by state and area, 46
Crime in the U.S., by volume and rate, 35
Crimes per 100,000 population, by population group, 252,
    257
Crime trends, additional information, 250
Crime trends, by population group, 247
Crime trends, cities by population group, 248
Crime trends, counties by population group, 249
Murder, by state and type of weapon, 259
Offense analysis, 83, 262
Offenses known to law enforcement, by counties, 190
Offenses known to law enforcement, by selected state, 84

Offenses known to law enforcement, by tribal, and other
    agencies, 222
Offenses known to law enforcement, by university and
    college, 181
Robbery, by state and type of weapon, 260

WASHINGTON
Aggravated assault, by state and type of weapon, 261
Arrests, numbers and types of offenses, 354
Crime, by metropolitan statistical area, 54
Crime, by state and area, 46
Hate crimes, 566, 567, 569
Law enforcement employees, 370–533
Murder, by state and type of weapon, 259
Offenses known to law enforcement, by agencies, 222
Offenses known to law enforcement, by counties, 190
Offenses known to law enforcement, by selected state, 84
Offenses known to law enforcement, by university and
    college, 181
Robbery, by state and type of weapon, 260

WEAPONS OFFENSES
Aggravated assault, by state and type of weapon, 261
Arrests, by geographic region, 284
Arrests, by population group, 285
Arrests, cities, distribution by age, 311
Arrests, cities, distribution by ethnicity, 318
Arrests, cities, distribution by race, 315
Arrests, cities, distribution by sex, 314
Arrests, cities, persons under 15, 18, 21, and 25, 313
Arrests, distribution by age, 293–302
Arrests, distribution by ethnicity, 307
Arrests, distribution by race, 304
Arrests, distribution by sex, 288, 290, 303
Arrests, estimated number of, 283
Arrests, females, distribution by age, 299
Arrests, males, distribution by age, 296
Arrests, metropolitan counties, distribution by age, 322
Arrests, metropolitan counties, distribution by ethnicity,
    329
Arrests, metropolitan counties, distribution by race, 326
Arrests, metropolitan counties, distribution by sex, 325
Arrests, metropolitan counties, persons under 15, 18, 21, and
    25, 324
Arrests, nonmetropolitan counties, distribution by age, 333
Arrests, nonmetropolitan counties, distribution by ethnicity,
    337
Arrests, nonmetropolitan counties, distribution by race, 339
Arrests, nonmetropolitan counties, distribution by sex, 336
Arrests, nonmetropolitan counties, persons under 15, 18, 21,
    and 25, 335
Arrests, suburban areas, distribution by age, 342–346
Arrests, suburban areas, distribution by ethnicity, 351
Arrests, suburban areas, distribution by race, 348
Arrests, suburban areas, distribution by sex, 347

Arrests, suburban areas, persons under 15, 18, 21, and 25, 346
Arrests of persons under 15, 18, 21, and 25, 302
Arrest trends, cities, 309
Arrest trends, current year over previous, 291, 292
Arrest trends, five-year, 289, 290
Arrest trends, metropolitan counties, 320, 321
Arrest trends, nonmetropolitan counties, 331, 332
Arrest trends, suburban areas, 342, 343
Arrest trends, ten-year, 287, 288
Incidents cleared by offense category, 269
Murder, by state and type of weapon, 259
Robbery, by state and type of weapon, 260

WEST VIRGINIA
Aggravated assault, by state and type of weapon, 261
Arrests, numbers and types of offenses, 354
Crime, by metropolitan statistical area, 54
Crime, by state and area, 46
Hate crimes, 566, 567, 569
Law enforcement employees, 370–533
Murder, by state and type of weapon, 259
Offenses known to law enforcement, by agencies, 222
Offenses known to law enforcement, by counties, 190
Offenses known to law enforcement, by selected state, 84
Offenses known to law enforcement, by university and
    college, 181
Robbery, by state and type of weapon, 260

WISCONSIN
Aggravated assault, by state and type of weapon, 261
Arrests, numbers and types of offenses, 354
Crime, by metropolitan statistical area, 54
Crime, by state and area, 46
Hate crimes, 566, 567, 569
Law enforcement employees, 370–533
Murder, by state and type of weapon, 259
Offenses known to law enforcement, by agencies, 222
Offenses known to law enforcement, by counties, 190
Offenses known to law enforcement, by selected state, 84
Offenses known to law enforcement, by university and
    college, 181
Robbery, by state and type of weapon, 260

WYOMING
Aggravated assault, by state and type of weapon, 261
Arrests, numbers and types of offenses, 354
Crime, by metropolitan statistical area, 54
Crime, by state and area, 46
Hate crimes, 566, 567, 569
Law enforcement employees, 370–533
Murder, by state and type of weapon, 259
Offenses known to law enforcement, by agencies, 222
Offenses known to law enforcement, by counties, 190
Offenses known to law enforcement, by selected state, 84
Offenses known to law enforcement, by university and
    college, 181
Robbery, by state and type of weapon, 260

Printed in the USA
CPSIA information can be obtained
at www.ICGtesting.com
CBHW080155010724
10714CB00004B/4

9 798892 050067